PHILIP'S

WORLD ATLAS

PHILIP'S

WORLD ATLAS

NEW EDITION

ICELAND
NORWAY
SWEDEN
FINLAND
GERMANY
Berlin
Warsaw
Prague
Vienna
ITALY
Rome
Belgrade
UKRAINE
Odessa
Danube
Rostov
Athens
Bursa
Izmir
Konya
Ankara
TURKEY
GEORGIA
Yerevan
ARMENIA
Tabriz
Nicosia
CYPRUS
Adana
Aleppo
SYRIA
Beirut
LEBANON
ISRAEL
Damascus
Amman
Jerusalem
JORDAN
Alexandria
CAIRO
Suez
EGYPT
Nile
Aswân
IRAQ
Mosul
Baghdād
Basra
KUWAIT
Kuwait
Shiraz
SAUDI ARABIA
Medina
Riyadh
BAHRAIN
QATAR
Al Manamah
Doha
UNITED ARAB EMIRATES
Abu Dhabi
Jedda
Mecca
Port Sudan
Khartoum
ERITREA
OMAN
Muscat
YEMEN
Aden
DJIBOUTI
Addis Ababa
ETHIOPIA
SOMALI REP.
UGANDA
KENYA
Mogadishu
Nairobi
TANZANIA
Mombasa
Murmansk
White Sea
Arkhangelsk
ST PETERSBURG
Khatanga
Norilsk
Verkhoyansk
Lena
Yakutsk
Okhotsk
Magadan
Sakhalin
Komsomolsk
Khabarovsk
Yuzhno-Sakhalinsk
L. Baikal
Chita
Amur
Blagoveshchensk
Hailar
Qiqihar
Harbin
Changchun
Vladivostok
Jilin
SHENYANG
Anshan
Jinzhou
Dalian
NORTH KOREA
P'yongyang
SEOUL
SOUTH KOREA
Pusan
Hiroshima
Kitakyushu
Baotou
BEIJING
TIANJIN
Taiyuan
Jinan
Hwang-ho
Lanzhou
Xi'an
Nanjing
SHANGHAI
Wuhan
HANGZHOU
Nanchang
Fuzhou
Chengdu
CHONGQING
Yangtze
Changsha
Kunming
Si Kiang
GUANGZHOU
HONG KONG
Macau
Brahmaputra
BURMA (MYANMAR)
Chittagong
CALCUTTA
DACCA
Irrawaddy
Salween
Mekong
Hanoi
Haiphong
Hainan
LAOS
Vientiane
VIETNAM
Rangoon
THAILAND
BANGKOK
CAMBODIA
Phnom Penh
Ho Chi Minh City
Ahmadabad
Vadodara
Indore
Nagpur
Surat
BOMBAY
KARACHI
Luzon
MANILA
Palawan
Zamboanga
SABAH
Bandar Seri Begawan
SARAWAK
Borneo
Celebes
MALAYSIA
Kuala Lumpur
Medan
Str. of Malacca
SINGAPORE

THE EARTH IN SPACE
Cartography by Philip's

Text
Keith Lye

Illustrations
Stefan Chabluk

Star Charts
John Cox
Richard Monkhouse

PICTURE ACKNOWLEDGEMENTS
Robert Harding Picture Library /PHOTRI 13, /Bill Ross 41, /Adam Woolfitt 43
Hutchison Library /Melanie Friend 47, /John Hatt 46
Image Bank /Peter Hendrie 20, /Daniel Hummel 34, /Image Makers 8 top, /Pete Turner 39
Images Colour Library Limited 15
Japan National Tourist Organisation 45
NASA/Galaxy Picture Library 8 bottom left
NPA Group, Edenbridge, UK 48
Panos Pictures /Howard Davies 35
Chris Rayner 19 top
Rex Features /SIPA Press /Scott Andrews 12
Science Photo Library /Martin Bond 14, /CNES, 1992 Distribution Spot Image 27 top, /Luke Dodd 3, 6, /Earth Satellite Corporation 25 bottom, /NASA 9 centre right, 9 top, 22, 23, 24, /David Parker 26, /Peter Ryan 27 below, /Jerry Schad 4, /Space Telescope Science Institute /NASA 9 centre left, 9 bottom right, /US Geological Survey 8 centre right
Space Telescope Science Institute /R. Williams /NASA 2
Starland Picture Library /NASA 8 centre left
Still Pictures /Francois Pierrel 28, /Heine Pedersen 31, 40
Tony Stone Images 33, /Glen Allison 38, /James Balog 16, /John Beatty 21, /Neil Beer 30, /Kristin Finnegan 11, /Jeremy Horner 42, /Gary Norman 36, /Frank Oberle 25 top, /Dennis Oda 17, /Nigel Press 37, /Donovan Reese 18, 19, /Hugh Sitton 32, /Richard Surman 44, /Michael Townsend 29, /World Perspectives 10
Telegraph Colour Library /Space Frontiers 9 bottom left

Published in Great Britain in 2001
by George Philip Limited,
a division of Octopus Publishing Group Limited,
2–4 Heron Quays, London E14 4JP

This edition produced for Lomond Books, 2001

Cartography by Philip's

ISBN 0-540-08161-2

A CIP catalogue record for this book is available from the British Library.

Printed in China

Details of other Philip's titles and services can be found on our website at:
www.philips-maps.co.uk

Philip's World Maps

The reference maps which form the main body of this atlas have been prepared in accordance with the highest standards of international cartography to provide an accurate and detailed representation of the Earth. The scales and projections used have been carefully chosen to give balanced coverage of the world, while emphasizing the most densely populated and economically significant regions. A hallmark of Philip's mapping is the use of hill shading and relief colouring to create a graphic impression of landforms: this makes the maps exceptionally easy to read. However, knowledge of the key features employed in the construction and presentation of the maps will enable the reader to derive the fullest benefit from the atlas.

MAP SEQUENCE

The atlas covers the Earth continent by continent: first Europe; then its land neighbour Asia (mapped north before south, in a clockwise sequence), then Africa, Australia and Oceania, North America and South America. This is the classic arrangement adopted by most cartographers since the 16th century. For each continent, there are maps at a variety of scales. First, physical relief and political maps of the whole continent; then a series of larger-scale maps

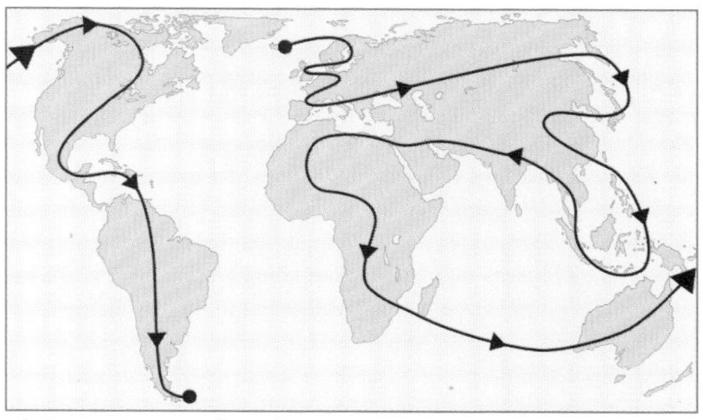

of the regions within the continent, each followed, where required, by still larger-scale maps of the most important or densely populated areas. The governing principle is that by turning the pages of the atlas, the reader moves steadily from north to south through each continent, with each map overlapping its neighbours. A key map showing this sequence, and the area covered by each map, can be found on the endpapers of the atlas.

MAP PRESENTATION

With very few exceptions (e.g. for the Arctic and Antarctic), the maps are drawn with north at the top, regardless of whether they are presented upright or sideways on the page. In the borders will be found the map title; a locator diagram showing the area covered and the page numbers for maps of adjacent areas; the scale; the projection used; the degrees of latitude and longitude; and the letters and figures used in the index for locating place names and geographical features. Physical relief maps also have a height reference panel identifying the colours used for each layer of contouring.

MAP SYMBOLS

Each map contains a vast amount of detail which can only be conveyed clearly and accurately by the use of symbols. Points and circles of varying sizes locate and identify the relative importance of towns and cities; different styles of type are employed for administrative, geographical and regional place names to aid identification. A variety of pictorial symbols denote landscape features such as glaciers, marshes and coral reefs, and man-made structures including roads, railways, airports, canals and dams. International borders are shown by red lines. Where neighbouring countries are in dispute, for example in parts of the Middle East, the maps show the *de facto* boundary between nations, regardless of the legal or historical situation. The symbols are explained on the first page of the World Maps section of the atlas.

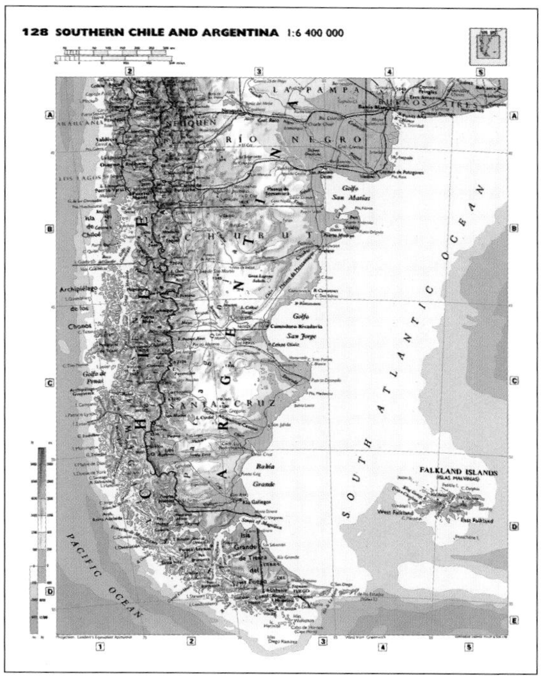

MAP SCALES

1:16 000 000
1 inch = 252 statute miles

The scale of each map is given in the numerical form known as the 'representative fraction'. The first figure is always one, signifying one unit of distance on the map; the second figure, usually in millions, is the number by which the map unit must be multiplied to give the equivalent distance on the Earth's surface. Calculations can easily be made in centimetres and kilometres, by dividing the Earth units figure by 100 000 (i.e. deleting the last five 0s). Thus 1:1 000 000 means 1 cm = 10 km. The calculation for inches and miles is more laborious, but 1 000 000 divided by 63 360 (the number of inches in a mile) shows that 1:1 000 000 means approximately 1 inch = 16 miles. The table below provides distance equivalents for scales down to 1:50 000 000.

LARGE SCALE

1:1 000 000	1 cm = 10 km	1 inch = 16 miles
1:2 500 000	1 cm = 25 km	1 inch = 39.5 miles
1:5 000 000	1 cm = 50 km	1 inch = 79 miles
1:6 000 000	1 cm = 60 km	1 inch = 95 miles
1:8 000 000	1 cm = 80 km	1 inch = 126 miles
1:10 000 000	1 cm = 100 km	1 inch = 158 miles
1:15 000 000	1 cm = 150 km	1 inch = 237 miles
1:20 000 000	1 cm = 200 km	1 inch = 316 miles
1:50 000 000	1 cm = 500 km	1 inch = 790 miles

SMALL SCALE

MEASURING DISTANCES

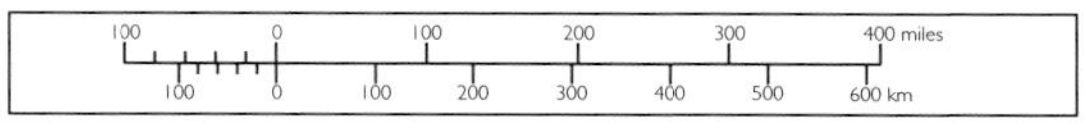

Although each map is accompanied by a scale bar, distances cannot always be measured with confidence because of the distortions involved in portraying the curved surface of the Earth on a flat page. As a general rule, the larger the map scale (i.e. the lower the number of Earth units in the representative fraction), the more accurate and reliable will be the distance measured. On small-scale maps such as those of the world and of entire continents, measurement may only be accurate along the 'standard parallels', or central axes, and should not be attempted without considering the map projection.

MAP PROJECTIONS

Unlike a globe, no flat map can give a true scale representation of the world in terms of area, shape and position of every region. Each of the numerous systems that have been devised for projecting the curved surface of the Earth on to a flat page involves the sacrifice of accuracy in one or more of these elements. The variations in shape and position of landmasses such as Alaska, Greenland and Australia, for example, can be quite dramatic when different projections are compared.

For this atlas, the guiding principle has been to select projections that involve the least distortion of size and distance. The projection used for each map is noted in the border. Most fall into one of three categories – conic, cylindrical or azimuthal – whose basic concepts are shown above. Each involves plotting the forms of the Earth's surface on a grid of latitude and longitude lines, which may be shown as parallels, curves or radiating spokes.

LATITUDE AND LONGITUDE

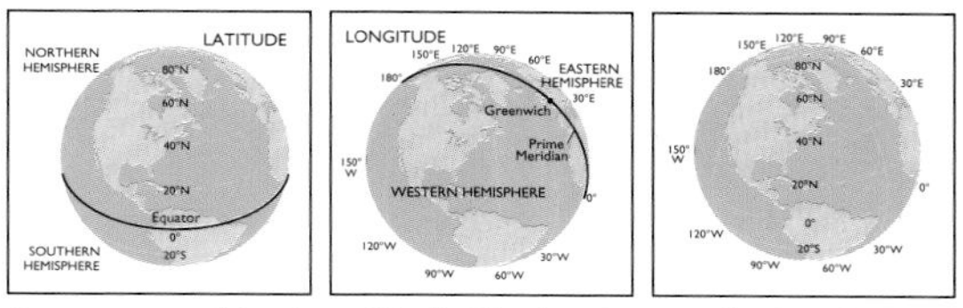

Accurate positioning of individual points on the Earth's surface is made possible by reference to the geometrical system of latitude and longitude. Latitude *parallels* are drawn west–east around the Earth and numbered by degrees north and south of the Equator, which is designated 0° of latitude. Longitude *meridians* are drawn north–south and numbered by degrees east and west of the *prime meridian*, 0° of longitude, which passes through Greenwich in England. By referring to these co-ordinates and their subdivisions of minutes (1/60th of a degree) and seconds (1/60th of a minute), any place on Earth can be located to within a few hundred yards. Latitude and longitude are indicated by blue lines on the maps; they are straight or curved according to the projection employed. Reference to these lines is the easiest way of determining the relative positions of places on different maps, and for plotting compass directions.

NAME FORMS

For ease of reference, both English and local name forms appear in the atlas. Oceans, seas and countries are shown in English throughout the atlas; country names may be abbreviated to their commonly accepted form (e.g. Germany, not The Federal Republic of Germany). Conventional English forms are also used for place names on the smaller-scale maps of the continents. However, local name forms are used on all large-scale and regional maps, with the English form given in brackets only for important cities – the large-scale map of Russia and Central Asia thus shows Moskva (Moscow). For countries which do not use a Roman script, place names have been transcribed according to the systems adopted by the British and US Geographic Names Authorities. For China, the Pin Yin system has been used, with some more widely known forms appearing in brackets, as with Beijing (Peking). Both English and local names appear in the index, the English form being cross-referenced to the local form.

Contents

World Statistics

Countries x
Cities xi
Climate xii
Physical Dimensions xiv
Regions in the News xvi

The Earth In Space

The Universe 2–3
Star Charts and Constellations 4–7
The Solar System 8–9
The Earth: Time and Motion 10–11
The Earth from Space 12–13
The Dynamic Earth 14–15
Earthquakes and Volcanoes 16–17
Forces of Nature 18–19
Oceans and Ice 20–21
The Earth's Atmosphere 22–23
Climate and Weather 24–25
Water and Land Use 26–27
The Natural World 28–29
The Human World 30–31
Languages and Religions 32–33
International Organizations 34–35
Agriculture 36–37
Energy and Minerals 38–39
World Economies 40–41
Trade and Commerce 42–43
Travel and Communications 44–45
The World Today 46–47

World Maps

Map Symbols **1**

The World: Political
1:71 100 000 **2–3**

Arctic Ocean
1:31 100 000 **4**

Antarctica
1:31 100 000 **5**

Europe

Europe: Physical
1:17 800 000 6

Europe: Political
1:17 800 000 7

Scandinavia
1:4 400 000

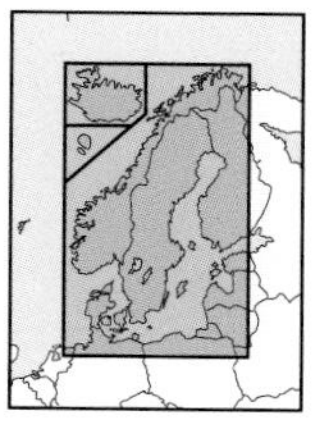

8–9

Denmark and Southern Sweden
1:2 200 000

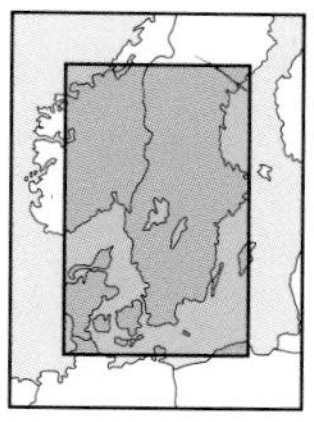

10–11

England and Wales
1:1 800 000

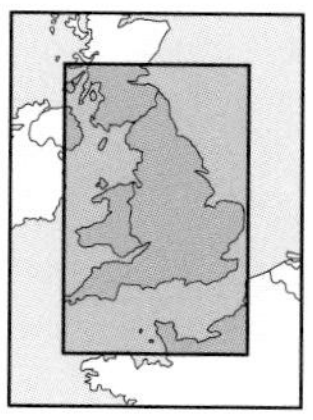

12–13

Scotland
1:1 800 000

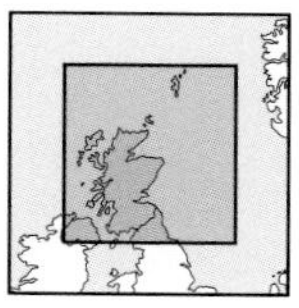

14

Ireland
1:1 800 000

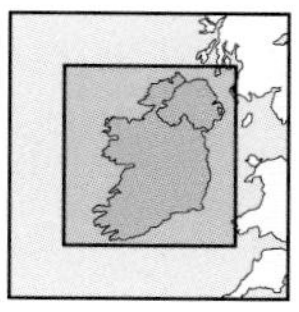

15

British Isles
1:4 400 000

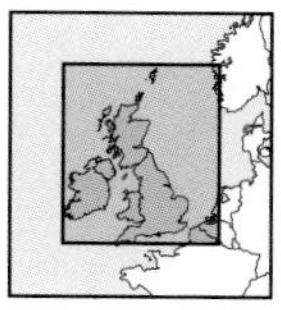

16

Netherlands, Belgium and Luxembourg
1:2 200 000

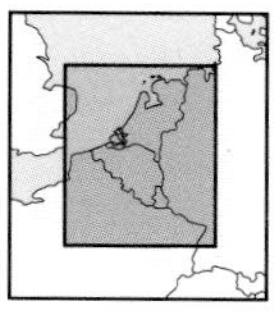

17

Northern France
1:2 200 000

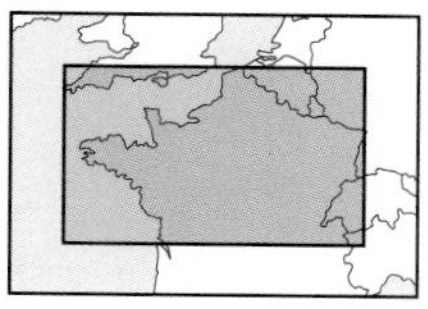

18–19

Southern France
1:2 200 000

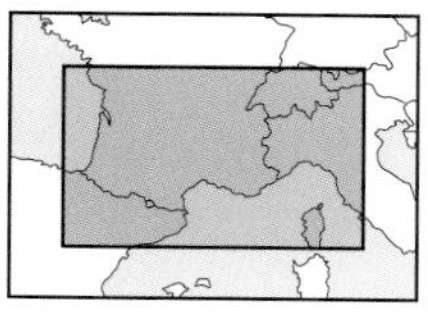

20–21

Middle Europe
1:4 400 000

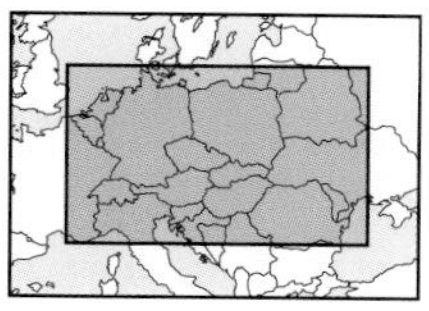

22–23

Germany and Switzerland
1:2 200 000

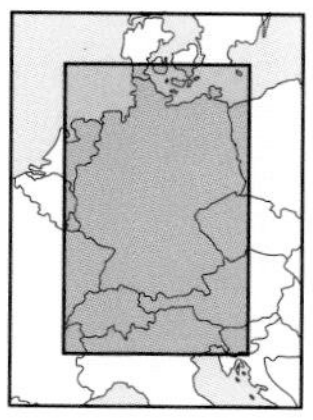

24–25

Austria, Czech Republic and Slovak Republic
1:2 200 000

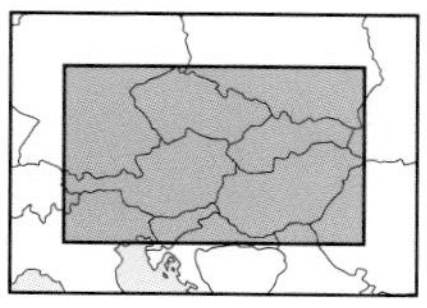

26–27

Northern Italy, Slovenia and Croatia
1:2 200 000

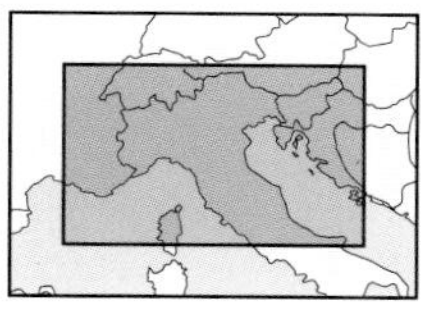

28–29

Southern Italy
1:2 200 000

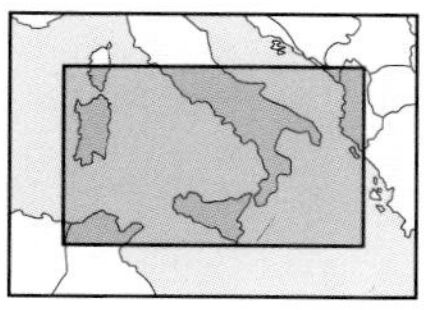

30–31

Eastern Spain
1:2 200 000

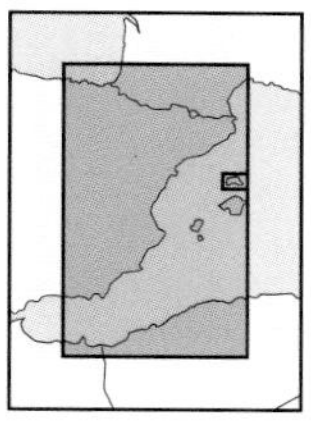

32–33

Western Spain and Portugal
1:2 200 000

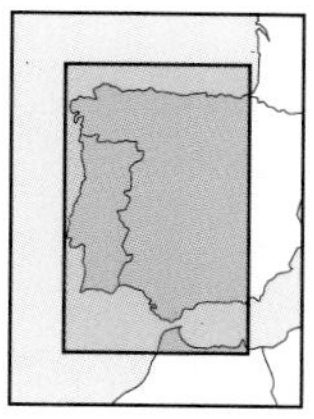

34–35

Malta, Crete, Corfu, Rhodes and Cyprus
1:900 000 / 1:1 200 000

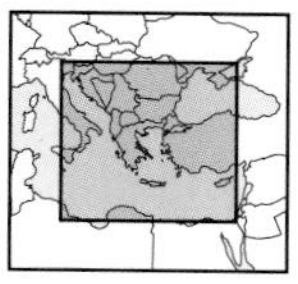

36

The Balearics, the Canaries and Madeira
1:900 000 / 1:1 800 000

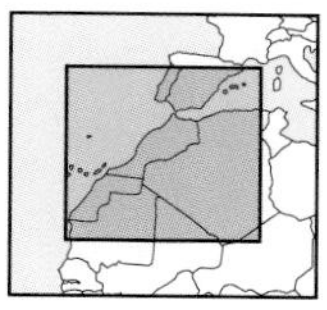

37

Southern Greece and Western Turkey
1:2 200 000

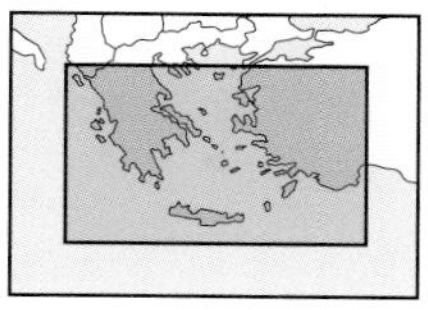

38–39

Northern Greece, Bulgaria and Yugoslavia
1:2 200 000

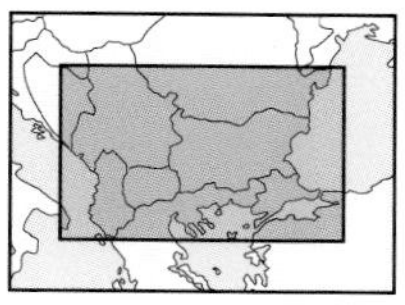

40–41

Hungary, Romania and the Lower Danube
1:2 200 000

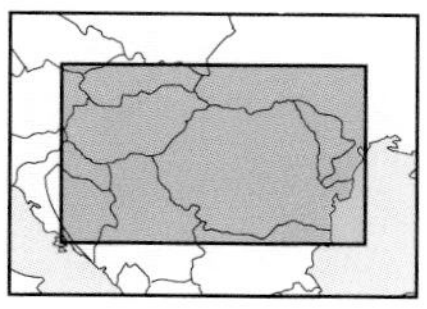

42–43

Poland and the Southern Baltic
1:2 200 000

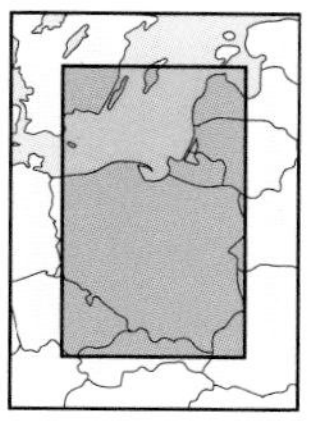

44–45

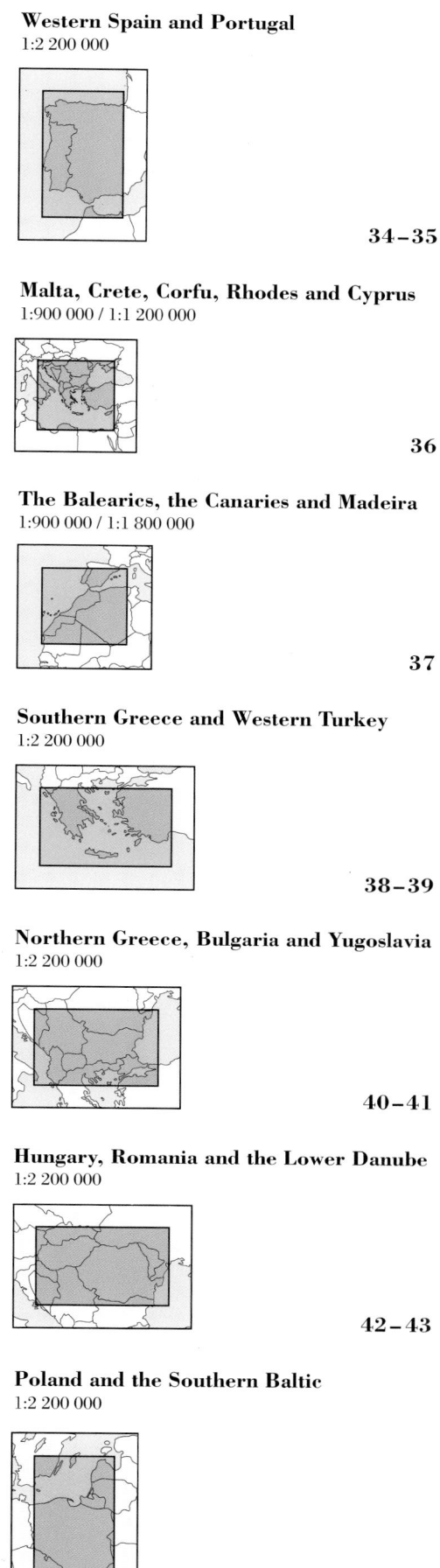

East Africa
1:7 100 000

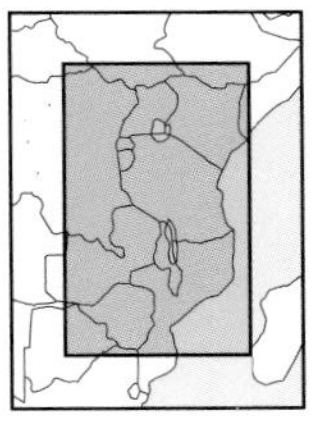

86–87

Southern Africa
1:7 100 000 / 1:7 100 000

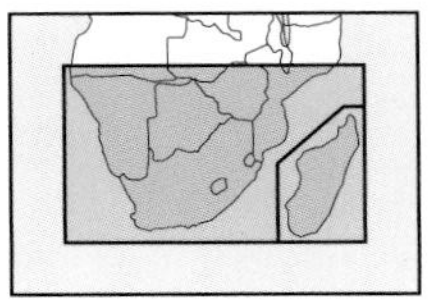

88–89

Australia and Oceania

Australia and Oceania: Physical and Political
1:44 400 000 — 90

New Zealand and Samoa, Fiji and Tonga
1:5 300 000 / 1:10 700 000

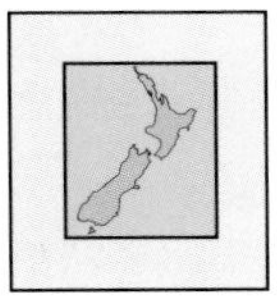

91

Western Australia
1:7 100 000

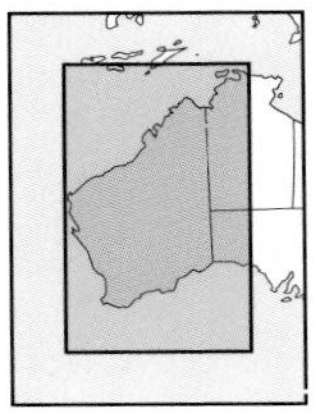

92–93

Eastern Australia
1:7 100 000

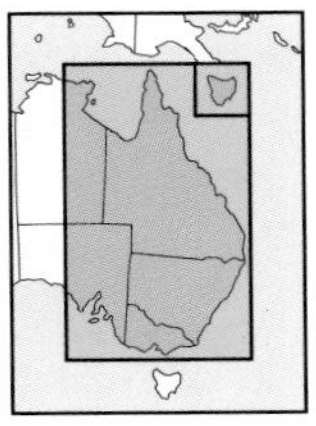

94–95

Pacific Ocean
1:48 000 000 — 96–97

North America

North America: Physical
1:31 100 000 — 98

North America: Political
1:31 100 000 — 99

Canada and Alaska
1:13 300 000 / 1:26 700 000

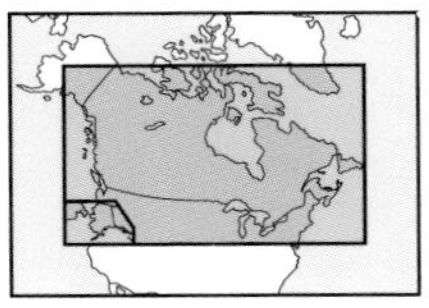

100–101

Eastern Canada
1:6 200 000

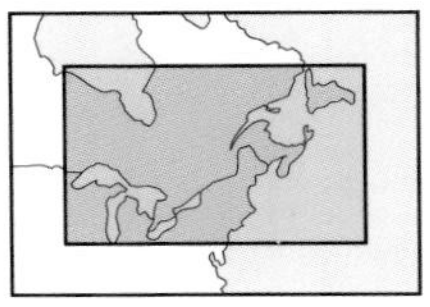

102–103

Western Canada
1:6 200 000

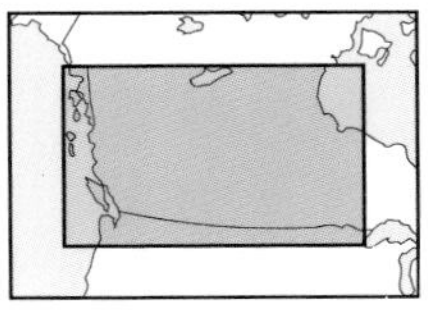

104–105

United States and Hawaii
1:10 700 000 / 1:8 900 000

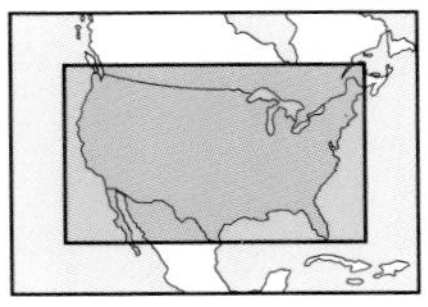

106–107

Eastern United States
1:5 300 000

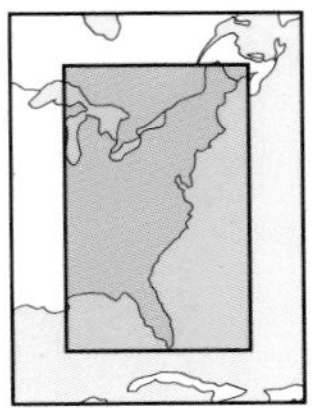

108–109

North-eastern United States
1:2 200 000

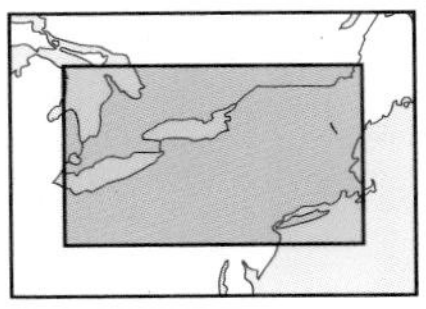

110–111

Middle United States
1:5 300 000

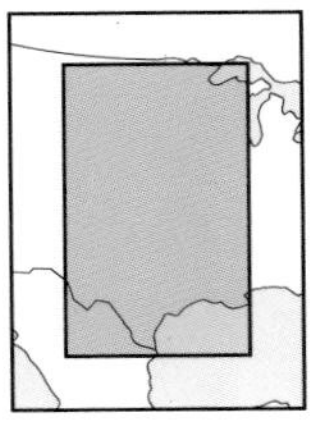

112–113

Western United States
1:5 300 000

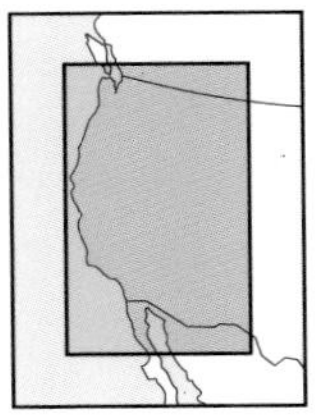

114–115

Central and Southern California and Western Washington
1:2 200 000

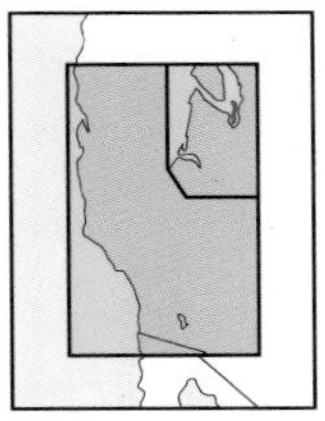

116–117

Mexico
1:7 100 000

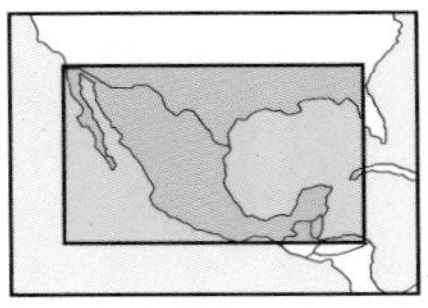

118–119

Central America and the West Indies
1:7 100 000

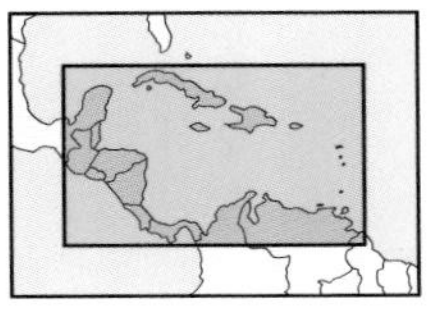

120–121

South America

South America: Physical
1:31 100 000 — 122

South America: Political
1:31 100 000 — 123

South America – North
1:14 200 000

124–125

Central South America
1:7 100 000

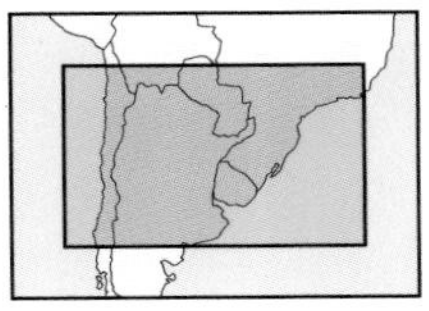

126–127

South America – South
1:14 200 000

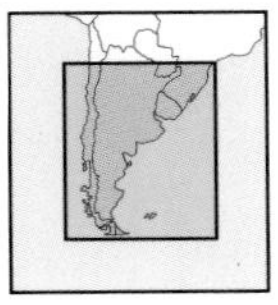

128

Index to World Maps

129–224

World Statistics: Countries

This alphabetical list includes all the countries and territories of the world. If a territory is not completely independent, then the country it is associated with is named. The area figures give the total area of land, inland water and ice.

Units for areas and populations are thousands. The population figures are 2000 estimates. The annual income is the Gross National Product per capita in US dollars. The figures are the latest available, usually 1999 estimates.

Country/Territory	Area km² Thousands	Area miles² Thousands	Population Thousands	Capital	Annual Income US $
Afghanistan	652	252	26,511	Kabul	800
Albania	28.8	11.1	3,795	Tirana	870
Algeria	2,382	920	32,904	Algiers	1,550
American Samoa (US)	0.20	0.08	39	Pago Pago	2,600
Andorra	0.45	0.17	49	Andorra La Vella	18,000
Angola	1,247	481	13,295	Luanda	220
Anguilla (UK)	0.1	0.04	8	The Valley	6,800
Antigua & Barbuda	0.44	0.17	79	St John's	8,520
Argentina	2,767	1,068	36,238	Buenos Aires	7,600
Armenia	29.8	11.5	3,968	Yerevan	490
Aruba (Netherlands)	0.19	0.07	58	Oranjestad	22,000
Australia	7,687	2,968	18,855	Canberra	20,050
Austria	83.9	32.4	7,613	Vienna	25,970
Azerbaijan	86.6	33.4	8,324	Baku	550
Azores (Portugal)	2.2	0.87	238	Ponta Delgada	–
Bahamas	13.9	5.4	295	Nassau	20,100
Bahrain	0.68	0.26	683	Manama	7,640
Bangladesh	144	56	150,589	Dhaka	370
Barbados	0.43	0.17	265	Bridgetown	7,890
Belarus	207.6	80.1	10,697	Minsk	2,630
Belgium	30.5	11.8	9,832	Brussels	24,510
Belize	23	8.9	230	Belmopan	2,730
Benin	113	43	6,369	Porto-Novo	380
Bermuda (UK)	0.05	0.02	62	Hamilton	35,590
Bhutan	47	18.1	1,906	Thimphu	510
Bolivia	1,099	424	9,724	La Paz/Sucre	1,010
Bosnia-Herzegovina	51	20	4,601	Sarajevo	1,720
Botswana	582	225	1,822	Gaborone	3,240
Brazil	8,512	3,286	179,487	Brasília	4,420
Brunei	5.8	2.2	333	Bandar Seri Begawan	24,630
Bulgaria	111	43	9,071	Sofia	1,380
Burkina Faso	274	106	12,092	Ouagadougou	240
Burma (= Myanmar)	677	261	51,129	Rangoon	1,200
Burundi	27.8	10.7	7,358	Bujumbura	120
Cambodia	181	70	10,046	Phnom Penh	260
Cameroon	475	184	16,701	Yaoundé	580
Canada	9,976	3,852	28,488	Ottawa	19,320
Canary Is. (Spain)	7.3	2.8	1,494	Las Palmas/Santa Cruz	–
Cape Verde Is.	4	1.6	515	Praia	1,330
Cayman Is. (UK)	0.26	0.10	35	George Town	20,000
Central African Republic	623	241	4,074	Bangui	290
Chad	1,284	496	7,337	Ndjaména	200
Chile	757	292	15,272	Santiago	4,740
China	9,597	3,705	1,299,180	Beijing	780
Colombia	1,139	440	39,397	Bogotá	2,250
Comoros	2.2	0.86	670	Moroni	350
Congo	342	132	3,167	Brazzaville	670
Congo (Dem. Rep. of the)	2,345	905	49,190	Kinshasa	110
Cook Is. (NZ)	0.24	0.09	17	Avarua	900
Costa Rica	51.1	19.7	3,711	San José	2,740
Croatia	56.5	21.8	4,960	Zagreb	4,580
Cuba	111	43	11,504	Havana	1,560
Cyprus	9.3	3.6	762	Nicosia	11,960
Czech Republic	78.9	30.4	10,500	Prague	5,060
Denmark	43.1	16.6	5,153	Copenhagen	32,030
Djibouti	23.2	9	552	Djibouti	790
Dominica	0.75	0.29	87	Roseau	3,170
Dominican Republic	48.7	18.8	8,621	Santo Domingo	1,910
Ecuador	284	109	13,319	Quito	1,310
Egypt	1,001	387	64,210	Cairo	1,400
El Salvador	21	8.1	6,739	San Salvador	1,900
Equatorial Guinea	28.1	10.8	455	Malabo	1,170
Eritrea	94	36	4,523	Asmara	200
Estonia	44.7	17.3	1,647	Tallinn	3,480
Ethiopia	1,128	436	61,841	Addis Ababa	100
Faroe Is. (Denmark)	1.4	0.54	49	Tórshavn	16,000
Fiji	18.3	7.1	883	Suva	2,210
Finland	338	131	5,077	Helsinki	23,780
France	552	213	58,145	Paris	23,480
French Guiana (France)	90	34.7	130	Cayenne	6,000
French Polynesia (France)	4	1.5	268	Papeete	18,050
Gabon	268	103	1,612	Libreville	3,350
Gambia, The	11.3	4.4	1,119	Banjul	340
Georgia	69.7	26.9	5,777	Tbilisi	620
Germany	357	138	76,962	Berlin	25,350
Ghana	239	92	20,564	Accra	390
Gibraltar (UK)	0.007	0.003	32	Gibraltar Town	5,000
Greece	132	51	10,193	Athens	11,770
Greenland (Denmark)	2,176	840	60	Nuuk (Godthåb)	16,100
Grenada	0.34	0.13	83	St George's	3,450
Guadeloupe (France)	1.7	0.66	365	Basse-Terre	9,200
Guam (US)	0.55	0.21	128	Agana	19,000
Guatemala	109	42	12,222	Guatemala City	1,660
Guinea	246	95	7,830	Conakry	510
Guinea-Bissau	36.1	13.9	1,197	Bissau	160
Guyana	215	83	891	Georgetown	760
Haiti	27.8	10.7	8,003	Port-au-Prince	460
Honduras	112	43	6,846	Tegucigalpa	760
Hong Kong (China)	1.1	0.40	6,336	–	23,520
Hungary	93	35.9	10,531	Budapest	4,650
Iceland	103	40	274	Reykjavik	29,280
India	3,288	1,269	1,041,543	New Delhi	450
Indonesia	1,905	735	218,661	Jakarta	580
Iran	1,648	636	68,759	Tehran	1,760
Iraq	438	169	26,339	Baghdad	2,400
Ireland	70.3	27.1	4,086	Dublin	19,160
Israel	27	10.3	5,321	Jerusalem	17,450
Italy	301	116	57,195	Rome	19,710
Ivory Coast (Côte d'Ivoire)	322	125	17,600	Yamoussoukro	710
Jamaica	11	4.2	2,735	Kingston	2,330
Japan	378	146	128,470	Tokyo	32,230
Jordan	89.2	34.4	5,558	Amman	1,500
Kazakstan	2,717	1,049	19,006	Astana	1,230
Kenya	580	224	35,060	Nairobi	360
Kiribati	0.72	0.28	72	Tarawa	910
Korea, North	121	47	26,117	Pyŏngyang	1,000
Korea, South	99	38.2	46,403	Seoul	8,490
Kuwait	17.8	6.9	2,639	Kuwait City	22,700
Kyrgyzstan	198.5	76.6	5,403	Bishkek	300
Laos	237	91	5,463	Vientiane	280
Latvia	65	25	2,768	Riga	2,470

Country/Territory	Area km² Thousands	Area miles² Thousands	Population Thousands	Capital	Annual Income US $
Lebanon	10.4	4	3,327	Beirut	3,700
Lesotho	30.4	11.7	2,370	Maseru	550
Liberia	111	43	3,575	Monrovia	1,000
Libya	1,760	679	6,500	Tripoli	6,700
Liechtenstein	0.16	0.06	28	Vaduz	50,000
Lithuania	65.2	25.2	3,935	Vilnius	2,620
Luxembourg	2.6	1	377	Luxembourg	44,640
Macau (China)	0.02	0.006	656	Macau	16,000
Macedonia	25.7	9.9	2,157	Skopje	1,690
Madagascar	587	227	16,627	Antananarivo	250
Madeira (Portugal)	0.81	0.31	253	Funchal	–
Malawi	118	46	12,458	Lilongwe	190
Malaysia	330	127	21,983	Kuala Lumpur	3,400
Maldives	0.30	0.12	283	Malé	1,160
Mali	1,240	479	12,685	Bamako	240
Malta	0.32	0.12	366	Valletta	9,210
Marshall Is.	0.18	0.07	70	Dalap-Uliga-Darrit	1,560
Martinique (France)	1.1	0.42	362	Fort-de-France	10,700
Mauritania	1,030	412	2,702	Nouakchott	380
Mauritius	2.0	0.72	1,201	Port Louis	3,590
Mayotte (France)	0.37	0.14	141	Mamoundzou	1,430
Mexico	1,958	756	107,233	Mexico City	4,400
Micronesia, Fed. States of	0.70	0.27	110	Palikir	1,810
Moldova	33.7	13	4,707	Chişinău	370
Monaco	0.002	0.0001	30	Monaco	25,000
Mongolia	1,567	605	2,847	Ulan Bator	350
Montserrat (UK)	0.10	0.04	13	Plymouth	4,500
Morocco	447	172	31,559	Rabat	1,200
Mozambique	802	309	20,493	Maputo	230
Namibia	825	318	2,437	Windhoek	1,890
Nauru	0.02	0.008	10	Yaren District	10,000
Nepal	141	54	24,084	Katmandu	220
Netherlands	41.5	16	15,829	Amsterdam/The Hague	24,320
Netherlands Antilles (Neths)	0.99	0.38	203	Willemstad	11,500
New Caledonia (France)	18.6	7.2	195	Nouméa	11,400
New Zealand	269	104	3,662	Wellington	13,780
Nicaragua	130	50	5,261	Managua	430
Niger	1,267	489	10,752	Niamey	190
Nigeria	924	357	105,000	Abuja	310
Northern Mariana Is. (US)	0.48	0.18	50	Saipan	11,500
Norway	324	125	4,331	Oslo	32,880
Oman	212	82	2,176	Muscat	7,900
Pakistan	796	307	162,409	Islamabad	470
Palau	0.46	0.18	18	Koror	5,000
Panama	77.1	29.8	2,893	Panama City	3,070
Papua New Guinea	463	179	4,845	Port Moresby	800
Paraguay	407	157	5,538	Asunción	1,580
Peru	1,285	496	26,276	Lima	2,390
Philippines	300	116	77,473	Manila	1,020
Poland	313	121	40,366	Warsaw	3,960
Portugal	92.4	35.7	10,587	Lisbon	10,600
Puerto Rico (US)	9	3.5	3,836	San Juan	8,200
Qatar	11	4.2	499	Doha	17,100
Réunion (France)	2.5	0.97	692	Saint-Denis	4,800
Romania	238	92	24,000	Bucharest	1,520
Russia	17,075	6,592	155,096	Moscow	2,270
Rwanda	26.3	10.2	10,200	Kigali	250
St Kitts & Nevis	0.36	0.14	44	Basseterre	6,420
St Lucia	0.62	0.24	177	Castries	3,770
St Vincent & Grenadines	0.39	0.15	128	Kingstown	2,700
Samoa	2.8	1.1	171	Apia	1,020
San Marino	0.06	0.02	25	San Marino	20,000
São Tomé & Príncipe	0.96	0.37	151	São Tomé	270
Saudi Arabia	2,150	830	20,697	Riyadh	6,910
Senegal	197	76	8,716	Dakar	510
Seychelles	0.46	0.18	75	Victoria	6,540
Sierra Leone	71.7	27.7	5,437	Freetown	130
Singapore	0.62	0.24	3,000	Singapore	29,610
Slovak Republic	49	18.9	5,500	Bratislava	3,590
Slovenia	20.3	7.8	2,055	Ljubljana	9,890
Solomon Is.	28.9	11.2	429	Honiara	750
Somalia	638	246	9,736	Mogadishu	600
South Africa	1,220	471	43,666	C. Town/Pretoria/Bloem.	3,160
Spain	505	195	40,667	Madrid	14,000
Sri Lanka	65.6	25.3	19,416	Colombo	820
Sudan	2,506	967	33,625	Khartoum	330
Surinam	163	63	497	Paramaribo	1,660
Swaziland	17.4	6.7	1,121	Mbabane	1,360
Sweden	450	174	8,560	Stockholm	25,040
Switzerland	41.3	15.9	6,762	Bern	38,350
Syria	185	71	17,826	Damascus	970
Taiwan	36	13.9	22,000	Taipei	12,400
Tajikistan	143.1	55.2	7,041	Dushanbe	290
Tanzania	945	365	39,639	Dodoma	240
Thailand	513	198	63,670	Bangkok	1,960
Togo	56.8	21.9	4,861	Lomé	320
Tonga	0.75	0.29	92	Nuku'alofa	1,720
Trinidad & Tobago	5.1	2	1,484	Port of Spain	4,390
Tunisia	164	63	9,924	Tunis	2,100
Turkey	779	301	66,789	Ankara	2,900
Turkmenistan	488.1	188.5	4,585	Ashkhabad	660
Turks & Caicos Is. (UK)	0.43	0.17	12	Cockburn Town	5,000
Tuvalu	0.03	0.01	11	Fongafale	600
Uganda	236	91	26,958	Kampala	320
Ukraine	603.7	233.1	52,558	Kiev	750
United Arab Emirates	83.6	32.3	1,951	Abu Dhabi	17,870
United Kingdom	243.3	94	58,393	London	22,640
United States of America	9,373	3,619	266,096	Washington, DC	30,600
Uruguay	177	68	3,274	Montevideo	5,900
Uzbekistan	447.4	172.7	26,044	Tashkent	720
Vanuatu	12.2	4.7	206	Port-Vila	1,170
Venezuela	912	352	24,715	Caracas	3,670
Vietnam	332	127	82,427	Hanoi	370
Virgin Is. (UK)	0.15	0.06	15	Road Town	–
Virgin Is. (US)	0.34	0.13	135	Charlotte Amalie	12,500
Wallis & Futuna Is. (France)	0.20	0.08	26	Mata-Utu	–
Western Sahara	266	103	228	El Aaiún	300
Yemen	528	204	13,219	Sana	350
Yugoslavia	102.3	39.5	10,761	Belgrade	2,300
Zambia	753	291	12,267	Lusaka	320
Zimbabwe	391	151	13,123	Harare	520

World Statistics: Cities

This list shows the principal cities with more than 500,000 inhabitants (for Brazil, China and India only cities with more than 1 million inhabitants are included). The figures are taken from the most recent census or population estimate available, and as far as possible are the population of the metropolitan area, e.g. greater New York, Mexico or Paris. All the figures are in thousands. Local name forms have been used for the smaller cities (e.g. Kraków).

AFGHANISTAN	
Kabul	1,565
ALGERIA	
Algiers	2,168
Oran	916
ANGOLA	
Luanda	2,418
ARGENTINA	
Buenos Aires	11,256
Córdoba	1,208
Rosario	1,118
Mendoza	773
La Plata	642
San Miguel de Tucumán	622
Mar del Plata	512
ARMENIA	
Yerevan	1,248
AUSTRALIA	
Sydney	3,770
Melbourne	3,217
Brisbane	1,489
Perth	1,262
Adelaide	1,080
AUSTRIA	
Vienna	1,595
AZERBAIJAN	
Baku	1,720
BANGLADESH	
Dhaka	6,105
Chittagong	2,041
Khulna	877
Rajshahi	517
BELARUS	
Minsk	1,700
Homyel	512
BELGIUM	
Brussels	948
BENIN	
Cotonou	537
BOLIVIA	
La Paz	1,126
Santa Cruz	767
BOSNIA-HERZEGOVINA	
Sarajevo	526
BRAZIL	
São Paulo	16,417
Rio de Janeiro	9,888
Salvador	2,211
Belo Horizonte	2,091
Fortaleza	1,965
Brasília	1,821
Curitiba	1,476
Recife	1,346
Pôrto Alegre	1,288
Manaus	1,157
Belém	1,144
Goiânia	1,004
BULGARIA	
Sofia	1,116
BURKINA FASO	
Ouagadougou	690
BURMA (MYANMAR)	
Rangoon	2,513
Mandalay	533
CAMBODIA	
Phnom Penh	920
CAMEROON	
Douala	1,200
Yaoundé	800
CANADA	
Toronto	4,344
Montréal	3,337
Vancouver	1,831
Ottawa–Hull	1,022
Edmonton	885
Calgary	831
Québec	693
Winnipeg	677
Hamilton	643
CENTRAL AFRICAN REP.	
Bangui	553
CHAD	
Ndjaména	530
CHILE	
Santiago	5,067
CHINA	
Shanghai	15,082
Beijing	12,362
Tianjin	10,687
Hong Kong (SAR)*	6,502
Chongqing	3,870
Shenyang	3,860
Wuhan	3,520
Guangzhou	3,114
Harbin	2,505
Nanjing	2,211
Xi'an	2,115
Chengdu	1,933
Dalian	1,855
Changchun	1,810
Jinan	1,660
Taiyuan	1,642
Qingdao	1,584
Fuzhou, Fujian	1,380
Zibo	1,346
Zhengzhou	1,324
Lanzhou	1,296
Anshan	1,252
Fushun	1,246
Kunming	1,242
Changsha	1,198
Hangzhou	1,185
Nanchang	1,169
Shijiazhuang	1,159
Guiyang	1,131
Ürümqi	1,130
Jilin	1,118
Tangshan	1,110
Qiqihar	1,104
Baotou	1,033
Hefei	1,000
COLOMBIA	
Bogotá	6,004
Cali	1,985
Medellín	1,970
Barranquilla	1,157
Cartagena	812
CONGO	
Brazzaville	937
Pointe-Noire	576
CONGO (DEM. REP.)	
Kinshasa	1,655
Lubumbashi	851
Mbuji-Mayi	806
COSTA RICA	
San José	1,220
CROATIA	
Zagreb	931
CUBA	
Havana	2,241
CZECH REPUBLIC	
Prague	1,209
DENMARK	
Copenhagen	1,362
DOMINICAN REPUBLIC	
Santo Domingo	2,135
Santiago	691
ECUADOR	
Guayaquil	1,973
Quito	1,487
EGYPT	
Cairo	9,900
Alexandria	3,431
El Gîza	2,144
Shubra el Kheima	834
EL SALVADOR	
San Salvador	1,522
ETHIOPIA	
Addis Ababa	2,112
FINLAND	
Helsinki	532
FRANCE	
Paris	9,319
Lyon	1,262
Marseille	1,087
Lille	959
Bordeaux	696
Toulouse	650
Nice	516
GEORGIA	
Tbilisi	1,300
GERMANY	
Berlin	3,470
Hamburg	1,706
Munich	1,240
Cologne	964
Frankfurt	651
Essen	616
Dortmund	600
Stuttgart	587
Düsseldorf	571
Bremen	549
Duisburg	535
Hanover	524
GHANA	
Accra	949
GREECE	
Athens	3,097
GUATEMALA	
Guatemala	1,167
GUINEA	
Conakry	1,508
HAITI	
Port-au-Prince	1,255
HONDURAS	
Tegucigalpa	813
HUNGARY	
Budapest	1,885
INDIA	
Bombay (Mumbai)	12,572
Calcutta (Kolkata)	10,916
Delhi	7,207
Madras (Chennai)	5,361
Hyderabad	4,280
Bangalore	4,087
Ahmadabad	3,298
Pune	2,485
Kanpur	2,111
Nagpur	1,661
Lucknow	1,642
Surat	1,517
Jaipur	1,514
Coimbatore	1,136
Vadodara	1,115
Indore	1,104
Patna	1,099
Madurai	1,094
Bhopal	1,064
Vishakhapatnam	1,052
Varanasi	1,026
Ludhiana	1,012
INDONESIA	
Jakarta	11,500
Surabaya	2,701
Bandung	2,368
Medan	1,910
Semarang	1,366
Palembang	1,352
Tangerang	1,198
Ujung Pandang	1,092
Bandar Lampung	832
Malang	763
Padang	721
Pakanbaru	558
Samarinda	536
Banjarmasin	535
Surakarta	516
IRAN	
Tehran	6,750
Mashhad	1,964
Esfahan	1,221
Tabriz	1,166
Shiraz	1,043
Ahvaz	828
Qom	780
Bakhtaran	666
Karaj	588
IRAQ	
Baghdad	3,841
Diyala	961
As Sulaymaniyah	952
Arbil	770
Al Mawsil	664
Kadhimain	521
IRELAND	
Dublin	952
ISRAEL	
Tel Aviv-Yafo	1,502
Jerusalem	591
ITALY	
Rome	2,775
Milan	1,369
Naples	1,067
Turin	962
Palermo	698
Genoa	678
IVORY COAST	
Abidjan	2,500
JAMAICA	
Kingston	644
JAPAN	
Tokyo–Yokohama	26,836
Osaka	10,601
Nagoya	2,152
Sapporo	1,757
Kyoto	1,464
Kobe	1,424
Fukuoka	1,285
Kawasaki	1,203
Hiroshima	1,109
Kitakyushu	1,020
Sendai	971
Chiba	857
Sakai	803
Kumamoto	650
Okayama	616
Sagamihara	571
Hamamatsu	562
Kagoshima	546
Funabashi	541
Higashiosaka	517
Hachioji	503
JORDAN	
Amman	1,300
Az-Zarqā	609
KAZAKSTAN	
Almaty	1,150
Qaraghandy	573
KENYA	
Nairobi	2,000
Mombasa	600
KOREA, NORTH	
Pyŏngyang	2,639
Hamhung	775
Chŏngjin	754
Chinnampo	691
Sinŭiju	500
KOREA, SOUTH	
Seoul	11,641
Pusan	3,814
Taegu	2,449
Inchon	2,308
Taejŏn	1,272
Kwangju	1,258
Ulsan	967
Sŏngnam	869
Puch'on	779
Suwŏn	756
Anyang	590
Chŏnju	563
Chŏngju	531
Ansan	510
P'ohang	509
KYRGYZSTAN	
Bishkek	584
LATVIA	
Riga	846
LEBANON	
Beirut	1,900
Tripoli	500
LIBYA	
Tripoli	1,083
LITHUANIA	
Vilnius	580
MACEDONIA	
Skopje	541
MADAGASCAR	
Antananarivo	1,053
MALAYSIA	
Kuala Lumpur	1,145
MALI	
Bamako	800
MAURITANIA	
Nouakchott	735
MEXICO	
Mexico City	15,048
Guadalajara	2,847
Monterrey	2,522
Puebla	1,055
León	872
Ciudad Juárez	798
Tijuana	743
Culiacán Rosales	602
Mexicali	602
Acapulco de Juárez	592
Mérida	557
Chihuahua	530
San Luis Potosí	526
Aguascalientés	506
MOLDOVA	
Chişinău	700
MONGOLIA	
Ulan Bator	627
MOROCCO	
Casablanca	3,079
Rabat-Salé	1,344
Fès	735
Marrakesh	621
MOZAMBIQUE	
Maputo	2,000
NEPAL	
Katmandu	535
NETHERLANDS	
Amsterdam	1,101
Rotterdam	1,076
The Hague	694
Utrecht	548
NEW ZEALAND	
Auckland	997
NICARAGUA	
Managua	864
NIGERIA	
Lagos	10,287
Ibadan	1,365
Ogbomosho	712
Kano	657
NORWAY	
Oslo	714
PAKISTAN	
Karachi	9,863
Lahore	5,085
Faisalabad	1,875
Peshawar	1,676
Gujranwala	1,663
Rawalpindi	1,290
Multan	1,257
Hyderabad	1,107
PARAGUAY	
Asunción	945
PERU	
Lima–Callao	6,601
Callao	638
Arequipa	620
Trujillo	509
PHILIPPINES	
Manila	9,280
Quezon City	1,989
Davao	1,191
Caloocan	1,023
Cebu	662
Zamboanga	511
POLAND	
Warsaw	1,638
Lódz	825
Kraków	745
Wroclaw	642
Poznań	581
PORTUGAL	
Lisbon	2,561
Oporto	1,174
ROMANIA	
Bucharest	2,060
RUSSIA	
Moscow	9,233
Petersburg	4,883
Nizhniy Novgorod	1,425
Novosibirsk	1,400
Yekaterinburg	1,300
Samara	1,200
Omsk	1,200
Chelyabinsk	1,100
Kazan	1,100
Ufa	1,100
Volgograd	1,003
Perm	1,000
Rostov	1,000
Voronezh	908
Saratov	895
Krasnoyarsk	869
Togliatti	689
Simbirsk	678
Izhevsk	654
Krasnodar	645
Vladivostok	632
Yaroslavl	629
Khabarovsk	618
Barnaul	596
Irkutsk	585
Novokuznetsk	572
Ryazan	536
Penza	534
Orenburg	532
Tula	532
Naberezhnyye-Chelny	526
Kemerovo	503
SAUDI ARABIA	
Riyadh	1,800
Jedda	1,500
Mecca	630
SENEGAL	
Dakar	1,571
SIERRA LEONE	
Freetown	505
SINGAPORE	
Singapore	3,104
SOMALIA	
Mogadishu	1,000
SOUTH AFRICA	
Cape Town	2,350
East Rand	1,379
Johannesburg	1,196
Durban	1,137
Pretoria	1,080
West Rand	870
Port Elizabeth	853
Vanderbijlpark–Vereeniging	774
Soweto	597
Sasolburg	540
SPAIN	
Madrid	3,029
Barcelona	1,614
Valencia	763
Sevilla	719
Zaragoza	607
Málaga	532
SRI LANKA	
Colombo	1,863
SUDAN	
Omdurman	1,267
Khartoum	925
Khartoum North	879
SWEDEN	
Stockholm	1,744
Göteborg	775
SWITZERLAND	
Zürich	1,175
Bern	942
SYRIA	
Aleppo	1,591
Damascus	1,549
Homs	644
TAIWAN	
Taipei	2,653
Kaohsiung	1,405
Taichung	817
Tainan	700
Panchiao	544
TAJIKISTAN	
Dushanbe	524
TANZANIA	
Dar-es-Salaam	1,361
THAILAND	
Bangkok	5,572
TOGO	
Lomé	590
TUNISIA	
Tunis	1,827
TURKEY	
Istanbul	7,490
Ankara	3,028
Izmir	2,333
Adana	1,472
Bursa	1,317
Konya	1,040
Gaziantep	930
Icel	908
Antalya	734
Diyarbakir	677
Kocaeli	661
Urfa	649
Kayseri	648
Manisa	641
Hatay	561
Samsun	557
Eskisehir	508
Balikesir	501
TURKMENISTAN	
Ashkhabad	536
UGANDA	
Kampala	773
UKRAINE	
Kiev	2,630
Kharkiv	1,555
Dnipropetrovsk	1,147
Donetsk	1,088
Odesa	1,046
Zaporizhzhya	887
Lviv	802
Kryvyy Rih	720
Mariupol	510
Mykolayiv	508
UNITED KINGDOM	
London	8,089
Birmingham	2,373
Manchester	2,353
Liverpool	852
Glasgow	832
Sheffield	661
Nottingham	649
Newcastle	617
Bristol	552
Leeds	529
UNITED STATES	
New York	16,329
Los Angeles	12,410
Chicago	7,668
Philadelphia	4,949
Washington, DC	4,466
Detroit	4,307
Houston	3,653
Atlanta	3,331
Boston	3,240
Dallas	2,898
Minneapolis–St Paul	2,688
San Diego	2,632
St Louis	2,536
Phoenix	2,473
Baltimore	2,458
Pittsburgh	2,402
Cleveland	2,222
San Francisco	2,182
Seattle	2,180
Tampa	2,157
Miami	2,025
Newark	1,934
Denver	1,796
Portland (Or.)	1,676
Kansas City (Mo.)	1,647
Cincinnati	1,581
San Jose	1,557
Norfolk	1,529
Indianapolis	1,462
Milwaukee	1,456
Sacramento	1,441
San Antonio	1,437
Columbus (Oh.)	1,423
New Orleans	1,309
Charlotte	1,260
Buffalo	1,189
Salt Lake City	1,178
Hartford	1,151
Oklahoma	1,007
Jacksonville (Fl.)	665
Omaha	663
Memphis	614
El Paso	579
Austin	514
Nashville	505
URUGUAY	
Montevideo	1,378
UZBEKISTAN	
Tashkent	2,107
VENEZUELA	
Caracas	2,784
Maracaibo	1,364
Valencia	1,032
Maracay	800
Barquisimeto	745
Ciudad Guayana	524
VIETNAM	
Ho Chi Minh City	4,322
Hanoi	3,056
Haiphong	783
YEMEN	
Sana	972
Aden	562
YUGOSLAVIA	
Belgrade	1,137
ZAMBIA	
Lusaka	982
ZIMBABWE	
Harare	1,189
Bulawayo	622

* SAR = Special Administrative Region of China

World Statistics: Climate

Rainfall and temperature figures are provided for more than 70 cities around the world. As climate is affected by altitude, the height of each city is shown in metres beneath its name. For each location, the top row of figures shows the total rainfall or snow in millimetres, and the bottom row the average temperature in degrees Celsius; the average annual temperature and total annual rainfall are at the end of the rows. The map opposite shows the city locations.

CITY	JAN.	FEB.	MAR.	APR.	MAY	JUNE	JULY	AUG.	SEPT.	OCT.	NOV.	DEC.	YEAR
EUROPE													
Athens, Greece	62	37	37	23	23	14	6	7	15	51	56	71	402
107 m	10	10	12	16	20	25	28	28	24	20	15	11	18
Berlin, Germany	46	40	33	42	49	65	73	69	48	49	46	43	603
55 m	–1	0	4	9	14	17	19	18	15	9	5	1	9
Istanbul, Turkey	109	92	72	46	38	34	34	30	58	81	103	119	816
14 m	5	6	7	11	16	20	23	23	20	16	12	8	14
Lisbon, Portugal	111	76	109	54	44	16	3	4	33	62	93	103	708
77 m	11	12	14	16	17	20	22	23	21	18	14	12	17
London, UK	54	40	37	37	46	45	57	59	49	57	64	48	593
5 m	4	5	7	9	12	16	18	17	15	11	8	5	11
Málaga, Spain	61	51	62	46	26	5	1	3	29	64	64	62	474
33 m	12	13	16	17	19	29	25	26	23	20	16	13	18
Moscow, Russia	39	38	36	37	53	58	88	71	58	45	47	54	624
156 m	–13	–10	–4	6	13	16	18	17	12	6	–1	–7	4
Odesa, Ukraine	57	62	30	21	34	34	42	37	37	13	35	71	473
64 m	–3	–1	2	9	15	20	22	22	18	12	9	1	10
Paris, France	56	46	35	42	57	54	59	64	55	50	51	50	619
75 m	3	4	8	11	15	18	20	19	17	12	7	4	12
Rome, Italy	71	62	57	51	46	37	15	21	63	99	129	93	744
17 m	8	9	11	14	18	22	25	25	22	17	13	10	16
Shannon, Ireland	94	67	56	53	61	57	77	79	86	86	96	117	929
2 m	5	5	7	9	12	14	16	16	14	11	8	6	10
Stockholm, Sweden	43	30	25	31	34	45	61	76	60	48	53	48	554
44 m	–3	–3	–1	5	10	15	18	17	12	7	3	0	7
ASIA													
Bahrain	8	18	13	8	<3	0	0	0	0	0	18	18	81
5 m	17	18	21	25	29	32	33	34	31	28	24	19	26
Bangkok, Thailand	8	20	36	58	198	160	160	175	305	206	66	5	1,397
2 m	26	28	29	30	29	29	28	28	28	28	26	25	28
Beirut, Lebanon	191	158	94	53	18	3	<3	<3	5	51	132	185	892
34 m	14	14	16	18	22	24	27	28	26	24	19	16	21
Bombay (Mumbai), India	3	3	3	<3	18	485	617	340	264	64	13	3	1,809
11 m	24	24	26	28	30	29	27	27	27	28	27	26	27
Calcutta, India	10	31	36	43	140	297	325	328	252	114	20	5	1,600
6 m	20	22	27	30	30	30	29	29	29	28	23	19	26
Colombo, Sri Lanka	89	69	147	231	371	224	135	109	160	348	315	147	2,365
7 m	26	26	27	28	28	27	27	27	27	27	26	26	27
Harbin, China	6	5	10	23	43	94	112	104	46	33	8	5	488
160 m	–18	–15	–5	6	13	19	22	21	14	4	–6	–16	3
ASIA (continued)													
Ho Chi Minh, Vietnam	15	3	13	43	221	330	315	269	335	269	114	56	1,984
9 m	26	27	29	30	29	28	28	28	27	27	27	26	28
Hong Kong, China	33	46	74	137	292	394	381	361	257	114	43	31	2,162
33 m	16	15	18	22	26	28	28	28	27	25	21	18	23
Jakarta, Indonesia	300	300	211	147	114	97	64	43	66	112	142	203	1,798
8 m	26	26	27	27	27	27	27	27	27	27	27	26	27
Kabul, Afghanistan	31	36	94	102	20	5	3	3	<3	15	20	10	338
1,815 m	–3	–1	6	13	18	22	25	24	20	14	7	3	12
Karachi, Pakistan	13	10	8	3	3	18	81	41	13	<3	3	5	196
4 m	19	20	24	28	30	31	30	29	28	28	24	20	26
Kazalinsk, Kazakstan	10	10	13	13	15	5	5	8	8	10	13	15	125
63 m	–12	–11	–3	6	18	23	25	23	16	8	–1	–7	7
New Delhi, India	23	18	13	8	13	74	180	172	117	10	3	10	640
218 m	14	17	23	28	33	34	31	30	29	26	20	15	25
Omsk, Russia	15	8	8	13	31	51	51	51	28	25	18	20	318
85 m	–22	–19	–12	–1	10	16	18	16	10	1	–11	–18	–1
Shanghai, China	48	58	84	94	94	180	147	142	130	71	51	36	1,135
7 m	4	5	9	14	20	24	28	28	23	19	12	7	16
Singapore	252	173	193	188	173	173	170	196	178	208	254	257	2,413
10 m	26	27	28	28	28	28	28	27	27	27	27	27	27
Tehran, Iran	46	38	46	36	13	3	3	3	3	8	20	31	246
1,220 m	2	5	9	16	21	26	30	29	25	18	12	6	17
Tokyo, Japan	48	74	107	135	147	165	142	152	234	208	97	56	1,565
6 m	3	4	7	13	17	21	25	26	23	17	11	6	14
Ulan Bator, Mongolia	<3	<3	3	5	10	28	76	51	23	5	5	3	208
1,325 m	–26	–21	–13	–1	6	14	16	14	8	–1	–13	–22	–3
Verkhoyansk, Russia	5	5	3	5	8	23	28	25	13	8	8	5	134
100 m	–50	–45	–32	–15	0	12	14	9	2	–15	–38	–48	–17
AFRICA													
Addis Ababa, Ethiopia	<3	3	25	135	213	201	206	239	102	28	<3	0	1,151
2,450 m	19	20	20	20	19	18	18	19	21	22	21	20	20
Antananarivo, Madag.	300	279	178	53	18	8	8	10	18	61	135	287	1,356
1,372 m	21	21	21	19	18	15	14	15	17	19	21	21	19
Cairo, Egypt	5	5	5	3	3	<3	0	0	<3	<3	3	5	28
116 m	13	15	18	21	25	28	28	28	26	24	20	15	22
Cape Town, S. Africa	15	8	18	48	79	84	89	66	43	31	18	10	508
17 m	21	21	20	17	14	13	12	13	14	16	18	19	17
Jo'burg, S. Africa	114	109	89	38	25	8	8	8	23	56	107	125	709
1,665 m	20	20	18	16	13	10	11	13	16	18	19	20	16

CITY	JAN.	FEB.	MAR.	APR.	MAY	JUNE	JULY	AUG.	SEPT.	OCT.	NOV.	DEC.	YEAR
AFRICA (continued)													
Khartoum, Sudan	<3	<3	<3	<3	3	8	53	71	18	5	<3	0	158
390 m	24	25	28	31	33	34	32	31	32	32	28	25	29
Kinshasa, Congo (D.R.)	135	145	196	196	158	8	3	3	31	119	221	142	1,354
325 m	26	26	27	27	26	24	23	24	25	26	26	26	25
Lagos, Nigeria	28	46	102	150	269	460	279	64	140	206	69	25	1,836
3 m	27	28	29	28	28	26	26	25	26	26	28	28	27
Lusaka, Zambia	231	191	142	18	3	<3	<3	0	<3	10	91	150	836
1,277 m	21	22	21	21	19	16	16	18	22	24	23	22	21
Monrovia, Liberia	31	56	97	216	516	973	996	373	744	772	236	130	5,138
23 m	26	26	27	27	26	25	24	25	25	25	26	26	26
Nairobi, Kenya	38	64	125	211	158	46	15	23	31	53	109	86	958
820 m	19	19	19	19	18	16	16	16	18	19	18	18	18
Timbuktu, Mali	<3	<3	3	<3	5	23	79	81	38	3	<3	<3	231
301 m	22	24	28	32	34	35	32	30	32	31	28	23	29
Tunis, Tunisia	64	51	41	36	18	8	3	8	33	51	48	61	419
66 m	10	11	13	16	19	23	26	27	25	20	16	11	18
Walvis Bay, Namibia	<3	5	8	3	3	<3	<3	3	<3	<3	<3	<3	23
7 m	19	19	19	18	17	16	15	14	14	15	17	18	18
AUSTRALIA, NEW ZEALAND AND ANTARCTICA													
Alice Springs, Aust.	43	33	28	10	15	13	8	8	8	18	31	38	252
579 m	29	28	25	20	15	12	12	14	18	23	26	28	21
Christchurch, N.Z.	56	43	48	48	66	66	69	48	46	43	48	56	638
10 m	16	16	14	12	9	6	6	7	9	12	14	16	11
Darwin, Australia	386	312	254	97	15	3	<3	3	13	51	119	239	1,491
30 m	29	29	29	29	28	26	25	26	28	29	30	29	28
Mawson, Antarctica	11	30	20	10	44	180	4	40	3	20	0	0	362
14 m	0	–5	–10	–14	–15	–16	–18	–18	–19	–13	–5	–1	–11
Perth, Australia	8	10	20	43	130	180	170	149	86	56	20	13	881
60 m	23	23	22	19	16	14	13	13	15	16	19	22	18
Sydney, Australia	89	102	127	135	127	117	117	76	73	71	73	73	1,181
42 m	22	22	21	18	15	13	12	13	15	18	19	21	17
NORTH AMERICA													
Anchorage, USA	20	18	15	10	13	18	41	66	66	56	25	23	371
40 m	–11	–8	–5	2	7	12	14	13	9	2	–5	–11	2
Chicago, USA	51	51	66	71	86	89	84	81	79	66	61	51	836
251 m	–4	–3	2	9	14	20	23	22	19	12	5	–1	10
Churchill, Canada	15	13	18	23	32	44	46	58	51	43	39	21	402
13 m	–28	–26	–20	–10	–2	6	12	11	5	–2	–12	–22	–7
Edmonton, Canada	25	19	19	22	43	77	89	78	39	17	16	25	466
676 m	–15	–10	–5	4	11	15	17	16	11	6	–4	–10	3
Honolulu, USA	104	66	79	48	25	18	23	28	36	48	64	104	643
12 m	23	18	19	20	22	24	25	26	26	24	22	19	22
Houston, USA	89	76	84	91	119	117	99	99	104	94	89	109	1,171
12 m	12	13	17	21	24	27	28	29	26	22	16	12	21

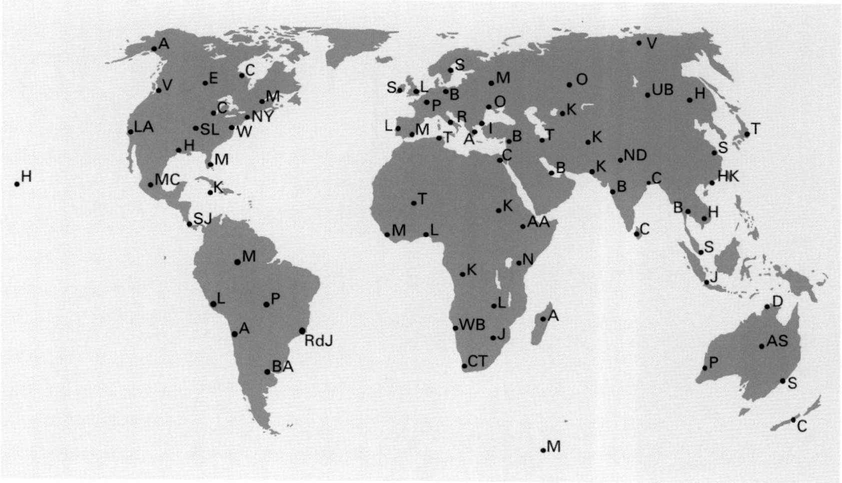

CITY	JAN.	FEB.	MAR.	APR.	MAY	JUNE	JULY	AUG.	SEPT.	OCT.	NOV.	DEC.	YEAR
NORTH AMERICA (continued)													
Kingston, Jamaica	23	15	23	31	102	89	38	91	99	180	74	36	800
34 m	25	25	25	26	26	28	28	28	27	27	26	26	26
Los Angeles, USA	79	76	71	25	10	3	<3	<3	5	15	31	66	381
95 m	13	14	14	16	17	19	21	22	21	18	16	14	17
Mexico City, Mexico	13	5	10	20	53	119	170	152	130	51	18	8	747
2,309 m	12	13	16	18	19	19	17	18	18	16	14	13	16
Miami, USA	71	53	64	81	173	178	155	160	203	234	71	51	1,516
8 m	20	20	22	23	25	27	28	28	27	25	22	21	24
Montréal, Canada	72	65	74	74	66	82	90	92	88	76	81	87	946
57 m	–10	–9	–3	–6	13	18	21	20	15	9	2	–7	6
New York City, USA	94	97	91	81	81	84	107	109	86	89	76	91	1,092
96 m	–1	–1	3	10	16	20	23	23	21	15	7	2	11
St Louis, USA	58	64	89	97	114	114	89	86	81	74	71	64	1,001
173 m	0	1	7	13	19	24	26	26	22	15	8	2	14
San José, Costa Rica	15	5	20	46	229	241	211	241	305	300	145	41	1,798
1,146 m	19	19	21	21	22	21	21	21	21	20	20	19	20
Vancouver, Canada	154	115	101	60	52	45	32	41	67	114	150	182	1,113
14 m	3	5	6	9	12	15	17	17	14	10	6	4	10
Washington, DC, USA	86	76	91	84	94	99	112	109	94	74	66	79	1,064
22 m	1	2	7	12	18	23	25	24	20	14	8	3	13
SOUTH AMERICA													
Antofagasta, Chile	0	0	0	<3	<3	3	5	3	<3	3	<3	0	13
94 m	21	21	20	18	16	15	14	14	15	16	18	19	17
Buenos Aires, Arg.	79	71	109	89	76	61	56	61	79	86	84	99	950
27 m	23	23	21	17	13	9	10	11	13	15	19	22	16
Lima, Peru	3	<3	<3	<3	5	5	8	8	8	3	3	<3	41
120 m	23	24	24	22	19	17	17	16	17	18	19	21	20
Manaus, Brazil	249	231	262	221	170	84	58	38	46	107	142	203	1,811
44 m	28	28	28	27	28	28	28	28	29	29	29	28	28
Paraná, Brazil	287	236	239	102	13	<3	3	5	28	127	231	310	1,582
260 m	23	23	23	23	23	21	21	22	24	24	24	23	23
Rio de Janeiro, Brazil	125	122	130	107	79	53	41	43	66	79	104	137	1,082
61 m	26	26	25	24	22	21	21	21	21	22	23	25	23

World Statistics: Physical Dimensions

Each topic list is divided into continents and within a continent the items are listed in order of size. The bottom part of many of the lists is selective in order to give examples from as many different countries as possible. The order of the continents is as in the atlas, Europe through to South America. The world top ten are shown in square brackets; in the case of mountains this has not been done because the world top 30 are all in Asia. The figures are rounded as appropriate.

WORLD, CONTINENTS, OCEANS

THE WORLD	km²	miles²	%
The World	509,450,000	196,672,000	–
Land	149,450,000	57,688,000	29.3
Water	360,000,000	138,984,000	70.7
Asia	44,500,000	17,177,000	29.8
Africa	30,302,000	11,697,000	20.3
North America	24,241,000	9,357,000	16.2
South America	17,793,000	6,868,000	11.9
Antarctica	14,100,000	5,443,000	9.4
Europe	9,957,000	3,843,000	6.7
Australia & Oceania	8,557,000	3,303,000	5.7
Pacific Ocean	179,679,000	69,356,000	49.9
Atlantic Ocean	92,373,000	35,657,000	25.7
Indian Ocean	73,917,000	28,532,000	20.5
Arctic Ocean	14,090,000	5,439,000	3.9

SEAS

PACIFIC	km²	miles²
South China Sea	2,974,600	1,148,500
Bering Sea	2,268,000	875,000
Sea of Okhotsk	1,528,000	590,000
East China & Yellow	1,249,000	482,000
Sea of Japan	1,008,000	389,000
Gulf of California	162,000	62,500
Bass Strait	75,000	29,000

ATLANTIC	km²	miles²
Caribbean Sea	2,766,000	1,068,000
Mediterranean Sea	2,516,000	971,000
Gulf of Mexico	1,543,000	596,000
Hudson Bay	1,232,000	476,000
North Sea	575,000	223,000
Black Sea	462,000	178,000
Baltic Sea	422,170	163,000
Gulf of St Lawrence	238,000	92,000

INDIAN	km²	miles²
Red Sea	438,000	169,000
The Gulf	239,000	92,000

MOUNTAINS

EUROPE		m	ft
Elbrus	Russia	5,642	18,510
Mont Blanc	France/Italy	4,807	15,771
Monte Rosa	Italy/Switzerland	4,634	15,203
Dom	Switzerland	4,545	14,911
Liskamm	Switzerland	4,527	14,852
Weisshorn	Switzerland	4,505	14,780
Taschorn	Switzerland	4,490	14,730
Matterhorn/Cervino	Italy/Switz.	4,478	14,691
Mont Maudit	France/Italy	4,465	14,649
Dent Blanche	Switzerland	4,356	14,291
Nadelhorn	Switzerland	4,327	14,196
Grandes Jorasses	France/Italy	4,208	13,806
Jungfrau	Switzerland	4,158	13,642
Barre des Ecrins	France	4,103	13,461
Gran Paradiso	Italy	4,061	13,323
Piz Bernina	Italy/Switzerland	4,049	13,284
Eiger	Switzerland	3,970	13,025
Monte Viso	Italy	3,841	12,602
Grossglockner	Austria	3,797	12,457
Wildspitze	Austria	3,772	12,382
Monte Disgrazia	Italy	3,678	12,066
Mulhacén	Spain	3,478	11,411
Pico de Aneto	Spain	3,404	11,168
Marmolada	Italy	3,342	10,964
Etna	Italy	3,340	10,958
Zugspitze	Germany	2,962	9,718
Musala	Bulgaria	2,925	9,596
Olympus	Greece	2,917	9,570
Triglav	Slovenia	2,863	9,393
Monte Cinto	France (Corsica)	2,710	8,891
Galdhöpiggen	Norway	2,468	8,100
Ben Nevis	UK	1,343	4,406

ASIA		m	ft
Everest	China/Nepal	8,850	29,035
K2 (Godwin Austen)	China/Kashmir	8,611	28,251
Kanchenjunga	India/Nepal	8,598	28,208
Lhotse	China/Nepal	8,516	27,939
Makalu	China/Nepal	8,481	27,824
Cho Oyu	China/Nepal	8,201	26,906
Dhaulagiri	Nepal	8,172	26,811
Manaslu	Nepal	8,156	26,758
Nanga Parbat	Kashmir	8,126	26,660
Annapurna	Nepal	8,078	26,502
Gasherbrum	China/Kashmir	8,068	26,469
Broad Peak	China/Kashmir	8,051	26,414
Xixabangma	China	8,012	26,286
Kangbachen	India/Nepal	7,902	25,925
Jannu	India/Nepal	7,902	25,925
Gayachung Kang	Nepal	7,897	25,909
Himalchuli	Nepal	7,893	25,896
Disteghil Sar	Kashmir	7,885	25,869
Nuptse	Nepal	7,879	25,849
Khunyang Chhish	Kashmir	7,852	25,761
Masherbrum	Kashmir	7,821	25,659
Nanda Devi	India	7,817	25,646
Rakaposhi	Kashmir	7,788	25,551
Batura	Kashmir	7,785	25,541
Namche Barwa	China	7,756	25,446
Kamet	India	7,756	25,446
Soltoro Kangri	Kashmir	7,742	25,400
Gurla Mandhata	China	7,728	25,354
Trivor	Pakistan	7,720	25,328
Kongur Shan	China	7,719	25,324
Tirich Mir	Pakistan	7,690	25,229
K'ula Shan	Bhutan/China	7,543	24,747
Pik Kommunizma	Tajikistan	7,495	24,590
Demavend	Iran	5,604	18,386
Ararat	Turkey	5,165	16,945
Gunong Kinabalu	Malaysia (Borneo)	4,101	13,455
Yu Shan	Taiwan	3,997	13,113
Fuji-San	Japan	3,776	12,388

AFRICA		m	ft
Kilimanjaro	Tanzania	5,895	19,340
Mt Kenya	Kenya	5,199	17,057
Ruwenzori (Margherita)	Uganda/Congo (D.R.)	5,109	16,762
Ras Dashan	Ethiopia	4,620	15,157
Meru	Tanzania	4,565	14,977
Karisimbi	Rwanda/Congo (D.R.)	4,507	14,787
Mt Elgon	Kenya/Uganda	4,321	14,176
Batu	Ethiopia	4,307	14,130
Guna	Ethiopia	4,231	13,882
Toubkal	Morocco	4,165	13,665
Irhil Mgoun	Morocco	4,071	13,356
Mt Cameroon	Cameroon	4,070	13,353
Amba Ferit	Ethiopia	3,875	13,042
Pico del Teide	Spain (Tenerife)	3,718	12,198
Thabana Ntlenyana	Lesotho	3,482	11,424
Emi Koussi	Chad	3,415	11,204
Mt aux Sources	Lesotho/S. Africa	3,282	10,768
Mt Piton	Réunion	3,069	10,069

OCEANIA		m	ft
Puncak Jaya	Indonesia	5,029	16,499
Puncak Trikora	Indonesia	4,750	15,584
Puncak Mandala	Indonesia	4,702	15,427
Mt Wilhelm	Papua NG	4,508	14,790
Mauna Kea	USA (Hawaii)	4,205	13,796
Mauna Loa	USA (Hawaii)	4,169	13,681
Mt Cook (Aoraki)	New Zealand	3,753	12,313
Mt Balbi	Solomon Is.	2,439	8,002
Orohena	Tahiti	2,241	7,352
Mt Kosciuszko	Australia	2,237	7,339

NORTH AMERICA		m	ft
Mt McKinley (Denali)	USA (Alaska)	6,194	20,321
Mt Logan	Canada	5,959	19,551
Citlaltepetl	Mexico	5,700	18,701
Mt St Elias	USA/Canada	5,489	18,008
Popocatepetl	Mexico	5,452	17,887
Mt Foraker	USA (Alaska)	5,304	17,401
Ixtaccihuatl	Mexico	5,286	17,342
Lucania	Canada	5,227	17,149
Mt Steele	Canada	5,073	16,644
Mt Bona	USA (Alaska)	5,005	16,420
Mt Blackburn	USA (Alaska)	4,996	16,391
Mt Sanford	USA (Alaska)	4,940	16,207
Mt Wood	Canada	4,848	15,905
Nevado de Toluca	Mexico	4,670	15,321
Mt Fairweather	USA (Alaska)	4,663	15,298
Mt Hunter	USA (Alaska)	4,442	14,573
Mt Whitney	USA	4,418	14,495
Mt Elbert	USA	4,399	14,432
Mt Harvard	USA	4,395	14,419
Mt Rainier	USA	4,392	14,409
Blanca Peak	USA	4,372	14,344
Longs Peak	USA	4,345	14,255
Tajumulco	Guatemala	4,220	13,845
Grand Teton	USA	4,197	13,770
Mt Waddington	Canada	3,994	13,104
Mt Robson	Canada	3,954	12,972
Chirripó Grande	Costa Rica	3,837	12,589
Pico Duarte	Dominican Rep.	3,175	10,417

SOUTH AMERICA		m	ft
Aconcagua	Argentina	6,960	22,834
Bonete	Argentina	6,872	22,546
Ojos del Salado	Argentina/Chile	6,863	22,516
Pissis	Argentina	6,779	22,241
Mercedario	Argentina/Chile	6,770	22,211
Huascaran	Peru	6,768	22,204
Llullaillaco	Argentina/Chile	6,723	22,057
Nudo de Cachi	Argentina	6,720	22,047
Yerupaja	Peru	6,632	21,758
N. de Tres Cruces	Argentina/Chile	6,620	21,719
Incahuasi	Argentina/Chile	6,601	21,654
Cerro Galan	Argentina	6,600	21,654
Tupungato	Argentina/Chile	6,570	21,555
Sajama	Bolivia	6,542	21,463
Illimani	Bolivia	6,485	21,276
Coropuna	Peru	6,425	21,079
Ausangate	Peru	6,384	20,945
Cerro del Toro	Argentina	6,380	20,932
Siula Grande	Peru	6,356	20,853
Chimborazo	Ecuador	6,267	20,561
Alpamayo	Peru	5,947	19,511
Cotapaxi	Ecuador	5,896	19,344
Pico Colon	Colombia	5,800	19,029
Pico Bolivar	Venezuela	5,007	16,427

ANTARCTICA		m	ft
Vinson Massif		4,897	16,066
Mt Kirkpatrick		4,528	14,855
Mt Markham		4,349	14,268

OCEAN DEPTHS

ATLANTIC OCEAN	m	ft	
Puerto Rico (Milwaukee) Deep	9,220	30,249	[7]
Cayman Trench	7,680	25,197	[10]
Gulf of Mexico	5,203	17,070	
Mediterranean Sea	5,121	16,801	
Black Sea	2,211	7,254	
North Sea	660	2,165	
Baltic Sea	463	1,519	
Hudson Bay	258	846	

INDIAN OCEAN	m	ft
Java Trench	7,450	24,442
Red Sea	2,635	8,454
Persian Gulf	73	239

PACIFIC OCEAN	m	ft	
Mariana Trench	11,022	36,161	[1]
Tonga Trench	10,882	35,702	[2]
Japan Trench	10,554	34,626	[3]
Kuril Trench	10,542	34,587	[4]
Mindanao Trench	10,497	34,439	[5]
Kermadec Trench	10,047	32,962	[6]

PACIFIC OCEAN (continued)	m	ft	
Peru–Chile Trench	8,050	26,410	[8]
Aleutian Trench	7,822	25,662	[9]

ARCTIC OCEAN	m	ft
Molloy Deep	5,608	18,399

LAND LOWS

		m	ft
Dead Sea	Asia	–411	–1,348
Lake Assal	Africa	–156	–512
Death Valley	N. America	–86	–282
Valdés Peninsula	S. America	–40	–131
Caspian Sea	Europe	–28	–92
Lake Eyre North	Oceania	–16	–52

RIVERS

EUROPE		km	miles	
Volga	Caspian Sea	3,700	2,300	
Danube	Black Sea	2,850	1,770	
Ural	Caspian Sea	2,535	1,575	
Dnepr (Dnipro)	Black Sea	2,285	1,420	
Kama	Volga	2,030	1,260	
Don	Black Sea	1,990	1,240	
Petchora	Arctic Ocean	1,790	1,110	
Oka	Volga	1,480	920	
Belaya	Kama	1,420	880	
Dnister (Dniester)	Black Sea	1,400	870	
Vyatka	Kama	1,370	850	
Rhine	North Sea	1,320	820	
N. Dvina	Arctic Ocean	1,290	800	
Desna	Dnepr (Dnipro)	1,190	740	
Elbe	North Sea	1,145	710	
Wisla	Baltic Sea	1,090	675	
Loire	Atlantic Ocean	1,020	635	

ASIA		km	miles	
Yangtze	Pacific Ocean	6,380	3,960	[3]
Yenisey–Angara	Arctic Ocean	5,550	3,445	[5]
Huang He	Pacific Ocean	5,464	3,395	[6]
Ob–Irtysh	Arctic Ocean	5,410	3,360	[7]
Mekong	Pacific Ocean	4,500	2,795	[9]
Amur	Pacific Ocean	4,400	2,730	[10]
Lena	Arctic Ocean	4,400	2,730	
Irtysh	Ob	4,250	2,640	
Yenisey	Arctic Ocean	4,090	2,540	
Ob	Arctic Ocean	3,680	2,285	
Indus	Indian Ocean	3,100	1,925	
Brahmaputra	Indian Ocean	2,900	1,800	
Syrdarya	Aral Sea	2,860	1,775	
Salween	Indian Ocean	2,800	1,740	
Euphrates	Indian Ocean	2,700	1,675	
Vilyuy	Lena	2,650	1,645	
Kolyma	Arctic Ocean	2,600	1,615	
Amudarya	Aral Sea	2,540	1,575	
Ural	Caspian Sea	2,535	1,575	
Ganges	Indian Ocean	2,510	1,560	
Si Kiang	Pacific Ocean	2,100	1,305	
Irrawaddy	Indian Ocean	2,010	1,250	
Tarim–Yarkand	Lop Nor	2,000	1,240	
Tigris	Indian Ocean	1,900	1,180	

AFRICA		km	miles	
Nile	Mediterranean	6,670	4,140	[1]
Congo	Atlantic Ocean	4,670	2,900	[8]
Niger	Atlantic Ocean	4,180	2,595	
Zambezi	Indian Ocean	3,540	2,200	
Oubangi/Uele	Congo (D.R.)	2,250	1,400	
Kasai	Congo (D.R.)	1,950	1,210	
Shaballe	Indian Ocean	1,930	1,200	
Orange	Atlantic Ocean	1,860	1,155	
Cubango	Okavango Swamps	1,800	1,120	
Limpopo	Indian Ocean	1,600	995	
Senegal	Atlantic Ocean	1,600	995	
Volta	Atlantic Ocean	1,500	930	

AUSTRALIA		km	miles
Murray–Darling	Indian Ocean	3,750	2,330
Darling	Murray	3,070	1,905
Murray	Indian Ocean	2,575	1,600
Murrumbidgee	Murray	1,690	1,050

NORTH AMERICA		km	miles	
Mississippi–Missouri	Gulf of Mexico	6,020	3,740	[4]
Mackenzie	Arctic Ocean	4,240	2,630	
Mississippi	Gulf of Mexico	3,780	2,350	
Missouri	Mississippi	3,780	2,350	
Yukon	Pacific Ocean	3,185	1,980	
Rio Grande	Gulf of Mexico	3,030	1,880	

NORTH AMERICA (continued)		km	miles
Arkansas	Mississippi	2,340	1,450
Colorado	Pacific Ocean	2,330	1,445
Red	Mississippi	2,040	1,270
Columbia	Pacific Ocean	1,950	1,210
Saskatchewan	Lake Winnipeg	1,940	1,205
Snake	Columbia	1,670	1,040
Churchill	Hudson Bay	1,600	990
Ohio	Mississippi	1,580	980
Brazos	Gulf of Mexico	1,400	870
St Lawrence	Atlantic Ocean	1,170	730

SOUTH AMERICA		km	miles	
Amazon	Atlantic Ocean	6,450	4,010	[2]
Paraná–Plate	Atlantic Ocean	4,500	2,800	
Purus	Amazon	3,350	2,080	
Madeira	Amazon	3,200	1,990	
São Francisco	Atlantic Ocean	2,900	1,800	
Paraná	Plate	2,800	1,740	
Tocantins	Atlantic Ocean	2,750	1,710	
Paraguay	Paraná	2,550	1,580	
Orinoco	Atlantic Ocean	2,500	1,550	
Pilcomayo	Paraná	2,500	1,550	
Araguaia	Tocantins	2,250	1,400	
Juruá	Amazon	2,000	1,240	
Xingu	Amazon	1,980	1,230	
Ucayali	Amazon	1,900	1,180	
Maranón	Amazon	1,600	990	
Uruguay	Plate	1,600	990	

LAKES

EUROPE		km^2	$miles^2$
Lake Ladoga	Russia	17,700	6,800
Lake Onega	Russia	9,700	3,700
Saimaa system	Finland	8,000	3,100
Vänern	Sweden	5,500	2,100
Rybinskoye Res.	Russia	4,700	1,800

ASIA		km^2	$miles^2$	
Caspian Sea	Asia	371,800	143,550	[1]
Lake Baykal	Russia	30,500	11,780	[8]
Aral Sea	Kazakstan/Uzbekistan	28,687	11,086	[10]
Tonlé Sap	Cambodia	20,000	7,700	
Lake Balqash	Kazakstan	18,500	7,100	
Lake Dongting	China	12,000	4,600	
Lake Ysyk	Kyrgyzstan	6,200	2,400	
Lake Orumiyeh	Iran	5,900	2,300	
Lake Koko	China	5,700	2,200	
Lake Poyang	China	5,000	1,900	
Lake Khanka	China/Russia	4,400	1,700	
Lake Van	Turkey	3,500	1,400	

AFRICA		km^2	$miles^2$	
Lake Victoria	E. Africa	68,000	26,000	[3]
Lake Tanganyika	C. Africa	33,000	13,000	[6]
Lake Malawi/Nyasa	E. Africa	29,600	11,430	[9]
Lake Chad	C. Africa	25,000	9,700	
Lake Turkana	Ethiopia/Kenya	8,500	3,300	
Lake Volta	Ghana	8,500	3,300	
Lake Bangweulu	Zambia	8,000	3,100	
Lake Rukwa	Tanzania	7,000	2,700	
Lake Mai-Ndombe	Congo (D.R.)	6,500	2,500	
Lake Kariba	Zambia/Zimbabwe	5,300	2,000	
Lake Albert	Uganda/Congo (D.R.)	5,300	2,000	
Lake Nasser	Egypt/Sudan	5,200	2,000	
Lake Mweru	Zambia/Congo (D.R.)	4,900	1,900	
Lake Cabora Bassa	Mozambique	4,500	1,700	
Lake Kyoga	Uganda	4,400	1,700	
Lake Tana	Ethiopia	3,630	1,400	

AUSTRALIA		km^2	$miles^2$
Lake Eyre	Australia	8,900	3,400
Lake Torrens	Australia	5,800	2,200
Lake Gairdner	Australia	4,800	1,900

NORTH AMERICA		km^2	$miles^2$	
Lake Superior	Canada/USA	82,350	31,800	[2]
Lake Huron	Canada/USA	59,600	23,010	[4]
Lake Michigan	USA	58,000	22,400	[5]
Great Bear Lake	Canada	31,800	12,280	[7]
Great Slave Lake	Canada	28,500	11,000	
Lake Erie	Canada/USA	25,700	9,900	
Lake Winnipeg	Canada	24,400	9,400	
Lake Ontario	Canada/USA	19,500	7,500	
Lake Nicaragua	Nicaragua	8,200	3,200	
Lake Athabasca	Canada	8,100	3,100	
Smallwood Reservoir	Canada	6,530	2,520	
Reindeer Lake	Canada	6,400	2,500	
Nettilling Lake	Canada	5,500	2,100	
Lake Winnipegosis	Canada	5,400	2,100	

SOUTH AMERICA		km^2	$miles^2$
Lake Titicaca	Bolivia/Peru	8,300	3,200
Lake Poopo	Bolivia	2,800	1,100

ISLANDS

EUROPE		km^2	$miles^2$	
Great Britain	UK	229,880	88,700	[8]
Iceland	Atlantic Ocean	103,000	39,800	
Ireland	Ireland/UK	84,400	32,600	
Novaya Zemlya (N.)	Russia	48,200	18,600	
W. Spitzbergen	Norway	39,000	15,100	
Novaya Zemlya (S.)	Russia	33,200	12,800	
Sicily	Italy	25,500	9,800	
Sardinia	Italy	24,000	9,300	
N.E. Spitzbergen	Norway	15,000	5,600	
Corsica	France	8,700	3,400	
Crete	Greece	8,350	3,200	
Zealand	Denmark	6,850	2,600	

ASIA		km^2	$miles^2$	
Borneo	S. E. Asia	744,360	287,400	[3]
Sumatra	Indonesia	473,600	182,860	[6]
Honshu	Japan	230,500	88,980	[7]
Sulawesi (Celebes)	Indonesia	189,000	73,000	
Java	Indonesia	126,700	48,900	
Luzon	Philippines	104,700	40,400	
Mindanao	Philippines	101,500	39,200	
Hokkaido	Japan	78,400	30,300	
Sakhalin	Russia	74,060	28,600	
Sri Lanka	Indian Ocean	65,600	25,300	
Taiwan	Pacific Ocean	36,000	13,900	
Kyushu	Japan	35,700	13,800	
Hainan	China	34,000	13,100	
Timor	Indonesia	33,600	13,000	
Shikoku	Japan	18,800	7,300	
Halmahera	Indonesia	18,000	6,900	
Ceram	Indonesia	17,150	6,600	
Sumbawa	Indonesia	15,450	6,000	
Flores	Indonesia	15,200	5,900	
Samar	Philippines	13,100	5,100	
Negros	Philippines	12,700	4,900	
Bangka	Indonesia	12,000	4,600	
Palawan	Philippines	12,000	4,600	
Panay	Philippines	11,500	4,400	
Sumba	Indonesia	11,100	4,300	
Mindoro	Philippines	9,750	3,800	

AFRICA		km^2	$miles^2$	
Madagascar	Indian Ocean	587,040	226,660	[4]
Socotra	Indian Ocean	3,600	1,400	
Réunion	Indian Ocean	2,500	965	
Tenerife	Atlantic Ocean	2,350	900	
Mauritius	Indian Ocean	1,865	720	

OCEANIA		km^2	$miles^2$	
New Guinea	Indon./Papua NG	821,030	317,000	[2]
New Zealand (S.)	Pacific Ocean	150,500	58,100	
New Zealand (N.)	Pacific Ocean	114,700	44,300	
Tasmania	Australia	67,800	26,200	
New Britain	Papua NG	37,800	14,600	
New Caledonia	Pacific Ocean	19,100	7,400	
Viti Levu	Fiji	10,500	4,100	
Hawaii	Pacific Ocean	10,450	4,000	
Bougainville	Papua NG	9,600	3,700	
Guadalcanal	Solomon Is.	6,500	2,500	
Vanua Levu	Fiji	5,550	2,100	
New Ireland	Papua NG	3,200	1,200	

NORTH AMERICA		km^2	$miles^2$	
Greenland	Atlantic Ocean	2,175,600	839,800	[1]
Baffin Is.	Canada	508,000	196,100	[5]
Victoria Is.	Canada	212,200	81,900	[9]
Ellesmere Is.	Canada	212,000	81,800	[10]
Cuba	Caribbean Sea	110,860	42,800	
Newfoundland	Canada	110,680	42,700	
Hispaniola	Dom. Rep./Haiti	76,200	29,400	
Banks Is.	Canada	67,000	25,900	
Devon Is.	Canada	54,500	21,000	
Melville Is.	Canada	42,400	16,400	
Vancouver Is.	Canada	32,150	12,400	
Somerset Is.	Canada	24,300	9,400	
Jamaica	Caribbean Sea	11,400	4,400	
Puerto Rico	Atlantic Ocean	8,900	3,400	
Cape Breton Is.	Canada	4,000	1,500	

SOUTH AMERICA		km^2	$miles^2$
Tierra del Fuego	Argentina/Chile	47,000	18,100
Falkland Is. (East)	Atlantic Ocean	6,800	2,600
South Georgia	Atlantic Ocean	4,200	1,600
Galapagos (Isabela)	Pacific Ocean	2,250	870

World: Regions in the News

YUGOSLAVIA
Population 10,761,000
(Serb 62.6%, Albanian 16.5%, Montenegrin 5%, Hungarian 3.3%, Muslim 3.2%)

Serbia Population: 5,799,800
(Serb 87.7%, excluding the provinces of Kosovo and Vojvodina)

Kosovo Population 2,084,4000
(Albanian 81.6%, Serb 9.9%)

Vojvodena Population: 1,980,800
(Serb 56.8%, Hungarian 16.9%)

Montenegro Population: 635,000
(Montenegrin 61.9%, Muslim 14.6%, Albanian 7%)

CROATIA
Population: 4,960,000
(Croat 78.1%, Serb 12.2%)

SLOVENIA
Population: 2,055,000
(Slovene 88%, Croat 3%, Serb 2%)

MACEDONIA (F. Y. R. O. M.)
Population: 2,157,000
(Macedonian 64%, Albanian 21.7%, Turkish 5%, Romanian 3%, Serb 2%)

BOSNIA-HERZEGOVINA
Population: 4,601,000
(Muslim 49%, Serb 31.2%, Croat 17.2%)

FORMER YUGOSLAVIA
AUSTRIA
HUNGARY
ROMANIA
SLOVENIA
CROATIA
BOSNIA-HERZEGOVINA
YUGOSLAVIA
SERBIA
Vojvodina
KOSOVO
MONTENEGRO
MACEDONIA
ALBANIA
BULGARIA
GREECE
ITALY
ADRIATIC SEA
Krajina
Maribor
Ljubljana
Zagreb
Rijeka
Osijek
Vukovar
Subotica
Novi Sad
Timişoara
Zrenjanin
Beograd (Belgrade)
Smederevo
Banja Luka
Bihać
Tuzla
Zenica
Srebrenica
Sarajevo
Goražde
Mostar
Split
Dubrovnik
Nikšić
Podgorica
Kragujevac
Kraljevo
Novi Pazar
Niš
Leskovac
Priština
Vranje
Dakovica
Prizren
Skopje
Tetovo
Kukës
Shkodër
Tirana
Durrës
Prilep
Bitola
Drava
Danube
Tisa
Morava
Ibar
16°E
18°E
20°E
14°E
46°N
44°N
42°N
0
100
200 km
International boundaries
Republic boundaries
Province boundaries
Capital cities
Dayton Peace Agreement Boundary
Muslim–Croat Federation
Bosnian Serb Republic

THREE NEW STATES IN INDIA
0
100
200 km
Chhattisgarh: Created 01/11/00
(formerly part of Madhya Pradesh)
Population: 17.6 million
Capital: Raipur
Uttaranchal: Created 09/11/00
(formerly part of Uttar Pradesh)
Population: 7.0 million
Provisional capital: Dehra Dun
Jharkhand: Created 15/11/00
(formerly part of Bihar)
Population: 26.9 million
Capital: Ranchi
HIMACHAL PRADESH
CHINA
UTTARANCHAL
Dehra Dun
Delhi
New Delhi
NEPAL
UTTAR PRADESH
Lucknow
Kanpur
Gwalior
Varanasi
Patna
BIHAR
INDIA
JHARKHAND
Ranchi
Jamshedpur
WEST BENGAL
MADHYA PRADESH
Jabalpur
CHHATTISGARH
Raipur
Nagpur
MAHARASHTRA
ORISSA
Cuttack
INDIAN OCEAN
ANDHRA PRADESH
Hyderabad
80°E
84°E
88°E
32°N
28°N
24°N
20°N

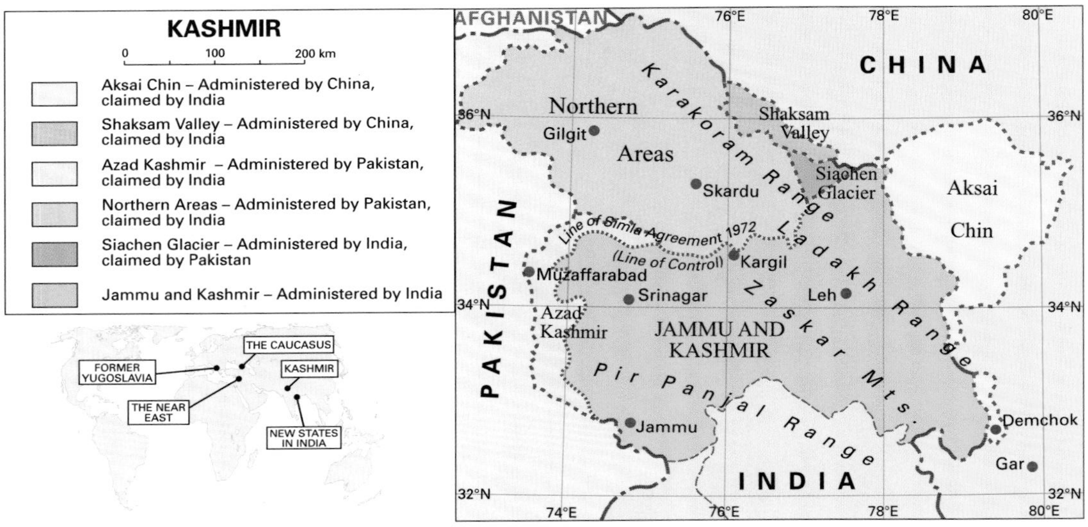

KASHMIR
0
100
200 km
Aksai Chin – Administered by China, claimed by India
Shaksam Valley – Administered by China, claimed by India
Azad Kashmir – Administered by Pakistan, claimed by India
Northern Areas – Administered by Pakistan, claimed by India
Siachen Glacier – Administered by India, claimed by Pakistan
Jammu and Kashmir – Administered by India
THE CAUCASUS
FORMER YUGOSLAVIA
KASHMIR
THE NEAR EAST
NEW STATES IN INDIA
AFGHANISTAN
CHINA
PAKISTAN
INDIA
Northern Areas
Gilgit
Shaksam Valley
Karakoram Range
Siachen Glacier
Skardu
Aksai Chin
Line of Simla Agreement 1972
(Line of Control)
Kargil
Ladakh Range
Muzaffarabad
Srinagar
Leh
Zaskar Mts.
Azad Kashmir
JAMMU AND KASHMIR
Pir Panjal Range
Jammu
Demchok
Gar
74°E
76°E
78°E
80°E
36°N
34°N
32°N

COUNTRIES AND REPUBLICS OF THE CAUCASUS REGION

RUSSIAN REPUBLICS

North Ossetia (Alania)
Population: 695,000
(Ossetian 53%, Russian 29%, Chechen 5.2%, Armenian 1.9%)

Chechenia Population: 1,308,000
(Chechen and Ingush 70.7%, Russian 23.1%, Armenian 1.2%)

Ingushetia (Split from Chechenia in June 1993) Population: 250,000

GEORGIA
Population: 5,777,000
(Georgian 70.1%, Armenian 8.1%, Russian 6.3%, Azerbaijani 5.7%, Ossetian 3%, Greek 2%, Abkhazian 2%)

Abkhazia Population: 537,500
(Georgian 45.7%, Abkhazian 17.8%, Armenian 14.6%, Russian 14.3%)

Ajaria Population: 382,000
(Georgian 82.8%, Russian 7.7%, Armenian 4%)

ARMENIA
Population: 3,968,000
(Armenian 93%, Azerbaijani 3%)

Nagorno-Karabakh
Population: 192,400 (Armenian 76.9%, Azerbaijani 21.5%)

AZERBAIJAN
Population: 8,324,000
(Azerbaijani 83%, Russian 6%, Armenian 6%, Lezgin 2%)

Naxçivan Population: 300,400

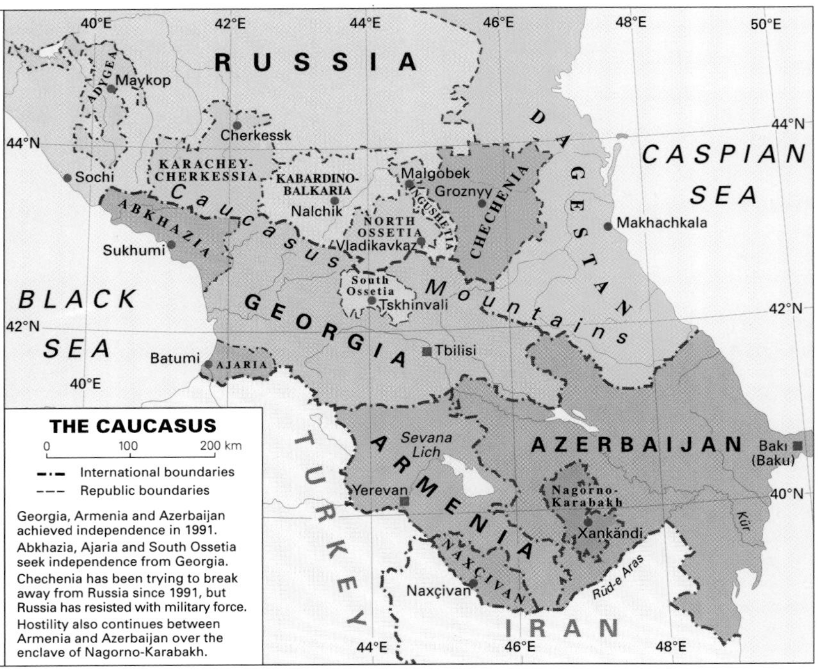

RUSSIA
ADYGEA
Maykop
Cherkessk
KARACHEY-CHERKESSIA
KABARDINO-BALKARIA
Nalchik
NORTH OSSETIA
Vladikavkaz
INGUSHETIA
Malgobek
Groznyy
CHECHENIA
DAGESTAN
Makhachkala
CASPIAN SEA
Sochi
ABKHAZIA
Sukhumi
Caucasus Mountains
South Ossetia
Tskhinvali
BLACK SEA
GEORGIA
Batumi
AJARIA
Tbilisi
TURKEY
Sevana Lich
Yerevan
ARMENIA
AZERBAIJAN
Baki (Baku)
Nagorno-Karabakh
Xankandi
NAXÇIVAN
Naxçivan
Kür
Rūd-e Aras
IRAN
40°E
42°E
44°E
46°E
48°E
50°E
44°N
42°N
40°N
THE CAUCASUS
0
100
200 km
International boundaries
Republic boundaries
Georgia, Armenia and Azerbaijan achieved independence in 1991. Abkhazia, Ajaria and South Ossetia seek independence from Georgia. Chechenia has been trying to break away from Russia since 1991, but Russia has resisted with military force. Hostility also continues between Armenia and Azerbaijan over the enclave of Nagorno-Karabakh.

THE NEAR EAST
0
25
50 km
1949 Armistice Line
1974 Cease-fire Line
Palestinian control
Joint Israeli/ Palestinian control
Efrata
Main Jewish settlements in the West Bank and Gaza Strip
Halhul
Main Palestinian Arab towns in the West Bank and Gaza Strip
Road corridor linking Gaza and West Bank
Saydā
Beqaa Valley
LEBANON
Lītani
Sūr (Tyre)
Qiryat Shemona
SYRIA
Golan Heights
Nahariyya
Zefat
Akko
Yam Kinneret
Hefa
Teverya
Nazerat
ISRAEL
Irbid
Jordan
Janin
Hadera
Tulkarm
Shavei Shomron
Tūbās
Netanya
Kedumim
Elon More
Qalqilya
Nabulus
Karne Shomron
Emanuel
Kfar Tapuah
Elkana
Ariel
Shiloh
Tel Aviv-Yafo
West Bank
As Salt
Rehovot
Ram Allah
Beit El
Al Birah
Arihā (Jericho)
'Ammān
Beit Horon
Ashdod
Jerusalem
Maale Adumim
Bayt Lahm (Bethlehem)
Ashqelon
Efrata
Tkoa
Halhul
Alei Sinai
Gaza
Nisanit
Al Khalil (Hebron)
Qiryat Arba
Dead Sea
Gaza Strip
Netzarin
Kfar Darom
Gadid
Khān Yūnis
Be'er Sheva
EGYPT
MEDITERRANEAN SEA
JORDAN
35°E
32°N
33°N

ISRAEL
Population: 5,321,000 (inc. East Jerusalem and Jewish settlers in the areas under Israeli administration. Jewish 82%, Arab Muslim 13.8%, Arab Christian 2.5%, Druze 1.7%)

West Bank
Population: 1,122,900 (Palestinian Arabs 97% [of whom Arab Muslim 85%, Jewish 7%, Christian 8%])

Gaza Strip
Population: 748,400 (Arab 98%)

JORDAN
Population: 5,558,000 (Arab 99% [of whom about 50% are Palestinian Arab])

LEBANON
Population: 3,327,000 (Arab 93% [of whom 83% are Lebanese Arab and 10% Palestinian Arab])

THE EARTH IN SPACE

The Universe 2

Star Charts and Constellations 4

The Solar System 8

The Earth: Time and Motion 10

The Earth from Space 12

The Dynamic Earth 14

Earthquakes and Volcanoes 16

Forces of Nature 18

Oceans and Ice 20

The Earth's Atmosphere 22

Climate and Weather 24

Water and Land Use 26

The Natural World 28

The Human World 30

Languages and Religions 32

International Organizations 34

Agriculture 36

Energy and Minerals 38

World Economies 40

Trade and Commerce 42

Travel and Communications 44

The World Today 46

The Universe

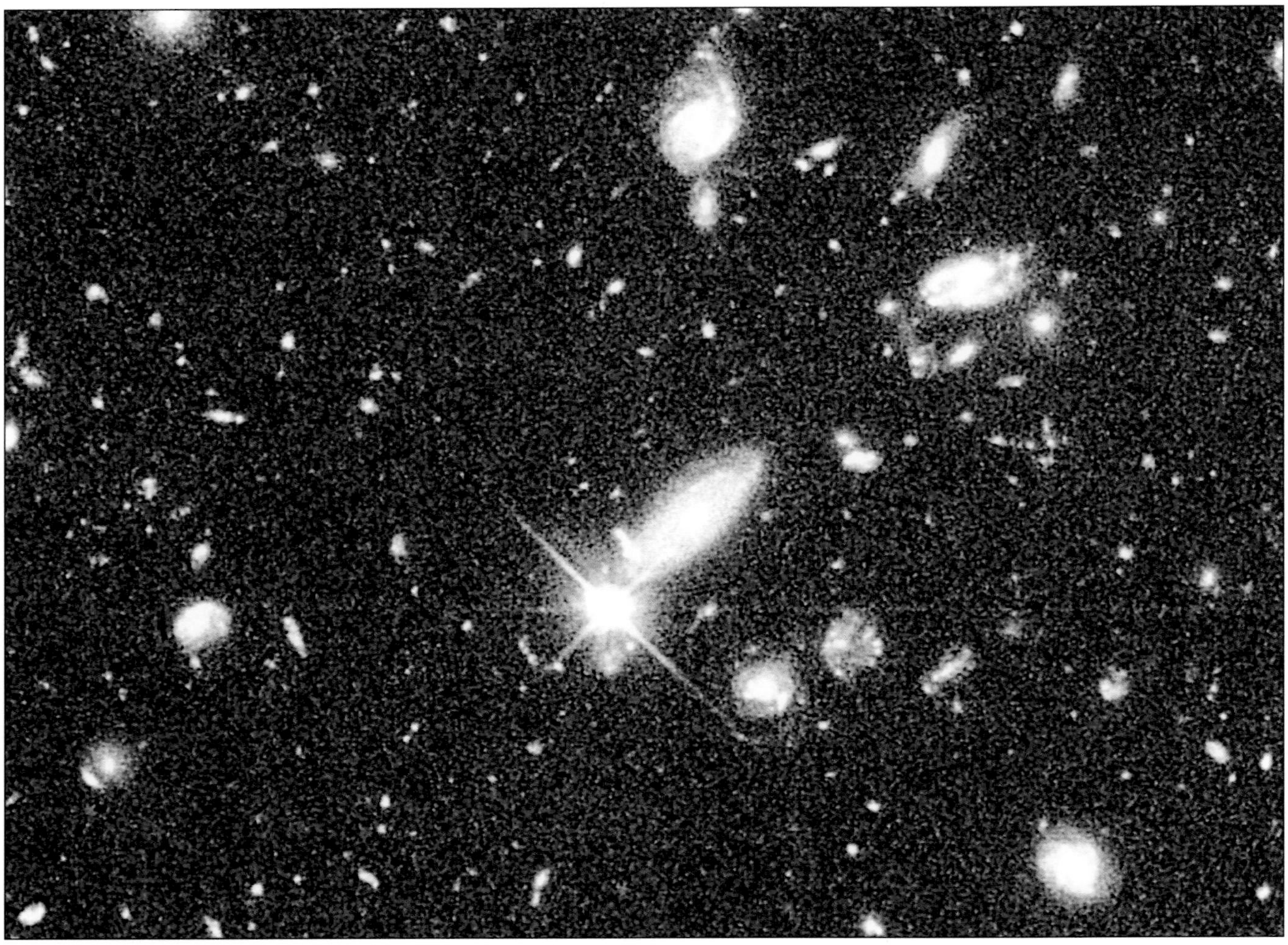

The depths of the Universe
This photograph shows some of the 1,500 or more galaxies that were recorded in the montage of photographs taken by the Hubble Space Telescope in 1995.

THE NEAREST STARS

The 20 nearest stars, excluding the Sun, with their distance from the Earth in light-years.*

Proxima Centauri	4.2
Alpha Centauri A	4.3
Alpha Centauri B	4.3
Barnard's Star	6.0
Wolf 359	7.8
Lalande 21185	8.3
Sirius A	8.7
Sirius B	8.7
UV Ceti A	8.7
UV Ceti B	8.7
Ross 154	9.4
Ross 248	10.3
Epsilon Eridani	10.7
Ross 128	10.9
61 Cygni A	11.1
61 Cygni B	11.1
Epsilon Indi	11.2
Groombridge 34 A	11.2
Groombridge 34 B	11.2
L789-6	11.2

** A light-year equals approximately 9,500 billion km [5,900 billion miles].*

Just before Christmas 1995, the Hubble Space Telescope, which is in orbit about 580 km [360 miles] above the Earth, focused on a tiny area in distant space. Over a ten-day period, photographs taken by the telescope revealed unknown galaxies billions of times fainter than the human eye can see.

Because the light from these distant objects has taken so long to reach us, the photographs transmitted from the telescope and released to the media were the deepest look into space that astronomers have ever seen. The features they revealed were in existence when the Universe was less than a billion years old.

The Hubble Space Telescope is operated by the Space Telescope Science Institute in America and was launched in April 1990. The photographs it took of the Hubble Deep Field have been described by NASA as the biggest advance in astronomy since the work of the Italian scientist Galileo in the early 17th century. US scientists described these astonishing photographs as 'postcards from the edge of space and time'.

The Big Bang

According to research published in 2001, the Universe was created, and 'time' began, about 12,500 million (or 12.5 billion) years ago, though earlier estimates have ranged from 8 to 24 billion years. Following a colossal explosion, called the 'Big Bang', the Universe expanded in the first millionth of a second of its existence

The End of the Universe
The diagram shows two theories concerning the fate of the Universe. One theory, top, suggests that the Universe will expand indefinitely, moving into an immense dark graveyard. Another theory, bottom, suggests that the galaxies will fall back until everything is again concentrated in one point in a so-called 'Big Crunch'. This might then be followed by a new 'Big Bang'.

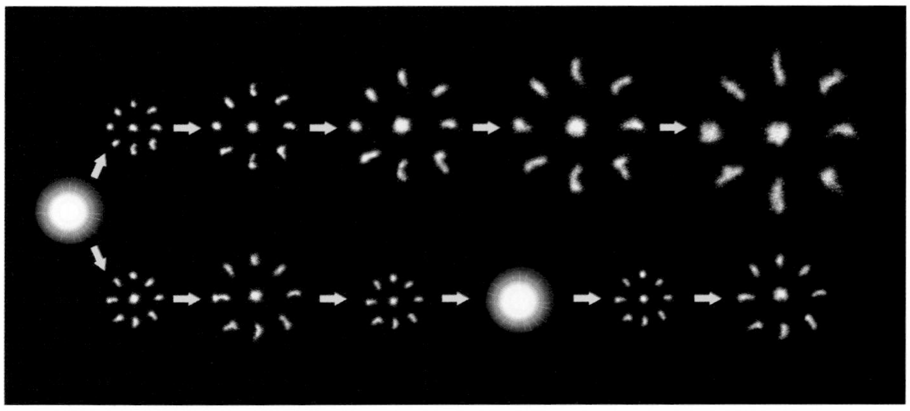

from a dimensionless point of infinite mass and density into a fireball about 30 billion km [19 million miles] across. The Universe has been expanding ever since, as demonstrated in the 1920s by Edwin Hubble, the American astronomer after whom the Hubble Space Telescope was named.

The temperature at the end of the first second was perhaps 10 billion degrees – far too hot for composite atomic nuclei to exist. As a result, the fireball consisted mainly of radiation mixed with microscopic particles of matter. Almost a million years passed before the Universe was cool enough for atoms to form.

The Home Galaxy
This schematic plan shows that our Solar System is located in one of the spiral arms of the Milky Way galaxy, a little less than 30,000 light-years from its centre. The centre of the Milky Way galaxy is not visible from Earth. Instead, it is masked by light-absorbing clouds of interstellar dust.

A few billion years later, atoms in regions where matter was relatively dense began, under the influence of gravity, to move together to form proto-galaxies – masses of gas separated by empty space. The proto-galaxies were dark, because the Universe had cooled. But a few billion years later, stars began to form within the proto-galaxies as particles were drawn together. The internal pressure produced as matter condensed created the high temperatures required to cause nuclear fusion. Stars were born and later destroyed. Each generation of stars fed on the debris of extinct ones. Each generation produced larger atoms, increasing the number of different chemical elements.

The Galaxies

At least a billion galaxies are scattered through the Universe, though the discoveries made by the Hubble Space Telescope suggest that there may be far more than once thought, and some estimates are as high as 100 billion. The largest galaxies contain trillions of stars, while small ones contain less than a billion.

Galaxies tend to occur in groups or clusters, while some clusters appear to be grouped in vast superclusters. Our Local Cluster includes the spiral Milky Way galaxy, whose diameter is about 100,000 light-years; one light-year, the distance that light travels in one year, measures about 9,500 billion km [5,900 billion miles]. The Milky Way is a huge galaxy, shaped like a disk with a bulge at the centre. It is larger, brighter and more massive than many other known galaxies. It contains about 100 billion stars which rotate around the centre of the galaxy in the same direction as the Sun does.

One medium-sized star in the Milky Way galaxy is the Sun. After its formation, about 5 billion years ago, there was enough leftover matter around it to create the planets, asteroids, moons and other bodies that together form our Solar System. The Solar System rotates around the centre of the Milky Way galaxy approximately every 225 million years.

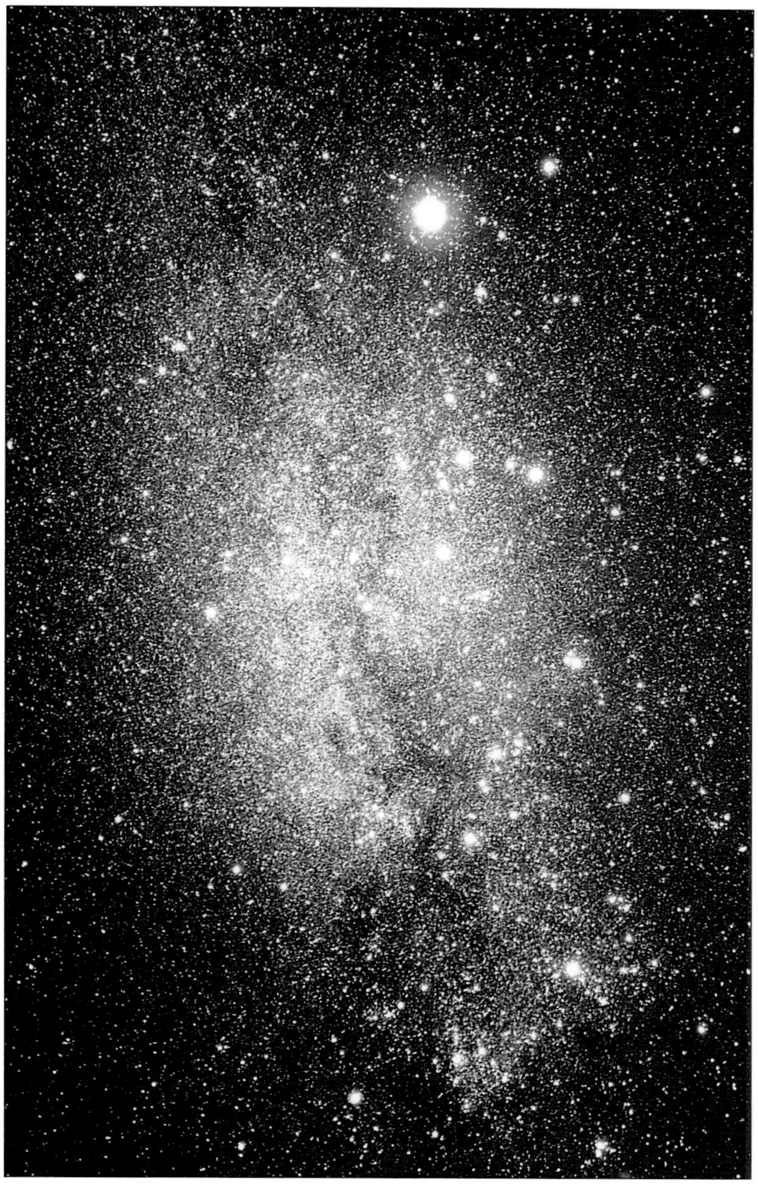

The Milky Way
This section of the Milky Way is dominated by Sirius, the Dog Star, top centre, in the constellation of Canis Major. Sirius is the brightest star in the sky.

Recent discoveries have revealed that other stars similar to our Sun have planets orbiting around them, while evidence from the Hubble Space Telescope suggests that the raw materials from which planets are formed is common in dusty disks around many stars. This provokes one of the most intriguing of all the questions that has ever faced humanity. If there are other planets in the Universe, then do living organisms exist elsewhere?

Before the time of Galileo, people thought that the Earth lay at the centre of the Universe. But we now know that our Solar System and even the Milky Way galaxy are tiny specks in the Universe as a whole. Perhaps our planet is also not unique in being the only one to support intelligent life.

Star Charts and Constellations

The Plough
The Plough, or Big Dipper, above glowing yellow clouds lit by city lights. It is part of a larger group called Ursa Major one of the best-known constellations of the northern hemisphere. The two bright stars to the lower right of the photograph (Merak and Dubhe) are known as the Pointers because they show the way to the Pole Star.

THE BRIGHTEST STARS

The 15 brightest stars visible from northern Europe. Magnitudes are given to the nearest tenth.

Sirius	−1.5
Arcturus	0.0
Vega	0.0
Capella	0.1
Rigel	0.1
Procyon	0.4
Betelgeuse	0.4
Altair	0.8
Aldebaran	0.8
Antares	1.0
Spica	1.0
Pollux	1.1
Fomalhaut	1.2
Deneb	1.2
Regulus	1.3

On a clear night, under the best conditions and far away from the glare of city lights, a person in northern Europe can look up and see about 2,500 stars. In a town, however, light pollution can reduce visibility to 200 stars or less. Over the whole celestial sphere it is possible to see about 8,500 stars with the naked eye and it is only when you look through a telescope that you begin to realize that the number of stars is countless.

Small and Large Stars

Stars come in several sizes. Some, called neutron stars, are compact, with the same mass as the Sun but with diameters of only about 20 km [12 miles]. Larger than neutron stars are the small white dwarfs. Our Sun is a medium-sized star, but many visible stars in the night sky are giants with diameters between 10 and 100 times that of the Sun, or supergiants with diameters over 100 times that of the Sun.

Two bright stars in the constellation Orion are Betelgeuse (also known as Alpha Orionis) and Rigel (or Beta Orionis). Betelgeuse is an orange-red supergiant, whose diameter is about 400 times that of the Sun. Rigel is also a supergiant. Its diameter is about 50 times that of the Sun, but its luminosity is estimated to be over 100,000 times that of the Sun.

The stars we see in the night sky all belong to our home galaxy, the Milky Way. This name is also used for the faint, silvery band that arches across the sky. This band, a slice through our

THE CONSTELLATIONS

The constellations and their English names. Constellations visible from both hemispheres are listed.

Andromeda	Andromeda	Delphinus	Dolphin	Perseus	Perseus
Antlia	Air Pump	Dorado	Swordfish	Phoenix	Phoenix
Apus	Bird of Paradise	Draco	Dragon	Pictor	Easel
Aquarius	Water Carrier	Equuleus	Little Horse	Pisces	Fishes
Aquila	Eagle	Eridanus	River Eridanus	Piscis Austrinus	Southern Fish
Ara	Altar	Fornax	Furnace	Puppis	Ship's Stern
Aries	Ram	Gemini	Twins	Pyxis	Mariner's Compass
Auriga	Charioteer	Grus	Crane	Reticulum	Net
Boötes	Herdsman	Hercules	Hercules	Sagitta	Arrow
Caelum	Chisel	Horologium	Clock	Sagittarius	Archer
Camelopardalis	Giraffe	Hydra	Water Snake	Scorpius	Scorpion
Cancer	Crab	Hydrus	Sea Serpent	Sculptor	Sculptor
Canes Venatici	Hunting Dogs	Indus	Indian	Scutum	Shield
Canis Major	Great Dog	Lacerta	Lizard	Serpens*	Serpent
Canis Minor	Little Dog	Leo	Lion	Sextans	Sextant
Capricornus	Sea Goat	Leo Minor	Little Lion	Taurus	Bull
Carina	Ship's Keel	Lepus	Hare	Telescopium	Telescope
Cassiopeia	Cassiopeia	Libra	Scales	Triangulum	Triangle
Centaurus	Centaur	Lupus	Wolf	Triangulum Australe	Southern Triangle
Cepheus	Cepheus	Lynx	Lynx		
Cetus	Whale	Lyra	Lyre	Tucana	Toucan
Chamaeleon	Chameleon	Mensa	Table	Ursa Major	Great Bear
Circinus	Compasses	Microscopium	Microscope	Ursa Minor	Little Bear
Columba	Dove	Monoceros	Unicorn	Vela	Ship's Sails
Coma Berenices	Berenice's Hair	Musca	Fly	Virgo	Virgin
Corona Australis	Southern Crown	Norma	Level	Volans	Flying Fish
Corona Borealis	Northern Crown	Octans	Octant	Vulpecula	Fox
Corvus	Crow	Ophiuchus	Serpent Bearer		
Crater	Cup	Orion	Hunter		
Crux	Southern Cross	Pavo	Peacock		
Cygnus	Swan	Pegasus	Winged Horse		

** In two halves: Serpens Caput, the head, and Serpens Cauda, the tail.*

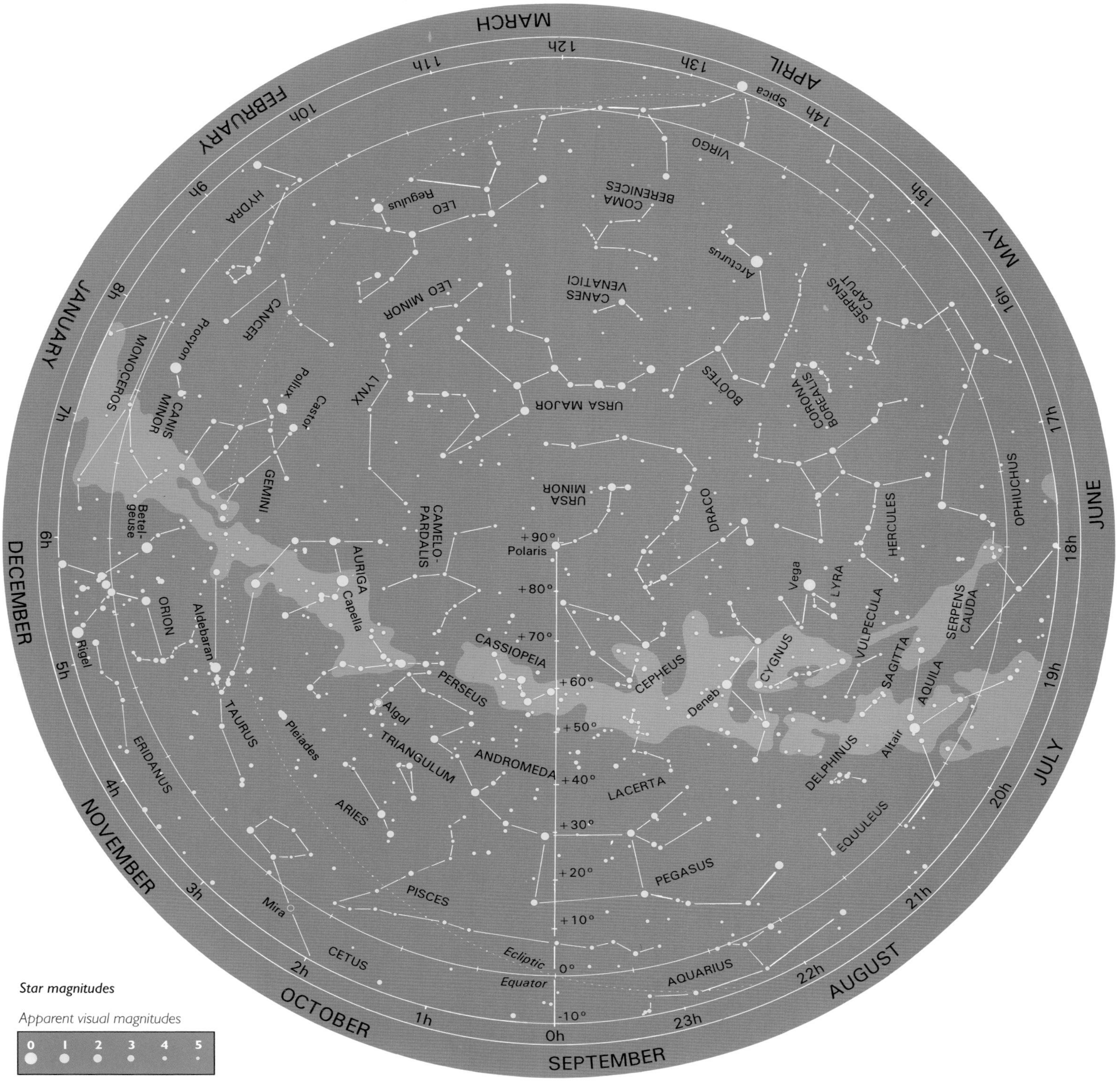

Star magnitudes

Apparent visual magnitudes

0 1 2 3 4 5

The Milky Way is shown in light blue on the above chart.

Star chart of the northern hemisphere

When you look into the sky, the stars seem to be on the inside of a huge dome. This gives astronomers a way of mapping them. This chart shows the sky as it would appear from the North Pole. To use the star chart above, an observer in the northern hemisphere should face south and turn the chart so that the current month appears at the bottom. The chart will then show the constellations on view at approximately 11pm Greenwich Mean Time. The map should be rotated clockwise 15° for each hour before 11pm and anticlockwise for each hour after 11pm.

galaxy, contains an enormous number of stars. The nucleus of the Milky Way galaxy cannot be seen from Earth. Lying in the direction of the constellation Sagittarius in the southern hemisphere, it is masked by clouds of dust.

The Brightness of Stars

Astronomers use a scale of magnitudes to measure the brightness of stars. The brightest visible to the naked eye were originally known as first-magnitude stars, ones not so bright were second-magnitude, down to the faintest visible, which were rated as sixth-magnitude. The brighter the star, the lower the magnitude. With the advent of telescopes and the development of accurate instruments for measuring brightnesses, the magnitude scale has been refined and extended. Very bright bodies such as Sirius, Venus and the Sun have negative magnitudes. The nearest star is Proxima Centauri, part of a multiple star system, which is 4.2 light-years away. Proxima Centauri is very faint and has a magnitude of 11.3. Alpha Centauri A, one of the two brighter members of the system, is the nearest visible star to Earth. It has a magnitude of 1.7.

These magnitudes are known as apparent magnitudes – measures of the brightnesses of the stars as they appear to us. These are the magnitudes shown on the charts on these pages. But the stars are at very different distances. The star Deneb, in the constellation Cygnus, for example, is over 1,200 light-years away. So astronomers also use absolute magnitudes – measures of how bright the stars really are. A star's absolute magnitude is the apparent magnitude it would have if it could be placed 32.6 light-years away. So Deneb, with an apparent magnitude of 1.2, has an absolute magnitude of –7.2.

The brightest star in the night sky is Sirius, the Dog Star, with a magnitude of –1.5. This medium-sized star is 8.64 light-years distant but it gives out about 20 times as much light as the Sun. After the Sun and the Moon, the brightest objects in the sky are the planets Venus, Mars and Jupiter. For example, Venus has a magnitude of up to –4. The planets have no light of their own however, and shine only because they reflect the Sun's rays. But whilst stars have fixed positions, the planets shift nightly in relation to the constellations, following a path called the Ecliptic (shown on the star charts). As they follow their orbits around the Sun, their distances from the Earth vary, and therefore so also do their magnitudes.

While atlas maps record the details of the Earth's surface, star charts are a guide to the heavens. An observer at the Equator can see the entire sky at some time during the year, but an observer at the poles can see only the stars in a single hemisphere. As a result, star charts of both hemispheres are produced. The northern hemisphere chart is centred on the North Celestial Pole, while the southern hemisphere chart is centred on the South Celestial Pole.

In the northern hemisphere, the North Pole is marked by the star Polaris, or North Star. Polaris lies within a degree of the point where an extension of the Earth's axis meets the sky. Polaris appears to be stationary and navigators throughout history have used it as a guide. Unfortunately, the South Pole has no convenient reference point.

Star charts of the two hemispheres are bounded by the Celestial Equator, an imaginary line in the sky directly above the terrestrial Equator. Astronomical co-ordinates, which give the location of stars, are normally stated in terms of right ascension (the equivalent of longitude) and declination (the equivalent of latitude). Because the stars appear to rotate around the Earth every 24 hours, right ascension is measured eastwards in hours and minutes. Declination is measured in degrees north or south of the Celestial Equator.

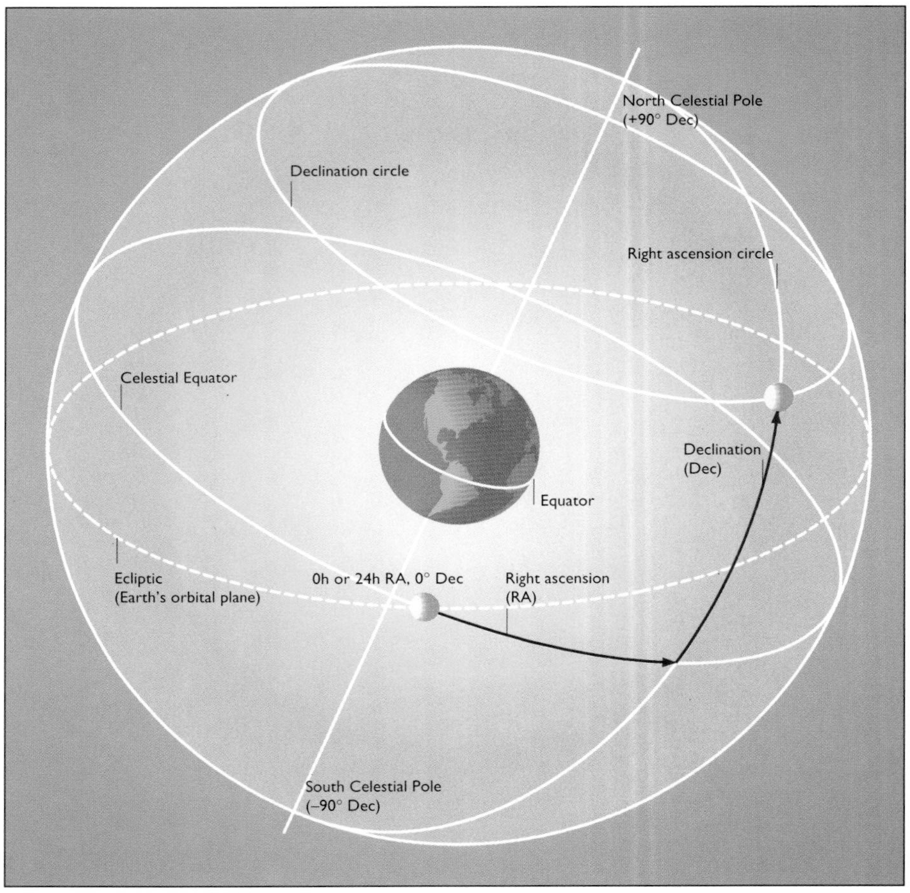

Celestial sphere
The diagram shows the imaginary surface on which astronomical positions are measured. The celestial sphere appears to rotate about the celestial poles, as though an extension of the Earth's own axis. The Earth's axis points towards the celestial poles.

The Southern Cross
The Southern Cross, or Crux, in the southern hemisphere, was classified as a constellation in the 17th century. It is as familiar to Australians and New Zealanders as the Plough (or Big Dipper) is to people in the northern hemisphere. The vertical axis of the Southern Cross points towards the South Celestial Pole.

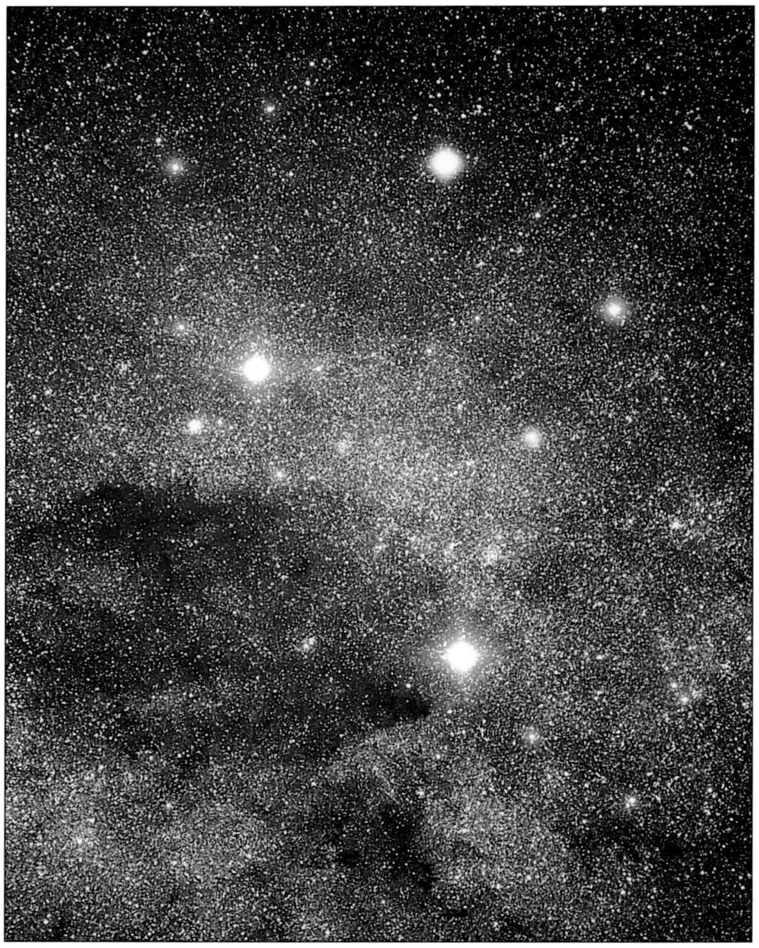

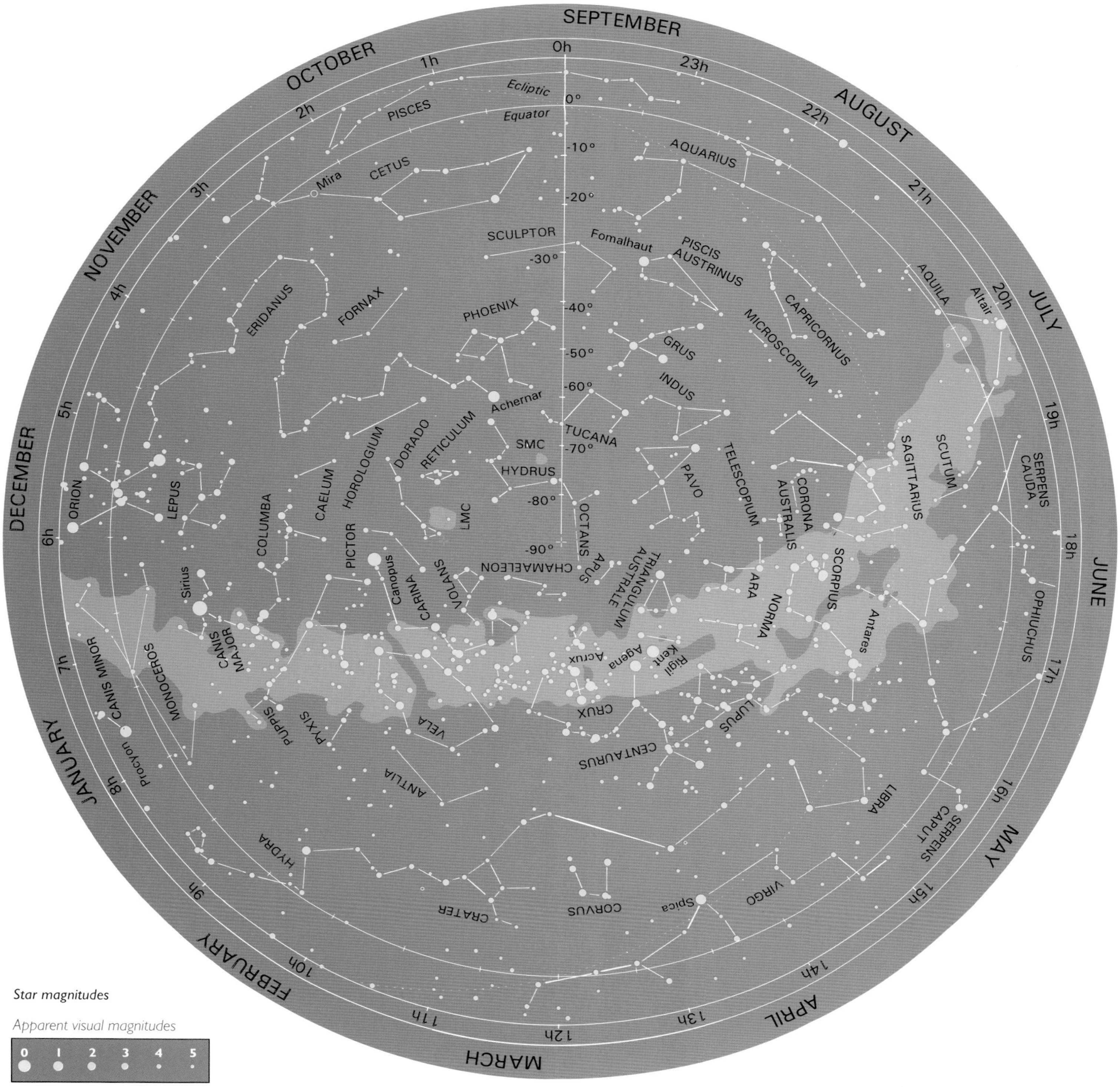

Star magnitudes

Apparent visual magnitudes

0 1 2 3 4 5

The Milky Way is shown in light blue on the above chart.

Star chart of the southern hemisphere

Many constellations in the southern hemisphere were named not by the ancients but by later astronomers. Some, including Antila (Air Pump) and Microscopium (Microscope), have modern names. The Large and Small Magellanic Clouds (LMC, SMC) are small 'satellite' galaxies of the Milky Way. To use the chart, an observer in the southern hemisphere should face north and turn the chart so that the current month appears at the bottom. The map will then show the constellations on view at approximately 11pm Greenwich Mean Time. The chart should be rotated clockwise 15° for each hour before 11pm and anticlockwise for each hour after 11pm.

Constellations

Every star is identifiable as a member of a constellation. The night sky contains 88 constellations, many of which were named by the ancient Greeks, Romans and other early peoples after animals and mythological characters, such as Orion and Perseus. More recently, astronomers invented names for constellations seen in the southern hemisphere, in areas not visible around the Mediterranean Sea.

Some groups of easily recognizable stars form parts of a constellation. For example, seven stars form the shape of the Plough or Big Dipper within the constellation Ursa Major. Such groups are called asterisms.

The stars in constellations lie in the same direction in space, but normally at vastly different distances. Hence, there is no real connection between them. The positions of stars seem fixed, but in fact the shapes of the constellations are changing slowly over very long periods of time. This is because the stars have their own 'proper motions', which because of the huge distances involved are imperceptible to the naked eye.

The Solar System

Although the origins of the Solar System are still a matter of debate, many scientists believe that it was formed from a cloud of gas and dust, the debris from some long-lost, exploded star. Around 5 billion years ago, material was drawn towards the hub of the rotating disk of gas and dust, where it was compressed to thermonuclear fusion temperatures. A new star, the Sun, was born, containing 99.8% of the mass of the Solar System. The remaining material was later drawn together to form the planets and the other bodies in the Solar System. Spacecraft, manned and unmanned, have greatly increased our knowledge of the Solar System since the start of the Space Age in 1957, when the Soviet Union launched the satellite Sputnik I.

The Planets

Mercury is the closest planet to the Sun and the fastest moving. Space probes have revealed that its surface is covered by craters, and looks much like our Moon. Mercury is a hostile place, with no significant atmosphere and temperatures ranging between 400°C [750°F] by day and –170°C [–275°F] by night. It seems unlikely that anyone will ever want to visit this planet.

Venus is much the same size as Earth, but it is the hottest of the planets, with temperatures reaching 475°C [885°F], even at night. The reason for this scorching heat is the atmosphere, which consists mainly of carbon dioxide, a gas that traps heat thus creating a greenhouse effect. The density of the atmosphere is about 90 times that of Earth and dense clouds permanently mask the surface. Active volcanic regions discharging sulphur dioxide may account for the haze of sulphuric acid droplets in the upper atmosphere.

From planet Earth, Venus is brighter than any other star or planet and is easy to spot. It is often the first object to be seen in the evening sky and the last to be seen in the morning sky. It can even be seen in daylight.

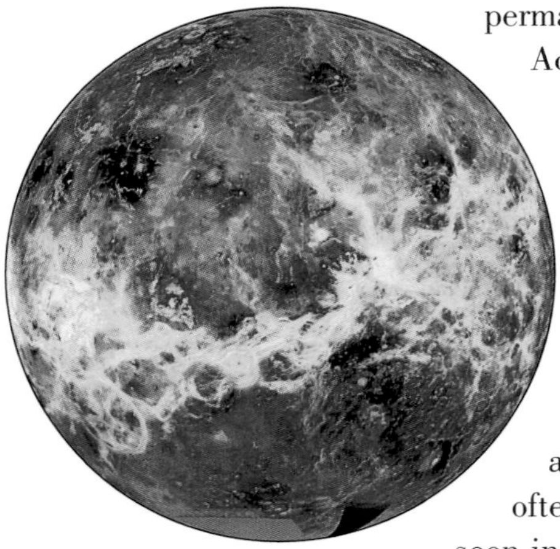

Earth, seen from space, looks blue (because of the oceans which cover more than 70% of the planet) and white (a result of clouds in the atmosphere). The atmosphere and water make Earth the only planet known to support life. The Earth's hard outer layers, including the crust and the top of the mantle, are divided into rigid plates. Forces inside the Earth move the plates, modifying the landscape and causing earthquakes and volcanic activity. Weathering and erosion also change the surface.

Mars has many features in common with Earth, including an atmosphere with clouds and polar caps that partly melt in summer. Scientists once considered that it was the most likely planet on which other life might exist, but the two Viking space probes that went there in the 1970s found only a barren rocky surface with no trace of water. But Mars did have flowing water at one time and there are many dry channels – but these are not the fictitious 'canals'. There are also giant, dormant volcanoes.

PLANETARY DATA

Planet	Mean distance from Sun (million km)	Mass (Earth=1)	Period of orbit (Earth yrs)	Period of rotation (Earth days)	Equatorial diameter (km)	Average density (water=1)	Surface gravity (Earth=1)	Number of known satellites
Sun	–	333,000	–	25.4	1,391,000	1.41	28	–
Mercury	57.9	0.055	0.2406	58.67	4,880	5.43	0.38	0
Venus	108.2	0.815	0.6152	243.0	12,104	5.20	0.90	0
Earth	149.6	1.0	1.00	1.00	12,756	5.52	1.00	1
Mars	227.9	0.107	1.88	1.028	6,792	3.91	0.38	2
Jupiter	778.3	317.8	11.86	0.411	142,800	1.33	2.69	28
Saturn	1,426.8	95.2	29.46	0.427	120,000	0.69	1.19	30
Uranus	2,869.4	14.53	84.01	0.748	51,118	1.29	0.79	21
Neptune	4,496.3	17.14	164.8	0.710	49,528	1.64	0.98	8
Pluto	5,900.1	0.002	2447.7	6.39	2,320	2.00	0.03	1

Asteroids are small, rocky bodies. Most of them orbit the Sun between Mars and Jupiter, but some small ones can approach the Earth. The largest is Ceres, 913 km [567 miles] in diameter. There may be around a million asteroids bigger than 1 km [0.6 miles].

Jupiter, the giant planet, lies beyond Mars and the asteroid belt. Its mass is almost three times as much as all the other planets combined and, because of its size, it shines more brightly than any other planet apart from Venus and, occasionally, Mars. The four largest moons of Jupiter were discovered by Galileo. Jupiter is made up mostly of hydrogen and helium, covered by a layer of clouds. Its Great Red Spot is a high-pressure storm. Jupiter made headline news when it was struck by fragments of Comet Shoemaker–Levy 9 in July 1994. This was the greatest collision ever seen by scientists between a planet and another heavenly body. The fragments of the comet that crashed into Jupiter created huge fireballs that caused scars on the planet that remained visible for months after the event.

Saturn is structurally similar to Jupiter but it is best known for its rings. The rings measure about 270,000 km [170,000 miles] across, yet they are no more than a few hundred metres thick. Seen from Earth, the rings seem divided into three main bands of varying brightness, but photographs sent back by the *Voyager* space probes in 1980 and 1981 showed that they are broken up into thousands of thin ringlets composed of ice particles ranging in size from a snowball to an iceberg. The origin of the rings is still a matter of debate.

Uranus was discovered in 1781 by William Herschel who first thought it was a comet. It is broadly similar to Jupiter and Saturn in composition, though its distance from the Sun makes its surface even colder. Uranus is circled by thin rings which were discovered in 1977. Unlike the rings of Saturn, the rings of Uranus are black, which explains why they cannot be seen from Earth.

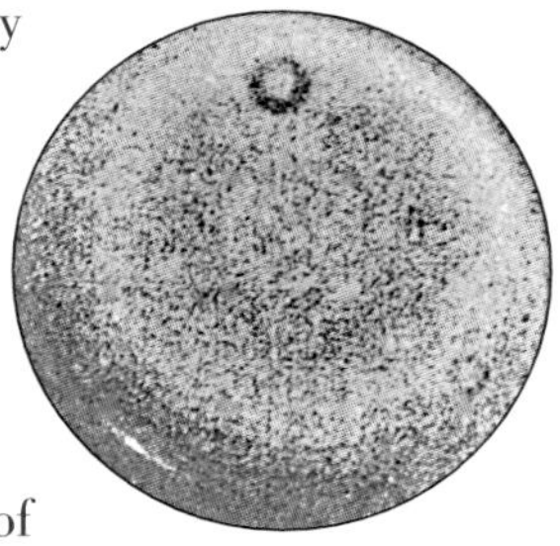

Neptune, named after the mythological sea god, was discovered in 1846 as the result of mathematical predictions made by astronomers to explain irregularities in the orbit of Uranus, its near twin. Little was known about this distant body until *Voyager 2* came close to it in 1989. Neptune has thin rings, like those of Uranus. Among its blue-green clouds is a prominent dark spot, which rotates anticlockwise every 18 hours or so.

Pluto is the smallest planet in the Solar System, even smaller than our Moon. The American astronomer Clyde Tombaugh discovered Pluto in 1930. Its orbit is odd and it sometimes comes closer to the Sun than Neptune. The nature of Pluto, a gloomy planet appropriately named after the Greek and Roman god of the underworld, is uncertain. At Pluto's distance and beyond are many small, asteroid-like bodies the first of which was found in 1992.

Comets are small icy bodies that orbit the Sun in highly elliptical orbits. When a comet swings in towards the Sun some of its ice evaporates, and the comet brightens and may become visible from Earth. The best known is Halley's Comet, which takes 76 years to orbit the Sun.

The Earth: Time and Motion

The Earth is constantly moving through space like a huge, self-sufficient spaceship. First, with the rest of the Solar System, it moves around the centre of the Milky Way galaxy. Second, it rotates around the Sun at a speed of more than 100,000 km/h [more than 60,000 mph], covering a distance of nearly 1,000 million km [600 million miles] in a little over 365 days. The Earth also spins on its axis, an imaginary line joining the North and South Poles, via the centre of the Earth, completing one turn in a day. The Earth's movements around the Sun determine our calendar, though accurate observations of the stars made by astronomers help to keep our clocks in step with the rotation of the Earth around the Sun.

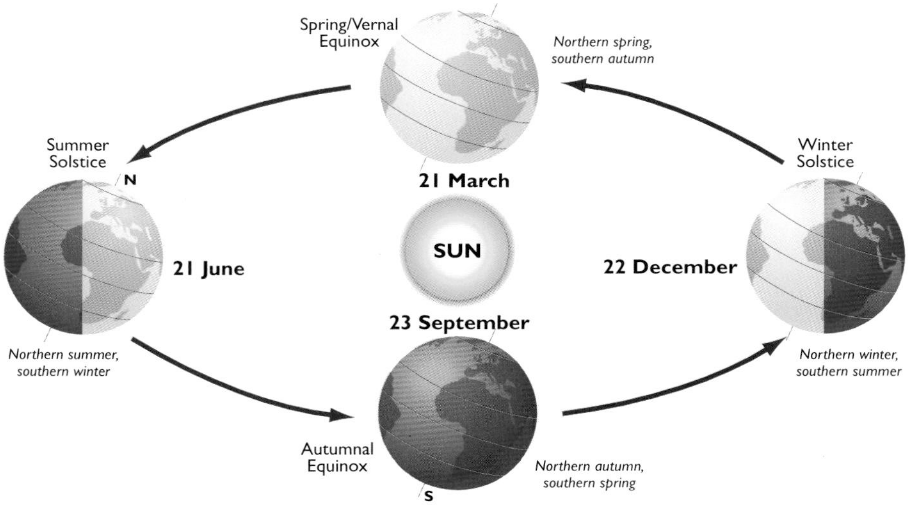
Spring/Vernal Equinox
Northern spring, southern autumn
Summer Solstice
N
21 March
Winter Solstice
SUN
21 June
22 December
23 September
Northern summer, southern winter
Northern winter, southern summer
Autumnal Equinox
Northern autumn, southern spring
S

The Seasons

The 23½° tilt of the Earth's axis remains constant as the Earth orbits around the Sun. As a result, first the northern and then the southern hemispheres lean towards the Sun. Annual variations in the amount of sunlight received in turn by each hemisphere are responsible for the four seasons experienced in the middle latitudes.

The Earth from the Moon

In 1969, Neil Armstrong and Edwin 'Buzz' Aldrin Junior were the first people to set foot on the Moon. This superb view of the Earth was taken by the crew of Apollo 11.

THE CHANGING YEAR

The Earth takes 365 days, 6 hours, 9 minutes and 9.54 seconds to complete one orbit around the Sun. We have a calendar year of 365 days, so allowance has to be made for the extra time over and above the 365 days. This is allowed for by introducing leap years of 366 days. Leap years are generally those, such as 1992 and 1996, which are divisible by four. Century years, however, are not leap years unless they are divisible by 400. Hence, 1700, 1800 and 1900 were not leap years, but the year 2000 was one. Leap years help to make the calendar conform with the solar year.

Because the Earth's axis is tilted by 23½°, the middle latitudes enjoy four distinct seasons. On 21 March, the vernal or spring equinox in the northern hemisphere, the Sun is directly overhead at the Equator and everywhere on Earth has about 12 hours of daylight and 12 hours of darkness. But as the Earth continues on its journey around the Sun, the northern hemisphere tilts more and more towards the Sun. Finally, on 21 June, the Sun is overhead at the Tropic of Cancer (latitude 23½° North). This is

Tides

The daily rises and falls of the ocean's waters are caused by the gravitational pull of the Moon and the Sun. The effect is greatest on the hemisphere facing the Moon, causing a 'tidal bulge'. The diagram below shows that the Sun, Moon and Earth are in line when the spring tides occur. This causes the greatest tidal ranges. On the other hand, the neap tides occur when the pull of the Moon and the Sun are opposed. Neap tides, when tidal ranges are at their lowest, occur near the Moon's first and third quarters.

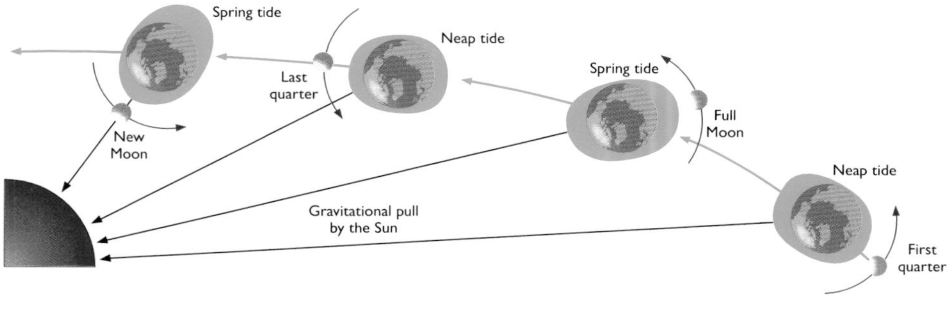
Spring tide
Neap tide
Last quarter
New Moon
Spring tide
Full Moon
Neap tide
Gravitational pull by the Sun
First quarter

SUN DATA	
DIAMETER	1.391×10^6 km
VOLUME	1.412×10^{18} km^3
VOLUME (EARTH=1)	1.303×10^6
MASS	1.989×10^{30} kg
MASS (EARTH=1)	3.329×10^5
MEAN DENSITY (WATER=1)	1.409
ROTATION PERIOD	
AT EQUATOR	25.4 days
AT POLES	about 35 days
SURFACE GRAVITY (EARTH=1)	28
MAGNITUDE	
APPARENT	–26.9
ABSOLUTE	+4.71
TEMPERATURE	
AT SURFACE	5,400°C [5,700 K]
AT CORE	15×10^6 K

MOON DATA	
DIAMETER	3,476 km
MASS (EARTH=1)	0.0123
DENSITY (WATER=1)	3.34
MEAN DISTANCE FROM EARTH	384,402 km
MAXIMUM DISTANCE (APOGEE)	406,740 km
MINIMUM DISTANCE (PERIGEE)	356,410 km
SIDERIAL ROTATION AND REVOLUTION PERIOD	27.322 days
SYNODIC MONTH (NEW MOON TO NEW MOON)	29.531 days
SURFACE GRAVITY (EARTH=1)	0.165
MAXIMUM SURFACE TEMPERATURE	+130°C [403 K]
MINIMUM SURFACE TEMPERATURE	–158°C [115 K]

the summer solstice in the northern hemisphere.

The overhead Sun then moves south again until on 23 September, the autumn equinox in the northern hemisphere, the Sun is again overhead at the Equator. The overhead Sun then moves south until, on around 22 December, it is overhead at the Tropic of Capricorn. This is the winter solstice in the northern hemisphere, and the summer solstice in the southern, where the seasons are reversed.

At the poles, there are two seasons. During half of the year, one of the poles leans towards the Sun and has continuous sunlight. For the other six months, the pole leans away from the Sun and is in continuous darkness.

Regions around the Equator do not have marked seasons. Because the Sun is high in the sky throughout the year, it is always hot or warm. When people talk of seasons in the tropics, they are usually referring to other factors, such as rainy and dry periods.

Day, Night and Tides

As the Earth rotates on its axis every 24 hours, first one side of the planet and then the other faces the Sun and enjoys daylight, while the opposite side is in darkness.

The length of daylight varies throughout the year. The longest day in the northern hemisphere falls on the summer solstice, 21 June, while the longest day in the southern hemisphere is on 22 December. At 40° latitude, the length of daylight on the longest day is 14 hours, 30 minutes. At 60° latitude, daylight on that day lasts 18 hours, 30 minutes. On the shortest day, 22 December in the northern hemisphere and 21 June in the southern, daylight hours at 40° latitude total 9 hours and 9 minutes. At latitude 60°, daylight lasts only 5 hours, 30 minutes in the 24-hour period.

Tides are caused by the gravitational pull of the Moon and, to a lesser extent, the Sun on the waters in the world's oceans. Tides occur twice every 24 hours, 50 minutes – one complete orbit of the Moon around the Earth.

The highest tides, the spring tides, occur when the Earth, Moon and Sun are in a straight line, so that the gravitational pulls of the Moon and Sun are combined. The lowest, or neap, tides occur when the Moon, Earth and Sun form a right angle. The gravitational pull of the Moon is then opposed by the gravitational pull of the Sun. The greatest tidal ranges occur in the Bay of Fundy in North America. The greatest mean spring range is 14.5 m [47.5 ft].

The speed at which the Earth is spinning on its axis is gradually slowing down, because of the movement of tides. As a result, experts have calculated that, in about 200 million years, the day will be 25 hours long.

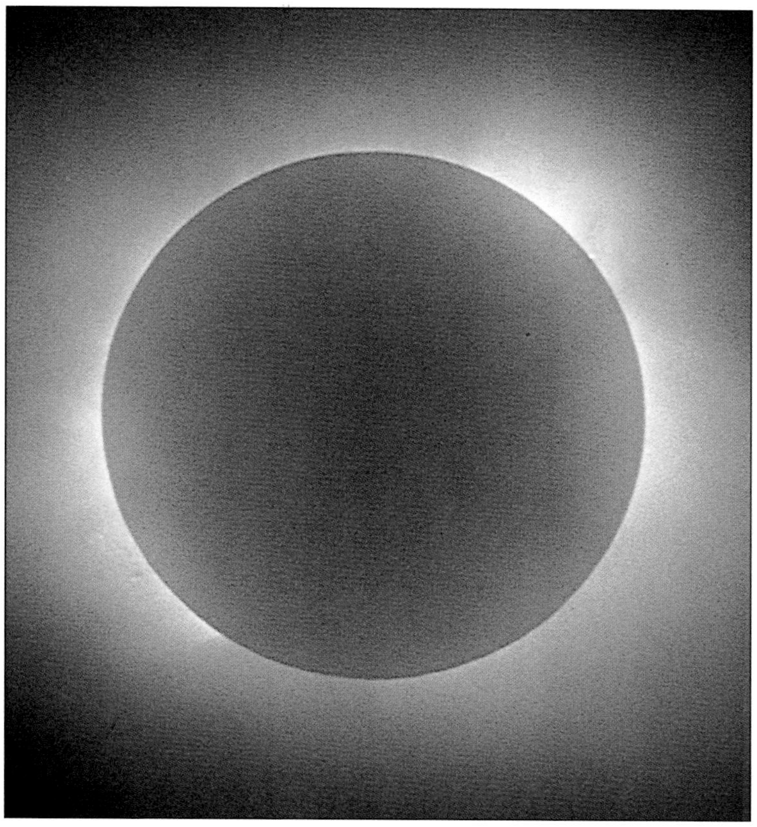

Total eclipse of the Sun

A total eclipse is caused when the Moon passes between the Sun and the Earth. With the Sun's bright disk completely obscured, the Sun's corona, or outer atmosphere, can be viewed.

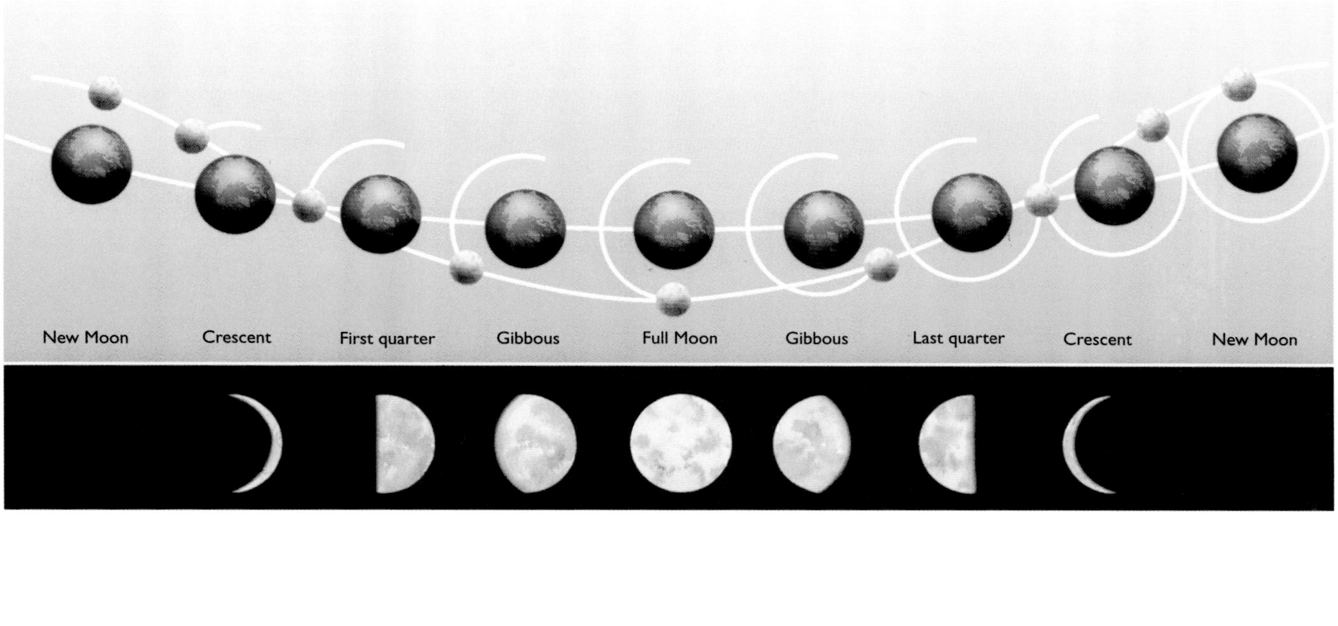
New Moon
Crescent
First quarter
Gibbous
Full Moon
Gibbous
Last quarter
Crescent
New Moon

Phases of the Moon

The Moon rotates more slowly than the Earth, making one complete turn on its axis in just over 27 days. This corresponds to its period of revolution around the Earth and, hence, the same hemisphere always faces us. The interval between one full Moon and the next (and also between new Moons) is about 29½ days, or one lunar month. The apparent changes in the appearance of the Moon are caused by its changing position in relation to Earth. Like the planets, the Moon produces no light of its own. It shines by reflecting the Sun's rays, varying from a slim crescent to a full circle and back again.

The Earth from Space

Any last doubts about whether the Earth was round or flat were finally resolved by the appearance of the first photographs of our planet taken at the start of the Space Age. Satellite images also confirmed that map- and globe-makers had correctly worked out the shapes of the continents and the oceans.

More importantly, images of our beautiful, blue, white and brown planet from space impressed on many people that the Earth and its resources are finite. They made people realize that if we allow our planet to be damaged by such factors as overpopulation, pollution and irresponsible over-use of resources, then its future and the survival of all the living things upon it may be threatened.

Views from Above

The first aerial photographs were taken from balloons in the mid-19th century and their importance in military reconnaissance was recognized as early as the 1860s during the American Civil War.

***Launch of the Space Shuttle* Atlantis**

Space Shuttles transport astronauts and equipment into orbit around the Earth. The American Space Shuttle Atlantis, *shown below, launched the Magellan probe, which undertook a radar mapping programme of the surface of Venus in the early 1990s.*

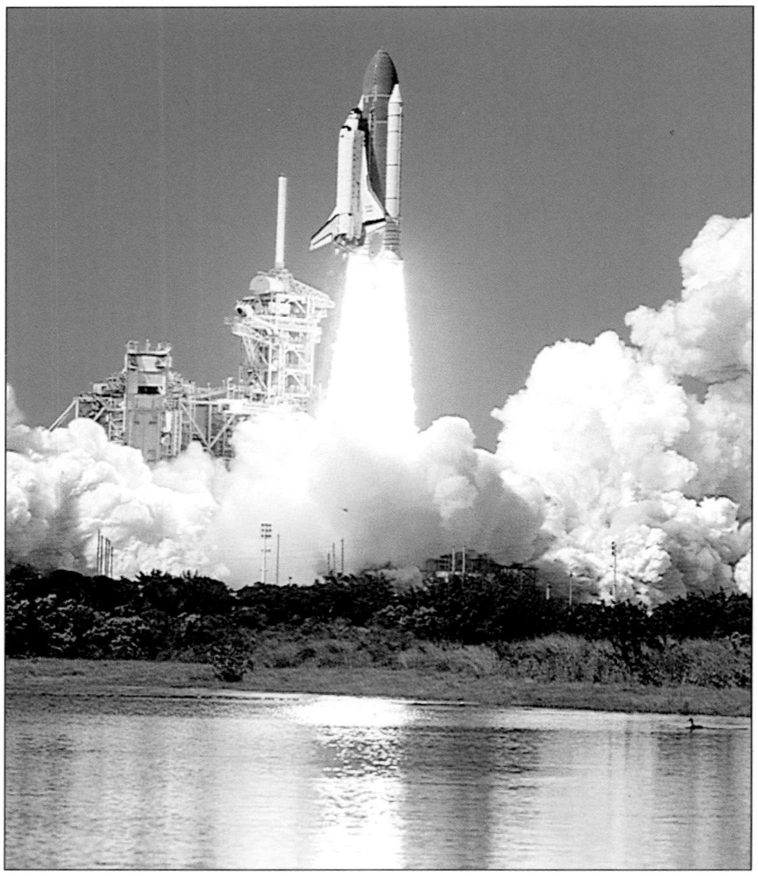

Since the end of World War II, photographs taken by aircraft have been widely used in map-making. The use of air photographs has greatly speeded up the laborious process of mapping land details and they have enabled cartographers to produce maps of the most remote parts of the world.

Aerial photographs have also proved useful because they reveal features that are not visible at ground level. For example, circles that appear on many air photographs do not correspond to visible features on the ground. Many of these mysterious shapes have turned out to be the sites of ancient settlements previously unknown to archaeologists.

Images from Space

Space probes equipped with cameras and a variety of remote sensing instruments have sent back images of distant planets and moons. From these images, detailed maps have been produced, rapidly expanding our knowledge of the Solar System.

Photographs from space are also proving invaluable in the study of the Earth. One of the best known uses of space imagery is the study of the atmosphere. Polar-orbiting weather satellites that circle the Earth, together with geostationary satellites, whose motion is synchronized with the Earth's rotation, now regularly transmit images showing the changing patterns of weather systems from above. Forecasters use these images to track the development and the paths taken by hurricanes, enabling them to issue storm warnings to endangered areas, saving lives and reducing damage to property.

Remote sensing devices are now monitoring changes in temperatures over the land and sea, while photographs indicate the melting of ice sheets. Such evidence is vital in the study of global warming. Other devices reveal polluted areas, patterns of vegetation growth, and areas suffering deforestation.

In recent years, remote sensing devices have been used to monitor the damage being done to the ozone layer in the stratosphere, which prevents most of the Sun's harmful ultraviolet radiation from reaching the surface. The discovery of 'ozone holes', where the protective layer of ozone is being thinned by chlorofluorocarbons (CFCs), chemicals used in the manufacture of such things as air conditioners and refrigerators, has enabled governments to take concerted action to save our planet from imminent danger.

Earth Data

MAXIMUM DISTANCE FROM SUN (APHELION)
152,007,016 km

MINIMUM DISTANCE FROM SUN (PERIHELION)
147,000,830 km

LENGTH OF YEAR – SOLAR TROPICAL (EQUINOX TO EQUINOX)
365.24 days

LENGTH OF YEAR – SIDEREAL (FIXED STAR TO FIXED STAR)
365.26 days

LENGTH OF DAY – MEAN SOLAR DAY
24 hours, 03 minutes, 56 seconds

LENGTH OF DAY – MEAN SIDEREAL DAY
23 hours, 56 minutes, 4 seconds

SUPERFICIAL AREA
510,000,000 km^2

LAND SURFACE
149,000,000 km^2 (29.3%)

WATER SURFACE
361,000,000 km^2 (70.7%)

EQUATORIAL CIRCUMFERENCE
40,077 km

POLAR CIRCUMFERENCE
40,009 km

EQUATORIAL DIAMETER
12,756.8 km

POLAR DIAMETER
12,713.8 km

EQUATORIAL RADIUS
6,378.4 km

POLAR RADIUS
6,356.9 km

VOLUME OF THE EARTH
$1,083,230 \times 10^6$ km^3

MASS OF THE EARTH
5.9×10^{21} tonnes

Satellite image of San Francisco Bay

Unmanned scientific satellites called ERTS (Earth Resources Technology Satellites), *or* Landsats, *were designed to collect information about the Earth's resources. The satellites transmitted images of the land using different wavelengths of light in order to identify, in false colours, such subtle features as areas that contain minerals or areas covered with growing crops, that are not identifiable on simple photographs using the visible range of the spectrum. They were also equipped to monitor conditions in the atmosphere and oceans, and also to detect pollution levels. This* Landsat *image of San Francisco Bay covers an area of great interest to geologists because it lies in an earthquake zone in the path of the San Andreas fault.*

The Dynamic Earth

The Earth was formed about 4.6 billion years [4,600 million years] ago from the ring of gas and dust left over after the formation of the Sun. As the Earth took shape, lighter elements, such as silicon, rose to the surface, while heavy elements, notably iron, sank towards the centre.

Gradually, the outer layers cooled to form a hard crust. The crust enclosed the dense mantle which, in turn, surrounded the even denser liquid outer and solid inner core. Around the Earth was an atmosphere, which contained abundant water vapour. When the surface cooled, rainwater began to fill hollows, forming the first lakes and seas. Since that time, our planet has been subject to constant change – the result of powerful internal and external forces that still operate today.

Lulworth Cove, southern England
When undisturbed by earth movements, sedimentary rock strata are generally horizontal. But lateral pressure has squeezed the Jurassic strata at Lulworth Cove into complex folds.

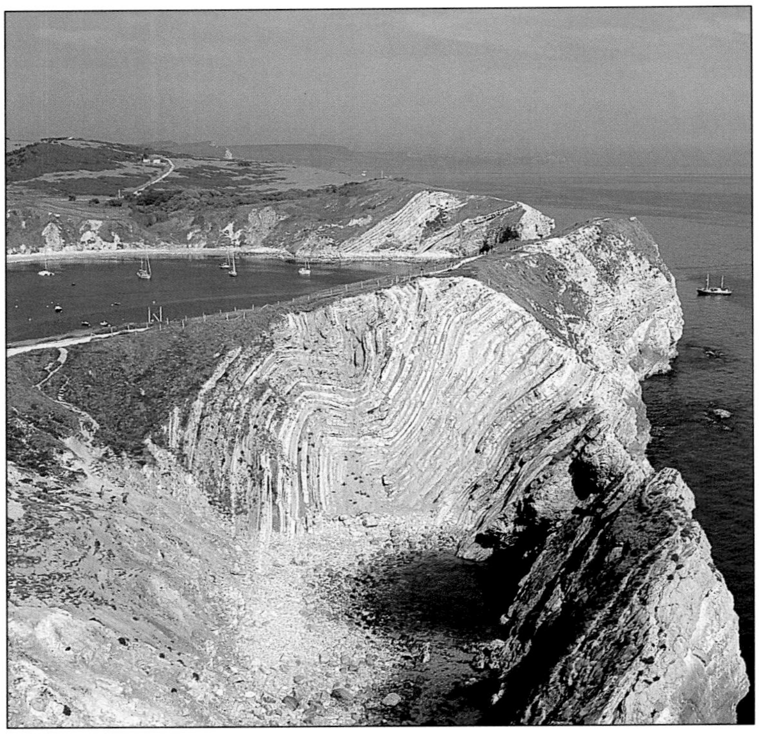

The History of the Earth

From their study of rocks, geologists have pieced together the history of our planet and the life forms that evolved upon it. They have dated the oldest known crystals, composed of the mineral zircon, at 4.2 billion years. But the oldest rocks are younger, less than 4 billion years old. This is because older rocks have been weathered away by natural processes.

The oldest rocks that contain fossils, which are evidence of once-living organisms, are around 3.5 billion years old. But fossils are rare in rocks formed in the first 4 billion years of Earth history. This vast expanse of time is called the Precambrian. This is because it precedes the Cambrian period, at the start of which, about 590 million years ago, life was abundant in the seas.

The Cambrian is the first period in the Paleozoic (or ancient life) era. The Paleozoic era is followed by the Mesozoic (middle life) era, which witnessed the spectacular rise and fall of the dinosaurs, and the Cenozoic (recent life) era, which was dominated by the evolution of mammals. Each of the eras is divided into periods, and the periods in the Cenozoic era, covering the last 65 million years, are further divided into epochs.

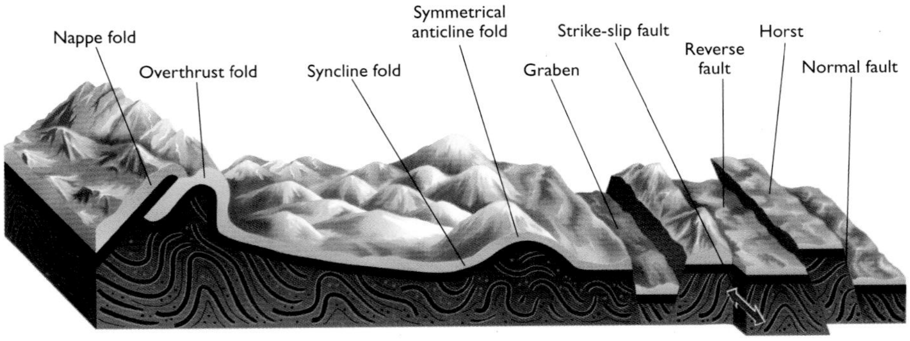

Mountain building
Lateral pressure, which occurs when plates collide, squeezes and compresses rocks into folds. Simple symmetrical upfolds are called anticlines, while downfolds are synclines. As the pressure builds up, strata become asymmetrical and they may be tilted over to form recumbent folds. The rocks often crack under the intense pressure and the folds are sheared away and pushed forward over other rocks. These features are called overthrust folds or nappes. Plate movements also create faults along which rocks move upwards, downwards and sideways. The diagram shows a downfaulted graben, or rift valley, and an uplifted horst, or block mountain.

The Earth's Changing Face

While life was gradually evolving, the face of the Earth was constantly changing. By piecing together evidence of rock structures and fossils, geologists have demonstrated that around 250 million years ago, all the world's land areas were grouped together in one huge landmass called Pangaea. Around 180 million years ago, the supercontinent Pangaea, began to break up. New oceans opened up as the continents began to move towards their present positions.

Evidence of how continents drift came from studies of the ocean floor in the 1950s and 1960s. Scientists discovered that the oceans are young features. By contrast with the continents, no part of the ocean floor is more than 200 million years old. The floors of oceans older than 200 million years have completely vanished.

Studies of long undersea ranges, called ocean ridges, revealed that the youngest rocks occur along their centres, which are the edges of huge plates – rigid blocks of the Earth's lithosphere, which is made up of the crust and the solid upper layer of the mantle. The Earth's lithosphere is split into six large and several smaller

The Himalayas seen from Nepal
The Himalayas are a young fold mountain range formed by a collision between two plates. The earthquakes felt in the region testify that the plate movements are still continuing.

plates. The ocean ridges are 'constructive' plate margins, because new crustal rock is being formed there from magma that wells up from the mantle as the plates gradually move apart. By contrast, the deep ocean trenches are 'destructive' plate edges. Here, two plates are pushing against each other and one plate is descending beneath the other into the mantle where it is melted and destroyed. Geologists call these areas subduction zones.

A third type of plate edge is called a transform fault. Here two plates are moving alongside each other. The best known of these plate edges is the San Andreas fault in California, which separates the Pacific plate from the North American plate.

Slow-moving currents in the partly molten asthenosphere, which underlies the solid lithosphere, are responsible for moving the plates, a process called plate tectonics.

Geological time scale
The geological time scale was first constructed by a study of the stratigraphic, or relative, ages of layers of rock. But the absolute ages of rock strata could not be fixed until the discovery of radioactivity in the early 20th century. Some names of periods, such as Cambrian (Latin for Wales), come from places where the rocks were first studied. Others, such as Carboniferous, refer to the nature of the rocks formed during the period. For example, coal seams (containing carbon) were formed from decayed plant matter during the Carboniferous period.

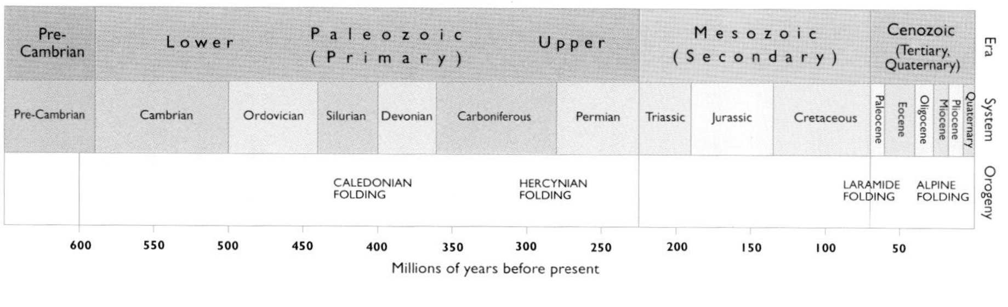

Pre-Cambrian
Lower
Paleozoic (Primary)
Upper
Mesozoic (Secondary)
Cenozoic (Tertiary, Quaternary)
Era
Pre-Cambrian
Cambrian
Ordovician
Silurian
Devonian
Carboniferous
Permian
Triassic
Jurassic
Cretaceous
Paleocene
Eocene
Oligocene
Miocene
Pliocene
Quaternary
System
CALEDONIAN FOLDING
HERCYNIAN FOLDING
LARAMIDE FOLDING
ALPINE FOLDING
Orogeny
600
550
500
450
400
350
300
250
200
150
100
50
Millions of years before present

Mountain Building

The study of plate tectonics has helped geologists to understand the mechanisms that are responsible for the creation of mountains. Many of the world's greatest ranges were created by the collision of two plates and the bending of the intervening strata into huge loops, or folds. For example, the Himalayas began to rise around 50 million years ago, when a plate supporting India collided with the huge Eurasian plate. Rocks on the floor of the intervening and long-vanished Tethys Sea were squeezed up to form the Himalayan Mountain Range.

Plate movements also create tension that cracks rocks, producing long faults along which rocks move upwards, downwards or sideways. Block mountains are formed when blocks of rock are pushed upwards along faults. Steep-sided rift valleys are formed when blocks of land sink down between faults. For example, the basin and range region of the south-western United States has both block mountains and down-faulted basins, such as Death Valley.

Earthquakes and Volcanoes

On 26 January, 2001, an earthquake rocked north-west India and south-east Pakistan. Bhuj, in Gujarat state, suffered the worst damage. The death toll was estimated at 20,000, and the 'quake was felt as far away as Karachi, Delhi and Mumbai. Earlier that month, an earthquake had struck El Salvador in Central America. Around 1,200 people died, 750 of them being buried by mudslides.

The Restless Earth

Earthquakes can occur anywhere, whenever rocks move along faults. But the most severe and most numerous earthquakes occur near the edges of the plates that make up the Earth's lithosphere. Japan, for example, lies in a particularly unstable region above subduction zones, where plates are descending into the Earth's mantle. It lies in a zone encircling the Pacific Ocean, called the 'Pacific ring of fire'.

Plates do not move smoothly. Their edges are jagged and for most of the time they are locked together. However, pressure gradually builds up until the rocks break and the plates lurch forward, setting off vibrations ranging from slight tremors to terrifying earthquakes. The greater the pressure released, the more destructive the earthquake.

Earthquakes are also common along the ocean trenches where plates are moving apart, but they mostly occur so far from land that they do little damage. Far more destructive are the earthquakes that occur where plates are moving alongside each other. For example, the earthquakes that periodically rock south-western California are caused by movements along the San Andreas Fault.

The spot where an earthquake originates is called the focus, while the point on the Earth's surface directly above the focus is called the epicentre. Two kinds of waves, P-waves or compressional waves and S-waves or shear waves, travel from the focus to the surface where they make the ground shake. P-waves travel faster than S-waves and the time difference between their arrival at recording stations enables scientists to calculate the distance from a station to the epicentre.

Earthquakes are measured on the Richter scale, which indicates the magnitude of the shock. The most destructive earthquakes are shallow-focus, that is, the focus is within 60 km [37 miles] of the surface. A magnitude of 7.0 is a major earthquake, but earthquakes with a somewhat lower magnitude can cause tremendous damage if their epicentres are on or close to densely populated areas.

San Andreas Fault, United States

Geologists call the San Andreas fault in south-western California a transform, or strike-slip, fault. Sudden movements along it cause earthquakes. In 1906, shifts of about 4.5 metres [15 ft] occurred near San Francisco, causing a massive earthquake.

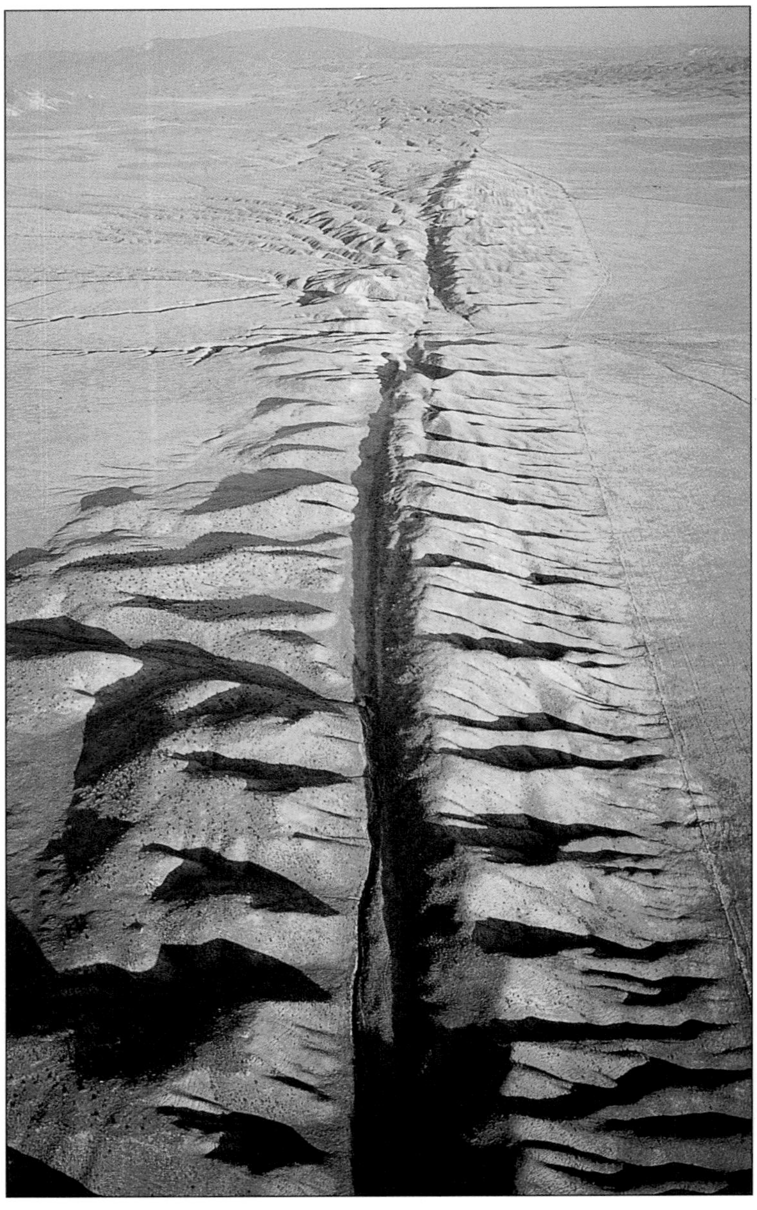

NOTABLE EARTHQUAKES
(since 1900)

Year	Location	Mag.
1906	San Francisco, USA	8.3
1906	Valparaiso, Chile	8.6
1908	Messina, Italy	7.5
1915	Avezzano, Italy	7.5
1920	Gansu, China	8.6
1923	Yokohama, Japan	8.3
1927	Nan Shan, China	8.3
1932	Gansu, China	7.6
1934	Bihar, India/Nepal	8.4
1935	Quetta, India†	7.5
1939	Chillan, Chile	8.3
1939	Erzincan, Turkey	7.9
1964	Anchorage, Alaska	8.4
1968	N. E. Iran	7.4
1970	N. Peru	7.7
1976	Guatemala	7.5
1976	Tangshan, China	8.2
1978	Tabas, Iran	7.7
1980	El Asnam, Algeria	7.3
1980	S. Italy	7.2
1985	Mexico City, Mexico	8.1
1988	N. W. Armenia	6.8
1990	N. Iran	7.7
1993	Maharashtra, India	6.4
1994	Los Angeles, USA	6.6
1995	Kobe, Japan	7.2
1995	Sakhalin Is., Russia	7.5
1996	Yunnan, China	7.0
1997	N. E. Iran	7.1
1998	N. Afghanistan	6.1
1998	N. E. Afghanistan	7.0
1999	Izmit, Turkey	7.4
1999	Taipei, Taiwan	7.6
2001	Gujarat, India	7.7
2001	El Salvador	6.6

† now Pakistan

Earthquakes in subduction zones

Along subduction zones, one plate is descending beneath another. The plates are locked together until the rocks break and the descending plate lurches forwards. From the point where the plate moves – the origin – seismic waves spread through the lithosphere, making the ground shake. The earthquake in Mexico City in 1985 occurred in this way.

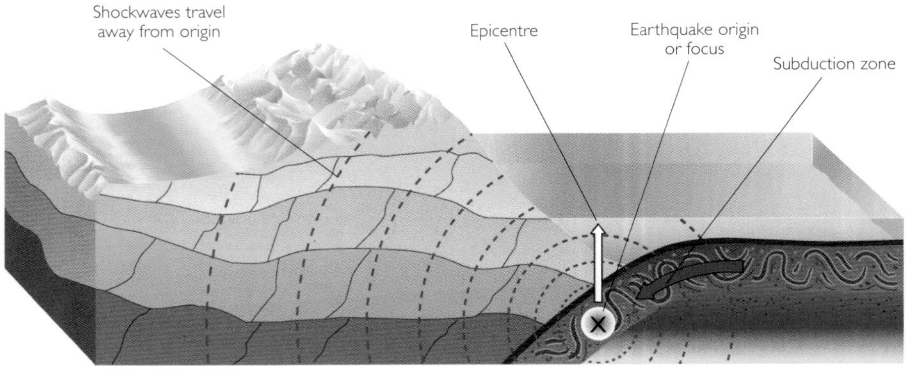
Shockwaves travel away from origin
Epicentre
Earthquake origin or focus
Subduction zone

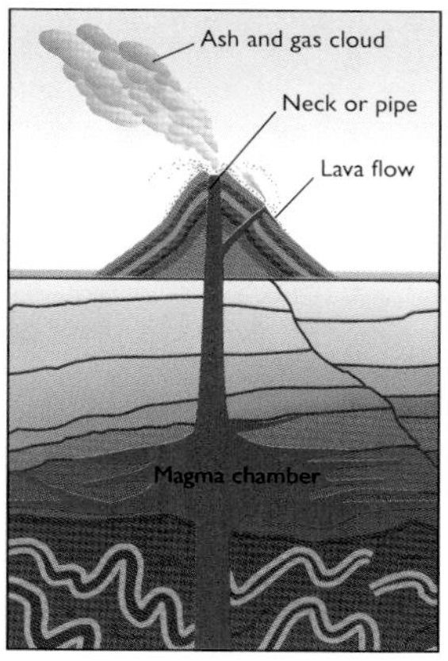

Cross-section of a volcano
Volcanoes are vents in the ground, through which magma reaches the surface. The term volcano is also used for the mountains formed from volcanic rocks. Beneath volcanoes are pockets of magma derived from the semi-molten asthenosphere in the mantle. The magma rises under pressure through the overlying rocks until it reaches the surface. There it emerges through vents as pyroclasts, ranging in size from large lumps of magma, called volcanic bombs, to fine volcanic ash and dust. In quiet eruptions, streams of liquid lava run down the side of the mountain. Side vents sometimes appear on the flanks of existing volcanoes.

Scientists have been working for years to find effective ways of forecasting earthquakes but with very limited success. Following the Kobe earthquake in 1995, many experts argued that they would be better employed developing techniques of reducing the damage caused by earthquakes, rather than pursuing an apparently vain attempt to predict them.

Volcanic Eruptions

Most active volcanoes also occur on or near plate edges. Many undersea volcanoes along the ocean ridges are formed from magma that wells up from the asthenosphere to fill the gaps created as the plates, on the opposite sides of the ridges, move apart. Some of these volcanoes reach the surface to form islands. Iceland is a country which straddles the Mid-Atlantic Ocean Ridge. It is gradually becoming wider as magma rises to the surface through faults and vents. Other volcanoes lie alongside subduction zones. The magma that fuels them comes from the melted edges of the descending plates.

A few volcanoes lie far from plate edges. For example, Mauna Loa and Kilauea on Hawaii are situated near the centre of the huge Pacific plate. The molten magma that reaches the surface is created by a source of heat, called a 'hot spot', in the Earth's mantle.

Magma is molten rock at temperatures of about 1,100°C to 1,200°C [2,012°F to 2,192°F]. It contains gases and superheated steam. The chemical composition of magma varies. Viscous magma is rich in silica and superheated steam, while runny magma contains less silica and steam. The chemical composition of the magma affects the nature of volcanic eruptions.

Explosive volcanoes contain thick, viscous magma. When they erupt, they usually hurl clouds of ash (shattered fragments of cooled magma) into the air. By contrast, quiet volcanoes emit long streams of runny magma, or lava. However, many volcanoes are intermediate in type, sometimes erupting explosively and sometimes emitting streams of fluid lava. Explosive and intermediate volcanoes usually have a conical shape, while quiet volcanoes are flattened, resembling upturned saucers. They are often called shield volcanoes.

One dangerous type of eruption is called a *nuée ardente*, or 'glowing cloud'. It occurs when a cloud of intensely hot volcanic gases and dust particles and superheated steam are exploded from a volcano. They move rapidly downhill, burning everything in their path and choking animals and people. The blast that creates the *nuée ardente* may release the pressure inside the volcano, resulting in a tremendous explosion that hurls tall columns of ash into the air.

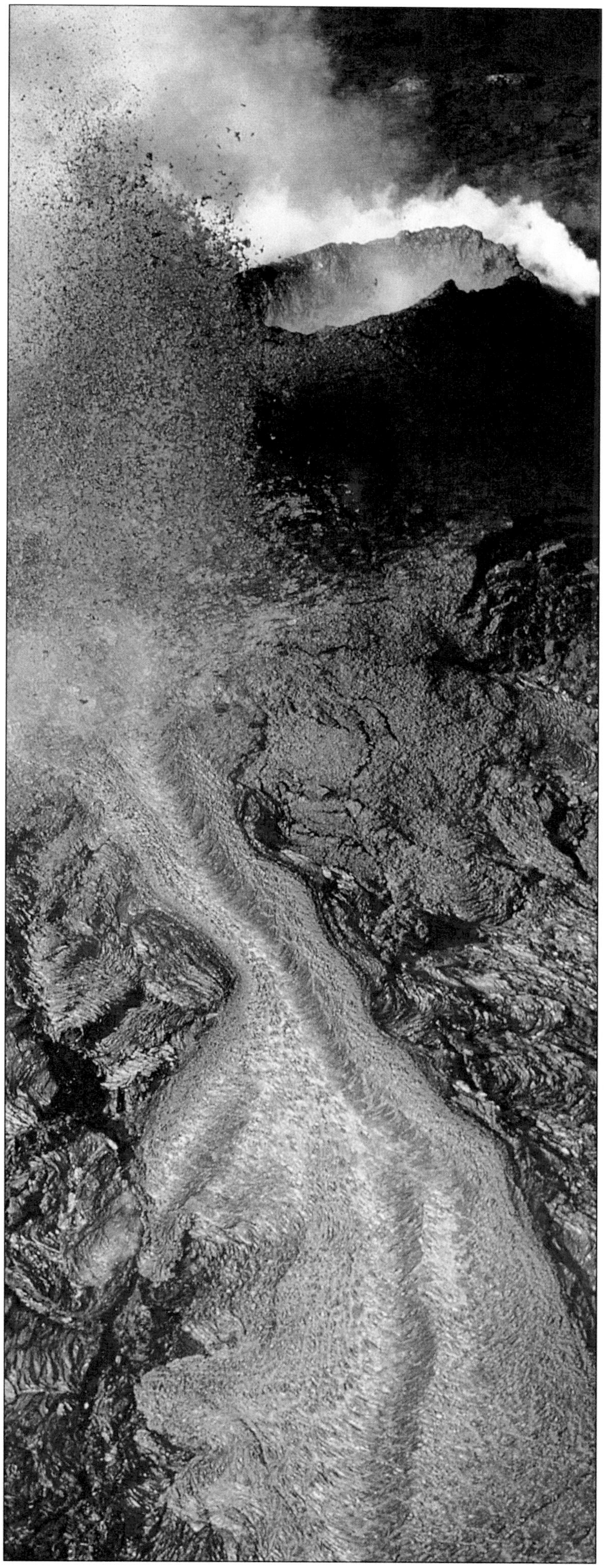

Kilauea Volcano, Hawaii
The volcanic Hawaiian islands in the North Pacific Ocean were formed as the Pacific plate moved over a 'hot spot' in the Earth's mantle. Kilauea on Hawaii emits blazing streams of liquid lava.

Forces of Nature

When the volcano Mount Pinatubo erupted in the Philippines in 1991, large areas around the mountain were covered by ash. Throughout the 1990s, rainwater mixed with the ash on sloping land, created lahars, or mudflows, which swept down river valleys burying many areas. Such incidents are not only reminders of the great forces that operate inside our planet but also of those natural forces operating on the surface, which can have dramatic effects on the land.

The chief forces acting on the surface of the Earth are weathering, running water, ice and winds. The forces of erosion seem to act slowly. One estimate suggests that an average of only 3.5 cm [1.4 in] of land is removed by natural processes every 1,000 years. This may not sound much, but over millions of years, it can reduce mountains to almost flat surfaces.

Weathering

Weathering occurs in all parts of the world, but the most effective type of weathering in any area depends on the climate and the nature of the rocks. For example, in cold mountain areas, when water freezes in cracks in rocks, the ice occupies 9% more space than the water. This exerts a force which, when repeated over and over again, can split boulders apart. By contrast, in hot deserts, intense heating by day and cooling by night causes the outer layers of rocks to expand and contract until they break up and peel away like layers of an onion. These are examples of what is called mechanical weathering.

Other kinds of weathering include chemical reactions usually involving water. Rainwater containing carbon dioxide dissolved from the air or the soil is a weak acid which reacts with limestone, wearing out pits, tunnels and networks of caves in layers of limestone rock. Water also combines with some minerals, such as the feldspars in granite, to create kaolin, a white

RATES OF EROSION

	SLOW ◄	WEATHERING RATE	► FAST
Mineral solubility	low (e.g. quartz)	moderate (e.g. feldspar)	high (e.g. calcite)
Rainfall	low	moderate	heavy
Temperature	cold	temperate	hot
Vegetation	sparse	moderate	lush
Soil cover	bare rock	thin to moderate soil	thick soil

Weathering is the breakdown and decay of rocks in situ. It may be mechanical (physical), chemical or biological.

Rates of erosion
The chart shows that the rates at which weathering takes place depend on the chemistry and hardness of rocks, climatic factors, especially rainfall and temperature, the vegetation and the nature of the soil cover in any area. The effects of weathering are increased by human action, particularly the removal of vegetation and the exposure of soils to the rain and wind.

Grand Canyon, Arizona, at dusk
The Grand Canyon in the United States is one of the world's natural wonders. Eroded by the Colorado River and its tributaries, it is up to 1.6 km [1 mile] deep and 29 km [18 miles] wide.

clay. These are examples of chemical weathering which constantly wears away rock.

Running Water, Ice and Wind

In moist regions, rivers are effective in shaping the land. They transport material worn away by weathering and erode the land. They wear out V-shaped valleys in upland regions, while vigorous meanders widen their middle courses. The work of rivers is at its most spectacular when earth movements lift up flat areas and rejuvenate the rivers, giving them a new erosive power capable of wearing out such features as the Grand Canyon. Rivers also have a constructive role. Some of the world's most fertile regions are deltas and flood plains composed of sediments periodically dumped there by such rivers as the Ganges, Mississippi and Nile.

Glaciers

During Ice Ages, ice spreads over large areas but, during warm periods, the ice retreats. The chart shows that the volume of ice in many glaciers is decreasing, possibly as a result of global warming. Experts estimate that, between 1850 and the early 21st century, more than half of the ice in Alpine glaciers has melted.

ANNUAL FLUCTUATIONS FOR SELECTED GLACIERS

Glacier name and location	Changes in the annual mass balance† 1970–1	1990–1	Cumulative total 1970–90
Alfotbreen, Norway	+940	+790	+12,110
Wolverine, USA	+770	–410	+2,320
Storglaciaren, Sweden	–190	+170	–120
Djankuat, Russia	–230	–310	–1,890
Grasubreen, Norway	+470	–520	–2,530
Ürümqi, China	+102	–706	–3,828
Golubin, Kyrgyzstan	–90	–722	–7,105
Hintereisferner, Austria	–600	–1,325	–9,081
Gries, Switzerland	–970	–1,480	–10,600
Careser, Italy	–650	–1,730	–11,610
Abramov, Tajikistan	–890	–420	–13,700
Sarennes, France	–1,100	–1,360	–15,020
Place, Canada	–343	–990	–15,175

† The annual mass balance is defined as the difference between glacier accumulation and ablation (melting) averaged over the whole glacier. Balances are expressed as water equivalent in millimetres. A plus indicates an increase in the depth or length of the glacier; a minus indicates a reduction.

Juneau Glacier, Alaska

Like huge conveyor belts, glaciers transport weathered debris from mountain regions. Rocks frozen in the ice give the glaciers teeth, enabling them to wear out typical glaciated land features.

Running water in the form of sea waves and currents shapes coastlines, wearing out caves, natural arches, and stacks. The sea also transports and deposits worn material to form such features as spits and bars.

Glaciers in cold mountain regions flow downhill, gradually deepening valleys and shaping dramatic landscapes. They erode steep-sided U-shaped valleys, into which rivers often plunge in large waterfalls. Other features include cirques, armchair-shaped basins bounded by knife-edged ridges called *arêtes*. When several glacial cirques erode to form radial *arêtes*, pyramidal peaks like the Matterhorn are created. Deposits of moraine, rock material dumped by the glacier, are further evidence that ice once covered large areas. The work of glaciers, like other agents of erosion, varies with the climate. In recent years, global warming has been making glaciers retreat in many areas, while several of the ice shelves in Antarctica have been breaking up.

Many land features in deserts were formed by running water at a time when the climate was much rainier than it is today. Water erosion also occurs when flash floods are caused by rare thunderstorms. But the chief agent of erosion in dry areas is wind-blown sand, which can strip the paint from cars, and undercut boulders to create mushroom-shaped rocks.

Oceans and Ice

Since the 1970s, oceanographers have found numerous hot vents on the ocean ridges. Called black smokers, the vents emit dark, mineral-rich water reaching 350°C [662°F]. Around the vents are chimney-like structures formed from minerals deposited from the hot water. The discovery of black smokers did not surprise scientists who already knew that the ridges were plate edges, where new crustal rock was being formed as molten magma welled up to the surface. But what was astonishing was that the hot water contained vast numbers of bacteria, which provided the base of a food chain that included many strange creatures, such as giant worms, eyeless shrimps and white clams. Many species were unknown to science.

Little was known about the dark world beneath the waves until about 50 years ago. But through the use of modern technology such as echo-sounders, magnetometers, research ships equipped with huge drills, submersibles that can carry scientists down to the ocean floor, and satellites, the secrets of the oceans have been gradually revealed.

The study of the ocean floor led to the discovery that the oceans are geologically young features – no more than 200 million years old. It also revealed evidence as to how oceans form and continents drift because of the action of plate tectonics.

Vava'u Island, Tonga
This small coral atoll in northern Tonga consists of a central island covered by rainforest. Low coral reefs washed by the waves surround a shallow central lagoon.

The Blue Planet

Water covers almost 71% of the Earth, which makes it look blue when viewed from space. Although the oceans are interconnected, geographers divide them into four main areas: the Pacific, Atlantic, Indian and Arctic oceans. The average depth of the oceans is 3,370 m [12,238 ft], but they are divided into several zones.

Around most continents are gently sloping continental shelves, which are flooded parts of the continents. The shelves end at the continental slope, at a depth of about 200 m [656 ft]. This slope leads steeply down to the abyss. The deepest parts of the oceans are the trenches, which reach a maximum depth of 11,033 m [36,198 ft] in the Mariana Trench in the western Pacific.

Most marine life is found in the top 200 m [656 ft], where there is sufficient sunlight for plants, called phytoplankton, to grow. Below this zone, life becomes more and more scarce, though no part of the ocean, even at the bottom of the deepest trenches, is completely without living things.

Continental islands, such as the British Isles, are high parts of the continental shelves. For example, until about 7,500 years ago, when the ice sheets formed during the Ice Ages were melting, raising the sea level and filling the North Sea and the Strait of Dover, Britain was linked to mainland Europe.

By contrast, oceanic islands, such as the Hawaiian chain in the North Pacific Ocean, rise from the ocean floor. All oceanic islands are of volcanic origin, although many of them in warm parts of the oceans have sunk and are capped by layers of coral to form ring- or horseshoe-shaped atolls and coral reefs.

Ocean Water

The oceans contain about 97% of the world's water. Seawater contains more than 70 dissolved elements, but chloride and sodium make up 85% of the total. Sodium chloride is common salt and it makes seawater salty. The salinity of the oceans is mostly between 3.3–3.7%. Ocean water fed by icebergs or large rivers is less saline than shallow seas in the tropics, where the evaporation rate is high. Seawater is a source of salt but the water is useless for agriculture or drinking unless it is desalinated. However, land

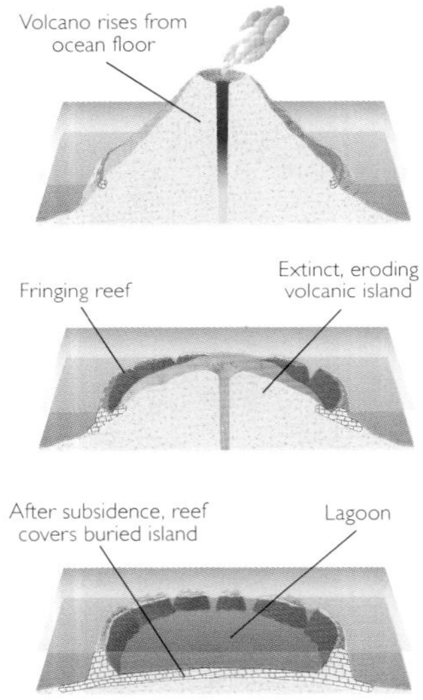
Volcano rises from ocean floor
Fringing reef
Extinct, eroding volcanic island
After subsidence, reef covers buried island
Lagoon

Development of an atoll
Some of the volcanoes that rise from the ocean floor reach the surface to form islands. Some of these islands subside and become submerged. As an island sinks, coral starts to grow around the rim of the volcano, building up layer upon layer of limestone deposits to form fringing reefs. Sometimes coral grows on the tip of a central cone to form an island in the middle of the atoll.

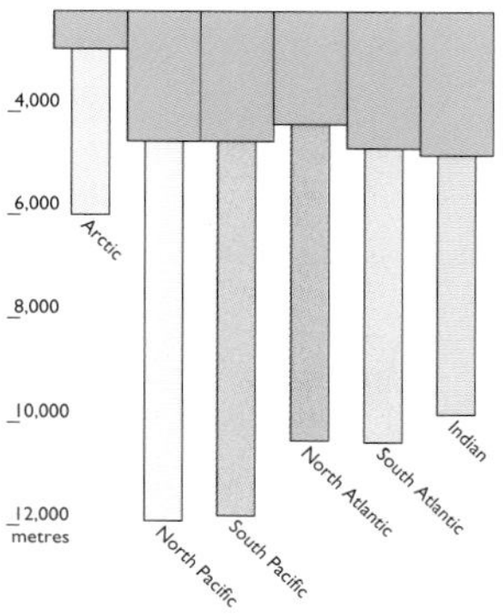

The ocean depths

The diagram shows the average depths (in dark blue) and the greatest depths in the four oceans. The North Pacific Ocean contains the world's deepest trenches, including the Mariana Trench, where the deepest manned descent was made by the bathyscaphe Trieste in 1960. It reached a depth of 10,916 metres [35,813 ft].

Relative sizes of the world's oceans:

PACIFIC	49%	ATLANTIC	26%
INDIAN	21%	ARCTIC	4%

Some geographers distinguish a fifth ocean, the Southern or Antarctic Ocean, but most authorities regard these waters as the southern extension of the Pacific, Atlantic and Indian oceans.

areas get a regular supply of fresh water through the hydrological cycle (see page 26).

The density of seawater depends on its salinity and temperature. Temperatures vary from –2°C [28°F], the freezing point of seawater at the poles, to around 30°C [86°F] in parts of the tropics. Density differences help to maintain the circulation of the world's oceans, especially deep-sea currents. But the main cause of currents within 350 m [1,148 ft] of the surface is the wind. Because of the Earth's rotation, currents are deflected, creating huge circular motions of surface water – clockwise in the northern hemisphere and anticlockwise in the southern hemisphere.

Ocean currents transport heat from the tropics to the polar regions and thus form part of the heat engine that drives the Earth's climates. Ocean currents have an especially marked effect on coastal climates, such as north-western Europe. In the mid-1990s, scientists warned that global warming may be weakening currents, including the warm Gulf Stream which is responsible for the mild winters experienced in north-western Europe.

Ice Sheets, Ice Caps and Glaciers

Global warming is also a threat to the world's ice sheets, ice caps and glaciers that together account for about 2% of the world's water. There are two ice sheets in the world, the largest covers most of Antarctica. With the ice reaching maximum depths of 4,800 m [15,748 ft], the Antarctic ice sheet contains about 70% of the world's fresh water, with a total volume about nine times greater than the Greenland ice sheet. Smaller bodies of ice include ice caps in northern Canada, Iceland and Scandinavia. Also throughout the world in high ranges are many valley glaciers, which help to shape dramatic mountain scenery.

Only about 11,000 years ago, during the final phase of the Pleistocene Ice Age, ice covered much of the northern hemisphere. The Ice Age, which began about 1.8 million years ago, was not a continuous period of cold. Instead, it consisted of glacial periods when the ice advanced and warmer interglacial periods when temperatures rose and the ice retreated.

Some scientists believe that we are now living in an inter-glacial period, and that glacial conditions will recur in the future. Others fear that global warming, caused mainly by pollution, may melt the world's ice, raising sea levels by up to 55 m [180 ft]. Many fertile and densely populated coastal plains, islands and cities would vanish from the map.

Weddell Sea, Antarctica

Antarctica contains two huge bays, occupied by the Ross and Weddell seas. Ice shelves extend from the ice sheet across parts of these seas. Researchers fear that warmer weather is melting Antarctica's ice sheets at a dangerous rate, after large chunks of the Larsen ice shelf and the Ronne ice shelf broke away in 1997 and 1998, respectively.

The Earth's Atmosphere

Since the discovery in 1985 of a thinning of the ozone layer, creating a so-called 'ozone hole', over Antarctica, many governments have worked to reduce the emissions of ozone-eating substances, notably the chlorofluorocarbons (CFCs) used in aerosols, refrigeration, air conditioning and dry cleaning.

Following forecasts that the ozone layer would rapidly repair itself as a result of controls on these emissions, scientists were surprised in early 1996 when a marked thinning of the ozone layer occurred over the Arctic, northern Europe, Russia and Canada. The damage, which was recorded as far south as southern Britain, was due to pollution combined with intense cold in the stratosphere. It was another sharp reminder of the dangers humanity faces when it interferes with and harms the environment.

The ozone layer in the stratosphere blocks out most of the dangerous ultraviolet B radiation in the Sun's rays. This radiation causes skin cancer and cataracts, as well as harming plants on the land and plankton in the oceans. The ozone layer is only one way in which the atmosphere protects life on Earth. The atmosphere also provides the air we breathe and the carbon dioxide required by plants. It is also a shield against meteors and it acts as a blanket to prevent heat radiated from the Earth escaping into space.

Layers of Air

The atmosphere is divided into four main layers. The troposphere at the bottom contains about 85% of the atmosphere's total mass, where most weather conditions occur. The troposphere is about 15 km [9 miles] thick over the Equator and 8 km [5 miles] thick at the poles. Temperatures decrease with height by approximately 1°C [2°F] for every 100 m [328 ft]. At the top of the troposphere is a level called the tropopause where temperatures are stable at around –55°C [–67°F]. Above the tropopause is the stratosphere, which contains the ozone layer. Here, at about 50 km [31 miles] above the Earth's surface, temperatures rise to about 0°C [32°F].

The ionosphere extends from the stratopause to about 600 km [373 miles] above the surface. Here temperatures fall up to about 80 km

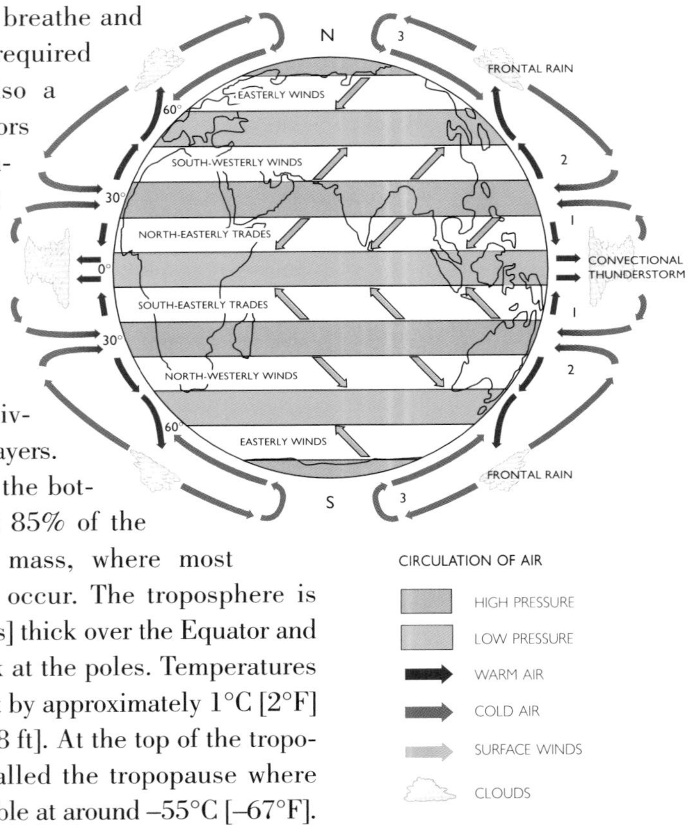

The circulation of the atmosphere can be divided into three rotating but interconnected air systems, or cells. The Hadley cell (figure 1 on the above diagram) is in the tropics; the Ferrel cell (2) lies between the subtropics and the mid-latitudes, and the Polar cell (3) is in the high latitudes.

Moonrise seen from orbit

This photograph taken by an orbiting Shuttle shows the crescent of the Moon. Silhouetted at the horizon is a dense cloud layer. The reddish-brown band is the tropopause, which separates the blue-white stratosphere from the yellow troposphere.

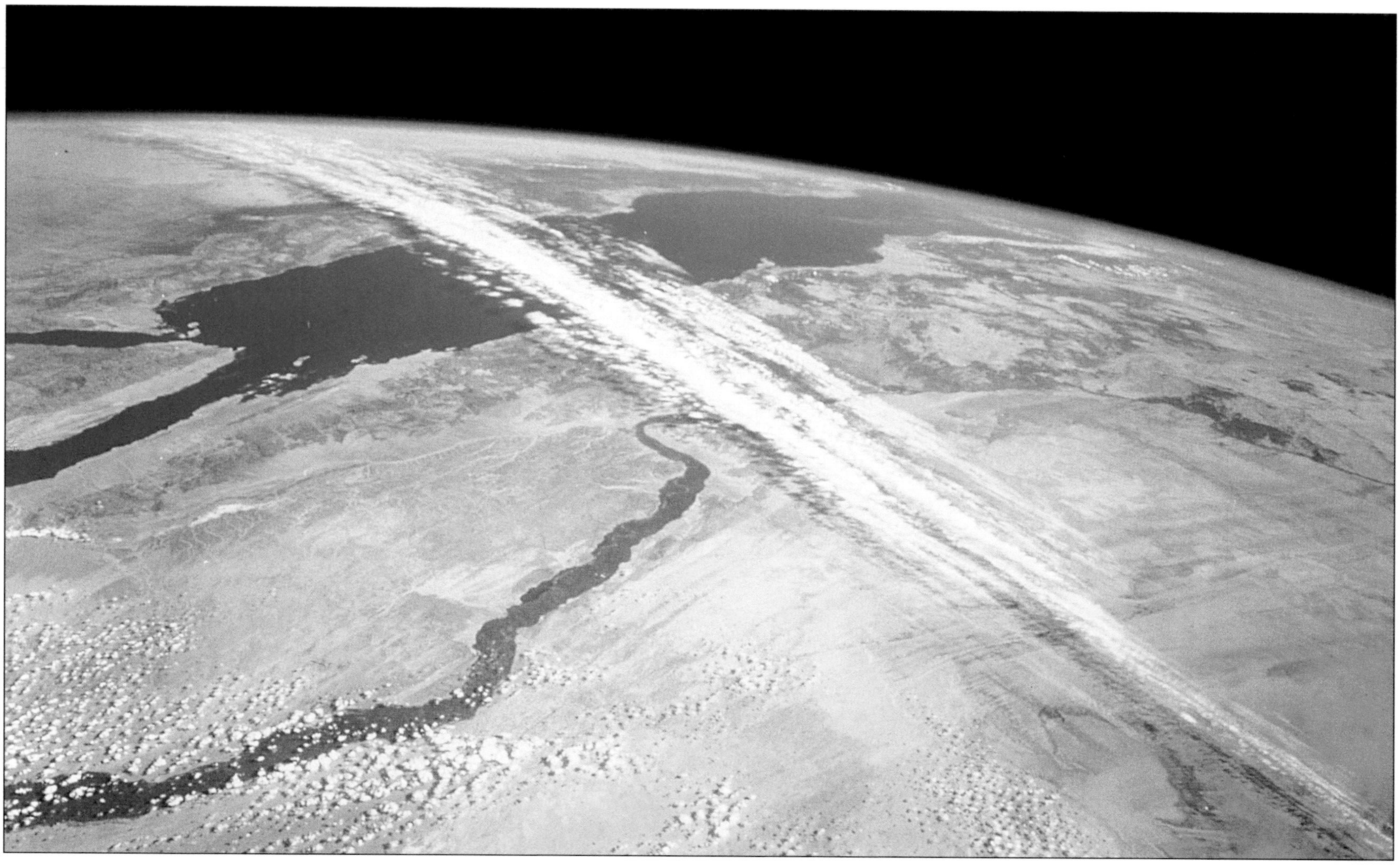

Jetstream from space

Jetstreams are strong winds that normally blow near the tropopause. Cirrus clouds mark the route of the jet stream in this photograph, which shows the Red Sea, North Africa and the Nile valley, which appears as a dark band crossing the desert.

[50 miles], but then rise. The aurorae, which occur in the ionosphere when charged particles from the Sun interact with the Earth's magnetic field, are strongest near the poles. In the exosphere, the outermost layer, the atmosphere merges into space.

Circulation of the Atmosphere

The heating of the Earth is most intense around the Equator where the Sun is high in the sky. Here warm, moist air rises in strong currents, creating a zone of low air pressure: the doldrums. The rising air eventually cools and spreads out north and south until it sinks back to the ground around latitudes 30° North and 30° South. This forms two zones of high air pressure called the horse latitudes.

From the horse latitudes, trade winds blow back across the surface towards the Equator, while westerly winds blow towards the poles. The warm westerlies finally meet the polar easterlies (cold dense air flowing from the poles). The line along which the warm and cold air streams meet is called the polar front. Depressions (or cyclones) are low air pressure frontal systems that form along the polar front.

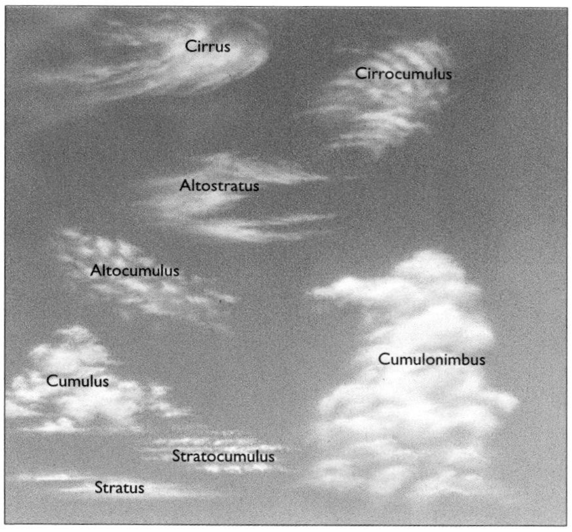
Cirrus
Cirrocumulus
Altostratus
Altocumulus
Cumulonimbus
Cumulus
Stratocumulus
Stratus

Classification of clouds

Clouds are classified broadly into cumuliform, or 'heap' clouds, and stratiform, or 'layer' clouds. Both types occur at all levels. The highest clouds, composed of ice crystals, are cirrus, cirrostratus and cirrocumulus. Medium-height clouds include altostratus, a grey cloud that often indicates the approach of a depression, and altocumulus, a thicker and fluffier version of cirrocumulus. Low clouds include stratus, which forms dull, overcast skies; nimbostratus, a dark grey layer cloud which brings almost continuous rain and snow; cumulus, a brilliant white heap cloud; and stratocumulus, a layer cloud arranged in globular masses or rolls. Cumulonimbus, a cloud associated with thunderstorms, lightning and heavy rain, often extends from low to medium altitudes. It has a flat base, a fluffy outline and often an anvil-shaped top.

Composition of the Atmosphere

The air in the troposphere is made up mainly of nitrogen (78%) and oxygen (21%). Argon makes up more than 0.9% and there are also minute amounts of carbon dioxide, helium, hydrogen, krypton, methane, ozone and xenon. The atmosphere also contains water vapour, the gaseous form of water, which, when it condenses around minute specks of dust and salt, forms tiny water droplets or ice crystals. Large masses of water droplets or ice crystals form clouds.

Climate and Weather

In 1992, Hurricane Andrew struck the Bahamas, Florida and Louisiana, causing record damage estimated at $30 billion. In September 1998, following heavy monsoon rains, floods submerged two-thirds of Bangladesh. The same month, in Central America, more than 7,000 people died in floods and mudslides caused by Hurricane Mitch. The economy of Honduras, already crippled by debt, was thought to have been put back by 15 to 20 years. In March 2000, the worst floods in Mozambique in 50 years devastated the country's economy.

Every year, exceptional weather conditions cause disasters around the world. Modern forecasting techniques now give people warning of advancing storms, but the toll of human deaths continues as people are powerless in the face of the awesome forces of nature.

Weather is the day-to-day condition of the atmosphere. In some places, the weather is normally stable, but in other areas, especially the middle latitudes, it is highly variable, changing with the passing of a depression. By contrast, climate is the average weather of a place, based on data obtained over a long period.

Hurricane Elena, 1995

Hurricanes form over warm oceans north and south of the Equator. Their movements are tracked by satellites, enabling forecasters to issue storm warnings as they approach land. In North America, forecasters identify them with boys' and girls' names.

Climatic Factors

Climate depends basically on the unequal heating of the Sun between the Equator and the poles. But ocean currents and terrain also affect climate. For example, despite their northerly positions, Norway's ports remain ice-free in winter. This is because of the warming effect of the North Atlantic Drift, an extension of the Gulf Stream which flows across the Atlantic Ocean from the Gulf of Mexico.

By contrast, the cold Benguela current which flows up the coast of south-western Africa cools the coast and causes arid conditions. This is because the cold onshore winds are warmed as they pass over the land. The warm air can hold more water vapour than cold air, giving the winds a drying effect.

The terrain affects climate in several ways. Because temperatures fall with altitude, highlands are cooler than lowlands in the same

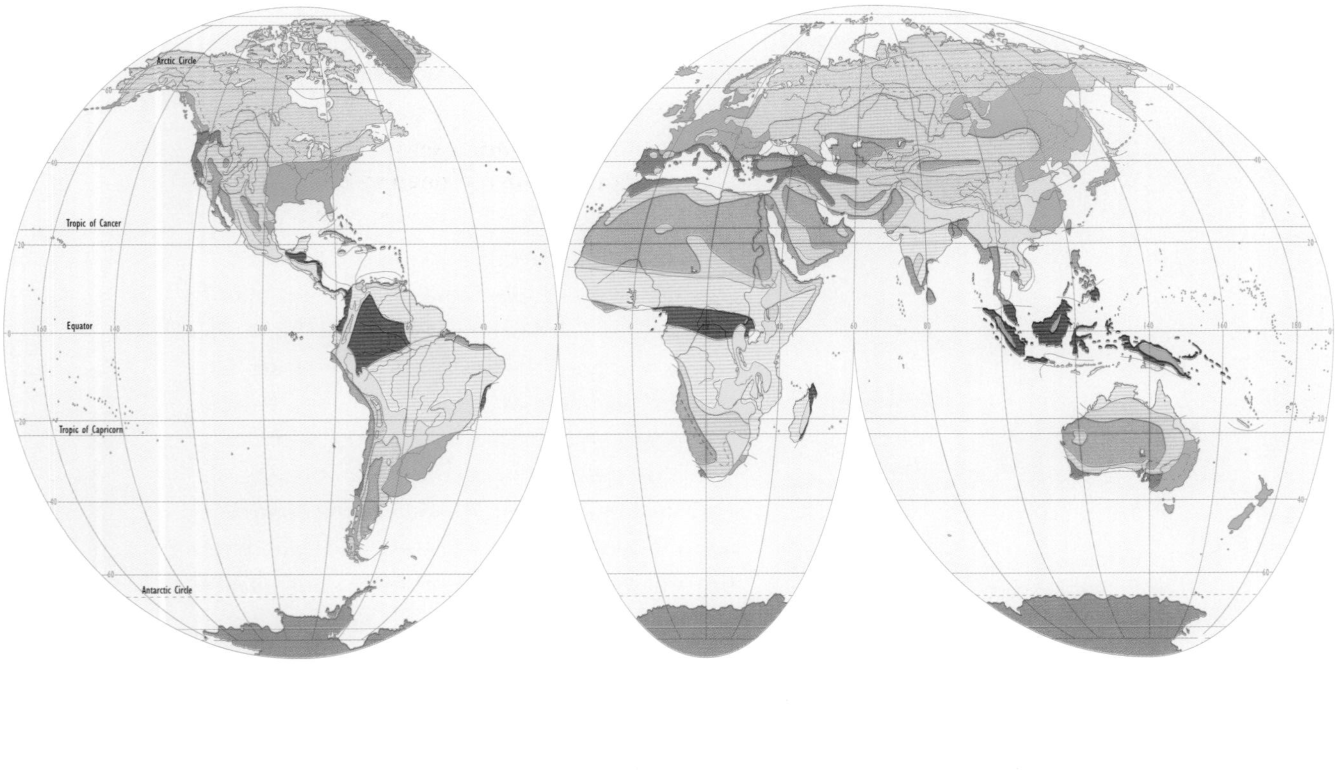

CLIMATIC REGIONS

Tropical rainy climates
All mean monthly temperatures above 18°C [64°F].

- RAINFOREST CLIMATE
- MONSOON CLIMATE
- SAVANNA CLIMATE

Dry climates
Low rainfall combined with a wide range of temperatures.

- STEPPE CLIMATE
- DESERT CLIMATE

Warm temperate rainy climates
The mean temperature is below 18°C [64°F] but above –3°C [26°F] and that of the warmest month is over 10°C [50°F].

- DRY WINTER CLIMATE
- DRY SUMMER CLIMATE
- CLIMATE WITH NO DRY SEASON

Cold temperate rainy climates
The mean temperature of the coldest month is below 3°C [37°F] but the warmest month is over 10°C [50°F].

- DRY WINTER CLIMATE
- CLIMATE WITH NO DRY SEASON

Polar climates
The temperature of the warmest month is below 10°C [50°F], giving permanently frozen subsoil.

- TUNDRA CLIMATE
- POLAR CLIMATE

Flood damage in the United States
In June and July 1993, the Mississippi River basin suffered record floods. The photograph shows a sunken church in Illinois. The flooding along the Mississippi, Missouri and other rivers caused great damage, amounting to about $12 billion. At least 48 people died in the floods.

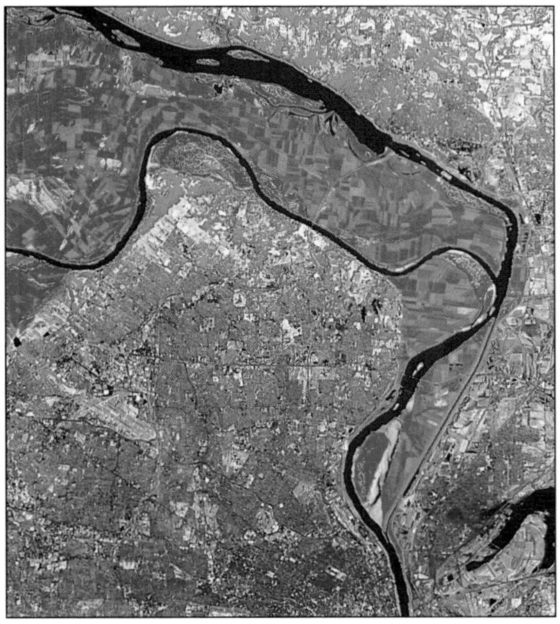

Floods in St Louis, United States
The satellite image, right, shows the extent of the floods at St Louis at the confluence of the Mississippi and the Missouri rivers in June and July 1993. The floods occurred when very heavy rainfall raised river levels by up to 14 m [46 ft]. The floods reached their greatest extent between Minneapolis in the north and a point approximately 150 km [93 miles] south of St Louis. In places, the width of the Mississippi increased to nearly 11 km [7 miles], while the Missouri reached widths of 32 km [20 miles]. In all, more than 28,000 sq km [10,800 sq miles] were inundated and hundreds of towns and cities were flooded. Damage to crops was estimated at $8 billion. The USA was hit again by flooding in early 1997, when heavy rainfall in North Dakota and Minnesota caused the Red River to flood. The flooding had a catastrophic effect on the city of Grand Forks, which was inundated for months.

latitude. Terrain also affects rainfall. When moist onshore winds pass over mountain ranges, they are chilled as they are forced to rise and the water vapour they contain condenses to form clouds which bring rain and snow. After the winds have crossed the mountains, the air descends and is warmed. These warm, dry winds create rain shadow (arid) regions on the lee side of the mountains.

Climatic Regions

The two major factors that affect climate are temperature and precipitation, including rain and snow. In addition, seasonal variations and other climatic features are also taken into account. Climatic classifications vary because of the weighting given to various features. Yet most classifications are based on five main climatic types: tropical rainy climates; dry climates; warm temperate rainy climates; cold temperate rainy climates; and very cold polar climates. Some classifications also allow for the effect of altitude. The main climatic regions are subdivided according to seasonal variations and also to the kind of vegetation associated with the climatic conditions. Thus, the rainforest climate, with rain throughout the year, differs from monsoon and savanna climates, which have marked dry seasons. Similarly, parched desert climates differ from steppe climates which have enough moisture for grasses to grow.

Water and Land Use

All life on land depends on fresh water. Yet about 80 countries now face acute water shortages. The world demand for fresh water is increasing by about 2.3% a year and this demand will double every 21 years. About a billion people, mainly in developing countries, do not have access to clean drinking water and around 10 million die every year from drinking dirty water. This problem is made worse in many countries by the pollution of rivers and lakes.

In 1995, a World Bank report suggested that wars will be fought over water in the 21st century. Relations between several countries are already soured by disputes over water resources. Egypt fears that Sudan and Ethiopia will appropriate the waters of the Nile, while Syria and Iraq are concerned that Turkish dams will hold back the waters of the Euphrates.

However, experts stress that while individual countries face water crises, there is no global crisis. The chief global problems are the uneven distribution of water and its inefficient and wasteful use.

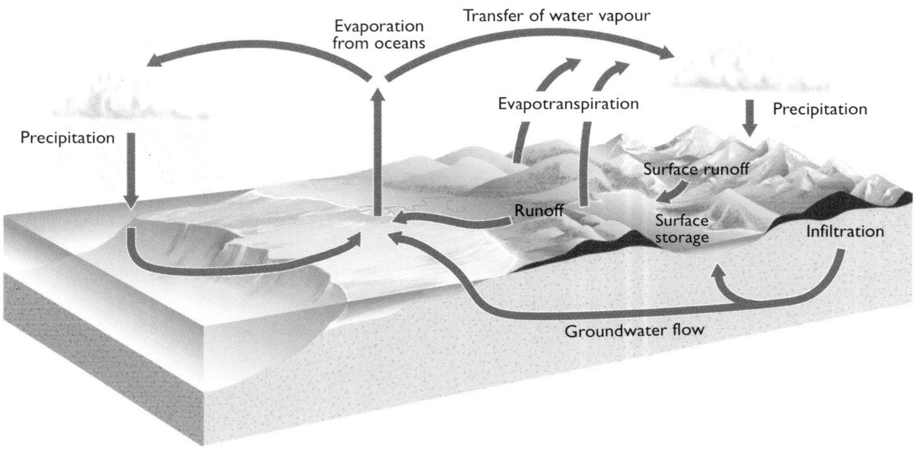

The hydrological cycle
The hydrological cycle is responsible for the continuous circulation of water around the planet. Water vapour contains and transports latent heat, or latent energy. When the water vapour condenses back into water (and falls as rain, hail or snow), the heat is released. When condensation takes place on cold nights, the cooling effect associated with nightfall is offset by the liberation of latent heat.

Hoover Dam, United States
The Hoover Dam in Arizona controls the Colorado River's flood waters. Its reservoir supplies domestic and irrigation water to the south-west, while a hydroelectric plant produces electricity.

THE WORLD'S WATER SUPPLY

Of the world's total water supply, 99.4% is in the oceans or frozen in bodies of ice. Most of the rest circulates through the rocks beneath our feet as ground water. Water in rivers and lakes, in the soil and in the atmosphere together make up only 0.013% of the world's water.

The freshwater supply on land is dependent on the hydrological, or water cycle which is driven by the Sun's heat. Water is evaporated from the oceans and carried into the air as invisible water vapour. Although this vapour averages less than 2% of the total mass of the atmosphere, it is the chief component from the standpoint of weather.

When air rises, water vapour condenses into visible water droplets or ice crystals, which eventually fall to earth as rain, snow, sleet, hail or frost. Some of the precipitation that reaches the ground returns directly to the atmosphere through evaporation or transpiration via plants. Much of the rest of the water flows into the rocks to become ground water or across the surface into rivers and, eventually, back to the oceans, so completing the hydrological cycle.

WATER DISTRIBUTION

The distribution of planetary water, by percentage.

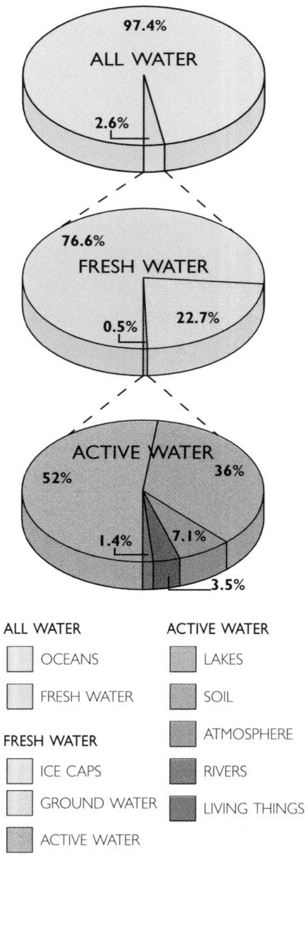

WATER AND AGRICULTURE

Only about a third of the world's land area is used for growing crops, while another third

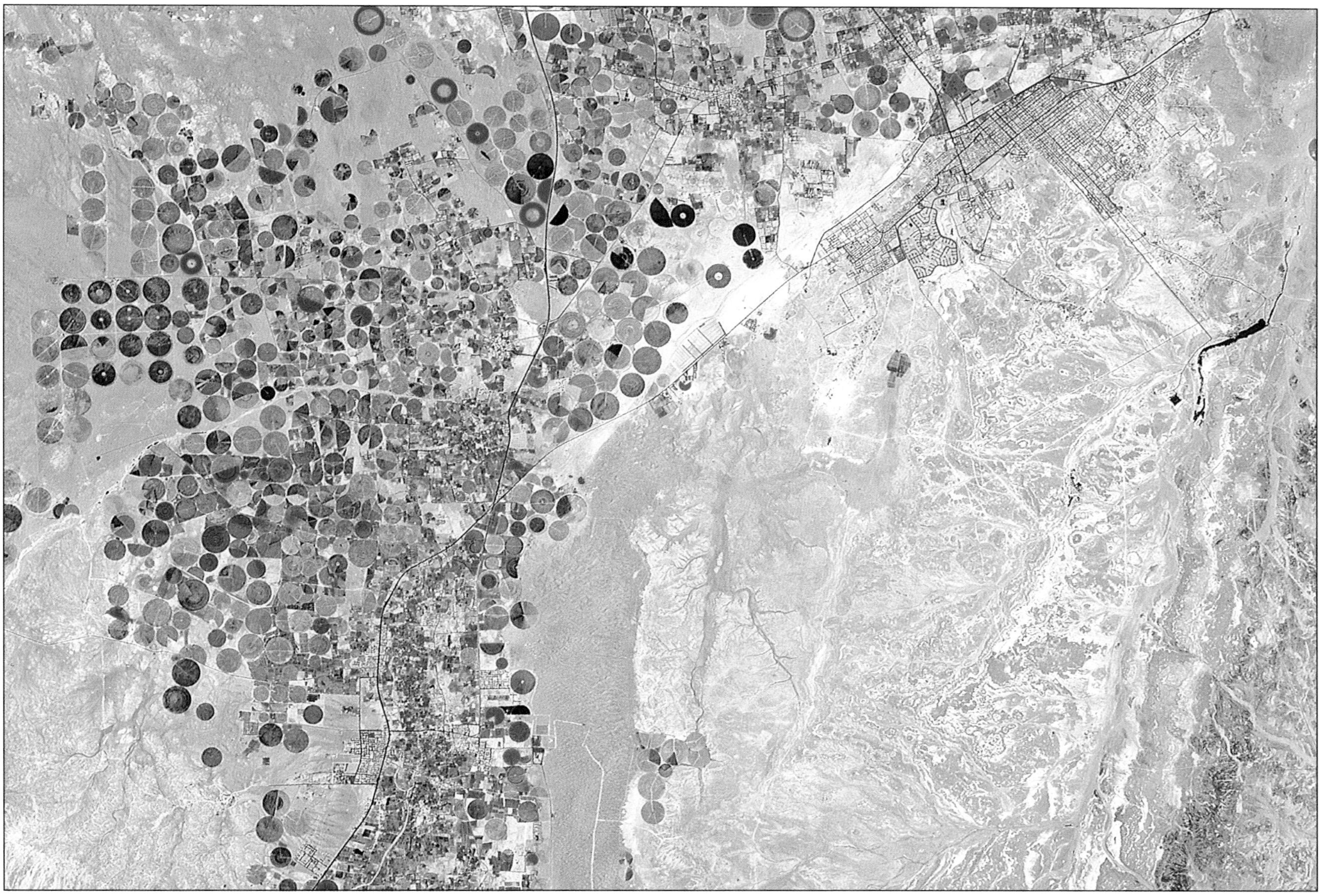

Irrigation in Saudi Arabia

Saudi Arabia is a desert country which gets its water from oases, which tap ground water supplies, and desalination plants. The sale of oil has enabled the arid countries of south-western Asia to develop their agriculture. In the above satellite image, vegetation appears brown and red.

Irrigation boom

The photograph shows a pivotal irrigation boom used to sprinkle water over a wheat field in Saudi Arabia. Irrigation in hot countries often takes place at night so that water loss through evaporation is reduced. Irrigation techniques vary from place to place. In monsoon areas with abundant water, the fields are often flooded, or the water is led to the crops along straight furrows. Sprinkler irrigation has become important since the 1940s. In other types of irrigation, the water is led through pipes which are on or under the ground. Underground pipes supply water directly to the plant roots and, as a result, water loss through evaporation is minimized.

consists of meadows and pasture. The rest of the world is unsuitable for farming, being too dry, too cold, too mountainous, or covered by dense forests. Although the demand for food increases every year, problems arise when attempts are made to increase the existing area of farmland. For example, the soils and climates of tropical forest and semi-arid regions of Africa and South America are not ideal for farming. Attempts to work such areas usually end in failure. To increase the world's food supply, scientists now concentrate on making existing farmland more productive rather than farming marginal land.

To grow crops, farmers need fertile, workable land, an equable climate, including a frost-free growing period, and an adequate supply of fresh water. In some areas, the water falls directly as rain. But many other regions depend on irrigation.

Irrigation involves water conservation through the building of dams which hold back storage reservoirs. In some areas, irrigation water comes from underground aquifers, layers of permeable and porous rocks through which ground water percolates. But in many cases, the water in the aquifers has been there for thousands of years, having accumulated at a time when the rainfall was much greater than it is today. As a result, these aquifers are not being renewed and will, one day, dry up.

Other sources of irrigation water are desalination plants, which remove salt from seawater and pump it to farms. This is a highly expensive process and is employed in areas where water supplies are extremely low, such as the island of Malta, or in the oil-rich desert countries around the Gulf, which can afford to build huge desalination plants.

LAND USE BY CONTINENT

	Forest	Permanent pasture	Permanent crops	Arable	Non-productive
North America	32.2%	17.3%	0.3%	12.6%	37.6%
South America	51.8%	26.7%	1.5%	6.6%	13.4%
Europe	33.4%	17.5%	3.0%	26.8%	19.3%
Africa	23.2%	26.6%	0.6%	5.6%	44.0%
Asia	20.2%	25.0%	1.2%	16.0%	37.8%
Oceania	23.5%	52.2%	0.1%	5.7%	18.5%

The Natural World

In 1995, a United Nations Environment Programme report stated that 11% of all mammal species, 18% of birds and 5% of fish are now threatened with extinction. Furthermore, it predicted that half of all bird and mammal species will become extinct within 300 years, or sooner if current trends continue. This will greatly reduce the biodiversity of our planet, causing the disappearance of unique combinations of genes that could be vital in improving food yields on farms or in the production of drugs to combat diseases.

Extinctions of species have occurred throughout Earth history, but today the extinction rate is estimated to be about 10,000 times the natural average. Some scientists have even compared it with the mass extinction that wiped out the dinosaurs 65 million years ago. However, the main cause of today's high extinction rate is not some natural disaster, such as the impact of an asteroid a few kilometres across, but it is the result of human actions, most notably the destruction of natural habitats for farming and other purposes. In some densely populated areas, such as Western Europe, the natural habitats were destroyed long ago. Today, the greatest damage is occurring in tropical rainforests, which contain more than half of the world's known species.

Modern technology has enabled people to live comfortably almost anywhere on Earth. But most plants and many animals are adapted to particular climatic conditions, and they live in association with and dependent on each other. Plant and animal communities that cover large areas are called biomes.

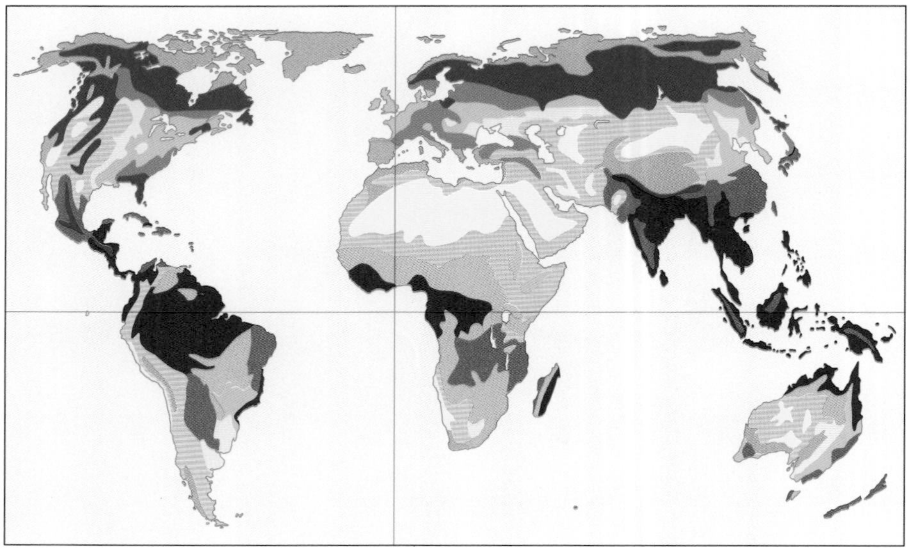
NATURAL VEGETATION
TUNDRA & MOUNTAIN VEGETATION
NEEDLELEAF EVERGREEN FOREST
MIXED NEEDLELEAF EVERGREEN & BROADLEAF DECIDUOUS TREES
BROADLEAF DECIDUOUS WOODLAND
MID-LATITUDE GRASSLAND
EVERGREEN BROADLEAF & DECIDUOUS TREES & SHRUBS
SEMI-DESERT SCRUB
DESERT
TROPICAL GRASSLAND (SAVANNA)
TROPICAL BROADLEAF RAINFOREST & MONSOON FOREST
SUBTROPICAL BROADLEAF & NEEDLELEAF FOREST

The map shows the world's main biomes. The classification is based on the natural 'climax' vegetation of regions, a result of the climate and the terrain. But human activities have greatly modified this basic division. For example, the original deciduous forests of Western Europe and the eastern United States have largely disappeared. In recent times, human development of some semi-arid areas has turned former dry grasslands into barren desert.

Rainforest in Rwanda

Rainforests are the most threatened of the world's biomes. Effective conservation policies must demonstrate to poor local people that they can benefit from the survival of the forests.

The World's Biomes

The world's biomes are defined mainly by climate and vegetation. They range from the tundra, in polar regions and high mountain regions, to the lush equatorial rainforests.

The Arctic tundra covers large areas in the polar regions of the northern hemisphere. Snow covers the land for more than half of the year and the subsoil, called permafrost, is permanently frozen. Comparatively few species can survive in this harsh, treeless environment. The main plants are hardy mosses, lichens, grasses, sedges and low shrubs. However, in summer, the tundra plays an important part in world animal geography, when its growing plants and swarms of insects provide food for migrating animals and birds that arrive from the south.

The tundra of the northern hemisphere merges in the south into a vast region of needleleaf evergreen forest, called the boreal forest or taiga. Such trees as fir, larch, pine and spruce are adapted to survive the long, bitterly cold winters of this region, but the number of plant and animal species is again small. South of the boreal forests is a zone of mixed needleleaf evergreens and broadleaf deciduous trees, which

Tundra in subarctic Alaska

The Denali National Park, Alaska, contains magnificent mountain scenery and tundra vegetation which flourishes during the brief summer. The park is open between 1 June and 15 September.

shed their leaves in winter. In warmer areas, this mixed forest merges into broadleaf deciduous forest, where the number and diversity of plant species is much greater.

Deciduous forests are adapted to temperate, humid regions. Evergreen broadleaf and deciduous trees grow in Mediterranean regions, with their hot, dry summers. But much of the original deciduous forest has been cut down and has given way to scrub and heathland. Grasslands occupy large areas in the middle latitudes, where the rainfall is insufficient to support forest growth. The moister grasslands are often called prairies, while drier areas are called steppe.

The tropics also contain vast dry areas of semi-desert scrub which merges into desert, as well as large areas of savanna, which is grassland with scattered trees. Savanna regions, with their marked dry season, support a wide range of mammals.

Tropical and subtropical regions contain three types of forest biomes. The tropical rainforest, the world's richest biome measured by its plant and animal species, experiences rain and high temperatures throughout the year. Similar forests occur in monsoon regions, which have a season of very heavy rainfall. They, too, are rich in plant species, though less so than the tropical rainforest. A third type of forest is the subtropical broadleaf and needleleaf forest, found in such places as south-eastern China, south-central Africa and eastern Brazil.

NET PRIMARY PRODUCTION OF EIGHT MAJOR BIOMES

- TROPICAL RAINFORESTS
- DECIDUOUS FORESTS
- TROPICAL GRASSLANDS
- CONIFEROUS FORESTS
- MEDITERRANEAN
- TEMPERATE GRASSLANDS
- TUNDRA
- DESERTS

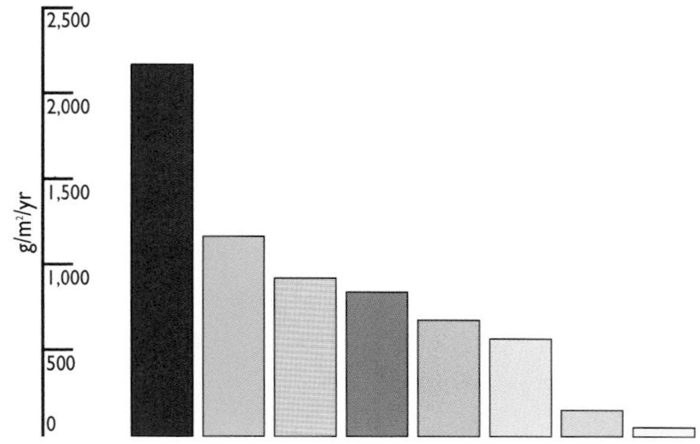

The net primary production of eight major biomes is expressed in grams of dry organic matter per square metre per year. The tropical rainforests produce the greatest amount of organic material. The tundra and deserts produce the least.

The Human World

Every minute, the world's population increases by between 160 and 170. While forecasts of future growth are difficult to make, most demographers are in agreement that the world's population, which passed the 6 billion mark in October 1999, would reach 8.9 billion by 2050. It was not expected to level out until 2200, when it would peak at around 11 billion. After 2200, it is expected to level out or even decline a little. The fastest rates of increase will take place in the developing countries of Africa, Asia and Latin America – the places least able to afford the enormous costs incurred by such a rapidly expanding population.

Elevated view of Ki Lung Street, Hong Kong

Urban areas of Hong Kong, a Special Administrative Region on the southern coast of China, contain busy streets overlooked by crowded apartments.

Average world population growth rates have declined from about 2% a year in the early 1960s to 1.4% in 1998. This was partly due to a decline in fertility rates – that is, the number of births to the number of women of child-bearing age – especially in developed countries where, as income has risen, the average size of families has fallen.

Declining fertility rates were also evident in many developing countries. Even Africa shows signs of such change, though its population is expected to triple before it begins to fall. Population growth is also dependent on death rates, which are affected by such factors as famine, disease and the quality of medical care.

The Population Explosion

The world's population has grown steadily throughout most of human history, though certain events triggered periods of population growth. The invention of agriculture around 10,000 years ago, led to great changes in human society. Before then, most people had obtained food by hunting animals and gathering plants. Average life expectancies were probably no more than 20 years and life was hard. However, when farmers began to produce food surpluses, people began to live settled lives. This major milestone in human history led to the development of the first cities and early civilizations.

From an estimated 8 million in 8000 BC, the world population rose to about 300 million by AD 1000. Between 1000 and 1750, the rate of world population increase was around 0.1% per year, but another period of major economic and social change – the Industrial Revolution – began in the late 18th century. The Industrial Revolution led to improvements in farm technology and increases in food production. The world population began to increase quickly as industrialization spread across Europe and into North America. By 1850, it had reached 1.2 billion. The 2 billion mark was passed in the 1920s, and then the population rapidly doubled to 4 billion by the 1970s.

Population Features

Population growth affects the structure of societies. In developing countries with high annual rates of population increase, the large majority of the people are young and soon to become parents themselves. For example, in Kenya, which had until recently an annual rate of population growth of around 4%, just over half

LARGEST CITIES

Within 10 years, for the first time ever, the majority of the world's population will live in urban areas. Almost all the urban growth will be in developing countries. Below is a list of cities with their estimated populations in the year 2015, in millions.

1	Tokyo	28.7
2	Mumbai (Bombay)	27.4
3	Lagos	24.1
4	Shanghai	23.2
5	Jakarta	21.5
6	São Paulo	21.0
7	Karachi	20.6
8	Beijing	19.6
9	Dhaka	19.2
10	Mexico City	19.1
11	Kolkata (Calcutta)	17.6
12	Delhi	17.5
13	New York City	17.4
14	Tianjin	17.1
15	Metro Manila	14.9
16	Cairo	14.7
17	Los Angeles	14.5
18	Seoul	13.1
19	Buenos Aires	12.5
20	Istanbul	12.1

These city populations are based on figures for urban agglomerations rather than actual city limits.

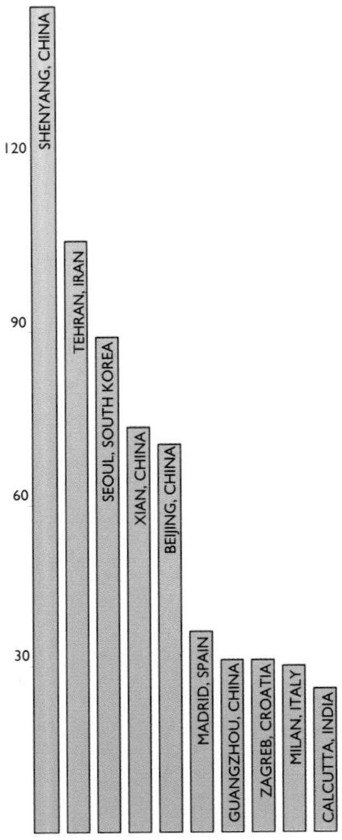

Urban air pollution

This diagram of the world's most polluted cities indicates the number of days per year when sulphur dioxide levels exceed the WHO threshhold of 150 micrograms per cubic metre.

Hong Kong's business district
By contrast with the picturesque old streets of Hong Kong, the business district of Hong Kong City, on the northern shore of Hong Kong Island, is a cluster of modern high-rise buildings. The glittering skyscrapers reflect the success of this tiny region, which has one of the strongest economies in Asia.

of the population is under 15 years of age. On the other hand, the populations of developed countries, with low population growth rates, have a fairly even spread across age groups.

Such differences are reflected in average life expectancies at birth. In rich countries, such as Australia and the United States, the average life expectancy is 77 years (74 years for men and 80 for women; women live longer, on average, than their male counterparts). As a result, an increasing proportion of the people are elderly and retired, contributing little to the economy. The reverse applies in many poor countries, where average life expectancies are below 60 years. In the early 21st century, life expectancies were falling in some southern African countries, such as Botswana, where they fell from nearly 70 to around 40 years because of the fast spread of HIV and AIDS.

Paralleling the population explosion has been a rapid growth in the number and size of cities and towns, which contained nearly half of the world's people by the 1990s. This proportion is expected to rise to nearly two-thirds by 2025.

Urbanization occurred first in areas undergoing the industrialization of their economies, but today it is also a feature of the developing world. In developing countries, people are leaving impoverished rural areas hoping to gain access to the education, health and other services available in cities. But many cities cannot provide the facilities necessitated by rapid population growth. Slums develop and pollution, crime and disease become features of everyday life.

The population explosion poses another probem for the entire world. No one knows how many people the world can support or how consumer demand will damage the fragile environments on our planet. The British economist Thomas Malthus argued in the late 18th century that overpopulation would lead to famine and war. But an increase in farm technology in the 19th and 20th centuries, combined with a green revolution, in which scientists developed high-yield crop varieties, has greatly increased food production since Malthus' time.

However, some modern scientists argue that overpopulation may become a problem in the 21st century. They argue that food shortages leading to disastrous famines will result unless population growth can be halted. Such people argue in favour of birth control programmes. China, one of the two countries with more than a billion people, has introduced a one-child family policy. Its action has slowed the growth of China's huge population.

POPULATION CHANGE 1990–2000

The population change for the years 1990–2000.

- OVER 40% POPULATION GAIN
- 30–40% POPULATION GAIN
- 20–30% POPULATION GAIN
- 10–20% POPULATION GAIN
- 0–10% POPULATION GAIN
- NO CHANGE OR LOSS

TOP 5 COUNTRIES	
Kuwait	+75.0%
Namibia	+62.5%
Afghanistan	+60.1%
Mali	+55.5%
Tanzania	+54.6%

BOTTOM 5 COUNTRIES	
Belgium	–0.1%
Hungary	–0.2%
Grenada	–2.4%
Germany	–3.2%
Tonga	–3.2%

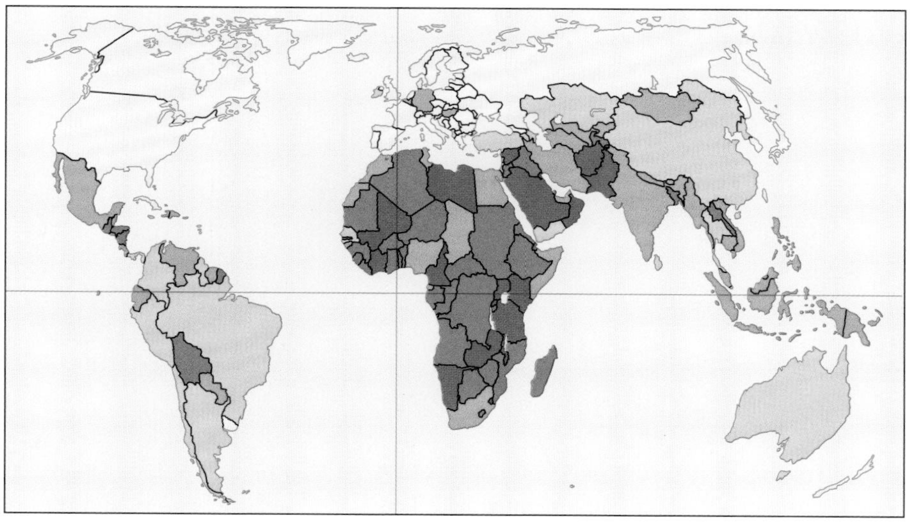

Languages and Religions

In 1995, 90-year-old Edna Guerro died in northern California. She was the last person able to speak Northern Pomo, one of about 50 Native American languages spoken in the state. Her death marked the extinction of one of the world's languages.

This event is not an isolated incident. Language experts regularly report the disappearance of languages and some of them predict that between 20 to 50% of the world's languages will no longer exist by the end of the 21st century. Improved transport and communications are partly to blame, because they bring people from various cultures into closer and closer contact. Many children no longer speak the language of their parents, preferring instead to learn the language used at their schools. The pressures on children to speak dominant rather than minority languages are often great. In the first part of the 20th century, Native American children were punished if they spoke their native language.

The disappearance of a language represents the extinction of a way of thinking, a unique expression of the experiences and knowledge of a group of people. Language and religion together give people an identity and a sense of belonging. However, there are others who argue that the disappearance of minority languages is a step towards international understanding and economic efficiency.

The World's Languages

Definitions of what is a language or a dialect vary and, hence, estimates of the number of languages spoken around the world range from about 3,000 to 6,000. But whatever the figure, it is clear that the number of languages far exceeds the number of countries.

RELIGIOUS ADHERENTS

Number of adherents to the world's major religions, in millions (1998).

Christian	1,980
Roman Catholic	1,300
Orthodox	240
African sects	110
Pentecostal	105
Others	225
Islam	1,300
Sunni	940
Shiite	120
Others	240
Hindu	900
Secular/Atheist/Agnostic/ Non-religious	850
Buddhist	360
Chinese Traditional	225
Indigenous/Animist	190
Sikh	23
Yoruba	20
Juche	19
Spiritism	14
Judaism	14
Baha'i	6
Jainism	4
Shinto	4

Buddhist monks in Katmandu, Nepal

Hinduism is Nepal's official religion, but the Nepalese observe the festivals of both Hinduism and Buddhism. They also regard Buddhist shrines and Hindu temples as equally sacred.

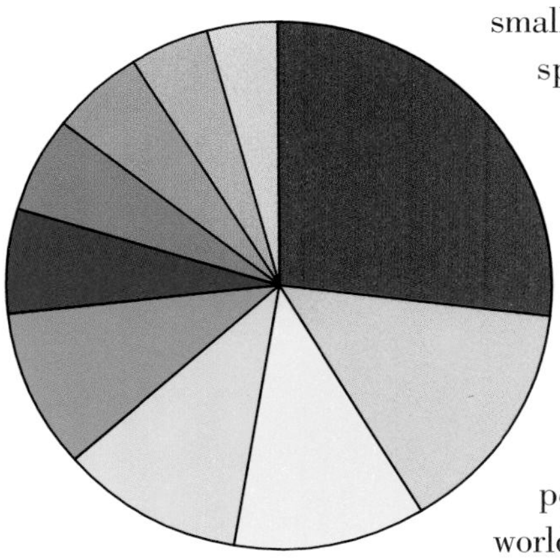

MOTHER TONGUES
First-language speakers of the major languages, in millions (1999).

- MANDARIN CHINESE 885M
- SPANISH 332M
- ENGLISH 322M
- BENGALI 189M
- HINDI 182M
- PORTUGUESE 170M
- RUSSIAN 170M
- JAPANESE 125M
- GERMAN 98M
- WU CHINESE 77M

Countries with only one language tend to be small. For example, in Liechtenstein, everyone speaks German. By contrast, more than 860 languages have been identified in Papua New Guinea, whose population is only about 4.3 million people. Hence, many of its languages are spoken by only small groups of people. In fact, scientists have estimated that about a third of the world's languages are now spoken by less than 1,000 people. By contrast, more than half of the world's population speak just seven languages.

The world's languages are grouped into families. The Indo-European family consists of languages spoken between Europe and the Indian subcontinent. The growth of European empires over the last 300 years led several Indo-European languages, most notably English, French, Portuguese and Spanish, to spread throughout much of North and South America, Africa, Australia and New Zealand.

English has become the official language in many countries which together contain more than a quarter of the world's population. It is now a major international language, surpassing in importance Mandarin Chinese, a member of the Sino-Tibetan family, which is the world's leading first language. Without a knowledge of English, businessmen face many problems when conducting international trade, especially with the United States or other English-speaking countries. But proposals that English, French, Russian or some other language should become a world language seem unlikely to be acceptable to a majority of the world's peoples.

World Religions

Religion is another fundamental aspect of human culture. It has inspired much of the world's finest architecture, literature, music and painting. It has also helped to shape human cultures since prehistoric times and is responsible for the codes of ethics by which most people live.

The world's major religions were all founded in Asia. Judaism, one of the first faiths to teach that there is only one god, is one of the world's oldest. Founded in south-western Asia, it influenced the more recent Christianity and Islam, two other monotheistic religions which now have the greatest number of followers. Hinduism, the third leading faith in terms of the numbers of followers, originated in the Indian subcontinent and most Hindus are now found in India. Another major religion, Buddhism, was founded in the subcontinent partly as a reaction to certain aspects of Hinduism. But unlike Hinduism, it has spread from India throughout much of eastern Asia.

Religion and language are powerful creative forces. They are also essential features of nationalism, which gives people a sense of belonging and pride. But nationalism is often also a cause of rivalry and tension. Cultural differences have led to racial hatred, the persecution of minorities, and to war between national groups.

The Church of San Giovanni, Dolomites, Italy
Christianity has done much to shape Western civilization. Christian churches were built as places of worship, but many of them are among the finest achievements of world architecture.

OFFICIAL LANGUAGES: % OF WORLD POPULATION	
English	27.0%
Chinese	19.0%
Hindi	13.5%
Spanish	5.4%
Russian	5.2%
French	4.2%
Arabic	3.3%
Portuguese	3.0%
Malay	3.0%
Bengali	2.9%
Japanese	2.3%

Polyglot nations
The graph, right, shows countries of the world with more than 200 languages. Although it has only about 4.3 million people, Papua New Guinea holds the record for the number of languages spoken.

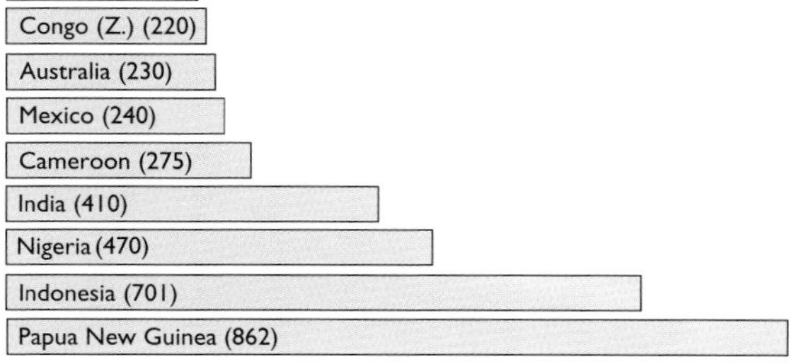
Brazil (210)
Congo (Z.) (220)
Australia (230)
Mexico (240)
Cameroon (275)
India (410)
Nigeria (470)
Indonesia (701)
Papua New Guinea (862)

International Organizations

Twelve days before the surrender of Germany and four months before the final end of World War II, representatives of 50 nations met in San Francisco to create a plan to set up a peace-keeping organization, the United Nations. Since its birth on 24 October 1945, its membership has grown from 51 to 188.

Its first 50 years have been marked by failures as well as successes. While it has helped to prevent some disputes from flaring up into full-scale wars, the Blue Berets, as the UN troops are called, have been forced, because of their policy of neutrality, to stand by when atrocities are committed by rival warring groups.

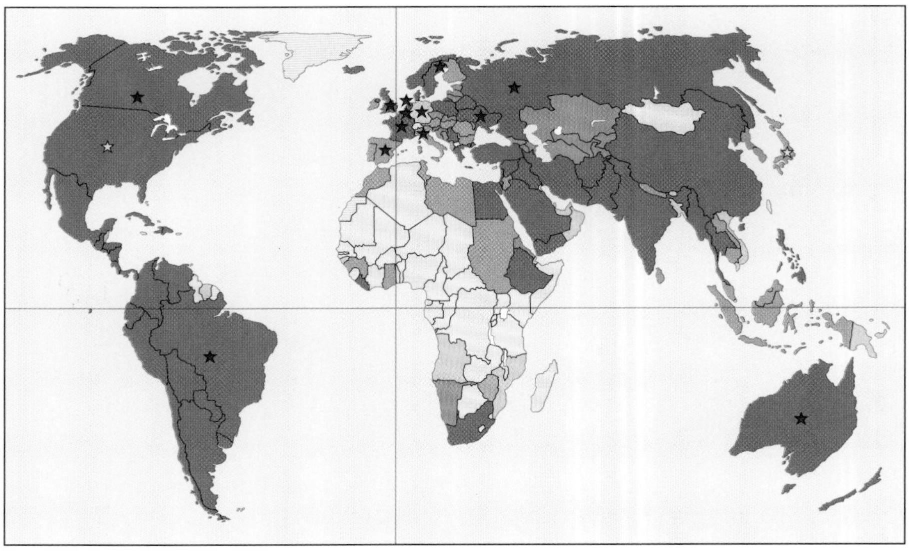

MEMBERS OF THE UN
Year of joining.

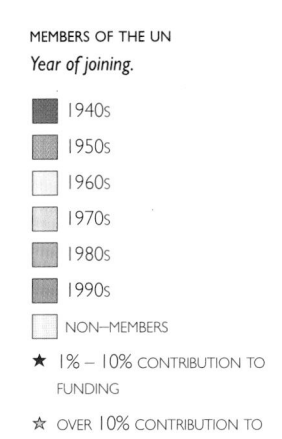

- 1940s
- 1950s
- 1960s
- 1970s
- 1980s
- 1990s
- NON–MEMBERS
- ★ 1% – 10% CONTRIBUTION TO FUNDING
- ☆ OVER 10% CONTRIBUTION TO FUNDING

The Work of the UN

The United Nations has six main organs. They include the General Assembly, where member states meet to discuss issues concerned with peace, security and development. The Security Council, containing 15 members, is concerned with maintaining world peace. The Secretariat, under the Secretary-General, helps the other organs to do their jobs effectively, while the Economic and Social Council works with specialized agencies to implement policies concerned with such matters as development, education and health. The International Court of Justice, or World Court, helps to settle disputes between member nations. The sixth organ of the UN, the Trusteeship Council, was designed to bring 11 UN trust territories to independence. Its task has now been completed.

The specialized agencies do much important work. For example, UNICEF (United Nations International Children's Fund) has provided health care and aid for children in many parts of the world. The ILO (International Labour Organization) has improved working conditions in many areas, while the FAO (Food and Agricultural Organization) has worked to improve the production and distribution of food. Among the other agencies are organizations to help refugees, to further human rights and to control the environment. The latest agency, set up in 1995, is the WTO (World Trade Organization), which took over the work of GATT (General Agreement on Tariffs and Trade).

Food aid

International organizations supply aid to people living in areas suffering from war or famine. In Bosnia-Herzegovina, the UN Protection Force supervised the movements of food aid, as did NATO on the borders of Kosovo a few years later.

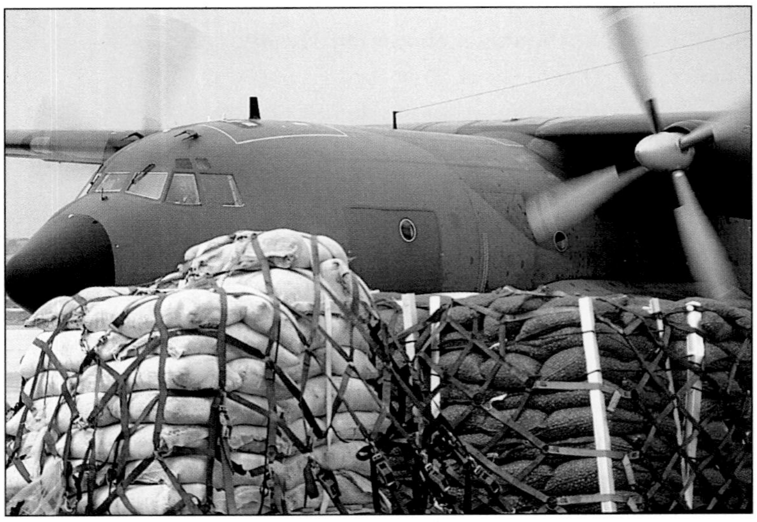

Other Organizations

In a world in which nations have become increasingly interdependent, many other organizations have been set up to deal with a variety of problems. Some, such as NATO (the North Atlantic Treaty Organization), are defence alliances. In the early 1990s, the end of the Cold War suggested that NATO's role might be finished, but the civil war in the former Yugoslavia showed that it still has a role in maintaining peace and security.

Other organizations encourage social and economic co-operation in various regions. Some are NGOs (non-governmental organizations), such as the Red Cross and its Muslim equivalent, the Red Crescent. Other NGOs raise funds to provide aid to countries facing major crises, such as famine.

Some major international organizations aim at economic co-operation and the removal of trade barriers. For example, the European Union has 15 members. Its economic success and the

INTERNATIONAL AID AND GNP
Aid provided as a percentage of GNP, with total aid in brackets (1997).

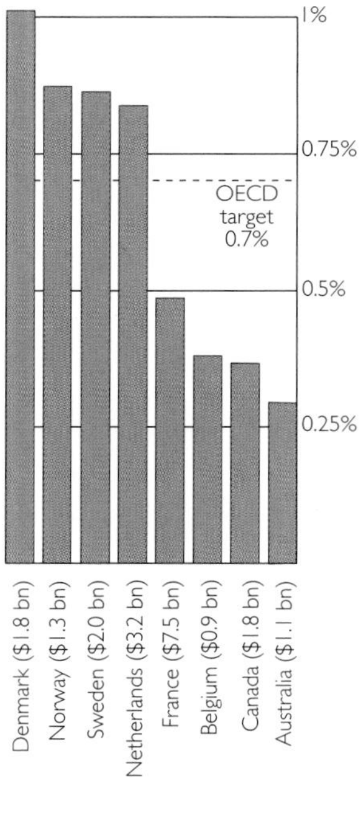
1%
0.75%
0.5%
0.25%
OECD target 0.7%
Denmark ($1.8 bn)
Norway ($1.3 bn)
Sweden ($2.0 bn)
Netherlands ($3.2 bn)
France ($7.5 bn)
Belgium ($0.9 bn)
Canada ($1.8 bn)
Australia ($1.1 bn)

UNHCR-funded jetty, Sri Lanka
In 1994, the UN High Commission for Refugees was responsible for 23 million people. Sometimes, it has to provide transport facilities, such as this jetty, to get aid to the refugees.

adoption of a single currency, the euro, by 12 of its members, has prompted some people to support the idea of a federal Europe. But others fear that political union might lead to a loss of national sovereignty by member states.

Other groupings include ASEAN (the Association of South-east Asian Nations) which aims to reduce trade barriers between its members (Brunei, Burma [Myanmar], Cambodia, Indonesia, Laos, Malaysia, the Philippines, Singapore, Thailand and Vietnam). APEC (the Asia-Pacific Co-operation Group), founded in 1989, aims to create a free trade zone between the countries of eastern Asia, North America, Australia and New Zealand by 2020. Meanwhile, Canada, Mexico and the United States have formed NAFTA (the North American Free Trade Agreement), while other economic groupings link most of the countries in Latin America. Another grouping with a more limited but important objective is OPEC (the Organization of Oil-Exporting Countries). OPEC works to unify policies concerning trade in oil on the world markets.

Some organizations exist to discuss matters of common interest between groups of nations. The Commonwealth of Nations, for example, grew out of links created by the British Empire. In North and South America, the OAS (Organization of American States) aims to increase understanding in the Western hemisphere. The OAU (Organization of African Unity) has a similar role in Africa, while the Arab League represents the Arab nations of North Africa and the Middle East.

COUNTRIES OF THE EUROPEAN UNION

	Total land area (sq km)	Total population (2000 est.)	GNP per capita, US$ (1999)	Unemployment rate, % (1996)	Year of accession to the EU	Seats in EU parliament (1998)
Austria	83,850	7,613,000	25,970	7%	1995	21
Belgium	30,510	9,832,000	24,510	12.7%	1958	25
Denmark	43,070	5,153,000	32,030	8.7%	1973	16
Finland	338,130	5,077,000	23,780	16.3%	1995	16
France	551,500	58,145,000	23,480	12.3%	1958	87
Germany	356,910	76,962,000	25,350	10.4%	1958	99
Greece	131,990	10,193,000	11,770	10.3%	1981	25
Ireland	70,280	4,086,000	19,160	11.9%	1973	15
Italy	301,270	57,195,000	19,710	12.1%	1958	87
Luxembourg	2,590	377,000	44,640	3.3%	1958	6
Netherlands	41,526	15,829,000	24,320	6.6%	1958	31
Portugal	92,390	10,587,000	10,600	7.3%	1986	24
Spain	504,780	40,667,000	14,000	22.2%	1986	64
Sweden	449,960	8,560,000	25,040	8.1%	1995	22
United Kingdom	243,368	58,393,000	22,640	7.6%	1973	87

Agriculture

In 1999, partly because of ongoing economic turmoil in Russia, the increase in food production was less than the rise in world population, creating a small per capita fall in food production. Downward trends in world food production in the 1990s reopened an old debate – whether food production will be able to keep pace with the rapidly rising world population in the 21st century.

Some experts argue that the lower than expected production figures in the 1990s heralded a period of relative scarcity and high prices of food, which will be felt most in the poorer developing countries. Others are more optimistic. They point to the successes of the 'green revolution' which, through the use of new crop varieties produced by scientists, irrigation and the extensive use of fertilizers and pesticides, has revolutionized food production since the 1950s and 1960s.

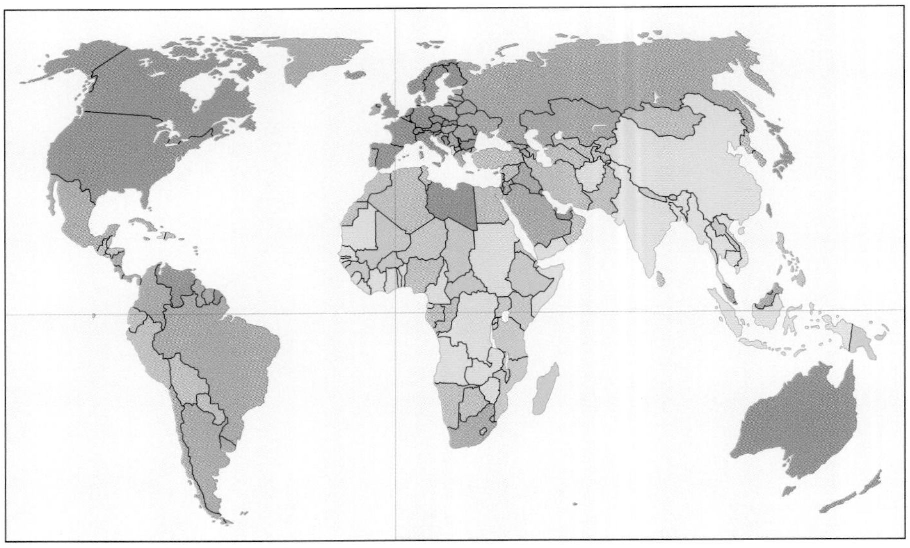

IMPORTANCE OF AGRICULTURE

Percentage of the population dependent on agriculture (1997).

- OVER 75% DEPENDENT
- 50–75% DEPENDENT
- 25–50% DEPENDENT
- 10–25% DEPENDENT
- UNDER 10% DEPENDENT

Rice harvest, Bali, Indonesia

More than half of the world's people eat rice as their basic food. Rice grows well in tropical and subtropical regions, such as in Indonesia, India and south-eastern China.

The green revolution has led to a great expansion in the production of many crops, including such basic foods as rice, maize and wheat. In India, its effects have been spectacular. Between 1955 and 1995, grain production trebled, giving the country sufficient food reserves to prevent famine in years when droughts or floods reduce the harvest. While once India had to import food, it is now self-sufficient.

Food Production

Agriculture, which supplies most of our food, together with materials to make clothes and other products, is the world's most important economic activity. But its relative importance has declined in comparison with manufacturing and service industries. As a result, the end of the 20th century marked the first time for 10,000 years when the vast majority of the people no longer had to depend for their living on growing crops and herding animals.

However, agriculture remains the dominant economic activity in many developing countries in Africa and Asia. For example, by the start of the 21st century, 80% or more of the people of Bhutan, Burundi, Nepal and Rwanda depended on farming for their living.

Many people in developing countries eke out the barest of livings by nomadic herding or shifting cultivation, combined with hunting, fishing and gathering plant foods. A large proportion of farmers live at subsistence level, producing little more than they require to provide the basic needs of their families.

The world's largest food producer and exporter is the United States, although agriculture employs

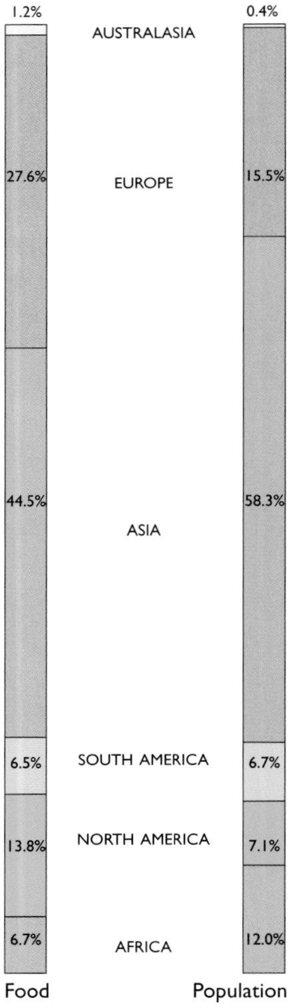
1.2%
0.4%
AUSTRALASIA
27.6%
EUROPE
15.5%
44.5%
ASIA
58.3%
6.5%
SOUTH AMERICA
6.7%
13.8%
NORTH AMERICA
7.1%
6.7%
AFRICA
12.0%
Food
Population

A comparison of world food production and population by continent.

Landsat ***image of the Nile delta, Egypt***

Most Egyptians live in the Nile valley and on its delta. Because much of the silt carried by the Nile now ends up on the floor of Lake Nasser, upstream of the Aswan Dam, the delta is now retreating and seawater is seeping inland. This eventuality was not foreseen when the Aswan High Dam was built in the 1960s.

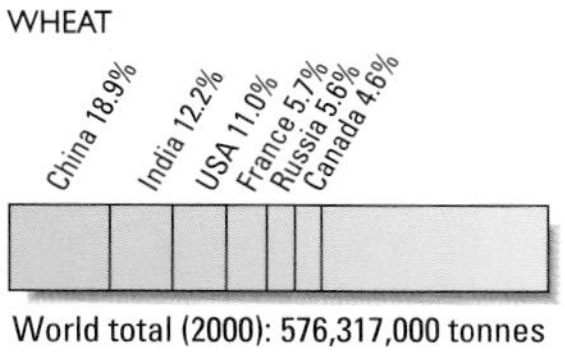
WHEAT
China 18.9%
India 12.2%
USA 11.0%
France 5.7%
Russia 5.6%
Canada 4.6%

World total (2000): 576,317,000 tonnes

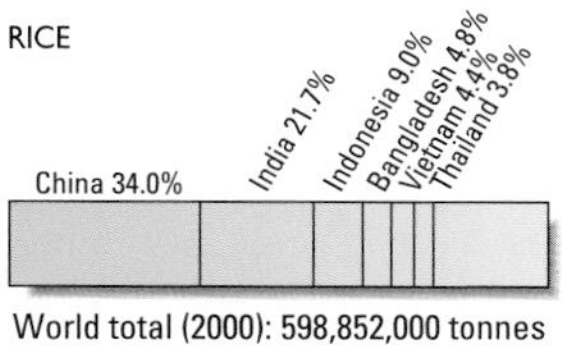
RICE
China 34.0%
India 21.7%
Indonesia 9.0%
Bangladesh 4.8%
Vietnam 4.4%
Thailand 3.8%

World total (2000): 598,852,000 tonnes

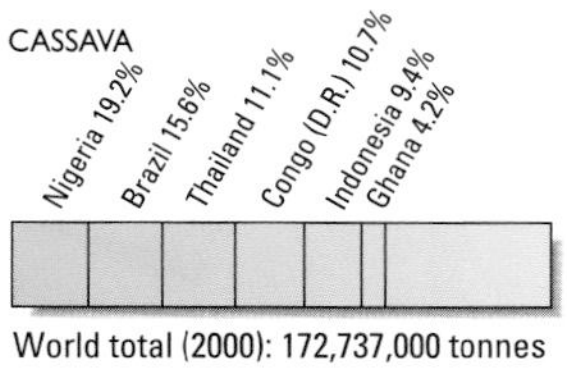
CASSAVA
Nigeria 19.2%
Brazil 15.6%
Thailand 11.1%
Congo (D.R.) 10.7%
Indonesia 9.4%
Ghana 4.2%

World total (2000): 172,737,000 tonnes

around 2% of its total workforce. The high production of the United States is explained by its use of scientific methods and mechanization, which are features of agriculture throughout the developed world.

Intensive or Organic Farming

In the early 21st century, some people were beginning to question the dependence of farmers on chemical fertilizers and pesticides. Many people became concerned that the widespread use of chemicals was seriously polluting and damaging the environment.

Others objected to the intensive farming of animals to raise production and lower prices. For example, the suggestion in Britain in 1996 that BSE, or 'mad cow disease', might be passed on to people causing CJD (Creuzfeldt-Jakob Disease) caused widespread alarm.

Such problems have led some farmers to return to organic farming, which is based on animal-welfare principles and the banning of chemical fertilizers and pesticides. The costs of organic foods are certainly higher than those produced by intensive farming, but an increasing number of consumers in the Western world are beginning to demand organic products from their retailers.

Energy and Minerals

In September 2000, Japan experienced its worst nuclear accident, when more than 400 people were exposed to harmful levels of radiation. This was the worst nuclear incident since the explosion at the Chernobyl nuclear power station, in Ukraine, in 1986. Nuclear power provides around 17% of the world's electricity and experts once thought that it would generate much of the world's energy supply. But concerns about safety and worries about the high costs make this seem unlikely. Some developed countries have already abandoned their nuclear programmes.

Fossil Fuels

Huge amounts of energy are needed for heating, generating electricity and for transport. In the early years of the Industrial Revolution, coal formed from organic matter buried beneath the Earth's surface, was the leading source of energy. It remains important as a raw material in the manufacture of drugs and other products and also as a fuel, despite the fact that burning coal causes air pollution and gives off carbon dioxide, an important greenhouse gas.

However, oil and natural gas, which came into wide use in the 20th century, are cheaper to produce and easier to handle than coal, while, kilogram for kilogram, they give out more heat. Oil is especially important in moving transport, supplying about 97% of the fuel required.

In 1995, proven reserves of oil were sufficient to supply the world, at current rates of production, for 43 years, while supplies of natural gas stood at about 66 years. Coal reserves are more abundant and known reserves would last 200 years at present rates of use. Although these figures must be regarded with caution, because they do not allow for future discoveries, it is clear that fossil fuel reserves will one day run out.

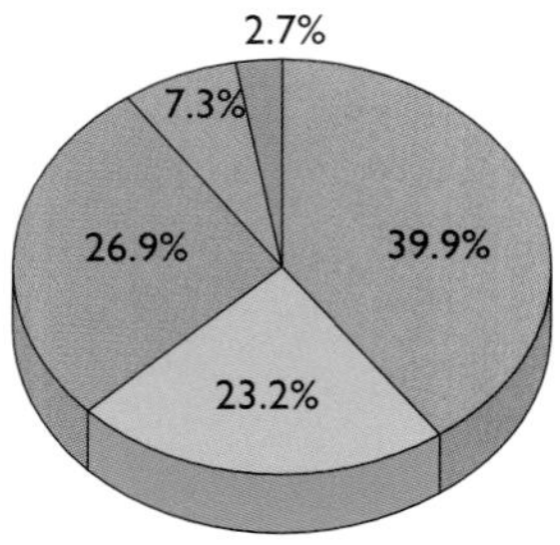
2.7%
7.3%
26.9%
39.9%
23.2%

WORLD ENERGY CONSUMPTION

- OIL
- GAS
- COAL
- NUCLEAR
- HYDRO

The diagram shows the proportion of world energy consumption in 1997 by form. Total energy consumption was 8,509.2 million tonnes of oil equivalent. Such fuels as wood, peat and animal wastes, together with renewable forms of energy, such as wind and geothermal power, are not included, although they are important in some areas.

Wind farms in California, United States

Wind farms using giant turbines can produce electricity at a lower cost than conventional power stations. But in many areas, winds are too light or too strong for wind farms to be effective.

SELECTED MINERAL PRODUCTION STATISTICS (1997)

Bauxite		Diamonds	
Australia	34.9%	Australia	33.9%
Guinea	15.1%	Congo (D.R.)	18.6%
Brazil	9.8%	Botswana	17.0%
Jamaica	9.4%	Russia	16.1%
China	7.1%	S. Africa	8.5%
Gold		**Iron ore**	
S. Africa	20.5%	China	22.1%
USA	14.9%	Brazil	17.4%
Australia	13.1%	Australia	14.0%
Canada	7.0%	Ukraine	10.3%
China	6.5%	Russia	6.7%
Manganese		**Zinc**	
Ukraine	27.0%	China	16.4%
China	25.6%	Canada	14.5%
S. Africa	11.4%	Australia	14.0%
Brazil	8.0%	Peru	11.7%
Australia	7.8%	USA	8.5%

Potash mines in Utah, United States
Potash is a mineral used mainly to make fertilizers. Much of it comes from mines where deposits formed when ancient seas dried up are exploited. Potash is also extracted from salt lakes.

MINERAL DISTRIBUTION
The map shows the richest sources of the most important minerals. Major mineral locations are named. Undersea deposits, most of which are considered inaccessible, are not shown.

- ▽ GOLD
- SILVER
- ◆ DIAMONDS
- ▽ TUNGSTEN
- ● IRON ORE
- ■ NICKEL
- CHROME
- ▲ MANGANESE
- □ COBALT
- ▲ MOLYBDENUM
- ■ COPPER
- ▲ LEAD
- ● BAUXITE
- ▽ TIN
- ◆ ZINC
- MERCURY

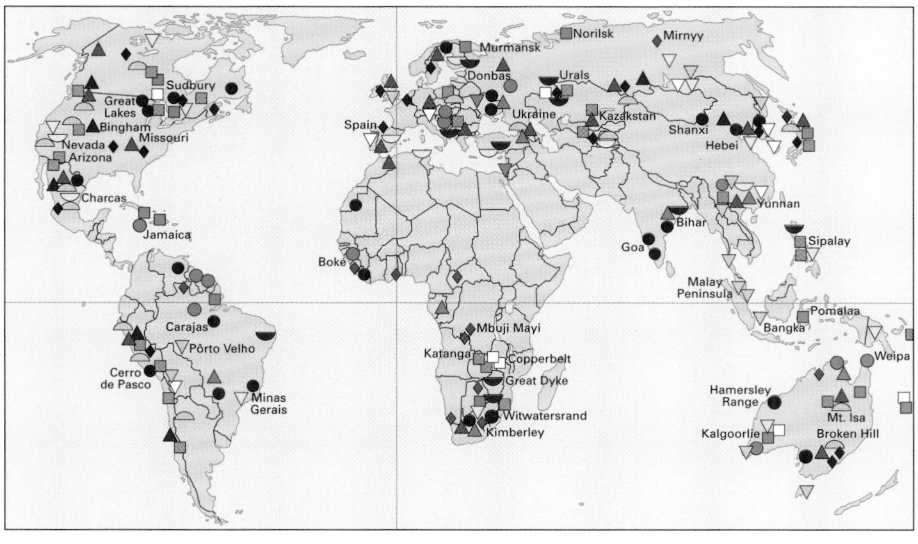

Alternative Energy

Other sources of energy are therefore required. Besides nuclear energy, the main alternative to fossil fuels is water power. The costs of building dams and hydroelectric power stations is high, though hydroelectric production is comparatively cheap and it does not cause pollution. But the creation of reservoirs uproots people and, in tropical rainforests, it destroys natural habitats. Hydroelectricity is also suitable only in areas with plenty of rivers and steep slopes, such as Norway, while it is unsuitable in flat areas, such as the Netherlands.

In Brazil, alcohol made from sugar has been used to fuel cars. Initially, this government-backed policy met with great success, but it has proved to be extremely expensive. Battery-run, electric cars have also been developed in the United States, but they appear to have limited use, because of the problems involved in regular and time-consuming recharging.

Other forms of energy, which are renewable and cleaner than fossil fuels, are winds, sea waves, the rise and fall of tides, and geothermal power. These forms of energy are already used to some extent. However, their contribution in global terms seems likely to remain small in the immediate future.

Minerals for Industry

In addition to energy, manufacturing industries need raw materials, including minerals, and these natural resources, like fossil fuels, are being used in such huge quantities that some experts have predicted shortages of some of them before long.

Manufacturers depend on supplies of about 80 minerals. Some, such as bauxite (aluminium ore) and iron, are abundant, but others are scarce or are found only in deposits that are uneconomical to mine. Many experts advocate a policy of recycling scrap metal, including aluminium, chromium, copper, lead, nickel and zinc. This practice would reduce pollution and conserve the energy required for extracting and refining mineral ores.

World Economies

In 1999, Tanzania had a per capita GNP (Gross National Product) of US$240, as compared with Switzerland, whose per capita GNP stood at $38,350. These figures indicate the vast gap between the economies and standards of living of the two countries.

The GNP includes the GDP (Gross Domestic Product), which consists of the total output of goods and services in a country in a given year, plus net exports – that is, the value of goods and services sold abroad less the value of foreign goods and services used in the country in the same year. The GNP divided by the population gives a country's GNP per capita. In low-income developing countries, agriculture makes a high contribution to the GNP. For example, in Tanzania, 56% of the GDP in 1995 came from agriculture. On the other hand, manufacturing was small-scale and contributed only 5% of the GDP. By comparison, in high-income economies, the percentage contribution of manufacturing far exceeds that of agriculture.

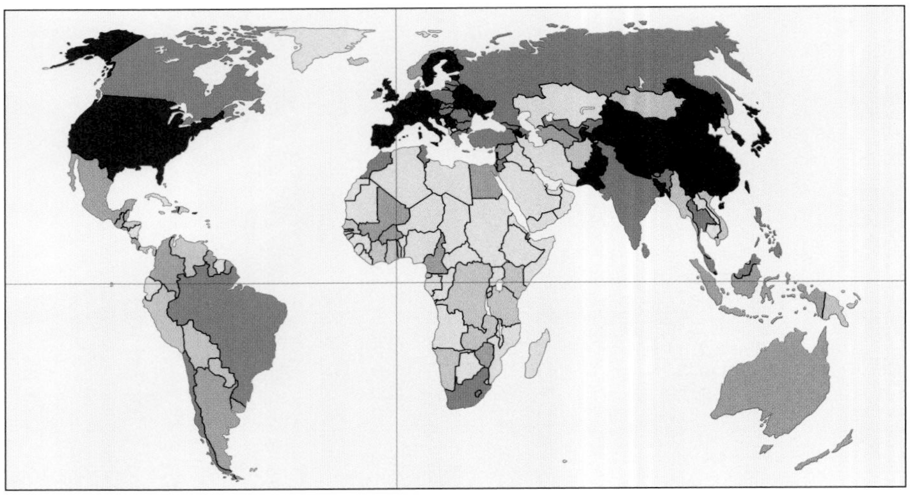

INDUSTRY AND TRADE

Manufactured goods (including machinery and transport) as a percentage of total exports.

- OVER 75%
- 50–75%
- 25–50%
- 10–25%
- UNDER 10%

Eastern Asia, including Japan (98.3%), Taiwan (92.7%) and Hong Kong (93.0%), contains countries whose exports are most dominated by manufactures. But some countries in Europe, such as Slovenia (92.5%), are also heavily dependent on manufacturing.

Microchip production, Taiwan

Despite its lack of resources, Taiwan is one of eastern Asia's 'tiger' economies. Its high-tech industries have helped it to achieve fast economic growth and to compete on the world market.

Industrialization

The Industrial Revolution began in Britain in the late 18th century. Before that time, most people worked on farms. But with the Industrial Revolution came factories, using machines that could manufacture goods much faster and more cheaply than those made by cottage industries which already existed.

The Industrial Revolution soon spread to several countries in mainland Europe and the United States and, by the late 19th century, it had reached Canada, Japan and Russia. At first, industrial development was based on such areas as coalfields or ironfields. But in the 20th century, the use of oil, which is easy to transport along pipelines, made it possible for industries to be set up anywhere.

Some nations, such as Switzerland, became industrialized even though they lacked natural resources. They depended instead on the specialized skills of their workers. This same pattern applies today. Some countries with rich natural resources, such as Mexico (with a per capita GNP in 1999 of $4,400), lag far behind Japan ($32,230) and Cyprus ($11,960), which lack resources and have to import many of the materials they need for their manufacturing industries.

Service Industries

Experts often refer to high-income countries as industrial economies. But manufacturing employs only one in six workers in the United

GROSS NATIONAL PRODUCT PER CAPITA US$ (1999 ESTIMATES)

1	Liechtenstein	50,000
2	Luxembourg	44,640
3	Switzerland	38,350
4	Bermuda	35,590
5	Norway	32,880
6	Japan	32,230
7	Denmark	32,030
8	USA	30,600
9	Singapore	29,610
10	Iceland	29,280
11	Austria	25,970
12	Germany	25,350
13	Sweden	25,040
14	Monaco	25,000
15	Belgium	24,510
16	Brunei	24,630
17	Netherlands	24,320
18	Finland	23,780
19	Hong Kong (China)	23,520
20	France	23,480

New cars awaiting transportation, Los Angeles, United States

Cars are the most important single manufactured item in world trade, followed by vehicle parts and engines. The world's leading car producers are Japan, the United States, Germany and France.

States, one in five in Britain, and one in three in Germany and Japan.

In most developed economies, the percentage of manufacturing jobs has fallen in recent years, while jobs in service industries have risen. For example, in Britain, the proportion of jobs in manufacturing fell from 37% in 1970 to 15% in 2000, while jobs in the service sector rose from just under 50% to 75%. While change in Britain was especially rapid, similar changes were taking place in most industrial economies. By the late 1990s, service industries accounted for well over half the jobs in the generally prosperous countries that made up the OECD (Organization for Economic Co-operation and Development). Instead of being called the 'industrial' economies, these countries might be better named the 'service' economies.

Service industries offer a wide range of jobs and many of them require high educational qualifications. These include finance, insurance and high-tech industries, such as computer programming, entertainment and telecommunications. Service industries also include marketing and advertising, which are essential if the cars and television sets made by manufacturers are to be sold. Another valuable service industry is tourism; in some countries, such as the Gambia, it is the major foreign exchange earner. Trade in services plays a crucial part in world economics. The share of services in world trade rose from 17% in 1980 to 22% in the 1990s.

THE WORKFORCE

Percentage of men and women between 15 and 64 years old in employment, selected countries (latest available year).

MEN

WOMEN

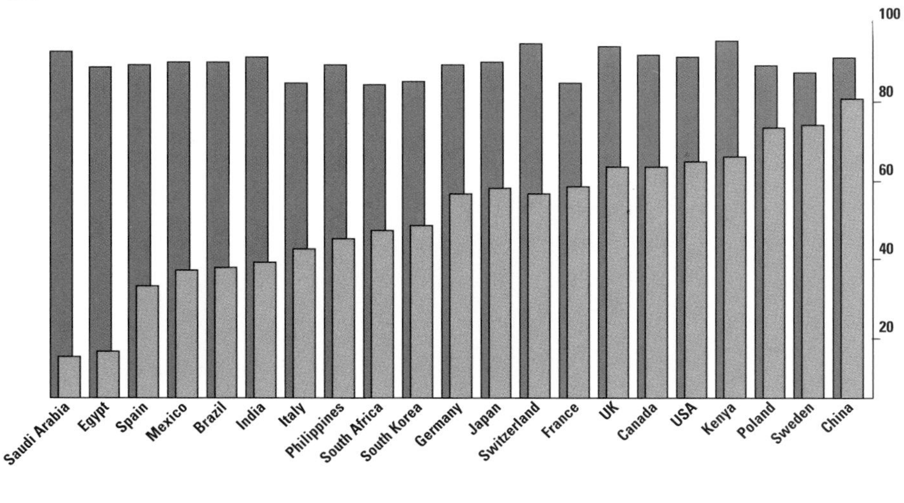
100
80
60
40
20
Saudi Arabia
Egypt
Spain
Mexico
Brazil
India
Italy
Philippines
South Africa
South Korea
Germany
Japan
Switzerland
France
UK
Canada
USA
Kenya
Poland
Sweden
China

Trade and Commerce

The establishment of the WTO (World Trade Organization) on 1 January 1995 was the latest step in the long history of world trade. The WTO was set up by the eighth round of negotiations, popularly called the 'Uruguay round', conducted by the General Agreement on Tariffs and Trade (GATT). This treaty was signed by representatives of 125 governments in April, 1994. By the end of 2000, the WTO had 140 members.

GATT was first established in 1948. Its initial aim was to produce a charter to create a body called the International Trade Organization. This body never came into being. Instead, GATT, acting as an *ad hoc* agency, pioneered a series of agreements aimed at liberalizing world trade by reducing tariffs on imports and other obstacles to free trade.

GATT's objectives were based on the belief that international trade creates wealth. Trade occurs because the world's resources are not distributed evenly between countries, and, in theory, free trade means that every country should concentrate on what it can do best and purchase from others goods and services that they can supply more cheaply. In practice, however, free trade may cause unemployment when imported goods are cheaper than those produced within the country.

Trade is sometimes an important factor in world politics, especially when trade sanctions are applied against countries whose actions incur the disapproval of the international community. For example, in the 1990s, worldwide trade sanctions were imposed on Serbia because of its involvement in the civil war in Bosnia-Herzegovina.

New York City Stock Exchange, United States

Stock exchanges, where stocks and shares are sold and bought, are important in channelling savings and investments to companies and governments. The world's largest stock exchange is in Tokyo, Japan.

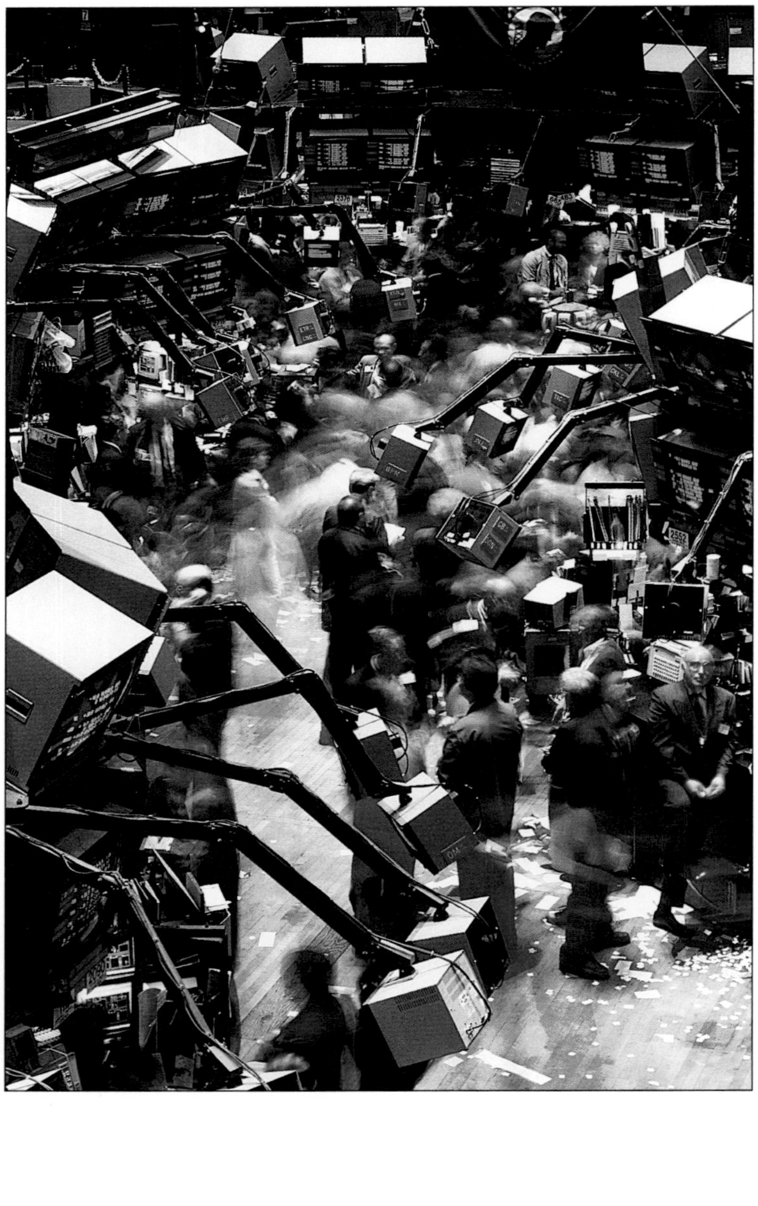

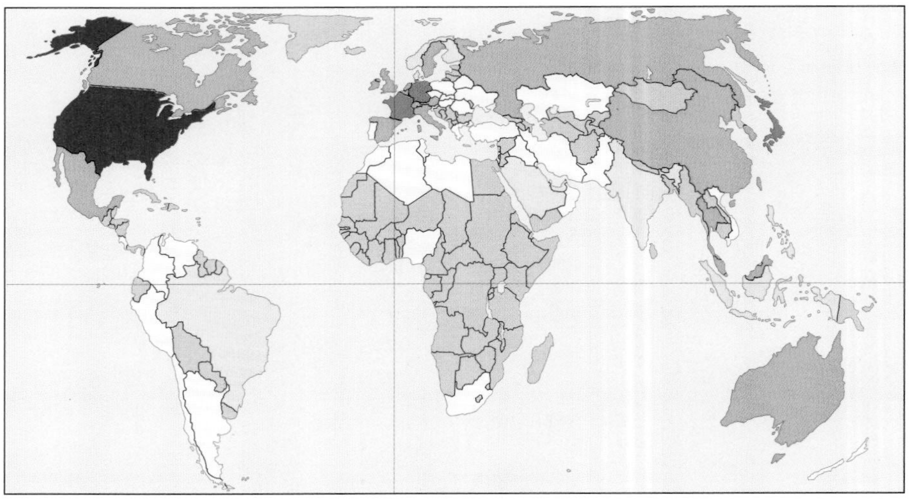

WORLD TRADE

Percentage share of total world exports by value (1999).

- OVER 10% OF WORLD TRADE
- 5–10% OF WORLD TRADE
- 1–5% OF WORLD TRADE
- 0.5–1% OF WORLD TRADE
- 0.1–0.5% OF WORLD TRADE
- UNDER 0.1% OF WORLD TRADE

The world's leading trading nations, according to the combined value of their exports and imports, are the United States, Germany, Japan, France and the United Kingdom.

Changing Trade Patterns

The early 16th century, when Europeans began to divide the world into huge empires, opened up a new era in international trade. By the 19th century, the colonial powers, who were among the first industrial powers, promoted trade with their colonies, from which they obtained unprocessed raw materials, such as food, natural fibres, minerals and timber. In return, they shipped clothes, shoes and other cheap items to the colonies.

From the late 19th century until the early 1950s, primary products dominated world trade, with oil becoming the leading item in the later part of this period. Many developing countries still depend heavily on the export of one or two primary products, such as coffee or iron ore, but overall the proportion of primary products in world trade has fallen since the 1950s. Today the most important elements in world trade are

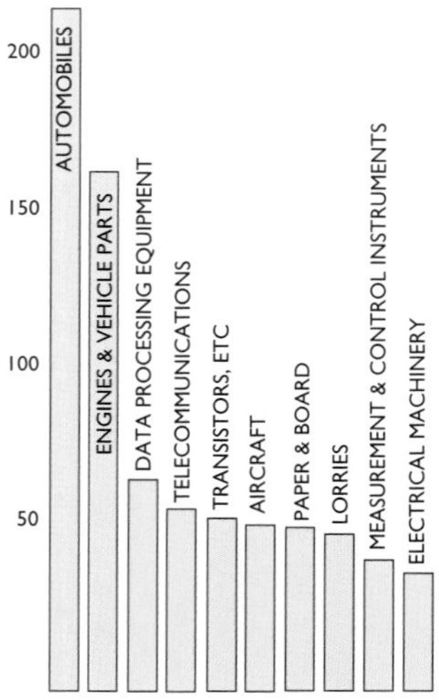

Traded products

Top ten manufactures traded by value in billions of US$ (latest available year).

Rotterdam, Netherlands

World trade depends on transport. Rotterdam, the world's largest port, serves not only the Netherlands, but also industrial areas in parts of Germany, France and Switzerland.

manufactures and semi-manufactures, exchanged mainly between the industrialized nations.

THE WORLD'S MARKETS

Private companies conduct most of world trade, but government policies affect it. Governments which believe that certain industries are strategic, or essential for the country's future, may impose tariffs on imports, or import quotas to limit the volume of imports, if they are thought to be undercutting the domestic industries.

For example, the United States has argued that Japan has greater access to its markets than the United States has to Japan's. This might have led the United States to resort to protectionism, but instead the United States remains committed to free trade.

Other problems in international trade occur when governments give subsidies to its producers, who can then export products at low prices. Another difficulty, called 'dumping', occurs when products are sold at below the market price in order to gain a market share. One of the aims of the newly-created WTO is the phasing out of government subsidies for agricultural products, though the world's poorest countries will be exempt from many of the WTO's most severe regulations.

Governments are also concerned about the volume of imports and exports and most countries keep records of international transactions. When the total value of goods and services imported exceeds the value of goods and services exported, then the country has a deficit in its balance of payments. Large deficits can weaken a country's economy.

DEPENDENCE ON TRADE

Value of exports as a percentage of GDP (Gross Domestic Product) 1997.

- OVER 50% GDP FROM EXPORTS
- 40–50% GDP FROM EXPORTS
- 30–40% GDP FROM EXPORTS
- 20–30% GDP FROM EXPORTS
- 10–20% GDP FROM EXPORTS
- UNDER 10% GDP FROM EXPORTS
- MOST DEPENDENT ON INDUSTRIAL EXPORTS (OVER 75% OF TOTAL)
- MOST DEPENDENT ON FUEL EXPORTS (OVER 75% OF TOTAL)
- MOST DEPENDENT ON METAL & MINERAL EXPORTS (OVER 75% OF TOTAL)

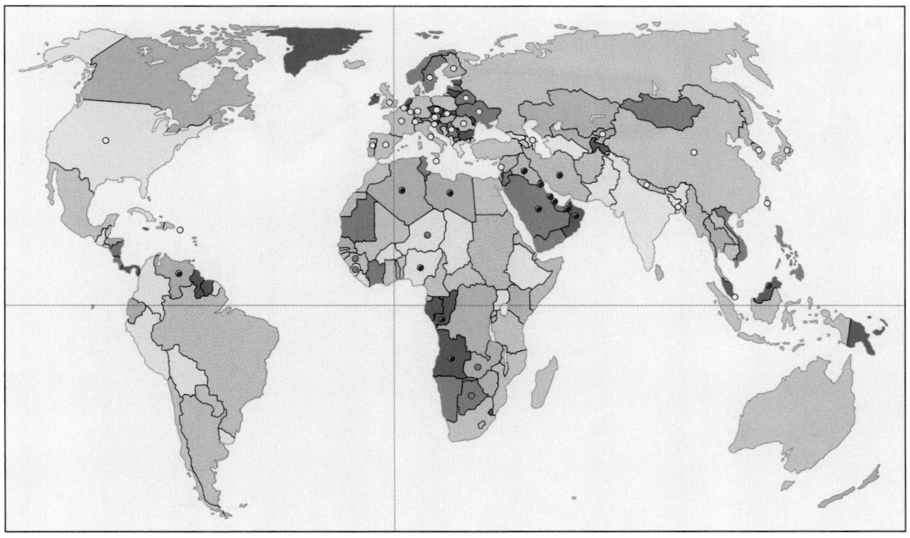

Travel and Communications

In the 1990s, millions of people became linked into an 'information superhighway' called the Internet. Equipped with a personal computer, an electricity supply, a telephone and a modem, people are able to communicate with others all over the world. People can now send messages by e-mail (electronic mail), they can engage in electronic discussions, contacting people with similar interests, and engage in 'chat lines', which are the latest equivalent of telephone conferences.

These new developments are likely to affect the working lives of people everywhere, enabling them to work at home whilst having many of the facilities that are available in an office. The Internet is part of an ongoing and astonishingly rapid evolution in the fields of communications and transport.

Transport

Around 200 years ago, most people never travelled far from their birthplace, but today we are much more mobile. Cars and buses now provide convenient forms of transport for many millions of people, huge ships transport massive cargoes around the world, and jet airliners, some travelling faster than the speed of sound, can transport high-value goods as well as holiday-makers to almost any part of the world.

Land transport of freight has developed greatly since the start of the Industrial Revolution. Canals, which became important in the 18th century, could not compete with rail transport in the 19th century. Rail transport remains important, but, during the 20th century, it suffered from competition with road transport, which is cheaper and has the advantage of carrying materials and goods from door to door.

Road transport causes pollution and the burning of fuels creates greenhouse gases that contribute to global warming. Yet privately owned cars are now the leading form of passenger traffic in developed nations, especially for journeys of less than around 400 km [250 miles]. Car owners do not have to suffer the inconvenience of waiting for public transport, such as buses, though they often have to endure traffic jams at peak travel times.

Ocean passenger traffic is now modest, but ships carry the bulk of international trade. Huge oil tankers and bulk grain carriers now ply the oceans with their cargoes, while container ships

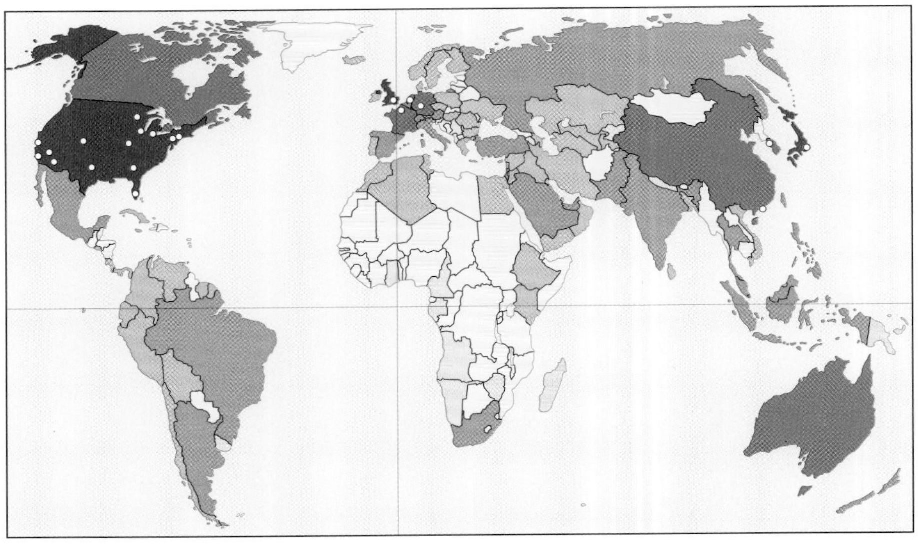

AIR TRAVEL – PASSENGER KILOMETRES* FLOWN (1997).

- OVER 100,000 MILLION
- 50,000–100,000 MILLION
- 10,000–50,000 MILLION
- 1,000–10,000 MILLION
- 500–1,000 MILLION
- UNDER 500 MILLION
- ○ MAJOR AIRPORTS (HANDLING OVER 25 MILLION PASSENGERS IN 2000)

** Passenger kilometres are the number of passengers (both international and domestic) multiplied by the distance flown by each passenger from the airport of origin.*

Jodrell Bank Observatory, Cheshire, England
The world's first giant radio telescope began operations at Jodrell Bank in 1957. Radio telescopes can explore the Universe as far as 16 billion light-years away.

SELECTED NEWSPAPER CIRCULATION FIGURES (1995)

France		**Russia**	
Le Monde	357,362	*Pravda*	1,373,795
Le Figaro	350,000	*Ivestia*	700,000
Germany		**Spain**	
Bild	4,500,000	*El Pais*	407,629
Süddeutsche Zeitung	402,866		
Italy		**United Kingdom**	
Corriera Della Sella	676,904	*The Sun*	4,061,253
La Republica	655,321	*Daily Mirror*	2,525,000
La Stampa	436,047	*Daily Express*	1,270,642
		The Times	672,802
		The Guardian	402,214
Japan		**United States**	
Yomiuri Shimbun (a.m. edition)	9,800,000	*New York Times*	1,724,705
(p.m. edition)	4,400,000	*Chicago Tribune*	1,110,552
Manichi Shimbun (a.m. edition)	3,200,000	*Houston Chronicle*	605,343
(p.m. edition)	1,900,000		

Kansai International Airport, Japan
The new airport, opened in September 1994, is built on an artificial island in Osaka Bay. The island holds the world's biggest airport terminal at nearly 2 km [1.2 miles] long.

carry mixed cargoes. Containers are boxes built to international standards that contain cargo. Containers are easy to handle, and so they reduce shipping costs, speed up deliveries and cut losses caused by breakages. Most large ports now have the facilities to handle containers.

Air transport is suitable for carrying goods that are expensive, light and compact, or perishable. However, because of the high costs of air freight, it is most suitable for carrying passengers along long-distance routes around the world. Through air travel, international tourism, with people sometimes flying considerable distances, has become a major and rapidly expanding industry.

Communications

After humans first began to communicate by using the spoken word, the next great stage in the development of communications was the invention of writing around 5,500 years ago.

The invention of movable type in the mid 15th century led to the mass production of books and, in the early 17th century, the first newspapers. Newspapers now play an important part in the mass communication of information, although today radio and, even more important, television have led to a decline in the circulation of newspapers in many parts of the world.

The most recent developments have occurred in the field of electronics. Artificial communications satellites now circle the planet, relaying radio, television, telegraph and telephone signals. This enables people to watch events on the far side of the globe as they are happening. Electronic equipment is also used in many other ways, such as in navigation systems used in air, sea and space, and also in modern weaponry, as shown vividly in the television coverage of the 1991 Gulf War.

The Age of Computers

One of the most remarkable applications of electronics is in the field of computers. Computers are now making a huge contribution to communications. They are able to process data at incredibly high speeds and can store vast quantities of information. For example, the work of weather forecasters has been greatly improved now that computers can process the enormous amount of data required for a single weather forecast. They also have many other applications in such fields as business, government, science and medicine.

Through the Internet, computers provide a free interchange of news and views around the world. But the dangers of misuse, such as the exchange of pornographic images, have led to calls for censorship. Censorship, however, is a blunt weapon, which can be used by authoritarian governments to suppress the free exchange of information that the new information superhighway makes possible.

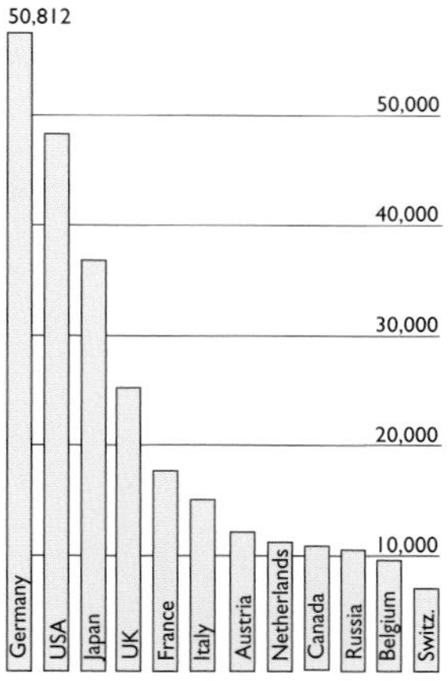

Spending on tourism
Countries spending the most on overseas tourism, US$ million (1996).

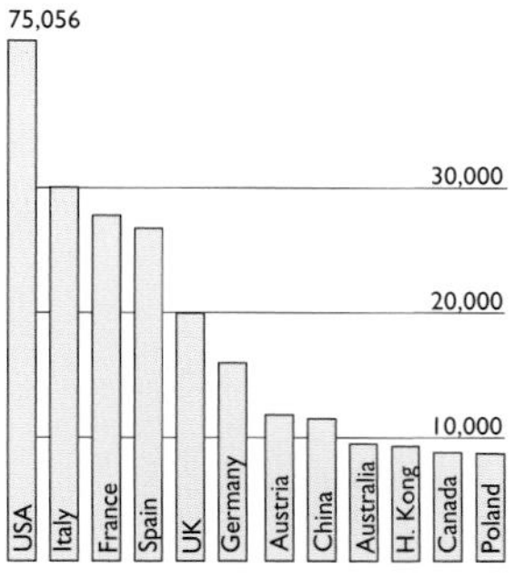

Receipts from tourism
Countries receiving the most from overseas tourism, US$ million (1996).

The World Today

The early years of the 20th century witnessed the exploration of Antarctica, the last uncharted continent. Today, less than 100 years later, tourists are able to take cruises to the icy southern continent, while almost no part of the globe is inaccessible to the determined traveller. Improved transport and images from space have made our world seem smaller.

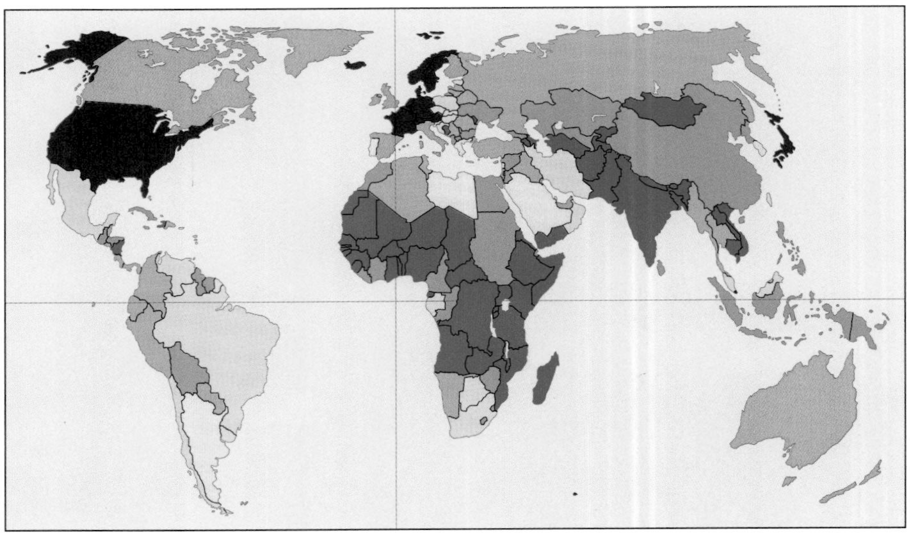

GROSS NATIONAL PRODUCT PER CAPITA

The value of total production divided by the population (1999).

- OVER 400% OF WORLD AVERAGE
- 200–400% OF WORLD AVERAGE
- 100–200% OF WORLD AVERAGE

[WORLD AVERAGE WEALTH PER PERSON US$6,316]

- 50–100% OF WORLD AVERAGE
- 25–50% OF WORLD AVERAGE
- 10–25% OF WORLD AVERAGE
- UNDER 10% OF WORLD AVERAGE

RICHEST COUNTRIES

Liechtenstein	$50,000
Luxembourg	$44,640
Switzerland	$38,350
Bermuda	$35,590
Norway	$32,880

POOREST COUNTRIES

Ethiopia	$100
Congo (Dem. Rep.)	$110
Burundi	$120
Sierra Leone	$130
Guinea-Bissau	$160

A Divided World

Between the end of World War II in 1945 and the late 1980s, the world was divided, politically and economically, into three main groups: the developed countries or Western democracies, with their free enterprise or mixed economies; the centrally planned or Communist countries; and the developing countries or Third World.

This division became obsolete when the former Soviet Union and its old European allies, together with the 'special economic zones' in eastern China, began the transition from centrally planned to free enterprise economies. This left the world divided into two broad camps: the prosperous developed countries and the poorer developing countries. The simplest way of distinguishing between the groups is with reference to their per capita Gross National Products (per capita GNPs).

The World Bank divides the developing countries into three main groups. At the bottom are the low-income economies, which include China, India and most of sub-Saharan Africa. In 1998, this group contained about 60% of the world's population, but its average per capita GNP was only US$410. The other two groups are the lower-middle-income economies, with an average per capita GNP of $1,200, and the upper-middle-income economies with an average per capita GNP of $4,900. By contrast, the high-income economies, also called the developed countries, contain only 15% of the world's population but have the high (and rising) average GNP per capita of $25,730.

Economic and Social Contrasts

Economic differences are coupled with other factors, such as rates of population growth. For example, in 1998, the low- and middle-income economies had a high population growth rate of 1.7%, while the growth rate in high-income economies was around 0.1%. No fewer than 18 countries in Europe experienced a natural decrease in population in 1998.

Stark contrasts exist worldwide in the quality

Porters carrying luggage for tourists, Selous Park, Tanzania

Improved and cheaper transport has led to a boom in tourism in many developing countries. Tourism provides jobs and foreign exchange, though it can undermine local cultures.

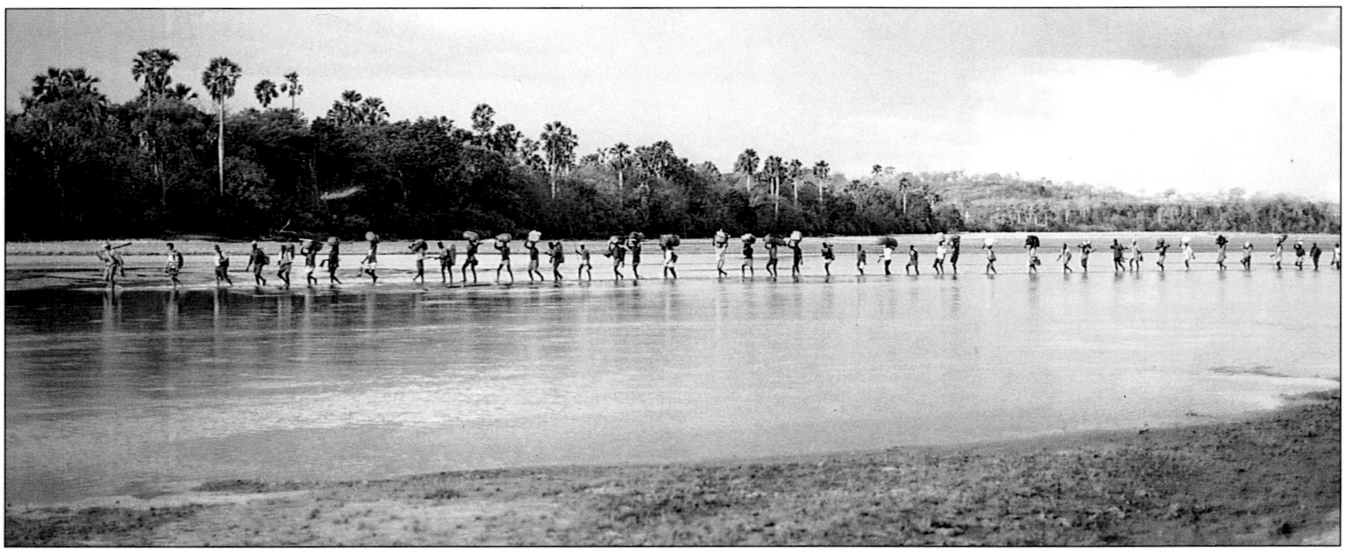

Birth control poster, China
China is the only country with more than a billion people. Central to its economic development policies is population control. Posters exhort the advantages of one-child families.

of life. Generally, the people in Western Europe and North America are better fed, healthier and have more cars and better homes than the people in low- and middle-income economies.

In 1998, the average life expectancy at birth in Africa was 50 years for men and 53 for women. By contrast, the average life expectancy in Europe was 69 for males and 72 for females. Illiteracy in low-income economies for people aged 15 and over was 39% in 1999. But for women, the percentage of those who could not read or write was 48%. Illiteracy is relatively rare for both sexes in high-income economies.

Future Development

In the last 50 years, despite all the aid supplied to developing countries, much of the world still suffers from poverty and economic backwardness. Some countries are even poorer now than they were a generation ago while others have become substantially richer.

The most remarkable success has been achieved in eastern Asia. Japan and the 'tiger economies' of Hong Kong, Indonesia, Malaysia, Singapore, South Korea, Thailand and Taiwan had an average annual economic growth rate of 5.5% between 1965 and 1993, while their share in the exports of manufactured goods more than doubled in the same period. In 1997, however, an Asian market crash temporarily halted this dramatic economic expansion.

Reasons advanced to explain the success of the eastern Asian countries include low wage scales, strong family structures, low state expenditure on welfare and large investment in education for both sexes. Some of the arguments are contradictory. For example, while some argue that the success of Hong Kong is due to free enterprise, the governments of Japan and South Korea have intervened substantially in the development of their economies.

Eastern Asia's economic growth has been exceptional and probably cannot be regarded as a model for the developing world. But several factors suggest that poor countries may find progress easier in the 21st century. For example, technology is now more readily transferable between countries, while improved transport and communications make it easier for countries to take part in the world economy. But industrial development and rising living standards could lead to an increase in global pollution. Hence, any strategy for global economic expansion must also take account of environmental factors.

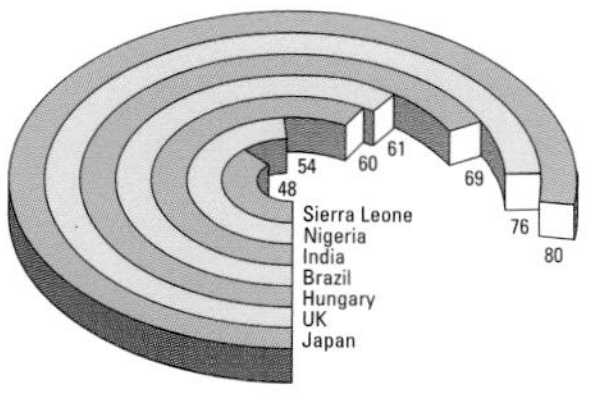

Years of life expectancy at birth, selected countries (1997).
The chart shows the contrasting range of average life expectancies at birth for a range of countries, including both low-income and high-income economies. Generally, improved health services are raising life expectancies. On average, women live longer than men, even in the poorer developing countries.

WESTERN CAPE, SOUTH AFRICA

WORLD MAPS

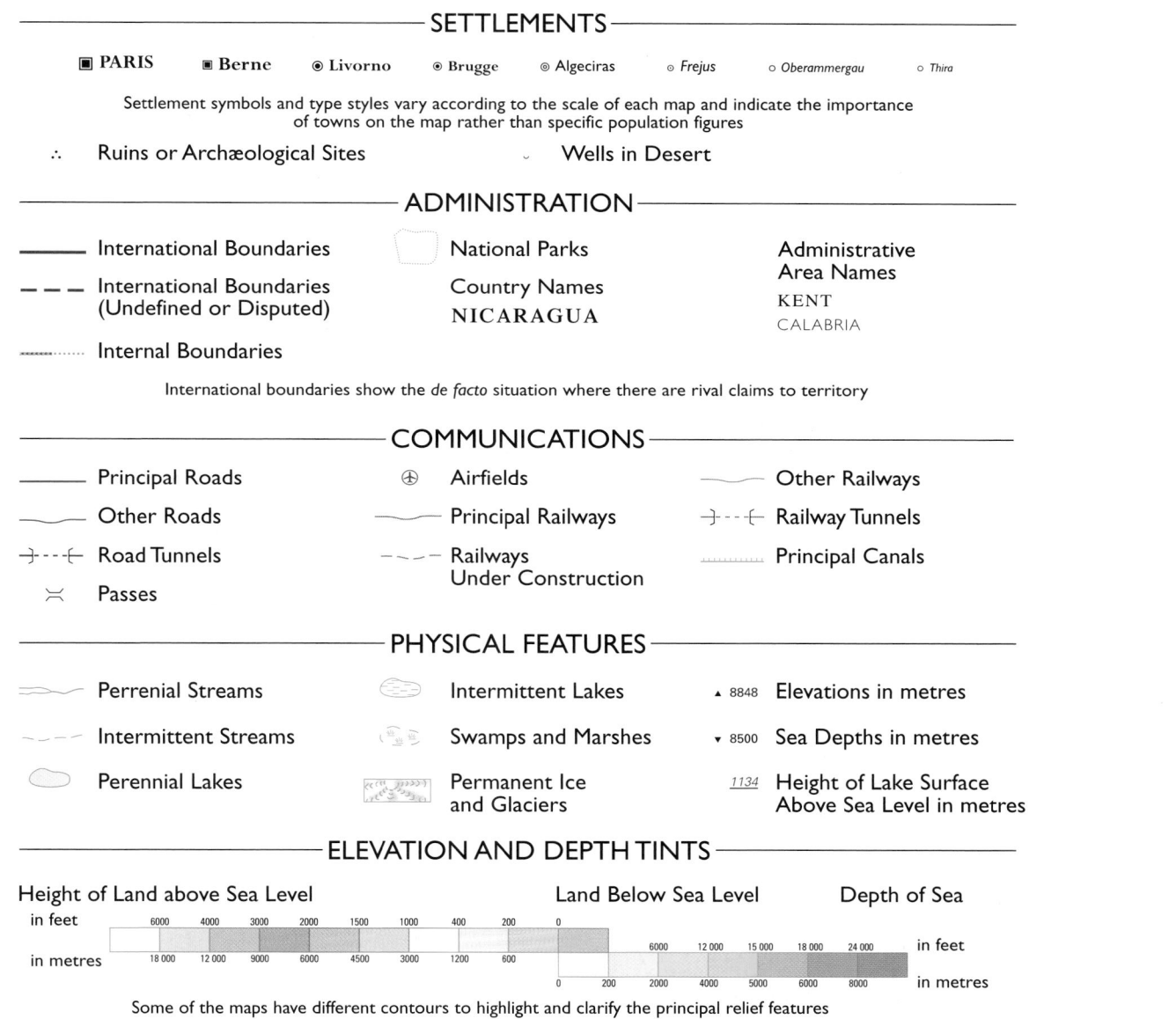

SETTLEMENTS

▣ **PARIS** ▪ **Berne** ⊙ **Livorno** ⊙ **Brugge** ⊚ Algeciras ○ *Frejus* ○ *Oberammergau* ○ *Thira*

Settlement symbols and type styles vary according to the scale of each map and indicate the importance of towns on the map rather than specific population figures

∴ Ruins or Archæological Sites

Wells in Desert

ADMINISTRATION

International Boundaries

International Boundaries (Undefined or Disputed)

Internal Boundaries

National Parks

Country Names
NICARAGUA

Administrative Area Names
KENT
CALABRIA

International boundaries show the *de facto* situation where there are rival claims to territory

COMMUNICATIONS

Principal Roads

Other Roads

Road Tunnels

Passes

Airfields

Principal Railways

Railways Under Construction

Other Railways

Railway Tunnels

Principal Canals

PHYSICAL FEATURES

Perrenial Streams

Intermittent Streams

Perennial Lakes

Intermittent Lakes

Swamps and Marshes

Permanent Ice and Glaciers

▲ 8848 Elevations in metres

▼ 8500 Sea Depths in metres

1134 Height of Lake Surface Above Sea Level in metres

ELEVATION AND DEPTH TINTS

Height of Land above Sea Level

in feet	6000	4000	3000	2000	1500	1000	400	200	0
in metres	18 000	12 000	9000	6000	4500	3000	1200	600	

Land Below Sea Level

Depth of Sea

in feet		6000	12 000	15 000	18 000	24 000
in metres	0	200	2000	4000	5000	6000	8000

Some of the maps have different contours to highlight and clarify the principal relief features

Beaufort Sea
Banks I.
Parry Is.
Queen Elizabeth Is.
Ellesmere I.
Devon I.
Victoria I.
Baffin Bay
Baffin I.
Davis Str.
GREENLAND (Denmark)
Nuuk
Denmark Str.
Reykjavík
ICELAND
Arctic Circle
Faroe Is. (Den.)
UNITED KINGDOM
Glasgow
Dublin
IRELAND
LONDON
Bering Strait
St. Lawrence I.
Yukon
Fairbanks
ALASKA (U.S.A.)
Anchorage
G. of Alaska
Kodiak I.
Mackenzie
Great Bear L.
Yellowknife
Great Slave L.
Hudson Bay
Churchill
Nelson
Aleutian Is. (U.S.A.)
Queen Charlotte Is.
Edmonton
Calgary
CANADA
L. Winnipeg
Winnipeg
Schefferville
Newfoundland
St. John's
Vancouver
Vancouver I.
Seattle
Portland
Missouri
UNITED STATES OF AMERICA
L. Superior
Ottawa
Québec
Montréal
Minneapolis
L. Michigan
L. Huron
Toronto
Milwaukee
Detroit
Halifax
Boston
Salt Lake City
CHICAGO
Denver
Pittsburgh
Cleveland
NEW YORK
PHILADELPHIA
Baltimore
Washington D.C.
SAN FRANCISCO
Sacramento
Colorado
Kansas City
St. Louis
Cincinnati
LOS ANGELES
San Diego
Phoenix
Memphis
Dallas
Atlanta
El Paso
Houston
Mississippi
Ciudad Juárez
Rio Grande
New Orleans
Jacksonville
Bermuda (U.K.)
NORTH ATLANTIC OCEAN
Azores (Port.)
PORTUGAL
Lisbon
Madrid
SPAIN
FRANCE
Bordeaux
Tangier
Rabat
Casablanca
Madeira (Port.)
Marrakesh
MOROCCO
Canary Is. (Sp.)
El Aaiún
WESTERN SAHARA
International Date Line
Midway Is.
Hawaiian Is. (U.S.A.)
Guadalupe I. (Mexico)
Monterrey
G. of California
Gulf of Mexico
Miami
BAHAMAS
Tropic of Cancer
Honolulu
Oahu
Hawaii
MEXICO
Havana
CUBA
Turks & Caicos Is. (U.K.)
León
Guadalajara
MÉXICO
Cayman Is. (U.K.)
Port-au-Prince
HAITI
DOMINICAN REP.
JAMAICA
Kingston
Santo Domingo
PUERTO RICO
Virgin Is. (U.S.A.)&(U.K.)
ANTIGUA & BARBUDA
ST. KITTS & NEVIS
Revilla Gigedo Is. (Mexico)
Puebla
Belmopan
BELIZE
GUATEMALA
Guatemala
HONDURAS
Tegucigalpa
San Salvador
EL SALVADOR
NICARAGUA
Managua
Caribbean Sea
GUADELOUPE (Fr.)
MARTINIQUE (Fr.)
DOMINICA
ST. LUCIA
ST. VINCENT & THE GRENADINES
BARBADOS
GRENADA
NETH. ANTILLES
TRINIDAD & TOBAGO
Barranquilla
San José
COSTA RICA
Panamá
PANAMA
Caracas
Orinoco
VENEZUELA
Georgetown
GUYANA
Paramaribo
SURINAM
Cayenne
FRENCH GUIANA
Clipperton I. (Fr.)
OCEAN
Nouakchott
MAURITANIA
Timbuktu
CAPE VERDE IS.
Dakar
SENEGAL
GAMBIA
GUINEA-BISSAU
Bissau
GUINEA
Bamako
BURKINA FASO
Ouagadougou
Conakry
SIERRA LEONE
Freetown
IVORY COAST
Yamoussoukro
Monrovia
LIBERIA
Abidjan
Gulf of
PACIFIC OCEAN
Palmyra Is. (U.S.A.)
Kiritimati
Howland I. (U.S.A.)
Baker I. (U.S.A.)
Jarvis I. (U.S.A.)
Equator
Medellín
Coco I. (C.Rica)
Malpelo (Colombia)
Cali
BOGOTÁ
COLOMBIA
São Paulo (Brazil)
Galápagos (Ecuador)
Quito
ECUADOR
Guayaquil
Negro
Japurá
Amazon
Manaus
Belém
Iquitos
Fortaleza
Fernando de Noronha (Brazil)
Natal
Recife
Abariringa
KIRIBATI
Phoenix Is.
Malden I.
Starbuck I.
Tokelau Is. (N.Z.)
Penrhyn Is.
Marquesas Is.
Manihiki
Flint I.
FRENCH POLYNESIA
Wallis & Futuna (Fr.)
SAMOA
AMERICAN SAMOA
FIJI
TONGA
Society Is.
Tahiti
Tuamotu Is.
Cook Is. (N.Z.)
Niue (N.Z.)
Tubuai Is.
Rapa
Pitcairn I. (U.K.)
Ducie I.
Ucayali
Marañón
Madeira
Xingu
Tocantins
São Francisco
BRAZIL
PERU
LIMA
Callao
Salvador
Ascension I. (U.K.)
Brasília
Arequipa
L. Titicaca
La Paz
BOLIVIA
Sucre
St. Helena (U.K.)
Belo Horizonte
SOUTH ATLANTIC OCEAN
Trindade (Brazil)
SÃO PAULO
RIO DE JANEIRO
Tropic of Capricorn
Antofagasta
PARAGUAY
Asunción
Santos
Curitiba
Easter I. (Chile)
Sala-y-Gómez (Chile)
San Felix (Chile)
San Ambrosio (Chile)
Tucumán
Paraná
Uruguay
Pôrto Alegre
Córdoba
Rio Grande
Valparaíso
Rosario
URUGUAY
Montevideo
Juan Fernández (Chile)
SANTIAGO
BUENOS AIRES
ARGENTINA
Talcahuano
CHILE
Bahía Blanca
Tristan da Cunha (U.K.)
Gough I. (U.K.)
Kermadec Is. (N.Z.)
Chiloé I.
Chatham Is. (N.Z.)
Falkland Is. (U.K.)
South Georgia (U.K.)
Punta Arenas
Tierra del Fuego
C. Horn
Scotia Sea
South Sandwich Is. (U.K.)
Drake Passage
South Orkney Is.
South Shetland Is.
Antarctic Circle
Bellingshausen Sea
Weddell Sea
Amundsen Sea
Antarctica
West from Greenwich

Projection: *Hammer Equal Area*

A R C T I C O C E A N
Barents Sea
Kara Sea
Laptev Sea
East Siberian Sea
New Siberian Is.
Severnaya Zemlya
Novaya Zemlya
Wrangel I.
Arctic Circle
R U S S I A
Murmansk
Arkhangelsk
Norilsk
Verkhoyansk
Yakutsk
Magadan
Okhotsk
Sea of Okhotsk
Bering Sea
Petropavlovsk-Kamchatskiy
International Date Line
Salekhard
ST.PETERSBURG
MOSCOW
Perm
Yekaterinburg
Kazan
Samara
Saratov
Volgograd
Chelyabinsk
Omsk
Novosibirsk
Tomsk
Krasnoyarsk
Barnaul
Irkutsk
Ulan Ude
L. Baikal
Sakhalin
Komsomolsk
Khabarovsk
Vladivostok
Kuril Is.
Sapporo
Astana
Qaraghandy
K A Z A K S T A N
L. Balkhash
Almaty
Bishkek
Tashkent
Dushanbe
Samarkand
Ashkhabad
Ulan Bator
M O N G O L I A
Ürümqi
C H I N A
Harbin
Changchun
SHENYANG
BEIJING
TIANJIN
Dalian
NORTH KOREA
P'yongyang
SEOUL
SOUTH KOREA
JAPAN
TŌKYŌ
Ōsaka
Kitakyūshu
Lanzhou
Taiyuan
Xi'an
Nanjing
SHANGHAI
East China Sea
Wuhan
Chengdu
CHONGQING
Lhasa
TIBET
Fuzhou
Taipei
TAIWAN
Ryukyu Is.
Kunming
GUANGZHOU
HONG KONG
Hanoi
Hainan
South China Sea
Vientiane
THAILAND
BANGKOK
VIET-NAM
CAMBODIA
Phnom Penh
Ho Chi Minh City
MANILA
PHILIPPINES
PACIFIC OCEAN
Bonin Is. (Japan)
Volcano Is. (Japan)
Marcus I. (Japan)
Tropic of Cancer
NORTHERN MARIANAS (U.S.A.)
Wake I. (U.S.A.)
GUAM (U.S.A.)
Yap
PALAU
FEDERATED STATES OF MICRONESIA
Caroline Is.
Truk
Pohnpei
MARSHALL IS.
Gilbert Is.
NAURU
KIRIBATI
TUVALU
SOLOMON IS.
Santa Cruz I.
VANUATU
FIJI
Suva
NEW CALEDONIA (Fr.)
FINLAND
Helsinki
SWEDEN
NORWAY
Oslo
Stockholm
Copenhagen
ESTONIA
LATVIA
LITH.
POLAND
Berlin
Warsaw
BELARUS
Minsk
Prague
Brussels
PARIS
Vienna
Budapest
UKRAINE
Kiev
Odessa
ROMANIA
Bucharest
Belgrade
BULGARIA
Sofia
ITALY
Milan
Rome
Naples
Black Sea
ISTANBUL
Ankara
TURKEY
Izmir
Athens
GREECE
GEORGIA
Tbilisi
Yerevan
ARM.
AZER.
Baku
Caspian Sea
Astrakhan
Aral Sea
UZBEKISTAN
TURKMENISTAN
KYRGYZSTAN
TAJIKISTAN
Tabriz
TEHRAN
Mashhad
I R A N
IRAQ
Baghdad
Esfahan
Shiraz
Kabul
AFGHANISTAN
Islamabad
Lahore
PAKISTAN
KARACHI
DELHI
New Delhi
Kanpur
NEPAL
Katmandu
BHUTAN
I N D I A
CALCUTTA (Kolkata)
Dacca
BANGLADESH
BURMA (MYANMAR)
Rangoon
Ahmadabad
Nagpur
MUMBAI (Bombay)
Arabian Sea
Bay of Bengal
Hyderabad
Bangalore
CHENNAI (Madras)
Andaman Is. (India)
Nicobar Is. (India)
SRI LANKA
Colombo
Lakshadweep Is. (India)
MALDIVES
SYRIA
Damascus
Beirut
Jerusalem
Amman
JORDAN
KUWAIT
BAHRAIN
QATAR
U.A.E.
Abu Dhabi
Muscat
OMAN
Riyadh
SAUDI ARABIA
Mecca
The Gulf
Red Sea
Sana'
YEMEN
Aden
G. of Aden
Socotra (Yemen)
Mediterranean Sea
Malta
Crete
Cyprus
Tunis
TUNISIA
Tripoli
Benghazi
LIBYA
Alexandria
CAIRO
EGYPT
Aswân
Nile
NIGER
Niamey
CHAD
L. Chad
Ndjamena
Kano
NIGERIA
Abuja
Ibadan
Lagos
SUDAN
Omdurmân
Khartoum
Asmara
ERITREA
DJIBOUTI
Addis Ababa
ETHIOPIA
SOMALI REP.
Mogadishu
CAMEROON
Douala
Yaoundé
CENTRAL AFRICAN REP.
Bangui
EQUATORIAL GUINEA
GABON
Libreville
CONGO
Brazzaville
Kinshasa
CONGO (DEM. REP. OF THE)
Kisangani
UGANDA
Kampala
KENYA
L. Turkana
Nairobi
RWANDA
Kigali
BURUNDI
Bujumbura
L. Victoria
Mombasa
Dodoma
Zanzibar
Dar es Salaam
TANZANIA
L. Tanganyika
Kananga
CABINDA (Angola)
Luanda
ANGOLA
Benguela
Lubumbashi
ZAMBIA
Lusaka
L. Malawi
Lilongwe
MALAWI
Harare
ZIMBABWE
MOZAMBIQUE
Bulawayo
Mozambique Channel
NAMIBIA
Windhoek
BOTSWANA
Gaborone
Pretoria
Johannesburg
Maputo
SWAZILAND
SOUTH AFRICA
LESOTHO
Durban
Cape Town
C. of Good Hope
Port Elizabeth
SEYCHELLES
Amirante Is.
Aldabra Is.
Agalega Is.
COMOROS
Mayotte (Fr.)
MADAGASCAR
Antananarivo
Cargados Carajos
Rodriguez
MAURITIUS
RÉUNION (Fr.)
Diego Garcia
Chagos Arch. (U.K.)
I N D I A N O C E A N
Equator
Tropic of Capricorn
Cocos Is. (Austral.)
Christmas I. (Austral.)
M A L A Y S I A
Kuala Lumpur
PEN. MALAYSIA
SABAH
SARAWAK
BRUNEI
Medan
Sumatra
SINGAPORE
Borneo
Palembang
Banjarmasin
I N D O N E S I A
JAKARTA
Bandung
Java
Surabaya
Ujung Pandang
IRIAN JAYA
EAST TIMOR
Timor
Arafura Sea
PAPUA NEW GUINEA
Port Moresby
New Ireland
New Britain
C. York
Darwin
Cairns
Townsville
Port Hedland
Alice Springs
AUSTRALIA
Rockhampton
Brisbane
Geraldton
Perth
Fremantle
Kalgoorlie-Boulder
Great Australian Bight
Adelaide
Darling
Newcastle
Sydney
Canberra
Melbourne
Tasmania
Hobart
Tasman Sea
Lord Howe I. (Austral.)
Norfolk I. (Austral.)
Auckland
North I.
NEW ZEALAND
Wellington
Christchurch
South I.
Stewart I.
Dunedin
Bounty Is. (N.Z.)
Antipodes Is.
Auckland Is. (N.Z.)
Campbell I. (N.Z.)
Macquarie Is. (Austral.)
Amsterdam I. (Fr.)
St.Paul (Fr.)
Prince Edward Is. (S.Africa)
Crozet Is. (Fr.)
Kerguelen (Fr.)
McDonald Is. (Austral.)
Heard I. (Austral.)
Bouvet I. (Norw.)
Svalbard (Norw.)
S O U T H E R N O C E A N
Antarctic Circle
Ross Sea
c t i c a
East from Greenwich
10 11 12 13 14 15 16 17 18
A B C D E F G H

Hanoi ◉ Capital Cities

ARCTIC OCEAN 1:31 100 000

COPYRIGHT GEORGE PHILIP LTD

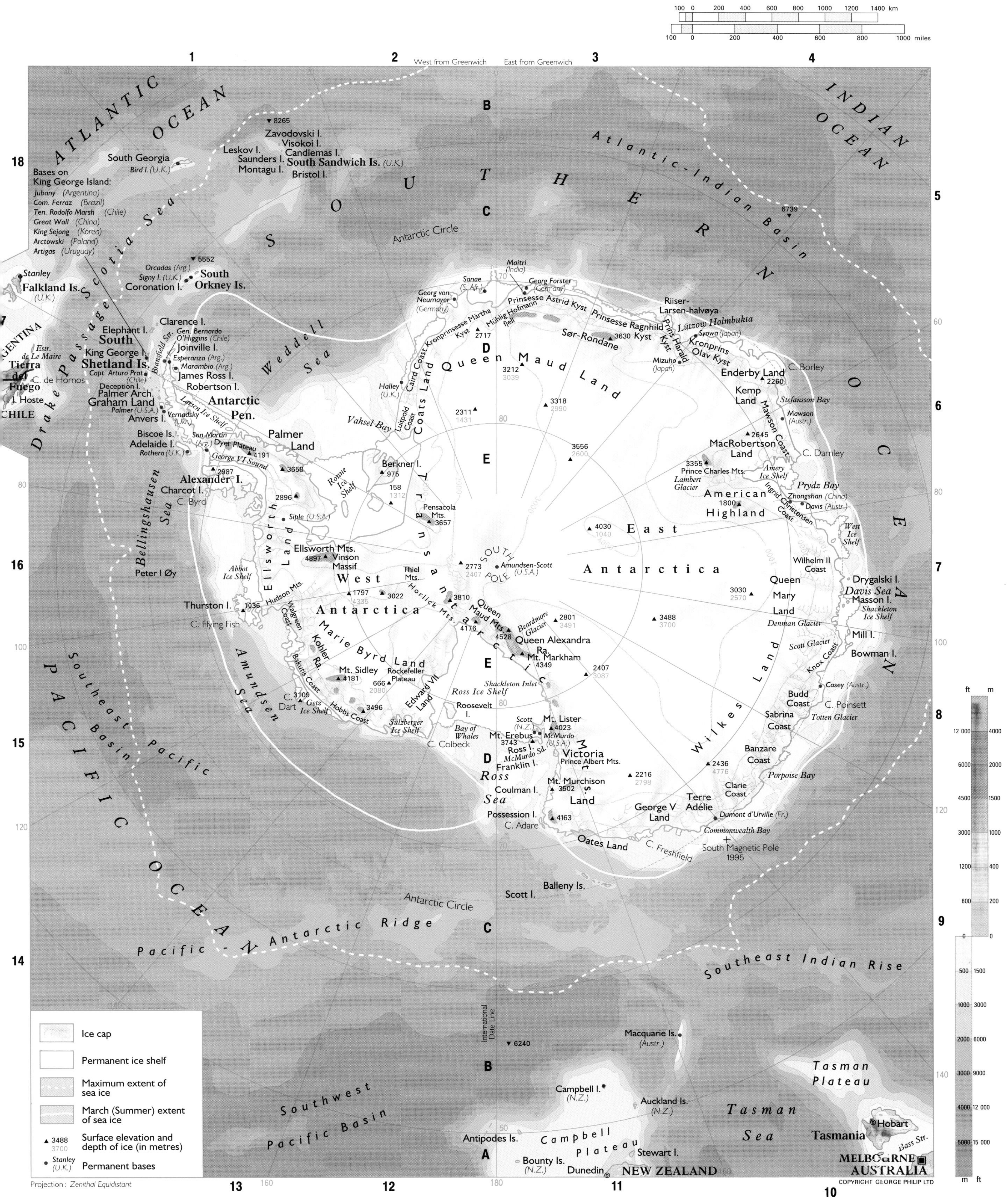
100 0 200 400 600 800 1000 1200 1400 km
100 0 200 400 600 800 1000 miles
West from Greenwich
East from Greenwich
ATLANTIC OCEAN
INDIAN OCEAN
SOUTHERN OCEAN
PACIFIC OCEAN
South Georgia
Bird I. (U.K.)
Bases on King George Island:
Jubany (Argentina)
Com. Ferraz (Brazil)
Ten. Rodolfo Marsh (Chile)
Great Wall (China)
King Sejong (Korea)
Arctowski (Poland)
Artigas (Uruguay)
Zavodovski I.
Visokoi I.
Candlemas I.
Leskov I.
Saunders I.
Montagu I.
South Sandwich Is. (U.K.)
Bristol I.
Scotia Sea
Drake Passage
Stanley
Falkland Is. (U.K.)
Orcadas (Arg.)
Signy I. (U.K.)
Coronation I.
South Orkney Is.
Clarence I.
Elephant I.
South Shetland Is.
King George I.
Joinville I.
James Ross I.
Robertson I.
Deception I.
Palmer Arch.
Graham Land
Anvers I.
Antarctic Pen.
Biscoe Is.
Adelaide I.
Rothera (U.K.)
Palmer Land
Alexander I.
Charcot I.
C. Byrd
Tierra del Fuego
C. de Hornos
I. Hoste
CHILE
Weddell Sea
Vahsel Bay
Larsen Ice Shelf
George VI Sound
Ronne Ice Shelf
Berkner I.
Bellingshausen Sea
Peter I Øy
Siple (U.S.A.)
Ellsworth Land
Ellsworth Mts.
Vinson Massif
Abbot Ice Shelf
Thurston I.
C. Flying Fish
Hudson Mts.
Walgreen Coast
West Antarctica
Marie Byrd Land
Kohler Ra.
Mt. Sidley
Rockefeller Plateau
Getz Ice Shelf
Hobbs Coast
Bakutis Coast
C. Dart
Amundsen Sea
Edward VII Land
Sulzberger Ice Shelf
Ross Ice Shelf
Roosevelt I.
Bay of Whales
C. Colbeck
Ross Sea
Shackleton Inlet
Scott (N.Z.)
McMurdo (U.S.A.)
Mt. Erebus
Ross I.
McMurdo Sd.
Franklin I.
Mt. Lister
Victoria Land
Prince Albert Mts.
Mt. Murchison
Coulman I.
Possession I.
C. Adare
Transantarctic Mts.
Thiel Mts.
Pensacola Mts.
Horlick Mts.
Queen Maud Mts.
Beardmore Glacier
Queen Alexandra Ra.
Mt. Markham
SOUTH POLE
Amundsen-Scott (U.S.A.)
Halley (U.K.)
Caird Coast
Luitpold Coast
Coats Land
Queen Maud Land
Sanae (S. Afr.)
Georg von Neumayer (Germany)
Maitri (India)
Georg Forster (Germany)
Kronprinsesse Märtha Kyst
Prinsesse Astrid Kyst
Prinsesse Ragnhild Kyst
Mühlig Hofmann fjell
Sør-Rondane
Riiser-Larsen-halvøya
Lützow Holmbukta
Prins Harald Kyst
Syowa (Japan)
Kronprins Olav Kyst
Mizuho (Japan)
Enderby Land
C. Borley
Kemp Land
Stefansson Bay
Mawson Coast
Mawson (Austr.)
MacRobertson Land
C. Darnley
Prince Charles Mts.
Lambert Glacier
Amery Ice Shelf
Prydz Bay
Zhongshan (China)
Davis (Austr.)
Ingrid Christensen Coast
American Highland
West Ice Shelf
East Antarctica
Wilhelm II Coast
Queen Mary Land
Drygalski I.
Davis Sea
Masson I.
Shackleton Ice Shelf
Denman Glacier
Mill I.
Scott Glacier
Knox Coast
Bowman I.
Casey (Austr.)
Budd Coast
C. Poinsett
Sabrina Coast
Totten Glacier
Wilkes Land
Banzare Coast
Porpoise Bay
Clarie Coast
Terre Adélie
Dumont d'Urville (Fr.)
George V Land
Commonwealth Bay
South Magnetic Pole 1995
Oates Land
C. Freshfield
Balleny Is.
Scott I.
Antarctic Circle
Atlantic-Indian Basin
Southeast Pacific Basin
Pacific-Antarctic Ridge
Southeast Indian Rise
International Date Line
Macquarie Is. (Austr.)
Tasman Plateau
Tasman Sea
Campbell I. (N.Z.)
Auckland Is. (N.Z.)
Southwest Pacific Basin
Campbell Plateau
Antipodes Is.
Bounty Is. (N.Z.)
Stewart I.
Dunedin
NEW ZEALAND
Tasmania
Hobart
Bass Str.
MELBOURNE
AUSTRALIA
Ice cap
Permanent ice shelf
Maximum extent of sea ice
March (Summer) extent of sea ice
3488 / 3700 Surface elevation and depth of ice (in metres)
Stanley (U.K.) Permanent bases
Projection: Zenithal Equidistant
COPYRIGHT GEORGE PHILIP LTD

The Antarctic Treaty was signed in Washington in 1959 so that scientific and technical research could continue unhampered by international politics.

All territorial claims covering land areas south of latitude 60°S have been suspended. Those claims were:

Norwegian claim	45°E - 20°W	French claim	136°E - 142°E	British claim	80°W - 20°W
Australian claims	45°E - 136°E	New Zealand claim	160°E - 150°W	Argentine claim	74°W - 53°W
	142°E - 160°E	Chilean claim	90°W - 53°W		

EUROPE : Physical 1:17 800 000

100 0 100 200 300 400 500 600 700 800 km
100 0 100 200 300 400 500 miles
Arctic Circle
Iceland
Hekla 1491
Öræfajökull 2119
Norwegian Sea
2851
Faroe Is.
Shetland Is.
Orkney Is.
Rockall
ATLANTIC OCEAN
British Isles
Hebrides
Ben Nevis 1347
Great Britain
Ireland
Irish Sea
Snowdon 1085
C. Clear
Celtic Sea
Land's End
Thames
English Channel
Ushant
Channel Is.
Brittany
Bay of Biscay
4817
Gironde
Loire
Seine
C. Finisterre
Cantabrian Mts.
Old Castile
New Castile
Iberian Peninsula
Douro
Serra da Estrêla
C. da Roca
Tagus
Guadiana
Sierra Morena
Guadalquivir
Andalusia
Sierra Nevada
Mulhacén 3748
C. de São Vicente
C. Trafalgar
Str. of Gibraltar
Er Rif
Africa
Plateau of the Shotts
Pyrenees
Pico de Aneto 3404
Ebro
Garonne
Massif Central
Puy de Sancy 1886
Cevennes
Rhône
G. of Lions
Balearic Is.
Minorca
Majorca
Ibiza
Mediterranean Sea
C. Blanc
C. Bon
Pantelleria
Malta
Sardinia
Corsica
Str. of Bonifacio
Ligurian Sea
Tyrrhenian Sea
Tiber
Sicily
Etna 3340
Str. of Messina
Calabria
Ionian Sea
4070
Ionian Is.
Str. of Otranto
Apennines
Gran Sasso d'Italia 2914
Vesuvius 1277
Adriatic Sea
Po
Alps
Mont Blanc 4807
Jura
Vosges
Black Forest
Hunsrück
Taunus
Westerwald
Rhine
Meuse
Ardennes
Weser
Elbe
Harz
Erzgebirge
Bohemian Forest
Moravian Hts.
Sudeten
Oder
Inn
Danube
Bakony Forest
Drava
Sava
Tisza
Mureş
Plain of Hungary
Carpathians
Tatra 2655
Transylvanian Alps
Wallachia
Danube
Balkans
Dinaric Alps
Rhodope
Pindus
Olympus 2917
Morea
C. Matapan
Crete
Ægean Sea
Dardanelles
Mt. Ida 1766
Sea of Marmara
Bosporus
Rhodes
Cyprus
Anatolia (Asia Minor)
L. Tuz
Kizil Irmak
Erciyas Daği 3770
Taurus Mts.
Asia
Pontine Mts.
Armenia
Ararat 5165
L. Van
L. Urmia
Araks
Kurdistan
Tigris
Euphrates
Mesopotamia
Caucasus
Elbrus 5642
Kura
Terek
Kuban
Black Sea
2211
Str. of Kerch
Crimea
Sea of Azov
Dniester
Prut
Bug
Dnieper
Ukraine
Donets
Don
Manych
Tsimlyansk Res.
Caspian Depression
Volga
Ural
-28
Caspian Sea
Volga Hts.
Obshchi Syrt
Kama
Ural Mountains
Narodnaya 1894
Telpos Iz 1617
Pechora
Ob
Central Russian Uplands
Oka
Volga
Rybinsk Res.
Pripet
North European Plain
Vistula
Niemen
W. Dvina
G. of Riga
Saaremaa
L. Chudskoye
Neva
G. of Finland
L. Ladoga
Svir
L. Onega
Onega
N. Dvina
Mezen
Kanin Pen.
White Sea
Kola Pen.
Finland
Aland
G. of Bothnia
Baltic Sea
Gotland
Öland
Bornholm
Mälaren
Vättern
Vänern
Kattegat
Skagerrak
Jutland
Helgoland
North Sea
15
Lindesnes
Scandinavia
Galdhøpiggen 2469
Indals
Ume
Lapland
Kebnekaise 2117
Torne
Inari
North Cape
Nordkinn
Vesterålen
Lofoten
ft m
15 000 5000
12 000 4000
6000 2000
3000 1000
1200 400
600 200
0 0
200 600
1000 3000
2000 6000
4000 12 000
m ft
Projection: Bonne
West from Greenwich
East from Greenwich
CARTOGRAPHY BY PHILIP'S

100 0 100 200 300 400 500 600 700 800 km

100 0 100 200 300 400 500 miles

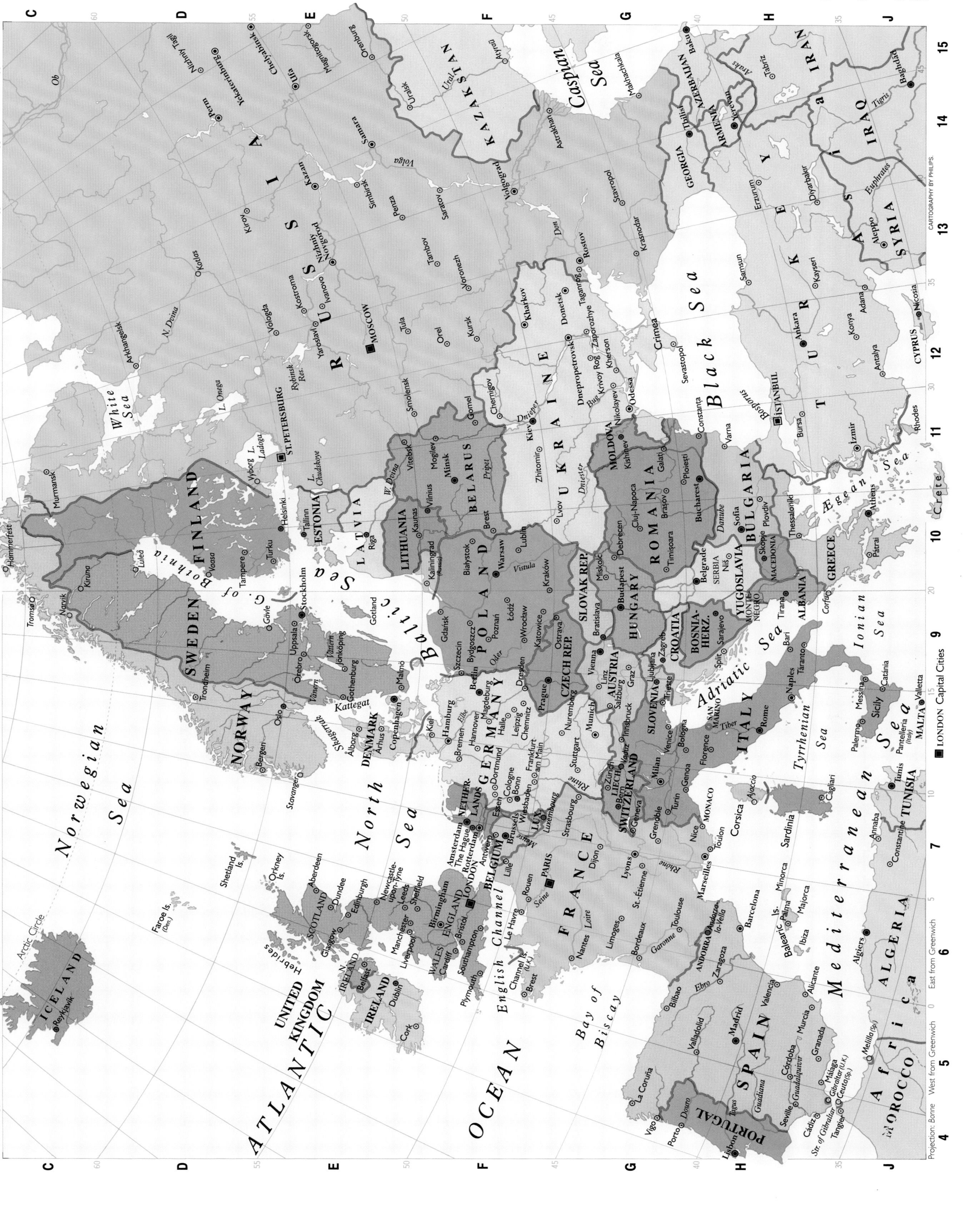

SCANDINAVIA 1:4 400 000

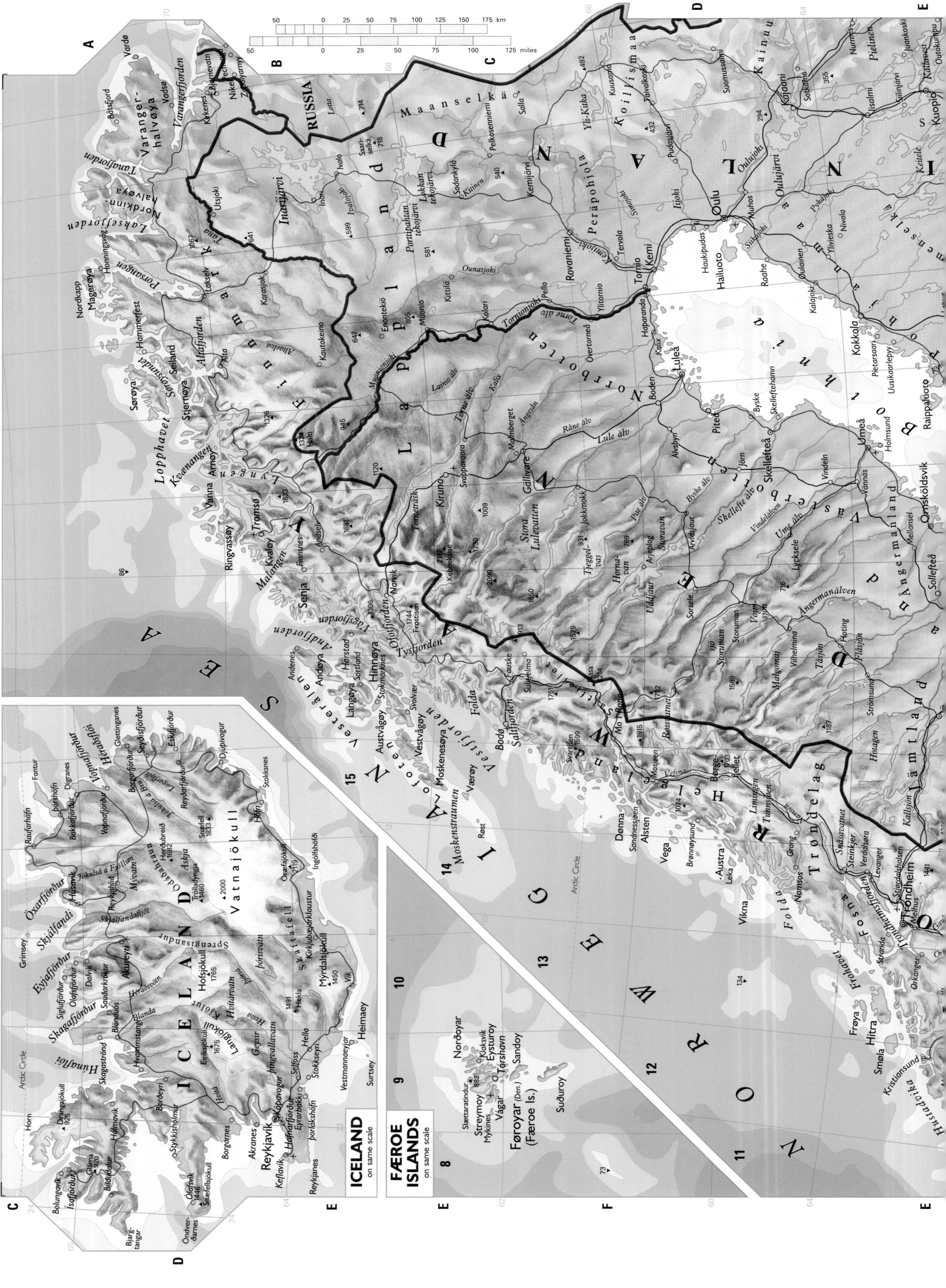

ICELAND
on same scale
FÆROE ISLANDS
on same scale
Føroyar (Den.) (Færoe Is.)
Nordoyar
Streymoy
Eysturoy
Tórshavn
Vágar
Sandoy
Suðuroy
I C E L A N D
Vatnajökull
Hofsjökull
Langjökull
Reykjavík
Akureyri
Keflavík
Húsavík
Heimaey
Arctic Circle
West from Greenwich
NORWEGIAN SEA
RUSSIA
Lofoten
Vesterålen
Finnmark
Lappland
Norrbotten
Västerbotten
Trøndelag
Jämtland
Ångermanland
Gulf of Bothnia
Nordkapp
Hammerfest
Vadsø
Vardø
Kirkenes
Tromsø
Narvik
Bodø
Trondheim
Kiruna
Gällivare
Luleå
Piteå
Skellefteå
Umeå
Örnsköldsvik
Oulu
Kemi
Tornio
Rovaniemi
Kajaani
Kuopio
Kokkola

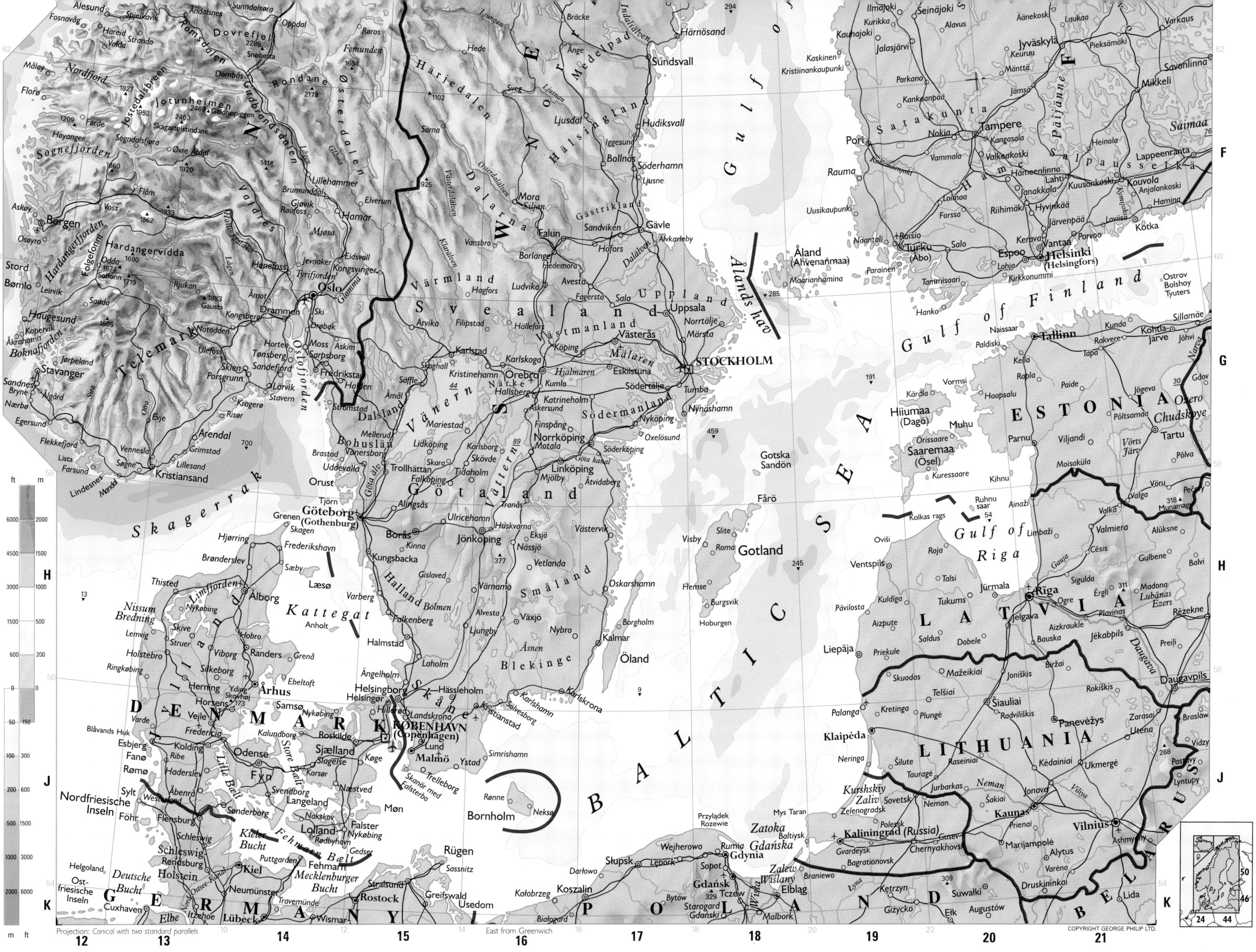

Gulf of Finland
Ålands hav
Gulf of Riga
BALTIC SEA
Skagerrak
Kattegat
NORWAY
SWEDEN
FINLAND
ESTONIA
LATVIA
LITHUANIA
DENMARK
POLAND
GERMANY
BELARUS
RUSSIA
Oslo
Bergen
Stavanger
Kristiansand
Göteborg (Gothenburg)
STOCKHOLM
Uppsala
Västerås
Helsinki (Helsingfors)
Turku (Åbo)
Tampere
Tallinn
Riga
Vilnius
Kaunas
Kaliningrad (Russia)
Gdańsk
Gdynia
KØBENHAVN (Copenhagen)
Malmö
Århus
Aalborg
Odense
Gotland
Öland
Bornholm
Åland (Ahvenanmaa)
Hiiumaa (Dagö)
Saaremaa (Ösel)
Sjælland
Fyn
Lolland
Rügen
Svealand
Götaland
Vänern
Vättern
Mälaren
Jotunheimen
Hardangervidda
Telemark
Dalarna
Värmland
Småland
Skåne
Halland
Blekinge
Saimaa
Zatoka Gdańska
Nordfriesische Inseln
Deutsche Bucht
Kieler Bucht
Mecklenburger Bucht
Projection: Conical with two standard parallels
East from Greenwich
COPYRIGHT GEORGE PHILIP LTD.

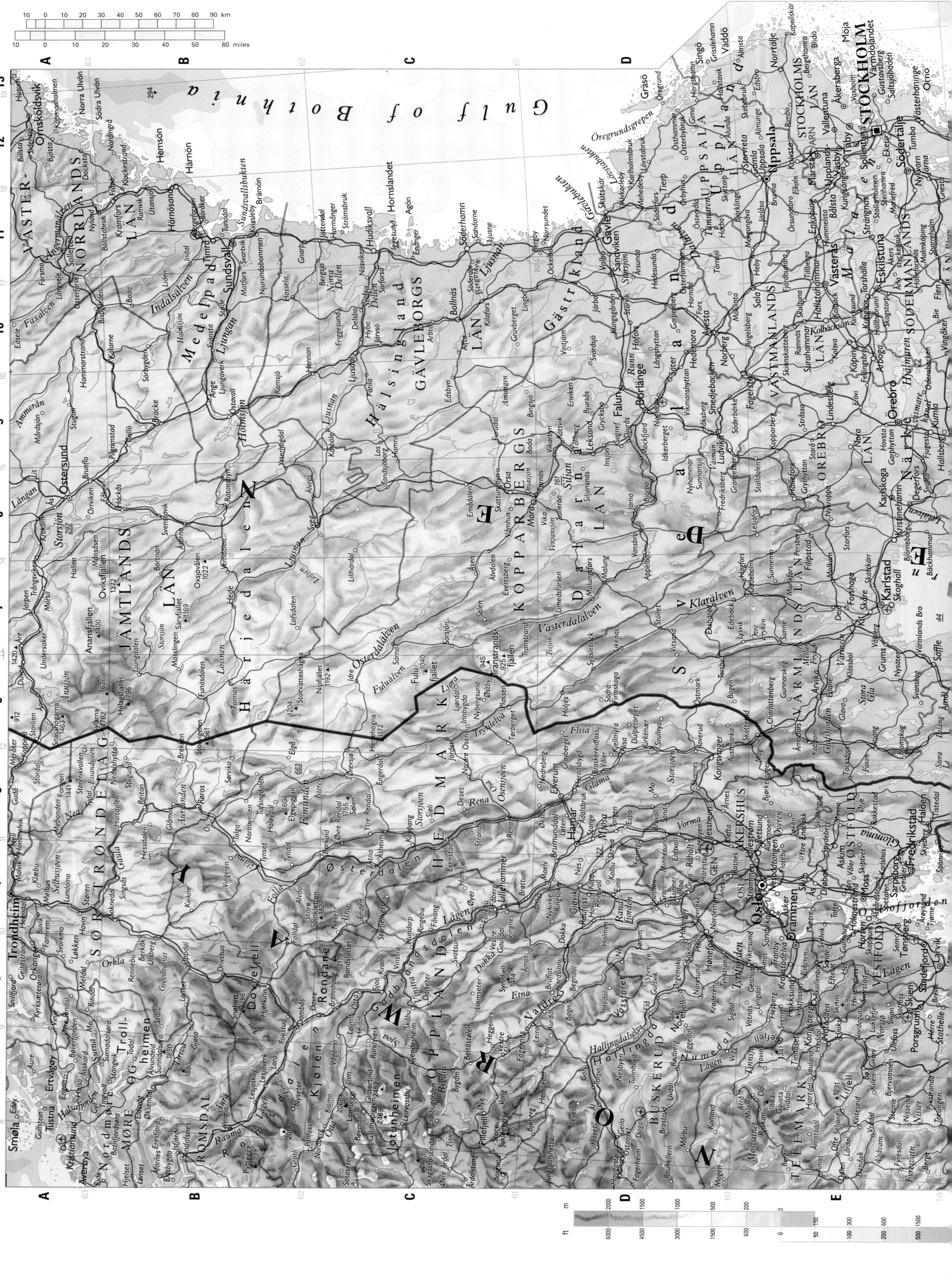
10 0 10 20 30 40 50 60 70 80 90 km
10 0 10 20 30 40 50 60 miles
Gulf of Bothnia
STOCKHOLM
Uppsala
Gävle
Sundsvall
Östersund
Trondheim
Oslo
Hamar
Lillehammer
Karlstad
Örebro
Falun
Borlänge
Västerås
Eskilstuna
Hudiksvall
Söderhamn
Härnösand
Bollnäs
Mora
Drammen
Fredrikstad
Halden
Tønsberg
Larvik
Kristiansund
Smøla
Siljan
JÄMTLANDS LÄN
GÄVLEBORGS LÄN
KOPPARBERGS LÄN
UPPSALA LÄN
STOCKHOLMS LÄN
VÄSTMANLANDS LÄN
ÖREBRO LÄN
VÄRMLANDS LÄN
SÖDERMANLANDS LÄN
VÄSTERNORRLANDS LÄN
SØR-TRØNDELAG
HEDMARK
OPPLAND
BUSKERUD
AKERSHUS
ØSTFOLD
VESTFOLD
TELEMARK
MØRE OG ROMSDAL
Jotunheimen
Dovrefjell
Rondane
Hälsingland
Härjedalen
Dalarna
Medelpad
Gästrikland
Uppland
Värmland
Närke
Mälaren
Klarälven
Glomma
m 2000 1500 1000 500 200 0
ft 6000 4500 3000 1500 600 0

Skagerrak
Kattegat
BALTIC SEA
DENMARK
GERMANY
POLAND
Jylland
Sjælland
Götaland
Småland
Skåne
Vättern
Västergötland
KØBENHAVN
Göteborg
Malmö
Århus
Odense
Ålborg
Jönköping
Norrköping
Linköping
Helsingborg
Kalmar
Växjö
Karlskrona
Visby
Gotland (Sweden)
Öland (Sweden)
Bornholm (Denmark)
Læsø (Denmark)
Anholt (Denmark)
Fehmarn Belt
Store Bælt
Lille Bælt
Øresund
Hanöbukten
Bornholmsgattet
Kalmarsund
Fyn
Lolland
Falster
Møn
Langeland
Ærø
Samsø
Sylt
Föhr
Amrum
Flensburg
Kiel
Slupsk
Ustka
Łeba
Lębork
AGDER
Arendal
Grimstad
Lillesand
Projection : Lambert's Conformal Conic
East from Greenwich
COPYRIGHT GEORGE PHILIP LTD.

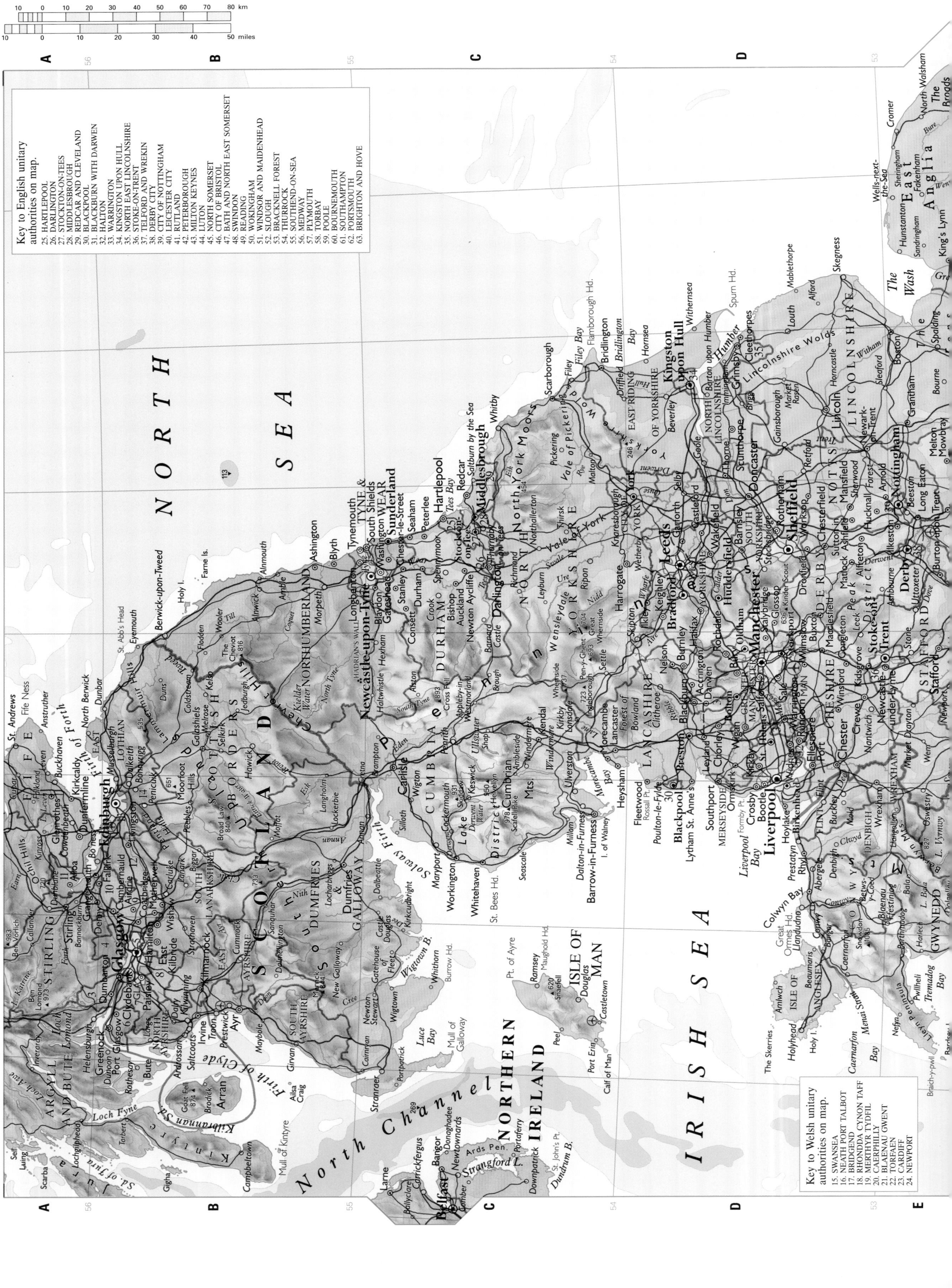
10 0 10 20 30 40 50 60 70 80 km
10 0 10 20 30 40 50 miles
Key to English unitary authorities on map.
25. HARTLEPOOL
26. DARLINGTON
27. STOCKTON-ON-TEES
28. MIDDLESBROUGH
29. REDCAR AND CLEVELAND
30. BLACKPOOL
31. BLACKBURN WITH DARWEN
32. HALTON
33. WARRINGTON
34. KINGSTON UPON HULL
35. NORTH EAST LINCOLNSHIRE
36. STOKE-ON-TRENT
37. TELFORD AND WREKIN
38. DERBY CITY
39. CITY OF NOTTINGHAM
40. LEICESTER CITY
41. RUTLAND
42. PETERBOROUGH
43. MILTON KEYNES
44. LUTON
45. NORTH SOMERSET
46. CITY OF BRISTOL
47. BATH AND NORTH EAST SOMERSET
48. SWINDON
49. READING
50. WOKINGHAM
51. WINDSOR AND MAIDENHEAD
52. SLOUGH
53. BRACKNELL FOREST
54. THURROCK
55. SOUTHEND-ON-SEA
56. MEDWAY
57. PLYMOUTH
58. TORBAY
59. POOLE
60. BOURNEMOUTH
61. SOUTHAMPTON
62. PORTSMOUTH
63. BRIGHTON AND HOVE
NORTH SEA
IRISH SEA
NORTHERN IRELAND
ISLE OF MAN
North Channel
Key to Welsh unitary authorities on map.
15. SWANSEA
16. NEATH PORT TALBOT
17. BRIDGEND
18. RHONDDA CYNON TAFF
19. MERTHYR TYDFIL
20. CAERPHILLY
21. BLAENAU GWENT
22. TORFAEN
23. CARDIFF
24. NEWPORT

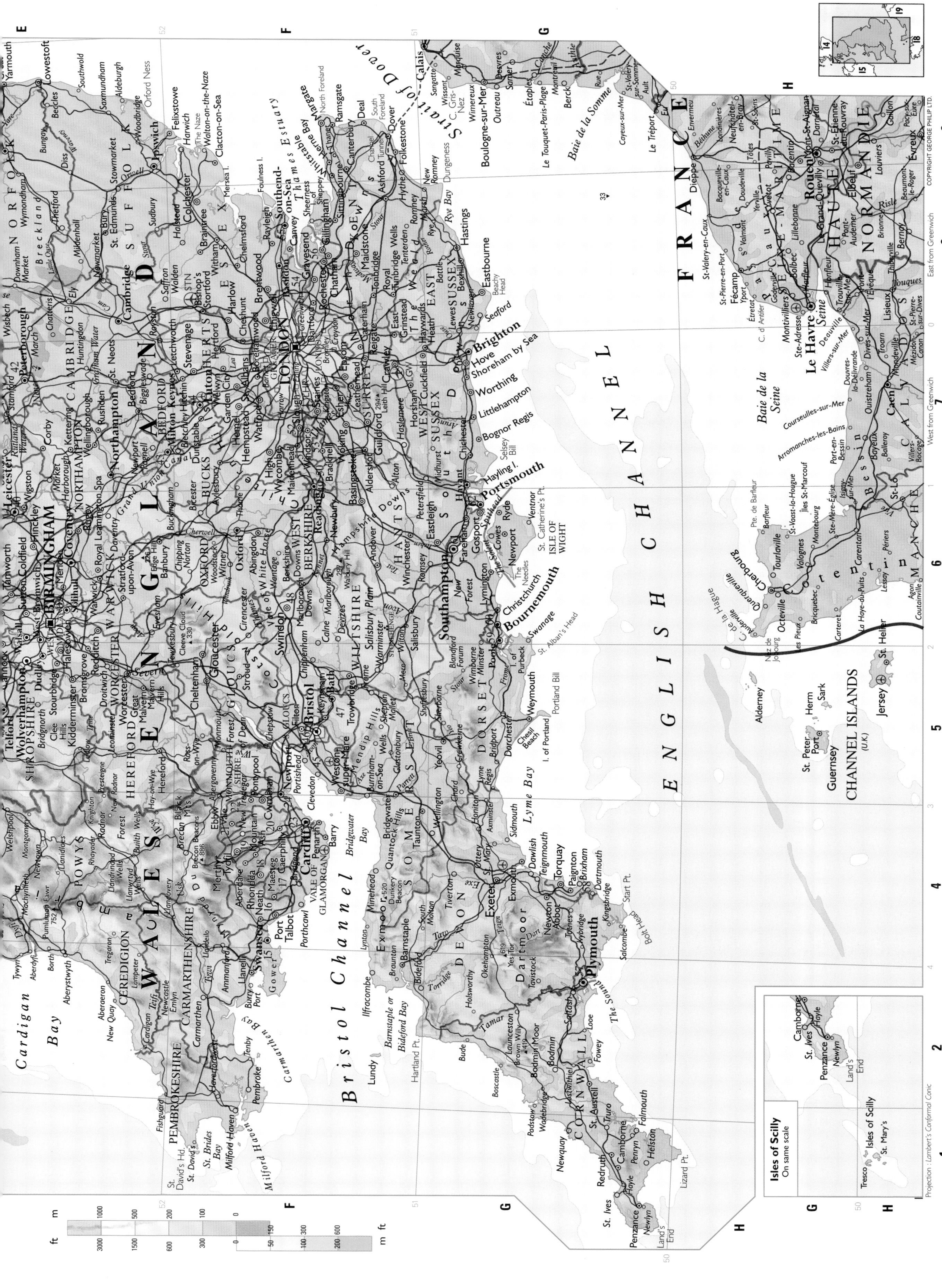
ENGLAND
WALES
FRANCE
ENGLISH CHANNEL
Bristol Channel
Cardigan Bay
Strait of Dover
Thames Estuary
Lyme Bay
Baie de la Seine
Baie de la Somme
CHANNEL ISLANDS (U.K.)
Alderney
Guernsey
Jersey
Sark
Herm
St. Peter Port
St. Helier
ISLE OF WIGHT
LONDON
BIRMINGHAM
Bristol
Cardiff
Swansea
Newport
Plymouth
Exeter
Southampton
Portsmouth
Bournemouth
Brighton
Oxford
Cambridge
Northampton
Gloucester
Reading
Dover
Calais
Boulogne-sur-Mer
Dieppe
Le Havre
Rouen
Caen
Cherbourg
NORMANDIE
HAUTE-NORMANDIE
Isles of Scilly
On same scale
Projection: Lambert's Conformal Conic
COPYRIGHT GEORGE PHILIP LTD.
West from Greenwich
East from Greenwich
m
ft
3000
1500
600
300
1000
500
200
100
0
50
150
100
300
200
600

SCOTLAND 1:1 800 000

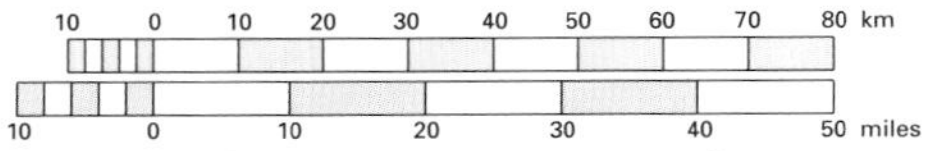
10 0 10 20 30 40 50 60 70 80 km
10 0 10 20 30 40 50 miles

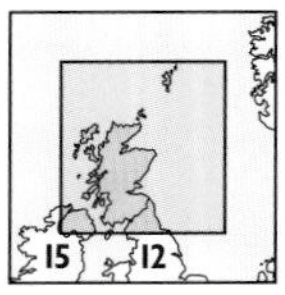
15
12

Key to Scottish unitary authorities on map
1. CITY OF ABERDEEN
2. DUNDEE CITY
3. WEST DUNBARTONSHIRE
4. EAST DUNBARTONSHIRE
5. CITY OF GLASGOW
6. INVERCLYDE
7. RENFREWSHIRE
8. EAST RENFREWSHIRE
9. NORTH LANARKSHIRE
10. FALKIRK
11. CLACKMANNANSHIRE
12. WEST LOTHIAN
13. CITY OF EDINBURGH
14. MIDLOTHIAN
ORKNEY IS.
On same scale
SHETLAND IS.
On same scale
SCOTLAND
ENGLAND
NORTHERN IRELAND
NORTH SEA
ATLANTIC OCEAN
North Channel
Pentland Firth
Moray Firth
Firth of Forth
Firth of Clyde
Solway Firth
North Minch
Little Minch
Outer Hebrides
Inner Hebrides
WESTERN ISLES
Lewis
Harris
North Uist
South Uist
Barra
Skye
Mull
Islay
Jura
Arran
Kintyre
Stornoway
Inverness
Aberdeen
Dundee
Perth
Stirling
Edinburgh
Glasgow
Fort William
Oban
Ayr
Dumfries
Carlisle
Newcastle-upon-Tyne
Belfast
Kirkwall
Lerwick
Wick
Thurso
Grampian Mountains
Cairngorm Mts.
Southern Uplands
Cheviot Hills
North West Highlands
Ben Nevis
1342
Cheviot Hills
HIGHLAND
MORAY
ABERDEENSHIRE
ANGUS
PERTH AND KINROSS
FIFE
STIRLING
ARGYLL AND BUTE
LOTHIAN
SCOTTISH BORDERS
SOUTH LANARKSHIRE
EAST AYRSHIRE
SOUTH AYRSHIRE
NORTH AYRSHIRE
DUMFRIES & GALLOWAY
NORTHUMBERLAND
CUMBRIA
DURHAM
SHETLAND
ORKNEY
Projection : Lambert's Conformal Conic
West from Greenwich
COPYRIGHT GEORGE PHILIP LTD.

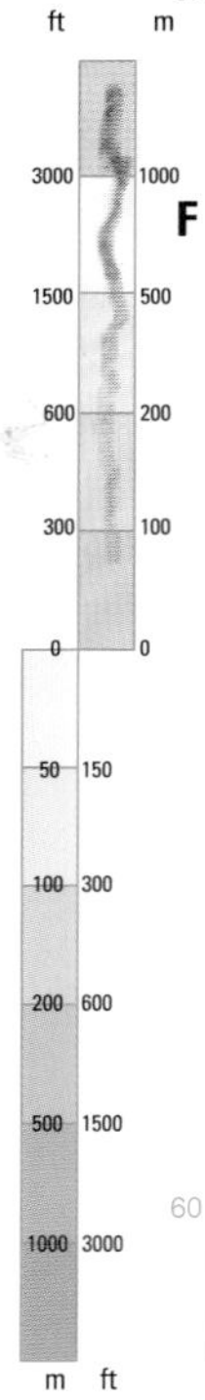
ft m
3000 1000
1500 500
600 200
300 100
0 0
50 150
100 300
200 600
500 1500
1000 3000
m ft

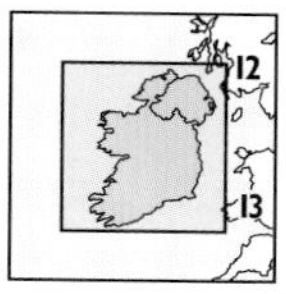

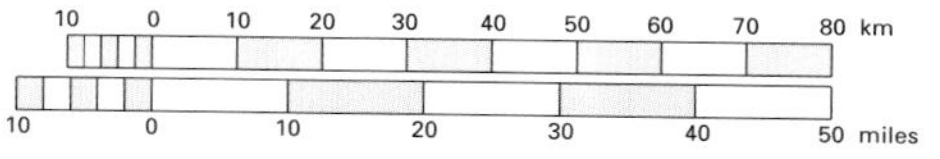

Projection : Lambert's Conformal Conic

West from Greenwich

50 0 25 50 75 100 125 150 175 km
50 0 25 50 75 100 125 miles
ATLANTIC OCEAN
NORTH SEA
IRISH SEA
CELTIC SEA
English Channel
Bristol Channel
St. George's Channel
North Channel
North Minch
Pentland Firth
Moray Firth
Firth of Clyde
Cardigan Bay
The Wash
Str. of Dover
UNITED KINGDOM
IRELAND
SCOTLAND
ENGLAND
WALES
NORTHERN IRELAND
FRANCE
BELGIUM
NETHERLANDS
NORWAY
Shetland Is.
Orkney Is.
Outer Hebrides
Inner Hebrides
Channel Is. (U.K.)
Isles of Scilly
I. of Man
Anglesey
North West Highlands
Grampian Mts.
Southern Uplands
Cheviot Hills
Pennines
Cambrian Mts.
Wicklow Mts.
Ben Nevis 1342
LONDON
Dublin
Belfast
Edinburgh
Glasgow
Cardiff
Aberdeen
Dundee
Inverness
Manchester
Liverpool
Leeds
Sheffield
BIRMINGHAM
Bristol
Newcastle-upon-Tyne
Southampton
Plymouth
Cork
Limerick
Galway
Waterford
Londonderry
Ulster
Connacht
Leinster
Munster
Projection: Conical with two standard parallels
East from Greenwich
West from Greenwich
COPYRIGHT GEORGE PHILIP LTD.

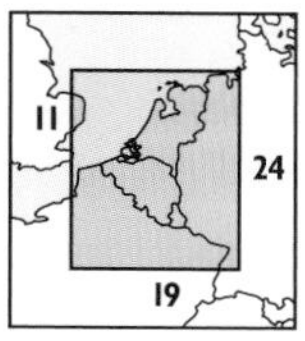

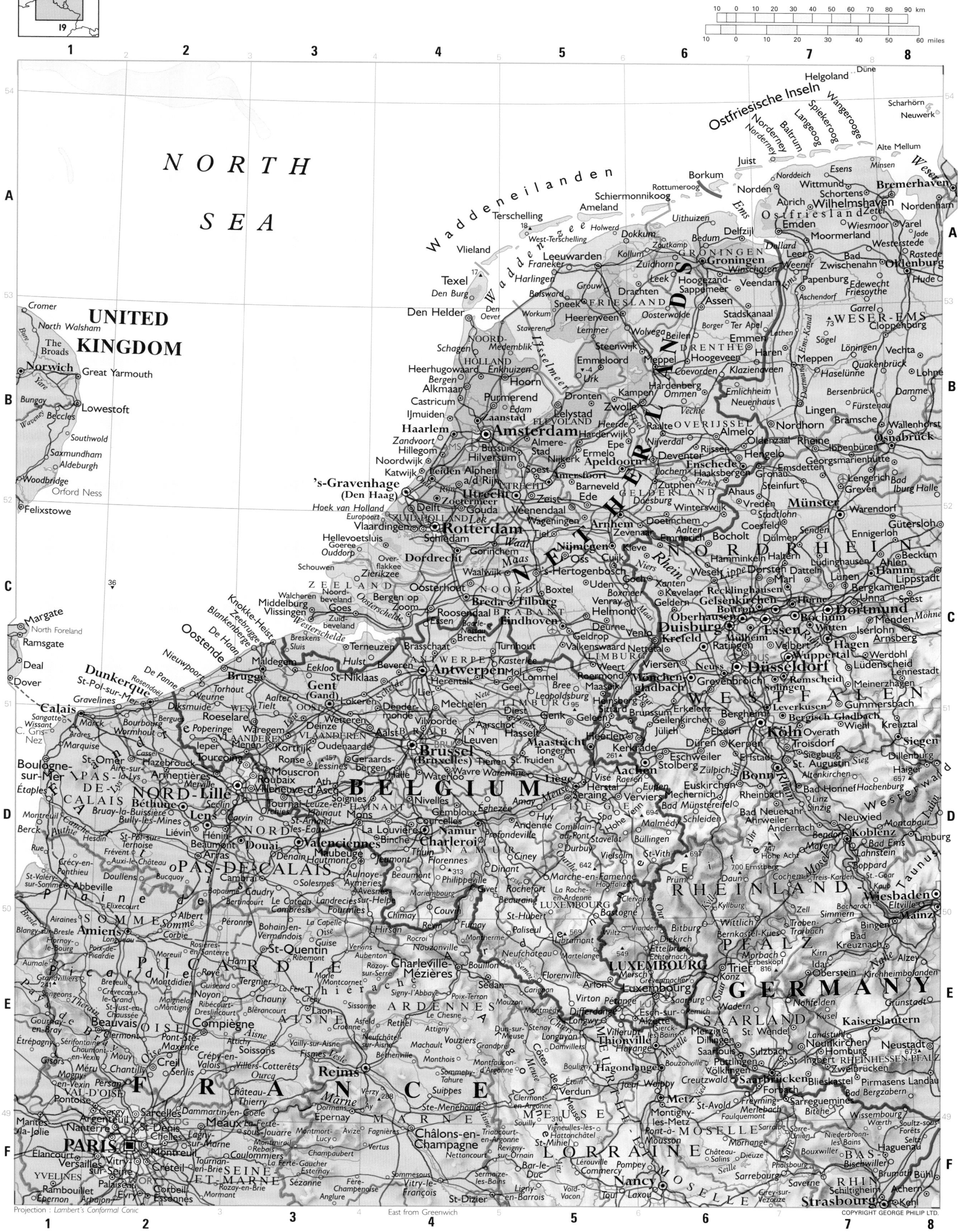

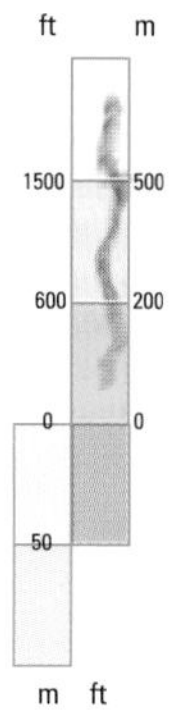

Underlined towns give their name to the administrative area in which they stand.

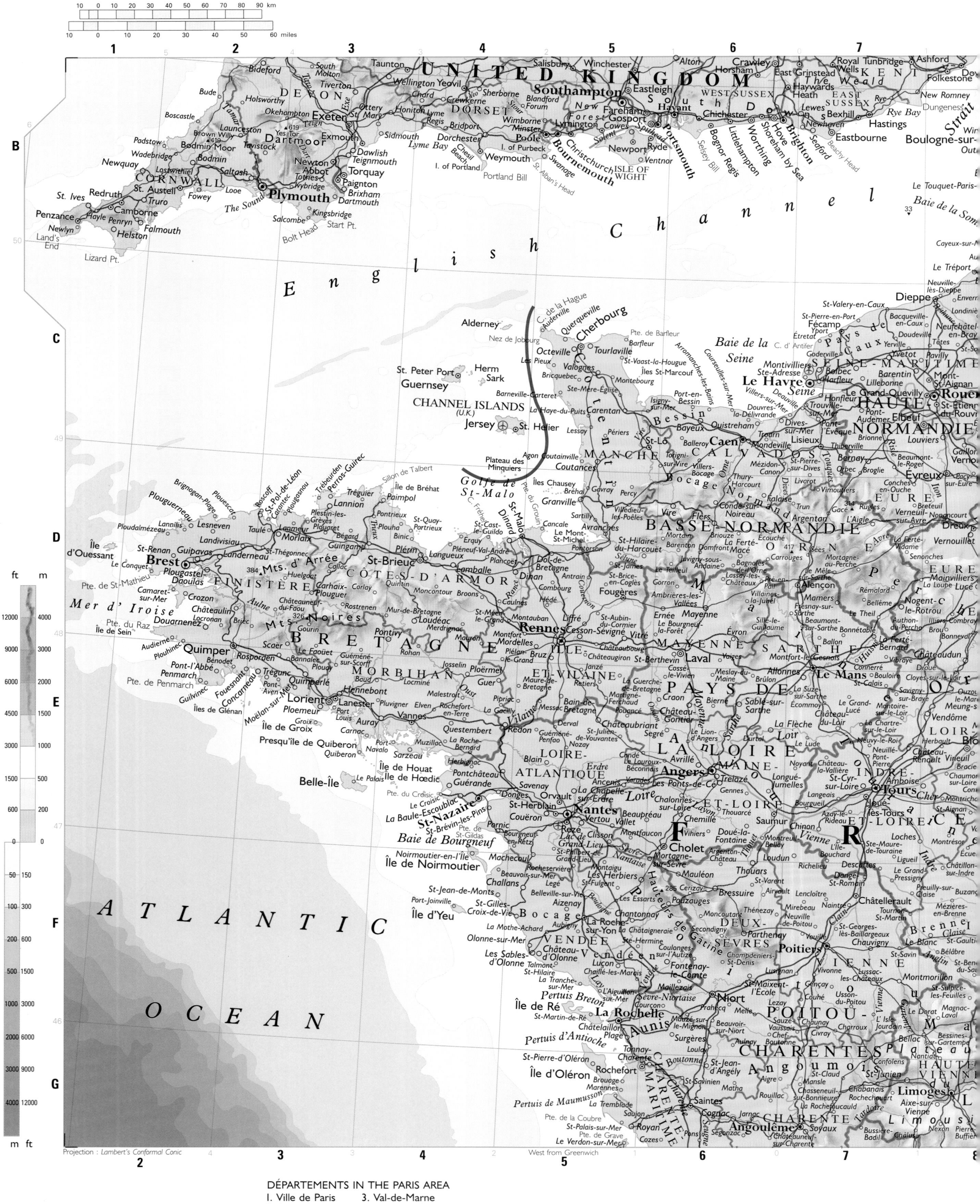

DÉPARTEMENTS IN THE PARIS AREA

1. Ville de Paris
2. Seine-St-Denis
3. Val-de-Marne
4. Hauts-de-Seine

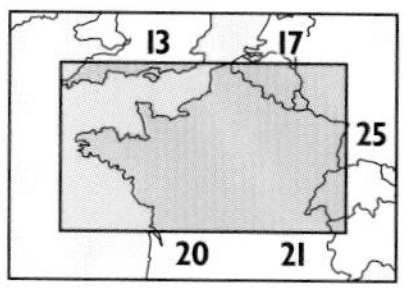

Underlined towns give their name to the administrative area in which they stand.

SOUTHERN FRANCE 1:2 200 000

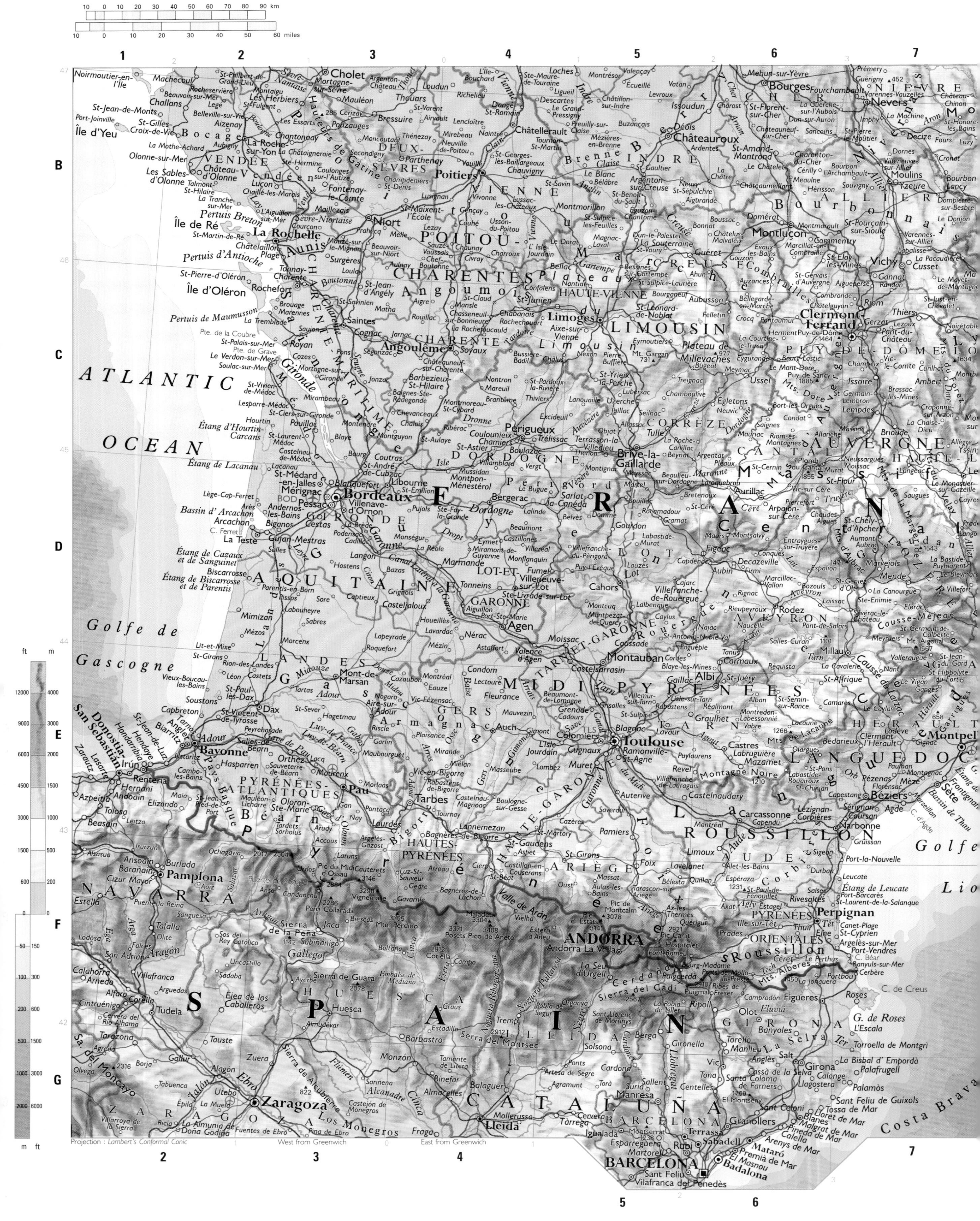

ATLANTIC OCEAN
Golfe de Gascogne
F R A N C E
S P A I N
ANDORRA
Bordeaux
Toulouse
Limoges
Poitiers
Clermont-Ferrand
Montpellier
Perpignan
Bayonne
Pau
Tarbes
Agen
Montauban
Périgueux
La Rochelle
Angoulême
Niort
Bourges
Nevers
Moulins
Vichy
Montluçon
Châteauroux
Cholet
Rodez
Albi
Carcassonne
Narbonne
Béziers
Sète
Nîmes
Pamplona
Zaragoza
Huesca
Lleida
Barcelona
Donostia-San Sebastián
Irun
Girona
Figueres
Sabadell
Terrassa
Badalona
Manresa
Île d'Yeu
Île de Ré
Île d'Oléron
Pertuis Breton
Pertuis d'Antioche
Pertuis de Maumusson
Bassin d'Arcachon
Étang de Lacanau
Étang d'Hourtin-Carcans
Étang de Cazaux et de Sanguinet
Étang de Biscarrosse et de Parentis
Gironde
Garonne
Dordogne
Lot
Tarn
Adour
Charente
Vienne
Creuse
Ebro
AQUITAINE
POITOU-CHARENTES
LIMOUSIN
AUVERGNE
MIDI-PYRÉNÉES
LANGUEDOC-ROUSSILLON
PYRÉNÉES-ATLANTIQUES
HAUTES-PYRÉNÉES
HAUTE-GARONNE
PYRÉNÉES-ORIENTALES
LANDES
GIRONDE
DORDOGNE
CORRÈZE
CANTAL
AVEYRON
GERS
TARN
ARIÈGE
AUDE
HÉRAULT
NAVARRA
HUESCA
LLEIDA
GIRONA
BARCELONA
CATALUÑA
ZARAGOZA
Massif Central
Plateau de Millevaches
Montagne Noire
Pic du Midi d'Ossau
Vignemale
Mte. Perdido
Pico de Aneto
Pic de Montcalm
Costa Brava
Golfe du Lion
C. de Creus
G. de Roses
Projection : Lambert's Conformal Conic
West from Greenwich
East from Greenwich

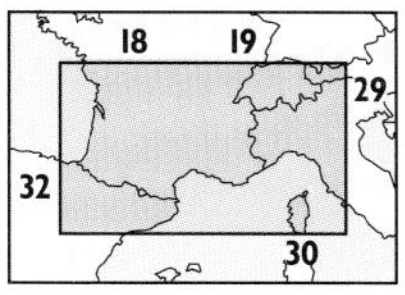

18
19
29
32
30

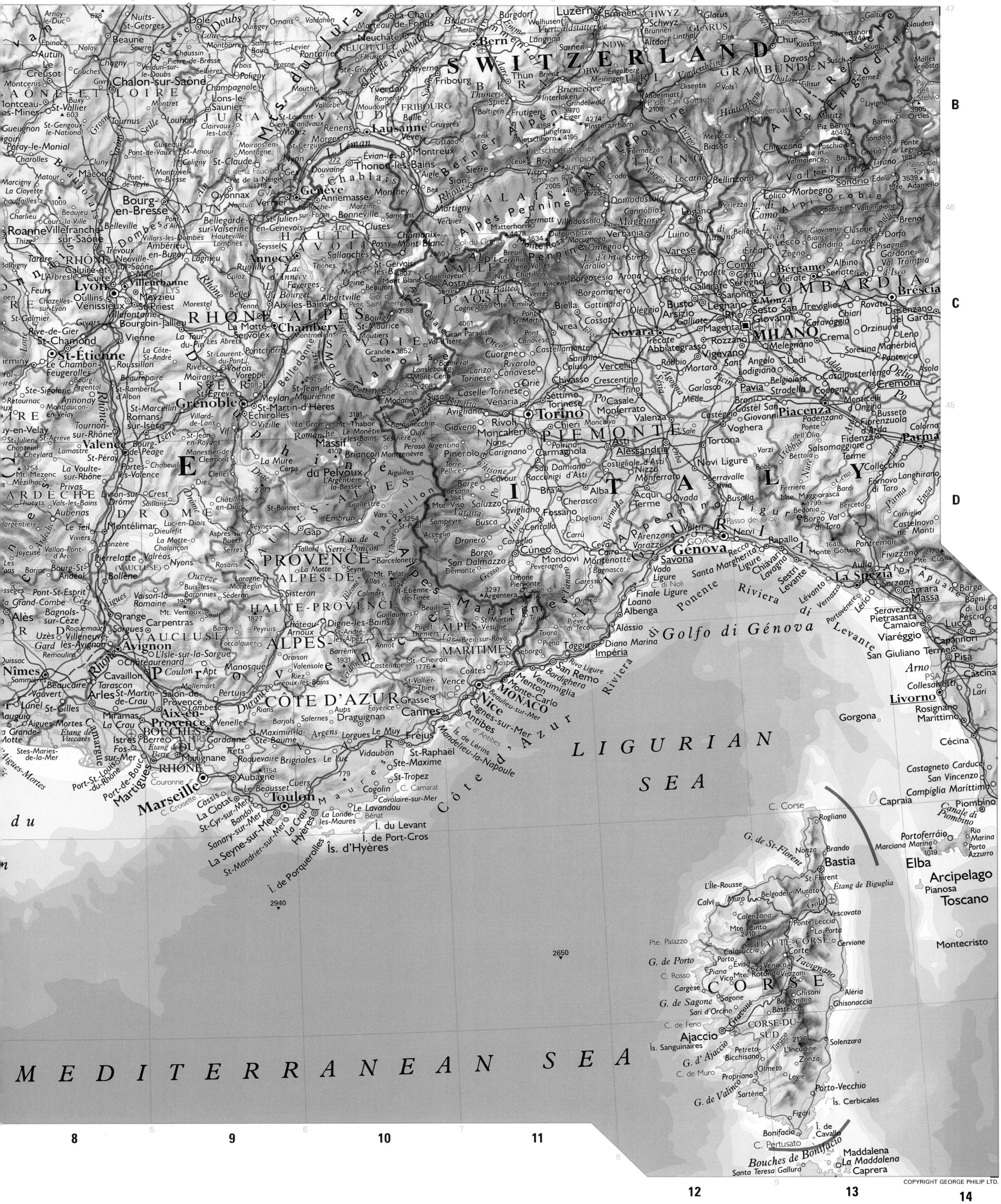

8
9
10
11
12
13
14
B
C
D
E
F
G
SWITZERLAND
ITALY
FRANCE
LIGURIAN SEA
MEDITERRANEAN SEA
Golfo di Génova
Riviera di Ponente
Riviera di Levante
Côte d'Azur
RHÔNE-ALPES
PROVENCE-ALPES-CÔTE D'AZUR
LOMBARDIA
PIEMONTE
VALLE D'AOSTA
LIGURIA
CORSE
HAUTE-CORSE
CORSE-DU-SUD
SAVOIE
HAUTE-SAVOIE
ISÈRE
DRÔME
ARDÈCHE
VAUCLUSE
BOUCHES-DU-RHÔNE
ALPES-DE-HAUTE-PROVENCE
HAUTES-ALPES
ALPES-MARITIMES
JURA
AIN
GRAUBÜNDEN
TICINO
VALAIS
BERN
VAUD
FRIBOURG
NEUCHÂTEL
Alpes Pennine
Alpi Lepontine
Alpi Marittime
Alpi Apuane
Alpi Orobie
Berner Alpen
Mts. du Jura
Massif du Pelvoux
Vanoise
Dauphiné
Apennino Ligure
Lac Léman
Lac de Neuchâtel
L. Maggiore
L. di Como
L. di Lugano
L. d'Iseo
L. d'Orta
Lago di Garda
Marseille
Toulon
Nice
MONACO
Cannes
Antibes
Grenoble
Lyon
St-Étienne
Valence
Avignon
Nîmes
Arles
Aix-en-Provence
Chambéry
Annecy
Genève
Lausanne
Bern
Luzern
MILANO
Torino
Genova
La Spezia
Livorno
Pisa
Lucca
Parma
Piacenza
Cremona
Brescia
Bergamo
Novara
Alessandria
Asti
Cuneo
Savona
Impéria
San Remo
Bastia
Ajaccio
Porto-Vecchio
Bonifacio
Elba
Arcipelago Toscano
Capraia
Gorgona
Montecristo
Pianosa
Îs. d'Hyères
Bouches de Bonifacio
Mt. Blanc 4807
Matterhorn 4478
Mte. Rosa 4634
Gran Paradiso 4061
Mte. Viso 3841
Mt. Cinto 2710
2940
2650

50 0 25 50 75 100 125 150 175 km
50 0 25 50 75 100 125 miles
NORTH SEA
BALTIC SEA
ADRIATIC SEA
UNITED KINGDOM
DENMARK
NETHERLANDS
BELGIUM
LUXEMBOURG
GERMANY
FRANCE
SWITZERLAND
LIECHTENSTEIN
AUSTRIA
CZECH
SLOVENIA
ITALY
MONACO
SAN MARINO
AMSTERDAM
ROTTERDAM
BRUSSEL (BRUXELLES)
PARIS
HAMBURG
BERLIN
PRAHA (Prague)
MÜNCHEN (Munich)
MILANO
TORINO (Turin)
LYON
MARSEILLE
Golfo di Venézia
Golfo di Génova
ft m
12000 4000
9000 3000
6000 2000
4500 1500
3000 1000
1500 500
600 200
0 0
50 150
100 300
200 600
500 1500
1000 3000
2000 6000
m ft
Projection: Conical with two standard parallels

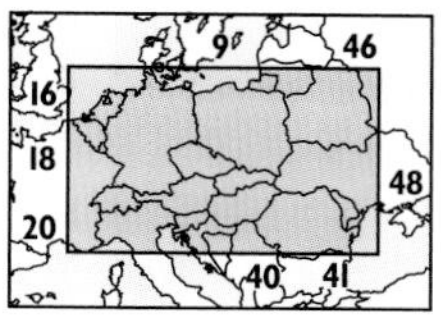
16
18
20
40
41
46
48

9
10
11
12
13
14
15
16
B
C
D
E
F
G
LITHUANIA
B E L A R U S
P O L A N D
U K R A I N E
SLOVAK REP.
H U N G A R Y
R O M A N I A
M O L D O V A
BOSNIA-HERZEGOVINA
YUGOSLAVIA
B U L G A R I A
C a r p a t h i a n s
Podilska Vysochyna
Pripet Marshes
Transilvania
Carpaţii Meridionali
Vojvodina
Wallachia
Kaliningrad (Russia)
Zatoka Gdańska
Zalew Wiślany
Pojezierze Mazurskie
Gdynia
Gdańsk
Elbląg
Olsztyn
Bydgoszcz
Toruń
Grudziądz
Białystok
Hrodna
Vilnius
Minsk
Maladzyechna
Barysaw
Mahilyow
Babruysk
Homyel
Baranavichy
Pinsk
Mazyr
Brest
Warszawa (Warsaw)
Płock
Łódź
Radom
Lublin
Kielce
Częstochowa
Katowice
Kraków
Tarnów
Rzeszów
Wrocław
Opole
Kalisz
Poznań
Lutsk
Rivne
Kovel
Lviv (Lvov)
Ternopil
Khmelnytskyy
Zhytomyr
Vinnytsya
Kyyiv (Kiev)
Bila Tserkva
Ivano-Frankivsk
Chernivtsi
Uzhhorod
Chişinău
Tiraspol
Bălţi
Uman
Bilhorod-Dnistrovskyy
Izmayil
Košice
Prešov
Žilina
Bratislava
Trnava
Nitra
Banská Bystrica
Ostrava
Miskolc
Debrecen
Nyíregyháza
Budapest
Székesfehérvár
Győr
Kecskemét
Szeged
Pécs
Satu Mare
Baia Mare
Oradea
Cluj-Napoca
Târgu Mureş
Suceava
Botoşani
Iaşi
Piatra Neamţ
Bacău
Braşov
Sibiu
Arad
Timişoara
Craiova
Piteşti
Ploieşti
Bucureşti (Bucharest)
Brăila
Galaţi
Constanţa
Tulcea
Ruse
Varna
Dobrich
Novi Sad
Beograd (Belgrade)
Osijek
Subotica
Sarajevo
Tuzla
Zenica
Dunaj
Duna
Dunărea (Danube)
Dnister
Wisła (Vistula)
Tisza
Mureş
Siret
Prut
Olt
Sava
Drava
Balaton
9
10
11
12
13
14
15
East from Greenwich
COPYRIGHT GEORGE PHILIP LTD.

10 0 10 20 30 40 50 60 70 80 90 km
10 0 10 20 30 40 50 60 miles
BALTIC SEA
NORTH SEA
DENMARK
POLAND
GERMANY
NETHERLANDS
MECKLENBURG-VORPOMMERN
BRANDENBURG
SCHLESWIG-HOLSTEIN
NIEDERSACHSEN
SACHSEN-ANHALT
SACHSEN
THÜRINGEN
NORDRHEIN-WESTFALEN
BERLIN
HAMBURG
Bremen
Hannover
Kiel
Rostock
Magdeburg
Leipzig
Dresden
Dortmund
Düsseldorf
Köln
Szczecin
Nordfriesische Inseln
Ostfriesische Inseln
Deutsche Bucht
Lübecker Bucht
Mecklenburger Bucht
Kieler Bucht
Fehmarn Belt
Rügen
Usedom
Fehmarn
Lolland
Falster
Helgoland

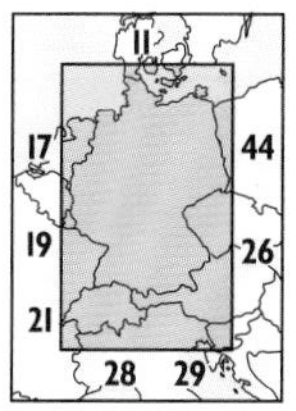

Projection : Lambert's Conformal Conic

East from Greenwich

COPYRIGHT GEORGE PHILIP LTD.

Underlined towns give their name to the administrative area in which they stand.

km
miles
GERMANY
CZECH REP.
AUSTRIA
SWITZERLAND
ITALY
SLOVENIA
THÜRINGEN
BAYERN
OBERFRANKEN
UNTERFRANKEN
MITTELFRANKEN
OBERPFALZ
NIEDERBAYERN
OBERBAYERN
SCHWABEN
ZÁPADOČESKÝ
STŘEDOČESKÝ
SEVEROČESKÝ
JIHOČESKÝ
NIEDERÖSTERREICH
OBERÖSTERREICH
SALZBURG
STEIERMARK
KÄRNTEN
OST TIROL
VORARLBERG
TRENTINO-ALTO ADIGE
FRIULI-VENEZIA GIULIA
VÉNETO
LOMBARDIA
PRAHA
München
Dresden
Nürnberg
Stuttgart
Augsburg
Regensburg
Linz
Salzburg
Innsbruck
Graz
Klagenfurt
Ljubljana
Zagreb
Trieste
Venézia
Golfo di Venézia
Plzeň
České Budějovice
Chemnitz
Erfurt
Würzburg
Bodensee
Projection : Lambert's Conformal Conic

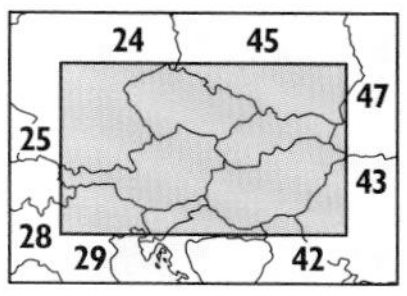

Underlined towns give their name to the administrative area in which they stand.

Underlined towns give their name to the administrative area in which they stand

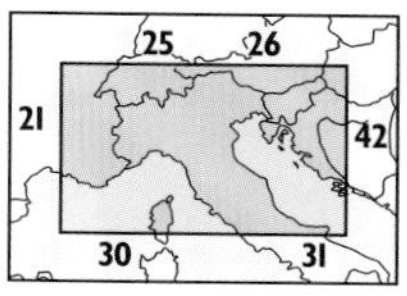

Administrative divisions in Croatia:

1. Brodsko-Posavska
2. Koprivničko-Križevačka
3. Krapinsko-Zagorska
4. Medimurska
6. Požeško-Slavonska
7. Varaždinska
8. Virovitičko-Podravska
10. Zagrebačka

– – – – Inter-entity boundaries as agreed at the 1995 Dayton Peace Agreement.

COPYRIGHT GEORGE PHILIP LTD.

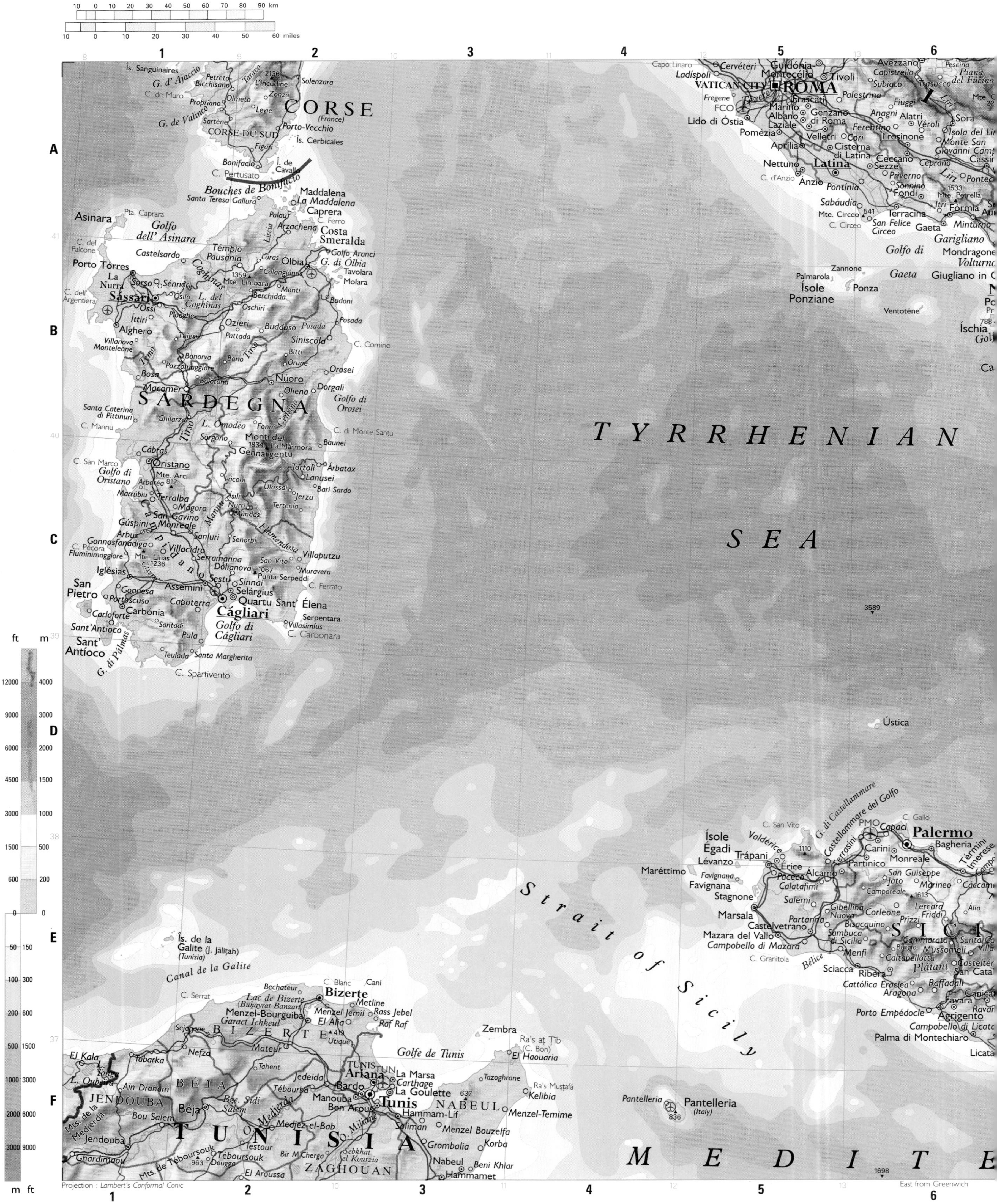
10 0 10 20 30 40 50 60 70 80 90 km
10 0 10 20 30 40 50 60 miles
TYRRHENIAN
SEA
Strait of Sicily
M E D I T E
CORSE
(France)
CORSE-DU-SUD
SARDEGNA
TUNISIA
SICI
G. d' Ajaccio
G. de Valinco
Bouches de Bonifacio
Golfo dell' Asinara
Golfo di Orosei
Golfo di Oristano
Golfo di Cágliari
G. di Palmas
Golfo di Gaeta
Golfe de Tunis
Canal de la Galite
G. di Castellammare
Ajaccio
Propriano
Sartène
Porto-Vecchio
Bonifacio
Asinara
Porto Torres
Sássari
Alghero
Ólbia
Témpio Pausánia
Nùoro
Oristano
Iglésias
Cágliari
Carbónia
San Pietro
Sant' Antíoco
C. Spartivento
ROMA
VATICAN CITY
Latina
Frosinone
Ísole Ponziane
Ponza
Íschia
Palermo
Trápani
Marsala
Ísole Egadi
Favignana
Maréttimo
Ústica
Agrigento
Pantelleria
Pantelleria (Italy)
Bizerte
Tunis
Ariana
Béja
Jendouba
Nabeul
Kelibia
Zembra
Îs. de la Galite (J. Jālīṭah) (Tunisia)
3589
1698
ft m
12000 4000
9000 3000
6000 2000
4500 1500
3000 1000
1500 500
600 200
0 0
50 150
100 300
200 600
500 1500
1000 3000
2000 6000
3000 9000
m ft
Projection : Lambert's Conformal Conic
East from Greenwich

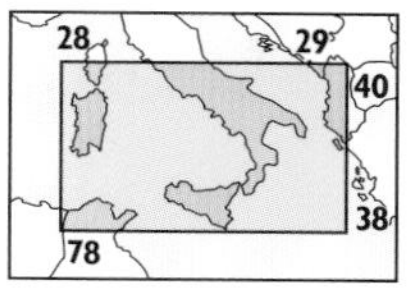

Underlined towns give their name to the administrative area in which they stand.

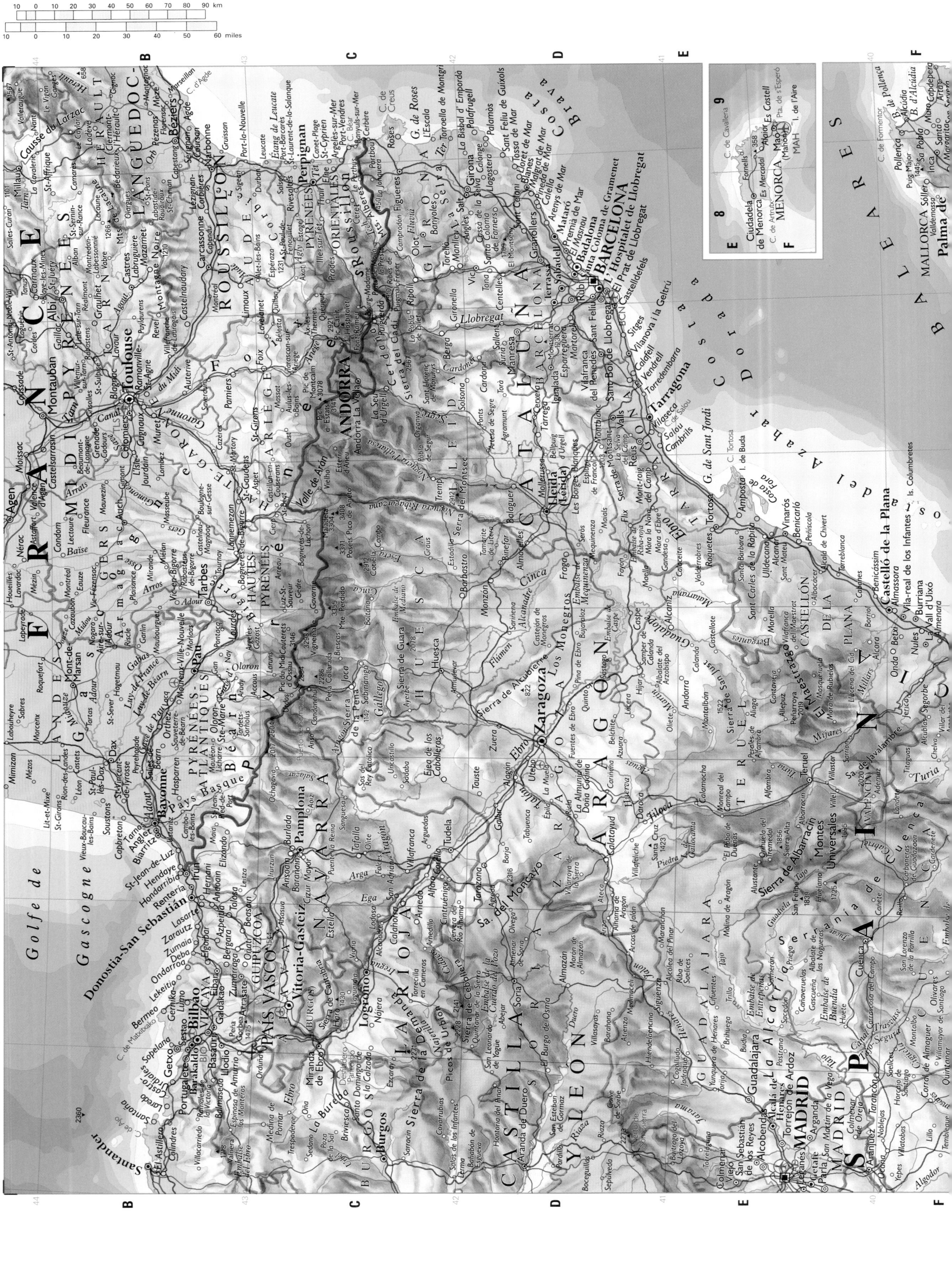
10 0 10 20 30 40 50 60 70 80 90 km
10 0 10 20 30 40 50 60 miles
FRANCE
MIDI-PYRÉNÉES
LANGUEDOC-ROUSSILLON
AQUITAINE
PYRÉNÉES-ATLANTIQUES
HAUTES-PYRÉNÉES
PYRÉNÉES-ORIENTALES
ANDORRA
CATALUÑA
BARCELONA
GIRONA
LLEIDA
TARRAGONA
ARAGÓN
HUESCA
ZARAGOZA
TERUEL
NAVARRA
PAÍS VASCO
LA RIOJA
CASTILLA Y LEÓN
CASTILLA-LA MANCHA
MADRID
CASTELLÓN
VALENCIA
ESPAÑA
Golfe de Gascogne
Costa Brava
Costa Daurada
Costa del Azahar
BALEARES
MENORCA
MALLORCA
Toulouse
Perpignan
Bilbao
Donostia-San Sebastián
Vitoria-Gasteiz
Pamplona
Logroño
Burgos
Soria
Guadalajara
Cuenca
Castelló de la Plana
Palma de Mallorca

MEDITERRANEAN SEA
ALGERIA
ALGER (Algiers)
Golfo de Valencia
Costa Blanca
Costa del Sol
Valencia
Alicante
Murcia
Cartagena
Almería
Granada
Albacete
Eivissa (Ibiza)
Formentera
Cabrera
Oran
Mostaganem
Ech Cheliff
Blida
Medea
Melilla
COPYRIGHT GEORGE PHILIP LTD.
Projection : Lambert's Conformal Conic

10 0 10 20 30 40 50 60 70 80 90 km

10 0 10 20 30 40 50 60 miles

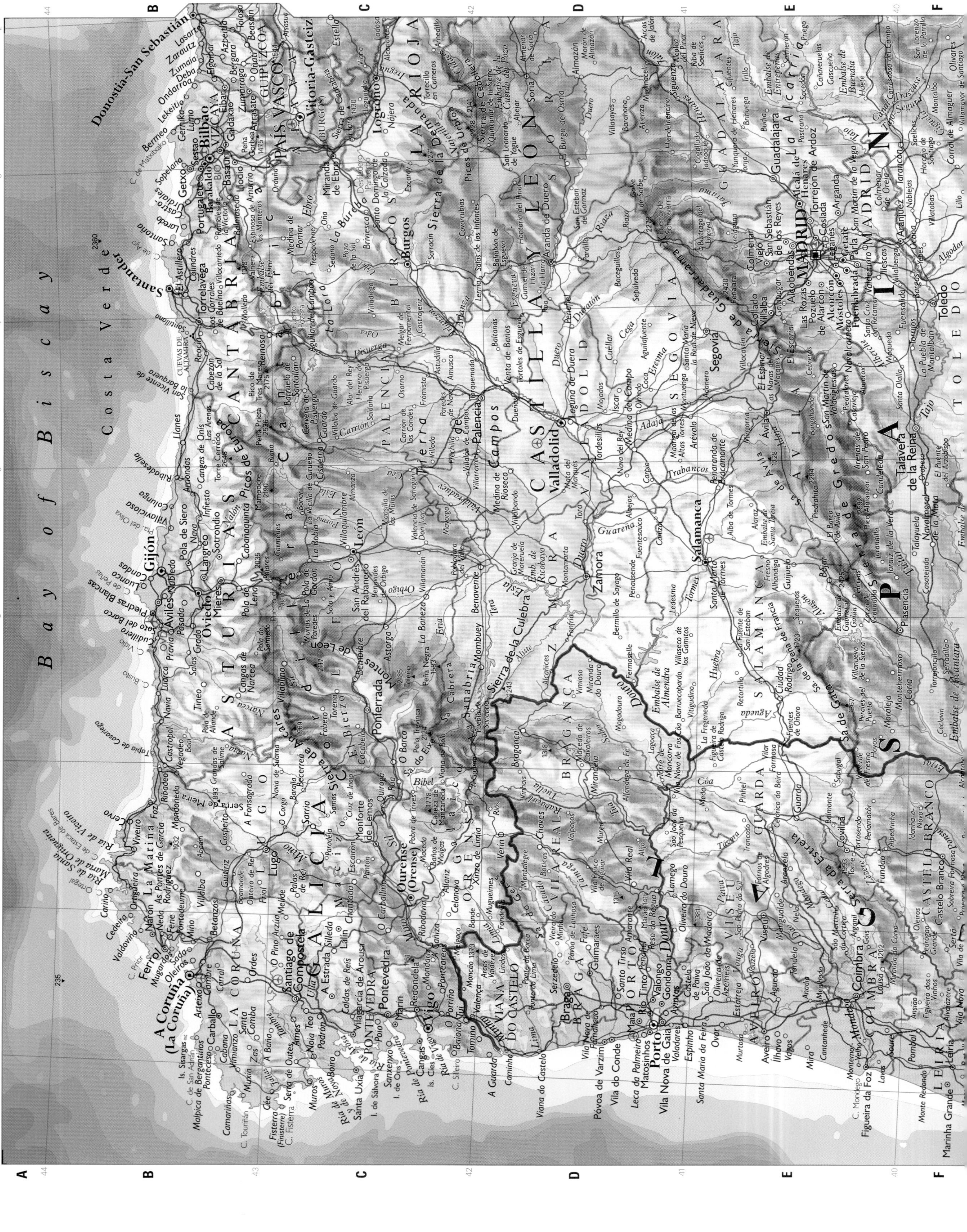

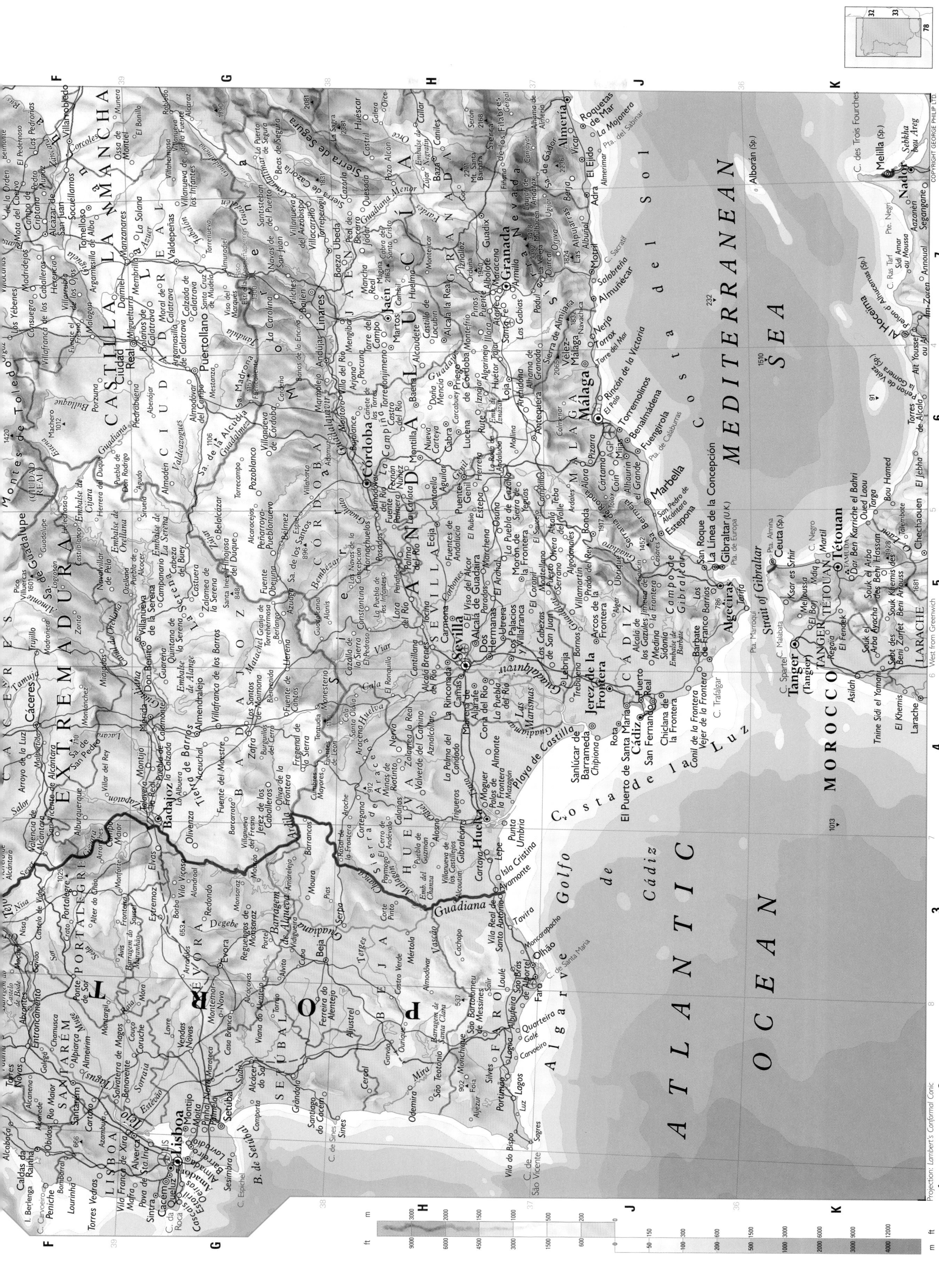
ATLANTIC OCEAN
MEDITERRANEAN SEA
Golfo de Cádiz
Costa de la Luz
Costa del Sol
Strait of Gibraltar
MOROCCO
EXTREMADURA
CASTILLA LA MANCHA
ANDALUCÍA
Algarve
Sierra de Segura
Sierra Nevada
Lisboa
Sevilla
Córdoba
Granada
Málaga
Cádiz
Huelva
Badajoz
Cáceres
Almería
Jaén
Gibraltar (U.K.)
Ceuta (Sp.)
Melilla (Sp.)
Tanger
Tétouan
Projection: Lambert's Conformal Conic
West from Greenwich
COPYRIGHT GEORGE PHILIP LTD.

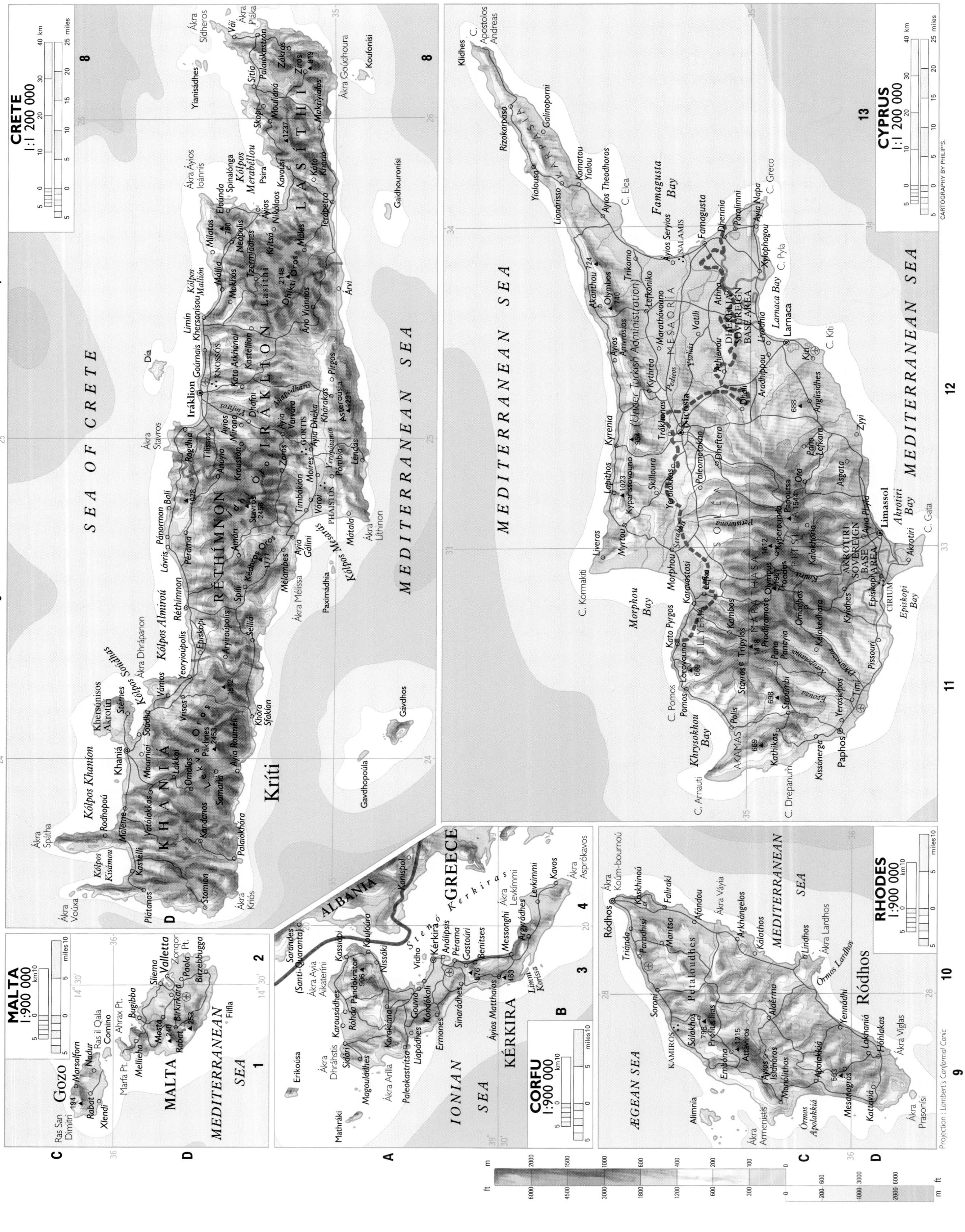
CRETE
1:1 200 000
CYPRUS
1:1 200 000
MALTA
1:900 000
CORFU
1:900 000
RHODES
1:900 000
SEA OF CRETE
MEDITERRANEAN SEA
Kríti
IONIAN SEA
ÆGEAN SEA
Projection: Lambert's Conformal Conic
CARTOGRAPHY BY PHILIP'S.

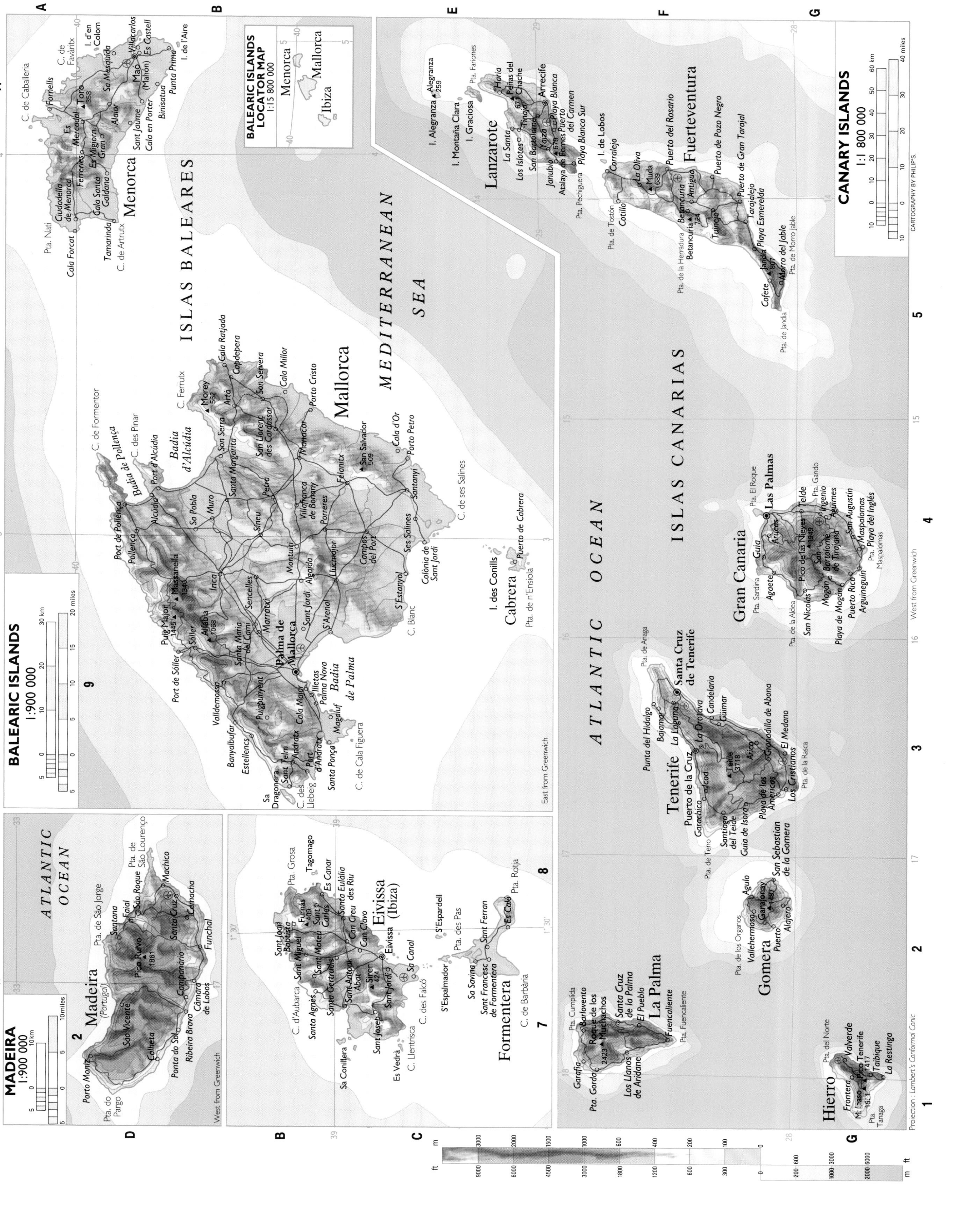
BALEARIC ISLANDS
1:900 000
BALEARIC ISLANDS LOCATOR MAP
1:15 800 000
Menorca
Mallorca
Ibiza
ISLAS BALEARES
MEDITERRANEAN SEA
Menorca
Ciudadella de Menorca
Ferreries
Es Mercadal
Es Migjorn Gran
Alaior
Fornells
Toro
358
Sa Mesquida
Maó (Mahón)
Villacarlos
Es Castell
Sant Jaume
Cala en Porter
Binisafua
Punta Prima
I. de l'Aire
I. d'en Colom
C. de Favàritx
C. de Cavalleria
Pta. Nati
Cala Forcat
Tamarinda
C. de Artrutx
Cala Santa Galdana
Mallorca
Palma de Mallorca
Badia de Palma
Badia de Pollença
Badia d'Alcúdia
C. de Formentor
C. des Pinar
C. Ferrutx
Port de Pollença
Pollença
Alcúdia
Port d'Alcúdia
Sa Pobla
Muro
Santa Margarita
Son Serra
Artà
Morey
562
Capdepera
Cala Ratjada
Son Servera
Sant Llorenç des Cardassar
Cala Millor
Porto Cristo
Manacor
Petra
Sineu
Inca
Felanitx
San Salvador
509
Cala d'Or
Porto Petro
Santanyí
Vilafranca de Bonany
Porreres
Montuïri
Campos del Port
Llucmajor
Algaida
Sant Jordi
S'Arenal
Ses Salines
Colònia de Sant Jordi
C. de ses Salines
S'Estanyol
C. Blanc
Sencelles
Marratxí
Santa Maria del Camí
Massanella
1340
Puig Major
1445
Alfàbia
1068
Sóller
Port de Sóller
Valldemossa
Banyalbufar
Estellencs
Puigpunyent
Illetas
Palma Nova
Magaluf
Cala Major
Andratx
Sant Telm
Port d'Andratx
Santa Ponça
Sa Dragonera
C. des Llebeig
C. de Cala Figuera
Cabrera
I. des Conills
Puerto de Cabrera
Pta. de n'Ensiola
East from Greenwich
Eivissa (Ibiza)
Eivissa
Sant Joan Baptista
Sant Miquel
Sant Mateu
Sant Carles
Santa Eulàlia des Riu
Es Canar
Tagomago
Pta. Grosa
Fumas
409
Can Clavo
Can Creu
Sant Antoni Abat
Santa Agnès
Santa Gertrudis
Sant Rafel
Sant Jordi
Sirer
424
Sant Josep
Sa Conillera
Es Vedrà
C. Llentrisca
C. des Falcó
C. d'Aubarca
Sa Canal
S'Espardell
S'Espalmador
Pta. des Pas
Formentera
Sant Ferran
Es Caló
Pta. Rotja
Sa Savina
Sant Francesc de Formentera
C. de Barbària
MADEIRA
1:900 000
Madeira (Portugal)
ATLANTIC OCEAN
Porto Moniz
Pta. do Pargo
São Vicente
Calheta
Ponta do Sol
Ribeira Brava
Câmara de Lobos
Funchal
Campanário
Pico Ruivo
1861
Santana
Faial
São Roque
Machico
Santa Cruz
Camacha
Pta. de São Jorge
Pta. de São Lourenço
West from Greenwich
CANARY ISLANDS
1:1 800 000
ISLAS CANARIAS
ATLANTIC OCEAN
Lanzarote
I. Alegranza
Alegranza
259
I. Montaña Clara
I. Graciosa
Pta. Fariones
Haría
Peñas del Chache
671
Arrecife
Tinajo
San Bartolomé
La Santa
Los Islotes
Yaiza
Playa Blanca
Puerto del Carmen
Playa Blanca Sur
Janubio
Atalaya de Femes
I. de Lobos
Fuerteventura
Corralejo
La Oliva
Muda
689
Puerto del Rosario
Cotillo
Pta. de Tostón
Betancuria
Antigua
Puerto de Pozo Negro
Puerto de Gran Tarajal
Tuineje
Tarajalejo
Playa Esmerelda
Jandía
807
Morro del Jable
Pta. de Morro Jable
Cofete
Pta. de Jandía
Pta. de la Herradura
Gran Canaria
Las Palmas
Pta. El Roque
Telde
Pta. Gando
Ingenio
Agüimes
San Augustin
Maspalomas
Playa del Inglés
Pico de las Nieves
1949
San Bartolomé de Tirajana
Arucas
Guía
Agaete
Pta. Sardina
San Nicolás
Mogán
Playa de Mogán
Puerto Rico
Arguineguín
Pta. de la Aldea
Tenerife
Santa Cruz de Tenerife
Pta. de Anaga
La Laguna
Candelaria
Güímar
La Orotava
Puerto de la Cruz
Punta del Hidalgo
Bajamar
Icod
Garachico
Teide
3718
Arico
Granadilla de Abona
El Medano
Los Cristianos
Playa de las Americas
Santiago del Teide
Guía de Isora
Pta. de Teno
Pta. de la Rasca
Gomera
San Sebastian de la Gomera
Agulo
Garajonay
1487
Vallehermoso
Alajeró
Pta. de los Organos
La Palma
Santa Cruz de la Palma
Barlovento
Roque de los Muchachos
2423
El Pueblo
Fuencaliente
Pta. Fuencaliente
Pta. Cumplida
Garafía
Pta. Gorda
Los Llanos de Aridane
Hierro
Valverde
Pico Tenerife
1417
Taibique
La Restinga
Frontera
Pta. del Norte
Pta. Tanaga
West from Greenwich
Projection : Lambert's Conformal Conic
CARTOGRAPHY BY PHILIP'S.

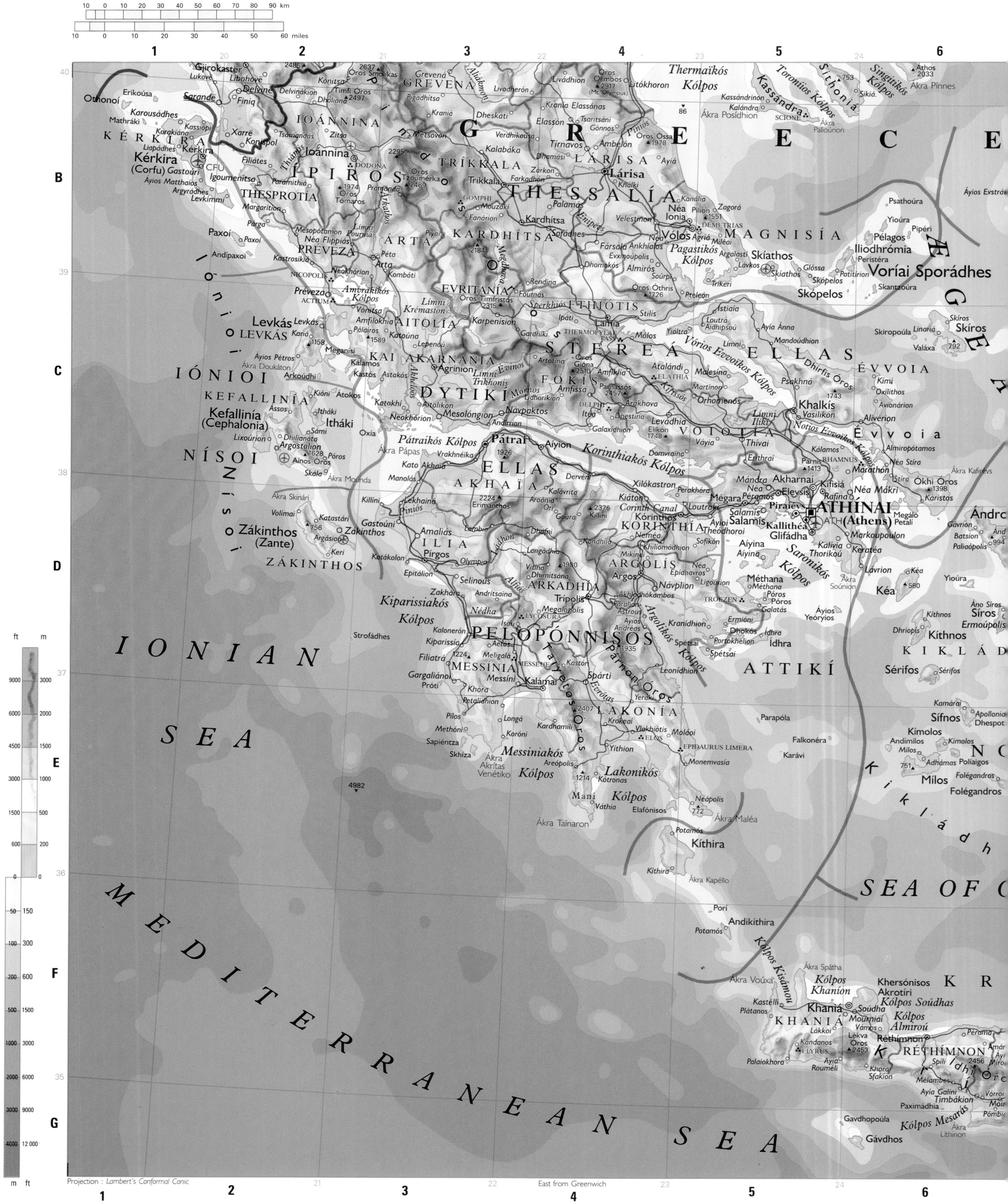
10 0 10 20 30 40 50 60 70 80 90 km
10 0 10 20 30 40 50 60 miles
ft m
9000 3000
6000 2000
4500 1500
3000 1000
1500 500
600 200
50 150
100 300
200 600
500 1500
1000 3000
2000 6000
3000 9000
4000 12 000
m ft
GREECE
IONIAN SEA
MEDITERRANEAN SEA
SEA OF
Thermaïkós Kólpos
Toronaíos Kólpos
Singitikós Kólpos
Kassándra
Sithonía
Ákra Pínnes
Áthos 2033
Kérkira (Corfu)
KÉRKIRA
Othonoí
Erikoúsa
Paxoí
Andípaxoi
Levkás
LEVKÁS
IÓNIOI
KEFALLINÍA
Kefallinía (Cephalonia)
Itháki
NÍSOI
Zákinthos (Zante)
ZÁKINTHOS
Ióniοi Nísoi
Gjirokastër
Sarandë
Ioánnina
IOÁNNINA
ÍPIROS
THESPROTÍA
PRÉVEZA
Préveza
ÁRTA
Árta
TRÍKKALA
Tríkkala
KARDHÍTSA
Kardhítsa
THESSALÍA
LÁRISA
Lárisa
MAGNISÍA
Vólos
Pagastikós Kólpos
Skíathos
Vóriai Sporádhes
Skópelos
Skíros
EVRITANÍA
FTHIÓTIS
Lamía
STERÉA
ELLAS
AITOLÍA KAI AKARNANÍA
DYTIKI ELLAS
FOKÍS
VOIOTÍA
ÉVVOIA
Évvoia
Khalkís
Pátrai
Pátraikós Kólpos
Korinthiakós Kólpos
AKHAÏA
ILIA
Pírgos
KORINTHÍA
Kórinthos
ARGOLÍS
Argos
Návplion
ARKADHÍA
Trípolis
PELOPÓNNISOS
MESSINÍA
Kalamáta
LAKONÍA
Spárti
Messiniakós Kólpos
Lakonikós Kólpos
Kiparissiakós Kólpos
Argolikós Kólpos
Saronikós Kólpos
ATHÍNAI (Athens)
Piraiévs
Elevsís
Mégara
Salamís
ATTIKÍ
Aíyina
Kéa
Kíthnos
Síros
Sérifos
Sífnos
Mílos
Kímolos
Folégandros
KIKLÁD
Kíthira
Andikíthira
Kólpos Kisámou
Kólpos Khaníon
Khaniá
KHANIÁ
Kólpos Soúdhas
Réthimnon
RÉTHIMNON
Kólpos Mesarás
Gávdhos
Gavdhopoúla
4982
Projection : Lambert's Conformal Conic
East from Greenwich
1 2 3 4 5 6
B C D E F G

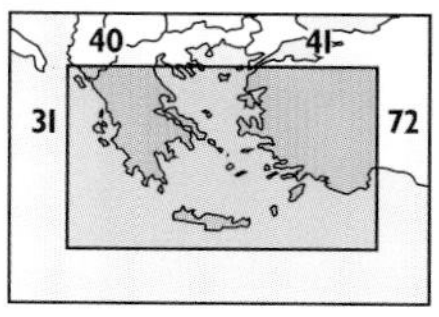
40
41
31
72

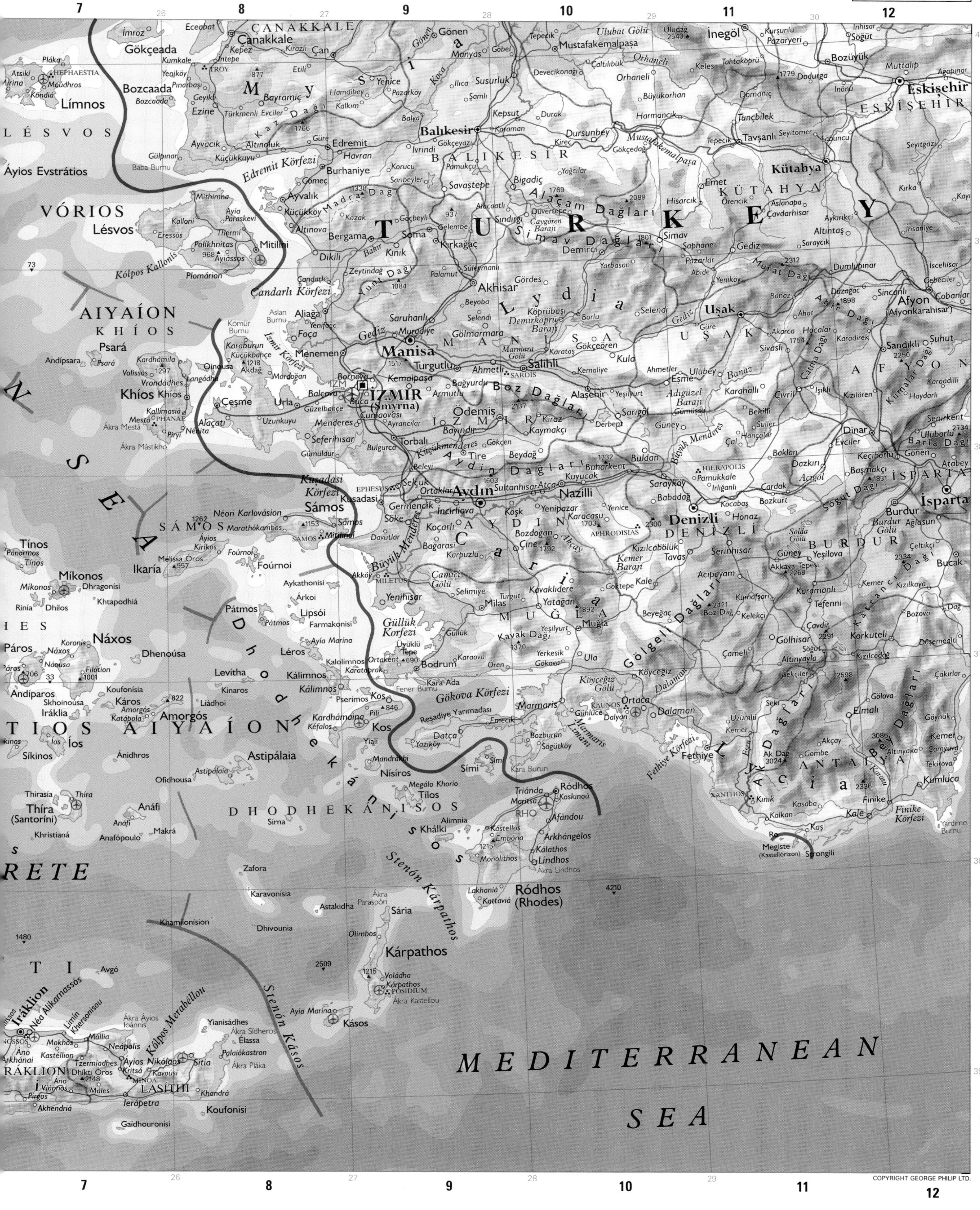
7
8
9
10
11
12
26
27
28
29
30
40
39
38
37
36
35
B
C
D
E
F
G
Çanakkale
Gökçeada
İmroz
Eceabat
Kepez
Intepe
Kumkale
Çan
Gönen
Manyas
Göbel
Tepecik
Mustafakemalpaşa
Ulubat Gölü
Uludağ 2543
İnegöl
Kurşunlu
Pazaryeri
İnhisar
Söğüt
Bozüyük
Muttalip
Eskişehir
ESKİŞEHİR
İnönü
Limnos
Límnos
Pláka
Atsikí
Mírina
Moúdhros
Kondiá
HEPHAESTIA
Bozcaada
Yeniköy
Pınarbaşı
TROY
Geyikli
Bayramiç
Ezine
Türkmenli
Evciler
M y s i a
Yenice
Pazarköy
Hamdibey
Kalkım
Ilıca
Susurluk
Şamlı
Balya
Kepsut
Durak
Devecikonağı
Çaltılıbük
Orhaneli
Büyükorhan
Keles
Tahtaköprü
Domaniç
Dodurga
Harmancık
Tunçbilek
Tavşanlı
Seyitömer
Sabuncu
Seyitgazi
LÉSVOS
Kaz Dağı
1766
Ayvacık
Altınoluk
Küçükkuyu
Güre
Edremit
Havran
Balıkesir
Karaman
Gökçeyazı
İvrindi
BALIKESİR
Dursunbey
Kireç
Mustafakemalpaşa
Gökçedağ
Tepecik
Kütahya
KÜTAHYA
Kırka
Gülpınar
Baba Burnu
Áyios Evstrátios
Edremit Körfezi
Burhaniye
Korucu
Pamukçu
Yağcılar
Bigadiç
Emet
Hisarcık
Örencik
Aslanapa
Çavdarhisar
Altıntaş
Aykırıkçı
İhsaniye
VÓRIOS
Lésvos
AIYAÍON
Mithimna
Kalloni
Ayía Paraskeví
Thermí
Eressós
Polikhnitas
Mitilíni
Ayiássos
Plomárion
Kólpos Kallonís
Gömeç
Sarıbeyler
Savaştepe
Madra Dağı
1338
Ayvalık
Küçükköy
Kozak
Altınova
Bergama
Dikili
Göçbeyli
Soma
Gelembe
Kırkağaç
Kınık
Alacaatlı
Düvertepe
Sındırgı
Çaygören Barajı
Alaçam Dağları
2089
Simav Dağları
Simav
Demirci
Şaphane
Gediz
Saraycık
TURKEY
Zeytindağ
Yunt Dağı
1084
Palamut
Süleymanlı
Akhisar
Gördes
Yorbasan
Pazarlar
Abide
Yeniköy
Murat Dağı
2312
Dumlupınar
İscehisar
Gebeciler
Çobanlar
Afyon
Afyonkarahisar
Sincanlı
Düzağaç
1898
73
Çandarlı
Çandarlı Körfezi
Aslan Burnu
Aliağa
Yenifoça
Foça
KHÍOS
Psará
Andípsara
Kömür Burnu
Karaburun
Küçükbahçe
Akdağ
1218
Oinoúsa
Menemen
Saruhanlı
Muradiye
Manisa
Gediz
Beyoba
Selendi
Köprübaşı
Demirköprü Barajı
Borlu
Selendi
Uşak
UŞAK
Banaz
Ahat
Ahır Dağı
Gure
Akarca
Hocalar
1754
Sivaslı
Karadirek
Sandıklı
Şuhut
2250
AFYON
Kumalar Dağı
Gölmarmara
MANİSA
Gökçeören
Marmara Gölü
Karataş
Kula
Turgutlu
Ahmetli
Salihli
SARDIS
Kemaliye
Ahmetler
Ulubey
Eşme
Banaz
Karadilli
Kardhámila
Volissós
1297
Vrondádhes
Langádha
Khíos
Mordoğan
İzmir Körfezi
Bornova
IZMIR
İZMİR
(Smyrna)
Kemalpaşa
Armutlu
Bağyurdu
Boz Dağları
Alaşehir
Yeşilyurt
Adıgüzel Barajı
Gümüşsu
Karahallı
Çivril
Işıklı
Kızılören
Haydarlı
Kallimasiá
Mestá
PHANAE
Pirgí
Nénita
Ákra Mestá
Ákra Mástikho
Çeşme
Urla
Balçova
Güzelbahçe
Buca
Cumaovası
Alaçatı
Uzunkuyu
Menderes
Ayrancılar
Ödemiş
2137
İZMİR
Kiraz
Kaymakçı
Sarıgöl
Derbent
Güney
Büyük Menderes
Bekilli
Süller
Hançalar
Çal
Dinar
Senirkent
Uluborlu
2734
Barla Dağı
Evciler
Seferihisar
Torbalı
Bayındır
Küçükmenderes
Gökçen
Tire
Beydağ
1732
Buharkent
Buldan
HIERAPOLIS
Pamukkale
Irlıganlı
Baklan
Dazkırı
Acıgöl
Keçiborlu
Gönen
Atabey
Başmakçı
1831
İSPARTA
Isparta
Gümüldür
Bulgurca
Belevi
Aydın Dağları
Kuşadası Körfezi
EPHESUS
Selçuk
Ortaklar
Aydın
1603
Sultanhisar
Atça
Kuyucak
Nazilli
Sarayköy
Babadağ
Kocabaş
Bozkurt
Çardak
Söğüt Dağı
Burdur
Ağlasun
Burdur Gölü
Çeltikçi
Sámos
Kuşadası
Germencik
İncirliova
Köşk
Yenipazar
Yenice
Denizli
Honaz
DENİZLİ
BURDUR
Néon Karlovásion
1262
SÁMOS
Marathókambos
1153
Sámos
Mitilínoi
Áyios Kírikos
Söke
Davutlar
Koçarlı
AYDIN
Karacasu
1703
APHRODISIAS
2300
Bozdoğan
Çine
1792
Akçay
Kızılcabölük
Tavas
Serinhisar
Solda Gölü
Güney
Yeşilova
2334
Bucak
Tínos
Pánormos
Tínos
Ikaría
Mélissa Óros
957
Foúrnoi
Foúrnoi
Bafa Gölü
Bağarası
Karpuzlu
C a r i a
Büyük Menderes
Akköy
MILETUS
Çamiçi Gölü
Kemer Barajı
Acıpayam
Kemer
Kızılkaya
Mikonos
Míkonos
Dhragonísi
Khtapodhiá
Rinía
Dhílos
Aykathonisi
Árkoi
Lipsói
Pátmos
Pátmos
Farmakonisi
Yenihisar
Selimiye
Milas
Turgut
Kavaklıdere
Yatağan
1892
Göktepe
Kale
Beyeğaç
Boz Dağ
2421
Kumafşarı
Kelekçi
Karamanlı
Tefenni
Bozova
Dağ
Çavdır
2291
Korkuteli
Döşemealtı
Náxos
Páros
Korónis
Náxos
Nóousa
Filotion
1001
706
33
Dhenoúsa
Ayía Marína
Léros
Güllük Körfezi
Güllük
Üyüklü Tepe
690
MUĞLA
Muğla
Yeşilyurt
Kavak Dağı
1370
Yerkesik
Gökova
Ula
Gölgeli Dağları
Köyceğiz
Gölhisar
Söğüt
Altınyayla
Kızılcadağ
Levítha
Kálimnos
Kálimnos
Kalolimnos
Ortakent
Karaova
Karatoprak
Bodrum
Ören
Köyceğiz Gölü
Dalaman
Bekçiler
2598
Çakırlar
Andíparos
Koufonísia
Kínaros
Káros
Amorgós
822
Skhoinousa
Iráklia
Amorgós
Katápola
Liádhoi
Pserimos
Kos
846
Kara Ada
Fener Burnu
Gökova Körfezi
Pili
Kardhámaina
Kéfalos
Reşadiye Yarımadası
Marmaris
Günlüce
KAUNOS
Ortaca
Dalyan
Dalaman
Seki
Gölova
Elmalı
Göynük
Kemer
Çamyuva
TIOS AIYAÍON
Kos
Emecik
Datça
Yazıköy
Yiali
Bozburun
Söğütköy
Marmaris Limanı
Fethiye Körfezi
Uzümlü
Kemer
Eşen
Fethiye
Ak Dağ
3024
Gombe
Akçay
Bey Dağları
3086
Altınyaka
Tekirova
ANTALYA
Íos
Íos
Síkinos
Ánidhros
Astipálaia
Astipálaia
Mandrákhi
Nísiros
Sími
Sími
Kara Burun
Ofidhousa
Megálo Khorío
Tílos
Triánda
Marítsa
Ródhos
Koskinoú
Afándou
Ly c i a
XANTHOS
Kınık
Kasaba
Kalkan
Kale
Finike
Kumluca
2336
Finike Körfezi
Yardımcı Burnu
Karasu
Thirasía
Thíra
Thíra
(Santoríni)
Anáfi
Anáfi
Khristianá
Anafópoulo
Makrá
Sírna
DHODHEKÁNISOS
Alimnia
Khálki
RHO
Kástellos
Embóna
1215
Monólithos
Arkhángelos
Kálathos
Líndhos
Ákra Líndhos
Kaş
Megiste
(Kastellórizon)
Strongili
RETE
Zafora
Stenón Kárpathos
Karavonísia
Ákra Paraspóri
Astakidha
Sária
Lakhaniá
Kattaviá
Ródhos
(Rhodes)
4210
Khamilonísion
Dhivounia
Ólimbos
1480
2509
Kárpathos
1215
Voládha
Kárpathos
POSIDIUM
Ákra Kastellou
TI
Avgó
Iráklion
Néa Alikarnassós
Límin Khersonísou
Kólpos Merabéllou
Stenón Kásos
Ákra Áyios Ioánnis
Yianisádhes
Ákra Sídheros
Élassa
Palaiókastron
Ákra Pláka
Ayía Marína
Kásos
Mália
Mokhós
Neápolis
Áno Arkhánai
Kastéllion
Tzermiadhes
Áyios Nikólaos
Sitía
Kritsá
Kavoúsi
MINOA
Dhikti Óros
2148
Áno Viánnos
Máles
LASÍTHI
Ierápetra
Pírgos
Akhendriá
Khandrá
Koufonísi
Gaidhouronísi
MEDITERRANEAN
SEA

Inter-entity boundaries as agreed at the 1995 Dayton Peace Agreement.

Underlined towns give their name to the administrative area in which they stand.

Administrative divisions in Croatia:
1. Brodsko-Posavska
2. Koprivničko-Križevačka
4. Međimurska
5. Osječko-Baranjska
6. Požeško-Slavonska
8. Virovitičko-Podravska
9. Vukovarsko-Srijemska

Inter-entity boundaries as agreed at the 1995 Dayton Peace Agreement.

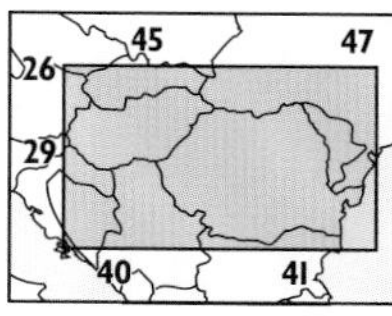

Underlined towns give their name to the administrative area in which they stand.

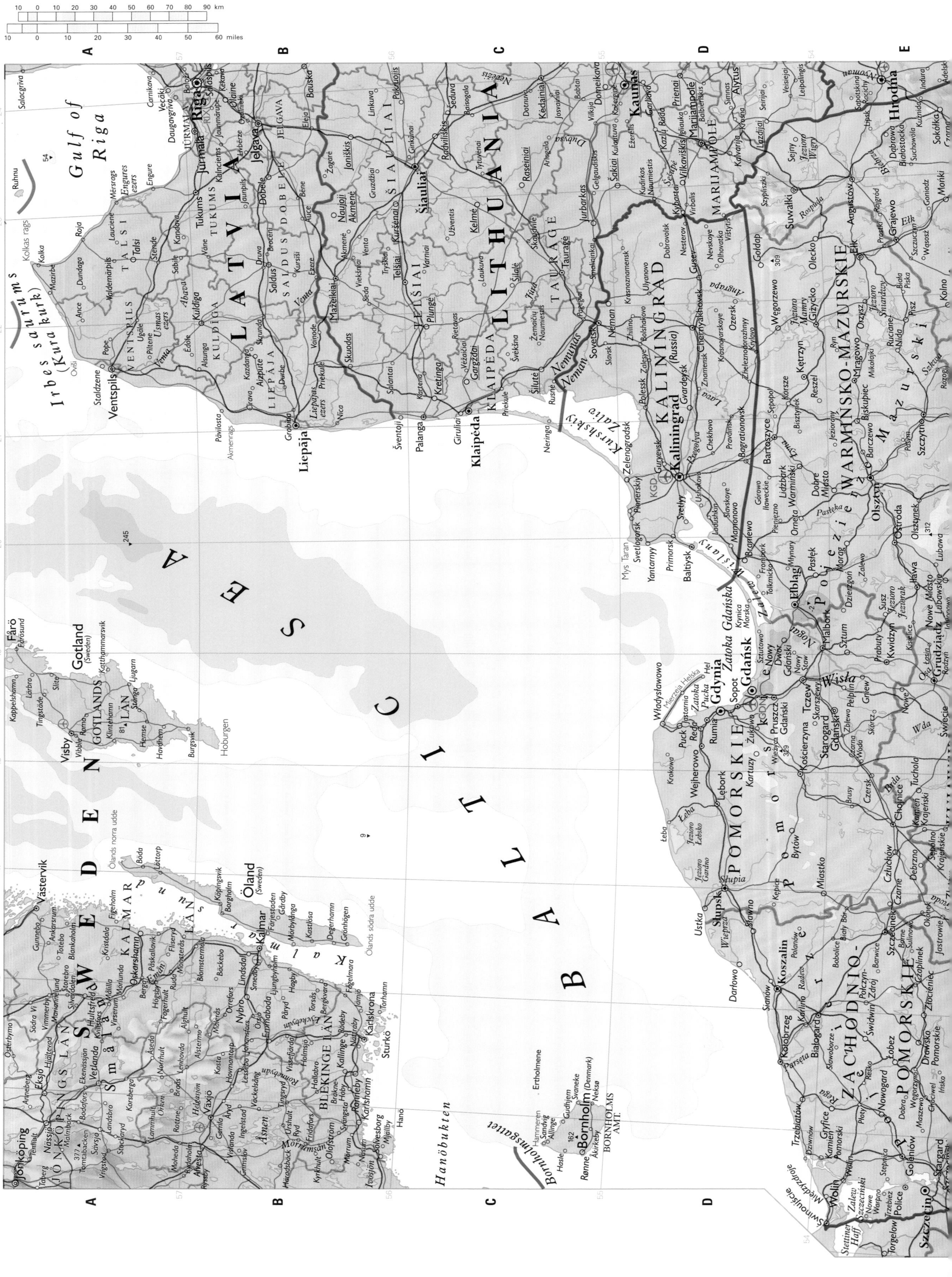

km
miles
Gulf of Riga
Irbes šaurums (Kura kurk)
LATVIA
LITHUANIA
KALININGRAD (Russia)
BALTIC SEA
SWEDEN
Gotland (Sweden)
Öland (Sweden)
Kalmarsund
Hanöbukten
Bornholmsgattet
Bornholm (Denmark)
POMORSKIE
WARMIŃSKO-MAZURSKIE
ZACHODNIO-POMORSKIE
Zatoka Gdańska
Kurshskiy Zaliv
Riga
Jūrmala
Jelgava
Ventspils
Liepāja
Klaipėda
Šiauliai
Kaunas
Kaliningrad
Gdańsk
Gdynia
Elbląg
Olsztyn
Słupsk
Koszalin
Szczecin
Hrodna
Kalmar
Karlskrona
Visby
Jönköping
Växjö

Underlined towns give their name to the administrative area in which they stand.

BALTIC STATES, BELARUS AND UKRAINE 1:4 400 000

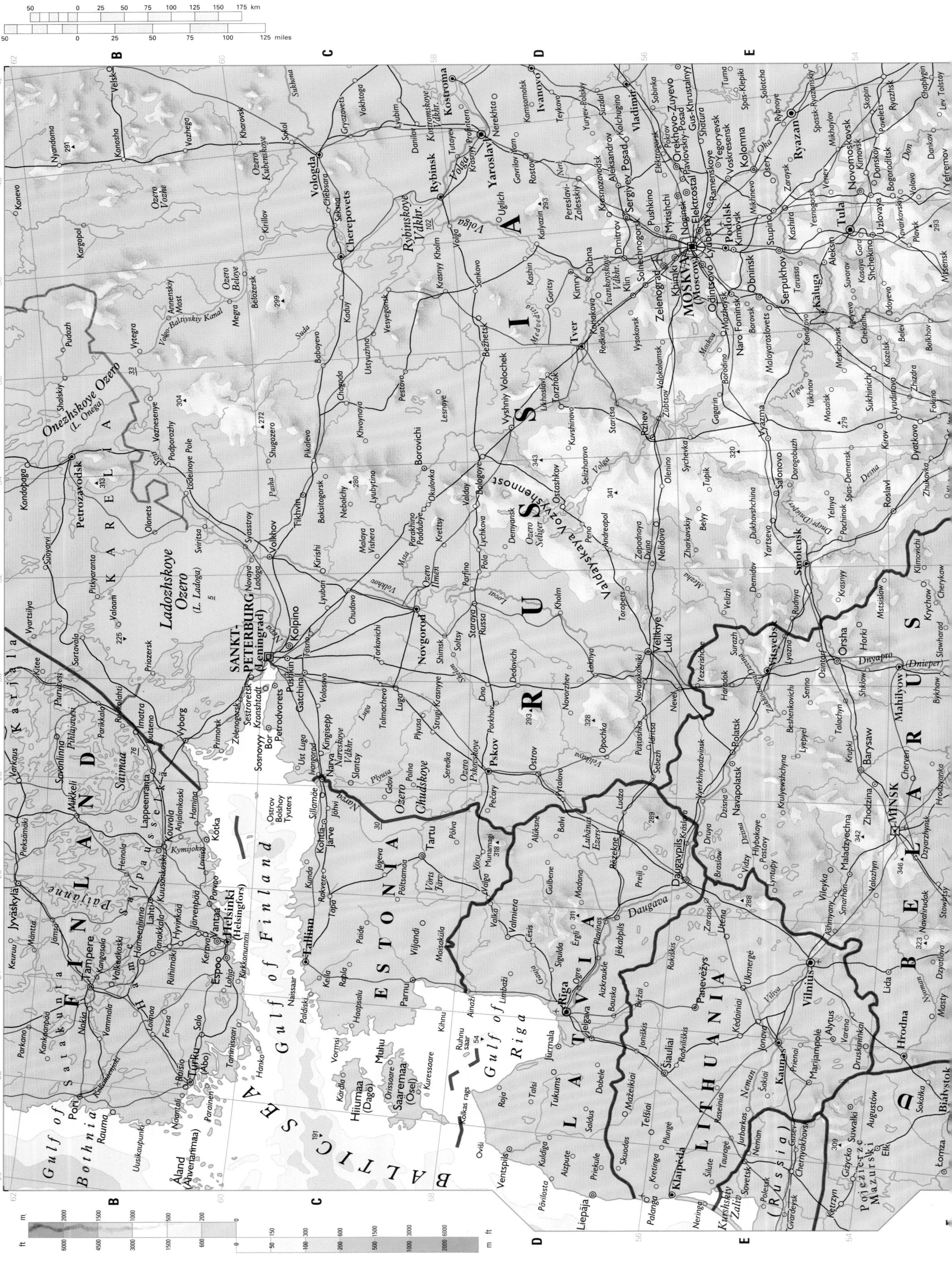

50 0 25 50 75 100 125 150 175 km
50 0 25 50 75 100 125 miles
FINLAND
ESTONIA
LATVIA
LITHUANIA
RUSSIA
KARELIA
BALTIC SEA
Gulf of Finland
Gulf of Riga
Gulf of Bothnia
Ladozhskoye Ozero
(L. Ladoga)
Onezhskoye Ozero
(L. Onega)
Ozero Chudskoye
SANKT-PETERBURG
(Leningrad)
MOSKVA
(Moscow)
Helsinki
(Helsingfors)
Tallinn
Riga
Vilnius
MINSK
Tartu
Parnu
Narva
Daugavpils
Kaunas
Klaipėda
Šiauliai
Panevėžys
Liepāja
Ventspils
Hrodna
Vitsyebsk
Mahilyow
Orsha
Pskov
Novgorod
Tver
Yaroslavl
Vologda
Cherepovets
Smolensk
Kaluga
Tula
Ryazan
Vladimir
Ivanovo
Kostroma
Rybinsk
Petrozavodsk
Vyborg
Tampere
Turku
(Åbo)
Lahti
Kotka
Pori
Hiiumaa
(Dagö)
Saaremaa
(Ösel)
Daugava
Volga
Neman
Dnyapro
(Dnieper)
Valdayskaya Vozvyshennost
Rybinskoye Vdkhr.
ft m
6000 2000
4500 1500
3000 1000
1500 500
600 200
50 150
100 300
200 600
500 1500
1000 3000
2000 6000

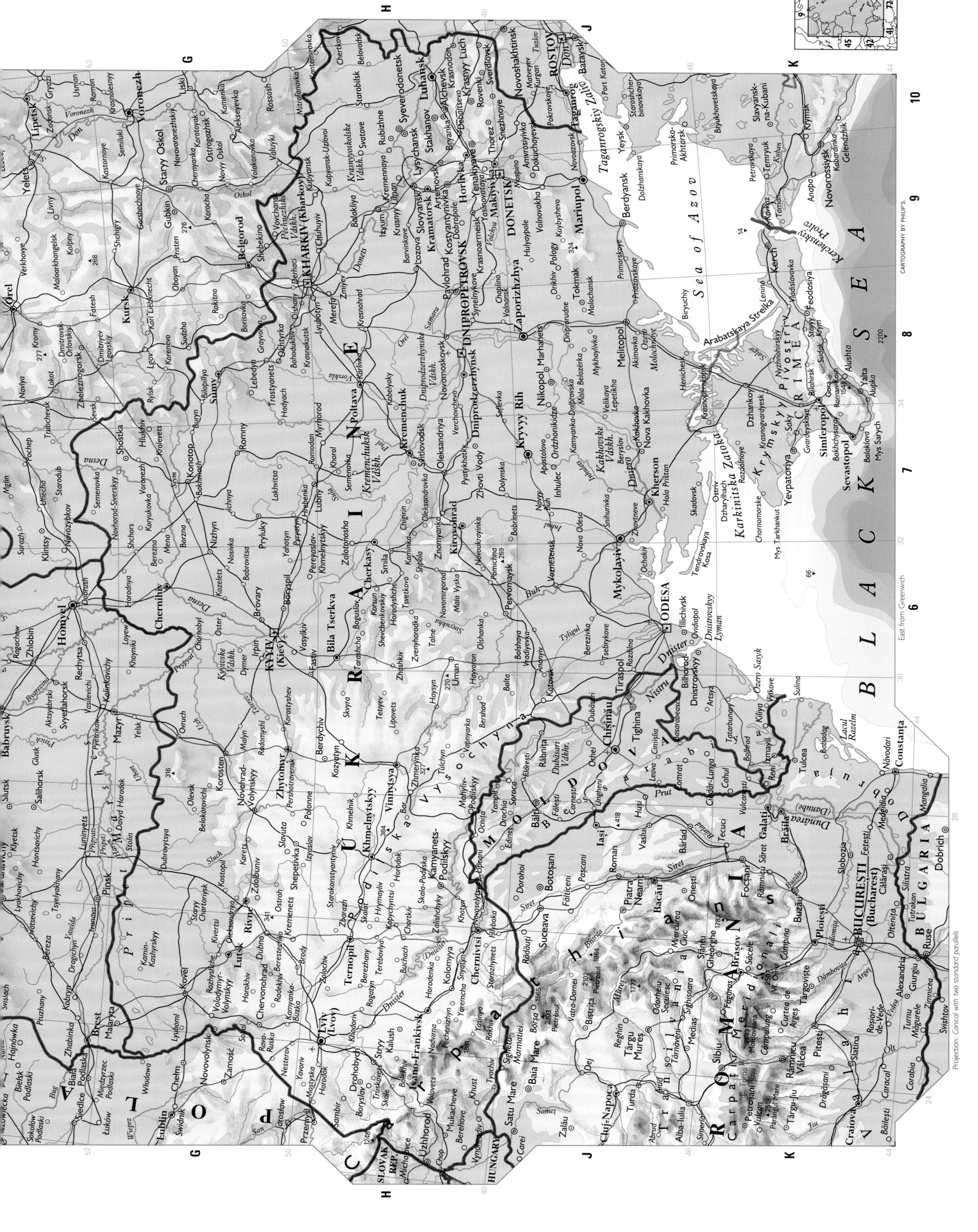
U K R A I N E
R O M A N I A
M O L D O V A
B L A C K   S E A
Sea of Azov
C R I M E A
Krymsky Pivostriv
P O L A N D
BULGARIA
HUNGARY
SLOVAK REP.
KYIV (Kiev)
KHARKIV (Kharkov)
DNIPROPETROVSK
DONETSK
ODESA
ROSTOV
BUCUREŞTI (Bucharest)
Chişinău
Lviv (Lvov)
Zaporizhzhya
Kryvyy Rih
Mykolayiv
Kherson
Sevastopol
Simferopol
Kerch
Mariupol
Luhansk
Voronezh
Kursk
Belgorod
Orel
Homyel
Brest
Pinsk
Lublin
Iaşi
Constanţa
Galaţi
Brăila
Cluj-Napoca
Braşov
Ploieşti
Craiova
Dobrich
Ruse
Poltava
Cherkasy
Chernihiv
Zhytomyr
Vinnytsya
Khmelnytskyy
Ternopil
Rivne
Lutsk
Chernivtsi
Ivano-Frankivsk
Uzhhorod
Sumy
Kremenchuk
Kirovohrad
Melitopol
Berdyansk
Taganrog
Tiraspol
Dnister
Dnipro
Desna
Pripet
Prut
Siret
Dunărea (Danube)
Buh
Donets
Karkinitska Zatoka
Taganrogskiy Zaliv
Kerchenskiy Proliv
Arabatskaya Strelka
East from Greenwich
CARTOGRAPHY BY PHILIP'S
Projection: Conical with two standard parallels

50 0 25 50 75 100 125 150 175 km

50 0 25 50 75 100 125 miles

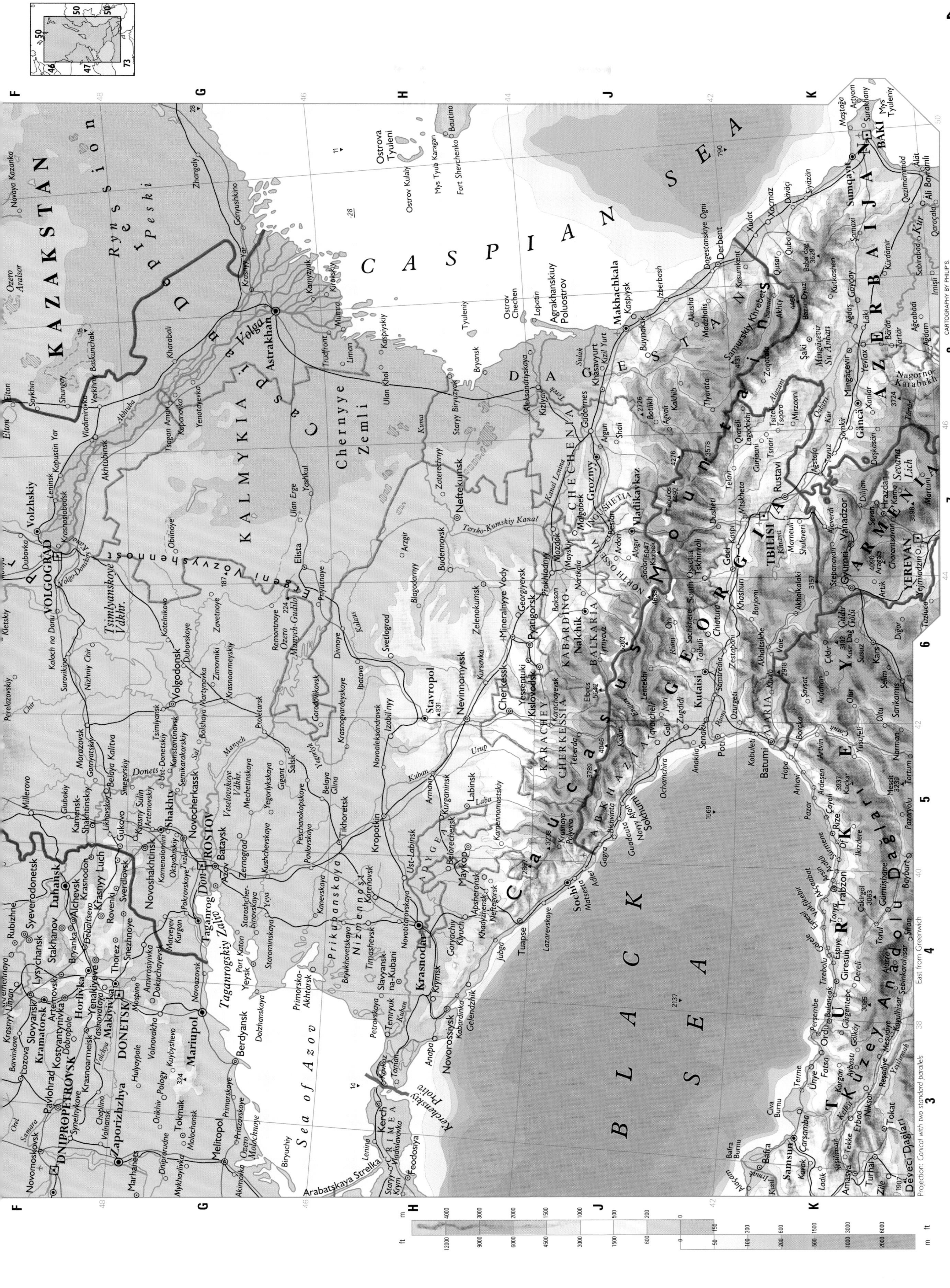

BLACK SEA
CASPIAN SEA
Sea of Azov
Taganrogskiy Zaliv
Caucasus
Caspian Depression
KAZAKSTAN
KALMYKIA
DAGESTAN
CHECHENIA
INGUSHETIA
NORTH OSSETIA
KABARDINO-BALKARIA
KARACHAY-CHERKESSIA
ADYGEA
ABKHAZIA
AJARIA
GEORGIA
ARMENIA
AZERBAIJAN
TURKEY
CRIMEA
Chernyye Zemli
Kuzey Anadolu Dağları
VOLGOGRAD
ROSTOV
DONETSK
DNIPROPETROVSK
TBILISI
YEREVAN
BAKI
Astrakhan
Krasnodar
Stavropol
Grozny
Makhachkala
Vladikavkaz
Nalchik
Elista
Sochi
Sokhumi
Kutaisi
Batumi
Trabzon
Samsun
Zaporizhzhya
Mariupol
Luhansk
Taganrog
Novorossiysk
Maykop
Derbent
Gäncä
Sumqayit
Elbrus 5642
Kazbek 5047
Volga
Don
Kuban
Terek
Kür
Projection: Conical with two standard parallels
East from Greenwich
CARTOGRAPHY BY PHILIP'S.

100 0 100 200 300 400 500 600 700 800 km
100 0 100 200 300 400 500 miles
RUSSIA
1 Adygea
2 Karachey-Cherkessia
3 Kabardino-Balkaria
4 North Ossetia
5 Ingushetia
6 Chechenia
7 Dagestan
8 Mordvinia
9 Chuvashia
10 Mari El
11 Tatarstan
12 Udmurtia
13 Khakassia
AZERBAIJAN
14 Naxçıvan
GEORGIA
15 Ajaria
16 Abkhazia
UKRAINE
17 Crimea
ft m
12 000 4000
9000 3000
6000 2000
3000 1000
1200 400
600 200
0 0
200 600
2000 6000
4000 12 000
m ft
RUSSIA
KAZAKSTAN
UZBEKISTAN
TURKMENISTAN
KYRGYZSTAN
TAJIKISTAN
AFGHANISTAN
IRAN
IRAQ
TURKEY
GEORGIA
ARMENIA
AZERBAIJAN
UKRAINE
BELARUS
POLAND
LITHUANIA
LATVIA
ESTONIA
FINLAND
SWEDEN
NORWAY
DENMARK
GERMANY
MOLDOVA
ROMANIA
MOSKVA
SANKT-PETERBURG
NIZHNIY NOVGOROD
KAZAN
SAMARA
VOLGOGRAD
ROSTOV
DONETSK
DNIPROPETROVSK
KHARKIV
KYYIV
ODESA
YEKATERINBURG
CHELYABINSK
OMSK
NOVOSIBIRSK
PERM
UFA
ALMATY
TOSHKENT
BAKI
TEHRĀN
TABRĪZ
MASHHAD
ESFAHAN
BAGHDAD
YEREVAN
TBILISI
ÜRÜMQI
STOCKHOLM
KØBENHAVN
HAMBURG
BERLIN
WARSZAWA
MINSK
Barents Sea
Kara Sea
Baltic Sea
Black Sea
Caspian Sea
Aral Sea
Gulf of Bothnia
Beloye More
Zemlya Frantsa Iosifa
Novaya Zemlya
Poluostrov Yamal
Ustyurt Plateau
Kyzyl Kum
Kara Kum
Dasht-e Kavir
Junggar Pendi
Projection: Conical Orthomorphic with two standard parallels
East from Greenwich

A
B
C
D
E
F
8 9 10 11 12 13 14 15 16 17 18 19
Mys Dezhneva (East C.)
Uelen
Chukchi Sea
St. Lawrence I. (U.S.A.)
Provideniya
Anadyrskiy Zaliv
Ostrov Vrangelya
East Siberian Sea
Ostrov Genriyetty
Ostrov Zhannetty
Ostrova Delonga
Ostrov Zhokhova
Ostrov Bennetta
Novosibirskiye Ostrova
Ostrov Faddeyevskiy
Ostrov Novaya Sibir
Ostrov Belkovskiy
Ostrov Kotelnyy
Ostrov Malyy Lyakhovskiy
Ostrov Bolshoy Lyakhovskiy
Lyakhovskiye Ostrova
Ostrov Stolbovoy
Proliv Dmitriya Lapteva
Laptev Sea
OCEAN
Mys Arkticheskiy
Ostrov Shmidta
Ostrov Komsomolets
Ostrov Pioner
Ostrov Oktyabrskoy Revolyutsii
Ostrov Bolshevik
Severnaya Zemlya
Proliv Vilkitskogo
Mys Chelyuskin
Poluostrov Taymyr
Gory Byrranga
Oz. Taymyr
Ostrov Bolshoy Begichev
Nordvik
Ostrova Medvezhi
Ostrov Ayon
Pevek
Chukotskoye Nagorye
Egvekinot
Vankarem
Beringovskiy
Anadyr
Koryakskoye Nagorye
Khatyrka
Bering Sea
Ambarchik
Cherskiy
Bilibino
Bolshoy Anyuy
Markovo
Penzhino
Yerepol
Nizhne Kolymsk
Omolon
Kamenskoye
Tilichiki
Korf
Kolymskoye Nagorye
Sredinnyy Khrebet
Poluostrov Kamchatka
Petropavlovsk-Kamchatskiy
Komandorskiye Ostrova
Ust-Kamchatsk
Klyuchevskaya Sopka
Sea of Okhotsk
Magadan
Khrebet Cherskogo
Verkhoyanskiy Khrebet
Tiksi
Ust Olenek
Saskylakh
Khatanga
Norilsk
Dudinka
Gory Putorana
Yakutsk
Vilyuysk
Mirnyy
Lensk
Olekminsk
Aldan
Neryungri
Stanovoy Khrebet
Khrebet Dzhugdzur
Okhotsk
Ayan
Sakhalin
Yuzhno-Sakhalinsk
Kurilskiye Ostrova
Nikolayevsk-na-Amur
Komsomolsk
Khabarovsk
Khrebet Sikhote Alin
Vladivostok
Nakhodka
Blagoveshchensk
Tynda
Bratsk
Ust-Ilimsk
Krasnoyarsk
Kansk
Achinsk
Abakan
Irkutsk
Angarsk
Ulan Ude
Chita
Yablonovyy Khrebet
Vostochnyy Sayan
Zabaykalsk
Manzhouli
Hailar
Da Hinggan Ling
Qiqihar
Harbin
Jiamusi
Jilin
Changchun
Shenyang
Anshan
Fushun
Dalian
Beijing
Baotou
Hohhot
Zhangjiakou
Chengde
Hami
Erenhot
Ulaanbaatar
MONGOLIA
Hangayn Nuruu
Hentiyn Nuruu
Gobi
CHINA
NORTH KOREA
SOUTH KOREA
P'yŏngyang
Soul
Inch'ŏn
Taejŏn
Taegu
Pusan
Chŏngjin
Sea of Japan
Hokkaidō
Sapporo
Hakodate
Aomori
Honshū
Niigata
Kanazawa
Ōsaka
JAPAN
Fuji-San 3776
RUSSIA
ASIA
Arctic Circle
COPYRIGHT GEORGE PHILIP LTD.

ASIA : Physical 1:44 400 000

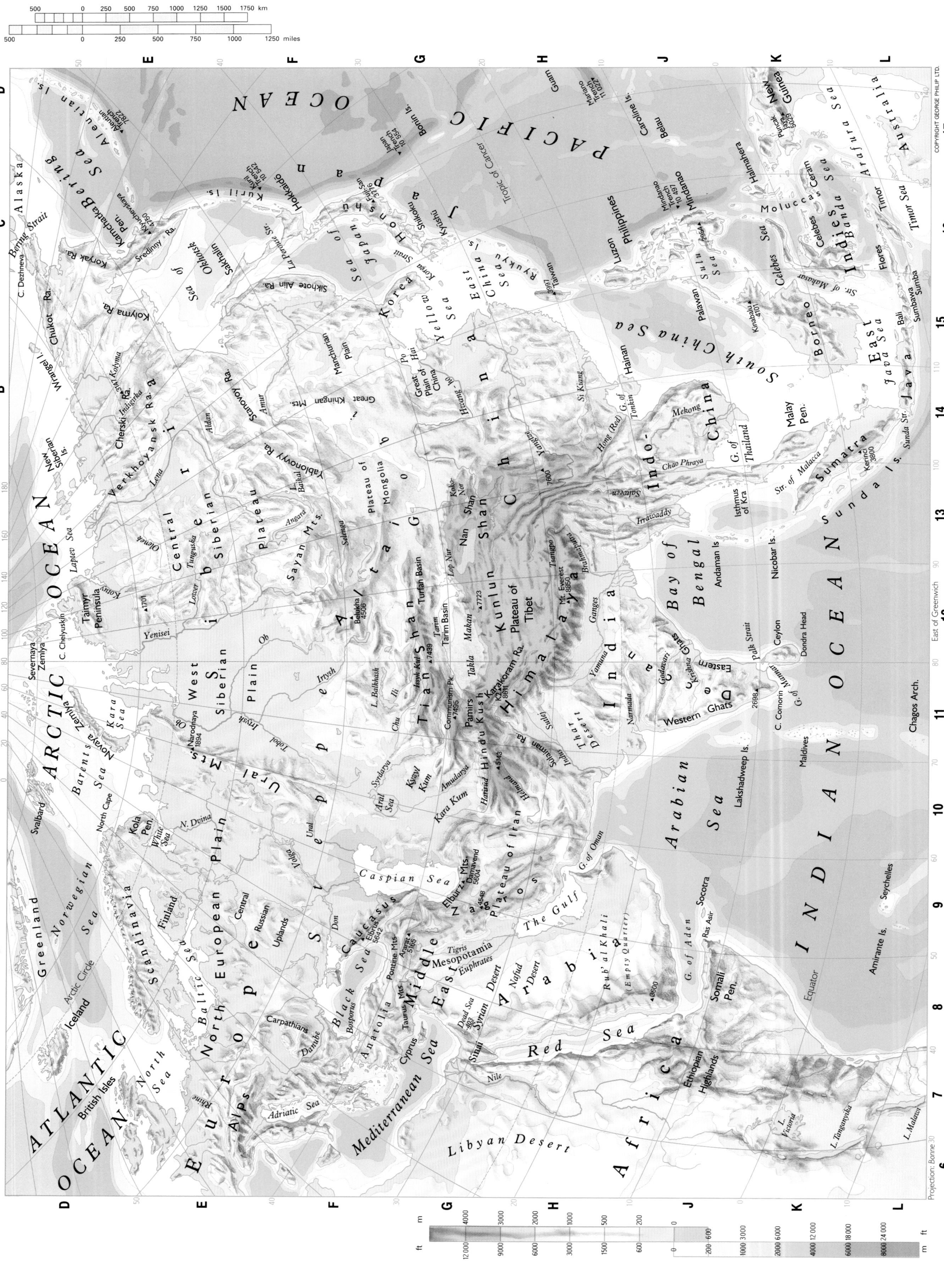

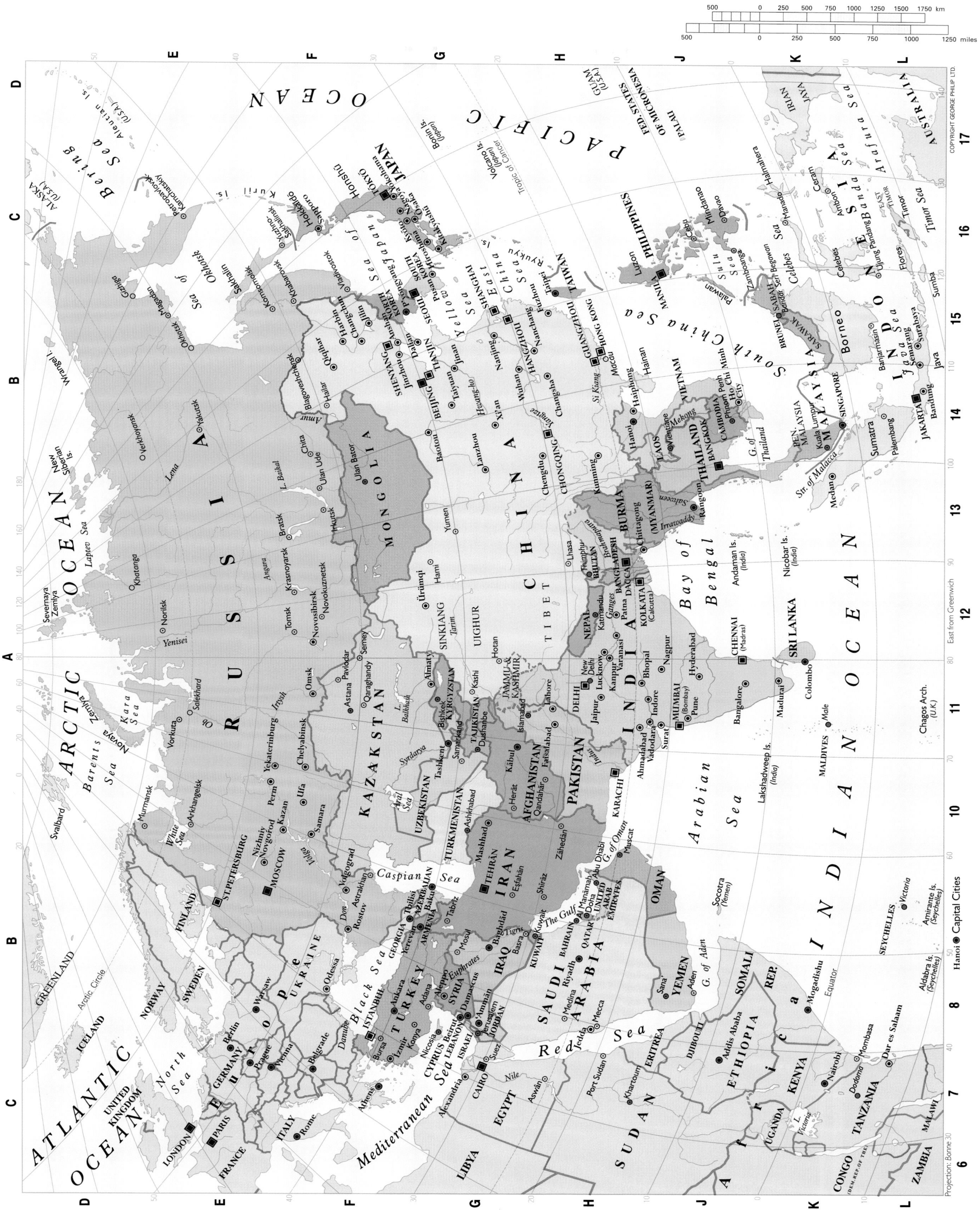

500 0 250 500 750 1000 1250 1500 1750 km
500 0 250 500 750 1000 1250 miles
ARCTIC OCEAN
PACIFIC OCEAN
INDIAN OCEAN
ATLANTIC OCEAN
RUSSIA
CHINA
INDIA
MONGOLIA
KAZAKSTAN
JAPAN
INDONESIA
IRAN
AFGHANISTAN
PAKISTAN
SAUDI ARABIA
TURKEY
Bay of Bengal
Arabian Sea
South China Sea
Hanoi Capital Cities
Projection: Bonne
COPYRIGHT GEORGE PHILIP LTD.
East from Greenwich

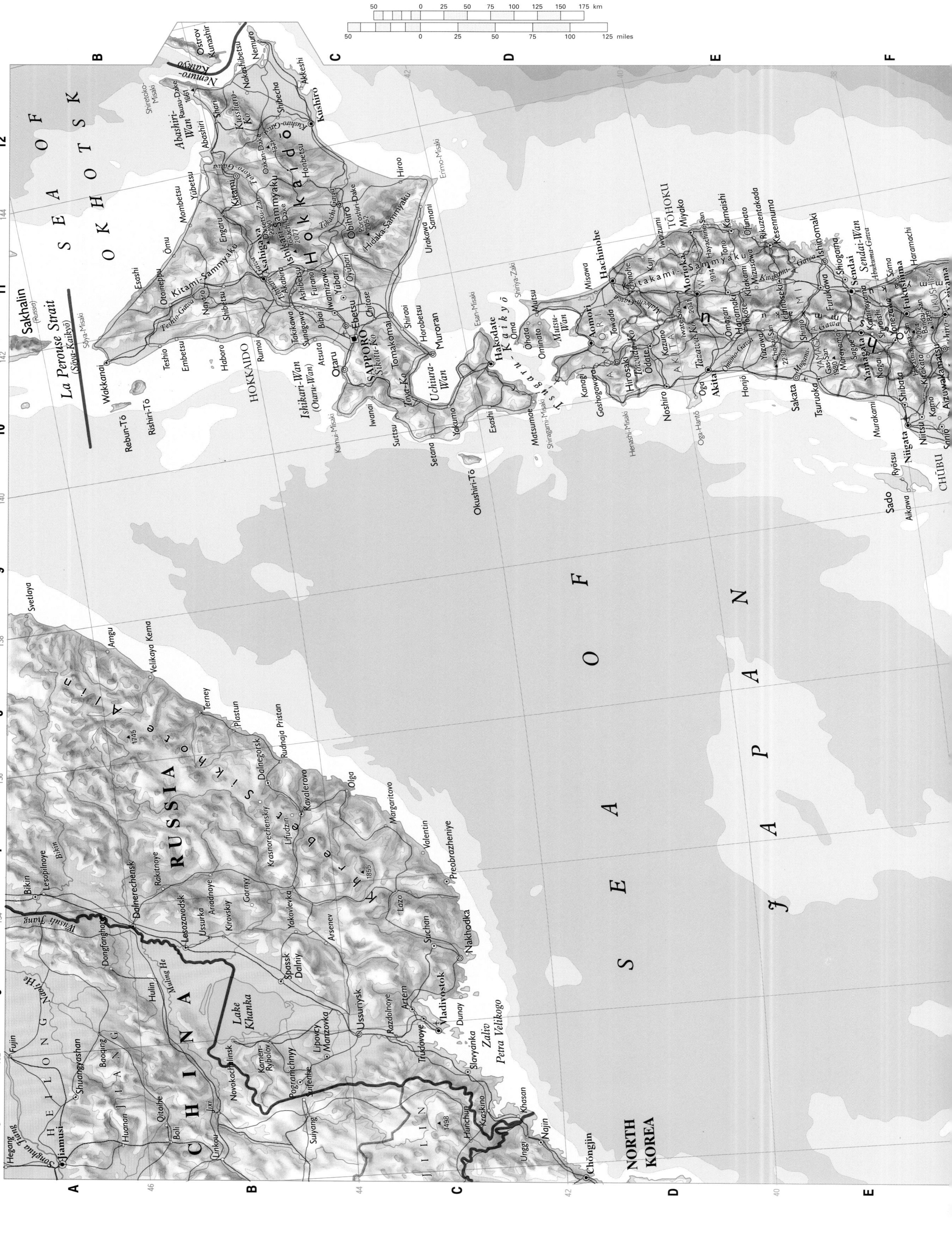

km
miles
SEA OF OKHOTSK
SEA OF JAPAN
Hokkaidō
HOKKAIDO
TŌHOKU
CHŪBU
RUSSIA
CHINA
NORTH KOREA
Sakhalin (Russia)
La Perouse Strait (Sōya-Kaikyō)
Tsugaru-Kaikyō
Nemuro-Kaikyō
Ostrov Kunashir
Nemuro
Kushiro
Abashiri-Wan
Abashiri
Rausu-Dake
Shiretoko-Misaki
Shari
Kitami
Kitami-Sammyaku
Asahigawa
Daisetsu-Zan
Tokachi-Dake
Ishikari-Sammyaku
Hidaka-Sammyaku
Obihiro
Hiroo
Erimo-Misaki
Samani
Urakawa
Wakkanai
Sōya-Misaki
Rebun-Tō
Rishiri-Tō
Teshio
Embetsu
Haboro
Rumoi
Esashi
Ōmu
Mombetsu
Yūbetsu
Ishikari-Wan (Otaru-Wan)
Otaru
SAPPORO
Ebetsu
Chitose
Tomakomai
Muroran
Uchiura-Wan
Hakodate
Esan-Misaki
Yakumo
Setana
Suttsu
Iwanai
Kamui-Misaki
Okushiri-Tō
Matsumae
Shirakami-Misaki
Ōma
Mutsu
Mutsu-Wan
Aomori
Hachinohe
Misawa
Towada
Hirosaki
Goshogawara
Noshiro
Akita
Oga
Oga-Hantō
Honjō
Sakata
Tsuruoka
Morioka
Miyako
Kamaishi
Ōfunato
Kesennuma
Ishinomaki
Sendai
Sendai-Wan
Shiogama
Yamagata
Fukushima
Niigata
Shibata
Murakami
Sado
Ryōtsu
Aikawa
Haramachi
Sōma
Svetlaya
Amgu
Velikaya Kema
Terney
Plastun
Rudnaja Pristan
Dalnegorsk
Kavalerovo
Olga
Margaritovo
Valentin
Preobrazheniye
Lazo
Nakhodka
Suchan
Arsenev
Vladivostok
Artem
Ussuriysk
Razdolnoye
Spassk Dalniy
Lake Khanka
Lesozavodsk
Dalnerechensk
Bikin
Lesopilnoye
Zaliv Petra Velikogo
Slavyanka
Kraskino
Khasan
Najin
Unggi
Chŏngjin
Hunchun
Suifenhe
Pogranichnyy
Jixi
Linkou
Jiamusi
Hegang
Fujin
Shuangyashan
Baoqing
Qitaihe
Boli
Huanan
Hulin
Dongfanghong
Wusuli Jiang
Muling He
Songhua Jiang
HEILONG JIANG
JILIN

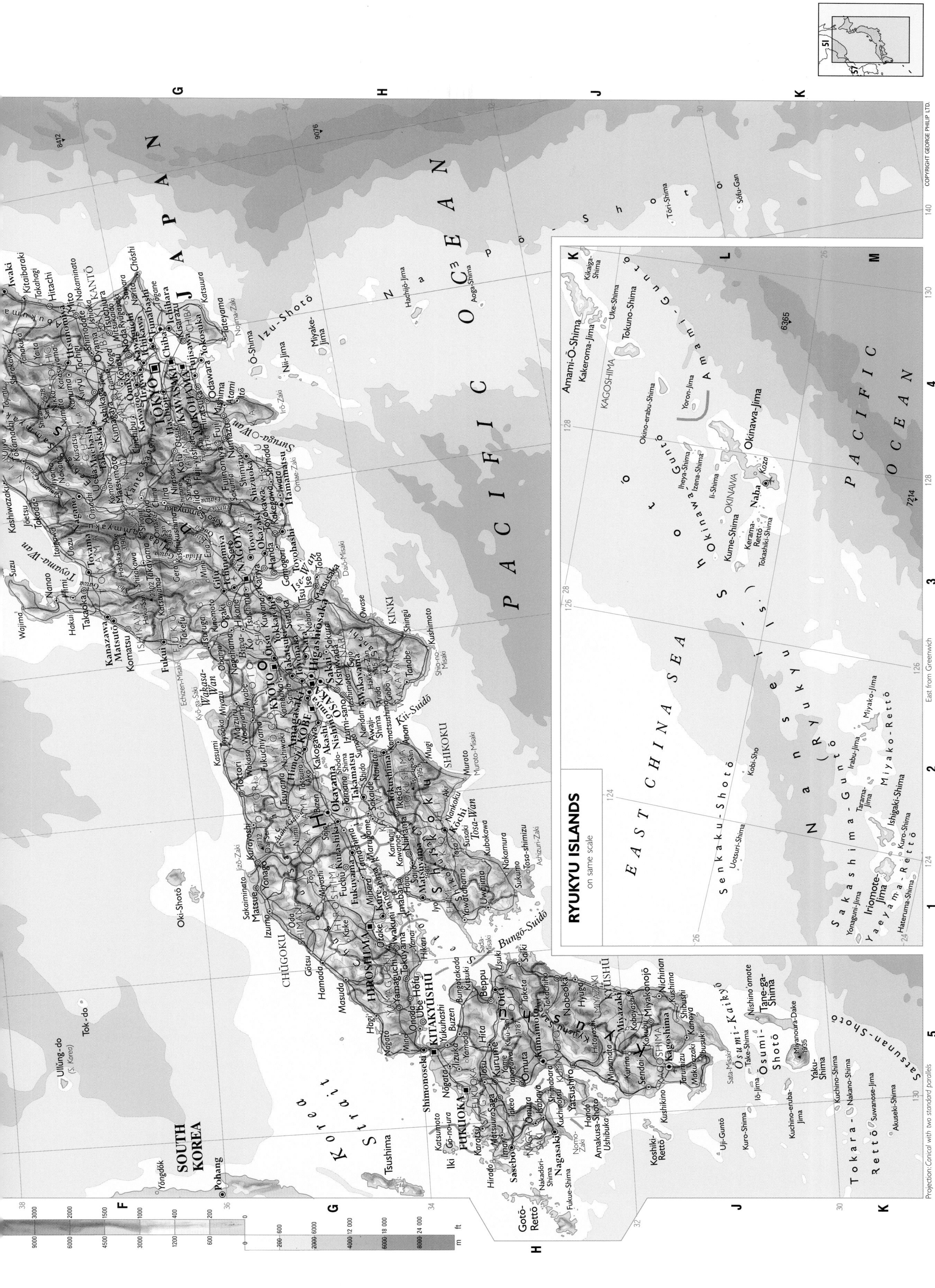
JAPAN
PACIFIC OCEAN
EAST CHINA SEA
RYUKYU ISLANDS
on same scale
SOUTH KOREA
Korea Strait
Projection: Conical with two standard parallels
COPYRIGHT GEORGE PHILIP LTD.
East from Greenwich

NORTHERN CHINA AND KOREA 1:5 300 000

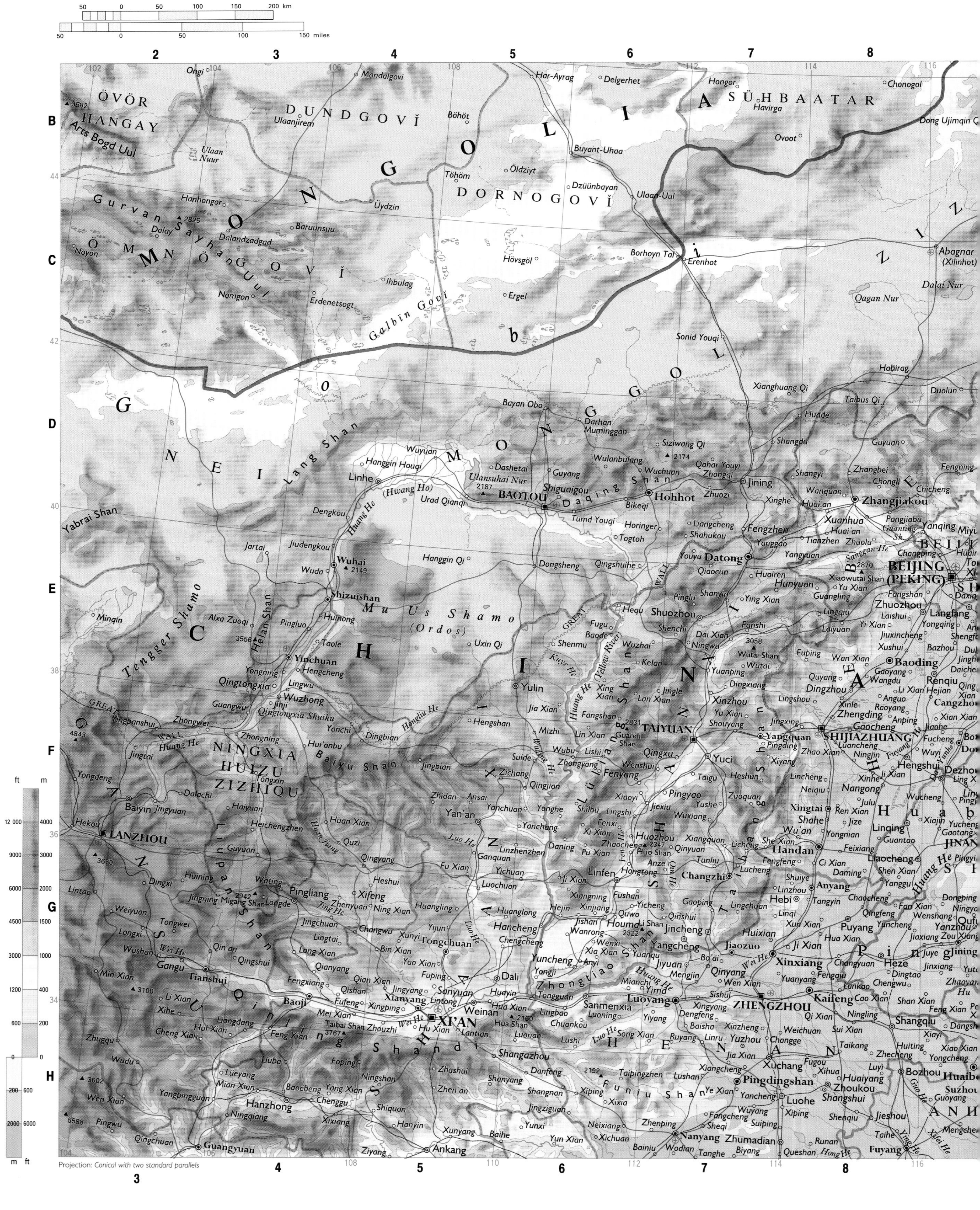

Projection: *Conical with two standard parallels*

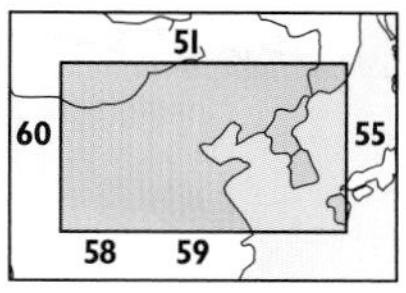
51
60
55
58
59

9
10
11
12
13
14
15
16
B
C
D
E
F
G
H
HARBIN
Bin Xian
Horqin Youyi Qianqi
(Ulanhot)
Zhenlai
Nen Jiang
Baicheng
Taoer He
Da'an
Maoxing
Zhaoyuan
Shuangcheng
Acheng
Yanshou
Linkou
Jixi
Turiy Rog
Ozero Khanka
Hulin He
Tuquan
Taonan
Anguang
Changchunling
Lalin
Shangzhi
Muling
Hulingol
Qagan Nur
Qian Gorlos
Fuyu
Sanchahe
Yimianpo
Hengdaohezi
Mudanjiang
Maqiaohe
Xiachengzi
Pogranichnyy
Qian'an
Shenjingzi
Beitaolaizhao
Yushu
Lalin He
Wuchang
Zhangguangcai Ling
1690
Hailin
Muling
Suiyang
Suifenhe
Golenki
Tongyu
Kaoshan
Shanhetun
Ning'an
Dongning
Nong'an
Dehui
Shulan
Beizhengzhen
Zhanyu
Jarud Qi
Fulongquan
Jiutai
Gangyao
Wulajie
Dongjingcheng
Ussuriysk
Changling
Jingpo Hu
Luozigou
1949
Xinkai He
Horqin Zuoyi Zhongqi
CHANGCHUN
JILIN
Xinzhan
Jiaohe
Emu
Huangsongdian
Chunyang
Razdolnoye
Artem
Maolin
Huaidezhen
Tavrichanka
Bairin Zuoqi
Fanjiatun
Songhua Hu
Dunhua
Daxinggou
Vladivostok
Kailu
Tongliao
Dongliao He
Gongzhuling
Shuangyang
Wangqing
Shixian
Linxi
Shuangliao
Yitong
Mingyuegue
Yanji
Tumen
Tumen Jiang
Hunchun
Slavyanka
2029
Bairin Youqi
Xiliao He
Lishu
Siping
Panshi
Huadian
Longjing
Namyang
Kraskino
Posyet
Jargalang
Bamiancheng
Liaoyuan
Erdao Jiang
Antu
Helong
Hoeamdong
Xar Moron He
Laoha He
Zhangwu
Xifeng
Huifa He
Ongniud Qi
Wutonghaolai
Kangping
Dongfeng
Huinan
Baishan
Baihe
1677
Hoeryong
Unggi
Sosura
Hure Qi
WALL
Tiefa
Kaiyuan
Meihekou
Fusong
Musan
Najin
Changbai Shan
2020
Xiawa
Faku
Liao He
Jingyu
Puryong
Pugodong
Liu He
Tieling
Shanchengzhen
Liuhe
2744
Paektu-san
Chongjin
Chifeng
Fuxin
Zhangwu
Qingyuan
Hunjiang
Linjiang
Pungsan
Nanam
Kyongsong
WILLOW
Xinlitun
Xinmin
Chunggang-up
2541
Chuuronjang
Heishui
Hachon
SHENYANG
FUSHUN
Xinbin
Weichang
Beipiao
Qinghemen
Heishan
Tonghua
Changbai
Irhyangdong
Ondaejin
1885
Ningcheng
THE
Liaozhong
Qinghecheng
Huch'ang
Hyesan
Hapsu
Simpungdong
Chaoyang
Beizhen
Dalian He
Inpundong
Kasan-dong
Kapsan
Kilchu
Yi Xian
Goubangzi
Liaoyang
Benxi
Huanren
1846
Manp'o
Musudan
Longhua
Anping
Tianshifu
Hun Jiang
Pujon-choshuji
P'ungsan
Kosongni
Kimch'aek
(Songjin)
Lingyuan
ANSHAN
Ji'an
Kanggye
Chail-bong
2522
Chengde
Pingquan
Jinzhou
Panjin
Lianshanguan
Yalu Jiang
Kuup-tong
Luanne
Jianchang
Jinxi
Niuzhuang
Haicheng
Supung Shuiku
Ch'osan
Changjin-choshuji
Kwangdaeri
Tanch'on
Luanping
Liugou
Tianzhuangtai
Kuandian
Pyoktong
Changhungni
Shangbancheng
Huludao
Yingkou
Dashiqiao
Koin-dong
Changjin
Pukch'ong
Kuancheng
Xingcheng
Fengcheng
Sinhung
Sinch'ang
Liaodong
Gaizhou
Xiuyan
Sakchu
Sinp'o
Xinglong
Shuangshanzi
Taegwan
NORTH
Oro
Sohori
Xiongyuecheng
Wanfu
1131
Dandong
Pukchin
Hongwon
Suizhong
Jianchangying
Buyun Shan
Sinuiju
Kujang
Hamhung
Hungnam
Gushan
Donggou
Yongamp'o
Kusong
Tokch'on
Tongchon-ni
SEA OF
Zunhua
Wan
Qinhuangdao
Chongju
Pakch'on
KOREA
Tongjoson
Fengrun
Lulong
Funing
Yalu Jiang
Sonch'on
Anju
Yonghung
Man
Yutian
Luan Xian
Sunch'on
Kowon
Baodi
Liaodong Bandao
Munch'on
TANGSHAN
Changli
Wafangdian
Zhuanghe
Sukch'on
Sinchang-ni
Wonsan
TIANJIN SHI
Luan He
Songch'on
Anbyon
Leting
Pulandian
Sunan
Kangdong
Tongyang
Kojo
Wuqing
Hangu
Pikou
P'YONGYANG
Chunghwa
Koksan
JAPAN
Singosan
Kosong
TIANJIN
Jin Xian
Hoeyang
1638
Tanggu
Korea
Namp'o
Songnim
Sepo-ri
Changdo-ri
Lushun
DALIAN
Suan
Chiha-ri
Kansong
Dagu
Bay
Sariwon
P'yonggang
Sokch'o
Oikou
Bo Hai
Cho-do
Chaeryong
Sinmak
Nam-ch'on
Kumhwa
Hwach'on choshui
Yangyang
Ch'orwon
Changyon
Sinch'on
Kumch'on
Chumunjin
Huanghua
Miaodao Qundao
Haeju
Kaesong
Panmunjom
Ch'unch'on
Kangnung
Ongjin
Yonan
Munsan
Uijongbu
Hongch'on
Yanshan
Paengnyong-do
Kanghwa
SOUL
Samch'ok
Ullung-do
Puch'on
Songnam
Hoengsong
Chongson
Qingyun
Penglai
INCH'ON
Anyang
Wonju
Wudi
Zhanhua
Huang He
Longkou
Daxindian
Yantai
Ansan
Han gang
Yongwol
Huimin
Laizhou
Huang Xian
Muping
Weihai
Suwon
Ich'on
Chech'on
Ulchin
Kenli
Fushan
Osan
Yoju
Chengshan Jiao
Dongying
Wan
Qixia
923
Wendeng
Ch'ungju
Yongju
Binzhou
Zhaoyuan
P'yongt'aek
Laizhou
Rongcheng
Ch'onan
SOUTH
Sosan
Chongju
Yech'on
Guangrao
Shandong Bandao
Naktong
Gaoyuan
Hongsong
Yesan
Andong
Yongdok
Huantai
Shouguang
Changyi
Laiyang
Rushan
KOREA
Linzi
Kongju
Uisong
Zhoucun
ZIBO
Yidu
Weifang
Pingdu
Laixi
Nanhuang
Shidao
Anmyon-do
TAEJON
Sangju
Ch'ongha
Haiyang
Sonsan
P'ohang
Boshan
Fangzi
Anqiu
Taechon-ni
Nonsan
Kimch'on
Changgi-Ap
Lancun
Kumi
Linqu
Gaomi
Kanggyong
Yongdong
Yongch'on
Jimo
Iri
Kyongju
Chengyang
Waegwan
Kunsan
Chonju
TAEGU
Jiaozhou
Laiwu
1108
QINGDAO
Chongdo
Kimje
Ulsan
Zhucheng
Jiaozhou Wan
Koch'ang
Koryong
Miryang
Puan
Hamyang
Xintai
Chongup
Yishui
Wulian
HUANG HAI
Namwon
Masan
Kimhae
Mengyin
Chii-san
Chinju
Tongnae
Sago-ri
1915
Tamyang
KWANGJU
PUSAN
Liangcheng
Songjong-ni
Ch'angwon
Pingyi
Yi He
Ju Xian
Rizhao
(Yellow Sea)
Naju
Hadong
Samch'onp'o
Tangtou
Shijiusuo
Sunch'on
Ch'ungmu
Sasuna
Fei Xian
Andongwei
Mokp'o
Posong
Yosu
Polgyo-ri
Linyi
Korea Strait
Saka
Tengzhou
Tsushima
Ganyu
Haizhou Wan
Changhung
Teng Xian
Haenam
Izuhara
Zaozhuang
Lianyungang
Huksan-chedo
Chindo
Tancheng
Lianyungang
Haizhou
Hanzhuang
Chenjiagang
Pizhou
Guanyun
Xinyi
Xiangshui
Iki
Xuzhou
Yaowan
Guannan
Karatsu
Imari
Suqian
Shuyang
Binhai
Cheju-do
Cheju
Onpyong-ni
JAPAN
Shuanggou
Lianshui
Da Yunhe
Hallim
Sasebo
Funing
Halla-san
Kashima
Suining
Sheyang
Taejong
1950
Omura
Lingbi
Huaiyin
Huai'an
Mosulpo
Sogwipo
Nakadori-Shima
Isahaya
Hongze Hu
Grand Canal
Yancheng
Nagasaki
Suzhou
Guzhen
Baoying
Liuzhuang
Wuhe
Fukue-Shima
Kuchinotsu
Xinghua
Bengbu
Gaoyou Hu
Fengyang
Dongtai
East from Greenwich
118
120
122
124
126
128
130
132
44
42
40
38
36
34

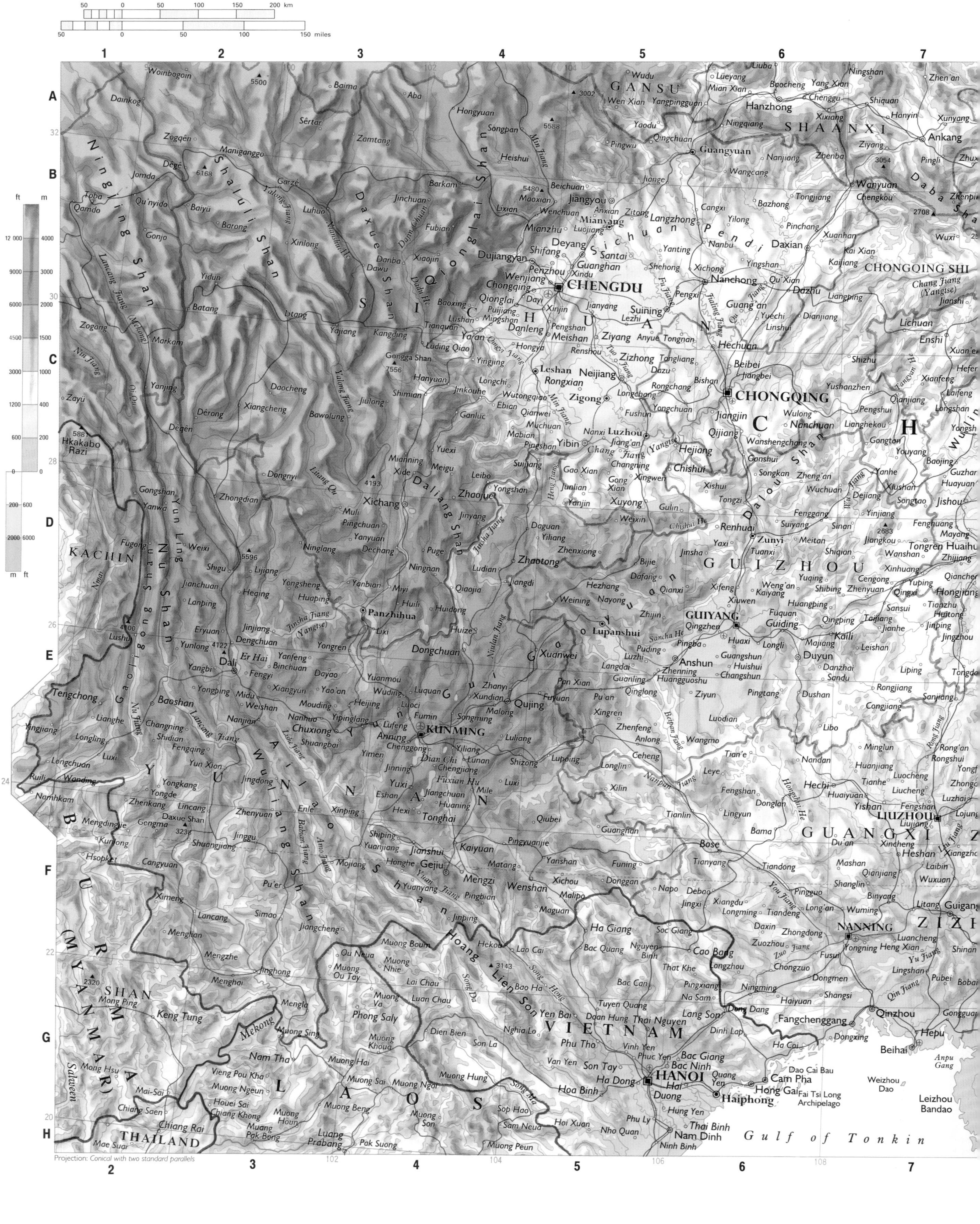

Projection: Conical with two standard parallels

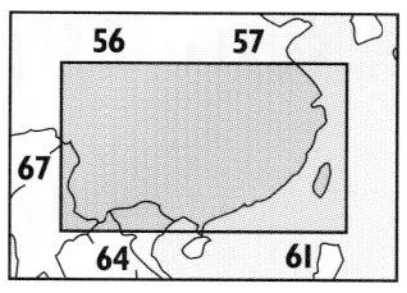
56
57
67
64
61

8
9
10
11
12
13
14
A
B
C
D
E
F
G
H
HENAN
HUBEI
HUNAN
ANHUI
JIANGSU
JIANGXI
ZHEJIANG
FUJIAN
GUANGDONG
GUANGZU
SHANGHAI SHI
TAIWAN
WUHAN
NANJING
SHANGHAI
HANGZHOU
CHANGSHA
NANCHANG
FUZHOU
GUANGZHOU
HONG KONG
(XIANGGANG)
T'AIPEI
KAOHSIUNG
Hefei
Anqing
Jiujiang
Yichang
Hengyang
Ganzhou
Shantou
Xiamen
Wenzhou
Ningbo
Shenzhen
Kowloon
Macau
Zhanjiang
Hainan
Changde
Yueyang
Dongting Hu
Poyang Hu
Tai Hu
Chang Jiang (Yangtse)
Dabie Shan
Jiuling Shan
Wuyi Shan
Nan Ling
Luoxiao Shan
Min Jiang
Gan Jiang
Xiang Jiang
Taiwan Strait
Luzon Strait
SOUTH CHINA SEA
Tropic of Cancer
Chungyang Shanmo
Matsu Tao
Penghu
Dangan Liedao
Tungsha Tao
Three Gorges Dam
East from Greenwich
112
114
116
118
120
122
32
30
28
26
24
22
20
COPYRIGHT GEORGE PHILIP LTD.

CHINA 1:17 800 000

RUSSIA
KAZAKSTAN
KYRGYZSTAN
MONGOLIA
CHINA
NEI MONGGOL ZIZHIQU
XINJIANG UYGUR ZIZHIQU
XIZANG ZIZHIQU (TIBET)
NEPAL
BHUTAN
BANGLADESH
INDIA
BURMA (MYANMAR)
THAILAND (SIAM)
LAOS
VIETNAM
NORTH KOREA
SOUTH KOREA
JAPAN
PHILIPPINES
TAIWAN (FORMOSA)
YELLOW SEA
EAST CHINA SEA
SOUTH CHINA SEA
BAY OF BENGAL
BEIJING (PEKING)
TIANJIN
SHANGHAI
HONG KONG
GUANGZHOU (CANTON)
KOLKATA (CALCUTTA)
Tarim Pendi
Tropic of Cancer
Projection: Bonne
East from Greenwich
COPYRIGHT GEORGE PHILIP LTD.

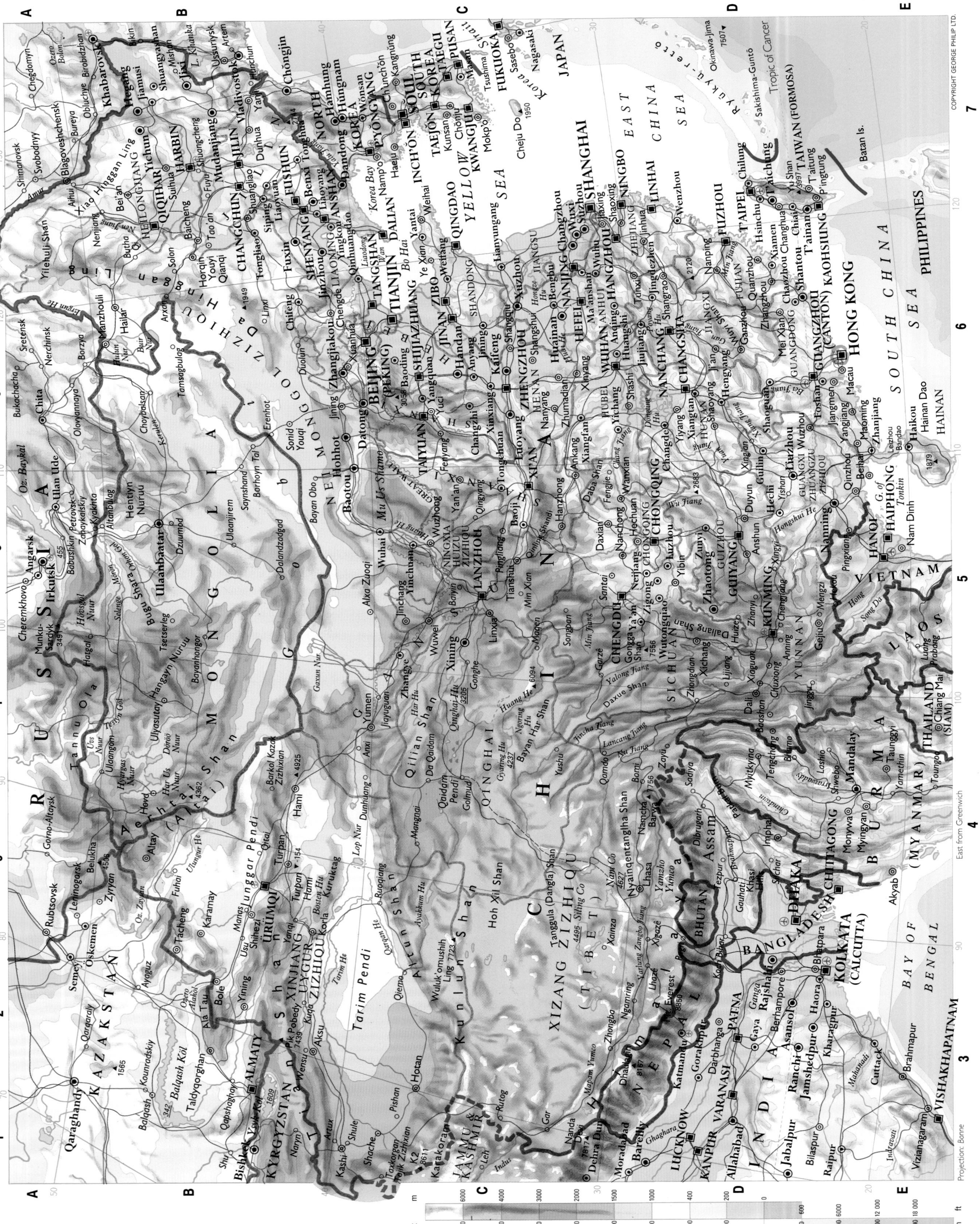

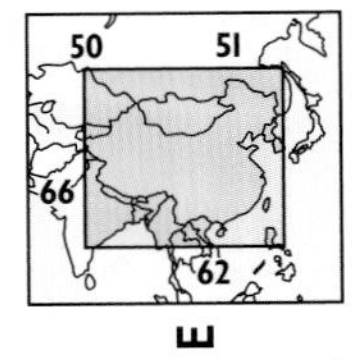

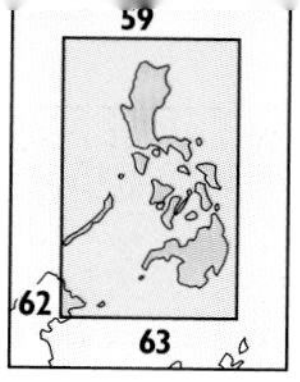
59
62
63

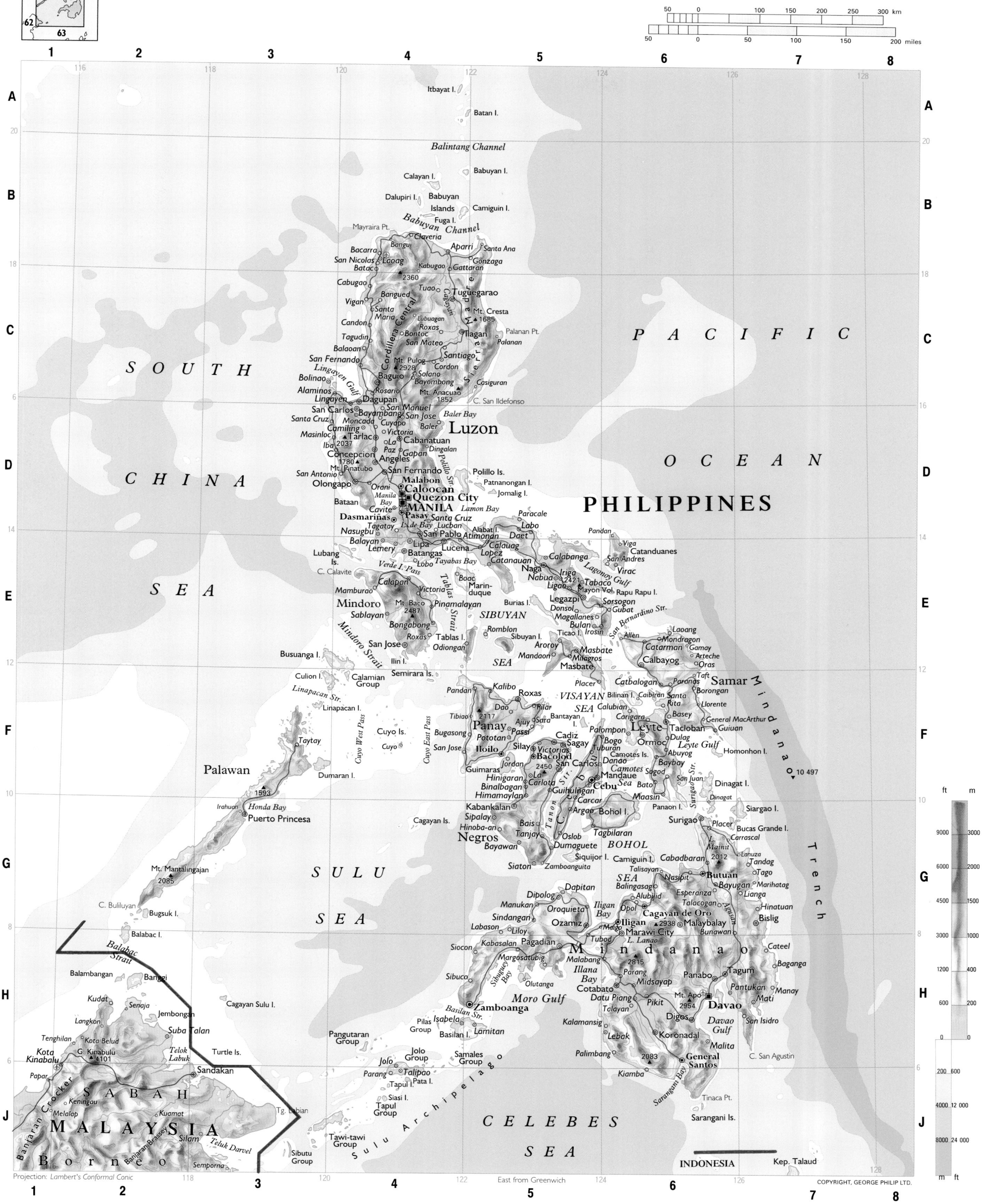
0 50 100 150 200 250 300 km
50 0 50 100 150 200 miles
A B C D E F G H J
1 2 3 4 5 6 7 8
116 118 120 122 124 126 128
20 18 16 14 12 10 8 6
Itbayat I.
Batan I.
Balintang Channel
Calayan I.
Babuyan I.
Dalupiri I.
Babuyan Islands
Camiguin I.
Fuga I.
Babuyan Channel
Mayraira Pt.
Claveria
Aparri
Santa Ana
Bangui
Bacarra
San Nicolas
Laoag
Batac
Kabugao
Gattaran
Gonzaga
2360
Cabugao
Tuao
Tuguegarao
Bangued
Vigan
Santa Maria
Cordillera Central
Cagayan
Mt. Cresta 1685
Sierra Madre
Candon
Lubuagan
Roxas
Palanan Pt.
Tagudin
Bontoc
Ilagan
Palanan
Balaoan
San Mateo
San Fernando
Mt. Pulog 2928
Santiago
Cordon
Bolinao
Lingayen Gulf
Baguio
Solano
Alaminos
Bayombong
Cosiguran
Rosario
Mt. Anacuao 1852
Lingayen
Dagupan
C. San Ildefonso
San Carlos
San Manuel
Santa Cruz
Bayambang
San Jose
Baler Bay
Moncada
Cuyapo
Baler
Luzon
Camiling
Victoria
Masinloc
Tarlac
Cabanatuan
2037
La Paz
Iba
Dingalan
Concepcion
Gapan
1780
Angeles
Polillo Str.
Mt. Pinatubo
San Fernando
Polillo Is.
San Antonio
Olongapo
Malabon
Patnanongan I.
Orani
Caloocan
Jomalig I.
Manila Bay
Quezon City
Bataan
MANILA
Lamon Bay
Cavite
Pasay
Paracale
Dasmariñas
Santa Cruz
Tagatay
L. de Bay
Lucban
Labo
Nasugbu
Alabat I.
Balayan
San Pablo
Atimonan
Daet
Lipa
Calauag
Lemery
Lucena
Pandan
Viga
Lubang Is.
Batangas
Lopez
Catanduanes
Tayabas Bay
Catanauan
Calabanga
San Andres
C. Calavite
Verde I. Pass
Lobo
Lagonoy Gulf
Boac
Naga
Iriga
Virac
Calapan
Marinduque
Nabua
2421
Tabaco
Victoria
Ligao
Mayon Vol.
Rapu Rapu I.
Mamburao
Legazpi
Mindoro
Mt. Baco 2487
Pinamalayan
Burias I.
Donsol
Sorsogon
Sablayan
Tablas Strait
SIBUYAN
Gubat
Magallanes
San Bernardino Str.
Bongabong
Romblon
Bulan
Mindoro Strait
Roxas
Tablas I.
Sibuyan I.
Ticao I.
Irosin
Laoang
Allen
Mondragon
San Jose
Odiongan
Aroroy
Catarman
Gamay
Mandaon
Masbate
Calbayog
Arteche
Busuanga I.
Ilin I.
SEA
Milagros
Masbate
Oras
Culion I.
Calamian Group
Semirara Is.
Placer
Catbalogan
Paranas
Taft
Samar
Linapacan Str.
Kalibo
VISAYAN
Bilinan I.
Caibiran
Santa
Borongan
Pandan
Roxas
Calubian
Rita
Linapacan I.
Dao
Pilar
SEA
Llorente
Tibiao
2117
Bantayan I.
Carigara
Basey
Cuyo West Pass
Cuyo East Pass
Ajuy
Sara
Palompon
Leyte
Tacloban
General MacArthur
Guiuan
Panay
Cuyo Is.
Bugasong
Passi
Cadiz
Bogo
Ormoc
Dulag
Taytay
Cuyo
Pototan
Sagay
Tuburan
Leyte Gulf
San Jose
Iloilo
Silay
Victorias
Danao
Abuyog
Homonhon I.
Jordan
Bacolod
Camotes Is.
Palawan
Guimaras
2450
San Carlos
Camotes Sea
Baybay
Mindanao Trench
Dumaran I.
Hinigaran
La Carlota
Mandaue
Sogod
10 497
Binalbagan
Cebu
Bato
San Juan
Dinagat I.
1593
Himamaylan
Guihulngan
Maasin
Dinagat
Surigao Str.
Irahuan
Honda Bay
Kabankalan
Carcar
Panaon I.
Siargao I.
Puerto Princesa
Sipalay
Tanon Str.
Argao
Bohol I.
Surigao
Cagayan Is.
Hinoba-an
Bais
Placer
Bucas Grande I.
Tanjay
Tagbilaran
Carrascal
Negros
Oslob
L. Mainit
Bayawan
Dumaguete
BOHOL
2012
Lanuza
Siquijor I.
Camiguin I.
Cabadbaran
Tandag
Mt. Mantalingajan 2085
SULU
Siaton
Zamboanguita
SEA
Talisayan
Butuan
Tago
Nasipit
Bayugan
Marihatag
Dapitan
Balingasag
Esperanza
Lianga
Dipolog
Alubijid
Talacogan
Manukan
Iligan Bay
Opol
Cagayan de Oro
Agusan
Hinatuan
C. Buliluyan
Bugsuk I.
Oroquieta
2938
Bislig
SEA
Sindangan
Ozamiz
Iligan
Malaybalay
Maigo
Marawi City
Bunawan
Labason
Liloy
Tubod
L. Lanao
Balabac I.
Balabac Strait
Siocon
Kabasalan
Pagadian
Mindanao
Cateel
Margosatubig
Malabang
2815
Sibuguey Bay
Illana Bay
Baganga
Balambangan
Sibuco
Olutanga
Parang
Tagum
Banggi
Moro Gulf
Midsayap
Panabo
Cotabato
Pantukan
Manay
Kudat
Cagayan Sulu I.
Mati
Datu Piang
Mt. Apo 2954
Senaja
Jembongan
Zamboanga
Pikit
Davao
Basilan Str.
Talayan
Langkon
Pilas Group
Isabela
Davao Gulf
Suba Talan
Digos
San Isidro
Basilan I.
Lamitan
Tenghilan
Koto Belud
Pangutaran Group
Kalamansig
Koronadal
Telok Labuk
Turtle Is.
Malita
Kota Kinabalu
G. Kinabalu 4101
Lebak
Jolo Group
Samales Group
Palimbang
2083
General Santos
C. San Agustin
Sandakan
Jolo
Papar
Parang
Talipao
Pata I.
Kiamba
SABAH
Tapul I.
Sarangani Bay
Crocker
Keningau
Siasi I.
Tinaca Pt.
Melalap
Kuamat
Tapul Group
Sulu Archipelago
Tg. Labian
CELEBES
Sarangani Is.
MALAYSIA
Silam
Tawi-tawi Group
Banjaran Brassey
Teluk Darvel
Sibutu Group
SEA
Banjaran Crocker
Borneo
Semporna
INDONESIA
Kep. Talaud
PACIFIC
OCEAN
PHILIPPINES
SOUTH
CHINA
SEA
ft m
9000 3000
6000 2000
4500 1500
3000 1000
1200 400
600 200
0 0
200 600
4000 12 000
8000 24 000
m ft
Projection: Lambert's Conformal Conic
East from Greenwich

COPYRIGHT, GEORGE PHILIP LTD.

100 0 100 200 300 400 500 km
100 0 50 100 150 200 250 300 350 miles
BURMA (MYANMAR)
RANGOON (YANGON)
G. of Martaban
THAILAND
BANGKOK
LAOS
Vientiane (Viangchan)
VIETNAM
Da Nang
Hue
Qui Nhon
Nha Trang
Cam Ranh
THANH PHO HO CHI MINH
Vung Tau
CAMBODIA
Phnom Penh (Phnum Penh)
Tonle Sap
Gulf of Thailand
ANDAMAN SEA
SOUTH CHINA SEA
Paracel Is.
Spratly Is.
Spratly I.
Amboyna Cay
Con Son
Ca Mau
Strait of Malacca
PENINSULAR MALAYSIA
MALAYSIA
KUALA LUMPUR
George Town
Ipoh
Kuala Terengganu
Kota Baharu
Kuantan
Johor Baharu
SINGAPORE
Kepulauan Natuna Besar
Kepulauan Anambas
Kepulauan Riau
Kepulauan Lingga
BRUNEI
Bandar Seri Begawan
SABAH
Kota Kinabalu
SARAWAK
Kuching
Pontianak
Borneo
KALIMANTAN
BARAT
TENGAH
TIMUR
SELATAN
Banjarmasin
Balikpapan
Samarinda
INDONESIA
SUMATERA
ACEH
UTARA
Banda Aceh
MEDAN
Simeulue
Nias
Kepulauan Batu
Siberut
Kepulauan Mentawai
Padang
Pekanbaru
RIAU
JAMBI
Jambi
PALEMBANG
BENGKULU
Bengkulu
LAMPUNG
Tanjungkarang Telukbetung
Bangka
Belitung
Selat Karimata
Greater Sunda Islands
JAVA SEA
JAKARTA
Bogor
BANDUNG
Cirebon
SEMARANG
Yogyakarta
Surakarta
SURABAYA
Malang
Madura
Jawa (Java)
BALI
Denpasar
Lombok
NUSA TENGGARA BARAT
Lesser
INDIAN OCEAN
Java Trench
Enggano
6073
6650
4424
Projection: Mercator
East from Greenwich
ft m
12 000 4000
9000 3000
6000 2000
4500 1500
3000 1000
1200 400
600 200
0 0
200 600
2000 6000
4000 12 000
6000 18 000
8000 24 000
m ft
1 2 3 4 5
A B C D E F

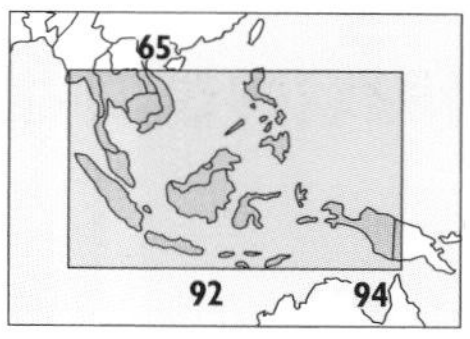

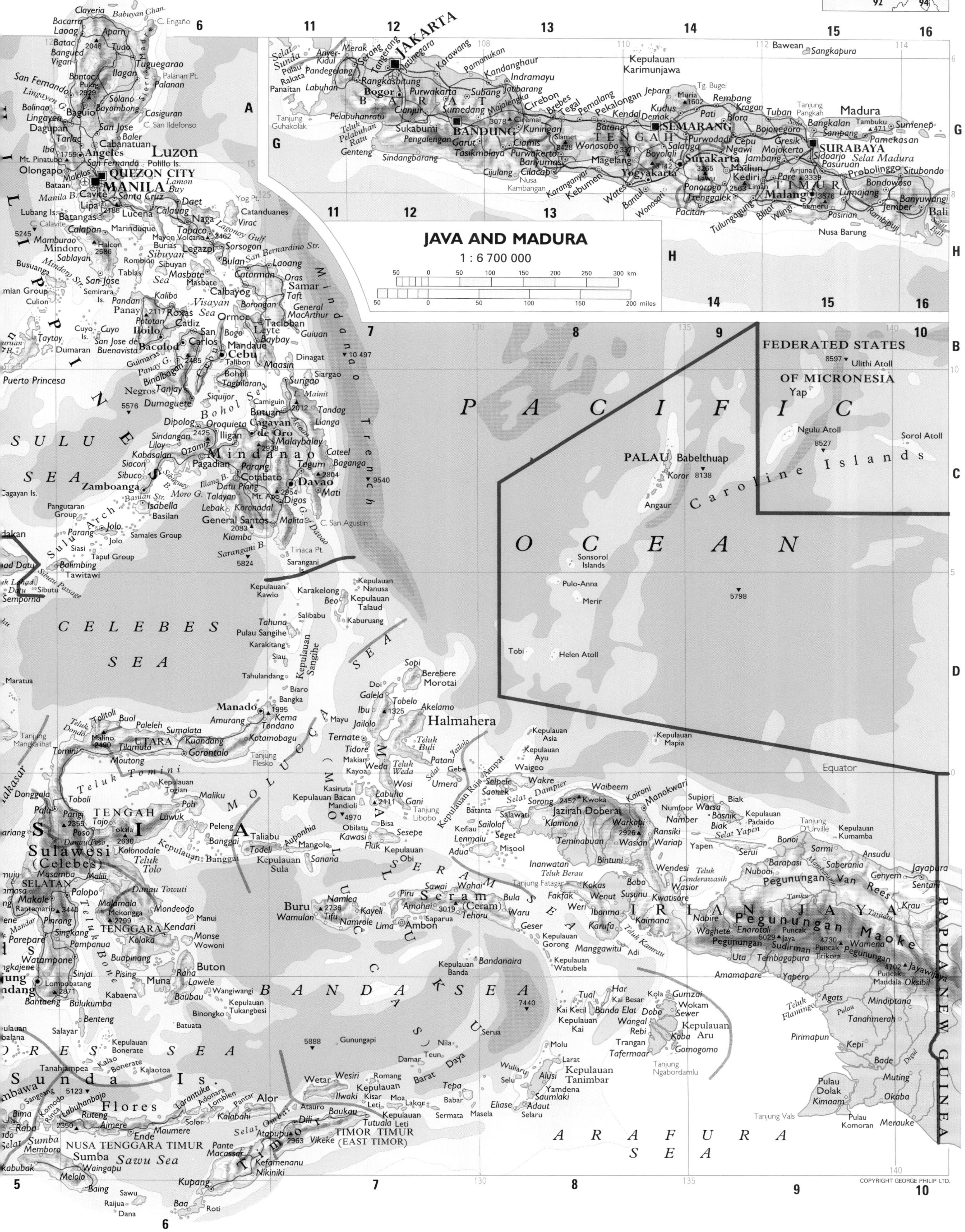
JAVA AND MADURA
1 : 6 700 000
JAKARTA
Bogor
Sukabumi
BANDUNG
Cirebon
Tegal
Pekalongan
SEMARANG
Yogyakarta
Surakarta
Madiun
Kediri
Malang
SURABAYA
Madura
Bali
Bawean
Kepulauan Karimunjawa
Selat Sunda
Selat Madura
Nusa Barung
Nusa Kambangan
FEDERATED STATES OF MICRONESIA
Yap
Ulithi Atoll
Ngulu Atoll
Sorol Atoll
Caroline Islands
PALAU
Babelthuap
Koror
Angaur
Sonsorol Islands
Pulo-Anna
Merir
Tobi
Helen Atoll
PACIFIC OCEAN
Equator
Luzon
QUEZON CITY
MANILA
Mindoro
Panay
Negros
Cebu
Samar
Leyte
Bohol
Mindanao
Zamboanga
Davao
General Santos
Mindanao Trench
SULU SEA
CELEBES SEA
Sulu Arch.
Jolo
Tawitawi
Kepulauan Talaud
Kepulauan Sangihe
Manado
Sulawesi (Celebes)
Teluk Tomini
Kendari
Buton
Muna
MOLUCCA SEA
Halmahera
Morotai
Ternate
Tidore
Kepulauan Sula
Buru
Seram (Ceram)
Ambon
SERAM SEA
BANDA SEA
FLORES SEA
Sunda Is.
Flores
Sumba
Sawu Sea
Timor
Kupang
Dili
TIMOR TIMUR (EAST TIMOR)
NUSA TENGGARA TIMUR
Wetar
Alor
Kepulauan Tanimbar
Kepulauan Kai
Kepulauan Aru
ARAFURA SEA
IRIAN JAYA
Jazirah Doberai
Manokwari
Sorong
Biak
Yapen
Teluk Cenderawasih
Pegunungan Maoke
Puncak Jaya
Jayapura
Merauke
Pulau Dolak
PAPUA NEW GUINEA
COPYRIGHT GEORGE PHILIP LTD.

50 0 50 100 150 200 km
50 0 50 100 150 miles
YUNNAN
GUANGXI ZHUANGZU ZIZHIQU
GUANGDONG
HAINAN
G. of Tonkin
VIETNAM
LAOS
THAILAND
CAMBODIA
BURMA (MYANMAR)
SHAN
KAYAH
MON
PEGU
HANOI
Haiphong
Vientiane (Viangchan)
BANGKOK
RANGOON (YANGON)
Mandalay
Chiang Mai
Luang Prabang
Da Nang
Hue
Haikou
Zhanjiang
Nanning
Mekong
Salween
Tonle Sap
Khorat
Phnom Dangrek
Dawna Range
TENASSERIM
G. of Martaban

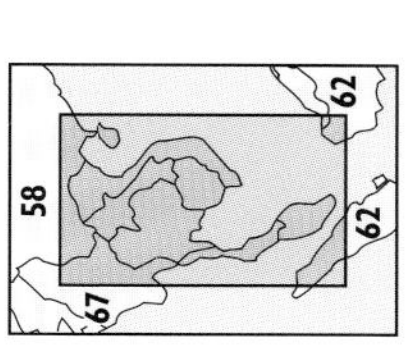

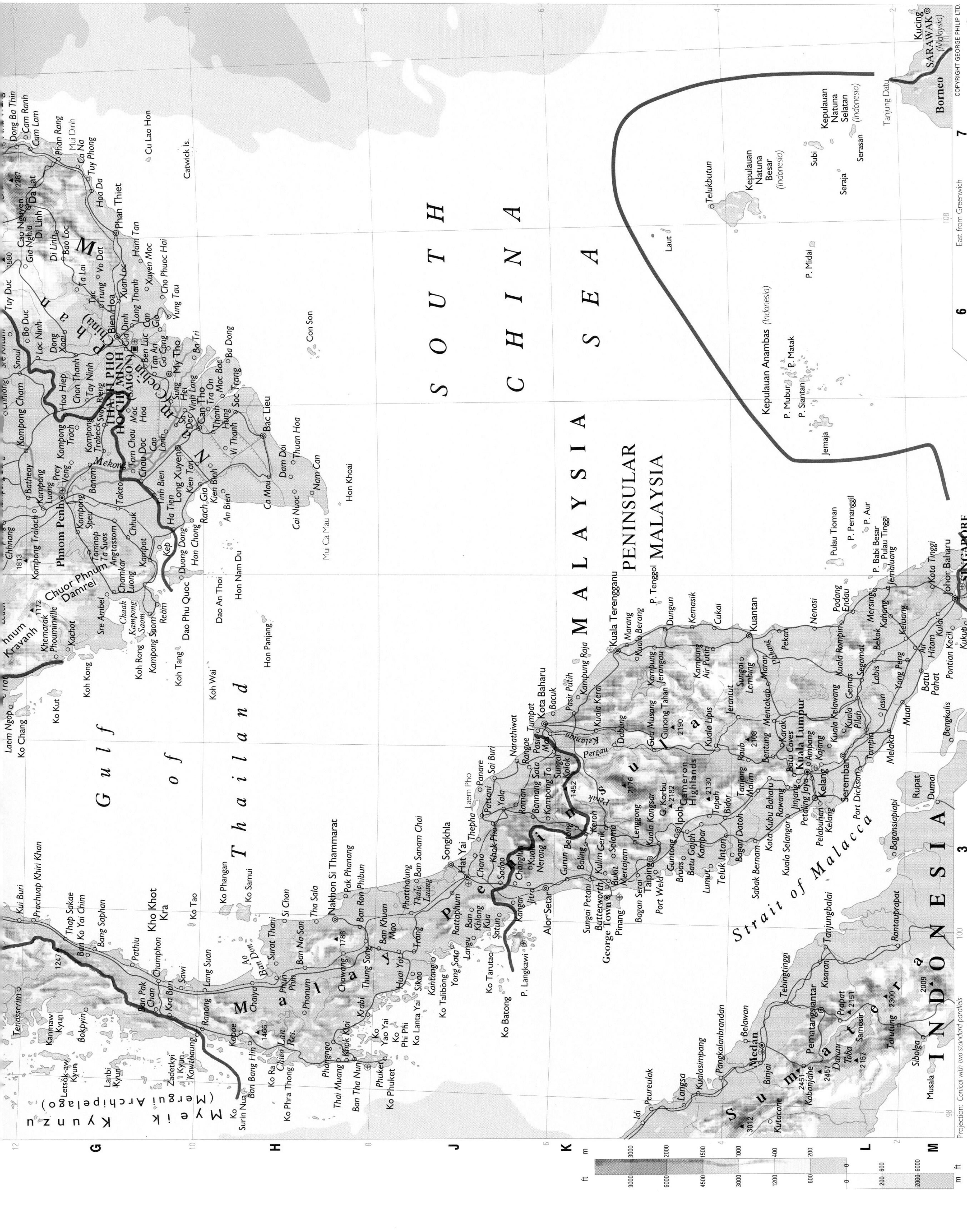

SOUTH CHINA SEA
Gulf of Thailand
MALAYSIA
PENINSULAR MALAYSIA
INDONESIA
SINGAPORE
Strait of Malacca
Sumatera
Borneo
SARAWAK (Malaysia)
Kuching
Mergui Archipelago (Myeik Kyunzu)
Kepulauan Natuna Besar (Indonesia)
Kepulauan Natuna Selatan (Indonesia)
Kepulauan Anambas (Indonesia)
THANH PHO HO CHI MINH (SAIGON)
Phnom Penh
Mekong
Kuala Lumpur
George Town
Kota Baharu
Kuala Terengganu
Kuantan
Johor Baharu
Melaka
Ipoh
Seremban
Hat Yai
Songkhla
Nakhon Si Thammarat
Surat Thani
Phuket
Medan
Pematangsiantar
Danau Toba
Ca Mau
Can Tho
Bac Lieu
Phan Thiet
Da Lat
Vung Tau
Con Son
Dao Phu Quoc
Cameron Highlands
Projection: Conical with two standard parallels
East from Greenwich
COPYRIGHT GEORGE PHILIP LTD.
m ft
3000 9000
2000 6000
1500 4500
1000 3000
400 1200
200 600
0 0
200 600
2000 6000

50 0 100 200 300 400 km
50 0 50 100 150 200 250 miles
TURKMENISTAN
AFGHANISTAN
PAKISTAN
IRAN
INDIA
ARABIAN SEA
SRI LANKA
Hindu Kush
Karakoram Range
JAMMU & KASHMIR
Aksai Chin
NORTH WEST FRONTIER
Northern Areas
BALUCHISTAN
SIND
PUNJAB
HARYANA
RAJASTHAN
GUJARAT
MADHYA PRADESH
MAHARASHTRA
KARNATAKA
TAMIL NADU
KERALA
ANDHRA PRADESH
HIMACHAL PRADESH
UTTARANCHAL
Thar Desert
(Great Indian Desert)
Rann of Kachchh
Gulf of Kachchh
Gulf of Khambhat
Gulf of Mannar
Palk Strait
Palk Bay
Adam's Bridge
Western Ghats
Eastern Ghats
Malabar Coast
Coromandel Coast
Vindhya Range
Satpura Range
Makran Coast Range
Central Makran Range
Siahan Range
Toba Kakar
Kirthar Range
Sulaiman Range
Safid Kuh
Dasht-e Khash
Dasht-e Margow
Rigestan
Kabul
Islamabad
Rawalpindi
Peshawar
Lahore
Faisalabad
Multan
Quetta
Hyderabad
Karachi
Amritsar
Delhi
New Delhi
Jaipur
Agra
Gwalior
Ahmadabad
Vadodara (Baroda)
Surat
Mumbai (Bombay)
Pune (Poona)
Nagpur
Bhopal
Indore
Jabalpur
Solapur
Hyderabad
Bangalore
Chennai (Madras)
Mysore
Coimbatore
Madurai
Tiruchchirappalli
Cochin (Kochi)
Trivandrum (Thiruvananthapuram)
Calicut (Kozhikode)
Mangalore
Pondicherry
Colombo
Kandy
Jaffna
Trincomalee
Srinagar
Gilgit
Herat
Qandahar
Zahedan
Tropic of Cancer
Mouths of the Indus
C. Comorin
C. Monze
Dondra Head
Continuation Southwards on same scale
Projection: Conical with two standard parallels

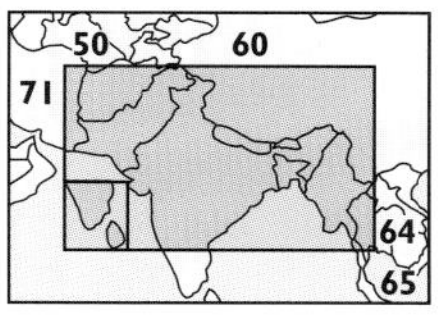

12 13 14 15 16 17 18 19 20 21 22

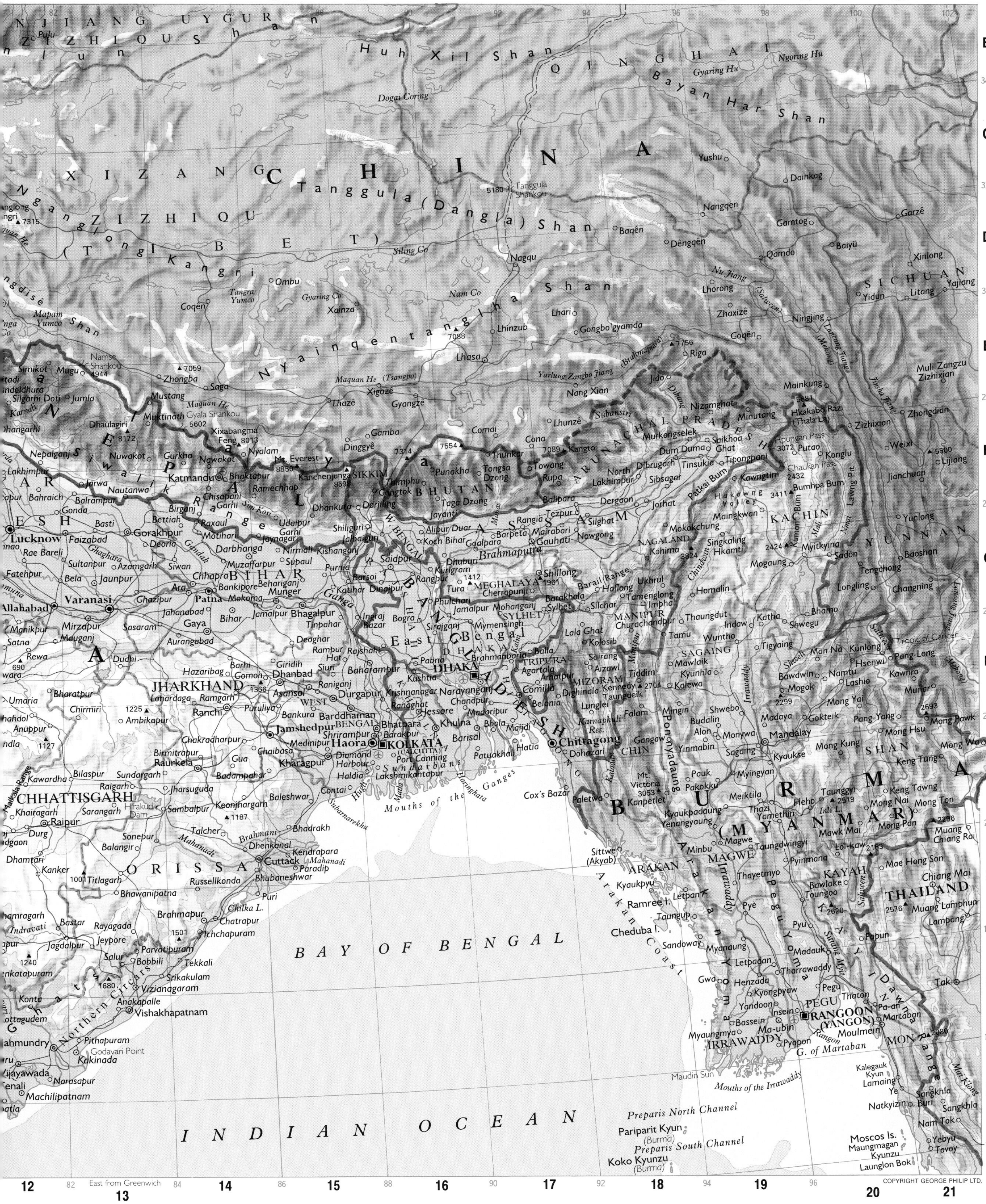

12 13 14 15 16 17 18 19 20 21

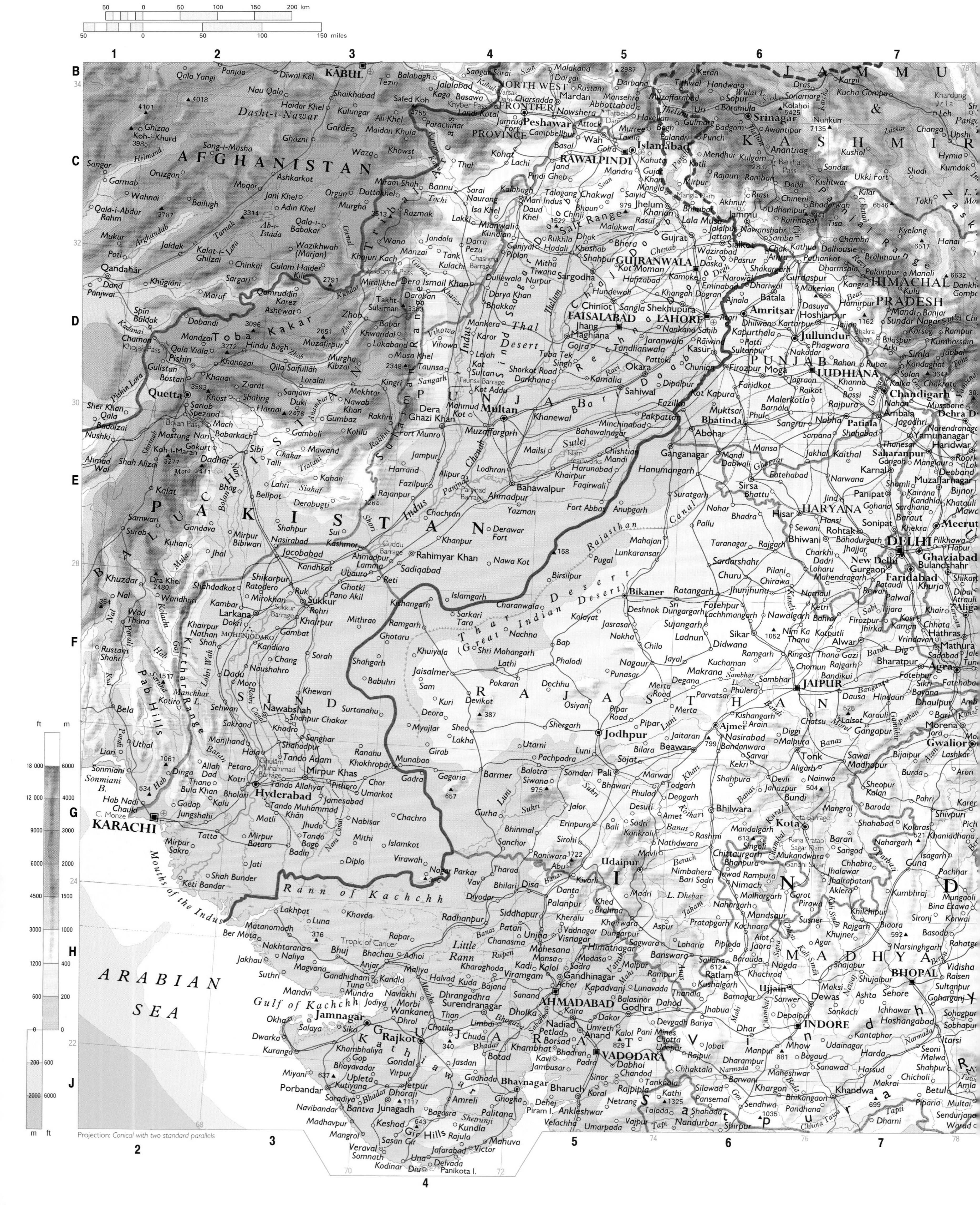

Projection: Conical with two standard parallels

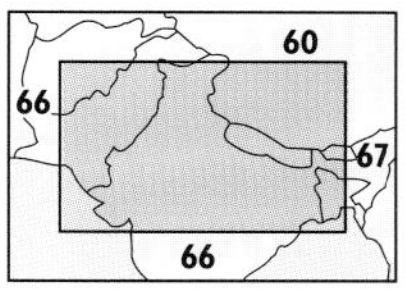
60
66
67
66

JAMMU AND KASHMIR
On same scale as Main Map
AFGHANISTAN
CHINA
NORTH WEST FRONTIER
Northern Areas
JAMMU & KASHMIR
PUNJAB
HIMACHAL PRADESH
Karakoram Ra.
Zaskar Mountains
Ladakh Range
Kunlun Shan
Aksai Chin
Srinagar
Islamabad
RAWALPINDI
K2 8611
Gasherbrum
Siachen Glacier
Nanga Parbat 8126
CHINA
Nganglong Kangri
Gangdisê Shan
XIZANG ZIZHIQU (TIBET)
Yarlung Zangbo Jiang (Brahmaputra)
NEPAL
Mahabharat Lekh
Siwalik Range
Mt. Everest 8850
Kanchenjunga
Annapurna 8078
Dhaulagiri 8172
Katmandu
SIKKIM
BHUTAN
Thimphu
UTTARANCHAL
UTTAR PRADESH
LUCKNOW
KANPUR
Allahabad
VARANASI
Bareilly
Moradabad
Gorakhpur
MADHYA PRADESH
Jabalpur
Kaimur Hills
BIHAR
PATNA
JHARKHAND
Ranchi
Dhanbad
Jamshedpur
CHHATTISGARH
WEST BENGAL
KOLKATA
Haora
BANGLADESH
DHAKA
RAJSHAHI
KHULNA
ASSAM
Garo Hills
Sundarbans
Mouths of the Ganges
The Sandheads
East from Greenwich
A B C D E F G H J
8 9 10 11 12 13

COPYRIGHT GEORGE PHILIP LTD.

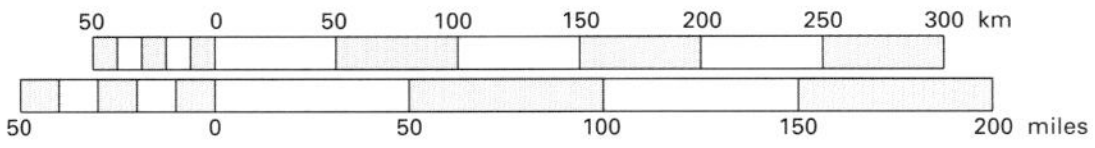
50 0 50 100 150 200 250 300 km
50 0 50 100 150 200 miles

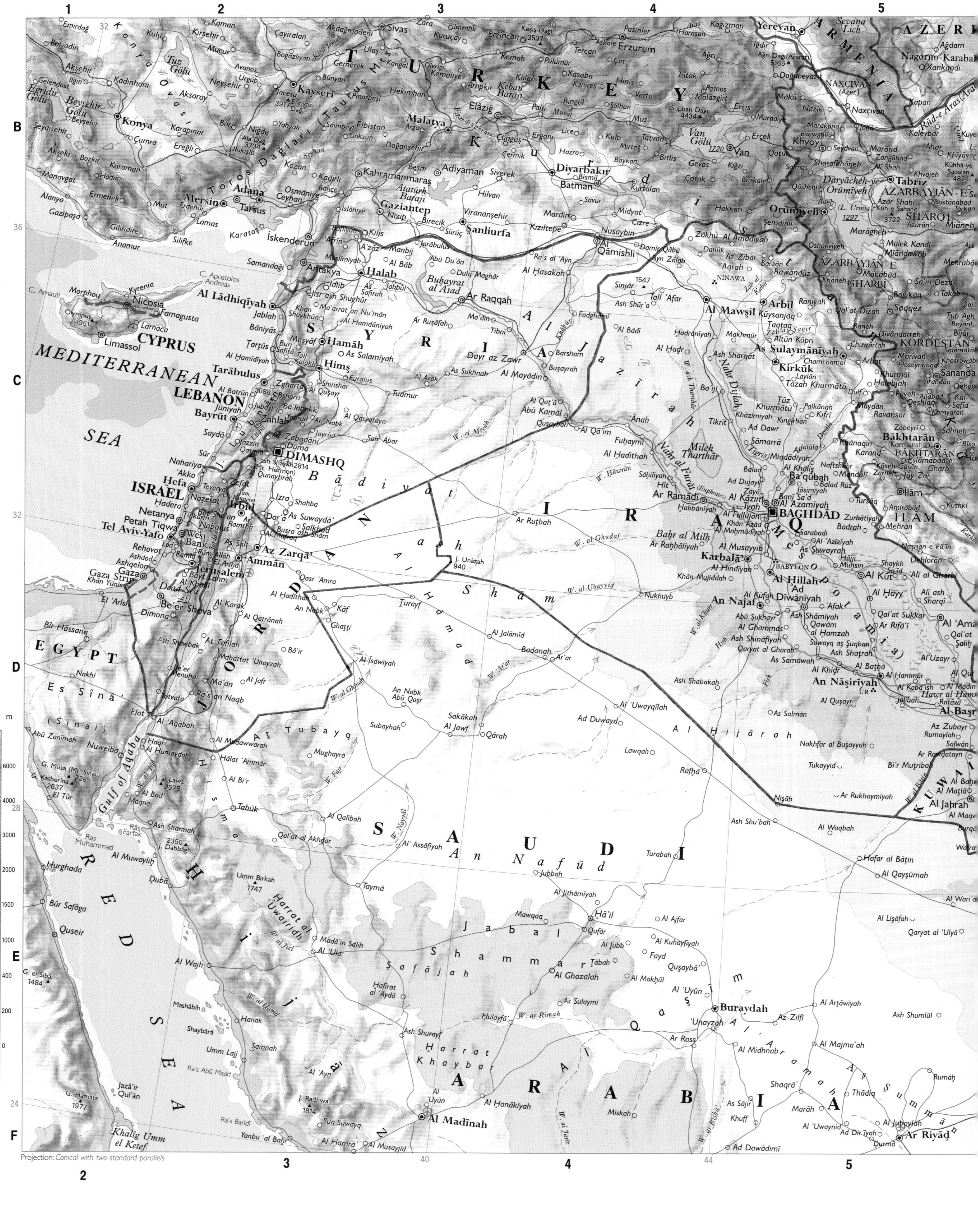
1
2
3
4
5
B
C
D
E
F
TURKEY
Konya
Kayseri
Sivas
Malatya
Erzurum
Van Gölü
Van
Diyarbakır
Adana
Mersin
Tarsus
Gaziantep
Şanlıurfa
İskenderun
Antakya
Halab
Al Lādhiqīyah
Ar Raqqah
Dayr az Zawr
Ḥamāh
Ḥimṣ
Tarābulus
LEBANON
Bayrūt
Zaḥlah
DIMASHQ
SYRIA
CYPRUS
Nicosia
Famagusta
Larnaca
Limassol
MEDITERRANEAN SEA
ISRAEL
Haifa
Tel Aviv-Yafo
Jerusalem
Gaza
Gaza Strip
West Bank
Dead Sea
Be'er Sheva
JORDAN
'Ammān
Az Zarqā'
Ma'ān
Al 'Aqabah
Elat
Gulf of Aqaba
EGYPT
(Sinai)
Es Sînâ'
Hurghada
Bûr Safâga
Quseir
RED SEA
IRAQ
BAGHDĀD
Al Mawṣil
Arbīl
Kirkūk
As Sulaymānīyah
Karbalā'
An Najaf
Al Ḥillah
Ar Ramādī
Tikrīt
Sāmarrā'
Ba'qūbah
Al Kūt
An Nāṣirīyah
Al Baṣrah
Nahr Dijlah (Tigris)
Nahr al Furāt (Euphrates)
Mesopotamia
Al Jazīrah
Bādiyat ash Shām
Al Ḥamād
Al Ḥijārah
SAUDI ARABIA
An Nafūd
Jabal Shammar
Ḥā'il
Buraydah
'Unayzah
Al Madīnah
Tabūk
Al Wajh
Yanbu' al Baḥr
Ar Riyāḍ
Al Jawf
Sakākah
Ḥarrat Khaybar
Al 'Ulā
Taymā
Al Ḥijāz
KUWAIT
Al Jahrah
ARMENIA
Yerevan
AZERBAIJAN
NAXÇIVAN (Azer.)
Tabrīz
Orūmīyeh
Daryācheh-ye Orūmīyeh
ĀZARBĀYJĀN-E SHARQĪ
ĀZARBĀYJĀN-E GHARBĪ
KORDESTĀN
Bākhtarān
ILAM
Ağrı Dağı (Ararat) 5165
J. Unāzah 940
Projection: Conical with two standard parallels
32
36
40
44
24
28

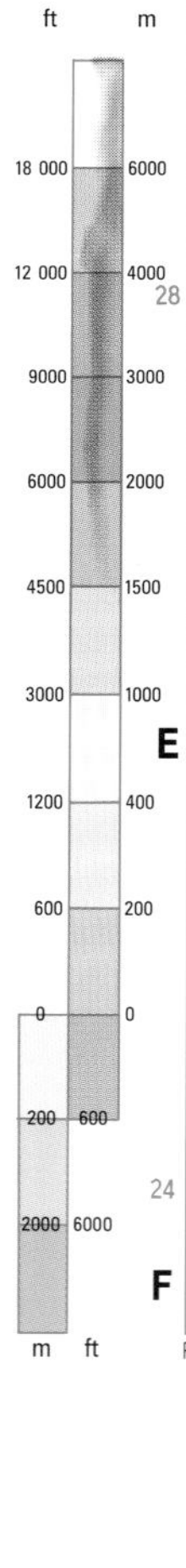
ft
m
18 000
6000
12 000
4000
9000
3000
6000
2000
4500
1500
3000
1000
1200
400
600
200
0
0
200
600
2000
6000
m
ft

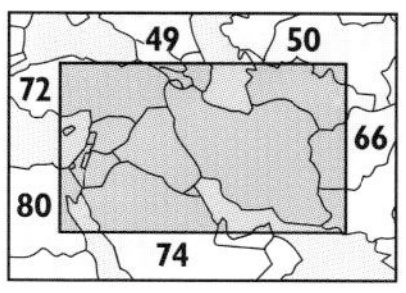
49
50
72
66
80
74

6
7
8
9
10
B
C
D
E
F
TURKMENISTAN
Türkmenbashi
Khrebet Bolshoy Balkhan 1880
Nebitdag
Gazanjyk
Gyzylarbat
Cheleken Yarymadasy
26 Bakinskikh Komissarov
Ostrov Ogurchinskiy
Kara Kum
Kopet Dagh
Ashgabat
Chärjew
Amudarya
Mary
Bayramaly
Yoloten
Murgab
Tejen
Sarakhs
Dashköpri
Uzboy
BAKI
Qazimämmäd
Älät
Neftçala
Kür Dili
995
Länkäran
Ästärä
CASPIAN SEA
-28
Ardabil
Tälesh
Bandar-e Anzalī
Rasht
Āstāneh
Lāhījān
Fowman
GĪLĀN
Rūd Sar
Rāmsar
Tonekābon
Now Shahr
Bābol Sar
Bābol
Sārī
Nekā
Behshahr
Bandar-e Torkeman
Gorgān
Gomishān
Gonbad-e Kāvūs
Gyzyletrek
Chāt
Atrak
Qapān
Āshkhāneh
Qatlīsh
Gīfān
Maneh
Bojnūrd
Shīrvān
Bājgīrān
Lotfābād
Mohammadābād
Dushak
Fārūj
Qūchān
3117
Kabūd Gonbad
Dowgha'ī
Esfarāyen
Ṣafīābād
Chanārān
Kūh-e Bīnālūd
3314
Mashhad
Kashaf
Mozdūrān
Soltānābād
Sabzevār
Neyshābūr
Ahmadābād
Farīmān
Dūkdamīn
Kūh-e Sorkh
3020
Robāt Sang
Shāmkūh
Torbat-e Heydārīyeh
Torbat-e Jām
Langar
Ahmadābād
Kashmar
Khorramābād
Roshkhvār
Khvāf
KHORĀSĀN
Kavīr-e Namak
Bejestān
Gonābād
Zūzan
Soltānābād
Mozhnābād
Daryācheh-i Namakzār
Reshteh-ye Kūhhā-ye Alborz
MĀZANDARĀN
Amol
Qā'emshahr
Kojūr
Baladeh
Gach Sar
Dāmghān
Bastām
Shāhrūd
Emāmrūd
Mayāmey
Mazīnān
Khānbāghī
Biārjmand
Sa'īdābād
Kalāteh
Kord Kūy
Rāmīān
Jājarm
Dasht
Nardīn
Qazvin
Takestān
Kahak
Ziārān
Hashtjerd
Karaj
TEHRĀN
Tajrish
Damāvand
5604
Fīrūzkūh
Lārīn
Eslamshahr
Rey
Eyvānki
Ātesḥān
Semnān
Lāsjerd
Ārādān
Miandarreh
Garmsār
SEMNĀN
Torūd
Garmāb
Tūrān
Dorūneh
MARKAZĪ
Qom
Daryācheh-ye Namak
Tūleh
Kāshān
Naṣrābād
Delījān
Abū Zeydābād
Mahallāt
Dasht-e Kavīr
Chāh-e Kavīr
Nagīneh
Abdolābād
Jandaq
IRAN
Khvor
Moṣṭafāābād
Mehr Jān
Shūrāb
Ḥalvān
Tabas
Karīt
Boshrūyeh
Ferdows
Nowghāb
Farrokhī
Qāyen
Seh Qal'eh
Esfideh
Shāhrakht
Yazdān
'Abbāsābād
Deyhūk
Sedeh
2896
Bīrjand
Tabas
Chāh Akhvor
Sarbīsheh
Homand
Behābād
Khūr
Khūsf
Māzhān
'Arābābād
'Alīābād
Nāy Band
Dasht-e Lūt
Shūsf
Qa'emābād
Nehbandān
Bandān
Zābol
Daryācheh-ye Sīstān
Sīstān
Dasht-e Mārgow
Zaranj
NĪMRŪZ
Chakhānsūr
Geng
Chahār Borjak
Rūdbār
Gowd-e Zirreh
AFGHANISTAN
HERĀT
Herāt
Kūhestān
Ghūrīān
Zendeh Jān
Rakhneh-ye Jamshīdī
Owbeh
Safīd Kūh
Kaoghān
Tūlak
Fārsī
Shīndand
Anār Darreh
Dowlatābād
FARĀH
Farāh
Kirteh
Lāsh-e Joveyn
Khāsh
Qal'eh-ye Valī
Bālā Morghāb
Gushgy
Qal'eh-ye Now
Kashk-e Kohneh
Harīrūd
Farāh
32
36
28
24
52
56
60
Abhar
Sa'īdīyeh
Kūhīn
Bīnāb
Manjīl
Marshūn
Qareh Tekān
Sīrdān
ZANJĀN
Zanjān
Nik Pey
Qezel Owzan
Āgh Kand
Khalkhāl
Ardabil
Qazvīn
Qaṭīābad
Heṣār
Nehāvand
Naqqāsh
Avej
Razan
Āsiā Bak
Zarand
Nowbarān
Row'ān
Zāreh
Jeyhunābād
Tafresh
Sāveh
Manzarīyeh
HAMADĀN
Hamadān
Tūyserkān
Āhū
Rāhjerd
Malāyer
Nahāvand
Zagheh
Shūr Āb
Arāk
Borūjerd
Khomeyn
Khorramābād
Dow Rūd
Alīgūdarz
Azna
Zāgheh
Safīd Dasht
Golpāyegān
Soh
Naṭanz
Ardestān
Zavāreh
Bād
Dorr
Zafarqand
Bāqerābād
Dāmaneh
Dārān
Khomeynī Shahr
Tīrān
Eṣfahān
EṢFAHĀN
Nā'īn
Kūhpāyeh
Najafābād
Jolfā
Zāyandeh
Varzaneh
Kūh-e Zard 4548
Ben
CHAHĀR MAHĀLL VA BAKHTIĀRĪ
Shahr-e Kord
Mobārakeh
Qomsheh
Boldājī
Sūlār
Lālī
Dezfūl
Andīmeshk
Sar Dasht
Rāzeh
Shūshtar
Masjed Soleymān
Meydān-e Naftūn
Darkhazīneh
Band Qīr
Naft-e Safīd
Veys
Haft Gel
Ahvāz
KHUZESTĀN
Rāmhormoz
Dehdez
Zāgros
Kūhhā-ye Zāgros
3723
Yazd-e Khvāst
Shūrjestān
Ābādeh
Sūrmaq
Abargū
Anārak
Ḥājjīābād-e Zarrīn
Posht-e Badam
Zarrīn
Ardakān
Khārānaq
Kalāntarī
Yazd
YAZD
Fahraj
Bāfq
Nadūshan
'Alīābād
Shīr Kūh 4075
Taft
Mehrīz
Deh-e Shīr
Kūlvand
Ḥasanābād
Bātlāq-e Gavkhūnī
'Aqdā
Dmān Āb
Kūh-e Darband 2499
Kūhbonān
Ravar
Tabas
Kāl Gūsheh
Shūr
Zarand
Ḥūr
Kūhpāyeh 3142
Namakzār-e Shahdād
Shahdād
Khenāmān
Kermān
Kūh-e Seh Konj 3992
Māhān
Rafsanjān
Kashkūīyeh
Anār
Dehaj
Ḥeydarābād
Golestānak
Marvast
Deh Bīd
Lāvar Meydān
Abdar
Shahr-e Bābak
Khātūnābād
Bavānāt
Tājābād
Shūzū
Khvānsār
Sa'ādatābād
KOHKĪLŪYEH VA BŪYER AḤMADĪ
Bahmanzād
Lendeh
Khosravī
Kūh-e Bul 3660
Sedeh
Kūh-e Dīnār 4431
Yāsūj
Āqā Jārī
Pāzanān
Behbehān
Gachsarān
Hendījān
Deylam
Qajarīyeh
Shādegān
Khalafābād
Kārūn
Khorramshahr
Ābādān
Bandar-e Ma'shur
Bandar-e Khomeynī
Khosrowābād
Al Fāw
Shatt al Arab
Būbīyān
Al Kuwayt
Mīnā' al Aḥmadī
Mīnā' Su'ūd
Al Khafjī
Ra's al Mish'āb
As Saffānīyah
Manīfah
Abū Ḥadrīyah
Abū 'Alī
Al Kharsānīyah
Al Jubayl
Najmah
Al Fāḍilī
Al Qaṭīf
Ad Dammām
Az Zahrān
Al Muḥarraq
Al Manāmah
BAHRAIN
Ra's Rakan
Ar Ru'ays
'Awālī
Ḥanīdh
'Uray'irah
Ayn Dār
Buqayq
Al Uqayr
Al Mubarraz
Al Hufūf
Al 'Udayliyah
Khurays
Al Hunayy
Al Jāfūrah
As Sal'wa
Nibāk
QATAR
Al Jamalīyah
Al Khawr
Dukhān
Umm Bāb
Ad Dawḥah
Al Wakrah
Musay'īd
THE GULF
Ḥālūl
Dās
Az Zarqā'
Abū Ẓaby
Dalmā
Ṣīr Banī Yās
Marāwīh
Abū al Abyad
Ruwais
Al Mughayrā
Ṭarīf
Ḥabshān
Bū Ḥasā
Khawr Duwayhin
UNITED ARAB EMIRATES
Sepīdān
Fahlīān
Bābā Kalū
Heṣār
Marv Dasht
PERSEPOLIS
Kāzerūn
Shīrāz
Tafīhān
Gavākān
Kavār
Sarvestān
Dāryācheh-ye Tashk
Neyrīz
FĀRS
Sa'ādatābād
Sa'īdābād
Mashīz
KERMĀN
Rāyen
Kūh-e Hazārān
Gūgher
Rābor 4419
Baft
Dar Mazār
Meydān-e Gel
Estahbānāt
Fasa
Fedeshkūh
Dārāb
Zāhedān
Fīrūzābād
Tal Ḥalal
Ganāveh
Bandar-e Rīg
Khārk
Dālakī
Borāzjān
Jazīreh-ye Shīf
Bāladeh
Farrāshband
Būshehr
BŪSHEHR
Ahram
Bāsht
Khvormūj
Senā
Bord
Konārī
Khūn-e Now
Mand
Kord Sheykh
Jahrom
Mobārakābād
Khosūyeh
Dehestān
Fūrg
Harvand
Ḥājjīābād
Ṭārom
Sa'ādatābād
Aḥmadī
3280
Nūrābād
Khvorgū
Shamīl
Makūyeh
Kangān
Deyyer
Ṭāherī
'Alamarvdasht
Evaz
Lār
Parak
Khalīlī
Anveh
Nakhl-e Taqī
Hormoz
Kūh-e Hormoz 2804
Rezvān
HORMOZGĀN
Bandar-e 'Abbās
Mīnāb
Khūnsorkh
Qeshm
Jaz-ye Hormoz
Bastak
Gāvbandī
Bandar-e Maqām
Bandar-e Chārak
Khamīr
Nāy Band
Lāvān
Hendorābī
Qeys
Bandar-e Lengeh
Bāsa'īdū
Forūr
Sirrī
Abū Mūsā
Str. of Hormuz
Al Khaṣab
Ra's Masandam (Oman)
J. al Ḥamīm 2057
Ra's al Khaymah
Dibā
Umm al Qaywayn
'Ajmān
Ash Shāriqah
Dubayy
Adh Dhayd
Al Fujayrah
Bū Baqarah
Shināṣ
Al Liwā'
Ṣuḥār
Maḥḍah
Al 'Ayn
Al Ḥajar al Gharbī
Aṣ Ṣaḥm
Al Khābūra
As Suwayq
Ḥafīt
1372
OMAN
Dank
Maskin
W. al 'Ayn
'Ibrī
Gulf of Oman
Nabīd
Keshit
Nosratābād
Golbaf
Tahrūd
Dārestān
Morghak
Bam
Shūr Gaz
Fahraj
Kūh-e Jebāl Bārez
3962
Rīgān
Biābān-e Kermān
Sabzvārān
Gav Koshī
Khabr
Kūshk
Dowsārī
Estārm
Dowlatābād
Golāshkerd
Kahnūj
Gāzbor
Dehnow-e Kūhestān
Kūh-e Bazmān 3489
Sīāreh
Dalgān
Ḥalīl
Hāmūn-e Jaz Mūrīān
Kalāteh-ye Ganj
Pūzeh Rīg
SĪSTĀN VA BALŪCHESTĀN
Bampūr
Īrānshahr
Kūhhā-ye Bashākerd
Remeshk
Kūh-e Kahran 2163
Kahnūj
Kūhestak
Shām
Fannūj
Mīr Shahdād
Jagīn
Gābrīk
Pūgūnzī
Parka Bandar
Kangān
Sogār
Rapch
Kalak
Band Boni
Jāsk
Ra's-e Meydānī
Ra's-e Tang
Nīkshahr
Bent
Qaṣr-e Qand
Pīshīn
Makrān
Teleng
Māch Kowr
Bāhū Kalāt
Pīr Sohrāb
Polān
Chāh Bahār
Gavāter
Ras Jiwani
Dasht
Tump
Sarbāz
Chānf
Īrafshān
Kūhīrī
Kont
Zābolī
Dāvar Panāh
Paskūh
Kārevandar
Jālq
Kūhak
Dehak
Eskān
Khāsh
Shāndak
Rod
Hamun-i Mashkel
Tahlab
Kūh-e Taftān 4042
Lādīz
Mīrjāveh
Mashki Chāh
PAKISTAN
Zāhedān
Hormak
Patambar
Gorg
East from Greenwich
COPYRIGHT GEORGE PHILIP LTD.

TURKEY AND TRANSCAUCASIA 1:4 400 000

Projection: *Conical with two standard parallels*

Division between Greeks and Turks in Cyprus; Turks to the North.

CASPIAN SEA
Caucasus Mountains
RUSSIA
GEORGIA
ARMENIA
AZERBAIJAN
IRAN
IRAQ
SYRIA
TURKEY
DAGESTAN
CHECHENIA
KABARDINO-BALKARIA
NORTH OSSETIA
INGUSHETIA
ABKHAZIA
AJARIA
South Ossetia
Nagorno-Karabakh
NAXÇIVAN (Azerbaijan)
Kurdistan
Al Jazīrah (Mesopotamia)
Bādiyat ash Shām
Anadolu Dağları
Güneydoğu Toroslar
Hakkâri Dağları
Bingöl Dağları
Munzur Dağları
Kūhhā-ye Ţālesh
Samurskiy Khrebet
Van Gölü
Daryācheh-ye Orūmīyeh (Lake Urmia)
Sevana Lich
Nahr al Furāt (Euphrates)
Nahr Dijlah (Tigris)
Fırat (Euphrates)
Rūd-e Aras (Araks)
Kür
TBILISI
YEREVAN
BAKI
BAGHDĀD
Sochi
Sokhumi
Batumi
Kutaisi
Poti
Trabzon
Rize
Erzurum
Kars
Gyumri
Vanadzor
Gäncä
Sumqayıt
Makhachkala
Derbent
Groznyy
Vladikavkaz
Tabrīz
Orūmīyeh (Urmia)
Ardabīl
Rasht
Zanjān
Hamadān
Sanandaj
Bākhtarān
Khorramābād
Dezfūl
Van
Diyarbakır
Malatya
Elâzığ
Şanlıurfa (Urfa)
Mardin
Al Mawşil (Mosul)
Arbīl
Kirkūk
As Sulaymānīyah
Dayr az Zawr
Ar Raqqah
Al Ḩasakah
Al Qāmishlī
Sāmarrā
Ar Ramādī
Al Fallūjah
Karbalā
Al Ḩillah
An Najaf
Al Kūt
Al 'Amārah
Ad Dīwānīyah
Tudmur PALMYRA
BABYLON
NĪNAWÁ
East from Greenwich
8 9 10 11 12 13
A B C D E F G
40 42 44 46 48 50
m ft

ARABIA AND THE HORN OF AFRICA 1:13 300 000

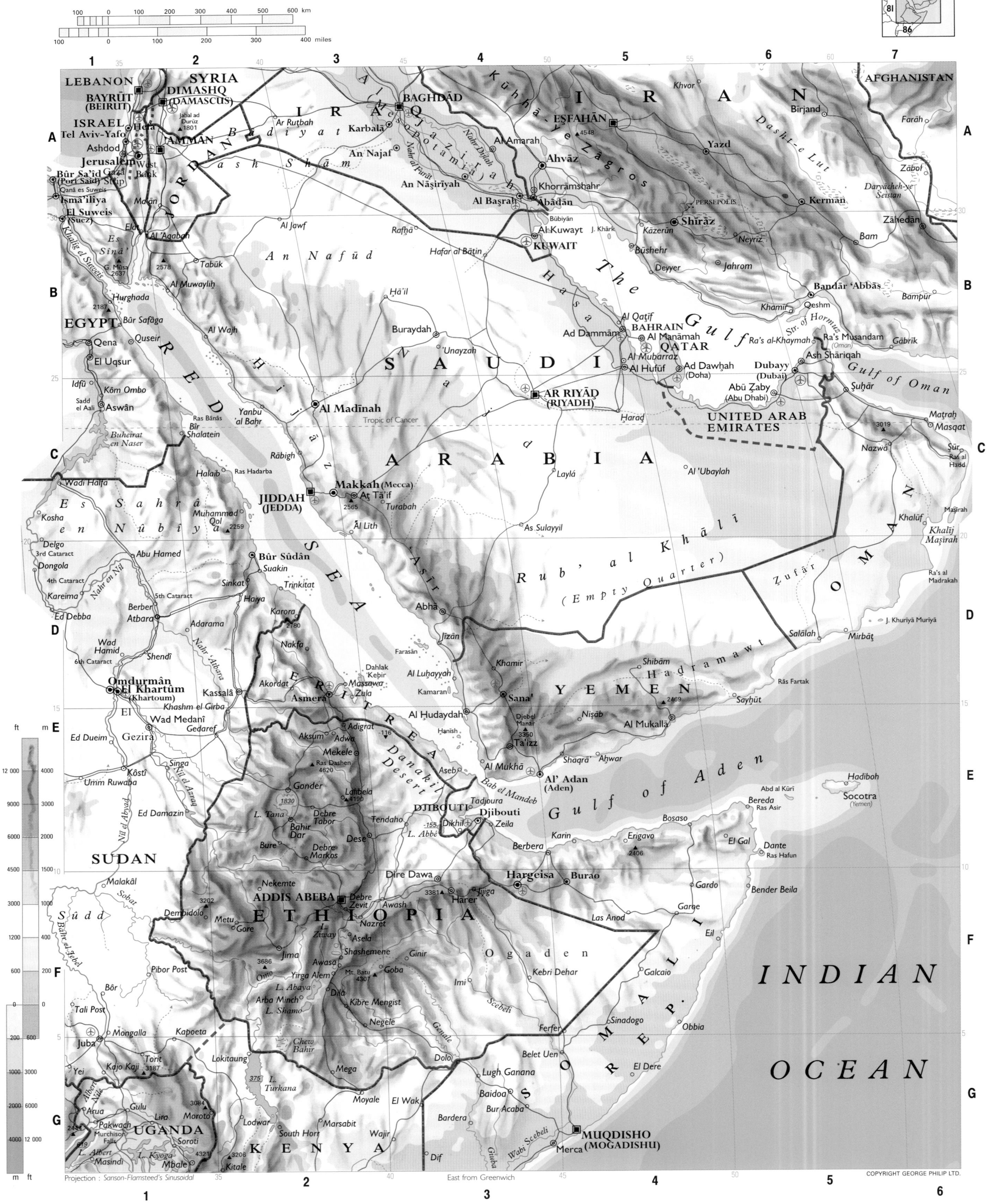

LEBANON
SYRIA
DIMASHQ (DAMASCUS)
BAYRŪT (BEIRUT)
ISRAEL
Tel Aviv-Yafo
Ashdod
Jerusalem
'AMMĀN
JORDAN
IRAQ
BAGHDĀD
IRAN
EŞFAHĀN
Yazd
Kermān
Shīrāz
Ahvāz
Al Başrah
KUWAIT
Al Kuwayt
Dasht-e Lut
Kūhhā-ye Zāgros
Bādiyat ash Shām
Al Jazīrah
An Nafūd
SAUDI ARABIA
AR RIYĀD (RIYADH)
Al Madīnah
Makkah (Mecca)
JIDDAH (JEDDA)
Hijāz
Najd
Rub' al Khālī (Empty Quarter)
The Gulf
BAHRAIN
Al Manāmah
QATAR
Ad Dawhah (Doha)
UNITED ARAB EMIRATES
Abū Zaby (Abu Dhabi)
Dubayy (Dubai)
Gulf of Oman
OMAN
Masqat
Şalālah
YEMEN
Sana'
Al Mukallā
Al' Adan (Aden)
Hadramawt
Gulf of Aden
Socotra (Yemen)
RED SEA
EGYPT
Bûr Sa'îd (Port Said)
El Suweis (Suez)
Aswân
Es Sahrâ en Nûbîya
SUDAN
Omdurmân
El Khartûm (Khartoum)
Bûr Sûdân
ERITREA
Asmera
Massawa
ETHIOPIA
ADDIS ABEBA
DJIBOUTI
Djibouti
Danakil Desert
Ogaden
Hargeisa
SOMALI REP.
MUQDISHO (MOGADISHU)
KENYA
UGANDA
AFGHANISTAN
INDIAN OCEAN
Tropic of Cancer
Projection : Sanson-Flamsteed's Sinusoidal
East from Greenwich
COPYRIGHT GEORGE PHILIP LTD.

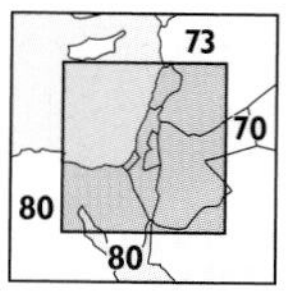
73
70
80
80

10 0 10 20 30 40 50 60 70 80 100 km
10 0 10 20 30 40 50 60 miles
CYPRUS
Paphos
Episkopi
Limassol
Episkopi Bay
Akrotiri Bay
C. Gata
MEDITERRANEAN SEA
LEBANON
ISRAEL
SYRIA
JORDAN
EGYPT
SAUDI ARABIA
Tarābulus (Tripoli)
BAYRŪT (Beirut)
Saydā (Sidon)
Sūr (Tyre)
Hims (Homs)
DIMASHQ (Damascus)
Naharıyya
'Akko (Acre)
Hefa (Haifa)
Netanya
Herzliyya
Tel Aviv-Yafo
Bat Yam
Rishon le Ziyyon
Ashdod
Ashqelon
Gaza
Gaza Strip
Khān Yūnis
Rafah
Jerusalem (Yerushalayim) (Al Quds)
Bayt Lahm (Bethlehem)
Al Khalīl (Hebron)
West Bank
Nāblus
El Arīhā (Jericho)
Be'er Sheva (Beersheba)
Dimona
Sedom
Mizpe Ramon
Hanegev
Elat
Al 'Aqabah
Gulf of Aqaba
Haql
'AMMĀN
Az Zarqā
Irbid
Al Mafraq
As Salt
Ma'dabā
Al Karak
At Tafilah
Ma'ān
PETRA
Ra's an Naqb
Al Mudawwarah
Bûr Sa'îd (Port Said)
Bûr Fu'ad
Ismâ'ilîya
El Suweis (Suez)
El Buheirat el Murrat el Kubra (Great Bitter L.)
Sînâ' (Sinai)
Gebel el Tîh
Shibh Jazīrat Sīnā'
Nakhl
El 'Arîsh
Sabkhet el Bardawîl
Golan Heights
Dead Sea
Jabal ash Shaykh (Mt. Hermon)
Al Qunaytirah
Yam Kinneret
Jabal Lubnān
Al Biqā' Valley
Jabal ad Durūz
AS SUWAYDĀ'
DAR'Ā
IRBID
AL BALQĀ
'AMMĀN
AL KARAK
MA'ĀN
HADAROM
HAMERKAZ
HAZAFON
HEFA
DIMASHQ
HIMS
AL JANŪB
ASH SHAMĀL
EL SUWEIS
Projection: Polyconic
East from Greenwich
COPYRIGHT GEORGE PHILIP LTD.
ft m
9000 3000
6000 2000
4500 1500
3000 1000
1200 400
600 200
200 600
2000 6000

1974 Cease Fire Lines

AFRICA : Physical 1:37 300 000

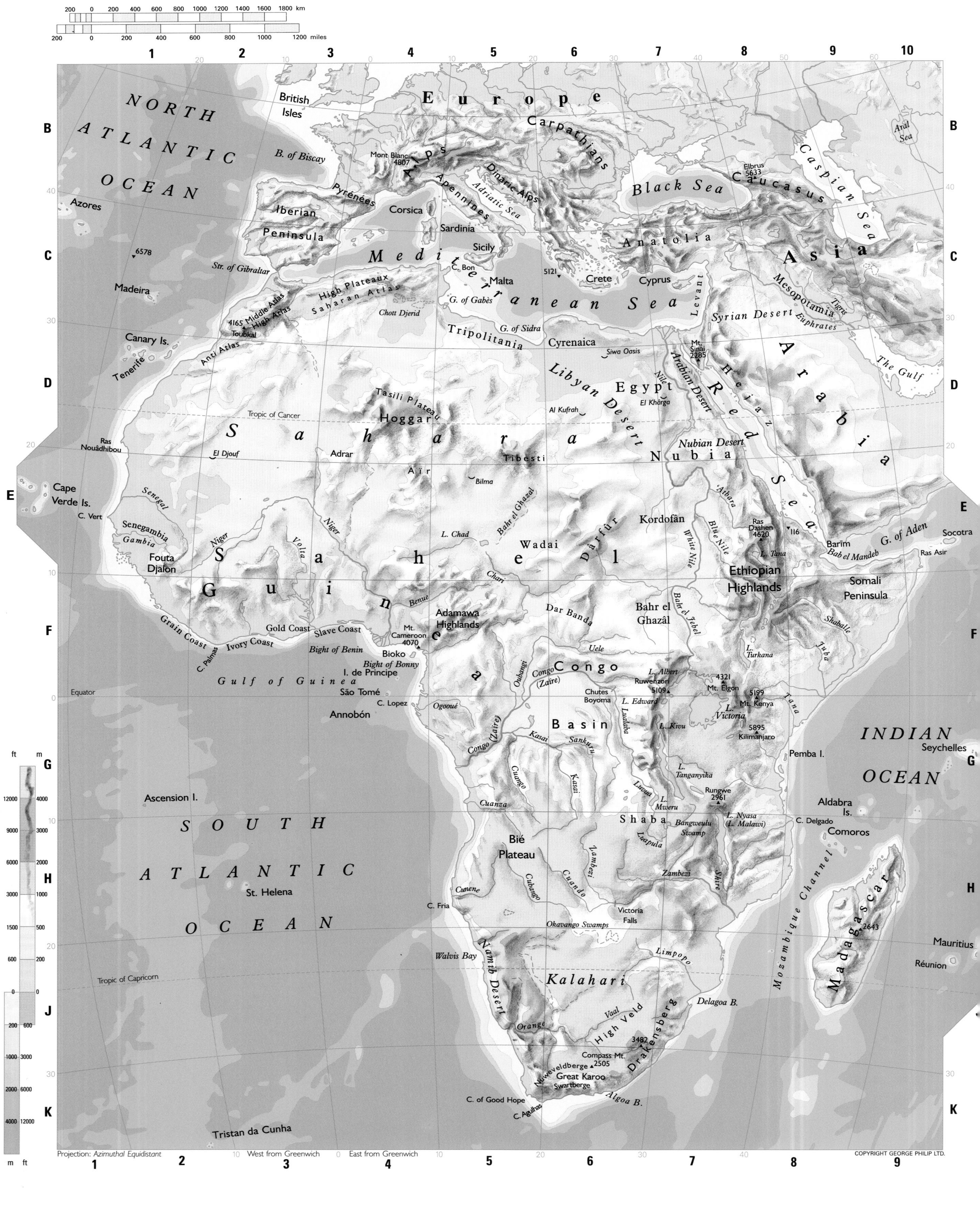

NORTH ATLANTIC OCEAN
British Isles
Europe
Carpathians
B. of Biscay
Mont Blanc 4807
Alps
Dinaric Alps
Apennines
Adriatic Sea
Black Sea
Elbrus 5633
Caucasus
Caspian Sea
Aral Sea
Azores
Pyrénées
Iberian Peninsula
Corsica
Sardinia
Sicily
Anatolia
Asia
Str. of Gibraltar
Madeira
Mediterranean Sea
C. Bon
Malta
Crete
Cyprus
Levant
Mesopotamia
Tigris
Euphrates
Syrian Desert
High Plateaux
Saharan Atlas
Middle Atlas
High Atlas
4165 Toubkal
Chott Djerid
G. of Gabès
G. of Sidra
Tripolitania
Cyrenaica
Canary Is.
Tenerife
Anti Atlas
Siwa Oasis
Mt. Sinai 2285
Arabian Desert
Hejaz
Arabia
The Gulf
Libyan Desert
Egypt
Nile
El Khârga
Red Sea
Tasili Plateau
Hoggar
Tropic of Cancer
Al Kufrah
Sahara
Ras Nouâdhibou
El Djouf
Adrar
Tibesti
Nubian Desert
Nubia
Aïr
Bilma
Cape Verde Is.
C. Vert
Senegal
Senegambia
Gambia
Fouta Djalon
Niger
Volta
Sahel
L. Chad
Bahr el Ghazal
Wadai
Darfur
Kordofân
'Atbara
Blue Nile
White Nile
Ras Dashen 4620
116
Barim
Bab el Mandeb
G. of Aden
Socotra
Ras Asir
L. Tana
Ethiopian Highlands
Somali Peninsula
Guinea
Chari
Benue
Dar Banda
Bahr el Ghazâl
Bahr el Jebel
Adamawa Highlands
Mt. Cameroon 4070
Grain Coast
Gold Coast
Slave Coast
Ivory Coast
C. Palmas
Bight of Benin
Bight of Bonny
Bioko
I. de Principe
São Tomé
Gulf of Guinea
Equator
C. Lopez
Annobón
Shaballe
Juba
L. Turkana
Uele
Ubangi
Congo (Zaïre)
Congo
L. Albert
Ruwenzori 5109
4321 Mt. Elgon
5199 Mt. Kenya
Tana
Chutes Boyoma
L. Edward
L. Victoria
Ogooué
Lualaba
L. Kivu
5895 Kilimanjaro
Basin
Kasai
Sankuru
INDIAN OCEAN
Seychelles
Pemba I.
Cuango
L. Tanganyika
Ascension I.
Rungwe 2961
Luvua
L. Mweru
Aldabra Is.
Cuanza
L. Nyasa (L. Malawi)
C. Delgado
Comoros
SOUTH ATLANTIC OCEAN
Shaba
Bangweulu Swamp
Luapula
Bié Plateau
Lambezi
Zambezi
Shire
Mozambique Channel
Madagascar
St. Helena
Cunene
Cubango
Cuando
C. Fria
Victoria Falls
Okavango Swamps
2643
Mauritius
Réunion
Namib Desert
Walvis Bay
Limpopo
Tropic of Capricorn
Kalahari
Delagoa B.
Vaal
Orange
High Veld
Drakensberg
3482
Compass Mt. 2505
Nuweveldberge
Great Karoo
Swartberge
Algoa B.
C. of Good Hope
C. Agulhas
Tristan da Cunha
6578
5121
Projection: Azimuthal Equidistant
West from Greenwich
East from Greenwich

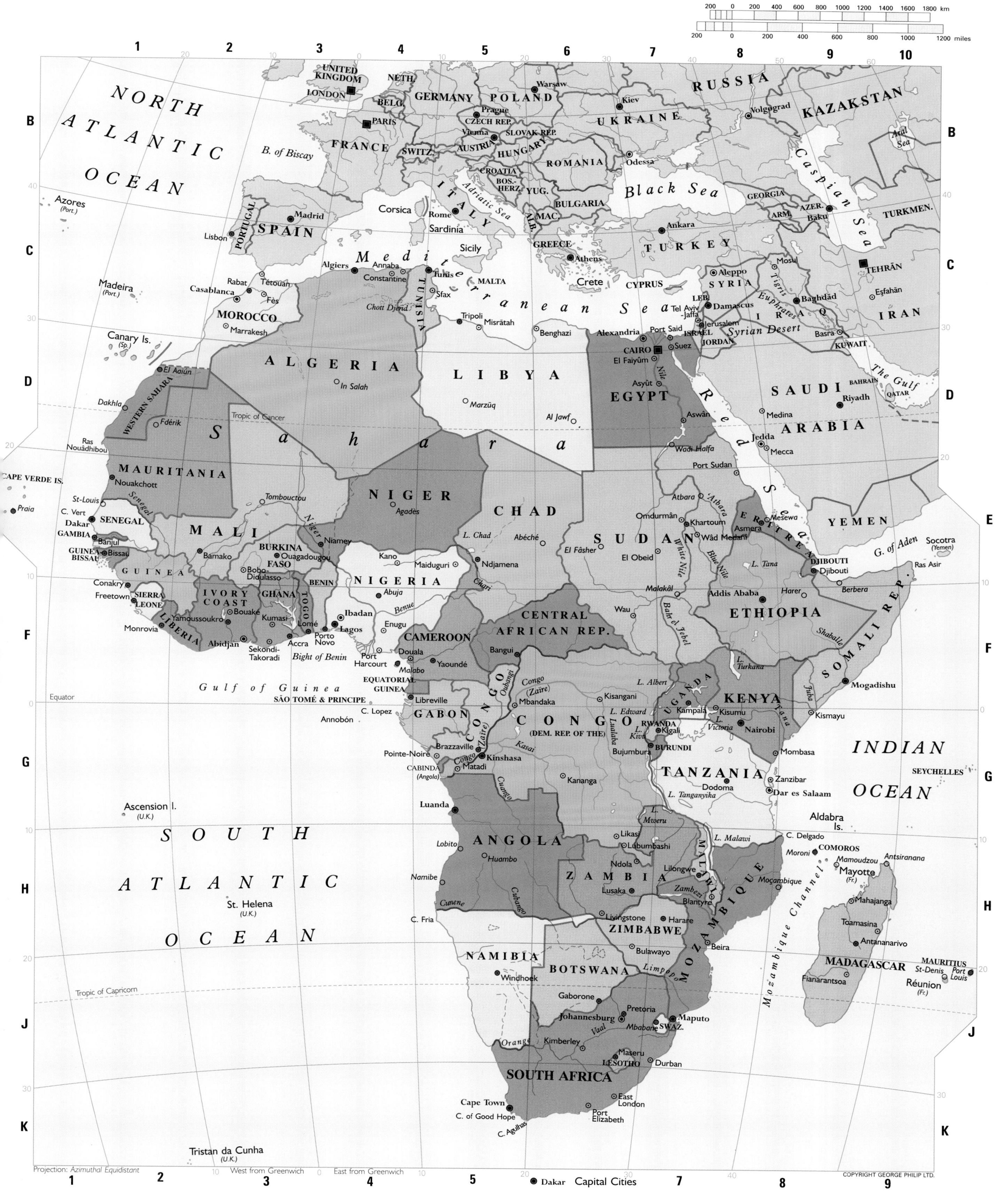
NORTH ATLANTIC OCEAN
Azores (Port.)
Madeira (Port.)
Canary Is. (Sp.)
CAPE VERDE IS.
Praia
B. of Biscay
UNITED KINGDOM
LONDON
NETH.
BELG.
PARIS
FRANCE
GERMANY
POLAND
Warsaw
Prague
CZECH REP.
Vienna
SLOVAK REP.
AUSTRIA
HUNGARY
SWITZ.
CROATIA
BOS.-HERZ.
YUG.
ROMANIA
BULGARIA
MAC.
ALB.
GREECE
Athens
ITALY
Rome
Corsica
Sardinia
Sicily
Adriatic Sea
RUSSIA
Kiev
UKRAINE
Odessa
Volgograd
KAZAKSTAN
Aral Sea
Caspian Sea
Black Sea
GEORGIA
ARM.
AZER.
Baku
TURKMEN.
Ankara
TURKEY
PORTUGAL
Lisbon
SPAIN
Madrid
Mediterranean Sea
Algiers
Annaba
Constantine
Tunis
TUNISIA
Sfax
MALTA
Chott Djerid
Tripoli
Misrātah
Benghazi
Crete
CYPRUS
Aleppo
SYRIA
Mosul
Tigris
Euphrates
Baghdād
IRAQ
TEHRĀN
Eşfahān
IRAN
LEB.
Damascus
Tel Aviv -Jaffa
Jerusalem
ISRAEL
JORDAN
Syrian Desert
Basra
KUWAIT
The Gulf
BAHRAIN
QATAR
Rabat
Tétouan
Casablanca
Fès
MOROCCO
Marrakesh
ALGERIA
In Salah
LIBYA
Marzūq
Al Jawf
Alexandria
Port Said
CAIRO
Suez
El Faiyûm
Nile
Asyût
EGYPT
Aswân
Red Sea
SAUDI ARABIA
Riyadh
Medina
Jedda
Mecca
El Aaiún
WESTERN SAHARA
Dakhla
Fdérik
Tropic of Cancer
Sahara
Ras Nouâdhibou
MAURITANIA
Nouakchott
St-Louis
Senegal
C. Vert
Dakar
SENEGAL
GAMBIA
Banjul
GUINEA-BISSAU
Bissau
Tombouctou
MALI
Bamako
Niger
Niamey
NIGER
Agades
CHAD
L. Chad
Abéché
Ndjamena
Chari
Wadi Halfa
Port Sudan
Atbara
Omdurmân
Khartoum
Wâd Medani
SUDAN
El Fâsher
El Obeid
White Nile
Blue Nile
Malakâl
Wau
Bahr el Jebel
ERITREA
Asmera
Mesewa
YEMEN
G. of Aden
Socotra (Yemen)
DJIBOUTI
Djibouti
Ras Asir
Berbera
L. Tana
Addis Ababa
Harer
ETHIOPIA
Shaballe
SOMALI REP.
Mogadishu
GUINEA
Conakry
SIERRA LEONE
Freetown
Monrovia
LIBERIA
BURKINA FASO
Ouagadougou
Bobo-Dioulasso
IVORY COAST
Yamoussoukro
Bouaké
Abidjan
GHANA
Kumasi
Sekondi-Takoradi
Accra
TOGO
Lomé
BENIN
Porto Novo
NIGERIA
Abuja
Kano
Maiduguri
Benue
Ibadan
Lagos
Enugu
Port Harcourt
Bight of Benin
Gulf of Guinea
CAMEROON
Douala
Yaoundé
Malabo
EQUATORIAL GUINEA
SÃO TOMÉ & PRINCIPE
Annobón
Equator
CENTRAL AFRICAN REP.
Bangui
Oubangui
Congo (Zaire)
Mbandaka
Libreville
C. Lopez
GABON
CONGO
Kisangani
L. Albert
UGANDA
Kampala
KENYA
Kisumu
Nairobi
Tana
Juba
Kismayu
L. Turkana
L. Edward
Lualaba
L. Kivu
RWANDA
Kigali
BURUNDI
Bujumbura
L. Victoria
Mombasa
CONGO (DEM. REP. OF THE)
Brazzaville
Kinshasa
Pointe-Noire
CABINDA (Angola)
Matadi
Kasai
Kananga
Cuango
TANZANIA
Dodoma
Zanzibar
Dar es Salaam
L. Tanganyika
INDIAN OCEAN
SEYCHELLES
Aldabra Is.
Luanda
ANGOLA
Huambo
Lobito
Namibe
Cunene
Cubango
C. Fria
L. Mweru
Likasi
Lubumbashi
Ndola
ZAMBIA
Lusaka
Lilongwe
MALAWI
L. Malawi
Zambezi
Blantyre
MOZAMBIQUE
Moçambique
C. Delgado
Moroni
COMOROS
Mamoudzou
Mayotte (Fr.)
Antsiranana
Mozambique Channel
Mahajanga
Toamasina
Antananarivo
MADAGASCAR
Fianarantsoa
Livingstone
Harare
ZIMBABWE
Bulawayo
Beira
Limpopo
NAMIBIA
Windhoek
BOTSWANA
Gaborone
Pretoria
Johannesburg
Maputo
Mbabane
SWAZ.
Vaal
Orange
Kimberley
Maseru
LESOTHO
Durban
SOUTH AFRICA
East London
Port Elizabeth
Cape Town
C. of Good Hope
C. Agulhas
MAURITIUS
St-Denis
Port Louis
Réunion (Fr.)
Tropic of Capricorn
Ascension I. (U.K.)
SOUTH ATLANTIC OCEAN
St. Helena (U.K.)
Tristan da Cunha (U.K.)
Projection: Azimuthal Equidistant
West from Greenwich
East from Greenwich
Dakar Capital Cities
COPYRIGHT GEORGE PHILIP LTD.
km
miles

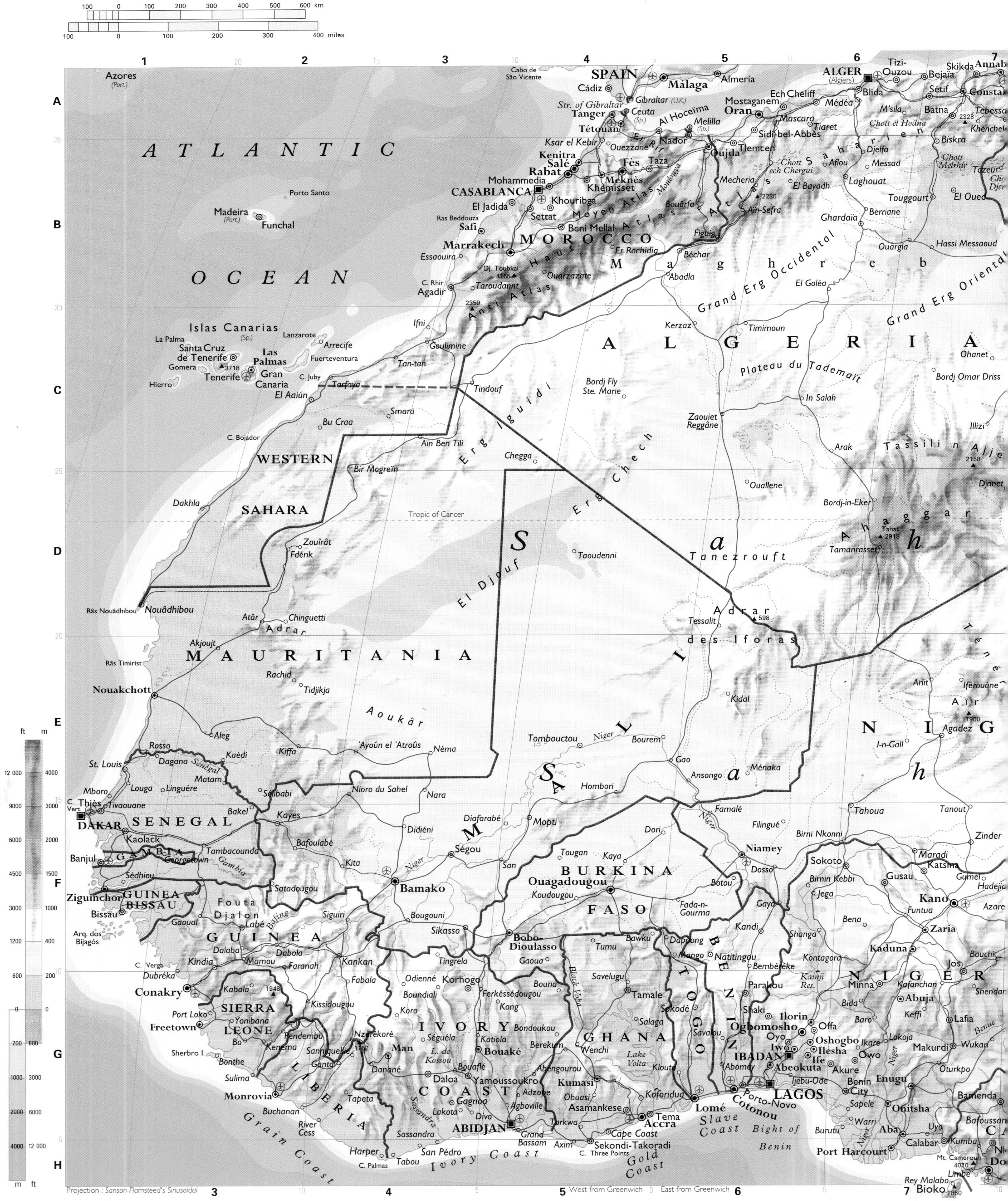

100 0 100 200 300 400 500 600 km
100 0 100 200 300 400 miles
ATLANTIC OCEAN
Azores (Port.)
Madeira (Port.)
Porto Santo
Funchal
Islas Canarias (Sp.)
La Palma
Santa Cruz de Tenerife
Gomera
Tenerife
3718
Hierro
Las Palmas
Gran Canaria
Lanzarote
Arrecife
Fuerteventura
C. Juby
Tarfaya
El Aaiún
SPAIN
Cabo de São Vicente
Cádiz
Málaga
Almería
Str. of Gibraltar
Gibraltar (U.K.)
Ceuta (Sp.)
Tanger
Tétouan
Al Hoceïma
Melilla (Sp.)
Nador
Ksar el Kebir
Ouezzane
Er Rif
Kenitra
Salé
Rabat
Fès
Taza
Oujda
Meknès
Khemisset
Mohammedia
CASABLANCA
Khouribga
El Jadida
Settat
Moyen Atlas
Moulouya
Beni Mellal
Bouârfa
Ras Beddouza
Safi
MOROCCO
Haut Atlas
Figuig
Marrakech
Essaouira
Er Rachidia
Béchar
Dj. Toubkal 4165
Ouarzazate
Abadla
C. Rhir
Agadir
Taroudannt
Anti Atlas
2359
Ifni
Goulimine
Tan-tan
Tindouf
Smara
Bu Craa
C. Bojador
Aïn Ben Tili
WESTERN SAHARA
Bir Mogreïn
Dakhla
Tropic of Cancer
Zouîrât
Fdérik
Râs Nouâdhibou
Nouâdhibou
Atâr
Chinguetti
Adrar
Akjoujt
Râs Timirist
MAURITANIA
Rachid
Tidjikja
Nouakchott
Aoukâr
Aleg
Rosso
Kaédi
Kiffa
'Ayoûn el 'Atroûs
Néma
St. Louis
Dagana
Senegal
Matam
Louga
Linguère
Mboro
Sélibabi
Nioro du Sahel
Nara
C. Vert
Thiès
Tivaouane
Bakel
DAKAR
SENEGAL
Kayes
Diafarabé
Kaolack
Didiéni
Bafoulabé
Banjul
GAMBIA
Georgetown
Tambacounda
Gambia
Kita
Ségou
Sédhiou
Ziguinchor
GUINEA-BISSAU
Satadougou
Bamako
Bissau
Fouta Djalon
Labé
Bafing
Siguiri
Gaoual
Bougouni
Arq. dos Bijagós
GUINEA
Dalaba
Dabola
Sikasso
Kindia
Mamou
Faranah
Kankan
C. Verga
Dubréka
Fabala
Conakry
Kabala
1948
SIERRA LEONE
Kissidougou
Port Loko
Yonibana
Freetown
Pendembu
Bo
Kenema
Nzérékoré
Sherbro I.
Sanniquellie
1752
Ganta
Bonthe
Sulima
LIBERIA
Monrovia
Tapeta
Buchanan
River Cess
Grain Coast
Harper
C. Palmas
Tabou
Ivory Coast
Odienné
Korhogo
Boundiali
Ferkéssédougou
Kong
Koro
IVORY COAST
Séguéla
Katiola
Bondoukou
Man
L. de Kossou
Bouaké
Danané
Bouaflé
Yamoussoukro
Daloa
Abengourou
Gagnoa
Adzopé
Agboville
Sassandra
Lakota
Divo
ABIDJAN
Grand Bassam
San Pédro
Tingréla
Bobo-Dioulasso
Gaoua
Bouna
Black Volta
ALGER (Algiers)
Blida
Tizi-Ouzou
Bejaïa
Skikda
Annaba
Sétif
Constantine
Médéa
Ech Cheliff
Mostaganem
Oran
Mascara
Tiaret
Sidi-bel-Abbès
Tlemcen
M'sila
Batna
Tebessa
Chott el Hodna
2328
Khenchela
Biskra
Djelfa
Chott Melrhir
Tozeur
Saharien
Aflou
Messad
Chott ech Chergui
Mecheria
El Bayadh
Laghouat
2235
Aïn-Sefra
Touggourt
El Oued
Berriane
Ghardaïa
Ouargla
Hassi Messaoud
Maghreb
Grand Erg Occidental
Grand Erg Oriental
El Goléa
Kerzaz
Timimoun
ALGERIA
Ohanet
Plateau du Tademaït
Bordj Omar Driss
Bordj Fly Ste. Marie
In Salah
Erg Iguidi
Zaouiet Reggâne
Illizi
Chegga
Arak
Tassili n Ajjer
2158
Erg Chech
Djanet
Ouallene
Bordj-in-Eker
Ahaggar
Tahat 2918
Tamanrasset
Sahara
Taoudenni
Tanezrouft
El Djouf
Adrar des Iforas
Tessalit
598
Ténéré
MALI
Arlit
Iférouâne
Kidal
Aïr
1900
Agadez
NIGER
Tombouctou
Niger
Bourem
I-n-Gall
Gao
Ansongo
Ménaka
Sahel
Hombori
Famalé
Tahoua
Tanout
Mopti
Dori
Filingué
Birni Nkonni
Zinder
Niamey
Maradi
Sokoto
Katsina
Tougan
Kaya
San
BURKINA FASO
Dosso
Birnin Kebbi
Gusau
Gumel
Hadejia
Ouagadougou
Botou
Koudougou
Jega
Fada-n-Gourma
Gaya
Kano
Funtua
Azare
Bena
Kandi
Zaria
Shanga
Tumu
Bawku
Dapaong
Kaduna
Mango
Natitingou
Kontagora
Bauchi
Bembéréké
Jos
Kainji Res.
Savelugu
Tamale
Parakou
Minna
Kafanchan
Shendam
TOGO
BENIN
NIGERIA
Sokodé
Salaga
Bida
Abuja
Shaki
Ilorin
Baro
Keffi
Lafia
Benue
GHANA
Savalou
Ogbomosho
Offa
Oyo
Oshogbo
Lokoja
Ikare
Makurdi
Wukari
Wenchi
Lake Volta
Iwo
Ilesha
Owo
Berekum
IBADAN
Ife
Kumasi
Kloute
Abomey
Abeokuta
Akure
Otukpo
Obuasi
Koforidua
Ijebu-Ode
Benin City
Enugu
Asamankese
LAGOS
Porto-Novo
Cotonou
Sapele
Onitsha
Bamenda
Lomé
Tema
Accra
Tarkwa
Cape Coast
Slave Coast
Bight of Benin
Warri
Bafoussam
Axim
Sekondi-Takoradi
C. Three Points
Gold Coast
Burutu
Aba
Uyo
Calabar
Kumba
Port Harcourt
Mt. Cameroun 4070
Limbe
Rey Malabo
Bioko
2850
ft m
12 000 4000
9000 3000
6000 2000
4500 1500
3000 1000
1200 400
600 200
0 0
200 600
1000 3000
2000 6000
4000 12 000
m ft
Projection : Sanson-Flamsteed's Sinusoidal
West from Greenwich
East from Greenwich

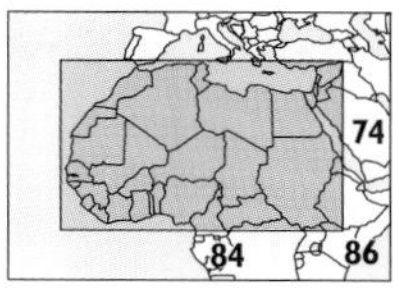
74
84
86

MEDITERRANEAN SEA
GREECE
TURKEY
CYPRUS
SYRIA
LEBANON
ISRAEL
IRAQ
JORDAN
SAUDI ARABIA
LIBYA
EGYPT
SUDAN
CHAD
CENTRAL AFRICAN REPUBLIC
ETHIOPIA
ERITREA
RED SEA
MALTA
Sicilia
Kríti
Iráklion
Ródhos
Antalya
ADANA
Antakya
HALAB
Al Lādhiqiyah
Nicosia
Ḩimş
Ṭarābulus
BAYRŪT
(Beirut)
DIMASHQ
(Damascus)
Tel Aviv-Yafo
Ashdod
Haifa
Jerusalem
West Bank
'AMMĀN
Ma'ān
Al 'Aqabah
Elat
Bizerte
TUNIS
CARTHAGE
Ariana
Béja
Nabeul
Sousse
Mahdia
Sfax
Golfe de Gabès
Île de Djerba
Zarzis
Médenine
Dehibat
Ghudāmis
Ṭarābulus (Tripoli)
Zuwārah
Az Zāwiyah
Al Khums
Misrātah
Gharyān
968
Mizdah
Tripolitania
Daraj
Surt
Khalij Surt
Banghāzī
Al Marj
Ẕāwiyat al Bayḍā
Darnah
Tubruq
Bardīyah
Suluq
Ajdābiyā
Cyrenaica
Al Jaghbūb
Awjilah
Hūn
Zillah
Idehan Awbārī
Brach
Sabhah
Awbārī
Marzūq
Fezzan
Ghat
Al Qaṭrūn
Wāw al Kabīr
Sahrâ' Rebiana
Al Kufrah
Al Jawf
Sahrâ' Lîbîya
1200
EL ISKANDARÎYA
(Alexandria)
Salûm
Marsâ Matrûh
El Alamein
Munkhafed el Qattâra
-133
Sîwa
Damanhûr
El Mahalla el Kubra
Dumyât
Bûr Sa'îd
El Mansûra
Tanta
Zagazig
Isma'iliya
EL GÎZA
EL QÂHIRA
(Cairo)
El Suweis
Helwân
El Faiyûm
Beni Suef
Maghâgha
El Minyâ
Mallawi
Manfalût
Asyût
Tahta
Sohâg
Girga
Qena
THEBES
KARNAK
El Uqsur
Qasr Farâfra
Mût
El Wâhât el-Dakhla
El Khârga
El Wâhât el-Khârga
Idfû
Kom Ombo
Sadd el Aali
Aswân
Buheirat en Naser
ABU SIMBEL
Es Sahrâ Esh Sharqîya
Nahr en Nîl
Khalîg el Suweis
Es Sinâ'
G. Mûsa 2637
Hurghada
2187
Bûr Safâga
Quseir
Ras Bânâs
Bîr Shalatein
Halaib
Ras Hadarba
Muhammad Qol
2259
Bûr Sûdân
Suakin
Trinkitat
Sinkat
Haiya
Karora
2760
Nakfa
Akordat
Kassalâ
Tabūk
2578
Al Muwayliḩ
Al Wajh
Yanbu 'al Bahr
Rābigh
Ḩijāz
Al Jawf
Ar Ruţbah
Bādiyat ash Shām
Jabal ad Durūz
1801
Nahr al Furāt
J. Uweinat 1893
1082
Wadi Halfa
El Wâhât el Selîma
Es Sahrâ en Nûbîya
Kosha
Delgo
3rd Cataract
Dongola
Abu Hamed
4th Cataract
5th Cataract
Kareima
Ed Debba
Berber
Atbara
Adarama
Nahr Atbara
Bir 'Atrun
Wad Hamid
Shendî
6th Cataract
Omdurmân
El Khartûm
(Khartoum)
El Wuz
Sodiri
Khashm el Girba
Gezira
Wâd Medanî
Gedaref
Ed Dueim
Umm Keddada
El Fâsher
El Obeid
Kôstî
Umm Ruwaba
Er Rahad
En Nahud
Abu Zabad
El Odaiya
Kordofân
1325
Kâdugli
Singa
Nîl el Azraq
Nîl el Abyad
Ed Damazin
Malha
1954
Kutum
Jebel Mara 3088
Nyâlâ
Dârfûr
Zalingei
Al Junaynah
Bahr el Arab
Sa'id Bundas
Raga
Bahr el Ghazâl
Gogriâl
Wâw
Tonj
Rumbêk
Bahr el Jebel
Sobat
Malakâl
Sudd
Bôr
Pibor Post
Toinya
Amadi
Tali Post
El Istiwa'iya
Mongalla
Kapoeta
Juba
Yei
Kajo Kaji
Torit
3187
Lokitaung
L. Turkana
Chew Bahir
L. Abaya
Arba Minch
L. Shamo
Omo
3686
Jima
Gore
Metu
Dembidolo
3202
Nekemte
Debre Markos
Bure
Bahir Dar
L. Tana
1830
Gonder
Aozou Strip
Toummo
Madama
Bardai
Aozou
Pic Toussidé 3265
3150 Tarso Emissi
Tibesti
Zouar
Emi Koussi 3415
Ma'tan as Sarra
Chirfa
Bilma
Grand Erg du Bilma
Fachi
Borkou
Ounianga Sérir
Dépression du Mourdi
Faya-Largeau
Fada
Ennedi
1310
Erg du Djourab
Zagaoua
Oum Chalouba
Biltine
Abéché
Zigey
Bahr el Ghazal
Mao
Lac Tchad
Nguigmi
Bosso
Moussoro
Ati
Oum Hadjer
Massakory
Gashua
Geidam
Maiduguri
Ndjamena
Kousseri
Bokoro
Mongo
Goz Beïda
Potiskum
Massenya
Abou-Deïa
Bama
Chari
Am Timan
Bajoga
Maroua
Bongor
Kumo
Biu
Mubi
Guider
Numan
Garoua
Yola
Logone
Laï
Pala
Moundou
Sarh
Koumra
Doba
Ndélé
Biraro
1256
Songo
Baïbokoum
Gashaka
Ngaoundéré
Banyo
Paoua
Kaga Bandoro
Bossangoa
Bozoum
Bouar
Bétaré Oya
Yoko
Foumban
Carnot
Bossembélé
Berbérati
Batouri
Bertoua
Nanga-Eboko
Abong-Mbang
Yaoundé
Bangui
Mbaïki
Zongo
Libenge
Bosobolo
Mobaye
Mobayi
Oubangi
Bangassou
Bomu
Bondo
Ango
Uele
Dungu
Faradje
Yambio
Obo
Sibut
Bambari
Ippy
Bakouma
Yalinga
Ouham
Sanaga
Fezzan
Niger
Ghazâl
COPYRIGHT GEORGE PHILIP LTD.

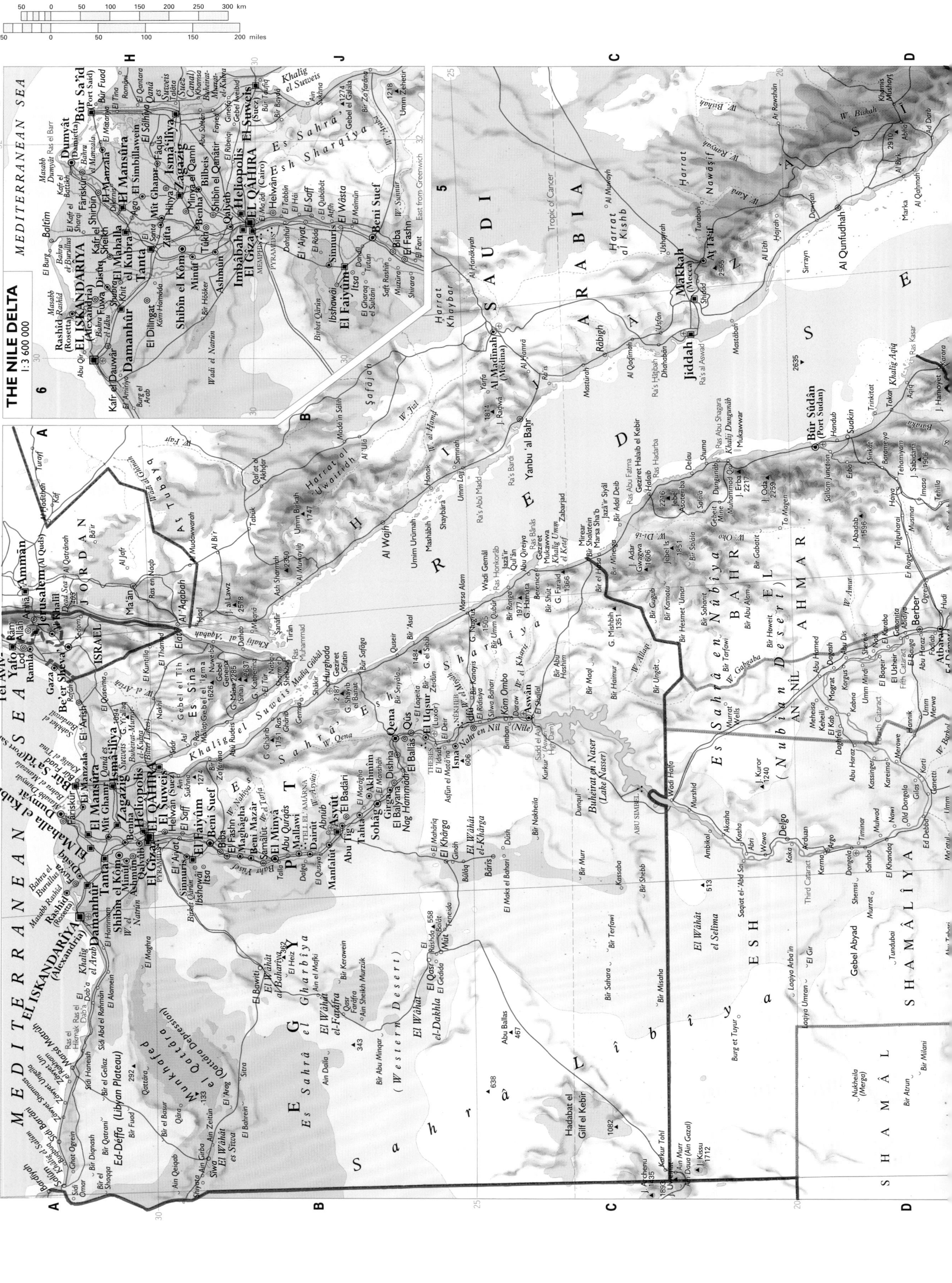

THE NILE DELTA
1:3 600 000
MEDITERRANEAN SEA
MEDITERRANEAN SEA
EL ISKANDARÎYA (Alexandria)
Bûr Sa'îd (Port Said)
Dumyât (Damietta)
EL QÂHIRA (Cairo)
El Gîza
El Suweis (Suez)
Heliopolis
Tanta
El Mansûra
Zagazig
Ismâ'ilîya
El Faiyûm
Beni Suef
Damanhûr
E G Y P T
Es Sahrâ el Gharbîya (Western Desert)
Es Sahrâ esh Sharqîya
Qena
El Uqsur (Luxor)
Aswân
Asyût
Sohâg
El Minya
Buheirat en Naser (Lake Nasser)
Wadi Halfa
Tel Aviv-Yafo
Jerusalem
'Ammân
ISRAEL
JORDAN
Al 'Aqabah
S A U D I   A R A B I A
Al Madinah (Medina)
Makkah (Mecca)
Jiddah
Yanbu 'al Bahr
Bûr Sûdân (Port Sudan)
Tropic of Cancer
Munkhafad el Qattâra (Qattara Depression)
Ed-Dêffa (Libyan Plateau)
Siwa
Es Sahrâ en Nûbîya
BAHR EL AHMAR
Sahrâ Lîbîya
ESH SHAMÂLÎYA
Berber
Atbara
Marsa Matruh
50 0 50 100 150 200 250 300 km
50 0 50 100 150 200 miles

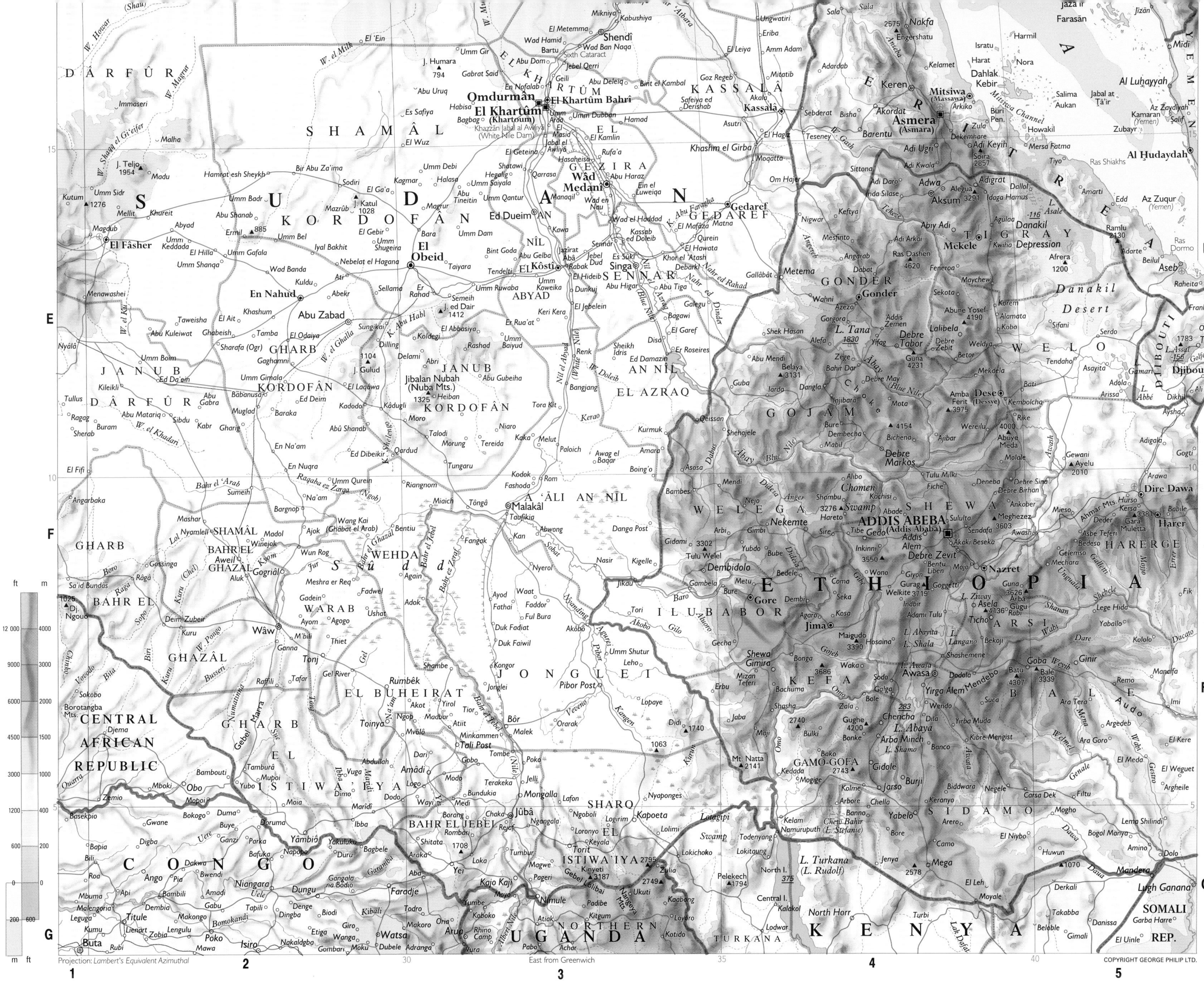

SUDAN
ETHIOPIA
ERITREA
DJIBOUTI
KENYA
UGANDA
CENTRAL AFRICAN REPUBLIC
CONGO
SOMALI REP.
YEMEN
DÂRFÛR
SHAMÂL
KORDOFÂN
KHARTÛM
KASSALÂ
GEZIRA
GEDAREF
SENNAR
ABYAD
JANUB KORDOFÂN
GHARB KORDOFÂN
JANUB DÂRFÛR
AN NÎL EL AZRAQ
A'ÂLI AN NÎL
WEHDA
SÛDD
JONGLEI
EL BUHEIRAT
WARAB
BAHR EL GHAZÂL
GHARB EL ISTIWA'IYA
SHARQ EL ISTIWA'IYA
BAHR EL JEBEL
TIGRAY
GONDER
GOJAM
WELO
SHEWA
WELEGA
ILUBABOR
KEFA
GAMO-GOFA
SIDAMO
BALE
ARSI
HARERGE
Danakil Desert
L. Tana
L. Turkana (L. Rudolf)
Projection: Lambert's Equivalent Azimuthal
East from Greenwich
COPYRIGHT GEORGE PHILIP LTD.
ft
m
12 000
9000
6000
4500
3000
1200
600
0
200
4000
3000
2000
1500
1000
400
200
0
600

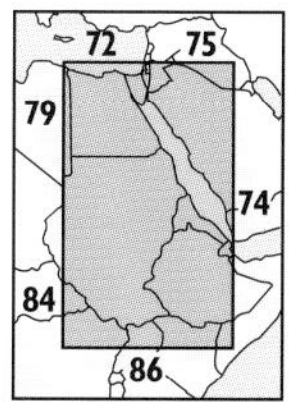

72
75
79
74
84
86

50 0 50 100 150 200 250 300 km
50 0 50 100 150 200 miles
MAURITANIA
Nouakchott
Trarza
Tagânt
Aoukâr
El Mreyyé
Tidjikja
Akjoujt
Boutilimit
Aleg
Kiffa
Néma
Timbedgha
Ayoûn el 'Akroûs
Oualâta
Kaédi
Rosso
Podor
St. Louis
Louga
Thiès
DAKAR
Rufisque
Diourbel
SENEGAL
Kaolack
Tambacounda
Kayes
Ziguinchor
Banjul
GAMBIA
GUINEA-BISSAU
Bissau
Arquipélago dos Bijagós
Bafatá
Boké
Fouta Djalon
Labé
Kindia
Conakry
Îles de Los
GUINEA
Kankan
Siguiri
Kouroussa
Faranah
Kissidougou
Guékédou
Macenta
Nzérékoré
SIERRA LEONE
Freetown
Makeni
Bo
Kenema
Bonthe
Sherbro I.
LIBERIA
Monrovia
Buchanan
Greenville
Harper
Cape Palmas
Grain Coast
MALI
Bamako
Ségou
Mopti
Djenné
Sikasso
Koutiala
Nioro du Sahel
Tombouctou (Timbuktu)
Goundam
Niafounké
Macina
Kita
IVORY COAST
Abidjan
Yamoussoukro
Bouaké
Korhogo
Daloa
Man
Odienné
Séguéla
Katiola
Gagnoa
Divo
Dabou
Grand Bassam
San Pédro
Sassandra
Tabou
Ivory Coast
Bobo-Dioulasso
Banfora
ATLANTIC OCEAN
GULF
Projection : Lambert's Equivalent Azimuthal
West from Greenwich
ft m
12 000 4000
9000 3000
6000 2000
4500 1500
3000 1000
1200 400
600 200
0 0
200 600
2000 6000
4000 12 000
6000 18 000
m ft

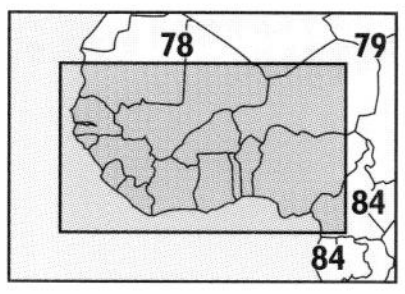
78
79
84
84

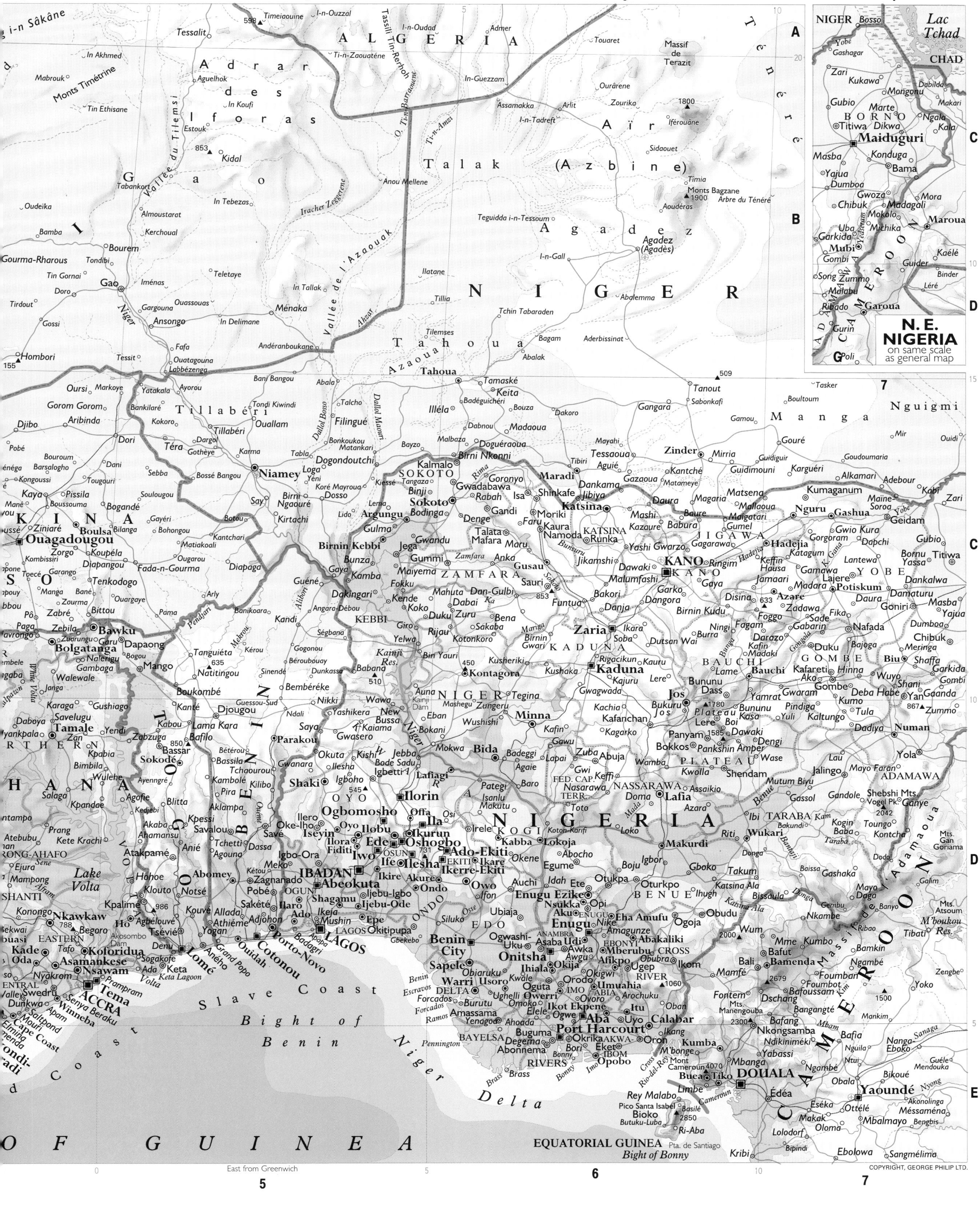
4
5
6
7
A
B
C
D
E
ALGERIA
NIGER
NIGERIA
BENIN
TOGO
GHANA
CAMEROON
CHAD
EQUATORIAL GUINEA
Adrar des Iforas
Aïr
Talak (Azbine)
Agadez
Ténéré
Tillabéri
Tahoua
Manga
Niamey
Agadez (Agadès)
Tahoua
Zinder
Maradi
Nguigmi
Sokoto
Katsina
KANO
Kaduna
Zaria
Jos
Bauchi
Maiduguri
Ouagadougou
Tamale
Kumasi
ACCRA
Tema
Lomé
Cotonou
Porto-Novo
LAGOS
IBADAN
Abeokuta
Ilorin
Ogbomosho
Oshogbo
Benin City
Onitsha
Enugu
Port Harcourt
Calabar
DOUALA
Yaoundé
Makurdi
Minna
Kontagora
Lake Volta
Kainji Res.
Lac Tchad
Slave Coast
Bight of Benin
Niger Delta
Bight of Bonny
GULF OF GUINEA
N.E. NIGERIA
on same scale
as general map
East from Greenwich
COPYRIGHT, GEORGE PHILIP LTD.

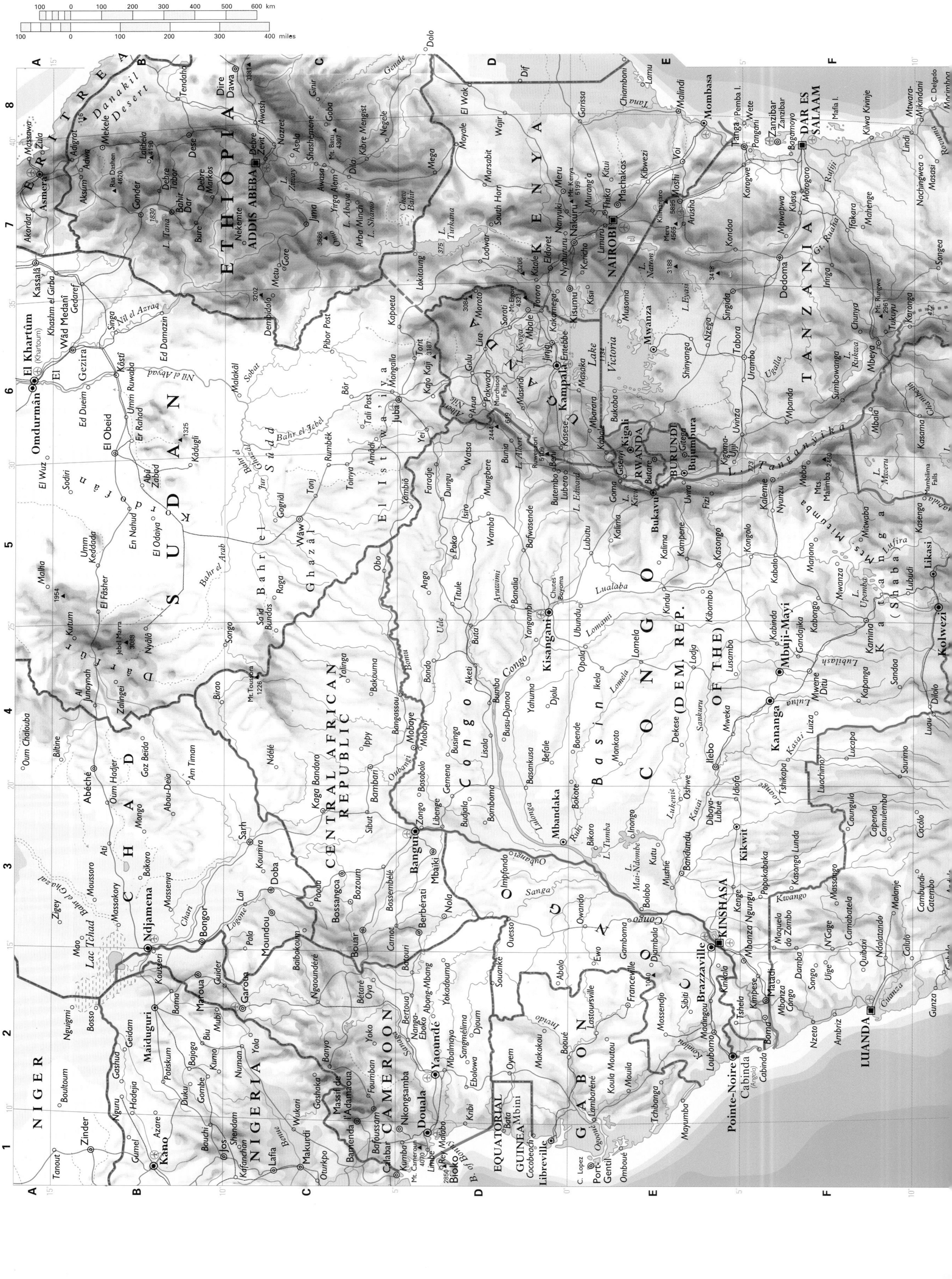
100 0 100 200 300 400 500 600 km
100 0 100 200 300 400 miles
ETHIOPIA
ADDIS ABEBA
ERITREA
Asmera
SUDAN
El Khartûm
Omdurmân
KENYA
NAIROBI
Mombasa
UGANDA
Kampala
TANZANIA
DAR ES SALAAM
Dodoma
RWANDA
Kigali
BURUNDI
Bujumbura
CONGO (DEM. REP. OF THE)
KINSHASA
Kisangani
Lubumbashi
CONGO
Brazzaville
Pointe-Noire
GABON
Libreville
EQUATORIAL GUINEA
CAMEROON
Yaoundé
Douala
CENTRAL AFRICAN REPUBLIC
Bangui
CHAD
Ndjamena
Lac Tchad
NIGERIA
NIGER
LUANDA
Cabinda
Lake Victoria
L. Tanganyika
Congo Basin
Bioko
Lake Kivu
Kolwezi
Mbuji-Mayi
Kananga

MADAGASCAR
On same scale as General Map
INDIAN OCEAN
ATLANTIC OCEAN
SOUTH AFRICA
BOTSWANA
NAMIBIA
ZIMBABWE
ZAMBIA
LESOTHO
SWAZILAND
Kalahari
Namib Desert
Skeleton Coast
Tropic of Capricorn
East from Greenwich
JOHANNESBURG
PRETORIA
CAPE TOWN
DURBAN
MAPUTO
HARARE
Lusaka
Bulawayo
Windhoek
Gaborone
Bloemfontein
Maseru
Port Elizabeth
East London
Kimberley
Beira
Antananarivo
Toamasina
Mahajanga
Fianarantsoa
Toliara
Taolanaro
Antsiranana
Livingstone
Victoria Falls
Walvis Bay
Swakopmund
Lüderitz
Projection : Sanson-Flamsteed's Sinusoidal
COPYRIGHT GEORGE PHILIP LTD.

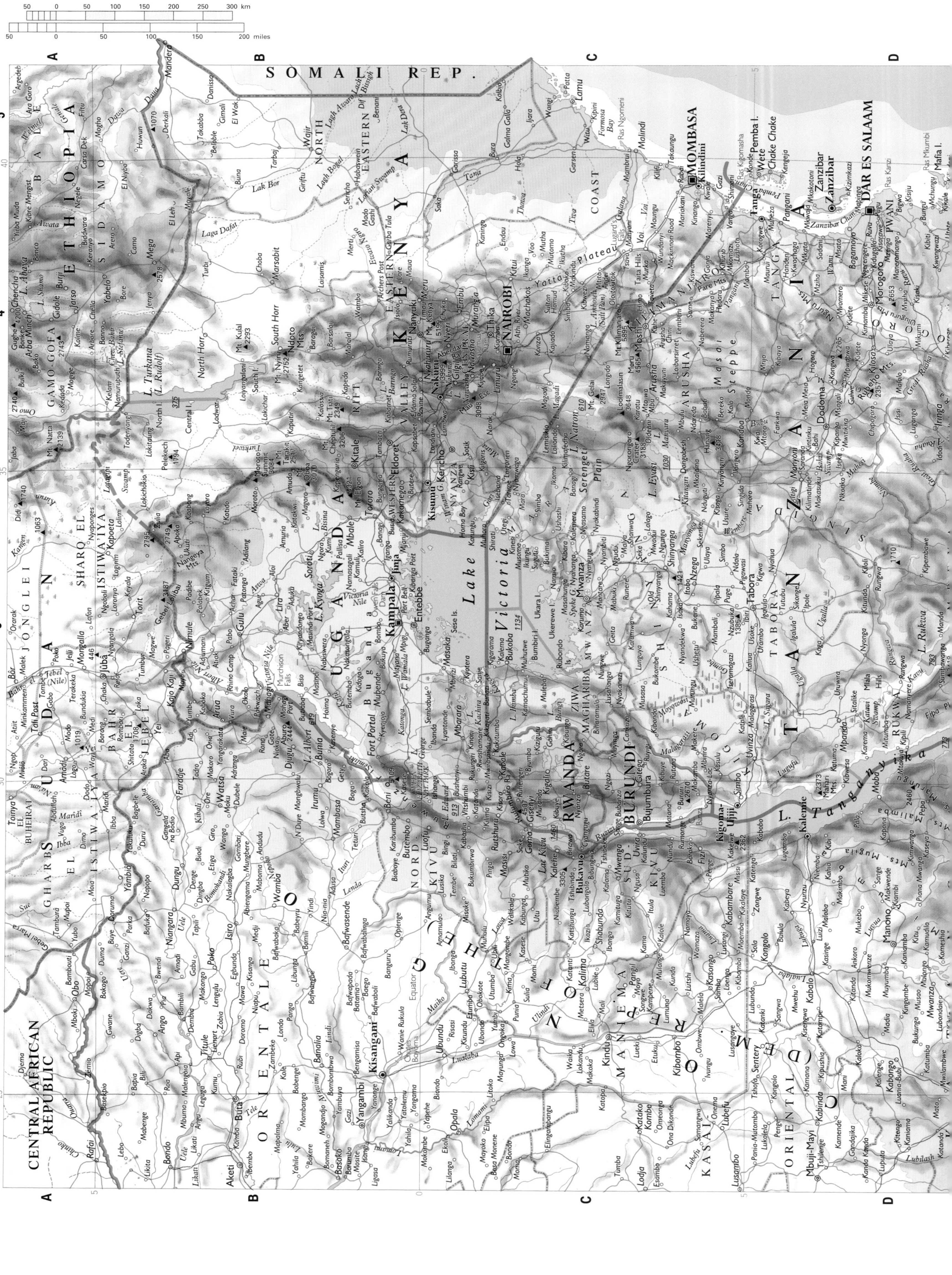
50 0 50 100 150 200 250 300 km
50 0 50 100 150 200 miles
SOMALI REP.
ETHIOPIA
KENYA
UGANDA
TANZANIA
RWANDA
BURUNDI
CENTRAL AFRICAN REPUBLIC
NAIROBI
MOMBASA
DAR ES SALAAM
Kampala
Kisangani
Zanzibar
Lake Victoria

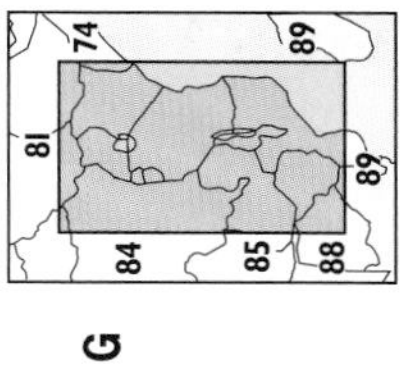
74
81
84
85
88
89
89

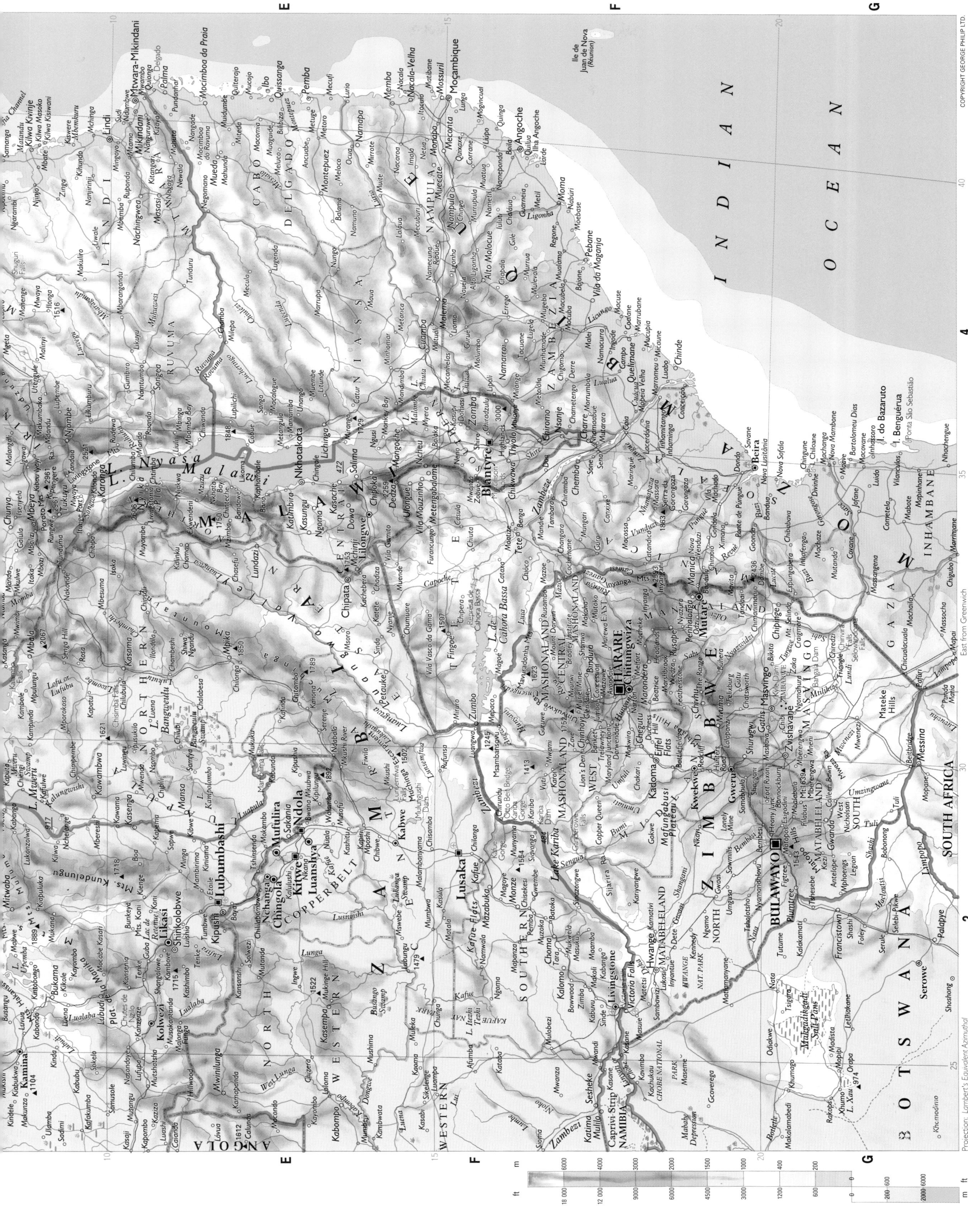
ZAMBIA
MALAWI
MOZAMBIQUE
ZIMBABWE
BOTSWANA
ANGOLA
NAMIBIA
SOUTH AFRICA
INDIAN OCEAN
L. Nyasa
Lake Kariba
Lusaka
HARARE
BULAWAYO
Blantyre
Lilongwe
Beira
Lubumbashi
Ndola
Kitwe
Kabwe
Livingstone
Victoria Falls
Tete
Quelimane
Nampula
Moçambique
Lindi
Mtwara-Mikindani
Gweru
Mutare
Masvingo
Chipata
Zomba
Karonga
Mbeya
Kolwezi
Likasi
Kamina
Francistown
Serowe
Palapye
Messina
Projection: Lambert's Equivalent Azimuthal
East from Greenwich
COPYRIGHT GEORGE PHILIP LTD.
m 6000 4000 3000 2000 1500 1000 400 200 0
ft 18 000 12 000 9000 6000 4500 3000 1200 600 0

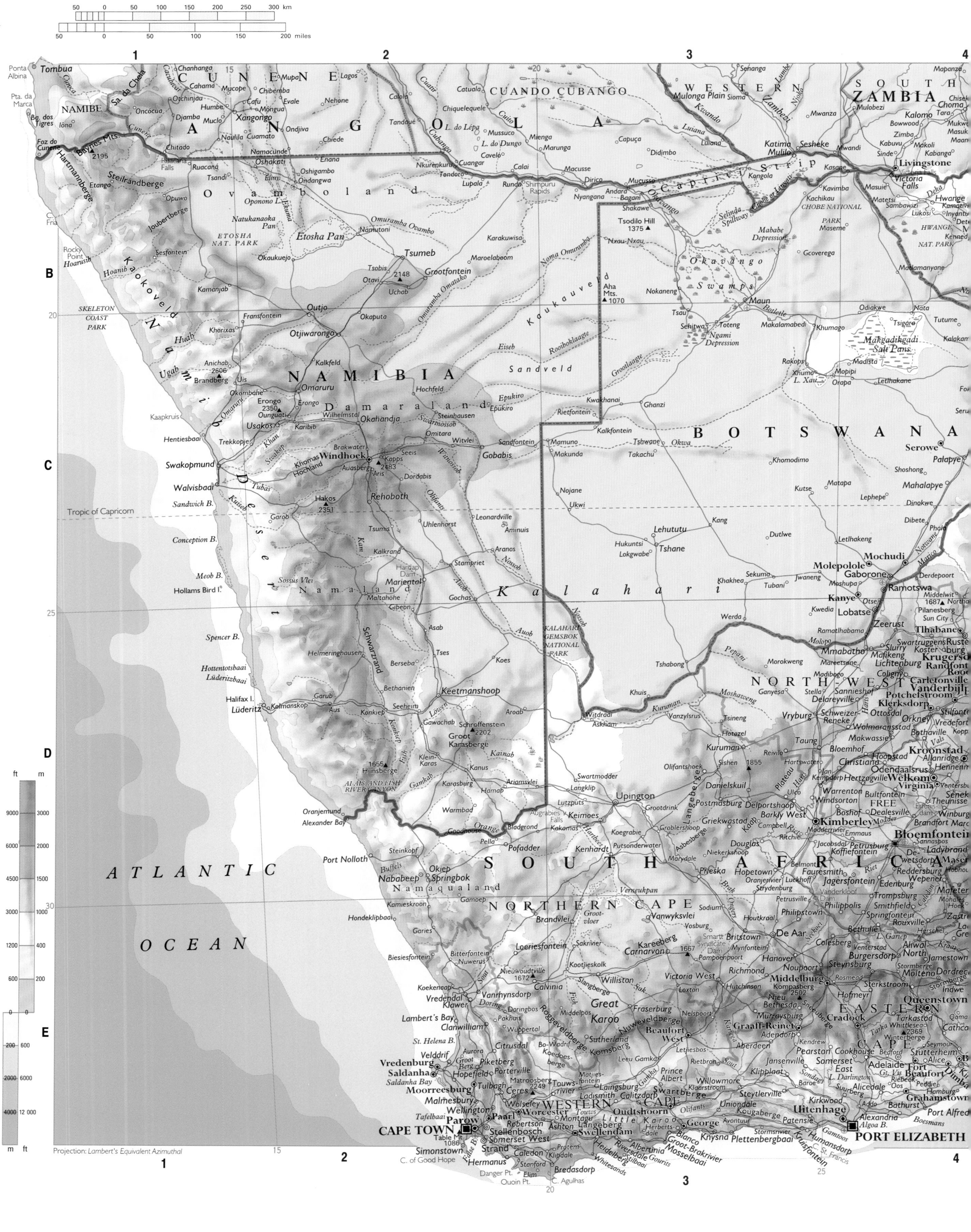

50 0 50 100 150 200 250 300 km
50 0 50 100 150 200 miles
ANGOLA
CUNENE
CUANDO CUBANGO
ZAMBIA
WESTERN
SOUTH
NAMIBIA
BOTSWANA
SOUTH AFRICA
NORTH WEST
NORTHERN CAPE
WESTERN CAPE
EASTERN CAPE
FREE
ATLANTIC OCEAN
Tropic of Capricorn
Namib Desert
Kalahari
Kaokoveld
Damaraland
Namaland
Ovamboland
Okavango Swamps
Caprivi Strip
Sandveld
Kaukauveld
Namaqualand
Great Karoo
Etosha Pan
Makgadikgadi Salt Pans
SKELETON COAST PARK
ETOSHA NAT. PARK
KALAHARI GEMSBOK NATIONAL PARK
CHOBE NATIONAL PARK
HWANGE NAT. PARK
Tombua
Namibe
Windhoek
Swakopmund
Walvisbaai
Lüderitz
Keetmanshoop
Rehoboth
Okahandja
Otjiwarongo
Outjo
Tsumeb
Grootfontein
Gobabis
Mariental
Oranjemund
Maun
Ghanzi
Serowe
Palapye
Mahalapye
Molepolole
Mochudi
Gaborone
Kanye
Lobatse
Ramotswa
Livingstone
Victoria Falls
Hwange
Kimberley
Bloemfontein
Upington
Springbok
Vryburg
Welkom
Kroonstad
De Aar
Colesberg
Beaufort West
Graaff-Reinet
Middelburg
Cradock
Queenstown
Oudtshoorn
George
Knysna
Uitenhage
Grahamstown
PORT ELIZABETH
CAPE TOWN
Parow
Stellenbosch
Paarl
Worcester
Swellendam
Hermanus
Saldanha
Vredenburg
Moorreesburg
C. of Good Hope
C. Agulhas
Projection: Lambert's Equivalent Azimuthal

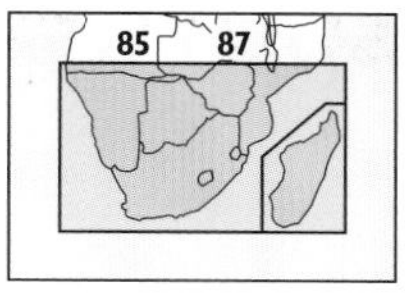
85
87

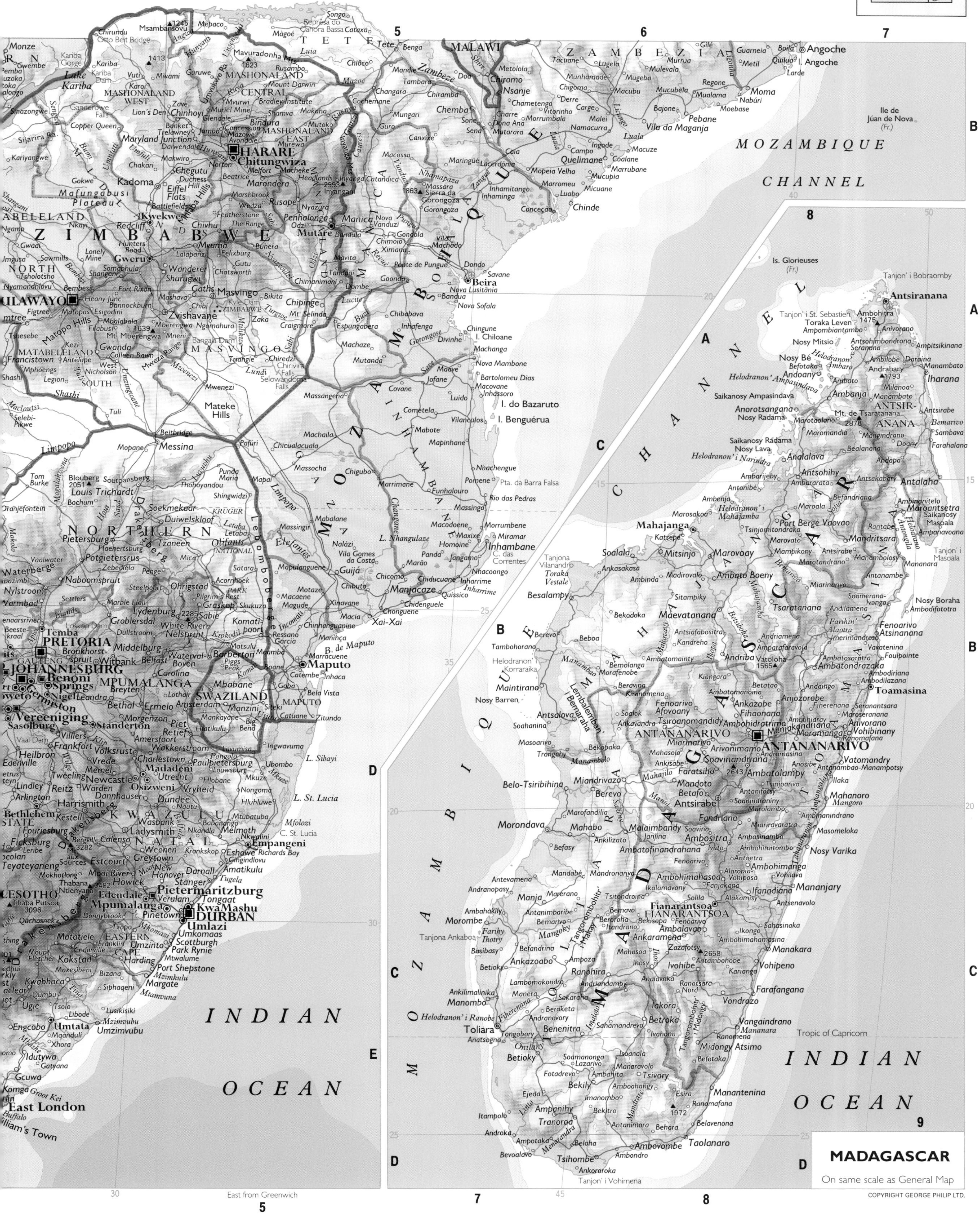
5
6
7
B
A
C
D
E
8
9
ZIMBABWE
MOZAMBIQUE
MALAWI
ZAMBEZIA
TETE
MASHONALAND CENTRAL
MASHONALAND WEST
MASHONALAND EAST
MANICA
SOFALA
MASVINGO
INHAMBANE
GAZA
MAPUTO
NORTHERN
MPUMALANGA
SWAZILAND
KWAZULU NATAL
LESOTHO
EASTERN CAPE
HARARE
Chitungwiza
Mutare
Masvingo
BULAWAYO
Gweru
Kwekwe
Kadoma
Zvishavane
Beira
Quelimane
Chinde
Angoche
I. Angoche
Moma
Pebane
Vila da Maganja
Chimoio
Manica
Dondo
Nova Sofala
I. Chiloane
Machanga
Nova Mambone
Bartolomeu Dias
I. do Bazaruto
I. Benguérua
Vilanculos
Inhambane
Maxixe
Homoine
Morrumbene
Massinga
Pomene
Pta. da Barra Falsa
Rio das Pedras
Inharrime
Quissico
Zavala
Manjacaze
Chibuto
Xai-Xai
Chonguene
Macia
Maputo
B. de Maputo
Marracuene
Catembe
Inhaca
Bela Vista
Zitundo
Messina
Beitbridge
Pafuri
Louis Trichardt
Tzaneen
Pietersburg
Potgietersrus
Nylstroom
Naboomspruit
Lydenburg
Nelspruit
Komatipoort
Barberton
PRETORIA
JOHANNESBURG
Benoni
Springs
Germiston
Vereeniging
Sasolburg
Middelburg
Witbank
Ermelo
Standerton
Piet Retief
Volksrust
Newcastle
Dundee
Ladysmith
Vryheid
Ulundi
Empangeni
Richards Bay
Stanger
Pietermaritzburg
DURBAN
KwaMashu
Umlazi
Umkomaas
Scottburgh
Port Shepstone
Margate
Kokstad
Umtata
Idutywa
East London
King William's Town
Harrismith
Bethlehem
Ficksburg
Maseru
L. St. Lucia
C. St. Lucia
L. Sibayi
Limpopo
Zambeze
Lake Kariba
Matopo Hills
Drakensberg
INDIAN OCEAN
MOZAMBIQUE CHANNEL
Ile de Júan de Nova (Fr.)
Is. Glorieuses (Fr.)
MADAGASCAR
ANTANANARIVO
Antsiranana
Tanjon' i Bobraomby
Ambohitra 1475
Nosy Bé
Ambanja
ANTSIRANANA
Mt. de Tsaratanana 2876
Sambava
Antalaha
Andapa
Mahajanga
Marovoay
Maevatanana
Soalala
Besalampy
Maintirano
Nosy Barren
Antsalova
Morondava
Mahabo
Belo-Tsiribihina
Miandrivazo
Antsirabe
Ambositra
Fianarantsoa
FIANARANTSOA
Ambalavao
Ihosy
Ranohira
Morombe
Manja
Toliara
Betioky
Ampanihy
Tranoroa
Tsihombe
Ambovombe
Taolanaro
Tanjon' i Vohimena
Tropic of Capricorn
Vangaindrano
Farafangana
Manakara
Mananjary
Nosy Varika
Mahanoro
Vatomandry
Toamasina
Fenoarivo Atsinanana
Foulpointe
Nosy Boraha
Mananara
Maroantsetra
Mandritsara
Port Bergé Vaovao
Tsaratanana
Ambatondrazaka
MADAGASCAR
On same scale as General Map
East from Greenwich
COPYRIGHT GEORGE PHILIP LTD.

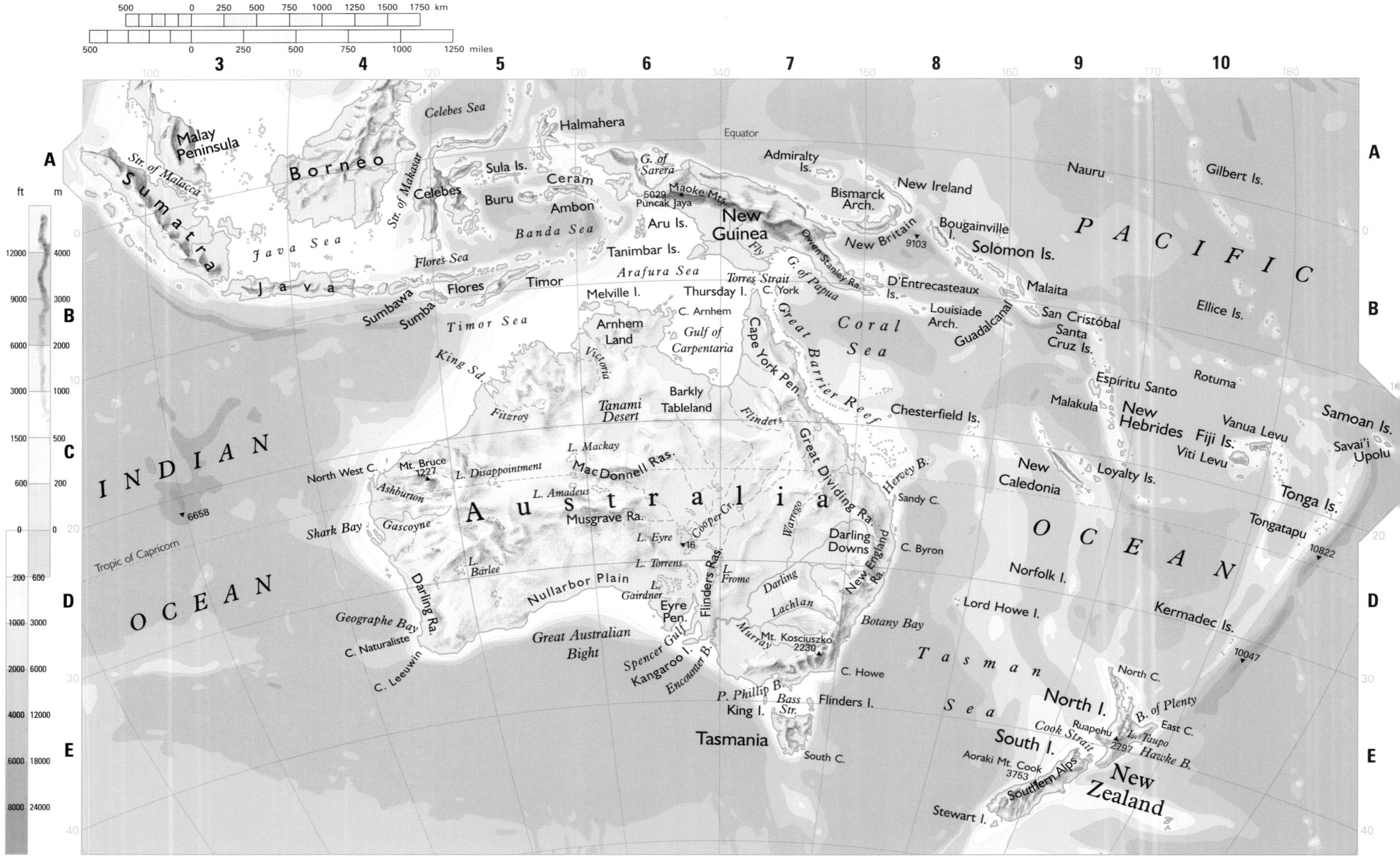
500 0 250 500 750 1000 1250 1500 1750 km
500 0 250 500 750 1000 1250 miles
ft m
12000 4000
9000 3000
6000 2000
3000 1000
1500 500
600 200
0 0
200 600
1000 3000
2000 6000
4000 12000
6000 18000
8000 24000
m ft
Malay Peninsula
Str. of Malacca
Sumatra
Borneo
Celebes Sea
Str. of Makasar
Celebes
Sula Is.
Halmahera
Ceram
Buru
Ambon
Banda Sea
Java Sea
Java
Flores Sea
Sumbawa
Sumba
Flores
Timor
Timor Sea
Equator
G. of Sarera
5029 Puncak Jaya
Maoke Mts.
Aru Is.
Tanimbar Is.
New Guinea
Fly
Owen Stanley Ra.
Admiralty Is.
Bismarck Arch.
New Ireland
New Britain
9103
Bougainville I.
Solomon Is.
Nauru
Gilbert Is.
PACIFIC
Arafura Sea
Torres Strait
C. York
G. of Papua
D'Entrecasteaux Is.
Louisiade Arch.
Malaita
Guadalcanal
San Cristóbal
Santa Cruz Is.
Ellice Is.
Melville I.
Thursday I.
C. Arnhem
Arnhem Land
Gulf of Carpentaria
Cape York Pen.
Great Barrier Reef
Coral Sea
Victoria
King Sd.
Fitzroy
Tanami Desert
Barkly Tableland
Flinders
Espíritu Santo
Rotuma
Malakula
New Hebrides
Fiji Is.
Vanua Levu
Viti Levu
Samoan Is.
Savai'i
Upolu
Chesterfield Is.
L. Mackay
L. Disappointment
MacDonnell Ras.
Mt. Bruce 1227
North West C.
Ashburton
L. Amadeus
Australia
Musgrave Ra.
Great Dividing Ra.
Hervey B.
Sandy C.
New Caledonia
Loyalty Is.
Tonga Is.
Tongatapu
10822
INDIAN
6658
Shark Bay
Gascoyne
Tropic of Capricorn
L. Eyre
Cooper Cr.
-16
Warrego
Darling Downs
C. Byron
New England Ra.
OCEAN
L. Barlee
L. Torrens
Nullarbor Plain
L. Gairdner
Flinders Ra.
L. Frome
Darling
Norfolk I.
Darling Ra.
OCEAN
Geographe Bay
C. Naturaliste
C. Leeuwin
Great Australian Bight
Eyre Pen.
Spencer Gulf
Kangaroo I.
Encounter B.
Lachlan
Murray
Mt. Kosciuszko 2230
Botany Bay
Lord Howe I.
Kermadec Is.
C. Howe
Tasman
10047
P. Phillip B.
Bass Str.
King I.
Flinders I.
Tasmania
South C.
Sea
North C.
North I.
B. of Plenty
East C.
Cook Strait
Ruapehu 2797
L. Taupo
Hawke B.
South I.
Aoraki Mt. Cook 3753
Southern Alps
New Zealand
Stewart I.
3 4 5 6 7 8 9 10
A B C D E
100 110 120 130 140 150 160 170 180
0 10 20 30 40

MALAYSIA
BRUNEI
PALAU
FEDERATED STATES OF MICRONESIA
MARSHALL IS.
Equator
Kuala Lumpur
SINGAPORE
Sumatra
Borneo
Celebes
Sula Is.
Buru
Ceram
IRIAN JAYA
PAPUA NEW GUINEA
New Ireland
Bairiki
KIRIBATI
NAURU
Ujung Pandang
INDONESIA
Java Sea
Banda Sea
Aru Is.
Tanimbar Is.
New Guinea
Madang
Lae
Fly
New Britain
Rabaul
Bougainville I.
PACIFIC
Choiseul
SOLOMON IS.
Santa Isabel
Malaita
Honiara
Guadalcanal
San Cristóbal
Santa Cruz Is.
TUVALU
Fongafale
JAKARTA
Java
Flores
Kupang
EAST TIMOR
Sumbawa
Sumba
Timor Sea
Arafura Sea
Torres Strait
Port Moresby
Darwin
Katherine
Gulf of Carpentaria
Cooktown
Cairns
CORAL SEA ISLANDS TERRITORY
Wyndham
Broome
NORTHERN TERRITORY
QUEENSLAND
Townsville
Mount Isa
Charters Towers
Espíritu Santo
VANUATU
Port Vila
Rotuma
Is. Wallis & Futuna (Fr.)
SAMOA
Apia
Chesterfield Is.
NEW CALEDONIA (Fr.)
Nouméa
Loyalty Is.
Viti Levu
Vanua Levu
Suva
FIJI
TONGA
Nuku'alofa
Dampier
Onslow
WESTERN AUSTRALIA
AUSTRALIA
Alice Springs
Longreach
Rockhampton
INDIAN
OCEAN
Wiluna
Oodnadatta
L. Eyre
SOUTH AUSTRALIA
Quilpie
Charleville
Toowoomba
Cunnamulla
Brisbane
Warwick
Tropic of Capricorn
Geraldton
Kalgoorlie-Boulder
Bourke
NEW SOUTH WALES
Norfolk I. (Aust.)
OCEAN
Perth
Fremantle
Esperance
Albany
Port Pirie
Broken Hill
Mildura
Newcastle
Sydney
A.C.T.
Canberra
Lord Howe I. (Aust.)
Kermadec Is. (N.Z.)
Great Australian Bight
Adelaide
VICTORIA
Ballarat
Geelong
Melbourne
Tasman
Sea
North I.
NEW ZEALAND
Auckland
King I.
Bass Str.
Launceston
Hobart
TASMANIA
New Plymouth
Hamilton
Napier
Wellington
South I.
Greymouth
Nelson
Christchurch
Invercargill
Dunedin
Chatham Is. (N.Z.)
International Date Line
A B C D E
0 10 20 30 40
Projection: Bonne
East from Greenwich
90 100 110 120 130 140 150 160 170
1 2 3 4 5 6 7 8 9 10 11
Canberra Capital Cities

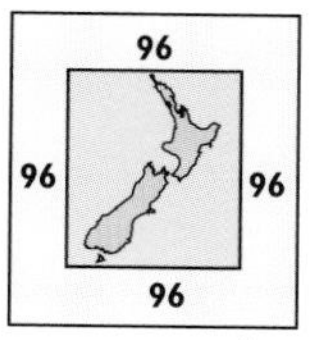
96
96
96
96

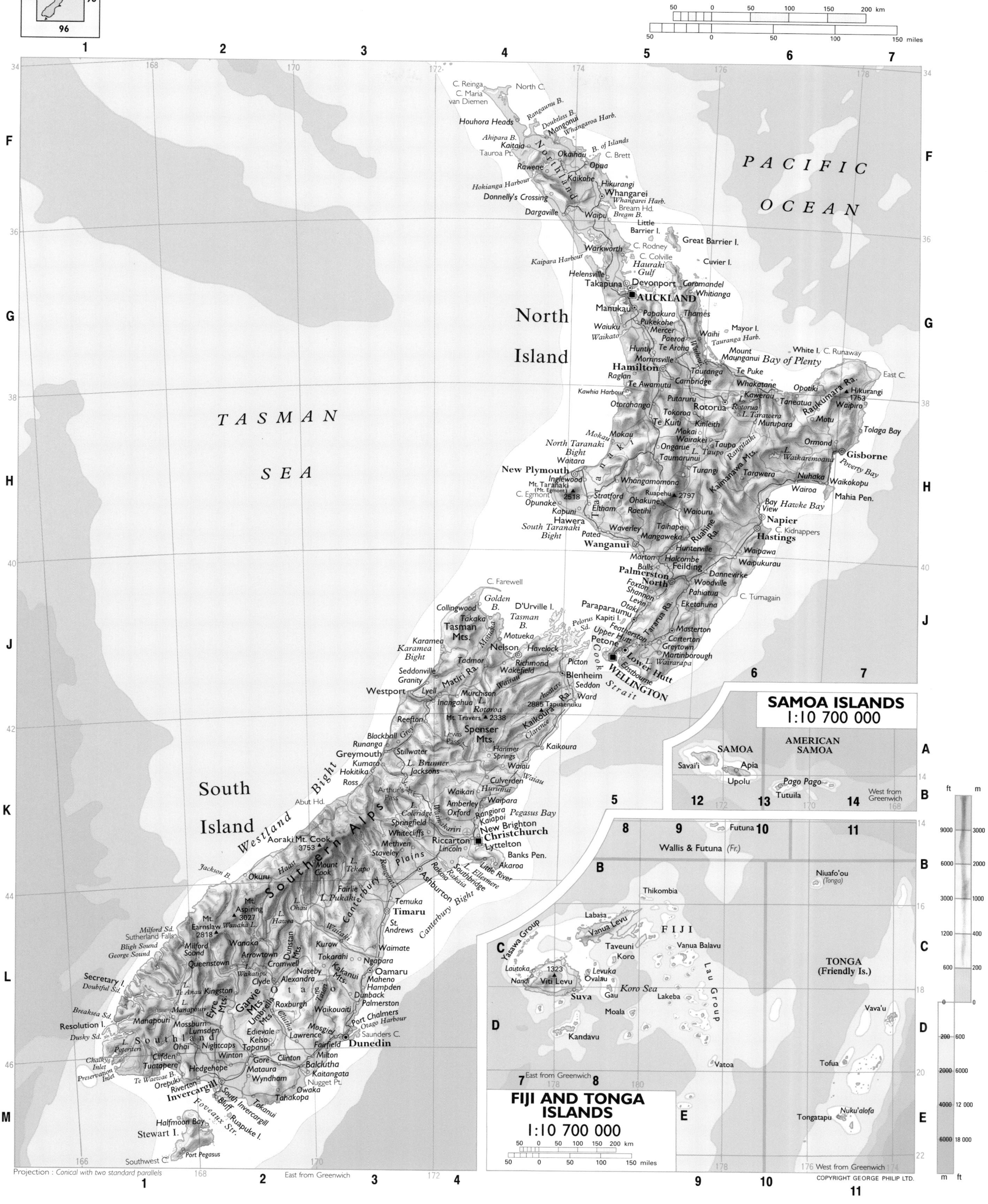
50 0 50 100 150 200 km
50 0 50 100 150 miles
PACIFIC OCEAN
TASMAN SEA
North Island
South Island
C. Reinga
C. Maria van Diemen
North C.
Rangaunu B.
Houhora Heads
Doubtless B.
Mangonui
Whangaroa Harb.
Ahipara B.
Kaitaia
Tauroa Pt.
B. of Islands
C. Brett
Okaihau
Rawene
Opua
Northland
Kaikohe
Hokianga Harbour
Hikurangi
Whangarei
Donnelly's Crossing
Whangarei Harb.
Bream Hd.
Bream B.
Dargaville
Waipu
Little Barrier I.
Great Barrier I.
Warkworth
C. Rodney
C. Colville
Kaipara Harbour
Hauraki Gulf
Cuvier I.
Helensville
Takapuna
Devonport
Coromandel
Whitianga
AUCKLAND
Manukau
Papakura
Thames
Pukekohe
Mayor I.
Waiuku
Mercer
Waihi
Waikato
Paeroa
Tauranga Harb.
Huntly
Te Aroha
Mount Maunganui
White I.
C. Runaway
Bay of Plenty
Morrinsville
Hamilton
Raglan
Tauranga
Te Puke
East C.
Cambridge
Whakatane
Opotiki
Hikurangi 1753
Kawhia Harbour
Te Awamutu
Kawerau
Raukumara Ra.
Putaruru
Rotorua
Taneatua
Waipiro
Otorohanga
L. Rotorua
L. Tarawera
Tokoroa
Murupara
Motu
Te Kuiti
Kinleith
Tolaga Bay
Mokau
Mokai
Wairakei
Taupo
Ormond
North Taranaki Bight
Ongarue
L. Taupo
Waitara
Taumarunui
L. Waikaremoana
Gisborne
New Plymouth
Turangi
Tarawera
Poverty Bay
Inglewood
Whangamomona
Nuhaka
Wairoa
Waikokopu
Mt. Taranaki (Mt. Egmont) 2518
Ruapehu 2797
Kaimanawa Mts.
C. Egmont
Opunake
Stratford
Ohakune
Mahia Pen.
Eltham
Raetihi
Bay View
Hawke Bay
Kapuni
Waiouru
Napier
Hawera
Taihape
South Taranaki Bight
Patea
Waverley
Mangaweka
Ruahine Ra.
Hastings
C. Kidnappers
Wanganui
Hunterville
Waipawa
Marton
Halcombe
Waipukurau
Bulls
Feilding
Palmerston North
Dannevirke
Foxton
Woodville
Shannon
Pahiatua
Levin
C. Turnagain
Paraparaumu
Otaki
Eketahuna
Kapiti I.
Featherston
Tararua Ra.
Masterton
Upper Hutt
Carterton
Petone
Greytown
Lower Hutt
Martinborough
WELLINGTON
L. Wairarapa
Eastbourne
Cook Strait
C. Farewell
Golden B.
Collingwood
D'Urville I.
Takaka
Tasman B.
Tasman Mts.
Motueka
Pelorus Sd.
Karamea
Karamea Bight
Havelock
Nelson
Tadmor
Richmond
Picton
Seddonville
Wakefield
Blenheim
Granity
Matiri Ra.
Seddon
Westport
Lyell
Wairau
Awatere
Ward
Murchison
Inangahua
L. Rotoroa
2885 Tapuaenuku
Mt. Travers 2338
Kaikoura Ra.
Reefton
Spenser Mts.
Clarence
Blackball
Runanga
Lewis Pass
Kaikoura
Greymouth
Stillwater
Hanmer Springs
Kumara
L. Brunner
Hokitika
Jacksons
Waiau
Ross
Culverden
Arthur's Pass
Hurunui
Abut Hd.
Waikari
Amberley
Waipara
Westland Bight
Coleridge
Oxford
Rangiora
Pegasus Bay
Kaiapoi
Springfield
New Brighton
Aoraki Mt. Cook 3753
Whitecliffs
Waimakariri
Christchurch
Riccarton
Lyttelton
Methven
Lincoln
Banks Pen.
Staveley
Plains
L. Ellesmere
Akaroa
Southern Alps
Mount Cook
L. Tekapo
Southbridge
Little River
Jackson B.
Okuru
Haast
Rakaia
Ashburton
Fairlie
L. Pukaki
Canterbury
Rangitata
Mt. Aspiring 3027
Temuka
L. Ohau
Timaru
Canterbury Bight
L. Hawea
Milford Sd.
Mt. Earnslaw 2818
L. Wanaka
St. Andrews
Sutherland Falls
Waitaki
Bligh Sound
Dunstan Mts.
Waimate
George Sound
Milford Sound
Wanaka
Kurow
Arrowtown
Tokarahi
Queenstown
Cromwell
Ngapara
Kakanui Mts.
Secretary I.
Naseby
Oamaru
Doubtful Sd.
L. Wakatipu
Clyde
Alexandra
Maheno
L. Te Anau
Kingston
Otago
Hampden
Dunback
Breaksea Sd.
L. Manapouri
Eyre Mts.
Garvie Mts.
Roxburgh
Palmerston
Resolution I.
Manapouri
Waikouaiti
Port Chalmers
Otago Harbour
Mossburn
Umbrella Mts.
Mosgiel
Saunders C.
Dusky Sd.
Lumsden
Edievale
Lawrence
L. Poteriteri
Southland
Ohai
Nightcaps
Kelso
Tapanui
Fairfield
Dunedin
Chalky Inlet
Clifden
Winton
Clutha
Milton
Tuatapere
Gore
Clinton
Balclutha
Preservation Inlet
Te Waewae B.
Hedgehope
Mataura
Kaitangata
Orepuki
Riverton
Wyndham
Nugget Pt.
Invercargill
Owaka
Bluff
Tahakopa
South Invercargill
Tokanui
Foveaux Str.
Ruapuke I.
Halfmoon Bay
Stewart I.
Port Pegasus
Southwest C.
Projection: Conical with two standard parallels
East from Greenwich
SAMOA ISLANDS 1:10 700 000
SAMOA
AMERICAN SAMOA
Savai'i
Apia
Upolu
Pago Pago
Tutuila
West from Greenwich
Futuna
Wallis & Futuna (Fr.)
Niuafo'ou (Tonga)
Thikombia
Labasa
Vanua Levu
FIJI
Yasawa Group
Taveuni
Vanua Balavu
Koro
Lautoka
1323
Viti Levu
Levuka
Ovalau
Lau Group
TONGA (Friendly Is.)
Nandi
Suva
Gau
Koro Sea
Lakeba
Moala
Vava'u
Kandavu
Tofua
Vatoa
East from Greenwich
FIJI AND TONGA ISLANDS 1:10 700 000
50 0 50 100 150 200 km
50 0 50 100 150 miles
Nuku'alofa
Tongatapu
West from Greenwich
ft m
9000 3000
6000 2000
3000 1000
1200 400
600 200
0 0
200 600
2000 6000
4000 12 000
6000 18 000
m ft

COPYRIGHT GEORGE PHILIP LTD.

km
miles
A
B
C
D
INDONESIA
TIMOR SEA
INDIAN OCEAN
NORTHERN TERRITORY
Tanami Desert
Great Sandy Desert
Gibson Desert
Timor
Kupang
Semau
Roti
Sawu
Raijua
Dana
Sumba
Waingapu
Melolo
Waikabubak
Sumbawa
Lombok
Bali
Melville I.
Bathurst I.
Darwin
Katherine
Kununurra
Wyndham
Derby
Broome
Port Hedland
Karratha
Dampier
Roebourne
Wickham
Onslow
Exmouth
Exmouth Gulf
Barrow I.
Monte Bello Is.
Newman
Halls Creek
Fitzroy Crossing
Kimberley
King Leopold Ranges
Durack Range
Hamersley Range
Joseph Bonaparte Gulf
Cambridge Gulf
Bonaparte Archipelago
Buccaneer Archipelago
Dampier Archipelago
King Sound
Eighty Mile Beach
Rowley Shoals
Mermaid Reef
Clerke Reef
Imperieuse Reef
Scott Reef
Seringapatam Reef
Ashmore Reef
Cartier I.
Hibernia Reef
Browse I.
Adele I.
Lacepede Is.
Lynher Reef
Lake Mackay
Lake Disappointment
L. Argyle
Tropic of Capricorn
Mt. Bruce 1236
Mt. Meharry 1251
Mt. Ord 937
Mt. Wells 970
Mt. Hann 776
Sandfire Roadhouse
Telfer Mine
Marble Bar
Nullagine
Tom Price
Paraburdoo
Wittenoom
Goldsworthy
Shay Gap
Lagrange
Gregory Lake
Billiluna
Tanami
Kalkarindji
Timber Creek
Top Springs
Jabiru
Kakadu Nat. Park
Mt. Zeil 1510
MacDonnell Ranges
Mt. Liebig 1524
Papunya
Yuendumu
Mt. Singleton 808
Mt. Leisler 901
L. Macdonald
L. Hopkins

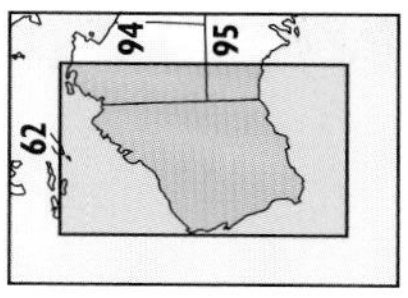

94
95
62

WESTERN AUSTRALIA
SOUTH AUSTRALIA
Great Victoria Desert
Nullarbor Plain
Great Australian Bight
SOUTHERN OCEAN
INDIAN OCEAN
PERTH
Fremantle
Kwinana
Rockingham
Mandurah
Bunbury
Busselton
Albany
Esperance
Geraldton
Carnarvon
Kalgoorlie-Boulder
Norseman
Merredin
Northam
Ayers Rock
Mt. Olga
Petermann Ranges
Musgrave Ranges
Everard Ranges
L. Carnegie
L. Barlee
L. Moore
L. Austin
L. Cowan
L. Dundas
Archipelago of the Recherche
Shark Bay
Houtman Abrolhos
Projection: Bonne
COPYRIGHT GEORGE PHILIP LTD.
East from Greenwich

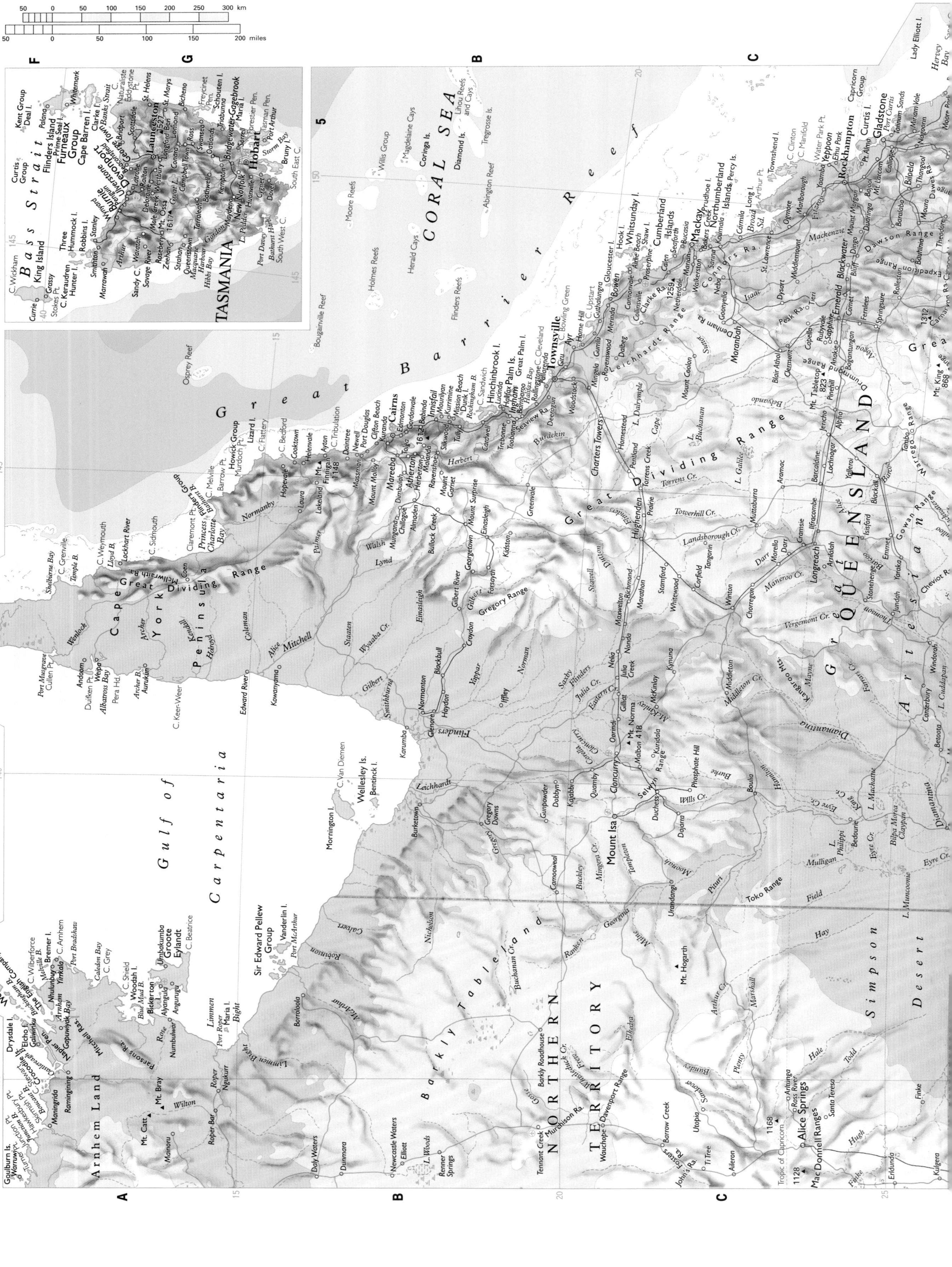
km
miles
TASMANIA
Bass Strait
CORAL SEA
Great Barrier Reef
Gulf of Carpentaria
Cape York Peninsula
Great Dividing Range
QUEENSLAND
NORTHERN TERRITORY
Great Artesian Basin
Simpson Desert
Barkly Tableland
Arnhem Land
Townsville
Cairns
Rockhampton
Mackay
Mount Isa
Alice Springs
Hobart
Launceston
Tropic of Capricorn

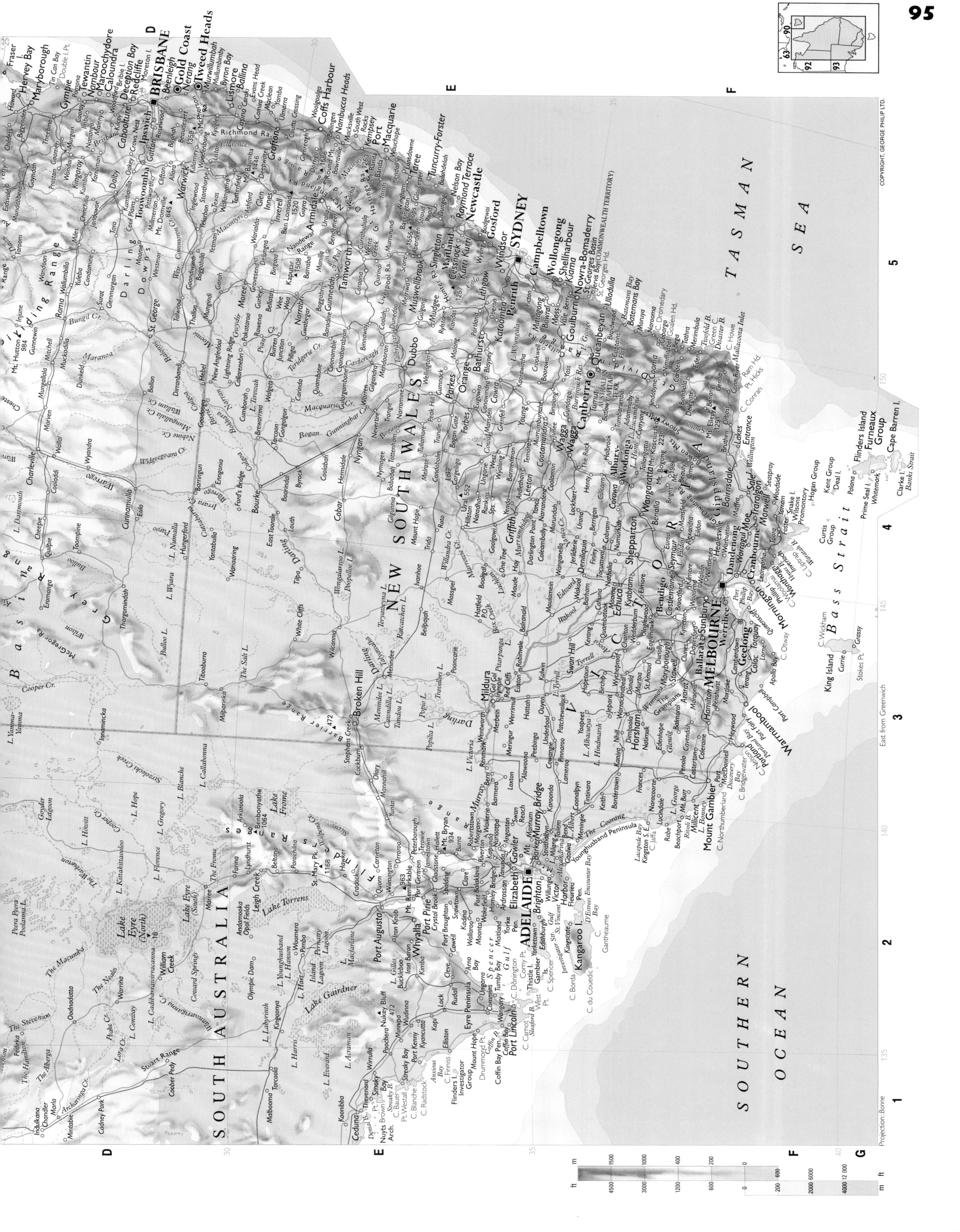
SOUTH AUSTRALIA
NEW SOUTH WALES
VICTORIA
TASMAN SEA
SOUTHERN OCEAN
Bass Strait
SYDNEY
MELBOURNE
ADELAIDE
BRISBANE
Canberra
Newcastle
Wollongong
Gold Coast
Tweed Heads
Coffs Harbour
Port Macquarie
Tamworth
Dubbo
Orange
Bathurst
Wagga Wagga
Albury-Wodonga
Bendigo
Ballarat
Geelong
Broken Hill
Mildura
Port Augusta
Whyalla
Port Pirie
Port Lincoln
Mount Gambier
Kangaroo I.
Lake Eyre (North)
Lake Eyre (South)
Lake Torrens
Lake Frome
Lake Gairdner
Great Dividing Range
Spencer Gulf
Eyre Peninsula
Gippsland
King Island
Flinders Island
Furneaux Group
Cape Barren I.
Projection: Bonne
East from Greenwich
COPYRIGHT, GEORGE PHILIP LTD.
m
ft

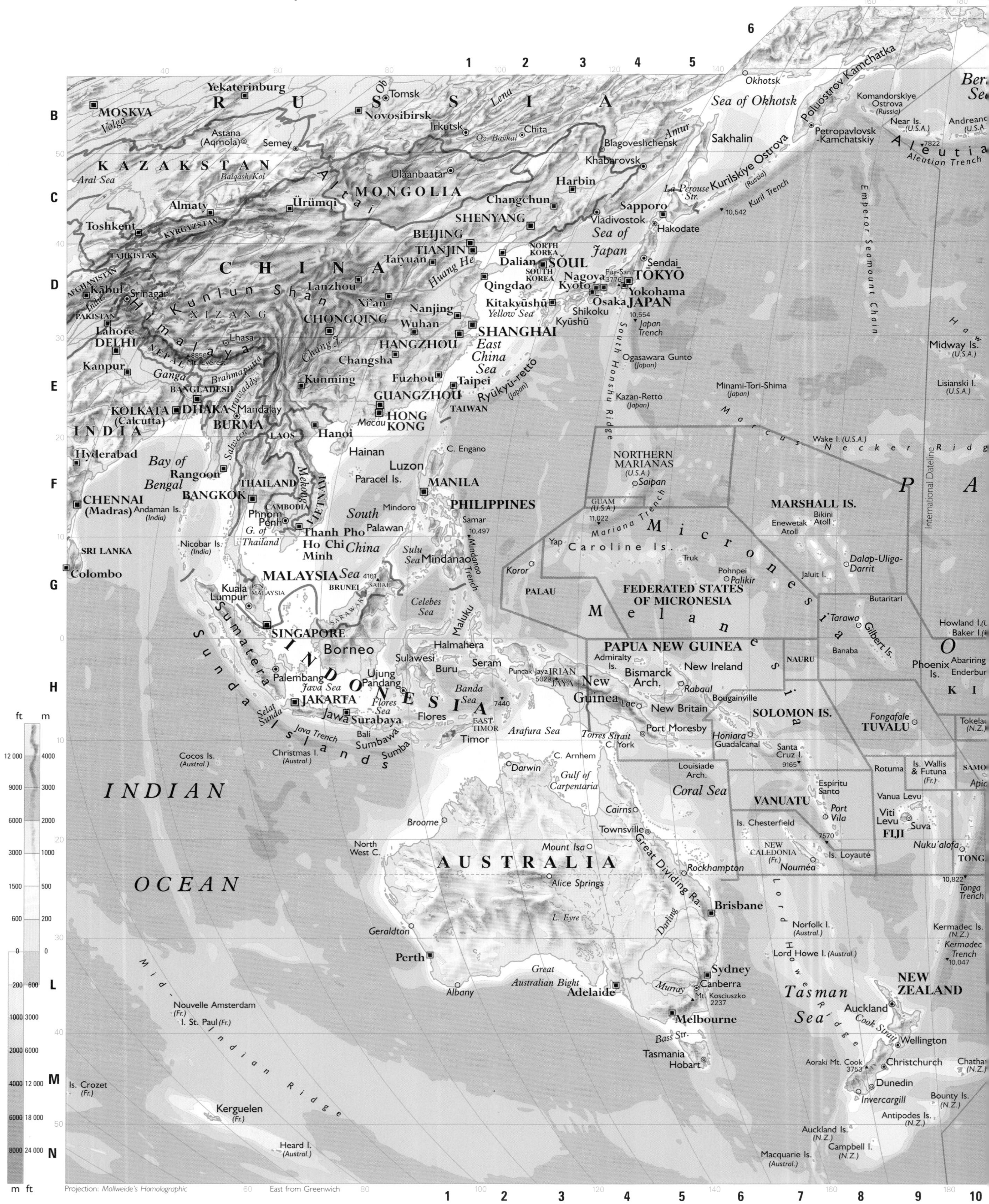
MOSKVA
Volga
Yekaterinburg
R U S S I A
Ob
Tomsk
Novosibirsk
Lena
Irkutsk
Oz. Baykal
Chita
Astana (Aqmola)
Semey
KAZAKSTAN
Balqash Köl
Aral Sea
Altai
Ulaanbaatar
MONGOLIA
Ürümqi
Almaty
KYRGYZSTAN
Toshkent
TAJIKISTAN
AFGHANISTAN
Kābul
Srinagar
Indus
PAKISTAN
Lahore
DELHI
Kanpur
Ganga
Himalaya
Kunlun Shan
XIZANG
Lhasa
NEPAL
8850 Mt. Everest
Brahmaputra
BANGLADESH
KOLKATA (Calcutta)
DHAKA
INDIA
Irrawaddy
Mandalay
BURMA
Salween
Hyderabad
Bay of Bengal
Rangoon
CHENNAI (Madras)
Andaman Is. (India)
Nicobar Is. (India)
SRI LANKA
Colombo
CHINA
Lanzhou
Xi'an
Taiyuan
BEIJING
TIANJIN
Huang He
Dalian
Qingdao
Nanjing
Wuhan
CHONGQING
Chang Jiang
Changsha
HANGZHOU
SHANGHAI
Kunming
Fuzhou
Taipei
TAIWAN
GUANGZHOU
Macau
HONG KONG
Hanoi
LAOS
Hainan
THAILAND
BANGKOK
Mekong
CAMBODIA
Phnom Penh
VIETNAM
G. of Thailand
Thanh Pho Ho Chi Minh
South China Sea
Paracel Is.
Luzon
C. Engano
MANILA
PHILIPPINES
Mindoro
Palawan
Samar
10,497
Sulu Sea
Mindanao
Mindanao Trench
MALAYSIA
4101
BRUNEI
SABAH
SARAWAK
Kuala Lumpur
PEN. MALAYSIA
SINGAPORE
Sumatera
Borneo
Celebes Sea
Maluku
Halmahera
Sulawesi
Buru
Seram
Palembang
INDONESIA
Ujung Pandang
Java Sea
JAKARTA
Flores Sea
Jawa
Surabaya
Flores
Banda Sea
7440
EAST TIMOR
Timor
Bali
Sumbawa
Sumba
Selat Sunda
Java Trench
Sunda Islands
Christmas I. (Austral.)
Cocos Is. (Austral.)
SHENYANG
Changchun
Harbin
Khabarovsk
Amur
Blagoveshchensk
Vladivostok
Sea of Japan
NORTH KOREA
SÖUL
SOUTH KOREA
Kitakyūshū
Yellow Sea
East China Sea
Ryūkyū-rettō (Japan)
Sapporo
Hakodate
Sendai
Fuji-San 3776
TŌKYŌ
Yokohama
Nagoya
Kyōto
Ōsaka
JAPAN
Shikoku
Kyūshū
10,554
Japan Trench
South Honshu Ridge
Ogasawara Gunto (Japan)
Kazan-Rettō (Japan)
Minami-Tori-Shima (Japan)
Okhotsk
Sea of Okhotsk
Sakhalin
La Perouse Str.
Kurilskiye Ostrova (Russia)
Kuril Trench
10,542
Poluostrov Kamchatka
Petropavlovsk-Kamchatskiy
Komandorskiye Ostrova (Russia)
Near Is. (U.S.A.)
Andreanof (U.S.A.)
Aleutian Is.
7822
Aleutian Trench
Bering Sea
Emperor Seamount Chain
Hawaiian Ridge
Midway Is. (U.S.A.)
Lisianski I. (U.S.A.)
Marcus Necker Ridge
Wake I. (U.S.A.)
International Dateline
PACIFIC OCEAN
NORTHERN MARIANAS (U.S.A.)
Saipan
GUAM (U.S.A.)
11,022
Mariana Trench
Micronesia
Caroline Is.
Yap
Koror
PALAU
Truk
Pohnpei
Palikir
FEDERATED STATES OF MICRONESIA
MARSHALL IS.
Enewetak Atoll
Bikini Atoll
Jaluit I.
Dalap-Uliga-Darrit
Butaritari
Tarawa
Gilbert Is.
Banaba
NAURU
Howland I. (U.S.A.)
Baker I.
Phoenix Is.
Abariringa
Enderbury
KIRIBATI
Melanesia
PAPUA NEW GUINEA
Admiralty Is.
Bismarck Arch.
New Ireland
Rabaul
Bougainville
New Britain
Puncak Jaya 5029
IRIAN JAYA
New Guinea
Lae
Port Moresby
Torres Strait
C. York
Arafura Sea
SOLOMON IS.
Honiara
Guadalcanal
Santa Cruz I.
9165
TUVALU
Fongafale
Tokelau (N.Z.)
Is. Wallis & Futuna (Fr.)
Rotuma
SAMOA
Apia
Louisiade Arch.
Coral Sea
VANUATU
Espíritu Santo
Port Vila
Vanua Levu
Viti Levu
Suva
FIJI
Is. Chesterfield
7570
NEW CALEDONIA (Fr.)
Nouméa
Is. Loyauté
Nuku'alofa
TONGA
10,822
Tonga Trench
Kermadec Is. (N.Z.)
Kermadec Trench
10,047
Lord Howe Rise
Norfolk I. (Austral.)
Lord Howe I. (Austral.)
Tasman Sea
NEW ZEALAND
Auckland
Cook Strait
Wellington
Aoraki Mt. Cook 3753
Christchurch
Chatham Is. (N.Z.)
Dunedin
Invercargill
Bounty Is. (N.Z.)
Antipodes Is. (N.Z.)
Auckland Is. (N.Z.)
Campbell I. (N.Z.)
Macquarie Is. (Austral.)
C. Arnhem
Darwin
Gulf of Carpentaria
Cairns
Townsville
Great Dividing Ra.
Mount Isa
Broome
North West C.
AUSTRALIA
Alice Springs
Rockhampton
Brisbane
L. Eyre
Darling
Geraldton
Perth
Great Australian Bight
Albany
Adelaide
Murray
Sydney
Canberra
Mt. Kosciuszko 2237
Melbourne
Bass Str.
Tasmania
Hobart
INDIAN OCEAN
Mid-Indian Ridge
Nouvelle Amsterdam (Fr.)
I. St. Paul (Fr.)
Is. Crozet (Fr.)
Kerguelen (Fr.)
Heard I. (Austral.)
ft m
12 000 4000
9000 3000
6000 2000
3000 1000
1500 500
600 200
0 0
200 600
1000 3000
2000 6000
4000 12 000
6000 18 000
8000 24 000
m ft
Projection: Mollweide's Homolographic
East from Greenwich

Arctic Circle
ALASKA
(U.S.A.)
Anchorage
Bristol Bay
Gulf of Alaska
Juneau
5959
Prince of Wales I.
(U.S.A.) Prince Rupert
Queen Charlotte Is.
(Canada)
C A N A D A
Edmonton
Calgary
Regina
Winnipeg
L. Winnipeg
Vancouver
Vancouver I.
Victoria
Seattle
Portland
R O C K Y M T S
Snake
Boise
Newfoundland
St. Lawrence
St. John's
N O R T H
Québec
Montréal
L. Superior
L. Huron
L. Michigan
Ottawa
Toronto
L. Ontario
Minneapolis
Missouri
Detroit
Buffalo
Boston
L. Erie
Salt Lake City
CHICAGO
Pittsburgh
NEW YORK CITY
PHILADELPHIA
Baltimore
Washington D.C.
C. Mendocino
Sacramento
SAN FRANCISCO
Denver
Kansas City
St. Louis
Cincinnati
Colorado
4418
UNITED STATES
Appalachian Mts.
A T L A N T I C
6741
Oklahoma City
Memphis
Mississippi
C. Hatteras
LOS ANGELES
San Diego
Phoenix
Dallas
Atlanta
Bermuda
(U.K.)
Ciudad Juárez
Houston
San Antonio
Jacksonville
Guadalupe
(Mex.)
Baja California
New Orleans
Sargasso Sea
Gulf of Mexico
Golfo de California
Miami
BAHAMAS
Florida Str.
O C E A N
Monterrey
Tropic of Cancer
M E X I C O
La Habana
CUBA
West Indies
Canal de Yucatan
Honolulu
Oahu
4205
HAWAIIAN IS.
(U.S.A.)
Hawaii
C. San Lucas
Guadalajara
MEXICO
5700
Puebla
Mérida
7680
JAMAICA
Kingston
HAITI
DOMINICAN REP.
9200
Leeward Is.
Is. Revilla Gigedo
(Mex.)
Acapulco
BELIZE
PUERTO RICO
(U.S.A.)
C I F I C
GUATEMALA
HONDURAS
Caribbean Sea
BARBADOS
Guatemala
San Salvador
EL SALVADOR
NICARAGUA
Windward Is.
Managua
Barranquilla
Maracaibo
North West Christmas I. Ridge
I. Clipperton
(Fr.)
San José
COSTA RICA
Colón
Panamá
PANAMA
Caracas
Orinoco
VENEZUELA
Palmyra Is.
(U.S.A.)
Teraina
Tabuaeran
Kiritimati
I. del Coco
(Costa Rica)
Medellín
Bogotá
I. de Malpelo
(Colombia)
Cali
COLOMBIA
Equator
Jarvis I.
(U.S.A.)
E A N
Galápagos
(Ecuador)
Quito
ECUADOR
Guayaquil
Iquitos
Amazonas
Malden I.
Starbuck I.
C. Paliñas
BRAZIL
East Pacific Ridge
Tongareva
Caroline I.
Is. Marquises
Trujillo
Pukapuka
Manihiki
Vostok I.
6369
PERU
Flint I.
LIMA
Cuzco
L. Titicaca
Nevada Ancohuma
6550
Suwarrow Is.
Is. de la Société
Tahiti
Papeete
Is. Tuamotu
Arequipa
La Paz
BOLIVIA
6866
Peru-
Arica
Cook Is.
(N.Z.)
FRENCH POLYNESIA
Tuamotu Ridge
Iquique
Chile
Austral Seamount Chain
Mururoa
Antofagasta
PARAGUAY
Rarotonga
Is. Tubuai
Tropic of Capricorn
Ducie I.
Pitcairn I.
(U.K.)
8050
Trench
Asunción
San Felix
(Chile)
San Ambrosio
(Chile)
San Miguel de Tucumán
Rapa
Sala-y-Gómez
(Chile)
I. de Pascua
(Chile)
Porto Alegre
Córdoba
Aconcagua
6960
Arch. de Juan Fernández
(Chile)
Valparaíso
Rosario
URUGUAY
SANTIAGO
BUENOS AIRES
Montevideo
Río de la Plata
Concepción
ARGENTINA
A N D E S
Chile Rise
SOUTH ATLANTIC OCEAN
Patagonia
6212
Pacific-Antarctic Ridge
Falkland Is.
(U.K.)
Punta Arenas
Est. de Magallanes
Tierra del Fuego
South Georgia
(U.K.)
C. de Hornos
West from Greenwich

100 0 200 400 600 800 1000 1200 1400 km
100 0 200 400 600 800 1000 miles
A
B
C
D
E
F
G
H
J
7
8
9
10
11
12
ARCTIC OCEAN
Asia
C. Dezhneva
St. Lawrence I.
Bering Strait
Bering Sea
Nunivak I.
C. Prince of Wales
Barrow Pt.
Beaufort Sea
Brooks Ra.
Yukon
Porcupine
Alaska
Mt. McKinley 6194
Alaska Range
Alaska Peninsula
Kodiak I.
Gulf of Alaska
Mt. St. Elias 5489
Mt. Logan 5959
C. Bathurst
Mackenzie Mts
Mackenzie
Arctic Circle
Great Bear L.
Great Slave L.
Liard
Back
Dubawnt
Banks I.
M'Clure Strait
Victoria I.
Melville I.
Viscount Melville Sd.
Parry Is.
Queen Elizabeth Is.
Sverdrup Is.
Axel Heiberg I.
Ellesmere I.
Nares Str.
Kane Basin
Bathurst I.
Devon I.
Lancaster Sd.
Bylot I.
Somerset I.
Prince of Wales I.
Gulf of Boothia
Boothia Pen.
Melville Pen.
Foxe Basin
Foxe Channel
Southampton I.
Baffin Island
Baffin Bay
Cumberland Sd.
Frobisher B.
Hudson Strait
C. Chidley
C. Wolstenholme
Ungava Peninsula
Greenland
Petermann's Peak 2940
Mt. Forel 3360
Denmark Strait
Iceland
2119
Disko I.
Davis Strait
Cape Farewell
Labrador Sea
Hamilton Inlet
Coast of Labrador
Str. of Belle Isle
Newfoundland
C. Race
Hudson Bay
Belcher Is.
C. Henrietta Maria
James Bay
Eastmain
Laurentian Plateau
St. Lawrence
Gulf of St. Lawrence
Pr. Edward I.
Cape Breton I.
Nova Scotia
Sable I.
B. of Fundy
C. Sable
C. Cod
Nantucket I.
Mt. Washington 1917
Hudson
Long I.
Alexander Archipelago
Stikine
Coast Mountains
Rocky Mountains
Queen Charlotte Islands
Skeena
Queen Charlotte Str.
Mt. Waddington 3994
Fraser
Mt. Robson 3954
Peace
Athabasca
L. Athabasca
Reindeer L.
Churchill
Nelson
L. Winnipeg
Great Plains
Saskatchewan
Selkirk Mts
Vancouver I.
Juan de Fuca Str.
C. Flattery
Mt. Rainier 4392
Cascade Range
Columbia
C. Blanco
C. Mendocino
Coast Ranges
Mt. Shasta 4317
Sacramento
Sierra Nevada
San Joaquin
Mt. Whitney 4418
Death Valley -86
Snake
Great Salt Lake
Great Basin
Wasatch Ra.
Missouri
Platte
Mt. Elbert 4399
Blanca Peak 4378
Grand Canyon
Colorado
Colorado Plateau
Gila
Arkansas
Ozark Plateau
Mississippi
Red
L. Superior
Great Lakes
L. Huron
L. Michigan
L. Erie
L. Ontario
Niagara Falls
Appalachian Mts.
Allegheny Mts.
Ohio
Cumberland Plateau
Tennessee
Blue Ridge Mts.
C. Charles
Chesapeake B.
C. Hatteras
Bermuda
Alabama
Florida
Florida Strait
NORTH ATLANTIC OCEAN
Sargasso Sea
Bahamas
Mississippi River Delta
Gulf of Mexico
Rio Grande
PACIFIC OCEAN
Guadalupe
Lower California
Gulf of California
Tropic of Cancer
C. San Lucas
Clarion Fracture Zone
Western Sierra Madre
Mexican Plateau
Eastern Sierra Madre
Santiago
C. Corrientes
Revilla Gigedo Is.
Balsas
Popocatepetl 5452
Citlaltepetl 5700
Isthmus of Tehuantepec
Gulf of Campeche
Yucatán Peninsula
Yucatan Channel
Yucatan Basin
Cuba
Greater Antilles
Cayman Trough
Jamaica
Hispaniola
9200
Puerto Rico
Caribbean Sea
G. of Honduras
C. Gracias a Dios
Coco
Colombian Basin
G. de Tehuantepec
Guatemala Trench
Central America
Sierra Nevada de Santa Marta 5800
G. de Venezuela
Maracaibo
G. of Darién
G. of Panamá
Andes
Magdalena
Cord. de Mérida
ft m
9000 3000
6000 2000
3000 1000
1500 500
600 200
0 0
200 600
1000 3000
2000 6000
4000 12000
6000 18000
8000 24000
m ft
Projection: Bonne
West from Greenwich
70
80
60
50
40
30
20
10
120
110
100
90

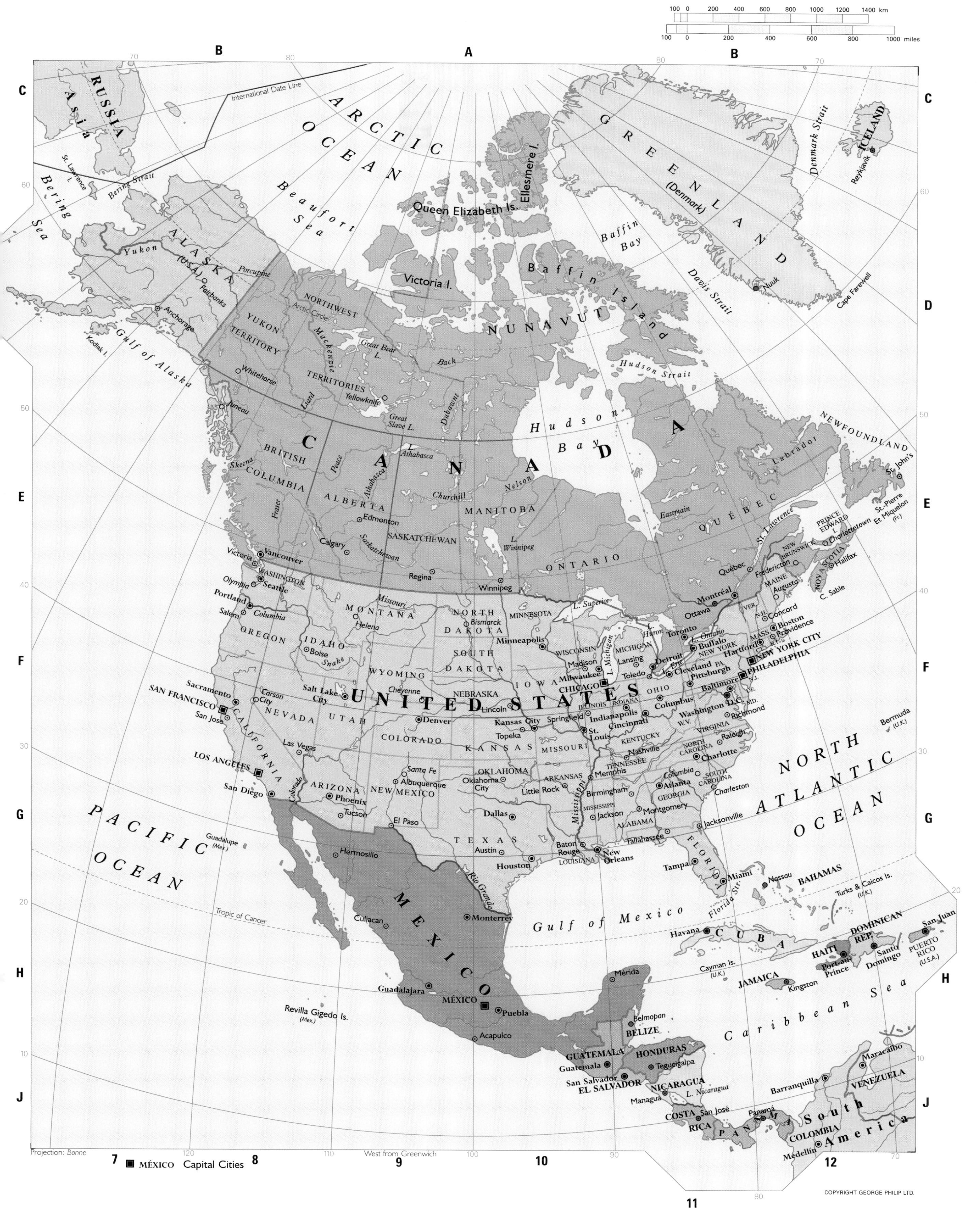
100 0 200 400 600 800 1000 1200 1400 km
100 0 200 400 600 800 1000 miles
ARCTIC OCEAN
International Date Line
RUSSIA
Asia
St. Lawrence I.
Bering Strait
Bering Sea
Beaufort Sea
Queen Elizabeth Is.
Ellesmere I.
GREENLAND (Denmark)
Denmark Strait
ICELAND
Reykjavik
Baffin Bay
Baffin Island
Davis Strait
Nuuk
Cape Farewell
Victoria I.
NUNAVUT
ALASKA (USA)
Yukon
Porcupine
Fairbanks
Anchorage
Kodiak I.
Gulf of Alaska
NORTHWEST TERRITORIES
Arctic Circle
YUKON TERRITORY
Mackenzie
Great Bear L.
Back
Whitehorse
Yellowknife
Liard
Great Slave L.
Dubawnt
Juneau
Hudson Strait
Hudson Bay
CANADA
NEWFOUNDLAND
Labrador
St John's
BRITISH COLUMBIA
Skeena
Peace
L. Athabasca
Athabasca
ALBERTA
Churchill
Nelson
MANITOBA
Eastmain
QUÉBEC
St. Lawrence
PRINCE EDWARD I.
Charlottetown
St.-Pierre Et Miquelon (Fr.)
Fraser
Edmonton
SASKATCHEWAN
Saskatchewan
Calgary
L. Winnipeg
NEW BRUNSWICK
NOVA SCOTIA
Halifax
Fredericton
Québec
ONTARIO
Victoria
Vancouver
Regina
Winnipeg
WASHINGTON
Olympia
Seattle
Missouri
MAINE
Augusta
C. Sable
Portland
Salem
Columbia
MONTANA
Helena
NORTH DAKOTA
Bismarck
MINNESOTA
L. Superior
Montréal
Ottawa
VER.
N.H.
Concord
Boston
Providence
MASS.
OREGON
IDAHO
Boise
Snake
SOUTH DAKOTA
Minneapolis
WISCONSIN
L. Michigan
MICHIGAN
L. Huron
Toronto
L. Ontario
Buffalo
NEW YORK
Hartford
NEW YORK CITY
PHILADELPHIA
WYOMING
Madison
Lansing
Detroit
L. Erie
Cleveland
PA.
Pittsburgh
Milwaukee
IOWA
CHICAGO
Toledo
OHIO
Baltimore
N.J.
DE.
MD.
Sacramento
SAN FRANCISCO
Carson City
San Jose
NEVADA
Salt Lake City
UNITED STATES
NEBRASKA
Lincoln
ILLINOIS
INDIANA
Indianapolis
Columbus
Washington D.C.
W.V.
Richmond
Bermuda (U.K.)
CALIFORNIA
UTAH
Denver
Kansas City
Springfield
St. Louis
Cincinnati
KENTUCKY
VIRGINIA
COLORADO
Topeka
KANSAS
MISSOURI
Nashville
Raleigh
NORTH CAROLINA
Charlotte
Las Vegas
LOS ANGELES
Santa Fe
Albuquerque
OKLAHOMA
Oklahoma City
ARKANSAS
TENNESSEE
Memphis
Little Rock
Mississippi
Birmingham
Columbia
Atlanta
SOUTH CAROLINA
GEORGIA
Charleston
NORTH ATLANTIC OCEAN
San Diego
Colorado
ARIZONA
Phoenix
NEW MEXICO
Tucson
El Paso
Dallas
MISSISSIPPI
Jackson
Montgomery
ALABAMA
Jacksonville
PACIFIC OCEAN
Guadalupe (Mex.)
TEXAS
Austin
Baton Rouge
LOUISIANA
New Orleans
Tallahassee
FLORIDA
Hermosillo
Houston
Tampa
Miami
Florida Str.
Nassau
BAHAMAS
Turks & Caicos Is. (U.K.)
Rio Grande
MEXICO
Tropic of Cancer
Culiacan
Monterrey
Gulf of Mexico
Havana
CUBA
DOMINICAN REP.
San Juan
PUERTO RICO (U.S.A.)
HAITI
Port-au-Prince
Santo Domingo
Cayman Is. (U.K.)
JAMAICA
Kingston
Mérida
Guadalajara
MÉXICO
Puebla
Revilla Gigedo Is. (Mex.)
Caribbean Sea
Belmopan
BELIZE
Acapulco
GUATEMALA
Guatemala
HONDURAS
Tegucigalpa
San Salvador
EL SALVADOR
NICARAGUA
L. Nicaragua
Managua
Maracaibo
VENEZUELA
Barranquilla
COSTA RICA
San José
Panamá
PANAMA
South America
COLOMBIA
Medellín
Projection: Bonne
■ MÉXICO Capital Cities
West from Greenwich

100 0 100 200 300 400 500 600 km
100 0 100 200 300 400 miles
Projection : Bonne
ALASKA
1:26 700 000
West from Greenwich
PACIFIC OCEAN
ALASKA
YUKON TERRITORY
NORTHWEST TERRITORIES
BRITISH COLUMBIA
ALBERTA
SASKATCHEWAN
MANITOBA
WASHINGTON
MONTANA
NORTH DAKOTA
SOUTH DAKOTA
NEBRASKA
MINNESOTA
IOWA
UNITED STATES
Anchorage
Fairbanks
Whitehorse
Dawson
Inuvik
Tuktoyaktuk
Aklavik
Old Crow
Fort McPherson
Norman Wells
Fort Good Hope
Yellowknife
Great Bear L.
Great Slave L.
Victoria Island
Banks Island
Amundsen Gulf
Coronation Gulf
Mackenzie Mountains
Selwyn Mts.
Cassiar Mountains
Rocky Mountains
Coast Mountains
Wrangell Mts.
St. Elias Mts.
Mt. Logan 5959
Mt. Lucania 5226
Mt. St. Elias 5489
Mt. Fairweather 4663
Juneau
Skagway
Sitka
Ketchikan
Prince Rupert
Queen Charlotte Is.
Alexander Archipelago
Vancouver I.
VANCOUVER
Victoria
SEATTLE
Tacoma
Olympia
Spokane
Kamloops
Prince George
Fort St. John
Dawson Creek
Grande Prairie
Peace River
Fort McMurray
Edmonton
Red Deer
Calgary
Lethbridge
Medicine Hat
Jasper
Banff
Mt. Robson 3954
Lake Athabasca
Uranium City
Fort Chipewyan
Fort Smith
Hay River
Fort Simpson
Fort Nelson
Fort Liard
Saskatoon
Regina
Moose Jaw
Swift Current
Prince Albert
North Battleford
Lloydminster
The Pas
Flin Flon
Thompson
Churchill
Gillam
Lake Winnipeg
L. Winnipegosis
L. Manitoba
Winnipeg
Brandon
Portage la Prairie
Selkirk
Kenora
Dryden
Fort Frances
L. of the Woods
Baker Lake
Rankin Inlet
Whale Cove
Arviat
Boothia Peninsula
King William I.
Gjoa Haven
Taloyoak
Kugluktuk
Cambridge Bay
Umingmaktok
Bismarck
Fargo
Minot
Williston
Pierre
Rapid City
Sioux Falls
Sioux City
Omaha
Des Moines
MINNEAPOLIS
ST. PAUL
Duluth
Rochester
Mason City
Waterloo
Dubuque
Cedar Rapids
North Platte
Grand Island
Bering Strait
BERING SEA
CHUKCHI SEA
GULF OF ALASKA
Aleutian Is.
Brooks Range
Alaska Range
Mt. McKinley 6194
Prudhoe Bay
Barrow
Nome
Kotzebue
Bethel
Kodiak I.
Dutch Harbor
Unalaska I.
Unimak I.
Alaska Peninsula
Provideniya
Anadyr
Koryakskoye Nagorye
RUSSIA
CANADA

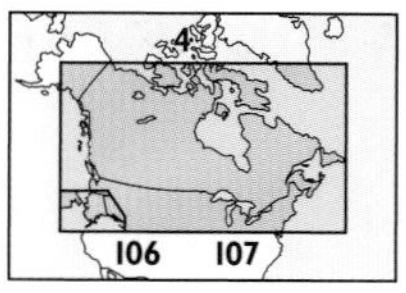
106
107

11
12
13
14
15
16
B
C
D
E
Devon I.
Lancaster Sound
Arctic Bay
Nanisivik
Borden Pen.
Bylot I.
Eclipse Sd.
Pond Inlet
Brodeur Peninsula
Baffin Bay
2136
1890
C. Adair
Clyde River
C. Raper
Baffin Island
Gulf of Boothia
Fury and Hecla Str.
Igloolik
Simpson Pen.
Pelly Bay
Committee B.
Melville Peninsula
Sanirajak
Prince Charles I.
Air Force I.
Foxe Basin
Nettilling L.
Home B.
Qikiqtarjuaq
C. Dyer
2591
Cumberland Peninsula
Pangnirtung
Hoare B.
Cumberland Sd.
Mercy C.
Rae Isthmus
Repulse Bay
Circle
NUNAVUT
C. Dorchester
Amadjuak L.
Foxe Pen.
Foxe Channel
Iqaluit
Hall Peninsula
Meta Incognita Peninsula
Kimmirut
Frobisher Bay
Resolution I.
Cape Dorset
Wager B.
Roes Welcome Sd.
Southampton I.
Salliq
Bell Pen.
Salisbury I.
Nottingham I.
Hudson Strait
Coats I.
Mansel I.
Ivujivik
Salluit
Kangiqsujuaq
Quaqtaq
Akpatok I.
C. Chidley
Kangirsuk
Ungava Bay
Péninsule d'Ungava
Puvirnituq
Arnaud
L. Payne
Hudson Bay
Ottawa Is.
257
Inukjuak
Feuilles
Koksoak
Kuujjuaq
Baleine
George
Kangiqsualujjuaq
1652
Hebron
Nain
Hopedale
C. Harrison
Rigolet
Cartwright
Port Hope Simpson
Belle Isle
C. Bauld
St. Anthony
L. Minto
Mélèzes
Caniapiscau
Sleeper Is.
King George Is.
Baker's Dozen Is.
Sanikiluaq
Belcher Is.
C. Tatnam
L. à l'Eau Claire
Grande Baleine
Kuujjuarapik
L. Bienville
Schefferville
Smallwood Res.
Labrador
North West River
Happy Valley-Goose Bay
Petitsikapau
Esker
Churchill Falls
Churchill
Rés. de Caniapiscau
Labrador City
Fermont
Ashuanipi
Natashquan
St-Augustin
Str. of Belle Isle
Notre Dame B.
Lewisporte
Gander
Bonavista
Baie Verte
Deer Lake
Grand Falls
Trinity B.
Carbonear
St. John's
Corner Brook
814
Newfoundland
Stephenville
Channel-Port aux Basques
Marystown
Placentia B.
Placentia
C. Race
C. Ray
C. Henrietta Maria
Peawanuck
Winisk
Severn
Pte. Louis XIV
Kanaaupscow
La Grande
Chisasibi
James Bay
Akimiski I.
Wemindji
Eastmain
1135
Gagnon
Moisie
Rés. Manicouagan
Manicouagan
Romaine
Havre-St-Pierre
I. d'Anticosti
Big Trout L.
Attawapiskat
Fort Albany
Albany
Charlton I.
Eastmain
Waskaganish
Rupert
Nottaway
L. Mistassini
L. Albanel
Peribonca
Sept-Îles
Port-Cartier
Gulf of St. Lawrence
Cabot Str.
North C.
ST.-PIERRE et MIQUELON (Fr.)
Moosonee
Harricana
L. St. Joseph
Missinaibi
Kenogami
Nakina
Hearst
Mattagami
Matagami
L. Matagami
Chibougamau
Baie Comeau
St. Lawrence
Matane
Gaspé
Pén. de Gaspé
Rimouski
Campbellton
Bathurst
Îs. de la Madeleine
Cape Breton I.
Glace Bay
Sydney
Port Hawkesbury
L. Nipigon
Nipigon
Geraldton
Marathon
Kapuskasing
Cochrane
Abitibi L.
Amos
Rés. Gouin
Roberval
Dolbeau
L. St-Jean
Chicoutmi
Jonquière
Rivière-du-Loup
Edmundston
Miramichi
PR. EDWARD I.
Summerside
Charlottetown
Northumberland Str.
Antigonish
New Glasgow
Oba
Timmins
Kirkland Lake
Rouyn-Noranda
Val-d'Or
La Tuque
1190
Québec
Grand Falls
NEW BRUNSWICK
Moncton
Amherst
Truro
NOVA SCOTIA
Sable I. (Nova Scotia)
Thunder Bay
Chapleau
New Liskeard
Wawa
Lake Superior
Rés. Cabonga
Mont-Laurier
Shawinigan
Trois-Rivières
Lévis
Thetford Mines
Woodstock
Fredericton
Saint John
Kentville
Dartmouth
Halifax
Bridgewater
Liverpool
Digby
B. of Fundy
Yarmouth
C. Sable
Houghton
183
Sault Ste. Marie
Elliot Lake
Sudbury
Outaouais
Joliette
St-Hyacinthe
Sherbrooke
MAINE
Bangor
Augusta
Lewiston
Portland
Ironwood
Marquette
L. Nipissing
North Bay
MONTRÉAL
Hull
Granby
L. Champlain
Ottawa
Cornwall
Montpelier
Burlington
6309
MICHIGAN
Manistique
Manitoulin I.
Parry Sound
Georgian Bay
Pembroke
Huntsville
Rhinelander
Escanaba
Menominee
Petoskey
Traverse City
Lake Huron
Barrie
Peterborough
Kingston
Belleville
VERMONT
NEW HAMPSHIRE
Concord
Manchester
WISCONSIN
Wausau
Green Bay
Appleton
Cadillac
Owen Sound
Oshawa
TORONTO
L. Ontario
75
Syracuse
MASS.
BOSTON
C. Cod
Sheboygan
Lake Michigan
Saginaw
Kitchener
Hamilton
Albany
Springfield
Providence
MILWAUKEE
Madison
Grand Rapids
Flint
London
Niagara Falls
Rochester
NEW YORK
HARTFORD
CONN.
R.I.
Lansing
Sarnia
BUFFALO
Elmira
Binghamton
New Haven
Rockford
Racine
Kenosha
174
Windsor
L. Erie
Erie
Jamestown
Scranton
Bridgeport
NEW YORK
CHICAGO
DETROIT
Toledo
CLEVELAND
Newark
N.J.
Gary
South Bend
ILLINOIS
INDIANA
OHIO
PENNSYLVANIA
Allentown
Trenton
Nunavik
Uummannaq
Qeqertarsuaq
Ilulissat
Qasigiannguit
Tasiilaq
GREENLAND (KALAALLIT NUNAAT) (Denmark)
Kangerlussuaq
Sisimiut
2850
Kong Frederik VI's Kyst
Maniitsoq
Nuuk
Qeqertarsuatsiaat
Paamiut
Arsuk
Qaqortoq
Alluitsup Paa
Nanortalik
Uummannarsuaq
Davis Strait
Labrador Sea
3809
ATLANTIC OCEAN
90
80
70
60
50
40
30
West from Greenwich
13
14
COPYRIGHT GEORGE PHILIP LTD.

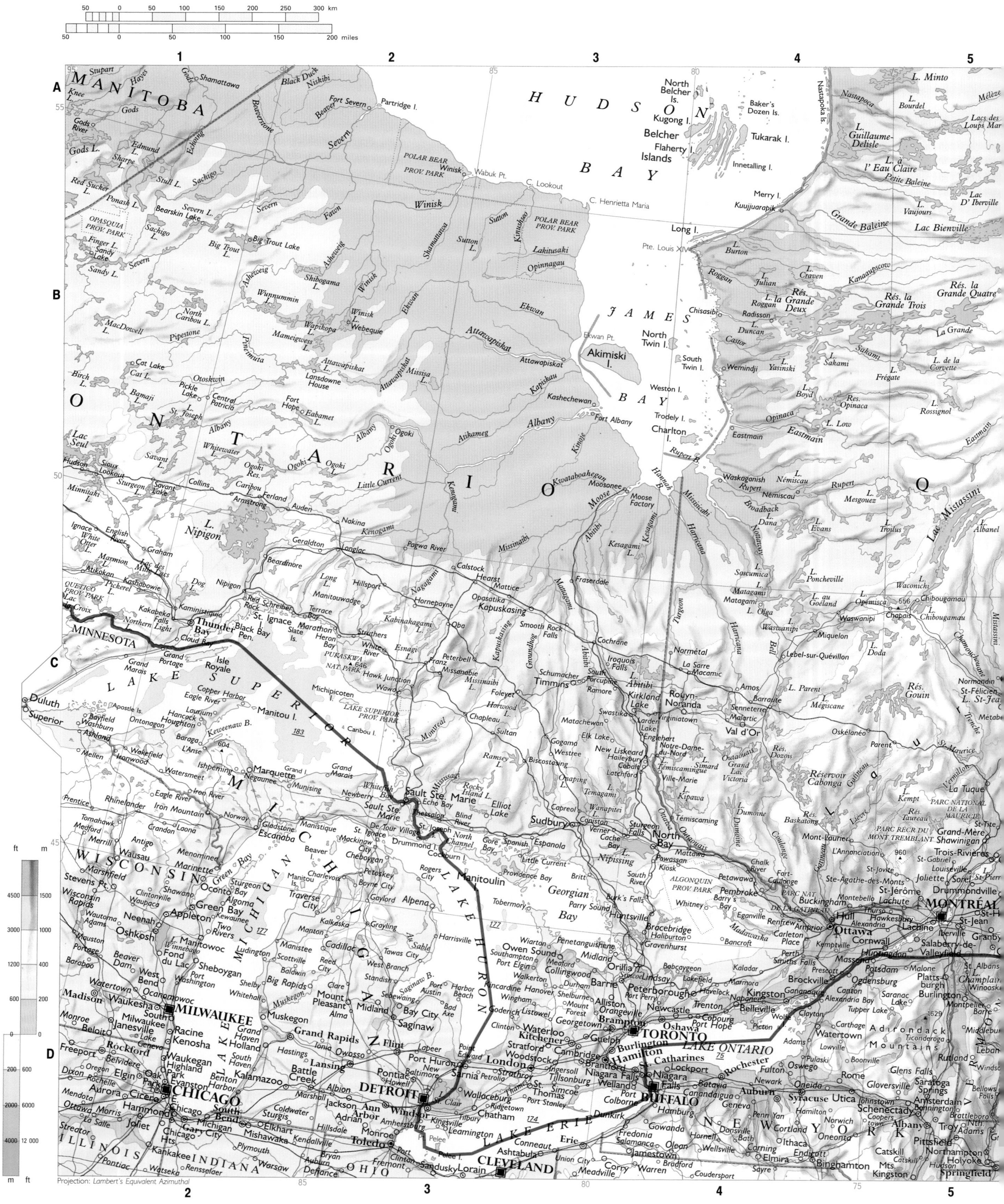

50 0 50 100 150 200 250 300 km
50 0 50 100 150 200 miles
HUDSON BAY
JAMES BAY
MANITOBA
ONTARIO
MINNESOTA
WISCONSIN
MICHIGAN
ILLINOIS
INDIANA
OHIO
NEW YORK
LAKE SUPERIOR
LAKE MICHIGAN
LAKE HURON
LAKE ONTARIO
LAKE ERIE
Georgian Bay
Belcher Islands
Akimiski I.
L. Nipigon
Lac Mistassini
Thunder Bay
Sault Ste. Marie
Sudbury
Timmins
North Bay
Rouyn-Noranda
Val d'Or
Ottawa
MONTRÉAL
TORONTO
Hamilton
London
Windsor
DETROIT
CLEVELAND
BUFFALO
MILWAUKEE
CHICAGO
Duluth
Kingston
Rochester
Syracuse
Albany
Manitoulin
Projection: Lambert's Equivalent Azimuthal
ft m
4500 1500
3000 1000
1200 400
600 200
0 0
200 600
2000 6000
4000 12 000
m ft

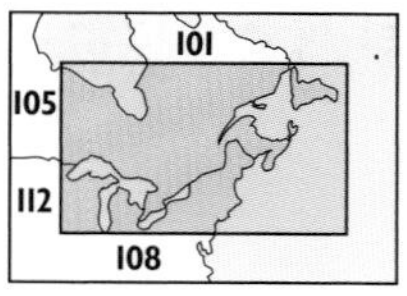
101
105
112
108

6
7
8
9
A
B
C
D
55
50
45
70
65
60
LABRADOR
SEA
NEWFOUNDLAND
Labrador
Newfoundland
QUÉBEC
GULF OF
ST. LAWRENCE
Î. d'Anticosti
Pén. de Gaspé
St. Lawrence
NEW
BRUNSWICK
PRINCE EDWARD
ISLAND
NOVA SCOTIA
Cape Breton
Island
Cabot Strait
Bay of Fundy
Smallwood Reservoir
Rés. Manicouagan
Rés. de Caniapiscau
Mealy Mts.
Long Range Mts.
Str. of Belle Isle
ST.-PIERRE
ET MIQUELON
(France)
MAINE
UNITED
STATES
NEW HAMPSHIRE
ATLANTIC
OCEAN
Sable I.
(Nova Scotia)
Îs. de la
Madeleine
(Québec)
Nain
Hopedale
Makkovik
Cartwright
Happy Valley-
Goose Bay
Churchill Falls
Schefferville
Labrador City
Fermont
Sept-Îles
Port-Cartier
Baie Comeau
Rimouski
Gaspé
Chicoutimi
Jonquière
Québec
Lévis
Sherbrooke
Moncton
Fredericton
Saint John
Bathurst
Edmundston
Charlottetown
Summerside
Halifax
Dartmouth
Truro
Yarmouth
Sydney
Corner Brook
Stephenville
Grand Falls
Windsor
Gander
St. John's
Channel-Port
aux Basques
Bangor
Augusta
Portland
Lewiston
Manchester
BOSTON
West from Greenwich
COPYRIGHT GEORGE PHILIP LTD.

50 0 50 100 150 200 250 300 km
50 0 50 100 150 200 miles
YUKON TERRITORY
NORTHWEST TERRITORIES
BRITISH COLUMBIA
ALBERTA
ALASKA (U.S.A.)
WASHINGTON
IDAHO
UNITED STATES
PACIFIC OCEAN
GREAT SLAVE LAKE
Whitehorse
Yellowknife
Fort Nelson
Fort St. John
Dawson Creek
Grande Prairie
Prince George
Prince Rupert
Kitimat
Kamloops
Kelowna
VANCOUVER
Victoria
SEATTLE
Edmonton
Calgary
Red Deer
Lethbridge
Juneau
Ketchikan
Queen Charlotte Islands
Vancouver Island
Queen Charlotte Sound
Dixon Entrance
Hecate Strait
Coast Mountains
Rocky Mountains
Cassiar Mountains
Skeena Mountains
Columbia Mts.
Monashee Mts.
Purcell Mts.
Cariboo Mts.
Caribou Mts.
Birch Mountains
Mackenzie
Peace
Liard
Projection: Lambert's Equivalent Azimuthal
West from Greenwich

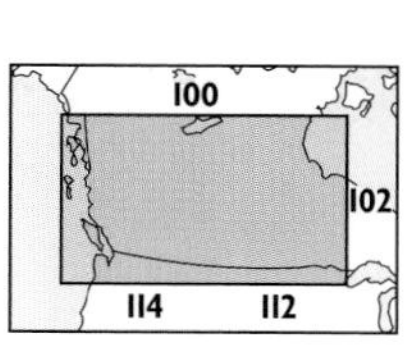
100
102
114
112

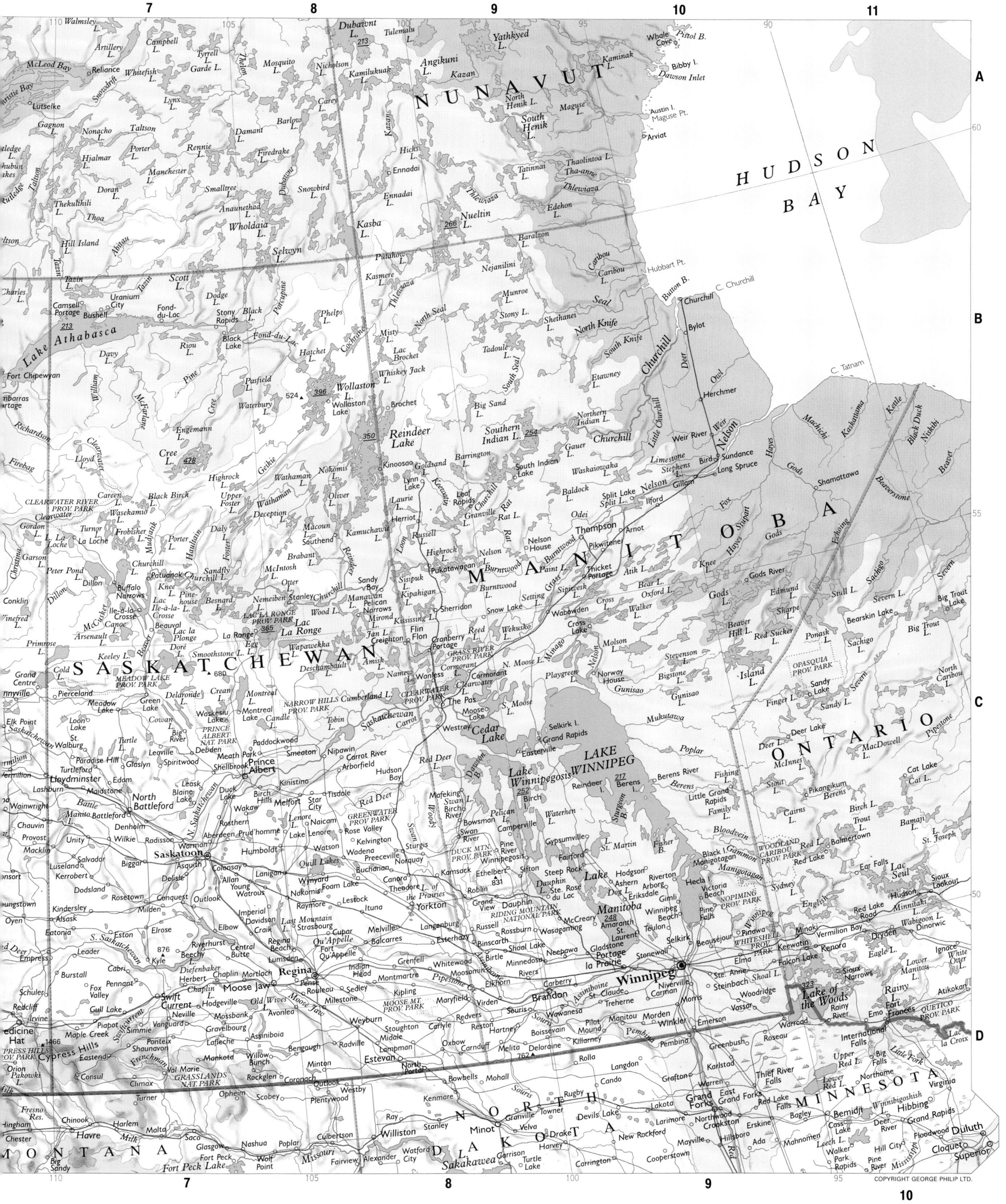
7
8
9
10
11
A
B
C
D
NUNAVUT
HUDSON BAY
SASKATCHEWAN
MANITOBA
ONTARIO
NORTH DAKOTA
MINNESOTA
MONTANA
Lake Athabasca
Reindeer Lake
Wollaston L.
Southern Indian L.
Cedar Lake
Lake Winnipegosis
LAKE WINNIPEG
Lake Manitoba
Lake of the Woods
Lac la Ronge
Kasba L.
Nueltin L.
Dubawnt L.
Yathkyed L.
Churchill
Thompson
The Pas
Flin Flon
Prince Albert
Saskatoon
Regina
Moose Jaw
Swift Current
Yorkton
Brandon
Winnipeg
Portage la Prairie
Dauphin
Kenora
Dryden
Lloydminster
North Battleford
Medicine Hat
Fort Chipewyan
Uranium City
Arviat
Minot
Williston
Grand Forks
Bemidji
Duluth
Superior
Hibbing
International Falls
Fort Frances
Lake Sakakawea
Fort Peck Lake
Havre
Cypress Hills
Nelson
Hayes
Saskatchewan
Assiniboine
Red
C. Churchill
C. Tatnam
COPYRIGHT GEORGE PHILIP LTD.

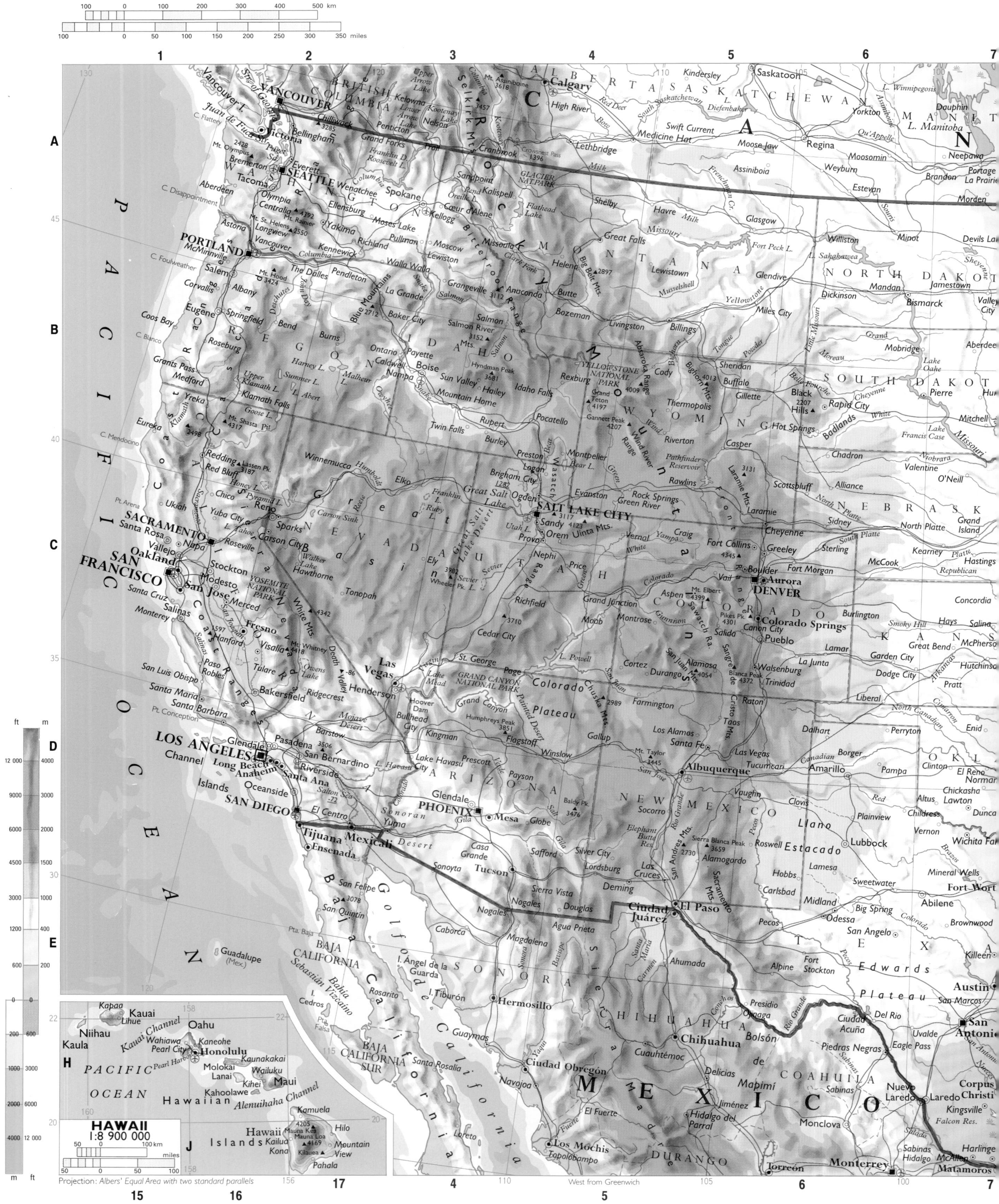

Projection: Albers' Equal Area with two standard parallels

West from Greenwich

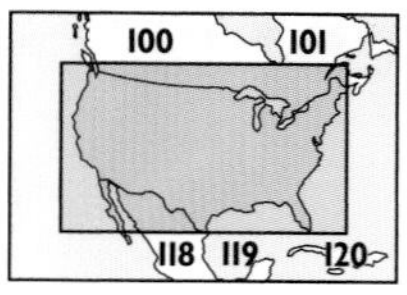
100
101
118
119
120

8
9
10
11
12
13
A
B
C
D
E
F
C A N A D A
O N T A R I O
Q U É B E C
Lake Winnipeg
Winnipeg
Lake of the Woods
Kenora
Dryden
Sioux Lookout
Nakina
Geraldton
Lake Nipigon
Nipigon
Marathon
Thunder Bay
Hearst
Moosonee
Cochrane
Timmins
Kirkland Lake
Rouyn-Noranda
Amos
L. Abitibi
L. Matagami
Chibougamau
L. Chibougamau
Baie-Comeau
Matane
Rimouski
Rivière-du-Loup
Edmundston
Chicoutimi
Jonquière
Alma
Roberval
La Tuque
Québec
Shawinigan
Trois-Rivières
Drummondville
Sherbrooke
MONTRÉAL
Hull
Ottawa
Pembroke
Sudbury
North Bay
Sault Ste. Marie
Wawa
Lake Superior
Lake Michigan
Lake Huron
Lake Erie
Lake Ontario
Georgian Bay
Manitoulin I.
Parry Sound
Owen Sound
Barrie
Orillia
Peterborough
Kingston
Oshawa
TORONTO
Kitchener
Hamilton
London
Windsor
DETROIT
Saint John
Calais
Houlton
Millinocket
Caribou
Presque Isle
Fort Kent
NEW BRUNSWICK
MAINE
Bangor
Belfast
Penobscot Bay
Waterville
Augusta
Lewiston
Brunswick
Portland
Farmington
Berlin
White Mts.
NEW HAMPSHIRE
VERMONT
Montpelier
Burlington
Plattsburgh
L. Champlain
Adirondack Mts.
Glens Falls
Rutland
Concord
Manchester
Nashua
Lowell
Lawrence
BOSTON
C. Cod
Worcester
Springfield
Providence
Fall River
New Bedford
Martha's Vineyard
Nantucket I.
HARTFORD
New Haven
Bridgeport
NEW YORK
Yonkers
Long I.
Paterson
Newark
Jersey City
Trenton
PHILADELPHIA
Allentown
Reading
Lancaster
Scranton
Wilkes-Barre
Williamsport
Elmira
Binghamton
Ithaca
Syracuse
Utica
Schenectady
Albany
Troy
Catskill Mts.
Poughkeepsie
Rochester
BUFFALO
Niagara Falls
Oswego
Watertown
Ogdensburg
Cornwall
Jamestown
Bradford
Erie
Warren
Oil City
PENNSYLVANIA
Altoona
Johnstown
Harrisburg
PITTSBURGH
Wheeling
Cumberland
Frederick
Wilmington
BALTIMORE
Dover
Atlantic City
C. May
Delaware B.
Annapolis
WASHINGTON D.C.
Salisbury
Chesapeake Bay
Morgantown
Clarksburg
Elkins
Parkersburg
WEST VIRGINIA
Charleston
Huntington
Harrisonburg
Charlottesville
Richmond
Petersburg
Lynchburg
Roanoke
Danville
Newport News
Virginia Beach
Norfolk
Elizabeth City
Albemarle Sd.
Pamlico Sd.
C. Hatteras
Rocky Mount
Greenville
Goldsboro
New Bern
Jacksonville
Onslow Bay
Wilmington
C. Fear
Raleigh
Durham
Greensboro
Winston-Salem
Hickory
NORTH CAROLINA
CHARLOTTE
Fayetteville
Rock Hill
Columbia
SOUTH CAROLINA
Florence
Sumter
Myrtle Beach
Long Bay
Georgetown
C. Romain
Charleston
Orangeburg
Augusta
Savannah
Statesboro
Brunswick
Waycross
Valdosta
Tifton
Albany
Douglas
Macon
Dublin
Cordele
GEORGIA
ATLANTA
Athens
Roswell
Gainesville
Rome
Columbus
La Grange
Auburn
Montgomery
ALABAMA
Birmingham
Tuscaloosa
Anniston
Gadsden
Decatur
Huntsville
Florence
Selma
Demopolis
Troy
Dothan
Andalusia
Mobile
Pensacola
Panama City
Tallahassee
Thomasville
Jacksonville
St. Augustine
Lake City
Gainesville
Ocala
Daytona Beach
Deltona
Orlando
C. Canaveral
Melbourne
Palm Bay
Fort Pierce
Lakeland
TAMPA
Clearwater
St. Petersburg
Tampa B.
Sarasota
L. Okeechobee
Charlotte Harbor
Cape Coral
Fort Myers
Naples
West Palm Beach
Fort Lauderdale
MIAMI
The Everglades
Florida Bay
Florida Keys
Key West
C. Sable
Straits of Florida
Apalachee B.
Apalachicola
C. San Blas
Grand Bahama I.
Freeport
Little Abaco I.
Great Abaco I.
N.E. Providence Channel
N.W. Providence Channel
BAHAMAS
Nassau
New Providence I.
Eleuthera I.
Cat I.
Exuma Sound
Andros I.
Great Exuma I.
Long I.
ATLANTIC OCEAN
GULF OF MEXICO
Mississippi River Delta
Breton Sd.
NEW ORLEANS
Houma
Morgan City
Atchafalaya B.
Marsh I.
Lafayette
Baton Rouge
L. Pontchartrain
Gulfport
Biloxi
Bogalusa
Hattiesburg
Laurel
Meridian
Jackson
McComb
Natchez
Vicksburg
MISSISSIPPI
Yazoo City
Greenwood
Greenville
Cleveland
Clarksdale
Oxford
Tupelo
Corinth
Columbus
Memphis
Jackson
TENNESSEE
Dyersburg
Nashville
Murfreesboro
Columbia
Chattanooga
Knoxville
Oak Ridge
Johnson City
Kingsport
Athens
Asheville
Spartanburg
Greenville
Anderson
Clarksville
Hopkinsville
Bowling Green
Paducah
Mayfield
Owensboro
Evansville
Henderson
KENTUCKY
Louisville
Frankfort
Lexington
Richmond
Danville
Somerset
Middlesboro
Hazard
Bluefield
Beckley
Radford
Pulaski
Blue Ridge
Appalachian Mountains
Cumberland Plateau
Allegheny Mountains
CINCINNATI
Dayton
Springfield
COLUMBUS
Zanesville
Marion
Lima
Mansfield
Canton
Akron
Youngstown
CLEVELAND
Toledo
Sandusky
Findlay
Fort Wayne
OHIO
INDIANA
INDIANAPOLIS
Richmond
Muncie
Kokomo
Marion
Lafayette
Bloomington
Terre Haute
Columbus
Vincennes
Elkhart
South Bend
Gary
CHICAGO
Joliet
Aurora
Elgin
Rockford
Kankakee
Bloomington
Champaign
Danville
Decatur
Springfield
Peoria
Galesburg
Rock Island
Davenport
Quincy
ILLINOIS
Effingham
Mattoon
Alton
East St. Louis
ST. LOUIS
Carbondale
Cape Girardeau
Mount Vernon
Midwest
Kalamazoo
Battle Creek
Jackson
Ann Arbor
Lansing
Grand Rapids
Muskegon
Flint
Saginaw
Bay City
Midland
Port Huron
Ludington
Manistee
Cadillac
Traverse City
Alpena
Petoskey
MICHIGAN
Escanaba
Manistique
Marquette
Ishpeming
Iron Mountain
Ironwood
Houghton
Keweenaw Bay
Apostle Is.
Ashland
Superior
Duluth
Two Harbors
Virginia
Hibbing
Bemidji
Grand Forks
Thief River Falls
International Falls
Fort Frances
Red Lake
Leech L.
Mille Lacs L.
Brainerd
Fargo
Moorhead
Fergus Falls
MINNESOTA
St. Cloud
Coon Rapids
MINNEAPOLIS
ST. PAUL
Willmar
Red Wing
Owatonna
Rochester
Winona
Mankato
Austin
Albert Lea
Worthington
Brookings
Madison
Watertown
Big Stone Lake
WISCONSIN
Eau Claire
Stevens Point
Wausau
Rhinelander
Rice Lake
Merrill
Menominee
Green Bay
Appleton
Manitowoc
Oshkosh
Sheboygan
La Crosse
Portage
Madison
MILWAUKEE
Racine
Kenosha
Janesville
Beloit
Dubuque
Clinton
Cedar Rapids
Iowa City
Waterloo
Charles City
Mason City
IOWA
Des Moines
Fort Dodge
Spencer
Cherokee
Sioux City
Council Bluffs
Ames
Ottumwa
Burlington
Creston
Red Oak
Maryville
Kirksville
Chillicothe
St. Joseph
Hannibal
MISSOURI
Columbia
Jefferson City
Sedalia
KANSAS CITY
Leavenworth
Lawrence
Topeka
Emporia
Wichita
Fort Scott
Pittsburg
Parsons
Nevada
Springfield
Joplin
Lebanon
Rolla
L. of the Ozarks
Ozark Plateau
West Plains
Poplar Bluff
Paragould
Blytheville
Jonesboro
Newport
ARKANSAS
Fayetteville
Boston Mts.
Russellville
Conway
Fort Smith
Little Rock
Hot Springs
Pine Bluff
Stuttgart
Ouachita Mts.
Camden
El Dorado
Texarkana
Hope
Paris
Sherman
Durant
McAlester
Muskogee
Tulsa
Bartlesville
Arkansas City
Ponca City
Oklahoma City
Shawnee
DALLAS
Arlington
Marshall
Longview
Tyler
Shreveport
Monroe
LOUISIANA
Alexandria
Natchitoches
Palestine
Nacogdoches
Lufkin
Toledo Bend Res.
De Ridder
Huntsville
Lake Charles
Beaumont
Port Arthur
New Iberia
HOUSTON
Pasadena
Galveston
Bryan
Corsicana
Freeport
Port Lavaca
Matagorda I.
Aransas Pass
Rio Grande
Laguna Madre
Beatrice
Moosehead L.
St. Lawrence
New Brunswick
95
90
85
80
75
70
65
45
40
35
30
25

km
miles
NEW YORK CITY
BOSTON
PHILADELPHIA
BALTIMORE
WASHINGTON D.C.
PITTSBURGH
CLEVELAND
DETROIT
CHICAGO
MILWAUKEE
TORONTO
MONTREAL
BUFFALO
COLUMBUS
CINCINNATI
INDIANAPOLIS
HARTFORD
LAKE ONTARIO
LAKE ERIE
LAKE HURON
LAKE MICHIGAN
LAKE SUPERIOR
Georgian Bay
Chesapeake Bay
Delaware Bay
NEW JERSEY
WEST VIRGINIA
KENTUCKY
INDIANA
OHIO
WISCONSIN
DELAWARE
MARYLAND

TENNESSEE
NORTH CAROLINA
SOUTH CAROLINA
GEORGIA
ALABAMA
MISSISSIPPI
FLORIDA
MAINE
NEW HAMPSHIRE
CANADA
BAHAMAS
ATLANTIC OCEAN
GULF OF MEXICO
Nashville
Knoxville
Chattanooga
Asheville
CHARLOTTE
Raleigh
Durham
Greensboro
Winston-Salem
Wilmington
Columbia
Charleston
Myrtle Beach
ATLANTA
Augusta
Macon
Columbus
Savannah
Birmingham
Huntsville
Montgomery
Mobile
Pensacola
Tallahassee
Jacksonville
Gainesville
Orlando
TAMPA
St. Petersburg
Daytona Beach
Fort Lauderdale
MIAMI
Florida Keys
Portland
Augusta
Bangor
Mt. Katahdin 1605
Pamlico Sound
Long Bay
Okefenokee Swamp
Lake Okeechobee
EVERGLADES NAT. PARK
BIG CYPRESS NAT. PRESERVE
GREAT SMOKY MTS. NAT. PARK
Grand Bahama
Great Abaco I.
Freeport
C. Hatteras
C. Lookout
C. Fear
C. Canaveral
C. San Blas
C. St. George
Continuation Eastwards On same scale.
ft
m
6000
4500
3000
1200
600
0
2000
1500
1000
400
200
0
200
2000
4000
600
6000
12 000
Projection: Albers' Equal Area with two standard parallels
West from Greenwich
COPYRIGHT.GEORGE PHILIP LTD.

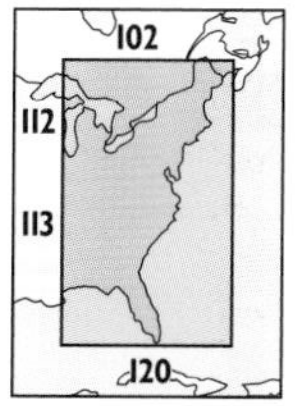
102
112
113
120

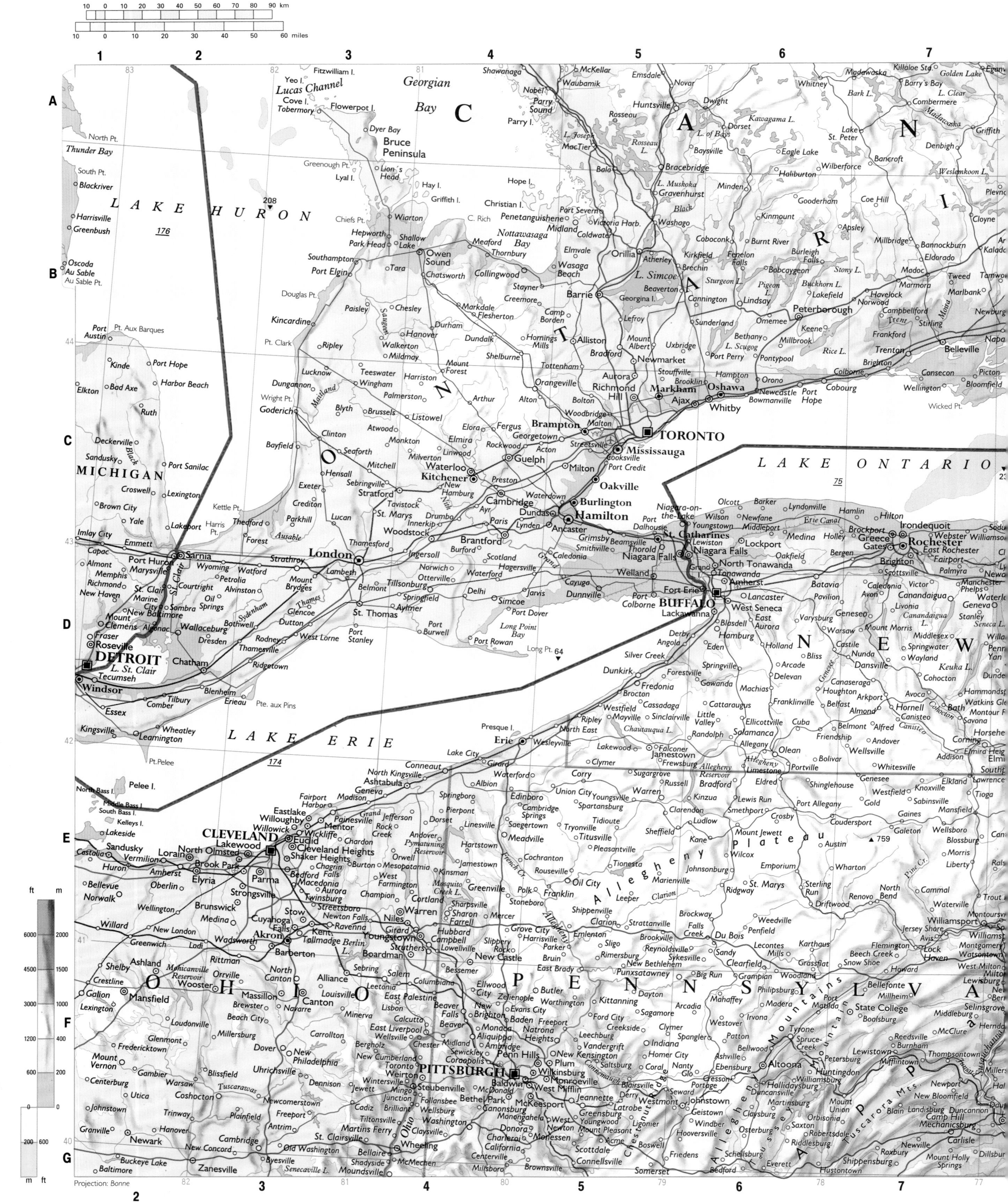
10 0 10 20 30 40 50 60 70 80 90 km
10 0 10 20 30 40 50 60 miles
1 2 3 4 5 6 7
A B C D E F G
Projection: Bonne
ft m
6000 2000
4500 1500
3000 1000
1200 400
600 200
0 0
200 600
m ft
LAKE HURON
176
208
Georgian Bay
Thunder Bay
LAKE ONTARIO
75
LAKE ERIE
174
64
MICHIGAN
ONTARIO
CANADA
NEW YORK
PENNSYLVANIA
OHIO
Allegheny Plateau
Allegheny Mountains
Appalachian Mountains
Tuscarora Mts.
Bruce Peninsula
Lucas Channel
Nottawasaga Bay
L. Simcoe
L. Muskoka
L. Joseph
Rosseau L.
L. Scugog
Rice L.
Chautauqua L.
Allegheny Reservoir
Pymatuning Reservoir
Mosquito Creek L.
Mohicanville Reservoir
L. St. Clair
Long Point Bay
Pt. Pelee
Pelee I.
North Bass I.
Middle Bass I.
South Bass I.
Kelleys I.
Tobermory
Flowerpot I.
Fitzwilliam I.
Cove I.
Yeo I.
Dyer Bay
Lion's Head
Wiarton
Owen Sound
Collingwood
Southampton
Port Elgin
Kincardine
Goderich
Bayfield
Sarnia
Port Huron
London
Strathroy
St. Thomas
Woodstock
Stratford
Kitchener
Waterloo
Guelph
Cambridge
Brantford
Hamilton
Burlington
Oakville
Mississauga
Brampton
TORONTO
Markham
Richmond Hill
Ajax
Whitby
Oshawa
Newmarket
Aurora
Barrie
Orillia
Gravenhurst
Bracebridge
Huntsville
Parry Sound
Midland
Penetanguishene
Peterborough
Lindsay
Cobourg
Port Hope
Trenton
Belleville
Niagara Falls
St. Catharines
Welland
Fort Erie
BUFFALO
Lackawanna
Lockport
Rochester
Irondequoit
Batavia
Dunkirk
Fredonia
Jamestown
Olean
Salamanca
Hornell
Erie
Meadville
Titusville
Oil City
Franklin
Warren
Bradford
Corry
Conneaut
Ashtabula
Painesville
Mentor
Willoughby
Euclid
CLEVELAND
Lakewood
Parma
Elyria
Lorain
Sandusky
Akron
Kent
Canton
Massillon
Youngstown
Warren
Niles
Sharon
New Castle
Butler
PITTSBURGH
Penn Hills
McKeesport
Washington
Wheeling
Steubenville
Weirton
Greensburg
Johnstown
Altoona
State College
Williamsport
Lock Haven
Huntingdon
Carlisle
Mansfield
Wooster
Zanesville
New Philadelphia
Newark
DETROIT
Windsor
Roseville
Chatham
Leamington
Kingsville
Port Sanilac
Harbor Beach
Port Austin
Oscoda
Harrisville
Greenbush
Orangeville
Alliston
Shelburne
Simcoe
Tillsonburg
Delhi
Dunnville
Port Colborne
Grimsby
Niagara-on-the-Lake
North Tonawanda
Tonawanda
Amherst
West Seneca
Hamburg
Medina
Albion
Brockport
Canandaigua
Geneva
Dansville
Wellsville
Bath
Corning
Elmira
Coudersport
Emporium
St. Marys
Ridgway
Du Bois
Clearfield
Punxsutawney
Indiana
Kittanning
Beaver Falls
Bellefonte
Tyrone
Hollidaysburg
Bedford
Somerset
Uniontown
Shippensburg
Chambersburg

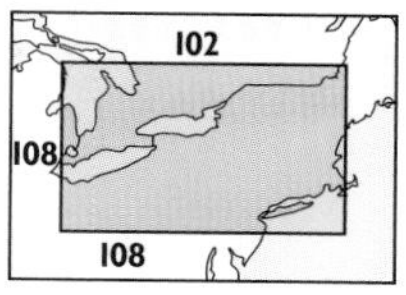
102
108
108

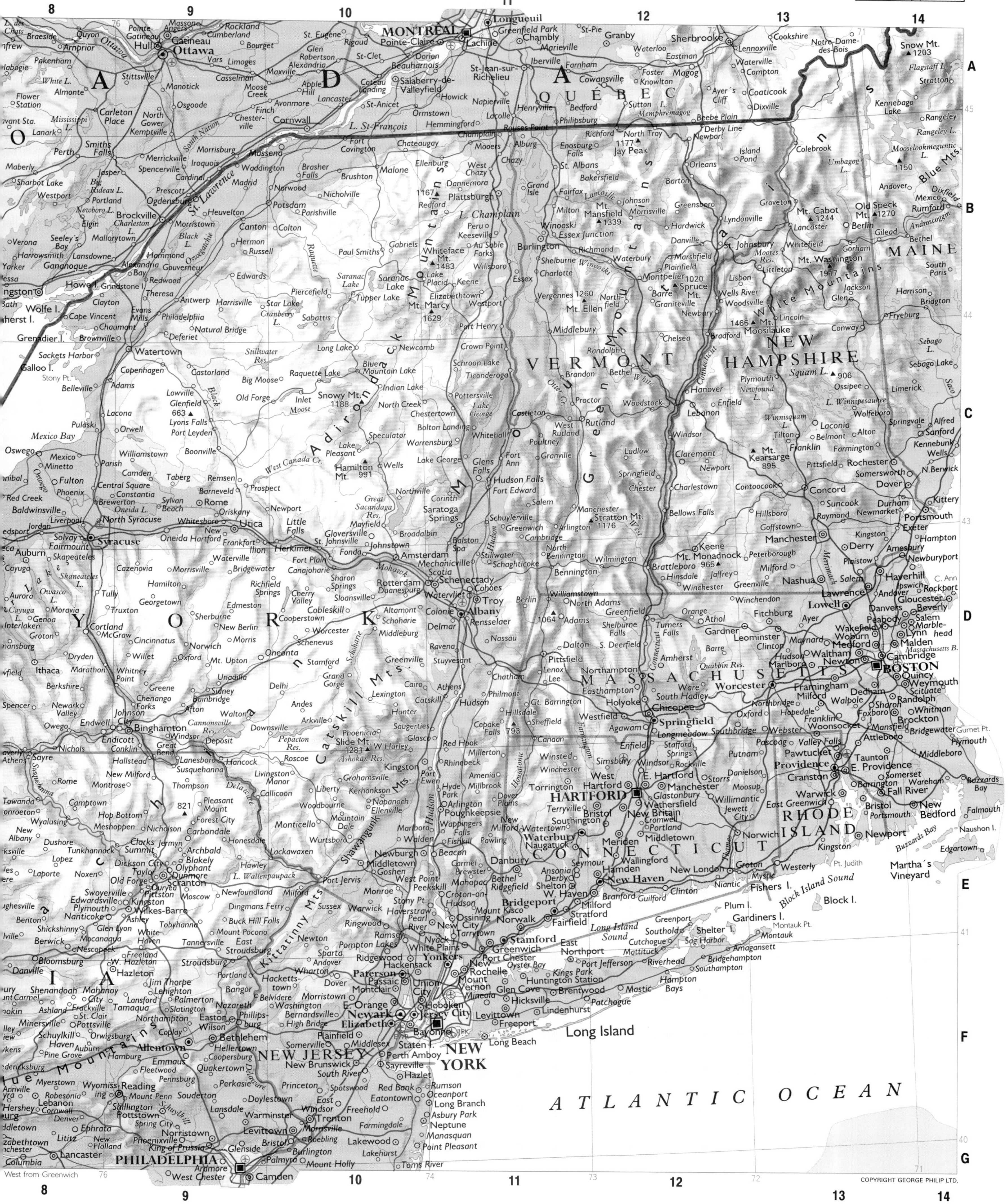
8
9
10
11
12
13
14
A
B
C
D
E
F
G
MONTREAL
Ottawa
Hull
QUÉBEC
VERMONT
NEW HAMPSHIRE
MAINE
MASSACHUSETTS
RHODE ISLAND
CONNECTICUT
NEW JERSEY
NEW YORK
BOSTON
HARTFORD
PHILADELPHIA
Providence
Springfield
Worcester
Albany
Syracuse
Utica
Binghamton
Burlington
Concord
Manchester
Portsmouth
New Haven
Bridgeport
Stamford
Newark
Jersey City
Trenton
Allentown
Bethlehem
Scranton
Wilkes-Barre
Sherbrooke
Granby
Adirondack Mountains
Catskill Mts.
Green Mountains
White Mountains
Blue Mountains
Kittatinny Mts.
Mt. Marcy 1629
Mt. Washington 1917
Mt. Mansfield 1339
L. Champlain
L. St-François
Long Island
Long Island Sound
Block Island Sound
Buzzards Bay
Martha's Vineyard
Nantucket
ATLANTIC OCEAN
West from Greenwich
76
75
74
73
72
71
45
44
43
41
40

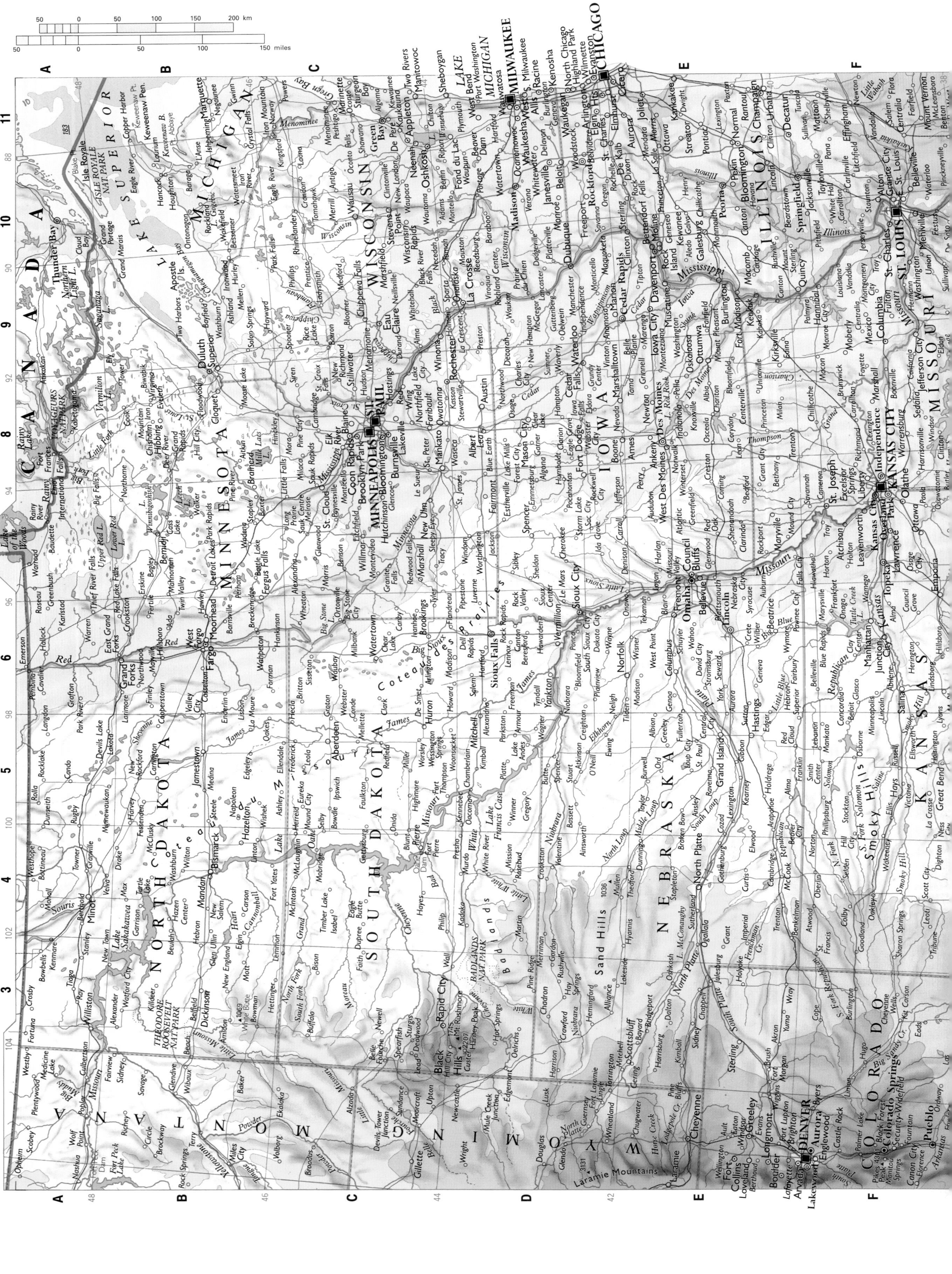

50 0 50 100 150 200 km
50 0 50 100 150 miles
C A N A D A
LAKE SUPERIOR
LAKE MICHIGAN
MICHIGAN
WISCONSIN
MINNESOTA
NORTH DAKOTA
SOUTH DAKOTA
IOWA
ILLINOIS
MISSOURI
NEBRASKA
KANSAS
COLORADO
WYOMING
MONTANA
CHICAGO
MILWAUKEE
MINNEAPOLIS
ST. PAUL
ST. LOUIS
KANSAS CITY
DENVER
Omaha
Des Moines
Sioux Falls
Fargo
Bismarck
Pierre
Lincoln
Topeka
Cheyenne
Duluth
Madison
Springfield
Jefferson City
Rapid City
Cedar Rapids
Davenport
Peoria
Green Bay
Thunder Bay
Sioux City
Aberdeen
Grand Forks
Mississippi
Missouri
Coteau des Prairies
Sand Hills
Black Hills
Laramie Mountains
ISLE ROYALE NAT. PARK
VOYAGEURS NAT. PARK
BADLANDS NAT. PARK
THEODORE ROOSEVELT NAT. PARK

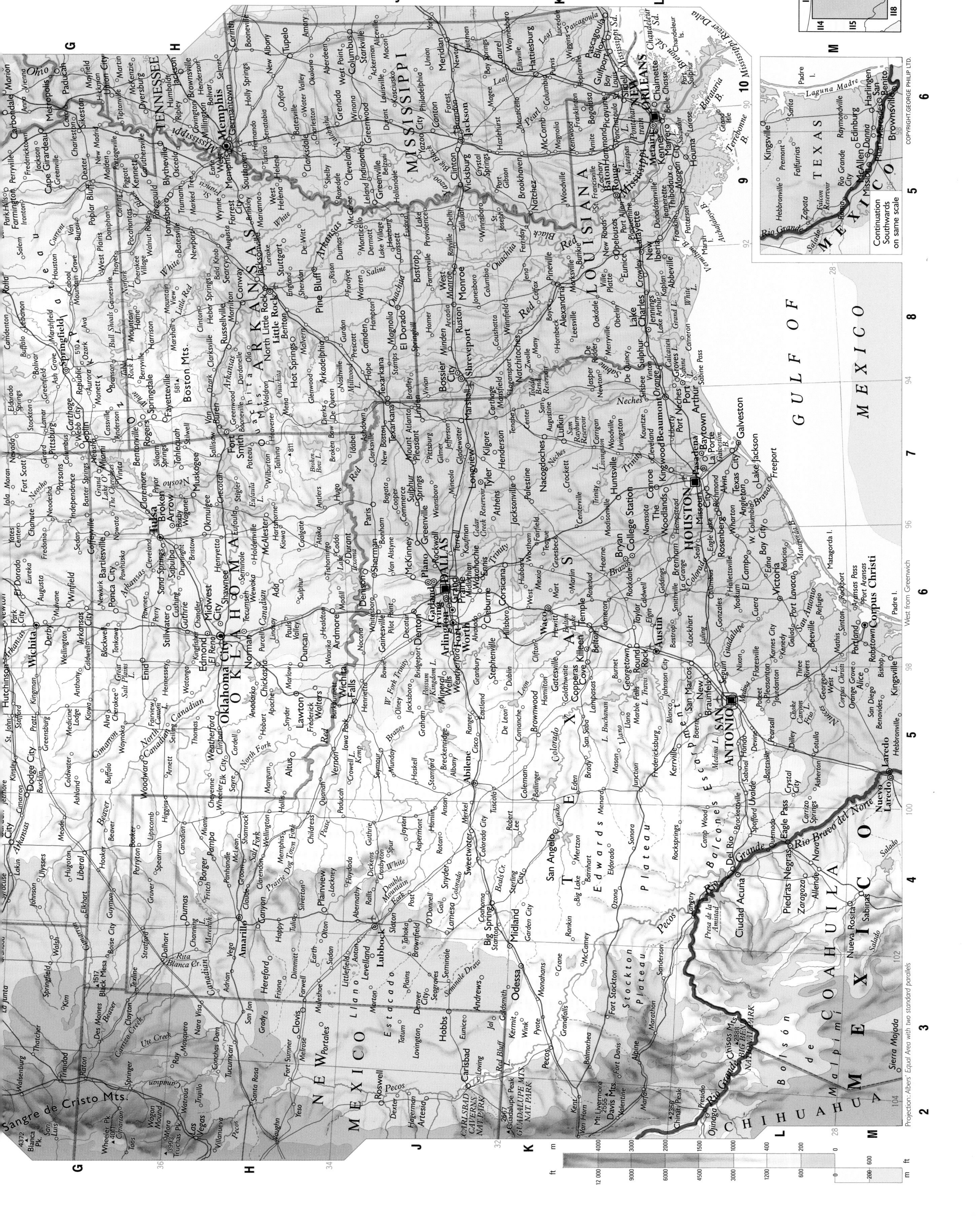
GULF OF MEXICO
TEXAS
OKLAHOMA
ARKANSAS
LOUISIANA
MISSISSIPPI
TENNESSEE
NEW MEXICO
COAHUILA
CHIHUAHUA
MEXICO
Dallas
Houston
San Antonio
New Orleans
Memphis
Oklahoma City
Tulsa
Little Rock
Shreveport
Jackson
Austin
Fort Worth
Corpus Christi
Lubbock
Amarillo
Wichita
Abilene
San Angelo
Odessa
Midland
Laredo
Baton Rouge
Galveston
Edwards Plateau
Llano Estacado
Stockton Plateau
Sangre de Cristo Mts.
Boston Mts.
Ouachita Mts.
Balcones Escarpment
Big Bend National Park
Continuation Southwards on same scale
Projection: Albers' Equal Area with two standard parallels
West from Greenwich
COPYRIGHT.GEORGE PHILIP LTD.

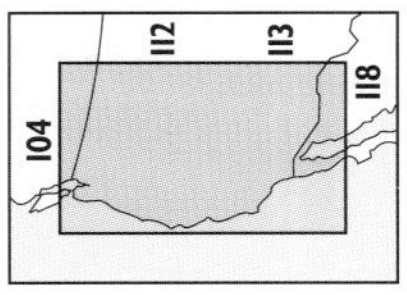
104
112
113
118

50 0 50 100 150 200 km

50 0 50 100 150 miles

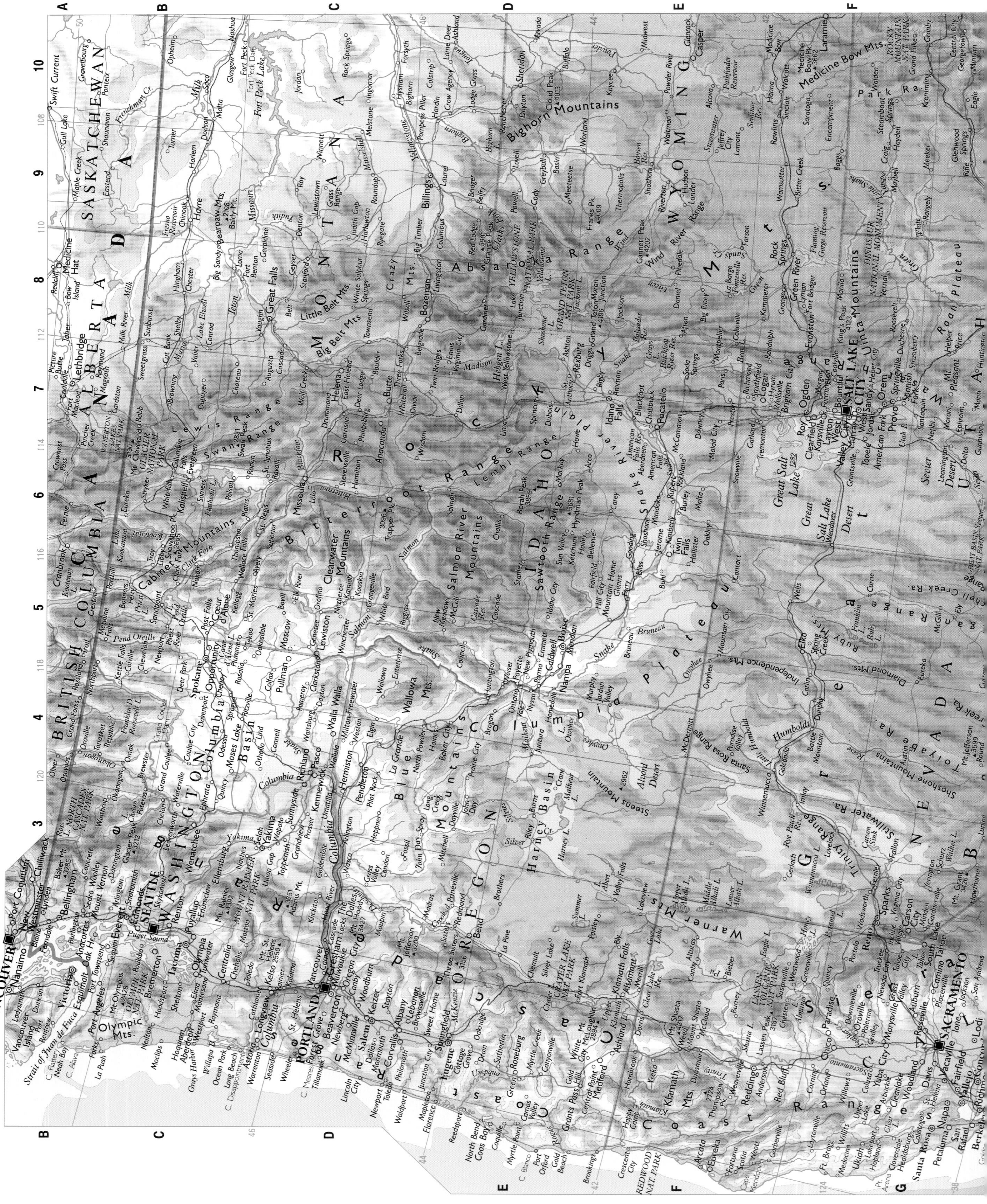
BRITISH COLUMBIA
ALBERTA
SASKATCHEWAN
CANADA
WASHINGTON
OREGON
IDAHO
MONTANA
WYOMING
NEVADA
UTAH
CALIFORNIA
VANCOUVER
SEATTLE
PORTLAND
SACRAMENTO
SALT LAKE CITY
Bighorn Mountains
Absaroka Range
Bitterroot Range
Salmon River Mountains
Blue Mountains
Cascade Range
Columbia Basin
Columbia Plateau
Great Salt Lake
Great Salt Lake Desert
Great Basin
Klamath Mts.
Olympic Mts.
Wind River Range
Lewis Range
Swan Range
Sawtooth Range
Wasatch Range
Uinta Mountains
Medicine Bow Mts.
Park Ra.
Wallowa Mts.
Steens Mountain
Warner Mts.
Ruby Mts.
Clearwater Mountains
Cabinet Mountains
Crazy Mts.
Little Belt Mts.
Big Belt Mts.
Harney Basin
Snake River Plain
Strait of Juan de Fuca
Puget Sound
YELLOWSTONE NATIONAL PARK
GRAND TETON NAT. PARK
GLACIER NATIONAL PARK
CRATER LAKE NAT. PARK
OLYMPIC NAT. PARK
NORTH CASCADES NAT. PARK
MOUNT RAINIER NAT. PARK
LASSEN VOLCANIC NAT. PARK
REDWOOD NAT. PARK
DINOSAUR NATIONAL MONUMENT
ROCKY MOUNTAIN NAT. PARK
WATERTON LAKES NAT. PARK

COLORADO
NEW MEXICO
ARIZONA
TEXAS
NEVADA
CALIFORNIA
UTAH
MEXICO
SONORA
CHIHUAHUA
BAJA CALIFORNIA
PACIFIC OCEAN
Golfo de California
Colorado Plateau
Sonoran Desert
Mojave Desert
Desierto de Altar
Sangre de Cristo Mts.
San Juan Mts.
Sawatch Range
Sacramento Mts.
San Andres Mts.
Chuska Mts.
Sierra de Juárez
Sierra de San Pedro Mártir
Coast Ranges
Santa Lucia Range
Channel Is.
Painted Desert
Grand Canyon
Death Valley
Mogollon Rim
Rio Grande
Rio Bravo del Norte
Salton Sea
SAN FRANCISCO
San Jose
Oakland
Fresno
Bakersfield
LOS ANGELES
SAN DIEGO
Tijuana
Mexicali
Ensenada
Las Vegas
PHOENIX
Tucson
Flagstaff
Yuma
Albuquerque
Santa Fe
El Paso
Ciudad Juárez
Las Cruces
Chihuahua
Hermosillo
Nogales
Agua Prieta
Grand Junction
Durango
Farmington
Gallup
Isla Guadalupe (Mexico)
Isla Cedros
I. Tiburón
I. Ángel de la Guarda
West from Greenwich
COPYRIGHT GEORGE PHILIP LTD.
Projection: Albers' Equal Area with two standard parallels

CENTRAL AND SOUTHERN CALIFORNIA AND WESTERN WASHINGTON 1:2 200 000

10 0 10 20 30 40 50 60 70 80 90 km
10 0 10 20 30 40 50 60 miles
NEVADA
ARIZONA
MEXICO
BAJA CALIFORNIA
PACIFIC OCEAN
Mojave Desert
Sonoran Desert
Channel Islands
Las Vegas
Henderson
North Las Vegas
Lake Mead
Death Valley
Amargosa Range
Bakersfield
LOS ANGELES
Santa Barbara
Ventura
Oxnard
Long Beach
Santa Ana
Riverside
San Bernardino
Palm Springs
Barstow
Lancaster
Palmdale
SAN DIEGO
Tijuana
Mexicali
Yuma
Salton Sea
Imperial Valley
Chocolate Mts.
Colorado
Needles
Lake Havasu City
Santa Catalina I.
San Clemente I.
San Nicolas I.
Santa Cruz I.
Santa Rosa I.
San Miguel I.
Santa Barbara Channel
San Pedro Channel
Gulf of Santa Catalina
Projection: Bonne
West from Greenwich
COPYRIGHT GEORGE PHILIP LTD.

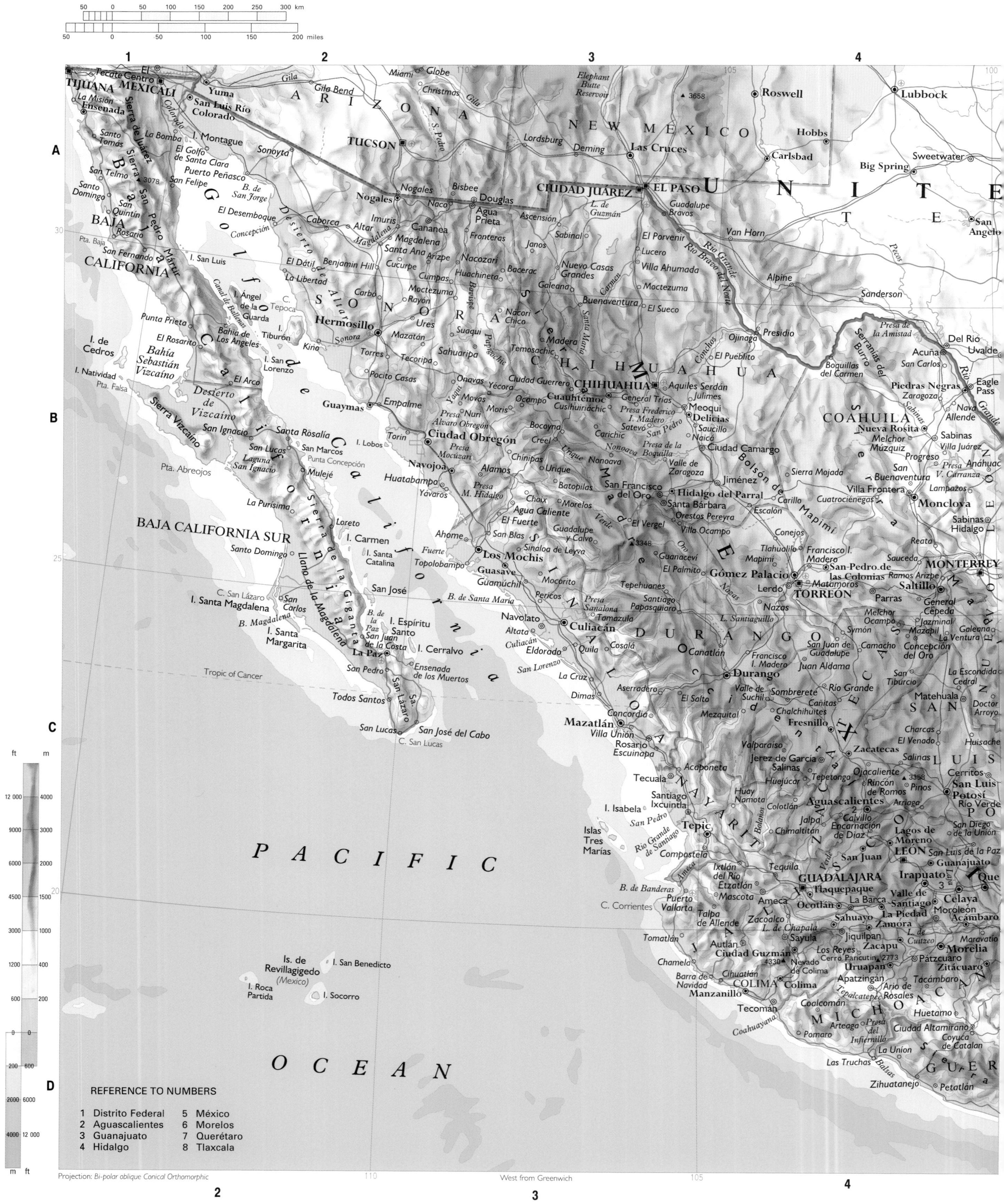
50 0 50 100 150 200 250 300 km
50 0 50 100 150 200 miles
1
2
3
4
A
B
C
D
ARIZONA
NEW MEXICO
UNITED STATES
SONORA
CHIHUAHUA
COAHUILA
DURANGO
SINALOA
NAYARIT
ZACATECAS
JALISCO
MICHOACAN
BAJA CALIFORNIA
BAJA CALIFORNIA SUR
Golfo de California
Sierra Madre Occidental
PACIFIC OCEAN
TIJUANA
MEXICALI
Ensenada
Yuma
San Luis Río Colorado
TUCSON
Nogales
Douglas
Las Cruces
CIUDAD JUÁREZ
EL PASO
Roswell
Lubbock
Hermosillo
Guaymas
Ciudad Obregón
Navojoa
Los Mochis
Culiacán
Mazatlán
CHIHUAHUA
Delicias
Hidalgo del Parral
Gómez Palacio
TORREÓN
Saltillo
MONTERREY
Monclova
Piedras Negras
Durango
Fresnillo
Zacatecas
Aguascalientes
San Luis Potosí
Tepic
GUADALAJARA
LEÓN
Irapuato
Morelia
Uruapan
Colima
Manzanillo
Santa Rosalía
Loreto
La Paz
San José del Cabo
San Lucas
Tropic of Cancer
Is. de Revillagigedo (Mexico)
I. San Benedicto
I. Socorro
I. Roca Partida
Islas Tres Marías
REFERENCE TO NUMBERS
1 Distrito Federal
2 Aguascalientes
3 Guanajuato
4 Hidalgo
5 México
6 Morelos
7 Querétaro
8 Tlaxcala
Projection: Bi-polar oblique Conical Orthomorphic
West from Greenwich
110
105
ft m
12 000 4000
9000 3000
6000 2000
4500 1500
3000 1000
1200 400
600 200
0 0
200 600
2000 6000
4000 12 000
m ft

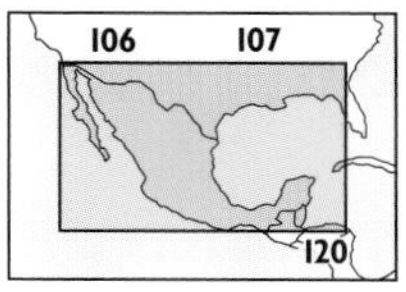

106
107
120

5
6
7
8
A
B
C
D
E
GULF OF MEXICO
Golfo de Campeche
Golfo de Tehuantepec
Golfo de Honduras
Canal de Yucatán
Tropic of Cancer
UNITED STATES
TEXAS
ARKANSAS
LOUISIANA
MISSISSIPPI
ALABAMA
GEORGIA
FLORIDA
MÉXICO
TAMAULIPAS
SAN LUIS POTOSÍ
VERACRUZ
PUEBLA
GUERRERO
OAXACA
CHIAPAS
TABASCO
CAMPECHE
YUCATÁN
QUINTANA ROO
GUATEMALA
BELIZE
HONDURAS
CUBA
Wichita Falls
Denison
Sherman
Paris
Hope
Camden
Texarkana
El Dorado
Greenville
Tuscaloosa
Opelika
Columbus
McRae
Denton
FORT WORTH
DALLAS
Marshall
Monroe
Vicksburg
Meridian
Selma
Phenix City
Montgomery
Americus
Cordele
Abilene
Ranger
Cleburne
Longview
Tyler
Shreveport
Tallulah
Jackson
Troy
Albany
Tifton
Waycross
Hillsboro
Corsicana
Palestine
Toledo Bend Res.
Natchez
Laurel
Hattiesburg
Flomaton
Dothan
Jim Woodruff Res.
Valdosta
Brownwood
Waco
Nacogdoches
Alexandria
McComb
Chattahoochee
Tallahassee
Lufkin
Sam Rayburn Reservoir
Jewett
Baton Rouge
Bogalusa
Hammond
Biloxi
Gulfport
MOBILE
Pensacola
Panama City
Lake City
Temple
Huntsville
Bryan
Lake Charles
Lafayette
L. Pontchartrain
NEW ORLEANS
Mobile Bay
Apalachee Bay
C. San Blas
Suwannee
Austin
Navasota
Beaumont
Port Arthur
Breton Sd.
HOUSTON
Atchafalaya Bay
Terrebonne Bay
Mississippi River Delta
Rosenberg
Galveston
Clearwater
SAN ANTONIO
Victoria
Dilley
Nueces
Alice
Corpus Christi
Laredo
Kingsville
Nuevo Laredo
Zapata
Presa Falcón
Nuevo Guerrero
Camargo
McAllen
Harlingen
Brownsville
Laguna Madre
Reynosa
Matamoros
Presa M. R. Gomez
China
Valle Hermoso
Santa Teresa
Montemorelos
Mendez
San Fernando
Linares
Villagrán
Hidalgo
Santander Jiménez
Zaragoza
La Pesca
Soto la Marina
Ciudad Victoria
Sierra de Tamaulipas
Llera
Aldama
Pta. Jerez
Ocampo
Ciudad Mante
Altamira
Ciudad Madero
Tampico
Ciudad de Valles
Cárdenas
Pánuco
L. de Tamiahua
Ozuluama
Tempoal
Tantoyuca
C. Rojo
Tamazunchale
Chicontepec
Tuxpan
Zimapán
Zacualtipan
Poza Rica
Papantla
San Juan del Río
Huichapan
Pachuca
Huauchinango
Nautla
Misantla
Tulancingo
Teziutlán
Tula
Zumpango
El Oro
Jalapa Enríquez
MÉXICO
Apizaco
Zempoala
Veracruz
Toluca
Tlaxcala
Amecameca
PUEBLA
Citlaltépetl
Coatepec
Tenango
Popocatépetl
Córdoba
Alvarado
Tlacotalpan
Orizaba
Cuernavaca
Tehuacán
Cosamaloapan
San Andrés Tuxtla
Jojutla
Izúcar de Matamoros
Chilac
Ajalpan
Tres Valles
Coatzacoalcos
Minatitlán
Acayucan
Iguala
Chiautla
Acatlán
Huautla de Jiménez
Presa Miguel Alemán
San Juan Bautista Valle Nacional
Istmo de Tehuantepec
Jesús Carranza
Chilpancingo
Chilapa
Huajuapan de León
Asunción Nochixtlán
Silacayoapan
Tlaxiaco
Oaxaca
Tlacolula
Monte Albán
Sierra Madre del Sur
Tierra Colorada
Ayutla
Ometepec
Acapulco
Ocotlán
Ejutla
San Jerónimo Taviche
Ixtepec
Tehuantepec
Juchitán
Salina Cruz
Pinotepa Nacional
Tututepec
San Pedro Mixtepec
Miahuatlán
Pochutla
Puerto Ángel
Puerto Escondido
Punta Maldonado
Jamiltepec
Papagayo
Verde
Progreso
Dzilam de Bravo
Pta. Yalkubul
Rio Lagartos
El Cuyo
C. Catoche
Cancún
Puerto Juárez
Motul
Temax
Tizimin
Espita
Izamal
Mérida
Dzibilchaltún
Valladolid
Chichen Itzá
Mayapán
Sotuta
Maxcanú
Ticul
Uxmal
Peto
Tekax
Puerto Morelos
Cozumel
Isla Cozumel
Tenabo
Bolonchenticul
Vigia Chico
B. de la Ascensión
Campeche
Edzná
Hopelchén
Felipe Carrillo Puerto
B. del Espíritu Santo
Champotón
Chenkán
Bacalar
Chetumal
B. de Chetumal
Banco Chinchorro
Ciudad del Carmen
L. de Términos
Matamoros
Corozal
Orange Walk
Ambergris Cay
Frontera
Paraiso
Comalcalco
Villahermosa
Cárdenas
Palizada
Concepción
Hondo
Balancán
Macuspana
La Venta
Belize City
Turneffe Is.
Tenosique
Uaxactún
San Ignacio
Tikal
Palenque
Belmopan
Benque Viejo
Dangriga
Raudales de Malpaso
Teapa
Presa Netzahualcoyotl
Simojovel
Ocosingo
L. Petén Itzá
La Libertad
Flores
Maya Mts.
Monkey River
Tuxtla Gutiérrez
Copainalá
Chiapa de Corzo
San Cristóbal de las Casas
La Independencia
Usumacinta
Lacantún
Salinas
San Luis
San Antonio
Punta Gorda
Puerto Barrios
Matías Romero
Comitán
Livingston
Arriaga
Tonalá
Sierra Madre
La Concordia
Sebol
Puerto Arista
Pijijiapan
Mapastepec
Motozintla
Cuilco
Huehuetenango
Cuchumatanes
Cobán
L. de Izabal
Sierra de las Minas
Huixtla
Tapachula
Coatepeque
Retalhuleu
San Marcos
Totonicapán
Sololá
Utatlán
Antigua
Mazatenango
GUATEMALA
Amatitlán
Jalapa
Chiquimula
Zacapa
Gualán
Copán
Santa Bárbara
Santa Rosa de Copán
La Esperanza
La Paz
L. de Yojoa
Comayagua
Tegucigalpa
Yuscarán
Danlí
San Pedro Sula
El Progreso
Arenal
Olanchito
Tela
Balfate
Savá
Trujillo
Is. de la Bahía
Roatán
Puerto Castilla
Iriona
Yoro
Juticalpa
Catacamas
Patuca
Sulaco
Motagua
La Esperanza
Guane
La Fe
C. San Antonio
C. Corrientes
I. Desterrada
I. Pérez (Mexico)
4220
3993
3703
3139
5452
5700
4282
4054
1879
100
95
90
85
30
25
20
15

COPYRIGHT GEORGE PHILIP LTD.

1:7 100 000

GULF OF MEXICO
PACIFIC OCEAN
CARIB
MEXICO
GUATEMALA
HONDURAS
EL SALVADOR
NICARAGUA
COSTA RICA
PANAMÁ
BELIZE
CUBA
JAMAICA
U.S.A.
YUCATÁN
CAMPECHE
QUINTANA ROO
Great Bahama Bank
Straits of Florida
Florida Keys
Canal de Yucatán
Canal Nicholás
Canal Viejo de Bahama
Santaren Channel
Northwest Providence Channel
Northeast Providence Channel
Golfo de Honduras
Golfo de Panamá
Golfo del Darién
G. de Papagayo
G. de Nicoya
G. de Fonseca
G. de Chiriquí
G. de los Mosquitos
Mosquitia
Cayman Islands (U.K.)
Grand Cayman
Little Cayman
Cayman Brac
Georgetown
7680
Swan Islands (U.S.A. & Honduras)
Pedro Cays (Jamaica)
Bajo Nuevo (Colombia)
Cayos Miskitos (Nicaragua)
Cayos Roncador (U.S.A. & Colombia)
I. de Providencia (Colombia)
I. de San Andrés (Colombia)
Cayos de Albuquerque (Colombia)
Is. del Maiz (Nicaragua. U.S.A.)
Dry Tortugas (U.S.A.)
Key West
MIAMI
Hialeah
Fort Lauderdale
Boca Raton
West Palm Beach
Fort Myers
Naples
L. Okeechobee
Everglades
C. Sable
Freeport
Grand Bahama
Nassau
New Providence
Andros Island
LA HABANA (Havana)
MARIANAO
Guanabacoa
Matanzas
Cárdenas
Pinar del Río
Cienfuegos
Santa Clara
Sancti Spíritus
Camagüey
HOLGUÍN
Bayamo
Manzanillo
SANTIAGO DE CUBA
Sierra Maestra
2000
I. de la Juventud
Nueva Gerona
Arch. de los Canarreos
Arch. de Jardines de la Reina
Montego Bay
KINGSTON
Spanish Town
Mandeville
Mérida
Progreso
Campeche
Ciudad del Carmen
Chetumal
Cancún
Isla Cozumel
Valladolid
Ambergris Cay
Belize City
Belmopan
Turneffe Is.
Dangriga
Is. de la Bahía
Roatán
Puerto Barrios
Puerto Cortés
San Pedro Sula
La Ceiba
Tegucigalpa
Choluteca
GUATEMALA
Quetzaltenango
Huehuetenango
Cobán
Flores
Tikal
Santa Ana
SAN SALVADOR
San Miguel
MANAGUA
León
Granada
Masaya
Matagalpa
Lago de Nicaragua
Bluefields
San Juan del Norte
Puerto Cabezas
C. Gracias a Dios
SAN JOSÉ
Cartago
Limón
Puntarenas
Alajuela
Liberia
3837
3374
Bocas del Toro
David
Colón
Panama Canal
PANAMÁ
Arch. de las Perlas
Archipiélago de San Blas
Serranía del Darién
Pen. de Azuero
I. de Coiba
CARTAGE
Projection: Conical with two standard parallels

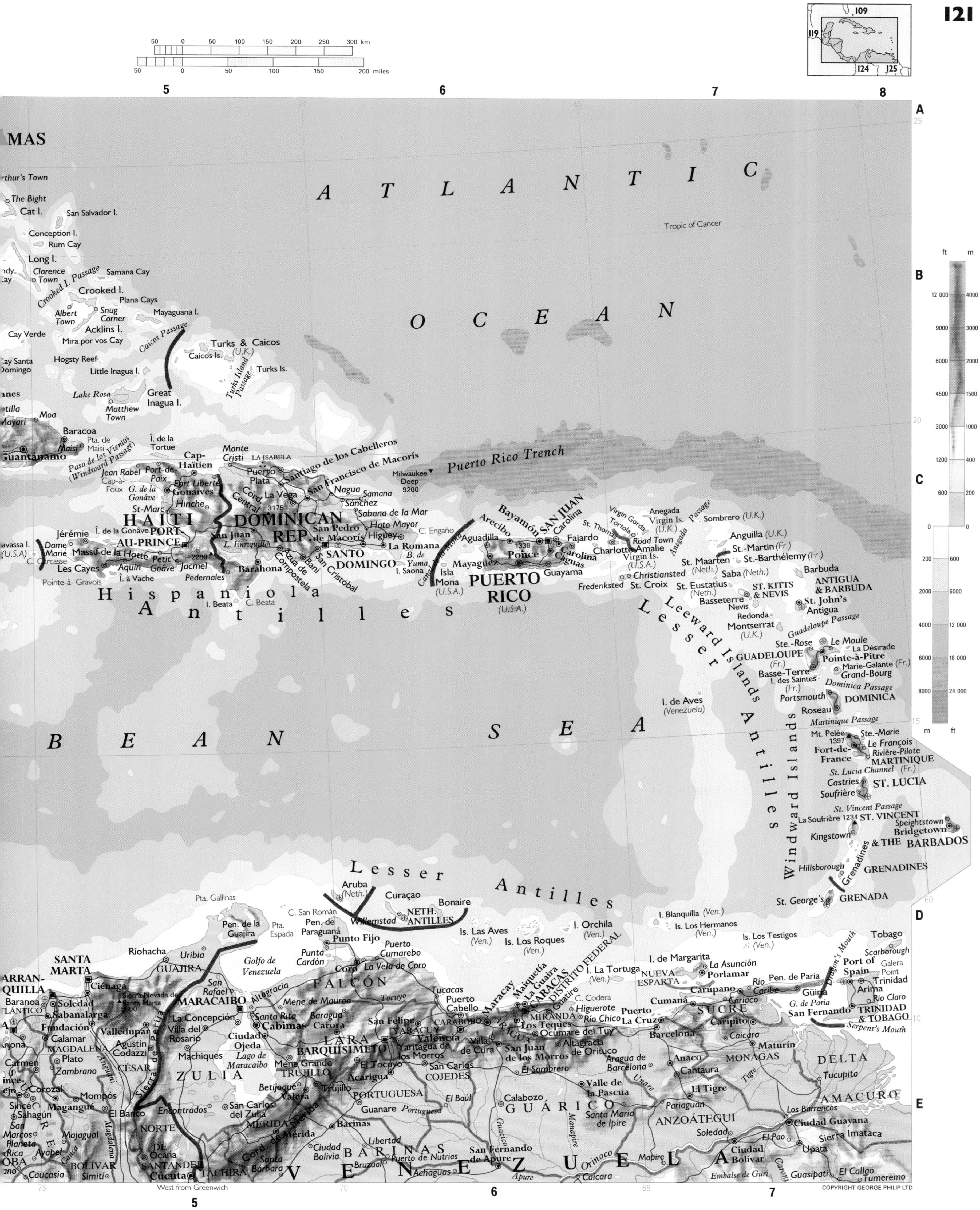
50 0 50 100 150 200 250 300 km
50 0 50 100 150 200 miles
109
119
124
125
5
6
7
8
A
B
C
D
E
A T L A N T I C
O C E A N
B E A N S E A
Tropic of Cancer
The Bight
Cat I.
San Salvador I.
Conception I.
Rum Cay
Long I.
Clarence Town
Samana Cay
Crooked I. Passage
Crooked I.
Plana Cays
Albert Town
Snug Corner
Mayaguana I.
Acklins I.
Cay Verde
Mira por vos Cay
Caicos Passage
Turks & Caicos
(U.K.)
Caicos Is.
Turks Is.
Turks Island Passage
Hogsty Reef
Little Inagua I.
Lake Rosa
Great Inagua I.
Matthew Town
Moa
Baracoa
Maisí
Pta. de Maisí
Paso de los Vientos
(Windward Passage)
Guantánamo
Î. de la Tortue
Cap-Haïtien
Monte Cristi
LA ISABELA
Jean Rabel
Port-de-Paix
Cap-à-Foux
G. de la Gonâve
Fort Liberté
Gonaïves
Hinche
St-Marc
Puerto Plata
Santiago de los Caballeros
San Francisco de Macorís
Milwaukee Deep 9200
Puerto Rico Trench
Cord. Central
La Vega
3175
Nagua
Samana
Sánchez
Sabana de la Mar
Hato Mayor
HAITI
DOMINICAN REP.
Jérémie
Î. de la Gonâve
PORT-AU-PRINCE
San Juan
L. Enriquillo
San Pedro de Macorís
Higüey
C. Engaño
Dame Marie
C. Carcasse
Massif de la Hotte
Les Cayes
Aquin
Petit Goâve
Jacmel
2280
Azua de Compostela
Baní
San Cristóbal
SANTO DOMINGO
La Romana
B. de Yuma
I. Saona
Î. à Vache
Pedernales
Barahona
Pointe-à-Gravois
Hispaniola
Antilles
I. Beata
C. Beata
Canal de la Mona
Isla Mona
(U.S.A.)
Aguadilla
Arecibo
Bayamón
SAN JUAN
Carolina
1338
Fajardo
Mayagüez
Ponce
Caguas
Guayama
PUERTO RICO
(U.S.A.)
Virgin Gorda
Tortola
Road Town
Anegada
Anegada Passage
Virgin Is.
(U.K.)
St. Thomas
Charlotte Amalie
Virgin Is.
(U.S.A.)
Christiansted
Frederiksted
St. Croix
Sombrero (U.K.)
Anguilla (U.K.)
St.-Martin (Fr.)
St. Maarten
(Neth.)
St.-Barthélemy (Fr.)
Saba (Neth.)
St. Eustatius
(Neth.)
Barbuda
ST. KITTS & NEVIS
Basseterre
Nevis
ANTIGUA & BARBUDA
St. John's
Antigua
Redonda
Montserrat
(U.K.)
Guadeloupe Passage
Leeward Islands
Lesser Antilles
Ste.-Rose
Le Moule
La Désirade
GUADELOUPE
(Fr.)
Pointe-à-Pitre
Basse-Terre
Marie-Galante (Fr.)
Grand-Bourg
I. des Saintes
(Fr.)
Dominica Passage
Portsmouth
DOMINICA
Roseau
I. de Aves
(Venezuela)
Martinique Passage
Mt. Pelée
1397
Ste.-Marie
Le François
Rivière-Pilote
Fort-de-France
MARTINIQUE
(Fr.)
St. Lucia Channel
Castries
Soufrière
ST. LUCIA
Windward Islands
St. Vincent Passage
La Soufrière 1234
ST. VINCENT
Kingstown
Speightstown
Bridgetown
BARBADOS
& THE GRENADINES
Grenadines
Hillsborough
GRENADINES
St. George's
GRENADA
Lesser Antilles
Aruba
(Neth.)
Curaçao
Bonaire
NETH. ANTILLES
Willemstad
Pta. Gallinas
C. San Román
Pen. de la Guajira
Pta. Espada
Pen. de Paraguaná
Punto Fijo
Is. Las Aves
(Ven.)
Is. Los Roques
(Ven.)
I. Orchila
(Ven.)
I. Blanquilla (Ven.)
Is. Los Hermanos
(Ven.)
Is. Los Testigos
(Ven.)
Tobago
Scarborough
Dragon's Mouth
Port of Spain
Galera Point
Trinidad
Arima
Río Claro
Río Caribe
Pen. de Paria
Güiria
G. de Paria
San Fernando
TRINIDAD & TOBAGO
Serpent's Mouth
I. de Margarita
La Asunción
Porlamar
NUEVA ESPARTA
I. La Tortuga
(Ven.)
DISTRITO FEDERAL
C. Codera
Carúpano
Cariaco
Cumaná
SUCRE
Caripito
Puerto La Cruz
Barcelona
Caicara
Maturín
Ríohacha
SANTA MARTA
Uribia
GUAJIRA
Golfo de Venezuela
Punta Cardón
Puerto Cumarebo
Coro
La Vela de Coro
FALCÓN
Ciénaga
Sierra Nevada de Santa Marta
5800
San Rafael
Altagracia
MARACAIBO
Mene de Mauroa
Tocuyo
Tucacas
Puerto Cabello
Maracay
Maiquetía
La Guaira
CARACAS
Guatire
Higuerote
Río Chico
MIRANDA
Los Teques
Ocumare del Tuy
Soledad
Sabanalarga
Fundación
Valledupar
La Concepción
Villa del Rosario
Santa Rita
Cabimas
Baragua
Carora
San Felipe
YARACUY
CARABOBO
Valencia
ARAGUA
Calamar
MAGDALENA
Agustín Codazzi
Ciudad Ojeda
LARA
BARQUISIMETO
Yaritagua de los Morros
Villa de Cura
San Juan de los Morros
Altagracia de Orituco
Plato
Zambrano
CÉSAR
Machiques
Lago de Maracaibo
Mene Grande
TRUJILLO
El Tocuyo
Acarigua
San Carlos
COJEDES
El Sombrero
Aragua de Barcelona
Unare
Anaco
Cantaura
MONAGAS
DELTA
Tucupita
ZULIA
Corozal
Mompós
Magangué
El Banco
Encontrados
San Carlos del Zulia
Betijoque
Valera
Trujillo
PORTUGUESA
Guanare
Portuguesa
El Baúl
Calabozo
GUÁRICO
Valle de la Pascua
Santa María de Ipire
Manapire
ANZOÁTEGUI
El Tigre
Pariaguán
Tigre
AMACURO
Los Barrancos
Ciudad Guayana
Sierra Imataca
Sincé
Sahagún
San Marcos
Planeta Rica
Majagual
Magdalena
Cauca
Ayapel
BOLÍVAR
Simití
Caucasia
NORTE DE SANTANDER
Ocaña
Cúcuta
TÁCHIRA
MÉRIDA
Cord. de Mérida
Mérida
Santa Bárbara
Barinas
Ciudad Bolivia
BARINAS
Libertad
Bruzual
Puerto de Nutrias
Achaguas
San Fernando de Apure
Apure
Guárico
Orinoco
Calcara
Mapire
Soledad
El Pao
Ciudad Bolívar
Caroní
Upata
Embalse de Guri
Guasipati
El Callao
Tumeremo
V E N E Z U E L A
Sierra de Perijá
Arigua
75
70
65
60
25
20
15
10
West from Greenwich
ft
m
12 000
9000
6000
4500
3000
1200
600
0
4000
3000
2000
1500
1000
400
200
200
2000
4000
6000
8000
600
6000
12 000
18 000
24 000

100 0 200 400 600 800 1000 1200 1400 km
100 0 200 400 600 800 1000 miles
Tropic of Cancer
Turks & Caicos Is.
Yucatan Channel
Cuba
Greater Antilles
Hispaniola
9200
Puerto Rico
Gulf of Campeche
Yucatán Peninsula
NORTH ATLANTIC OCEAN
Isthmus of Tehuantepec
G. de Honduras
Jamaica
Lesser Antilles
Guadeloupe
Dominica
Martinique
St. Lucia
Barbados
St. Vincent
Grenada
Tobago
Trinidad
C. Gracias a Dios
Caribbean Sea
Guatemala Trench
Coco
L. Nicaragua
C. de la Aguja
5800
Sierra Nevada de Santa Marta
L. Maracaibo
I. Margarita
Panama Canal
G. of Darién
Orinoco
Llanos
Meta
Cord. de Mérida
Magdalena
Gulf of Panamá
Cordillera Occidental
Cordillera Central
Cordillera Oriental
Guiana Highlands
2810
Mt. Roraima
Sierra Pacaraima
Essequibo
Courantyne
Serra Tumucumaque
C. Orange
Guaviare
Branco
C. de San Francisco
Caquetá
Negro
Equator
Cotopaxi 5897
Chimborazo 6267
Japurá
Putumayo
Marajó I.
Amazon
Galapagos Is.
Napo
G. of Guayaquil
Marañón
Pta. Pariñas
Pta. Negra
Tocantins
Xingu
Tapajós
Juruá
Purus
Madeira
Selvas
Parnaíba
C. de São Roque
Ucayali
Huascarán 6768
Aripuanã
Roosevelt
Teles Pires
Plat. of Borborema
São Francisco
Araguaia
Madre de Dios
Arinos
Chile Peru Trench
Guaporé
Plateau of Mato Grosso
Brazilian Highlands
Mamoré
Chincha Alta
L. Titicaca
Nevada Ancohuma 6550
Bolivian Plateau
L. de Poopó
PACIFIC OCEAN
Abrolhos Bank
Gran Chaco
Paraguay
Paraná
Serra da Mantiqueira
2890
Pico da Bandeira
Pilcomayo
C. Frio
Tropic of Capricorn
8050
Atacama Desert
Cerro Ojos del Salado 6863
Iguaçu Falls
San Félix
San Ambrosio
Uruguay
Serra do Mar
Andes
Salado
Salinas Grandes
Entre Rios
L. Mar Chiquita
Sierra de Córdoba
Pampas
L. dos Patos
Mt. Aconcagua 6960
Arch. de Juan Fernández
Río de la Plata
SOUTH ATLANTIC OCEAN
Colorado
Bahía Blanca
Negro
G. San Matías
40
Valdés Peninsula
Chile Rise
Chiloé I.
Chubut
Patagonia
Argentine Basin
Chonos Archipelago
Mte. San Valentín 4058
Taitao Peninsula
Gulf of San Jorge
Gulf of Penas
6212
Wellington I.
Madre de Dios I.
West Falkland
Falkland Is.
East Falkland
Magellan's Str.
Santa Inés I.
Tierra del Fuego
Staten I.
Canal Cockburn
Canal Beagle
C. Horn
South Georgia
ft m
12000 4000
9000 3000
6000 2000
3000 1000
1500 500
600 200
0 0
200 600
1000 3000
2000 6000
4000 12000
6000 18000
8000 24000
m ft
Projection: Lambert's Azimuthal Equal Area
West from Greenwich
CARTOGRAPHY BY PHILIP'S.

100 0 200 400 600 800 1000 1200 1400 km
100 0 200 400 600 800 1000 miles
1 2 3 4 5 6 7
A B C D E F G H
90 80 70 60 50 40 30 20
Tropic of Cancer
Equator
Tropic of Capricorn
Havana
CUBA
BAHAMAS
Turks & Caicos Is. (U.K.)
MEXICO
BELIZE
JAMAICA
Kingston
HAITI
Port-au-Prince
DOMINICAN REP.
San Juan
PUERTO RICO (U.S.A.)
Virgin Is. (U.K.)
ST. KITTS & NEVIS
Basse-Terre
ANTIGUA & BARBUDA
GUADELOUPE (Fr.)
DOMINICA
Fort-de-France
MARTINIQUE (Fr.)
Castries
ST. LUCIA
ST. VINCENT
Kingstown
BARBADOS
Bridgetown
GRENADA
St. George's
Port of Spain
TRINIDAD & TOBAGO
GUATEMALA
Guatemala
HONDURAS
Tegucigalpa
San Salvador
EL SALVADOR
NICARAGUA
Managua
COSTA RICA
San José
Panamá
PANAMA
Caribbean Sea
Aruba
Curaçao
C. de la Aguja
Barranquilla
Cartagena
G. of Darién
Maracaibo
Caracas
Barquisimeto
Valencia
Cúcuta
San Cristóbal
Orinoco
Ciudad Guayana
Bucaramanga
VENEZUELA
Georgetown
Medellín
Paramaribo
Gulf of Panamá
Magdalena
Bogotá
GUYANA
Cayenne
C. Orange
Cali
SURINAM
FRENCH GUIANA
Essequibo
COLOMBIA
RORAIMA
Branco
AMAPÁ
Galapagos Is. (Ecuador)
Quito
ECUADOR
Napo
Putumayo
Japurá
Amazon
Marajó I.
Belém
Guayaquil
G. of Guayaquil
Manaus
Santarém
Iquitos
Marañón
AMAZONAS
PARÁ
Tapajós
Xingu
Tocantins
São Luís
Fortaleza
Juruá
Madeira
Purus
MARANHÃO
Teresina
CEARÁ
C. de São Roque
RIO G. DO NORTE
Natal
Chiclayo
Ucayali
Parnaíba
PIAUÍ
PARAÍBA
Campina Grande
Trujillo
ACRE
Pôrto Velho
Araguaia
Recife
PERNAMBUCO
Chimbote
PERU
Madre de Dios
RONDÔNIA
TOCANTINS
ALAGOAS
Maceió
BRAZIL
SERGIPE
Aracaju
Callao
LIMA
Mamoré
MATO GROSSO
BAHÍA
São Francisco
Salvador
Cuzco
L. Titicaca
BOLIVIA
GOIÁS
Cuiabá
DIS. FED.
Brasília
Arequipa
La Paz
Cochabamba
Santa Cruz
Goiânia
PACIFIC
Paraguay
MINAS GERAIS
Sucre
MATO GROSSO DO SUL
Belo Horizonte
ESPÍRITO SANTO
Iquique
Ribeirão Prêto
Vitória
Paraná
SÃO PAULO
Juiz de Fora
PARAGUAY
Campos
Campinas
R. DE J.
Antofagasta
Pilcomayo
SÃO PAULO
Niterói
RIO DE JANEIRO
Salta
Asunción
PARANÁ
Curitiba
San Félix (Chile)
San Ambrosio (Chile)
San Miguel de Tucumán
Resistencia
Corrientes
SANTA CATARINA
Uruguay
Salado
RIO GRANDE DO SUL
Pôrto Alegre
OCEAN
Córdoba
Santa Fe
San Juan
Paraná
Pelotas
Viña del Mar
Mendoza
Rosario
URUGUAY
Valparaíso
SANTIAGO
Arch. de Juan Fernández (Chile)
BUENOS AIRES
Montevideo
La Plata
Río de la Plata
Talca
ARGENTINA
CHILE
Concepción
Bahía Blanca
Mar del Plata
SOUTH
Colorado
Valdivia
Negro
Viedma
Puerto Montt
ATLANTIC
Chubut
OCEAN
Comodoro Rivadavia
Gulf of San Jorge
Gulf of Penas
West Falkland
FALKLAND IS. (U.K.)
Stanley
East Falkland
Magellan's Str.
Punta Arenas
Tierra del Fuego
South Georgia (U.K.)
C. Horn
West from Greenwich
Projection: Lambert's Azimuthal Equal Area
LIMA Capital Cities
CARTOGRAPHY BY PHILIP'S.
NORTH ATLANTIC OCEAN

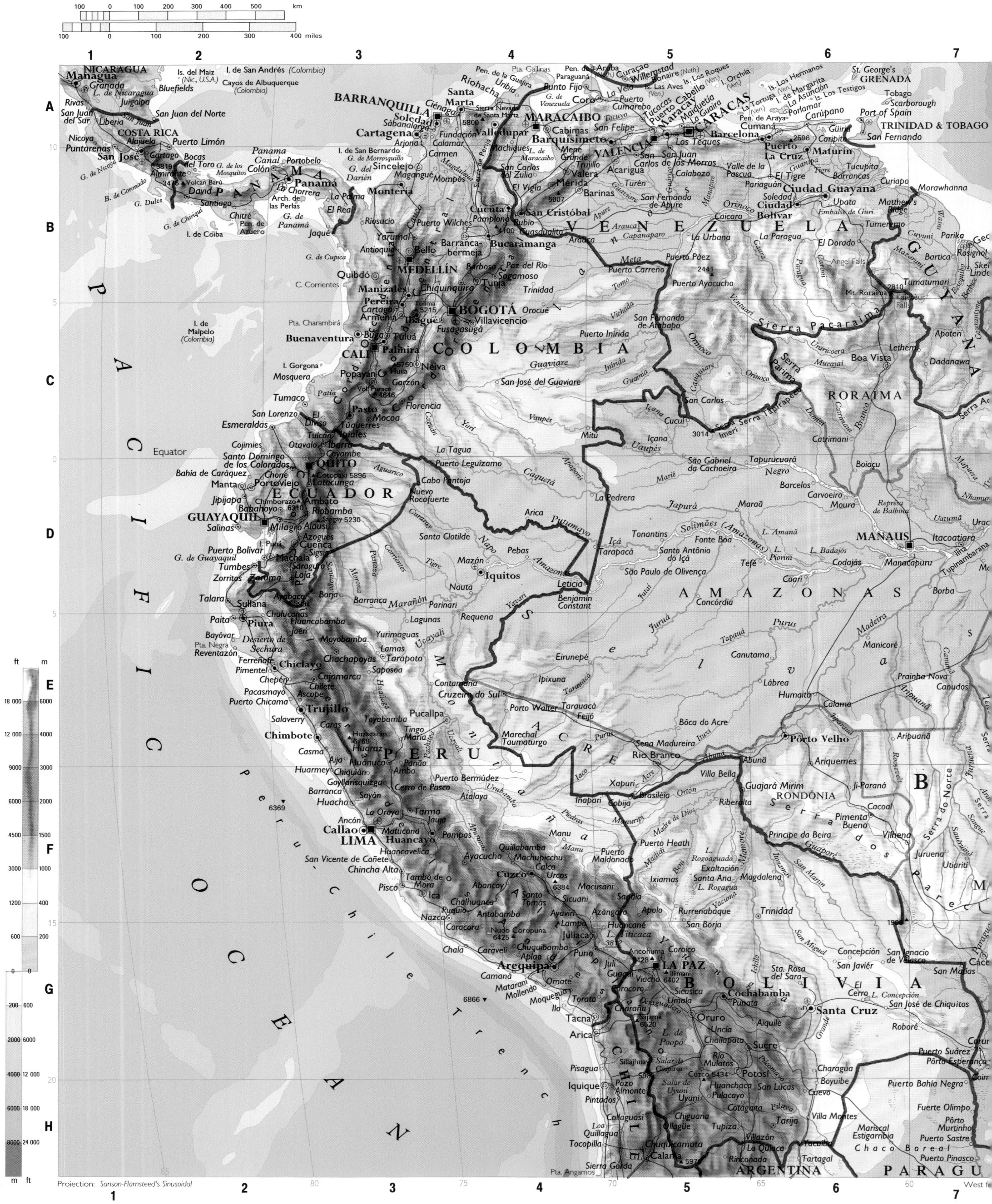
km
miles
PACIFIC OCEAN
Peru-Chile Trench
Equator
NICARAGUA
COSTA RICA
PANAMA
COLOMBIA
VENEZUELA
GUYANA
ECUADOR
PERU
BOLIVIA
CHILE
ARGENTINA
PARAGU
TRINIDAD & TOBAGO
GRENADA
AMAZONAS
RORAIMA
RONDÔNIA
ACRE
Chaco Boreal
Managua
San José
Panamá
BARRANQUILLA
Cartagena
MARACAIBO
CARACAS
VALENCIA
Barquisimeto
MEDELLÍN
BOGOTÁ
CALI
QUITO
GUAYAQUIL
LIMA
Callao
Arequipa
LA PAZ
Cochabamba
Santa Cruz
Sucre
Potosí
Iquitos
MANAUS
Porto Velho
Rio Branco
Ciudad Guayana
Cuzco
Trujillo
Chiclayo
Piura
L. Titicaca
Projection: Sanson-Flamsteed's Sinusoidal

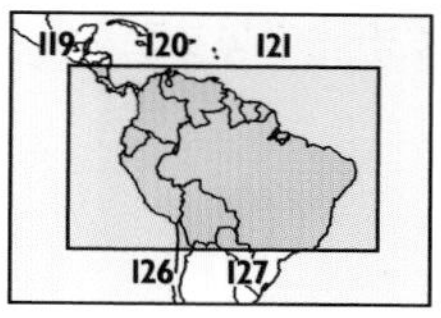
119
120
121
126
127

8
9
10
11
12
13
A
B
C
D
E
F
G
H
ATLANTIC
OCEAN
Equator
São Paulo (Braz.)
Fernando de Noronha (Braz.)
Rocas
Trindade (Braz.)
6059
Nickerie
Paramaribo
Nieuw Amsterdam
Moengo
Totness
Albina
St-Laurent
Iracoubo
Sinnamary
Kourou
Cayenne
Kaw
C. Orange
St-Georges
Oiapoque
FRENCH GUIANA
Camopi
Serra Tumucumaque
Amapá
I. de Maracá
AMAPÁ
Meriruma
Serra do Navio
Macapá
I. Caviana
I. Mexiana
Mazagão
C. Maguarinho
Afuá
Chaves
Soure
I. de Marajó
Curuçá
Salinópolis
Vigia
Bragança
BELÉM
Breves
Gurupá
Almeirim
Prainha
Monte Alegre
Óbidos
Alenquer
Santarém
Belterra
Aveiro
Amazonas (Amazon)
Xingu
Pôrto de Móz
Curralinho
Abaetetuba
Castanhal
Cametá
Baião
Capanema
Viseu
Turiaçu
Cururupu
B. de São Marcos
Alcântara
São Luís
Barreirinhas
Tutóia
Luís Correia
Camocim
Granja
Itapipoca
Caucaia
FORTALEZA
Pinheiro
Rosário
Itapecuru-Mirim
Viana
Parnaíba
Santa Inês
Bacabal
Brejo
Coroatá
Codó
Caxias
Piracuruca
Piripiri
Sobral
Maranguape
Cascavel
Baturité
Aracati
Russas
Quixadá
Ipu
Campo Maior
Oiticica
Areia Branca
Macau
Mossoró
Ceará Mirim
C. de São Roque
Natal
Altamira
PARÁ
Brasília Legal
Tucuruí
Represa de Tucuruí
Itaituba
Iriri
Açailândia
Pedreiras
MARANHÃO
Imperatriz
Marabá
Carajás
Serra dos Carajás
São João do Araguaia
Tocantinópolis
Grajaú
Pôrto Franco
Barra do Corda
Estreito
Carolina
Colinas
Teresina
Amarante
Crateús
CEARÁ
Senador Pompeu
Valença do Piauí
Floriano
Oeiras
Picos
Iguatu
Crato
Cajàzeiras
Sousa
Patos
Caicó
Currais Novos
Alagoa Grande
Canguaretama
Mamanguape
Cabedelo
João Pessoa
Campina Grande
Olinda
RECIFE
Jaboatão
PARAÍBA
RIO GRANDE DO NORTE
Juàzeiro do Norte
Ouricuri
Chapada do Araripe
Paulistana
Salgueiro
PERNAMBUCO
Caruaru
Pesqueira
Garanhuns
Palmares
Vitória de Santo Antão
Petrolândia
Palmeira dos Índios
Rio Largo
Maceió
Arapiraca
Penedo
ALAGOAS
Própria
SERGIPE
Capela
Aracaju
São Cristóvão
Estância
Loreto
Nova Iorque
PIAUÍ
Uruçuí
Riachão
Araguaína
Conceição do Araguaia
Araguacema
Pedro Afonso
Serra do Estrondo
Serra do Penitente
Santa Filomena
Caracol
Novo Remanso
São João do Piauí
Serra Dois Irmãos
Petrolina
Juàzeiro
Nova Casa Nova
Represa de Sobradinho
Paulo Afonso
Senhor-do-Bonfim
Chapada das Mangabeiras
Parnaguá
Palmas
Pôrto Nacional
TOCANTINS
BRAZIL
Serra do Cachimbo
Serra Formosa
Santa Isabel do Morro
I. do Bananal
Gurupi
Peixe
Serra do Roncador
Barra
Xique-Xique
Jacobina
Mundo Novo
Queimadas
Serrinha
Alagoinhas
Feira de Santana
Cachoeira
Santo Amaro
SALVADOR
BAHIA
Taguatinga
Barreiras
Ibotirama
Itaberaba
Castro Alves
Bom Jesus da Lapa
Serra do Sincorá
Valença
Nazaré
B. de Todos os Santos
Jequié
Paraná
Campos Belos
São Domingos
Santa Maria da Vitória
Serra Geral de Goiás
Posse
Carinhanha
Caetité
Brumado
Ubaitaba
Itabuna
Ilhéus
Vitória da Conquista
Canavieiras
Condeúba
MATO GROSSO
Planalto do Mato Grosso
Niquelândia
1678
Uruaçu
Aruanã
Formosa
DIST. FED.
BRASÍLIA
Taguatinga
Luziânia
Anápolis
Goiânia
GOIÁS
Goiás
Barra do Garças
Rondonópolis
Santo Antonio
Januária
Monte Azul
São Francisco
Janaúba
Pedra Azul
Montes Claros
Salinas
Jequitinhonha
Belmonte
Pôrto Seguro
Itamaraju
Prado
Caravelas
Nanuque
Mucuri
Conceição da Barra
São Mateus
Linhares
Araçuaí
Teófilo Otoni
Pirapora
Paracatu
Vianópolis
Morrinhos
Ipameri
Catalão
Patos de Minas
Alto Araguaia
Jataí
Rio Verde
Quirinópolis
Itumbiara
Araguari
Uberlândia
Patrocínio
Diamantina
1340
Corinto
Curvelo
Governador Valadares
Nova Venécia
Colatina
MINAS GERAIS
Serra do Espinhaço
Ipatinga
Itabira
Sete Lagoas
Caratinga
BELO HORIZONTE
Sabará
ESPÍRITO SANTO
Cariacica
Vitória
Vila Velha
Cachoeiro de Itapemirim
Coxim
DO SUL
MATO GROSSO DO SUL
Campo Grande
Miranda
Aquidauana
Paranaíba
Ituiutaba
Prata
Uberaba
Araxá
Ibiá
Frutal
Santa Fé do Sul
Água Clara
Ribas do Rio Pardo
Três Lagoas
São José do Rio Prêto
Andradina
Araçatuba
Panorama
Presidente Epitácio
Penápolis
Lins
Catanduva
Igarapava
Franca
Passos
Divinópolis
Nova Lima
Ouro Prêto
Conselheiro Lafaiete
Barbacena
Ubá
Juiz de Fora
Itaperuna
Campos
Ponte Nova
2890
Ribeirão Prêto
Araraquara
Poços de Caldas
Guaxupé
São João del Rei
São Lourenço
Três Rios
Nova Friburgo
Petrópolis
Dourados
Ponta Porã
Presidente Prudente
Marília
Bauru
Jaú
SÃO PAULO
São Carlos
Moji-Mirim
Limeira
Piracicaba
Botucatu
Assis
Campinas
2787
Volta Redonda
RIO DE JANEIRO
Niterói
Cabo Frio
55
50
45
40
35
30
10
5
0
15
20
COPYRIGHT GEORGE PHILIP LTD.

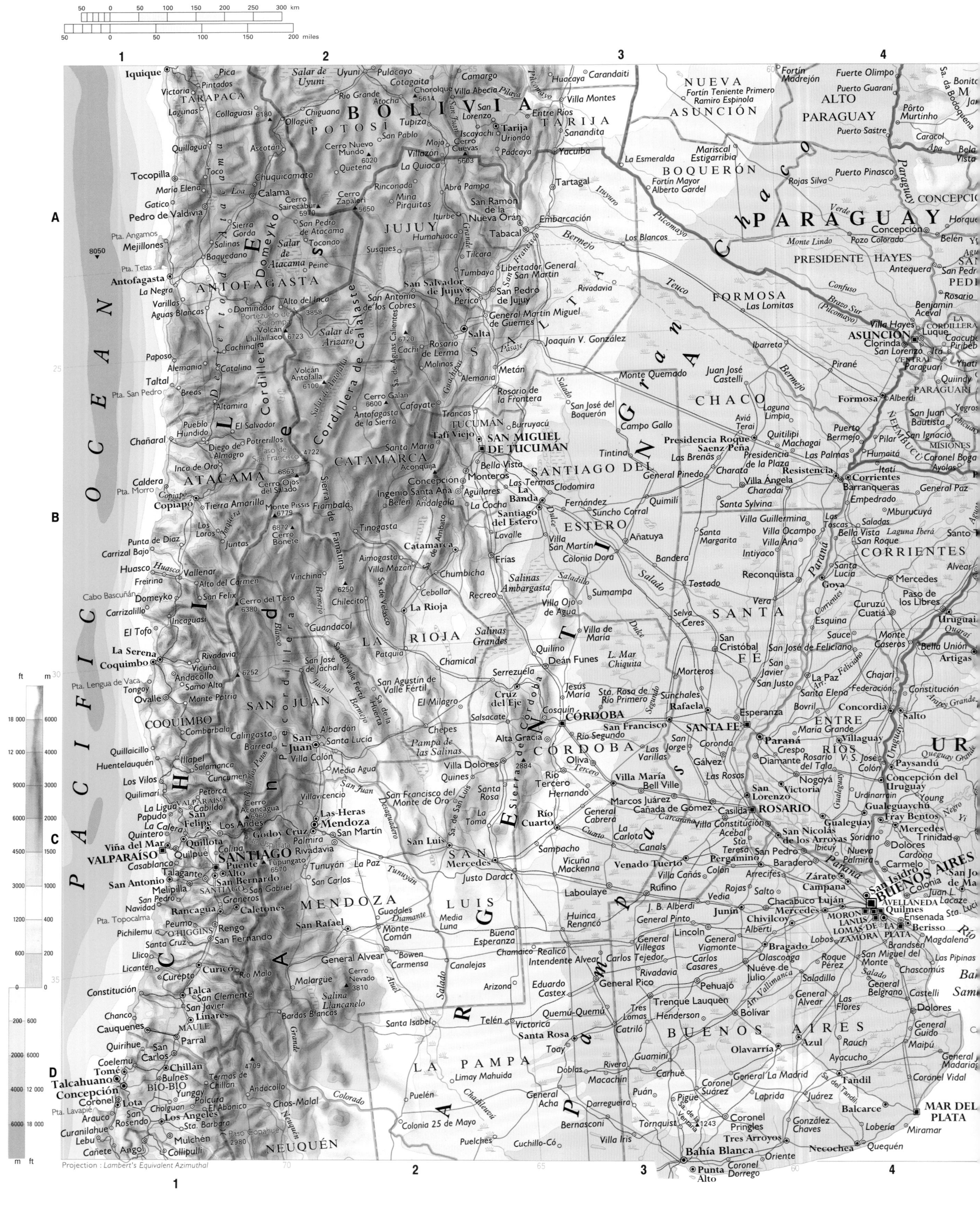
50 0 50 100 150 200 250 300 km
50 0 50 100 150 200 miles
1 2 3 4
A B C D
ft m
18 000 6000
12 000 4000
9000 3000
6000 2000
4500 1500
3000 1000
1200 400
600 200
0 0
200 600
2000 6000
4000 12 000
6000 18 000
m ft
PACIFIC OCEAN
BOLIVIA
PARAGUAY
ARGENTINA
CHILE
URUGUAY
Gran Chaco
Pampas
Cordillera de los Andes
Atacama
POTOSÍ
TARIJA
TARAPACÁ
ANTOFAGASTA
ATACAMA
COQUIMBO
VALPARAÍSO
SANTIAGO
O'HIGGINS
MAULE
BÍO-BÍO
JUJUY
SALTA
CATAMARCA
TUCUMÁN
SANTIAGO DEL ESTERO
LA RIOJA
SAN JUAN
MENDOZA
SAN LUIS
CÓRDOBA
SANTA FÉ
ENTRE RÍOS
CORRIENTES
CHACO
FORMOSA
LA PAMPA
NEUQUÉN
BUENOS AIRES
NUEVA ASUNCIÓN
ALTO PARAGUAY
BOQUERÓN
PRESIDENTE HAYES
ASUNCIÓN
SAN MIGUEL DE TUCUMÁN
CÓRDOBA
ROSARIO
SANTA FE
MENDOZA
SANTIAGO
VALPARAÍSO
BUENOS AIRES
MAR DEL PLATA
Bahía Blanca
Antofagasta
Salta
Concepción
Talcahuano
Projection : Lambert's Equivalent Azimuthal

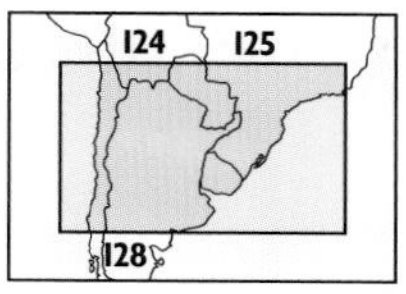
124
125
128

5
6
7
A
B
C
D
BELO HORIZONTE
Vitória
RIO DE JANEIRO
NITERÓI
NOVA IGUAÇU
DUQUE DE CAXIAS
SÃO GONÇALO
CAMPOS
SÃO PAULO
SANTO ANDRÉ
SANTOS
CAMPINAS
Ribeirão Prêto
Sorocaba
Jundiaí
Londrina
Maringá
Ponta Grossa
CURITIBA
Joinville
Blumenau
Florianópolis
Caxias do Sul
PÔRTO ALEGRE
Pelotas
Rio Grande
Santa Maria
Foz do Iguaçu
Ciudad del Este
Encarnación
B R A Z I L
P A R A N Á
SÃO PAULO
SANTA CATARINA
RIO GRANDE DO SUL
MISIONES
Lagoa dos Patos
Lagoa Mirim
Tropic of Capricorn
A T L A N T I C
O C E A N
5304
West from Greenwich

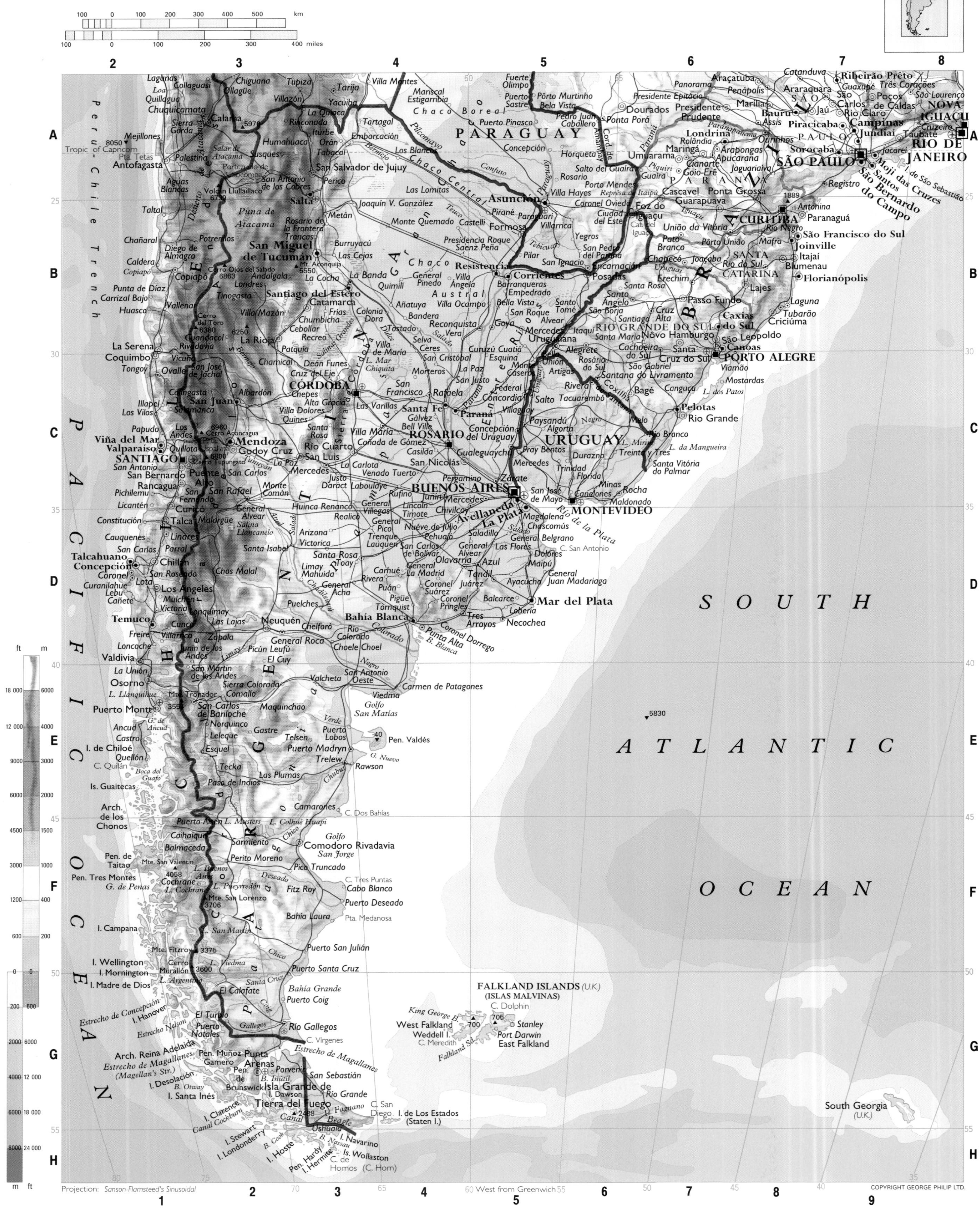

PARAGUAY
URUGUAY
SOUTH ATLANTIC OCEAN
PACIFIC OCEAN
Peru-Chile Trench
Tropic of Capricorn
FALKLAND ISLANDS (U.K.)
(ISLAS MALVINAS)
West Falkland
East Falkland
Stanley
South Georgia (U.K.)
BUENOS AIRES
MONTEVIDEO
SANTIAGO
Asunción
CÓRDOBA
ROSARIO
Mendoza
San Miguel de Tucumán
Mar del Plata
Bahía Blanca
Comodoro Rivadavia
Río Gallegos
Punta Arenas
Ushuaia
Tierra del Fuego
Estrecho de Magallanes
Isla Grande de Tierra del Fuego
PÔRTO ALEGRE
CURITIBA
SÃO PAULO
RIO DE JANEIRO
Antofagasta
Valparaíso
Concepción
Puerto Montt
Mte. Aconcagua 6960
Gran Chaco
Chaco Boreal
Chaco Central
Chaco Austral
Puna de Atacama
Desierto de Atacama
Río de la Plata
Pen. Valdés
Golfo San Matías
Golfo San Jorge
I. de Chiloé
Arch. de los Chonos
Arch. Reina Adelaida
I. de Los Estados (Staten I.)
C. de Hornos (C. Horn)
5830
ft
m
Projection: Sanson-Flamsteed's Sinusoidal
West from Greenwich
COPYRIGHT GEORGE PHILIP LTD.

INDEX

The index contains the names of all the principal places and features shown on the World Maps. Each name is followed by an additional entry in italics giving the country or region within which it is located. The alphabetical order of names composed of two or more words is governed primarily by the first word and then by the second. This is an example of the rule:

Mīr Kūh, *Iran* **71** **E8**
Mīr Shahdād, *Iran* **71** **E8**
Mira, *Italy* **29** **C9**
Mira por vos Cay, *Bahamas* . . **121** **B5**
Miraj, *India* **66** **L9**

Physical features composed of a proper name (Erie) and a description (Lake) are positioned alphabetically by the proper name. The description is positioned after the proper name and is usually abbreviated:

Erie, L., *N. Amer.* **110** **D4**

Where a description forms part of a settlement or administrative name however, it is always written in full and put in its true alphabetic position:

Mount Morris, *U.S.A.* **110** **D7**

Names beginning with M' and Mc are indexed as if they were spelled Mac. Names beginning St. are alphabetised under Saint, but Sankt, Sint, Sant', Santa and San are all spelt in full and are alphabetised accordingly. If the same place name occurs two or more times in the index and all are in the same country, each is followed by the name of the administrative subdivision in which it is located. The names are placed in the alphabetical order of the subdivisions. For example:

Jackson, *Ky., U.S.A.* **108** **G4**
Jackson, *Mich., U.S.A.* **108** **D3**
Jackson, *Minn., U.S.A.* **112** **D7**

The number in bold type which follows each name in the index refers to the number of the map page where that feature or place will be found. This is usually the largest scale at which the place or feature appears.

The letter and figure which are in bold type immediately after the page number give the grid square on the map page, within which the feature is situated. The letter represents the latitude and the figure the longitude.

In some cases the feature itself may fall within the specified square, while the name is outside. This is usually the case only with features which are larger than a grid square.

Rivers are indexed to their mouths or confluences, and carry the symbol → after their names. A solid square ■ follows the name of a country, while an open square □ refers to a first order administrative area.

ABBREVIATIONS USED IN THE INDEX

A.C.T. – Australian Capital Territory
Afghan. – Afghanistan
Ala. – Alabama
Alta. – Alberta
Amer. – America(n)
Arch. – Archipelago
Ariz. – Arizona
Ark. – Arkansas
Atl. Oc. – Atlantic Ocean
B. – Baie, Bahía, Bay, Bucht, Bugt
B.C. – British Columbia
Bangla. – Bangladesh
Barr. – Barrage
Bos.-H. – Bosnia-Herzegovina
C. – Cabo, Cap, Cape, Coast
C.A.R. – Central African Republic
C. Prov. – Cape Province
Calif. – California
Cent. – Central
Chan. – Channel
Colo. – Colorado
Conn. – Connecticut
Cord. – Cordillera
Cr. – Creek
Czech. – Czech Republic
D.C. – District of Columbia
Del. – Delaware
Dep. – Dependency
Des. – Desert
Dist. – District
Dj. – Djebel
Domin. – Dominica
Dom. Rep. – Dominican Republic
E. – East
E. Salv. – El Salvador
Eq. Guin. – Equatorial Guinea
Fla. – Florida
Falk. Is. – Falkland Is.
G. – Golfe, Golfo, Gulf, Guba, Gebel
Ga. – Georgia
Gt. – Great, Greater
Guinea-Biss. – Guinea-Bissau
H.K. – Hong Kong
H.P. – Himachal Pradesh
Hants. – Hampshire
Harb. – Harbor, Harbour
Hd. – Head
Hts. – Heights
I.(s). – Île, Ilha, Insel, Isla, Island, Isle
Ill. – Illinois
Ind. – Indiana
Ind. Oc. – Indian Ocean
Ivory C. – Ivory Coast
J. – Jabal, Jebel, Jazira
Junc. – Junction
K. – Kap, Kapp
Kans. – Kansas
Kep. – Kepulauan
Ky. – Kentucky
L. – Lac, Lacul, Lago, Lagoa, Lake, Limni, Loch, Lough
La. – Louisiana
Liech. – Liechtenstein
Lux. – Luxembourg
Mad. P. – Madhya Pradesh
Madag. – Madagascar
Man. – Manitoba
Mass. – Massachusetts
Md. – Maryland
Me. – Maine
Medit. S. – Mediterranean Sea
Mich. – Michigan
Minn. – Minnesota
Miss. – Mississippi
Mo. – Missouri
Mont. – Montana
Mozam. – Mozambique
Mt.(e) – Mont, Monte, Monti, Montaña, Mountain
N. – Nord, Norte, North, Northern, Nouveau
N.B. – New Brunswick
N.C. – North Carolina
N. Cal. – New Caledonia
N. Dak. – North Dakota
N.H. – New Hampshire
N.I. – North Island
N.J. – New Jersey
N. Mex. – New Mexico
N.S. – Nova Scotia
N.S.W. – New South Wales
N.W.T. – North West Territory
N.Y. – New York
N.Z. – New Zealand
Nebr. – Nebraska
Neths. – Netherlands
Nev. – Nevada
Nfld. – Newfoundland
Nic. – Nicaragua
O. – Oued, Ouadi
Occ. – Occidentale
Okla. – Oklahoma
Ont. – Ontario
Or. – Orientale
Oreg. – Oregon
Os. – Ostrov
Oz. – Ozero
P. – Pass, Passo, Pasul, Pulau
P.E.I. – Prince Edward Island
Pa. – Pennsylvania
Pac. Oc. – Pacific Ocean
Papua N.G. – Papua New Guinea
Pass. – Passage
Pen. – Peninsula, Péninsule
Phil. – Philippines
Pk. – Park, Peak
Plat. – Plateau
Prov. – Province, Provincial
Pt. – Point
Pta. – Ponta, Punta
Pte. – Pointe
Qué. – Québec
Queens. – Queensland
R. – Rio, River
R.I. – Rhode Island
Ra.(s). – Range(s)
Raj. – Rajasthan
Reg. – Region
Rep. – Republic
Res. – Reserve, Reservoir
S. – San, South, Sea
Si. Arabia – Saudi Arabia
S.C. – South Carolina
S. Dak. – South Dakota
S.I. – South Island
S. Leone – Sierra Leone
Sa. – Serra, Sierra
Sask. – Saskatchewan
Scot. – Scotland
Sd. – Sound
Sev. – Severnaya
Sib. – Siberia
Sprs. – Springs
St. – Saint
Sta. – Santa, Station
Ste. – Sainte
Sto. – Santo
Str. – Strait, Stretto
Switz. – Switzerland
Tas. – Tasmania
Tenn. – Tennessee
Tex. – Texas
Tg. – Tanjung
Trin. & Tob. – Trinidad & Tobago
U.A.E. – United Arab Emirates
U.K. – United Kingdom
U.S.A. – United States of America
Ut. P. – Uttar Pradesh
Va. – Virginia
Vdkhr. – Vodokhranilishche
Vf. – Vîrful
Vic. – Victoria
Vol. – Volcano
Vt. – Vermont
W. – Wadi, West
W. Va. – West Virginia
Wash. – Washington
Wis. – Wisconsin
Wlkp. – Wielkopolski
Wyo. – Wyoming
Yorks. – Yorkshire
Yug. – Yugoslavia

A

A Baña, *Spain* 34 C2
A Cañiza, *Spain* 34 C2
A Coruña, *Spain* 34 B2
A Estrada, *Spain* 34 C2
A Fonsagrada, *Spain* 34 B3
A Guarda, *Spain* 34 D2
A Gudiña, *Spain* 34 C3
A Rúa, *Spain* 34 C3
Aachen, *Germany* 24 E2
Aalborg = Ålborg, *Denmark* 11 G3
Aalen, *Germany* 25 G6
A'âli an Nîl □, *Sudan* 81 F3
Aalst, *Belgium* 17 D4
Aalten, *Neths.* 17 C6
Aalter, *Belgium* 17 C3
Äänekoski, *Finland* 9 E21
Aarau, *Switz.* 25 H4
Aarberg, *Switz.* 25 H3
Aare →, *Switz.* 25 H4
Aargau □, *Switz.* 25 H4
Aarhus = Århus, *Denmark* 11 H4
Aarschot, *Belgium* 17 D4
Aba, *China* 58 A3
Aba, *Dem. Rep. of the Congo* 86 B3
Aba, *Nigeria* 83 D6
Âbâ, Jazîrat, *Sudan* 81 E3
Abadab, J., *Sudan* 80 D4
Ābādān, *Iran* 71 D6
Abade, *Ethiopia* 81 F4
Ābādeh, *Iran* 71 D7
Abadin, *Spain* 34 B3
Abadla, *Algeria* 78 B5
Abaetetuba, *Brazil* 125 D9
Abagnar Qi, *China* 56 C9
Abai, *Paraguay* 127 B4
Abak, *Nigeria* 83 E6
Abakaliki, *Nigeria* 83 D6
Abakan, *Russia* 51 D10
Abala, *Niger* 83 C5
Abalak, *Niger* 83 B6
Abalemma, *Niger* 83 B6
Abana, *Turkey* 72 B6
Abancay, *Peru* 124 F4
Abano Terme, *Italy* 29 C8
Abarán, *Spain* 33 G3
Abariringa, *Kiribati* 96 H10
Abarqū, *Iran* 71 D7
Abashiri, *Japan* 54 B12
Abashiri-Wan, *Japan* 54 C12
Abaújszántó, *Hungary* 42 B6
Abava →, *Latvia* 44 A8
Ābay = Nîl el Azraq →, *Sudan* 81 D3
Abay, *Kazakstan* 50 E8
Abaya, L., *Ethiopia* 81 F4
Abaza, *Russia* 50 D9
Abbadia San Salvatore, *Italy* 29 F8
'Abbāsābād, *Iran* 71 C8
Abbay = Nîl el Azraq →, *Sudan* 81 D3
Abbaye, Pt., *U.S.A.* 108 B1
Abbé, L., *Ethiopia* 81 E5
Abbeville, *France* 19 B8
Abbeville, *Ala., U.S.A.* 109 K3
Abbeville, *La., U.S.A.* 113 L8
Abbeville, *S.C., U.S.A.* 109 H4
Abbiategrasso, *Italy* 28 C5
Abbot Ice Shelf, *Antarctica* 5 D16
Abbottabad, *Pakistan* 68 B5
Abd al Kūrī, *Ind. Oc.* 74 E5
Ābdar, *Iran* 71 D7
'Abdolābād, *Iran* 71 C8
Abdulpur, *Bangla.* 69 G13
Abéché, *Chad* 79 F10
Abejar, *Spain* 32 D2
Abekr, *Sudan* 81 E2
Abengourou, *Ivory C.* 82 D4
Abenójar, *Spain* 35 G6
Åbenrå, *Denmark* 11 J3
Abensberg, *Germany* 25 G7
Abeokuta, *Nigeria* 83 D5
Aber, *Uganda* 86 B3
Aberaeron, *U.K.* 13 E3
Aberayron = Aberaeron, *U.K.* 13 E3
Aberchirder, *U.K.* 14 D6
Abercorn = Mbala, *Zambia* 87 D3
Abercorn, *Australia* 95 D5
Aberdare, *U.K.* 13 F4
Aberdare Ra., *Kenya* 86 C4
Aberdeen, *Canada* 105 C7
Aberdeen, *S. Africa* 88 E3
Aberdeen, *U.K.* 14 D6
Aberdeen, *Ala., U.S.A.* 109 J1
Aberdeen, *Idaho, U.S.A.* 114 E7
Aberdeen, *Md., U.S.A.* 108 F7
Aberdeen, *S. Dak., U.S.A.* 112 C5
Aberdeen, *Wash., U.S.A.* 116 D3
Aberdeen, City of □, *U.K.* 14 D6
Aberdeenshire □, *U.K.* 14 D6
Aberdovey = Aberdyfi, *U.K.* 13 E3
Aberdyfi, *U.K.* 13 E3
Aberfeldy, *U.K.* 14 E5
Abergavenny, *U.K.* 13 F4
Abergele, *U.K.* 12 D4
Abernathy, *U.S.A.* 113 J4
Abert, L., *U.S.A.* 114 E3
Aberystwyth, *U.K.* 13 E3
Abhā, *Si. Arabia* 74 D3
Abhar, *Iran* 71 B6
Abhayapuri, *India* 69 F14
Abia □, *Nigeria* 83 D6
Abide, *Turkey* 39 C11
Abidiya, *Sudan* 80 D3
Abidjan, *Ivory C.* 82 D4
Abilene, *Kans., U.S.A.* 112 F6
Abilene, *Tex., U.S.A.* 113 J5
Abingdon, *U.K.* 13 F6
Abingdon, *U.S.A.* 109 G5
Abington Reef, *Australia* 94 B4
Abitau →, *Canada* 105 B7
Abitibi →, *Canada* 102 B3
Abitibi, L., *Canada* 102 C4
Abiy Adi, *Ethiopia* 81 E4
Abkhaz Republic = Abkhazia □, *Georgia* 49 J5
Abkhazia □, *Georgia* 49 J5
Abminga, *Australia* 95 D1
Abnûb, *Egypt* 80 B3
Åbo = Turku, *Finland* 9 F20
Abocho, *Nigeria* 83 D6
Abohar, *India* 68 D6
Aboisso, *Ivory C.* 82 D4
Abomey, *Benin* 83 D5
Abong-Mbang, *Cameroon* 84 D2
Abonnema, *Nigeria* 83 E6
Abony, *Hungary* 42 C5
Aboso, *Ghana* 82 D4
Abou-Deïa, *Chad* 79 F9
Aboyne, *U.K.* 14 D6
Abra Pampa, *Argentina* 126 A2
Abraham L., *Canada* 104 C5
Abrantes, *Portugal* 35 F2
Abreojos, Pta., *Mexico* 118 B2
Abri, *Esh Shamâliya, Sudan* 80 C3
Abri, *Janub Kordofân, Sudan* 81 E3
Abrud, *Romania* 42 D8
Abruzzo □, *Italy* 29 F10
Absaroka Range, *U.S.A.* 114 D9
Abtenau, *Austria* 26 D6
Abu, *India* 68 G5
Abū al Abyad, *U.A.E.* 71 E7
Abū al Khaṣīb, *Iraq* 71 D6
Abū 'Alī, *Si. Arabia* 71 E6
Abū 'Alī →, *Lebanon* 75 A4
Abu Ballas, *Egypt* 80 C2
Abu Deleiq, *Sudan* 81 D3
Abu Dhabi = Abū Ẓāby, *U.A.E.* 71 E7
Abu Dis, *Sudan* 80 D3
Abu Dom, *Sudan* 81 D3
Abū Du'ān, *Syria* 70 B3
Abu el Gairi, W. →, *Egypt* 75 F2
Abu Fatma, Ras, *Sudan* 80 C4
Abu Gabra, *Sudan* 81 E2
Abu Ga'da, W. →, *Egypt* 75 F1
Abu Gelba, *Sudan* 81 E3
Abu Gubeiha, *Sudan* 81 E3
Abu Habl, Khawr →, *Sudan* 81 E3
Abū Ḥadrīyah, *Si. Arabia* 71 E6
Abu Hamed, *Sudan* 80 D3
Abu Haraz, *An Nîl el Azraq, Sudan* 80 D3
Abu Haraz, *El Gezira, Sudan* 81 E3
Abu Haraz, *Esh Shamâliya, Sudan* 80 D3
Abu Higar, *Sudan* 81 E3
Abū Kamāl, *Syria* 70 C4
Abu Kuleiwat, *Sudan* 81 E2
Abū Madd, Ra's, *Si. Arabia* 70 E3
Abu Matariq, *Sudan* 81 E2
Abu Mendi, *Ethiopia* 81 E4
Abū Mūsā, *U.A.E.* 71 E7
Abū Qaṣr, *Si. Arabia* 70 D3
Abu Qir, *Egypt* 80 H7
Abu Qireiya, *Egypt* 80 C4
Abu Qurqâs, *Egypt* 80 B3
Abu Şafāt, W. →, *Jordan* 75 E5
Abu Shagara, Ras, *Sudan* 80 C4
Abu Shanab, *Sudan* 81 E2
Abu Simbel, *Egypt* 80 C3
Abū Şukhayr, *Iraq* 70 D5
Abu Sultân, *Egypt* 80 H8
Abu Tabari, *Sudan* 80 D2
Abu Tig, *Egypt* 80 B3
Abu Tiga, *Sudan* 81 E3
Abu Tineitin, *Sudan* 81 E3
Abu Uruq, *Sudan* 81 D3
Abu Zabad, *Sudan* 81 E2
Abū Ẓāby, *U.A.E.* 71 E7
Abū Zeydābād, *Iran* 71 C6
Abuja, *Nigeria* 83 D6
Abukuma-Gawa →, *Japan* 54 E10
Abukuma-Sammyaku, *Japan* 54 F10
Abunã, *Brazil* 124 E5
Abunã →, *Brazil* 124 E5
Abune Yosef, *Ethiopia* 81 E4
Aburo, *Dem. Rep. of the Congo* 86 B3
Abut Hd., *N.Z.* 91 K3
Abuye Meda, *Ethiopia* 81 E4
Abwong, *Sudan* 81 F3
Åby, *Sweden* 11 F10
Aby, Lagune, *Ivory C.* 82 D4
Abyad, *Sudan* 81 E2
Åbybro, *Denmark* 11 G3
Acadia National Park, *U.S.A.* 109 C11
Açailândia, *Brazil* 125 D9
Acajutla, *El Salv.* 120 D2
Acámbaro, *Mexico* 118 D4
Acanthus, *Greece* 40 F7
Acaponeta, *Mexico* 118 C3
Acapulco, *Mexico* 119 D5
Acarai, Serra, *Brazil* 124 C7
Acarigua, *Venezuela* 124 B5
Acatlán, *Mexico* 119 D5
Acayucan, *Mexico* 119 D6
Accéglio, *Italy* 28 D4
Accomac, *U.S.A.* 108 G8
Accous, *France* 20 E3
Accra, *Ghana* 83 D4
Accrington, *U.K.* 12 D5
Acebal, *Argentina* 126 C3
Aceh □, *Indonesia* 62 D1
Acerra, *Italy* 31 B7
Aceuchal, *Spain* 35 G4
Achalpur, *India* 66 J10
Acheng, *China* 57 B14
Achenkirch, *Austria* 26 D4
Achensee, *Austria* 26 D4
Acher, *India* 68 H5
Achern, *Germany* 25 G4
Achill Hd., *Ireland* 15 C1
Achill I., *Ireland* 15 C1
Achim, *Germany* 24 B5
Achinsk, *Russia* 51 D10
Acıgöl, *Turkey* 39 D11
Acıpayam, *Turkey* 39 D11
Acireale, *Italy* 31 E8
Ackerman, *U.S.A.* 113 J10
Acklins I., *Bahamas* 121 B5
Acme, *Canada* 104 C6
Acme, *U.S.A.* 110 F5
Aconcagua, Cerro, *Argentina* 126 C2
Aconquija, Mt., *Argentina* 126 B2
Açores, Is. dos = Azores, *Atl. Oc.* 78 A1
Acornhoek, *S. Africa* 89 C5
Acquapendente, *Italy* 29 F8
Acquasanta Terme, *Italy* 29 F10
Acquasparta, *Italy* 29 F9
Acquaviva delle Fonti, *Italy* 31 B9
Ácqui Terme, *Italy* 28 D5
Acraman, L., *Australia* 95 E2
Acre = 'Akko, *Israel* 75 C4
Acre □, *Brazil* 124 E4
Acre →, *Brazil* 124 E5
Acri, *Italy* 31 C9
Acs, *Hungary* 42 C3
Actium, *Greece* 38 C2
Acton, *Canada* 110 C4
Acuña, *Mexico* 118 B4
Ad Dammām, *Si. Arabia* 71 E6
Ad Dāmūr, *Lebanon* 75 B4
Ad Dawādimī, *Si. Arabia* 70 E5
Ad Dawḥah, *Qatar* 71 E6
Ad Dawr, *Iraq* 70 C4
Ad Dir'īyah, *Si. Arabia* 70 E5
Ad Dīwānīyah, *Iraq* 70 D5
Ad Dujayl, *Iraq* 70 C5
Ad Duwayd, *Si. Arabia* 70 D4
Ada, *Ghana* 83 D5
Ada, *Serbia, Yug.* 42 E5
Ada, *Minn., U.S.A.* 112 B6
Ada, *Okla., U.S.A.* 113 H6
Adabiya, *Egypt* 75 F1
Adair, C., *Canada* 101 A12
Adaja →, *Spain* 34 D6
Adak I., *U.S.A.* 100 C2
Adamaoua, Massif de l', *Cameroon* 83 D7
Adamawa □, *Nigeria* 83 D7
Adamawa Highlands = Adamaoua, Massif de l', *Cameroon* 83 D7
Adamello, Mte., *Italy* 28 B7
Adami Tulu, *Ethiopia* 81 F4
Adams, *Mass., U.S.A.* 111 D11
Adams, *N.Y., U.S.A.* 111 C8
Adams, *Wis., U.S.A.* 112 D10
Adam's Bridge, *Sri Lanka* 66 Q11
Adams L., *Canada* 104 C5
Adams Mt., *U.S.A.* 116 D5
Adam's Peak, *Sri Lanka* 66 R12
Adamuz, *Spain* 35 G6
Adana, *Turkey* 70 B2
Adanero, *Spain* 34 E6
Adapazarı = Sakarya, *Turkey* 72 B4
Adar Gwagwa, J., *Sudan* 80 C4
Adarama, *Sudan* 81 D3
Adare, C., *Antarctica* 5 D11
Adarte, *Eritrea* 81 E5
Adaut, *Indonesia* 63 F8
Adavale, *Australia* 95 D3
Adda →, *Italy* 28 C6
Addis Ababa = Addis Abeba, *Ethiopia* 81 F4
Addis Abeba, *Ethiopia* 81 F4
Addis Alem, *Ethiopia* 81 F4
Addis Zemen, *Ethiopia* 81 E4
Addison, *U.S.A.* 110 D7
Addo, *S. Africa* 88 E4
Adebour, *Niger* 83 C7
Ādeh, *Iran* 70 B5
Adel, *U.S.A.* 109 K4
Adelaide, *Australia* 95 E2
Adelaide, *Bahamas* 120 A4
Adelaide, *S. Africa* 88 E4
Adelaide I., *Antarctica* 5 C17
Adelaide Pen., *Canada* 100 B10
Adelaide River, *Australia* 92 B5
Adelanto, *U.S.A.* 117 L9
Adele I., *Australia* 92 C3
Adélie, Terre, *Antarctica* 5 C10
Adélie Land = Adélie, Terre, *Antarctica* 5 C10
Ademuz, *Spain* 32 E3
Aden = Al 'Adan, *Yemen* 74 E4
Aden, G. of, *Asia* 74 E4
Adendorp, *S. Africa* 88 E3
Aderbissinat, *Niger* 83 B6
Adh Dhayd, *U.A.E.* 71 E7
Adhoi, *India* 68 H4
Adi, *Indonesia* 63 E8
Adi Arkai, *Ethiopia* 81 E4
Adi Daro, *Ethiopia* 81 E4
Adi Keyih, *Eritrea* 81 E4
Adi Kwala, *Eritrea* 81 E4
Adi Ugri, *Eritrea* 81 E4
Adieu, C., *Australia* 93 F5
Adieu Pt., *Australia* 92 C3
Adigala, *Ethiopia* 81 E5
Adige →, *Italy* 29 C9
Adigrat, *Ethiopia* 81 E4
Adıgüzel Barajı, *Turkey* 39 C11
Adilabad, *India* 66 K11
Adilcevaz, *Turkey* 73 C10
Adirondack Mts., *U.S.A.* 111 C10
Adıyaman, *Turkey* 73 D8
Adjohon, *Benin* 83 D5
Adjud, *Romania* 43 D12
Adjumani, *Uganda* 86 B3
Adlavik Is., *Canada* 103 A8
Adler, *Russia* 49 J4
Admer, *Algeria* 83 A6
Admiralty G., *Australia* 92 B4
Admiralty I., *U.S.A.* 104 B2
Admiralty Is., *Papua N. G.* 96 H6
Ado, *Nigeria* 83 D5
Ado-Ekiti, *Nigeria* 83 D6
Adok, *Sudan* 81 F3
Adola, *Ethiopia* 81 E5
Adonara, *Indonesia* 63 F6
Adoni, *India* 66 M10
Adony, *Hungary* 42 C3
Adour →, *France* 20 E2
Adra, *India* 69 H12
Adra, *Spain* 35 J7
Adrano, *Italy* 31 E7
Adrar, *Mauritania* 78 D3
Adrar des Iforas, *Algeria* 78 C5
Ádria, *Italy* 29 C9
Adrian, *Mich., U.S.A.* 108 E3
Adrian, *Tex., U.S.A.* 113 H3
Adriatic Sea, *Medit. S.* 6 G9
Adua, *Indonesia* 63 E7
Adwa, *Ethiopia* 81 E4
Adygea □, *Russia* 49 H5
Adzhar Republic = Ajaria □, *Georgia* 49 K6
Adzopé, *Ivory C.* 82 D4
Ægean Sea, *Medit. S.* 39 C7
Aerhtai Shan, *Mongolia* 60 B4
Ærø, *Denmark* 11 K4
Ærøskøbing, *Denmark* 11 K4
Aëtós, *Greece* 38 D3
'Afak, *Iraq* 70 C5
Afándou, *Greece* 36 C10
Afghanistan ■, *Asia* 66 C4
Afikpo, *Nigeria* 83 D6
Aflou, *Algeria* 78 B6
Afragóla, *Italy* 31 B7
Afram →, *Ghana* 83 D4
Afrera, *Ethiopia* 81 E5
Africa 76 E6
'Afrīn, *Syria* 70 B3
Afşin, *Turkey* 72 C7
Afton, *N.Y., U.S.A.* 111 D9
Afton, *Wyo., U.S.A.* 114 E8
Afuá, *Brazil* 125 D8
'Afula, *Israel* 75 C4
Afyon, *Turkey* 39 C12
Afyon □, *Turkey* 39 C12
Afyonkarahisar = Afyon, *Turkey* 39 C12
Aga, *Egypt* 80 H7
Agadès = Agadez, *Niger* 83 B6
Agadez, *Niger* 83 B6
Agadir, *Morocco* 78 B4
Agaete, *Canary Is.* 37 F4
Agaie, *Nigeria* 83 D6
Again, *Sudan* 81 F2
Ağapınar, *Turkey* 39 B12
Agar, *India* 68 H7
Agaro, *Ethiopia* 81 F4
Agartala, *India* 67 H17
Agăş, *Romania* 43 D11
Agassiz, *Canada* 104 D4
Agats, *Indonesia* 63 F9
Agawam, *U.S.A.* 111 D12
Agbélouvé, *Togo* 83 D5
Agboville, *Ivory C.* 82 D4
Ağcabädi, *Azerbaijan* 49 K8
Ağdam, *Azerbaijan* 49 L8
Ağdaş, *Azerbaijan* 49 K8
Agde, *France* 20 E7
Agde, C. d', *France* 20 E7
Agdzhabedi = Ağcabädi, *Azerbaijan* 49 K8
Agen, *France* 20 D4
Agerbæk, *Denmark* 11 J2
Agersø, *Denmark* 11 J5
Ageyevo, *Russia* 46 E9
Āgh Kand, *Iran* 71 B6
Aghireşu, *Romania* 43 D8
Aginskoye, *Russia* 51 D12
Ağlasun, *Turkey* 39 D12
Agly →, *France* 20 F7
Agnew, *Australia* 93 E3
Agnibilékrou, *Ivory C.* 82 D4
Agnita, *Romania* 43 E9
Agnone, *Italy* 29 G11
Agofie, *Ghana* 83 D5
Agogna →, *Italy* 28 C5
Agogo, *Sudan* 81 F2
Agön, *Sweden* 10 C11
Agon Coutainville, *France* 18 C5
Ágordo, *Italy* 29 B9
Agori, *India* 69 G10
Agouna, *Benin* 83 D5
Agout →, *France* 20 E5
Agra, *India* 68 F7
Agrakhanskiuy Poluostrov, *Russia* 49 J8
Agramunt, *Spain* 32 D6
Agreda, *Spain* 32 D3
Ağri, *Turkey* 73 C10
Agri →, *Italy* 31 B9
Ağrı Dağı, *Turkey* 70 B5
Ağri Karakose = Ağri, *Turkey* 73 C10
Agriá, *Greece* 38 B5
Agrigento, *Italy* 30 E6
Agrínion, *Greece* 38 C3
Agrópoli, *Italy* 31 B7
Ağstafa, *Azerbaijan* 49 K7
Agua Caliente, *Baja Calif., Mexico* 117 N10
Agua Caliente, *Sinaloa, Mexico* 118 B3
Agua Caliente Springs, *U.S.A.* 117 N10
Água Clara, *Brazil* 125 H8
Agua Hechicero, *Mexico* 117 N10
Agua Prieta, *Mexico* 118 A3
Aguadilla, *Puerto Rico* 121 C6
Aguadulce, *Panama* 120 E3
Aguanga, *U.S.A.* 117 M10
Aguanish, *Canada* 103 B7
Aguanus →, *Canada* 103 B7
Aguapey →, *Argentina* 126 B4
Aguaray Guazú →, *Paraguay* 126 A4
Aguarico →, *Ecuador* 124 D3
Aguas →, *Spain* 32 D4
Aguas Blancas, *Chile* 126 A2
Aguas Calientes, Sierra de, *Argentina* 126 B2
Aguascalientes, *Mexico* 118 C4
Aguascalientes □, *Mexico* 118 C4
Agudo, *Spain* 35 G6
Águeda, *Portugal* 34 E2
Agueda →, *Spain* 34 D4
Aguelhok, *Mali* 83 B5
Aguié, *Niger* 83 C6
Aguilafuente, *Spain* 34 D6
Aguilar, *Spain* 35 H6
Aguilar de Campóo, *Spain* 34 C6
Aguilares, *Argentina* 126 B2
Aguilas, *Spain* 33 H3
Agüimes, *Canary Is.* 37 G4
Aguja, C. de la, *Colombia* 122 B3
Agulaa, *Ethiopia* 81 E4
Agulhas, C., *S. Africa* 88 E3
Agulo, *Canary Is.* 37 F2
Agung, *Indonesia* 62 F5
Agur, *Uganda* 86 B3
Agusan →, *Phil.* 61 G6
Ağva, *Turkey* 41 E13
Agvali, *Russia* 49 J8
Aha Mts., *Botswana* 88 B3
Ahaggar, *Algeria* 78 D7
Ahamansu, *Ghana* 83 D5
Ahar, *Iran* 70 B5
Ahat, *Turkey* 39 C11
Ahaus, *Germany* 24 C2
Ahipara B., *N.Z.* 91 F4
Ahir Dağı, *Turkey* 39 C12
Ahiri, *India* 66 K12
Ahlat, *Turkey* 73 C10
Ahlen, *Germany* 24 D3
Ahmad Wal, *Pakistan* 68 E1
Ahmadabad, *India* 68 H5
Aḥmadābād, *Khorāsān, Iran* 71 C9
Aḥmadābād, *Khorāsān, Iran* 71 C8
Aḥmadī, *Iran* 71 E8
Ahmadnagar, *India* 66 K9
Ahmadpur, *Pakistan* 68 E4
Ahmadpur Lamma, *Pakistan* 68 E4
Ahmar, *Ethiopia* 81 F5
Ahmedabad = Ahmadabad, *India* 68 H5
Ahmednagar = Ahmadnagar, *India* 66 K9
Ahmetbey, *Turkey* 41 E11
Ahmetler, *Turkey* 39 C11
Ahmetli, *Turkey* 39 C9
Ahoada, *Nigeria* 83 D6
Ahome, *Mexico* 118 B3
Ahoskie, *U.S.A.* 109 G7
Ahr →, *Germany* 24 E3
Ahram, *Iran* 71 D6
Ahrax Pt., *Malta* 36 D1
Ahrensbök, *Germany* 24 A6
Ahrensburg, *Germany* 24 B6
Āhū, *Iran* 71 C6
Ahuachapán, *El Salv.* 120 D2
Ahun, *France* 19 F9
Åhus, *Sweden* 11 J8
Ahvāz, *Iran* 71 D6
Ahvenanmaa = Åland, *Finland* 9 F19
Aḥwar, *Yemen* 74 E4
Ahzar →, *Mali* 83 B5
Ai →, *India* 69 F14
Ai-Ais, *Namibia* 88 D2
Aichach, *Germany* 25 G7
Aichi □, *Japan* 55 G8
Aigle, *Switz.* 25 J2
Aignay-le-Duc, *France* 19 E11
Aigoual, Mt., *France* 20 D7
Aigre, *France* 20 C4
Aigua, *Uruguay* 127 C5
Aigueperse, *France* 19 F10
Aigues →, *France* 21 D8
Aigues-Mortes, *France* 21 E8
Aigues-Mortes, G. d', *France* 21 E8
Aiguilles, *France* 21 D10
Aiguillon, *France* 20 D4
Aigurande, *France* 19 F8
Aihui, *China* 60 A7
Aija, *Peru* 124 E3
Aikawa, *Japan* 54 E9
Aiken, *U.S.A.* 109 J5
Ailao Shan, *China* 58 F3

Aileron, *Australia* 94 C1
Aillant-sur-Tholon, *France* 19 E10
Aillik, *Canada* 103 A8
Ailsa Craig, *U.K.* 14 F3
'Ailūn, *Jordan* 75 C4
Aim, *Russia* 51 D14
Aimere, *Indonesia* 63 F6
Aimogasta, *Argentina* 126 B2
Ain □, *France* 19 F12
Ain →, *France* 21 C9
Aïn Ben Tili, *Mauritania* 78 C4
Ain Dalla, *Egypt* 80 B2
Ain el Mafki, *Egypt* 80 B2
Ain Girba, *Egypt* 80 B2
Ain Murr, *Sudan* 80 C2
Ain Qeiqab, *Egypt* 80 B1
Aïn Sefra, *Algeria* 78 B5
Ain Sheikh Murzûk, *Egypt* 80 B2
Ain Sudr, *Egypt* 75 F2
Ain Sukhna, *Egypt* 80 J8
Ain Zeitûn, *Egypt* 80 B2
Ainaži, *Latvia* 9 H21
Aínos Óros, *Greece* 38 C2
Ainsworth, *U.S.A.* 112 D5
Aiquile, *Bolivia* 124 G5
Aïr, *Niger* 83 B6
Air Force I., *Canada* 101 B12
Air Hitam, *Malaysia* 65 M4
Airaines, *France* 19 C8
Airdrie, *Canada* 104 C6
Airdrie, *U.K.* 14 F5
Aire →, *France* 19 C11
Aire →, *U.K.* 12 D7
Aire, I. de l', *Spain* 37 B11
Aire-sur-la-Lys, *France* 19 B9
Aire-sur-l'Adour, *France* 20 E3
Airlie Beach, *Australia* 94 C4
Airvault, *France* 18 F6
Aisch →, *Germany* 25 F6
Aisne □, *France* 19 C10
Aisne →, *France* 19 C9
Ait, *India* 69 G8
Aitana, Sierra de, *Spain* 33 G4
Aitkin, *U.S.A.* 112 B8
Aitolía Kai Akarnanía □, *Greece* 38 C3
Aitolikón, *Greece* 38 C3
Aiud, *Romania* 43 D8
Aix-en-Provence, *France* 21 E9
Aix-la-Chapelle = Aachen, *Germany* 24 E2
Aix-les-Bains, *France* 21 C9
Aixe-sur-Vienne, *France* 20 C5
Áíyina, *Greece* 38 D5
Aiyínion, *Greece* 40 F6
Aíyion, *Greece* 38 C4
Aizawl, *India* 67 H18
Aizenay, *France* 18 F5
Aizkraukle, *Latvia* 9 H21
Aizpute, *Latvia* 9 H19
Aizuwakamatsu, *Japan* 54 F9
Ajaccio, *France* 21 G12
Ajaccio, G. d', *France* 21 G12
Ajaigarh, *India* 69 G9
Ajalpan, *Mexico* 119 D5
Ajanta Ra., *India* 66 J9
Ajari Rep. = Ajaria □, *Georgia* 49 K6
Ajaria □, *Georgia* 49 K6
Ajax, *Canada* 110 C5
Ajdābiyā, *Libya* 79 B10
Ajdovščina, *Slovenia* 29 C10
Ajibar, *Ethiopia* 81 E4
Ajka, *Hungary* 42 C2
'Ajmān, *U.A.E.* 71 E7
Ajmer, *India* 68 F6
Ajnala, *India* 68 D6
Ajo, *U.S.A.* 115 K7
Ajo, C. de, *Spain* 34 B7
Ajok, *Sudan* 81 F2
Ajuy, *Phil.* 61 F5
Ak Dağ, *Turkey* 39 E11
Ak Dağları, *Muğla, Turkey* 39 E11
Ak Dağları, *Sivas, Turkey* 72 C7
Akaba, *Togo* 83 D5
Akabira, *Japan* 54 C11
Akaki Beseka, *Ethiopia* 81 F4
Akala, *Sudan* 81 D4
Akamas □, *Cyprus* 36 D11
Akanthou, *Cyprus* 36 D12
Akarca, *Turkey* 39 C11
Akaroa, *N.Z.* 91 K4
Akasha, *Sudan* 80 C3
Akashi, *Japan* 55 G7
Akbarpur, *Bihar, India* 69 G10
Akbarpur, *Ut. P., India* 69 F10
Akçaabat, *Turkey* 73 B8
Akçadağ, *Turkey* 72 C7
Akçakale, *Turkey* 73 D8
Akçakoca, *Turkey* 72 B4
Akçaova, *Turkey* 41 E13
Akçay, *Turkey* 39 E11
Akçay →, *Turkey* 39 D10
Akdağ, *Turkey* 39 C8
Akdağmadeni, *Turkey* 72 C6
Akelamo, *Indonesia* 63 D7
Åkers styckebruk, *Sweden* 10 E11
Åkersberga, *Sweden* 10 E12
Aketi, *Dem. Rep. of the Congo* 84 D4
Akhaïa □, *Greece* 38 C3
Akhalkalaki, *Georgia* 49 K6
Akhaltsikhe, *Georgia* 49 K6
Akharnaí, *Greece* 38 C5
Akhelóös →, *Greece* 38 C3
Akhendriá, *Greece* 39 G7
Akhisar, *Turkey* 39 C9
Akhladhókambos, *Greece* 38 D4
Akhmîm, *Egypt* 80 B3
Akhnur, *India* 69 C6
Akhtopol, *Bulgaria* 41 D11
Akhtuba →, *Russia* 49 G8
Akhtubinsk, *Russia* 49 F8
Akhty, *Russia* 49 K8
Akhtyrka = Okhtyrka, *Ukraine* 47 G8
Aki, *Japan* 55 H6
Akimiski I., *Canada* 102 B3
Akimovka, *Ukraine* 47 J8
Åkirkeby, *Denmark* 11 J8
Akita, *Japan* 54 E10
Akita □, *Japan* 54 E10
Akjoujt, *Mauritania* 82 B2
Akka, *Mali* 82 B4
Akkaya Tepesi, *Turkey* 39 D11
Akkeshi, *Japan* 54 C12
'Akko, *Israel* 75 C4
Akköy, *Turkey* 39 D9
Aklampa, *Benin* 83 D5
Aklavik, *Canada* 100 B6
Aklera, *India* 68 G7
Akmenė, *Lithuania* 44 B9
Akmenrags, *Latvia* 44 B8
Akmolinsk = Astana, *Kazakstan* 50 D8
Akmonte = Almonte, *Spain* 35 H4
Akō, *Japan* 55 G7
Ako, *Nigeria* 83 C7
Akôbô, *Sudan* 81 F3
Akobo →, *Ethiopia* 81 F3
Akola, *India* 66 J10
Akonolinga, *Cameroon* 83 E7
Akor, *Mali* 82 C3
Akordat, *Eritrea* 81 D4
Akosombo Dam, *Ghana* 83 D5
Akot, *Sudan* 81 F3
Akoupé, *Ivory C.* 82 D4
Akpatok I., *Canada* 101 B13
Åkrahamn, *Norway* 9 G11
Akranes, *Iceland* 8 D2
Akreïjit, *Mauritania* 82 B3
Akrítas Venétiko, Ákra, *Greece* 38 E3
Akron, *Colo., U.S.A.* 112 E3
Akron, *Ohio, U.S.A.* 110 E3
Akrotiri, *Cyprus* 36 E11
Akrotíri, Ákra, *Greece* 41 F9
Akrotiri Bay, *Cyprus* 36 E12
Aksai Chin, *India* 69 B8
Aksaray, *Turkey* 70 B2
Aksay, *Kazakstan* 50 D6
Akşehir, *Turkey* 70 B1
Akşehir Gölü, *Turkey* 72 C4
Akstafa = Ağstafa, *Azerbaijan* 49 K7
Aksu, *China* 60 B3
Aksu →, *Turkey* 72 D4
Aksum, *Ethiopia* 81 E4
Aktash, *Russia* 48 C11
Aktogay, *Kazakstan* 50 E8
Aktsyabrski, *Belarus* 47 F5
Aktyubinsk = Aqtöbe, *Kazakstan* 50 D6
Aku, *Nigeria* 83 D6
Akure, *Nigeria* 83 D6
Akureyri, *Iceland* 8 D4
Akuseki-Shima, *Japan* 55 K4
Akusha, *Russia* 49 J8
Akwa-Ibom □, *Nigeria* 83 E6
Akyab = Sittwe, *Burma* 67 J18
Akyazı, *Turkey* 72 B4
Al 'Adan, *Yemen* 74 E4
Al Aḩsā = Hasa □, *Si. Arabia* 71 E6
Al Ajfar, *Si. Arabia* 70 E4
Al Amādīyah, *Iraq* 70 B4
Al 'Amārah, *Iraq* 70 D5
Al 'Aqabah, *Jordan* 75 F4
Al Arak, *Syria* 70 C3
Al 'Aramah, *Si. Arabia* 70 E5
Al Arţāwīyah, *Si. Arabia* 70 E5
Al 'Āşimah = 'Ammān □, *Jordan* 75 D5
Al 'Assāfīyah, *Si. Arabia* 70 D3
Al 'Ayn, *Oman* 71 E7
Al 'Ayn, *Si. Arabia* 70 E3
Al 'Azamīyah, *Iraq* 70 C5
Al 'Azīzīyah, *Iraq* 70 C5
Al Bāb, *Syria* 70 B3
Al Bad', *Si. Arabia* 70 D2
Al Bādī, *Iraq* 70 C4
Al Baḩrah, *Kuwait* 70 D5
Al Baḩral Mayyit = Dead Sea, *Asia* 75 D4
Al Balqā' □, *Jordan* 75 C4
Al Bārūk, J., *Lebanon* 75 B4
Al Başrah, *Iraq* 70 D5
Al Baṭḩā, *Iraq* 70 D5
Al Batrūn, *Lebanon* 75 A4
Al Bayḑā, *Libya* 79 B10
Al Biqā, *Lebanon* 75 A5
Al Bi'r, *Si. Arabia* 70 D3
Al Burayj, *Syria* 75 A5
Al Faḑilī, *Si. Arabia* 71 E6
Al Fallūjah, *Iraq* 70 C4
Al Fāw, *Iraq* 71 D6
Al Fujayrah, *U.A.E.* 71 E8
Al Ghadaf, W. →, *Jordan* 75 D5
Al Ghammās, *Iraq* 70 D5
Al Ghazālah, *Si. Arabia* 70 E4
Al Ḩadīthah, *Iraq* 70 C4
Al Ḩadīthah, *Si. Arabia* 75 D6
Al Ḩaḑr, *Iraq* 70 C4
Al Ḩājānah, *Syria* 75 B5
Al Hajar al Gharbi, *Oman* 71 E8
Al Hāmad, *Si. Arabia* 70 D3
Al Hamdānīyah, *Syria* 70 C3
Al Ḩamīdīyah, *Syria* 75 A4
Al Ḩammār, *Iraq* 70 D5
Al Ḩamrā', *Si. Arabia* 70 E3
Al Ḩanākīyah, *Si. Arabia* 70 E4
Al Harīr, W. →, *Syria* 75 C4
Al Ḩasā, W. →, *Jordan* 75 D4
Al Ḩasakah, *Syria* 70 B4
Al Haydān, W. →, *Jordan* 75 D4
Al Ḩayy, *Iraq* 70 C5
Al Ḩijarah, *Asia* 70 D4
Al Ḩillah, *Iraq* 70 C5
Al Ḩillah, *Si. Arabia* 74 B4
Al Hindīyah, *Iraq* 70 C5
Al Hirmil, *Lebanon* 75 A5
Al Hoceïma, *Morocco* 78 A5
Al Ḩudaydah, *Yemen* 74 E3
Al Hufūf, *Si. Arabia* 71 E6
Al Ḩumayḑah, *Si. Arabia* 70 D2
Al Ḩunayy, *Si. Arabia* 71 E6
Al Īsāwīyah, *Si. Arabia* 70 D3
Al Jafr, *Jordan* 75 E5
Al Jāfūrah, *Si. Arabia* 71 E7
Al Jaghbūb, *Libya* 79 C10
Al Jahrah, *Kuwait* 70 D5
Al Jalāmīd, *Si. Arabia* 70 D3
Al Jamalīyah, *Qatar* 71 E6
Al Janūb □, *Lebanon* 75 B4
Al Jawf, *Libya* 79 D10
Al Jawf, *Si. Arabia* 70 D3
Al Jazirah, *Iraq* 70 C5
Al Jithāmīyah, *Si. Arabia* 70 E4
Al Jubayl, *Si. Arabia* 71 E6
Al Jubaylah, *Si. Arabia* 70 E5
Al Jubb, *Si. Arabia* 70 E4
Al Junaynah, *Sudan* 79 F10
Al Kabā'ish, *Iraq* 70 D5
Al Karak, *Jordan* 75 D4
Al Karak □, *Jordan* 75 E5
Al Kāzim Tyah, *Iraq* 70 C5
Al Khābūra, *Oman* 71 F8
Al Khafji, *Si. Arabia* 71 E6
Al Khalīl, *West Bank* 75 D4
Al Khāliş, *Iraq* 70 C5
Al Kharsānīyah, *Si. Arabia* 71 E6
Al Khaşab, *Oman* 71 E8
Al Khawr, *Qatar* 71 E6
Al Khiḑr, *Iraq* 70 D5
Al Khiyām, *Lebanon* 75 B4
Al Kiswah, *Syria* 75 B5
Al Kūfah, *Iraq* 70 C5
Al Kufrah, *Libya* 79 D10
Al Kuhayfīyah, *Si. Arabia* 70 E4
Al Kūt, *Iraq* 70 C5
Al Kuwayt, *Kuwait* 70 D5
Al Labwah, *Lebanon* 75 A5
Al Lādhiqīyah, *Syria* 70 C2
Al Līth, *Si. Arabia* 74 C3
Al Liwā', *Oman* 71 E8
Al Luḩayyah, *Yemen* 74 D3
Al Madīnah, *Iraq* 70 D5
Al Madīnah, *Si. Arabia* 70 E3
Al Mafraq, *Jordan* 75 C5
Al Maḩmūdīyah, *Iraq* 70 C5
Al Majma'ah, *Si. Arabia* 70 E5
Al Makhruq, W. →, *Jordan* 75 D6
Al Makḩūl, *Si. Arabia* 70 E4
Al Manāmah, *Bahrain* 71 E6
Al Maqwa', *Kuwait* 70 D5
Al Marj, *Libya* 79 B10
Al Maţlā, *Kuwait* 70 D5
Al Mawjib, W. →, *Jordan* 75 D4
Al Mawşil, *Iraq* 70 B4
Al Mayādin, *Syria* 70 C4
Al Mazār, *Jordan* 75 D4
Al Midhnab, *Si. Arabia* 70 E5
Al Minā', *Lebanon* 75 A4
Al Miqdādīyah, *Iraq* 70 C5
Al Mubarraz, *Si. Arabia* 71 E6
Al Mudawwarah, *Jordan* 75 F5
Al Mughayrā', *U.A.E.* 71 E7
Al Muḩarraq, *Bahrain* 71 E6
Al Mukallā, *Yemen* 74 E4
Al Mukhā, *Yemen* 74 E3
Al Musayjīd, *Si. Arabia* 70 E3
Al Musayyib, *Iraq* 70 C5
Al Muwayh, *Si. Arabia* 80 C5
Al Muwayliḩ, *Si. Arabia* 70 E2
Al Owuho = Otukpa, *Nigeria* 83 D6
Al Qā'im, *Iraq* 70 C4
Al Qalībah, *Si. Arabia* 70 D3
Al Qāmishlī, *Syria* 70 B4
Al Qaryatayn, *Syria* 75 A6
Al Qaşīm, *Si. Arabia* 70 E4
Al Qaţ'ā, *Syria* 70 C4
Al Qaţīf, *Si. Arabia* 71 E6
Al Qatrānah, *Jordan* 75 D5
Al Qaţrūn, *Libya* 79 D9
Al Qayşūmah, *Si. Arabia* 70 D5
Al Quds = Jerusalem, *Israel* 75 D4
Al Qunayţirah, *Syria* 75 C4
Al Qunfudhah, *Si. Arabia* 80 D5
Al Qurnah, *Iraq* 70 D5
Al Quşayr, *Iraq* 70 D5
Al Quşayr, *Syria* 75 A5
Al Qutayfah, *Syria* 75 B5
Al 'Ubaylah, *Si. Arabia* 74 C5
Al 'Uḑaylīyah, *Si. Arabia* 71 E6
Al 'Ulā, *Si. Arabia* 70 E3
Al 'Uqayr, *Si. Arabia* 71 E6
Al 'Uwaynid, *Si. Arabia* 70 E5
Al 'Uwayqīlah, *Si. Arabia* 70 D4
Al 'Uyūn, *Ḩijāz, Si. Arabia* 70 E3
Al 'Uyūn, *Najd, Si. Arabia* 70 E4
Al 'Uzayr, *Iraq* 70 D5
Al Wajh, *Si. Arabia* 70 E3
Al Wakrah, *Qatar* 71 E6
Al Waqbah, *Si. Arabia* 70 D5
Al Wari'āh, *Si. Arabia* 70 E5
Ala, *Italy* 28 C8
Ala Dağ, *Turkey* 70 B2
Ala Dağları, *Turkey* 73 C10
Alabama □, *U.S.A.* 109 J2
Alabama →, *U.S.A.* 109 K2
Alabaster, *U.S.A.* 109 J2
Alaca, *Turkey* 72 B6
Alacaatlı, *Turkey* 39 B10
Alaçam, *Turkey* 72 B6
Alaçam Dağları, *Turkey* 39 B10
Alaçatı, *Turkey* 39 C8
Alachua, *U.S.A.* 109 L4
Alaejos, *Spain* 34 D5
Alaérma, *Greece* 36 C9
Alagir, *Russia* 49 J7
Alagna Valsésia, *Italy* 28 C4
Alagoa Grande, *Brazil* 125 E11
Alagoas □, *Brazil* 125 E11
Alagoinhas, *Brazil* 125 F11
Alagón, *Spain* 32 D3
Alagón →, *Spain* 34 F4
Alaior, *Spain* 37 B11
Alajero, *Canary Is.* 37 F2
Alajuela, *Costa Rica* 120 D3
Alakamisy, *Madag.* 89 C8
Alaknanda →, *India* 69 D8
Alakol, Ozero, *Kazakstan* 60 B3
Alamarvdasht, *Iran* 71 E7
Alamata, *Ethiopia* 81 E4
Alameda, *Calif., U.S.A.* 116 H4
Alameda, *N. Mex., U.S.A.* 115 J10
Alaminos, *Phil.* 61 C3
Alamo, *U.S.A.* 117 J11
Alamo Crossing, *U.S.A.* 117 L13
Alamogordo, *U.S.A.* 115 K11
Alamos, *Mexico* 118 B3
Alamosa, *U.S.A.* 115 H11
Åland, *Finland* 9 F19
Alandroal, *Portugal* 35 G3
Ålands hav, *Sweden* 9 F18
Alange, Presa de, *Spain* 35 G4
Alania = North Ossetia □, *Russia* 49 J7
Alanís, *Spain* 35 G5
Alanya, *Turkey* 70 B1
Alaotra, Farihin', *Madag.* 89 B8
Alapayevsk, *Russia* 50 D7
Alappuzha = Alleppey, *India* 66 Q10
Alar del Rey, *Spain* 34 C6
Alaraz, *Spain* 34 E5
Alarcón, Embalse de, *Spain* 32 F2
Alarobia-Vohiposa, *Madag.* 89 C8
Alaşehir, *Turkey* 39 C10
Alaska □, *U.S.A.* 100 B5
Alaska, G. of, *Pac. Oc.* 100 C5
Alaska Peninsula, *U.S.A.* 100 C4
Alaska Range, *U.S.A.* 100 B4
Alássio, *Italy* 28 E5
Älät, *Azerbaijan* 49 L9
Alatri, *Italy* 29 G10
Alatyr, *Russia* 48 C8
Alatyr →, *Russia* 48 C8
Alausi, *Ecuador* 124 D3
Álava □, *Spain* 32 C2
Alava, C., *U.S.A.* 114 B1
Alaverdi, *Armenia* 49 K7
Alavus, *Finland* 9 E20
'Alayh, *Lebanon* 75 B4
Alazani →, *Azerbaijan* 49 K8
Alba, *Italy* 28 D5
Alba □, *Romania* 43 D8
Alba Adriática, *Italy* 29 F10
Alba de Tormes, *Spain* 34 E5
Alba-Iulia, *Romania* 43 D8
Albac, *Romania* 42 D7
Albacete, *Spain* 33 F3
Albacete □, *Spain* 33 G3
Ålbæk, *Denmark* 11 G4
Ålbæk Bugt, *Denmark* 11 G4
Albaida, *Spain* 33 G4
Albalate de las Nogueras, *Spain* 32 E2
Albalate del Arzobispo, *Spain* 32 D4
Alban, *France* 20 E6
Albanel, L., *Canada* 102 B5
Albania ■, *Europe* 40 E4
Albano Laziale, *Italy* 29 G9
Albany, *Australia* 93 G2
Albany, *Ga., U.S.A.* 109 K3
Albany, *N.Y., U.S.A.* 111 D11
Albany, *Oreg., U.S.A.* 114 D2
Albany, *Tex., U.S.A.* 113 J5
Albany →, *Canada* 102 B3
Albardón, *Argentina* 126 C2
Albarracín, *Spain* 32 E3
Albarracín, Sierra de, *Spain* 32 E3
Albatera, *Spain* 33 G4
Albatross B., *Australia* 94 A3
Albegna →, *Italy* 29 F8
Albemarle, *U.S.A.* 109 H5
Albemarle Sd., *U.S.A.* 109 H7
Albenga, *Italy* 28 D5
Alberche →, *Spain* 34 F6
Alberdi, *Paraguay* 126 B4
Alberes, Mts., *France* 20 F6
Ålberga, *Sweden* 11 F10
Albersdorf, *Germany* 24 A5
Albert, *France* 19 C9
Albert, L., *Africa* 86 B3
Albert Edward Ra., *Australia* 92 C4
Albert Lea, *U.S.A.* 112 D8
Albert Nile →, *Uganda* 86 B3
Albert Town, *Bahamas* 121 B5
Alberta □, *Canada* 104 C6
Alberti, *Argentina* 126 D3
Albertinia, *S. Africa* 88 E3
Albertirsa, *Hungary* 42 C4
Alberton, *Canada* 103 C7
Albertville = Kalemie, *Dem. Rep. of the Congo* 86 D2
Albertville, *France* 21 C10
Albertville, *U.S.A.* 109 H2
Albi, *France* 20 E6
Albia, *U.S.A.* 112 E8
Albina, *Surinam* 125 B8
Albina, Ponta, *Angola* 88 B1
Albino, *Italy* 28 C6
Albion, *Mich., U.S.A.* 108 D3
Albion, *Nebr., U.S.A.* 112 E6
Albion, *Pa., U.S.A.* 110 E4
Albocácer, *Spain* 32 E5
Albolote, *Spain* 35 H7
Alborán, *Medit. S.* 35 K7
Alborea, *Spain* 33 F3
Ålborg, *Denmark* 11 G3
Ålborg Bugt, *Denmark* 11 H4
Alborz, Reshteh-ye Kūhhā-ye, *Iran* 71 C7
Albox, *Spain* 33 H2
Albufeira, *Portugal* 35 H2
Albula →, *Switz.* 25 J5
Albuñol, *Spain* 35 J7
Albuquerque, *U.S.A.* 115 J10
Albuquerque, Cayos de, *Caribbean* 120 D3
Alburg, *U.S.A.* 111 B11
Alburno, Mte., *Italy* 31 B8
Alburquerque, *Spain* 35 F4
Alcácer do Sal, *Portugal* 35 G2
Alcáçovas, *Portugal* 35 G2
Alcalá de Chivert, *Spain* 32 E5
Alcalá de Guadaira, *Spain* 35 H5
Alcalá de Henares, *Spain* 34 E7
Alcalá de los Gazules, *Spain* 35 J5
Alcalá del Júcar, *Spain* 33 F3
Alcalá del Río, *Spain* 35 H5
Alcalá del Valle, *Spain* 35 J5
Alcalá la Real, *Spain* 35 H7
Álcamo, *Italy* 30 E5
Alcanadre, *Spain* 32 C2
Alcanadre →, *Spain* 32 D4
Alcanar, *Spain* 32 E5
Alcanede, *Portugal* 35 F2
Alcanena, *Portugal* 35 F2
Alcañices, *Spain* 34 D4
Alcañiz, *Spain* 32 D4
Alcântara, *Brazil* 125 D10
Alcántara, *Spain* 34 F4
Alcántara, Embalse de, *Spain* 34 F4
Alcantarilla, *Spain* 33 H3
Alcaracejos, *Spain* 35 G6
Alcaraz, *Spain* 33 G2
Alcaraz, Sierra de, *Spain* 33 G2
Alcaudete, *Spain* 35 H6
Alcázar de San Juan, *Spain* 35 F7
Alchevsk, *Ukraine* 47 H10
Alcira = Alzira, *Spain* 33 F4
Alcobaça, *Portugal* 35 F2
Alcobendas, *Spain* 34 E7
Alcolea del Pinar, *Spain* 32 D2
Alcora, *Spain* 32 E4
Alcorcón, *Spain* 34 E7
Alcoutim, *Portugal* 35 H3
Alcova, *U.S.A.* 114 E10
Alcoy, *Spain* 33 G4
Alcubierre, Sierra de, *Spain* 32 D4
Alcublas, *Spain* 32 F4
Alcúdia, *Spain* 37 B10
Alcúdia, B. d', *Spain* 37 B10
Alcudia, Sierra de la, *Spain* 35 G6
Aldabra Is., *Seychelles* 77 G8
Aldama, *Mexico* 119 C5
Aldan, *Russia* 51 D13
Aldan →, *Russia* 51 C13
Aldea, Pta. de la, *Canary Is.* 37 G4
Aldeburgh, *U.K.* 13 E9
Alder Pk., *U.S.A.* 116 K5
Alderney, *U.K.* 13 H5
Aldershot, *U.K.* 13 F7
Åled, *Sweden* 11 H6
Aledo, *U.S.A.* 112 E9
Alefa, *Ethiopia* 81 E4
Aleg, *Mauritania* 82 B2
Alegranza, *Canary Is.* 37 E6
Alegranza, I., *Canary Is.* 37 E6
Alegre, *Brazil* 127 A7
Alegrete, *Brazil* 127 B4
Aleisk, *Russia* 50 D9
Aleksandriya = Oleksandriya, *Kirovohrad, Ukraine* 47 H7
Aleksandriya = Oleksandriya, *Rivne, Ukraine* 47 G4
Aleksandriyskaya, *Russia* 49 J8
Aleksandrov, *Russia* 46 D10
Aleksandrov Gay, *Russia* 48 E9
Aleksandrovac, *Serbia, Yug.* 40 C5
Aleksandrovac, *Serbia, Yug.* 40 B5
Aleksandrovka = Oleksandrovka, *Ukraine* 47 H7
Aleksandrovo, *Bulgaria* 41 C8
Aleksandrovsk-Sakhalinskiy, *Russia* 51 D15
Aleksandrów Kujawski, *Poland* 45 F5
Aleksandrów Łódźki, *Poland* 45 G6
Alekseyevka, *Samara, Russia* 48 D10
Alekseyevka, *Voronezh, Russia* 47 G10
Aleksin, *Russia* 46 E9
Aleksinac, *Serbia, Yug.* 40 C5
Além Paraíba, *Brazil* 127 A7

Alemania, *Argentina* 126 **B2**
Alemania, *Chile* 126 **B2**
Alençon, *France* 18 **D7**
Alenquer, *Brazil* 125 **D8**
Alenuihaha Channel, *U.S.A.* 106 **H17**
Alépé, *Ivory C.* 82 **D4**
Aleppo = Ḩalab, *Syria* 70 **B3**
Aléria, *France* 21 **F13**
Alès, *France* 21 **D8**
Aleşd, *Romania* 42 **C7**
Alessândria, *Italy* 28 **D5**
Ålestrup, *Denmark* 11 **H3**
Ålesund, *Norway* 9 **E12**
Alet-les-Bains, *France* 20 **F6**
Aletschhorn, *Switz.* 25 **J4**
Aleutian Is., *Pac. Oc.* 100 **C2**
Aleutian Trench, *Pac. Oc.* 96 **C10**
Alexander, *U.S.A.* 112 **B3**
Alexander, Mt., *Australia* 93 **E3**
Alexander Arch., *U.S.A.* 100 **C6**
Alexander Bay, *S. Africa* 88 **D2**
Alexander City, *U.S.A.* 109 **J3**
Alexander I., *Antarctica* 5 **C17**
Alexandra, *N.Z.* 91 **L2**
Alexandra Falls, *Canada* 104 **A5**
Alexandria = El Iskandarîya, *Egypt* 80 **H7**
Alexandria, *B.C., Canada* 104 **C4**
Alexandria, *Ont., Canada* 102 **C5**
Alexandria, *Romania* 43 **G10**
Alexandria, *S. Africa* 88 **E4**
Alexandria, *U.K.* 14 **F4**
Alexandria, *La., U.S.A.* 113 **K8**
Alexandria, *Minn., U.S.A.* 112 **C7**
Alexandria, *S. Dak., U.S.A.* 112 **D6**
Alexandria, *Va., U.S.A.* 108 **F7**
Alexandria Bay, *U.S.A.* 111 **B9**
Alexandroúpolis, *Greece* 41 **F9**
Alexis →, *Canada* 103 **B8**
Alexis Creek, *Canada* 104 **C4**
Alfabia, *Spain* 37 **B9**
Alfambra, *Spain* 32 **E3**
Alfândega da Fé, *Portugal* 34 **D4**
Alfaro, *Spain* 32 **C3**
Alfatar, *Bulgaria* 41 **C11**
Alfaz del Pi, *Spain* 33 **G4**
Alfeld, *Germany* 24 **D5**
Alfenas, *Brazil* 127 **A6**
Alfiós →, *Greece* 38 **D3**
Alföld, *Hungary* 42 **D5**
Alfonsine, *Italy* 29 **D9**
Alford, *Aberds., U.K.* 14 **D6**
Alford, *Lincs., U.K.* 12 **D8**
Alfred, *Maine, U.S.A.* 111 **C14**
Alfred, *N.Y., U.S.A.* 110 **D7**
Alfreton, *U.K.* 12 **D6**
Alfta, *Sweden* 10 **C10**
Alga, *Kazakstan* 50 **E6**
Algaida, *Spain* 37 **B9**
Algar, *Spain* 35 **J5**
Ålgård, *Norway* 9 **G11**
Algarinejo, *Spain* 35 **H6**
Algarve, *Portugal* 35 **J2**
Algeciras, *Spain* 35 **J5**
Algemesí, *Spain* 33 **F4**
Alger, *Algeria* 78 **A6**
Algeria ■, *Africa* 78 **C6**
Alghero, *Italy* 30 **B1**
Älghult, *Sweden* 11 **G9**
Algiers = Alger, *Algeria* 78 **A6**
Algoa B., *S. Africa* 88 **E4**
Algodonales, *Spain* 35 **J5**
Algodor →, *Spain* 34 **F7**
Algoma, *U.S.A.* 108 **C2**
Algona, *U.S.A.* 112 **D7**
Algonac, *U.S.A.* 110 **D2**
Algonquin Prov. Park, *Canada* 102 **C4**
Algorta, *Uruguay* 128 **C5**
Alhama de Almería, *Spain* 35 **J8**
Alhama de Aragón, *Spain* 32 **D3**
Alhama de Granada, *Spain* 35 **H7**
Alhama de Murcia, *Spain* 33 **H3**
Alhambra, *U.S.A.* 117 **L8**
Alhaurín el Grande, *Spain* 35 **J6**
Alhucemas = Al Hoceïma, *Morocco* 78 **A5**
'Alī al Gharbī, *Iraq* 70 **C5**
'Alī ash Sharqī, *Iraq* 70 **C5**
Äli Bayramlı, *Azerbaijan* 49 **L9**
'Alī Khēl, *Afghan.* 68 **C3**
Ali Sahîh, *Djibouti* 81 **E5**
Alī Shāh, *Iran* 70 **B5**
Ália, *Italy* 30 **E6**
'Alīābād, *Khorāsān, Iran* 71 **C8**
'Alīābād, *Kordestān, Iran* 70 **C5**
'Alīābād, *Yazd, Iran* 71 **D7**
Aliaga, *Spain* 32 **E4**
Aliağa, *Turkey* 39 **C8**
Aliákmon →, *Greece* 40 **F6**
Alibo, *Ethiopia* 81 **F4**
Alibori →, *Benin* 83 **C5**
Alibunar, *Serbia, Yug.* 42 **E5**
Alicante, *Spain* 33 **G4**
Alicante □, *Spain* 33 **G4**
Alice, *S. Africa* 88 **E4**
Alice, *U.S.A.* 113 **M5**
Alice →, *Queens., Australia* 94 **C3**
Alice →, *Queens., Australia* 94 **B3**
Alice, Punta, *Italy* 31 **C10**
Alice Arm, *Canada* 104 **B3**
Alice Springs, *Australia* 94 **C1**
Alicedale, *S. Africa* 88 **E4**
Aliceville, *U.S.A.* 109 **J1**
Alicudi, *Italy* 31 **D7**
Aliganj, *India* 69 **F8**
Aligarh, *Raj., India* 68 **G7**
Aligarh, *Ut. P., India* 68 **F8**
Alīgūdarz, *Iran* 71 **C6**
Alijó, *Portugal* 34 **D3**
Alimnía, *Greece* 36 **C9**
Alingsås, *Sweden* 11 **G6**
Alipur, *Pakistan* 68 **E4**
Alipur Duar, *India* 67 **F16**
Aliquippa, *U.S.A.* 110 **F4**
Alishan, *Taiwan* 59 **F13**
Aliste →, *Spain* 34 **D5**
Alitus = Alytus, *Lithuania* 9 **J21**
Alivérion, *Greece* 38 **C6**
Aliwal North, *S. Africa* 88 **E4**
Alix, *Canada* 104 **C6**
Aljezur, *Portugal* 35 **H2**
Aljustrel, *Portugal* 35 **H2**
Alkamari, *Niger* 83 **C7**
Alkmaar, *Neths.* 17 **B4**
All American Canal, *U.S.A.* 115 **K6**
Allada, *Benin* 83 **D5**
Allagash →, *U.S.A.* 109 **B11**
Allah Dad, *Pakistan* 68 **G2**
Allahabad, *India* 69 **G9**
Allan, *Canada* 105 **C7**
Allanche, *France* 20 **C6**
Allanridge, *S. Africa* 88 **D4**
Allaqi, Wadi →, *Egypt* 80 **C3**
Allariz, *Spain* 34 **C3**
Allassac, *France* 20 **C5**
Ålleberg, *Sweden* 11 **F7**
Allegany, *U.S.A.* 110 **D6**
Allegheny →, *U.S.A.* 110 **F5**
Allegheny Mts., *U.S.A.* 108 **G6**
Allegheny Reservoir, *U.S.A.* 110 **E6**
Allègre, *France* 20 **C7**
Allen, Bog of, *Ireland* 15 **C5**
Allen, L., *Ireland* 15 **B3**
Allendale, *U.S.A.* 109 **J5**
Allende, *Mexico* 118 **B4**
Allentown, *U.S.A.* 111 **F9**
Allentsteig, *Austria* 26 **C8**
Alleppey, *India* 66 **Q10**
Allepuz, *Spain* 32 **E4**
Aller →, *Germany* 24 **C5**
Alliance, *Nebr., U.S.A.* 112 **D3**
Alliance, *Ohio, U.S.A.* 110 **F3**
Allier □, *France* 19 **F9**
Allier →, *France* 19 **F10**
Alliford Bay, *Canada* 104 **C2**
Allinge, *Denmark* 11 **J8**
Alliston, *Canada* 102 **D4**
Alloa, *U.K.* 14 **E5**
Allones, *France* 18 **D8**
Allora, *Australia* 95 **D5**
Allos, *France* 21 **D10**
Alluitsup Paa, *Greenland* 4 **C5**
Alma, *Canada* 103 **C5**
Alma, *Ga., U.S.A.* 109 **K4**
Alma, *Kans., U.S.A.* 112 **F6**
Alma, *Mich., U.S.A.* 108 **D3**
Alma, *Nebr., U.S.A.* 112 **E5**
Alma Ata = Almaty, *Kazakstan* 50 **E8**
Almacelles, *Spain* 32 **D5**
Almada, *Portugal* 35 **G1**
Almaden, *Australia* 94 **B3**
Almadén, *Spain* 35 **G6**
Almanor, L., *U.S.A.* 114 **F3**
Almansa, *Spain* 33 **G3**
Almanza, *Spain* 34 **C5**
Almanzor, Pico, *Spain* 34 **E5**
Almanzora →, *Spain* 33 **H3**
Almaş, Munţii, *Romania* 42 **F7**
Almassora, *Spain* 32 **F4**
Almaty, *Kazakstan* 50 **E8**
Almazán, *Spain* 32 **D2**
Almeirim, *Brazil* 125 **D8**
Almeirim, *Portugal* 35 **F2**
Almelo, *Neths.* 17 **B6**
Almenar de Soria, *Spain* 32 **D2**
Almenara, *Spain* 32 **F4**
Almenara, Sierra de la, *Spain* 33 **H3**
Almendra, Embalse de, *Spain* 34 **D4**
Almendralejo, *Spain* 35 **G4**
Almere-Stad, *Neths.* 17 **B5**
Almería, *Spain* 35 **J8**
Almería □, *Spain* 33 **H2**
Almerìa, G. de, *Spain* 33 **J2**
Almetyevsk, *Russia* 48 **C11**
Älmhult, *Sweden* 11 **H8**
Almirante, *Panama* 120 **E3**
Almiropótamos, *Greece* 38 **C6**
Almirós, *Greece* 38 **B4**
Almiroú, Kólpos, *Greece* 36 **D6**
Almodôvar, *Portugal* 35 **H2**
Almodóvar del Campo, *Spain* 35 **G6**
Almodóvar del Río, *Spain* 35 **H5**
Almond, *U.S.A.* 110 **D7**
Almont, *U.S.A.* 110 **D1**
Almonte, *Canada* 111 **A8**
Almonte, *Spain* 35 **H4**
Almora, *India* 69 **E8**
Almoradí, *Spain* 33 **G4**
Almorox, *Spain* 34 **E6**
Almoustarat, *Mali* 83 **B5**
Älmsta, *Sweden* 10 **E12**
Almudévar, *Spain* 32 **C4**
Almuñécar, *Spain* 35 **J7**
Almunge, *Sweden* 10 **E12**
Almuradiel, *Spain* 35 **G7**
Alness, *U.K.* 14 **D4**
Alnmouth, *U.K.* 12 **B6**
Alnwick, *U.K.* 12 **B6**
Aloi, *Uganda* 86 **B3**
Alon, *Burma* 67 **H19**
Alor, *Indonesia* 63 **F6**
Alor Setar, *Malaysia* 65 **J3**
Álora, *Spain* 35 **J6**
Alosno, *Spain* 35 **H3**
Alot, *India* 68 **H6**
Aloysius, Mt., *Australia* 93 **E4**
Alpaugh, *U.S.A.* 116 **K7**
Alpedrinha, *Portugal* 34 **E3**
Alpena, *U.S.A.* 108 **C4**
Alpes-de-Haute-Provence □, *France* 21 **D10**
Alpes-Maritimes □, *France* 21 **E11**
Alpha, *Australia* 94 **C4**
Alphen aan den Rijn, *Neths.* 17 **B4**
Alpiarça, *Portugal* 35 **F2**
Alpine, *Ariz., U.S.A.* 115 **K9**
Alpine, *Calif., U.S.A.* 117 **N10**
Alpine, *Tex., U.S.A.* 113 **K3**
Alps, *Europe* 6 **F7**
Alpu, *Turkey* 72 **C4**
Alqueta, Barragem do, *Portugal* 35 **G3**
Alrø, *Denmark* 11 **J4**
Als, *Denmark* 11 **K3**
Alsace, *France* 19 **D14**
Alsask, *Canada* 105 **C7**
Alsasua, *Spain* 32 **C2**
Alsek →, *U.S.A.* 104 **B1**
Alsfeld, *Germany* 24 **E5**
Alsten, *Norway* 8 **D15**
Alstermo, *Sweden* 11 **H9**
Alston, *U.K.* 12 **C5**
Alta, *Norway* 8 **B20**
Alta, Sierra, *Spain* 32 **E3**
Alta Gracia, *Argentina* 126 **C3**
Alta Sierra, *U.S.A.* 117 **K8**
Altaelva →, *Norway* 8 **B20**
Altafjorden, *Norway* 8 **A20**
Altai = Aerhtai Shan, *Mongolia* 60 **B4**
Altamaha →, *U.S.A.* 109 **K5**
Altamira, *Brazil* 125 **D8**
Altamira, *Chile* 126 **B2**
Altamira, *Mexico* 119 **C5**
Altamira, Cuevas de, *Spain* 34 **B6**
Altamont, *U.S.A.* 111 **D10**
Altamura, *Italy* 31 **B9**
Altanbulag, *Mongolia* 60 **A5**
Altar, *Mexico* 118 **A2**
Altar, Desierto de, *Mexico* 118 **B2**
Altata, *Mexico* 118 **C3**
Altavista, *U.S.A.* 108 **G6**
Altay, *China* 60 **B3**
Altdorf, *Switz.* 25 **J4**
Alte Mellum, *Germany* 24 **B4**
Altea, *Spain* 33 **G4**
Altenberg, *Germany* 24 **E9**
Altenbruch, *Germany* 24 **B4**
Altenburg, *Germany* 24 **E8**
Altenkirchen, *Mecklenburg-Vorpommern, Germany* 24 **A9**
Altenkirchen, *Rhld-Pfz., Germany* 24 **E3**
Altenmarkt, *Austria* 26 **D7**
Alter do Chão, *Portugal* 35 **F3**
Altınoluk, *Turkey* 39 **B8**
Altınova, *Turkey* 39 **B8**
Altıntaş, *Turkey* 39 **B12**
Altınyaka, *Turkey* 39 **E12**
Altınyayla, *Turkey* 39 **D11**
Altiplano = Bolivian Plateau, *S. Amer.* 122 **E4**
Altkirch, *France* 19 **E14**
Altmark, *Germany* 24 **C7**
Altmühl →, *Germany* 25 **G7**
Altmunster, *Austria* 26 **D6**
Alto Adige = Trentino-Alto Adige □, *Italy* 29 **B8**
Alto Araguaia, *Brazil* 125 **G8**
Alto Cuchumatanes = Cuchumatanes, Sierra de los, *Guatemala* 120 **C1**
Alto del Carmen, *Chile* 126 **B1**
Alto del Inca, *Chile* 126 **A2**
Alto Ligonha, *Mozam.* 87 **F4**
Alto Molocue, *Mozam.* 87 **F4**
Alto Paraguay □, *Paraguay* 126 **A4**
Alto Paraná □, *Paraguay* 127 **B5**
Alton, *Canada* 110 **C4**
Alton, *U.K.* 13 **F7**
Alton, *Ill., U.S.A.* 112 **F9**
Alton, *N.H., U.S.A.* 111 **C13**
Altoona, *U.S.A.* 110 **F6**
Altötting, *Germany* 25 **G8**
Altstätten, *Switz.* 25 **H5**
Altūn Kūprī, *Iraq* 70 **C5**
Altun Shan, *China* 60 **C3**
Alturas, *U.S.A.* 114 **F3**
Altus, *U.S.A.* 113 **H5**
Alubijid, *Phil.* 61 **G6**
Alucra, *Turkey* 73 **B8**
Aluk, *Sudan* 81 **F2**
Alūksne, *Latvia* 9 **H22**
Alunda, *Sweden* 10 **D12**
Alunite, *U.S.A.* 117 **K12**
Aluoro →, *Ethiopia* 81 **F3**
Alupka, *Ukraine* 47 **K8**
Alushta, *Ukraine* 47 **K8**
Alusi, *Indonesia* 63 **F8**
Alustante, *Spain* 32 **E3**
Alva, *U.S.A.* 113 **G5**
Alvaiázere, *Portugal* 34 **F2**
Älvängen, *Sweden* 11 **G6**
Alvarado, *Mexico* 119 **D5**
Alvarado, *U.S.A.* 113 **J6**
Alvaro Obregón, Presa, *Mexico* 118 **B3**
Älvdalen, *Sweden* 10 **C8**
Alvear, *Argentina* 126 **B4**
Alverca, *Portugal* 35 **G1**
Alvesta, *Sweden* 11 **H8**
Alvin, *U.S.A.* 113 **L7**
Alvinston, *Canada* 110 **D3**
Alvito, *Portugal* 35 **G3**
Älvkarleby, *Sweden* 10 **D11**
Alvord Desert, *U.S.A.* 114 **E4**
Älvros, *Sweden* 10 **B8**
Älvsbyn, *Sweden* 8 **D19**
Alwar, *India* 68 **F7**
Alxa Zuoqi, *China* 56 **E3**
Alyangula, *Australia* 94 **A2**
Alyata = Älät, *Azerbaijan* 49 **L9**
Alyth, *U.K.* 14 **E5**
Alytus, *Lithuania* 9 **J21**
Alzada, *U.S.A.* 112 **C2**
Alzey, *Germany* 25 **F4**
Alzira, *Spain* 33 **F4**
Am Timan, *Chad* 79 **F10**
Amadeus, L., *Australia* 93 **D5**
Amadi, *Dem. Rep. of the Congo* 86 **B2**
Amâdi, *Sudan* 81 **F3**
Amadjuak L., *Canada* 101 **B12**
Amadora, *Portugal* 35 **G1**
Amagansett, *U.S.A.* 111 **F12**
Amagasaki, *Japan* 55 **G7**
Amager, *Denmark* 11 **J6**
Amagunze, *Nigeria* 83 **D6**
Amahai, *Indonesia* 63 **E7**
Amakusa-Shotō, *Japan* 55 **H5**
Åmål, *Sweden* 10 **E6**
Amalfi, *Italy* 31 **B7**
Amaliás, *Greece* 38 **D3**
Amalner, *India* 66 **J9**
Amamapare, *Indonesia* 63 **E9**
Amambaí, *Brazil* 127 **A4**
Amambaí →, *Brazil* 127 **A5**
Amambay □, *Paraguay* 127 **A4**
Amambay, Cordillera de, *S. Amer.* 127 **A4**
Amami-Guntō, *Japan* 55 **L4**
Amami-Ō-Shima, *Japan* 55 **L4**
Amaná, L., *Brazil* 124 **D6**
Amanat →, *India* 69 **G11**
Amanda Park, *U.S.A.* 116 **C3**
Amangeldy, *Kazakstan* 50 **D7**
Amantea, *Italy* 31 **C9**
Amapá, *Brazil* 125 **C8**
Amapá □, *Brazil* 125 **C8**
Amara, *Sudan* 81 **E3**
Amarante, *Brazil* 125 **E10**
Amarante, *Portugal* 34 **D2**
Amaranth, *Canada* 105 **C9**
Amareleja, *Portugal* 35 **G3**
Amargosa →, *U.S.A.* 117 **J10**
Amargosa Range, *U.S.A.* 117 **J10**
Amári, *Greece* 36 **D6**
Amarillo, *U.S.A.* 113 **H4**
Amarkantak, *India* 69 **H9**
Amârna, Tell el', *Sudan* 80 **B3**
Amaro, Mte., *Italy* 29 **F11**
Amarpur, *India* 69 **G12**
Amarti, *Eritrea* 81 **E5**
Amarwara, *India* 69 **H8**
Amasra, *Turkey* 72 **B5**
Amassama, *Nigeria* 83 **D6**
Amasya, *Turkey* 72 **B6**
Amata, *Australia* 93 **E5**
Amatikulu, *S. Africa* 89 **D5**
Amatitlán, *Guatemala* 120 **D1**
Amatrice, *Italy* 29 **F10**
Amay, *Belgium* 17 **D5**
Amazon = Amazonas →, *S. Amer.* 122 **D5**
Amazonas □, *Brazil* 124 **E6**
Amazonas →, *S. Amer.* 122 **D5**
Amba Ferit, *Ethiopia* 81 **E4**
Ambah, *India* 68 **F8**
Ambahakily, *Madag.* 89 **C7**
Ambahita, *Madag.* 89 **C8**
Ambala, *India* 68 **D7**
Ambalavao, *Madag.* 89 **C8**
Ambanja, *Madag.* 89 **A8**
Ambararata, *Madag.* 89 **B8**
Ambarchik, *Russia* 51 **C17**
Ambarijeby, *Madag.* 89 **A8**
Ambaro, Helodranon', *Madag.* 89 **A8**
Ambato, *Ecuador* 124 **D3**
Ambato, *Madag.* 89 **A8**
Ambato, Sierra de, *Argentina* 126 **B2**
Ambato Boeny, *Madag.* 89 **B8**
Ambatofinandrahana, *Madag.* 89 **C8**
Ambatolampy, *Madag.* 89 **B8**
Ambatomainty, *Madag.* 89 **B8**
Ambatomanoina, *Madag.* 89 **B8**
Ambatondrazaka, *Madag.* 89 **B8**
Ambatosoratra, *Madag.* 89 **B8**
Ambelón, *Greece* 38 **B4**
Ambenja, *Madag.* 89 **B8**
Amberg, *Germany* 25 **F7**
Ambergris Cay, *Belize* 119 **D7**
Ambérieu-en-Bugey, *France* 21 **C9**
Amberley, *N.Z.* 91 **K4**
Ambert, *France* 20 **C7**
Ambidédi, *Mali* 82 **C2**
Ambikapur, *India* 69 **H10**
Ambikol, *Sudan* 80 **C3**
Ambilobé, *Madag.* 89 **A8**
Ambinanindrano, *Madag.* 89 **C8**
Ambinanitelo, *Madag.* 89 **B8**
Ambinda, *Madag.* 89 **B8**
Amble, *U.K.* 12 **B6**
Ambleside, *U.K.* 12 **C5**
Ambo, *Peru* 124 **F3**
Amboahangy, *Madag.* 89 **C8**
Ambodifototra, *Madag.* 89 **B8**
Ambodilazana, *Madag.* 89 **B8**
Ambodiriana, *Madag.* 89 **B8**
Ambohidratrimo, *Madag.* 89 **B8**
Ambohidray, *Madag.* 89 **B8**
Ambohimahamasina, *Madag.* 89 **C8**
Ambohimahasoa, *Madag.* 89 **C8**
Ambohimanga, *Madag.* 89 **C8**
Ambohimitombo, *Madag.* 89 **C8**
Ambohitra, *Madag.* 89 **A8**
Amboise, *France* 18 **E8**
Ambon, *Indonesia* 63 **E7**
Ambondro, *Madag.* 89 **D8**
Amboseli, L., *Kenya* 86 **C4**
Ambositra, *Madag.* 89 **C8**
Ambovombe, *Madag.* 89 **D8**
Amboy, *U.S.A.* 117 **L11**
Amboyna Cay, *S. China Sea* 62 **C4**
Ambridge, *U.S.A.* 110 **F4**
Ambriz, *Angola* 84 **F2**
Amchitka I., *U.S.A.* 100 **C1**
Amderma, *Russia* 50 **C7**
Amdhi, *India* 69 **H9**
Ameca, *Mexico* 118 **C4**
Ameca →, *Mexico* 118 **C3**
Amecameca, *Mexico* 119 **D5**
Ameland, *Neths.* 17 **A5**
Amélia, *Italy* 29 **F9**
Amendolara, *Italy* 31 **C9**
Amenia, *U.S.A.* 111 **E11**
American Falls, *U.S.A.* 114 **E7**
American Falls Reservoir, *U.S.A.* 114 **E7**
American Fork, *U.S.A.* 114 **F8**
American Highland, *Antarctica* 5 **D6**
American Samoa ■, *Pac. Oc.* 91 **B13**
Americana, *Brazil* 127 **A6**
Americus, *U.S.A.* 109 **K3**
Amersfoort, *Neths.* 17 **B5**
Amersfoort, *S. Africa* 89 **D4**
Amery Ice Shelf, *Antarctica* 5 **C6**
Ames, *Spain* 34 **C2**
Ames, *U.S.A.* 112 **E8**
Amesbury, *U.S.A.* 111 **D14**
Amet, *India* 68 **G5**
Amfíklia, *Greece* 38 **C4**
Amfilokhía, *Greece* 38 **C3**
Amfípolis, *Greece* 40 **F7**
Ámfissa, *Greece* 38 **C4**
Amga, *Russia* 51 **C14**
Amga →, *Russia* 51 **C14**
Amgu, *Russia* 51 **E14**
Amgun →, *Russia* 51 **D14**
Amherst, *Canada* 103 **C7**
Amherst, *Mass., U.S.A.* 111 **D12**
Amherst, *N.Y., U.S.A.* 110 **D6**
Amherst, *Ohio, U.S.A.* 110 **E2**
Amherst I., *Canada* 111 **B8**
Amherstburg, *Canada* 102 **D3**
Amiata, Mte., *Italy* 29 **F8**
Amidon, *U.S.A.* 112 **B3**
Amiens, *France* 19 **C9**
Amindaion, *Greece* 40 **F5**
Åminne, *Sweden* 11 **G7**
Amino, *Ethiopia* 81 **G5**
Aminuis, *Namibia* 88 **C2**
Amīrābād, *Iran* 70 **C5**
Amirante Is., *Seychelles* 52 **K9**
Amisk L., *Canada* 105 **C8**
Amistad, Presa de la, *Mexico* 118 **B4**
Amite, *U.S.A.* 113 **K9**
Amla, *India* 68 **J8**
Amlia I., *U.S.A.* 100 **C2**
Amlwch, *U.K.* 12 **D3**
Amm Adam, *Sudan* 81 **D4**
'Ammān, *Jordan* 75 **D4**
'Ammān □, *Jordan* 75 **D5**
Ammanford, *U.K.* 13 **F4**
Ammassalik = Tasiilaq, *Greenland* 4 **C6**
Ammerån →, *Sweden* 10 **A10**
Ammersee, *Germany* 25 **G7**
Ammon, *U.S.A.* 114 **E8**
Amnat Charoen, *Thailand* 64 **E5**
Amnura, *Bangla.* 69 **G13**
Amo Jiang →, *China* 58 **F3**
Āmol, *Iran* 71 **B7**
Amorgós, *Greece* 39 **E7**
Amory, *U.S.A.* 109 **J1**
Amos, *Canada* 102 **C4**
Åmot, *Norway* 9 **G13**
Åmotfors, *Sweden* 10 **E6**
Amoy = Xiamen, *China* 59 **E12**
Ampanavoana, *Madag.* 89 **B9**
Ampang, *Malaysia* 65 **L3**
Ampangalana, Lakandranon', *Madag.* 89 **C8**
Ampanihy, *Madag.* 89 **C7**
Ampanafaravola, *Madag.* 89 **B8**
Ampasinambo, *Madag.* 89 **C8**
Ampasindava, Helodranon', *Madag.* 89 **A8**
Ampasindava, Saikanosy, *Madag.* 89 **A8**
Ampenan, *Indonesia* 62 **F5**
Amper, *Nigeria* 83 **D6**
Amper →, *Germany* 25 **G7**
Ampezzo, *Italy* 29 **B9**
Ampitsikinana, *Réunion* 89 **A8**
Ampombiantambo, *Madag.* 89 **A8**
Amposta, *Spain* 32 **E5**
Ampotaka, *Madag.* 89 **D7**
Ampoza, *Madag.* 89 **C7**

Amqui, Canada 103 C6
Amravati, India 66 J10
Amreli, India 68 J4
Amritsar, India 68 D6
Amroha, India 69 E8
Amrum, Germany 24 A4
Amsterdam, Neths. 17 B4
Amsterdam, U.S.A. 111 D10
Amsterdam, I. = Nouvelle-Amsterdam, I., Ind. Oc. 3 F13
Amstetten, Austria 26 C7
Amudarya →, Uzbekistan 50 E6
Amundsen Gulf, Canada 100 A7
Amundsen Sea, Antarctica 5 D15
Amungen, Sweden 10 C9
Amuntai, Indonesia 62 E5
Amur →, Russia 51 D15
Amur, W. →, Sudan 80 D3
Amurang, Indonesia 63 D6
Amurrio, Spain 32 B1
Amursk, Russia 51 D14
Amusco, Spain 34 C6
Amvrakikós Kólpos, Greece 38 C2
Amvrosiyivka, Ukraine 47 J10
Amyderya = Amudarya →, Uzbekistan 50 E6
An Bien, Vietnam 65 H5
An Hoa, Vietnam 64 E7
An Nabatīyah at Tahta, Lebanon 75 B4
An Nabk, Si. Arabia 70 D3
An Nabk, Syria 75 A5
An Nafūd, Si. Arabia 70 D4
An Najaf, Iraq 70 C5
An Nāşirīyah, Iraq 70 D5
An Nhon, Vietnam 64 F7
An Nîl □, Sudan 80 D3
An Nîl el Abyad □, Sudan 81 E3
An Nîl el Azraq □, Sudan 81 E3
An Nu'ayrīyah, Si. Arabia 71 E6
An Nu'mānīyah, Iraq 73 F11
An Nuwayb'ī, W. →, Si. Arabia 75 F3
An Thoi, Dao, Vietnam 65 H4
An Uaimh, Ireland 15 C5
Anabar →, Russia 51 B12
'Anabtā, West Bank 75 C4
Anaconda, U.S.A. 114 C7
Anacortes, U.S.A. 116 B4
Anacuao, Mt., Phil. 61 C4
Anadarko, U.S.A. 113 H5
Anadia, Portugal 34 E2
Anadolu, Turkey 72 C5
Anadyr, Russia 51 C18
Anadyr →, Russia 51 C18
Anadyrskiy Zaliv, Russia 51 C19
Anáfi, Greece 39 E7
Anafópoulo, Greece 39 E7
Anaga, Pta. de, Canary Is. 37 F3
Anagni, Italy 29 G10
'Ānah, Iraq 70 C4
Anaheim, U.S.A. 117 M9
Anahim Lake, Canada 104 C3
Anáhuac, Mexico 118 B4
Anakapalle, India 67 L13
Anakie, Australia 94 C4
Anaklia, Georgia 49 J5
Analalava, Madag. 89 A8
Analavoka, Madag. 89 C8
Análipsis, Greece 36 A3
Anambar →, Pakistan 68 D3
Anambas, Kepulauan, Indonesia 65 L6
Anambas Is. = Anambas, Kepulauan, Indonesia 65 L6
Anambra □, Nigeria 83 D6
Anamosa, U.S.A. 112 D9
Anamur, Turkey 70 B2
Anamur Burnu, Turkey 72 D5
Anan, Japan 55 H7
Anand, India 68 H5
Anánes, Greece 38 E6
Anantnag, India 69 C6
Ananyiv, Ukraine 47 J5
Anapa, Russia 47 K9
Anapodháris →, Greece 36 E7
Anápolis, Brazil 125 G9
Anapu →, Brazil 125 D8
Anār, Iran 71 D7
Anārak, Iran 71 C7
Anarisfjällen, Sweden 10 A7
Anas →, India 68 H5
Anatolia = Anadolu, Turkey 72 C5
Anatsogno, Madag. 89 C7
Añatuya, Argentina 126 B3
Anaunethad L., Canada 105 A8
Anbyŏn, N. Korea 57 E14
Ancares, Sierra de, Spain 34 C4
Ancaster, Canada 110 C5
Ancenis, France 18 E5
Anchor Bay, U.S.A. 116 G3
Anchorage, U.S.A. 100 B5
Anci, China 56 E9
Ancohuma, Nevada, Bolivia 122 E4
Ancón, Peru 124 F3
Ancona, Italy 29 E10
Ancud, Chile 128 E2
Ancud, G. de, Chile 128 E2
Ancy-le-Franc, France 19 E11
Andacollo, Argentina 126 D1
Andacollo, Chile 126 C1
Andaingo, Madag. 89 B8
Andalgalá, Argentina 126 B2
Åndalsnes, Norway 9 E12
Andalucía □, Spain 35 H6
Andalusia = Andalucía □, Spain 35 H6
Andalusia, U.S.A. 109 K2
Andaman Is., Ind. Oc. 52 H13
Andaman Sea, Ind. Oc. 62 B1
Andamooka Opal Fields, Australia 95 E2
Andapa, Madag. 89 A8
Andara, Namibia 88 B3
Andelot-Blancheville, France 19 D12
Andenes, Norway 8 B17
Andenne, Belgium 17 D5
Andéranboukane, Mali 83 B5
Andermatt, Switz. 25 J4
Andernach, Germany 24 E3
Andernos-les-Bains, France 20 D2
Anderslöv, Sweden 11 J7
Anderson, Alaska, U.S.A. 100 B5
Anderson, Calif., U.S.A. 114 F2
Anderson, Ind., U.S.A. 108 E3
Anderson, Mo., U.S.A. 113 G7
Anderson, S.C., U.S.A. 109 H4
Anderson →, Canada 100 B7
Anderstorp, Sweden 11 G7
Andes, U.S.A. 111 D10
Andes, Cord. de los, S. Amer. 122 F4
Andfjorden, Norway 8 B17
Andhra Pradesh □, India 66 L11
Andijon, Uzbekistan 50 E8
Andikíthira, Greece 38 F5
Andilamena, Madag. 89 B8
Andīmeshk, Iran 71 C6
Andímilos, Greece 38 E6
Andíparos, Greece 39 D7
Andípaxoi, Greece 38 B2
Andípsara, Greece 39 C7
Andírrion, Greece 38 C3
Andizhan = Andijon, Uzbekistan 50 E8
Andoain, Spain 32 B2
Andoany, Madag. 89 A8
Andong, S. Korea 57 F15
Andongwei, China 57 G10
Andoom, Australia 94 A3
Andorra, Spain 32 E4
Andorra ■, Europe 20 F5
Andorra La Vella, Andorra 20 F5
Andover, U.K. 13 F6
Andover, Maine, U.S.A. 111 B14
Andover, Mass., U.S.A. 111 D13
Andover, N.J., U.S.A. 111 F10
Andover, N.Y., U.S.A. 110 D7
Andover, Ohio, U.S.A. 110 E4
Andøya, Norway 8 B16
Andradina, Brazil 125 H8
Andrahary, Mt., Madag. 89 A8
Andramasina, Madag. 89 B8
Andranopasy, Madag. 89 C7
Andranovory, Madag. 89 C7
Andratx, Spain 37 B9
Andreanof Is., U.S.A. 100 C2
Andreapol, Russia 46 D7
Andrews, S.C., U.S.A. 109 J6
Andrews, Tex., U.S.A. 113 J3
Andreyevka, Russia 48 D10
Ándria, Italy 31 A9
Andriamena, Madag. 89 B8
Andriandampy, Madag. 89 C8
Andriba, Madag. 89 B8
Andrijevica, Montenegro, Yug. 40 D3
Andrítsaina, Greece 38 D3
Androka, Madag. 89 C7
Andropov = Rybinsk, Russia 46 C10
Ándros, Greece 38 D6
Andros I., Bahamas 120 B4
Andros Town, Bahamas 120 B4
Androscoggin →, U.S.A. 111 C14
Andrychów, Poland 45 J6
Andselv, Norway 8 B18
Andújar, Spain 35 G6
Andulo, Angola 84 G3
Aneby, Sweden 11 G8
Anegada I., U.S. Virgin Is. 121 C7
Anegada Passage, W. Indies 121 C7
Anécho, Togo 83 D5
Anenni-Noi, Moldova 43 D14
Aneto, Pico de, Spain 32 C5
Anfu, China 59 D10
Ang Thong, Thailand 64 E3
Angamos, Punta, Chile 126 A1
Angara →, Russia 51 D10
Angara-Débou, Benin 83 C5
Angarab, Ethiopia 81 E4
Angarbaka, Sudan 81 F1
Angarsk, Russia 51 D11
Angas Hills, Australia 92 D4
Angaur I., Pac. Oc. 63 C8
Ånge, Sweden 10 B9
Ángel, Salto = Angel Falls, Venezuela 124 B6
Ángel de la Guarda, I., Mexico 118 B2
Angel Falls, Venezuela 124 B6
Angeles, Phil. 61 D4
Ängelholm, Sweden 11 H6
Angels Camp, U.S.A. 116 G6
Ängelsberg, Sweden 10 E10
Anger →, Ethiopia 81 F4
Angereb →, Ethiopia 81 E4
Ångermanälven →, Sweden 10 B11
Ångermanland, Sweden 8 E18
Angermünde, Germany 24 B9
Angers, Canada 111 A9
Angers, France 18 E6
Angerville, France 19 D9
Ängesån →, Sweden 8 C20
Angikuni L., Canada 105 A9
Angkor, Cambodia 64 F4
Anglès, Spain 32 D7
Anglesey, Isle of □, U.K. 12 D3
Anglet, France 20 E2
Angleton, U.S.A. 113 L7
Anglin →, France 20 B4
Anglisidhes, Cyprus 36 E12
Anglure, France 19 D10
Angmagssalik = Tasiilaq, Greenland 4 C6
Ango, Dem. Rep. of the Congo 86 B2
Angoche, Mozam. 87 F4
Angoche, I., Mozam. 87 F4
Angol, Chile 126 D1
Angola, Ind., U.S.A. 108 E3
Angola, N.Y., U.S.A. 110 D5
Angola ■, Africa 85 G3
Angoulême, France 20 C4
Angoumois, France 20 C4
Angra dos Reis, Brazil 127 A7
Angren, Uzbekistan 50 E8
Angtassom, Cambodia 65 G5
Angu, Dem. Rep. of the Congo 86 B1
Anguang, China 57 B12
Anguilla ■, W. Indies 121 C7
Anguo, China 56 E8
Angurugu, Australia 94 A2
Angus □, U.K. 14 E6
Angwa →, Zimbabwe 89 B5
Anhanduí →, Brazil 127 A5
Anholt, Denmark 11 H5
Anhua, China 59 C8
Anhui □, China 59 B11
Anhwei = Anhui □, China 59 B11
Anichab, Namibia 88 C1
Ánidhros, Greece 39 E7
Anié, Togo 83 D5
Animas →, U.S.A. 115 H9
Anina, Romania 42 E6
Aninoasa, Romania 43 F9
Anivorano, Madag. 89 B8
Anjalankoski, Finland 9 F22
Anjar, India 68 H4
Anji, China 59 B12
Anjou, France 18 E6
Anjozorobe, Madag. 89 B8
Anju, N. Korea 57 E13
Anka, Nigeria 83 C6
Ankaboa, Tanjona, Madag. 89 C7
Ankang, China 56 H5
Ankara, Turkey 72 C5
Ankaramena, Madag. 89 C8
Ankaratra, Madag. 85 H9
Ankarsrum, Sweden 11 G10
Ankasakasa, Madag. 89 B7
Ankavandra, Madag. 89 B8
Ankazoabo, Madag. 89 C7
Ankazobe, Madag. 89 B8
Ankeny, U.S.A. 112 E8
Ankilimalinika, Madag. 89 C7
Ankilizato, Madag. 89 C8
Ankisabe, Madag. 89 B8
Anklam, Germany 24 B9
Ankober, Ethiopia 81 F4
Ankoro, Dem. Rep. of the Congo 86 D2
Ankororoka, Madag. 89 D8
Anlong, China 58 E5
Anlu, China 59 B9
Anmyŏn-do, S. Korea 57 F14
Ånn, Sweden 10 A6
Ann, C., U.S.A. 111 D14
Ann Arbor, U.S.A. 108 D4
Anna, Russia 48 E5
Anna, U.S.A. 113 G10
Annaba, Algeria 78 A7
Annaberg-Buchholz, Germany 24 E9
Annalee →, Ireland 15 B4
Annam, Vietnam 64 E7
Annamitique, Chaîne, Asia 64 D6
Annan, U.K. 14 G5
Annan →, U.K. 14 G5
Annapolis, U.S.A. 108 F7
Annapolis Royal, Canada 103 D6
Annapurna, Nepal 69 E10
Annean, L., Australia 93 E2
Anneberg, Sweden 11 G8
Annecy, France 21 C10
Annecy, Lac d', France 21 C10
Annemasse, France 19 F13
Annenskiy Most, Russia 46 B9
Anning, China 58 E4
Anniston, U.S.A. 109 J3
Annobón, Atl. Oc. 77 G4
Annonay, France 21 C8
Annot, France 21 E10
Annotto Bay, Jamaica 120 C4
Annsjön, Sweden 10 A6
Annville, U.S.A. 111 F8
Annweiler, Germany 25 F3
Áno Arkhánai, Greece 39 F7
Áno Porróia, Greece 40 E7
Áno Síros, Greece 38 D6
Áno Viánnos, Greece 36 D7
Anorotsangana, Madag. 89 A8
Anosibe, Madag. 89 B8
Anou Mellene, Mali 83 B5
Anoumaba, Ivory C. 82 D4
Anóyia, Greece 36 D6
Anping, Hebei, China 56 E8
Anping, Liaoning, China 57 D12
Anpu Gang, China 58 G7
Anqing, China 59 B11
Anqiu, China 57 F10
Anren, China 59 D9
Ansager, Denmark 11 J2
Ansai, China 56 F5
Ansbach, Germany 25 F6
Anseba →, Eritrea 81 D4
Ansfelden, Austria 26 C7
Anshan, China 57 D12
Anshun, China 58 D5
Ansião, Portugal 34 F2
Ansley, U.S.A. 112 E5
Ansó, Spain 32 C4
Ansoain, Spain 32 C3
Anson, U.S.A. 113 J5
Anson B., Australia 92 B5
Ansongo, Mali 83 B5
Ansonia, U.S.A. 111 E11
Anstruther, U.K. 14 E6
Ansudu, Indonesia 63 E9
Antabamba, Peru 124 F4
Antakya, Turkey 70 B3
Antalaha, Madag. 89 A9
Antalya, Turkey 72 D4
Antalya □, Turkey 39 E12
Antalya Körfezi, Turkey 72 D4
Antambohobe, Madag. 89 C8
Antanambao-Manampotsy, Madag. 89 B8
Antanambe, Madag. 89 B8
Antananarivo, Madag. 89 B8
Antananarivo □, Madag. 89 B8
Antanifotsy, Madag. 89 B8
Antanimbaribe, Madag. 89 C7
Antanimora, Madag. 89 C8
Antarctic Pen., Antarctica 5 C18
Antarctica 5 E3
Antelope, Zimbabwe 87 G2
Antequera, Paraguay 126 A4
Antequera, Spain 35 H6
Antero, Mt., U.S.A. 115 G10
Antevamena, Madag. 89 C7
Anthemoús, Greece 40 F7
Anthony, Kans., U.S.A. 113 G5
Anthony, N. Mex., U.S.A. 115 K10
Anti Atlas, Morocco 78 C4
Anti-Lebanon = Ash Sharqi, Al Jabal, Lebanon 75 B5
Antibes, France 21 E11
Antibes, C. d', France 21 E11
Anticosti, Î. d', Canada 103 C7
Antifer, C. d', France 18 C7
Antigo, U.S.A. 112 C10
Antigonish, Canada 103 C7
Antigua, Canary Is. 37 F5
Antigua, W. Indies 121 C7
Antigua & Barbuda ■, W. Indies 121 C7
Antigua Guatemala, Guatemala 120 D1
Antilla, Cuba 120 B4
Antilles = West Indies, Cent. Amer. 121 D7
Antioch, U.S.A. 116 G5
Antioche, Pertuis d', France 20 B2
Antioquia, Colombia 124 B3
Antipodes Is., Pac. Oc. 96 M9
Antlers, U.S.A. 113 H7
Antoetra, Madag. 89 C8
Antofagasta, Chile 126 A1
Antofagasta □, Chile 126 A2
Antofagasta de la Sierra, Argentina 126 B2
Antofalla, Argentina 126 B2
Antofalla, Salar de, Argentina 126 B2
Anton, U.S.A. 113 J3
Antongila, Helodrano, Madag. 89 B8
Antonibé, Madag. 89 B8
Antonibé, Presqu'île d', Madag. 89 A8
Antonina, Brazil 127 B6
Antrain, France 18 D5
Antrim, U.K. 15 B5
Antrim, U.S.A. 110 F3
Antrim □, U.K. 15 B5
Antrim, Mts. of, U.K. 15 A5
Antrim Plateau, Australia 92 C4
Antrodoco, Italy 29 F10
Antropovo, Russia 48 A6
Antsakabary, Madag. 89 B8
Antsalova, Madag. 89 B7
Antsenavolo, Madag. 89 C8
Antsiafabositra, Madag. 89 B8
Antsirabe, Antananarivo, Madag. 89 B8
Antsirabe, Antsiranana, Madag. 89 A8
Antsirabe, Mahajanga, Madag. 89 B8
Antsiranana, Madag. 89 A8
Antsiranana □, Madag. 89 A8
Antsohihy, Madag. 89 A8
Antsohimbondrona Seranana, Madag. 89 A8
Antu, China 57 C15
Antwerp = Antwerpen, Belgium 17 C4
Antwerp, U.S.A. 111 B9
Antwerpen, Belgium 17 C4
Antwerpen □, Belgium 17 C4
Anupgarh, India 68 E5
Anuppur, India 69 H9
Anuradhapura, Sri Lanka 66 Q12
Anveh, Iran 71 E7
Anvers = Antwerpen, Belgium 17 C4
Anvers I., Antarctica 5 C17
Anwen, China 59 C13
Anxi, Fujian, China 59 E12
Anxi, Gansu, China 60 B4
Anxian, China 58 B5
Anxiang, China 59 C9
Anxious B., Australia 95 E1
Anyama, Ivory C. 82 D4
Anyang, China 56 F8
Anyer-Kidul, Indonesia 63 G11
Anyi, Jiangxi, China 59 C10
Anyi, Shanxi, China 56 G6
Anyuan, China 59 E10
Anyue, China 58 B5
Anza, U.S.A. 117 M10
Anze, China 56 F7
Anzhero-Sudzhensk, Russia 50 D9
Ánzio, Italy 30 A5
Aoga-Shima, Japan 55 H9
Aoiz, Spain 32 C3
Aomen = Macau □, China 59 F9
Aomori, Japan 54 D10
Aomori □, Japan 54 D10
Aonla, India 69 E8
Aoraki Mount Cook, N.Z. 91 K3
Aosta, Italy 28 C4
Aoudéras, Niger 83 B6
Aoukâr, Mauritania 82 B3
Apa →, S. Amer. 126 A4
Apache, U.S.A. 113 H5
Apache Junction, U.S.A. 115 K8
Apalachee B., U.S.A. 109 L4
Apalachicola, U.S.A. 109 L3
Apalachicola →, U.S.A. 109 L3
Apam, Ghana 83 D4
Apapa, Nigeria 83 D5
Apaporis →, Colombia 124 D5
Aparri, Phil. 61 B4
Apateu, Romania 42 D6
Apatin, Serbia, Yug. 42 E4
Apatity, Russia 50 C4
Apatzingán, Mexico 118 D4
Apeldoorn, Neths. 17 B5
Apen, Germany 24 B3
Apennines = Appennini, Italy 28 E7
Aphrodisias, Turkey 39 D10
Apia, Samoa 91 A13
Apiacás, Serra dos, Brazil 124 E7
Apies →, S. Africa 89 D4
Apizaco, Mexico 119 D5
Aplao, Peru 124 G4
Apo, Mt., Phil. 63 C7
Apolakkiá, Greece 36 C9
Apolakkiá, Órmos, Greece 36 C9
Apolda, Germany 24 D7
Apollonia, Greece 38 E6
Apolo, Bolivia 124 F5
Aporé →, Brazil 125 G8
Apostle Is., U.S.A. 112 B9
Apóstoles, Argentina 127 B4
Apostolos Andreas, C., Cyprus 36 D13
Apostolovo, Ukraine 47 J7
Apoteri, Guyana 124 C7
Appalachian Mts., U.S.A. 108 G6
Äppelbo, Sweden 10 D8
Appennini, Italy 28 E7
Appennino Ligure, Italy 28 D6
Appenzell-Ausser Rhoden □, Switz. 25 H5
Appenzell-Inner Rhoden □, Switz. 25 H5
Appiano, Italy 29 B8
Apple Hill, Canada 111 A10
Apple Valley, U.S.A. 117 L9
Appleby-in-Westmorland, U.K. 12 C5
Appleton, U.S.A. 108 C1
Approuague →, Fr. Guiana 125 C8
Apricena, Italy 29 G12
Aprília, Italy 30 A5
Apsheronsk, Russia 49 H4
Apsley, Canada 110 B6
Apt, France 21 E9
Apuane, Alpi, Italy 28 D7
Apucarana, Brazil 127 A5
Apulia = Púglia □, Italy 31 A9
Apure →, Venezuela 124 B5
Apurimac →, Peru 124 F4
Apuseni, Munţii, Romania 42 D7
Āqā Jarī, Iran 71 D6
Aqaba = Al 'Aqabah, Jordan 75 F4
Aqaba, G. of, Red Sea 70 D2
'Aqabah, Khalīj al = Aqaba, G. of, Red Sea 70 D2
'Aqdā, Iran 71 C7
Aqīq, Sudan 80 D4
Aqīq, Khalīg, Sudan 80 D4
Aqmola = Astana, Kazakstan 50 D8
'Aqrah, Iraq 70 B4
Aqtaū, Kazakstan 50 E6
Aqtöbe, Kazakstan 50 D6
Aquidauana, Brazil 125 H7
Aquiles Serdán, Mexico 118 B3
Aquin, Haiti 121 C5
Aquitaine □, France 20 D3
Aqviligjuaq = Pelly Bay, Canada 101 B11
Ar Rachidiya = Er Rachidia, Morocco 78 B5
Ar Rafīd, Syria 75 C4
Ar Raḩḩālīyah, Iraq 70 C4
Ar Ramādī, Iraq 70 C4
Ar Ramthā, Jordan 75 C5
Ar Raqqah, Syria 70 C3
Ar Rass, Si. Arabia 70 E4
Ar Rawshān, Si. Arabia 80 C5
Ar Rifā'ī, Iraq 70 D5
Ar Riyāḑ, Si. Arabia 70 E5
Ar Ru'ays, Qatar 71 E6
Ar Rukhaymīyah, Iraq 70 D5
Ar Ruşāfah, Syria 70 C3
Ar Ruţbah, Iraq 70 C4
Ara, India 69 G11
Ara Goro, Ethiopia 81 F5
Ara Tera, Ethiopia 81 F5
Arab, U.S.A. 109 H2
'Arab, Bahr el →, Sudan 81 F2
Arab, Khalîg el, Egypt 80 A2
Arab, Shatt al →, Asia 71 D6
'Araba, W. →, Egypt 80 J8

'Arabābād, *Iran* 71 C8
Araban, *Turkey* 72 D7
Arabatskaya Strelka, *Ukraine* 47 K8
Arabba, *Italy* 29 B8
Arabia, *Asia* 52 G8
Arabian Desert = Es Sahrâ' Esh Sharqîya, *Egypt* 80 B3
Arabian Gulf = Gulf, The, *Asia* 71 E6
Arabian Sea, *Ind. Oc.* 52 H10
Araç, *Turkey* 72 B5
Aracaju, *Brazil* 125 F11
Aracati, *Brazil* 125 D11
Araçatuba, *Brazil* 127 A5
Aracena, *Spain* 35 H4
Aracena, Sierra de, *Spain* 35 H4
Aračinovo, *Macedonia* 40 D5
Araçuaí, *Brazil* 125 G10
'Arad, *Israel* 75 D4
Arad, *Romania* 42 D6
Arad □, *Romania* 42 D6
Arādān, *Iran* 71 C7
Aradhippou, *Cyprus* 36 E12
Arafura Sea, *E. Indies* 52 K17
Aragats, *Armenia* 49 K7
Aragón □, *Spain* 32 D4
Aragón →, *Spain* 32 C3
Aragona, *Italy* 30 E6
Araguacema, *Brazil* 125 E9
Araguaia →, *Brazil* 122 D6
Araguaína, *Brazil* 125 E9
Araguari, *Brazil* 125 G9
Araguari →, *Brazil* 125 C9
Arain, *India* 68 F6
Arak, *Algeria* 78 C6
Arāk, *Iran* 71 C6
Araka, *Sudan* 81 G3
Arakan Coast, *Burma* 67 K19
Arakan Yoma, *Burma* 67 K19
Arákhova, *Greece* 38 C4
Arakli, *Turkey* 73 B8
Araks = Aras, Rūd-e →, *Asia* 49 K9
Aral, *Kazakstan* 50 E7
Aral Sea, *Asia* 50 E7
Aral Tengizi = Aral Sea, *Asia* 50 E7
Aralsk = Aral, *Kazakstan* 50 E7
Aralskoye More = Aral Sea, *Asia* 50 E7
Aralsor, Ozero, *Kazakstan* 49 F9
Aramac, *Australia* 94 C4
Aran I., *Ireland* 15 A3
Aran Is., *Ireland* 15 C2
Aranda de Duero, *Spain* 34 D7
Arandān, *Iran* 70 C5
Arandelovac, *Serbia, Yug.* 40 B4
Aranjuez, *Spain* 34 E7
Aranos, *Namibia* 88 C2
Aransas Pass, *U.S.A.* 113 M6
Aranyaprathet, *Thailand* 64 F4
Araouane, *Mali* 82 B4
Arapahoe, *U.S.A.* 112 E5
Arapey Grande →, *Uruguay* 126 C4
Arapgir, *Turkey* 70 B3
Arapiraca, *Brazil* 125 E11
Arapongas, *Brazil* 127 A5
Ar'ar, *Si. Arabia* 70 D4
Araranguá, *Brazil* 127 B6
Araraquara, *Brazil* 125 H9
Ararás, Serra das, *Brazil* 127 B5
Ararat, *Armenia* 73 C11
Ararat, Mt. = Ağrı Dağı, *Turkey* 70 B5
Araria, *India* 69 F12
Araripe, Chapada do, *Brazil* 125 E11
Araruama, L. de, *Brazil* 127 A7
Aras, Rūd-e →, *Asia* 49 K9
Aratâne, *Mauritania* 82 B3
Arauca, *Colombia* 124 B4
Arauca →, *Venezuela* 124 B5
Arauco, *Chile* 126 D1
Arawa, *Ethiopia* 81 F5
Araxá, *Brazil* 125 G9
Araya, Pen. de, *Venezuela* 124 A6
Arba Gugu, *Ethiopia* 81 F5
Arba Minch, *Ethiopia* 81 F4
Arbat, *Iraq* 70 C5
Árbatax, *Italy* 30 C2
Arbi, *Ethiopia* 81 F4
Arbīl, *Iraq* 70 B5
Arboga, *Sweden* 10 E9
Arbois, *France* 19 F12
Arbore, *Ethiopia* 81 F4
Arboréa, *Italy* 30 C1
Arborfield, *Canada* 105 C8
Arborg, *Canada* 105 C9
Arbre du Ténéré, *Niger* 83 B7
Arbroath, *U.K.* 14 E6
Arbuckle, *U.S.A.* 116 F4
Arbus, *Italy* 30 C1
Arc →, *France* 21 C10
Arc-lès-Gray, *France* 19 E12
Arcachon, *France* 20 D2
Arcachon, Bassin d', *France* 20 D2
Arcade, *Calif., U.S.A.* 117 L8
Arcade, *N.Y., U.S.A.* 110 D6
Arcadia, *Fla., U.S.A.* 109 M5
Arcadia, *La., U.S.A.* 113 J8
Arcadia, *Pa., U.S.A.* 110 F6
Arcata, *U.S.A.* 114 F1
Arcévia, *Italy* 29 E9
Archangel = Arkhangelsk, *Russia* 50 C5
Archar, *Bulgaria* 40 C6
Archbald, *U.S.A.* 111 E9
Archena, *Spain* 33 G3
Archer →, *Australia* 94 A3
Archer B., *Australia* 94 A3
Archers Post, *Kenya* 86 B4
Arches National Park, *U.S.A.* 115 G9
Archidona, *Spain* 35 H6
Arci, Mte., *Italy* 30 C1
Arcidosso, *Italy* 29 F8
Arcis-sur-Aube, *France* 19 D11
Arckaringa Cr. →, *Australia* 95 D2
Arco, *Italy* 28 C7
Arco, *U.S.A.* 114 E7
Arcos = Arcos de Jalón, *Spain* 32 D2
Arcos de Jalón, *Spain* 32 D2
Arcos de la Frontera, *Spain* 35 J5
Arcos de Valdevez, *Portugal* 34 D2
Arcot, *India* 66 N11
Arcozelo, *Portugal* 34 E3
Arctic Bay, *Canada* 101 A11
Arctic Ocean, *Arctic* 4 B18
Arctic Red River = Tsiigehtchic, *Canada* 100 B6
Arda →, *Bulgaria* 41 E10
Arda →, *Italy* 28 C7
Ardabīl, *Iran* 71 B6
Ardahan, *Turkey* 73 B10
Ardakān = Sepīdān, *Iran* 71 D7
Ardakān, *Iran* 71 C7
Ardala, *Sweden* 11 F7
Ardales, *Spain* 35 J6
Ardèche □, *France* 21 D8
Ardèche →, *France* 21 D8
Ardee, *Ireland* 15 C5
Arden, *Canada* 110 B8
Arden, *Denmark* 11 H3
Arden, *Calif., U.S.A.* 116 G5
Arden, *Nev., U.S.A.* 117 J11
Ardenne, *Belgium* 6 F7
Ardennes = Ardenne, *Belgium* 6 F7
Ardennes □, *France* 19 C11
Ardentes, *France* 19 F8
Arderin, *Ireland* 15 C4
Ardeşen, *Turkey* 73 B9
Ardestān, *Iran* 71 C7
Árdhas →, *Greece* 41 E10
Ardhéa, *Greece* 40 F6
Ardila →, *Portugal* 35 G3
Ardino, *Bulgaria* 41 E9
Ardivachar Pt., *U.K.* 14 D1
Ardmore, *Okla., U.S.A.* 113 H6
Ardmore, *Pa., U.S.A.* 111 G9
Ardnamurchan, Pt. of, *U.K.* 14 E2
Ardnave Pt., *U.K.* 14 F2
Ardon, *Russia* 49 J7
Ardore, *Italy* 31 D9
Ardres, *France* 19 B8
Ardrossan, *U.K.* 14 F4
Ards Pen., *U.K.* 15 B6
Arduan, *Sudan* 80 D3
Ardud, *Romania* 42 C7
Åre, *Sweden* 10 A7
Arecibo, *Puerto Rico* 121 C6
Areia Branca, *Brazil* 125 E11
Arena, Pt., *U.S.A.* 116 G3
Arenal, *Honduras* 120 C2
Arenas = Las Arenas, *Spain* 34 B6
Arenas de San Pedro, *Spain* 34 E5
Arendal, *Norway* 9 G13
Arendsee, *Germany* 24 C7
Arenys de Mar, *Spain* 32 D7
Arenzano, *Italy* 28 D5
Areópolis, *Greece* 38 E4
Arequipa, *Peru* 124 G4
Arero, *Ethiopia* 81 G4
Arès, *France* 20 D2
Arévalo, *Spain* 34 D6
Arezzo, *Italy* 29 E8
Arga, *Turkey* 70 B3
Arga →, *Spain* 32 C3
Argalastí, *Greece* 38 B5
Argamasilla de Alba, *Spain* 35 F7
Argamasilla de Calatrava, *Spain* 35 G6
Arganda, *Spain* 34 E7
Arganil, *Portugal* 34 E2
Argedeb, *Ethiopia* 81 F5
Argelès-Gazost, *France* 20 E3
Argelès-sur-Mer, *France* 20 F7
Argens →, *France* 21 E10
Argent-sur-Sauldre, *France* 19 E9
Argenta, *Canada* 104 C5
Argenta, *Italy* 29 D8
Argentan, *France* 18 D6
Argentário, Mte., *Italy* 29 F8
Argentat, *France* 20 C5
Argentera, *Italy* 28 D4
Argenteuil, *France* 19 D9
Argentia, *Canada* 103 C9
Argentiera, C. dell', *Italy* 30 B1
Argentina ■, *S. Amer.* 128 D3
Argentina Is., *Antarctica* 5 C17
Argentino, L., *Argentina* 128 G2
Argenton-Château, *France* 18 F6
Argenton-sur-Creuse, *France* 19 F8
Argeş □, *Romania* 43 F9
Argeş →, *Romania* 43 F11
Arghandab →, *Afghan.* 68 D1
Argheile, *Ethiopia* 81 F5
Argo, *Sudan* 80 D3
Argolikós Kólpos, *Greece* 38 D4
Argolís □, *Greece* 38 D4
Argonne, *France* 19 C12
Árgos, *Greece* 38 D4
Árgos Orestikón, *Greece* 40 F5
Argostólion, *Greece* 38 C2
Arguedas, *Spain* 32 C3
Arguello, Pt., *U.S.A.* 117 L6
Arguineguín, *Canary Is.* 37 G4
Argun, *Russia* 49 J7
Argun →, *Russia* 51 D13
Argungu, *Nigeria* 83 C5
Argus Pk., *U.S.A.* 117 K9
Argyle, L., *Australia* 92 C4
Argyll & Bute □, *U.K.* 14 E3
Arhavi, *Turkey* 73 B9
Århus, *Denmark* 11 H4
Århus Amtskommune □, *Denmark* 11 H4
Ariadnoye, *Russia* 54 B7
Ariamsvlei, *Namibia* 88 D2
Ariano Irpino, *Italy* 31 A8
Aribinda, *Burkina Faso* 83 C4
Arica, *Chile* 124 G4
Arica, *Colombia* 124 D4
Arico, *Canary Is.* 37 F3
Arid, C., *Australia* 93 F3
Arida, *Japan* 55 G7
Ariège □, *France* 20 F5
Ariège →, *France* 20 E5
Arieş →, *Romania* 43 D8
Arihā, *Israel* 80 A4
Arilje, *Serbia, Yug.* 40 C4
Arílla, Ákra, *Greece* 36 A3
Arima, *Trin. & Tob.* 121 D7
Arinos →, *Brazil* 122 E5
Ario de Rosales, *Mexico* 118 D4
Ariogala, *Lithuania* 44 C10
Aripuanã, *Brazil* 124 E6
Aripuanã →, *Brazil* 122 D4
Ariquemes, *Brazil* 124 E6
Arisaig, *U.K.* 14 E3
Arîsh, W. el →, *Egypt* 80 A3
Arissa, *Ethiopia* 81 E5
Aristazabal I., *Canada* 104 C3
Arivonimamo, *Madag.* 89 B8
Ariza, *Spain* 32 D2
Arizaro, Salar de, *Argentina* 126 A2
Arizona, *Argentina* 126 D2
Arizona □, *U.S.A.* 115 J8
Arizpe, *Mexico* 118 A2
Årjäng, *Sweden* 10 E6
Arjeplog, *Sweden* 8 D18
Arjona, *Colombia* 124 A3
Arjona, *Spain* 35 H6
Arjuna, *Indonesia* 63 G15
Arka, *Russia* 51 C15
Arkadak, *Russia* 48 E6
Arkadelphia, *U.S.A.* 113 H8
Arkadhía □, *Greece* 38 D4
Arkaig, L., *U.K.* 14 E3
Arkalyk = Arqalyk, *Kazakstan* 50 D7
Arkansas □, *U.S.A.* 113 H8
Arkansas →, *U.S.A.* 113 J9
Arkansas City, *U.S.A.* 113 G6
Arkaroola, *Australia* 95 E2
Árkathos →, *Greece* 38 B3
Arkhángelos, *Greece* 36 C10
Arkhangelsk, *Russia* 50 C5
Arkhangelskoye, *Russia* 48 E5
Arki, *India* 68 D7
Arkiko, *Eritrea* 81 D4
Arklow, *Ireland* 15 D5
Arkoi, *Greece* 39 D8
Arkona, Kap, *Germany* 24 A9
Arkösund, *Sweden* 11 F10
Arkoúdhi, *Greece* 38 C2
Arkport, *U.S.A.* 110 D7
Arkticheskiy, Mys, *Russia* 51 A10
Arkul, *Russia* 48 B10
Arkville, *U.S.A.* 111 D10
Årla, *Sweden* 10 E10
Arlanza →, *Spain* 34 C6
Arlanzón →, *Spain* 34 C6
Arlbergpass, *Austria* 26 D3
Arles, *France* 21 E8
Arlington, *S. Africa* 89 D4
Arlington, *N.Y., U.S.A.* 111 E11
Arlington, *Oreg., U.S.A.* 114 D3
Arlington, *S. Dak., U.S.A.* 112 C6
Arlington, *Tex., U.S.A.* 113 J6
Arlington, *Va., U.S.A.* 108 F7
Arlington, *Vt., U.S.A.* 111 C11
Arlington, *Wash., U.S.A.* 116 B4
Arlington Heights, *U.S.A.* 108 D2
Arlit, *Niger* 78 E7
Arlon, *Belgium* 17 E5
Arltunga, *Australia* 94 C1
Arly, *Burkina Faso* 83 C5
Armagh, *U.K.* 15 B5
Armagh □, *U.K.* 15 B5
Armagnac, *France* 20 E4
Armançon →, *France* 19 E10
Armavir, *Russia* 49 H5
Armenia, *Colombia* 124 C3
Armenia ■, *Asia* 49 K7
Armeniş, *Romania* 42 E7
Armenistís, Ákra, *Greece* 36 C9
Armentières, *France* 19 B9
Armilla, *Spain* 35 H7
Armour, *U.S.A.* 112 D5
Armstrong, *B.C., Canada* 104 C5
Armstrong, *Ont., Canada* 102 B2
Armutlu, *Bursa, Turkey* 41 F12
Armutlu, *İzmir, Turkey* 39 C9
Arnaía, *Greece* 40 F7
Arnarfjörður, *Iceland* 8 D2
Arnaud →, *Canada* 101 B12
Arnauti, C., *Cyprus* 36 D11
Arnay-le-Duc, *France* 19 E11
Arnedillo, *Spain* 32 C2
Arnedo, *Spain* 32 C2
Arnett, *U.S.A.* 113 G5
Arnhem, *Neths.* 17 C5
Arnhem, C., *Australia* 94 A2
Arnhem B., *Australia* 94 A2
Arnhem Land, *Australia* 94 A1
Árnissa, *Greece* 40 F5
Arno →, *Italy* 28 E7
Arnold, *U.K.* 12 D6
Arnold, *U.S.A.* 116 G6
Arnoldstein, *Austria* 26 E6
Arnon →, *France* 19 E9
Arnot, *Canada* 105 B9
Arnøy, *Norway* 8 A19
Arnprior, *Canada* 102 C4
Arnsberg, *Germany* 24 D4
Arnstadt, *Germany* 24 E6
Aroab, *Namibia* 88 D2
Aroánia Óri, *Greece* 38 D4
Aroche, *Spain* 35 H4
Arochuku, *Nigeria* 83 D6
Arolsen, *Germany* 24 D5
Aron, *India* 68 G6
Aron →, *France* 19 F10
Arona, *Italy* 28 C5
Aroroy, *Phil.* 61 E5
Arosa, Ría de, *Spain* 34 C2
Arpajon, *France* 19 D9
Arpajon-sur-Cère, *France* 20 D6
Arpaşu de Jos, *Romania* 43 E9
Arqalyk, *Kazakstan* 50 D7
Arrah = Ara, *India* 69 G11
Arrah, *Ivory C.* 82 D4
Arraiolos, *Portugal* 35 G3
Arran, *U.K.* 14 F3
Arras, *France* 19 B9
Arrasate, *Spain* 32 B2
Arrats →, *France* 20 D4
Arreau, *France* 20 F4
Arrecife, *Canary Is.* 37 F6
Arrecifes, *Argentina* 126 C3
Arrée, Mts. d', *France* 18 D3
Arresø, *Denmark* 11 J6
Arriaga, *Chiapas, Mexico* 119 D6
Arriaga, *San Luis Potosí, Mexico* 118 C4
Arrilalah, *Australia* 94 C3
Arrino, *Australia* 93 E2
Arriondas, *Spain* 34 B5
Arromanches-les-Bains, *France* 18 C6
Arronches, *Portugal* 35 F3
Arros →, *France* 20 E3
Arrow, L., *Ireland* 15 B3
Arrowhead, L., *U.S.A.* 117 L9
Arrowtown, *N.Z.* 91 L2
Arroyo de la Luz, *Spain* 35 F4
Arroyo Grande, *U.S.A.* 117 K6
Års, *Denmark* 11 H3
Ars, *Iran* 70 B5
Ars-sur-Moselle, *France* 19 C13
Arsenault L., *Canada* 105 B7
Arsenev, *Russia* 54 B6
Arsi □, *Ethiopia* 81 F4
Arsiero, *Italy* 29 C8
Arsin, *Turkey* 73 B8
Arsk, *Russia* 48 B9
Årsunda, *Sweden* 10 D10
Árta, *Greece* 38 B3
Artà, *Spain* 37 B10
Árta □, *Greece* 38 B3
Arteaga, *Mexico* 118 D4
Arteche, *Phil.* 61 E6
Arteijo = Arteixo, *Spain* 34 B2
Arteixo, *Spain* 34 B2
Artem = Artyom, *Azerbaijan* 49 K10
Artem, *Russia* 54 C6
Artemovsk, *Russia* 51 D10
Artemovsk, *Ukraine* 47 H9
Artemovskiy, *Russia* 49 G5
Artenay, *France* 19 D8
Artern, *Germany* 24 D7
Artesa de Segre, *Spain* 32 D6
Artesia = Mosomane, *Botswana* 88 C4
Artesia, *U.S.A.* 113 J2
Arthington, *Liberia* 82 D2
Arthur, *Canada* 110 C4
Arthur →, *Australia* 94 G3
Arthur Cr. →, *Australia* 94 C2
Arthur Pt., *Australia* 94 C5
Arthur River, *Australia* 93 F2
Arthur's Pass, *N.Z.* 91 K3
Arthur's Town, *Bahamas* 121 B4
Artigas, *Uruguay* 126 C4
Artik, *Armenia* 49 K6
Artillery L., *Canada* 105 A7
Artois, *France* 19 B9
Artotína, *Greece* 38 C4
Artrutx, C. de, *Spain* 37 B10
Artsyz, *Ukraine* 47 J5
Artvin, *Turkey* 73 B9
Artyom, *Azerbaijan* 49 K10
Aru, Kepulauan, *Indonesia* 63 F8
Aru Is. = Aru, Kepulauan, *Indonesia* 63 F8
Arua, *Uganda* 86 B3
Aruanã, *Brazil* 125 F8
Aruba ■, *W. Indies* 121 D6
Arucas, *Canary Is.* 37 F4
Arudy, *France* 20 E3
Arun →, *Nepal* 69 F12
Arun →, *U.K.* 13 G7
Arunachal Pradesh □, *India* 67 F19
Arusha, *Tanzania* 86 C4
Arusha □, *Tanzania* 86 C4
Arusha Chini, *Tanzania* 86 C4
Aruwimi →, *Dem. Rep. of the Congo* 86 B1
Arvada, *Colo., U.S.A.* 112 F2
Arvada, *Wyo., U.S.A.* 114 D10
Arve →, *France* 19 F13
Árvi, *Greece* 36 E7
Arviat, *Canada* 105 A10
Arvidsjaur, *Sweden* 8 D18
Arvika, *Sweden* 10 E6
Arvin, *U.S.A.* 117 K8
Arwal, *India* 69 G11
Arxan, *China* 60 B6
Åryd, *Sweden* 11 H8
Aryirádhes, *Greece* 36 B3
Aryiroúpolis, *Greece* 36 D6
Arys, *Kazakstan* 50 E7
Arzachena, *Italy* 30 A2
Arzamas, *Russia* 48 C6
Arzgir, *Russia* 49 H7
Arzignano, *Italy* 29 C8
Arzúa, *Spain* 34 C2
Aš, *Czech Rep.* 26 A5
Ås, *Sweden* 10 A8
As Pontes de García Rodríguez, *Spain* 34 B3
Aş Şafā, *Syria* 75 B6
As Saffānīyah, *Si. Arabia* 71 E6
As Safīrah, *Syria* 70 B3
Aş Şahm, *Oman* 71 E8
As Sājir, *Si. Arabia* 70 E5
As Salamīyah, *Syria* 70 C3
As Salmān, *Iraq* 70 D5
As Salt, *Jordan* 75 C4
As Sal'w'a, *Qatar* 71 E6
As Samāwah, *Iraq* 70 D5
As Sanamayn, *Syria* 75 B5
As Sohar = Şuḩār, *Oman* 71 E8
As Sukhnah, *Syria* 70 C3
As Sulaymānīyah, *Iraq* 70 C5
As Sulaymī, *Si. Arabia* 70 E4
As Sulayyil, *Si. Arabia* 74 C4
As Summān, *Si. Arabia* 70 E5
As Suwaydā', *Syria* 75 C5
As Suwaydā' □, *Syria* 75 C5
As Suwayq, *Oman* 71 F8
Aş Şuwayrah, *Iraq* 70 C5
Åsa, *Sweden* 11 G6
Asab, *Namibia* 88 D2
Asaba, *Nigeria* 83 D6
Asad, Buḩayrat al, *Syria* 70 C3
Asadābād, *Iran* 73 E13
Asafo, *Ghana* 82 D4
Asahi-Gawa →, *Japan* 55 G6
Asahigawa, *Japan* 54 C11
Asale, L., *Ethiopia* 81 E5
Asamankese, *Ghana* 83 D4
Asan →, *India* 69 F8
Asansol, *India* 69 H12
Åsarna, *Sweden* 10 B8
Asayita, *Ethiopia* 81 E5
Asbe Teferi, *Ethiopia* 81 F5
Asbesberge, *S. Africa* 88 D3
Asbestos, *Canada* 103 C5
Asbury Park, *U.S.A.* 111 F10
Ascea, *Italy* 31 B8
Ascensión, *Mexico* 118 A3
Ascensión, B. de la, *Mexico* 119 D7
Ascension I., *Atl. Oc.* 77 G2
Aschach an der Donau, *Austria* 26 C7
Aschaffenburg, *Germany* 25 F5
Aschendorf, *Germany* 24 B3
Aschersleben, *Germany* 24 D7
Asciano, *Italy* 29 E8
Áscoli Piceno, *Italy* 29 F10
Áscoli Satriano, *Italy* 31 A8
Ascope, *Peru* 124 E3
Ascotán, *Chile* 126 A2
Aseb, *Eritrea* 81 E5
Åseda, *Sweden* 11 G9
Asela, *Ethiopia* 81 F4
Åsen, *Sweden* 10 C7
Asenovgrad, *Bulgaria* 41 D8
Aserradero, *Mexico* 118 C3
Asfeld, *France* 19 C11
Asfûn el Matâ'na, *Egypt* 80 B3
Asgata, *Cyprus* 36 E12
Ash Fork, *U.S.A.* 115 J7
Ash Grove, *U.S.A.* 113 G8
Ash Shabakah, *Iraq* 70 D4
Ash Shamāl □, *Lebanon* 75 A5
Ash Shāmīyah, *Iraq* 70 D5
Ash Shāriqah, *U.A.E.* 71 E7
Ash Sharmah, *Si. Arabia* 70 D2
Ash Sharqāt, *Iraq* 70 C4
Ash Sharqi, Al Jabal, *Lebanon* 75 B5
Ash Shaţrah, *Iraq* 70 D5
Ash Shawbak, *Jordan* 70 D2
Ash Shawmari, J., *Jordan* 75 E5
Ash Shināfīyah, *Iraq* 70 D5
Ash Shu'bah, *Si. Arabia* 70 D5
Ash Shumlūl, *Si. Arabia* 70 E5
Ash Shūr'a, *Iraq* 70 C4
Ash Shurayf, *Si. Arabia* 70 E3
Ash Shuwayfāt, *Lebanon* 75 B4
Ashanti □, *Ghana* 83 D4
Ashau, *Vietnam* 64 D6
Ashbourne, *U.K.* 12 D6
Ashburn, *U.S.A.* 109 K4
Ashburton, *N.Z.* 91 K3
Ashburton →, *Australia* 92 D1
Ashcroft, *Canada* 104 C4
Ashdod, *Israel* 75 D3
Ashdown, *U.S.A.* 113 J7
Asheboro, *U.S.A.* 109 H6
Ashern, *Canada* 105 C9
Asherton, *U.S.A.* 113 L5
Asheville, *U.S.A.* 109 H4
Ashewat, *Pakistan* 68 D3
Asheweig →, *Canada* 102 B2
Ashford, *Australia* 95 D5

Ashford, U.K. 13 F8
Ashgabat, Turkmenistan 50 F6
Ashibetsu, Japan 54 C11
Ashikaga, Japan 55 F9
Ashington, U.K. 12 B6
Ashizuri-Zaki, Japan 55 H6
Ashkarkot, Afghan. 68 C2
Ashkhabad = Ashgabat, Turkmenistan 50 F6
Āshkhāneh, Iran 71 B8
Ashland, Kans., U.S.A. 113 G5
Ashland, Ky., U.S.A. 108 F4
Ashland, Mont., U.S.A. 114 D10
Ashland, Ohio, U.S.A. 110 F2
Ashland, Oreg., U.S.A. 114 E2
Ashland, Pa., U.S.A. 111 F8
Ashland, Va., U.S.A. 108 G7
Ashland, Wis., U.S.A. 112 B9
Ashley, N. Dak., U.S.A. 112 B5
Ashley, Pa., U.S.A. 111 E9
Ashmore Reef, Australia 92 B3
Ashmûn, Egypt 80 H7
Ashmyany, Belarus 9 J21
Ashokan Reservoir, U.S.A. 111 E10
Ashqelon, Israel 75 D3
Ashta, India 68 H7
Ashtabula, U.S.A. 110 E4
Ashton, S. Africa 88 E3
Ashton, U.S.A. 114 D8
Ashuanipi, L., Canada 103 B6
Ashville, U.S.A. 110 F6
'Āṣī →, Asia 72 D6
Asia 52 E11
Asia, Kepulauan, Indonesia 63 D8
Āsīā Bak, Iran 71 C6
Asiago, Italy 29 C8
Asifabad, India 66 K11
Asinara, Italy 30 A1
Asinara, G. dell', Italy 30 A1
Asino, Russia 50 D9
Asipovichy, Belarus 46 F5
'Asīr □, Si. Arabia 74 D3
Asir, Ras, Somali Rep. 74 E5
Aşkale, Turkey 73 C9
Askersund, Sweden 11 F8
Askham, S. Africa 88 D3
Askim, Norway 9 G14
Askja, Iceland 8 D5
Askøy, Norway 9 F11
Asl, Egypt 80 B3
Aslan Burnu, Turkey 39 C8
Aslanapa, Turkey 39 B11
Asmara = Asmera, Eritrea 81 D4
Asmera, Eritrea 81 D4
Asnæs, Denmark 11 J4
Åsnen, Sweden 11 H8
Ásola, Italy 28 C7
Asosa, Ethiopia 81 E3
Asoteriba, Jebel, Sudan 80 C4
Aspe, Spain 33 G4
Aspen, U.S.A. 115 G10
Aspendos, Turkey 72 D4
Aspermont, U.S.A. 113 J4
Aspet, France 20 E4
Aspiring, Mt., N.Z. 91 L2
Aspres-sur-Buëch, France 21 D9
Asprókavos, Ákra, Greece 36 B4
Aspromonte, Italy 31 D9
Aspur, India 68 H6
Asquith, Canada 105 C7
Assâba, Massif de l', Mauritania 82 B2
Assaikio, Nigeria 83 D6
Assal, L., Djibouti 81 E5
Assam □, India 67 G18
Assamakka, Niger 83 B6
Asse, Belgium 17 D4
Assémini, Italy 30 C1
Assen, Neths. 17 A6
Assens, Denmark 11 J3
Assini, Ivory C. 82 D4
Assiniboia, Canada 105 D7
Assiniboine →, Canada 105 D9
Assiniboine, Mt., Canada 104 C5
Assis, Brazil 127 A5
Assisi, Italy 29 E9
Ássos, Greece 38 C2
Assynt, L., U.K. 14 C3
Astaffort, France 20 D4
Astakidha, Greece 39 F8
Astakós, Greece 38 C3
Astana, Kazakstan 50 D8
Āstāneh, Iran 71 B6
Astara, Azerbaijan 71 B6
Āstārā, Iran 73 C13
Asteroúsia, Greece 36 E7
Asti, Italy 28 D5
Astipálaia, Greece 39 E8
Astorga, Spain 34 C4
Astoria, U.S.A. 116 D3
Åstorp, Sweden 11 H6
Astrakhan, Russia 49 G9
Astudillo, Spain 34 C6
Asturias □, Spain 34 B5
Asunción, Paraguay 126 B4
Asunción Nochixtlán, Mexico 119 D5
Åsunden, Sweden 11 F9
Asutri, Sudan 81 D4
Aswa →, Uganda 86 B3
Aswad, Ra's al, Si. Arabia 80 C4
Aswân, Egypt 80 C3
Aswân High Dam = Sadd el Aali, Egypt 80 C3
Asyût, Egypt 80 B3
Asyûti, Wadi →, Egypt 80 B3
Aszód, Hungary 42 C4
At Ṭafīlah, Jordan 75 E4
Aṭ Ṭā'if, Si. Arabia 74 C3
Aṭ Ṭirāq, Si. Arabia 70 E5
Aṭ Tubayq, Si. Arabia 70 D3
Atabey, Turkey 39 D12
Atacama □, Chile 126 B2
Atacama, Desierto de, Chile 126 A2
Atacama, Salar de, Chile 126 A2
Atakpamé, Togo 83 D5
Atalándi, Greece 38 C4
Atalaya, Peru 124 F4
Atalaya de Femes, Canary Is. 37 F6
Atami, Japan 55 G9
Atapupu, Indonesia 63 F6
Atâr, Mauritania 78 D3
Atarfe, Spain 35 H7
Atari, Pakistan 68 D6
Atascadero, U.S.A. 116 K6
Atasu, Kazakstan 50 E8
Atatürk Barajı, Turkey 73 D8
Atauro, Indonesia 63 F7
'Atbara, Sudan 80 D3
'Atbara, Nahr →, Sudan 80 D3
Atbasar, Kazakstan 50 D7
Atça, Turkey 39 D10
Atchafalaya B., U.S.A. 113 L9
Atchison, U.S.A. 112 F7
Atebubu, Ghana 83 D4
Ateca, Spain 32 D3
Aterno →, Italy 29 F10
Āteshān, Iran 71 C7
Atesine, Alpi, Italy 29 B8
Atessa, Italy 29 F11
Atfîh, Egypt 80 J7
Ath, Belgium 17 D3
Athabasca, Canada 104 C6
Athabasca →, Canada 105 B6
Athabasca, L., Canada 105 B7
Athboy, Ireland 15 C5
Athenry, Ireland 15 C3
Athens = Athínai, Greece 38 D5
Athens, Ala., U.S.A. 109 H2
Athens, Ga., U.S.A. 109 J4
Athens, N.Y., U.S.A. 111 D11
Athens, Ohio, U.S.A. 108 F4
Athens, Pa., U.S.A. 111 E8
Athens, Tenn., U.S.A. 109 H3
Athens, Tex., U.S.A. 113 J7
Atherley, Canada 110 B5
Atherton, Australia 94 B4
Athiéme, Benin 83 D5
Athienou, Cyprus 36 D12
Athínai, Greece 38 D5
Athlone, Ireland 15 C4
Athna, Cyprus 36 D12
Athol, U.S.A. 111 D12
Atholl, Forest of, U.K. 14 E5
Atholville, Canada 103 C6
Áthos, Greece 41 F8
Athy, Ireland 15 C5
Ati, Chad 79 F9
Ati, Sudan 81 E2
Atiak, Uganda 86 B3
Atienza, Spain 32 D2
Atiit, Sudan 81 F3
Atik L., Canada 105 B9
Atikameg →, Canada 102 B3
Atikokan, Canada 102 C1
Atikonak L., Canada 103 B7
Atimonan, Phil. 61 E4
Atka, Russia 51 C16
Atka I., U.S.A. 100 C2
Atkarsk, Russia 48 E7
Atkinson, U.S.A. 112 D5
Atlanta, Ga., U.S.A. 109 J3
Atlanta, Tex., U.S.A. 113 J7
Atlantic, U.S.A. 112 E7
Atlantic City, U.S.A. 108 F8
Atlantic Ocean 2 E9
Atlas Mts. = Haut Atlas, Morocco 78 B4
Atlin, Canada 104 B2
Atlin, L., Canada 104 B2
Atlin Prov. Park, Canada 104 B2
Atmore, U.S.A. 109 K2
Atoka, U.S.A. 113 H6
Atokos, Greece 38 C2
Atolia, U.S.A. 117 K9
Atrai →, Bangla. 69 G13
Atrak = Atrek →, Turkmenistan 71 B8
Ätran, Sweden 11 G6
Ätran →, Sweden 11 H6
Atrauli, India 68 E8
Atrek →, Turkmenistan 71 B8
Atri, Italy 29 F10
Atsikí, Greece 39 B7
Atsoum, Mts., Cameroon 83 D7
Atsuta, Japan 54 C10
Attalla, U.S.A. 109 H2
Attapu, Laos 64 E6
Attáviros, Greece 36 C9
Attawapiskat, Canada 102 B3
Attawapiskat →, Canada 102 B3
Attawapiskat L., Canada 102 B2
Attersee, Austria 26 D6
Attica, Ind., U.S.A. 108 E2
Attica, Ohio, U.S.A. 110 E2
Attichy, France 19 C10
Attigny, France 19 C11
Attika = Attikí □, Greece 38 D5
Attikamagen L., Canada 103 B6
Attikí □, Greece 38 D5
Attleboro, U.S.A. 111 E13
Attock, Pakistan 68 C5
Attopeu = Attapu, Laos 64 E6
Attu I., U.S.A. 100 C1
Attur, India 66 P11
Atuel →, Argentina 126 D2
Åtvidaberg, Sweden 11 F10
Atwater, U.S.A. 116 H6
Atwood, Canada 110 C3
Atwood, U.S.A. 112 F4
Atyraū, Kazakstan 50 E6
Au Sable, U.S.A. 110 B1
Au Sable →, U.S.A. 108 C4
Au Sable Forks, U.S.A. 111 B11
Au Sable Pt., U.S.A. 110 B1
Aubagne, France 21 E9
Aubarca, C. d', Spain 37 B7
Aube □, France 19 D11
Aube →, France 19 D10
Aubenas, France 21 D8
Aubenton, France 19 C11
Auberry, U.S.A. 116 H7
Aubigny-sur-Nère, France 19 E9
Aubin, France 20 D6
Aubrac, Mts. d', France 20 D7
Auburn, Ala., U.S.A. 109 J3
Auburn, Calif., U.S.A. 116 G5
Auburn, Ind., U.S.A. 108 E3
Auburn, Maine, U.S.A. 109 C10
Auburn, N.Y., U.S.A. 111 D8
Auburn, Nebr., U.S.A. 112 E7
Auburn, Pa., U.S.A. 111 F8
Auburn, Wash., U.S.A. 116 C4
Auburn Ra., Australia 95 D5
Auburndale, U.S.A. 109 L5
Aubusson, France 20 C6
Auce, Latvia 44 B9
Auch, France 20 E4
Auchi, Nigeria 83 D6
Auckland, N.Z. 91 G5
Auckland Is., Pac. Oc. 96 N8
Aude □, France 20 E6
Aude →, France 20 E7
Auden, Canada 102 B2
Auderville, France 18 C5
Audierne, France 18 D2
Audincourt, France 19 E13
Audo, Ethiopia 81 F5
Audubon, U.S.A. 112 E7
Aue, Germany 24 E8
Auerbach, Germany 24 E8
Augathella, Australia 95 D4
Aughnacloy, U.K. 15 B5
Augrabies Falls, S. Africa 88 D3
Augsburg, Germany 25 G6
Augusta, Australia 93 F2
Augusta, Italy 31 E8
Augusta, Ark., U.S.A. 113 H9
Augusta, Ga., U.S.A. 109 J5
Augusta, Kans., U.S.A. 113 G6
Augusta, Maine, U.S.A. 101 D13
Augusta, Mont., U.S.A. 114 C7
Augustenborg, Denmark 11 K3
Augustów, Poland 44 E9
Augustus, Mt., Australia 93 D2
Augustus I., Australia 92 C3
Aukan, Eritrea 81 D5
Aukum, U.S.A. 116 G6
Auld, L., Australia 92 D3
Aulla, Italy 28 D6
Aulnay, France 20 B3
Aulne →, France 18 D2
Aulnoye-Aymeries, France 19 B10
Ault, France 18 B8
Ault, U.S.A. 112 E2
Aulus-les-Bains, France 20 F5
Aumale, France 19 C8
Aumont-Aubrac, France 20 D7
Auna, Nigeria 83 C5
Auning, Denmark 11 H4
Aunis, France 20 B3
Auponhia, Indonesia 63 E7
Aups, France 21 E10
Aur, Pulau, Malaysia 65 L5
Auraiya, India 69 F8
Aurangabad, Bihar, India 69 G11
Aurangabad, Maharashtra, India 66 K9
Auray, France 18 E4
Aurich, Germany 24 B3
Aurillac, France 20 D6
Auronzo di Cadore, Italy 29 B9
Aurora, Canada 110 C5
Aurora, S. Africa 88 E2
Aurora, Colo., U.S.A. 112 F2
Aurora, Ill., U.S.A. 108 E1
Aurora, Mo., U.S.A. 113 G8
Aurora, N.Y., U.S.A. 111 D8
Aurora, Nebr., U.S.A. 112 E6
Aurora, Ohio, U.S.A. 110 E3
Aurukun, Australia 94 A3
Aus, Namibia 88 D2
Ausable →, Canada 110 C3
Auschwitz = Oświęcim, Poland 45 H6
Austerlitz = Slavkov u Brna, Czech Rep. 27 B9
Austin, Minn., U.S.A. 112 D8
Austin, Nev., U.S.A. 114 G5
Austin, Pa., U.S.A. 110 E6
Austin, Tex., U.S.A. 113 K6
Austin, L., Australia 93 E2
Austin I., Canada 105 A10
Austra, Norway 8 D14
Austral Is. = Tubuai Is., Pac. Oc. 97 K13
Austral Seamount Chain, Pac. Oc. 97 K13
Australia ■, Oceania 96 K5
Australind, Australia 93 F2
Austria ■, Europe 26 E7
Austvågøy, Norway 8 B16
Auterive, France 20 E5
Authie →, France 19 B8
Authon-du-Perche, France 18 D7
Autlán, Mexico 118 D4
Autun, France 19 F11
Auvergne, France 20 C7
Auvergne, Mts. d', France 20 C6
Auvézère →, France 20 C4
Auxerre, France 19 E10
Auxi-le-Château, France 19 B9
Auxonne, France 19 E12
Auzances, France 19 F9
Ava, U.S.A. 113 G8
Avallon, France 19 E10
Avalon, U.S.A. 117 M8
Avalon Pen., Canada 103 C9
Avanos, Turkey 70 B2
Avaré, Brazil 127 A6
Ávas, Greece 41 F9
Avawatz Mts., U.S.A. 117 K10
Avdan Dağı, Turkey 41 F13
Aveiro, Brazil 125 D7
Aveiro, Portugal 34 E2
Aveiro □, Portugal 34 E2
Āvej, Iran 71 C6
Avellaneda, Argentina 126 C4
Avellino, Italy 31 B7
Avenal, U.S.A. 116 K6
Aversa, Italy 31 B7
Avery, U.S.A. 114 C6
Aves, Is. las, Venezuela 121 D6
Avesnes-sur-Helpe, France 19 B10
Avesta, Sweden 10 D10
Aveyron □, France 20 D6
Aveyron →, France 20 D5
Avezzano, Italy 29 F10
Avgó, Greece 39 F7
Aviá Terai, Argentina 126 B3
Aviano, Italy 29 B9
Aviemore, U.K. 14 D5
Avigliana, Italy 28 C4
Avigliano, Italy 31 B8
Avignon, France 21 E8
Ávila, Spain 34 E6
Ávila □, Spain 34 E6
Ávila, Sierra de, Spain 34 E5
Avila Beach, U.S.A. 117 K6
Avilés, Spain 34 B5
Avintes, Portugal 34 D2
Avionárion, Greece 38 C6
Avis, Portugal 35 F3
Avis, U.S.A. 110 E7
Avísio →, Italy 28 B8
Aviz = Avis, Portugal 35 F3
Avize, France 19 D11
Avlum, Denmark 11 H2
Avoca, U.S.A. 110 D7
Avoca →, Ireland 15 D5
Avola, Canada 104 C5
Avola, Italy 31 F8
Avon, U.S.A. 110 D7
Avon →, Australia 93 F2
Avon →, Bristol, U.K. 13 F5
Avon →, Dorset, U.K. 13 G6
Avon →, Warks., U.K. 13 E5
Avon Park, U.S.A. 109 M5
Avondale, Zimbabwe 87 F3
Avonlea, Canada 105 D8
Avonmore, Canada 111 A10
Avramov, Bulgaria 41 D10
Avranches, France 18 D5
Avre →, France 18 D8
Avrig, Romania 43 E9
Avrillé, France 18 E6
Avtovac, Bos.-H. 40 C2
Awag el Baqar, Sudan 81 E3
A'waj →, Syria 75 B5
Awaji-Shima, Japan 55 G7
'Awālī, Bahrain 71 E6
Awantipur, India 69 C6
Awasa, Ethiopia 81 F4
Awasa, L., Ethiopia 81 F4
Awash, Ethiopia 81 F5
Awash →, Ethiopia 81 E5
Awaso, Ghana 82 D4
Awatere →, N.Z. 91 J5
Awbārī, Libya 79 C8
Awe, L., U.K. 14 E3
Aweil, Sudan 81 F2
Awgu, Nigeria 83 D6
Awjilah, Libya 79 C10
Awka, Nigeria 83 D6
Ax-les-Thermes, France 20 F5
Axat, France 20 F6
Axe →, U.K. 13 F5
Axel Heiberg I., Canada 4 B3
Axim, Ghana 82 E4
Axintele, Romania 43 F11
Axiós →, Greece 40 F6
Axminster, U.K. 13 G4
Axvall, Sweden 11 F7
Ay, France 19 C11
Ayabaca, Peru 124 D3
Ayabe, Japan 55 G7
Ayacucho, Argentina 126 D4
Ayacucho, Peru 124 F4
Ayaguz, Kazakstan 50 E9
Ayamé, Ivory C. 82 D4
Ayamonte, Spain 35 H3
Ayan, Russia 51 D14
Ayancık, Turkey 72 B6
Ayas, Turkey 72 B5
Ayaviri, Peru 124 F4
Aybastı, Turkey 72 B7
Aydın, Turkey 72 D2
Aydin □, Turkey 39 D9
Aydin Dağları, Turkey 39 D10
Ayelu, Ethiopia 81 E5
Ayenngré, Togo 83 D5
Ayer, U.S.A. 111 D13
Ayerbe, Spain 32 C4
Ayer's Cliff, Canada 111 A12
Ayers Rock, Australia 93 E5
Ayiá, Greece 38 B4
Ayia Aikateríni, Ákra, Greece 36 A3
Ayía Ánna, Greece 38 C5
Ayia Dhéka, Greece 36 D6
Ayia Gálini, Greece 36 D6
Ayía Marína, Kásos, Greece 39 F8
Ayía Marína, Léros, Greece 39 D8
Áyia Napa, Cyprus 36 E13
Ayía Paraskeví, Greece 39 B8
Áyia Phyla, Cyprus 36 E12
Ayía Rouméli, Greece 38 F5
Ayia Varvára, Greece 36 D7
Ayiássos, Greece 39 B8
Áyioi Theódhoroi, Greece 38 D5
Áyion Óros □, Greece 41 F8
Áyios Amvrósios, Cyprus 36 D12
Áyios Andréas, Greece 38 D4
Áyios Evstrátios, Greece 38 B6
Áyios Ioánnis, Ákra, Greece 36 D7
Áyios Isidhoros, Greece 36 C9
Áyios Kiríkos, Greece 39 D8
Áyios Matthaíos, Greece 36 B3
Áyios Mírono, Greece 39 F7
Áyios Nikólaos, Greece 36 D7
Áyios Pétros, Greece 38 C2
Áyios Seryios, Cyprus 36 D12
Áyios Theodhoros, Cyprus 36 D13
Áyios Yeóryios, Greece 38 D5
Aykathonisi, Greece 39 D8
Aykirikçi, Turkey 39 B12
Aylesbury, U.K. 13 F7
Aylmer, Canada 110 D4
Aylmer, L., Canada 100 B8
'Ayn, Wādī al, Oman 71 F7
Ayn Dār, Si. Arabia 71 E7
Ayn Zālah, Iraq 70 B4
Ayna, Spain 33 G2
Ayod, Sudan 81 F3
Ayolas, Paraguay 126 B4
Ayom, Sudan 81 F2
Ayon, Ostrov, Russia 51 C17
Ayora, Spain 33 F3
Ayorou, Niger 83 C5
'Ayoûn el 'Atroûs, Mauritania 82 B3
Ayr, Australia 94 B4
Ayr, Canada 110 C4
Ayr, U.K. 14 F4
Ayr →, U.K. 14 F4
Ayrancı, Turkey 72 D5
Ayrancılar, Turkey 39 C9
Ayre, Pt. of, U.K. 12 C3
Aysha, Ethiopia 81 E5
Ayton, Australia 94 B4
Aytos, Bulgaria 41 D11
Aytoska Planina, Bulgaria 41 D11
Ayu, Kepulauan, Indonesia 63 D8
Ayutla, Guatemala 120 D1
Ayutla, Mexico 119 D5
Ayvacık, Turkey 72 C2
Ayvalık, Turkey 39 B8
Az Zabadānī, Syria 75 B5
Az Ẓāhirīyah, West Bank 75 D3
Aẓ Ẓahrān, Si. Arabia 71 E6
Az Zarqā, Jordan 75 C5
Az Zarqā', U.A.E. 71 E7
Az Zībār, Iraq 70 B5
Az Zilfī, Si. Arabia 70 E5
Az Zubayr, Iraq 70 D5
Az Zuqur, Yemen 81 E5
Azambuja, Portugal 35 F2
Azamgarh, India 69 F10
Azangaro, Peru 124 F4
Azaoua, Niger 83 B5
Azaouad, Mali 82 B4
Azaouak, Vallée de l', Mali 83 B5
Āzār Shahr, Iran 70 B5
Azara, Nigeria 83 D6
Azarān, Iran 70 B5
Azärbayjan = Azerbaijan ■, Asia 49 K9
Āzarbāyjān-e Gharbī □, Iran 70 B5
Āzarbāyjān-e Sharqī □, Iran 70 B5
Azare, Nigeria 83 C7
Azay-le-Rideau, France 18 E7
A'zāz, Syria 70 B3
Azbine = Aïr, Niger 83 B6
Azerbaijan ■, Asia 49 K9
Azerbaijchan = Azerbaijan ■, Asia 49 K9
Azezo, Ethiopia 81 E4
Azimganj, India 69 G13
Aznalcóllar, Spain 35 H4
Azogues, Ecuador 124 D3
Azores, Atl. Oc. 78 A1
Azov, Russia 49 G4
Azov, Sea of, Europe 47 J9
Azovskoye More = Azov, Sea of, Europe 47 J9
Azpeitia, Spain 32 B2
Azraq ash Shīshān, Jordan 75 D5
Aztec, U.S.A. 115 H10
Azúa de Compostela, Dom. Rep. 121 C5
Azuaga, Spain 35 G5
Azuara, Spain 32 D4
Azuer →, Spain 35 F7
Azuero, Pen. de, Panama 120 E3
Azuga, Romania 43 E10
Azul, Argentina 126 D4
Azusa, U.S.A. 117 L9
Azzano Décimo, Italy 29 C9

B

Ba Don, *Vietnam* 64 D6
Ba Dong, *Vietnam* 65 H6
Ba Ngoi = Cam Lam, *Vietnam* 65 G7
Ba Tri, *Vietnam* 65 G6
Ba Xian = Bazhou, *China* 56 E9
Baa, *Indonesia* 63 F6
Baamonde, *Spain* 34 B3
Baarle-Nassau, *Belgium* 17 C4
Bab el Mandeb, *Red Sea* 74 E3
Baba, *Bulgaria* 40 D7
Bābā, Koh-i-, *Afghan.* 66 B5
Baba Burnu, *Turkey* 39 B8
Baba dag, *Azerbaijan* 49 K9
Bābā Kalū, *Iran* 71 D6
Babadag, *Romania* 43 F13
Babadağ, *Turkey* 39 D10
Babadayhan, *Turkmenistan* 50 F7
Babaeski, *Turkey* 41 E11
Babahoyo, *Ecuador* 124 D3
Babai = Sarju →, *India* 69 F9
Babana, *Nigeria* 83 C5
Babanusa, *Sudan* 81 E2
Babar, *Indonesia* 63 F7
Babar, *Pakistan* 68 D3
Babarkach, *Pakistan* 68 E3
Babayevo, *Russia* 46 C8
Babb, *U.S.A.* 114 B7
Babelthuap, *Pac. Oc.* 63 C8
Babenhausen, *Germany* 25 F4
Băbeni, *Romania* 43 F9
Baberu, *India* 69 G9
Babi Besar, Pulau, *Malaysia* 65 L4
Babia Gora, *Europe* 45 J6
Babian Jiang →, *China* 58 F3
Babile, *Ethiopia* 81 F5
Babimost, *Poland* 45 F2
Babinda, *Australia* 94 B4
Babine, *Canada* 104 B3
Babine →, *Canada* 104 B3
Babine L., *Canada* 104 C3
Babo, *Indonesia* 63 E8
Babócsa, *Hungary* 42 D2
Bābol, *Iran* 71 B7
Bābol Sar, *Iran* 71 B7
Baborów, *Poland* 45 H5
Babruysk, *Belarus* 47 F5
Babuhri, *India* 68 F3
Babuna, *Macedonia* 40 E5
Babura, *Nigeria* 83 C6
Babusar Pass, *Pakistan* 69 B5
Babushkin, *Russia* 60 A5
Babušnica, *Serbia, Yug.* 40 C6
Babuyan Chan., *Phil.* 61 B4
Babylon, *Iraq* 70 C5
Bač, *Serbia, Yug.* 42 E4
Bâc →, *Moldova* 43 D14
Bac Can, *Vietnam* 58 F5
Bac Giang, *Vietnam* 58 G6
Bac Lieu, *Vietnam* 65 H5
Bac Ninh, *Vietnam* 58 G6
Bac Phan, *Vietnam* 64 B5
Bac Quang, *Vietnam* 58 F5
Bacabal, *Brazil* 125 D10
Bacalar, *Mexico* 119 D7
Bacan, Kepulauan, *Indonesia* 63 E7
Bacarra, *Phil.* 61 B4
Bacău, *Romania* 43 D11
Bacău □, *Romania* 43 D11
Baccarat, *France* 19 D13
Bacerac, *Mexico* 118 A3
Băceşti, *Romania* 43 D12
Bach Long Vi, Dao, *Vietnam* 64 B6
Bacharach, *Germany* 25 E3
Bachelina, *Russia* 50 D7
Bachhwara, *India* 69 G11
Bachuma, *Ethiopia* 81 F4
Bačina, *Serbia, Yug.* 40 C5
Back →, *Canada* 100 B9
Bačka Palanka, *Serbia, Yug.* 42 E4
Bačka Topola, *Serbia, Yug.* 42 E4
Bäckebo, *Sweden* 11 H10
Bäckefors, *Sweden* 11 F6
Bäckhammar, *Sweden* 10 E8
Bački Petrovac, *Serbia, Yug.* 42 E4
Backnang, *Germany* 25 G5
Baco, Mt., *Phil.* 61 E4
Bacolod, *Phil.* 61 F5
Bacqueville-en-Caux, *France* 18 C8
Bács-Kiskun □, *Hungary* 42 D4
Bácsalmás, *Hungary* 42 D4
Bacuag = Placer, *Phil.* 61 G6
Bacuk, *Malaysia* 65 J4
Bād, *Iran* 71 C7
Bad →, *U.S.A.* 112 C4
Bad Aussee, *Austria* 26 D6
Bad Axe, *U.S.A.* 110 C2
Bad Bergzabern, *Germany* 25 F3
Bad Berleburg, *Germany* 24 D4
Bad Bevensen, *Germany* 24 B6
Bad Bramstedt, *Germany* 24 B5
Bad Brückenau, *Germany* 25 E5
Bad Doberan, *Germany* 24 A7
Bad Driburg, *Germany* 24 D5
Bad Ems, *Germany* 25 E3
Bad Frankenhausen, *Germany* 24 D7
Bad Freienwalde, *Germany* 24 C10
Bad Goisern, *Austria* 26 D6
Bad Harzburg, *Germany* 24 D6
Bad Hersfeld, *Germany* 24 E5
Bad Hofgastein, *Austria* 26 D6
Bad Homburg, *Germany* 25 E4
Bad Honnef, *Germany* 24 E3
Bad Iburg, *Germany* 24 C4
Bad Ischl, *Austria* 26 D6
Bad Kissingen, *Germany* 25 E6
Bad Königshofen, *Germany* 25 E6
Bad Kreuznach, *Germany* 25 F3
Bad Krozingen, *Germany* 25 H3
Bad Laasphe, *Germany* 24 E4
Bad Lands, *U.S.A.* 112 D3
Bad Langensalza, *Germany* 24 D6
Bad Lauterberg, *Germany* 24 D6
Bad Leonfelden, *Austria* 26 C7
Bad Liebenwerda, *Germany* 24 D9
Bad Mergentheim, *Germany* 25 F5
Bad Münstereifel, *Germany* 24 E2
Bad Nauheim, *Germany* 25 E4
Bad Neuenahr-Ahrweiler, *Germany* 24 E3
Bad Neustadt, *Germany* 25 E6
Bad Oeynhausen, *Germany* 24 C4
Bad Oldesloe, *Germany* 24 B6
Bad Orb, *Germany* 25 E5
Bad Pyrmont, *Germany* 24 D5
Bad Reichenhall, *Germany* 25 H8
Bad Säckingen, *Germany* 25 H3
Bad Salzuflen, *Germany* 24 C4
Bad Salzungen, *Germany* 24 E6
Bad Schwartau, *Germany* 24 B6
Bad Segeberg, *Germany* 24 B6
Bad St. Leonhard, *Austria* 26 E7
Bad Tölz, *Germany* 25 H7
Bad Urach, *Germany* 25 G5
Bad Vöslau, *Austria* 27 D9
Bad Waldsee, *Germany* 25 H5
Bad Wildungen, *Germany* 24 D5
Bad Wimpfen, *Germany* 25 F5
Bad Windsheim, *Germany* 25 F6
Bad Zwischenahn, *Germany* 24 B4
Bada Barabil, *India* 69 H11
Badagara, *India* 66 P9
Badagri, *Nigeria* 83 D5
Badajós, L., *Brazil* 124 D6
Badajoz, *Spain* 35 G4
Badajoz □, *Spain* 35 G4
Badalona, *Spain* 32 D7
Badalzai, *Afghan.* 68 E1
Badampahar, *India* 67 H15
Badanah, *Si. Arabia* 70 D4
Badarinath, *India* 69 D8
Badas, Kepulauan, *Indonesia* 62 D3
Baddo →, *Pakistan* 66 F4
Bade, *Indonesia* 63 F9
Badeggi, *Nigeria* 83 D6
Badéguichéri, *Niger* 83 C6
Baden, *Austria* 27 C9
Baden, *Switz.* 25 H4
Baden, *U.S.A.* 110 F4
Baden-Baden, *Germany* 25 G4
Baden-Württemberg □, *Germany* 25 G4
Badgastein, *Austria* 26 D6
Badger, *Canada* 103 C8
Badger, *U.S.A.* 116 J7
Bādghīsāt □, *Afghan.* 66 B3
Badgom, *India* 69 B6
Badia Polésine, *Italy* 29 C8
Badin, *Pakistan* 68 G3
Badlands National Park, *U.S.A.* 112 D3
Badogo, *Mali* 82 C3
Badoumbé, *Mali* 82 C2
Badrah, *Iraq* 70 C5
Badrinath, *India* 69 D8
Badulla, *Sri Lanka* 66 R12
Baena, *Spain* 35 H6
Baeza, *Spain* 35 H7
Bafang, *Cameroon* 83 D7
Bafatá, *Guinea-Biss.* 82 C2
Baffin B., *Canada* 101 A13
Baffin I., *Canada* 101 B12
Bafia, *Cameroon* 83 E7
Bafilo, *Togo* 83 D5
Bafing →, *Mali* 82 C2
Bafliyūn, *Syria* 70 B3
Bafoulabé, *Mali* 82 C2
Bafoussam, *Cameroon* 83 D7
Bāfq, *Iran* 71 D7
Bafra, *Turkey* 72 B6
Bafra Burnu, *Turkey* 72 B7
Bāft, *Iran* 71 D8
Bafut, *Cameroon* 83 D7
Bafwasende, *Dem. Rep. of the Congo* 86 B2
Bagam, *Niger* 83 B6
Bagamoyo, *Tanzania* 86 D4
Bagan Datoh, *Malaysia* 65 L3
Bagan Serai, *Malaysia* 65 K3
Baganga, *Phil.* 61 H7
Bagani, *Namibia* 88 B3
Bagansiapiapi, *Indonesia* 62 D2
Bagasra, *India* 68 J4
Bagaud, *India* 68 H6
Bagawi, *Sudan* 81 E3
Bagbag, *Sudan* 81 D3
Bagdad, *U.S.A.* 117 L11
Bagdarin, *Russia* 51 D12
Bagé, *Brazil* 127 C5
Bagenalstown = Muine Bheag, *Ireland* 15 D5
Baggs, *U.S.A.* 114 F10
Bagh, *Pakistan* 69 C5
Baghain →, *India* 69 G9
Baghdād, *Iraq* 70 C5
Bagheria, *Italy* 30 D6
Baghlān, *Afghan.* 66 A6
Bagley, *U.S.A.* 112 B7
Bagnara Cálabra, *Italy* 31 D8
Bagnasco, *Italy* 28 D5
Bagnères-de-Bigorre, *France* 20 E4
Bagnères-de-Luchon, *France* 20 F4
Bagni di Lucca, *Italy* 28 D7
Bagno di Romagna, *Italy* 29 E8
Bagnoles-de-l'Orne, *France* 18 D6
Bagnols-sur-Cèze, *France* 21 D8
Bagnorégio, *Italy* 29 F9
Bago = Pegu, *Burma* 67 L20
Bagodar, *India* 69 G11
Bagrationovsk, *Russia* 9 J19
Bagrdan, *Serbia, Yug.* 40 B5
Baguio, *Phil.* 61 C4
Bağyurdu, *Turkey* 39 C9
Bagzane, Monts, *Niger* 83 B6
Bah, *India* 69 F8
Bahabón de Esgueva, *Spain* 34 D7
Bahadurganj, *India* 69 F12
Bahadurgarh, *India* 68 E7
Bahama, Canal Viejo de, *W. Indies* 120 B4
Bahamas ■, *N. Amer.* 121 B5
Bahār, *Iran* 73 E13
Baharampur, *India* 69 G13
Baharîya, El Wâhât al, *Egypt* 80 B2
Bahawalnagar, *Pakistan* 68 E5
Bahawalpur, *Pakistan* 68 E4
Bahçe, *Turkey* 72 D7
Bahçecik, *Turkey* 41 F13
Baheri, *India* 69 E8
Bahgul →, *India* 69 F8
Bahi, *Tanzania* 86 D4
Bahi Swamp, *Tanzania* 86 D4
Bahía = Salvador, *Brazil* 125 F11
Bahía □, *Brazil* 125 F10
Bahía, Is. de la, *Honduras* 120 C2
Bahía Blanca, *Argentina* 126 D3
Bahía de Caráquez, *Ecuador* 124 D2
Bahía Honda, *Cuba* 120 B3
Bahía Laura, *Argentina* 128 F3
Bahía Negra, *Paraguay* 124 H7
Bahir Dar, *Ethiopia* 81 E4
Bahmanzād, *Iran* 71 D6
Bahr el Ahmar □, *Sudan* 80 D4
Bahr el Ghazâl □, *Sudan* 81 F2
Bahr el Jabal □, *Sudan* 81 G3
Bahr Yûsef →, *Egypt* 80 B3
Bahraich, *India* 69 F9
Bahrain ■, *Asia* 71 E6
Bahror, *India* 68 F7
Bāhū Kalāt, *Iran* 71 E9
Bai, *Mali* 82 C4
Bai Bung, Mui = Ca Mau, Mui, *Vietnam* 65 H5
Bai Duc, *Vietnam* 64 C5
Bai Thuong, *Vietnam* 64 C5
Baia de Aramă, *Romania* 42 E7
Baia Mare, *Romania* 43 C8
Baia-Sprie, *Romania* 43 C8
Baião, *Brazil* 125 D9
Baïbokoum, *Chad* 79 G9
Baicheng, *China* 57 B12
Băicoi, *Romania* 43 E10
Baidoa, *Somali Rep.* 74 G3
Baie Comeau, *Canada* 103 C6
Baie-St-Paul, *Canada* 103 C5
Baie Trinité, *Canada* 103 C6
Baie Verte, *Canada* 103 C8
Baignes-Ste-Radegonde, *France* 20 C3
Baigneux-les-Juifs, *France* 19 E11
Baihar, *India* 69 H9
Baihe, *China* 56 H6
Ba'ījī, *Iraq* 70 C4
Baijnath, *India* 69 E8
Baikal, L. = Baykal, Oz., *Russia* 51 D11
Baikunthpur, *India* 69 H10
Baile Atha Cliath = Dublin, *Ireland* 15 C5
Băile Govora, *Romania* 43 E9
Băile Herculane, *Romania* 42 F7
Băile Olăneşti, *Romania* 43 E9
Băile Tuşnad, *Romania* 43 D10
Bailén, *Spain* 35 G7
Băileşti, *Romania* 43 F8
Baima, *China* 58 A3
Bain-de-Bretagne, *France* 18 E5
Bainbridge, *Ga., U.S.A.* 109 K3
Bainbridge, *N.Y., U.S.A.* 111 D9
Baing, *Indonesia* 63 F6
Bainiu, *China* 56 H7
Baiona, *Spain* 34 C2
Bā'ir, *Jordan* 75 E5
Bairin Youqi, *China* 57 C10
Bairin Zuoqi, *China* 57 C10
Bais, *Phil.* 61 G5
Baisha, *China* 56 G7
Baissa, *Nigeria* 83 D7
Baitadi, *Nepal* 69 E9
Baiyin, *China* 56 F3
Baiyü, *China* 58 B2
Baiyu Shan, *China* 56 F4
Baiyuda, *Sudan* 80 D3
Baj Baj, *India* 69 H13
Baja, *Hungary* 42 D3
Baja, Pta., *Mexico* 118 B1
Baja California, *Mexico* 118 A1
Baja California □, *Mexico* 118 B2
Baja California Sur □, *Mexico* 118 B2
Bajag, *India* 69 H9
Bajamar, *Canary Is.* 37 F3
Bajana, *India* 68 H4
Bājgīrān, *Iran* 71 B8
Bajimba, Mt., *Australia* 95 D5
Bajina Bašta, *Serbia, Yug.* 40 C3
Bajmok, *Serbia, Yug.* 42 E4
Bajo Nuevo, *Caribbean* 120 C4
Bajoga, *Nigeria* 83 C7
Bajool, *Australia* 94 C5
Bak, *Hungary* 42 D1
Bakar, *Croatia* 29 C11
Bakel, *Senegal* 82 C2
Baker, *Calif., U.S.A.* 117 K10
Baker, *Mont., U.S.A.* 112 B2
Baker, L., *Canada* 100 B10
Baker City, *U.S.A.* 114 D5
Baker I., *Pac. Oc.* 96 G10
Baker I., *U.S.A.* 104 B2
Baker L., *Australia* 93 E4
Baker Lake, *Canada* 100 B10
Baker Mt., *U.S.A.* 114 B3
Bakers Creek, *Australia* 94 C4
Baker's Dozen Is., *Canada* 102 A4
Bakersfield, *Calif., U.S.A.* 117 K8
Bakersfield, *Vt., U.S.A.* 111 B12
Bakhchysaray, *Ukraine* 47 K7
Bakhmach, *Ukraine* 47 G7
Bākhtarān, *Iran* 70 C5
Bākhtarān □, *Iran* 70 C5
Bakı, *Azerbaijan* 49 K9
Bakır →, *Turkey* 39 C9
Bakırdaği, *Turkey* 72 C6
Bakkafjörður, *Iceland* 8 C6
Baklan, *Turkey* 39 C11
Bako, *Ethiopia* 81 F4
Bako, *Ivory C.* 82 D3
Bakony, *Hungary* 42 C2
Bakony Forest = Bakony, *Hungary* 42 C2
Bakori, *Nigeria* 83 C6
Bakouma, *C.A.R.* 84 C4
Baksan, *Russia* 49 J6
Bakswaho, *India* 69 G8
Baku = Bakı, *Azerbaijan* 49 K9
Bakundi, *Nigeria* 83 D7
Bakutis Coast, *Antarctica* 5 D15
Baky = Bakı, *Azerbaijan* 49 K9
Bala, *Canada* 110 A5
Bala, *Senegal* 82 C2
Bâlâ, *Turkey* 72 C5
Bala, *U.K.* 12 E4
Bala, L., *U.K.* 12 E4
Balabac I., *Phil.* 62 C5
Balabac Str., *E. Indies* 62 C5
Balabagh, *Afghan.* 68 B4
Ba'labakk, *Lebanon* 75 B5
Balabalangan, Kepulauan, *Indonesia* 62 E5
Bălăciţa, *Romania* 43 F8
Balad, *Iraq* 70 C5
Balad Rūz, *Iraq* 70 C5
Bālādeh, *Fārs, Iran* 71 D6
Bālādeh, *Māzandaran, Iran* 71 B6
Balaghat, *India* 66 J12
Balaghat Ra., *India* 66 K10
Balaguer, *Spain* 32 D5
Balakhna, *Russia* 48 B6
Balaklava, *Ukraine* 47 K7
Balakliya, *Ukraine* 47 H9
Balakovo, *Russia* 48 D8
Balamau, *India* 69 F9
Bălan, *Romania* 43 D10
Balancán, *Mexico* 119 D6
Balashov, *Russia* 48 E6
Balasinor, *India* 68 H5
Balasore = Baleshwar, *India* 67 J15
Balassagyarmat, *Hungary* 42 B4
Balât, *Egypt* 80 B2
Balaton, *Hungary* 42 D2
Balatonboglár, *Hungary* 42 D2
Balatonfüred, *Hungary* 42 D2
Balatonszentgyörgy, *Hungary* 42 D2
Balayan, *Phil.* 61 E4
Balazote, *Spain* 33 G2
Balbieriškis, *Lithuania* 44 D10
Balbigny, *France* 21 C8
Balbina, Reprêsa de, *Brazil* 124 D7
Balboa, *Panama* 120 E4
Balbriggan, *Ireland* 15 C5
Balcarce, *Argentina* 126 D4
Balcarres, *Canada* 105 C8
Bălceşti, *Romania* 43 F8
Balchik, *Bulgaria* 41 C12
Balclutha, *N.Z.* 91 M2
Balcones Escarpment, *U.S.A.* 113 L5
Balçova, *Turkey* 39 C9
Bald Hd., *Australia* 93 G2
Bald I., *Australia* 93 F2
Bald Knob, *U.S.A.* 113 H9
Baldock L., *Canada* 105 B9
Baldwin, *Mich., U.S.A.* 108 D3
Baldwin, *Pa., U.S.A.* 110 F5
Baldwinsville, *U.S.A.* 111 C8
Baldy Mt., *U.S.A.* 114 B9
Baldy Peak, *U.S.A.* 115 K9
Bale, *Croatia* 29 C10
Bale, *Ethiopia* 81 F5
Bale □, *Ethiopia* 81 F5
Baleares, Is., *Spain* 37 B10
Balearic Is. = Baleares, Is., *Spain* 37 B10
Baleine = Whale →, *Canada* 103 A6
Băleni, *Romania* 43 E12
Baler, *Phil.* 61 D4
Baler Bay, *Phil.* 61 D4
Baleshare, *U.K.* 14 D1
Baleshwar, *India* 67 J15
Balezino, *Russia* 48 B11
Balfate, *Honduras* 120 C2
Bali, *Cameroon* 83 D7
Balí, *Greece* 36 D6
Bali, *India* 68 G5
Bali, *Indonesia* 62 F4
Bali □, *Indonesia* 62 F5
Bali, Selat, *Indonesia* 63 H16
Balia, *S. Leone* 82 D2
Baliapal, *India* 69 J12
Baligród, *Poland* 45 J9
Balikeşir, *Turkey* 39 B9
Balikeşir □, *Turkey* 39 B9
Balıklıçeşme, *Turkey* 41 F11
Balikpapan, *Indonesia* 62 E5
Balimbing, *Phil.* 63 C5
Baling, *Malaysia* 65 K3
Balingen, *Germany* 25 G4
Balinţ, *Romania* 42 E6
Balintang Channel, *Phil.* 61 B4
Balipara, *India* 67 F18
Balkan Mts. = Stara Planina, *Bulgaria* 40 C7
Balkhash = Balqash, *Kazakstan* 50 E8
Balkhash, Ozero = Balqash Köl, *Kazakstan* 50 E8
Balla, *Bangla.* 67 G17
Ballachulish, *U.K.* 14 E3
Balladonia, *Australia* 93 F3
Ballaghaderreen, *Ireland* 15 C3
Ballard, L., *Australia* 93 E3
Ballater, *U.K.* 14 D5
Ballé, *Mali* 82 B3
Ballenas, Canal de, *Mexico* 118 B2
Balleny Is., *Antarctica* 5 C11
Balleroy, *France* 18 C6
Ballerup, *Denmark* 11 J6
Ballı, *Turkey* 41 F11
Ballia, *India* 69 G11
Ballina, *Australia* 95 D5
Ballina, *Ireland* 15 B2
Ballinasloe, *Ireland* 15 C3
Ballinger, *U.S.A.* 113 K5
Ballinrobe, *Ireland* 15 C2
Ballinskelligs B., *Ireland* 15 E1
Ballon, *France* 18 D7
Ballsh, *Albania* 40 F3
Ballston Spa, *U.S.A.* 111 D11
Ballycastle, *U.K.* 15 A5
Ballyclare, *U.K.* 15 B5
Ballyhaunis, *Ireland* 15 C3
Ballymena, *U.K.* 15 B5
Ballymoney, *U.K.* 15 A5
Ballymote, *Ireland* 15 B3
Ballynahinch, *U.K.* 15 B6
Ballyquintin Pt., *U.K.* 15 B6
Ballyshannon, *Ireland* 15 B3
Balmaceda, *Chile* 128 F2
Balmaseda, *Spain* 32 B1
Balmazújváros, *Hungary* 42 C6
Balmertown, *Canada* 105 C10
Balmorhea, *U.S.A.* 113 K3
Balonne →, *Australia* 95 D4
Balotra, *India* 68 G5
Balqash, *Kazakstan* 50 E8
Balqash Köl, *Kazakstan* 50 E8
Balrampur, *India* 69 F10
Balş, *Romania* 43 F9
Balsas, *Mexico* 119 D5
Balsas →, *Brazil* 125 E9
Balsas →, *Mexico* 118 D4
Bålsta, *Sweden* 10 E11
Balston Spa, *U.S.A.* 111 D11
Balta, *Romania* 42 F7
Balta, *Ukraine* 47 H5
Baltanás, *Spain* 34 D6
Bălţi, *Moldova* 43 C12
Baltic Sea, *Europe* 9 H18
Baltîm, *Egypt* 80 H7
Baltimore, *Ireland* 15 E2
Baltimore, *Md., U.S.A.* 108 F7
Baltimore, *Ohio, U.S.A.* 110 G2
Baltit, *Pakistan* 69 A6
Baltiysk, *Russia* 9 J18
Baltrum, *Germany* 24 B3
Baluchistan □, *Pakistan* 66 F4
Balurghat, *India* 69 G13
Balvi, *Latvia* 9 H22
Balya, *Turkey* 39 B9
Bam, *Iran* 71 D8
Bama, *China* 58 E6
Bama, *Nigeria* 83 C7
Bamaga, *Australia* 94 A3
Bamaji L., *Canada* 102 B1
Bamako, *Mali* 82 C3
Bamba, *Mali* 83 B4
Bambara Maoundé, *Mali* 82 B4
Bambari, *C.A.R.* 84 C4
Bambaroo, *Australia* 94 B4
Bambaya, *Guinea* 82 D2
Bamberg, *Germany* 25 F6
Bamberg, *U.S.A.* 109 J5
Bambesi, *Ethiopia* 81 F3
Bambey, *Senegal* 82 C1
Bambili, *Dem. Rep. of the Congo* 86 B2
Bamboi, *Ghana* 82 D4
Bamenda, *Cameroon* 83 D7
Bamfield, *Canada* 104 D3
Bāmīān □, *Afghan.* 66 B5
Bamiancheng, *China* 57 C13
Bamkin, *Cameroon* 83 D7
Bampūr, *Iran* 71 E9
Ban, *Burkina Faso* 82 C4
Ban Ban, *Laos* 64 C4
Ban Bang Hin, *Thailand* 65 H2
Ban Chiang Klang, *Thailand* 64 C3
Ban Chik, *Laos* 64 D4
Ban Choho, *Thailand* 64 E4
Ban Dan Lan Hoi, *Thailand* 64 D2
Ban Don = Surat Thani, *Thailand* 65 H2

Ban Don, *Vietnam* 64 F6
Ban Don, Ao →, *Thailand* 65 H2
Ban Dong, *Thailand* 64 C3
Ban Hong, *Thailand* 64 C2
Ban Kaeng, *Thailand* 64 D3
Ban Kantang, *Thailand* 65 J2
Ban Keun, *Laos* 64 C4
Ban Khai, *Thailand* 64 F3
Ban Kheun, *Laos* 64 B3
Ban Khlong Kua, *Thailand* 65 J3
Ban Khuan Mao, *Thailand* 65 J2
Ban Ko Yai Chim, *Thailand* 65 G2
Ban Kok, *Thailand* 64 D4
Ban Laem, *Thailand* 64 F2
Ban Lao Ngam, *Laos* 64 E6
Ban Le Kathe, *Thailand* 64 E2
Ban Mae Chedi, *Thailand* 64 C2
Ban Mae Laeng, *Thailand* 64 B2
Ban Mae Sariang, *Thailand* 64 C1
Ban Mê Thuôt = Buon Ma Thuot, *Vietnam* 64 F7
Ban Mi, *Thailand* 64 E3
Ban Muong Mo, *Laos* 64 C4
Ban Na Mo, *Laos* 64 D5
Ban Na San, *Thailand* 65 H2
Ban Na Tong, *Laos* 64 B3
Ban Nam Bac, *Laos* 64 B4
Ban Nam Ma, *Laos* 64 A3
Ban Ngang, *Laos* 64 E6
Ban Nong Bok, *Laos* 64 D5
Ban Nong Boua, *Laos* 64 E6
Ban Nong Pling, *Thailand* 64 E3
Ban Pak Chan, *Thailand* 65 G2
Ban Phai, *Thailand* 64 D4
Ban Pong, *Thailand* 64 F2
Ban Ron Phibun, *Thailand* 65 H2
Ban Sanam Chai, *Thailand* 65 J3
Ban Sangkha, *Thailand* 64 E4
Ban Tak, *Thailand* 64 D2
Ban Tako, *Thailand* 64 E4
Ban Tha Dua, *Thailand* 64 D2
Ban Tha Li, *Thailand* 64 D3
Ban Tha Nun, *Thailand* 65 H2
Ban Thahine, *Laos* 64 E5
Ban Xien Kok, *Laos* 64 B3
Ban Yen Nhan, *Vietnam* 64 B6
Banaba, *Kiribati* 96 H8
Banalia, *Dem. Rep. of the Congo* 86 B2
Banam, *Cambodia* 65 G5
Banamba, *Mali* 82 C3
Banana Is., *S. Leone* 82 D2
Bananal, I. do, *Brazil* 125 F8
Banaras = Varanasi, *India* 69 G10
Banas →, *Gujarat, India* 68 H4
Banas →, *Mad. P., India* 69 G9
Bânâs, Ras, *Egypt* 80 C4
Banaz, *Turkey* 39 C11
Banaz →, *Turkey* 39 C11
Banbridge, *U.K.* 15 B5
Banbury, *U.K.* 13 E6
Banchory, *U.K.* 14 D6
Banco, *Ethiopia* 81 F4
Bancroft, *Canada* 102 C4
Band, *Romania* 43 D9
Band Bonī, *Iran* 71 E8
Band Qīr, *Iran* 71 D6
Banda, *Mad. P., India* 69 G8
Banda, *Ut. P., India* 69 G9
Banda, Kepulauan, *Indonesia* 63 E7
Banda Aceh, *Indonesia* 62 C1
Banda Elat, *Indonesia* 63 F8
Banda Is. = Banda, Kepulauan, *Indonesia* 63 E7
Banda Sea, *Indonesia* 63 F7
Bandai-San, *Japan* 54 F10
Bandama →, *Ivory C.* 82 D3
Bandama Blanc →, *Ivory C.* 82 D3
Bandama Rouge →, *Ivory C.* 82 D4
Bandān, *Iran* 71 D9
Bandanaira, *Indonesia* 63 E7
Bandanwara, *India* 68 F6
Bandar = Machilipatnam, *India* 67 L12
Bandār 'Abbās, *Iran* 71 E8
Bandar-e Anzalī, *Iran* 71 B6
Bandar-e Bushehr = Būshehr, *Iran* 71 D6
Bandar-e Chārak, *Iran* 71 E7
Bandar-e Deylam, *Iran* 71 D6
Bandar-e Khomeynı, *Iran* 71 D6
Bandar-e Lengeh, *Iran* 71 E7
Bandar-e Maqām, *Iran* 71 E7
Bandar-e Ma'shur, *Iran* 71 D6
Bandar-e Rīg, *Iran* 71 D6
Bandar-e Torkeman, *Iran* 71 B7
Bandar Maharani = Muar, *Malaysia* 65 L4
Bandar Penggaram = Batu Pahat, *Malaysia* 65 M4
Bandar Seri Begawan, *Brunei* 62 C4
Bandar Sri Aman, *Malaysia* 62 D4
Bandawe, *Malawi* 87 E3
Bande, *Spain* 34 C3
Bandeira, Pico da, *Brazil* 127 A7
Bandera, *Argentina* 126 B3
Banderas, B. de, *Mexico* 118 C3
Bandhogarh, *India* 69 H9
Bandi →, *India* 68 F6
Bandiagara, *Mali* 82 C4
Bandikui, *India* 68 F7
Bandırma, *Turkey* 41 F11
Bandol, *France* 21 E9
Bandon, *Ireland* 15 E3
Bandon →, *Ireland* 15 E3
Bandula, *Mozam.* 87 F3
Bandundu, *Dem. Rep. of the Congo* 84 E3
Bandung, *Indonesia* 62 F3
Bané, *Burkina Faso* 83 C4
Băneasa, *Romania* 43 E12
Bāneh, *Iran* 70 C5
Bañeres, *Spain* 33 G4
Banes, *Cuba* 121 B4
Banff, *Canada* 104 C5
Banff, *U.K.* 14 D6
Banff Nat. Park, *Canada* 104 C5
Banfora, *Burkina Faso* 82 C4
Bang Fai →, *Laos* 64 D5
Bang Hieng →, *Laos* 64 D5
Bang Krathum, *Thailand* 64 D3
Bang Lamung, *Thailand* 64 F3
Bang Mun Nak, *Thailand* 64 D3
Bang Pa In, *Thailand* 64 E3
Bang Rakam, *Thailand* 64 D3
Bang Saphan, *Thailand* 65 G2
Bangaduni I., *India* 69 J13
Bangala Dam, *Zimbabwe* 87 G3
Bangalore, *India* 66 N10
Banganga →, *India* 68 F6
Bangangté, *Cameroon* 83 D7
Bangaon, *India* 69 H13
Bangassou, *C.A.R.* 84 D4
Banggai, *Indonesia* 63 E6
Banggai, Kepulauan, *Indonesia* 63 E6
Banggai Arch. = Banggai, Kepulauan, *Indonesia* 63 E6
Banggi, *Malaysia* 62 C5
Banghāzī, *Libya* 79 B10
Bangjang, *Sudan* 81 E3
Bangka, *Sulawesi, Indonesia* 63 D7
Bangka, *Sumatera, Indonesia* 62 E3
Bangka, Selat, *Indonesia* 62 E3
Bangkalan, *Indonesia* 63 G15
Bangkinang, *Indonesia* 62 D2
Bangko, *Indonesia* 62 E2
Bangkok, *Thailand* 64 F3
Bangladesh ■, *Asia* 67 H17
Bangolo, *Ivory C.* 82 D3
Bangong Co, *India* 69 B8
Bangor, *Down, U.K.* 15 B6
Bangor, *Gwynedd, U.K.* 12 D3
Bangor, *Maine, U.S.A.* 101 D13
Bangor, *Pa., U.S.A.* 111 F9
Bangued, *Phil.* 61 C4
Bangui, *C.A.R.* 84 D3
Bangui, *Phil.* 61 B4
Banguru, *Dem. Rep. of the Congo* 86 B2
Bangweulu, L., *Zambia* 87 E3
Bangweulu Swamp, *Zambia* 87 E3
Bani, *Dom. Rep.* 121 C5
Bani →, *Mali* 82 C4
Bani Bangou, *Niger* 83 B5
Banī Sa'd, *Iraq* 70 C5
Bania, *Ivory C.* 82 D4
Banihal Pass, *India* 69 C6
Banikoara, *Benin* 83 C5
Bāniyās, *Syria* 70 C3
Banja Luka, *Bos.-H.* 42 F2
Banjar, *India* 68 D7
Banjar →, *India* 69 H9
Banjarmasin, *Indonesia* 62 E4
Banjul, *Gambia* 82 C1
Banka, *India* 69 G12
Bankas, *Mali* 82 C4
Bankeryd, *Sweden* 11 G8
Banket, *Zimbabwe* 87 F3
Bankilaré, *Niger* 83 C5
Bankipore, *India* 67 G14
Banks I., *B.C., Canada* 104 C3
Banks I., *N.W.T., Canada* 100 A7
Banks Pen., *N.Z.* 91 K4
Banks Str., *Australia* 94 G4
Bankura, *India* 69 H12
Bankya, *Bulgaria* 40 D7
Banmankhi, *India* 69 G12
Bann →, *Arm., U.K.* 15 B5
Bann →, *L'derry., U.K.* 15 A5
Bannalec, *France* 18 E3
Bannang Sata, *Thailand* 65 J3
Banning, *U.S.A.* 117 M10
Banningville = Bandundu, *Dem. Rep. of the Congo* 84 E3
Banno, *Ethiopia* 81 G4
Bannockburn, *Canada* 110 B7
Bannockburn, *U.K.* 14 E5
Bannockburn, *Zimbabwe* 87 G2
Bannu, *Pakistan* 66 C7
Bano, *India* 69 H11
Bañolas = Banyoles, *Spain* 32 C7
Banon, *France* 21 D9
Baños de la Encina, *Spain* 35 G7
Baños de Molgas, *Spain* 34 C3
Bánovce nad Bebravou, *Slovak Rep.* 27 C11
Banoviči, *Bos.-H.* 42 F3
Bansgaon, *India* 69 F10
Banská Bystrica, *Slovak Rep.* 27 C12
Banská Štiavnica, *Slovak Rep.* 27 C11
Bansko, *Bulgaria* 40 E7
Banskobystrický □, *Slovak Rep.* 27 C12
Banswara, *India* 68 H6
Bantaeng, *Indonesia* 63 F5
Bantaji, *Nigeria* 83 D7
Bantayan, *Phil.* 61 F5
Bantry, *Ireland* 15 E2
Bantry B., *Ireland* 15 E2
Bantul, *Indonesia* 63 G14
Bantva, *India* 68 J4
Banya, *Bulgaria* 41 D8
Banyak, Kepulauan, *Indonesia* 62 D1
Banyalbufar, *Spain* 37 B9
Banyo, *Cameroon* 83 D7
Banyoles, *Spain* 32 C7
Banyuls-sur-Mer, *France* 20 F7
Banyumas, *Indonesia* 63 G13
Banyuwangi, *Indonesia* 63 H16
Banzare Coast, *Antarctica* 5 C9
Banzyville = Mobayi, *Dem. Rep. of the Congo* 84 D4
Bao Ha, *Vietnam* 58 F5
Bao Lac, *Vietnam* 64 A5
Bao Loc, *Vietnam* 65 G6
Bao'an = Shenzhen, *China* 59 F10
Baocheng, *China* 56 H4
Baode, *China* 56 E6
Baodi, *China* 57 E9
Baoding, *China* 56 E8
Baoji, *China* 56 G4
Baojing, *China* 58 C7
Baokang, *China* 59 B8
Baoshan, *Shanghai, China* 59 B13
Baoshan, *Yunnan, China* 58 E2
Baotou, *China* 56 D6
Baoxing, *China* 58 B4
Baoying, *China* 57 H10
Bap, *India* 68 F5
Bapatla, *India* 67 M12
Bapaume, *France* 19 B9
Bāqerābād, *Iran* 71 C6
Ba'qūbah, *Iraq* 70 C5
Baquedano, *Chile* 126 A2
Bar, *Montenegro, Yug.* 40 D3
Bar, *Ukraine* 47 H4
Bar Bigha, *India* 69 G11
Bar Harbor, *U.S.A.* 109 C11
Bar-le-Duc, *France* 19 D12
Bar-sur-Aube, *France* 19 D11
Bar-sur-Seine, *France* 19 D11
Bara, *India* 69 G9
Bâra, *Romania* 43 C12
Bara Banki, *India* 69 F9
Barabai, *Indonesia* 62 E5
Baraboo, *U.S.A.* 112 D10
Baracoa, *Cuba* 121 B5
Baradā →, *Syria* 75 B5
Baradero, *Argentina* 126 C4
Baraga, *U.S.A.* 112 B10
Bărăganul, *Romania* 43 F12
Barah →, *India* 68 F6
Barahona, *Dom. Rep.* 121 C5
Barahona, *Spain* 32 D2
Barail Range, *India* 67 G18
Baraka, *Sudan* 81 E2
Baraka →, *Sudan* 80 D4
Barakaldo, *Spain* 32 B2
Barakar →, *India* 69 G12
Barakhola, *India* 67 G18
Barakot, *India* 69 J11
Barakpur, *India* 69 H13
Baralaba, *Australia* 94 C4
Baralla, *Spain* 34 C3
Baralzon L., *Canada* 105 B9
Barameiya, *Sudan* 80 D4
Baramula, *India* 69 B6
Baran, *India* 68 G7
Baran →, *Pakistan* 68 G3
Barañain, *Spain* 32 C3
Baranavichy, *Belarus* 47 F4
Barani, *Burkina Faso* 82 C4
Baranof, *U.S.A.* 104 B2
Baranof I., *U.S.A.* 100 C6
Baranów Sandomierski, *Poland* 45 H8
Baranya □, *Hungary* 42 E3
Baraolt, *Romania* 43 D10
Barapasi, *Indonesia* 63 E9
Barasat, *India* 69 H13
Barat Daya, Kepulauan, *Indonesia* 63 F7
Barataria B., *U.S.A.* 113 L10
Barauda, *India* 68 H6
Baraut, *India* 68 E7
Barbacena, *Brazil* 127 A7
Barbados ■, *W. Indies* 121 D8
Barban, *Croatia* 29 C11
Barbària, C. de, *Spain* 37 C7
Barbaros, *Turkey* 41 F11
Barbastro, *Spain* 32 C5
Barbate = Barbate de Franco, *Spain* 35 J5
Barbate de Franco, *Spain* 35 J5
Barberino di Mugello, *Italy* 29 E8
Barberton, *S. Africa* 89 D5
Barberton, *U.S.A.* 110 E3
Barbezieux-St-Hilaire, *France* 20 C3
Barbosa, *Colombia* 124 B4
Barbourville, *U.S.A.* 109 G4
Barbuda, *W. Indies* 121 C7
Bârca, *Romania* 43 G8
Barcaldine, *Australia* 94 C4
Barcarrota, *Spain* 35 G4
Barcellona Pozzo di Gotto, *Italy* 31 D8
Barcelona, *Spain* 32 D7
Barcelona, *Venezuela* 124 A6
Barcelona □, *Spain* 32 D7
Barcelonette, *France* 21 D10
Barcelos, *Brazil* 124 D6
Barcin, *Poland* 45 F4
Barclayville, *Liberia* 82 E3
Barcoo →, *Australia* 94 D3
Barcs, *Hungary* 42 E2
Barczewo, *Poland* 44 E7
Bärdä, *Azerbaijan* 49 K8
Bardaï, *Chad* 79 D9
Bardas Blancas, *Argentina* 126 D2
Barddhaman, *India* 69 H12
Bardejov, *Slovak Rep.* 27 B14
Bardera, *Somali Rep.* 74 G3
Bardi, *Italy* 28 D6
Bardīyah, *Libya* 79 B10
Bardolino, *Italy* 28 C7
Bardonécchia, *Italy* 28 C3
Bardsey I., *U.K.* 12 E3
Bardstown, *U.S.A.* 108 G3
Bareilly, *India* 69 E8
Barela, *India* 69 H9
Barentin, *France* 18 C7
Barenton, *France* 18 D6
Barents Sea, *Arctic* 4 B9
Barentu, *Eritrea* 81 D4
Barfleur, *France* 18 C5
Barfleur, Pte. de, *France* 18 C5
Barga, *Italy* 28 D7
Bargara, *Australia* 94 C5
Bargas, *Spain* 34 F6
Bârgăului Bistriţa, *Romania* 43 C9
Barge, *Italy* 28 D4
Bargnop, *Sudan* 81 F2
Bargteheide, *Germany* 24 B6
Barguzin, *Russia* 51 D11
Barh, *India* 69 G11
Barhaj, *India* 69 F10
Barharwa, *India* 69 G12
Barhi, *India* 69 G11
Bari, *India* 68 F7
Bari, *Italy* 31 A9
Bari Doab, *Pakistan* 68 D5
Bari Sadri, *India* 68 G6
Bari Sardo, *Italy* 30 C2
Barīdī, Ra's, *Si. Arabia* 70 E3
Barīm, *Yemen* 76 E8
Barinas, *Venezuela* 124 B4
Baring, C., *Canada* 100 B8
Baringo, *Kenya* 86 B4
Baringo, L., *Kenya* 86 B4
Bârîs, *Egypt* 80 C3
Barisal, *Bangla.* 67 H17
Barisan, Bukit, *Indonesia* 62 E2
Barito →, *Indonesia* 62 E4
Barjac, *France* 21 D8
Barjols, *France* 21 E10
Bark L., *Canada* 110 A7
Barka = Baraka →, *Sudan* 80 D4
Barkakana, *India* 69 H11
Barkam, *China* 58 B4
Barker, *U.S.A.* 110 C6
Barkley, L., *U.S.A.* 109 G2
Barkley Sound, *Canada* 104 D3
Barkly East, *S. Africa* 88 E4
Barkly Roadhouse, *Australia* 94 B2
Barkly Tableland, *Australia* 94 B2
Barkly West, *S. Africa* 88 D3
Barkol, Wadi →, *Sudan* 80 D3
Barla Dağı, *Turkey* 39 C12
Bârlad, *Romania* 43 D12
Bârlad →, *Romania* 43 E12
Barlee, L., *Australia* 93 E2
Barlee, Mt., *Australia* 93 D4
Barletta, *Italy* 31 A9
Barlinek, *Poland* 45 F2
Barlovento, *Canary Is.* 37 F2
Barlow L., *Canada* 105 A8
Barmer, *India* 68 G4
Barmouth, *U.K.* 12 E3
Barmstedt, *Germany* 24 B5
Barna →, *India* 69 G10
Barnagar, *India* 68 H6
Barnala, *India* 68 D6
Barnard Castle, *U.K.* 12 C6
Barnaul, *Russia* 50 D9
Barnesville, *U.S.A.* 109 J3
Barnet □, *U.K.* 13 F7
Barneveld, *Neths.* 17 B5
Barneveld, *U.S.A.* 111 C9
Barneville-Cartevert, *France* 18 C5
Barnhart, *U.S.A.* 113 K4
Barnsley, *U.K.* 12 D6
Barnstaple, *U.K.* 13 F3
Barnstaple Bay = Bideford Bay, *U.K.* 13 F3
Barnsville, *U.S.A.* 112 B6
Barnwell, *U.S.A.* 109 J5
Baro, *Nigeria* 83 D6
Baro →, *Ethiopia* 81 F3
Baroda = Vadodara, *India* 68 H5
Baroda, *India* 68 G7
Baroe, *S. Africa* 88 E3
Baron Ra., *Australia* 92 D4
Barong, *China* 58 B2
Barotseland, *Zambia* 85 H4
Barouéli, *Mali* 82 C3
Barpeta, *India* 67 F17
Barques, Pt. Aux, *U.S.A.* 110 B2
Barquísimeto, *Venezuela* 124 A5
Barr, Ras el, *Egypt* 80 H7
Barr Smith Range, *Australia* 93 E3
Barra, *Brazil* 125 F10
Barra, *U.K.* 14 E1
Barra, Sd. of, *U.K.* 14 D1
Barra de Navidad, *Mexico* 118 D4
Barra do Corda, *Brazil* 125 E9
Barra do Piraí, *Brazil* 127 A7
Barra Falsa, Pta. da, *Mozam.* 89 C6
Barra Hd., *U.K.* 14 E1
Barra Mansa, *Brazil* 127 A7
Barrackpur = Barakpur, *India* 69 H13
Barradale Roadhouse, *Australia* 92 D1
Barrafranca, *Italy* 31 E7
Barraigh = Barra, *U.K.* 14 E1
Barranca, *Lima, Peru* 124 F3
Barranca, *Loreto, Peru* 124 D3
Barrancabermeja, *Colombia* 124 B4
Barrancas, *Venezuela* 124 B6
Barrancos, *Portugal* 35 G4
Barranqueras, *Argentina* 126 B4
Barranquilla, *Colombia* 124 A4
Barraute, *Canada* 102 C4
Barre, *Mass., U.S.A.* 111 D12
Barre, *Vt., U.S.A.* 111 B12
Barreal, *Argentina* 126 C2
Barreiras, *Brazil* 125 F10
Barreirinhas, *Brazil* 125 D10
Barreiro, *Portugal* 35 G1
Barrême, *France* 21 E10
Barren, Nosy, *Madag.* 89 B7
Barretos, *Brazil* 125 H9
Barrhead, *Canada* 104 C6
Barrie, *Canada* 102 D4
Barrière, *Canada* 104 C4
Barrington, *U.S.A.* 111 E13
Barrington L., *Canada* 105 B8
Barringun, *Australia* 95 D4
Barro do Garças, *Brazil* 125 G8
Barron, *U.S.A.* 112 C9
Barrow, *U.S.A.* 100 A4
Barrow →, *Ireland* 15 D5
Barrow, Pt., *U.S.A.* 98 B4
Barrow Creek, *Australia* 94 C1
Barrow I., *Australia* 92 D2
Barrow-in-Furness, *U.K.* 12 C4
Barrow Pt., *Australia* 94 A3
Barrow Ra., *Australia* 93 E4
Barrow Str., *Canada* 4 B3
Barruecopardo, *Spain* 34 D4
Barruelo de Santullán, *Spain* 34 C6
Barry, *U.K.* 13 F4
Barry's Bay, *Canada* 102 C4
Barsalogho, *Burkina Faso* 83 C4
Barsat, *Pakistan* 69 A5
Barsham, *Syria* 70 C4
Barsi, *India* 66 K9
Barsinghausen, *Germany* 24 C5
Barsoi, *India* 67 G15
Barstow, *U.S.A.* 117 L9
Barth, *Germany* 24 A8
Barthélemy, Col, *Vietnam* 64 C5
Bartica, *Guyana* 124 B7
Bartin, *Turkey* 72 B5
Bartlesville, *U.S.A.* 113 G7
Bartlett, *U.S.A.* 116 J8
Bartlett, L., *Canada* 104 A5
Bartolomeu Dias, *Mozam.* 87 G4
Barton, *U.S.A.* 111 B12
Barton upon Humber, *U.K.* 12 D7
Bartoszyce, *Poland* 44 D7
Bartow, *U.S.A.* 109 M5
Barú, Volcan, *Panama* 120 E3
Barumba, *Dem. Rep. of the Congo* 86 B1
Baruth, *Germany* 24 C9
Baruunsuu, *Mongolia* 56 C3
Barvinkove, *Ukraine* 47 H9
Barwani, *India* 68 H6
Barwice, *Poland* 44 E3
Barycz →, *Poland* 45 G3
Barysaw, *Belarus* 46 E5
Barysh, *Russia* 48 D8
Barzān, *Iraq* 70 B5
Bârzava, *Romania* 42 D6
Bas-Rhin □, *France* 19 D14
Bašaid, *Serbia, Yug.* 42 E5
Bāsa'idū, *Iran* 71 E7
Basal, *Pakistan* 68 C5
Basankusa, *Dem. Rep. of the Congo* 84 D3
Basarabeasca, *Moldova* 43 D13
Basarabi, *Romania* 43 F13
Basauri, *Spain* 32 B2
Basawa, *Afghan.* 68 B4
Bascuñán, C., *Chile* 126 B1
Basel, *Switz.* 25 H3
Basel-Landschaft □, *Switz.* 25 H3
Basento →, *Italy* 31 B9
Bashākerd, Kūhhā-ye, *Iran* 71 E8
Bashaw, *Canada* 104 C6
Bāshī, *Iran* 71 D6
Bashkir Republic = Bashkortostan □, *Russia* 50 D6
Bashkortostan □, *Russia* 50 D6
Basibasy, *Madag.* 89 C7
Basilan I., *Phil.* 61 H5
Basilan Str., *Phil.* 61 H5
Basildon, *U.K.* 13 F8
Basile, *Eq. Guin.* 83 E6
Basilicata □, *Italy* 31 B9
Basim = Washim, *India* 66 J10
Basin, *U.S.A.* 114 D9
Basingstoke, *U.K.* 13 F6
Baška, *Croatia* 29 D11
Başkale, *Turkey* 73 C10
Baskatong, Rés., *Canada* 102 C4
Basle = Basel, *Switz.* 25 H3
Başmakçı, *Turkey* 39 D12
Basoda, *India* 68 H7
Basoka, *Dem. Rep. of the Congo* 86 B1
Basque, Pays, *France* 20 E2
Basque Provinces = País Vasco □, *Spain* 32 C2
Basra = Al Başrah, *Iraq* 70 D5
Bass Str., *Australia* 94 F4
Bassano, *Canada* 104 C6
Bassano del Grappa, *Italy* 29 C8
Bassar, *Togo* 83 D5
Bassas da India, *Ind. Oc.* 85 J7
Basse-Normandie □, *France* 18 D6
Basse Santa-Su, *Gambia* 82 C2
Basse-Terre, *Guadeloupe* 121 C7

Bassein, *Burma* 67 L19
Basseterre, *St. Kitts & Nevis* ... 121 C7
Bassett, *U.S.A.* 112 D5
Bassi, *India* 68 D7
Bassigny, *France* 19 E12
Bassikounou, *Mauritania* 82 B3
Bassila, *Benin* 83 D5
Bassum, *Germany* 24 C4
Båstad, *Sweden* 11 H6
Bastak, *Iran* 71 E7
Baştām, *Iran* 71 B7
Bastar, *India* 67 K12
Bastelica, *France* 21 F13
Basti, *India* 69 F10
Bastia, *France* 21 F13
Bastogne, *Belgium* 17 D5
Bastrop, *La., U.S.A.* 113 J9
Bastrop, *Tex., U.S.A.* 113 K6
Bat Yam, *Israel* 75 C3
Bata, *Eq. Guin.* 84 D1
Bata, *Romania* 42 D7
Bataan □, *Phil.* 61 D4
Batabanó, *Cuba* 120 B3
Batabanó, G. de, *Cuba* 120 B3
Batac, *Phil.* 61 B4
Batagai, *Russia* 51 C14
Batajnica, *Serbia, Yug.* 40 B4
Batak, *Bulgaria* 41 E8
Batala, *India* 68 D6
Batalha, *Portugal* 34 F2
Batama, *Dem. Rep. of the Congo* 86 B2
Batamay, *Russia* 51 C13
Batang, *China* 58 B2
Batang, *Indonesia* 63 G13
Batangas, *Phil.* 61 E4
Batanta, *Indonesia* 63 E8
Batatais, *Brazil* 127 A6
Batavia, *U.S.A.* 110 D6
Bataysk, *Russia* 47 J10
Batchelor, *Australia* 92 B5
Batdambang, *Cambodia* 64 F4
Bates Ra., *Australia* 93 E3
Batesburg-Leesville, *U.S.A.* ... 109 J5
Batesville, *Ark., U.S.A.* 113 H9
Batesville, *Miss., U.S.A.* 113 H10
Batesville, *Tex., U.S.A.* 113 L5
Bath, *Canada* 111 B8
Bath, *U.K.* 13 F5
Bath, *Maine, U.S.A.* 109 D11
Bath, *N.Y., U.S.A.* 110 D7
Bath & North East Somerset □, *U.K.* 13 F5
Batheay, *Cambodia* 65 G5
Bathurst = Banjul, *Gambia* 82 C1
Bathurst, *Canada* 103 C6
Bathurst, *S. Africa* 88 E4
Bathurst, C., *Canada* 100 A7
Bathurst B., *Australia* 94 A3
Bathurst Harb., *Australia* 94 G4
Bathurst I., *Australia* 92 B5
Bathurst I., *Canada* 4 B2
Bathurst Inlet, *Canada* 100 B9
Bati, *Ethiopia* 81 E5
Batie, *Burkina Faso* 82 D4
Batman, *Turkey* 70 B4
Baṭn al Ghūl, *Jordan* 75 F4
Batna, *Algeria* 78 A7
Batobato = San Isidro, *Phil.* ... 61 H7
Batočina, *Serbia, Yug.* 40 B5
Batoka, *Zambia* 87 F2
Baton Rouge, *U.S.A.* 113 K9
Batong, Ko, *Thailand* 65 J2
Bátonyterenye, *Hungary* 42 C4
Batopilas, *Mexico* 118 B3
Batouri, *Cameroon* 84 D2
Båtsfjord, *Norway* 8 A23
Battambang = Batdambang, *Cambodia* 64 F4
Batticaloa, *Sri Lanka* 66 R12
Battipáglia, *Italy* 31 B7
Battle, *U.K.* 13 G8
Battle →, *Canada* 105 C7
Battle Creek, *U.S.A.* 108 D3
Battle Ground, *U.S.A.* 116 E4
Battle Harbour, *Canada* 103 B8
Battle Lake, *U.S.A.* 112 B7
Battle Mountain, *U.S.A.* 114 F5
Battlefields, *Zimbabwe* 87 F2
Battleford, *Canada* 105 C7
Battonya, *Hungary* 42 D6
Batu, *Ethiopia* 81 F4
Batu, Kepulauan, *Indonesia* ... 62 E1
Batu Caves, *Malaysia* 65 L3
Batu Gajah, *Malaysia* 65 K3
Batu Is. = Batu, Kepulauan, *Indonesia* 62 E1
Batu Pahat, *Malaysia* 65 M4
Batuata, *Indonesia* 63 F6
Batumi, *Georgia* 49 K5
Baturaja, *Indonesia* 62 E2
Baturité, *Brazil* 125 D11
Bau, *Malaysia* 62 D4
Baubau, *Indonesia* 63 F6
Bauchi, *Nigeria* 83 C6
Bauchi □, *Nigeria* 83 C7
Baud, *France* 18 E3
Baudette, *U.S.A.* 112 A7
Bauer, C., *Australia* 95 E1
Bauhinia, *Australia* 94 C4
Baukau, *E. Timor* 63 F7
Bauld, C., *Canada* 101 C14
Baume-les-Dames, *France* 19 E13
Baunatal, *Germany* 24 D5
Baunei, *Italy* 30 B2
Baure, *Nigeria* 83 C6
Bauru, *Brazil* 127 A6
Bausi, *India* 69 G12
Bauska, *Latvia* 9 H21
Bautino, *Kazakstan* 49 H10
Bautzen, *Germany* 24 D10
Bauya, *S. Leone* 82 D2
Bavānāt, *Iran* 71 D7
Bavanište, *Serbia, Yug.* 42 F5
Bavaria = Bayern □, *Germany* . 25 G7
Båven, *Sweden* 10 E10
Bavispe →, *Mexico* 118 B3
Bawdwin, *Burma* 67 H20
Bawean, *Indonesia* 62 F4
Bawku, *Ghana* 83 C4
Bawlake, *Burma* 67 K20
Bawolung, *China* 58 C3
Baxley, *U.S.A.* 109 K4
Baxoi, *China* 58 B1
Baxter, *U.S.A.* 112 B7
Baxter Springs, *U.S.A.* 113 G7
Bay, L. de, *Phil.* 61 D4
Bay City, *Mich., U.S.A.* 108 D4
Bay City, *Tex., U.S.A.* 113 L7
Bay Minette, *U.S.A.* 109 K2
Bay Roberts, *Canada* 103 C9
Bay St. Louis, *U.S.A.* 113 K10
Bay Springs, *U.S.A.* 113 K10
Bay View, *N.Z.* 91 H6
Baya, *Dem. Rep. of the Congo* . 87 E2
Bayamo, *Cuba* 120 B4
Bayamón, *Puerto Rico* 121 C6
Bayan Har Shan, *China* 60 C4
Bayan Hot = Alxa Zuoqi, *China* 56 E3
Bayan Obo, *China* 56 D5
Bayan-Ovoo = Erdenetsogt, *Mongolia* 56 C4
Bayana, *India* 68 F7
Bayanaūyl, *Kazakstan* 50 D8
Bayandalay, *Mongolia* 56 C2
Bayanhongor, *Mongolia* 60 B5
Bayard, *N. Mex., U.S.A.* 115 K9
Bayard, *Nebr., U.S.A.* 112 E3
Bayawan, *Phil.* 61 G5
Baybay, *Phil.* 61 F6
Bayburt, *Turkey* 73 B9
Bayelsa □, *Nigeria* 83 E6
Bayerische Alpen, *Germany* ... 25 H7
Bayerischer Wald, *Germany* ... 25 G8
Bayern □, *Germany* 25 G7
Bayeux, *France* 18 C6
Bayfield, *Canada* 110 C3
Bayfield, *U.S.A.* 112 B9
Bayındır, *Turkey* 39 C9
Baykal, Oz., *Russia* 51 D11
Baykan, *Turkey* 70 B4
Baykonur = Bayqongyr, *Kazakstan* 50 E7
Baynes Mts., *Namibia* 88 B1
Bayombong, *Phil.* 61 C4
Bayon, *France* 19 D13
Bayona = Baiona, *Spain* 34 C2
Bayonne, *France* 20 E2
Bayonne, *U.S.A.* 111 F10
Bayovar, *Peru* 124 E2
Bayqongyr, *Kazakstan* 50 E7
Bayram-Ali = Bayramaly, *Turkmenistan* 50 F7
Bayramaly, *Turkmenistan* 50 F7
Bayramiç, *Turkey* 39 B8
Bayreuth, *Germany* 25 F7
Bayrischzell, *Germany* 25 H8
Bayrūt, *Lebanon* 75 B4
Bays, L. of, *Canada* 110 A5
Baysville, *Canada* 110 A5
Bayt Lahm, *West Bank* 75 D4
Baytown, *U.S.A.* 113 L7
Bayzo, *Niger* 83 C5
Baza, *Spain* 35 H8
Bazar Dyuzi, *Russia* 49 K8
Bazardüzü = Bazar Dyuzi, *Russia* 49 K8
Bazarny Karabulak, *Russia* 48 D8
Bazarnyy Syzgan, *Russia* 48 D8
Bazaruto, I. do, *Mozam.* 89 C6
Bazas, *France* 20 D3
Bazhong, *China* 58 B6
Bazhou, *China* 56 E9
Bazmān, Kūh-e, *Iran* 71 D9
Beach, *U.S.A.* 112 B3
Beach City, *U.S.A.* 110 F3
Beachy Hd., *U.K.* 13 G8
Beacon, *Australia* 93 F2
Beacon, *U.S.A.* 111 E11
Beaconsfield, *Australia* 94 G4
Beagle, Canal, *S. Amer.* 122 J4
Beagle Bay, *Australia* 92 C3
Bealanana, *Madag.* 89 A8
Beals Cr. →, *U.S.A.* 113 J4
Beamsville, *Canada* 110 C5
Bear →, *Calif., U.S.A.* 116 G5
Bear →, *Utah, U.S.A.* 106 B4
Béar, C., *France* 20 F7
Bear I., *Ireland* 15 E2
Bear L., *Canada* 105 B9
Bear L., *U.S.A.* 114 F8
Beardmore, *Canada* 102 C2
Beardmore Glacier, *Antarctica* . 5 E11
Beardstown, *U.S.A.* 112 F9
Bearma →, *India* 69 G8
Béarn, *France* 20 E3
Bearpaw Mts., *U.S.A.* 114 B9
Bearskin Lake, *Canada* 102 B1
Beas →, *India* 68 D6
Beas de Segura, *Spain* 35 G8
Beasain, *Spain* 32 B2
Beata, C., *Dom. Rep.* 121 C5
Beata, I., *Dom. Rep.* 121 C5
Beatrice, *U.S.A.* 112 E6
Beatrice, *Zimbabwe* 87 F3
Beatrice, C., *Australia* 94 A2
Beatton →, *Canada* 104 B4
Beatton River, *Canada* 104 B4
Beatty, *U.S.A.* 116 J10
Beaucaire, *France* 21 E8
Beauce, Plaine de la, *France* ... 19 D8
Beauceville, *Canada* 103 C5
Beaudesert, *Australia* 95 D5
Beaufort, *France* 21 C10
Beaufort, *Malaysia* 62 C5
Beaufort, *N.C., U.S.A.* 109 H7
Beaufort, *S.C., U.S.A.* 109 J5
Beaufort Sea, *Arctic* 4 B1
Beaufort West, *S. Africa* 88 E3
Beaugency, *France* 19 E8
Beauharnois, *Canada* 111 A11
Beaujeu, *France* 19 F11
Beaujolais, *France* 19 F11
Beaulieu →, *Canada* 104 A6
Beaulieu-sur-Dordogne, *France* 20 D5
Beaulieu-sur-Mer, *France* 21 E11
Beauly, *U.K.* 14 D4
Beauly →, *U.K.* 14 D4
Beaumaris, *U.K.* 12 D3
Beaumont, *Belgium* 17 D4
Beaumont, *France* 20 D4
Beaumont, *U.S.A.* 113 K7
Beaumont-de-Lomagne, *France* 20 E5
Beaumont-le-Roger, *France* ... 18 C7
Beaumont-sur-Sarthe, *France* .. 18 D7
Beaune, *France* 19 E11
Beaune-la-Rolande, *France* ... 19 D9
Beaupré, *Canada* 103 C5
Beaupréau, *France* 18 E6
Beauraing, *Belgium* 17 D4
Beaurepaire, *France* 21 C9
Beauséjour, *Canada* 105 C9
Beauvais, *France* 19 C9
Beauval, *Canada* 105 B7
Beauvoir-sur-Mer, *France* 18 F4
Beauvoir-sur-Niort, *France* 20 B3
Beaver, *Okla., U.S.A.* 113 G4
Beaver, *Pa., U.S.A.* 110 F4
Beaver, *Utah, U.S.A.* 115 G7
Beaver →, *B.C., Canada* 104 B4
Beaver →, *Ont., Canada* 102 A2
Beaver →, *Sask., Canada* 105 B7
Beaver →, *U.S.A.* 113 G5
Beaver City, *U.S.A.* 112 E5
Beaver Creek, *Canada* 100 B5
Beaver Dam, *U.S.A.* 112 D10
Beaver Falls, *U.S.A.* 110 F4
Beaver Hill L., *Canada* 105 C10
Beaver I., *U.S.A.* 108 C3
Beaverhill L., *Canada* 104 C6
Beaverlodge, *Canada* 104 B5
Beaverstone →, *Canada* 102 B2
Beaverton, *Canada* 110 B5
Beaverton, *U.S.A.* 116 E4
Beawar, *India* 68 F6
Bebedouro, *Brazil* 127 A6
Beboa, *Madag.* 89 B7
Bebra, *Germany* 24 E5
Beccles, *U.K.* 13 E9
Bečej, *Serbia, Yug.* 42 E5
Beceni, *Romania* 43 E11
Becerreá, *Spain* 34 C3
Béchar, *Algeria* 78 B5
Bechyně, *Czech Rep.* 26 B7
Beckley, *U.S.A.* 108 G5
Beckum, *Germany* 24 D4
Beclean, *Romania* 43 C9
Bečov nad Teplou, *Czech Rep.* . 26 A5
Bečva →, *Czech Rep.* 27 B10
Bédar, *Spain* 33 H3
Bédarieux, *France* 20 E7
Beddouza, Ras, *Morocco* 78 B4
Bedele, *Ethiopia* 81 F4
Bederkesa, *Germany* 24 B4
Bedeso, *Ethiopia* 81 F5
Bedford, *Canada* 111 A12
Bedford, *S. Africa* 88 E4
Bedford, *U.K.* 13 E7
Bedford, *Ind., U.S.A.* 108 F2
Bedford, *Iowa, U.S.A.* 112 E7
Bedford, *Ohio, U.S.A.* 110 E3
Bedford, *Pa., U.S.A.* 110 F6
Bedford, *Va., U.S.A.* 108 G6
Bedford, C., *Australia* 94 B4
Bedfordshire □, *U.K.* 13 E7
Będków, *Poland* 45 G6
Bednja →, *Croatia* 29 B13
Bednodemyanovsk, *Russia* 48 D6
Bedónia, *Italy* 28 D6
Bedourie, *Australia* 94 C2
Bedum, *Neths.* 17 A6
Będzin, *Poland* 45 H6
Beebe Plain, *Canada* 111 A12
Beech Creek, *U.S.A.* 110 E7
Beelitz, *Germany* 24 C8
Beenleigh, *Australia* 95 D5
Be'er Menuha, *Israel* 70 D2
Be'er Sheva, *Israel* 75 D3
Beersheba = Be'er Sheva, *Israel* 75 D3
Beeskow, *Germany* 24 C10
Beestekraal, *S. Africa* 89 D4
Beeston, *U.K.* 12 E6
Beetzendorf, *Germany* 24 C7
Beeville, *U.S.A.* 113 L6
Befale, *Dem. Rep. of the Congo* 84 D4
Befandriana, *Mahajanga, Madag.* 89 B8
Befandriana, *Toliara, Madag.* .. 89 C7
Befasy, *Madag.* 89 C7
Befotaka, *Antsiranana, Madag.* 89 A8
Befotaka, *Fianarantsoa, Madag.* 89 C8
Bega, Canalul, *Romania* 42 E5
Bégard, *France* 18 D3
Beğendik, *Turkey* 41 F10
Begoro, *Ghana* 83 D4
Begusarai, *India* 69 G12
Behābād, *Iran* 71 C8
Behala, *India* 69 H13
Behara, *Madag.* 89 C8
Behbehān, *Iran* 71 D6
Behm Canal, *U.S.A.* 104 B2
Behshahr, *Iran* 71 B7
Bei Jiang →, *China* 59 F9
Bei'an, *China* 60 B7
Beibei, *China* 58 C6
Beichuan, *China* 58 B5
Beihai, *China* 58 G7
Beijing, *China* 56 E9
Beijing □, *China* 56 E9
Beilen, *Neths.* 17 B6
Beiliu, *China* 59 F8
Beilngries, *Germany* 25 F7
Beilul, *Eritrea* 81 E5
Beinn na Faoghla = Benbecula, *U.K.* 14 D1
Beipan Jiang, *China* 58 E5
Beipiao, *China* 57 D11
Beira, *Mozam.* 87 F3
Beirut = Bayrūt, *Lebanon* 75 B4
Beiseker, *Canada* 104 C6
Beitaolaizhao, *China* 57 B13
Beitbridge, *Zimbabwe* 87 G3
Beiuş, *Romania* 42 D7
Beizhen = Binzhou, *China* 57 F10
Beizhen, *China* 57 D11
Beizhengzhen, *China* 57 B12
Beja, *Portugal* 35 G3
Béja, *Tunisia* 79 A7
Beja □, *Portugal* 35 H3
Bejaïa, *Algeria* 78 A7
Béjar, *Spain* 34 E5
Bejestān, *Iran* 71 C8
Bekçiler, *Turkey* 39 E11
Békés, *Hungary* 42 D6
Békés □, *Hungary* 42 D6
Békéscsaba, *Hungary* 42 D6
Bekilli, *Turkey* 39 C11
Bekily, *Madag.* 89 C8
Bekisopa, *Madag.* 89 C8
Bekitro, *Madag.* 89 C8
Bekodoka, *Madag.* 89 B8
Bekoji, *Ethiopia* 81 F4
Bekok, *Malaysia* 65 L4
Bekopaka, *Madag.* 89 B7
Bekwai, *Ghana* 83 D4
Bela, *India* 69 G10
Bela, *Pakistan* 68 F2
Bela Crkva, *Serbia, Yug.* 42 F6
Bela Palanka, *Serbia, Yug.* 40 C6
Bela Vista, *Brazil* 126 A4
Bela Vista, *Mozam.* 89 D5
Bélâbre, *France* 20 B5
Belalcázar, *Spain* 35 G5
Belan →, *India* 69 G9
Belanovica, *Serbia, Yug.* 40 B4
Belarus ■, *Europe* 46 F4
Belau = Palau ■, *Pac. Oc.* 52 J17
Belavenona, *Madag.* 89 C8
Belawan, *Indonesia* 62 D1
Belaya, *Ethiopia* 81 E4
Belaya Glina, *Russia* 49 G5
Belaya Kalitva, *Russia* 49 F5
Belaya Tserkov = Bila Tserkva, *Ukraine* 47 H6
Belceşti, *Romania* 43 C12
Bełchatów, *Poland* 45 G6
Belcher Is., *Canada* 102 A3
Belchite, *Spain* 32 D4
Belden, *U.S.A.* 116 E5
Belém, *Brazil* 125 D9
Belén, *Argentina* 126 B2
Belén, *Paraguay* 126 A4
Belen, *U.S.A.* 115 J10
Belene, *Bulgaria* 41 C9
Beleni, *Turkey* 72 D7
Bélesta, *France* 20 F5
Belet Uen, *Somali Rep.* 74 G4
Belev, *Russia* 46 F9
Belevi, *Turkey* 39 C9
Belfair, *U.S.A.* 116 C4
Belfast, *S. Africa* 89 D5
Belfast, *U.K.* 15 B6
Belfast, *Maine, U.S.A.* 109 C11
Belfast, *N.Y., U.S.A.* 110 D6
Belfast L., *U.K.* 15 B6
Belfield, *U.S.A.* 112 B3
Belfort, *France* 19 E13
Belfort, Territoire de □, *France* 19 E13
Belfry, *U.S.A.* 114 D9
Belgaum, *India* 66 M9
Belgioioso, *Italy* 28 C6
Belgium ■, *Europe* 17 D4
Belgodère, *France* 21 F13
Belgorod, *Russia* 47 G9
Belgorod-Dnestrovskiy = Bilhorod-Dnistrovskyy, *Ukraine* 47 J6
Belgrade = Beograd, *Serbia, Yug.* 40 B4
Belgrade, *U.S.A.* 114 D8
Belhaven, *U.S.A.* 109 H7
Beli Drim →, *Europe* 40 D4
Beli Manastir, *Croatia* 42 E3
Beli Timok →, *Serbia, Yug.* ... 40 C6
Bélice →, *Italy* 30 E5
Belinskiy, *Russia* 48 D6
Belinyu, *Indonesia* 62 E3
Beliton Is. = Belitung, *Indonesia* 62 E3
Belitung, *Indonesia* 62 E3
Beliu, *Romania* 42 D6
Belize ■, *Cent. Amer.* 119 D7
Belize City, *Belize* 119 D7
Beljakovci, *Macedonia* 40 D5
Beljanica, *Serbia, Yug.* 40 B5
Belkovskiy, Ostrov, *Russia* 51 B14
Bell →, *Canada* 102 C4
Bell I., *Canada* 103 B8
Bell-Irving →, *Canada* 104 B3
Bell Peninsula, *Canada* 101 B11
Bell Ville, *Argentina* 126 C3
Bella, *Italy* 31 B8
Bella Bella, *Canada* 104 C3
Bella Coola, *Canada* 104 C3
Bella Unión, *Uruguay* 126 C4
Bella Vista, *Corrientes, Argentina* 126 B4
Bella Vista, *Tucuman, Argentina* 126 B2
Bellac, *France* 20 B5
Bellágio, *Italy* 28 C6
Bellaire, *U.S.A.* 110 F4
Bellária, *Italy* 29 D9
Bellary, *India* 66 M10
Bellata, *Australia* 95 D4
Belle-Chasse, *U.S.A.* 113 L10
Belle Fourche, *U.S.A.* 112 C3
Belle Fourche →, *U.S.A.* 112 C3
Belle Glade, *U.S.A.* 109 M5
Belle-Île, *France* 18 E3
Belle Isle, *Canada* 103 B8
Belle Isle, Str. of, *Canada* 103 B8
Belle Plaine, *U.S.A.* 112 E8
Belle Yella, *Liberia* 82 D3
Belledonne, *France* 21 C10
Bellefontaine, *U.S.A.* 108 E4
Bellefonte, *U.S.A.* 110 F7
Bellegarde, *France* 19 E9
Bellegarde-en-Marche, *France* . 20 C6
Bellegarde-sur-Valserine, *France* 19 F12
Bellême, *France* 18 D7
Belleoram, *Canada* 103 C8
Belleville, *Canada* 102 D4
Belleville, *France* 19 F11
Belleville, *Ill., U.S.A.* 112 F10
Belleville, *Kans., U.S.A.* 112 F6
Belleville, *N.Y., U.S.A.* 111 C8
Belleville-sur-Vie, *France* 18 F5
Bellevue, *Canada* 104 D6
Bellevue, *Idaho, U.S.A.* 114 E6
Bellevue, *Nebr., U.S.A.* 112 E7
Bellevue, *Ohio, U.S.A.* 110 E2
Bellevue, *Wash., U.S.A.* 116 C4
Belley, *France* 21 C9
Bellin = Kangirsuk, *Canada* ... 101 B13
Bellinge, *Denmark* 11 J4
Bellingham, *U.S.A.* 100 D7
Bellingshausen Sea, *Antarctica* . 5 C17
Bellinzona, *Switz.* 25 J5
Bello, *Colombia* 124 B3
Bellows Falls, *U.S.A.* 111 C12
Bellpat, *Pakistan* 68 E3
Bellpuig d'Urgell, *Spain* 32 D6
Belluno, *Italy* 29 B9
Bellwood, *U.S.A.* 110 F6
Bélmez, *Spain* 35 G5
Belmont, *Canada* 110 D3
Belmont, *S. Africa* 88 D3
Belmont, *U.S.A.* 110 D6
Belmonte, *Brazil* 125 G11
Belmonte, *Portugal* 34 E3
Belmonte, *Spain* 33 F2
Belmopan, *Belize* 119 D7
Belmullet, *Ireland* 15 B2
Belo Horizonte, *Brazil* 125 G10
Belo-sur-Mer, *Madag.* 89 C7
Belo-Tsiribihina, *Madag.* 89 B7
Belogorsk = Bilohirsk, *Ukraine* 47 K8
Belogorsk, *Russia* 51 D13
Belogradchik, *Bulgaria* 40 C6
Belogradets, *Bulgaria* 41 C11
Beloha, *Madag.* 89 D8
Beloit, *Kans., U.S.A.* 112 F5
Beloit, *Wis., U.S.A.* 112 D10
Belokorovichi, *Ukraine* 47 G5
Belomorsk, *Russia* 50 C4
Belonia, *India* 67 H17
Belopolye = Bilopillya, *Ukraine* 47 G8
Belorechensk, *Russia* 49 H4
Belorussia = Belarus ■, *Europe* 46 F4
Beloslav, *Bulgaria* 41 C11
Belovo, *Bulgaria* 41 D8
Belovo, *Russia* 50 D9
Belovodsk, *Ukraine* 47 H10
Beloye, Ozero, *Russia* 46 B9
Beloye More, *Russia* 50 C4
Belozem, *Bulgaria* 41 D9
Belozersk, *Russia* 46 B9
Belpasso, *Italy* 31 E7
Belpre, *U.S.A.* 108 F5
Belrain, *India* 69 E9
Belt, *U.S.A.* 114 C8
Belterra, *Brazil* 125 D8
Beltinci, *Slovenia* 29 B13
Belton, *U.S.A.* 113 K6
Belton L., *U.S.A.* 113 K6
Beltsy = Bălţi, *Moldova* 43 C12
Belturbet, *Ireland* 15 B4
Belukha, *Russia* 50 E9

Beluran, Malaysia 62 C5
Beluša, Slovak Rep. 27 B11
Belušić, Serbia, Yug. 40 C5
Belvedere Maríttimo, Italy 31 C8
Belvès, France 20 D5
Belvidere, Ill., U.S.A. 112 D10
Belvidere, N.J., U.S.A. 111 F9
Belvis de la Jara, Spain 34 F6
Belyando →, Australia 94 C4
Belyy, Russia 46 E7
Belyy, Ostrov, Russia 50 B8
Belyy Yar, Russia 50 D9
Bełżec, Poland 45 H10
Belzig, Germany 24 C8
Belzoni, U.S.A. 113 J9
Bełżyce, Poland 45 G9
Bemaraha, Lembalemban' i, Madag. 89 B7
Bemarivo, Madag. 89 C7
Bemarivo →, Antsiranana, Madag. 89 A9
Bemarivo →, Mahajanga, Madag. 89 B8
Bemavo, Madag. 89 C8
Bembéréke, Benin 83 C5
Bembesi, Zimbabwe 87 G2
Bembesi →, Zimbabwe 87 F2
Bembézar →, Spain 35 H5
Bembibre, Spain 34 C4
Bemetara, India 69 J9
Bemidji, U.S.A. 112 B7
Bemolanga, Madag. 89 B8
Ben, Iran 71 C6
Ben Cruachan, U.K. 14 E3
Ben Dearg, U.K. 14 D4
Ben Hope, U.K. 14 C4
Ben Lawers, U.K. 14 E4
Ben Lomond, N.S.W., Australia 95 E5
Ben Lomond, Tas., Australia 94 G4
Ben Lomond, U.K. 14 E4
Ben Luc, Vietnam 65 G6
Ben Macdhui, U.K. 14 D5
Ben Mhor, U.K. 14 D1
Ben More, Arg. & Bute, U.K. 14 E2
Ben More, Stirl., U.K. 14 E4
Ben More Assynt, U.K. 14 C4
Ben Nevis, U.K. 14 E3
Ben Quang, Vietnam 64 D6
Ben Vorlich, U.K. 14 E4
Ben Wyvis, U.K. 14 D4
Bena, Nigeria 83 C6
Benāb, Iran 73 D12
Benalmádena, Spain 35 J6
Benares = Varanasi, India 69 G10
Bénat, C., France 21 E10
Benavente, Portugal 35 G2
Benavente, Spain 34 C5
Benavides, U.S.A. 113 M5
Benavides de Órbigo, Spain 34 C5
Benbecula, U.K. 14 D1
Bend, U.S.A. 114 D3
Bender Beila, Somali Rep. 74 F5
Bendery = Tighina, Moldova 43 D14
Bendorf, Germany 24 E3
Benē Beraq, Israel 75 C3
Bénéna, Mali 82 C4
Benenitra, Madag. 89 C8
Benešov, Czech Rep. 26 B7
Benevento, Italy 31 A7
Benfeld, France 19 D14
Benga, Mozam. 87 F3
Bengal, Bay of, Ind. Oc. 67 M17
Bengbis, Cameroon 83 E7
Bengbu, China 57 H9
Benghazi = Banghāzī, Libya 79 B10
Bengkalis, Indonesia 62 D2
Bengkulu, Indonesia 62 E2
Bengkulu □, Indonesia 62 E2
Bengough, Canada 105 D7
Bengtsfors, Sweden 10 E6
Benguela, Angola 85 G2
Benguérua, I., Mozam. 89 C6
Benha, Egypt 80 H7
Beni, Dem. Rep. of the Congo 86 B2
Beni →, Bolivia 124 F5
Beni Mazâr, Egypt 80 B3
Beni Mellal, Morocco 78 B4
Beni Suef, Egypt 80 J7
Beniah L., Canada 104 A6
Benicarló, Spain 32 E5
Benicássim, Spain 32 E5
Benicia, U.S.A. 116 G4
Benidorm, Spain 33 G4
Benin ■, Africa 83 D5
Benin →, Nigeria 83 D6
Benin, Bight of, W. Afr. 83 E5
Benin City, Nigeria 83 D6
Benisa, Spain 33 G5
Benitses, Greece 36 A3
Benjamin Aceval, Paraguay 126 A4
Benjamin Constant, Brazil 124 D4
Benjamin Hill, Mexico 118 A2
Benkelman, U.S.A. 112 E4
Benkovac, Croatia 29 D12
Bennett, Canada 104 B2
Bennett, L., Australia 92 D5
Bennetta, Ostrov, Russia 51 B15
Bennettsville, U.S.A. 109 H6
Bennichchāb, Mauritania 82 B1
Bennington, N.H., U.S.A. 111 D11
Bennington, Vt., U.S.A. 111 D11
Bénodet, France 18 E2
Benoni, S. Africa 89 D4
Benque Viejo, Belize 119 D7
Bensheim, Germany 25 F4
Benson, Ariz., U.S.A. 115 L8
Benson, Minn., U.S.A. 112 C7
Bent, Iran 71 E8
Benteng, Indonesia 63 F6
Bentinck I., Australia 94 B2
Bentiu, Sudan 81 F2
Bento Gonçalves, Brazil 127 B5
Benton, Ark., U.S.A. 113 H8
Benton, Calif., U.S.A. 116 H8
Benton, Ill., U.S.A. 112 G10
Benton, Pa., U.S.A. 111 E8
Benton Harbor, U.S.A. 108 D2
Bentonville, U.S.A. 113 G7
Bentu Liben, Ethiopia 81 F4
Bentung, Malaysia 65 L3
Benue □, Nigeria 83 D6
Benue →, Nigeria 83 D6
Benxi, China 57 D12
Beo, Indonesia 63 D7
Beograd, Serbia, Yug. 40 B4
Beoumi, Ivory C. 82 D3
Bepan Jiang →, China 58 E6
Beppu, Japan 55 H5
Beqaa Valley = Al Biqā, Lebanon 75 A5
Ber Mota, India 68 H3
Berach →, India 68 G6
Beraketa, Madag. 89 C7
Berane, Montenegro, Yug. 40 D3
Berat, Albania 40 F3
Berau, Teluk, Indonesia 63 E8
Beravina, Madag. 89 B8
Berber, Sudan 80 D3
Berbera, Somali Rep. 74 E4
Berbérati, C.A.R. 84 D3
Berbice →, Guyana 124 B7
Berceto, Italy 28 D6
Berchidda, Italy 30 B2
Berchtesgaden, Germany 25 H8
Berck, France 19 B8
Berdichev = Berdychiv, Ukraine 47 H5
Berdsk, Russia 50 D9
Berdyansk, Ukraine 47 J9
Berdychiv, Ukraine 47 H5
Berea, U.S.A. 108 G3
Berebere, Indonesia 63 D7
Bereda, Somali Rep. 74 E5
Berehove, Ukraine 47 H2
Berekum, Ghana 82 D4
Berenice, Egypt 80 C4
Berens →, Canada 105 C9
Berens I., Canada 105 C9
Berens River, Canada 105 C9
Beresford, U.S.A. 112 D6
Berestechko, Ukraine 47 G3
Bereşti, Romania 43 D12
Beretău →, Romania 42 C6
Berettyó →, Hungary 42 D6
Berettyóújfalu, Hungary 42 C6
Berevo, Mahajanga, Madag. 89 B7
Berevo, Toliara, Madag. 89 B7
Bereza = Byaroza, Belarus 47 F3
Berezhany, Ukraine 47 H3
Berezina = Byarezina →, Belarus 47 F6
Berezivka, Ukraine 47 J6
Berezna, Ukraine 47 G6
Berezniki, Russia 50 C5
Berezniki, Russia 50 D6
Berezovo, Russia 50 C7
Berga, Spain 32 C6
Berga, Sweden 11 G10
Bergama, Turkey 39 B9
Bérgamo, Italy 28 C6
Bergara, Spain 32 B2
Bergby, Sweden 10 D11
Bergedorf, Germany 24 B6
Bergeforsen, Sweden 10 B11
Bergen, Mecklenburg-Vorpommern, Germany 24 A9
Bergen, Niedersachsen, Germany 24 C5
Bergen, Neths. 17 B4
Bergen, Norway 9 F11
Bergen, U.S.A. 110 C7
Bergen op Zoom, Neths. 17 C4
Bergerac, France 20 D4
Bergheim, Germany 24 E2
Bergholz, U.S.A. 110 F4
Bergisch Gladbach, Germany 17 D7
Bergkamen, Germany 24 D3
Bergkvara, Sweden 11 H10
Bergshamra, Sweden 10 E12
Bergsjö, Sweden 10 C11
Bergues, France 19 B9
Bergviken, Sweden 10 C10
Bergville, S. Africa 89 D4
Berhala, Selat, Indonesia 62 E2
Berhampore = Baharampur, India 69 G13
Berhampur = Brahmapur, India 67 K14
Berheci →, Romania 43 E12
Bering Sea, Pac. Oc. 100 C1
Bering Strait, Pac. Oc. 100 B3
Beringovskiy, Russia 51 C18
Berisso, Argentina 126 C4
Berja, Spain 35 J8
Berkeley, U.S.A. 116 H4
Berkner I., Antarctica 5 D18
Berkovitsa, Bulgaria 40 C7
Berkshire, U.S.A. 111 D8
Berkshire Downs, U.K. 13 F6
Berlanga, Spain 35 G5
Berlenga, I., Portugal 35 F1
Berlin, Germany 24 C9
Berlin, Md., U.S.A. 108 F8
Berlin, N.H., U.S.A. 111 B13
Berlin, N.Y., U.S.A. 111 D11
Berlin, Wis., U.S.A. 108 D1
Berlin □, Germany 24 C9
Berlin L., U.S.A. 110 E4
Bermeja, Sierra, Spain 35 J5
Bermejo →, Formosa, Argentina 126 B4
Bermejo →, San Juan, Argentina 126 C2
Bermen, L., Canada 103 B6
Bermeo, Spain 32 B2
Bermillo de Sayago, Spain 34 D4
Bermuda ■, Atl. Oc. 98 F13
Bern, Switz. 25 J3
Bern □, Switz. 25 J3
Bernalda, Italy 31 B9
Bernalillo, U.S.A. 115 J10
Bernardo de Irigoyen, Argentina 127 B5
Bernardo O'Higgins □, Chile 126 C1
Bernardsville, U.S.A. 111 F10
Bernasconi, Argentina 126 D3
Bernau, Bayern, Germany 25 H8
Bernau, Brandenburg, Germany 24 C9
Bernay, France 18 C7
Bernburg, Germany 24 D7
Berndorf, Austria 26 D9
Berne = Bern, Switz. 25 J3
Berne = Bern □, Switz. 25 J3
Berner Alpen, Switz. 25 J3
Berneray, U.K. 14 D1
Bernier I., Australia 93 D1
Bernina, Piz, Switz. 25 J5
Bernkastel-Kues, Germany 25 F3
Beroroha, Madag. 89 C8
Béroubouay, Benin 83 C5
Beroun, Czech Rep. 26 B7
Berounka →, Czech Rep. 26 B7
Berovo, Macedonia 40 E6
Berre, Étang de, France 21 E9
Berre-l'Étang, France 21 E9
Berriane, Algeria 78 B6
Berry, France 19 F8
Berry Is., Bahamas 120 A4
Berryessa L., U.S.A. 116 G4
Berryville, U.S.A. 113 G8
Berseba, Namibia 88 D2
Bersenbrück, Germany 24 C3
Bershad, Ukraine 47 H5
Berthold, U.S.A. 112 A4
Berthoud, U.S.A. 112 E2
Bertincourt, France 19 B9
Bertoua, Cameroon 84 D2
Bertraghboy B., Ireland 15 C2
Berwick, U.S.A. 111 E8
Berwick-upon-Tweed, U.K. 12 B6
Berwyn Mts., U.K. 12 E4
Beryslav, Ukraine 47 J7
Berzasca, Romania 42 F6
Berzence, Hungary 42 D2
Besal, Pakistan 69 B5
Besalampy, Madag. 89 B7
Besançon, France 19 E13
Besar, Indonesia 62 E5
Beshenkovichi, Belarus 46 E5
Beška, Serbia, Yug. 42 E5
Beslan, Russia 49 J7
Besna Kobila, Serbia, Yug. 40 D6
Besnard L., Canada 105 B7
Besni, Turkey 70 B3
Besor, N. →, Egypt 75 D3
Bessarabiya, Moldova 47 J5
Bessarabka = Basarabeasca, Moldova 43 D13
Bessèges, France 21 D8
Bessemer, Ala., U.S.A. 109 J2
Bessemer, Mich., U.S.A. 112 B9
Bessemer, Pa., U.S.A. 110 F4
Bessin, France 18 C6
Bessines-sur-Gartempe, France 20 B5
Beswick, Australia 92 B5
Bet She'an, Israel 75 C4
Bet Shemesh, Israel 75 D4
Betafo, Madag. 89 B8
Betancuria, Canary Is. 37 F5
Betanzos, Spain 34 B2
Bétaré Oya, Cameroon 84 C2
Betatao, Madag. 89 B8
Bétera, Spain 33 F4
Bétérou, Benin 83 D5
Bethal, S. Africa 89 D4
Bethanien, Namibia 88 D2
Bethany, Canada 110 B6
Bethany, U.S.A. 112 E7
Bethel, Alaska, U.S.A. 100 B3
Bethel, Conn., U.S.A. 111 E11
Bethel, Maine, U.S.A. 111 B14
Bethel, Vt., U.S.A. 111 C12
Bethel Park, U.S.A. 110 F4
Béthenville, France 19 C11
Bethlehem = Bayt Lahm, West Bank 75 D4
Bethlehem, S. Africa 89 D4
Bethlehem, U.S.A. 111 F9
Bethulie, S. Africa 88 E4
Béthune, France 19 B9
Béthune →, France 18 C8
Betioky, Madag. 89 C7
Betong, Thailand 65 K3
Betoota, Australia 94 D3
Betor, Ethiopia 81 E4
Betroka, Madag. 89 C8
Betsiamites, Canada 103 C6
Betsiamites →, Canada 103 C6
Betsiboka →, Madag. 89 B8
Bettendorf, U.S.A. 112 E9
Bettiah, India 69 F11
Bettna, Sweden 11 F10
Béttola, Italy 28 D6
Betul, India 66 J10
Betung, Malaysia 62 D4
Betws-y-Coed, U.K. 12 D4
Betxi, Spain 32 F4
Betzdorf, Germany 24 E3
Beuil, France 21 D10
Beulah, Mich., U.S.A. 108 C2
Beulah, N. Dak., U.S.A. 112 B4
Beuvron →, France 18 E8
Beveren, Belgium 17 C4
Beverley, Australia 93 F2
Beverley, U.K. 12 D7
Beverley Hills, U.S.A. 109 L4
Beverly, U.S.A. 111 D14
Beverly Hills, U.S.A. 117 L8
Beverungen, Germany 24 D5
Bevoalavo, Madag. 89 D7
Bewas →, India 69 H8
Bex, Switz. 25 J3
Bexhill, U.K. 13 G8
Bey Dağları, Turkey 39 E12
Beyānlū, Iran 70 C5
Beyazköy, Turkey 41 E11
Beyçayırı, Turkey 41 F10
Beydağ, Turkey 39 C10
Beyeğaç, Turkey 39 D10
Beyin, Ghana 82 D4
Beykoz, Turkey 41 E13
Beyla, Guinea 82 D3
Beynat, France 20 C5
Beyneu, Kazakstan 50 E6
Beyoba, Turkey 39 C9
Beyoğlu, Turkey 41 E12
Beypazarı, Turkey 72 B4
Beyşehir, Turkey 72 D4
Beyşehir Gölü, Turkey 70 B1
Beytüşşebap, Turkey 73 D10
Bezdan, Serbia, Yug. 42 E3
Bezhetsk, Russia 46 D9
Béziers, France 20 E7
Bezwada = Vijayawada, India 67 L12
Bhabua, India 69 G10
Bhachau, India 66 H7
Bhadar →, Gujarat, India 68 H5
Bhadar →, Gujarat, India 68 J3
Bhadarwah, India 69 C6
Bhadohi, India 69 G10
Bhadra, India 68 E6
Bhadrakh, India 67 J15
Bhadran, India 68 H5
Bhadravati, India 66 N9
Bhag, Pakistan 68 E2
Bhagalpur, India 69 G12
Bhagirathi →, Ut. P., India 69 D8
Bhagirathi →, W. Bengal, India 69 H13
Bhakkar, Pakistan 68 D4
Bhakra Dam, India 68 D7
Bhamo, Burma 67 G20
Bhandara, India 66 J11
Bhanpura, India 68 G6
Bhanrer Ra., India 69 H8
Bhaptiahi, India 69 F12
Bharat = India ■, Asia 66 K11
Bharatpur, Mad. P., India 69 H9
Bharatpur, Raj., India 68 F7
Bharno, India 69 H11
Bhatinda, India 68 D6
Bhatpara, India 69 H13
Bhattu, India 68 E6
Bhaun, Pakistan 68 C5
Bhaunagar = Bhavnagar, India 66 J8
Bhavnagar, India 66 J8
Bhawari, India 68 G5
Bhayavadar, India 68 J4
Bhera, Pakistan 68 C5
Bhikangaon, India 68 J6
Bhilsa = Vidisha, India 68 H7
Bhilwara, India 68 G6
Bhima →, India 66 L10
Bhimbar, Pakistan 69 C6
Bhind, India 69 F8
Bhinga, India 69 F9
Bhinmal, India 68 G5
Bhiwandi, India 66 K8
Bhiwani, India 68 E7
Bhogava →, India 68 H5
Bhola, Bangla. 67 H17
Bholari, Pakistan 68 G3
Bhopal, India 68 H7
Bhubaneshwar, India 67 J14
Bhuj, India 68 H3
Bhusaval, India 66 J9
Bhutan ■, Asia 67 F17
Biafra, B. of = Bonny, Bight of, Africa 83 E6
Biak, Indonesia 63 E9
Biała, Poland 45 H4
Biała →, Poland 45 H7
Biała Piska, Poland 44 E9
Biała Podlaska, Poland 45 F10
Biała Rawska, Poland 45 G7
Białobrzegi, Poland 45 G7
Białogard, Poland 44 D2
Białowieża, Poland 45 F10
Biały Bór, Poland 44 E3
Białystok, Poland 45 E10
Biancavilla, Italy 31 E7
Bianco, Italy 31 D9
Biankouma, Ivory C. 82 D3
Biaora, India 68 H7
Bīārjmand, Iran 71 B7
Biaro, Indonesia 63 D7
Biarritz, France 20 E2
Biasca, Switz. 25 J4
Biba, Egypt 80 J7
Bibai, Japan 54 C10
Bibbiena, Italy 29 E8
Bibby I., Canada 105 A10
Bibel →, Spain 34 C3
Biberach, Germany 25 G5
Bibiani, Ghana 82 D4
Bibungwa, Dem. Rep. of the Congo 86 C2
Bic, Canada 103 C6
Bicaj, Albania 40 E4
Bicaz, Romania 43 D11
Bicazu Ardelean, Romania 43 D10
Bíccari, Italy 31 A8
Bicester, U.K. 13 F6
Bichena, Ethiopia 81 E4
Bicheno, Australia 94 G4
Bichia, India 69 H9
Bichvinta, Georgia 49 J5
Bickerton I., Australia 94 A2
Bicske, Hungary 42 C3
Bida, Nigeria 83 D6
Bidar, India 66 L10
Biddeford, U.S.A. 109 D10
Biddwara, Ethiopia 81 F4
Bideford, U.K. 13 F3
Bideford Bay, U.K. 13 F3
Bidhuna, India 69 F8
Bidor, Malaysia 65 K3
Bie, Sweden 10 E10
Bié, Planalto de, Angola 85 G3
Bieber, U.S.A. 114 F3
Biebrza →, Poland 45 E9
Biecz, Poland 45 J8
Biel, Switz. 25 H3
Bielawa, Poland 45 H3
Bielefeld, Germany 24 C4
Bielersee, Switz. 25 H3
Biella, Italy 28 C5
Bielsk Podlaski, Poland 45 F10
Bielsko-Biała, Poland 45 J6
Bien Hoa, Vietnam 65 G6
Bienne = Biel, Switz. 25 H3
Bienvenida, Spain 35 G4
Bienville, L., Canada 102 A5
Bierné, France 18 E6
Bierun, Poland 45 H6
Bierutów, Poland 45 G4
Biescas, Spain 32 C4
Biese →, Germany 24 C7
Biesiesfontein, S. Africa 88 E2
Bietigheim-Bissingen, Germany 25 G5
Bieżuń, Poland 45 F6
Biferno →, Italy 29 G12
Big →, Canada 103 B8
Big B., Canada 103 A7
Big Bear City, U.S.A. 117 L10
Big Bear Lake, U.S.A. 117 L10
Big Belt Mts., U.S.A. 114 C8
Big Bend, Swaziland 89 D5
Big Bend National Park, U.S.A. 113 L3
Big Black →, U.S.A. 113 K9
Big Blue →, U.S.A. 112 F6
Big Creek, U.S.A. 116 H7
Big Cypress National Preserve, U.S.A. 109 M5
Big Cypress Swamp, U.S.A. 109 M5
Big Falls, U.S.A. 112 A8
Big Fork →, U.S.A. 112 A8
Big Horn Mts. = Bighorn Mts., U.S.A. 114 D10
Big I., Canada 104 A5
Big Lake, U.S.A. 113 K4
Big Moose, U.S.A. 111 C10
Big Muddy Cr. →, U.S.A. 112 A2
Big Pine, U.S.A. 116 H8
Big Piney, U.S.A. 114 E8
Big Rapids, U.S.A. 108 D3
Big Rideau L., Canada 111 B8
Big River, Canada 105 C7
Big Run, U.S.A. 110 F6
Big Sable Pt., U.S.A. 108 C2
Big Salmon →, Canada 104 A2
Big Sand L., Canada 105 B9
Big Sandy, U.S.A. 114 B8
Big Sandy →, U.S.A. 108 F4
Big Sandy Cr. →, U.S.A. 112 F3
Big Sioux →, U.S.A. 112 D6
Big Spring, U.S.A. 113 J4
Big Stone City, U.S.A. 112 C6
Big Stone Gap, U.S.A. 109 G4
Big Stone L., U.S.A. 112 C6
Big Sur, U.S.A. 116 J5
Big Timber, U.S.A. 114 D9
Big Trout L., Canada 102 B2
Big Trout Lake, Canada 102 B2
Biğa, Turkey 41 F11
Biga →, Turkey 41 F11
Bigadiç, Turkey 39 B10
Biganos, France 20 D3
Biggar, Canada 105 C7
Biggar, U.K. 14 F5
Bigge I., Australia 92 B4
Biggenden, Australia 95 D5
Biggleswade, U.K. 13 E7
Biggs, U.S.A. 116 F5
Bighorn, U.S.A. 114 C10
Bighorn →, U.S.A. 114 C10
Bighorn L., U.S.A. 114 D9
Bighorn Mts., U.S.A. 114 D10
Bignona, Senegal 82 C1
Bigorre, France 20 E4

Bigstone L., Canada 105 C9
Biguglia, Étang de, France 21 F13
Bigwa, Tanzania 86 D4
Bihać, Bos.-H. 29 D12
Bihar, India 69 G11
Bihar □, India 69 G12
Biharamulo, Tanzania 86 C3
Bihariganj, India 69 G12
Biharkeresztes, Hungary 42 C6
Bihor □, Romania 42 D7
Bihor, Munţii, Romania 42 D7
Bijagós, Arquipélago dos, Guinea-Biss. 82 C1
Bijaipur, India 68 F7
Bijapur, Karnataka, India 66 L9
Bijapur, Mad. P., India 67 K12
Bījār, Iran 70 C5
Bijawar, India 69 G8
Bijeljina, Bos.-H. 42 F4
Bijelo Polje, Montenegro, Yug. 40 C3
Bijie, China 58 D5
Bijnor, India 68 E8
Bikaner, India 68 E5
Bikapur, India 69 F10
Bikeqi, China 56 D6
Bikfayyā, Lebanon 75 B4
Bikin, Russia 51 E14
Bikin →, Russia 54 A7
Bikini Atoll, Marshall Is. 96 F8
Bikita, Zimbabwe 89 C5
Bikoué, Cameroon 83 E7
Bila Tserkva, Ukraine 47 H6
Bilanga, Burkina Faso 83 C4
Bilara, India 68 F5
Bilaspur, Mad. P., India 69 H10
Bilaspur, Punjab, India 68 D7
Biläsuvar, Azerbaijan 73 C13
Bilauk Taungdan, Thailand 64 F2
Bilbao, Spain 32 B2
Bilbeis, Egypt 80 H7
Bilbo = Bilbao, Spain 32 B2
Bilbor, Romania 43 C10
Bilciureşti, Romania 43 F10
Bíldudalur, Iceland 8 D2
Bílé Karpaty, Europe 27 B11
Bileća, Bos.-H. 40 D2
Bilecik, Turkey 72 B4
Biłgoraj, Poland 45 H9
Bilgram, India 69 F9
Bilhaur, India 69 F9
Bilhorod-Dnistrovskyy, Ukraine 47 J6
Bilibino, Russia 51 C17
Bilibiza, Mozam. 87 E5
Bilisht, Albania 40 F5
Billabalong Roadhouse, Australia 93 E2
Billdal, Sweden 11 G5
Billiluna, Australia 92 C4
Billings, U.S.A. 114 D9
Billiton Is. = Belitung, Indonesia 62 E3
Billsta, Sweden 10 A12
Billund, Denmark 11 J3
Bilma, Niger 79 E8
Bilo Gora, Croatia 42 E2
Biloela, Australia 94 C5
Bilohirsk, Ukraine 47 K8
Bilopillya, Ukraine 47 G8
Biloxi, U.S.A. 113 K10
Bilpa Morea Claypan, Australia 94 D3
Biltine, Chad 79 F10
Bilyarsk, Russia 48 C10
Bima, Indonesia 63 F5
Bimban, Egypt 80 C3
Bimbila, Ghana 83 D5
Bimini Is., Bahamas 120 A4
Bin Xian, Heilongjiang, China 57 B14
Bin Xian, Shaanxi, China 56 G5
Bin Yauri, Nigeria 83 C5
Bina-Etawah, India 68 G8
Bināb, Iran 71 B6
Binalbagan, Phil. 61 F5
Bīnālūd, Kūh-e, Iran 71 B8
Binatang = Bintangor, Malaysia 62 D4
Binche, Belgium 17 D4
Binchuan, China 58 E3
Binder, Chad 83 D7
Bindki, India 69 F9
Bindslev, Denmark 11 G4
Bindura, Zimbabwe 87 F3
Binefar, Spain 32 D5
Bingara, Australia 95 D5
Bingen, Germany 25 F3
Bingerville, Ivory C. 82 D4
Bingham, U.S.A. 109 C11
Binghamton, U.S.A. 111 D9
Bingöl, Turkey 70 B4
Bingöl Dağları, Turkey 73 C9
Bingsjö, Sweden 10 C9
Binh Dinh = An Nhon, Vietnam 64 F7
Binh Khe, Vietnam 64 F7
Binh Son, Vietnam 64 E7
Binhai, China 57 G10
Binic, France 18 D4
Binisatua, Spain 37 B11
Binjai, Indonesia 62 D3
Binji, Nigeria 83 C5
Binongko, Indonesia 63 F6
Binscarth, Canada 105 C8
Bint Goda, Sudan 81 E3
Bintan, Indonesia 62 D2
Bintangor, Malaysia 62 D4
Bintulu, Malaysia 62 D4
Bintuni, Indonesia 63 E8
Binyang, China 58 F7
Binz, Germany 24 A9
Binzert = Bizerte, Tunisia 79 A7
Binzhou, China 57 F10
Bío Bío □, Chile 126 D1
Biograd na Moru, Croatia 29 E12
Bioko, Eq. Guin. 83 E6
Biokovo, Croatia 29 E14
Bipindi, Cameroon 83 E7
Bir, India 66 K9
Bir, Ras, Djibouti 81 E5
Bîr Abu Hashim, Egypt 80 C3
Bîr Abu Minqar, Egypt 80 B2
Bîr Abu Muḥammad, Egypt 75 F3
Bi'r ad Dabbāghāt, Jordan 75 E4
Bîr Adal Deib, Sudan 80 C4
Bi'r al Butayyihāt, Jordan 75 F4
Bi'r al Mārī, Jordan 75 E4
Bi'r al Qattār, Jordan 75 F4
Bîr 'Asal, Egypt 80 B3
Bir Atrun, Sudan 80 D2
Bîr Beiḍa, Egypt 75 E3
Bîr Diqnash, Egypt 80 A2
Bîr el 'Abd, Egypt 75 D2
Bîr el Basur, Egypt 80 B2
Bîr el Biarât, Egypt 75 F3
Bîr el Duweidar, Egypt 75 E1
Bîr el Garârât, Egypt 75 D2
Bîr el Gellaz, Egypt 80 A2
Bîr el Heisi, Egypt 75 F3
Bîr el Jafir, Egypt 75 E1
Bîr el Mâlḥi, Egypt 75 E2
Bîr el Shaqqa, Egypt 80 A2
Bîr el Thamâda, Egypt 75 E2
Bîr Fuad, Egypt 80 A2
Bîr Gebeil Ḥiṣn, Egypt 75 E2
Bi'r Ghadīr, Syria 75 A6
Bîr Haimur, Egypt 80 C3
Bîr Ḥasana, Egypt 75 E2
Bîr Hôôker, Egypt 80 H7
Bîr Kanayis, Egypt 80 C3
Bîr Kaseiba, Egypt 75 E2
Bîr Kerawein, Egypt 80 B2
Bîr Lahfân, Egypt 75 E2
Bîr Madkûr, Egypt 75 E1
Bîr Maql, Egypt 80 C3
Bîr Mîneiga, Sudan 80 C4
Bîr Misaha, Egypt 80 C2
Bîr Mogreïn, Mauritania 78 C3
Bîr Murr, Egypt 80 C3
Bi'r Muţribah, Kuwait 70 D5
Bîr Nakheila, Egypt 80 C3
Bîr Qatia, Egypt 75 E1
Bîr Qatrani, Egypt 80 A2
Bîr Ranga, Egypt 80 C4
Bîr Sahara, Egypt 80 C2
Bîr Seiyâla, Egypt 80 B3
Bîr Shalatein, Egypt 80 C4
Bîr Shebb, Egypt 80 C2
Bîr Shût, Egypt 80 C4
Bîr Terfawi, Egypt 80 C2
Bîr Umm Qubûr, Egypt 80 C3
Bîr Ungât, Egypt 80 C3
Bîr Za'farâna, Egypt 80 J8
Bîr Zeidûn, Egypt 80 B3
Biramféro, Guinea 82 C3
Biratnagar, Nepal 69 F12
Birawa, Dem. Rep. of the Congo 86 C2
Birch →, Canada 104 B6
Birch Hills, Canada 105 C7
Birch I., Canada 105 C9
Birch L., N.W.T., Canada 104 A5
Birch L., Ont., Canada 102 B1
Birch Mts., Canada 104 B6
Birch River, Canada 105 C8
Birchiş, Romania 42 E7
Bird, Canada 105 B10
Bird I. = Las Aves, Is., W. Indies 121 C7
Birdsville, Australia 94 D2
Birdum Cr. →, Australia 92 C5
Birecik, Turkey 70 B3
Bireuen, Indonesia 62 C1
Birein, Israel 75 E3
Biri →, Sudan 81 F2
Birifo, Gambia 82 C2
Birigui, Brazil 127 A5
Birjand, Iran 71 C8
Birkenfeld, Germany 25 F3
Birkenhead, U.K. 12 D4
Birkerød, Denmark 11 J6
Birket Qârûn, Egypt 80 J7
Birkfeld, Austria 26 D8
Bîrlad = Bârlad, Romania 43 D12
Birmingham, U.K. 13 E6
Birmingham, U.S.A. 109 J2
Birmitrapur, India 67 H14
Birni Ngaouré, Niger 83 C5
Birni Nkonni, Niger 83 C6
Birnin Gwari, Nigeria 83 C6
Birnin Kebbi, Nigeria 83 C5
Birnin Kudu, Nigeria 83 C6
Birobidzhan, Russia 51 E14
Birr, Ireland 15 C4
Birrie →, Australia 95 D4
Birsilpur, India 68 E5
Birsk, Russia 50 D6
Birštonas, Lithuania 44 D11
Birtle, Canada 105 C8
Birur, India 66 N9
Biryuchiy, Ukraine 47 J8
Biržai, Lithuania 9 H21
Birzebbugga, Malta 36 D2
Bisa, Indonesia 63 E7
Bisáccia, Italy 31 A8
Bisacquino, Italy 30 E6
Bisalpur, India 69 E8
Bisbee, U.S.A. 115 L9
Biscarrosse, France 20 D2
Biscarrosse et de Parentis, Étang de, France 20 D2
Biscay, B. of, Atl. Oc. 6 F5
Biscayne B., U.S.A. 109 N5
Biscéglie, Italy 31 A9
Bischheim, France 19 D14
Bischofshofen, Austria 26 D6
Bischofswerda, Germany 24 D10
Bischwiller, France 19 D14
Biscoe Bay, Antarctica 5 D13
Biscoe Is., Antarctica 5 C17
Biscostasing, Canada 102 C3
Biševo, Croatia 29 F13
Bisha, Eritrea 81 D4
Bishah, W. →, Si. Arabia 80 C5
Bishan, China 58 C6
Bishkek, Kyrgyzstan 50 E8
Bishnupur, India 69 H12
Bisho, S. Africa 89 E4
Bishop, Calif., U.S.A. 116 H8
Bishop, Tex., U.S.A. 113 M6
Bishop Auckland, U.K. 12 C6
Bishop's Falls, Canada 103 C8
Bishop's Stortford, U.K. 13 F8
Bisignano, Italy 31 C9
Bisina, L., Uganda 86 B3
Biskra, Algeria 78 B7
Biskupiec, Poland 44 E7
Bismarck, U.S.A. 112 B4
Bismarck Arch., Papua N. G. 96 H7
Bismark, Germany 24 C7
Bismil, Turkey 73 D9
Biso, Uganda 86 B3
Bison, U.S.A. 112 C3
Bīsotūn, Iran 70 C5
Bispgården, Sweden 10 A10
Bissagos = Bijagós, Arquipélago dos, Guinea-Biss. 82 C1
Bissau, Guinea-Biss. 82 C1
Bissaula, Nigeria 83 D7
Bissikrima, Guinea 82 C2
Bissorã, Guinea-Biss. 82 C1
Bistcho L., Canada 104 B5
Bistreţ, Romania 43 G8
Bistrica = Ilirska-Bistrica, Slovenia 29 C11
Bistriţa, Romania 43 C9
Bistriţa →, Romania 43 D11
Bistriţa Năsăud □, Romania 43 C9
Bistriţei, Munţii, Romania 43 C10
Biswan, India 69 F9
Bisztynek, Poland 44 D7
Bitburg, Germany 25 F2
Bitche, France 19 C14
Bithynia, Turkey 72 B4
Bitlis, Turkey 70 B4
Bitola, Macedonia 40 E5
Bitolj = Bitola, Macedonia 40 E5
Bitonto, Italy 31 A9
Bitter Creek, U.S.A. 114 F9
Bitter L. = Buheirat-Murrat-el-Kubra, Egypt 80 H8
Bitterfeld, Germany 24 D8
Bitterfontein, S. Africa 88 E2
Bitterroot →, U.S.A. 114 C6
Bitterroot Range, U.S.A. 114 D6
Bitterwater, U.S.A. 116 J6
Bitti, Italy 30 B2
Bittou, Burkina Faso 83 C4
Biu, Nigeria 83 C7
Bivolari, Romania 43 C12
Bivolu, Vf., Romania 43 C10
Biwa-Ko, Japan 55 G8
Biwabik, U.S.A. 112 B8
Bixad, Romania 43 C8
Bixby, U.S.A. 113 H7
Biyang, China 56 H7
Biysk, Russia 50 D9
Bizana, S. Africa 89 E4
Bizen, Japan 55 G7
Bizerte, Tunisia 79 A7
Bjargtangar, Iceland 8 D1
Bjärnum, Sweden 11 H7
Bjästa, Sweden 10 A12
Bjelasica, Montenegro, Yug. 40 D3
Bjelašnica, Bos.-H. 42 G3
Bjelovar, Croatia 29 C13
Bjerringbro, Denmark 11 H3
Björbo, Sweden 10 D8
Björklinge, Sweden 10 D11
Björneborg, Sweden 10 E8
Bjørnevatn, Norway 8 B23
Bjørnøya, Arctic 4 B8
Bjursås, Sweden 10 D9
Bjuv, Sweden 11 H6
Bla, Mali 82 C3
Blace, Serbia, Yug. 40 C5
Blachownia, Poland 45 H5
Black = Da →, Vietnam 58 G5
Black →, Canada 110 B5
Black →, Ariz., U.S.A. 115 K8
Black →, Ark., U.S.A. 113 H9
Black →, Mich., U.S.A. 110 D2
Black →, N.Y., U.S.A. 111 C8
Black →, Wis., U.S.A. 112 D9
Black Bay Pen., Canada 102 C2
Black Birch L., Canada 105 B7
Black Diamond, Canada 104 C6
Black Duck →, Canada 102 A2
Black Forest = Schwarzwald, Germany 25 G4
Black Forest, U.S.A. 112 F2
Black Hd., Ireland 15 C2
Black Hills, U.S.A. 112 D3
Black I., Canada 105 C9
Black L., Canada 105 B7
Black L., Mich., U.S.A. 108 C3
Black L., N.Y., U.S.A. 111 B9
Black Lake, Canada 105 B7
Black Mesa, U.S.A. 113 G3
Black Mt. = Mynydd Du, U.K. 13 F4
Black Mts., U.K. 13 F4
Black Range, U.S.A. 115 K10
Black River, Jamaica 120 C4
Black River Falls, U.S.A. 112 C9
Black Sea, Eurasia 6 G12
Black Tickle, Canada 103 B8
Black Volta →, Africa 82 D4
Black Warrior →, U.S.A. 109 J2
Blackall, Australia 94 C4
Blackball, N.Z. 91 K3
Blackbull, Australia 94 B3
Blackburn, U.K. 12 D5
Blackburn with Darwen □, U.K. 12 D5
Blackfoot, U.S.A. 114 E7
Blackfoot →, U.S.A. 114 C7
Blackfoot River Reservoir, U.S.A. 114 E8
Blackpool, U.K. 12 D4
Blackpool □, U.K. 12 D4
Blackriver, U.S.A. 110 B1
Blacks Harbour, Canada 103 C6
Blacksburg, U.S.A. 108 G5
Blacksod B., Ireland 15 B1
Blackstone, U.S.A. 108 G7
Blackstone Ra., Australia 93 E4
Blackwater, Australia 94 C4
Blackwater →, Meath, Ireland 15 C4
Blackwater →, Waterford, Ireland 15 D4
Blackwater →, U.K. 15 B5
Blackwell, U.S.A. 113 G6
Blackwells Corner, U.S.A. 117 K7
Blaenau Ffestiniog, U.K. 12 E4
Blaenau Gwent □, U.K. 13 F4
Blagaj, Bos.-H. 40 C1
Blagnac, France 20 E5
Blagodarnoye = Blagodarnyy, Russia 49 H6
Blagodarnyy, Russia 49 H6
Blagoevgrad, Bulgaria 40 D7
Blagoveshchensk, Russia 51 D13
Blain, France 18 E5
Blain, U.S.A. 110 F7
Blaine, Minn., U.S.A. 112 C8
Blaine, Wash., U.S.A. 116 B4
Blaine Lake, Canada 105 C7
Blair, U.S.A. 112 E6
Blair Athol, Australia 94 C4
Blair Atholl, U.K. 14 E5
Blairgowrie, U.K. 14 E5
Blairsden, U.S.A. 116 F6
Blairsville, U.S.A. 110 F5
Blaj, Romania 43 D8
Blake Pt., U.S.A. 112 A10
Blakely, Ga., U.S.A. 109 K3
Blakely, Pa., U.S.A. 111 E9
Blâmont, France 19 D13
Blanc, C., Spain 37 B9
Blanc, Mont, Alps 21 C10
Blanc-Sablon, Canada 103 B8
Blanca, B., Argentina 122 G4
Blanca Peak, U.S.A. 115 H11
Blanche, C., Australia 95 E1
Blanche, L., S. Austral., Australia 95 D2
Blanche, L., W. Austral., Australia 92 D3
Blanco, S. Africa 88 E3
Blanco, U.S.A. 113 K5
Blanco →, Argentina 126 C2
Blanco, C., Costa Rica 120 E2
Blanco, C., U.S.A. 114 E1
Blanda →, Iceland 8 D3
Blandford Forum, U.K. 13 G5
Blanding, U.S.A. 115 H9
Blanes, Spain 32 D7
Blangy-sur-Bresle, France 19 C8
Blanice →, Czech Rep. 26 B7
Blankaholm, Sweden 11 G10
Blankenberge, Belgium 17 C3
Blankenburg, Germany 24 D6
Blanquefort, France 20 D3
Blanquilla, I., Venezuela 121 D7
Blanquillo, Uruguay 127 C4
Blansko, Czech Rep. 27 B9
Blantyre, Malawi 87 F4
Blarney, Ireland 15 E3
Blasdell, U.S.A. 110 D6
Błaszki, Poland 45 G5
Blatná, Czech Rep. 26 B6
Blato, Croatia 29 F13
Blaubeuren, Germany 25 G5
Blaustein, Germany 25 G5
Blåvands Huk, Denmark 11 J2
Blaydon, U.K. 12 C6
Blaye, France 20 C3
Blaye-les-Mines, France 20 D6
Blaze, Pt., Australia 92 B5
Błażowa, Poland 45 J9
Bleckede, Germany 24 B6
Bled, Slovenia 29 B11
Bleiburg, Austria 26 E7
Blejeşti, Romania 43 F10
Blekinge, Sweden 9 H16
Blekinge län □, Sweden 11 H9
Blenheim, Canada 110 D3
Blenheim, N.Z. 91 J4
Bléone →, France 21 D10
Blérancourt, France 19 C10
Bletchley, U.K. 13 F7
Blida, Algeria 78 A6
Blidö, Sweden 10 E12
Blidsberg, Sweden 11 G7
Blieskastel, Germany 25 F3
Bligh Sound, N.Z. 91 L1
Blind River, Canada 102 C3
Blinisht, Albania 40 E3
Bliss, Idaho, U.S.A. 114 E6
Bliss, N.Y., U.S.A. 110 D6
Blissfield, U.S.A. 110 F3
Blitar, Indonesia 63 H15
Blitta, Togo 83 D5
Block I., U.S.A. 111 E13
Block Island Sd., U.S.A. 111 E13
Blodgett Iceberg Tongue, Antarctica 5 C9
Bloemfontein, S. Africa 88 D4
Bloemhof, S. Africa 88 D4
Blois, France 18 E8
Blomskog, Sweden 10 E6
Blomstermåla, Sweden 11 H10
Blönduós, Iceland 8 D3
Błonie, Poland 45 F7
Bloodvein →, Canada 105 C9
Bloody Foreland, Ireland 15 A3
Bloomer, U.S.A. 112 C9
Bloomfield, Canada 110 C7
Bloomfield, Iowa, U.S.A. 112 E8
Bloomfield, N. Mex., U.S.A. 115 H10
Bloomfield, Nebr., U.S.A. 112 D6
Bloomington, Ill., U.S.A. 112 E10
Bloomington, Ind., U.S.A. 108 F2
Bloomington, Minn., U.S.A. 112 C8
Bloomsburg, U.S.A. 111 F8
Blora, Indonesia 63 G14
Blossburg, U.S.A. 110 E7
Blouberg, S. Africa 89 C4
Blountstown, U.S.A. 109 K3
Bludenz, Austria 26 D2
Blue Earth, U.S.A. 112 D8
Blue Mesa Reservoir, U.S.A. 115 G10
Blue Mountain Lake, U.S.A. 111 C10
Blue Mts., Maine, U.S.A. 111 B14
Blue Mts., Oreg., U.S.A. 114 D4
Blue Mts., Pa., U.S.A. 111 F8
Blue Mud B., Australia 94 A2
Blue Nile = Nîl el Azraq →, Sudan 81 D3
Blue Rapids, U.S.A. 112 F6
Blue Ridge Mts., U.S.A. 109 G5
Blue River, Canada 104 C5
Bluefield, U.S.A. 108 G5
Bluefields, Nic. 120 D3
Bluff, Australia 94 C4
Bluff, N.Z. 91 M2
Bluff, U.S.A. 115 H9
Bluff Knoll, Australia 93 F2
Bluff Pt., Australia 93 E1
Bluffton, U.S.A. 108 E3
Blumenau, Brazil 127 B6
Blunt, U.S.A. 112 C5
Bly, U.S.A. 114 E3
Blyth, Canada 110 C3
Blyth, U.K. 12 B6
Blythe, U.S.A. 117 M12
Blytheville, U.S.A. 113 H10
Bo, S. Leone 82 D2
Bo Duc, Vietnam 65 G6
Bo Hai, China 57 E10
Bo Xian = Bozhou, China 56 H8
Boa Vista, Brazil 124 C6
Boac, Phil. 61 E4
Boaco, Nic. 120 D2
Bo'ai, China 56 G7
Boal, Spain 34 B4
Boalsburg, U.S.A. 110 F7
Boane, Mozam. 89 D5
Boardman, U.S.A. 110 E4
Bobai, China 58 F7
Bobbili, India 67 K13
Bóbbio, Italy 28 D6
Bobcaygeon, Canada 102 D4
Böblingen, Germany 25 G5
Bobo-Dioulasso, Burkina Faso 82 C4
Bobolice, Poland 44 E3
Boboshevo, Bulgaria 40 D7
Bobov Dol, Bulgaria 40 D6
Bóbr →, Poland 45 F2
Bobraomby, Tanjon' i, Madag. 89 A8
Bobrinets, Ukraine 47 H7
Bobrov, Russia 48 E5
Bobrovitsa, Ukraine 47 G6
Bobruysk = Babruysk, Belarus 47 F5
Boby, Pic, Madag. 85 J9
Bôca do Acre, Brazil 124 E5
Boca Raton, U.S.A. 109 M5
Bocanda, Ivory C. 82 D4
Bocas del Toro, Panama 120 E3
Boceguillas, Spain 34 D7
Bochnia, Poland 45 J7
Bocholt, Germany 24 D2
Bochum, Germany 24 D3
Bockenem, Germany 24 C6
Boćki, Poland 45 F10
Bocognano, France 21 F13
Bocoyna, Mexico 118 B3
Bocşa, Romania 42 E6
Boda, Dalarnas, Sweden 10 C9
Böda, Kalmar, Sweden 11 G11
Boda, Västernorrland, Sweden 10 B10
Bodafors, Sweden 11 G8
Bodaybo, Russia 51 D12
Boddam, U.K. 14 B7

Boddington, *Australia* 93 F2
Bode Sadu, *Nigeria* 83 D5
Bodega Bay, *U.S.A.* 116 G3
Boden, *Sweden* 8 D19
Bodensee, *Europe* 25 H5
Bodenteich, *Germany* 24 C6
Bodhan, *India* 66 K10
Bodinga, *Nigeria* 83 C6
Bodmin, *U.K.* 13 G3
Bodmin Moor, *U.K.* 13 G3
Bodø, *Norway* 8 C16
Bodrog →, *Hungary* 42 B6
Bodrum, *Turkey* 39 D9
Bódva →, *Hungary* 42 B5
Boën, *France* 21 C8
Boende, *Dem. Rep. of the Congo* 84 E4
Boerne, *U.S.A.* 113 L5
Boesmans →, *S. Africa* 88 E4
Boffa, *Guinea* 82 C2
Bogalusa, *U.S.A.* 113 K10
Bogan →, *Australia* 95 D4
Bogandé, *Burkina Faso* 83 C4
Bogantungan, *Australia* 94 C4
Bogata, *U.S.A.* 113 J7
Bogatić, *Serbia, Yug.* 40 B3
Boğazkale, *Turkey* 72 B6
Boğazlıyan, *Turkey* 72 C6
Bogen, *Sweden* 10 D6
Bogense, *Denmark* 11 J4
Bogetići, *Montenegro, Yug.* 40 D2
Boggabilla, *Australia* 95 D5
Boggeragh Mts., *Ireland* 15 D3
Boglan = Solhan, *Turkey* 70 B4
Bognor Regis, *U.K.* 13 G7
Bogo, *Phil.* 61 F6
Bogodukhov = Bohodukhiv, *Ukraine* 47 G8
Bogol Manya, *Ethiopia* 81 G5
Bogor, *Indonesia* 62 F3
Bogoroditsk, *Russia* 46 F10
Bogorodsk, *Russia* 48 B6
Bogoso, *Ghana* 82 D4
Bogotá, *Colombia* 124 C4
Bogotol, *Russia* 50 D9
Bogou, *Togo* 83 C5
Bogra, *Bangla.* 67 G16
Boguchany, *Russia* 51 D10
Boguchar, *Russia* 48 F5
Bogué, *Mauritania* 82 B2
Boguslav, *Ukraine* 47 H6
Boguszów-Gorce, *Poland* 45 H3
Bohain-en-Vermandois, *France* 19 C10
Bohemian Forest = Böhmerwald, *Germany* 25 F9
Bohinjska Bistrica, *Slovenia* 29 B11
Böhmerwald, *Germany* 25 F9
Bohmte, *Germany* 24 C4
Bohodukhiv, *Ukraine* 47 G8
Bohol □, *Phil.* 61 G6
Bohol Sea, *Phil.* 63 C6
Bohongou, *Burkina Faso* 83 C5
Böhönye, *Hungary* 42 D2
Bohuslän, *Sweden* 11 F5
Boi, *Nigeria* 83 D6
Boi, Pta. de, *Brazil* 127 A6
Boiaçu, *Brazil* 124 D6
Boileau, C., *Australia* 92 C3
Boing'o, *Sudan* 81 F3
Boiro, *Spain* 34 C2
Boise, *U.S.A.* 114 E5
Boise City, *U.S.A.* 113 G3
Boissevain, *Canada* 105 D8
Bóite →, *Italy* 29 B9
Boitzenburg, *Germany* 24 B9
Boizenburg, *Germany* 24 B6
Bojador C., *W. Sahara* 78 C3
Bojana →, *Albania* 40 E3
Bojano, *Italy* 31 A7
Bojanowo, *Poland* 45 G3
Bøjden, *Denmark* 11 J4
Bojnūrd, *Iran* 71 B8
Bojonegoro, *Indonesia* 63 G14
Boju, *Nigeria* 83 D6
Boka, *Serbia, Yug.* 42 E5
Boka Kotorska, *Montenegro, Yug.* 40 D2
Bokala, *Ivory C.* 82 D4
Bokani, *Nigeria* 83 D6
Bokaro, *India* 69 H11
Boké, *Guinea* 82 C2
Bokhara →, *Australia* 95 D4
Bokkos, *Nigeria* 83 D6
Boknafjorden, *Norway* 9 G11
Bokoro, *Chad* 79 F9
Bokpyin, *Burma* 65 G2
Boksitogorsk, *Russia* 46 C7
Bol, *Croatia* 29 E13
Bolama, *Guinea-Biss.* 82 C1
Bolan →, *Pakistan* 68 E2
Bolan Pass, *Pakistan* 66 E5
Bolaños →, *Mexico* 118 C4
Bolaños de Calatrava, *Spain* 35 G7
Bolayır, *Turkey* 41 F10
Bolbec, *France* 18 C7
Boldājī, *Iran* 71 D6
Boldeşti-Scăeni, *Romania* 43 E11
Bole, *China* 60 B3
Bole, *Ethiopia* 81 F4
Bole, *Ghana* 82 D4
Bolekhiv, *Ukraine* 47 H2
Bolesławiec, *Poland* 45 G2
Bolgatanga, *Ghana* 83 C4
Bolgrad = Bolhrad, *Ukraine* 47 K5
Bolhrad, *Ukraine* 47 K5
Bolinao, *Phil.* 61 C3
Bolintin-Vale, *Romania* 43 F10
Bolívar, *Argentina* 126 D3
Bolivar, *Mo., U.S.A.* 113 G8
Bolivar, *N.Y., U.S.A.* 110 D6
Bolivar, *Tenn., U.S.A.* 113 H10
Bolivia ■, *S. Amer.* 124 G6
Bolivian Plateau, *S. Amer.* 122 E4
Boljevac, *Serbia, Yug.* 40 C5
Bolkhov, *Russia* 46 F9
Bolków, *Poland* 45 H3
Bollebygd, *Sweden* 11 G6
Bollène, *France* 21 D8
Bollnäs, *Sweden* 10 C10
Bollon, *Australia* 95 D4
Bollstabruk, *Sweden* 10 B11
Bolmen, *Sweden* 11 H7
Bolobo, *Dem. Rep. of the Congo* 84 E3
Bologna, *Italy* 29 D8
Bologoye, *Russia* 46 D8
Bolon, Ozero, *Russia* 60 B8
Bolonchenticul, *Mexico* 119 D7
Bolótana, *Italy* 30 B1
Boloven, Cao Nguyen, *Laos* 64 E6
Bolpur, *India* 69 H12
Bolsena, *Italy* 29 F8
Bolsena, L. di, *Italy* 29 F8
Bolshaya Chernigovka, *Russia* 48 D10
Bolshaya Glushitsa, *Russia* 48 D10
Bolshaya Martynovka, *Russia* 49 G5
Bolshaya Vradiyevka, *Ukraine* 47 J6
Bolshevik, Ostrov, *Russia* 51 B11
Bolshoi Kavkas = Caucasus Mountains, *Eurasia* 49 J7
Bolshoy Anyuy →, *Russia* 51 C17
Bolshoy Begichev, Ostrov, *Russia* 51 B12
Bolshoy Lyakhovskiy, Ostrov, *Russia* 51 B15
Bolshoy Tokmak = Tokmak, *Ukraine* 47 J8
Bolshoy Tyuters, Ostrov, *Russia* 9 G22
Bolsward, *Neths.* 17 A5
Bolt Head, *U.K.* 13 G4
Boltaña, *Spain* 32 C5
Boltigen, *Switz.* 25 J3
Bolton, *Canada* 110 C5
Bolton, *U.K.* 12 D5
Bolton Landing, *U.S.A.* 111 C11
Bolu, *Turkey* 72 B4
Bolungavík, *Iceland* 8 C2
Boluo, *China* 59 F10
Bolvadin, *Turkey* 70 B1
Bolzano, *Italy* 29 B8
Bom Jesus da Lapa, *Brazil* 125 F10
Boma, *Dem. Rep. of the Congo* 84 F2
Bombarral, *Portugal* 35 F1
Bombay = Mumbai, *India* 66 K8
Bomboma, *Dem. Rep. of the Congo* 84 D3
Bombombwa, *Dem. Rep. of the Congo* 86 B2
Bomi Hills, *Liberia* 82 D2
Bomili, *Dem. Rep. of the Congo* 86 B2
Bømlo, *Norway* 9 G11
Bomokandi →, *Dem. Rep. of the Congo* 86 B2
Bomu →, *C.A.R.* 84 D4
Bon, C., *Tunisia* 76 C5
Bon Sar Pa, *Vietnam* 64 F6
Bonaigarh, *India* 69 J11
Bonaire, *Neth. Ant.* 121 D6
Bonanza, *Nic.* 120 D3
Bonaparte Arch., *Australia* 92 B3
Boñar, *Spain* 34 C5
Bonaventure, *Canada* 103 C6
Bonavista, *Canada* 103 C9
Bonavista, C., *Canada* 103 C9
Bonavista B., *Canada* 103 C9
Bondeno, *Italy* 29 D8
Bondo, *Dem. Rep. of the Congo* 86 B1
Bondoukou, *Ivory C.* 82 D4
Bondowoso, *Indonesia* 63 G15
Bone, Teluk, *Indonesia* 63 E6
Bonerate, *Indonesia* 63 F6
Bonerate, Kepulauan, *Indonesia* 63 F6
Bo'ness, *U.K.* 14 E5
Bonete, Cerro, *Argentina* 126 B2
Bong Son = Hoai Nhon, *Vietnam* 64 E7
Bonga, *Ethiopia* 81 F4
Bongabong, *Phil.* 61 E4
Bongor, *Chad* 79 F9
Bongouanou, *Ivory C.* 82 D4
Bonham, *U.S.A.* 113 J6
Boni, *Mali* 82 B4
Bonifacio, *France* 21 G13
Bonifacio, Bouches de, *Medit. S.* 30 A2
Bonin Is. = Ogasawara Gunto, *Pac. Oc.* 52 G18
Bonke, *Ethiopia* 81 F4
Bonkoukou, *Niger* 83 C5
Bonn, *Germany* 24 E3
Bonnat, *France* 19 F8
Bonne Terre, *U.S.A.* 113 G9
Bonners Ferry, *U.S.A.* 114 B5
Bonnétable, *France* 18 D7
Bonneval, *Eure-et-Loir, France* 18 D8
Bonneval, *Savoie, France* 21 C11
Bonneville, *France* 19 F13
Bonnie Rock, *Australia* 93 F2
Bonny, *Nigeria* 83 E6
Bonny →, *Nigeria* 83 E6
Bonny, Bight of, *Africa* 83 E6
Bonny-sur-Loire, *France* 19 E9
Bonnyrigg, *U.K.* 14 F5
Bonnyville, *Canada* 105 C6
Bono, *Italy* 30 B2
Bonoi, *Indonesia* 63 E9
Bonorva, *Italy* 30 B1
Bonsall, *U.S.A.* 117 M9
Bontang, *Indonesia* 62 D5
Bonthe, *S. Leone* 82 D2
Bontoc, *Phil.* 61 C4
Bonyeri, *Ghana* 82 D4
Bonyhád, *Hungary* 42 D3
Bonython Ra., *Australia* 92 D4
Bookabie, *Australia* 93 F5
Booker, *U.S.A.* 113 G4
Boola, *Guinea* 82 D3
Boonah, *Australia* 95 D5
Boone, *Iowa, U.S.A.* 112 D8
Boone, *N.C., U.S.A.* 109 G5
Booneville, *Ark., U.S.A.* 113 H8
Booneville, *Miss., U.S.A.* 109 H1
Boonville, *Calif., U.S.A.* 116 F3
Boonville, *Ind., U.S.A.* 108 F2
Boonville, *Mo., U.S.A.* 112 F8
Boonville, *N.Y., U.S.A.* 111 C9
Boorindal, *Australia* 95 E4
Boothia, Gulf of, *Canada* 101 A11
Boothia Pen., *Canada* 100 A10
Bootle, *U.K.* 12 D4
Booué, *Gabon* 84 E2
Boppard, *Germany* 25 E3
Boquete, *Panama* 120 E3
Boquilla, Presa de la, *Mexico* 118 B3
Boquillas del Carmen, *Mexico* 118 B4
Bor, *Czech Rep.* 26 B5
Bor, *Russia* 48 B7
Bor, *Serbia, Yug.* 40 B6
Bôr, *Sudan* 81 F3
Bor, *Sweden* 11 G8
Bor, *Turkey* 72 D6
Bor Mashash, *Israel* 75 D3
Borah Peak, *U.S.A.* 114 D7
Borang, *Sudan* 81 G3
Borås, *Sweden* 11 G6
Borāzjān, *Iran* 71 D6
Borba, *Brazil* 124 D7
Borba, *Portugal* 35 G3
Borborema, Planalto da, *Brazil* 122 D7
Borcea, *Romania* 43 F12
Borçka, *Turkey* 73 B9
Bord Khūn-e Now, *Iran* 71 D6
Bordeaux, *France* 20 D3
Borden, *Australia* 93 F2
Borden, *Canada* 103 C7
Borden I., *Canada* 4 B2
Borden Pen., *Canada* 101 A11
Borders = Scottish Borders □, *U.K.* 14 F6
Borðeyri, *Iceland* 8 D3
Bordighera, *Italy* 28 E4
Bordj Fly Ste. Marie, *Algeria* 78 C5
Bordj-in-Eker, *Algeria* 78 D7
Bordj Omar Driss, *Algeria* 78 C7
Bore, *Ethiopia* 81 G4
Borehamwood, *U.K.* 13 F7
Borek Wielkopolski, *Poland* 45 G4
Borensberg, *Sweden* 11 F9
Borgå = Porvoo, *Finland* 9 F21
Borgarfjörður, *Iceland* 8 D7
Borgarnes, *Iceland* 8 D3
Børgefjellet, *Norway* 8 D15
Borger, *Neths.* 17 B6
Borger, *U.S.A.* 113 H4
Borgholm, *Sweden* 11 H10
Bórgia, *Italy* 31 D9
Borgo San Dalmazzo, *Italy* 28 D4
Borgo San Lorenzo, *Italy* 29 E8
Borgo Val di Taro, *Italy* 28 D6
Borgo Valsugana, *Italy* 29 B8
Borgomanero, *Italy* 28 C5
Borgorose, *Italy* 29 F10
Borgosésia, *Italy* 28 C5
Borhoyn Tal, *Mongolia* 56 C6
Bori, *Nigeria* 83 E6
Borikhane, *Laos* 64 C4
Borisoglebsk, *Russia* 48 E6
Borisov = Barysaw, *Belarus* 46 E5
Borisovka, *Russia* 47 G9
Borja, *Peru* 124 D3
Borja, *Spain* 32 D3
Borjas Blancas = Les Borges Blanques, *Spain* 32 D5
Borjomi, *Georgia* 49 K6
Børkop, *Denmark* 11 J3
Borkou, *Chad* 79 E9
Borkum, *Germany* 24 B2
Borlänge, *Sweden* 10 D9
Borley, C., *Antarctica* 5 C5
Borlu, *Turkey* 39 C10
Bormida →, *Italy* 28 D5
Bórmio, *Italy* 28 B7
Borna, *Germany* 24 D8
Borne Sulinowo, *Poland* 44 E3
Borneo, *E. Indies* 62 D5
Bornholm, *Denmark* 11 J8
Bornholms Amtskommune □, *Denmark* 11 J8
Bornholmsgattet, *Europe* 11 J8
Borno □, *Nigeria* 83 C7
Bornos, *Spain* 35 J5
Bornova, *Turkey* 39 C9
Bornu Yassa, *Nigeria* 83 C7
Boro →, *Sudan* 81 F2
Borodino, *Russia* 46 E8
Borogontsy, *Russia* 51 C14
Boromo, *Burkina Faso* 82 C4
Boron, *U.S.A.* 117 L9
Borongan, *Phil.* 61 F6
Borotangba Mts., *C.A.R.* 81 F2
Borotou, *Ivory C.* 82 D3
Borovan, *Bulgaria* 40 C7
Borovichi, *Russia* 46 C7
Borovsk, *Russia* 46 E9
Borrby, *Sweden* 11 J8
Borrego Springs, *U.S.A.* 117 M10
Borriol, *Spain* 32 E4
Borroloola, *Australia* 94 B2
Borşa, *Cluj, Romania* 43 D8
Borşa, *Maramureş, Romania* 43 C9
Borsad, *India* 68 H5
Borsec, *Romania* 43 D10
Borsod-Abaúj-Zemplén □, *Hungary* 42 B6
Bort-les-Orgues, *France* 20 C6
Borth, *U.K.* 13 E3
Börtnan, *Sweden* 10 B7
Borūjerd, *Iran* 71 C6
Boryslav, *Ukraine* 47 H2
Boryspil, *Ukraine* 47 G6
Borzhomi = Borjomi, *Georgia* 49 K6
Borzna, *Ukraine* 47 G7
Borzya, *Russia* 51 D12
Bosa, *Italy* 30 B1
Bosanska Dubica, *Bos.-H.* 29 C13
Bosanska Gradiška, *Bos.-H.* 42 E2
Bosanska Kostajnica, *Bos.-H.* 29 C13
Bosanska Krupa, *Bos.-H.* 29 D13
Bosanski Brod, *Bos.-H.* 42 E2
Bosanski Novi, *Bos.-H.* 29 C13
Bosanski Petrovac, *Bos.-H.* 29 D13
Bosanski Šamac, *Bos.-H.* 42 E3
Bosansko Grahovo, *Bos.-H.* 29 D13
Bosaso, *Somali Rep.* 74 E4
Boscastle, *U.K.* 13 G3
Bose, *China* 58 F6
Boshan, *China* 57 F9
Boshof, *S. Africa* 88 D4
Boshrūyeh, *Iran* 71 C8
Bosilegrad, *Serbia, Yug.* 40 D6
Boskovice, *Czech Rep.* 27 B9
Bosna →, *Bos.-H.* 42 E3
Bosna i Hercegovina = Bosnia-Herzegovina ■, *Europe* 42 G2
Bosnia-Herzegovina ■, *Europe* 42 G2
Bosnik, *Indonesia* 63 E9
Bosobolo, *Dem. Rep. of the Congo* 84 D3
Bosporus = İstanbul Boğazı, *Turkey* 41 E13
Bosque Farms, *U.S.A.* 115 J10
Bossangoa, *C.A.R.* 84 C3
Bossé Bangou, *Niger* 83 C5
Bossier City, *U.S.A.* 113 J8
Bosso, *Niger* 83 C7
Bosso, Dallol →, *Niger* 83 C5
Bostan, *Pakistan* 68 D2
Bostānābād, *Iran* 70 B5
Bosten Hu, *China* 60 B3
Boston, *U.K.* 12 E7
Boston, *U.S.A.* 111 D13
Boston Bar, *Canada* 104 D4
Boston Mts., *U.S.A.* 113 H8
Bosut →, *Croatia* 42 E3
Boswell, *Canada* 104 D5
Boswell, *U.S.A.* 110 F5
Botad, *India* 68 H4
Botan →, *Turkey* 73 D10
Botene, *Laos* 64 D3
Botev, *Bulgaria* 41 D8
Botevgrad, *Bulgaria* 40 D7
Bothaville, *S. Africa* 88 D4
Bothnia, G. of, *Europe* 8 E19
Bothwell, *Australia* 94 G4
Bothwell, *Canada* 110 D3
Boticas, *Portugal* 34 D3
Botletle →, *Botswana* 88 C3
Botlikh, *Russia* 49 J8
Botna →, *Moldova* 43 D14
Botoroaga, *Romania* 43 F10
Botoşani, *Romania* 43 C11
Botoşani □, *Romania* 43 C11
Botou, *Burkina Faso* 83 C5
Botricello, *Italy* 31 D9
Botro, *Ivory C.* 82 D3
Botswana ■, *Africa* 88 C3
Bottineau, *U.S.A.* 112 A4
Bottnaryd, *Sweden* 11 G7
Bottrop, *Germany* 17 C6
Botucatu, *Brazil* 127 A6
Botwood, *Canada* 103 C8
Bou Djébéha, *Mali* 82 B4
Bou Rjeïmât, *Mauritania* 82 B1
Bouaflé, *Ivory C.* 82 D3
Bouaké, *Ivory C.* 82 D3
Bouar, *C.A.R.* 84 C3
Bouârfa, *Morocco* 78 B5
Boucaut B., *Australia* 94 A1
Bouches-du-Rhône □, *France* 21 E9
Bougainville, C., *Australia* 92 B4
Bougainville I., *Papua N. G.* 96 H7
Bougainville Reef, *Australia* 94 B4
Bougie = Bejaïa, *Algeria* 78 A7
Bougouni, *Mali* 82 C3
Bouillon, *Belgium* 17 E5
Boukombé, *Benin* 83 C5
Boulal, *Mali* 82 B3
Boulazac, *France* 20 C4
Boulder, *Colo., U.S.A.* 112 E2
Boulder, *Mont., U.S.A.* 114 C7
Boulder City, *U.S.A.* 117 K12
Boulder Creek, *U.S.A.* 116 H4
Boulder Dam = Hoover Dam, *U.S.A.* 117 K12
Bouli, *Mauritania* 82 B2
Boulia, *Australia* 94 C2
Bouligny, *France* 19 C12
Boulogne →, *France* 18 E5
Boulogne-sur-Gesse, *France* 20 E4
Boulogne-sur-Mer, *France* 19 B8
Bouloire, *France* 18 E7
Boulouli, *Mali* 82 B3
Boulsa, *Burkina Faso* 83 C4
Boultoum, *Niger* 83 C7
Boûmdeïd, *Mauritania* 82 B2
Boun Neua, *Laos* 64 B3
Boun Tai, *Laos* 64 B3
Bouna, *Ivory C.* 82 D4
Boundary Peak, *U.S.A.* 116 H8
Boundiali, *Ivory C.* 82 D3
Bountiful, *U.S.A.* 114 F8
Bounty Is., *Pac. Oc.* 96 M9
Boura, *Mali* 82 C4
Bourbon-Lancy, *France* 19 F10
Bourbon-l'Archambault, *France* 19 F10
Bourbonnais, *France* 19 F10
Bourbonne-les-Bains, *France* 19 E12
Bourbourg, *France* 19 B9
Bourdel L., *Canada* 102 A5
Bourem, *Mali* 83 B4
Bourg, *France* 20 C3
Bourg-Argental, *France* 21 C8
Bourg-de-Péage, *France* 21 C9
Bourg-en-Bresse, *France* 19 F12
Bourg-Lastic, *France* 20 C6
Bourg-Madame, *France* 20 F5
Bourg-St-Andéol, *France* 21 D8
Bourg-St-Maurice, *France* 21 C10
Bourganeuf, *France* 20 C5
Bourges, *France* 19 E9
Bourget, *Canada* 111 A9
Bourget, Lac du, *France* 21 C9
Bourgneuf, B. de, *France* 18 E4
Bourgneuf-en-Retz, *France* 18 E5
Bourgogne, *France* 19 F11
Bourgoin-Jallieu, *France* 21 C9
Bourgueil, *France* 18 E7
Bourke, *Australia* 95 E4
Bourne, *U.K.* 12 E7
Bournemouth, *U.K.* 13 G6
Bournemouth □, *U.K.* 13 G6
Bouroum, *Burkina Faso* 83 C4
Bouse, *U.S.A.* 117 M13
Boussac, *France* 19 F9
Boussé, *Burkina Faso* 83 C4
Boussouma, *Burkina Faso* 83 C4
Boutilimit, *Mauritania* 82 B2
Boutonne →, *France* 20 C3
Bouvet I. = Bouvetøya, *Antarctica* 3 G10
Bouvetøya, *Antarctica* 3 G10
Bouxwiller, *France* 19 D14
Bouza, *Niger* 83 C6
Bouzonville, *France* 19 C13
Bova Marina, *Italy* 31 E8
Bovalino Marina, *Italy* 31 D9
Bovec, *Slovenia* 29 B10
Bovill, *U.S.A.* 114 C5
Bovino, *Italy* 31 A8
Bovril, *Argentina* 126 C4
Bow →, *Canada* 104 C6
Bow Island, *Canada* 104 D6
Bowbells, *U.S.A.* 112 A3
Bowdle, *U.S.A.* 112 C5
Bowelling, *Australia* 93 F2
Bowen, *Argentina* 126 D2
Bowen, *Australia* 94 C4
Bowie, *Ariz., U.S.A.* 115 K9
Bowie, *Tex., U.S.A.* 113 J6
Bowkān, *Iran* 70 B5
Bowland, Forest of, *U.K.* 12 D5
Bowling Green, *Ky., U.S.A.* 108 G2
Bowling Green, *Ohio, U.S.A.* 108 E4
Bowling Green, C., *Australia* 94 B4
Bowman, *U.S.A.* 112 B3
Bowman I., *Antarctica* 5 C8
Bowmanville, *Canada* 110 C6
Bowmore, *U.K.* 14 F2
Bowraville, *Australia* 95 E5
Bowron →, *Canada* 104 C4
Bowron Lake Prov. Park, *Canada* 104 C4
Bowser L., *Canada* 104 B3
Bowsman, *Canada* 105 C8
Bowwood, *Zambia* 87 F2
Box Cr. →, *Australia* 95 E3
Boxholm, *Sweden* 11 F9
Boxmeer, *Neths.* 17 C5
Boxtel, *Neths.* 17 C5
Boyabat, *Turkey* 72 B6
Boyalıca, *Turkey* 41 F13
Boyang, *China* 59 C11
Boyce, *U.S.A.* 113 K8
Boyd L., *Canada* 102 B4
Boyle, *Canada* 104 C6
Boyle, *Ireland* 15 C3
Boyne →, *Ireland* 15 C5
Boyne City, *U.S.A.* 108 C3
Boynitsa, *Bulgaria* 40 C6
Boynton Beach, *U.S.A.* 109 M5
Boyolali, *Indonesia* 63 G14
Boyoma, Chutes, *Dem. Rep. of the Congo* 86 B2
Boysen Reservoir, *U.S.A.* 114 E9
Boyuibe, *Bolivia* 124 G6
Boyup Brook, *Australia* 93 F2
Boz Burun, *Turkey* 41 F12
Boz Dağ, *Turkey* 39 D11
Boz Dağları, *Turkey* 39 C10

Bozburun, *Turkey* 39 E10
Bozcaada, *Turkey* 72 C2
Bozdoğan, *Turkey* 39 D10
Bozeman, *U.S.A.* 114 D8
Bozen = Bolzano, *Italy* 29 B8
Boževac, *Serbia, Yug.* 40 B5
Bozhou, *China* 56 H8
Bozkır, *Turkey* 72 D5
Bozkurt, *Turkey* 39 D11
Bozouls, *France* 20 D6
Bozoum, *C.A.R.* 84 C3
Bozova, *Antalya, Turkey* 39 D12
Bozova, *Sanliurfa, Turkey* 73 D8
Bozovici, *Romania* 42 F7
Bozüyük, *Turkey* 39 B12
Bra, *Italy* 28 D4
Braås, *Sweden* 11 G9
Brabant □, *Belgium* 17 D4
Brabant L., *Canada* 105 B8
Brabrand, *Denmark* 11 H4
Brač, *Croatia* 29 E13
Bracadale, L., *U.K.* 14 D2
Bracciano, *Italy* 29 F9
Bracciano, L. di, *Italy* 29 F9
Bracebridge, *Canada* 102 C4
Brach, *Libya* 79 C8
Bracieux, *France* 18 E8
Bräcke, *Sweden* 10 B9
Brackettville, *U.S.A.* 113 L4
Bracki Kanal, *Croatia* 29 E13
Bracknell, *U.K.* 13 F7
Bracknell Forest □, *U.K.* 13 F7
Brad, *Romania* 42 D7
Brádano →, *Italy* 31 B9
Bradenton, *U.S.A.* 109 M4
Bradford, *Canada* 110 B5
Bradford, *U.K.* 12 D6
Bradford, *Pa., U.S.A.* 110 E6
Bradford, *Vt., U.S.A.* 111 C12
Bradley, *Ark., U.S.A.* 113 J8
Bradley, *Calif., U.S.A.* 116 K6
Bradley Institute, *Zimbabwe* 87 F3
Brady, *U.S.A.* 113 K5
Brædstrup, *Denmark* 11 J3
Braeside, *Canada* 111 A8
Braga, *Portugal* 34 D2
Braga □, *Portugal* 34 D2
Bragadiru, *Romania* 43 G10
Bragado, *Argentina* 126 D3
Bragança, *Brazil* 125 D9
Bragança, *Portugal* 34 D4
Bragança □, *Portugal* 34 D4
Bragança Paulista, *Brazil* 127 A6
Brahmanbaria, *Bangla.* 67 H17
Brahmani →, *India* 67 J15
Brahmapur, *India* 67 K14
Brahmaputra →, *India* 69 H13
Braich-y-pwll, *U.K.* 12 E3
Brăila, *Romania* 43 E12
Brăila □, *Romania* 43 E12
Brainerd, *U.S.A.* 112 B7
Braintree, *U.K.* 13 F8
Braintree, *U.S.A.* 111 D14
Brak →, *S. Africa* 88 D3
Brake, *Germany* 24 B4
Brakel, *Germany* 24 D5
Bräkne-Hoby, *Sweden* 11 H9
Brakwater, *Namibia* 88 C2
Brålanda, *Sweden* 11 F6
Bramberg, *Germany* 25 E6
Bramdrupdam, *Denmark* 11 J3
Bramming, *Denmark* 11 J2
Brämön, *Sweden* 10 B11
Brampton, *Canada* 102 D4
Brampton, *U.K.* 12 C5
Bramsche, *Germany* 24 C3
Branco →, *Brazil* 122 D4
Brandberg, *Namibia* 88 B2
Brande, *Denmark* 11 J3
Brandenburg = Neubrandenburg, *Germany* 24 B9
Brandenburg, *Germany* 24 C8
Brandenburg □, *Germany* 24 C9
Brandfort, *S. Africa* 88 D4
Brando, *France* 21 F13
Brandon, *Canada* 105 D9
Brandon, *U.S.A.* 111 C11
Brandon B., *Ireland* 15 D1
Brandon Mt., *Ireland* 15 D1
Brandsen, *Argentina* 126 D4
Brandvlei, *S. Africa* 88 E3
Brandýs nad Labem, *Czech Rep.* 26 A7
Brănești, *Romania* 43 F11
Branford, *U.S.A.* 111 E12
Braniewo, *Poland* 44 D6
Bransfield Str., *Antarctica* 5 C18
Brańsk, *Poland* 45 F9
Branson, *U.S.A.* 113 G8
Brantford, *Canada* 102 D3
Brantôme, *France* 20 C4
Branzi, *Italy* 28 B6
Bras d'Or L., *Canada* 103 C7
Brasher Falls, *U.S.A.* 111 B10
Brasil, Planalto, *Brazil* 122 E6
Brasiléia, *Brazil* 124 F5
Brasília, *Brazil* 125 G9
Brasília Legal, *Brazil* 125 D7
Braslaw, *Belarus* 9 J22
Braslovče, *Slovenia* 29 B12
Brașov, *Romania* 43 E10
Brașov □, *Romania* 43 E10
Brass, *Nigeria* 83 E6
Brass →, *Nigeria* 83 E6
Brassac-les-Mines, *France* 20 C7
Brasschaat, *Belgium* 17 C4
Brassey, Banjaran, *Malaysia* 62 D5
Brassey Ra., *Australia* 93 E3
Brasstown Bald, *U.S.A.* 109 H4
Brastad, *Sweden* 11 F5
Brastavățu, *Romania* 43 G9
Bratan = Morozov, *Bulgaria* 41 D9
Brateș, *Romania* 43 E11
Bratislava, *Slovak Rep.* 27 C10
Bratislavský □, *Slovak Rep.* 27 C10
Bratsigovo, *Bulgaria* 41 D8
Bratsk, *Russia* 51 D11
Brattleboro, *U.S.A.* 111 D12
Bratunac, *Bos.-H.* 42 F4
Braunau, *Austria* 26 C6
Braunschweig, *Germany* 24 C6
Braunton, *U.K.* 13 F3
Bravicea, *Moldova* 43 C13
Bråviken, *Sweden* 11 F10
Bravo del Norte, Rio = Grande, Rio →, *U.S.A.* 113 N6
Brawley, *U.S.A.* 117 N11
Bray, *Ireland* 15 C5
Bray, Mt., *Australia* 94 A1
Bray-sur-Seine, *France* 19 D10
Brazeau →, *Canada* 104 C5
Brazil, *U.S.A.* 108 F2
Brazil ■, *S. Amer.* 125 F9
Brazilian Highlands = Brasil, Planalto, *Brazil* 122 E6
Brazo Sur →, *S. Amer.* 126 B4
Brazos →, *U.S.A.* 113 L7
Brazzaville, *Congo* 84 E3
Brčko, *Bos.-H.* 42 F3
Brda →, *Poland* 45 E5
Brdy, *Czech Rep.* 26 B6
Breaden, L., *Australia* 93 E4
Breaksea Sd., *N.Z.* 91 L1
Bream B., *N.Z.* 91 F5
Bream Hd., *N.Z.* 91 F5
Breas, *Chile* 126 B1
Breaza, *Romania* 43 E10
Brebes, *Indonesia* 63 G13
Brechin, *Canada* 110 B5
Brechin, *U.K.* 14 E6
Brecht, *Belgium* 17 C4
Breckenridge, *Colo., U.S.A.* 114 G10
Breckenridge, *Minn., U.S.A.* 112 B6
Breckenridge, *Tex., U.S.A.* 113 J5
Breckland, *U.K.* 13 E8
Břeclav, *Czech Rep.* 27 C9
Brecon, *U.K.* 13 F4
Brecon Beacons, *U.K.* 13 F4
Breda, *Neths.* 17 C4
Bredaryd, *Sweden* 11 G7
Bredasdorp, *S. Africa* 88 E3
Bredebro, *Denmark* 11 J2
Bredstedt, *Germany* 24 A4
Bree, *Belgium* 17 C5
Bregalnica →, *Macedonia* 40 E6
Bregenz, *Austria* 26 D2
Bregovo, *Bulgaria* 40 B6
Bréhal, *France* 18 D5
Bréhat, Î. de, *France* 18 D4
Breiðafjörður, *Iceland* 8 D2
Breil-sur-Roya, *France* 21 E11
Breisach, *Germany* 25 G3
Brejo, *Brazil* 125 D10
Bremen, *Germany* 24 B4
Bremen □, *Germany* 24 B4
Bremer Bay, *Australia* 93 F2
Bremer I., *Australia* 94 A2
Bremerhaven, *Germany* 24 B4
Bremerton, *U.S.A.* 116 C4
Bremervörde, *Germany* 24 B5
Brenes, *Spain* 35 H5
Brenham, *U.S.A.* 113 K6
Brenne, *France* 20 B5
Brennerpass, *Austria* 26 D4
Breno, *Italy* 28 C7
Brent, *U.S.A.* 109 J2
Brenta →, *Italy* 29 C9
Brentwood, *U.K.* 13 F8
Brentwood, *Calif., U.S.A.* 116 H5
Brentwood, *N.Y., U.S.A.* 111 F11
Bréscia, *Italy* 28 C7
Breskens, *Neths.* 17 C3
Breslau = Wrocław, *Poland* 45 G4
Bresle →, *France* 18 B8
Bressanone, *Italy* 29 B8
Bressay, *U.K.* 14 A7
Bresse, *France* 19 F12
Bressuire, *France* 18 F6
Brest, *Belarus* 47 F2
Brest, *France* 18 D2
Brest-Litovsk = Brest, *Belarus* 47 F2
Bretagne, *France* 18 D3
Bretçu, *Romania* 43 D11
Bretenoux, *France* 20 D5
Breteuil, *Eure, France* 18 D7
Breteuil, *Oise, France* 19 C9
Breton, *Canada* 104 C6
Breton, Pertuis, *France* 20 B2
Breton Sd., *U.S.A.* 113 L10
Brett, C., *N.Z.* 91 F5
Bretten, *Germany* 25 F4
Breuil-Cervínia, *Italy* 28 C4
Brevard, *U.S.A.* 109 H4
Breves, *Brazil* 125 D8
Brewarrina, *Australia* 95 E4
Brewer, *U.S.A.* 109 C11
Brewer, Mt., *U.S.A.* 116 J8
Brewerville, *Liberia* 82 D2
Brewster, *N.Y., U.S.A.* 111 E11
Brewster, *Ohio, U.S.A.* 110 F3
Brewster, *Wash., U.S.A.* 114 B4
Brewster, Kap = Kangikajik, *Greenland* 4 B6
Brewton, *U.S.A.* 109 K2
Breyten, *S. Africa* 89 D5
Breza, *Bos.-H.* 42 F3
Brezhnev = Naberezhnyye Chelny, *Russia* 48 C11
Brežice, *Slovenia* 29 C12
Březnice, *Czech Rep.* 26 B6
Breznik, *Bulgaria* 40 D6
Brezno, *Slovak Rep.* 27 C12
Brezoi, *Romania* 43 E9
Brezovica, *Kosovo, Yug.* 40 D5
Brezovo, *Bulgaria* 41 D9
Briançon, *France* 21 D10
Briare, *France* 19 E9
Briático, *Italy* 31 D9
Bribie I., *Australia* 95 D5
Bribri, *Costa Rica* 120 E3
Briceni, *Moldova* 43 B12
Bricquebec, *France* 18 C5
Bridgehampton, *U.S.A.* 111 F12
Bridgend, *U.K.* 13 F4
Bridgend □, *U.K.* 13 F4
Bridgeport, *Calif., U.S.A.* 116 G7
Bridgeport, *Conn., U.S.A.* 111 E11
Bridgeport, *Nebr., U.S.A.* 112 E3
Bridgeport, *Tex., U.S.A.* 113 J6
Bridger, *U.S.A.* 114 D9
Bridgeton, *U.S.A.* 108 F8
Bridgetown, *Australia* 93 F2
Bridgetown, *Barbados* 121 D8
Bridgetown, *Canada* 103 D6
Bridgewater, *Canada* 103 D7
Bridgewater, *Mass., U.S.A.* 111 E14
Bridgewater, *N.Y., U.S.A.* 111 D9
Bridgewater-Gagebrook, *Australia* 94 G4
Bridgnorth, *U.K.* 13 E5
Bridgton, *U.S.A.* 111 B14
Bridgwater, *U.K.* 13 F5
Bridgwater B., *U.K.* 13 F4
Bridlington, *U.K.* 12 C7
Bridlington B., *U.K.* 12 C7
Bridport, *Australia* 94 G4
Bridport, *U.K.* 13 G5
Briec, *France* 18 D2
Brienne-le-Château, *France* 19 D11
Brienon-sur-Armançon, *France* 19 E10
Brienz, *Switz.* 25 J4
Brienzersee, *Switz.* 25 J3
Brig, *Switz.* 25 J3
Brigg, *U.K.* 12 D7
Brigham City, *U.S.A.* 114 F7
Brighton, *Canada* 110 B7
Brighton, *U.K.* 13 G7
Brighton, *Colo., U.S.A.* 112 F2
Brighton, *N.Y., U.S.A.* 110 C7
Brignogan-Plage, *France* 18 D2
Brignoles, *France* 21 E10
Brihuega, *Spain* 32 E2
Brikama, *Gambia* 82 C1
Brilliant, *U.S.A.* 110 F4
Brilon, *Germany* 24 D4
Bríndisi, *Italy* 31 B10
Brinje, *Croatia* 29 D12
Brinkley, *U.S.A.* 113 H9
Brinnon, *U.S.A.* 116 C4
Brion, I., *Canada* 103 C7
Brionne, *France* 18 C7
Brionski, *Croatia* 29 D10
Brioude, *France* 20 C7
Briouze, *France* 18 D6
Brisbane, *Australia* 95 D5
Brisbane →, *Australia* 95 D5
Brisighella, *Italy* 29 D8
Bristol, *U.K.* 13 F5
Bristol, *Conn., U.S.A.* 111 E12
Bristol, *Pa., U.S.A.* 111 F10
Bristol, *R.I., U.S.A.* 111 E13
Bristol, *Tenn., U.S.A.* 109 G4
Bristol, City of □, *U.K.* 13 F5
Bristol B., *U.S.A.* 100 C4
Bristol Channel, *U.K.* 13 F3
Bristol I., *Antarctica* 5 B1
Bristol L., *U.S.A.* 115 J5
Bristow, *U.S.A.* 113 H6
Britain = Great Britain, *Europe* 6 E5
British Columbia □, *Canada* 104 C3
British Indian Ocean Terr. = Chagos Arch., *Ind. Oc.* 52 K11
British Isles, *Europe* 6 E5
Brits, *S. Africa* 89 D4
Britstown, *S. Africa* 88 E3
Britt, *Canada* 102 C3
Brittany = Bretagne, *France* 18 D3
Britton, *U.S.A.* 112 C6
Brive-la-Gaillarde, *France* 20 C5
Briviesca, *Spain* 34 C7
Brixen = Bressanone, *Italy* 29 B8
Brixham, *U.K.* 13 G4
Brnaze, *Croatia* 29 E13
Brno, *Czech Rep.* 27 B9
Broad →, *U.S.A.* 109 J5
Broad Arrow, *Australia* 93 F3
Broad B., *U.K.* 14 C2
Broad Haven, *Ireland* 15 B2
Broad Law, *U.K.* 14 F5
Broad Sd., *Australia* 94 C4
Broadalbin, *U.S.A.* 111 C10
Broadback →, *Canada* 102 B4
Broadhurst Ra., *Australia* 92 D3
Broads, The, *U.K.* 12 E9
Broadus, *U.S.A.* 112 C2
Broager, *Denmark* 11 K3
Broby, *Sweden* 11 H8
Broćeni, *Latvia* 44 B9
Brochet, *Canada* 105 B8
Brochet, L., *Canada* 105 B8
Brocken, *Germany* 24 D6
Brockport, *U.S.A.* 110 C7
Brockton, *U.S.A.* 111 D13
Brockville, *Canada* 102 D4
Brockway, *Mont., U.S.A.* 112 B2
Brockway, *Pa., U.S.A.* 110 E6
Brocton, *U.S.A.* 110 D5
Brod, *Macedonia* 40 E5
Brodarevo, *Serbia, Yug.* 40 C3
Brodeur Pen., *Canada* 101 A11
Brodhead, Mt., *U.S.A.* 110 E7
Brodick, *U.K.* 14 F3
Brodnica, *Poland* 45 E6
Brody, *Ukraine* 47 G3
Brogan, *U.S.A.* 114 D5
Broglie, *France* 18 C7
Brok, *Poland* 45 F8
Broken Arrow, *U.S.A.* 113 G7
Broken Bow, *Nebr., U.S.A.* 112 E5
Broken Bow, *Okla., U.S.A.* 113 H7
Broken Bow Lake, *U.S.A.* 113 H7
Broken Hill = Kabwe, *Zambia* 87 E2
Brokind, *Sweden* 11 F9
Bromley □, *U.K.* 13 F8
Bromölla, *Sweden* 11 H8
Bromsgrove, *U.K.* 13 E5
Brønderslev, *Denmark* 11 G3
Brong-Ahafo □, *Ghana* 82 D4
Broni, *Italy* 28 C6
Bronkhorstspruit, *S. Africa* 89 D4
Brønnøysund, *Norway* 8 D15
Bronte, *Italy* 31 E7
Brook Park, *U.S.A.* 110 E4
Brookhaven, *U.S.A.* 113 K9
Brookings, *Oreg., U.S.A.* 114 E1
Brookings, *S. Dak., U.S.A.* 112 C6
Brooklin, *Canada* 110 C6
Brooklyn Park, *U.S.A.* 112 C8
Brooks, *Canada* 104 C6
Brooks Range, *U.S.A.* 100 B5
Brooksville, *U.S.A.* 109 L4
Brookton, *Australia* 93 F2
Brookville, *U.S.A.* 110 E5
Broom, L., *U.K.* 14 D3
Broome, *Australia* 92 C3
Broons, *France* 18 D4
Brora, *U.K.* 14 C5
Brora →, *U.K.* 14 C5
Brørup, *Denmark* 11 J2
Brösarp, *Sweden* 11 J8
Brosna →, *Ireland* 15 C4
Broșteni, *Mehedinți, Romania* 42 F7
Broșteni, *Suceava, Romania* 43 C10
Brothers, *U.S.A.* 114 E3
Brou, *France* 18 D8
Brouage, *France* 20 C2
Brough, *U.K.* 12 C5
Brough Hd., *U.K.* 14 B5
Broughton Island = Qikiqtarjuaq, *Canada* 101 B13
Broumov, *Czech Rep.* 27 A9
Brovary, *Ukraine* 47 G6
Brovst, *Denmark* 11 G3
Brown, L., *Australia* 93 F2
Brown, Pt., *Australia* 95 E1
Brown City, *U.S.A.* 110 C2
Brown Willy, *U.K.* 13 G3
Brownfield, *U.S.A.* 113 J3
Browning, *U.S.A.* 114 B7
Brownsville, *Oreg., U.S.A.* 114 D2
Brownsville, *Pa., U.S.A.* 110 F5
Brownsville, *Tenn., U.S.A.* 113 H10
Brownsville, *Tex., U.S.A.* 113 N6
Brownville, *U.S.A.* 111 C9
Brownwood, *U.S.A.* 113 K5
Browse I., *Australia* 92 B3
Bruas, *Malaysia* 65 K3
Bruay-la-Buissière, *France* 19 B9
Bruce, Mt., *Australia* 92 D2
Bruce Pen., *Canada* 110 B3
Bruce Rock, *Australia* 93 F2
Bruche →, *France* 19 D14
Bruchsal, *Germany* 25 F4
Bruck an der Leitha, *Austria* 27 C9
Bruck an der Mur, *Austria* 26 D8
Brue →, *U.K.* 13 F5
Bruges = Brugge, *Belgium* 17 C3
Brugg, *Switz.* 25 H4
Brugge, *Belgium* 17 C3
Bruin, *U.S.A.* 110 E5
Brûlé, *Canada* 104 C5
Brûlon, *France* 18 E6
Brumado, *Brazil* 125 F10
Brumath, *France* 19 D14
Brumunddal, *Norway* 9 F14
Bruneau, *U.S.A.* 114 E6
Bruneau →, *U.S.A.* 114 E6
Bruneck = Brunico, *Italy* 29 B8
Brunei = Bandar Seri Begawan, *Brunei* 62 C4
Brunei ■, *Asia* 62 D4
Brunflo, *Sweden* 10 A8
Brunico, *Italy* 29 B8
Brunna, *Sweden* 10 E11
Brunnen, *Switz.* 25 J4
Brunner, L., *N.Z.* 91 K3
Brunsbüttel, *Germany* 24 B5
Brunssum, *Neths.* 17 D5
Brunswick = Braunschweig, *Germany* 24 C6
Brunswick, *Ga., U.S.A.* 109 K5
Brunswick, *Maine, U.S.A.* 109 D11
Brunswick, *Md., U.S.A.* 108 F7
Brunswick, *Mo., U.S.A.* 112 F8
Brunswick, *Ohio, U.S.A.* 110 E3
Brunswick, Pen. de, *Chile* 128 G2
Brunswick B., *Australia* 92 C3
Brunswick Junction, *Australia* 93 F2
Bruntál, *Czech Rep.* 27 B10
Bruny I., *Australia* 94 G4
Brus Laguna, *Honduras* 120 C3
Brusartsi, *Bulgaria* 40 C7
Brush, *U.S.A.* 112 E3
Brushton, *U.S.A.* 111 B10
Brusio, *Switz.* 25 J6
Brusque, *Brazil* 127 B6
Brussel, *Belgium* 17 D4
Brussels = Brussel, *Belgium* 17 D4
Brussels, *Canada* 110 C3
Brusy, *Poland* 44 E4
Bruxelles = Brussel, *Belgium* 17 D4
Bruyères, *France* 19 D13
Bruz, *France* 18 D5
Brwinów, *Poland* 45 F7
Bryagovo, *Bulgaria* 41 E9
Bryan, *Ohio, U.S.A.* 108 E3
Bryan, *Tex., U.S.A.* 113 K6
Bryan, Mt., *Australia* 95 E2
Bryanka, *Ukraine* 47 H10
Bryansk, *Bryansk, Russia* 47 F8
Bryansk, *Dagestan, Russia* 49 H8
Bryanskoye = Bryansk, *Russia* 49 H8
Bryce Canyon National Park, *U.S.A.* 115 H7
Bryne, *Norway* 9 G11
Bryson City, *U.S.A.* 109 H4
Bryukhovetskaya, *Russia* 47 K10
Brza Palanka, *Serbia, Yug.* 40 B6
Brzeg, *Poland* 45 H4
Brzeg Dolny, *Poland* 45 G3
Brześć Kujawski, *Poland* 45 F5
Brzesko, *Poland* 45 J7
Brzeziny, *Poland* 45 G6
Brzozów, *Poland* 45 J9
Bsharri, *Lebanon* 75 A5
Bū Baqarah, *U.A.E.* 71 E8
Bu Craa, *W. Sahara* 78 C3
Bū Ḩasā, *U.A.E.* 71 F7
Bua, *Sweden* 11 G6
Bua Yai, *Thailand* 64 E4
Buapinang, *Indonesia* 63 E6
Buba, *Guinea-Biss.* 82 C2
Bubanza, *Burundi* 86 C2
Bubaque, *Guinea-Biss.* 82 C1
Bube, *Ethiopia* 81 F4
Būbiyān, *Kuwait* 71 D6
Buca, *Turkey* 39 C9
Bucak, *Turkey* 39 D12
Bucaramanga, *Colombia* 124 B4
Bucas Grande I., *Phil.* 61 G6
Bucasia, *Australia* 94 C4
Buccaneer Arch., *Australia* 92 C3
Buccino, *Italy* 31 B8
Bucecea, *Romania* 43 C11
Buchach, *Ukraine* 47 H3
Buchan, *U.K.* 14 D6
Buchan Ness, *U.K.* 14 D7
Buchanan, *Canada* 105 C8
Buchanan, *Liberia* 82 D2
Buchanan, L., *Queens., Australia* 94 C4
Buchanan, L., *W. Austral., Australia* 93 E3
Buchanan, L., *U.S.A.* 113 K5
Buchanan Cr. →, *Australia* 94 B2
Buchans, *Canada* 103 C8
Bucharest = București, *Romania* 43 F11
Buchen, *Germany* 25 F5
Buchholz, *Germany* 24 B5
Buchloe, *Germany* 25 G6
Buchon, Pt., *U.S.A.* 116 K6
Buciumi, *Romania* 42 C8
Buck Hill Falls, *U.S.A.* 111 E9
Bückeburg, *Germany* 24 C5
Buckeye, *U.S.A.* 115 K7
Buckeye Lake, *U.S.A.* 110 G2
Buckhannon, *U.S.A.* 108 F5
Buckhaven, *U.K.* 14 E5
Buckhorn L., *Canada* 110 B6
Buckie, *U.K.* 14 D6
Buckingham, *Canada* 102 C4
Buckingham, *U.K.* 13 F7
Buckingham B., *Australia* 94 A2
Buckinghamshire □, *U.K.* 13 F7
Buckle Hd., *Australia* 92 B4
Buckley, *U.K.* 12 D4
Buckley →, *Australia* 94 C2
Bucklin, *U.S.A.* 113 G5
Bucks L., *U.S.A.* 116 F5
Bucquoy, *France* 19 B9
Buctouche, *Canada* 103 C7
București, *Romania* 43 F11
Bucyrus, *U.S.A.* 108 E4
Budacu, Vf., *Romania* 43 C10
Budalin, *Burma* 67 H19
Budaörs, *Hungary* 42 C3
Budapest, *Hungary* 42 C4
Budapest □, *Hungary* 42 C4
Budaun, *India* 69 E8
Budd Coast, *Antarctica* 5 C8
Buddusò, *Italy* 30 B2
Bude, *U.K.* 13 G3
Budennovsk, *Russia* 49 H7
Budești, *Romania* 43 F11
Budge Budge = Baj Baj, *India* 69 H13
Budia, *Spain* 32 E2
Büdingen, *Germany* 25 E5
Budjala, *Dem. Rep. of the Congo* 84 D3
Budoni, *Italy* 30 B2
Búdrio, *Italy* 29 D8
Budva, *Montenegro, Yug.* 40 D2
Budzyń, *Poland* 45 F3
Buea, *Cameroon* 83 E6

Buellton, U.S.A. 117 L6
Buena Esperanza, Argentina 126 C2
Buena Park, U.S.A. 117 M9
Buena Vista, Colo., U.S.A. 115 G10
Buena Vista, Va., U.S.A. 108 G6
Buena Vista Lake Bed, U.S.A. 117 K7
Buenaventura, Colombia 124 C3
Buenaventura, Mexico 118 B3
Buendía, Embalse de, Spain 32 E2
Buenos Aires, Argentina 126 C4
Buenos Aires, Costa Rica 120 E3
Buenos Aires □, Argentina 126 D4
Buenos Aires, L., Chile 128 F2
Buffalo, Mo., U.S.A. 113 G8
Buffalo, N.Y., U.S.A. 110 D6
Buffalo, Okla., U.S.A. 113 G5
Buffalo, S. Dak., U.S.A. 112 C3
Buffalo, Wyo., U.S.A. 114 D10
Buffalo →, Canada 104 A5
Buffalo →, S. Africa 89 D5
Buffalo Head Hills, Canada 104 B5
Buffalo L., Alta., Canada 104 C6
Buffalo L., N.W.T., Canada 104 A5
Buffalo Narrows, Canada 105 B7
Buffels →, S. Africa 88 D2
Buford, U.S.A. 109 H4
Bug = Buh →, Ukraine 47 J6
Bug →, Poland 45 F8
Buga, Colombia 124 C3
Buganda, Uganda 86 C3
Buganga, Uganda 86 C3
Bugasong, Phil. 61 F5
Bugeat, France 20 C5
Bugel, Tanjung, Indonesia 63 G14
Bugibba, Malta 36 D1
Bugojno, Bos.-H. 42 F2
Bugsuk, Phil. 62 C5
Buguma, Nigeria 83 E6
Bugun Shara, Mongolia 60 B5
Buguruslan, Russia 50 D6
Buh →, Ukraine 47 J6
Buharkent, Turkey 39 D10
Buheirat-Murrat-el-Kubra, Egypt 80 H8
Buhera, Zimbabwe 89 B5
Bühl, Germany 25 G4
Buhl, U.S.A. 114 E6
Buhuşi, Romania 43 D11
Builth Wells, U.K. 13 E4
Buinsk, Russia 48 C9
Buir Nur, Mongolia 60 B6
Buis-les-Baronnies, France 21 D9
Buitrago = Buitrago del Lozoya, Spain 34 E7
Buitrago del Lozoya, Spain 34 E7
Bujalance, Spain 35 H6
Bujanovac, Serbia, Yug. 40 D5
Bujaraloz, Spain 32 D4
Buje, Croatia 29 C10
Bujumbura, Burundi 86 C2
Bük, Hungary 42 C1
Buk, Poland 45 F3
Bukachacha, Russia 51 D12
Bukama, Dem. Rep. of the Congo 87 D2
Bukavu, Dem. Rep. of the Congo 86 C2
Bukene, Tanzania 86 C3
Bukhara = Bukhoro, Uzbekistan 50 F7
Bukhoro, Uzbekistan 50 F7
Bukima, Tanzania 86 C3
Bukit Mertajam, Malaysia 65 K3
Bukittinggi, Indonesia 62 E2
Bükk, Hungary 42 B5
Bukoba, Tanzania 86 C3
Bukuru, Nigeria 83 D6
Bukuya, Uganda 86 B3
Būl, Kuh-e, Iran 71 D7
Bula, Guinea-Biss. 82 C1
Bula, Indonesia 63 E8
Bülach, Switz. 25 H4
Bulan, Phil. 61 E5
Bulancak, Turkey 73 B8
Bulandshahr, India 68 E7
Bulanık, Turkey 73 C10
Bûlâq, Egypt 80 B3
Bulawayo, Zimbabwe 87 G2
Buldan, Turkey 39 C10
Bulgar, Russia 48 C9
Bulgaria ■, Europe 41 D9
Bulgheria, Monte, Italy 31 B8
Bulgurca, Turkey 39 C9
Buli, Teluk, Indonesia 63 D7
Buliluyan, C., Phil. 61 G2
Bulki, Ethiopia 81 F4
Bulkley →, Canada 104 B3
Bull Shoals L., U.S.A. 113 G8
Bullaque →, Spain 35 G6
Bullas, Spain 33 G3
Bulle, Switz. 25 J3
Bullhead City, U.S.A. 117 K12
Büllingen, Belgium 17 D6
Bullock Creek, Australia 94 B3
Bulloo →, Australia 95 D3
Bulloo L., Australia 95 D3
Bulls, N.Z. 91 J5
Bully-les-Mines, France 19 B9
Bulnes, Chile 126 D1
Bulqizë, Albania 40 E4
Bulsar = Valsad, India 66 J8
Bultfontein, S. Africa 88 D4
Bulukumba, Indonesia 63 F6
Bulun, Russia 51 B13
Bumba, Dem. Rep. of the Congo 84 D4
Bumbeşti-Jiu, Romania 43 E8
Bumbiri I., Tanzania 86 C3
Bumbuna, S. Leone 82 D2
Bumhpa Bum, Burma 67 F20
Bumi →, Zimbabwe 87 F2
Buna, Kenya 86 B4
Bunawan, Phil. 61 G6
Bunazi, Tanzania 86 C3
Bunbury, Australia 93 F2
Bunclody, Ireland 15 D5
Buncrana, Ireland 15 A4
Bundaberg, Australia 95 C5
Bünde, Germany 24 C4
Bundey →, Australia 94 C2
Bundi, India 68 G6
Bundoran, Ireland 15 B3
Bundukia, Sudan 81 F3
Bung Kan, Thailand 64 C4
Bunga →, Nigeria 83 C6
Bungay, U.K. 13 E9
Bungil Cr. →, Australia 95 D4
Bungo-Suidō, Japan 55 H6
Bungoma, Kenya 86 B3
Bungotakada, Japan 55 H5
Bungu, Tanzania 86 D4
Bunia, Dem. Rep. of the Congo 86 B3
Bunji, Pakistan 69 B6
Bunkie, U.S.A. 113 K8
Bunnell, U.S.A. 109 L5
Buñol, Spain 33 F4
Bunsuru, Nigeria 83 C5
Buntok, Indonesia 62 E4
Bununu Dass, Nigeria 83 C6
Bununu Kasa, Nigeria 83 D6
Bünyan, Turkey 72 C6
Bunyu, Indonesia 62 D5
Bunza, Nigeria 83 C5
Buol, Indonesia 63 D6
Buon Brieng, Vietnam 64 F7
Buon Ma Thuot, Vietnam 64 F7
Buong Long, Cambodia 64 F6
Buorkhaya, Mys, Russia 51 B14
Buqayq, Si. Arabia 71 E6
Buqbuq, Egypt 80 A2
Bur Acaba, Somali Rep. 74 G3
Bûr Fuad, Egypt 80 H8
Bûr Safâga, Egypt 70 E2
Bûr Sa'îd, Egypt 80 H8
Bûr Sûdân, Sudan 80 D4
Bûr Taufiq, Egypt 80 J8
Bura, Kenya 86 C4
Burakin, Australia 93 F2
Buram, Sudan 81 E2
Burao, Somali Rep. 74 F4
Burāq, Syria 75 B5
Buraydah, Si. Arabia 70 E4
Burbank, U.S.A. 117 L8
Burda, India 68 G6
Burdekin →, Australia 94 B4
Burdur, Turkey 39 D12
Burdur □, Turkey 39 D12
Burdur Gölü, Turkey 39 D12
Burdwan = Barddhaman, India 69 H12
Bure, Gojam, Ethiopia 81 E4
Bure, Ilubabor, Ethiopia 81 F4
Bure →, U.K. 12 E9
Büren, Germany 24 D4
Bureya →, Russia 51 E13
Burford, Canada 110 C4
Burg, Germany 24 C7
Burg auf Fehmarn, Germany 24 A7
Burg el Arab, Egypt 80 H6
Burg et Tuyur, Sudan 80 C2
Burg Stargard, Germany 24 B9
Burgas, Bulgaria 41 D11
Burgas □, Bulgaria 41 D10
Burgaski Zaliv, Bulgaria 41 D11
Burgdorf, Germany 24 C6
Burgdorf, Switz. 25 H3
Burgenland □, Austria 27 D9
Burgeo, Canada 103 C8
Burgersdorp, S. Africa 88 E4
Burges, Mt., Australia 93 F3
Burghausen, Germany 25 G8
Búrgio, Italy 30 E6
Burglengenfeld, Germany 25 F8
Burgohondo, Spain 34 E6
Burgos, Spain 34 C7
Burgos □, Spain 34 C7
Burgstädt, Germany 24 E8
Burgsvik, Sweden 11 G12
Burguillos del Cerro, Spain 35 G4
Burgundy = Bourgogne, France 19 F11
Burhaniye, Turkey 39 B8
Burhanpur, India 66 J10
Burhi Gandak →, India 69 G12
Burhner →, India 69 H9
Buri Pen., Eritrea 81 D4
Burias I., Phil. 61 E5
Burica, Pta., Costa Rica 120 E3
Burien, U.S.A. 116 C4
Burigi, L., Tanzania 86 C3
Burin, Canada 103 C8
Buriram, Thailand 64 E4
Burj Sāfitā, Syria 70 C3
Burji, Ethiopia 81 F4
Burkburnett, U.S.A. 113 H5
Burke →, Australia 94 C2
Burke Chan., Canada 104 C3
Burketown, Australia 94 B2
Burkina Faso ■, Africa 82 C4
Burk's Falls, Canada 102 C4
Burlada, Spain 32 C3
Burleigh Falls, Canada 110 B6
Burley, U.S.A. 114 E7
Burlingame, U.S.A. 116 H4
Burlington, Canada 102 D4
Burlington, Colo., U.S.A. 112 F3
Burlington, Iowa, U.S.A. 112 E9
Burlington, Kans., U.S.A. 112 F7
Burlington, N.C., U.S.A. 109 G6
Burlington, N.J., U.S.A. 111 F10
Burlington, Vt., U.S.A. 111 B11
Burlington, Wash., U.S.A. 116 B4
Burlington, Wis., U.S.A. 108 D1
Burlyu-Tyube, Kazakstan 50 E8
Burma ■, Asia 67 J20
Burnaby I., Canada 104 C2
Burnet, U.S.A. 113 K5
Burney, U.S.A. 114 F3
Burnham, U.S.A. 110 F7
Burnham-on-Sea, U.K. 13 F5
Burnie, Australia 94 G4
Burnley, U.K. 12 D5
Burns, U.S.A. 114 E4
Burns Lake, Canada 104 C3
Burnside →, Canada 100 B9
Burnside, L., Australia 93 E3
Burnsville, U.S.A. 112 C8
Burnt L., Canada 103 B7
Burnt River, Canada 110 B6
Burntwood →, Canada 105 B9
Burntwood L., Canada 105 B8
Burqān, Kuwait 70 D5
Burra, Nigeria 83 C6
Burray, U.K. 14 C6
Burrel, Albania 40 E4
Burren Junction, Australia 95 E4
Burriana, Spain 32 F4
Burro, Serranías del, Mexico 118 B4
Burrow Hd., U.K. 14 G4
Burruyacú, Argentina 126 B3
Burry Port, U.K. 13 F3
Bursa, Turkey 41 F13
Burseryd, Sweden 11 G7
Burstall, Canada 105 C7
Burton, Ohio, U.S.A. 110 E3
Burton, S.C., U.S.A. 109 J5
Burton, L., Canada 102 B4
Burton upon Trent, U.K. 12 E6
Buru, Indonesia 63 E7
Burullus, Bahra el, Egypt 80 H7
Burûn, Râs, Egypt 75 D2
Burundi ■, Africa 86 C3
Bururi, Burundi 86 C2
Burutu, Nigeria 83 D6
Burwell, U.S.A. 112 E5
Burwick, U.K. 14 C5
Bury, U.K. 12 D5
Bury St. Edmunds, U.K. 13 E8
Buryatia □, Russia 51 D11
Buryn, Ukraine 47 G7
Burzenin, Poland 45 G5
Busalla, Italy 28 D5
Busango Swamp, Zambia 87 E2
Buşayrah, Syria 70 C4
Busca, Italy 28 D4
Bushat, Albania 40 E3
Būshehr, Iran 71 D6
Būshehr □, Iran 71 D6
Bushell, Canada 105 B7
Bushenyi, Uganda 86 C3
Bushire = Būshehr, Iran 71 D6
Busie, Ghana 82 C4
Businga, Dem. Rep. of the Congo 84 D4
Busko-Zdrój, Poland 45 H7
Busovača, Bos.-H. 42 F2
Buşra ash Shām, Syria 75 C5
Busselton, Australia 93 F2
Busseri →, Sudan 81 F2
Busseto, Italy 28 D7
Bussière-Badil, France 20 C4
Bussolengo, Italy 28 C7
Bussum, Neths. 17 B5
Buşteni, Romania 43 E10
Busto, C., Spain 34 B4
Busto Arsízio, Italy 28 C5
Busu-Djanoa, Dem. Rep. of the Congo 84 D4
Busuanga I., Phil. 61 E3
Büsum, Germany 24 A4
Buta, Dem. Rep. of the Congo 86 B1
Butare, Rwanda 86 C2
Butaritari, Kiribati 96 G9
Bute, U.K. 14 F3
Bute Inlet, Canada 104 C4
Butemba, Uganda 86 B3
Butembo, Dem. Rep. of the Congo 86 B2
Buteni, Romania 42 D7
Butera, Italy 31 E7
Butha Qi, China 60 B7
Butiaba, Uganda 86 B3
Butler, Mo., U.S.A. 112 F7
Butler, Pa., U.S.A. 110 F5
Buton, Indonesia 63 E6
Butte, Mont., U.S.A. 114 C7
Butte, Nebr., U.S.A. 112 D5
Butte Creek →, U.S.A. 116 F5
Butterworth = Gcuwa, S. Africa 89 E4
Butterworth, Malaysia 65 K3
Buttevant, Ireland 15 D3
Buttfield, Mt., Australia 93 D4
Button B., Canada 105 B10
Buttonwillow, U.S.A. 117 K7
Butty Hd., Australia 93 F3
Butuan, Phil. 61 G6
Butuku-Luba, Eq. Guin. 83 E6
Butung = Buton, Indonesia 63 E6
Buturlinovka, Russia 48 E5
Butzbach, Germany 25 E4
Bützow, Germany 24 B7
Buxa Duar, India 69 F13
Buxar, India 69 G10
Buxtehude, Germany 24 B5
Buxton, U.K. 12 D6
Buxy, France 19 F11
Buy, Russia 48 A5
Buynaksk, Russia 49 J8
Buyo, Ivory C. 82 D3
Buyo, L. de, Ivory C. 82 D3
Büyük Menderes →, Turkey 39 D9
Büyükçekmece, Turkey 41 E12
Büyükkarıştıran, Turkey 41 E11
Büyükkemikli Burnu, Turkey 41 F10
Büyükorhan, Turkey 39 B10
Büyükyoncalı, Turkey 41 E11
Buzançais, France 18 F8
Buzău, Romania 43 E11
Buzău □, Romania 43 E11
Buzău →, Romania 43 E12
Buzău, Pasul, Romania 43 E11
Buzen, Japan 55 H5
Buzet, Croatia 29 C10
Buzi →, Mozam. 87 F3
Buziaş, Romania 42 E6
Buzuluk, Russia 50 D6
Buzuluk →, Russia 48 E6
Buzzards B., U.S.A. 111 E14
Buzzards Bay, U.S.A. 111 E14
Bwana Mkubwe, Dem. Rep. of the Congo 87 E2
Byala, Ruse, Bulgaria 41 C9
Byala, Varna, Bulgaria 41 D11
Byala Slatina, Bulgaria 40 C7
Byarezina →, Belarus 47 F6
Byaroza, Belarus 47 F3
Bychawa, Poland 45 G9
Byczyna, Poland 45 G5
Bydgoszcz, Poland 45 E5
Byelarus = Belarus ■, Europe 46 F4
Byelorussia = Belarus ■, Europe 46 F4
Byers, U.S.A. 112 F2
Byesville, U.S.A. 110 G3
Byford, Australia 93 F2
Bykhaw, Belarus 46 F6
Bykhov = Bykhaw, Belarus 46 F6
Bykovo, Russia 48 F7
Bylas, U.S.A. 115 K8
Bylot, Canada 105 B10
Bylot I., Canada 101 A12
Byrd, C., Antarctica 5 C17
Byron Bay, Australia 95 D5
Byrranga, Gory, Russia 51 B11
Byrranga Mts. = Byrranga, Gory, Russia 51 B11
Byrum, Denmark 11 G5
Byske, Sweden 8 D19
Byske älv →, Sweden 8 D19
Bystrzyca →, Dolnośląskie, Poland 45 G3
Bystrzyca →, Lubelskie, Poland 45 G9
Bystrzyca Kłodzka, Poland 45 H3
Bytča, Slovak Rep. 27 B11
Bytom, Poland 45 H5
Bytom Odrzański, Poland 45 G2
Bytów, Poland 44 D4
Byumba, Rwanda 86 C3
Bzenec, Czech Rep. 27 C10
Bzura →, Poland 45 F7

C

Ca →, Vietnam 64 C5
Ca Mau, Vietnam 65 H5
Ca Mau, Mui, Vietnam 65 H5
Ca Na, Vietnam 65 G7
Caacupé, Paraguay 126 B4
Caála, Angola 85 G3
Caamano Sd., Canada 104 C3
Caazapá, Paraguay 126 B4
Caazapá □, Paraguay 127 B4
Cabadbaran, Phil. 61 G6
Cabalian = San Juan, Phil. 61 F6
Cabana, Spain 34 B2
Cabañaquinta, Spain 34 B5
Cabanatuan, Phil. 61 D4
Cabanes, Spain 32 E5
Cabano, Canada 103 C6
Čabar, Croatia 29 C11
Cabazon, U.S.A. 117 M10
Cabedelo, Brazil 125 E12
Cabeza del Buey, Spain 35 G5
Cabezón de la Sal, Spain 34 B6
Cabildo, Chile 126 C1
Cabimas, Venezuela 124 A4
Cabinda, Angola 84 F2
Cabinda □, Angola 84 F2
Cabinet Mts., U.S.A. 114 C6
Cabo Blanco, Argentina 128 F3
Cabo Frio, Brazil 127 A7
Cabo Pantoja, Peru 124 D3
Cabonga, Réservoir, Canada 102 C4
Cabool, U.S.A. 113 G8
Caboolture, Australia 95 D5
Cabora Bassa Dam = Cahora Bassa, Représa de, Mozam. 87 F3
Caborca, Mexico 118 A2
Cabot, Mt., U.S.A. 111 B13
Cabot Hd., Canada 110 A3
Cabot Str., Canada 103 C8
Cabra, Spain 35 H6
Cabra del Santo Cristo, Spain 35 H7
Cábras, Italy 30 C1
Cabrera, Spain 37 B9
Cabrera, Sierra, Spain 34 C4
Cabri, Canada 105 C7
Cabriel →, Spain 33 F3
Cabugao, Phil. 61 C4
Cacabelos, Spain 34 C4
Caçador, Brazil 127 B5
Čačak, Serbia, Yug. 40 C4
Caçapava do Sul, Brazil 127 C5
Cáccamo, Italy 30 E6
Cacém, Portugal 35 G1
Cáceres, Brazil 124 G7
Cáceres, Spain 35 F4
Cáceres □, Spain 34 F5
Cache Bay, Canada 102 C4
Cache Cr. →, U.S.A. 116 G5
Cache Creek, Canada 104 C4
Cacheu, Guinea-Biss. 82 C1
Cachi, Argentina 126 B2
Cachimbo, Serra do, Brazil 125 E7
Cachinal de la Sierra, Chile 126 A2
Cachoeira, Brazil 125 F11
Cachoeira do Sul, Brazil 127 C5
Cachoeiro de Itapemirim, Brazil 127 A7
Cachopo, Portugal 35 H3
Cacine, Guinea-Biss. 82 C1
Cacoal, Brazil 124 F6
Cacólo, Angola 84 G3
Caconda, Angola 85 G3
Čadca, Slovak Rep. 27 B11
Caddo, U.S.A. 113 H6
Cader Idris, U.K. 13 E4
Cadereyta, Mexico 118 B5
Cadí, Sierra del, Spain 32 C6
Cadibarrawirracanna, L., Australia 95 D2
Cadillac, France 20 D3
Cadillac, U.S.A. 108 C3
Cadiz, Phil. 61 F5
Cádiz, Spain 35 J4
Cadiz, Calif., U.S.A. 117 L11
Cadiz, Ohio, U.S.A. 110 F4
Cádiz □, Spain 35 J5
Cádiz, G. de, Spain 35 J3
Cadiz L., U.S.A. 115 J6
Cadney Park, Australia 95 D1
Cadomin, Canada 104 C5
Cadotte Lake, Canada 104 B5
Cadours, France 20 E5
Cadoux, Australia 93 F2
Caen, France 18 C6
Caernarfon, U.K. 12 D3
Caernarfon B., U.K. 12 D3
Caernarvon = Caernarfon, U.K. 12 D3
Caerphilly, U.K. 13 F4
Caerphilly □, U.K. 13 F4
Caesarea, Israel 75 C3
Caetité, Brazil 125 F10
Cafayate, Argentina 126 B2
Cafu, Angola 88 B2
Cagayan →, Phil. 61 B4
Cagayan de Oro, Phil. 61 G6
Cagayan Is., Phil. 61 G4
Cagayan Sulu I., Phil. 61 H3
Cagli, Italy 29 E9
Cágliari, Italy 30 C2
Cágliari, G. di, Italy 30 C2
Cagnano Varano, Italy 29 G12
Cagnes-sur-Mer, France 21 E11
Caguán →, Colombia 124 D4
Caguas, Puerto Rico 121 C6
Caha Mts., Ireland 15 E2
Cahama, Angola 88 B1
Caher, Ireland 15 D4
Caherciveen, Ireland 15 E1
Cahora Bassa, Représa de, Mozam. 87 F3
Cahore Pt., Ireland 15 D5
Cahors, France 20 D5
Cahul, Moldova 43 E13
Cai Bau, Dao, Vietnam 58 G6
Cai Nuoc, Vietnam 65 H5
Caia, Mozam. 87 F4
Caianda, Angola 87 E1
Caibarién, Cuba 120 B4
Caibiran, Phil. 61 F6
Caicara, Venezuela 124 B5
Caicó, Brazil 125 E11
Caicos Is., Turks & Caicos 121 B5
Caicos Passage, W. Indies 121 B5
Caidian, China 59 B10
Căinari, Moldova 43 D14
Caird Coast, Antarctica 5 D1
Cairn Gorm, U.K. 14 D5
Cairngorm Mts., U.K. 14 D5
Cairnryan, U.K. 14 G3
Cairns, Australia 94 B4
Cairns L., Canada 105 C10
Cairo = El Qâhira, Egypt 80 H7
Cairo, Ga., U.S.A. 109 K3
Cairo, Ill., U.S.A. 113 G10
Cairo, N.Y., U.S.A. 111 D11
Cairo Montenotte, Italy 28 D5
Caithness, Ord of, U.K. 14 C5
Cajamarca, Peru 124 E3
Cajarc, France 20 D5
Cajàzeiras, Brazil 125 E11
Čajetina, Serbia, Yug. 40 C3
Çakirgol, Turkey 73 B8
Çakırlar, Turkey 39 E12
Čakovec, Croatia 29 B13
Çal, Turkey 39 C11
Cala, Spain 35 H4
Cala →, Spain 35 H4
Cala Cadolar, Punta de = Rotja, Pta., Spain 33 G6
Cala d'Or, Spain 37 B10
Cala en Porter, Spain 37 B11
Cala Figuera, C. de, Spain 37 B9
Cala Forcat, Spain 37 B10
Cala Major, Spain 37 B9

Cala Mezquida = Sa Mesquida, *Spain* 37 B11
Cala Millor, *Spain* 37 B10
Cala Ratjada, *Spain* 37 B10
Cala Santa Galdana, *Spain* 37 B10
Calabanga, *Phil.* 61 E5
Calabar, *Nigeria* 83 E6
Calabogie, *Canada* 111 A8
Calabozo, *Venezuela* 124 B5
Calábria □, *Italy* 31 C9
Calaburras, Pta. de, *Spain* 35 J6
Calaceite, *Spain* 32 D5
Calacuccia, *France* 21 F13
Calafat, *Romania* 42 G7
Calafate, *Argentina* 128 G2
Calafell, *Spain* 32 D6
Calahorra, *Spain* 32 C3
Calais, *France* 19 B8
Calais, *U.S.A.* 109 C12
Calalaste, Cord. de, *Argentina* 126 B2
Calama, *Brazil* 124 E6
Calama, *Chile* 126 A2
Calamar, *Colombia* 124 A4
Calamian Group, *Phil.* 61 F3
Calamocha, *Spain* 32 E3
Calamonte, *Spain* 35 G4
Călan, *Romania* 42 E7
Calañas, *Spain* 35 H4
Calanda, *Spain* 32 E4
Calang, *Indonesia* 62 D1
Calangiánus, *Italy* 30 B2
Calapan, *Phil.* 61 E4
Călărasi, *Moldova* 43 C13
Călăraşi, *Romania* 43 F12
Călăraşi □, *Romania* 43 F12
Calasparra, *Spain* 33 G3
Calatafimi, *Italy* 30 E5
Calatayud, *Spain* 32 D3
Călăţele, *Romania* 42 D8
Calato = Kálathos, *Greece* 39 E10
Calauag, *Phil.* 61 E5
Calavà, C., *Italy* 31 D7
Calavite, C., *Phil.* 61 E4
Calayan, *Phil.* 61 B4
Calbayog, *Phil.* 61 E6
Calca, *Peru* 124 F4
Calcasieu L., *U.S.A.* 113 L8
Calcutta = Kolkata, *India* 69 H13
Calcutta, *U.S.A.* 110 F4
Caldaro, *Italy* 29 B8
Caldas da Rainha, *Portugal* 35 F1
Caldas de Reis, *Spain* 34 C2
Calder →, *U.K.* 12 D6
Caldera, *Chile* 126 B1
Caldwell, *Idaho, U.S.A.* 114 E5
Caldwell, *Kans., U.S.A.* 113 G6
Caldwell, *Tex., U.S.A.* 113 K6
Caledon, *S. Africa* 88 E2
Caledon →, *S. Africa* 88 E4
Caledon B., *Australia* 94 A2
Caledonia, *Canada* 110 C5
Caledonia, *U.S.A.* 110 D7
Calella, *Spain* 32 D7
Calemba, *Angola* 88 B2
Calen, *Australia* 94 C4
Calenzana, *France* 21 F12
Caletones, *Chile* 126 C1
Calexico, *U.S.A.* 117 N11
Calf of Man, *U.K.* 12 C3
Calgary, *Canada* 104 C6
Calheta, *Madeira* 37 D2
Calhoun, *U.S.A.* 109 H3
Cali, *Colombia* 124 C3
Calicut, *India* 66 P9
Caliente, *U.S.A.* 115 H6
California, *Mo., U.S.A.* 112 F8
California, *Pa., U.S.A.* 110 F5
California □, *U.S.A.* 116 H7
California, Baja, *Mexico* 118 A1
California, Baja, T.N. = Baja California □, *Mexico* 118 B2
California, Baja, T.S. = Baja California Sur □, *Mexico* 118 B2
California, G. de, *Mexico* 118 B2
California City, *U.S.A.* 117 K9
California Hot Springs, *U.S.A.* 117 K8
Călimăneşti, *Romania* 43 E9
Călimani, Munţii, *Romania* 43 C10
Calingasta, *Argentina* 126 C2
Calipatria, *U.S.A.* 117 M11
Calistoga, *U.S.A.* 116 G4
Calitri, *Italy* 31 B8
Calitzdorp, *S. Africa* 88 E3
Callabonna, L., *Australia* 95 D3
Callac, *France* 18 D3
Callan, *Ireland* 15 D4
Callander, *U.K.* 14 E4
Callao, *Peru* 124 F3
Calles, *Mexico* 119 C5
Callicoon, *U.S.A.* 111 E9
Calling Lake, *Canada* 104 B6
Calliope, *Australia* 94 C5
Callosa de Ensarriá, *Spain* 33 G4
Callosa de Segura, *Spain* 33 G4
Calne, *U.K.* 13 F6
Calola, *Angola* 88 B2
Calolbon = San Andres, *Phil.* 61 E6
Calonge, *Spain* 32 D8
Caloocan, *Phil.* 61 D4
Calore →, *Italy* 31 A7
Caloundra, *Australia* 95 D5
Calpe, *Spain* 33 G5
Calpella, *U.S.A.* 116 F3
Calpine, *U.S.A.* 116 F6
Calstock, *Canada* 102 C3
Caltabellotta, *Italy* 30 E6
Caltagirone, *Italy* 31 E7
Caltanissetta, *Italy* 31 E7
Çaltılıbük, *Turkey* 41 G12
Caluire-et-Cuire, *France* 19 G11
Calulo, *Angola* 84 G2
Caluso, *Italy* 28 C4
Calvados □, *France* 18 C6
Calvert →, *Australia* 94 B2
Calvert I., *Canada* 104 C3
Calvert Ra., *Australia* 92 D3
Calvi, *France* 21 F12
Calviá, *Spain* 33 F7
Calvillo, *Mexico* 118 C4
Calvinia, *S. Africa* 88 E2
Calvo = Calvo, Mte., *Italy* 29 G12
Calvo, Mte., *Italy* 29 G12
Calwa, *U.S.A.* 116 J7
Calzada Almuradiel = Almuradiel, *Spain* 35 G7
Calzada de Calatrava, *Spain* 35 G7
Cam →, *U.K.* 13 E8
Cam Lam, *Vietnam* 65 G7
Cam Pha, *Vietnam* 58 G6
Cam Ranh, *Vietnam* 65 G7
Cam Xuyen, *Vietnam* 64 C6
Camabatela, *Angola* 84 F3
Camacha, *Madeira* 37 D3
Camacho, *Mexico* 118 C4
Camacupa, *Angola* 85 G3
Camagüey, *Cuba* 120 B4
Camaiore, *Italy* 28 E7
Camaná, *Peru* 124 G4
Camanche Reservoir, *U.S.A.* 116 G6
Camaquã, *Brazil* 127 C5
Camaquã →, *Brazil* 127 C5
Câmara de Lobos, *Madeira* 37 D3
Camarat, C., *France* 21 E10
Camarès, *France* 20 E6
Camaret-sur-Mer, *France* 18 D2
Camargo, *Mexico* 119 B5
Camargue, *France* 21 E8
Camarillo, *U.S.A.* 117 L7
Camariñas, *Spain* 34 B1
Camarón, C., *Honduras* 120 C2
Camarones, *Argentina* 128 E3
Camas, *Spain* 35 H4
Camas, *U.S.A.* 116 E4
Camas Valley, *U.S.A.* 114 E2
Camballin, *Australia* 92 C3
Cambará, *Brazil* 127 A5
Cambay = Khambhat, *India* 68 H5
Cambay, G. of = Khambhat, G. of, *India* 66 J8
Cambil, *Spain* 35 H7
Cambo-les-Bains, *France* 20 E2
Cambodia ■, *Asia* 64 F5
Camborne, *U.K.* 13 G2
Cambrai, *France* 19 B10
Cambre, *Spain* 34 B2
Cambria, *U.S.A.* 116 K5
Cambrian Mts., *U.K.* 13 E4
Cambridge, *Canada* 102 D3
Cambridge, *Jamaica* 120 C4
Cambridge, *N.Z.* 91 G5
Cambridge, *U.K.* 13 E8
Cambridge, *Mass., U.S.A.* 111 D13
Cambridge, *Minn., U.S.A.* 112 C8
Cambridge, *N.Y., U.S.A.* 111 C11
Cambridge, *Nebr., U.S.A.* 112 E4
Cambridge, *Ohio, U.S.A.* 110 F3
Cambridge Bay = Ikaluktutiak, *Canada* 100 B9
Cambridge G., *Australia* 92 B4
Cambridge Springs, *U.S.A.* 110 E4
Cambridgeshire □, *U.K.* 13 E7
Cambrils, *Spain* 32 D6
Cambuci, *Brazil* 127 A7
Cambundi-Catembo, *Angola* 84 G3
Camden, *Ala., U.S.A.* 109 K2
Camden, *Ark., U.S.A.* 113 J8
Camden, *Maine, U.S.A.* 109 C11
Camden, *N.J., U.S.A.* 111 G9
Camden, *N.Y., U.S.A.* 111 C9
Camden, *S.C., U.S.A.* 109 H5
Camden Sd., *Australia* 92 C3
Camdenton, *U.S.A.* 113 F8
Çameli, *Turkey* 39 D11
Camenca, *Moldova* 43 B13
Camerino, *Italy* 29 E10
Cameron, *Ariz., U.S.A.* 115 J8
Cameron, *La., U.S.A.* 113 L8
Cameron, *Mo., U.S.A.* 112 F7
Cameron, *Tex., U.S.A.* 113 K6
Cameron Highlands, *Malaysia* 65 K3
Cameron Hills, *Canada* 104 B5
Cameroon ■, *Africa* 84 C2
Camerota, *Italy* 31 B8
Cameroun →, *Cameroon* 83 E6
Cameroun, Mt., *Cameroon* 83 E6
Cametá, *Brazil* 125 D9
Çamiçi Gölü, *Turkey* 39 D9
Camiguin □, *Phil.* 61 G6
Camiguin I., *Phil.* 61 B4
Camiling, *Phil.* 61 D4
Camilla, *U.S.A.* 109 K3
Caminha, *Portugal* 34 D2
Camino, *U.S.A.* 116 G6
Camira Creek, *Australia* 95 D5
Cammal, *U.S.A.* 110 E7
Cammarata, *Italy* 30 E6
Camocim, *Brazil* 125 D10
Camooweal, *Australia* 94 B2
Camopi, *Fr. Guiana* 125 C8
Camotes Is., *Phil.* 61 F6
Camotes Sea, *Phil.* 61 F6
Camp Borden, *Canada* 110 B5
Camp Hill, *U.S.A.* 110 F8
Camp Nelson, *U.S.A.* 117 J8
Camp Pendleton, *U.S.A.* 117 M9
Camp Verde, *U.S.A.* 115 J8
Camp Wood, *U.S.A.* 113 L5
Campagna, *Italy* 31 B8
Campana, *Argentina* 126 C4
Campana, I., *Chile* 128 F1
Campanário, *Madeira* 37 D2
Campanario, *Spain* 35 G5
Campánia □, *Italy* 31 B7
Campbell, *S. Africa* 88 D3
Campbell, *Calif., U.S.A.* 116 H5
Campbell, *Ohio, U.S.A.* 110 E4
Campbell I., *Pac. Oc.* 96 N8
Campbell L., *Canada* 105 A7
Campbell River, *Canada* 104 C3
Campbell Town, *Australia* 94 G4
Campbellford, *Canada* 110 B7
Campbellpur, *Pakistan* 68 C5
Campbellsville, *U.S.A.* 108 G3
Campbellton, *Canada* 103 C6
Campbeltown, *U.K.* 14 F3
Campeche, *Mexico* 119 D6
Campeche □, *Mexico* 119 D6
Campeche, Golfo de, *Mexico* 119 D6
Campello, *Spain* 33 G4
Câmpeni, *Romania* 42 D8
Camperville, *Canada* 105 C8
Campi Salentina, *Italy* 31 B11
Câmpia Turzii, *Romania* 43 D8
Campidano, *Italy* 30 C1
Campíglia Maríttima, *Italy* 28 E7
Campillo de Altobuey, *Spain* 33 F3
Campillos, *Spain* 35 H6
Câmpina, *Romania* 43 E10
Campina Grande, *Brazil* 125 E11
Campinas, *Brazil* 127 A6
Campli, *Italy* 29 F10
Campo, *Spain* 32 C5
Campo de Criptana, *Spain* 35 F7
Campo de Gibraltar, *Spain* 35 J5
Campo Grande, *Brazil* 125 H8
Campo Maíor, *Brazil* 125 D10
Campo Maior, *Portugal* 35 F3
Campo Mourão, *Brazil* 127 A5
Campo Túres, *Italy* 29 B8
Campobasso, *Italy* 31 A7
Campobello di Licata, *Italy* 30 E6
Campobello di Mazara, *Italy* 30 E5
Campofelice di Roccella, *Italy* 30 E6
Campomarino, *Italy* 29 G12
Camporeale, *Italy* 30 E6
Camporrobles, *Spain* 32 F3
Campos, *Brazil* 127 A7
Campos Belos, *Brazil* 125 F9
Campos del Puerto, *Spain* 37 B10
Campos Novos, *Brazil* 127 B5
Camprodón, *Spain* 32 C7
Camptonville, *U.S.A.* 116 F5
Camptown, *U.S.A.* 111 E8
Câmpulung, *Argeş, Romania* 43 E10
Câmpulung, *Suceava, Romania* 43 C10
Câmpuri, *Romania* 43 D11
Camrose, *Canada* 104 C6
Camsell Portage, *Canada* 105 B7
Çamyuva, *Turkey* 39 E12
Çan, *Turkey* 41 F11
Can Clavo, *Spain* 37 C7
Can Creu, *Spain* 37 C7
Can Gio, *Vietnam* 65 G6
Can Tho, *Vietnam* 65 G5
Canaan, *U.S.A.* 111 D11
Canada ■, *N. Amer.* 100 C10
Cañada de Gómez, *Argentina* 126 C3
Canadian, *U.S.A.* 113 H4
Canadian →, *U.S.A.* 113 H7
Canajoharie, *U.S.A.* 111 D10
Çanakkale, *Turkey* 41 F10
Çanakkale □, *Turkey* 41 F10
Çanakkale Boğazı, *Turkey* 41 F10
Canal Flats, *Canada* 104 C5
Canalejas, *Argentina* 126 D2
Canals, *Argentina* 126 C3
Canals, *Spain* 33 G4
Canandaigua, *U.S.A.* 110 D7
Canandaigua L., *U.S.A.* 110 D7
Cananea, *Mexico* 118 A2
Canarias, Is., *Atl. Oc.* 37 F4
Canarreos, Arch. de los, *Cuba* 120 B3
Canary Is. = Canarias, Is., *Atl. Oc.* 37 F4
Canaseraga, *U.S.A.* 110 D7
Canatlán, *Mexico* 118 C4
Canaveral, C., *U.S.A.* 109 L5
Cañaveruelas, *Spain* 32 E2
Canavieiras, *Brazil* 125 G11
Canby, *Calif., U.S.A.* 114 F3
Canby, *Minn., U.S.A.* 112 C6
Canby, *Oreg., U.S.A.* 116 E4
Cancale, *France* 18 D5
Canche →, *France* 19 B8
Cancún, *Mexico* 119 C7
Candanchu, *Spain* 32 C4
Çandarlı, *Turkey* 39 C8
Çandarlı Körfezi, *Turkey* 39 C8
Candas, *Spain* 34 B5
Candé, *France* 18 E5
Candela, *Italy* 31 A8
Candelaria, *Argentina* 127 B4
Candelaria, *Canary Is.* 37 F3
Candeleda, *Spain* 34 E5
Candia = Iráklion, *Greece* 36 D7
Candia, Sea of = Crete, Sea of, *Greece* 39 E7
Candle L., *Canada* 105 C7
Candlemas I., *Antarctica* 5 B1
Cando, *U.S.A.* 112 A5
Candon, *Phil.* 61 C4
Canea = Khaniá, *Greece* 36 D6
Canelli, *Italy* 28 D5
Canelones, *Uruguay* 127 C4
Canet-Plage, *France* 20 F7
Cañete, *Chile* 126 D1
Cañete, *Peru* 124 F3
Cañete, *Spain* 32 E3
Cañete de las Torres, *Spain* 35 H6
Cangas, *Spain* 34 C2
Cangas de Narcea, *Spain* 34 B4
Cangas de Onís, *Spain* 34 B5
Cangnan, *China* 59 D13
Canguaretama, *Brazil* 125 E11
Canguçu, *Brazil* 127 C5
Canguçu, Serra do, *Brazil* 127 C5
Cangwu, *China* 59 F8
Cangxi, *China* 58 B5
Cangyuan, *China* 58 F2
Cangzhou, *China* 56 E9
Caniapiscau →, *Canada* 103 A6
Caniapiscau, Rés. de, *Canada* 103 B6
Canicattì, *Italy* 30 E6
Canicattini Bagni, *Italy* 31 E8
Caniles, *Spain* 35 H8
Canim Lake, *Canada* 104 C4
Canindeyu □, *Paraguay* 127 A5
Canino, *Italy* 29 F8
Canisteo, *U.S.A.* 110 D7
Canisteo →, *U.S.A.* 110 D7
Cañitas, *Mexico* 118 C4
Cañizal, *Spain* 34 D5
Canjáyar, *Spain* 35 H8
Çankırı, *Turkey* 72 B5
Cankuzo, *Burundi* 86 C3
Canmore, *Canada* 104 C5
Canna, *U.K.* 14 D2
Cannanore, *India* 66 P9
Cannes, *France* 21 E11
Canning Town = Port Canning, *India* 69 H13
Cannington, *Canada* 110 B5
Cannóbio, *Italy* 28 B5
Cannock, *U.K.* 13 E5
Cannon Ball →, *U.S.A.* 112 B4
Cannondale Mt., *Australia* 94 D4
Cannonsville Reservoir, *U.S.A.* 111 D9
Cannonvale, *Australia* 94 C4
Canoas, *Brazil* 127 B5
Canoe L., *Canada* 105 B7
Canon City, *U.S.A.* 112 F2
Canora, *Canada* 105 C8
Canosa di Púglia, *Italy* 31 A9
Canso, *Canada* 103 C7
Cantabria □, *Spain* 34 B7
Cantabria, Sierra de, *Spain* 32 C2
Cantabrian Mts. = Cantábrica, Cordillera, *Spain* 34 C5
Cantábrica, Cordillera, *Spain* 34 C5
Cantal □, *France* 20 C6
Cantal, Plomb du, *France* 20 C6
Cantanhede, *Portugal* 34 E2
Cantavieja, *Spain* 32 E4
Čantavir, *Serbia, Yug.* 42 E4
Cantemir, *Moldova* 43 D13
Canterbury, *Australia* 94 D3
Canterbury, *U.K.* 13 F9
Canterbury Bight, *N.Z.* 91 L3
Canterbury Plains, *N.Z.* 91 K3
Cantil, *U.S.A.* 117 K9
Cantillana, *Spain* 35 H5
Canton = Guangzhou, *China* 59 F9
Canton, *Ga., U.S.A.* 109 H3
Canton, *Ill., U.S.A.* 112 E9
Canton, *Miss., U.S.A.* 113 J9
Canton, *Mo., U.S.A.* 112 E9
Canton, *N.Y., U.S.A.* 111 B9
Canton, *Ohio, U.S.A.* 110 F3
Canton, *Pa., U.S.A.* 110 E8
Canton, *S. Dak., U.S.A.* 112 D6
Canton L., *U.S.A.* 113 G5
Cantù, *Italy* 28 C6
Canudos, *Brazil* 124 E7
Canumã →, *Brazil* 124 D7
Canutama, *Brazil* 124 E6
Canutillo, *U.S.A.* 115 L10
Canvey, *U.K.* 13 F8
Canyon, *U.S.A.* 113 H4
Canyonlands National Park, *U.S.A.* 115 G9
Canyonville, *U.S.A.* 114 E2
Cao Bang, *Vietnam* 58 F6
Cao He →, *China* 57 D13
Cao Lanh, *Vietnam* 65 G5
Cao Xian, *China* 56 G8
Cáorle, *Italy* 29 C9
Cap-aux-Meules, *Canada* 103 C7
Cap-Chat, *Canada* 103 C6
Cap-de-la-Madeleine, *Canada* 102 C5
Cap-Haïtien, *Haiti* 121 C5
Capac, *U.S.A.* 110 C2
Capáccio, *Italy* 31 B8
Capaci, *Italy* 30 D6
Capanaparo →, *Venezuela* 124 B5
Capánnori, *Italy* 28 E7
Capbreton, *France* 20 E2
Capdenac, *France* 20 D6
Capdepera, *Spain* 32 F8
Cape →, *Australia* 94 C4
Cape Barren I., *Australia* 94 G4
Cape Breton Highlands Nat. Park, *Canada* 103 C7
Cape Breton I., *Canada* 103 C7
Cape Charles, *U.S.A.* 108 G8
Cape Coast, *Ghana* 83 D4
Cape Coral, *U.S.A.* 109 M5
Cape Dorset, *Canada* 101 B12
Cape Fear →, *U.S.A.* 109 H6
Cape Girardeau, *U.S.A.* 113 G10
Cape May, *U.S.A.* 108 F8
Cape May Point, *U.S.A.* 108 F8
Cape Province, *S. Africa* 85 L3
Cape Tormentine, *Canada* 103 C7
Cape Town, *S. Africa* 88 E2
Cape Verde Is. ■, *Atl. Oc.* 77 E1
Cape Vincent, *U.S.A.* 111 B8
Cape York Peninsula, *Australia* 94 A3
Capela, *Brazil* 125 F11
Capella, *Australia* 94 C4
Capendu, *France* 20 E6
Capestang, *France* 20 E7
Capim →, *Brazil* 125 D9
Capistrello, *Italy* 29 G10
Capitan, *U.S.A.* 115 K11
Capitol Reef National Park, *U.S.A.* 115 G8
Capitola, *U.S.A.* 116 J5
Capizzi, *Italy* 31 E7
Capoche →, *Mozam.* 87 F3
Capoterra, *Italy* 30 C1
Cappadocia, *Turkey* 72 C6
Capraia, *Italy* 28 E6
Caprara, Pta., *Italy* 30 A1
Caprarola, *Italy* 29 F9
Capreol, *Canada* 102 C3
Caprera, *Italy* 30 A2
Capri, *Italy* 31 B7
Capricorn Group, *Australia* 94 C5
Capricorn Ra., *Australia* 92 D2
Caprino Veronese, *Italy* 28 C7
Caprivi Strip, *Namibia* 88 B3
Captieux, *France* 20 D3
Caquetá →, *Colombia* 122 D4
Caracal, *Romania* 43 F9
Caracas, *Venezuela* 124 A5
Caracol, *Mato Grosso do Sul, Brazil* 126 A4
Caracol, *Piauí, Brazil* 125 E10
Caráglio, *Italy* 28 D4
Carajas, *Brazil* 125 E8
Carajás, Serra dos, *Brazil* 125 E8
Carangola, *Brazil* 127 A7
Caransebeş, *Romania* 42 E7
Carantec, *France* 18 D3
Caraquet, *Canada* 103 C6
Caras, *Peru* 124 E3
Caraş Severin □, *Romania* 42 E7
Caraşova, *Romania* 42 E6
Caratasca, L., *Honduras* 120 C3
Caratinga, *Brazil* 125 G10
Caraúbas, *Brazil* 125 E11
Caravaca = Caravaca de la Cruz, *Spain* 33 G3
Caravaca de la Cruz, *Spain* 33 G3
Caravággio, *Italy* 28 C6
Caravela, *Guinea-Biss.* 82 C1
Caravelas, *Brazil* 125 G11
Caraveli, *Peru* 124 G4
Caràzinho, *Brazil* 127 B5
Carballino = O Carballiño, *Spain* 34 C2
Carballo, *Spain* 34 B2
Carberry, *Canada* 105 D9
Carbó, *Mexico* 118 B2
Carbonara, C., *Italy* 30 C2
Carbondale, *Colo., U.S.A.* 114 G10
Carbondale, *Ill., U.S.A.* 113 G10
Carbondale, *Pa., U.S.A.* 111 E9
Carbonear, *Canada* 103 C9
Carboneras, *Spain* 33 J3
Carboneras de Guadazaón, *Spain* 32 F3
Carbónia, *Italy* 30 C1
Carcabuey, *Spain* 35 H6
Carcagente = Carcaixent, *Spain* 33 F4
Carcaixent, *Spain* 33 F4
Carcajou, *Canada* 104 B5
Carcar, *Phil.* 61 F5
Carcarana →, *Argentina* 126 C3
Carcasse, C., *Haiti* 121 C5
Carcassonne, *France* 20 E6
Carcross, *Canada* 104 A2
Çardak, *Çanakkale, Turkey* 41 F10
Çardak, *Denizli, Turkey* 39 D11
Cardamon Hills, *India* 66 Q10
Cardeña, *Spain* 35 G6
Cárdenas, *Cuba* 120 B3
Cárdenas, *San Luis Potosí, Mexico* 119 C5
Cárdenas, *Tabasco, Mexico* 119 D6
Cardenete, *Spain* 32 F3
Cardiff, *U.K.* 13 F4
Cardiff □, *U.K.* 13 F4
Cardiff-by-the-Sea, *U.S.A.* 117 M9
Cardigan, *U.K.* 13 E3
Cardigan B., *U.K.* 13 E3
Cardinal, *Canada* 111 B9
Cardona, *Spain* 32 D6
Cardona, *Uruguay* 126 C4
Cardoner →, *Spain* 32 D6
Cardoso, Ilha do, *Brazil* 127 B5
Cardston, *Canada* 104 D6
Cardwell, *Australia* 94 B4
Careen L., *Canada* 105 B7
Carei, *Romania* 42 C7
Careme = Ciremai, *Indonesia* 63 G13
Carentan, *France* 18 C5
Carey, *U.S.A.* 114 E7
Carey, L., *Australia* 93 E3
Carey L., *Canada* 105 A8
Careysburg, *Liberia* 82 D2

Cargèse, *France* 21 F12
Carhaix-Plouguer, *France* 18 D3
Carhué, *Argentina* 126 D3
Caria, *Turkey* 39 D10
Cariacica, *Brazil* 125 H10
Cariati, *Italy* 31 C9
Caribbean Sea, *W. Indies* 121 D5
Cariboo Mts., *Canada* 104 C4
Caribou, *U.S.A.* 109 B12
Caribou →, *Man., Canada* 105 B10
Caribou →, *N.W.T., Canada* 104 A3
Caribou I., *Canada* 102 C2
Caribou Is., *Canada* 104 A6
Caribou L., *Man., Canada* 105 B9
Caribou L., *Ont., Canada* 102 B2
Caribou Mts., *Canada* 104 B5
Carichic, *Mexico* 118 B3
Carigara, *Phil.* 61 F6
Carignan, *France* 19 C12
Carignano, *Italy* 28 D4
Carillo, *Mexico* 118 B4
Cariñena, *Spain* 32 D3
Carinhanha, *Brazil* 125 F10
Carinhanha →, *Brazil* 125 F10
Carini, *Italy* 30 D6
Cariño, *Spain* 34 B3
Carínola, *Italy* 30 A6
Carinthia = Kärnten □, *Austria* 26 E6
Caripito, *Venezuela* 124 A6
Carlbrod = Dimitrovgrad, *Serbia, Yug.* 40 C6
Carlet, *Spain* 33 F4
Carleton, Mt., *Canada* 103 C6
Carleton Place, *Canada* 102 C4
Carletonville, *S. Africa* 88 D4
Cârlibaba, *Romania* 43 C10
Carlin, *U.S.A.* 114 F5
Carlingford L., *U.K.* 15 B5
Carlinville, *U.S.A.* 112 F10
Carlisle, *U.K.* 12 C5
Carlisle, *U.S.A.* 110 F7
Carlit, Pic, *France* 20 F5
Carloforte, *Italy* 30 C1
Carlos Casares, *Argentina* 126 D3
Carlos Tejedor, *Argentina* 126 D3
Carlow, *Ireland* 15 D5
Carlow □, *Ireland* 15 D5
Carlsbad, *Calif., U.S.A.* 117 M9
Carlsbad, *N. Mex., U.S.A.* 113 J2
Carlsbad Caverns National Park, *U.S.A.* 113 J2
Carluke, *U.K.* 14 F5
Carlyle, *Canada* 105 D8
Carmacks, *Canada* 100 B6
Carmagnola, *Italy* 28 D4
Carman, *Canada* 105 D9
Carmarthen, *U.K.* 13 F3
Carmarthen B., *U.K.* 13 F3
Carmarthenshire □, *U.K.* 13 F3
Carmaux, *France* 20 D6
Carmel, *U.S.A.* 111 E11
Carmel-by-the-Sea, *U.S.A.* 116 J5
Carmel Valley, *U.S.A.* 116 J5
Carmelo, *Uruguay* 126 C4
Carmen, *Colombia* 124 B3
Carmen, *Paraguay* 127 B4
Carmen →, *Mexico* 118 A3
Carmen, I., *Mexico* 118 B2
Carmen de Patagones, *Argentina* 128 E4
Cármenes, *Spain* 34 C5
Carmensa, *Argentina* 126 D2
Carmi, *Canada* 104 D5
Carmi, *U.S.A.* 108 F1
Carmichael, *U.S.A.* 116 G5
Carmila, *Australia* 94 C4
Carmona, *Costa Rica* 120 E2
Carmona, *Spain* 35 H5
Carn Ban, *U.K.* 14 D4
Carn Eige, *U.K.* 14 D3
Carnamah, *Australia* 93 E2
Carnarvon, *Australia* 93 D1
Carnarvon, *S. Africa* 88 E3
Carnarvon Ra., *Queens., Australia* 94 D4
Carnarvon Ra., *W. Austral., Australia* 93 E3
Carnation, *U.S.A.* 116 C5
Carndonagh, *Ireland* 15 A4
Carnduff, *Canada* 105 D8
Carnegie, *U.S.A.* 110 F4
Carnegie, L., *Australia* 93 E3
Carnic Alps = Karnische Alpen, *Europe* 26 E6
Carniche Alpi = Karnische Alpen, *Europe* 26 E6
Carnot, *C.A.R.* 84 D3
Carnot, C., *Australia* 95 E2
Carnot B., *Australia* 92 C3
Carnoustie, *U.K.* 14 E6
Carnsore Pt., *Ireland* 15 D5
Caro, *U.S.A.* 108 D4
Carol City, *U.S.A.* 109 N5
Carolina, *Brazil* 125 E9
Carolina, *Puerto Rico* 121 C6
Carolina, *S. Africa* 89 D5
Caroline I., *Kiribati* 97 H12
Caroline Is., *Micronesia* 52 J17
Caroni →, *Venezuela* 124 B6
Caronie = Nébrodi, Monti, *Italy* 31 E7
Carpathians, *Europe* 6 F10
Carpaţii Meridionali, *Romania* 43 E9
Carpentaria, G. of, *Australia* 94 A2
Carpentras, *France* 21 D9
Carpi, *Italy* 28 D7
Cărpineni, *Moldova* 43 D13
Carpinteria, *U.S.A.* 117 L7
Carpio, *Spain* 34 D5
Carr Boyd Ra., *Australia* 92 C4
Carrabelle, *U.S.A.* 109 L3
Carral, *Spain* 34 B2
Carranza, Presa V., *Mexico* 118 B4
Carrara, *Italy* 28 D7
Carrascal, *Phil.* 61 G6
Carrascosa del Campo, *Spain* 32 E2
Carrauntoohill, *Ireland* 15 D2
Carrick-on-Shannon, *Ireland* 15 C3
Carrick-on-Suir, *Ireland* 15 D4
Carrickfergus, *U.K.* 15 B6
Carrickmacross, *Ireland* 15 C5
Carrington, *U.S.A.* 112 B5
Carrión →, *Spain* 34 D6
Carrión de los Condes, *Spain* 34 C6
Carrizal Bajo, *Chile* 126 B1
Carrizalillo, *Chile* 126 B1
Carrizo Cr. →, *U.S.A.* 113 G3
Carrizo Springs, *U.S.A.* 113 L5
Carrizozo, *U.S.A.* 115 K11
Carroll, *U.S.A.* 112 D7
Carrollton, *Ga., U.S.A.* 109 J3
Carrollton, *Ill., U.S.A.* 112 F9
Carrollton, *Ky., U.S.A.* 108 F3
Carrollton, *Mo., U.S.A.* 112 F8
Carrollton, *Ohio, U.S.A.* 110 F3
Carron →, *U.K.* 14 D4
Carron, L., *U.K.* 14 D3
Carrot →, *Canada* 105 C8
Carrot River, *Canada* 105 C8
Carrouges, *France* 18 D6
Carrù, *Italy* 28 D4
Carruthers, *Canada* 105 C7
Carsa Dek, *Ethiopia* 81 F4
Çarşamba, *Turkey* 72 B7
Carsóli, *Italy* 29 F10
Carson, *Calif., U.S.A.* 117 M8
Carson, *N. Dak., U.S.A.* 112 B4
Carson →, *U.S.A.* 116 F8
Carson City, *U.S.A.* 116 F7
Carson Sink, *U.S.A.* 114 G4
Cartagena, *Colombia* 124 A3
Cartagena, *Spain* 33 H4
Cartago, *Colombia* 124 C3
Cartago, *Costa Rica* 120 E3
Cártama, *Spain* 35 J6
Cartaxo, *Portugal* 35 F2
Cartaya, *Spain* 35 H3
Cartersville, *U.S.A.* 109 H3
Carterton, *N.Z.* 91 J5
Carthage, *Tunisia* 30 F3
Carthage, *Ill., U.S.A.* 112 E9
Carthage, *Mo., U.S.A.* 113 G7
Carthage, *N.Y., U.S.A.* 108 D8
Carthage, *Tex., U.S.A.* 113 J7
Cartier I., *Australia* 92 B3
Cartwright, *Canada* 103 B8
Caruaru, *Brazil* 125 E11
Carúpano, *Venezuela* 124 A6
Caruthersville, *U.S.A.* 113 G10
Carvin, *France* 19 B9
Carvoeiro, *Brazil* 124 D6
Carvoeiro, C., *Portugal* 35 F1
Cary, *U.S.A.* 109 H6
Casa Branca, *Portugal* 35 G2
Casa Grande, *U.S.A.* 115 K8
Casablanca, *Chile* 126 C1
Casablanca, *Morocco* 78 B4
Casacalenda, *Italy* 29 G11
Casalbordino, *Italy* 29 F11
Casale Monferrato, *Italy* 28 C5
Casalmaggiore, *Italy* 28 D7
Casalpusterlengo, *Italy* 28 C6
Casamance →, *Senegal* 82 C1
Casarano, *Italy* 31 B11
Casares, *Spain* 35 J5
Casas Ibáñez, *Spain* 33 F3
Casasimarro, *Spain* 33 F2
Casatejada, *Spain* 34 F5
Casavieja, *Spain* 34 E6
Cascade, *Idaho, U.S.A.* 114 D5
Cascade, *Mont., U.S.A.* 114 C8
Cascade Locks, *U.S.A.* 116 E5
Cascade Ra., *U.S.A.* 116 D5
Cascade Reservoir, *U.S.A.* 114 D5
Cascais, *Portugal* 35 G1
Cascavel, *Brazil* 127 A5
Cáscina, *Italy* 28 E7
Casco B., *U.S.A.* 109 D10
Caselle Torinese, *Italy* 28 C4
Caserta, *Italy* 31 A7
Cashel, *Ireland* 15 D4
Casiguran, *Phil.* 61 C5
Casilda, *Argentina* 126 C3
Casimcea, *Romania* 43 F13
Casino, *Australia* 95 D5
Casiquiare →, *Venezuela* 124 C5
Čáslav, *Czech Rep.* 26 B8
Casma, *Peru* 124 E3
Casmalia, *U.S.A.* 117 L6
Cásola Valsénio, *Italy* 29 D8
Cásoli, *Italy* 29 F11
Caspe, *Spain* 32 D4
Casper, *U.S.A.* 114 E10
Caspian Depression, *Eurasia* 49 G9
Caspian Sea, *Eurasia* 50 E6
Cass Lake, *U.S.A.* 112 B7
Cassà de la Selva, *Spain* 32 D7
Cassadaga, *U.S.A.* 110 D5
Cassano allo Iónio, *Italy* 31 C9
Casse, Grande, *France* 21 C10
Cassel, *France* 19 B9
Casselman, *Canada* 111 A9
Casselton, *U.S.A.* 112 B6
Cassiar, *Canada* 104 B3
Cassiar Mts., *Canada* 104 B2
Cassino, *Italy* 30 A6
Cassis, *France* 21 E9
Cassville, *U.S.A.* 113 G8
Castagneto Carducci, *Italy* 28 E7
Castaic, *U.S.A.* 117 L8
Castalia, *U.S.A.* 110 E2
Castanhal, *Brazil* 125 D9
Castéggio, *Italy* 28 C6
Castejón de Monegros, *Spain* 32 D4
Castèl di Sangro, *Italy* 29 G11
Castèl San Giovanni, *Italy* 28 C6
Castèl San Pietro Terme, *Italy* 29 D8
Castelbuono, *Italy* 31 E7
Castelfidardo, *Italy* 29 E10
Castelfiorentino, *Italy* 28 E7
Castelfranco Emília, *Italy* 28 D8
Castelfranco Véneto, *Italy* 29 C8
Casteljaloux, *France* 20 D4
Castellabate, *Italy* 31 B7
Castellammare, G. di, *Italy* 30 D5
Castellammare del Golfo, *Italy* 30 D5
Castellammare di Stábia, *Italy* 31 B7
Castellamonte, *Italy* 28 C4
Castellane, *France* 21 E10
Castellaneta, *Italy* 31 B9
Castelli, *Argentina* 126 D4
Castelló de la Plana, *Spain* 32 F4
Castellón de la Plana □, *Spain* 32 E4
Castellote, *Spain* 32 E4
Castelmáuro, *Italy* 29 G11
Castelnau-de-Médoc, *France* 20 C3
Castelnau-Magnoac, *France* 20 E4
Castelnaudary, *France* 20 E5
Castelnovo ne' Monti, *Italy* 28 D7
Castelnuovo di Val di Cécina, *Italy* 28 E7
Castelo, *Brazil* 127 A7
Castelo Branco, *Portugal* 34 F3
Castelo Branco □, *Portugal* 34 F3
Castelo de Paiva, *Portugal* 34 D2
Castelo de Vide, *Portugal* 35 F3
Castelsardo, *Italy* 30 B1
Castelsarrasin, *France* 20 D5
Casteltérmini, *Italy* 30 E6
Castelvetrano, *Italy* 30 E5
Castets, *France* 20 E2
Castiglion Fiorentino, *Italy* 29 E8
Castiglione del Lago, *Italy* 29 E9
Castiglione della Pescáia, *Italy* 28 F7
Castiglione delle Stiviere, *Italy* 28 C7
Castilblanco, *Spain* 35 F5
Castile, *U.S.A.* 110 D6
Castilla, Playa de, *Spain* 35 J4
Castilla-La Mancha □, *Spain* 6 H5
Castilla y Leon □, *Spain* 34 D6
Castillo de Locubín, *Spain* 35 H7
Castillon-en-Couserans, *France* 20 F5
Castillonès, *France* 20 D4
Castillos, *Uruguay* 127 C5
Castle Dale, *U.S.A.* 114 G8
Castle Douglas, *U.K.* 14 G5
Castle Rock, *Colo., U.S.A.* 112 F2
Castle Rock, *Wash., U.S.A.* 116 D4
Castlebar, *Ireland* 15 C2
Castleblaney, *Ireland* 15 B5
Castlederg, *U.K.* 15 B4
Castleford, *U.K.* 12 D6
Castlegar, *Canada* 104 D5
Castlepollard, *Ireland* 15 C4
Castlerea, *Ireland* 15 C3
Castlereagh →, *Australia* 95 E4
Castlereagh B., *Australia* 94 A2
Castleton, *U.S.A.* 111 C11
Castletown, *U.K.* 12 C3
Castletown Bearhaven, *Ireland* 15 E2
Castor, *Canada* 104 C6
Castor →, *Canada* 102 B4
Castorland, *U.S.A.* 111 C9
Castres, *France* 20 E6
Castricum, *Neths.* 17 B4
Castries, *St. Lucia* 121 D7
Castril, *Spain* 35 H8
Castro, *Brazil* 127 A6
Castro, *Chile* 128 E2
Castro Alves, *Brazil* 125 F11
Castro del Río, *Spain* 35 H6
Castro-Urdiales, *Spain* 34 B7
Castro Verde, *Portugal* 35 H2
Castrojeriz, *Spain* 34 C6
Castropol, *Spain* 34 B4
Castroreale, *Italy* 31 D8
Castrovíllari, *Italy* 31 C9
Castroville, *U.S.A.* 116 J5
Castuera, *Spain* 35 G5
Çat, *Turkey* 73 C9
Cat Ba, Dao, *Vietnam* 64 B6
Cat I., *Bahamas* 121 B4
Cat L., *Canada* 102 B1
Cat Lake, *Canada* 102 B1
Čata, *Slovak Rep.* 27 D11
Catacamas, *Honduras* 120 D2
Cataguases, *Brazil* 127 A7
Çatak, *Turkey* 73 C10
Catalão, *Brazil* 125 G9
Çatalca, *Turkey* 41 E12
Catalina, *Canada* 103 C9
Catalina, *Chile* 126 B2
Catalina, *U.S.A.* 115 K8
Catalonia = Cataluña □, *Spain* 32 D6
Cataluña □, *Spain* 32 D6
Çatalzeytin, *Turkey* 72 B6
Catamarca, *Argentina* 126 B2
Catamarca □, *Argentina* 126 B2
Catanauan, *Phil.* 61 E5
Catanduanes □, *Phil.* 61 E6
Catanduva, *Brazil* 127 A6
Catánia, *Italy* 31 E8
Catánia, G. di, *Italy* 31 E8
Catanzaro, *Italy* 31 D9
Catarman, *Phil.* 61 E6
Catbalogan, *Phil.* 61 F6
Cateel, *Phil.* 61 H7
Catembe, *Mozam.* 89 D5
Caterham, *U.K.* 13 F7
Cathcart, *S. Africa* 88 E4
Cathlamet, *U.S.A.* 116 D3
Catio, *Guinea-Biss.* 82 C1
Catlettsburg, *U.S.A.* 108 F4
Çatma Dağı, *Turkey* 39 C11
Catoche, C., *Mexico* 119 C7
Cátria, Mte., *Italy* 29 E9
Catriló, *Argentina* 126 D3
Catrimani, *Brazil* 124 C6
Catrimani →, *Brazil* 124 C6
Catskill, *U.S.A.* 111 D11
Catskill Mts., *U.S.A.* 111 D10
Catt, Mt., *Australia* 94 A1
Cattaraugus, *U.S.A.* 110 D6
Cattólica, *Italy* 29 E9
Cattólica Eraclea, *Italy* 30 E6
Catuala, *Angola* 88 B2
Catuane, *Mozam.* 89 D5
Catur, *Mozam.* 87 E4
Catwick Is., *Vietnam* 65 G7
Cauca →, *Colombia* 124 B4
Caucaia, *Brazil* 125 D11
Caucasus Mountains, *Eurasia* 49 J7
Caudete, *Spain* 33 G3
Caudry, *France* 19 B10
Caulnes, *France* 18 D4
Caulónia, *Italy* 31 D9
Caungula, *Angola* 84 F3
Cauquenes, *Chile* 126 D1
Caura →, *Venezuela* 124 B6
Cauresi →, *Mozam.* 87 F3
Căuşani, *Moldova* 43 D14
Causapscal, *Canada* 103 C6
Caussade, *France* 20 D5
Causse-Méjean, *France* 20 D7
Cauterets, *France* 20 F3
Cauvery →, *India* 66 P11
Caux, Pays de, *France* 18 C7
Cava de' Tirreni, *Italy* 31 B7
Cávado →, *Portugal* 34 D2
Cavaillon, *France* 21 E9
Cavalaire-sur-Mer, *France* 21 E10
Cavalese, *Italy* 29 B8
Cavalier, *U.S.A.* 112 A6
Cavalla = Cavally →, *Africa* 82 E3
Cavalleria, C. de, *Spain* 37 A11
Cavallo, I. de, *France* 21 G13
Cavally →, *Africa* 82 E3
Cavan, *Ireland* 15 B4
Cavan □, *Ireland* 15 C4
Cavárzere, *Italy* 29 C9
Çavdarhisar, *Turkey* 39 B11
Çavdır, *Turkey* 39 D11
Cave Creek, *U.S.A.* 115 K7
Cavenagh Ra., *Australia* 93 E4
Caviana, I., *Brazil* 125 C8
Cavite, *Phil.* 61 D4
Cavnic, *Romania* 43 C8
Cavour, *Italy* 28 D4
Cavtat, *Croatia* 40 D2
Cawnpore = Kanpur, *India* 69 F9
Caxias, *Brazil* 125 D10
Caxias do Sul, *Brazil* 127 B5
Çay, *Turkey* 72 C4
Cay Sal Bank, *Bahamas* 120 B4
Cayambe, *Ecuador* 124 C3
Çaycuma, *Turkey* 72 B5
Çayeli, *Turkey* 73 B9
Cayenne, *Fr. Guiana* 125 B8
Caygören Barajı, *Turkey* 39 B10
Cayiralan, *Turkey* 72 C6
Caylus, *France* 20 D5
Cayman Brac, *Cayman Is.* 120 C4
Cayman Is. ■, *W. Indies* 120 C3
Cayo Romano, *Cuba* 120 B4
Cayres, *France* 20 D7
Cayuga, *Canada* 110 D5
Cayuga, *U.S.A.* 111 D8
Cayuga L., *U.S.A.* 111 D8
Cazalla de la Sierra, *Spain* 35 H5
Căzăneşti, *Romania* 43 F12
Cazaubon, *France* 20 E3
Cazaux et de Sanguinet, Étang de, *France* 20 D2
Cazenovia, *U.S.A.* 111 D9
Cazères, *France* 20 E5
Cazin, *Bos.-H.* 29 D12
Čazma, *Croatia* 29 C13
Cazombo, *Angola* 85 G4
Cazorla, *Spain* 35 H7
Cazorla, Sierra de, *Spain* 35 G8
Cea →, *Spain* 34 C5
Ceamurlia de Jos, *Romania* 43 F13
Ceanannus Mor, *Ireland* 15 C5
Ceará = Fortaleza, *Brazil* 125 D11
Ceará □, *Brazil* 125 E11
Ceará Mirim, *Brazil* 125 E11
Ceauru, L., *Romania* 43 F8
Cebaco, I. de, *Panama* 120 E3
Cebollar, *Argentina* 126 B2
Cebollera, Sierra de, *Spain* 32 D2
Cebreros, *Spain* 34 E6
Cebu, *Phil.* 61 F5
Čečava, *Bos.-H.* 42 F2
Ceccano, *Italy* 30 A6
Cece, *Hungary* 42 D3
Cechi, *Ivory C.* 82 D4
Cecil Plains, *Australia* 95 D5
Cécina, *Italy* 28 E7
Cécina →, *Italy* 28 E7
Ceclavín, *Spain* 34 F4
Cedar →, *U.S.A.* 112 E9
Cedar City, *U.S.A.* 115 H7
Cedar Creek Reservoir, *U.S.A.* 113 J6
Cedar Falls, *Iowa, U.S.A.* 112 D8
Cedar Falls, *Wash., U.S.A.* 116 C5
Cedar Key, *U.S.A.* 109 L4
Cedar L., *Canada* 105 C9
Cedar Rapids, *U.S.A.* 112 E9
Cedartown, *U.S.A.* 109 H3
Cedarvale, *Canada* 104 B3
Cedarville, *S. Africa* 89 E4
Cedeira, *Spain* 34 B2
Cedral, *Mexico* 118 C4
Cedrino →, *Italy* 30 B2
Cedro, *Brazil* 125 E11
Cedros, I. de, *Mexico* 118 B1
Ceduna, *Australia* 95 E1
Cedynia, *Poland* 45 F1
Cée, *Spain* 34 C1
Cefalù, *Italy* 31 D7
Cega →, *Spain* 34 D6
Cegléd, *Hungary* 42 C4
Céglie Messápico, *Italy* 31 B10
Cehegín, *Spain* 33 G3
Ceheng, *China* 58 E5
Cehu-Silvaniei, *Romania* 43 C8
Ceica, *Romania* 42 D7
Ceira →, *Portugal* 34 E2
Čelákovice, *Czech Rep.* 26 A7
Celano, *Italy* 29 F10
Celanova, *Spain* 34 C3
Celaya, *Mexico* 118 C4
Celebes Sea, *Indonesia* 63 D6
Čelić, *Bos.-H.* 42 F3
Celina, *U.S.A.* 108 E3
Celinac, *Bos.-H.* 42 F2
Celje, *Slovenia* 29 B12
Celldömölk, *Hungary* 42 C2
Celle, *Germany* 24 C6
Celorico da Beira, *Portugal* 34 E3
Çeltikçi, *Turkey* 39 D12
Çemişgezek, *Turkey* 73 C8
Cenderwasih, Teluk, *Indonesia* 63 E9
Cengong, *China* 58 D7
Ceno →, *Italy* 28 D7
Centallo, *Italy* 28 D4
Centelles, *Spain* 32 D7
Center, *N. Dak., U.S.A.* 112 B4
Center, *Tex., U.S.A.* 113 K7
Centerburg, *U.S.A.* 110 F2
Centerville, *Calif., U.S.A.* 116 J7
Centerville, *Iowa, U.S.A.* 112 E8
Centerville, *Pa., U.S.A.* 110 F5
Centerville, *Tenn., U.S.A.* 109 H2
Centerville, *Tex., U.S.A.* 113 K7
Cento, *Italy* 29 D8
Central □, *Ghana* 83 D4
Central □, *Kenya* 86 C4
Central □, *Malawi* 87 E3
Central □, *Zambia* 87 E2
Central, Cordillera, *Colombia* 122 C3
Central, Cordillera, *Costa Rica* 120 D3
Central, Cordillera, *Dom. Rep.* 121 C5
Central, Cordillera, *Phil.* 61 C4
Central African Rep. ■, *Africa* 84 C4
Central America, *America* 98 H11
Central Butte, *Canada* 105 C7
Central City, *Colo., U.S.A.* 114 G11
Central City, *Ky., U.S.A.* 108 G2
Central City, *Nebr., U.S.A.* 112 E6
Central I., *Kenya* 86 B4
Central Makran Range, *Pakistan* 66 F4
Central Patricia, *Canada* 102 B1
Central Point, *U.S.A.* 114 E2
Central Russian Uplands, *Europe* 6 E13
Central Siberian Plateau, *Russia* 52 C14
Central Square, *U.S.A.* 111 C8
Centralia, *Ill., U.S.A.* 112 F10
Centralia, *Mo., U.S.A.* 112 F8
Centralia, *Wash., U.S.A.* 116 D4
Cenxi, *China* 59 F8
Čeotina →, *Bos.-H.* 40 C2
Cephalonia = Kefallinía, *Greece* 38 C2
Čepin, *Croatia* 42 E3
Ceprano, *Italy* 30 A6
Ceptura, *Romania* 43 E11
Cepu, *Indonesia* 63 G14
Ceram = Seram, *Indonesia* 63 E7
Ceram Sea = Seram Sea, *Indonesia* 63 E7
Cerbère, *France* 20 F7
Cerbicales, Is., *France* 21 G13
Cercal, *Portugal* 35 H2
Cerdaña, *Spain* 32 C6
Cère →, *France* 20 D5
Cerea, *Italy* 29 C8
Ceredigion □, *U.K.* 13 E3
Ceres, *Argentina* 126 B3
Ceres, *S. Africa* 88 E2
Ceres, *U.S.A.* 116 H6
Céret, *France* 20 F6
Cergy, *France* 19 C9
Cerignola, *Italy* 31 A8
Cerigo = Kíthira, *Greece* 38 E5
Cérilly, *France* 19 F9
Cerisiers, *France* 19 D10
Cerizay, *France* 18 F6
Çerkeş, *Turkey* 72 B5
Çerkezköy, *Turkey* 41 E12
Cerknica, *Slovenia* 29 C11
Cerkovica, *Bulgaria* 41 C8

Cermerno, Serbia, Yug. 40 C4
Çermik, Turkey 73 C8
Cerna, Romania 43 E13
Cerna →, Romania 43 F8
Cernavodă, Romania 43 F13
Cernay, France 19 E14
Cernik, Croatia 42 E2
Cerralvo, I., Mexico 118 C3
Cërrik, Albania 40 E3
Cerritos, Mexico 118 C4
Cerro Chato, Uruguay 127 C4
Certaldo, Italy 28 E8
Cervaro →, Italy 31 A8
Cervati, Monte, Italy 31 B8
Cerventes, Australia 93 F2
Cervera, Spain 32 D6
Cervera de Pisuerga, Spain 34 C6
Cervera del Río Alhama, Spain 32 C3
Cervéteri, Italy 29 F9
Cérvia, Italy 29 D9
Cervignano del Friuli, Italy 29 C10
Cervinara, Italy 31 A7
Cervione, France 21 F13
Cervo, Spain 34 B3
Cesarò, Italy 31 E7
Cesena, Italy 29 D9
Cesenático, Italy 29 D9
Cēsis, Latvia 9 H21
Česká Lípa, Czech Rep. 26 A7
Česká Třebová, Czech Rep. 27 B9
České Budějovice, Czech Rep. 26 C7
České Velenice, Czech Rep. 26 C7
Českomoravská Vrchovina, Czech Rep. 26 B8
Český Brod, Czech Rep. 26 A7
Český Krumlov, Czech Rep. 26 C7
Český Těšín, Czech Rep. 27 B11
Česma →, Croatia 29 C13
Çeşme, Turkey 39 C8
Cesson-Sévigné, France 18 D5
Cestas, France 20 D3
Cestos →, Liberia 82 D3
Cetate, Romania 42 F8
Cetin Grad, Croatia 29 C12
Cetina →, Croatia 29 E13
Cetinje, Montenegro, Yug. 40 D2
Cetraro, Italy 31 C8
Ceuta, N. Afr. 78 A4
Ceva, Italy 28 D5
Cévennes, France 20 D7
Ceyhan, Turkey 70 B2
Ceyhan →, Turkey 72 D6
Ceylânpınar, Turkey 73 D9
Ceylon = Sri Lanka ■, Asia 66 R12
Cèze →, France 21 D8
Cha-am, Thailand 64 F2
Cha Pa, Vietnam 64 A4
Chabanais, France 20 C4
Chabeuil, France 21 D9
Chablais, France 19 F13
Chablis, France 19 E10
Chacabuco, Argentina 126 C3
Chachapoyas, Peru 124 E3
Chachoengsao, Thailand 64 F3
Chachran, Pakistan 66 E7
Chachro, Pakistan 68 G4
Chaco □, Argentina 126 B3
Chaco □, Paraguay 126 B4
Chaco →, U.S.A. 115 H9
Chaco Austral, S. Amer. 128 B4
Chaco Boreal, S. Amer. 124 H6
Chaco Central, S. Amer. 128 A4
Chacon, C., U.S.A. 104 C2
Chad ■, Africa 79 F8
Chad, L. = Tchad, L., Chad 79 F8
Chadan, Russia 51 D10
Chadileuvú →, Argentina 126 D2
Chadiza, Zambia 87 E3
Chadron, U.S.A. 112 D3
Chadyr-Lunga = Ciadâr-Lunga, Moldova 43 D13
Chae Hom, Thailand 64 C2
Chaem →, Thailand 64 C2
Chaeryŏng, N. Korea 57 E13
Chagai Hills = Chāh Gay, Afghan. 66 E3
Chagda, Russia 51 D14
Chagny, France 19 F11
Chagoda, Russia 46 C8
Chagos Arch., Ind. Oc. 52 K11
Chagrin Falls, U.S.A. 110 E3
Chāh Ākhvor, Iran 71 C8
Chāh Bahar, Iran 71 E9
Chāh-e Kavīr, Iran 71 C8
Chāh Gay, Afghan. 66 E3
Chahar Burjak, Afghan. 66 D3
Chahār Mahāll va Bakhtīarī □, Iran 71 C6
Chaibasa, India 67 H14
Chaillé-les-Marais, France 20 B2
Chainat, Thailand 64 E3
Chaiya, Thailand 65 H2
Chaj Doab, Pakistan 68 C5
Chajari, Argentina 126 C4
Chak Amru, Pakistan 68 C6
Chaka, Sudan 81 G3
Chakar →, Pakistan 68 E3
Chakari, Zimbabwe 89 B4
Chake Chake, Tanzania 86 D4
Chakhānsūr, Afghan. 66 D3
Chakonipau, L., Canada 103 A6
Chakradharpur, India 69 H11
Chakrata, India 68 D7
Chakwal, Pakistan 68 C5
Chala, Peru 124 G4
Chalais, France 20 C4
Chalchihuites, Mexico 118 C4
Chalcis = Khalkís, Greece 38 C5
Châlette-sur-Loing, France 19 D9
Chaleur B., Canada 103 C6
Chalfant, U.S.A. 116 H8
Chalhuanca, Peru 124 F4
Chalindrey, France 19 E12
Chaling, China 59 D9
Chalisgaon, India 66 J9
Chalk River, Canada 102 C4
Chalky Inlet, N.Z. 91 M1
Challans, France 18 F5
Challapata, Bolivia 124 G5
Challis, U.S.A. 114 D6
Chalmette, U.S.A. 113 L10
Chalon-sur-Saône, France 19 F11
Chalonnes-sur-Loire, France 18 E6
Châlons-en-Champagne, France 19 D11
Châlus, France 20 C4
Chalyaphum, Thailand 64 E4
Cham, Germany 25 F8
Cham, Cu Lao, Vietnam 64 E7
Chama, U.S.A. 115 H10
Chamaicó, Argentina 126 D3
Chaman, Pakistan 66 D5
Chamba, India 68 C7
Chamba, Tanzania 87 E4
Chambal →, India 69 F8
Chamberlain, U.S.A. 112 D5
Chamberlain →, Australia 92 C4
Chamberlain L., U.S.A. 109 B11
Chambers, U.S.A. 115 J9
Chambersburg, U.S.A. 108 F7
Chambéry, France 21 C9
Chambeshi →, Zambia 84 G6
Chambly, Canada 111 A11
Chambord, Canada 103 C5
Chamboulive, France 20 C5
Chamchamal, Iraq 70 C5
Chamela, Mexico 118 D3
Chamical, Argentina 126 C2
Chamkar Luong, Cambodia 65 G4
Chamoli, India 69 D8
Chamonix-Mont Blanc, France 21 C10
Chamouchouane →, Canada 102 C5
Champa, India 69 H10
Champagne, Canada 104 A1
Champagne, France 19 D11
Champagnole, France 19 F12
Champaign, U.S.A. 108 E1
Champassak, Laos 64 E5
Champaubert, France 19 D10
Champawat, India 69 E9
Champdeniers-St-Denis, France 20 B3
Champdoré, L., Canada 103 A6
Champeix, France 20 C7
Champion, U.S.A. 110 E4
Champlain, U.S.A. 111 B11
Champlain, L., U.S.A. 111 B11
Champlitte, France 19 E12
Champotón, Mexico 119 D6
Champua, India 69 H11
Chamusca, Portugal 35 F2
Chana, Thailand 65 J3
Chañaral, Chile 126 B1
Chanārān, Iran 71 B8
Chanasma, India 68 H5
Chanco, Chile 126 D1
Chand, India 69 J8
Chandan, India 69 G12
Chandan Chauki, India 69 E9
Chandannagar, India 69 H13
Chandausi, India 69 E8
Chandeleur Is., U.S.A. 113 L10
Chandeleur Sd., U.S.A. 113 L10
Chandigarh, India 68 D7
Chandil, India 69 H12
Chandler, Australia 95 D1
Chandler, Canada 103 C7
Chandler, Ariz., U.S.A. 115 K8
Chandler, Okla., U.S.A. 113 H6
Chandod, India 68 J5
Chandpur, Bangla. 67 H17
Chandrapur, India 66 K11
Chānf, Iran 71 E9
Chang, Pakistan 68 F3
Chang, Ko, Thailand 65 F4
Ch'ang Chiang = Chang Jiang →, China 59 B13
Chang Jiang →, China 59 B13
Changa, India 69 C7
Changanacheri, India 66 Q10
Changane →, Mozam. 89 C5
Changbai, China 57 D15
Changbai Shan, China 57 C15
Changchiak'ou = Zhangjiakou, China 56 D8
Ch'angchou = Changzhou, China 59 B12
Changchun, China 57 C13
Changchunling, China 57 B13
Changde, China 59 C8
Changdo-ri, N. Korea 57 E14
Changfeng, China 59 A11
Changhai = Shanghai, China 59 B13
Changhua, China 59 B12
Changhua, Taiwan 59 E13
Changhŭng, S. Korea 57 G14
Changhŭngni, N. Korea 57 D15
Changjiang, China 64 C7
Changjin, N. Korea 57 D14
Changjin-chŏsuji, N. Korea 57 D14
Changle, China 59 E12
Changli, China 57 E10
Changling, China 57 B12
Changlun, Malaysia 65 J3
Changning, Hunan, China 59 D9
Changning, Sichuan, China 58 C5
Changning, Yunnan, China 58 E2
Changping, China 56 D9
Changsha, China 59 C9
Changshan, China 59 C12
Changshu, China 59 B13
Changshun, China 58 D6
Changtai, China 59 E11
Changting, China 59 E11
Changwu, China 56 G4
Changxing, China 59 B12
Changyang, China 59 B8
Changyi, China 57 F10
Changyŏn, N. Korea 57 E13
Changyuan, China 56 G8
Changzhi, China 56 F7
Changzhou, China 59 B12
Chanhanga, Angola 88 B1
Chanlar = Xanlar, Azerbaijan 49 K8
Channapatna, India 66 N10
Channel Is., U.K. 13 H5
Channel Is., U.S.A. 117 M7
Channel Islands National Park, U.S.A. 117 M8
Channel-Port aux Basques, Canada 103 C8
Channel Tunnel, Europe 13 F9
Channing, U.S.A. 113 H3
Chantada, Spain 34 C3
Chanthaburi, Thailand 64 F4
Chantilly, France 19 C9
Chantonnay, France 18 F5
Chantrey Inlet, Canada 100 B10
Chanute, U.S.A. 113 G7
Chanza →, Spain 35 H3
Chao Hu, China 59 B11
Chao Phraya →, Thailand 64 F3
Chao Phraya Lowlands, Thailand 64 E3
Chaocheng, China 56 F8
Chaohu, China 59 B11
Chaoyang, Guangdong, China 59 F11
Chaoyang, Liaoning, China 57 D11
Chaozhou, China 59 F11
Chapais, Canada 102 C5
Chapala, Mozam. 87 F4
Chapala, L. de, Mexico 118 C4
Chapayev, Kazakstan 48 E10
Chapayevsk, Russia 48 D9
Chapecó, Brazil 127 B5
Chapel Hill, U.S.A. 109 H6
Chapleau, Canada 102 C3
Chaplin, Canada 105 C7
Chaplin L., Canada 105 C7
Chaplino, Ukraine 47 H9
Chaplygin, Russia 46 F11
Chappell, U.S.A. 112 E3
Chapra = Chhapra, India 69 G11
Chara, Russia 51 D12
Charadai, Argentina 126 B4
Charagua, Bolivia 124 G6
Charambirá, Punta, Colombia 124 C3
Charaña, Bolivia 124 G5
Charantsavan, Armenia 49 K7
Charanwala, India 68 F5
Charata, Argentina 126 B3
Charcas, Mexico 118 C4
Chard, U.K. 13 G5
Chardon, U.S.A. 110 E3
Chardzhou = Chärjew, Turkmenistan 50 F7
Charente □, France 20 C4
Charente →, France 20 C2
Charente-Maritime □, France 20 C3
Charenton-du-Cher, France 19 F9
Chari →, Chad 79 F8
Chārīkār, Afghan. 66 B6
Chariton →, U.S.A. 112 F8
Chärjew, Turkmenistan 50 F7
Charkhari, India 69 G8
Charkhi Dadri, India 68 E7
Charleroi, Belgium 17 D4
Charleroi, U.S.A. 110 F5
Charles, C., U.S.A. 108 G8
Charles City, U.S.A. 112 D8
Charles L., Canada 105 B6
Charles Town, U.S.A. 108 F7
Charleston, Ill., U.S.A. 108 F1
Charleston, Miss., U.S.A. 113 H9
Charleston, Mo., U.S.A. 113 G10
Charleston, S.C., U.S.A. 109 J6
Charleston, W. Va., U.S.A. 108 F5
Charleston L., Canada 111 B9
Charleston Peak, U.S.A. 117 J11
Charlestown, Ireland 15 C3
Charlestown, S. Africa 89 D4
Charlestown, Ind., U.S.A. 108 F3
Charlestown, N.H., U.S.A. 111 C12
Charleville = Rath Luirc, Ireland 15 D3
Charleville, Australia 95 D4
Charleville-Mézières, France 19 C11
Charlevoix, U.S.A. 108 C3
Charlieu, France 19 F11
Charlotte, Mich., U.S.A. 108 D3
Charlotte, N.C., U.S.A. 109 H5
Charlotte, Vt., U.S.A. 111 B11
Charlotte Amalie, U.S. Virgin Is. 121 C7
Charlotte Harbor, U.S.A. 109 M4
Charlotte L., Canada 104 C3
Charlottenberg, Sweden 10 E6
Charlottesville, U.S.A. 108 F6
Charlottetown, Nfld., Canada 103 B8
Charlottetown, P.E.I., Canada 103 C7
Charlton, U.S.A. 112 E8
Charlton I., Canada 102 B4
Charmes, France 19 D13
Charny, Canada 103 C5
Charolles, France 19 F11
Chârost, France 19 F9
Charre, Mozam. 87 F4
Charroux, France 20 B4
Charsadda, Pakistan 68 B4
Charters Towers, Australia 94 C4
Chartres, France 18 D8
Chascomús, Argentina 126 D4
Chasefu, Zambia 87 E3
Chashma Barrage, Pakistan 68 C4
Chasseneuil-sur-Bonnieure, France 20 C4
Chāt, Iran 71 B7
Chatal Balkan = Udvoy Balkan, Bulgaria 41 D10
Château-Arnoux, France 21 D10
Château-Chinon, France 19 E10
Château-d'Olonne, France 20 B2
Château-du-Loir, France 18 E7
Château-Gontier, France 18 E6
Château-la-Vallière, France 18 E7
Château-Landon, France 19 D9
Château-Renault, France 18 E7
Château-Salins, France 19 D13
Château-Thierry, France 19 C10
Châteaubourg, France 18 D5
Châteaubriant, France 18 E5
Châteaudun, France 18 D8
Chateaugay, U.S.A. 111 B10
Châteaugiron, France 18 D5
Châteauguay, L., Canada 103 A5
Châteaulin, France 18 D2
Châteaumeillant, France 19 F9
Châteauneuf-du-Faou, France 18 D3
Châteauneuf-sur-Charente, France 20 C3
Châteauneuf-sur-Cher, France 19 F9
Châteauneuf-sur-Loire, France 19 E9
Châteaurenard, Bouches-du-Rhône, France 21 E8
Châteaurenard, Loiret, France 19 E9
Châteauroux, France 19 F8
Châteauvillain, France 19 D11
Châtelaillon-Plage, France 20 B2
Châtelguyon, France 20 C7
Châtellerault, France 18 F7
Châtelus-Malvaleix, France 19 F9
Chatham = Miramichi, Canada 103 C6
Chatham, Canada 102 D3
Chatham, U.K. 13 F8
Chatham, U.S.A. 111 D11
Chatham Is., Pac. Oc. 96 M10
Châtillon, Italy 28 C4
Châtillon-Coligny, France 19 E9
Châtillon-en-Diois, France 21 D9
Châtillon-sur-Indre, France 18 F8
Châtillon-sur-Loire, France 19 E9
Châtillon-sur-Seine, France 19 E11
Chatmohar, Bangla. 69 G13
Chatra, India 69 G11
Chatrapur, India 67 K14
Chats, L. des, Canada 111 A8
Chatsu, India 68 F6
Chatsworth, Canada 110 B4
Chatsworth, Zimbabwe 87 F3
Chattahoochee, U.S.A. 109 K3
Chattahoochee →, U.S.A. 109 K3
Chattanooga, U.S.A. 109 H3
Chatteris, U.K. 13 E8
Chaturat, Thailand 64 E3
Chau Doc, Vietnam 65 G5
Chaudes-Aigues, France 20 D7
Chauffailles, France 19 F11
Chaukan Pass, Burma 67 F20
Chaumont, France 19 D12
Chaumont, U.S.A. 111 B8
Chaumont-en-Vexin, France 19 C8
Chaumont-sur-Loire, France 18 E8
Chaunay, France 20 B4
Chauny, France 19 C10
Chausey, Îs., France 18 D5
Chaussin, France 19 F12
Chautauqua L., U.S.A. 110 D5
Chauvigny, France 18 F7
Chauvin, Canada 105 C6
Chavanges, France 19 D11
Chaves, Brazil 125 D9
Chaves, Portugal 34 D3
Chawang, Thailand 65 H2
Chazelles-sur-Lyon, France 21 C8
Chazy, U.S.A. 111 B11
Cheb, Czech Rep. 26 A5
Cheboksarskoye Vdkhr., Russia 48 B8
Cheboksary, Russia 48 B8
Cheboygan, U.S.A. 108 C3
Chebsara, Russia 46 C10
Chech, Erg, Africa 78 D5
Chechen, Ostrov, Russia 49 H8
Chechenia □, Russia 49 J7
Checheno-Ingush Republic = Chechenia □, Russia 49 J7
Chechnya = Chechenia □, Russia 49 J7
Ch'ech'ŏn, S. Korea 57 F15
Chęciny, Poland 45 H7
Checotah, U.S.A. 113 H7
Chedabucto B., Canada 103 C7
Cheduba I., Burma 67 K18
Cheepie, Australia 95 D4
Chef-Boutonne, France 20 B3
Chegdomyn, Russia 51 D14
Chegga, Mauritania 78 C4
Chegutu, Zimbabwe 87 F3
Chehalis, U.S.A. 116 D4
Chehalis →, U.S.A. 116 D3
Cheiron, Mt., France 21 E10
Cheju do, S. Korea 57 H14
Chekalin, Russia 46 E9
Chekiang = Zhejiang □, China 59 C13
Chel = Kuru, Bahr el →, Sudan 81 F2
Chela, Sa. da, Angola 88 B1
Chelan, U.S.A. 114 C4
Chelan, L., U.S.A. 114 B3
Cheleken, Turkmenistan 50 F6
Cheleken Yarymadasy, Turkmenistan 71 B7
Chelforó, Argentina 128 D3
Chelkar = Shalqar, Kazakstan 50 E6
Chelkar Tengiz, Solonchak, Kazakstan 50 E7
Chella, Ethiopia 81 F4
Chelles, France 19 D9
Chełm, Poland 45 G10
Chełmno, Poland 45 E5
Chelmsford, U.K. 13 F8
Chełmża, Poland 45 E5
Chelsea, U.S.A. 111 C12
Cheltenham, U.K. 13 F5
Chelva, Spain 32 F4
Chelyabinsk, Russia 50 D7
Chelyuskin, C., Russia 52 B14
Chemainus, Canada 116 B3
Chemba, Mozam. 85 H6
Chembar = Belinskiy, Russia 48 D6
Chemillé, France 18 E6
Chemnitz, Germany 24 E8
Chemult, U.S.A. 114 E3
Chen, Gora, Russia 51 C15
Chenab →, Pakistan 68 D4
Chenango Forks, U.S.A. 111 D9
Chencha, Ethiopia 81 F4
Chenchiang = Zhenjiang, China 59 A12
Cheney, U.S.A. 114 C5
Cheng Xian, China 56 H3
Chengbu, China 59 D8
Chengcheng, China 56 G5
Chengchou = Zhengzhou, China 56 G7
Chengde, China 57 D9
Chengdong Hu, China 59 A11
Chengdu, China 58 B5
Chenggong, China 58 E4
Chenggu, China 56 H4
Chenghai, China 59 F11
Chengjiang, China 58 E4
Chengkou, China 58 B7
Ch'engmai, China 64 C7
Ch'engtu = Chengdu, China 58 B5
Chengwu, China 56 G8
Chengxi Hu, China 59 A11
Chengyang, China 57 F11
Chenjiagang, China 57 G10
Chenkán, Mexico 119 D6
Chennai, India 66 N12
Chenôve, France 19 E12
Chenxi, China 59 C8
Chenzhou, China 59 E9
Cheo Reo, Vietnam 62 B3
Cheom Ksan, Cambodia 64 E5
Chepelare, Bulgaria 41 E8
Chepén, Peru 124 E3
Chepes, Argentina 126 C2
Chepo, Panama 120 E4
Chepstow, U.K. 13 F5
Cheptulil, Mt., Kenya 86 B4
Chequamegon B., U.S.A. 112 B9
Cher □, France 19 E9
Cher →, France 18 E7
Chéradi, Italy 31 B10
Cherasco, Italy 28 D4
Cheraw, U.S.A. 109 H6
Cherbourg, France 18 C5
Cherdakly, Russia 48 C9
Cherdyn, Russia 50 C6
Cheremkhovo, Russia 51 D11
Cherepanovo, Russia 50 D9
Cherepovets, Russia 46 C9
Chergui, Chott ech, Algeria 78 B6
Cherikov = Cherykaw, Belarus 46 F6
Cherkasy, Ukraine 47 H7
Cherkessk, Russia 49 H6
Cherlak, Russia 50 D8
Chernaya, Russia 51 B9
Cherni, Bulgaria 40 D7
Chernigov = Chernihiv, Ukraine 47 G6
Chernihiv, Ukraine 47 G6
Chernivtsi, Ukraine 47 H3
Chernobyl = Chornobyl, Ukraine 47 G6
Chernogorsk, Russia 51 D10
Chernomorskoye = Chornomorske, Ukraine 47 K7
Chernovtsy = Chernivtsi, Ukraine 47 H3
Chernyakhovsk, Russia 9 J19
Chernyanka, Russia 47 G9
Chernysheyskiy, Russia 51 C12
Chernyye Zemli, Russia 49 H8
Cherokee, Iowa, U.S.A. 112 D7
Cherokee, Okla., U.S.A. 113 G5
Cherokee Village, U.S.A. 113 G9
Cherokees, Grand Lake O' The, U.S.A. 113 G7
Cherrapunji, India 67 G17
Cherry Valley, Calif., U.S.A. 117 M10
Cherry Valley, N.Y., U.S.A. 111 D10
Cherskiy, Russia 51 C17
Cherskogo Khrebet, Russia 51 C15
Chertkovo, Russia 47 H11
Cherven, Belarus 46 F5
Cherven-Bryag, Bulgaria 41 C8
Chervonohrad, Ukraine 47 G3
Cherwell →, U.K. 13 F6

Cherykaw, *Belarus* 46 **F6**
Chesapeake, *U.S.A.* 108 **G7**
Chesapeake B., *U.S.A.* 108 **G7**
Cheshire □, *U.K.* 12 **D5**
Cheshskaya Guba, *Russia* 50 **C5**
Cheshunt, *U.K.* 13 **F7**
Chesil Beach, *U.K.* 13 **G5**
Chesley, *Canada* 110 **B3**
Cheste, *Spain* 33 **F4**
Chester, *U.K.* 12 **D5**
Chester, *Calif., U.S.A.* 114 **F3**
Chester, *Ill., U.S.A.* 113 **G10**
Chester, *Mont., U.S.A.* 114 **B8**
Chester, *Pa., U.S.A.* 108 **F8**
Chester, *S.C., U.S.A.* 109 **H5**
Chester, *Vt., U.S.A.* 111 **C12**
Chester, *W. Va., U.S.A.* 110 **F4**
Chester-le-Street, *U.K.* 12 **C6**
Chesterfield, *U.K.* 12 **D6**
Chesterfield, Is., *N. Cal.* 96 **J7**
Chesterfield Inlet, *Canada* 100 **B10**
Chesterton Ra., *Australia* 95 **D4**
Chestertown, *U.S.A.* 111 **C11**
Chesterville, *Canada* 111 **A9**
Chestnut Ridge, *U.S.A.* 110 **F5**
Chesuncook L., *U.S.A.* 109 **C11**
Chéticamp, *Canada* 103 **C7**
Chetrosu, *Moldova* 43 **B12**
Chetumal, *Mexico* 119 **D7**
Chetumal, B. de, *Mexico* 119 **D7**
Chetwynd, *Canada* 104 **B4**
Chevanceaux, *France* 20 **C3**
Cheviot, The, *U.K.* 12 **B5**
Cheviot Hills, *U.K.* 12 **B5**
Cheviot Ra., *Australia* 94 **D3**
Chew Bahir, *Ethiopia* 81 **G4**
Chewelah, *U.S.A.* 114 **B5**
Cheyenne, *Okla., U.S.A.* 113 **H5**
Cheyenne, *Wyo., U.S.A.* 112 **E2**
Cheyenne →, *U.S.A.* 112 **C4**
Cheyenne Wells, *U.S.A.* 112 **F3**
Cheyne B., *Australia* 93 **F2**
Chhabra, *India* 68 **G7**
Chhaktala, *India* 68 **H6**
Chhapra, *India* 69 **G11**
Chhata, *India* 68 **F7**
Chhatarpur, *Bihar, India* 69 **G11**
Chhatarpur, *Mad. P., India* 69 **G8**
Chhattisgarh □, *India* 69 **J10**
Chhep, *Cambodia* 64 **F5**
Chhindwara, *Mad. P., India* 69 **H8**
Chhindwara, *Mad. P., India* 69 **H8**
Chhlong, *Cambodia* 65 **F5**
Chhota Tawa →, *India* 68 **H7**
Chhoti Kali Sindh →, *India* 68 **G6**
Chhuikhadan, *India* 69 **J9**
Chhuk, *Cambodia* 65 **G5**
Chi →, *Thailand* 64 **E5**
Chiai, *Taiwan* 59 **F13**
Chiali, *Taiwan* 59 **F13**
Chiamboni, *Somali Rep.* 84 **E8**
Chiamussu = Jiamusi, *China* 60 **B8**
Chianciano Terme, *Italy* 29 **E8**
Chiang Dao, *Thailand* 64 **C2**
Chiang Kham, *Thailand* 64 **C3**
Chiang Khan, *Thailand* 64 **D3**
Chiang Khong, *Thailand* 58 **G3**
Chiang Mai, *Thailand* 64 **C2**
Chiang Rai, *Thailand* 58 **H2**
Chiang Saen, *Thailand* 58 **G3**
Chiapa →, *Mexico* 119 **D6**
Chiapa de Corzo, *Mexico* 119 **D6**
Chiapas □, *Mexico* 119 **D6**
Chiaramonte Gulfi, *Italy* 31 **E7**
Chiaravalle, *Italy* 29 **E10**
Chiaravalle Centrale, *Italy* 31 **D9**
Chiari, *Italy* 28 **C6**
Chiatura, *Georgia* 49 **J6**
Chiautla, *Mexico* 119 **D5**
Chiávari, *Italy* 28 **D6**
Chiavenna, *Italy* 28 **B6**
Chiba, *Japan* 55 **G10**
Chiba □, *Japan* 55 **G10**
Chibabava, *Mozam.* 89 **C5**
Chibemba, *Cunene, Angola* 85 **H2**
Chibemba, *Huila, Angola* 88 **B2**
Chibi, *Zimbabwe* 89 **C5**
Chibia, *Angola* 85 **H2**
Chibougamau, *Canada* 102 **C5**
Chibougamau, L., *Canada* 102 **C5**
Chibuk, *Nigeria* 83 **C7**
Chibuto, *Mozam.* 89 **C5**
Chic-Chocs, Mts., *Canada* 103 **C6**
Chicacole = Srikakulam, *India* 67 **K13**
Chicago, *U.S.A.* 108 **E2**
Chicago Heights, *U.S.A.* 108 **E2**
Chichagof I., *U.S.A.* 100 **C6**
Chichén-Itzá, *Mexico* 119 **C7**
Chicheng, *China* 56 **D8**
Chichester, *U.K.* 13 **G7**
Chichester Ra., *Australia* 92 **D2**
Chichibu, *Japan* 55 **F9**
Ch'ich'ihaerh = Qiqihar, *China* 51 **E13**
Chicholi, *India* 68 **H8**
Chickasha, *U.S.A.* 113 **H6**
Chiclana de la Frontera, *Spain* 35 **J4**
Chiclayo, *Peru* 124 **E3**
Chico, *U.S.A.* 116 **F5**
Chico →, *Chubut, Argentina* 128 **E3**
Chico →, *Santa Cruz, Argentina* 128 **G3**
Chicomo, *Mozam.* 89 **C5**
Chicontepec, *Mexico* 119 **C5**
Chicopee, *U.S.A.* 111 **D12**
Chicoutimi, *Canada* 103 **C5**
Chicualacuala, *Mozam.* 89 **C5**
Chidambaram, *India* 66 **P11**
Chidenguele, *Mozam.* 89 **C5**
Chidley, C., *Canada* 101 **B13**
Chiducuane, *Mozam.* 89 **C5**
Chiede, *Angola* 88 **B2**
Chiefs Pt., *Canada* 110 **B3**
Chiem Hoa, *Vietnam* 64 **A5**
Chiemsee, *Germany* 25 **H8**
Chiengi, *Zambia* 87 **D2**
Chiengmai = Chiang Mai, *Thailand* 64 **C2**
Chienti →, *Italy* 29 **E10**
Chieri, *Italy* 28 **C4**
Chiers →, *France* 19 **C11**
Chiesa in Valmalenco, *Italy* 28 **B6**
Chiese →, *Italy* 28 **C7**
Chieti, *Italy* 29 **F11**
Chifeng, *China* 57 **C10**
Chigirin, *Ukraine* 47 **H7**
Chignecto B., *Canada* 103 **C7**
Chiguana, *Bolivia* 126 **A2**
Chigwell, *U.K.* 13 **F8**
Chiha-ri, *N. Korea* 57 **E14**
Chihli, G. of = Bo Hai, *China* 57 **E10**
Chihuahua, *Mexico* 118 **B3**
Chihuahua □, *Mexico* 118 **B3**
Chiili = Shīeli, *Kazakstan* 50 **E7**
Chik Bollapur, *India* 66 **N10**
Chikmagalur, *India* 66 **N9**
Chikwawa, *Malawi* 87 **F3**
Chilac, *Mexico* 119 **D5**
Chilam Chavki, *Pakistan* 69 **B6**
Chilanga, *Zambia* 87 **F2**
Chilapa, *Mexico* 119 **D5**
Chilas, *Pakistan* 69 **B6**
Chilaw, *Sri Lanka* 66 **R11**
Chilcotin →, *Canada* 104 **C4**
Childers, *Australia* 95 **D5**
Childress, *U.S.A.* 113 **H4**
Chile ■, *S. Amer.* 128 **D2**
Chile Rise, *Pac. Oc.* 97 **L18**
Chilecito, *Argentina* 126 **B2**
Chilete, *Peru* 124 **E3**
Chilia, Braţul →, *Romania* 43 **E14**
Chililabombwe, *Zambia* 87 **E2**
Chilin = Jilin, *China* 57 **C14**
Chilka L., *India* 67 **K14**
Chilko →, *Canada* 104 **C4**
Chilko L., *Canada* 104 **C4**
Chillagoe, *Australia* 94 **B3**
Chillán, *Chile* 126 **D1**
Chillicothe, *Ill., U.S.A.* 112 **E10**
Chillicothe, *Mo., U.S.A.* 112 **F8**
Chillicothe, *Ohio, U.S.A.* 108 **F4**
Chilliwack, *Canada* 104 **D4**
Chilo, *India* 68 **F5**
Chiloane, I., *Mozam.* 89 **C5**
Chiloé, I. de, *Chile* 122 **H3**
Chilpancingo, *Mexico* 119 **D5**
Chiltern Hills, *U.K.* 13 **F7**
Chilton, *U.S.A.* 108 **C1**
Chilubi, *Zambia* 87 **E2**
Chilubula, *Zambia* 87 **E3**
Chilumba, *Malawi* 87 **E3**
Chilung, *Taiwan* 59 **E13**
Chilwa, L., *Malawi* 87 **F4**
Chimaltitán, *Mexico* 118 **C4**
Chimán, *Panama* 120 **E4**
Chimanimani, *Zimbabwe* 89 **B5**
Chimay, *Belgium* 17 **D4**
Chimayo, *U.S.A.* 115 **H11**
Chimbay, *Uzbekistan* 50 **E6**
Chimborazo, *Ecuador* 122 **D3**
Chimbote, *Peru* 124 **E3**
Chimkent = Shymkent, *Kazakstan* 50 **E7**
Chimoio, *Mozam.* 87 **F3**
Chimpembe, *Zambia* 87 **D2**
Chin □, *Burma* 67 **J18**
Chin Ling Shan = Qinling Shandi, *China* 56 **H5**
China, *Mexico* 119 **B5**
China ■, *Asia* 60 **D6**
China Lake, *U.S.A.* 117 **K9**
Chinan = Jinan, *China* 56 **F9**
Chinandega, *Nic.* 120 **D2**
Chinati Peak, *U.S.A.* 113 **L2**
Chincha Alta, *Peru* 122 **E3**
Chinchaga →, *Canada* 104 **B5**
Chinchilla, *Australia* 95 **D5**
Chinchilla de Monte Aragón, *Spain* 33 **G3**
Chinchorro, Banco, *Mexico* 119 **D7**
Chinchou = Jinzhou, *China* 57 **D11**
Chincoteague, *U.S.A.* 108 **G8**
Chinde, *Mozam.* 87 **F4**
Chindo, *S. Korea* 57 **G14**
Chindwin →, *Burma* 67 **J19**
Chineni, *India* 69 **C6**
Chinga, *Mozam.* 87 **F4**
Chingola, *Zambia* 87 **E2**
Chingole, *Malawi* 87 **E3**
Ch'ingtao = Qingdao, *China* 57 **F11**
Chinguetti, *Mauritania* 78 **D3**
Chingune, *Mozam.* 89 **C5**
Chinhae, *S. Korea* 57 **G15**
Chinhanguanine, *Mozam.* 89 **D5**
Chinhoyi, *Zimbabwe* 87 **F3**
Chini, *India* 68 **D8**
Chiniot, *Pakistan* 68 **D5**
Chínipas, *Mexico* 118 **B3**
Chinji, *Pakistan* 68 **C5**
Chinju, *S. Korea* 57 **G15**
Chinle, *U.S.A.* 115 **H9**
Chinmen, *Taiwan* 59 **E13**
Chinmen Tao, *Taiwan* 59 **E12**
Chinnampo = Namp'o, *N. Korea* 57 **E13**
Chino, *Japan* 55 **G9**
Chino, *U.S.A.* 117 **L9**
Chino Valley, *U.S.A.* 115 **J7**
Chinon, *France* 18 **E7**
Chinook, *U.S.A.* 114 **B9**
Chinsali, *Zambia* 87 **E3**
Chióggia, *Italy* 29 **C9**
Chíos = Khíos, *Greece* 39 **C8**
Chipata, *Zambia* 87 **E3**
Chiperceni, *Moldova* 43 **C13**
Chipinge, *Zimbabwe* 87 **G3**
Chipiona, *Spain* 35 **J4**
Chipley, *U.S.A.* 109 **K3**
Chipman, *Canada* 103 **C6**
Chipoka, *Malawi* 87 **E3**
Chippenham, *U.K.* 13 **F5**
Chippewa →, *U.S.A.* 112 **C8**
Chippewa Falls, *U.S.A.* 112 **C9**
Chipping Norton, *U.K.* 13 **F6**
Chiprovtsi, *Bulgaria* 40 **C6**
Chiputneticook Lakes, *U.S.A.* 109 **C11**
Chiquián, *Peru* 124 **F3**
Chiquimula, *Guatemala* 120 **D2**
Chiquinquira, *Colombia* 124 **B4**
Chir →, *Russia* 49 **F6**
Chirala, *India* 66 **M12**
Chiramba, *Mozam.* 87 **F3**
Chirawa, *India* 68 **E6**
Chirchiq, *Uzbekistan* 50 **E7**
Chiredzi, *Zimbabwe* 89 **C5**
Chiricahua Peak, *U.S.A.* 115 **L9**
Chiriquí, G. de, *Panama* 120 **E3**
Chiriquí, L. de, *Panama* 120 **E3**
Chirivira Falls, *Zimbabwe* 87 **G3**
Chirmiri, *India* 67 **H13**
Chirnogi, *Romania* 43 **F11**
Chirpan, *Bulgaria* 41 **D9**
Chirripó Grande, Cerro, *Costa Rica* 120 **E3**
Chirundu, *Zimbabwe* 89 **B4**
Chisamba, *Zambia* 87 **E2**
Chisapani Garhi, *Nepal* 67 **F14**
Chisasibi, *Canada* 102 **B4**
Ch'ishan, *Taiwan* 59 **F13**
Chisholm, *Canada* 104 **C6**
Chisholm, *U.S.A.* 112 **B8**
Chishtian Mandi, *Pakistan* 68 **E5**
Chishui, *China* 58 **C5**
Chishui He →, *China* 58 **C5**
Chisimaio, *Somali Rep.* 77 **G8**
Chisimba Falls, *Zambia* 87 **E3**
Chişinău, *Moldova* 43 **C13**
Chişineu Criş, *Romania* 42 **D6**
Chisone →, *Italy* 28 **D4**
Chisos Mts., *U.S.A.* 113 **L3**
Chistopol, *Russia* 48 **C10**
Chita, *Russia* 51 **D12**
Chitipa, *Malawi* 87 **D3**
Chitose, *Japan* 54 **C10**
Chitral, *Pakistan* 66 **B7**
Chitré, *Panama* 120 **E3**
Chittagong, *Bangla.* 67 **H17**
Chittagong □, *Bangla.* 67 **G17**
Chittaurgarh, *India* 68 **G6**
Chittoor, *India* 66 **N11**
Chitungwiza, *Zimbabwe* 87 **F3**
Chiusi, *Italy* 29 **E8**
Chiva, *Spain* 33 **F4**
Chivasso, *Italy* 28 **C4**
Chivhu, *Zimbabwe* 87 **F3**
Chivilcoy, *Argentina* 126 **C4**
Chiwanda, *Tanzania* 87 **E3**
Chixi, *China* 59 **G9**
Chizera, *Zambia* 87 **E2**
Chkalov = Orenburg, *Russia* 50 **D6**
Chkolovsk, *Russia* 48 **B6**
Chloride, *U.S.A.* 117 **K12**
Chlumec nad Cidlinou, *Czech Rep.* 26 **A8**
Chmielnik, *Poland* 45 **H7**
Cho Bo, *Vietnam* 58 **G5**
Cho-do, *N. Korea* 57 **E13**
Cho Phuoc Hai, *Vietnam* 65 **G6**
Choba, *Kenya* 86 **B4**
Chobe National Park, *Botswana* 88 **B4**
Choch'iwŏn, *S. Korea* 57 **F14**
Chocianów, *Poland* 45 **G2**
Chociwel, *Poland* 44 **E2**
Chocolate Mts., *U.S.A.* 117 **M11**
Choctawhatchee →, *U.S.A.* 109 **K3**
Chodecz, *Poland* 45 **F6**
Chodov, *Czech Rep.* 26 **A5**
Chodziez, *Poland* 45 **F3**
Choele Choel, *Argentina* 128 **D3**
Choix, *Mexico* 118 **B3**
Chojna, *Poland* 45 **F1**
Chojnice, *Poland* 44 **E4**
Chojnów, *Poland* 45 **G2**
Chōkai-San, *Japan* 54 **E10**
Choke, *Ethiopia* 81 **E4**
Choke Canyon L., *U.S.A.* 113 **L5**
Chokurdakh, *Russia* 51 **B15**
Cholame, *U.S.A.* 116 **K6**
Cholet, *France* 18 **E6**
Cholguan, *Chile* 126 **D1**
Choluteca, *Honduras* 120 **D2**
Choluteca →, *Honduras* 120 **D2**
Chom Bung, *Thailand* 64 **F2**
Chom Thong, *Thailand* 64 **C2**
Choma, *Zambia* 87 **F2**
Chomen Swamp, *Ethiopia* 81 **F4**
Chomun, *India* 68 **F6**
Chomutov, *Czech Rep.* 26 **A6**
Chon Buri, *Thailand* 64 **F3**
Chon Thanh, *Vietnam* 65 **G6**
Ch'onan, *S. Korea* 57 **F14**
Chone, *Ecuador* 124 **D3**
Chong Kai, *Cambodia* 64 **F4**
Chong Mek, *Thailand* 64 **E5**
Chongde, *China* 59 **B13**
Chŏngdo, *S. Korea* 57 **G15**
Chŏngha, *S. Korea* 57 **F15**
Chŏngjin, *N. Korea* 57 **D15**
Chŏngjiu, *S. Korea* 57 **F14**
Chŏngju, *N. Korea* 57 **E13**
Chongli, *China* 56 **D8**
Chongming, *China* 59 **B13**
Chongming Dao, *China* 59 **B13**
Chongqing, *Chongqing, China* 58 **C6**
Chongqing, *Sichuan, China* 58 **B4**
Chongqing Shi □, *China* 58 **C6**
Chongren, *China* 59 **D11**
Chonguene, *Mozam.* 89 **C5**
Chŏngŭp, *S. Korea* 57 **G14**
Chongyi, *China* 59 **E10**
Chongzuo, *China* 58 **F6**
Chŏnju, *S. Korea* 57 **G14**
Chonos, Arch. de los, *Chile* 122 **H3**
Chop, *Ukraine* 47 **H2**
Chopim →, *Brazil* 127 **B5**
Chor, *Pakistan* 68 **G3**
Chorbat La, *India* 69 **B7**
Chorley, *U.K.* 12 **D5**
Chornobyl, *Ukraine* 47 **G6**
Chornomorske, *Ukraine* 47 **K7**
Chorolque, Cerro, *Bolivia* 126 **A2**
Choroszcz, *Poland* 45 **E9**
Chorregon, *Australia* 94 **C3**
Chortkiv, *Ukraine* 47 **H3**
Ch'ŏrwon, *S. Korea* 57 **E14**
Chorzele, *Poland* 45 **E7**
Chorzów, *Poland* 45 **H5**
Chos-Malal, *Argentina* 126 **D1**
Ch'osan, *N. Korea* 57 **D13**
Choszczno, *Poland* 45 **E2**
Choteau, *U.S.A.* 114 **C7**
Chotěboř, *Czech Rep.* 26 **B8**
Chotila, *India* 68 **H4**
Chotta Udepur, *India* 68 **H6**
Chowchilla, *U.S.A.* 116 **H6**
Choybalsan, *Mongolia* 60 **B6**
Christchurch, *N.Z.* 91 **K4**
Christchurch, *U.K.* 13 **G6**
Christian I., *Canada* 110 **B4**
Christiana, *S. Africa* 88 **D4**
Christiansfeld, *Denmark* 11 **J3**
Christiansted, *U.S. Virgin Is.* 121 **C7**
Christie B., *Canada* 105 **A6**
Christina →, *Canada* 105 **B6**
Christmas Cr. →, *Australia* 92 **C4**
Christmas I. = Kiritimati, *Kiribati* 97 **G12**
Christmas I., *Ind. Oc.* 96 **J2**
Christopher L., *Australia* 93 **D4**
Chrudim, *Czech Rep.* 26 **B8**
Chrzanów, *Poland* 45 **H6**
Chtimba, *Malawi* 87 **E3**
Chu = Shū, *Kazakstan* 50 **E8**
Chu →, *Vietnam* 64 **C5**
Chu Lai, *Vietnam* 64 **E7**
Ch'uanchou = Quanzhou, *China* 59 **E12**
Chuankou, *China* 56 **G6**
Chubbuck, *U.S.A.* 114 **E7**
Chūbu □, *Japan* 55 **F8**
Chubut →, *Argentina* 122 **H4**
Chuchi L., *Canada* 104 **B4**
Chuda, *India* 68 **H4**
Chudovo, *Russia* 46 **C6**
Chudskoye, Ozero, *Russia* 9 **G22**
Chūgoku □, *Japan* 55 **G6**
Chūgoku-Sanchi, *Japan* 55 **G6**
Chuguyev = Chuhuyiv, *Ukraine* 47 **H9**
Chugwater, *U.S.A.* 112 **E2**
Chuhuyiv, *Ukraine* 47 **H9**
Chukchi Sea, *Russia* 51 **C19**
Chukotskoye Nagorye, *Russia* 51 **C18**
Chula Vista, *U.S.A.* 117 **N9**
Chulucanas, *Peru* 124 **E2**
Chulym →, *Russia* 50 **D9**
Chum Phae, *Thailand* 64 **D4**
Chum Saeng, *Thailand* 64 **E3**
Chumar, *India* 69 **C8**
Chumbicha, *Argentina* 126 **B2**
Chumerna, *Bulgaria* 41 **D9**
Chumikan, *Russia* 51 **D14**
Chumphon, *Thailand* 65 **G2**
Chumuare, *Mozam.* 87 **E3**
Chumunjin, *S. Korea* 57 **F15**
Chuna →, *Russia* 51 **D10**
Chun'an, *China* 59 **C12**
Ch'unch'ŏn, *S. Korea* 57 **F14**
Chunchura, *India* 69 **H13**
Chunga, *Zambia* 87 **F2**
Chunggang-ŭp, *N. Korea* 57 **D14**
Chunghwa, *N. Korea* 57 **E13**
Ch'ungju, *S. Korea* 57 **F14**
Chungking = Chongqing, *China* 58 **C6**
Chungli, *Taiwan* 59 **E13**
Ch'ungmu, *S. Korea* 57 **G15**
Chungt'iaoshan = Zhongtiao Shan, *China* 56 **G6**
Chungyang Shanmo, *Taiwan* 59 **F13**
Chunian, *Pakistan* 68 **D6**
Chunya, *Tanzania* 87 **D3**
Chunyang, *China* 57 **C15**
Chuquibamba, *Peru* 124 **G4**
Chuquicamata, *Chile* 126 **A2**
Chur, *Switz.* 25 **J5**
Churachandpur, *India* 67 **G18**
Churchill, *Canada* 105 **B10**
Churchill →, *Man., Canada* 105 **B10**
Churchill →, *Nfld., Canada* 103 **B7**
Churchill, C., *Canada* 105 **B10**
Churchill Falls, *Canada* 103 **B7**
Churchill L., *Canada* 105 **B7**
Churchill Pk., *Canada* 104 **B3**
Churki, *India* 69 **H10**
Churu, *India* 68 **E6**
Churún Merú = Angel Falls, *Venezuela* 124 **B6**
Chushal, *India* 69 **C8**
Chuska Mts., *U.S.A.* 115 **H9**
Chusovoy, *Russia* 50 **D6**
Chute-aux-Outardes, *Canada* 103 **C6**
Chuuronjang, *N. Korea* 57 **D15**
Chuvash Republic = Chuvashia □, *Russia* 48 **C8**
Chuvashia □, *Russia* 48 **C8**
Chuwārtah, *Iraq* 70 **C5**
Chuxiong, *China* 58 **E3**
Chüy = Shū →, *Kazakstan* 52 **E10**
Chuy, *Uruguay* 127 **C5**
Chuzhou, *China* 59 **A12**
Ci Xian, *China* 56 **F8**
Ciacova, *Romania* 42 **E6**
Ciadâr-Lunga, *Moldova* 43 **D13**
Ciamis, *Indonesia* 63 **G13**
Cianjur, *Indonesia* 63 **G12**
Cianorte, *Brazil* 127 **A5**
Cibola, *U.S.A.* 117 **M12**
Cicero, *U.S.A.* 108 **E2**
Cidacos →, *Spain* 32 **C3**
Cide, *Turkey* 72 **B5**
Ciechanów, *Poland* 45 **F7**
Ciechanowiec, *Poland* 45 **F9**
Ciechocinek, *Poland* 45 **F5**
Ciego de Avila, *Cuba* 120 **B4**
Ciénaga, *Colombia* 124 **A4**
Cienfuegos, *Cuba* 120 **B3**
Cierp, *France* 20 **F4**
Cíes, Is., *Spain* 34 **C2**
Cieszanów, *Poland* 45 **H10**
Cieszyn, *Poland* 45 **J5**
Cieza, *Spain* 33 **G3**
Çifteler, *Turkey* 72 **C4**
Cifuentes, *Spain* 32 **E2**
Cihanbeyli, *Turkey* 72 **C5**
Cihuatlán, *Mexico* 118 **D4**
Cijara, Embalse de, *Spain* 35 **F6**
Cijulang, *Indonesia* 63 **G13**
Cilacap, *Indonesia* 63 **G13**
Çıldır, *Turkey* 73 **B10**
Çıldır Gölü, *Turkey* 73 **B10**
Cili, *China* 59 **C8**
Cilibia, *Romania* 43 **E12**
Cilicia, *Turkey* 72 **D5**
Cill Chainnigh = Kilkenny, *Ireland* 15 **D4**
Cilo Dağı, *Turkey* 73 **D10**
Cima, *U.S.A.* 117 **K11**
Cimarron, *Kans., U.S.A.* 113 **G4**
Cimarron, *N. Mex., U.S.A.* 113 **G2**
Cimarron →, *U.S.A.* 113 **G6**
Cimişlia, *Moldova* 43 **D13**
Cimone, Mte., *Italy* 28 **D7**
Çınar, *Turkey* 73 **D9**
Çınarcık, *Turkey* 41 **F13**
Cinca →, *Spain* 32 **D5**
Cincar, *Bos.-H.* 42 **G2**
Cincinnati, *U.S.A.* 108 **F3**
Cincinnatus, *U.S.A.* 111 **D9**
Çine, *Turkey* 39 **D10**
Ciney, *Belgium* 17 **D5**
Cíngoli, *Italy* 29 **E10**
Cinigiano, *Italy* 29 **F8**
Cinto, Mte., *France* 21 **F12**
Cintruénigo, *Spain* 32 **C3**
Ciocile, *Romania* 43 **F12**
Ciolănești din Deal, *Romania* 43 **F10**
Ciorani, *Romania* 43 **F11**
Čiovo, *Croatia* 29 **E13**
Circeo, Mte., *Italy* 30 **A6**
Çirçir, *Turkey* 72 **C7**
Circle, *Alaska, U.S.A.* 100 **B5**
Circle, *Mont., U.S.A.* 112 **B2**
Circleville, *U.S.A.* 108 **F4**
Cirebon, *Indonesia* 62 **F3**
Ciremai, *Indonesia* 63 **G13**
Cirencester, *U.K.* 13 **F6**
Cireşu, *Romania* 42 **F7**
Cirey-sur-Vezouze, *France* 19 **D13**
Ciriè, *Italy* 28 **C4**
Cirium, *Cyprus* 36 **E11**
Cirò, *Italy* 31 **C10**
Cirò Marina, *Italy* 31 **C10**
Ciron →, *France* 20 **D3**
Cisco, *U.S.A.* 113 **J5**
Cislău, *Romania* 43 **E11**
Cisna, *Poland* 45 **J9**
Cisnădie, *Romania* 43 **E9**
Cisterna di Latina, *Italy* 30 **A5**
Cisternino, *Italy* 31 **B10**
Cistierna, *Spain* 34 **C5**
Citeli-Ckaro = Tsiteli-Tsqaro, *Georgia* 49 **K8**
Citlaltépetl, *Mexico* 119 **D5**
Citrus Heights, *U.S.A.* 116 **G5**
Citrusdal, *S. Africa* 88 **E2**
Città della Pieve, *Italy* 29 **F9**
Città di Castello, *Italy* 29 **E9**
Città Sant' Angelo, *Italy* 29 **F11**
Cittadella, *Italy* 29 **C8**
Cittaducale, *Italy* 29 **F9**
Cittanova, *Italy* 31 **D9**
Ciuc, Munţii, *Romania* 43 **D11**
Ciucaş, Vf., *Romania* 43 **E10**
Ciucea, *Romania* 42 **D7**
Ciuciulea, *Moldova* 43 **C12**

Ciuciuleni, Moldova 43 C13
Ciudad Altamirano, Mexico 118 D4
Ciudad Bolívar, Venezuela 124 B6
Ciudad Camargo, Mexico 118 B3
Ciudad de Valles, Mexico 119 C5
Ciudad del Carmen, Mexico 119 D6
Ciudad del Este, Paraguay 127 B5
Ciudad Delicias = Delicias, Mexico 118 B3
Ciudad Guayana, Venezuela 124 B6
Ciudad Guerrero, Mexico 118 B3
Ciudad Guzmán, Mexico 118 D4
Ciudad Juárez, Mexico 118 A3
Ciudad Madero, Mexico 119 C5
Ciudad Mante, Mexico 119 C5
Ciudad Obregón, Mexico 118 B3
Ciudad Real, Spain 35 G7
Ciudad Real □, Spain 35 G7
Ciudad Rodrigo, Spain 34 E4
Ciudad Trujillo = Santo Domingo, Dom. Rep. 121 C6
Ciudad Victoria, Mexico 119 C5
Ciudadela, Spain 37 B10
Ciulnița, Romania 43 F12
Ciumeghiu, Romania 42 D6
Ciuperceni, Romania 42 F8
Civa Burnu, Turkey 72 B7
Cividale del Friuli, Italy 29 B10
Civita Castellana, Italy 29 F9
Civitanova Marche, Italy 29 E10
Civitavécchia, Italy 29 F8
Civray, France 20 B4
Çivril, Turkey 39 C11
Cixerri →, Italy 30 C1
Cixi, China 59 B13
Cizre, Turkey 70 B4
Cizur Mayor, Spain 32 C3
Clackmannanshire □, U.K. 14 E5
Clacton-on-Sea, U.K. 13 F9
Clain →, France 18 F7
Claire, L., Canada 104 B6
Clairton, U.S.A. 110 F5
Clairvaux-les-Lacs, France 19 F12
Claise →, France 20 B5
Clallam Bay, U.S.A. 116 B2
Clamecy, France 19 E10
Clanton, U.S.A. 109 J2
Clanwilliam, S. Africa 88 E2
Clara, Ireland 15 C4
Claraville, U.S.A. 117 K8
Clare, U.S.A. 108 D3
Clare □, Ireland 15 D3
Clare →, Ireland 15 C2
Clare I., Ireland 15 C1
Claremont, Calif., U.S.A. 117 L9
Claremont, N.H., U.S.A. 111 C12
Claremont Pt., Australia 94 A3
Claremore, U.S.A. 113 G7
Claremorris, Ireland 15 C3
Clarence →, Australia 95 D5
Clarence →, N.Z. 91 K4
Clarence, I., Chile 128 G2
Clarence I., Antarctica 5 C18
Clarence Str., Australia 92 B5
Clarence Town, Bahamas 121 B5
Clarendon, Pa., U.S.A. 110 E5
Clarendon, Tex., U.S.A. 113 H4
Clarenville, Canada 103 C9
Claresholm, Canada 104 D6
Clarie Coast, Antarctica 5 C9
Clarinda, U.S.A. 112 E7
Clarion, Iowa, U.S.A. 112 D8
Clarion, Pa., U.S.A. 110 E5
Clarion →, U.S.A. 110 E5
Clark, U.S.A. 112 C6
Clark, Pt., Canada 110 B3
Clark Fork, U.S.A. 114 B5
Clark Fork →, U.S.A. 114 B5
Clarkdale, U.S.A. 115 J7
Clarke City, Canada 103 B6
Clarke I., Australia 94 G4
Clarke Ra., Australia 94 C4
Clark's Fork →, U.S.A. 114 D9
Clark's Harbour, Canada 103 D6
Clarks Hill L., U.S.A. 109 J4
Clarks Summit, U.S.A. 111 E9
Clarksburg, U.S.A. 108 F5
Clarksdale, U.S.A. 113 H9
Clarksville, Ark., U.S.A. 113 H8
Clarksville, Tenn., U.S.A. 109 G2
Clarksville, Tex., U.S.A. 113 J7
Clatskanie, U.S.A. 116 D3
Claude, U.S.A. 113 H4
Claveria, Phil. 61 B4
Clay, U.S.A. 116 G5
Clay Center, U.S.A. 112 F6
Claypool, U.S.A. 115 K8
Claysburg, U.S.A. 110 F6
Claysville, U.S.A. 110 F4
Clayton, N. Mex., U.S.A. 113 G3
Clayton, N.Y., U.S.A. 111 B8
Clear, C., Ireland 15 E2
Clear, L., Canada 110 A7
Clear Hills, Canada 104 B5
Clear I., Ireland 15 E2
Clear L., U.S.A. 116 F4
Clear Lake, Iowa, U.S.A. 112 D8
Clear Lake, S. Dak., U.S.A. 112 C6
Clear Lake Reservoir, U.S.A. 114 F3
Clearfield, Pa., U.S.A. 110 E6
Clearfield, Utah, U.S.A. 114 F8
Clearlake, U.S.A. 114 G2
Clearlake Highlands, U.S.A. 116 G4
Clearwater, Canada 104 C4
Clearwater, U.S.A. 109 M4
Clearwater →, Alta., Canada 104 C6
Clearwater →, Alta., Canada 105 B6
Clearwater L., Canada 105 C9
Clearwater Mts., U.S.A. 114 C6
Clearwater Prov. Park, Canada 105 C8
Clearwater River Prov. Park, Canada 105 B7
Cleburne, U.S.A. 113 J6
Clee Hills, U.K. 13 E5
Cleethorpes, U.K. 12 D7
Cleeve Cloud, U.K. 13 F6
Clelles, France 21 D9
Clemson, U.S.A. 109 H4
Clerke Reef, Australia 92 C2
Clermont, Australia 94 C4
Clermont, France 19 C9
Clermont, U.S.A. 109 L5
Clermont-en-Argonne, France 19 C12
Clermont-Ferrand, France 20 C7
Clermont-l'Hérault, France 20 E7
Clerval, France 19 E13
Clervaux, Lux. 17 D6
Cles, Italy 28 B8
Clevedon, U.K. 13 F5
Cleveland, Miss., U.S.A. 113 J9
Cleveland, Ohio, U.S.A. 110 E3
Cleveland, Okla., U.S.A. 113 G6
Cleveland, Tenn., U.S.A. 109 H3
Cleveland, Tex., U.S.A. 113 K7
Cleveland, C., Australia 94 B4
Cleveland, Mt., U.S.A. 114 B7
Cleveland Heights, U.S.A. 110 E3
Clevelândia, Brazil 127 B5
Clew B., Ireland 15 C2
Clewiston, U.S.A. 109 M5
Clifden, Ireland 15 C1
Clifden, N.Z. 91 M1
Cliffdell, U.S.A. 116 D5
Cliffy Hd., Australia 93 G2
Clifton, Australia 95 D5
Clifton, Ariz., U.S.A. 115 K9
Clifton, Colo., U.S.A. 115 G9
Clifton, Tex., U.S.A. 113 K6
Clifton Beach, Australia 94 B4
Climax, Canada 105 D7
Clinch →, U.S.A. 109 H3
Clingmans Dome, U.S.A. 109 H4
Clint, U.S.A. 115 L10
Clinton, B.C., Canada 104 C4
Clinton, Ont., Canada 102 D3
Clinton, N.Z. 91 M2
Clinton, Ark., U.S.A. 113 H8
Clinton, Conn., U.S.A. 111 E12
Clinton, Ill., U.S.A. 112 E10
Clinton, Ind., U.S.A. 108 F2
Clinton, Iowa, U.S.A. 112 E9
Clinton, Mass., U.S.A. 111 D13
Clinton, Miss., U.S.A. 113 J9
Clinton, Mo., U.S.A. 112 F8
Clinton, N.C., U.S.A. 109 H6
Clinton, Okla., U.S.A. 113 H5
Clinton, S.C., U.S.A. 109 H5
Clinton, Tenn., U.S.A. 109 G3
Clinton, Wash., U.S.A. 116 C4
Clinton C., Australia 94 C5
Clinton Colden L., Canada 100 B9
Clintonville, U.S.A. 112 C10
Clipperton, I., Pac. Oc. 97 F17
Clisham, U.K. 14 D2
Clisson, France 18 E5
Clitheroe, U.K. 12 D5
Clo-oose, Canada 116 B2
Cloates, Pt., Australia 92 D1
Clocolan, S. Africa 89 D4
Clodomira, Argentina 126 B3
Clogher Hd., Ireland 15 C5
Clonakilty, Ireland 15 E3
Clonakilty B., Ireland 15 E3
Cloncurry, Australia 94 C3
Cloncurry →, Australia 94 B3
Clondalkin, Ireland 15 C5
Clones, Ireland 15 B4
Clonmel, Ireland 15 D4
Cloppenburg, Germany 24 C4
Cloquet, U.S.A. 112 B8
Clorinda, Argentina 126 B4
Cloud Bay, Canada 102 C2
Cloud Peak, U.S.A. 114 D10
Cloudcroft, U.S.A. 115 K11
Cloverdale, U.S.A. 116 G4
Clovis, Calif., U.S.A. 116 J7
Clovis, N. Mex., U.S.A. 113 H3
Cloyes-sur-le-Loir, France 18 E8
Cloyne, Canada 110 B7
Cluj □, Romania 43 D8
Cluj-Napoca, Romania 43 D8
Cluny, France 19 F11
Cluses, France 19 F13
Clusone, Italy 28 C6
Clutha →, N.Z. 91 M2
Clwyd →, U.K. 12 D4
Clyde, Canada 104 C6
Clyde, N.Z. 91 L2
Clyde, U.S.A. 110 C8
Clyde →, U.K. 14 F4
Clyde, Firth of, U.K. 14 F3
Clyde River, Canada 101 A13
Clydebank, U.K. 14 F4
Clymer, N.Y., U.S.A. 110 D5
Clymer, Pa., U.S.A. 110 D5
Ćmielów, Poland 45 H8
Côa →, Portugal 34 D3
Coachella, U.S.A. 117 M10
Coachella Canal, U.S.A. 117 N12
Coahoma, U.S.A. 113 J4
Coahuayana →, Mexico 118 D4
Coahuila □, Mexico 118 B4
Coal →, Canada 104 B3
Coalane, Mozam. 87 F4
Coalcomán, Mexico 118 D4
Coaldale, Canada 104 D6
Coalgate, U.S.A. 113 H6
Coalinga, U.S.A. 116 J6
Coalisland, U.K. 15 B5
Coalville, U.K. 12 E6
Coalville, U.S.A. 114 F8
Coari, Brazil 124 D6
Coast □, Kenya 86 C4
Coast Mts., Canada 104 C3
Coast Ranges, U.S.A. 116 G4
Coatbridge, U.K. 14 F4
Coatepec, Mexico 119 D5
Coatepeque, Guatemala 120 D1
Coatesville, U.S.A. 108 F8
Coaticook, Canada 103 C5
Coats I., Canada 101 B11
Coats Land, Antarctica 5 D1
Coatzacoalcos, Mexico 119 D6
Cobadin, Romania 43 F13
Cobalt, Canada 102 C4
Cobán, Guatemala 120 C1
Çobanlar, Turkey 39 C12
Cóbh, Ireland 15 E3
Cobija, Bolivia 124 F5
Cobleskill, U.S.A. 111 D10
Coboconk, Canada 110 B6
Cobourg, Canada 102 D4
Cobourg Pen., Australia 92 B5
Cóbué, Mozam. 87 E3
Coburg, Germany 25 E6
Coca, Spain 34 D6
Cocanada = Kakinada, India 67 L13
Cocentaina, Spain 33 G4
Cochabamba, Bolivia 124 G5
Cochem, Germany 25 E3
Cochemane, Mozam. 87 F3
Cochin, India 66 Q10
Cochin China = Nam-Phan, Vietnam 65 G6
Cochran, U.S.A. 109 J4
Cochrane, Alta., Canada 104 C6
Cochrane, Ont., Canada 102 C3
Cochrane, Chile 128 F2
Cochrane →, Canada 105 B8
Cochrane, L., Chile 128 F2
Cochranton, U.S.A. 110 E4
Cockburn, Canal, Chile 122 J3
Cockburn I., Canada 102 C3
Cockburn Ra., Australia 92 C4
Cockermouth, U.K. 12 C4
Cocklebiddy, Australia 93 F4
Coco →, Cent. Amer. 120 D3
Coco, I. del, Pac. Oc. 97 G19
Cocoa, U.S.A. 109 L5
Cocobeach, Gabon 84 D1
Cocora, Romania 43 F12
Cocos Is., Ind. Oc. 96 J1
Cod, C., U.S.A. 108 D10
Codajás, Brazil 124 D6
Codigoro, Italy 29 D9
Codlea, Romania 43 E10
Codó, Brazil 125 D10
Codogno, Italy 28 C6
Codróipo, Italy 29 C10
Codru, Munții, Romania 42 D7
Cody, U.S.A. 114 D9
Coe Hill, Canada 110 B7
Coelemu, Chile 126 D1
Coen, Australia 94 A3
Coesfeld, Germany 24 D3
Cœur d'Alene, U.S.A. 114 C5
Cœur d'Alene L., U.S.A. 114 C5
Coevorden, Neths. 17 B6
Cofete, Canary Is. 37 F5
Coffeyville, U.S.A. 113 G7
Coffin B., Australia 95 E2
Coffin Bay, Australia 95 E2
Coffin Bay Peninsula, Australia 95 E2
Cofrentes, Spain 33 F3
Cogalnic →, Moldova 43 E14
Cogealac, Romania 43 F13
Coghinas →, Italy 30 B1
Coghinas, L. del, Italy 30 B2
Cognac, France 20 C3
Cogne, Italy 28 C4
Cogolin, France 21 E10
Cogolludo, Spain 32 E1
Cohocton, U.S.A. 110 D7
Cohocton →, U.S.A. 110 D7
Cohoes, U.S.A. 111 D11
Cohuna, Australia 95 F3
Coiba, I., Panama 120 E3
Coig →, Argentina 128 G3
Coigeach, Rubha, U.K. 14 C3
Coihaique, Chile 128 F2
Coimbatore, India 66 P10
Coimbra, Brazil 124 G7
Coimbra, Portugal 34 E2
Coimbra □, Portugal 34 E2
Coín, Spain 35 J6
Coipasa, Salar de, Bolivia 124 G5
Cojimies, Ecuador 124 C3
Cojocna, Romania 43 D8
Cojutepequé, El Salv. 120 D2
Čoka, Serbia, Yug. 42 E5
Cokeville, U.S.A. 114 E8
Colatina, Brazil 125 G10
Colbeck, C., Antarctica 5 D13
Colborne, Canada 110 C7
Colby, U.S.A. 112 F4
Colchester, U.K. 13 F8
Cold L., Canada 105 C7
Coldstream, Canada 104 C5
Coldstream, U.K. 14 F6
Coldwater, Canada 110 B5
Coldwater, Kans., U.S.A. 113 G5
Coldwater, Mich., U.S.A. 108 E3
Colebrook, U.S.A. 111 B13
Coleman, U.S.A. 113 K5
Coleman →, Australia 94 B3
Colenso, S. Africa 89 D4
Coleraine, U.K. 15 A5
Coleridge, L., N.Z. 91 K3
Colesberg, S. Africa 88 E4
Coleville, U.S.A. 116 G7
Colfax, Calif., U.S.A. 116 F6
Colfax, La., U.S.A. 113 K8
Colfax, Wash., U.S.A. 114 C5
Colhué Huapi, L., Argentina 128 F3
Colibași, Moldova 43 E13
Colibași, Romania 43 F9
Cólico, Italy 28 B6
Coligny, France 19 F12
Coligny, S. Africa 89 D4
Colima, Mexico 118 D4
Colima □, Mexico 118 D4
Colima, Nevado de, Mexico 118 D4
Colina, Chile 126 C1
Colina do Norte, Guinea-Biss. 82 C2
Colinas, Brazil 125 E10
Colindres, Spain 34 B7
Coll, U.K. 14 E2
Collaguasi, Chile 126 A2
Collarada, Peña, Spain 32 C4
Collarenebri, Australia 95 D4
Colle di Val d'Elsa, Italy 28 E8
Collécchio, Italy 28 D7
Colleen Bawn, Zimbabwe 87 G2
College Park, U.S.A. 109 J3
College Station, U.S.A. 113 K6
Collesalvetti, Italy 28 E7
Collie, Australia 93 F2
Collier B., Australia 92 C3
Collier Ra., Australia 93 D2
Collina, Passo di, Italy 28 D7
Collingwood, Canada 102 D3
Collingwood, N.Z. 91 J4
Collins, Canada 102 B2
Collinsville, Australia 94 C4
Collipulli, Chile 126 D1
Collooney, Ireland 15 B3
Colmar, France 19 D14
Colmars, France 21 D10
Colmenar, Spain 35 J6
Colmenar de Oreja, Spain 34 E7
Colmenar Viejo, Spain 34 E7
Cologne = Köln, Germany 24 E2
Colom, I. d'en, Spain 37 B11
Coloma, U.S.A. 116 G6
Colomb-Béchar = Béchar, Algeria 78 B5
Colombey-les-Belles, France 19 D12
Colombey-les-Deux-Églises, France 19 D11
Colombia ■, S. Amer. 124 C4
Colombian Basin, S. Amer. 98 H12
Colombo, Sri Lanka 66 R11
Colomiers, France 20 E5
Colón, Buenos Aires, Argentina 126 C3
Colón, Entre Ríos, Argentina 126 C4
Colón, Cuba 120 B3
Colón, Panama 120 E4
Colonia de Sant Jordi, Spain 37 B9
Colonia del Sacramento, Uruguay 126 C4
Colonia Dora, Argentina 126 B3
Colonial Beach, U.S.A. 108 F7
Colonie, U.S.A. 111 D11
Colonna, C., Italy 31 C10
Colonsay, Canada 105 C7
Colonsay, U.K. 14 E2
Colorado □, U.S.A. 115 G10
Colorado →, Argentina 128 D4
Colorado →, N. Amer. 115 L6
Colorado →, U.S.A. 113 L7
Colorado City, U.S.A. 113 J4
Colorado Plateau, U.S.A. 115 H8
Colorado River Aqueduct, U.S.A. 117 L12
Colorado Springs, U.S.A. 112 F2
Colorno, Italy 28 D7
Colotlán, Mexico 118 C4
Colstrip, U.S.A. 114 D10
Colton, U.S.A. 111 B10
Columbia, Ky., U.S.A. 108 G3
Columbia, La., U.S.A. 113 J8
Columbia, Miss., U.S.A. 113 K10
Columbia, Mo., U.S.A. 112 F8
Columbia, Pa., U.S.A. 111 F8
Columbia, S.C., U.S.A. 109 J5
Columbia, Tenn., U.S.A. 109 H2
Columbia →, N. Amer. 116 D2
Columbia, C., Canada 4 A4
Columbia, District of □, U.S.A. 108 F7
Columbia, Mt., Canada 104 C5
Columbia Basin, U.S.A. 114 C4
Columbia Falls, U.S.A. 114 B6
Columbia Mts., Canada 104 C5
Columbia Plateau, U.S.A. 114 D5
Columbiana, U.S.A. 110 F4
Columbretes, Is., Spain 32 F5
Columbus, Ga., U.S.A. 109 J3
Columbus, Ind., U.S.A. 108 F3
Columbus, Kans., U.S.A. 113 G7
Columbus, Miss., U.S.A. 109 J1
Columbus, Mont., U.S.A. 114 D9
Columbus, N. Mex., U.S.A. 115 L10
Columbus, Nebr., U.S.A. 112 E6
Columbus, Ohio, U.S.A. 108 F4
Columbus, Tex., U.S.A. 113 L6
Colunga, Spain 34 B5
Colusa, U.S.A. 116 F4
Colville, U.S.A. 114 B5
Colville →, U.S.A. 100 A4
Colville, C., N.Z. 91 G5
Colwood, Canada 116 B3
Colwyn Bay, U.K. 12 D4
Coma, Ethiopia 81 F4
Comácchio, Italy 29 D9
Comalcalco, Mexico 119 D6
Comallo, Argentina 128 E2
Comana, Romania 43 F11
Comanche, U.S.A. 113 K5
Comănești, Romania 43 D11
Comarnic, Romania 43 E10
Comayagua, Honduras 120 D2
Combahee →, U.S.A. 109 J5
Combarbalá, Chile 126 C1
Combeaufontaine, France 19 E12
Comber, Canada 110 D2
Comber, U.K. 15 B6
Combermere, Canada 110 A7
Comblain-au-Pont, Belgium 17 D5
Combourg, France 18 D5
Combrailles, France 19 F9
Combronde, France 20 C7
Comeragh Mts., Ireland 15 D4
Comet, Australia 94 C4
Comilla, Bangla. 67 H17
Comino, Malta 36 C1
Comino, C., Italy 30 B2
Cómiso, Italy 31 F7
Comitán, Mexico 119 D6
Commentry, France 19 F9
Commerce, Ga., U.S.A. 109 H4
Commerce, Tex., U.S.A. 113 J7
Commercy, France 19 D12
Committee B., Canada 101 B11
Commonwealth B., Antarctica 5 C10
Commoron Cr. →, Australia 95 D5
Communism Pk. = Kommunizma, Pik, Tajikistan 50 F8
Como, Italy 28 C6
Como, Lago di, Italy 28 B6
Comodoro Rivadavia, Argentina 128 F3
Comorâște, Romania 42 E6
Comorin, C., India 66 Q10
Comoro Is. = Comoros ■, Ind. Oc. 77 H8
Comoros ■, Ind. Oc. 77 H8
Comox, Canada 104 D4
Compiègne, France 19 C9
Comporta, Portugal 35 G2
Compostela, Mexico 118 C4
Comprida, I., Brazil 127 A6
Compton, Canada 111 A13
Compton, U.S.A. 117 M8
Comrat, Moldova 43 D13
Con Cuong, Vietnam 64 C5
Con Son, Vietnam 65 H6
Conakry, Guinea 82 D2
Conara, Australia 94 G4
Concarneau, France 18 E3
Conceição, Mozam. 87 F4
Conceição da Barra, Brazil 125 G11
Conceição do Araguaia, Brazil 125 E9
Concepción, Argentina 126 B2
Concepción, Bolivia 124 G6
Concepción, Chile 126 D1
Concepción, Mexico 119 D6
Concepción, Paraguay 126 A4
Concepción □, Chile 126 D1
Concepción →, Mexico 118 A2
Concepción, Est. de, Chile 128 G2
Concepción, L., Bolivia 124 G6
Concepción, Punta, Mexico 118 B2
Concepción del Oro, Mexico 118 C4
Concepción del Uruguay, Argentina 126 C4
Conception, Pt., U.S.A. 117 L6
Conception B., Canada 103 C9
Conception B., Namibia 88 C1
Conception I., Bahamas 121 B4
Concession, Zimbabwe 87 F3
Conchas Dam, U.S.A. 113 H2
Conches-en-Ouche, France 18 D7
Concho, U.S.A. 115 J9
Concho →, U.S.A. 113 K5
Conchos →, Chihuahua, Mexico 118 B4
Conchos →, Tamaulipas, Mexico 119 B5
Concord, Calif., U.S.A. 116 H4
Concord, N.C., U.S.A. 109 H5
Concord, N.H., U.S.A. 111 C13
Concordia, Argentina 126 C4
Concórdia, Brazil 124 D5
Concordia, Mexico 118 C3
Concordia, U.S.A. 112 F6
Concrete, U.S.A. 114 B3
Condamine, Australia 95 D5
Condat, France 20 C6
Conde, U.S.A. 112 C5
Condé-sur-Noireau, France 18 D6
Condeúba, Brazil 125 F10
Condom, France 20 E4
Condon, U.S.A. 114 D3
Conegliano, Italy 29 C9
Conejera, I. = Conills, I. des, Spain 37 B9
Conejos, Mexico 118 B4
Confolens, France 20 B4
Confuso →, Paraguay 126 B4
Congaz, Moldova 43 D13
Conghua, China 59 F9
Congjiang, China 58 E7
Congleton, U.K. 12 D5

Congo (Kinshasa) = Congo, Dem. Rep. of the ■, Africa 84 E4
Congo ■, Africa 84 E3
Congo →, Africa 84 F2
Congo, Dem. Rep. of the ■, Africa 84 E4
Congo Basin, Africa 84 E4
Congonhas, Brazil 127 A7
Congress, U.S.A. 115 J7
Conil = Conil de la Frontera, Spain 35 J4
Conil de la Frontera, Spain 35 J4
Conills, I. des, Spain 37 B9
Coniston, Canada 102 C3
Conjeeveram = Kanchipuram, India 66 N11
Conklin, Canada 105 B6
Conklin, U.S.A. 111 D9
Conn, L., Ireland 15 B2
Connacht □, Ireland 15 C2
Conneaut, U.S.A. 110 E4
Connecticut □, U.S.A. 111 E12
Connecticut →, U.S.A. 111 E12
Connell, U.S.A. 114 C4
Connellsville, U.S.A. 110 F5
Connemara, Ireland 15 C2
Connemaugh →, U.S.A. 110 F5
Connerré, France 18 D7
Connersville, U.S.A. 108 F3
Connors Ra., Australia 94 C4
Conques, France 20 D6
Conquest, Canada 105 C7
Conrad, U.S.A. 114 B8
Conroe, U.S.A. 113 K7
Consecon, Canada 110 C7
Conselheiro Lafaiete, Brazil 127 A7
Conselve, Italy 29 C8
Consett, U.K. 12 C6
Consort, Canada 105 C6
Constance = Konstanz, Germany 25 H5
Constance, L. = Bodensee, Europe 25 H5
Constanţa, Romania 43 F13
Constanţa □, Romania 43 F13
Constantia, U.S.A. 111 C8
Constantina, Spain 35 H5
Constantine, Algeria 78 A7
Constitución, Chile 126 D1
Constitución, Uruguay 126 C4
Consuegra, Spain 35 F7
Consul, Canada 105 D7
Contact, U.S.A. 114 F6
Contai, India 69 J12
Contamana, Peru 124 E4
Contarina, Italy 29 C9
Contas →, Brazil 125 F11
Contes, France 21 E11
Contoocook, U.S.A. 111 C13
Contra Costa, Mozam. 89 D5
Contres, France 18 E8
Contrexéville, France 19 D12
Contwoyto L., Canada 100 B8
Conversano, Italy 31 B10
Conway = Conwy, U.K. 12 D4
Conway = Conwy →, U.K. 12 D4
Conway, Ark., U.S.A. 113 H8
Conway, N.H., U.S.A. 111 C13
Conway, S.C., U.S.A. 109 J6
Conway, L., Australia 95 D2
Conwy, U.K. 12 D4
Conwy □, U.K. 12 D4
Conwy →, U.K. 12 D4
Coober Pedy, Australia 95 D1
Cooch Behar = Koch Bihar, India 67 F16
Cooinda, Australia 92 B5
Cook, Australia 93 F5
Cook, U.S.A. 112 B8
Cook, B., Chile 128 H3
Cook, C., Canada 104 C3
Cook, Mt. = Aoraki Mount Cook, N.Z. 91 K3
Cook Inlet, U.S.A. 100 C4
Cook Is., Pac. Oc. 97 J12
Cook Strait, N.Z. 91 J5
Cookeville, U.S.A. 109 G3
Cookhouse, S. Africa 88 E4
Cookshire, Canada 111 A13
Cookstown, U.K. 15 B5
Cooksville, Canada 110 C5
Cooktown, Australia 94 B4
Cooladdi, Australia 95 D4
Coolgardie, Australia 93 F3
Coolidge, U.S.A. 115 K8
Coolidge Dam, U.S.A. 115 K8
Coon Rapids, U.S.A. 112 C8
Coonana, Australia 93 F3
Coondapoor, India 66 N9
Cooninie, L., Australia 95 D2
Cooper, U.S.A. 113 J7
Cooper Cr. →, Australia 95 D2
Cooperstown, N. Dak., U.S.A. 112 B5
Cooperstown, N.Y., U.S.A. 111 D10
Coorabie, Australia 93 F5
Coorow, Australia 93 E2
Cooroy, Australia 95 D5
Coos Bay, U.S.A. 114 E1
Coosa →, U.S.A. 109 J2
Cootehill, Ireland 15 B4
Copahue Paso, Argentina 126 D1
Copainalá, Mexico 119 D6
Copake Falls, U.S.A. 111 D11
Copalnic Mănăştur, Romania 43 C8
Copán, Honduras 120 D2
Cope, U.S.A. 112 F3
Cope, C., Spain 33 H3
Copenhagen = København, Denmark 11 J6
Copenhagen, U.S.A. 111 C9
Copertino, Italy 31 B11
Copiapó, Chile 126 B1
Copiapó →, Chile 126 B1
Coplay, U.S.A. 111 F9
Copp L., Canada 104 A6
Copparo, Italy 29 D8
Coppename →, Surinam 125 B7
Copper Harbor, U.S.A. 108 B2
Copper Queen, Zimbabwe 87 F2
Copperas Cove, U.S.A. 113 K6
Copperbelt □, Zambia 87 E2
Coppermine = Kugluktuk, Canada 100 B8
Coppermine →, Canada 100 B8
Copperopolis, U.S.A. 116 H6
Copşa Mică, Romania 43 D9
Coquet →, U.K. 12 B6
Coquille, U.S.A. 114 E1
Coquimbo, Chile 126 C1
Coquimbo □, Chile 126 C1
Corabia, Romania 43 G9
Coracora, Peru 124 G4
Coraki, Australia 95 D5
Coral, U.S.A. 110 F5
Coral Gables, U.S.A. 109 N5
Coral Harbour = Salliq, Canada 101 B11
Coral Sea, Pac. Oc. 96 J7
Coral Springs, U.S.A. 109 M5
Coraopolis, U.S.A. 110 F4
Corato, Italy 31 A9
Corbeil-Essonnes, France 19 D9
Corbie, France 19 C9
Corbières, France 20 F6
Corbigny, France 19 E10
Corbin, U.S.A. 108 G3
Corbones →, Spain 35 H5
Corbu, Romania 43 F13
Corby, U.K. 13 E7
Corcaigh = Cork, Ireland 15 E3
Corcoran, U.S.A. 116 J7
Cordele, U.S.A. 109 K4
Cordell, U.S.A. 113 H5
Cordenòns, Italy 29 C9
Cordes, France 20 D5
Córdoba, Argentina 126 C3
Córdoba, Mexico 119 D5
Córdoba, Spain 35 H6
Córdoba □, Argentina 126 C3
Córdoba □, Spain 35 G6
Córdoba, Sierra de, Argentina 126 C3
Cordon, Phil. 61 C4
Cordova, U.S.A. 100 B5
Corella, Spain 32 C3
Corella →, Australia 94 B3
Corfield, Australia 94 C3
Corfu = Kérkira, Greece 36 A3
Corfu, Str. of, Greece 36 A4
Corgo = O Corgo, Spain 34 C3
Cori, Italy 30 A5
Coria, Spain 34 F4
Coria del Río, Spain 35 H4
Corigliano Cálabro, Italy 31 C9
Coringa Is., Australia 94 B4
Corinth = Kórinthos, Greece 38 D4
Corinth, Miss., U.S.A. 109 H1
Corinth, N.Y., U.S.A. 111 C11
Corinth, G. of = Korinthiakós Kólpos, Greece 38 C4
Corinth Canal, Greece 38 D4
Corinto, Brazil 125 G10
Corinto, Nic. 120 D2
Cork, Ireland 15 E3
Cork □, Ireland 15 E3
Cork Harbour, Ireland 15 E3
Corlay, France 18 D3
Corleone, Italy 30 E6
Corleto Perticara, Italy 31 B9
Çorlu, Turkey 41 E11
Cormack L., Canada 104 A4
Cormòns, Italy 29 C10
Cormorant, Canada 105 C8
Cormorant L., Canada 105 C8
Corn Is. = Maiz, Is. del, Nic. 120 D3
Cornélio Procópio, Brazil 127 A5
Corner Brook, Canada 103 C8
Corneşti, Moldova 43 C13
Corníglio, Italy 28 D7
Corning, Ark., U.S.A. 113 G9
Corning, Calif., U.S.A. 114 G2
Corning, Iowa, U.S.A. 112 E7
Corning, N.Y., U.S.A. 110 D7
Corno Grande, Italy 29 F10
Cornwall, Canada 102 C5
Cornwall, U.S.A. 111 F8
Cornwall □, U.K. 13 G3
Coro, Venezuela 124 A5
Coroatá, Brazil 125 D10
Corocoro, Bolivia 124 G5
Coroico, Bolivia 124 G5
Coromandel, N.Z. 91 G5
Coromandel Coast, India 66 N12
Corona, Calif., U.S.A. 117 M9
Corona, N. Mex., U.S.A. 115 J11
Coronach, Canada 105 D7
Coronado, U.S.A. 117 N9
Coronado, B. de, Costa Rica 120 E3
Coronados, Is. los, U.S.A. 117 N9
Coronation, Canada 104 C6
Coronation Gulf, Canada 100 B8
Coronation I., Antarctica 5 C18
Coronation Is., Australia 92 B3
Coronda, Argentina 126 C3
Coronel, Chile 126 D1
Coronel Bogado, Paraguay 126 B4
Coronel Dorrego, Argentina 126 D3
Coronel Oviedo, Paraguay 126 B4
Coronel Pringles, Argentina 126 D3
Coronel Suárez, Argentina 126 D3
Coronel Vidal, Argentina 126 D4
Coropuna, Nevado, Peru 124 G4
Çorovodë, Albania 40 F4
Corozal, Belize 119 D7
Corps, France 21 D9
Corpus, Argentina 127 B4
Corpus Christi, U.S.A. 113 M6
Corpus Christi, L., U.S.A. 113 L6
Corral de Almaguer, Spain 34 F7
Corralejo, Canary Is. 37 F6
Corraun Pen., Ireland 15 C2
Corréggio, Italy 28 D7
Correntes, C. das, Mozam. 89 C6
Corrèze □, France 20 C5
Corrèze →, France 20 C5
Corrib, L., Ireland 15 C2
Corridónia, Italy 29 E10
Corrientes, Argentina 126 B4
Corrientes □, Argentina 126 B4
Corrientes →, Argentina 126 C4
Corrientes →, Peru 124 D4
Corrientes, C., Colombia 124 B3
Corrientes, C., Cuba 120 B3
Corrientes, C., Mexico 118 C3
Corrigan, U.S.A. 113 K7
Corrigin, Australia 93 F2
Corry, U.S.A. 110 E5
Corse, France 21 G13
Corse, C., France 21 E13
Corse-du-Sud □, France 21 G13
Corsica = Corse, France 21 G13
Corsicana, U.S.A. 113 J6
Corte, France 21 F13
Corte Pinto, Portugal 35 H3
Cortegana, Spain 35 H4
Cortez, U.S.A. 115 H9
Cortina d'Ampezzo, Italy 29 B9
Cortland, N.Y., U.S.A. 111 D8
Cortland, Ohio, U.S.A. 110 E4
Cortona, Italy 29 E8
Corubal →, Guinea-Biss. 82 C2
Coruche, Portugal 35 G2
Çoruh →, Turkey 49 K5
Çorum, Turkey 72 B6
Corumbá, Brazil 124 G7
Corund, Romania 43 D10
Corunna = A Coruña, Spain 34 B2
Corvallis, U.S.A. 114 D2
Corvette, L. de la, Canada 102 B5
Corydon, U.S.A. 112 E8
Cosalá, Mexico 118 C3
Cosamaloapan, Mexico 119 D5
Cosenza, Italy 31 C9
Coşereni, Romania 43 F11
Coshocton, U.S.A. 110 F3
Cosmo Newberry, Australia 93 E3
Cosne-Cours-sur-Loire, France 19 E9
Coso Junction, U.S.A. 117 J9
Coso Pk., U.S.A. 117 J9
Cospeito, Spain 34 B3
Cosquín, Argentina 126 C3
Cossato, Italy 28 C5
Cossé-le-Vivien, France 18 E6
Cosson →, France 18 E8
Costa Blanca, Spain 33 G4
Costa Brava, Spain 32 D8
Costa del Sol, Spain 35 J6
Costa Dorada, Spain 32 D6
Costa Mesa, U.S.A. 117 M9
Costa Rica ■, Cent. Amer. 120 E3
Costa Smeralda, Italy 30 A2
Costeşti, Romania 43 F9
Costigliole d'Asti, Italy 28 D5
Cosumnes →, U.S.A. 116 G5
Coswig, Sachsen, Germany 24 D9
Coswig, Sachsen-Anhalt, Germany 24 D8
Cotabato, Phil. 61 H6
Cotagaita, Bolivia 126 A2
Côte d'Azur, France 21 E11
Côte-d'Ivoire = Ivory Coast ■, Africa 82 D4
Côte d'Or, France 19 E11
Côte-d'Or □, France 19 E11
Coteau des Prairies, U.S.A. 112 C6
Coteau du Missouri, U.S.A. 112 B4
Coteau Landing, Canada 111 A10
Cotentin, France 18 C5
Côtes-d'Armor □, France 18 D4
Côtes de Meuse, France 19 C12
Côtes-du-Nord = Côtes-d'Armor □, France 18 D4
Cotiella, Spain 32 C5
Cotillo, Canary Is. 37 F5
Cotiujeni, Moldova 43 C13
Cotonou, Benin 83 D5
Cotopaxi, Ecuador 122 D3
Cotronei, Italy 31 C9
Cotswold Hills, U.K. 13 F5
Cottage Grove, U.S.A. 114 E2
Cottbus, Germany 24 D10
Cottonwood, U.S.A. 115 J7
Cotulla, U.S.A. 113 L5
Coubre, Pte. de la, France 20 C2
Couches, France 19 F11
Couço, Portugal 35 G2
Coudersport, U.S.A. 110 E6
Couëron, France 18 E5
Couesnon →, France 18 D5
Couhé, France 20 B4
Coulanges-sur-Yonne, France 19 E10
Coulee City, U.S.A. 114 C4
Coulman I., Antarctica 5 D11
Coulommiers, France 19 D10
Coulon →, France 21 E9
Coulonge →, Canada 102 C4
Coulonges-sur-l'Autize, France 20 B3
Coulounieix-Chamiers, France 20 C4
Coulterville, U.S.A. 116 H6
Council, U.S.A. 114 D5
Council Bluffs, U.S.A. 112 E7
Council Grove, U.S.A. 112 F6
Coupeville, U.S.A. 116 B4
Courantyne →, S. Amer. 122 C5
Courcelles, Belgium 17 D4
Courçon, France 20 B3
Courmayeur, Italy 28 C3
Couronne, C., France 21 E9
Cours-la-Ville, France 19 F11
Coursan, France 20 E7
Courseulles-sur-Mer, France 18 C6
Courtenay, Canada 104 D4
Courtenay, France 19 D10
Courtland, U.S.A. 116 G5
Courtrai = Kortrijk, Belgium 17 D3
Courtright, Canada 110 D2
Coushatta, U.S.A. 113 J8
Coutances, France 18 C5
Coutras, France 20 C3
Coutts Crossing, Australia 95 D5
Couvin, Belgium 17 D4
Covarrubias, Spain 34 C7
Covasna, Romania 43 E11
Covasna □, Romania 43 E10
Cove I., Canada 110 A3
Coventry, U.K. 13 E6
Covilhã, Portugal 34 E3
Covington, Ga., U.S.A. 109 J4
Covington, Ky., U.S.A. 108 F3
Covington, Okla., U.S.A. 113 G6
Covington, Tenn., U.S.A. 113 H10
Covington, Va., U.S.A. 108 G5
Cowan, L., Australia 93 F3
Cowan L., Canada 105 C7
Cowansville, Canada 102 C5
Coward Springs, Australia 95 D2
Cowcowing Lakes, Australia 93 F2
Cowdenbeath, U.K. 14 E5
Cowes, U.K. 13 G6
Cowichan L., Canada 116 B2
Cowlitz →, U.S.A. 116 D4
Cox, Spain 33 G4
Coxilha Grande, Brazil 127 B5
Coxim, Brazil 125 G8
Cox's Bazar, Bangla. 67 J17
Coyote Wells, U.S.A. 117 N11
Coyuca de Benítez, Mexico 119 D4
Coyuca de Catalan, Mexico 118 D4
Cozad, U.S.A. 112 E5
Cozes, France 20 C3
Cozumel, Mexico 119 C7
Cozumel, Isla, Mexico 119 C7
Cracow = Kraków, Poland 45 H6
Cracow, Australia 95 D5
Cradock, Australia 95 E2
Cradock, S. Africa 88 E4
Craig, U.S.A. 114 F10
Craigavon, U.K. 15 B5
Craigmore, Zimbabwe 87 G3
Craik, Canada 105 C7
Crailsheim, Germany 25 F6
Craiova, Romania 43 F8
Cramsie, Australia 94 C3
Cranberry L., U.S.A. 111 B10
Cranberry Portage, Canada 105 C8
Cranbrook, Australia 93 F2
Cranbrook, Canada 104 D5
Crandon, U.S.A. 112 C10
Crane, Oreg., U.S.A. 114 E4
Crane, Tex., U.S.A. 113 K3
Cranston, U.S.A. 111 E13
Craon, France 18 E6
Craonne, France 19 C10
Craponne-sur-Arzon, France 20 C7
Crasna, Romania 43 D12
Crasna →, Romania 42 C7
Crasnei, Munţii, Romania 43 C8
Crater L., U.S.A. 114 E2
Crater Lake National Park, U.S.A. 114 E2
Crateús, Brazil 125 E10
Crati →, Italy 31 C9
Crato, Brazil 125 E11
Crato, Portugal 35 F3
Craven, L., Canada 102 B4
Crawford, U.S.A. 112 D3
Crawfordsville, U.S.A. 108 E2
Crawley, U.K. 13 F7
Crazy Mts., U.S.A. 114 C8
Crean L., Canada 105 C7
Crécy-en-Ponthieu, France 19 B8
Crediton, Canada 110 C3
Cree →, Canada 105 B7
Cree →, U.K. 14 G4
Cree L., Canada 105 B7
Creede, U.S.A. 115 H10
Creekside, U.S.A. 110 F5
Creel, Mexico 118 B3
Creemore, Canada 110 B4
Creighton, Canada 105 C8
Creighton, U.S.A. 112 D6
Creil, France 19 C9
Crema, Italy 28 C6
Cremona, Italy 28 C7
Crepaja, Serbia, Yug. 42 E5
Crépy, France 19 C10
Crépy-en-Valois, France 19 C9
Cres, Croatia 29 D11
Crescent City, U.S.A. 114 F1
Crescentino, Italy 28 C5
Crespo, Argentina 126 C3
Cresson, U.S.A. 110 F6
Crest, France 21 D9
Cresta, Mt., Phil. 61 C5
Crestline, Calif., U.S.A. 117 L9
Crestline, Ohio, U.S.A. 110 F2
Creston, Canada 104 D5
Creston, Calif., U.S.A. 116 K6
Creston, Iowa, U.S.A. 112 E7
Crestview, Calif., U.S.A. 116 H8
Crestview, Fla., U.S.A. 109 K2
Crêt de la Neige, France 19 F12
Crete = Kríti, Greece 36 D7
Crete, U.S.A. 112 E6
Crete, Sea of, Greece 39 E7
Créteil, France 19 D9
Creus, C. de, Spain 32 C8
Creuse □, France 19 F9
Creuse →, France 20 B4
Creutzwald, France 19 C13
Creuzburg, Germany 24 D6
Crèvecœur-le-Grand, France 19 C9
Crevillente, Spain 33 G4
Crewe, U.K. 12 D5
Crewkerne, U.K. 13 G5
Criciúma, Brazil 127 B6
Cricova, Moldova 43 C13
Crieff, U.K. 14 E5
Crikvenica, Croatia 29 C11
Crimea □, Ukraine 47 K8
Crimean Pen. = Krymskyy Pivostriv, Ukraine 47 K8
Crimmitschau, Germany 24 E8
Cristuru Secuiesc, Romania 43 D10
Crişul Alb →, Romania 42 D6
Crişul Negru →, Romania 42 D6
Crişul Repede →, Romania 42 D5
Criuleni, Moldova 43 C14
Crivitz, Germany 24 B7
Crna →, Macedonia 40 E5
Crna Gora = Montenegro □, Yugoslavia 40 D3
Crna Gora, Macedonia 40 D5
Crna Reka = Crna →, Macedonia 40 E5
Crna Trava, Serbia, Yug. 40 D6
Crni Drim →, Macedonia 40 E4
Crni Timok →, Serbia, Yug. 40 C6
Crnoljeva Planina, Kosovo, Yug. 40 D5
Črnomelj, Slovenia 29 C12
Croagh Patrick, Ireland 15 C2
Croatia ■, Europe 29 C13
Crocker, Banjaran, Malaysia 62 C5
Crockett, U.S.A. 113 K7
Crocodile = Krokodil →, Mozam. 89 D5
Crocodile Is., Australia 94 A1
Crocq, France 20 C6
Crodo, Italy 28 B5
Crohy Hd., Ireland 15 B3
Croisette, C., France 21 E9
Croisic, Pte. du, France 18 E4
Croix, L. La, Canada 102 C1
Croker, C., Australia 92 B5
Croker, C., Canada 110 B4
Croker I., Australia 92 B5
Cromarty, U.K. 14 D4
Cromer, U.K. 12 E9
Cromwell, N.Z. 91 L2
Cromwell, U.S.A. 111 E12
Cronat, France 19 F10
Crook, U.K. 12 C6
Crooked →, Canada 104 C4
Crooked →, U.S.A. 114 D3
Crooked I., Bahamas 121 B5
Crooked Island Passage, Bahamas 121 B5
Crookston, Minn., U.S.A. 112 B6
Crookston, Nebr., U.S.A. 112 D4
Crosby, U.K. 12 D4
Crosby, N. Dak., U.S.A. 112 A3
Crosby, Pa., U.S.A. 110 E6
Crosbyton, U.S.A. 113 J4
Crosía, Italy 31 C9
Cross →, Nigeria 83 E6
Cross City, U.S.A. 109 L4
Cross Fell, U.K. 12 C5
Cross L., Canada 105 C9
Cross Lake, Canada 105 C9
Cross River □, Nigeria 83 D6
Cross Sound, U.S.A. 100 C6
Crossett, U.S.A. 113 J9
Crosshaven, Ireland 15 E3
Crossville, U.S.A. 109 G3
Croswell, U.S.A. 110 C2
Croton-on-Hudson, U.S.A. 111 E11
Crotone, Italy 31 C10
Crow →, Canada 104 B4
Crow Agency, U.S.A. 114 D10
Crow Hd., Ireland 15 E1
Crowell, U.S.A. 113 J5
Crowley, U.S.A. 113 K8
Crowley, L., U.S.A. 116 H8
Crown Point, Ind., U.S.A. 108 E2
Crown Point, N.Y., U.S.A. 111 C11
Crownpoint, U.S.A. 115 J9
Crows Landing, U.S.A. 116 H5
Crows Nest, Australia 95 D5
Crowsnest Pass, Canada 104 D6
Croydon, Australia 94 B3
Croydon □, U.K. 13 F7
Crozet, Is., Ind. Oc. 3 G12
Crozon, France 18 D2

Cruz, C., *Cuba* 120 C4
Cruz Alta, *Brazil* 127 B5
Cruz de Incio, *Spain* 34 C3
Cruz del Eje, *Argentina* 126 C3
Cruzeiro, *Brazil* 127 A7
Cruzeiro do Oeste, *Brazil* 127 A5
Cruzeiro do Sul, *Brazil* 124 E4
Cry L., *Canada* 104 B3
Crystal Bay, *U.S.A.* 116 F7
Crystal City, *U.S.A.* 113 L5
Crystal Falls, *U.S.A.* 108 B1
Crystal River, *U.S.A.* 109 L4
Crystal Springs, *U.S.A.* 113 K9
Csenger, *Hungary* 42 C7
Csongrád, *Hungary* 42 D5
Csongrád □, *Hungary* 42 D5
Csorna, *Hungary* 42 C2
Csurgo, *Hungary* 42 D2
Cu Lao Hon, *Vietnam* 65 G7
Cua Rao, *Vietnam* 64 C5
Cuácua →, *Mozam.* 87 F4
Cuamato, *Angola* 88 B2
Cuamba, *Mozam.* 87 E4
Cuando →, *Angola* 85 H4
Cuando Cubango □, *Angola* 88 B3
Cuangar, *Angola* 88 B2
Cuango = Kwango →, *Dem. Rep. of the Congo* 84 E3
Cuanza →, *Angola* 84 F2
Cuarto →, *Argentina* 126 C3
Cuatrociénegas, *Mexico* 118 B4
Cuauhtémoc, *Mexico* 118 B3
Cuba, *Portugal* 35 G3
Cuba, *N. Mex., U.S.A.* 115 J10
Cuba, *N.Y., U.S.A.* 110 D6
Cuba ■, *W. Indies* 120 B4
Cubango →, *Africa* 88 B3
Çubuk, *Turkey* 72 B5
Cuchumatanes, Sierra de los, *Guatemala* 120 C1
Cuckfield, *U.K.* 13 F7
Cucuí, *Brazil* 124 C5
Cucurpe, *Mexico* 118 A2
Cúcuta, *Colombia* 124 B4
Cudalbi, *Romania* 43 E12
Cuddalore, *India* 66 P11
Cuddapah, *India* 66 M11
Cuddapan, L., *Australia* 94 D3
Cudillero, *Spain* 34 B4
Cue, *Australia* 93 E2
Cuéllar, *Spain* 34 D6
Cuenca, *Ecuador* 124 D3
Cuenca, *Spain* 32 E2
Cuenca □, *Spain* 32 F3
Cuenca, Serranía de, *Spain* 32 F3
Cuerdo del Pozo, Embalse de la, *Spain* 32 D2
Cuernavaca, *Mexico* 119 D5
Cuero, *U.S.A.* 113 L6
Cuers, *France* 21 E10
Cuevas del Almanzora, *Spain* 33 H3
Cuevo, *Bolivia* 124 H6
Cugir, *Romania* 43 E8
Cugnaux, *France* 20 E5
Cuhai-Bakony →, *Hungary* 42 C2
Cuiabá, *Brazil* 125 G7
Cuiabá →, *Brazil* 125 G7
Cuijk, *Neths.* 17 C5
Cuilco, *Guatemala* 120 C1
Cuillin Hills, *U.K.* 14 D2
Cuillin Sd., *U.K.* 14 D2
Cuiseaux, *France* 19 F12
Cuito →, *Angola* 88 B3
Cuitzeo, L. de, *Mexico* 118 D4
Cujmir, *Romania* 42 F7
Cukai, *Malaysia* 65 K4
Culbertson, *U.S.A.* 112 A2
Culebra, Sierra de la, *Spain* 34 D4
Culfa, *Azerbaijan* 73 C11
Culgoa →, *Australia* 95 D4
Culiacán, *Mexico* 118 C3
Culiacán →, *Mexico* 118 C3
Culion, *Phil.* 61 F4
Cúllar, *Spain* 35 H8
Cullen, *U.K.* 14 D6
Cullen Pt., *Australia* 94 A3
Cullera, *Spain* 33 F4
Cullman, *U.S.A.* 109 H2
Culoz, *France* 21 C9
Culpeper, *U.S.A.* 108 F7
Culuene →, *Brazil* 125 F8
Culver, Pt., *Australia* 93 F3
Culverden, *N.Z.* 91 K4
Cumaná, *Venezuela* 124 A6
Cumaovası, *Turkey* 39 C9
Cumberland, *B.C., Canada* 104 D4
Cumberland, *Ont., Canada* 111 A9
Cumberland, *U.S.A.* 108 F6
Cumberland →, *U.S.A.* 109 G2
Cumberland, L., *U.S.A.* 109 G3
Cumberland I., *U.S.A.* 109 K5
Cumberland Is., *Australia* 94 C4
Cumberland L., *Canada* 105 C8
Cumberland Pen., *Canada* 101 B13
Cumberland Plateau, *U.S.A.* 109 H3
Cumberland Sd., *Canada* 101 B13
Cumbernauld, *U.K.* 14 F5
Cumborah, *Australia* 95 D4
Cumbres Mayores, *Spain* 35 G4
Cumbria □, *U.K.* 12 C5
Cumbrian Mts., *U.K.* 12 C5
Cumbum, *India* 66 M11
Cuminá →, *Brazil* 125 D7
Cummings Mt., *U.S.A.* 117 K8
Cummins, *Australia* 95 E2
Cumnock, *U.K.* 14 F4
Cumpas, *Mexico* 118 B3
Cumplida, Pta., *Canary Is.* 37 F2
Çumra, *Turkey* 72 D5
Cunco, *Chile* 128 D2
Cuncumén, *Chile* 126 C1
Cunderdin, *Australia* 93 F2
Cunene →, *Angola* 88 B1
Cúneo, *Italy* 28 D4
Çüngüş, *Turkey* 70 B3
Cunillera, I. = Sa Conillera, *Spain* 37 C7
Cunlhat, *France* 20 C7
Cunnamulla, *Australia* 95 D4
Cuorgnè, *Italy* 28 C4
Cupar, *Canada* 105 C8
Cupar, *U.K.* 14 E5
Cupcini, *Moldova* 43 B12
Cupica, G. de, *Colombia* 124 B3
Ćuprija, *Serbia, Yug.* 40 C5
Curaçao, *Neth. Ant.* 121 D6
Curanilahue, *Chile* 126 D1
Curaray →, *Peru* 124 D4
Cure →, *France* 19 E10
Curepto, *Chile* 126 D1
Curiapo, *Venezuela* 124 B6
Curicó, *Chile* 126 C1
Curinga, *Italy* 31 D9
Curitiba, *Brazil* 127 B6
Curitibanos, *Brazil* 127 B5
Currais Novos, *Brazil* 125 E11
Curralinho, *Brazil* 125 D9
Currant, *U.S.A.* 114 G6
Current →, *U.S.A.* 113 G9
Currie, *Australia* 94 F3
Currie, *U.S.A.* 114 F6
Curtea de Argeş, *Romania* 43 E9
Curtici, *Romania* 42 D6
Curtis, *U.S.A.* 112 E4
Curtis Group, *Australia* 94 F4
Curtis I., *Australia* 94 C5
Curuápanema →, *Brazil* 125 D7
Curuçá, *Brazil* 125 D9
Curuguaty, *Paraguay* 127 A4
Curup, *Indonesia* 62 E2
Cururupu, *Brazil* 125 D10
Curuzú Cuatiá, *Argentina* 126 B4
Curvelo, *Brazil* 125 G10
Cushing, *U.S.A.* 113 H6
Cushing, Mt., *Canada* 104 B3
Cusihuiriáchic, *Mexico* 118 B3
Cusna, Mte., *Italy* 28 D7
Cusset, *France* 19 F10
Custer, *U.S.A.* 112 D3
Cut Bank, *U.S.A.* 114 B7
Cutchogue, *U.S.A.* 111 E12
Cuthbert, *U.S.A.* 109 K3
Cutler, *U.S.A.* 116 J7
Cutro, *Italy* 31 C9
Cuttaburra →, *Australia* 95 D3
Cuttack, *India* 67 J14
Cuvier, C., *Australia* 93 D1
Cuvier I., *N.Z.* 91 G5
Cuxhaven, *Germany* 24 B4
Cuyahoga Falls, *U.S.A.* 110 E3
Cuyapo, *Phil.* 61 D4
Cuyo, *Phil.* 61 F4
Cuyo East Pass, *Phil.* 61 F4
Cuyo West Pass, *Phil.* 61 F4
Cuyuni →, *Guyana* 124 B7
Cuzco, *Bolivia* 124 H5
Cuzco, *Peru* 124 F4
Čvrsnica, *Bos.-H.* 42 G2
Cwmbran, *U.K.* 13 F4
Cyangugu, *Rwanda* 86 C2
Cybinka, *Poland* 45 F1
Cyclades = Kikládhes, *Greece* 38 E6
Cygnet, *Australia* 94 G4
Cynthiana, *U.S.A.* 108 F3
Cypress Hills, *Canada* 105 D7
Cypress Hills Prov. Park, *Canada* 105 D7
Cyprus ■, *Asia* 36 E12
Cyrenaica, *Libya* 79 C10
Czaplinek, *Poland* 44 E3
Czar, *Canada* 105 C6
Czarna →, *Łódzkie, Poland* 45 G6
Czarna →, *Świętokrzyskie, Poland* 45 H8
Czarna Białostocka, *Poland* 45 E10
Czarna Woda, *Poland* 44 E5
Czarne, *Poland* 44 E3
Czarnków, *Poland* 45 F3
Czech Rep. ■, *Europe* 26 B8
Czechowice-Dziedzice, *Poland* 45 J5
Czempiń, *Poland* 45 F3
Czeremcha, *Poland* 45 F10
Czerniejewo, *Poland* 45 F4
Czersk, *Poland* 44 E4
Czerwieńsk, *Poland* 45 F2
Czerwionka-Leszczyny, *Poland* 45 H5
Częstochowa, *Poland* 45 H6
Człopa, *Poland* 45 E3
Człuchów, *Poland* 44 E4
Czyżew-Osada, *Poland* 45 F9

D

Da →, *Vietnam* 58 G5
Da Hinggan Ling, *China* 60 B7
Da Lat, *Vietnam* 65 G7
Da Nang, *Vietnam* 64 D7
Da Qaidam, *China* 60 C4
Da Yunhe →, *China* 57 G11
Da'an, *China* 57 B13
Dab'a, Ras el, *Egypt* 80 H6
Daba Shan, *China* 58 B7
Dabai, *Nigeria* 83 C6
Dabakala, *Ivory C.* 82 D4
Dabas, *Hungary* 42 C4
Dabat, *Ethiopia* 81 E4
Dabbagh, Jabal, *Si. Arabia* 70 E2
Dabhoi, *India* 68 H5
Dąbie, *Poland* 45 F5
Dabie Shan, *China* 59 B10
Dabilda, *Cameroon* 83 C7
Dabnou, *Niger* 83 C6
Dabo = Pasirkuning, *Indonesia* 62 E2
Dabola, *Guinea* 82 C2
Dabou, *Ivory C.* 82 D4
Daboya, *Ghana* 83 D4
Dąbrowa Białostocka, *Poland* 44 E10
Dąbrowa Górnicza, *Poland* 45 H6
Dąbrowa Tarnowska, *Poland* 45 H7
Dabu, *China* 59 E11
Dabung, *Malaysia* 65 K4
Dabus →, *Ethiopia* 81 E4
Dacato →, *Ethiopia* 81 F5
Dacca = Dhaka, *Bangla.* 69 H14
Dacca = Dhaka □, *Bangla.* 69 G14
Dachau, *Germany* 25 G7
Dachstein, Hoher, *Austria* 26 D6
Dačice, *Czech Rep.* 26 B8
Dadanawa, *Guyana* 124 C7
Daday, *Turkey* 72 B5
Dade City, *U.S.A.* 109 L4
Dadhar, *Pakistan* 68 E2
Dadiya, *Nigeria* 83 D7
Dadra & Nagar Haveli □, *India* 66 J8
Dadri = Charkhi Dadri, *India* 68 E7
Dadu, *Pakistan* 68 F2
Dadu He →, *China* 58 C4
Daet, *Phil.* 61 D5
Dafang, *China* 58 D5
Dağ, *Turkey* 39 D12
Dagana, *Senegal* 82 B1
Dagash, *Sudan* 80 D3
Dagestan □, *Russia* 49 J8
Dagestanskiye Ogni, *Russia* 49 J9
Daggett, *U.S.A.* 117 L10
Daghestan Republic = Dagestan □, *Russia* 49 J8
Daghfeli, *Sudan* 80 D3
Dağlıq Qarabağ = Nagorno-Karabakh, *Azerbaijan* 70 B5
Dagö = Hiiumaa, *Estonia* 9 G20
Dagu, *China* 57 E9
Daguan, *China* 58 D4
Dagupan, *Phil.* 61 C4
Daguragu, *Australia* 92 C5
Dahab, *Egypt* 80 B3
Dahlak Kebir, *Eritrea* 81 D5
Dahlenburg, *Germany* 24 B6
Dahlonega, *U.S.A.* 109 H4
Dahme, *Germany* 24 D9
Dahod, *India* 68 H6
Dahomey = Benin ■, *Africa* 83 D5
Dahong Shan, *China* 59 B9
Dahra, *Senegal* 82 B1
Dahshûr, *Egypt* 80 J7
Dahūk, *Iraq* 70 B3
Dai Hao, *Vietnam* 64 C6
Dai-Sen, *Japan* 55 G6
Dai Shan, *China* 59 B14
Dai Xian, *China* 56 E7
Daicheng, *China* 56 E9
Daimiel, *Spain* 35 F7
Daingean, *Ireland* 15 C4
Dainkog, *China* 58 A1
Daintree, *Australia* 94 B4
Daiō-Misaki, *Japan* 55 G8
Dair, J. ed, *Sudan* 81 E3
Dairût, *Egypt* 80 B3
Daisetsu-Zan, *Japan* 54 C11
Dajarra, *Australia* 94 C2
Dajin Chuan →, *China* 58 B3
Dak Dam, *Cambodia* 64 F6
Dak Nhe, *Vietnam* 64 E6
Dak Pek, *Vietnam* 64 E6
Dak Song, *Vietnam* 65 F6
Dak Sui, *Vietnam* 64 E6
Dakar, *Senegal* 82 C1
Dakhla, *W. Sahara* 78 D2
Dakhla, El Wâhât el-, *Egypt* 80 B2
Dakingari, *Nigeria* 83 C5
Dakor, *India* 68 H5
Dakoro, *Niger* 83 C6
Dakota City, *U.S.A.* 112 D6
Đakovica, *Kosovo, Yug.* 40 D4
Đakovo, *Croatia* 42 E3
Dalaba, *Guinea* 82 C2
Dalachi, *China* 56 F3
Dalai Nur, *China* 56 C9
Dālakī, *Iran* 71 D6
Dalälven →, *Sweden* 10 D10
Dalaman, *Turkey* 39 E10
Dalaman →, *Turkey* 39 E10
Dalandzadgad, *Mongolia* 56 C3
Dalap-Uliga-Darrit, *Marshall Is.* 96 G9
Dalarna, *Sweden* 10 D8
Dalarnas län □, *Sweden* 10 C8
Dālbandīn, *Pakistan* 66 E4
Dalbeattie, *U.K.* 14 G5
Dalbeg, *Australia* 94 C4
Dalbosjön, *Sweden* 11 F6
Dalby, *Australia* 95 D5
Dalby, *Sweden* 11 J7
Dale City, *U.S.A.* 108 F7
Dale Hollow L., *U.S.A.* 109 G3
Dalga, *Egypt* 80 B3
Dalgān, *Iran* 71 E8
Dalhart, *U.S.A.* 113 G3
Dalhousie, *Canada* 103 C6
Dalhousie, *India* 68 C6
Dali, *Shaanxi, China* 56 G5
Dali, *Yunnan, China* 58 E3
Dalian, *China* 57 E11
Daliang Shan, *China* 58 D4
Daling He →, *China* 57 D11
Dāliyat el Karmel, *Israel* 75 C4
Dalj, *Croatia* 42 E3
Dalkeith, *U.K.* 14 F5
Dallas, *Oreg., U.S.A.* 114 D2
Dallas, *Tex., U.S.A.* 113 J6
Dallol, *Ethiopia* 81 E5
Dalmā, *U.A.E.* 71 E7
Dalmacija, *Croatia* 29 E13
Dalmas, L., *Canada* 103 B5
Dalmatia = Dalmacija, *Croatia* 29 E13
Dalmau, *India* 69 F9
Dalmellington, *U.K.* 14 F4
Dalnegorsk, *Russia* 51 E14
Dalnerechensk, *Russia* 51 E14
Daloa, *Ivory C.* 82 D3
Dalou Shan, *China* 58 C6
Dalry, *U.K.* 14 F4
Dalrymple, L., *Australia* 94 C4
Dals Långed, *Sweden* 11 F6
Dalsjöfors, *Sweden* 11 G7
Dalsland, *Sweden* 11 F6
Daltenganj, *India* 69 H11
Dalton, *Ga., U.S.A.* 109 H3
Dalton, *Mass., U.S.A.* 111 D11
Dalton, *Nebr., U.S.A.* 112 E3
Dalton Iceberg Tongue, *Antarctica* 5 C9
Dalton-in-Furness, *U.K.* 12 C4
Dalupiri I., *Phil.* 61 B4
Dalvík, *Iceland* 8 D4
Dalwallinu, *Australia* 93 F2
Daly →, *Australia* 92 B5
Daly City, *U.S.A.* 116 H4
Daly L., *Canada* 105 B7
Daly River, *Australia* 92 B5
Daly Waters, *Australia* 94 B1
Dalyan, *Turkey* 39 E10
Dam Doi, *Vietnam* 65 H5
Dam Ha, *Vietnam* 64 B6
Daman, *India* 66 J8
Dāmaneh, *Iran* 71 C6
Damanhûr, *Egypt* 80 H7
Damant L., *Canada* 105 A7
Damanzhuang, *China* 56 E9
Damar, *Indonesia* 63 F7
Damaraland, *Namibia* 88 C2
Damascus = Dimashq, *Syria* 75 B5
Damaturu, *Nigeria* 83 C7
Damāvand, *Iran* 71 C7
Damāvand, Qolleh-ye, *Iran* 71 C7
Damba, *Angola* 84 F3
Dâmboviţa □, *Romania* 43 F10
Dâmboviţa →, *Romania* 43 F11
Dâmbovnic →, *Romania* 43 F10
Dame Marie, *Haiti* 121 C5
Dāmghān, *Iran* 71 B7
Dămienesti, *Romania* 43 D11
Damietta = Dumyât, *Egypt* 80 H7
Daming, *China* 56 F8
Damīr Qābū, *Syria* 70 B4
Dammam = Ad Dammām, *Si. Arabia* 71 E6
Dammarie-les-Lys, *France* 19 D9
Dammartin-en-Goële, *France* 19 C9
Damme, *Germany* 24 C4
Damodar →, *India* 69 H12
Damoh, *India* 69 H8
Dampier, *Australia* 92 D2
Dampier, Selat, *Indonesia* 63 E8
Dampier Arch., *Australia* 92 D2
Damrei, Chuor Phnum, *Cambodia* 65 G4
Damvillers, *France* 19 C12
Dan-Gulbi, *Nigeria* 83 C6
Dan Xian, *China* 64 C7
Dana, *Indonesia* 63 F6
Dana, L., *Canada* 102 B4
Dana, Mt., *U.S.A.* 116 H7
Danakil Desert, *Ethiopia* 81 E5
Danané, *Ivory C.* 82 D3
Danao, *Phil.* 61 F6
Danau Poso, *Indonesia* 63 E6
Danba, *China* 58 B3
Danbury, *U.S.A.* 111 E11
Danby L., *U.S.A.* 115 J6
Dand, *Afghan.* 68 D1
Dandeldhura, *Nepal* 69 E9
Dandeli, *India* 66 M9
Dandîl, *Egypt* 80 J7
Dandong, *China* 57 D13
Danfeng, *China* 56 H6
Dangan Liedao, *China* 59 F10
Dangé-St-Romain, *France* 20 B4
Dângeni, *Romania* 43 C11
Danger Is. = Pukapuka, *Cook Is.* 97 J11
Danger Pt., *S. Africa* 88 E2
Dangla, *Ethiopia* 81 E4
Dangla Shan = Tanggula Shan, *China* 60 C4
Dangora, *Nigeria* 83 C6
Dangouadougou, *Burkina Faso* 82 D4
Dangrek, Phnom, *Thailand* 64 E5
Dangriga, *Belize* 119 D7
Dangshan, *China* 56 G9
Dangtu, *China* 59 B12
Dangyang, *China* 59 B8
Dani, *Burkina Faso* 83 C4
Daniel, *U.S.A.* 114 E8
Daniel's Harbour, *Canada* 103 B8
Danielskuil, *S. Africa* 88 D3
Danielson, *U.S.A.* 111 E13
Danilov, *Russia* 46 C11
Danilovgrad, *Montenegro, Yug.* 40 D3
Danilovka, *Russia* 48 E7
Daning, *China* 56 F6
Danissa, *Kenya* 86 B5
Danja, *Nigeria* 83 C6
Danjiangkou, *China* 59 A8
Danjiangkou Shuiku, *China* 59 A8
Dank, *Oman* 71 F8
Dankalwa, *Nigeria* 83 C7
Dankama, *Nigeria* 83 C6
Dankhar Gompa, *India* 66 C11
Dankov, *Russia* 46 F10
Danleng, *China* 58 B4
Danlí, *Honduras* 120 D2
Dannemora, *U.S.A.* 111 B11
Dannenberg, *Germany* 24 B7
Dannevirke, *N.Z.* 91 J6
Dannhauser, *S. Africa* 89 D5
Dansville, *U.S.A.* 110 D7
Danta, *India* 68 G5
Dantan, *India* 69 J12
Dante, *Somali Rep.* 74 E5
Danube = Dunărea →, *Europe* 43 E14
Danvers, *U.S.A.* 111 D14
Danville, *Ill., U.S.A.* 108 E2
Danville, *Ky., U.S.A.* 108 G3
Danville, *Pa., U.S.A.* 111 F8
Danville, *Va., U.S.A.* 109 G6
Danville, *Vt., U.S.A.* 111 B12
Danyang, *China* 59 B12
Danzhai, *China* 58 D6
Danzig = Gdańsk, *Poland* 44 D5
Dão →, *Portugal* 34 E2
Dao Xian, *China* 59 E8
Daocheng, *China* 58 C3
Daoukro, *Ivory C.* 82 D4
Dapaong, *Togo* 83 C5
Dapchi, *Nigeria* 83 C7
Dapitan, *Phil.* 61 G5
Daqing Shan, *China* 56 D6
Daqu Shan, *China* 59 B14
Dar Banda, *Africa* 76 F6
Dar el Beida = Casablanca, *Morocco* 78 B4
Dar es Salaam, *Tanzania* 86 D4
Dar Mazār, *Iran* 71 D8
Dar'ā, *Syria* 75 C5
Dar'ā □, *Syria* 75 C5
Dārāb, *Iran* 71 D7
Daraban, *Pakistan* 68 D4
Darabani, *Romania* 43 B11
Daraina, *Madag.* 89 A8
Daraj, *Libya* 79 B8
Dārān, *Iran* 71 C6
Daravica, *Kosovo, Yug.* 40 D4
Daraw, *Egypt* 80 C3
Dārayyā, *Syria* 75 B5
Darazo, *Nigeria* 83 C7
Darband, *Pakistan* 68 B5
Darband, Kūh-e, *Iran* 71 D8
Darbhanga, *India* 69 F11
D'Arcy, *Canada* 104 C4
Darda, *Croatia* 42 E3
Dardanelle, *Ark., U.S.A.* 113 H8
Dardanelle, *Calif., U.S.A.* 116 G7
Dardanelles = Çanakkale Boğazı, *Turkey* 41 F10
Dare →, *Ethiopia* 81 F5
Darende, *Turkey* 72 C7
Dārestān, *Iran* 71 D8
Darfo, *Italy* 28 C7
Dârfûr, *Sudan* 79 F10
Dargai, *Pakistan* 68 B4
Dargan Ata, *Turkmenistan* 50 E7
Dargaville, *N.Z.* 91 F4
Dargol, *Niger* 83 C5
Darhan Muminggan Lianheqi, *China* 56 D6
Dari, *Sudan* 81 F3
Darıca, *Turkey* 72 B3
Darién, G. del, *Colombia* 122 C3
Dariganga = Ovoot, *Mongolia* 56 B7
Darinskoye, *Kazakstan* 48 E10
Darjeeling = Darjiling, *India* 69 F13
Darjiling, *India* 69 F13
Darkan, *Australia* 93 F2
Darkhana, *Pakistan* 68 D5
Darkhazīneh, *Iran* 71 D6
Darkot Pass, *Pakistan* 69 A5
Darling Downs, *Australia* 95 D5
Darling Ra., *Australia* 93 F2
Darlington, *U.K.* 12 C6
Darlington, *U.S.A.* 109 H6
Darlington □, *U.K.* 12 C6
Darlington, L., *S. Africa* 88 E4
Darlot, L., *Australia* 93 E3
Darłowo, *Poland* 44 D3
Dărmăneşti, *Bacău, Romania* 43 D11
Dărmăneşti, *Suceava, Romania* 43 C11
Darmstadt, *Germany* 25 F4
Darnah, *Libya* 79 B10
Darnall, *S. Africa* 89 D5
Darney, *France* 19 D13
Darnley, C., *Antarctica* 5 C6
Darnley B., *Canada* 100 B7
Daroca, *Spain* 32 D3
Darou-Mousti, *Senegal* 82 B1
Darr →, *Australia* 94 C3
Darra Pezu, *Pakistan* 68 C4
Darrequeira, *Argentina* 126 D3
Darrington, *U.S.A.* 114 B3
Darsser Ort, *Germany* 24 A8

Dart →, *U.K.* 13 G4
Dart, C., *Antarctica* 5 D14
Dartford, *U.K.* 13 F8
Dartmoor, *U.K.* 13 G4
Dartmouth, *Canada* 103 D7
Dartmouth, *U.K.* 13 G4
Dartmouth, L., *Australia* 95 D4
Dartuch, C. = Artrutx, C. de, *Spain* 37 B10
Daruvar, *Croatia* 42 E2
Darvaza, *Turkmenistan* 50 E6
Darvel, Teluk = Lahad Datu, Teluk, *Malaysia* 63 D5
Darwen, *U.K.* 12 D5
Darwendale, *Zimbabwe* 89 B5
Darwha, *India* 66 J10
Darwin, *Australia* 92 B5
Darwin, *U.S.A.* 117 J9
Darya Khan, *Pakistan* 68 D4
Daryoi Amu = Amudarya →, *Uzbekistan* 50 E6
Dās, *U.A.E.* 71 E7
Dashen, Ras, *Ethiopia* 81 E4
Dashetai, *China* 56 D5
Dashhowuz, *Turkmenistan* 50 E6
Dashkesan = Daşkäsän, *Azerbaijan* 49 K7
Dashköpri, *Turkmenistan* 71 B9
Dasht, *Iran* 71 B8
Dasht →, *Pakistan* 66 G2
Daska, *Pakistan* 68 C6
Daşkäsän, *Azerbaijan* 49 K7
Dassa, *Benin* 83 D5
Dasuya, *India* 68 D6
Datça, *Turkey* 39 E9
Datia, *India* 69 G8
Datian, *China* 59 E11
Datong, *Anhui, China* 59 B11
Datong, *Shanxi, China* 56 D7
Dattakhel, *Pakistan* 68 C3
Datteln, *Germany* 24 D3
Datu, Tanjung, *Indonesia* 62 D3
Datu Piang, *Phil.* 61 H6
Datuk, Tanjong = Datu, Tanjung, *Indonesia* 62 D3
Daud Khel, *Pakistan* 68 C4
Daudnagar, *India* 69 G11
Daugava →, *Latvia* 9 H21
Daugavpils, *Latvia* 9 J22
Daulpur, *India* 68 F7
Daun, *Germany* 25 E2
Dauphin, *Canada* 105 C8
Dauphin, *U.S.A.* 110 F8
Dauphin L., *Canada* 105 C9
Dauphiné, *France* 21 C9
Daura, *Borno, Nigeria* 83 C7
Daura, *Katsina, Nigeria* 83 C6
Dausa, *India* 68 F7
Däväçi, *Azerbaijan* 49 K9
Davangere, *India* 66 M9
Davao, *Phil.* 61 H6
Davao G., *Phil.* 61 H6
Dāvar Panāh, *Iran* 71 E9
Davenport, *Calif., U.S.A.* 116 H4
Davenport, *Iowa, U.S.A.* 112 E9
Davenport, *Wash., U.S.A.* 114 C4
Davenport Ra., *Australia* 94 C1
Daventry, *U.K.* 13 E6
David, *Panama* 120 E3
David City, *U.S.A.* 112 E6
David Gorodok = Davyd Haradok, *Belarus* 47 F4
Davidson, *Canada* 105 C7
Davis, *U.S.A.* 116 G5
Davis Dam, *U.S.A.* 117 K12
Davis Inlet, *Canada* 103 A7
Davis Mts., *U.S.A.* 113 K2
Davis Sea, *Antarctica* 5 C7
Davis Str., *N. Amer.* 101 B14
Davo →, *Ivory C.* 82 D3
Davos, *Switz.* 25 J5
Davutlar, *Turkey* 39 D9
Davy L., *Canada* 105 B7
Davyd Haradok, *Belarus* 47 F4
Dawa →, *Ethiopia* 81 G5
Dawaki, *Bauchi, Nigeria* 83 D6
Dawaki, *Kano, Nigeria* 83 C6
Dawei, *Burma* 64 E2
Dawes Ra., *Australia* 94 C5
Dawlish, *U.K.* 13 G4
Dawna Ra., *Burma* 64 D2
Dawros Hd., *Ireland* 15 B3
Dawson, *Canada* 100 B6
Dawson, *U.S.A.* 109 K3
Dawson, I., *Chile* 128 G2
Dawson B., *Canada* 105 C8
Dawson Creek, *Canada* 104 B4
Dawson Inlet, *Canada* 105 A10
Dawson Ra., *Australia* 94 C4
Dawu, *Hubei, China* 59 B9
Dawu, *Sichuan, China* 58 B3
Dax, *France* 20 E2
Daxian, *China* 58 B6
Daxin, *China* 58 F6
Daxindian, *China* 57 F11
Daxinggou, *China* 57 C15
Daxue Shan, *Sichuan, China* 58 B3
Daxue Shan, *Yunnan, China* 58 F2
Dayao, *China* 58 E3
Daye, *China* 59 B10
Dayet en Naharat, *Mali* 82 B4
Dayi, *China* 58 B4
Dayong, *China* 59 C8
Dayr az Zawr, *Syria* 70 C4
Daysland, *Canada* 104 C6
Dayton, *Nev., U.S.A.* 116 F7
Dayton, *Ohio, U.S.A.* 108 F3
Dayton, *Pa., U.S.A.* 110 F5
Dayton, *Tenn., U.S.A.* 109 H3
Dayton, *Wash., U.S.A.* 114 C4
Dayton, *Wyo., U.S.A.* 114 D10
Daytona Beach, *U.S.A.* 109 L5
Dayu, *China* 59 E10
Dayville, *U.S.A.* 114 D4
Dazhu, *China* 58 B6
Dazkırı, *Turkey* 39 D11
Dazu, *China* 58 C5
De Aar, *S. Africa* 88 E3
De Funiak Springs, *U.S.A.* 109 K2
De Grey →, *Australia* 92 D2
De Haan, *Belgium* 17 C3
De Kalb, *U.S.A.* 112 E10
De Land, *U.S.A.* 109 L5
De Leon, *U.S.A.* 113 J5
De Panne, *Belgium* 17 C2
De Pere, *U.S.A.* 108 C1
De Queen, *U.S.A.* 113 H7
De Quincy, *U.S.A.* 113 K8
De Ridder, *U.S.A.* 113 K8
De Smet, *U.S.A.* 112 C6
De Soto, *U.S.A.* 112 F9
De Tour Village, *U.S.A.* 108 C4
De Witt, *U.S.A.* 113 H9
Dead Sea, *Asia* 75 D4
Deadwood, *U.S.A.* 112 C3
Deadwood L., *Canada* 104 B3
Deal, *U.K.* 13 F9
Deal I., *Australia* 94 F4
Dealesville, *S. Africa* 88 D4
De'an, *China* 59 C10
Dean →, *Canada* 104 C3
Dean, Forest of, *U.K.* 13 F5
Dean Chan., *Canada* 104 C3
Deán Funes, *Argentina* 126 C3
Dease →, *Canada* 104 B3
Dease L., *Canada* 104 B2
Dease Lake, *Canada* 104 B2
Death Valley, *U.S.A.* 117 J10
Death Valley Junction, *U.S.A.* 117 J10
Death Valley National Park, *U.S.A.* 117 J10
Deauville, *France* 18 C7
Deba, *Spain* 32 B2
Deba Habe, *Nigeria* 83 C7
Debaltsevo, *Ukraine* 47 H10
Debao, *China* 58 F6
Debar, *Macedonia* 40 E4
Debden, *Canada* 105 C7
Dębica, *Poland* 45 H8
Dęblin, *Poland* 45 G8
Dębno, *Poland* 45 F1
Débo, L., *Mali* 82 B4
Debolt, *Canada* 104 B5
Deborah East, L., *Australia* 93 F2
Deborah West, L., *Australia* 93 F2
Debrc, *Serbia, Yug.* 40 B3
Debre Birhan, *Ethiopia* 81 F4
Debre Markos, *Ethiopia* 81 E4
Debre May, *Ethiopia* 81 E4
Debre Sina, *Ethiopia* 81 F4
Debre Tabor, *Ethiopia* 81 E4
Debre Zevit, *Ethiopia* 81 F4
Debre Zeyit, *Ethiopia* 81 E4
Debrecen, *Hungary* 42 C6
Debrzno, *Poland* 44 E4
Dečani, *Kosovo, Yug.* 40 D4
Decatur, *Ala., U.S.A.* 109 H2
Decatur, *Ga., U.S.A.* 109 J3
Decatur, *Ill., U.S.A.* 112 F10
Decatur, *Ind., U.S.A.* 108 E3
Decatur, *Tex., U.S.A.* 113 J6
Decazeville, *France* 20 D6
Deccan, *India* 66 L11
Deception Bay, *Australia* 95 D5
Deception L., *Canada* 105 B8
Dechang, *China* 58 D4
Dechhu, *India* 68 F5
Děčín, *Czech Rep.* 26 A7
Decize, *France* 19 F10
Deckerville, *U.S.A.* 110 C2
Decollatura, *Italy* 31 C9
Decorah, *U.S.A.* 112 D9
Deda, *Romania* 43 D9
Dedéagach = Alexandroúpolis, *Greece* 41 F9
Deder, *Ethiopia* 81 F5
Dedham, *U.S.A.* 111 D13
Dédougou, *Burkina Faso* 82 C4
Dedovichi, *Russia* 46 D5
Dedza, *Malawi* 87 E3
Dee →, *Aberds., U.K.* 14 D6
Dee →, *Dumf. & Gall., U.K.* 14 G4
Dee →, *Wales, U.K.* 12 D4
Deep B., *Canada* 104 A5
Deepwater, *Australia* 95 D5
Deer →, *Canada* 105 B10
Deer L., *Canada* 105 C10
Deer Lake, *Nfld., Canada* 103 C8
Deer Lake, *Ont., Canada* 105 C10
Deer Lodge, *U.S.A.* 114 C7
Deer Park, *U.S.A.* 114 C5
Deer River, *U.S.A.* 112 B8
Deeragun, *Australia* 94 B4
Deerdepoort, *S. Africa* 88 C4
Deferiet, *U.S.A.* 111 B9
Defiance, *U.S.A.* 108 E3
Degana, *India* 68 F6
Dêgê, *China* 58 B2
Degebe →, *Portugal* 35 G3
Degeberga, *Sweden* 11 J8
Dégelis, *Canada* 103 C6
Degema, *Nigeria* 83 E6
Degerfors, *Sweden* 10 E8
Degerhamn, *Sweden* 11 H10
Deggendorf, *Germany* 25 G8
Degh →, *Pakistan* 68 D5
Değirmendere, *Turkey* 41 F13
Deh Bīd, *Iran* 71 D7
Deh-e Shīr, *Iran* 71 D7
Dehaj, *Iran* 71 D7
Dehak, *Iran* 71 E9
Dehdez, *Iran* 71 D6
Dehej, *India* 68 J5
Dehestān, *Iran* 71 D7
Dehgolān, *Iran* 70 C5
Dehibat, *Tunisia* 79 B8
Dehlorān, *Iran* 70 C5
Dehnow-e Kūhestān, *Iran* 71 E8
Dehra Dun, *India* 68 D8
Dehri, *India* 69 G11
Dehua, *China* 59 E12
Dehui, *China* 57 B13
Deim Zubeir, *Sudan* 81 F2
Deinze, *Belgium* 17 D3
Dej, *Romania* 43 C8
Deje, *Sweden* 10 E7
Dejiang, *China* 58 C7
Deka →, *Zimbabwe* 88 B4
Dekemhare, *Eritrea* 81 D4
Dekese, *Dem. Rep. of the Congo* 84 E4
Del Mar, *U.S.A.* 117 N9
Del Norte, *U.S.A.* 115 H10
Del Rio, *U.S.A.* 113 L4
Delai, *Sudan* 80 D4
Delambre I., *Australia* 92 D2
Delami, *Sudan* 81 E3
Delano, *U.S.A.* 117 K7
Delano Peak, *U.S.A.* 115 G7
Delareyville, *S. Africa* 88 D4
Delaronde L., *Canada* 105 C7
Delavan, *U.S.A.* 112 D10
Delaware, *U.S.A.* 108 E4
Delaware □, *U.S.A.* 108 F8
Delaware →, *U.S.A.* 111 G9
Delaware B., *U.S.A.* 108 F8
Delay →, *Canada* 103 A5
Delbrück, *Germany* 24 D4
Delčevo, *Macedonia* 40 E6
Delémont, *Switz.* 25 H3
Delevan, *U.S.A.* 110 D6
Delft, *Neths.* 17 B4
Delfzijl, *Neths.* 17 A6
Delgado, C., *Mozam.* 87 E5
Delgerhet, *Mongolia* 56 B6
Delgo, *Sudan* 80 C3
Delhi, *Canada* 110 D4
Delhi, *India* 68 E7
Delhi, *La., U.S.A.* 113 J9
Delhi, *N.Y., U.S.A.* 111 D10
Deli Jovan, *Serbia, Yug.* 40 B6
Delia, *Canada* 104 C6
Delice, *Turkey* 72 C6
Delicias, *Mexico* 118 B3
Delījān, *Iran* 71 C6
Déline, *Canada* 100 B7
Delisle, *Canada* 105 C7
Delitzsch, *Germany* 24 D8
Dell City, *U.S.A.* 115 L11
Dell Rapids, *U.S.A.* 112 D6
Delle, *France* 19 E14
Delmar, *U.S.A.* 111 D11
Delmenhorst, *Germany* 24 B4
Delnice, *Croatia* 29 C11
Delonga, Ostrova, *Russia* 51 B15
Deloraine, *Australia* 94 G4
Deloraine, *Canada* 105 D8
Delphi, *Greece* 38 C4
Delphi, *U.S.A.* 108 E2
Delphos, *U.S.A.* 108 E3
Delportshoop, *S. Africa* 88 D3
Delray Beach, *U.S.A.* 109 M5
Delsbo, *Sweden* 10 C10
Delta, *Colo., U.S.A.* 115 G9
Delta, *Utah, U.S.A.* 114 G7
Delta □, *Nigeria* 83 D6
Delta Junction, *U.S.A.* 100 B5
Deltona, *U.S.A.* 109 L5
Delungra, *Australia* 95 D5
Delvada, *India* 68 J4
Delvinákion, *Greece* 38 B2
Delvinë, *Albania* 40 G4
Demak, *Indonesia* 63 G14
Demanda, Sierra de la, *Spain* 32 C2
Demavand = Damāvand, *Iran* 71 C7
Dembecha, *Ethiopia* 81 E4
Dembi, *Ethiopia* 81 F4
Dembia, *Dem. Rep. of the Congo* 86 B2
Dembidolo, *Ethiopia* 81 F3
Demchok, *India* 69 C8
Demer →, *Belgium* 17 D4
Demetrias, *Greece* 38 B5
Demidov, *Russia* 46 E6
Deming, *N. Mex., U.S.A.* 115 K10
Deming, *Wash., U.S.A.* 116 B4
Demini →, *Brazil* 124 D6
Demirci, *Turkey* 39 B10
Demirköprü Barajı, *Turkey* 39 C10
Demirköy, *Turkey* 41 E11
Demmin, *Germany* 24 B9
Demonte, *Italy* 28 D4
Demopolis, *U.S.A.* 109 J2
Dempo, *Indonesia* 62 E2
Demyansk, *Russia* 46 D7
Den Burg, *Neths.* 17 A4
Den Chai, *Thailand* 64 D3
Den Haag = 's-Gravenhage, *Neths.* 17 B4
Den Helder, *Neths.* 17 B4
Den Oever, *Neths.* 17 B5
Denain, *France* 19 B10
Denair, *U.S.A.* 116 H6
Denau, *Uzbekistan* 50 F7
Denbigh, *Canada* 110 A7
Denbigh, *U.K.* 12 D4
Denbighshire □, *U.K.* 12 D4
Dendang, *Indonesia* 62 E3
Dendermonde, *Belgium* 17 C4
Deneba, *Ethiopia* 81 F4
Dengchuan, *China* 58 E3
Denge, *Nigeria* 83 C6
Dengfeng, *China* 56 G7
Dengi, *Nigeria* 83 D6
Dengkou, *China* 56 D4
Dengzhou, *China* 59 A9
Denham, *Australia* 93 E1
Denham Ra., *Australia* 94 C4
Denham Sd., *Australia* 93 E1
Denholm, *Canada* 105 C7
Denia, *Spain* 33 G5
Denial B., *Australia* 95 E1
Denison, *Iowa, U.S.A.* 112 E7
Denison, *Tex., U.S.A.* 113 J6
Denison Plains, *Australia* 92 C4
Denizli, *Turkey* 39 D11
Denizli □, *Turkey* 39 D11
Denman Glacier, *Antarctica* 5 C7
Denmark, *Australia* 93 F2
Denmark ■, *Europe* 11 J3
Denmark Str., *Atl. Oc.* 4 C6
Dennison, *U.S.A.* 110 F3
Denny, *U.K.* 14 E5
Denpasar, *Indonesia* 62 F5
Denton, *Mont., U.S.A.* 114 C9
Denton, *Tex., U.S.A.* 113 J6
D'Entrecasteaux, Pt., *Australia* 93 F2
Denu, *Ghana* 83 D5
Denver, *Colo., U.S.A.* 112 F2
Denver, *Pa., U.S.A.* 111 F8
Denver City, *U.S.A.* 113 J3
Deoband, *India* 68 E7
Deogarh, *India* 68 G5
Deoghar, *India* 69 G12
Deolali, *India* 66 K8
Deoli = Devli, *India* 68 G6
Déols, *France* 19 F8
Deora, *India* 68 F4
Deori, *India* 69 H8
Deoria, *India* 69 F10
Deosai Mts., *Pakistan* 69 B6
Deosri, *India* 69 F14
Depalpur, *India* 68 H6
Deping, *China* 57 F9
Deposit, *U.S.A.* 111 D9
Depuch I., *Australia* 92 D2
Deputatskiy, *Russia* 51 C14
Dêqên, *China* 58 C2
Deqing, *China* 59 F8
Dera Ghazi Khan, *Pakistan* 68 D4
Dera Ismail Khan, *Pakistan* 68 D4
Derabugti, *Pakistan* 68 E3
Derawar Fort, *Pakistan* 68 E4
Derbent, *Russia* 49 J9
Derbent, *Turkey* 39 C10
Derby, *Australia* 92 C3
Derby, *U.K.* 12 E6
Derby, *Conn., U.S.A.* 111 E11
Derby, *Kans., U.S.A.* 113 G6
Derby, *N.Y., U.S.A.* 110 D6
Derby City □, *U.K.* 12 E6
Derby Line, *U.S.A.* 111 B12
Derbyshire □, *U.K.* 12 D6
Derecske, *Hungary* 42 C6
Dereköy, *Turkey* 41 E11
Dereli, *Turkey* 73 B8
Derg →, *U.K.* 15 B4
Derg, L., *Ireland* 15 D3
Dergachi = Derhaci, *Ukraine* 47 G9
Dergaon, *India* 67 F19
Derhaci, *Ukraine* 47 G9
Derik, *Turkey* 73 D9
Derinkuyu, *Turkey* 72 C6
Dermantsi, *Bulgaria* 41 C8
Dermott, *U.S.A.* 113 J9
Dêrong, *China* 58 C2
Derry = Londonderry, *U.K.* 15 B4
Derry = Londonderry □, *U.K.* 15 B4
Derry, *N.H., U.S.A.* 111 D13
Derry, *Pa., U.S.A.* 110 F5
Derryveagh Mts., *Ireland* 15 B3
Derudub, *Sudan* 80 D4
Derval, *France* 18 E5
Dervéni, *Greece* 38 C4
Derventa, *Bos.-H.* 42 F2
Derwent →, *Cumb., U.K.* 12 C4
Derwent →, *Derby, U.K.* 12 E6
Derwent →, *N. Yorks., U.K.* 12 D7
Derwent Water, *U.K.* 12 C4
Des Moines, *Iowa, U.S.A.* 112 E8
Des Moines, *N. Mex., U.S.A.* 113 G3
Des Moines →, *U.S.A.* 112 E9
Desa, *Romania* 42 G8
Desaguadero →, *Argentina* 126 C2
Desaguadero →, *Bolivia* 124 G5
Descanso, Pta., *Mexico* 117 N9
Descartes, *France* 20 B4
Deschaillons, *Canada* 103 C5
Deschambault L., *Canada* 105 C8
Deschutes →, *U.S.A.* 114 D3
Dese, *Ethiopia* 81 E4
Deseado →, *Argentina* 128 F3
Desenzano del Garda, *Italy* 28 C7
Desert Center, *U.S.A.* 117 M11
Desert Hot Springs, *U.S.A.* 117 M10
Deshnok, *India* 68 F5
Desna →, *Ukraine* 47 G6
Desnătui →, *Romania* 43 G8
Desolación, I., *Chile* 128 G2
Despeñaperros, Paso, *Spain* 35 G7
Despotovac, *Serbia, Yug.* 40 B5
Dessau, *Germany* 24 D8
Dessye = Dese, *Ethiopia* 81 E4
Desuri, *India* 68 G5
Desvres, *France* 19 B8
Det Udom, *Thailand* 64 E5
Deta, *Romania* 42 E6
Dete, *Zimbabwe* 88 B4
Đetinja →, *Serbia, Yug.* 40 C4
Detmold, *Germany* 24 D4
Detour, Pt., *U.S.A.* 108 C2
Detroit, *U.S.A.* 110 D1
Detroit Lakes, *U.S.A.* 112 B7
Detva, *Slovak Rep.* 27 C12
Deurne, *Neths.* 17 C5
Deutsche Bucht, *Germany* 24 A4
Deutschlandsberg, *Austria* 26 E8
Deux-Sèvres □, *France* 18 F6
Deva, *Romania* 42 E7
Devakottai, *India* 66 Q11
Devaprayag, *India* 69 D8
Dévaványa, *Hungary* 42 C5
Deveci Dağları, *Turkey* 72 B7
Devecikonağı, *Turkey* 41 G12
Devecser, *Hungary* 42 C2
Develi, *Turkey* 72 C6
Deventer, *Neths.* 17 B6
Deveron →, *U.K.* 14 D6
Devesel, *Romania* 42 F7
Devgadh Bariya, *India* 68 H5
Devikot, *India* 68 F4
Devils Den, *U.S.A.* 116 K7
Devils Lake, *U.S.A.* 112 A5
Devils Paw, *Canada* 104 B2
Devils Tower Junction, *U.S.A.* 112 C2
Devin, *Bulgaria* 41 E8
Devine, *U.S.A.* 113 L5
Devizes, *U.K.* 13 F6
Devli, *India* 68 G6
Devnya, *Bulgaria* 41 C11
Devoll →, *Albania* 40 F4
Devon, *Canada* 104 C6
Devon □, *U.K.* 13 G4
Devon I., *Canada* 4 B3
Devonport, *Australia* 94 G4
Devonport, *N.Z.* 91 G5
Devrek, *Turkey* 72 B4
Devrekâni, *Turkey* 72 B5
Devrez →, *Turkey* 72 B6
Dewas, *India* 68 H7
Dewetsdorp, *S. Africa* 88 D4
Dexing, *China* 59 C11
Dexter, *Maine, U.S.A.* 109 C11
Dexter, *Mo., U.S.A.* 113 G10
Dexter, *N. Mex., U.S.A.* 113 J2
Dey-Dey, L., *Australia* 93 E5
Deyang, *China* 58 B5
Deyhūk, *Iran* 71 C8
Deyyer, *Iran* 71 E6
Dezadeash L., *Canada* 104 A1
Dezfūl, *Iran* 71 C6
Dezhneva, Mys, *Russia* 51 C19
Dezhou, *China* 56 F9
Dhadhar →, *India* 69 G11
Dháfni, *Kríti, Greece* 36 D7
Dháfni, *Pelóponnisos, Greece* 38 D4
Dhahabān, *Si. Arabia* 80 C4
Dhahiriya = Az̧ Z̧āhirīyah, *West Bank* 75 D3
Dhahran = Az̧ Z̧ahrān, *Si. Arabia* 71 E6
Dhak, *Pakistan* 68 C5
Dhaka, *Bangla.* 69 H14
Dhaka □, *Bangla.* 69 G14
Dhali, *Cyprus* 36 D12
Dhamási, *Greece* 38 B4
Dhampur, *India* 69 E8
Dhamtari, *India* 67 J12
Dhanbad, *India* 69 H12
Dhangarhi, *Nepal* 67 E12
Dhankuta, *Nepal* 69 F12
Dhar, *India* 68 H6
Dharampur, *India* 68 H6
Dharamsala = Dharmsala, *India* 68 C7
Dhariwal, *India* 68 D6
Dharla →, *Bangla.* 69 G13
Dharmapuri, *India* 66 N11
Dharmjaygarh, *India* 69 H10
Dharmsala, *India* 68 C7
Dharni, *India* 68 J7
Dharwad, *India* 66 M9
Dhasan →, *India* 69 G8
Dhaulagiri, *Nepal* 69 E10
Dhebar, L., *India* 68 G6
Dheftera, *Cyprus* 36 D12
Dhenkanal, *India* 67 J14
Dhenoúsa, *Greece* 39 D7
Dherinia, *Cyprus* 36 D12
Dheskáti, *Greece* 40 G5
Dhespotikó, *Greece* 38 E6
Dhestina, *Greece* 38 C4
Dhiarrizos →, *Cyprus* 36 E11
Dhībān, *Jordan* 75 D4
Dhidhimótikhon, *Greece* 41 E10
Dhíkti Óros, *Greece* 36 D7
Dhilianáta, *Greece* 38 C2
Dhílos, *Greece* 39 D7
Dhilwan, *India* 68 D6
Dhimarkhera, *India* 69 H9
Dhimitsána, *Greece* 38 D4
Dhírfis Óros, *Greece* 38 C5
Dhodhekánisos, *Greece* 39 E8

Dhodhekánisos □, *Greece* 39 E8
Dhokós, *Greece* 38 D5
Dholiana, *Greece* 38 B2
Dholka, *India* 68 H5
Dhomokós, *Greece* 38 B4
Dhoraji, *India* 68 J4
Dhoxáton, *Greece* 41 E8
Dhragonísi, *Greece* 39 D7
Dhráhstis, Ákra, *Greece* 36 A3
Dhrangadhra, *India* 68 H4
Dhrápanon, Ákra, *Greece* 36 D6
Dhriopís, *Greece* 38 D6
Dhrol, *India* 68 H4
Dhuburi, *India* 67 F16
Dhule, *India* 66 J9
Di-ib, W. →, *Sudan* 80 C4
Di Linh, *Vietnam* 65 G7
Di Linh, Cao Nguyen, *Vietnam* 65 G7
Día, *Greece* 36 D7
Diabakania, *Guinea* 82 C2
Diablo, Mt., *U.S.A.* 116 H5
Diablo Range, *U.S.A.* 116 J5
Diafarabé, *Mali* 82 C4
Diala, *Mali* 82 C3
Dialakoro, *Mali* 82 C3
Dialakoto, *Senegal* 82 C2
Diallassagou, *Mali* 82 C4
Diamante, *Argentina* 126 C3
Diamante, *Italy* 31 C8
Diamante →, *Argentina* 126 C2
Diamantina, *Brazil* 125 G10
Diamantina →, *Australia* 95 D2
Diamantino, *Brazil* 125 F7
Diamond Bar, *U.S.A.* 117 L9
Diamond Harbour, *India* 69 H13
Diamond Is., *Australia* 94 B5
Diamond Mts., *U.S.A.* 114 G6
Diamond Springs, *U.S.A.* 116 G6
Dian Chi, *China* 58 E4
Dianalund, *Denmark* 11 J5
Dianbai, *China* 59 G8
Diancheng, *China* 59 G8
Dianjiang, *China* 58 B6
Diano Marina, *Italy* 28 E5
Dianra, *Ivory C.* 82 D3
Diapaga, *Burkina Faso* 83 C5
Diapangou, *Burkina Faso* 83 C5
Diariguila, *Guinea* 82 C2
Dībā, *Oman* 71 E8
Dibai, *India* 68 E8
Dibaya-Lubue, *Dem. Rep. of the Congo* 84 E3
Dibete, *Botswana* 88 C4
Dibrugarh, *India* 67 F19
Dickens, *U.S.A.* 113 J4
Dickinson, *U.S.A.* 112 B3
Dickson = Dikson, *Russia* 50 B9
Dickson, *U.S.A.* 109 G2
Dickson City, *U.S.A.* 111 E9
Dicle Nehri →, *Turkey* 73 D9
Dicomano, *Italy* 29 E8
Didesa, W. →, *Ethiopia* 81 E4
Didi, *Sudan* 81 F3
Didiéni, *Mali* 82 C3
Didsbury, *Canada* 104 C6
Didwana, *India* 68 F6
Die, *France* 21 D9
Diébougou, *Burkina Faso* 82 C4
Diecke, *Guinea* 82 D3
Diefenbaker, L., *Canada* 105 C7
Diego de Almagro, *Chile* 126 B1
Diego Garcia, *Ind. Oc.* 3 E13
Diekirch, *Lux.* 17 E6
Diéma, *Mali* 82 C3
Diembéring, *Senegal* 82 C1
Dien Ban, *Vietnam* 64 E7
Dien Bien, *Vietnam* 58 G4
Dien Khanh, *Vietnam* 65 F7
Diepholz, *Germany* 24 C4
Dieppe, *France* 18 C8
Dierks, *U.S.A.* 113 H8
Diest, *Belgium* 17 D5
Dietikon, *Switz.* 25 H4
Dieulefit, *France* 21 D9
Dieuze, *France* 19 D13
Dif, *Somali Rep.* 74 G3
Differdange, *Lux.* 17 E5
Dig, *India* 68 F7
Digba, *Dem. Rep. of the Congo* 86 B2
Digby, *Canada* 103 D6
Diggi, *India* 68 F6
Dighinala, *Bangla.* 67 H18
Dighton, *U.S.A.* 112 F4
Digna, *Mali* 82 C3
Digne-les-Bains, *France* 21 D10
Digoin, *France* 19 F11
Digor, *Turkey* 73 B10
Digos, *Phil.* 61 H6
Digranes, *Iceland* 8 C6
Digul →, *Indonesia* 63 F9
Dihang →, *India* 67 F19
Dijlah, Nahr →, *Asia* 70 D5
Dijon, *France* 19 E12
Dikhil, *Djibouti* 81 E5
Dikili, *Turkey* 39 B8
Dikirnis, *Egypt* 80 H7
Dikkil = Dikhil, *Djibouti* 81 E5
Dikodougou, *Ivory C.* 82 D3
Diksmuide, *Belgium* 17 C2
Dikson, *Russia* 50 B9
Dikwa, *Nigeria* 83 C7
Dila, *Ethiopia* 81 F4
Dili, *E. Timor* 63 F7
Dilijan, *Armenia* 49 K7
Dilizhan = Dilijan, *Armenia* 49 K7
Dilj, *Croatia* 42 E3
Dillenburg, *Germany* 24 E4
Dilley, *U.S.A.* 113 L5
Dilling, *Sudan* 81 E2
Dillingen, *Bayern, Germany* 25 G6
Dillingen, *Saarland, Germany* 25 F2
Dillingham, *U.S.A.* 100 C4
Dillon, *Canada* 105 B7
Dillon, *Mont., U.S.A.* 114 D7
Dillon, *S.C., U.S.A.* 109 H6
Dillon →, *Canada* 105 B7
Dillsburg, *U.S.A.* 110 F7
Dilly, *Mali* 82 C3
Dilolo, *Dem. Rep. of the Congo* 84 G4
Dimas, *Mexico* 118 C3
Dimashq, *Syria* 75 B5
Dimashq □, *Syria* 75 B5
Dimbaza, *S. Africa* 89 E4
Dimbokro, *Ivory C.* 82 D4
Dîmbovița = Dâmbovița →, *Romania* 43 F11
Dimbulah, *Australia* 94 B4
Dimitrovgrad, *Bulgaria* 41 D9
Dimitrovgrad, *Russia* 48 C9
Dimitrovgrad, *Serbia, Yug.* 40 C6
Dimitrovo = Pernik, *Bulgaria* 40 D7
Dimmitt, *U.S.A.* 113 H3
Dimo, *Sudan* 81 F2
Dimona, *Israel* 75 D4
Dimovo, *Bulgaria* 40 C6
Dinagat, *Phil.* 61 F6
Dinajpur, *Bangla.* 67 G16
Dinan, *France* 18 D4
Dīnān Āb, *Iran* 71 C8
Dinant, *Belgium* 17 D4
Dinapur, *India* 69 G11
Dinar, *Turkey* 39 C12
Dīnār, Kūh-e, *Iran* 71 D6
Dinara Planina, *Croatia* 29 D13
Dinard, *France* 18 D4
Dinaric Alps = Dinara Planina, *Croatia* 29 D13
Dindanko, *Mali* 82 C3
Dinder, Nahr ed →, *Sudan* 81 E3
Dindigul, *India* 66 P11
Dindori, *India* 69 H9
Ding Xian = Dingzhou, *China* 56 E8
Dinga, *Pakistan* 68 G2
Dingalan, *Phil.* 61 D4
Dingbian, *China* 56 F4
Dingelstädt, *Germany* 24 D6
Dingle, *Ireland* 15 D1
Dingle, *Sweden* 11 F5
Dingle B., *Ireland* 15 D1
Dingmans Ferry, *U.S.A.* 111 E10
Dingnan, *China* 59 E10
Dingo, *Australia* 94 C4
Dingolfing, *Germany* 25 G8
Dingtao, *China* 56 G8
Dinguira, *Mali* 82 C2
Dinguiraye, *Guinea* 82 C2
Dingwall, *U.K.* 14 D4
Dingxi, *China* 56 G3
Dingxiang, *China* 56 E7
Dingyuan, *China* 59 A11
Dingzhou, *China* 56 E8
Dinh, Mui, *Vietnam* 65 G7
Dinh Lap, *Vietnam* 58 G6
Dinokwe, *Botswana* 88 C4
Dinorwic, *Canada* 105 D10
Dinosaur National Monument, *U.S.A.* 114 F9
Dinosaur Prov. Park, *Canada* 104 C6
Dinuba, *U.S.A.* 116 J7
Diö, *Sweden* 11 H8
Dioïla, *Mali* 82 C3
Dioka, *Mali* 82 C2
Diongoï, *Mali* 82 C3
Diósgyör, *Hungary* 42 B5
Diosig, *Romania* 42 C7
Diougani, *Mali* 82 C4
Diouloulou, *Senegal* 82 C1
Dioura, *Mali* 82 C3
Diourbel, *Senegal* 82 C1
Dipalpur, *Pakistan* 68 D5
Diplo, *Pakistan* 68 G3
Dipolog, *Phil.* 61 G5
Dir, *Pakistan* 66 B7
Diré, *Mali* 82 B4
Dire Dawa, *Ethiopia* 81 F5
Diriamba, *Nic.* 120 D2
Dirk Hartog I., *Australia* 93 E1
Dirranbandi, *Australia* 95 D4
Disa, *India* 68 G5
Disa, *Sudan* 81 E3
Disappointment, C., *U.S.A.* 114 C2
Disappointment, L., *Australia* 92 D3
Disentis Muster, *Switz.* 25 J4
Dishna, *Egypt* 80 B3
Disina, *Nigeria* 83 C6
Disko = Qeqertarsuaq, *Greenland* 101 B5
Disko Bugt, *Greenland* 4 C5
Disna = Dzisna →, *Belarus* 46 E5
Diss, *U.K.* 13 E9
Disteghil Sar, *Pakistan* 69 A6
Distrito Federal □, *Brazil* 125 G9
Distrito Federal □, *Mexico* 119 D5
Disûq, *Egypt* 80 H7
Diu, *India* 68 J4
Dīvāndarreh, *Iran* 70 C5
Dives →, *France* 18 C6
Dives-sur-Mer, *France* 18 C6
Divichi = Däväçi, *Azerbaijan* 49 K9
Divide, *U.S.A.* 114 D7
Dividing Ra., *Australia* 93 E2
Divinópolis, *Brazil* 125 H10
Divjake, *Albania* 40 F3
Divnoye, *Russia* 49 H6
Divo, *Ivory C.* 82 D3
Divriği, *Turkey* 73 C8
Dīwāl Kol, *Afghan.* 68 B2
Dixie Mt., *U.S.A.* 116 F6
Dixon, *Calif., U.S.A.* 116 G5
Dixon, *Ill., U.S.A.* 112 E10
Dixon Entrance, *U.S.A.* 100 C6
Dixville, *Canada* 111 A13
Diyadin, *Turkey* 73 C10
Diyālā →, *Iraq* 70 C5
Diyarbakır, *Turkey* 70 B4
Diyodar, *India* 68 G4
Djakarta = Jakarta, *Indonesia* 62 F3
Djamba, *Angola* 88 B1
Djambala, *Congo* 84 E2
Djanet, *Algeria* 78 D7
Djawa = Jawa, *Indonesia* 62 F3
Djelfa, *Algeria* 78 B6
Djema, *C.A.R.* 86 A2
Djenné, *Mali* 82 C4
Djerba, I. de, *Tunisia* 79 B8
Djerid, Chott, *Tunisia* 78 B7
Djibo, *Burkina Faso* 83 C4
Djibouti, *Djibouti* 81 E5
Djibouti ■, *Africa* 81 E5
Djolu, *Dem. Rep. of the Congo* 84 D4
Djougou, *Benin* 83 D5
Djoum, *Cameroon* 84 D2
Djourab, Erg du, *Chad* 79 E9
Djugu, *Dem. Rep. of the Congo* 86 B3
Djúpivogur, *Iceland* 8 D6
Djurås, *Sweden* 10 D9
Djursland, *Denmark* 11 H4
Dmitriya Lapteva, Proliv, *Russia* 51 B15
Dmitriyev Lgovskiy, *Russia* 47 F8
Dmitrov, *Russia* 46 D9
Dmitrovsk-Orlovskiy, *Russia* 47 F8
Dnepr → = Dnipro →, *Ukraine* 47 J7
Dneprodzerzhinsk = Dniprodzerzhynsk, *Ukraine* 47 H8
Dneprodzerzhinskoye Vdkhr. = Dniprodzerzhynske Vdskh., *Ukraine* 47 H8
Dnepropetrovsk = Dnipropetrovsk, *Ukraine* 47 H8
Dneprorudnoye = Dniprorudne, *Ukraine* 47 J8
Dnestr → = Dnister →, *Europe* 47 J6
Dnestrovski = Belgorod, *Russia* 47 G9
Dnieper = Dnipro →, *Ukraine* 47 J7
Dniester = Dnister →, *Europe* 47 J6
Dnipro →, *Ukraine* 47 J7
Dniprodzerzhynsk, *Ukraine* 47 H8
Dniprodzerzhynske Vdskh., *Ukraine* 47 H8
Dnipropetrovsk, *Ukraine* 47 H8
Dniprorudne, *Ukraine* 47 J8
Dnister →, *Europe* 47 J6
Dnistrovskyy Lyman, *Ukraine* 47 J6
Dno, *Russia* 46 D5
Dnyapro = Dnipro →, *Ukraine* 47 J7
Doaktown, *Canada* 103 C6
Doan Hung, *Vietnam* 58 G5
Doany, *Madag.* 89 A8
Doba, *Chad* 79 G9
Dobandi, *Pakistan* 68 D2
Dobbiaco, *Italy* 29 B9
Dobbyn, *Australia* 94 B3
Dobczyce, *Poland* 45 J7
Dobele, *Latvia* 9 H20
Dobele □, *Latvia* 44 B10
Döbeln, *Germany* 24 D9
Doberai, Jazirah, *Indonesia* 63 E8
Dobiegniew, *Poland* 45 F2
Doblas, *Argentina* 126 D3
Dobo, *Indonesia* 63 F8
Doboj, *Bos.-H.* 42 F3
Dobra, *Wielkopolskie, Poland* 45 G5
Dobra, *Zachodnio-Pomorskie, Poland* 44 E2
Dobra, *Dîmbovita, Romania* 43 F10
Dobra, *Hunedoara, Romania* 42 E7
Dobre Miasto, *Poland* 44 E7
Dobrești, *Romania* 42 D7
Dobrich, *Bulgaria* 41 C11
Dobrinishta, *Bulgaria* 40 E7
Dobříš, *Czech Rep.* 26 B7
Dobrodzień, *Poland* 45 H5
Dobropole, *Ukraine* 47 H9
Dobruja, *Europe* 43 F13
Dobrush, *Belarus* 47 F6
Dobrzany, *Poland* 44 E2
Dobrzyń nad Wisłą, *Poland* 45 F6
Doc, Mui, *Vietnam* 64 D6
Docker River, *Australia* 93 D4
Dockstа, *Sweden* 10 A12
Doctor Arroyo, *Mexico* 118 C4
Doda, *India* 69 C6
Doda, L., *Canada* 102 C4
Dodecanese = Dhodhekánisos, *Greece* 39 E8
Dodge City, *U.S.A.* 113 G5
Dodge L., *Canada* 105 B7
Dodgeville, *U.S.A.* 112 D9
Dodo, *Cameroon* 83 D7
Dodo, *Sudan* 81 F2
Dodola, *Ethiopia* 81 F4
Dodoma, *Tanzania* 86 D4
Dodoma □, *Tanzania* 86 D4
Dodona, *Greece* 38 B2
Dodsland, *Canada* 105 C7
Dodson, *U.S.A.* 114 B9
Dodurga, *Turkey* 39 B11
Doesburg, *Neths.* 17 B6
Doetinchem, *Neths.* 17 C6
Dog Creek, *Canada* 104 C4
Dog L., *Man., Canada* 105 C9
Dog L., *Ont., Canada* 102 C2
Doğanşehir, *Turkey* 72 C7
Dogliani, *Italy* 28 D4
Dogondoutchi, *Niger* 83 C5
Dogran, *Pakistan* 68 D5
Doğubayazıt, *Turkey* 70 B5
Doguéraoua, *Niger* 83 C6
Doha = Ad Dawḩah, *Qatar* 71 E6
Dohazari, *Bangla.* 67 H18
Dohrighat, *India* 69 F10
Doi, *Indonesia* 63 D7
Doi Luang, *Thailand* 64 C3
Doi Saket, *Thailand* 64 C2
Dois Irmãos, Sa., *Brazil* 125 E10
Dojransko Jezero, *Macedonia* 40 E6
Dokkum, *Neths.* 17 A5
Dokri, *Pakistan* 68 F3
Dokuchayevsk, *Ukraine* 47 J9
Dol-de-Bretagne, *France* 18 D5
Dolac, *Kosovo, Yug.* 40 D4
Dolak, Pulau, *Indonesia* 63 F9
Dolbeau, *Canada* 103 C5
Dole, *France* 19 E12
Doleib, Wadi →, *Sudan* 81 E3
Dolenji Logatec, *Slovenia* 29 C11
Dolgellau, *U.K.* 12 E4
Dolgelley = Dolgellau, *U.K.* 12 E4
Dolhasca, *Romania* 43 C11
Dolianova, *Italy* 30 C2
Dolinskaya = Dolynska, *Ukraine* 47 H7
Dolj □, *Romania* 43 F8
Dollard, *Neths.* 17 A7
Dolna Banya, *Bulgaria* 40 D7
Dolni Chiflik, *Bulgaria* 41 D11
Dolni Dŭbnik, *Bulgaria* 41 C8
Dolnośląskie □, *Poland* 45 G3
Dolný Kubín, *Slovak Rep.* 27 B12
Dolo, *Ethiopia* 81 G5
Dolo, *Italy* 29 C9
Dolomites = Dolomiti, *Italy* 29 B8
Dolomiti, *Italy* 29 B8
Dolores, *Argentina* 126 D4
Dolores, *Uruguay* 126 C4
Dolores, *U.S.A.* 115 H9
Dolores →, *U.S.A.* 115 G9
Dolovo, *Serbia, Yug.* 42 F5
Dolphin, C., *Falk. Is.* 128 G5
Dolphin and Union Str., *Canada* 100 B8
Dolsk, *Poland* 45 G4
Dolynska, *Ukraine* 47 H7
Dolzhanskaya, *Russia* 47 J9
Dom Pedrito, *Brazil* 127 C5
Doma, *Nigeria* 83 D6
Domaniç, *Turkey* 39 B11
Domariaganj →, *India* 69 F10
Domasi, *Malawi* 87 F4
Domažlice, *Czech Rep.* 26 B5
Dombarovskiy, *Russia* 50 D6
Dombås, *Norway* 9 E13
Dombasle-sur-Meurthe, *France* 19 D13
Dombes, *France* 21 C9
Dombóvár, *Hungary* 42 D3
Dombrád, *Hungary* 42 B6
Domel I. = Letsôk-aw Kyun, *Burma* 65 G2
Domérat, *France* 19 F9
Domeyko, *Chile* 126 B1
Domeyko, Cordillera, *Chile* 126 A2
Domfront, *France* 18 D6
Dominador, *Chile* 126 A2
Dominica ■, *W. Indies* 121 C7
Dominica Passage, *W. Indies* 121 C7
Dominican Rep. ■, *W. Indies* 121 C5
Dömitz, *Germany* 24 B7
Domme, *France* 20 D5
Domnești, *Romania* 43 E9
Domodóssola, *Italy* 28 B5
Dompaire, *France* 19 D13
Dompierre-sur-Besbre, *France* 19 F10
Dompim, *Ghana* 82 D4
Domrémy-la-Pucelle, *France* 19 D12
Domville, Mt., *Australia* 95 D5
Domvraína, *Greece* 38 C4
Domžale, *Slovenia* 29 B11
Don →, *Russia* 47 J10
Don →, *Aberds., U.K.* 14 D6
Don →, *S. Yorks., U.K.* 12 D7
Don, C., *Australia* 92 B5
Don Benito, *Spain* 35 G5
Dona Ana = Nhamaabué, *Mozam.* 87 F4
Doña Mencía, *Spain* 35 H6
Donaghadee, *U.K.* 15 B6
Donaldsonville, *U.S.A.* 113 K9
Donalsonville, *U.S.A.* 109 K3
Donau = Dunărea →, *Europe* 43 E14
Donau →, *Austria* 17 D3
Donaueschingen, *Germany* 25 H4
Donauwörth, *Germany* 25 G6
Doncaster, *U.K.* 12 D6
Dondo, *Mozam.* 87 F3
Dondo, Teluk, *Indonesia* 63 D6
Dondra Head, *Sri Lanka* 66 S12
Donduşeni, *Moldova* 43 B12
Donegal, *Ireland* 15 B3
Donegal □, *Ireland* 15 B4
Donegal B., *Ireland* 15 B3
Donets →, *Russia* 49 G5
Donetsk, *Ukraine* 47 J9
Dong Ba Thin, *Vietnam* 65 F7
Dong Dang, *Vietnam* 58 G6
Dong Giam, *Vietnam* 64 C5
Dong Ha, *Vietnam* 64 D6
Dong Hene, *Laos* 64 D5
Dong Hoi, *Vietnam* 64 D6
Dong Jiang →, *China* 59 F10
Dong Khe, *Vietnam* 64 A6
Dong Ujimqin Qi, *China* 56 B9
Dong Van, *Vietnam* 64 A5
Dong Xoai, *Vietnam* 65 G6
Donga, *Nigeria* 83 D7
Donga →, *Nigeria* 83 D7
Dong'an, *China* 59 D8
Dongara, *Australia* 93 E1
Dongbei, *China* 57 D13
Dongchuan, *China* 58 D4
Donges, *France* 18 E4
Dongfang, *China* 64 C7
Dongfeng, *China* 57 C13
Donggala, *Indonesia* 63 E5
Donggan, *China* 58 F5
Donggou, *China* 57 E13
Dongguan, *China* 59 F9
Dongguang, *China* 56 F9
Donghai Dao, *China* 59 G8
Dongjingcheng, *China* 57 B15
Dongkou, *China* 59 D8
Donglan, *China* 58 E6
Dongliu, *China* 59 B11
Dongmen, *China* 58 F6
Dongning, *China* 57 B16
Dongnyi, *China* 58 C3
Dongola, *Sudan* 80 D3
Dongping, *China* 56 G9
Dongshan, *China* 59 F11
Dongsheng, *China* 56 E6
Dongtai, *China* 57 H11
Dongting Hu, *China* 59 C9
Dongtou, *China* 59 D13
Dongxiang, *China* 59 C11
Dongxing, *China* 58 G7
Dongyang, *China* 59 C13
Dongzhi, *China* 59 B11
Doniphan, *U.S.A.* 113 G9
Donja Stubica, *Croatia* 29 C12
Donji Dušnik, *Serbia, Yug.* 40 C6
Donji Miholjac, *Croatia* 42 E3
Donji Milanovac, *Serbia, Yug.* 40 B6
Donji Vakuf, *Bos.-H.* 42 F2
Dønna, *Norway* 8 C15
Donna, *U.S.A.* 113 M5
Donnaconna, *Canada* 103 C5
Donnelly's Crossing, *N.Z.* 91 F4
Donnybrook, *Australia* 93 F2
Donnybrook, *S. Africa* 89 D4
Donora, *U.S.A.* 110 F5
Donostia = Donostia-San Sebastián, *Spain* 32 B3
Donostia-San Sebastián, *Spain* 32 B3
Donskoy, *Russia* 46 F10
Donsol, *Phil.* 61 E5
Donzère, *France* 21 D8
Donzy, *France* 19 E10
Doon →, *U.K.* 14 F4
Dora, L., *Australia* 92 D3
Dora Báltea →, *Italy* 28 C5
Dora Ripária →, *Italy* 28 C4
Doran L., *Canada* 105 A7
Dorchester, *U.K.* 13 G5
Dorchester, C., *Canada* 101 B12
Dordabis, *Namibia* 88 C2
Dordogne □, *France* 20 C4
Dordogne →, *France* 20 C3
Dordrecht, *Neths.* 17 C4
Dordrecht, *S. Africa* 88 E4
Dore →, *France* 20 C7
Dore, Mts., *France* 20 C6
Doré L., *Canada* 105 C7
Doré Lake, *Canada* 105 C7
Dorfen, *Germany* 25 G8
Dorgali, *Italy* 30 B2
Dori, *Burkina Faso* 83 C4
Doring →, *S. Africa* 88 E2
Doringbos, *S. Africa* 88 E2
Dorion, *Canada* 111 A10
Dormaa-Ahenkro, *Ghana* 82 D4
Dormans, *France* 19 C10
Dormo, Ras, *Eritrea* 81 E5
Dornbirn, *Austria* 26 D2
Dornes, *France* 19 F10
Dornești, *Romania* 43 C11
Dornie, *U.K.* 14 D3
Dornoch, *U.K.* 14 D4
Dornoch Firth, *U.K.* 14 D4
Dornogovĭ □, *Mongolia* 56 C6
Doro, *Mali* 83 B4
Dorog, *Hungary* 42 C3
Dorogobuzh, *Russia* 46 E7
Dorohoi, *Romania* 43 C11
Döröö Nuur, *Mongolia* 60 B4
Dorr, *Iran* 71 C6
Dorre I., *Australia* 93 E1
Dorris, *U.S.A.* 114 F3
Dorset, *Canada* 110 A6
Dorset, *U.S.A.* 110 E4
Dorset □, *U.K.* 13 G5
Dorsten, *Germany* 24 D2
Dortmund, *Germany* 24 D3
Dortmund-Ems-Kanal →, *Germany* 24 D3
Dörtyol, *Turkey* 72 D7
Dorum, *Germany* 24 B4
Doruma, *Dem. Rep. of the Congo* 86 B2
Dorūneh, *Iran* 71 C8
Dos Bahías, C., *Argentina* 128 E3
Dos Hermanas, *Spain* 35 H5
Dos Palos, *U.S.A.* 116 J6
Döşemealtı, *Turkey* 39 D12

Dosso, *Niger* 83 C5
Dothan, *U.S.A.* 109 K3
Doty, *U.S.A.* 116 D3
Douai, *France* 19 B10
Douako, *Guinea* 82 D2
Douala, *Cameroon* 83 E6
Douarnenez, *France* 18 D2
Doubabougou, *Mali* 82 C3
Double Island Pt., *Australia* 95 D5
Double Mountain Fork →, *U.S.A.* 113 J4
Doubrava →, *Czech Rep.* 26 A8
Doubs □, *France* 19 E13
Doubs →, *France* 19 F12
Doubtful Sd., *N.Z.* 91 L1
Doubtless B., *N.Z.* 91 F4
Doudeville, *France* 18 C7
Doué-la-Fontaine, *France* 18 E6
Douentza, *Mali* 82 C4
Douglas, *S. Africa* 88 D3
Douglas, *U.K.* 12 C3
Douglas, *Ariz., U.S.A.* 115 L9
Douglas, *Ga., U.S.A.* 109 K4
Douglas, *Wyo., U.S.A.* 112 D2
Douglas Chan., *Canada* 104 C3
Douglas Pt., *Canada* 110 B3
Douglasville, *U.S.A.* 109 J3
Doukáton, Ákra, *Greece* 38 C2
Doulevant-le-Château, *France* 19 D11
Doullens, *France* 19 B9
Doumen, *China* 59 F9
Douna, *Mali* 82 C3
Douna, *Mali* 83 C4
Dounreay, *U.K.* 14 C5
Dourada, Serra, *Brazil* 125 F9
Dourados, *Brazil* 127 A5
Dourados →, *Brazil* 127 A5
Dourados, Serra dos, *Brazil* 127 A5
Dourdan, *France* 19 D9
Douro →, *Europe* 34 D2
Douvaine, *France* 19 F13
Douvres-la-Délivrande, *France* 18 C6
Douze →, *France* 20 E3
Dove →, *U.K.* 12 E6
Dove Creek, *U.S.A.* 115 H9
Dover, *Australia* 94 G4
Dover, *U.K.* 13 F9
Dover, *Del., U.S.A.* 108 F8
Dover, *N.H., U.S.A.* 111 C14
Dover, *N.J., U.S.A.* 111 F10
Dover, *Ohio, U.S.A.* 110 F3
Dover, Pt., *Australia* 93 F4
Dover, Str. of, *Europe* 13 G9
Dover-Foxcroft, *U.S.A.* 109 C11
Dover Plains, *U.S.A.* 111 E11
Dovey = Dyfi →, *U.K.* 13 E3
Dovrefjell, *Norway* 9 E13
Dow Rūd, *Iran* 71 C6
Dowa, *Malawi* 87 E3
Dowagiac, *U.S.A.* 108 E2
Dowerin, *Australia* 93 F2
Dowgha'i, *Iran* 71 B8
Dowlatābād, *Iran* 71 D8
Down □, *U.K.* 15 B5
Downey, *Calif., U.S.A.* 117 M8
Downey, *Idaho, U.S.A.* 114 E7
Downham Market, *U.K.* 13 E8
Downieville, *U.S.A.* 116 F6
Downpatrick, *U.K.* 15 B6
Downpatrick Hd., *Ireland* 15 B2
Downsville, *U.S.A.* 111 D10
Downton, Mt., *Canada* 104 C4
Dowsārī, *Iran* 71 D8
Doyle, *U.S.A.* 116 E6
Doylestown, *U.S.A.* 111 F9
Dozois, Rés., *Canada* 102 C4
Dra Khel, *Pakistan* 68 F2
Drac →, *France* 21 C9
Dračevo, *Macedonia* 40 E5
Drachten, *Neths.* 17 A6
Drăgăneşti, *Moldova* 43 C13
Drăgăneşti-Olt, *Romania* 43 F9
Drăgăneşti-Vlaşca, *Romania* 43 F10
Dragaš, *Kosovo, Yug.* 40 D4
Drăgăşani, *Romania* 43 F9
Dragichyn, *Belarus* 47 F3
Dragocvet, *Serbia, Yug.* 40 C5
Dragovishtitsa, *Bulgaria* 40 D6
Draguignan, *France* 21 E10
Drain, *U.S.A.* 114 E2
Drake, *U.S.A.* 112 B4
Drake Passage, *S. Ocean* 5 B17
Drakensberg, *S. Africa* 89 D4
Dráma, *Greece* 41 E8
Dráma □, *Greece* 41 E8
Drammen, *Norway* 9 G14
Drangajökull, *Iceland* 8 C2
Dranov, Ostrov, *Romania* 43 F14
Dras, *India* 69 B6
Drau = Drava →, *Croatia* 42 E3
Drava →, *Croatia* 42 E3
Dravograd, *Slovenia* 29 B12
Drawa →, *Poland* 45 F2
Drawno, *Poland* 45 E2
Drawsko Pomorskie, *Poland* 44 E2
Drayton Valley, *Canada* 104 C6
Dreieich, *Germany* 25 E4
Dren, *Kosovo, Yug.* 40 C4
Drenthe □, *Neths.* 17 B6
Drepanum, C., *Cyprus* 36 E11
Dresden, *Canada* 110 D2
Dresden, *Germany* 24 D9
Dreux, *France* 18 D8
Drezdenko, *Poland* 45 F2
Driffield, *U.K.* 12 C7
Driftwood, *U.S.A.* 110 E6
Driggs, *U.S.A.* 114 E8
Drin →, *Albania* 40 D3
Drin i Zi →, *Albania* 40 E4
Drina →, *Bos.-H.* 40 B3
Drincea →, *Romania* 42 F7
Drinjača →, *Bos.-H.* 42 F4
Drissa = Vyerkhnyadzvinsk, *Belarus* 46 E4
Drniš, *Croatia* 29 E13
Drøbak, *Norway* 9 G14
Drobeta-Turnu Severin, *Romania* 42 F7
Drobin, *Poland* 45 F6
Drochia, *Moldova* 43 B12
Drogheda, *Ireland* 15 C5
Drogichin = Dragichyn, *Belarus* 47 F3
Drogobych = Drohobych, *Ukraine* 47 H2
Drohiczyn, *Poland* 45 F9
Drohobych, *Ukraine* 47 H2
Droichead Atha = Drogheda, *Ireland* 15 C5
Droichead Nua, *Ireland* 15 C5
Droitwich, *U.K.* 13 E5
Drôme □, *France* 21 D9
Drôme →, *France* 21 D8
Dromore, *U.K.* 15 B4
Dromore West, *Ireland* 15 B3
Dronero, *Italy* 28 D4
Dronfield, *U.K.* 12 D6
Dronne →, *France* 20 C3
Dronninglund, *Denmark* 11 G4
Dronten, *Neths.* 17 B5
Dropt →, *France* 20 D3
Drosendorf, *Austria* 26 C8
Droué, *France* 18 D8
Drumbo, *Canada* 110 C4
Drumheller, *Canada* 104 C6
Drummond, *U.S.A.* 114 C7
Drummond I., *U.S.A.* 108 C4
Drummond Pt., *Australia* 95 E2
Drummond Ra., *Australia* 94 C4
Drummondville, *Canada* 102 C5
Drumright, *U.S.A.* 113 H6
Druskininkai, *Lithuania* 9 J20
Drut →, *Belarus* 47 F6
Druya, *Belarus* 46 E4
Druzhba, *Bulgaria* 41 C12
Druzhina, *Russia* 51 C15
Drvar, *Bos.-H.* 29 D13
Drvenik, *Croatia* 29 E13
Drwęca →, *Poland* 45 E5
Dry Tortugas, *U.S.A.* 120 B3
Dryanovo, *Bulgaria* 41 D9
Dryden, *Canada* 105 D10
Dryden, *U.S.A.* 111 D8
Drygalski I., *Antarctica* 5 C7
Drysdale →, *Australia* 92 B4
Drysdale I., *Australia* 94 A2
Drzewica, *Poland* 45 G7
Drzewiczka →, *Poland* 45 G7
Dschang, *Cameroon* 83 D7
Du Bois, *U.S.A.* 110 E6
Du Gué →, *Canada* 102 A5
Du He, *China* 59 A8
Du Quoin, *U.S.A.* 112 G10
Du'an, *China* 58 F7
Duanesburg, *U.S.A.* 111 D10
Duaringa, *Australia* 94 C4
Ḑubā, *Si. Arabia* 70 E2
Dubai = Dubayy, *U.A.E.* 71 E7
Dubăsari, *Moldova* 43 C14
Dubăsari Vdkhr., *Moldova* 43 C13
Dubawnt →, *Canada* 105 A8
Dubawnt, L., *Canada* 105 A8
Dubayy, *U.A.E.* 71 E7
Dubele, *Dem. Rep. of the Congo* 86 B2
Dübendorf, *Switz.* 25 H4
Dubica, *Croatia* 29 C13
Dublin, *Ireland* 15 C5
Dublin, *Ga., U.S.A.* 109 J4
Dublin, *Tex., U.S.A.* 113 J5
Dublin □, *Ireland* 15 C5
Dubna, *Russia* 46 D9
Dubnica nad Váhom, *Slovak Rep.* 27 C11
Dubno, *Ukraine* 47 G3
Dubois, *U.S.A.* 114 D7
Dubossary = Dubăsari, *Moldova* 43 C14
Dubossary Vdkhr. = Dubăsari Vdkhr., *Moldova* 43 C13
Dubovka, *Russia* 49 F7
Dubovskoye, *Russia* 49 G6
Dubrajpur, *India* 69 H12
Dubréka, *Guinea* 82 D2
Dubrovitsa = Dubrovytsya, *Ukraine* 47 G4
Dubrovnik, *Croatia* 40 D2
Dubrovytsya, *Ukraine* 47 G4
Dubuque, *U.S.A.* 112 D9
Dubysa →, *Lithuania* 44 C10
Duchang, *China* 59 C11
Duchesne, *U.S.A.* 114 F8
Duchess, *Australia* 94 C2
Ducie I., *Pac. Oc.* 97 K15
Duck →, *U.S.A.* 109 G2
Duck Cr. →, *Australia* 92 D2
Duck Lake, *Canada* 105 C7
Duck Mountain Prov. Park, *Canada* 105 C8
Duckwall, Mt., *U.S.A.* 116 H6
Duderstadt, *Germany* 24 D6
Dudhi, *India* 67 G13
Dudinka, *Russia* 51 C9
Dudley, *U.K.* 13 E5
Dudwa, *India* 69 E9
Duékoué, *Ivory C.* 82 D3
Dueñas, *Spain* 34 D6
Duero = Douro →, *Europe* 34 D2
Dufftown, *U.K.* 14 D5
Dufourspitz, *Switz.* 25 K3
Dūghī Kalā, *Afghan.* 66 C3
Dugi Otok, *Croatia* 29 D11
Dugo Selo, *Croatia* 29 C13
Duifken Pt., *Australia* 94 A3
Duisburg, *Germany* 24 D2
Duiwelskloof, *S. Africa* 89 C5
Dujiangyan, *China* 58 B4
Duk Fadiat, *Sudan* 81 F3
Duk Faiwil, *Sudan* 81 F3
Dukat, *Albania* 40 F3
Dūkdamīn, *Iran* 71 C8
Dukelský Průsmyk, *Slovak Rep.* 27 B14
Dukhān, *Qatar* 71 E6
Dukhovshchina, *Russia* 46 E7
Duki, *Pakistan* 66 D6
Dukla, *Poland* 45 J8
Duku, *Bauchi, Nigeria* 83 C7
Duku, *Sokoto, Nigeria* 83 C5
Dulag, *Phil.* 61 F6
Dulce, *U.S.A.* 115 H10
Dulce →, *Argentina* 126 C3
Dulce, G., *Costa Rica* 120 E3
Dulf, *Iraq* 70 C5
Dŭlgopol, *Bulgaria* 41 C11
Dulit, Banjaran, *Malaysia* 62 D4
Duliu, *China* 56 E9
Dullewala, *Pakistan* 68 D4
Dullstroom, *S. Africa* 89 D5
Dülmen, *Germany* 24 D3
Dulovo, *Bulgaria* 41 C11
Dulq Maghār, *Syria* 70 B3
Duluth, *U.S.A.* 112 B8
Dum Dum, *India* 69 H13
Dum Duma, *India* 67 F19
Dūmā, *Syria* 75 B5
Dumaguete, *Phil.* 61 G5
Dumai, *Indonesia* 62 D2
Dumaran, *Phil.* 61 F3
Dumas, *Ark., U.S.A.* 113 J9
Dumas, *Tex., U.S.A.* 113 H4
Ḑumayr, *Syria* 75 B5
Dumbarton, *U.K.* 14 F4
Ďumbier, *Slovak Rep.* 27 C12
Dumbleyung, *Australia* 93 F2
Dumboa, *Nigeria* 83 C7
Dumbrăveni, *Romania* 43 D9
Dumfries, *U.K.* 14 F5
Dumfries & Galloway □, *U.K.* 14 F5
Dumitreşti, *Romania* 43 E11
Dumka, *India* 69 G12
Dumlupınar, *Turkey* 39 C12
Dümmer, *Germany* 24 C4
Dumoine →, *Canada* 102 C4
Dumoine, L., *Canada* 102 C4
Dumraon, *India* 69 G11
Dumyât, *Egypt* 80 H7
Dumyât, Masabb, *Egypt* 80 H7
Dún Dealgan = Dundalk, *Ireland* 15 B5
Dun Laoghaire, *Ireland* 15 C5
Dun-le-Palestel, *France* 19 F8
Dun-sur-Auron, *France* 19 F9
Dun-sur-Meuse, *France* 19 C12
Duna = Dunărea →, *Europe* 43 E14
Duna →, *Hungary* 42 E3
Duna-völgyi-főcsatorna, *Hungary* 42 D4
Dunaföldvár, *Hungary* 42 D3
Dunagiri, *India* 69 D8
Dunaj = Dunărea →, *Europe* 43 E14
Dunaj →, *Slovak Rep.* 27 D11
Dunajec →, *Poland* 45 H7
Dunajská Streda, *Slovak Rep.* 27 C10
Dunakeszi, *Hungary* 42 C4
Dunapataj, *Hungary* 42 D4
Dunărea →, *Europe* 43 E14
Dunaszekcső, *Hungary* 42 D3
Dunaújváros, *Hungary* 42 D3
Dunav = Dunărea →, *Europe* 43 E14
Dunavaţu de Jos, *Romania* 43 F14
Dunavtsi, *Bulgaria* 40 C6
Dunay, *Russia* 54 C6
Dunback, *N.Z.* 91 L3
Dunbar, *U.K.* 14 E6
Dunblane, *U.K.* 14 E5
Duncan, *Canada* 104 D4
Duncan, *Ariz., U.S.A.* 115 K9
Duncan, *Okla., U.S.A.* 113 H6
Duncan, L., *Canada* 102 B4
Duncan L., *Canada* 104 A6
Duncan Town, *Bahamas* 120 B4
Duncannon, *U.S.A.* 110 F7
Duncansby Head, *U.K.* 14 C5
Duncansville, *U.S.A.* 110 F6
Dundaga, *Latvia* 44 A9
Dundalk, *Canada* 110 B4
Dundalk, *Ireland* 15 B5
Dundalk, *U.S.A.* 108 F7
Dundalk Bay, *Ireland* 15 C5
Dundas, *Canada* 110 C5
Dundas, L., *Australia* 93 F3
Dundas I., *Canada* 104 C2
Dundas Str., *Australia* 92 B5
Dundee, *S. Africa* 89 D5
Dundee, *U.K.* 14 E6
Dundee, *U.S.A.* 110 D8
Dundee City □, *U.K.* 14 E6
Dundgovĭ □, *Mongolia* 56 B4
Dundrum, *U.K.* 15 B6
Dundrum B., *U.K.* 15 B6
Dunedin, *N.Z.* 91 L3
Dunedin, *U.S.A.* 109 L4
Dunfermline, *U.K.* 14 E5
Dungannon, *Canada* 110 C3
Dungannon, *U.K.* 15 B5
Dungarpur, *India* 68 H5
Dungarvan, *Ireland* 15 D4
Dungarvan Harbour, *Ireland* 15 D4
Dungeness, *U.K.* 13 G8
Dungo, L. do, *Angola* 88 B2
Dungu, *Dem. Rep. of the Congo* 86 B2
Dungun, *Malaysia* 65 K4
Dunguṉâb, *Sudan* 80 C4
Dunguṉâb, Khalij, *Sudan* 80 C4
Dunhua, *China* 57 C15
Dunhuang, *China* 60 B4
Dunk I., *Australia* 94 B4
Dunkassa, *Benin* 83 C5
Dunkeld, *Australia* 95 E4
Dunkeld, *U.K.* 14 E5
Dunkerque, *France* 19 A9
Dunkery Beacon, *U.K.* 13 F4
Dunkirk = Dunkerque, *France* 19 A9
Dunkirk, *U.S.A.* 110 D5
Dunkuj, *Sudan* 81 E3
Dunkwa, *Central, Ghana* 82 D4
Dunkwa, *Central, Ghana* 83 D4
Dúnleary = Dun Laoghaire, *Ireland* 15 C5
Dunleer, *Ireland* 15 C5
Dunmanus B., *Ireland* 15 E2
Dunmanway, *Ireland* 15 E2
Dunmara, *Australia* 94 B1
Dunmore, *U.S.A.* 111 E9
Dunmore Hd., *Ireland* 15 D1
Dunmore Town, *Bahamas* 120 A4
Dunn, *U.S.A.* 109 H6
Dunnellon, *U.S.A.* 109 L4
Dunnet Hd., *U.K.* 14 C5
Dunning, *U.S.A.* 112 E4
Dunnville, *Canada* 110 D5
Dunoon, *U.K.* 14 F4
Dunphy, *U.S.A.* 114 F5
Dunqul, *Egypt* 80 C3
Duns, *U.K.* 14 F6
Dunseith, *U.S.A.* 112 A4
Dunsmuir, *U.S.A.* 114 F2
Dunstable, *U.K.* 13 F7
Dunstan Mts., *N.Z.* 91 L2
Dunster, *Canada* 104 C5
Dunvegan L., *Canada* 105 A7
Duolun, *China* 56 C9
Duong Dong, *Vietnam* 65 G4
Dupree, *U.S.A.* 112 C4
Dupuyer, *U.S.A.* 114 B7
Duque de Caxias, *Brazil* 127 A7
Durack →, *Australia* 92 C4
Durack Ra., *Australia* 92 C4
Durağan, *Turkey* 72 B6
Durak, *Turkey* 39 B10
Đurakovac, *Kosovo, Yug.* 40 D4
Durance →, *France* 21 E8
Durand, *U.S.A.* 112 C9
Durango, *Mexico* 118 C4
Durango, *Spain* 32 B2
Durango, *U.S.A.* 115 H10
Durango □, *Mexico* 118 C4
Durankulak, *Bulgaria* 41 C12
Durant, *Miss., U.S.A.* 113 J10
Durant, *Okla., U.S.A.* 113 J6
Duratón →, *Spain* 34 D6
Durazno, *Uruguay* 126 C4
Durazzo = Durrës, *Albania* 40 E3
Durban, *France* 20 F6
Durban, *S. Africa* 89 D5
Durbuy, *Belgium* 17 D5
Dúrcal, *Spain* 35 J7
Đurđevac, *Croatia* 42 D2
Düren, *Germany* 24 E2
Durg, *India* 67 J12
Durgapur, *India* 69 H12
Durham, *Canada* 102 D3
Durham, *U.K.* 12 C6
Durham, *Calif., U.S.A.* 116 F5
Durham, *N.C., U.S.A.* 109 H6
Durham, *N.H., U.S.A.* 111 C14
Durham □, *U.K.* 12 C6
Durleşti, *Moldova* 43 C13
Ḑurmā, *Si. Arabia* 70 E5
Durmitor, *Montenegro, Yug.* 40 C2
Durness, *U.K.* 14 C4
Durrës, *Albania* 40 E3
Durrow, *Ireland* 15 D4
Dursey I., *Ireland* 15 E1
Dursunbey, *Turkey* 39 B10
Durtal, *France* 18 E6
Duru, *Dem. Rep. of the Congo* 86 B2
Duru Gölü, *Turkey* 41 E12
Durusu, *Turkey* 41 E12
Durūz, Jabal ad, *Jordan* 75 C5
D'Urville, Tanjung, *Indonesia* 63 E9
D'Urville I., *N.Z.* 91 J4
Duryea, *U.S.A.* 111 E9
Dûsh, *Egypt* 80 C3
Dushak, *Turkmenistan* 50 F7
Dushan, *China* 58 E6
Dushanbe, *Tajikistan* 50 F7
Dusheti, *Georgia* 49 J7
Dushore, *U.S.A.* 111 E8
Dusky Sd., *N.Z.* 91 L1
Dussejour, C., *Australia* 92 B4
Düsseldorf, *Germany* 24 D2
Duszniki-Zdrój, *Poland* 45 H3
Dutch Harbor, *U.S.A.* 100 C3
Dutlwe, *Botswana* 88 C3
Dutsan Wai, *Nigeria* 83 C6
Dutton, *Canada* 110 D3
Dutton →, *Australia* 94 C3
Duved, *Sweden* 10 A6
Düvertepe, *Turkey* 39 B10
Duwayhin, Khawr, *U.A.E.* 71 E6
Duyun, *China* 58 D6
Düzağac, *Turkey* 39 C12
Düzce, *Turkey* 72 B4
Duzdab = Zāhedān, *Iran* 71 D9
Dve Mogili, *Bulgaria* 41 C9
Dvina, Severnaya →, *Russia* 50 C5
Dvinsk = Daugavpils, *Latvia* 9 J22
Dvor, *Croatia* 29 C13
Dvůr Králové nad Labem, *Czech Rep.* 26 A8
Dwarka, *India* 68 H3
Dwellingup, *Australia* 93 F2
Dwight, *Canada* 110 A5
Dwight, *U.S.A.* 108 E1
Dyatkovo, *Russia* 46 F8
Dyatlovo = Dzyatlava, *Belarus* 46 F3
Dyce, *U.K.* 14 D6
Dyer, C., *Canada* 101 B13
Dyer Bay, *Canada* 110 A3
Dyer Plateau, *Antarctica* 5 D17
Dyersburg, *U.S.A.* 113 G10
Dyfi →, *U.K.* 13 E3
Dyje →, *Czech Rep.* 27 C9
Dymer, *Ukraine* 47 G6
Dynów, *Poland* 45 J9
Dysart, *Australia* 94 C4
Dzamin Üüd = Borhoyn Tal, *Mongolia* 56 C6
Dzerzhinsk, *Russia* 48 B6
Dzhalinda, *Russia* 51 D13
Dzhambul = Taraz, *Kazakstan* 50 E8
Dzhankoy, *Ukraine* 47 K8
Dzhanybek, *Kazakstan* 48 F8
Dzharylhach, Ostriv, *Ukraine* 47 J7
Dzhezkazgan = Zhezqazghan, *Kazakstan* 50 E7
Dzhizak = Jizzakh, *Uzbekistan* 50 E7
Dzhugdzur, Khrebet, *Russia* 51 D14
Dzhvari = Jvari, *Georgia* 49 J6
Działdowo, *Poland* 45 E7
Działoszyce, *Poland* 45 H7
Działoszyn, *Poland* 45 G5
Dzibilchaltun, *Mexico* 119 C7
Dzierzgoń, *Poland* 44 E6
Dzierżoniów, *Poland* 45 H3
Dzilam de Bravo, *Mexico* 119 C7
Dzisna, *Belarus* 46 E5
Dzisna →, *Belarus* 46 E5
Dziwnów, *Poland* 44 D1
Dzungaria = Junggar Pendi, *China* 60 B3
Dzuumod, *Mongolia* 60 B5
Dzyarzhynsk, *Belarus* 46 F4
Dzyatlava, *Belarus* 46 F3

E

Eabamet L., *Canada* 102 B2
Eads, *U.S.A.* 112 F3
Eagar, *U.S.A.* 115 J9
Eagle, *Alaska, U.S.A.* 100 B5
Eagle, *Colo., U.S.A.* 114 G10
Eagle →, *Canada* 103 B8
Eagle Butte, *U.S.A.* 112 C4
Eagle Grove, *U.S.A.* 112 D8
Eagle L., *Canada* 105 D10
Eagle L., *Calif., U.S.A.* 114 F3
Eagle L., *Maine, U.S.A.* 109 B11
Eagle Lake, *Canada* 110 A6
Eagle Lake, *Maine, U.S.A.* 109 B11
Eagle Lake, *Tex., U.S.A.* 113 L6
Eagle Mountain, *U.S.A.* 117 M11
Eagle Nest, *U.S.A.* 115 H11
Eagle Pass, *U.S.A.* 113 L4
Eagle Pk., *U.S.A.* 116 G7
Eagle Pt., *Australia* 92 C3
Eagle River, *Mich., U.S.A.* 108 B1
Eagle River, *Wis., U.S.A.* 112 C10
Eaglehawk, *Australia* 95 F3
Eagles Mere, *U.S.A.* 111 E8
Ealing □, *U.K.* 13 F7
Ear Falls, *Canada* 105 C10
Earle, *U.S.A.* 113 H9
Earlimart, *U.S.A.* 117 K7
Earn →, *U.K.* 14 E5
Earn, L., *U.K.* 14 E4
Earnslaw, Mt., *N.Z.* 91 L2
Earth, *U.S.A.* 113 H3
Easley, *U.S.A.* 109 H4
East Anglia, *U.K.* 12 E9
East Angus, *Canada* 103 C5
East Aurora, *U.S.A.* 110 D6
East Ayrshire □, *U.K.* 14 F4
East Bengal, *Bangla.* 67 H17
East Beskids = Vychodné Beskydy, *Europe* 27 B15
East Brady, *U.S.A.* 110 F5
East C., *N.Z.* 91 G7
East Chicago, *U.S.A.* 108 E2
East China Sea, *Asia* 60 C7
East Coulee, *Canada* 104 C6
East Dereham, *U.K.* 13 E8
East Dunbartonshire □, *U.K.* 14 F4
East Falkland, *Falk. Is.* 122 J5
East Grand Forks, *U.S.A.* 112 B6
East Greenwich, *U.S.A.* 111 E13
East Grinstead, *U.K.* 13 F8
East Hartford, *U.S.A.* 111 E12
East Helena, *U.S.A.* 114 C8
East Indies, *Asia* 52 K15
East Kilbride, *U.K.* 14 F4

East Lansing, *U.S.A.* 108 D3
East Liverpool, *U.S.A.* 110 F4
East London, *S. Africa* 89 E4
East Lothian □, *U.K.* 14 F6
East Main = Eastmain, *Canada* 102 B4
East Northport, *U.S.A.* 111 F11
East Orange, *U.S.A.* 111 F10
East Pacific Ridge, *Pac. Oc.* 97 J17
East Palestine, *U.S.A.* 110 F4
East Pine, *Canada* 104 B4
East Point, *U.S.A.* 109 J3
East Providence, *U.S.A.* 111 E13
East Pt., *Canada* 103 C7
East Renfrewshire □, *U.K.* 14 F4
East Retford = Retford, *U.K.* 12 D7
East Riding of Yorkshire □, *U.K.* 12 D7
East Rochester, *U.S.A.* 110 C7
East St. Louis, *U.S.A.* 112 F9
East Schelde = Oosterschelde →, *Neths.* 17 C4
East Sea = Japan, Sea of, *Asia* 54 E7
East Siberian Sea, *Russia* 51 B17
East Stroudsburg, *U.S.A.* 111 E9
East Sussex □, *U.K.* 13 G8
East Tawas, *U.S.A.* 108 C4
East Timor ■, *Asia* 63 F7
East Toorale, *Australia* 95 E4
East Walker →, *U.S.A.* 116 G7
East Windsor, *U.S.A.* 111 F10
Eastbourne, *N.Z.* 91 J5
Eastbourne, *U.K.* 13 G8
Eastend, *Canada* 105 D7
Easter I. = Pascua, I. de, *Pac. Oc.* 97 K17
Eastern □, *Ghana* 83 D4
Eastern □, *Kenya* 86 C4
Eastern Cape □, *S. Africa* 88 E4
Eastern Cr. →, *Australia* 94 C3
Eastern Ghats, *India* 66 N11
Eastern Group = Lau Group, *Fiji* 91 C9
Eastern Group, *Australia* 93 F3
Eastern Province □, *S. Leone* 82 D2
Eastern Transvaal = Mpumalanga □, *S. Africa* 89 B5
Easterville, *Canada* 105 C9
Easthampton, *U.S.A.* 111 D12
Eastlake, *U.S.A.* 110 E3
Eastland, *U.S.A.* 113 J5
Eastleigh, *U.K.* 13 G6
Eastmain, *Canada* 102 B4
Eastmain →, *Canada* 102 B4
Eastman, *Canada* 111 A12
Eastman, *U.S.A.* 109 J4
Easton, *Md., U.S.A.* 108 F7
Easton, *Pa., U.S.A.* 111 F9
Easton, *Wash., U.S.A.* 116 C5
Eastpointe, *U.S.A.* 110 D2
Eastport, *U.S.A.* 109 C12
Eastsound, *U.S.A.* 116 B4
Eaton, *U.S.A.* 112 E2
Eatonia, *Canada* 105 C7
Eatonton, *U.S.A.* 109 J4
Eatontown, *U.S.A.* 111 F10
Eatonville, *U.S.A.* 116 D4
Eau Claire, *U.S.A.* 112 C9
Eau Claire, L. à l', *Canada* 102 A5
Eauze, *France* 20 E4
Eban, *Nigeria* 83 D5
Ebbw Vale, *U.K.* 13 F4
Ebeltoft, *Denmark* 11 H4
Ebeltoft Vig, *Denmark* 11 H4
Ebensburg, *U.S.A.* 110 F6
Ebensee, *Austria* 26 D6
Eber Gölü, *Turkey* 72 C4
Eberbach, *Germany* 25 F4
Eberswalde-Finow, *Germany* 24 C9
Ebetsu, *Japan* 54 C10
Ebian, *China* 58 C4
Ebingen, *Germany* 25 G5
Éboli, *Italy* 31 B8
Ebolowa, *Cameroon* 83 E7
Ebonyi □, *Nigeria* 83 D6
Ebrach, *Germany* 25 F6
Ébrié, Lagune, *Ivory C.* 82 D4
Ebro →, *Spain* 32 E5
Ebro, Embalse del, *Spain* 34 C7
Ebstorf, *Germany* 24 B6
Eceabat, *Turkey* 41 F10
Ech Cheliff, *Algeria* 78 A6
Echigo-Sammyaku, *Japan* 55 F9
Échirolles, *France* 21 C9
Echizen-Misaki, *Japan* 55 G7
Echmiadzin = Yejmiadzin, *Armenia* 49 K7
Echo Bay, *N.W.T., Canada* 100 B8
Echo Bay, *Ont., Canada* 102 C3
Echoing →, *Canada* 102 B1
Echternach, *Lux.* 17 E6
Ecija, *Spain* 35 H5
Eckental, *Germany* 25 F7
Eckernförde, *Germany* 24 A5
Eclipse Is., *Australia* 92 B4
Eclipse Sd., *Canada* 101 A11
Écommoy, *France* 18 E7
Écouché, *France* 18 D6
Ecuador ■, *S. Amer.* 124 D3
Écueillé, *France* 18 E8
Ed, *Sweden* 11 F5
Ed Dabbura, *Sudan* 80 D3
Ed Da'ein, *Sudan* 81 E2
Ed Damazin, *Sudan* 79 F12
Ed Dâmer, *Sudan* 80 D3
Ed Debba, *Sudan* 80 D3
Ed-Déffa, *Egypt* 80 A2
Ed Deim, *Sudan* 81 E2
Ed Dueim, *Sudan* 81 E3
Edam, *Canada* 105 C7
Edam, *Neths.* 17 B5
Edane, *Sweden* 10 E6
Eday, *U.K.* 14 B6
Edd, *Eritrea* 81 E5
Eddrachillis B., *U.K.* 14 C3
Eddystone Pt., *Australia* 94 G4
Ede, *Neths.* 17 B5
Ede, *Nigeria* 83 D5
Edéa, *Cameroon* 83 E7
Edebäck, *Sweden* 10 D7
Edehon L., *Canada* 105 A9
Edelény, *Hungary* 42 B5
Eden, *N.C., U.S.A.* 109 G6
Eden, *N.Y., U.S.A.* 110 D6
Eden, *Tex., U.S.A.* 113 K5
Eden →, *U.K.* 12 C4
Edenburg, *S. Africa* 88 D4
Edendale, *S. Africa* 89 D5
Edenderry, *Ireland* 15 C4
Edenton, *U.S.A.* 109 G7
Edenville, *S. Africa* 89 D4
Eder →, *Germany* 24 D5
Eder-Stausee, *Germany* 24 D4
Edewecht, *Germany* 24 B3
Edgar, *U.S.A.* 112 E6
Edgartown, *U.S.A.* 111 E14
Edge Hill, *U.K.* 13 E6
Edgefield, *U.S.A.* 109 J5
Edgeley, *U.S.A.* 112 B5
Edgemont, *U.S.A.* 112 D3
Edgeøya, *Svalbard* 4 B9
Édhessa, *Greece* 40 F6
Edievale, *N.Z.* 91 L2
Edina, *Liberia* 82 D2
Edina, *U.S.A.* 112 E8
Edinboro, *U.S.A.* 110 E4
Edinburg, *U.S.A.* 113 M5
Edinburgh, *U.K.* 14 F5
Edinburgh, City of □, *U.K.* 14 F5
Edineţ, *Moldova* 43 B12
Edirne, *Turkey* 41 E10
Edirne □, *Turkey* 41 E10
Edison, *U.S.A.* 116 B4
Edmeston, *U.S.A.* 111 D9
Edmond, *U.S.A.* 113 H6
Edmonds, *U.S.A.* 116 C4
Edmonton, *Australia* 94 B4
Edmonton, *Canada* 104 C6
Edmund L., *Canada* 102 B1
Edmundston, *Canada* 103 C6
Edna, *U.S.A.* 113 L6
Edo □, *Nigeria* 83 D6
Edolo, *Italy* 28 B7
Edremit, *Turkey* 39 B9
Edremit Körfezi, *Turkey* 39 B8
Edsbro, *Sweden* 10 E12
Edsbyn, *Sweden* 10 C9
Edson, *Canada* 104 C5
Eduardo Castex, *Argentina* 126 D3
Edward, L., *Africa* 86 C2
Edward River, *Australia* 94 A3
Edward VII Land, *Antarctica* 5 E13
Edwards, *Calif., U.S.A.* 117 L9
Edwards, *N.Y., U.S.A.* 111 B9
Edwards Air Force Base, *U.S.A.* 117 L9
Edwards Plateau, *U.S.A.* 113 K4
Edwardsville, *U.S.A.* 111 E9
Edzo, *Canada* 104 A5
Eeklo, *Belgium* 17 C3
Eferding, *Austria* 26 C7
Effingham, *U.S.A.* 108 F1
Eforie, *Romania* 43 F13
Ega →, *Spain* 32 C3
Égadi, Ísole, *Italy* 30 E5
Egan Range, *U.S.A.* 114 G6
Eganville, *Canada* 102 C4
Eger = Cheb, *Czech Rep.* 26 A5
Eger, *Hungary* 42 C5
Eger →, *Hungary* 42 C5
Egersund, *Norway* 9 G12
Egg L., *Canada* 105 B7
Eggenburg, *Austria* 26 C8
Eggenfelden, *Germany* 25 G8
Éghezée, *Belgium* 17 D4
Égletons, *France* 20 C6
Egmont, *Canada* 104 D4
Egmont, C., *N.Z.* 91 H4
Egmont, Mt. = Taranaki, Mt., *N.Z.* 91 H5
Egra, *India* 69 J12
Eğridir, *Turkey* 72 D4
Eğridir Gölü, *Turkey* 70 B1
Egtved, *Denmark* 11 J3
Egume, *Nigeria* 83 D6
Éguzon-Chantôme, *France* 19 F8
Egvekinot, *Russia* 51 C19
Egyek, *Hungary* 42 C5
Egypt ■, *Africa* 80 B3
Eha Amufu, *Nigeria* 83 D6
Ehime □, *Japan* 55 H6
Ehingen, *Germany* 25 G5
Ehrenberg, *U.S.A.* 117 M12
Ehrwald, *Austria* 26 D3
Eibar, *Spain* 32 B2
Eichstätt, *Germany* 25 G7
Eider →, *Germany* 24 A4
Eidsvold, *Australia* 95 D5
Eidsvoll, *Norway* 9 F14
Eifel, *Germany* 25 E2
Eiffel Flats, *Zimbabwe* 87 F3
Eiger, *Switz.* 28 B5
Eigg, *U.K.* 14 E2
Eighty Mile Beach, *Australia* 92 C3
Eil, *Somali Rep.* 74 F4
Eil, L., *U.K.* 14 E3
Eilenburg, *Germany* 24 D8
Ein el Luweiqa, *Sudan* 81 E3
Einasleigh, *Australia* 94 B3
Einasleigh →, *Australia* 94 B3
Einbeck, *Germany* 24 D5
Eindhoven, *Neths.* 17 C5
Einsiedeln, *Switz.* 25 H4
Eire = Ireland ■, *Europe* 15 C4
Eiríksjökull, *Iceland* 8 D3
Eirunepé, *Brazil* 124 E5
Eiseb →, *Namibia* 88 C2
Eisenach, *Germany* 24 E6
Eisenberg, *Germany* 24 E7
Eisenerz, *Austria* 26 D7
Eisenhüttenstadt, *Germany* 24 C10
Eisenkappel, *Austria* 26 E7
Eisenstadt, *Austria* 27 D9
Eisfeld, *Germany* 25 E6
Eisleben, *Germany* 24 D7
Eislingen, *Germany* 25 G5
Eivissa, *Spain* 37 C7
Eixe, Serra do, *Spain* 34 C4
Ejea de los Caballeros, *Spain* 32 C3
Ejeda, *Madag.* 89 C7
Ejura, *Ghana* 83 D4
Ejutla, *Mexico* 119 D5
Ekalaka, *U.S.A.* 112 C2
Ekenässjön, *Sweden* 11 G9
Ekerö, *Sweden* 10 E11
Eket, *Nigeria* 83 E6
Eketahuna, *N.Z.* 91 J5
Ekhínos, *Greece* 41 E9
Ekibastuz, *Kazakstan* 50 D8
Ekiti □, *Nigeria* 83 D6
Ekoli, *Dem. Rep. of the Congo* 86 C1
Ekoln, *Sweden* 10 E11
Ekshärad, *Sweden* 10 D7
Eksjö, *Sweden* 11 G8
Ekuma →, *Namibia* 88 B2
Ekwan →, *Canada* 102 B3
Ekwan Pt., *Canada* 102 B3
El Aaiún, *W. Sahara* 78 C3
El Abanico, *Chile* 126 D1
El Abbasiya, *Sudan* 81 E3
El 'Agrûd, *Egypt* 75 E3
El Ait, *Sudan* 81 E2
El 'Aiyat, *Egypt* 80 J7
El Alamein, *Egypt* 80 A2
El 'Aqaba, W. →, *Egypt* 75 E2
El 'Arag, *Egypt* 80 B2
El Arahal, *Spain* 35 H5
El Arīḥā, *West Bank* 75 D4
El 'Arîsh, *Egypt* 75 D2
El 'Arîsh, W. →, *Egypt* 75 D2
El Asnam = Ech Cheliff, *Algeria* 78 A6
El Astillero, *Spain* 34 B7
El Badâri, *Egypt* 80 B3
El Bahrein, *Egypt* 80 B2
El Ballâs, *Egypt* 80 B3
El Balyana, *Egypt* 80 B3
El Baqeir, *Sudan* 80 D3
El Barco de Ávila, *Spain* 34 E5
El Barco de Valdeorras = O Barco, *Spain* 34 C4
El Bauga, *Sudan* 80 D3
El Bawiti, *Egypt* 80 B2
El Bayadh, *Algeria* 78 B6
El Bierzo, *Spain* 34 C4
El Bluff, *Nic.* 120 D3
El Bonillo, *Spain* 33 G2
El Brûk, W. →, *Egypt* 75 E2
El Buheirat □, *Sudan* 81 F3
El Burgo de Osma, *Spain* 32 D1
El Cajon, *U.S.A.* 117 N10
El Campo, *U.S.A.* 113 L6
El Centro, *U.S.A.* 117 N11
El Cerro, *Bolivia* 124 G6
El Cerro de Andévalo, *Spain* 35 H4
El Compadre, *Mexico* 117 N10
El Coronil, *Spain* 35 H5
El Cuy, *Argentina* 128 D3
El Cuyo, *Mexico* 119 C7
El Dab'a, *Egypt* 80 H6
El Daheir, *Egypt* 75 D3
El Dátil, *Mexico* 118 B2
El Deir, *Egypt* 80 B3
El Dere, *Somali Rep.* 74 G4
El Descanso, *Mexico* 117 N10
El Desemboque, *Mexico* 118 A2
El Dilingat, *Egypt* 80 H7
El Diviso, *Colombia* 124 C3
El Djouf, *Mauritania* 78 D4
El Dorado, *Ark., U.S.A.* 113 J8
El Dorado, *Kans., U.S.A.* 113 G6
El Dorado, *Venezuela* 124 B6
El 'Ein, *Sudan* 81 D2
El Ejido, *Spain* 35 J8
El Escorial, *Spain* 34 E6
El Espinar, *Spain* 34 D6
El Faiyûm, *Egypt* 80 J7
El Fâsher, *Sudan* 81 E2
El Fashn, *Egypt* 80 J7
El Ferrol = Ferrol, *Spain* 34 B2
El Fifi, *Sudan* 81 E2
El Fuerte, *Mexico* 118 B3
El Ga'a, *Sudan* 81 E2
El Gal, *Somali Rep.* 74 E5
El Garef, *Sudan* 81 E3
El Gebir, *Sudan* 81 E2
El Gedida, *Egypt* 80 B2
El Geneina = Al Junaynah, *Sudan* 79 F10
El Geteina, *Sudan* 81 E3
El Gezira □, *Sudan* 81 E3
El Gir, *Sudan* 80 D2
El Gîza, *Egypt* 80 J7
El Goléa, *Algeria* 78 B6
El Grau, *Spain* 33 G4
El Hagiz, *Sudan* 81 D4
El Hâi, *Egypt* 80 J7
El Hammam, *Egypt* 80 A2
El Hawata, *Sudan* 81 E3
El Heiz, *Egypt* 80 B2
El Hideib, *Sudan* 81 E3
El Hilla, *Sudan* 81 E2
El 'Idisât, *Egypt* 80 B3
El Iskandarîya, *Egypt* 80 H7
El Istiwa'iya, *Sudan* 79 G11
El Jadida, *Morocco* 78 B4
El Jardal, *Honduras* 120 D2
El Jebelein, *Sudan* 81 E3
El Kab, *Sudan* 80 D3
El Kabrît, G., *Egypt* 75 F2
El Kafr el Sharqi, *Egypt* 80 H7
El Kamlin, *Sudan* 81 D3
El Karaba, *Sudan* 80 D3
El Kere, *Ethiopia* 81 F5
El Khandaq, *Sudan* 80 D3
El Khârga, *Egypt* 80 B3
El Khartûm, *Sudan* 81 D3
El Khartûm □, *Sudan* 81 D3
El Khartûm Bahrî, *Sudan* 81 D3
El Kuntilla, *Egypt* 75 E3
El Laqâwa, *Sudan* 81 E2
El Laqeita, *Egypt* 80 B3
El Leh, *Ethiopia* 81 G4
El Leiya, *Sudan* 81 D4
El Maestrazgo, *Spain* 32 E4
El Mafâza, *Sudan* 81 E3
El Maghra, *Egypt* 80 A2
El Mahalla el Kubra, *Egypt* 80 H7
El Mahârîq, *Egypt* 80 B3
El Maîmûn, *Egypt* 80 J7
El Maks el Bahari, *Egypt* 80 C3
El Manshâh, *Egypt* 80 B3
El Mansûra, *Egypt* 80 H7
El Manzala, *Egypt* 80 H7
El Marâgha, *Egypt* 80 B3
El Masid, *Sudan* 81 D3
El Masnou, *Spain* 32 D7
El Matariya, *Egypt* 80 H8
El Meda, *Ethiopia* 81 F5
El Medano, *Canary Is.* 37 F3
El Metemma, *Sudan* 81 D3
El Milagro, *Argentina* 126 C2
El Minyâ, *Egypt* 80 B3
El Monte, *U.S.A.* 117 L8
El Montseny, *Spain* 32 D7
El Mreyye, *Mauritania* 82 B3
El Niybo, *Ethiopia* 81 G4
El Obeid, *Sudan* 81 E3
El Odaiya, *Sudan* 81 E2
El Oro, *Mexico* 119 D4
El Oued, *Algeria* 78 B7
El Palmito, Presa, *Mexico* 118 B3
El Paso, *U.S.A.* 115 L10
El Paso Robles, *U.S.A.* 116 K6
El Pedernoso, *Spain* 33 F2
El Pedroso, *Spain* 35 H5
El Pobo de Dueñas, *Spain* 32 E3
El Portal, *U.S.A.* 116 H7
El Porvenir, *Mexico* 118 A3
El Prat de Llobregat, *Spain* 32 D7
El Progreso, *Honduras* 120 C2
El Pueblito, *Mexico* 118 B3
El Pueblo, *Canary Is.* 37 F2
El Puente del Arzobispo, *Spain* 34 F5
El Puerto de Santa María, *Spain* 35 J4
El Qâhira, *Egypt* 80 H7
El Qantara, *Egypt* 75 E1
El Qasr, *Egypt* 80 B2
El Qubâbât, *Egypt* 80 J7
El Quseima, *Egypt* 75 E3
El Qusîya, *Egypt* 80 B3
El Râshda, *Egypt* 80 B2
El Real, *Panama* 124 B3
El Reno, *U.S.A.* 113 H6
El Ridisiya, *Egypt* 80 C3
El Rio, *U.S.A.* 117 L7
El Ronquillo, *Spain* 35 H4
El Roque, Pta., *Canary Is.* 37 F4
El Rosarito, *Mexico* 118 B2
El Rubio, *Spain* 35 H5
El Saff, *Egypt* 80 J7
El Saheira, W. →, *Egypt* 75 E2
El Salto, *Mexico* 118 C3
El Salvador ■, *Cent. Amer.* 120 D2
El Sauce, *Nic.* 120 D2
El Saucejo, *Spain* 35 H5
El Shallal, *Egypt* 80 C3
El Simbillawein, *Egypt* 80 H7
El Sueco, *Mexico* 118 B3
El Suweis, *Egypt* 80 J8
El Tabbîn, *Egypt* 80 J7
El Tamarâni, W. →, *Egypt* 75 E3
El Thamad, *Egypt* 75 F3
El Tigre, *Venezuela* 124 B6
El Tîh, Gebal, *Egypt* 75 F2
El Tîna, *Egypt* 80 H8
El Tîna, Khalîg, *Egypt* 75 D1
El Tofo, *Chile* 126 B1
El Tránsito, *Chile* 126 B1
El Tûr, *Egypt* 70 D2
El Turbio, *Argentina* 128 G2
El Uqsur, *Egypt* 80 B3
El Venado, *Mexico* 118 C4
El Vendrell, *Spain* 32 D6
El Vergel, *Mexico* 118 B3
El Vigía, *Venezuela* 124 B4
El Viso del Alcor, *Spain* 35 H5
El Wabeira, *Egypt* 75 F2
El Wak, *Kenya* 86 B5
El Waqf, *Egypt* 80 B3
El Weguet, *Ethiopia* 81 F5
El Wuz, *Sudan* 81 D3
Elafónisos, *Greece* 38 E4
Élancourt, *France* 19 D8
Élassa, *Greece* 39 F8
Elassón, *Greece* 38 B4
Elat, *Israel* 75 F3
Eláthia, *Greece* 38 C4
Elâzığ, *Turkey* 70 B3
Elba, *Italy* 28 F7
Elba, *U.S.A.* 109 K2
Elbasan, *Albania* 40 E4
Elbe, *U.S.A.* 116 D4
Elbe →, *Europe* 24 B4
Elbe-Seitenkanal, *Germany* 24 C6
Elbert, Mt., *U.S.A.* 115 G10
Elberton, *U.S.A.* 109 H4
Elbeuf, *France* 18 C8
Elbidtan, *Turkey* 70 B3
Elbing = Elbląg, *Poland* 44 D6
Elbistan, *Turkey* 72 C7
Elbląg, *Poland* 44 D6
Elbow, *Canada* 105 C7
Elbrus, *Asia* 49 J6
Elburz Mts. = Alborz, Reshteh-ye Kūhhā-ye, *Iran* 71 C7
Elche, *Spain* 33 G4
Elche de la Sierra, *Spain* 33 G2
Elcho I., *Australia* 94 A2
Elda, *Spain* 33 G4
Elde →, *Germany* 24 B7
Eldon, *Mo., U.S.A.* 112 F8
Eldon, *Wash., U.S.A.* 116 C3
Eldora, *U.S.A.* 112 D8
Eldorado, *Argentina* 127 B5
Eldorado, *Canada* 110 B7
Eldorado, *Mexico* 118 C3
Eldorado, *Ill., U.S.A.* 108 G1
Eldorado, *Tex., U.S.A.* 113 K4
Eldorado Springs, *U.S.A.* 113 G8
Eldoret, *Kenya* 86 B4
Eldred, *U.S.A.* 110 E6
Elea, C., *Cyprus* 36 D13
Eleanora, Pk., *Australia* 93 F3
Elefantes →, *Mozam.* 89 C5
Elektrogorsk, *Russia* 46 E10
Elektrostal, *Russia* 46 E10
Elele, *Nigeria* 83 D6
Elena, *Bulgaria* 41 D9
Elephant Butte Reservoir, *U.S.A.* 115 K10
Elephant I., *Antarctica* 5 C18
Eleshnitsa, *Bulgaria* 40 E7
Eleşkirt, *Turkey* 73 C10
Eleuthera, *Bahamas* 120 B4
Elevsís, *Greece* 38 C5
Elevtheroúpolis, *Greece* 41 F8
Elgin, *Canada* 111 B8
Elgin, *U.K.* 14 D5
Elgin, *Ill., U.S.A.* 108 D1
Elgin, *N. Dak., U.S.A.* 112 B4
Elgin, *Oreg., U.S.A.* 114 D5
Elgin, *Tex., U.S.A.* 113 K6
Elgoibar, *Spain* 32 B2
Elgon, Mt., *Africa* 86 B3
Eliase, *Indonesia* 63 F8
Elikón, *Greece* 38 C4
Elim, *Namibia* 88 B2
Elim, *S. Africa* 88 E2
Elin Pelin, *Bulgaria* 40 D7
Elista, *Russia* 49 G7
Elizabeth, *N.J., U.S.A.* 111 F10
Elizabeth, *N.J., U.S.A.* 111 F10
Elizabeth City, *U.S.A.* 109 G7
Elizabethton, *U.S.A.* 109 G4
Elizabethtown, *Ky., U.S.A.* 108 G3
Elizabethtown, *N.Y., U.S.A.* 111 B11
Elizabethtown, *Pa., U.S.A.* 111 F8
Elizondo, *Spain* 32 B3
Ełk, *Poland* 44 E9
Elk →, *Canada* 104 C5
Ełk →, *Poland* 44 E9
Elk →, *U.S.A.* 109 H2
Elk City, *U.S.A.* 113 H5
Elk Creek, *U.S.A.* 116 F4
Elk Grove, *U.S.A.* 116 G5
Elk Island Nat. Park, *Canada* 104 C6
Elk Lake, *Canada* 102 C3
Elk Point, *Canada* 105 C6
Elk River, *Idaho, U.S.A.* 114 C5
Elk River, *Minn., U.S.A.* 112 C8
Elkedra →, *Australia* 94 C2
Elkhart, *Ind., U.S.A.* 108 E3
Elkhart, *Kans., U.S.A.* 113 G4
Elkhorn, *Canada* 105 D8
Elkhorn →, *U.S.A.* 112 E6
Elkhovo, *Bulgaria* 41 D10
Elkin, *U.S.A.* 109 G5
Elkins, *U.S.A.* 108 F6
Elkland, *U.S.A.* 110 E7
Elko, *Canada* 104 D5
Elko, *U.S.A.* 114 F6
Elkton, *U.S.A.* 110 C1
Ell, L., *Australia* 93 E4
Ellef Ringnes I., *Canada* 4 B2
Ellen, Mt., *U.S.A.* 111 B12
Ellenburg, *U.S.A.* 111 B11
Ellendale, *U.S.A.* 112 B5
Ellensburg, *U.S.A.* 114 C3
Ellenville, *U.S.A.* 111 E10
Ellesmere, L., *N.Z.* 91 M4
Ellesmere I., *Canada* 4 B4
Ellesmere Port, *U.K.* 12 D5

Ellice Is. = Tuvalu ■, Pac. Oc. 96 H9
Ellicottville, U.S.A. 110 D6
Elliot, Australia 94 B1
Elliot, S. Africa 89 E4
Elliot Lake, Canada 102 C3
Elliotdale = Xhora, S. Africa 89 E4
Ellis, U.S.A. 112 F5
Elliston, Australia 95 E1
Ellisville, U.S.A. 113 K10
Ellon, U.K. 14 D6
Ellore = Eluru, India 67 L12
Ellsworth, Kans., U.S.A. 112 F5
Ellsworth, Maine, U.S.A. 109 C11
Ellsworth Land, Antarctica 5 D16
Ellsworth Mts., Antarctica 5 D16
Ellwangen, Germany 25 G6
Ellwood City, U.S.A. 110 F4
Elm, Switz. 25 J5
Elma, Canada 105 D9
Elma, U.S.A. 116 D3
Elmadağ, Turkey 72 C5
Elmalı, Turkey 39 E11
Elmhurst, U.S.A. 108 E2
Elmina, Ghana 83 D4
Elmira, Canada 110 C4
Elmira, U.S.A. 110 D8
Elmira Heights, U.S.A. 110 D8
Elmore, U.S.A. 117 M11
Elmshorn, Germany 24 B5
Elmvale, Canada 110 B5
Elne, France 20 F6
Elora, Canada 110 C4
Elos, Greece 38 E4
Eloúnda, Greece 36 D7
Eloy, U.S.A. 115 K8
Éloyes, France 19 D13
Elrose, Canada 105 C7
Elsdorf, Germany 24 E2
Elsie, U.S.A. 116 E3
Elsinore = Helsingør, Denmark 11 H6
Elster →, Germany 24 D7
Elsterwerda, Germany 24 D9
Eltham, N.Z. 91 H5
Elton, Russia 49 F8
Elton, Ozero, Russia 49 F8
Eltville, Germany 25 E4
Eluru, India 67 L12
Elvas, Portugal 35 G3
Elven, France 18 E4
Elverum, Norway 9 F14
Elvire →, Australia 92 C4
Elvire, Mt., Australia 93 E2
Elvo →, Italy 28 C5
Elwell, L., U.S.A. 114 B8
Elwood, Ind., U.S.A. 108 E3
Elwood, Nebr., U.S.A. 112 E5
Elx = Elche, Spain 33 G4
Ely, U.K. 13 E8
Ely, Minn., U.S.A. 112 B9
Ely, Nev., U.S.A. 114 G6
Elyria, U.S.A. 110 E2
Elyrus, Greece 38 F5
Elz →, Germany 25 G3
Emådalen, Sweden 10 C8
Emāmrūd, Iran 71 B7
Emån →, Sweden 11 G10
Emba, Kazakstan 50 E6
Emba →, Kazakstan 50 E6
Embarcación, Argentina 126 A3
Embarras Portage, Canada 105 B6
Embetsu, Japan 54 B10
Embi = Emba, Kazakstan 50 E6
Embi = Emba →, Kazakstan 50 E6
Embóna, Greece 36 C9
Embrun, France 21 D10
Embu, Kenya 86 C4
Emden, Germany 24 B3
Emecik, Turkey 39 E9
Emerald, Australia 94 C4
Emerson, Canada 105 D9
Emet, Turkey 39 B11
Emi Koussi, Chad 79 E9
Emília-Romagna □, Italy 28 D8
Emilius, Mte., Italy 28 C4
Eminabad, Pakistan 68 C6
Emine, Nos, Bulgaria 41 D11
Emirdağ, Turkey 72 C4
Emlenton, U.S.A. 110 E5
Emlichheim, Germany 24 C2
Emmaboda, Sweden 11 H9
Emmaus, S. Africa 88 D4
Emmaus, U.S.A. 111 F9
Emme →, Switz. 25 H3
Emmeloord, Neths. 17 B5
Emmen, Neths. 17 B6
Emmen, Switz. 25 H4
Emmendingen, Germany 25 G3
Emmental, Switz. 25 J3
Emmerich, Germany 24 D2
Emmet, Australia 94 C3
Emmetsburg, U.S.A. 112 D7
Emmett, Idaho, U.S.A. 114 E5
Emmett, Mich., U.S.A. 110 D2
Emmonak, U.S.A. 100 B3
Emo, Canada 105 D10
Emőd, Hungary 42 C5
Emona, Bulgaria 41 D11
Empalme, Mexico 118 B2
Empangeni, S. Africa 89 D5
Empedrado, Argentina 126 B4
Emperor Seamount Chain, Pac. Oc. 96 D9
Empoli, Italy 28 E7
Emporia, Kans., U.S.A. 112 F6
Emporia, Va., U.S.A. 109 G7
Emporium, U.S.A. 110 E6
Empress, Canada 105 C7
Empty Quarter = Rub' al Khālī, Si. Arabia 74 D4
Ems →, Germany 24 B3
Emsdale, Canada 110 A5
Emsdetten, Germany 24 C3
Emu, China 57 C15
Emu Park, Australia 94 C5
'En 'Avrona, Israel 75 F4
En Nahud, Sudan 81 E2
En Nofalab, Sudan 81 D3
Ena, Japan 55 G8
Enana, Namibia 88 B2
Enånger, Sweden 10 C11
Enard B., U.K. 14 C3
Enare = Inarijärvi, Finland 8 B22
Enarotali, Indonesia 63 E9
Encampment, U.S.A. 114 F10
Encantadas, Serra, Brazil 127 C5
Encarnación, Paraguay 127 B4
Encarnación de Diaz, Mexico 118 C4
Enchi, Ghana 82 D4
Encinitas, U.S.A. 117 M9
Encino, U.S.A. 115 J11
Encs, Hungary 42 B6
Endako, Canada 104 C3
Ende, Indonesia 63 F6
Endeavour Str., Australia 94 A3
Endelave, Denmark 11 J4
Enderbury I., Kiribati 96 H10
Enderby, Canada 104 C5
Enderby I., Australia 92 D2
Enderby Land, Antarctica 5 C5
Enderlin, U.S.A. 112 B6
Endicott, U.S.A. 111 D8
Endwell, U.S.A. 111 D8
Endyalgout I., Australia 92 B5
Eneabba, Australia 93 E2
Enewetak Atoll, Marshall Is. 96 F8
Enez, Turkey 41 F10
Enfield, Canada 103 D7
Enfield, Conn., U.S.A. 111 E12
Enfield, N.H., U.S.A. 111 C12
Engadin, Switz. 25 J6
Engaño, C., Dom. Rep. 121 C6
Engaño, C., Phil. 63 A6
Engaru, Japan 54 B11
Engcobo, S. Africa 89 E4
Engelberg, Switz. 25 J4
Engels, Russia 48 E8
Engemann L., Canada 105 B7
Engershatu, Eritrea 81 D4
Enggano, Indonesia 62 F2
England, U.S.A. 113 H9
England □, U.K. 12 D7
Englee, Canada 103 B8
Englehart, Canada 102 C4
Englewood, U.S.A. 112 F2
English →, Canada 105 C10
English Bazar = Ingraj Bazar, India 69 G13
English Channel, Europe 13 G6
English River, Canada 102 C1
Engures ezers, Latvia 44 A10
Enguri →, Georgia 49 J5
Enid, U.S.A. 113 G6
Enipévs →, Greece 38 B4
Enkhuizen, Neths. 17 B5
Enköping, Sweden 10 E11
Enle, China 58 F3
Enna, Italy 31 E7
Ennadai, Canada 105 A8
Ennadai L., Canada 105 A8
Ennedi, Chad 79 E10
Enngonia, Australia 95 D4
Ennigerloh, Germany 24 D4
Ennis, Ireland 15 D3
Ennis, Mont., U.S.A. 114 D8
Ennis, Tex., U.S.A. 113 J6
Enniscorthy, Ireland 15 D5
Enniskillen, U.K. 15 B4
Ennistimon, Ireland 15 D2
Enns, Austria 26 C7
Enns →, Austria 26 C7
Enontekiö, Finland 8 B20
Enosburg Falls, U.S.A. 111 B12
Enping, China 59 F9
Enriquillo, L., Dom. Rep. 121 C5
Enschede, Neths. 17 B6
Ensenada, Argentina 126 C4
Ensenada, Mexico 118 A1
Ensenada de los Muertos, Mexico 118 C2
Enshi, China 58 B7
Ensiola, Pta. de n', Spain 37 B9
Ensisheim, France 19 E14
Entebbe, Uganda 86 B3
Enterprise, Canada 104 A5
Enterprise, Ala., U.S.A. 109 K3
Enterprise, Oreg., U.S.A. 114 D5
Entraygues-sur-Truyère, France 20 D6
Entre Ríos, Bolivia 126 A3
Entre Ríos □, Argentina 126 C4
Entrepeñas, Embalse de, Spain 32 E2
Entroncamento, Portugal 35 F2
Enugu, Nigeria 83 D6
Enugu □, Nigeria 83 D6
Enugu Ezike, Nigeria 83 D6
Enumclaw, U.S.A. 116 C5
Envermeu, France 18 C8
Enviken, Sweden 10 D9
Enying, Hungary 42 D3
Enza →, Italy 28 D7
Eólie, Ís., Italy 31 D7
Epanomí, Greece 40 F6
Epe, Neths. 17 B5
Epe, Nigeria 83 D5
Épernay, France 19 C10
Épernon, France 19 D8
Ephesus, Turkey 39 D9
Ephraim, U.S.A. 114 G8
Ephrata, Pa., U.S.A. 111 F8
Ephrata, Wash., U.S.A. 114 C4
Epidaurus Limera, Greece 38 E5
Épila, Spain 32 D3
Épinac, France 19 F11
Épinal, France 19 D13
Episkopi, Cyprus 36 E11
Episkopí, Greece 36 D6
Episkopi Bay, Cyprus 36 E11
Epitálion, Greece 38 D3
Eppan = Appiano, Italy 29 B8
Eppingen, Germany 25 F4
Epsom, U.K. 13 F7
Epukiro, Namibia 88 C2
Equatorial Guinea ■, Africa 84 D1
Er Hai, China 58 E3
Er Rachidia, Morocco 78 B5
Er Rahad, Sudan 81 E3
Er Rif, Morocco 78 A5
Er Rogel, Sudan 80 D4
Er Roseires, Sudan 81 E3
Er Rua'at, Sudan 81 E3
Eraclea, Italy 29 C9
Erāwadī Myit = Irrawaddy →, Burma 67 M19
Erāwadī Myitwanya = Irrawaddy, Mouths of the, Burma 67 M19
Erba, Italy 28 C6
Erba, Sudan 80 D4
Erba, J., Sudan 80 C4
Erbaa, Turkey 72 B7
Erbeskopf, Germany 25 F3
Erbil = Arbīl, Iraq 70 B5
Erbu, Ethiopia 81 E3
Erçek, Turkey 70 B4
Erçiş, Turkey 73 C10
Erciyaş Dağı, Turkey 70 B2
Érd, Hungary 42 C3
Erdao Jiang →, China 57 C14
Erdek, Turkey 41 F11
Erdemli, Turkey 72 D6
Erdene = Ulaan-Uul, Mongolia 56 B6
Erdenetsogt, Mongolia 56 C4
Erding, Germany 25 G7
Erdre →, France 18 E5
Erebus, Mt., Antarctica 5 D11
Erechim, Brazil 127 B5
Ereğli, Konya, Turkey 70 B2
Ereğli, Zonguldak, Turkey 72 B4
Erei, Monti, Italy 31 E7
Erenhot, China 56 C7
Eresma →, Spain 34 D6
Eressós, Greece 39 B7
Erfenisdam, S. Africa 88 D4
Erftstadt, Germany 24 E2
Erft →, Germany 24 D2
Erfurt, Germany 24 E7
Erg Iguidi, Africa 78 C4
Ergani, Turkey 70 B3
Ergel, Mongolia 56 C5
Ergene →, Turkey 41 E10
Ergeni Vozvyshennost, Russia 49 G7
Ērgli, Latvia 9 H21
Erhlin, Taiwan 59 F13
Eria →, Spain 34 C5
Eriba, Sudan 81 D4
Eriboll, L., U.K. 14 C4
Érice, Italy 30 D5
Erie, U.S.A. 110 D4
Erie, L., N. Amer. 110 D4
Erie Canal, U.S.A. 110 C7
Erieau, Canada 110 D3
Erigavo, Somali Rep. 74 E4
Erikoúsa, Greece 36 A3
Eriksdale, Canada 105 C9
Erímanthos, Greece 38 D3
Erimo-misaki, Japan 54 D11
Erinpura, India 68 G5
Eriskay, U.K. 14 D1
Erithraí, Greece 38 C5
Eritrea ■, Africa 81 E4
Erjas →, Portugal 34 F3
Erkelenz, Germany 24 D2
Erkner, Germany 24 C9
Erlangen, Germany 25 F6
Erldunda, Australia 94 D1
Ermelo, Neths. 17 B5
Ermelo, S. Africa 89 D4
Ermenek, Turkey 70 B2
Ermil, Sudan 81 E2
Ermióni, Greece 38 D5
Ermones, Greece 36 A3
Ermoúpolis = Síros, Greece 38 D6
Ernakulam = Cochin, India 66 Q10
Erne →, Ireland 15 B3
Erne, Lower L., U.K. 15 B4
Erne, Upper L., U.K. 15 B4
Ernée, France 18 D6
Ernest Giles Ra., Australia 93 E3
Ernstberg, Germany 25 E2
Erode, India 66 P10
Eromanga, Australia 95 D3
Erongo, Namibia 88 C2
Erquy, France 18 D4
Erramala Hills, India 66 M11
Errer →, Ethiopia 81 F5
Errigal, Ireland 15 A3
Erris Hd., Ireland 15 B1
Ersekë, Albania 40 F4
Erskine, U.S.A. 112 B7
Erstein, France 19 D14
Ertholmene, Denmark 11 J9
Ertil, Russia 48 E5
Ertis = Irtysh →, Russia 50 C7
Eruh, Turkey 73 D10
Eruwa, Nigeria 83 D5
Ervy-le-Châtel, France 19 D10
Erwin, U.S.A. 109 G4
Eryuan, China 58 D2
Erzgebirge, Germany 24 E8
Erzin, Russia 51 D10
Erzincan, Turkey 70 B3
Erzurum, Turkey 70 B4
Es Caló, Spain 37 C8
Es Canar, Spain 37 B8
Es Mercadal, Spain 37 B11
Es Migjorn Gran, Spain 37 B11
Es Safiya, Sudan 81 D3
Es Sahrâ' Esh Sharqîya, Egypt 80 B3
Es Sînâ', Egypt 75 F3
Es Sûkî, Sudan 81 E3
Es Vedrà, Spain 37 C7
Esambo, Dem. Rep. of the Congo 86 C1
Esan-Misaki, Japan 54 D10
Esashi, Hokkaidō, Japan 54 B11
Esashi, Hokkaidō, Japan 54 D10
Esbjerg, Denmark 11 J2
Escalante, U.S.A. 115 H8
Escalante →, U.S.A. 115 H8
Escalón, Mexico 118 B4
Escambia →, U.S.A. 109 K2
Escanaba, U.S.A. 108 C2
Esch-sur-Alzette, Lux. 17 E6
Eschede, Germany 24 C6
Eschwege, Germany 24 D6
Eschweiler, Germany 24 E2
Escondido, U.S.A. 117 M9
Escravos →, Nigeria 83 D6
Escuinapa, Mexico 118 C3
Escuintla, Guatemala 120 D1
Eséka, Cameroon 83 E7
Eşen →, Turkey 39 E11
Esenguly, Turkmenistan 50 F6
Esens, Germany 24 B3
Esenyurt, Turkey 41 E12
Esera →, Spain 32 C5
Eşfahān, Iran 71 C6
Eşfahān □, Iran 71 C6
Esfarāyen, Iran 71 B8
Esfīdeh, Iran 71 C8
Esgueva →, Spain 34 D6
Esh Sham = Dimashq, Syria 75 B5
Esh Shamâliya □, Sudan 80 D2
Esha Ness, U.K. 14 A7
Eshan, China 58 E4
Esher, U.K. 13 F7
Eshowe, S. Africa 89 D5
Esiama, Ghana 82 E4
Esigodini, Zimbabwe 89 C4
Esil = Ishim →, Russia 50 D8
Esino →, Italy 29 E10
Esira, Madag. 89 C8
Esk →, Cumb., U.K. 14 G5
Esk →, N. Yorks., U.K. 12 C7
Eskān, Iran 71 E9
Esker, Canada 103 B6
Eskifjörður, Iceland 8 D7
Eskilsäter, Sweden 11 F7
Eskilstuna, Sweden 10 E10
Eskimalatya, Turkey 73 C8
Eskimo Pt., Canada 100 B10
Eskişehir, Turkey 39 B12
Eskişehir □, Turkey 39 B12
Esla →, Spain 34 D4
Eslāmābād-e Gharb, Iran 70 C5
Eslāmshahr, Iran 71 C6
Eslöv, Sweden 11 J7
Eşme, Turkey 39 C10
Esmeraldas, Ecuador 124 C3
Esnagi L., Canada 102 C3
Espalion, France 20 D6
Espanola, Canada 102 C3
Espanola, U.S.A. 115 H10
Esparreguera, Spain 32 D6
Esparta, Costa Rica 120 E3
Espelkamp, Germany 24 C4
Esperance, Australia 93 F3
Esperance B., Australia 93 F3
Esperanza, Argentina 126 C3
Esperanza, Phil. 61 G6
Espéraza, France 20 F6
Espichel, C., Portugal 35 G1
Espiel, Spain 35 G5
Espigão, Serra do, Brazil 127 B5
Espinazo, Sierra del = Espinhaço, Serra do, Brazil 125 G10
Espinhaço, Serra do, Brazil 125 G10
Espinho, Portugal 34 D2
Espinilho, Serra do, Brazil 127 B5
Espinosa de los Monteros, Spain 34 B7
Espírito Santo □, Brazil 125 H10
Espíritu Santo, Vanuatu 96 J8
Espíritu Santo, B. del, Mexico 119 D7
Espíritu Santo, I., Mexico 118 C2
Espita, Mexico 119 C7
Espiye, Turkey 73 B8
Espluga de Francolí, Spain 32 D6
Espoo, Finland 9 F21
Espuña, Sierra de, Spain 33 H3
Espungabera, Mozam. 89 C5
Esquel, Argentina 128 E2
Esquimalt, Canada 104 D4
Esquina, Argentina 126 C4
Essaouira, Morocco 78 B4
Essebie, Dem. Rep. of the Congo 86 B3
Essen, Belgium 17 C4
Essen, Germany 24 D3
Essendon, Mt., Australia 93 E3
Essequibo →, Guyana 122 C5
Essex, Canada 110 D2
Essex, Calif., U.S.A. 117 L11
Essex, N.Y., U.S.A. 111 B11
Essex □, U.K. 13 F8
Essex Junction, U.S.A. 111 B11
Esslingen, Germany 25 G5
Essonne □, France 19 D9
Estaca de Bares, C. de, Spain 34 B3
Estadilla, Spain 32 C5
Estados, I. de Los, Argentina 122 J4
Estagel, France 20 F6
Eşţahbānāt, Iran 71 D7
Estância, Brazil 125 F11
Estancia, U.S.A. 115 J10
Estārm, Iran 71 D8
Estarreja, Portugal 34 E2
Estats, Pic d', Spain 32 C6
Estcourt, S. Africa 89 D4
Este, Italy 29 C8
Estelí, Nic. 120 D2
Estella, Spain 32 C2
Estellencs, Spain 37 B9
Estena →, Spain 35 F6
Estepa, Spain 35 H6
Estepona, Spain 35 J5
Esterhazy, Canada 105 C8
Esternay, France 19 D10
Esterri d'Aneu, Spain 32 C6
Estevan, Canada 105 D8
Estevan Group, Canada 104 C3
Estherville, U.S.A. 112 D7
Estissac, France 19 D10
Eston, Canada 105 C7
Estonia ■, Europe 9 G21
Estoril, Portugal 35 G1
Estouk, Mali 83 B5
Estreito, Brazil 125 E9
Estrela, Serra da, Portugal 34 E3
Estrella, Spain 35 G7
Estremoz, Portugal 35 G3
Estrondo, Serra do, Brazil 125 E9
Esztergom, Hungary 42 C3
Et Tîdra, Mauritania 82 B1
Etah, India 69 F8
Étain, France 19 C12
Étampes, France 19 D9
Etanga, Namibia 88 B1
Étaples, France 19 B8
Etawah, India 69 F8
Etawney L., Canada 105 B9
Ete, Nigeria 83 D6
Ethel, U.S.A. 116 D4
Ethelbert, Canada 105 C8
Ethiopia ■, Africa 74 F3
Ethiopian Highlands, Ethiopia 52 J7
Etili, Turkey 41 G10
Etive, L., U.K. 14 E3
Etna, Italy 31 E7
Etoile, Dem. Rep. of the Congo 87 E2
Etosha Nat. Park, Namibia 88 B2
Etosha Pan, Namibia 88 B2
Etowah, U.S.A. 109 H3
Étréchy, France 19 D9
Étrépagny, France 19 C8
Étretat, France 18 C7
Etropole, Bulgaria 41 D8
Ettelbruck, Lux. 17 E6
Ettlingen, Germany 25 G4
Ettrick Water →, U.K. 14 F6
Etuku, Dem. Rep. of the Congo 86 C2
Etulia, Moldova 43 E13
Etzatlán, Mexico 118 C4
Etzná, Mexico 119 D6
Eu, France 18 B8
Euboea = Évvoia, Greece 38 C6
Eucla, Australia 93 F4
Euclid, U.S.A. 110 E3
Eudora, U.S.A. 113 J9
Eufaula, Ala., U.S.A. 109 K3
Eufaula, Okla., U.S.A. 113 H7
Eufaula L., U.S.A. 113 H7
Eugene, U.S.A. 114 E2
Eulo, Australia 95 D4
Eunice, La., U.S.A. 113 K8
Eunice, N. Mex., U.S.A. 113 J3
Eupen, Belgium 17 D6
Euphrates = Furāt, Nahr al →, Asia 70 D5
Eure □, France 18 C8
Eure →, France 18 C8
Eure-et-Loir □, France 18 D8
Eureka, Canada 4 B3
Eureka, Calif., U.S.A. 114 F1
Eureka, Kans., U.S.A. 113 G6
Eureka, Mont., U.S.A. 114 B6
Eureka, Nev., U.S.A. 114 G5
Eureka, S. Dak., U.S.A. 112 C5
Eureka, Mt., Australia 93 E3
Europa, Île, Ind. Oc. 85 J8
Europa, Picos de, Spain 34 B6
Europa, Pta. de, Gib. 35 J5
Europe 6 E10
Europoort, Neths. 17 C4
Euskirchen, Germany 24 E2
Eustis, U.S.A. 109 L5
Eutin, Germany 24 A6
Eutsuk L., Canada 104 C3
Evale, Angola 88 B2
Evans, U.S.A. 112 E2
Evans, L., Canada 102 B4
Evans City, U.S.A. 110 F4
Evans Head, Australia 95 D5

Evans Mills, U.S.A. 111 B9
Evansburg, Canada 104 C5
Evanston, Ill., U.S.A. 108 E2
Evanston, Wyo., U.S.A. 114 F8
Evansville, U.S.A. 108 G2
Évaux-les-Bains, France 19 F9
Evaz, Iran 71 E7
Evciler, Afyon, Turkey 39 C11
Evciler, Çanakkale, Turkey 39 B8
Eveleth, U.S.A. 112 B8
Evensk, Russia 51 C16
Everard, L., Australia 95 E2
Everard Ranges, Australia 93 E5
Everest, Mt., Nepal 69 E12
Everett, Pa., U.S.A. 110 F6
Everett, Wash., U.S.A. 116 C4
Everglades, The, U.S.A. 109 N5
Everglades City, U.S.A. 109 N5
Everglades National Park, U.S.A. 109 N5
Evergreen, Ala., U.S.A. 109 K2
Evergreen, Mont., U.S.A. 114 B6
Everöd, Sweden 11 J8
Evertsberg, Sweden 10 C7
Evesham, U.K. 13 E6
Évian-les-Bains, France 19 F13
Évinos →, Greece 38 C3
Évisa, France 21 F12
Evje, Norway 9 G12
Évora, Portugal 35 G3
Évora □, Portugal 35 G3
Evowghlī, Iran 70 B5
Évreux, France 18 C8
Evritanía □, Greece 38 B3
Évron, France 18 D6
Évros □, Greece 41 E10
Évros →, Greece 72 B2
Evrótas →, Greece 38 E4
Évry, France 19 D9
Évvoia, Greece 38 C6
Évvoia □, Greece 38 C5
Evxinoúpolis, Greece 38 B4
Ewe, L., U.K. 14 D3
Ewing, U.S.A. 112 D5
Ewo, Congo 84 E2
Exaltación, Bolivia 124 F5
Excelsior Springs, U.S.A. 112 F7
Excideuil, France 20 C5
Exe →, U.K. 13 G4
Exeter, Canada 110 C3
Exeter, U.K. 13 G4
Exeter, Calif., U.S.A. 116 J7
Exeter, N.H., U.S.A. 111 D14
Exmoor, U.K. 13 F4
Exmouth, Australia 92 D1
Exmouth, U.K. 13 G4
Exmouth G., Australia 92 D1
Expedition Ra., Australia 94 C4
Extremadura □, Spain 35 F4
Exuma Sound, Bahamas 120 B4
Eyasi, L., Tanzania 86 C4
Eye Pen., U.K. 14 C2
Eyemouth, U.K. 14 F6
Eygurande, France 19 G9
Eyjafjörður, Iceland 8 C4
Eymet, France 20 D4
Eymoutiers, France 20 C5
Eynesil, Turkey 73 B8
Eyre (North), L., Australia 95 D2
Eyre (South), L., Australia 95 D2
Eyre Mts., N.Z. 91 L2
Eyre Pen., Australia 95 E2
Eysturoy, Færoe Is. 8 E9
Eyvānkī, Iran 71 C6
Ez Zeidab, Sudan 80 D3
Ezcaray, Spain 32 C1
Ežerėlis, Lithuania 44 D10
Ezhou, China 59 B10
Ezine, Turkey 39 B8
Ezouza →, Cyprus 36 E11

F

F.Y.R.O.M. = Macedonia ■, Europe 40 E5
Fabala, Guinea 82 D3
Fabens, U.S.A. 115 L10
Fabero, Spain 34 C4
Fåborg, Denmark 11 J4
Fabriano, Italy 29 E9
Făcăeni, Romania 43 F12
Fachi, Niger 79 E8
Fada, Chad 79 E10
Fada-n-Gourma, Burkina Faso 83 C5
Fadd, Hungary 42 D3
Faddeyevskiy, Ostrov, Russia 51 B15
Faddor, Sudan 81 F3
Fadghāmī, Syria 70 C4
Fadlab, Sudan 80 D3
Faenza, Italy 29 D8
Færoe Is. = Føroyar, Atl. Oc. 8 F9
Fafa, Mali 83 B5
Fafe, Portugal 34 D2
Fagam, Nigeria 83 C7
Făgăras, Romania 43 E9
Făgăras, Munţii, Romania 43 E9
Fågelmara, Sweden 11 H9
Fagerhult, Sweden 11 G9
Fagersta, Sweden 10 D9
Făget, Romania 42 E7
Făget, Munţii, Romania 43 C8
Fagnano, L., Argentina 128 G3
Fagnières, France 19 D11
Faguibine, L., Mali 82 B4
Fahlīān, Iran 71 D6
Fahraj, Kermān, Iran 71 D8
Fahraj, Yazd, Iran 71 D7
Fai Tsi Long Archipelago, Vietnam 58 G6
Faial, Madeira 37 D3
Fair Haven, U.S.A. 108 D9
Fair Hd., U.K. 15 A5
Fair Oaks, U.S.A. 116 G5
Fairbanks, U.S.A. 100 B5
Fairbury, U.S.A. 112 E6
Fairfax, U.S.A. 111 B11
Fairfield, Ala., U.S.A. 109 J2
Fairfield, Calif., U.S.A. 116 G4
Fairfield, Conn., U.S.A. 111 E11
Fairfield, Idaho, U.S.A. 114 E6
Fairfield, Ill., U.S.A. 108 F1
Fairfield, Iowa, U.S.A. 112 E9
Fairfield, Tex., U.S.A. 113 K7
Fairford, Canada 105 C9
Fairhope, U.S.A. 109 K2
Fairlie, N.Z. 91 L3
Fairmead, U.S.A. 116 H6
Fairmont, Minn., U.S.A. 112 D7
Fairmont, W. Va., U.S.A. 108 F5
Fairmont, Calif., U.S.A. 117 L8
Fairmount, N.Y., U.S.A. 111 C8
Fairplay, U.S.A. 115 G11
Fairport, U.S.A. 110 C7
Fairport Harbor, U.S.A. 110 E3
Fairview, Canada 104 B5
Fairview, Mont., U.S.A. 112 B2
Fairview, Okla., U.S.A. 113 G5
Fairweather, Mt., U.S.A. 104 B1
Faisalabad, Pakistan 68 D5
Faith, U.S.A. 112 C3
Faizabad, India 69 F10
Fajardo, Puerto Rico 121 C6
Fajr, W. →, Si. Arabia 70 D3
Fakenham, U.K. 12 E8
Fåker, Sweden 10 A8
Fakfak, Indonesia 63 E8
Fakiya, Bulgaria 41 D11
Fakobli, Ivory C. 82 D3
Fakse, Denmark 11 J6
Fakse Bugt, Denmark 11 J6
Fakse Ladeplads, Denmark 11 J6
Faku, China 57 C12
Falaba, S. Leone 82 D2
Falaise, France 18 D6
Falaise, Mui, Vietnam 64 C5
Falakrón Óros, Greece 40 E7
Falam, Burma 67 H18
Falces, Spain 32 C3
Fălciu, Romania 43 D13
Falcó, C. des, Spain 37 C7
Falcón, Presa, Mexico 119 B5
Falcon Lake, Canada 105 D9
Falcon Reservoir, U.S.A. 113 M5
Falconara Marittima, Italy 29 E10
Falcone, C. del, Italy 30 B1
Falconer, U.S.A. 110 D5
Faléa, Mali 82 C2
Falémé →, Senegal 82 C2
Falerum, Sweden 11 F10
Faleshty = Făleşti, Moldova 43 C12
Făleşti, Moldova 43 C12
Falfurrias, U.S.A. 113 M5
Falher, Canada 104 B5
Falirakí, Greece 36 C10
Falkenberg, Germany 24 D9
Falkenberg, Sweden 11 H6
Falkensee, Germany 24 C9
Falkirk, U.K. 14 F5
Falkirk □, U.K. 14 F5
Falkland, U.K. 14 E5
Falkland Is. □, Atl. Oc. 128 G5
Falkland Sd., Falk. Is. 128 G5
Falkonéra, Greece 38 E5
Falköping, Sweden 11 F7
Fall River, U.S.A. 111 E13
Fallbrook, U.S.A. 117 M9
Fallon, U.S.A. 114 G4
Falls City, U.S.A. 112 E7
Falls Creek, U.S.A. 110 E6
Falmouth, Jamaica 120 C4
Falmouth, U.K. 13 G2
Falmouth, U.S.A. 111 E14
Falsa, Pta., Mexico 118 B1
False B., S. Africa 88 E2
Falso, C., Honduras 120 C3
Falster, Denmark 11 K5
Falsterbo, Sweden 9 J15
Fălticeni, Romania 43 C11
Falun, Sweden 10 D9
Famagusta, Cyprus 36 D12
Famagusta Bay, Cyprus 36 D13
Famalé, Niger 78 F6
Famatina, Sierra de, Argentina 126 B2
Family L., Canada 105 C9
Famoso, U.S.A. 117 K7
Fan Xian, China 56 G8
Fana, Mali 82 C3
Fanad Hd., Ireland 15 A4
Fanárion, Greece 38 B3
Fandriana, Madag. 89 C8
Fang, Thailand 58 H2
Fang Xian, China 59 A8
Fangaga, Sudan 80 D4
Fangak, Sudan 81 F3
Fangchang, China 59 B12
Fangcheng, China 56 H7
Fangchenggang, China 58 G7
Fangliao, Taiwan 59 F13
Fangshan, China 56 E6
Fangzi, China 57 F10
Fani i Madh →, Albania 40 E4
Fanjakana, Madag. 89 C8
Fanjiatun, China 57 C13
Fannich, L., U.K. 14 D4
Fannūj, Iran 71 E8
Fanø, Denmark 11 J2
Fano, Italy 29 E10
Fanshi, China 56 E7
Fao = Al Fāw, Iraq 71 D6
Faqirwali, Pakistan 68 E5
Fâqûs, Egypt 80 H7
Fara in Sabina, Italy 29 F9
Faradje, Dem. Rep. of the Congo 86 B2
Farafangana, Madag. 89 C8
Farâfra, El Wâhât el-, Egypt 80 B2
Farāh, Afghan. 66 C3
Farāh □, Afghan. 66 C3
Farahalana, Madag. 89 A9
Faraid, Gebel, Egypt 80 C4
Farako, Ivory C. 82 D4
Faramana, Burkina Faso 82 C4
Faranah, Guinea 82 C2
Farasān, Jazā'ir, Si. Arabia 74 D3
Farasan Is. = Farasān, Jazā'ir, Si. Arabia 74 D3
Faratsiho, Madag. 89 B8
Fardes →, Spain 35 H7
Fareham, U.K. 13 G6
Farewell, C., N.Z. 91 J4
Farewell C. = Nunap Isua, Greenland 101 C15
Färgelanda, Sweden 11 F5
Farghona, Uzbekistan 50 E8
Fargo, U.S.A. 112 B6
Fār'iah, W. al →, West Bank 75 C4
Faribault, U.S.A. 112 C8
Faridabad, India 68 E6
Faridkot, India 68 D6
Faridpur, Bangla. 69 H13
Faridpur, India 69 E8
Färila, Sweden 10 C9
Farim, Guinea-Biss. 82 C1
Farīmān, Iran 71 C8
Farina, Australia 95 E2
Fariones, Pta., Canary Is. 37 E6
Fâriskûr, Egypt 80 H7
Färjestaden, Sweden 11 H10
Farkadhón, Greece 38 B4
Farmakonisi, Greece 39 D9
Farmerville, U.S.A. 113 J8
Farmingdale, U.S.A. 111 F10
Farmington, Canada 104 B4
Farmington, Calif., U.S.A. 116 H6
Farmington, Maine, U.S.A. 109 C10
Farmington, Mo., U.S.A. 113 G9
Farmington, N.H., U.S.A. 111 C13
Farmington, N. Mex., U.S.A. 115 H9
Farmington, Utah, U.S.A. 114 F8
Farmington →, U.S.A. 111 E12
Farmville, U.S.A. 108 G6
Färnäs, Sweden 10 D8
Farne Is., U.K. 12 B6
Farnham, Canada 111 A12
Farnham, Mt., Canada 104 C5
Faro, Brazil 125 D7
Faro, Canada 100 B6
Faro, Portugal 35 H3
Fårö, Sweden 9 H18
Faro □, Portugal 35 H2
Fårösund, Sweden 11 G13
Farquhar, C., Australia 93 D1
Farrars Cr. →, Australia 94 D3
Farrāshband, Iran 71 D7
Farrell, U.S.A. 110 E4
Farrokhī, Iran 71 C8
Farruch, C. = Ferrutx, C., Spain 37 B10
Fārs □, Iran 71 D7
Fársala, Greece 38 B4
Farsø, Denmark 11 H3
Farson, U.S.A. 114 E9
Farsund, Norway 9 G12
Fartak, Râs, Si. Arabia 70 D2
Fartak, Ra's, Yemen 74 D5
Fârţăneşti, Romania 43 E12
Fartura, Serra da, Brazil 127 B5
Faru, Nigeria 83 C6
Fārūj, Iran 71 B8
Fårup, Denmark 11 H3
Farvel, Kap = Nunap Isua, Greenland 101 C15
Farwell, U.S.A. 113 H3
Fasā, Iran 71 D7
Fasano, Italy 31 B10
Fashoda, Sudan 81 F3
Fassa, Mali 82 C3
Fastiv, Ukraine 47 G5
Fastov = Fastiv, Ukraine 47 G5
Fatagar, Tanjung, Indonesia 63 E8
Fatehabad, Haryana, India 68 E6
Fatehabad, Ut. P., India 68 F8
Fatehgarh, India 69 F8
Fatehpur, Bihar, India 69 G11
Fatehpur, Raj., India 68 F6
Fatehpur, Ut. P., India 69 G9
Fatehpur, Ut. P., India 69 F9
Fatehpur Sikri, India 68 F6
Fatesh, Russia 47 F8
Fathai, Sudan 81 F3
Fatick, Senegal 82 C1
Fatima, Canada 103 C7
Fátima, Portugal 35 F2
Fatoya, Guinea 82 C3
Fatsa, Turkey 72 B7
Faucille, Col de la, France 19 F13
Faulkton, U.S.A. 112 C5
Faulquemont, France 19 C13
Faure I., Australia 93 E1
Făurei, Romania 43 E12
Fauresmith, S. Africa 88 D4
Fauske, Norway 8 C16
Favara, Italy 30 E6
Favàritx, C. de, Spain 37 B11
Faverges, France 21 C10
Favignana, Italy 30 E5
Favignana, I., Italy 30 E5
Fawcett, Pt., Australia 92 B5
Fawn →, Canada 102 A2
Fawnskin, U.S.A. 117 L10
Faxaflói, Iceland 8 D2
Faxälven →, Sweden 10 A10
Faya-Largeau, Chad 79 E9
Fayd, Si. Arabia 70 E4
Fayence, France 21 E10
Fayette, Ala., U.S.A. 109 J2
Fayette, Mo., U.S.A. 112 F8
Fayetteville, Ark., U.S.A. 113 G7
Fayetteville, N.C., U.S.A. 109 H6
Fayetteville, Tenn., U.S.A. 109 H2
Fayied, Egypt 80 H8
Fayón, Spain 32 D5
Fazilka, India 68 D6
Fazilpur, Pakistan 68 E4
Fdérik, Mauritania 78 D3
Feale →, Ireland 15 D2
Fear, C., U.S.A. 109 J7
Feather →, U.S.A. 114 G3
Feather Falls, U.S.A. 116 F5
Featherston, N.Z. 91 J5
Featherstone, Zimbabwe 87 F3
Fécamp, France 18 C7
Fedala = Mohammedia, Morocco 78 B4
Federación, Argentina 126 C4
Féderal, Argentina 128 C5
Federal Capital Terr. □, Nigeria 83 D6
Federal Way, U.S.A. 116 C4
Fedeshkūh, Iran 71 D7
Fehérgyarmat, Hungary 42 C7
Fehmarn, Germany 24 A7
Fehmarn Bælt, Europe 11 K5
Fehmarn Belt = Fehmarn Bælt, Europe 11 K5
Fei Xian, China 57 G9
Feijó, Brazil 124 E4
Feilding, N.Z. 91 J5
Feira de Santana, Brazil 125 F11
Feixi, China 59 B11
Feixiang, China 56 F8
Fejér □, Hungary 42 C3
Fejø, Denmark 11 K5
Feke, Turkey 72 D6
Fekete →, Hungary 42 E3
Felanitx, Spain 37 B10
Feldbach, Austria 26 E8
Feldberg, Baden-W., Germany 25 H3
Feldberg, Mecklenburg-Vorpommern, Germany 24 B9
Feldkirch, Austria 26 D2
Feldkirchen, Austria 26 E7
Felipe Carrillo Puerto, Mexico 119 D7
Felixburg, Zimbabwe 89 B5
Felixstowe, U.K. 13 F9
Felletin, France 20 C6
Fellingsbro, Sweden 10 E9
Felton, U.S.A. 116 H4
Feltre, Italy 29 B8
Femer Bælt = Fehmarn Bælt, Europe 11 K5
Femø, Denmark 11 K5
Femunden, Norway 9 E14
Fen He →, China 56 G6
Fene, Spain 34 B2
Fenelon Falls, Canada 110 B6
Fener Burnu, Turkey 39 E9
Feneroa, Ethiopia 81 E4
Feng Xian, Jiangsu, China 56 G9
Feng Xian, Shaanxi, China 56 H4
Fengári, Greece 41 F9
Fengcheng, Jiangxi, China 59 C10
Fengcheng, Liaoning, China 57 D13
Fengfeng, China 56 F8
Fenggang, China 58 D6
Fenghua, China 59 C13
Fenghuang, China 58 D7
Fengkai, China 59 F8
Fengkang, Taiwan 59 F13
Fengle, China 59 B9
Fenglin, Taiwan 59 F13
Fengning, China 56 D9
Fengqing, China 58 E2
Fengqiu, China 56 G8
Fengrun, China 57 E10
Fengshan, Guangxi Zhuangzu, China 58 E7
Fengshan, Guangxi Zhuangzu, China 58 E6
Fengshan, Taiwan 59 F13
Fengshun, China 59 F11
Fengtai, Anhui, China 59 A11
Fengtai, Beijing, China 56 E9
Fengxian, China 59 B13
Fengxiang, China 56 G4
Fengxin, China 59 C10
Fengyang, China 57 H9
Fengyi, China 58 E3
Fengyüan, Taiwan 59 E13
Fengzhen, China 56 D7
Feno, C. de, France 21 G12
Fenoarivo, Fianarantsoa, Madag. 89 C8
Fenoarivo, Fianarantsoa, Madag. 89 C8
Fenoarivo Afovoany, Madag. 89 B8
Fenoarivo Atsinanana, Madag. 89 B8
Fens, The, U.K. 12 E7
Fensmark, Denmark 11 J5
Fenton, U.S.A. 108 D4
Fenxi, China 56 F6
Fenyang, China 56 F6
Fenyi, China 59 D10
Feodosiya, Ukraine 47 K8
Ferdows, Iran 71 C8
Fère-Champenoise, France 19 D10
Fère-en-Tardenois, France 19 C10
Ferentino, Italy 29 G10
Ferfer, Somali Rep. 74 F4
Fergana = Farghona, Uzbekistan 50 E8
Fergus, Canada 110 C4
Fergus Falls, U.S.A. 112 B6
Feričanci, Croatia 42 E2
Ferkéssédougou, Ivory C. 82 D3
Ferlach, Austria 26 E7
Ferland, Canada 102 B2
Ferlo, Vallée du, Senegal 82 B2
Fermanagh □, U.K. 15 B4
Fermo, Italy 29 E10
Fermont, Canada 103 B6
Fermoselle, Spain 34 D4
Fermoy, Ireland 15 D3
Fernán Nuñéz, Spain 35 H6
Fernández, Argentina 126 B3
Fernandina Beach, U.S.A. 109 K5
Fernando de Noronha, Brazil 125 D12
Fernando Póo = Bioko, Eq. Guin. 83 E6
Ferndale, U.S.A. 116 B4
Fernie, Canada 104 D5
Fernlees, Australia 94 C4
Fernley, U.S.A. 114 G4
Ferozepore = Firozpur, India 68 D6
Férrai, Greece 41 F10
Ferrandina, Italy 31 B9
Ferrara, Italy 29 D8
Ferrato, C., Italy 30 C2
Ferreira do Alentejo, Portugal 35 G2
Ferreñafe, Peru 124 E3
Ferrerías, Spain 37 B11
Ferret, C., France 20 D2
Ferrette, France 19 E14
Ferriday, U.S.A. 113 K9
Ferriere, Italy 28 D6
Ferrières, France 19 D9
Ferro, Capo, Italy 30 A2
Ferrol, Spain 34 B2
Ferron, U.S.A. 115 G8
Ferrutx, C., Spain 37 B10
Ferryland, Canada 103 C9
Fertile, U.S.A. 112 B6
Fertőszentmiklós, Hungary 42 C1
Fès, Morocco 78 B5
Fessenden, U.S.A. 112 B5
Festus, U.S.A. 112 F9
Feté Bowé, Senegal 82 C2
Feteşti, Romania 43 F12
Fethiye, Turkey 39 E11
Fethiye Körfezi, Turkey 39 E10
Fetlar, U.K. 14 A8
Feuilles →, Canada 101 C12
Feurs, France 21 C8
Fez = Fès, Morocco 78 B5
Fezzan, Libya 79 C8
Fiambalá, Argentina 126 B2
Fianarantsoa, Madag. 89 C8
Fianarantsoa □, Madag. 89 B8
Fiche, Ethiopia 81 F4
Fichtelgebirge, Germany 25 E7
Ficksburg, S. Africa 89 D4
Fidenza, Italy 28 D7
Fiditi, Nigeria 83 D5
Field →, Australia 94 C2
Field I., Australia 92 B5
Fieni, Romania 43 E10
Fier, Albania 40 F3
Fierzë, Albania 40 D4
Fife □, U.K. 14 E5
Fife Ness, U.K. 14 E6
Fifth Cataract, Sudan 80 D3
Figari, France 21 G13
Figeac, France 20 D6
Figeholm, Sweden 11 G10
Figline Valdarno, Italy 29 E8
Figtree, Zimbabwe 87 G2
Figueira Castelo Rodrigo, Portugal 34 E4
Figueira da Foz, Portugal 34 E2
Figueiró dos Vinhos, Portugal 34 F2
Figueres, Spain 32 C7
Figuig, Morocco 78 B5
Fihaonana, Madag. 89 B8
Fiherenana, Madag. 89 B8
Fiherenana →, Madag. 89 C7
Fiji ■, Pac. Oc. 91 C8
Fik, Ethiopia 81 F5
Fika, Nigeria 83 C7
Filabres, Sierra de los, Spain 35 H8
Filabusi, Zimbabwe 89 C4
Filadélfia, Italy 31 D9
Fil'akovo, Slovak Rep. 27 C12
Filey, U.K. 12 C7
Filey B., U.K. 12 C7
Filfla, Malta 36 D1
Filiaşi, Romania 43 F8
Filiátes, Greece 38 B2
Filiatrá, Greece 38 D3
Filicudi, Italy 31 D7
Filingué, Niger 83 C5
Filiourí →, Greece 41 E9
Filipstad, Sweden 10 E8
Filisur, Switz. 25 J5

Fillmore, *Calif., U.S.A.* 117 L8
Fillmore, *Utah, U.S.A.* 115 G7
Filótion, *Greece* 39 D7
Filottrano, *Italy* 29 E10
Filtu, *Ethiopia* 81 F5
Finale Emília, *Italy* 29 D8
Finale Lígure, *Italy* 28 D5
Fiñana, *Spain* 35 H8
Finch, *Canada* 111 A9
Findhorn →, *U.K.* 14 D5
Findlay, *U.S.A.* 108 E4
Finger L., *Canada* 102 B1
Finger Lakes, *U.S.A.* 111 D8
Fíngoè, *Mozam.* 87 E3
Finike, *Turkey* 39 E12
Finike Körfezi, *Turkey* 39 E12
Finiq, *Albania* 40 G4
Finistère □, *France* 18 D3
Finisterre = Fisterra, *Spain* 34 C1
Finisterre, C. = Fisterra, C., *Spain* 34 C1
Finke, *Australia* 94 D1
Finland ■, *Europe* 8 E22
Finland, G. of, *Europe* 9 G21
Finlay →, *Canada* 104 B3
Finley, *U.S.A.* 112 B6
Finn →, *Ireland* 15 B4
Finnerödja, *Sweden* 11 F8
Finnigan, Mt., *Australia* 94 B4
Finniss, C., *Australia* 95 E1
Finnmark, *Norway* 8 B20
Finnsnes, *Norway* 8 B18
Finspång, *Sweden* 11 F9
Finsteraarhorn, *Switz.* 25 J4
Finsterwalde, *Germany* 24 D9
Fiora →, *Italy* 29 F8
Fiorenzuola d'Arda, *Italy* 28 D6
Fiq, *Syria* 75 C4
Firat = Furāt, Nahr al →, *Asia* 70 D5
Firebag →, *Canada* 105 B6
Firebaugh, *U.S.A.* 116 J6
Firedrake L., *Canada* 105 A8
Firenze, *Italy* 29 E8
Firenzuola, *Italy* 29 D8
Firk →, *Iraq* 70 D5
Firmi, *France* 20 D6
Firminy, *France* 21 C8
Firozabad, *India* 69 F8
Firozpur, *India* 68 D6
Firozpur-Jhirka, *India* 68 F7
Fīrūzābād, *Iran* 71 D7
Fīrūzkūh, *Iran* 71 C7
Firvale, *Canada* 104 C3
Fish →, *Namibia* 88 D2
Fish →, *S. Africa* 88 E3
Fish River Canyon, *Namibia* 88 D2
Fisher, *Australia* 93 F5
Fisher B., *Canada* 105 C9
Fishers I., *U.S.A.* 111 E13
Fishguard, *U.K.* 13 E3
Fishing L., *Canada* 105 C9
Fishkill, *U.S.A.* 111 E11
Fismes, *France* 19 C10
Fisterra, *Spain* 34 C1
Fisterra, C., *Spain* 34 C1
Fitchburg, *U.S.A.* 111 D13
Fitz Roy, *Argentina* 128 F3
Fitzgerald, *Canada* 104 B6
Fitzgerald, *U.S.A.* 109 K4
Fitzmaurice →, *Australia* 92 B5
Fitzroy →, *Queens., Australia* 94 C5
Fitzroy →, *W. Austral., Australia* 92 C3
Fitzroy, Mte., *Argentina* 128 F2
Fitzroy Crossing, *Australia* 92 C4
Fitzwilliam I., *Canada* 110 A3
Fiuggi, *Italy* 29 G10
Fiume = Rijeka, *Croatia* 29 C11
Five Points, *U.S.A.* 116 J6
Fivizzano, *Italy* 28 D7
Fizi, *Dem. Rep. of the Congo* 86 C2
Fjällbacka, *Sweden* 11 F5
Fjärdhundra, *Sweden* 10 E10
Fjellerup, *Denmark* 11 H4
Fjerritslev, *Denmark* 11 G3
Fjugesta, *Sweden* 10 E8
Flagstaff, *U.S.A.* 115 J8
Flagstaff L., *U.S.A.* 109 C10
Flaherty I., *Canada* 102 A4
Flåm, *Norway* 9 F12
Flambeau →, *U.S.A.* 112 C9
Flamborough Hd., *U.K.* 12 C7
Fläming, *Germany* 24 C8
Flaming Gorge Reservoir, *U.S.A.* 114 F9
Flamingo, Teluk, *Indonesia* 63 F9
Flanders = Flandre, *Europe* 19 B9
Flandre, *Europe* 19 B9
Flandre Occidentale = West-Vlaanderen □, *Belgium* 17 D2
Flandre Orientale = Oost-Vlaanderen □, *Belgium* 17 C3
Flandreau, *U.S.A.* 112 C6
Flanigan, *U.S.A.* 116 E7
Flannan Is., *U.K.* 14 C1
Flåsjön, *Sweden* 8 D16
Flat →, *Canada* 104 A3
Flathead L., *U.S.A.* 114 C7
Flattery, C., *Australia* 94 A4
Flattery, C., *U.S.A.* 116 B2
Flatwoods, *U.S.A.* 108 F4
Fleetwood, *U.K.* 12 D4
Fleetwood, *U.S.A.* 111 F9
Flekkefjord, *Norway* 9 G12
Flemington, *U.S.A.* 110 E7
Flen, *Sweden* 10 E10
Flensburg, *Germany* 24 A5
Flers, *France* 18 D6
Flesherton, *Canada* 110 B4
Flesko, Tanjung, *Indonesia* 63 D6
Fleurance, *France* 20 E4
Fleurier, *Switz.* 25 J2
Fleurieu Pen., *Australia* 95 F2
Flevoland □, *Neths.* 17 B5
Flin Flon, *Canada* 105 C8
Flinders →, *Australia* 94 B3
Flinders B., *Australia* 93 F2
Flinders Group, *Australia* 94 A3
Flinders I., *S. Austral., Australia* 95 E1
Flinders I., *Tas., Australia* 94 G4
Flinders Reefs, *Australia* 94 B4
Flint, *U.K.* 12 D4
Flint, *U.S.A.* 108 D4
Flint →, *U.S.A.* 109 K3
Flint I., *Kiribati* 97 J12
Flintshire □, *U.K.* 12 D4
Fliseryd, *Sweden* 11 G10
Flix, *Spain* 32 D5
Flixecourt, *France* 19 B9
Floby, *Sweden* 11 F7
Floda, *Sweden* 11 G6
Flodden, *U.K.* 12 B5
Flogny-la-Chapelle, *France* 19 E10
Floodwood, *U.S.A.* 112 B8
Flora, *U.S.A.* 108 F1
Florac, *France* 20 D7
Florala, *U.S.A.* 109 K2
Florence = Firenze, *Italy* 29 E8
Florence, *Ala., U.S.A.* 109 H2
Florence, *Ariz., U.S.A.* 115 K8
Florence, *Colo., U.S.A.* 112 F2
Florence, *Oreg., U.S.A.* 114 E1
Florence, *S.C., U.S.A.* 109 H6
Florence, L., *Australia* 95 D2
Florencia, *Colombia* 124 C3
Florennes, *Belgium* 17 D4
Florensac, *France* 20 E7
Florenville, *Belgium* 17 E5
Flores, *Guatemala* 120 C2
Flores, *Indonesia* 63 F6
Flores I., *Canada* 104 D3
Flores Sea, *Indonesia* 63 F6
Floreşti, *Moldova* 43 C13
Floresville, *U.S.A.* 113 L5
Floriano, *Brazil* 125 E10
Florianópolis, *Brazil* 127 B6
Florida, *Cuba* 120 B4
Florida, *Uruguay* 127 C4
Florida □, *U.S.A.* 109 L5
Florida, Straits of, *U.S.A.* 120 B4
Florida B., *U.S.A.* 120 B3
Florida Keys, *U.S.A.* 109 N5
Florídia, *Italy* 31 E8
Flórina, *Greece* 40 F5
Flórina □, *Greece* 40 F5
Florø, *Norway* 9 F11
Flower Station, *Canada* 111 A8
Flowerpot I., *Canada* 110 A3
Floydada, *U.S.A.* 113 J4
Fluk, *Indonesia* 63 E7
Flúmen →, *Spain* 32 D4
Flumendosa →, *Italy* 30 C2
Fluminimaggiore, *Italy* 30 C1
Flushing = Vlissingen, *Neths.* 17 C3
Fluviá →, *Spain* 32 C8
Flying Fish, C., *Antarctica* 5 D15
Foam Lake, *Canada* 105 C8
Foča, *Bos.-H.* 40 C2
Foça, *Turkey* 39 C8
Focşani, *Romania* 43 E12
Fodécontéa, *Guinea* 82 C2
Fogang, *China* 59 F9
Fóggia, *Italy* 31 A8
Foggo, *Nigeria* 83 C6
Foglia →, *Italy* 29 E9
Fogo, *Canada* 103 C9
Fogo I., *Canada* 103 C9
Fohnsdorf, *Austria* 26 D7
Föhr, *Germany* 24 A4
Foia, *Portugal* 35 H2
Foix, *France* 20 E5
Fojnica, *Bos.-H.* 42 G2
Fokino, *Russia* 46 F8
Fokís □, *Greece* 38 C4
Fokku, *Nigeria* 83 C5
Folda, *Nord-Trøndelag, Norway* 8 D14
Folda, *Nordland, Norway* 8 C16
Főldeák, *Hungary* 42 D5
Folégandros, *Greece* 38 E6
Foley, *Botswana* 88 C4
Foley, *U.S.A.* 109 K2
Foleyet, *Canada* 102 C3
Folgefonni, *Norway* 9 F12
Foligno, *Italy* 29 F9
Folkestone, *U.K.* 13 F9
Folkston, *U.S.A.* 109 K5
Follansbee, *U.S.A.* 110 F4
Follónica, *Italy* 28 F7
Follónica, G. di, *Italy* 28 F7
Folsom L., *U.S.A.* 116 G5
Folteşti, *Romania* 43 E13
Fond-du-Lac, *Canada* 105 B7
Fond du Lac, *U.S.A.* 112 D10
Fond-du-Lac →, *Canada* 105 B7
Fonda, *U.S.A.* 111 D10
Fondi, *Italy* 30 A6
Fonfría, *Spain* 34 D4
Fongafale, *Tuvalu* 96 H9
Fonni, *Italy* 30 B2
Fonsagrada = A Fonsagrada, *Spain* 34 B3
Fonseca, G. de, *Cent. Amer.* 120 D2
Font-Romeu, *France* 20 F5
Fontaine-Française, *France* 19 E12
Fontainebleau, *France* 19 D9
Fontana, *U.S.A.* 117 L9
Fontas →, *Canada* 104 B4
Fonte Boa, *Brazil* 124 D5
Fontem, *Cameroon* 83 D6
Fontenay-le-Comte, *France* 20 B3
Fontenelle Reservoir, *U.S.A.* 114 E8
Fontur, *Iceland* 8 C6
Fonyód, *Hungary* 42 D2
Foochow = Fuzhou, *China* 59 D12
Foping, *China* 56 H5
Forbach, *France* 19 C13
Forbesganj, *India* 69 F12
Forcados, *Nigeria* 83 D6
Forcados →, *Nigeria* 83 D6
Forcalquier, *France* 21 E9
Forchheim, *Germany* 25 F7
Ford City, *Calif., U.S.A.* 117 K7
Ford City, *Pa., U.S.A.* 110 F5
Førde, *Norway* 9 F11
Ford's Bridge, *Australia* 95 D4
Fordyce, *U.S.A.* 113 J8
Forécariah, *Guinea* 82 D2
Forel, Mt., *Greenland* 4 C6
Foremost, *Canada* 104 D6
Forest, *Canada* 110 C3
Forest, *U.S.A.* 113 J10
Forest City, *Iowa, U.S.A.* 112 D8
Forest City, *N.C., U.S.A.* 109 H5
Forest City, *Pa., U.S.A.* 111 E9
Forest Grove, *U.S.A.* 116 E3
Forestburg, *Canada* 104 C6
Foresthill, *U.S.A.* 116 F6
Forestier Pen., *Australia* 94 G4
Forestville, *Canada* 103 C6
Forestville, *Calif., U.S.A.* 116 G4
Forestville, *N.Y., U.S.A.* 110 D5
Forez, Mts. du, *France* 20 C7
Forfar, *U.K.* 14 E6
Forks, *U.S.A.* 116 C2
Forksville, *U.S.A.* 111 E8
Forlì, *Italy* 29 D9
Forman, *U.S.A.* 112 B6
Formazza, *Italy* 28 B5
Formby Pt., *U.K.* 12 D4
Formentera, *Spain* 37 C7
Formentor, C. de, *Spain* 37 B10
Former Yugoslav Republic of Macedonia = Macedonia ■, *Europe* 40 E5
Fórmia, *Italy* 30 A6
Formígine, *Italy* 28 D7
Formosa = Taiwan ■, *Asia* 59 F13
Formosa, *Argentina* 126 B4
Formosa, *Brazil* 125 G9
Formosa □, *Argentina* 126 B4
Formosa, Serra, *Brazil* 125 F8
Formosa Bay, *Kenya* 86 C5
Formosa Strait = Taiwan Strait, *Asia* 59 E12
Fornells, *Spain* 37 A11
Fornos de Algodres, *Portugal* 34 E3
Fornovo di Taro, *Italy* 28 D7
Føroyar, *Atl. Oc.* 8 F9
Forres, *U.K.* 14 D5
Forrest, *Australia* 93 F4
Forrest, Mt., *Australia* 93 D4
Forrest City, *U.S.A.* 113 H9
Fors, *Sweden* 10 D10
Forsayth, *Australia* 94 B3
Forshaga, *Sweden* 10 E7
Förslöv, *Sweden* 11 H6
Forsmo, *Sweden* 10 A11
Forssa, *Finland* 9 F20
Forst, *Germany* 24 D10
Forsvik, *Sweden* 11 F8
Forsyth, *U.S.A.* 114 C10
Fort Abbas, *Pakistan* 68 E5
Fort Albany, *Canada* 102 B3
Fort Ann, *U.S.A.* 111 C11
Fort Assiniboine, *Canada* 104 C6
Fort Augustus, *U.K.* 14 D4
Fort Beaufort, *S. Africa* 88 E4
Fort Benton, *U.S.A.* 114 C8
Fort Bragg, *U.S.A.* 114 G2
Fort Bridger, *U.S.A.* 114 F8
Fort Chipewyan, *Canada* 105 B6
Fort Collins, *U.S.A.* 112 E2
Fort-Coulonge, *Canada* 102 C4
Fort Covington, *U.S.A.* 111 B10
Fort Davis, *U.S.A.* 113 K3
Fort-de-France, *Martinique* 121 D7
Fort Defiance, *U.S.A.* 115 J9
Fort Dodge, *U.S.A.* 112 D7
Fort Edward, *U.S.A.* 111 C11
Fort Erie, *Canada* 110 D6
Fort Fairfield, *U.S.A.* 109 B12
Fort Frances, *Canada* 105 D10
Fort Garland, *U.S.A.* 115 H11
Fort George = Chisasibi, *Canada* 102 B4
Fort Good-Hope, *Canada* 100 B7
Fort Hancock, *U.S.A.* 115 L11
Fort Hertz = Putao, *Burma* 67 F20
Fort Hope, *Canada* 102 B2
Fort Irwin, *U.S.A.* 117 K10
Fort Kent, *U.S.A.* 109 B11
Fort Klamath, *U.S.A.* 114 E3
Fort Laramie, *U.S.A.* 112 D2
Fort Lauderdale, *U.S.A.* 109 M5
Fort Liard, *Canada* 104 A4
Fort Liberté, *Haiti* 121 C5
Fort Lupton, *U.S.A.* 112 E2
Fort Mackay, *Canada* 104 B6
Fort Macleod, *Canada* 104 D6
Fort McMurray, *Canada* 104 B6
Fort McPherson, *Canada* 100 B6
Fort Madison, *U.S.A.* 112 E9
Fort Meade, *U.S.A.* 109 M5
Fort Morgan, *U.S.A.* 112 E3
Fort Myers, *U.S.A.* 109 M5
Fort Nelson, *Canada* 104 B4
Fort Nelson →, *Canada* 104 B4
Fort Norman = Tulita, *Canada* 100 B7
Fort Payne, *U.S.A.* 109 H3
Fort Peck, *U.S.A.* 114 B10
Fort Peck Dam, *U.S.A.* 114 C10
Fort Peck L., *U.S.A.* 114 C10
Fort Pierce, *U.S.A.* 109 M5
Fort Pierre, *U.S.A.* 112 C4
Fort Pierre Bordes = Ti-n-Zaouatene, *Algeria* 83 B5
Fort Plain, *U.S.A.* 111 D10
Fort Portal, *Uganda* 86 B3
Fort Providence, *Canada* 104 A5
Fort Qu'Appelle, *Canada* 105 C8
Fort Resolution, *Canada* 104 A6
Fort Rixon, *Zimbabwe* 87 G2
Fort Ross, *U.S.A.* 116 G3
Fort Rupert = Waskaganish, *Canada* 102 B4
Fort St. James, *Canada* 104 C4
Fort St. John, *Canada* 104 B4
Fort Saskatchewan, *Canada* 104 C6
Fort Scott, *U.S.A.* 113 G7
Fort Severn, *Canada* 102 A2
Fort Shevchenko, *Kazakstan* 49 H10
Fort Simpson, *Canada* 104 A4
Fort Smith, *Canada* 104 B6
Fort Smith, *U.S.A.* 113 H7
Fort Stockton, *U.S.A.* 113 K3
Fort Sumner, *U.S.A.* 113 H2
Fort Thompson, *U.S.A.* 112 C5
Fort Valley, *U.S.A.* 109 J4
Fort Vermilion, *Canada* 104 B5
Fort Walton Beach, *U.S.A.* 109 K2
Fort Wayne, *U.S.A.* 108 E3
Fort William, *U.K.* 14 E3
Fort Worth, *U.S.A.* 113 J6
Fort Yates, *U.S.A.* 112 B4
Fort Yukon, *U.S.A.* 100 B5
Fortaleza, *Brazil* 125 D11
Forteau, *Canada* 103 B8
Fortescue →, *Australia* 92 D2
Forth →, *U.K.* 14 E5
Forth, Firth of, *U.K.* 14 E6
Fortore →, *Italy* 29 G12
Fortrose, *U.K.* 14 D4
Fortuna, *Spain* 33 G3
Fortuna, *Calif., U.S.A.* 114 F1
Fortuna, *N. Dak., U.S.A.* 112 A3
Fortune, *Canada* 103 C8
Fortune B., *Canada* 103 C8
Forūr, *Iran* 71 E7
Fos-sur-Mer, *France* 21 E8
Foshan, *China* 59 F9
Fosna, *Norway* 8 E14
Fosnavåg, *Norway* 9 E11
Foso, *Ghana* 83 D4
Fossano, *Italy* 28 D4
Fossil, *U.S.A.* 114 D3
Fossombrone, *Italy* 29 E9
Foster, *Canada* 111 A12
Foster →, *Canada* 105 B7
Fosters Ra., *Australia* 94 C1
Fostoria, *U.S.A.* 108 E4
Fotadrevo, *Madag.* 89 C8
Fouesnant, *France* 18 E2
Fougères, *France* 18 D5
Foul Pt., *Sri Lanka* 66 Q12
Foula, *U.K.* 14 A6
Foulalaba, *Mali* 82 C3
Foulness I., *U.K.* 13 F8
Foulpointe, *Madag.* 89 B8
Foulweather, C., *U.S.A.* 106 B2
Foumban, *Cameroon* 83 D7
Foumbot, *Cameroon* 83 D7
Foundiougne, *Senegal* 82 C1
Fountain, *U.S.A.* 112 F2
Fountain Springs, *U.S.A.* 117 K8
Fourchambault, *France* 19 E10
Fouriesburg, *S. Africa* 88 D4
Fourmies, *France* 19 B11
Fournás, *Greece* 38 B3
Foúrnoi, *Greece* 39 D8
Fours, *France* 19 F10
Fourth Cataract, *Sudan* 80 D3
Fouta Djalon, *Guinea* 82 C2
Foux, Cap-à-, *Haiti* 121 C5
Foveaux Str., *N.Z.* 91 M2
Fowey, *U.K.* 13 G3
Fowler, *Calif., U.S.A.* 116 J7
Fowler, *Colo., U.S.A.* 112 F3
Fowlers B., *Australia* 93 F5
Fowman, *Iran* 71 B6
Fox →, *Canada* 105 B10
Fox Creek, *Canada* 104 C5
Fox Lake, *Canada* 104 B6
Fox Valley, *Canada* 105 C7
Foxboro, *U.S.A.* 111 D13
Foxe Basin, *Canada* 101 B12
Foxe Chan., *Canada* 101 B11
Foxe Pen., *Canada* 101 B12
Foxen, *Sweden* 10 E5
Foxton, *N.Z.* 91 J5
Foyle, Lough, *U.K.* 15 A4
Foynes, *Ireland* 15 D2
Foz, *Spain* 34 B3
Foz do Cunene, *Angola* 88 B1
Foz do Iguaçu, *Brazil* 127 B5
Frackville, *U.S.A.* 111 F8
Fraga, *Spain* 32 D5
Fraile Muerto, *Uruguay* 127 C5
Framingham, *U.S.A.* 111 D13
Frampol, *Poland* 45 H9
Franca, *Brazil* 125 H9
Francavilla al Mare, *Italy* 29 F11
Francavilla Fontana, *Italy* 31 B10
France ■, *Europe* 7 F6
Frances →, *Canada* 104 A3
Frances L., *Canada* 104 A3
Franceville, *Gabon* 84 E2
Franche-Comté, *France* 19 F12
Francis Case, L., *U.S.A.* 112 D5
Francisco Beltrão, *Brazil* 127 B5
Francisco I. Madero, *Coahuila, Mexico* 118 B4
Francisco I. Madero, *Durango, Mexico* 118 C4
Francistown, *Botswana* 89 C4
Francofonte, *Italy* 31 E7
François, *Canada* 103 C8
François L., *Canada* 104 C3
Franeker, *Neths.* 17 A5
Frankado, *Djibouti* 81 E5
Frankenberg, *Germany* 24 D4
Frankenwald, *Germany* 25 E7
Frankford, *Canada* 110 B7
Frankfort, *S. Africa* 89 D4
Frankfort, *Ind., U.S.A.* 108 E2
Frankfort, *Kans., U.S.A.* 112 F6
Frankfort, *Ky., U.S.A.* 108 F3
Frankfort, *N.Y., U.S.A.* 111 C9
Frankfurt, *Brandenburg, Germany* 24 C10
Frankfurt, *Hessen, Germany* 25 E4
Fränkische Alb, *Germany* 25 F7
Fränkische Rezat →, *Germany* 25 F7
Fränkische Saale →, *Germany* 25 E5
Fränkische Schweiz, *Germany* 25 F7
Frankland →, *Australia* 93 G2
Franklin, *Ky., U.S.A.* 109 G2
Franklin, *La., U.S.A.* 113 L9
Franklin, *Mass., U.S.A.* 111 D13
Franklin, *N.H., U.S.A.* 111 C13
Franklin, *Nebr., U.S.A.* 112 E5
Franklin, *Pa., U.S.A.* 110 E5
Franklin, *Va., U.S.A.* 109 G7
Franklin, *W. Va., U.S.A.* 108 F6
Franklin B., *Canada* 100 B7
Franklin D. Roosevelt L., *U.S.A.* 114 B4
Franklin I., *Antarctica* 5 D11
Franklin L., *U.S.A.* 114 F6
Franklin Mts., *Canada* 100 B7
Franklin Str., *Canada* 100 A10
Franklinton, *U.S.A.* 113 K9
Franklinville, *U.S.A.* 110 D6
Franks Pk., *U.S.A.* 114 E9
Frånö, *Sweden* 10 B11
Fransfontein, *Namibia* 88 C2
Fränsta, *Sweden* 10 B10
Frantsa Iosifa, Zemlya, *Russia* 50 A6
Franz, *Canada* 102 C3
Franz Josef Land = Frantsa Iosifa, Zemlya, *Russia* 50 A6
Franzburg, *Germany* 24 A8
Frascati, *Italy* 29 G9
Fraser, *U.S.A.* 110 D2
Fraser →, *B.C., Canada* 104 D4
Fraser →, *Nfld., Canada* 103 A7
Fraser, Mt., *Australia* 93 E2
Fraser I., *Australia* 95 D5
Fraser Lake, *Canada* 104 C4
Fraserburg, *S. Africa* 88 E3
Fraserburgh, *U.K.* 14 D6
Fraserdale, *Canada* 102 C3
Frashër, *Albania* 40 F4
Frasne, *France* 19 F13
Frăteşti, *Romania* 43 G10
Frauenfeld, *Switz.* 25 H4
Fray Bentos, *Uruguay* 126 C4
Frechilla, *Spain* 34 C6
Fredericia, *Denmark* 11 J3
Frederick, *Md., U.S.A.* 108 F7
Frederick, *Okla., U.S.A.* 113 H5
Frederick, *S. Dak., U.S.A.* 112 C5
Fredericksburg, *Pa., U.S.A.* 111 F8
Fredericksburg, *Tex., U.S.A.* 113 K5
Fredericksburg, *Va., U.S.A.* 108 F7
Fredericktown, *Mo., U.S.A.* 113 G9
Fredericktown, *Ohio, U.S.A.* 110 F2
Frederico I. Madero, Presa, *Mexico* 118 B3
Frederico Westphalen, *Brazil* 127 B5
Fredericton, *Canada* 103 C6
Fredericton Junction, *Canada* 103 C6
Frederiksborg Amtskommune □, *Denmark* 11 J6
Frederikshåb = Paamiut, *Greenland* 4 C5
Frederikshavn, *Denmark* 11 G4
Frederikssund, *Denmark* 11 J6
Frederiksted, *U.S. Virgin Is.* 121 C7
Frederiksværk, *Denmark* 11 J6
Fredonia, *Ariz., U.S.A.* 115 H7
Fredonia, *Kans., U.S.A.* 113 G7
Fredonia, *N.Y., U.S.A.* 110 D5
Fredriksberg, *Sweden* 10 D8
Fredrikstad, *Norway* 9 G14
Free State □, *S. Africa* 88 D4
Freehold, *U.S.A.* 111 F10
Freel Peak, *U.S.A.* 116 G7
Freeland, *U.S.A.* 111 E9
Freels, C., *Canada* 103 C9
Freeman, *Calif., U.S.A.* 117 K9
Freeman, *S. Dak., U.S.A.* 112 D6
Freeport, *Bahamas* 120 A4
Freeport, *Ill., U.S.A.* 112 D10

Freeport, *N.Y., U.S.A.* 111 **F11**
Freeport, *Ohio, U.S.A.* 110 **F3**
Freeport, *Pa., U.S.A.* 110 **F5**
Freeport, *Tex., U.S.A.* 113 **L7**
Freetown, *S. Leone* 82 **D2**
Frégate, L., *Canada* 102 **B5**
Fregenal de la Sierra, *Spain* 35 **G4**
Fregene, *Italy* 29 **G9**
Fréhel, C., *France* 18 **D4**
Freiberg, *Germany* 24 **E9**
Freibourg = Fribourg, *Switz.* 25 **J3**
Freiburg, *Baden-W., Germany* 25 **H3**
Freiburg, *Niedersachsen, Germany* 24 **B5**
Freilassing, *Germany* 25 **H8**
Freire, *Chile* 128 **D2**
Freirina, *Chile* 126 **B1**
Freising, *Germany* 25 **G7**
Freistadt, *Austria* 26 **C7**
Freital, *Germany* 24 **D9**
Fréjus, *France* 21 **E10**
Fremantle, *Australia* 93 **F2**
Fremont, *Calif., U.S.A.* 116 **H4**
Fremont, *Mich., U.S.A.* 108 **D3**
Fremont, *Nebr., U.S.A.* 112 **E6**
Fremont, *Ohio, U.S.A.* 108 **E4**
Fremont →, *U.S.A.* 115 **G8**
French Camp, *U.S.A.* 116 **H5**
French Creek →, *U.S.A.* 110 **E5**
French Guiana ■, *S. Amer.* 125 **C8**
French Polynesia ■, *Pac. Oc.* 97 **K13**
Frenchman Cr. →, *N. Amer.* 114 **B10**
Frenchman Cr. →, *U.S.A.* 112 **E4**
Frenštát pod Radhoštěm, *Czech Rep.* 27 **B11**
Fresco, *Ivory C.* 82 **D3**
Fresco →, *Brazil* 125 **E8**
Freshfield, C., *Antarctica* 5 **C10**
Fresnay-sur-Sarthe, *France* 18 **D7**
Fresnillo, *Mexico* 118 **C4**
Fresno, *U.S.A.* 116 **J7**
Fresno Alhandiga, *Spain* 34 **E5**
Fresno Reservoir, *U.S.A.* 114 **B9**
Freudenstadt, *Germany* 25 **G4**
Frévent, *France* 19 **B9**
Frew →, *Australia* 94 **C2**
Frewsburg, *U.S.A.* 110 **D5**
Freycinet Pen., *Australia* 94 **G4**
Freyming-Merlebach, *France* 19 **C13**
Freyung, *Germany* 25 **G9**
Fria, *Guinea* 82 **C2**
Fria, C., *Namibia* 88 **B1**
Friant, *U.S.A.* 116 **J7**
Frías, *Argentina* 126 **B2**
Fribourg, *Switz.* 25 **J3**
Fribourg □, *Switz.* 25 **J3**
Fridafors, *Sweden* 11 **H8**
Friday Harbor, *U.S.A.* 116 **B3**
Friedberg, *Bayern, Germany* 25 **G6**
Friedberg, *Hessen, Germany* 25 **E4**
Friedens, *U.S.A.* 110 **F6**
Friedland, *Germany* 24 **B9**
Friedrichshafen, *Germany* 25 **H5**
Friedrichskoog, *Germany* 24 **A4**
Friedrichstadt, *Germany* 24 **A5**
Friendly Is. = Tonga ■, *Pac. Oc.* 91 **D11**
Friendship, *U.S.A.* 110 **D6**
Friesach, *Austria* 26 **E7**
Friesack, *Germany* 24 **C8**
Friesland □, *Neths.* 17 **A5**
Friesoythe, *Germany* 24 **B3**
Friggesund, *Sweden* 10 **C10**
Frillesås, *Sweden* 11 **G6**
Frinnaryd, *Sweden* 11 **G8**
Frio →, *U.S.A.* 113 **L5**
Frio, C., *Brazil* 122 **F6**
Friol, *Spain* 34 **B3**
Friona, *U.S.A.* 113 **H3**
Fristad, *Sweden* 11 **G6**
Fritch, *U.S.A.* 113 **H4**
Fritsla, *Sweden* 11 **G6**
Fritzlar, *Germany* 24 **D5**
Friuli-Venézia Giulia □, *Italy* 29 **B9**
Frobisher B., *Canada* 101 **B13**
Frobisher Bay = Iqaluit, *Canada* 101 **B13**
Frobisher L., *Canada* 105 **B7**
Frohavet, *Norway* 8 **E13**
Frohnleiten, *Austria* 26 **D8**
Frolovo, *Russia* 48 **F6**
Frombork, *Poland* 44 **D6**
Frome, *U.K.* 13 **F5**
Frome →, *U.K.* 13 **G5**
Frómista, *Spain* 34 **C6**
Front Range, *U.S.A.* 106 **C5**
Front Royal, *U.S.A.* 108 **F6**
Fronteira, *Portugal* 35 **F3**
Frontera, *Canary Is.* 37 **G2**
Frontera, *Mexico* 119 **D6**
Fronteras, *Mexico* 118 **A3**
Frontignan, *France* 20 **E7**
Frosinone, *Italy* 30 **A6**
Frostburg, *U.S.A.* 108 **F6**
Frostisen, *Norway* 8 **B17**
Frouard, *France* 19 **D13**
Frövi, *Sweden* 10 **E9**
Frøya, *Norway* 8 **E13**
Frumoasa, *Romania* 43 **D10**
Frunze = Bishkek, *Kyrgyzstan* 50 **E8**
Fruška Gora, *Serbia, Yug.* 42 **E4**
Frutal, *Brazil* 125 **H9**
Frutigen, *Switz.* 25 **J3**
Frýdek-Místek, *Czech Rep.* 27 **B11**
Frýdlant, *Czech Rep.* 26 **A8**
Fryeburg, *U.S.A.* 111 **B14**
Fryvaldov = Jeseník, *Czech Rep.* 27 **A10**
Fthiótis □, *Greece* 38 **C4**
Fu Jiang →, *China* 58 **C6**
Fu Xian = Wafangdian, *China* 57 **E11**
Fu Xian, *China* 56 **G5**
Fu'an, *China* 59 **D12**
Fubian, *China* 58 **B4**
Fucécchio, *Italy* 28 **E7**
Fucheng, *China* 56 **F9**
Fuchou = Fuzhou, *China* 59 **D12**
Fuchū, *Japan* 55 **G6**
Fuchuan, *China* 59 **E8**
Fuchun Jiang →, *China* 59 **B13**
Fúcino, Piana del, *Italy* 29 **F10**
Fuding, *China* 59 **D13**
Fuencaliente, *Canary Is.* 37 **F2**
Fuencaliente, *Spain* 35 **G6**
Fuencaliente, Pta., *Canary Is.* 37 **F2**
Fuengirola, *Spain* 35 **J6**
Fuenlabrada, *Spain* 34 **E7**
Fuensalida, *Spain* 34 **E6**
Fuente-Alamo, *Spain* 33 **G3**
Fuente-Álamo de Murcia, *Spain* 33 **H3**
Fuente de Cantos, *Spain* 35 **G4**
Fuente del Maestre, *Spain* 35 **G4**
Fuente el Fresno, *Spain* 35 **F7**
Fuente Obejuna, *Spain* 35 **G5**
Fuente Palmera, *Spain* 35 **H5**
Fuentes de Andalucía, *Spain* 35 **H5**
Fuentes de Ebro, *Spain* 32 **D4**
Fuentes de León, *Spain* 35 **G4**
Fuentes de Oñoro, *Spain* 34 **E4**
Fuentesaúco, *Spain* 34 **D5**
Fuerte →, *Mexico* 118 **B3**
Fuerte Olimpo, *Paraguay* 126 **A4**
Fuerteventura, *Canary Is.* 37 **F6**
Fufeng, *China* 56 **G5**
Fuga I., *Phil.* 61 **B4**
Fugong, *China* 58 **D2**
Fugou, *China* 56 **G8**
Fugu, *China* 56 **E6**
Fuhai, *China* 60 **B3**
Fuḩaymī, *Iraq* 70 **C4**
Fuji, *Japan* 55 **G9**
Fuji-San, *Japan* 55 **G9**
Fuji-Yoshida, *Japan* 55 **G9**
Fujian □, *China* 59 **E12**
Fujinomiya, *Japan* 55 **G9**
Fujisawa, *Japan* 55 **G9**
Fujiyama, Mt. = Fuji-San, *Japan* 55 **G9**
Fukien = Fujian □, *China* 59 **E12**
Fukuchiyama, *Japan* 55 **G7**
Fukue-Shima, *Japan* 55 **H4**
Fukui, *Japan* 55 **F8**
Fukui □, *Japan* 55 **G8**
Fukuoka, *Japan* 55 **H5**
Fukuoka □, *Japan* 55 **H5**
Fukushima, *Japan* 54 **F10**
Fukushima □, *Japan* 54 **F10**
Fukuyama, *Japan* 55 **G6**
Fulacunda, *Guinea-Biss.* 82 **C1**
Fulda, *Germany* 24 **E5**
Fulda →, *Germany* 24 **D5**
Fulford Harbour, *Canada* 116 **B3**
Fuliang, *China* 59 **C11**
Fullerton, *Calif., U.S.A.* 117 **M9**
Fullerton, *Nebr., U.S.A.* 112 **E6**
Fulongquan, *China* 57 **B13**
Fülöpszállás, *Hungary* 42 **D4**
Fulton, *Mo., U.S.A.* 112 **F9**
Fulton, *N.Y., U.S.A.* 111 **C8**
Fuluälven →, *Sweden* 10 **C7**
Fulufjället, *Sweden* 10 **C6**
Fumay, *France* 19 **C11**
Fumel, *France* 20 **D4**
Fumin, *China* 58 **E4**
Funabashi, *Japan* 55 **G10**
Funafuti = Fongafale, *Tuvalu* 96 **H9**
Funäsdalen, *Sweden* 10 **B6**
Funchal, *Madeira* 37 **D3**
Fundación, *Colombia* 124 **A4**
Fundão, *Portugal* 34 **E3**
Fundu Moldovei, *Romania* 43 **C10**
Fundulea, *Romania* 43 **F11**
Fundy, B. of, *Canada* 103 **D6**
Funhalouro, *Mozam.* 89 **C5**
Funing, *Hebei, China* 57 **E10**
Funing, *Jiangsu, China* 57 **H10**
Funing, *Yunnan, China* 58 **F5**
Funiu Shan, *China* 56 **H7**
Funsi, *Ghana* 82 **C4**
Funtua, *Nigeria* 83 **C6**
Fuping, *Hebei, China* 56 **E8**
Fuping, *Shaanxi, China* 56 **G5**
Fuqing, *China* 59 **E12**
Fuquan, *China* 58 **D6**
Furano, *Japan* 54 **C11**
Furāt, Nahr al →, *Asia* 70 **D5**
Fūrg, *Iran* 71 **D7**
Furmanov, *Russia* 48 **B5**
Furmanovo, *Kazakstan* 48 **F9**
Furnás, *Spain* 37 **B8**
Furnas, Represa de, *Brazil* 127 **A6**
Furneaux Group, *Australia* 94 **G4**
Furqlus, *Syria* 75 **A6**
Fürstenau, *Germany* 24 **C3**
Fürstenberg, *Germany* 24 **B9**
Fürstenfeld, *Austria* 26 **D9**
Fürstenfeldbruck, *Germany* 25 **G7**
Fürstenwalde, *Germany* 24 **C10**
Fürth, *Germany* 25 **F6**
Furth im Wald, *Germany* 25 **F8**
Furtwangen, *Germany* 25 **G4**
Furudal, *Sweden* 10 **C9**
Furukawa, *Japan* 54 **E10**
Furulund, *Sweden* 11 **J7**
Fury and Hecla Str., *Canada* 101 **B11**
Fusagasuga, *Colombia* 124 **C4**
Fuscaldo, *Italy* 31 **C9**
Fushan, *Shandong, China* 57 **F11**
Fushan, *Shanxi, China* 56 **G6**
Fushë Arrëz, *Albania* 40 **D4**
Fushë-Krujë, *Albania* 40 **E3**
Fushun, *Liaoning, China* 57 **D12**
Fushun, *Sichuan, China* 58 **C5**
Fusong, *China* 57 **C14**
Füssen, *Germany* 25 **H6**
Fusui, *China* 58 **F6**
Futog, *Yugoslavia* 42 **E4**
Futuna, *Wall. & F. Is.* 91 **B8**
Fuwa, *Egypt* 80 **H7**
Fuxian Hu, *China* 58 **E4**
Fuxin, *China* 57 **C11**
Fuyang, *Anhui, China* 56 **H8**
Fuyang, *Zhejiang, China* 59 **B12**
Fuyang He →, *China* 56 **E9**
Fuying Dao, *China* 59 **D13**
Fuyu, *China* 57 **B13**
Fuyuan, *China* 58 **E5**
Füzesgyarmat, *Hungary* 42 **C6**
Fuzhou, *China* 59 **D12**
Fylde, *U.K.* 12 **D5**
Fyn, *Denmark* 11 **J4**
Fyne, L., *U.K.* 14 **F3**
Fyns Amtskommune □, *Denmark* 11 **J4**
Fynshav, *Denmark* 11 **K3**

G

Ga, *Ghana* 82 **D4**
Gaanda, *Nigeria* 83 **C7**
Gabarin, *Nigeria* 83 **C7**
Gabas →, *France* 20 **E3**
Gabela, *Angola* 84 **G2**
Gabès, *Tunisia* 79 **B8**
Gabès, G. de, *Tunisia* 79 **B8**
Gabgaba, W. →, *Egypt* 80 **C3**
Gąbin, *Poland* 45 **F6**
Gabon ■, *Africa* 84 **E2**
Gaborone, *Botswana* 88 **C4**
Gabriels, *U.S.A.* 111 **B10**
Gābrīk, *Iran* 71 **E8**
Gabrovo, *Bulgaria* 41 **D9**
Gacé, *France* 18 **D7**
Gāch Sār, *Iran* 71 **B6**
Gachsārān, *Iran* 71 **D6**
Gacko, *Bos.-H.* 40 **C2**
Gadag, *India* 66 **M9**
Gadamai, *Sudan* 81 **D4**
Gadap, *Pakistan* 68 **G2**
Gadarwara, *India* 69 **H8**
Gadebusch, *Germany* 24 **B7**
Gadein, *Sudan* 81 **F2**
Gadhada, *India* 68 **J4**
Gádor, Sierra de, *Spain* 35 **J8**
Gadra, *Pakistan* 68 **G4**
Gadsden, *U.S.A.* 109 **H3**
Gadwal, *India* 66 **L10**
Gadyach = Hadyach, *Ukraine* 47 **G8**
Găeşti, *Romania* 43 **F10**
Gaeta, *Italy* 30 **A6**
Gaeta, G. di, *Italy* 30 **A6**
Gaffney, *U.S.A.* 109 **H5**
Gafsa, *Tunisia* 78 **B7**
Gagarawa, *Nigeria* 83 **C6**
Gagaria, *India* 68 **G4**
Gagarin, *Russia* 46 **E8**
Gaggenau, *Germany* 25 **G4**
Gaghamni, *Sudan* 81 **E2**
Gagino, *Russia* 48 **C7**
Gagliano del Capo, *Italy* 31 **C11**
Gagnef, *Sweden* 10 **D9**
Gagnoa, *Ivory C.* 82 **D3**
Gagnon, *Canada* 103 **B6**
Gagnon, L., *Canada* 105 **A6**
Gagra, *Georgia* 49 **J5**
Gahini, *Rwanda* 86 **C3**
Gahmar, *India* 69 **G10**
Gai Xian = Gaizhou, *China* 57 **D12**
Gaïdhouronísi, *Greece* 36 **E7**
Gail, *U.S.A.* 113 **J4**
Gail →, *Austria* 26 **E6**
Gaillac, *France* 20 **E5**
Gaillimh = Galway, *Ireland* 15 **C2**
Gaillon, *France* 18 **C8**
Gaines, *U.S.A.* 110 **E7**
Gainesville, *Fla., U.S.A.* 109 **L4**
Gainesville, *Ga., U.S.A.* 109 **H4**
Gainesville, *Mo., U.S.A.* 113 **G8**
Gainesville, *Tex., U.S.A.* 113 **J6**
Gainsborough, *U.K.* 12 **D7**
Gairloch, L., *U.K.* 14 **D3**
Gaizhou, *China* 57 **D12**
Gaj, *Croatia* 42 **E2**
Gaj →, *Pakistan* 68 **F2**
Gakuch, *Pakistan* 69 **A5**
Galala, Gebel el, *Egypt* 80 **J8**
Galán, Cerro, *Argentina* 126 **B2**
Galana →, *Kenya* 86 **C5**
Galanta, *Slovak Rep.* 27 **C10**
Galapagar, *Spain* 34 **E7**
Galápagos, *Pac. Oc.* 122 **D1**
Galashiels, *U.K.* 14 **F6**
Galatás, *Greece* 38 **D5**
Galaţi, *Romania* 43 **E13**
Galaţi □, *Romania* 43 **E12**
Galatia, *Turkey* 72 **C5**
Galatina, *Italy* 31 **B11**
Galátone, *Italy* 31 **B11**
Galax, *U.S.A.* 109 **G5**
Galaxídhion, *Greece* 38 **C4**
Galcaio, *Somali Rep.* 74 **F4**
Galdhøpiggen, *Norway* 9 **F12**
Galeana, *Chihuahua, Mexico* 118 **A3**
Galeana, *Nuevo León, Mexico* 118 **A3**
Galegu, *Sudan* 81 **E4**
Galela, *Indonesia* 63 **D7**
Galena, *U.S.A.* 100 **B4**
Galera, *Spain* 33 **H2**
Galera Pt., *Trin. & Tob.* 121 **D7**
Galesburg, *U.S.A.* 112 **E9**
Galeton, *U.S.A.* 110 **E7**
Galga, *Ethiopia* 81 **F4**
Gali, *Georgia* 49 **J5**
Galicea Mare, *Romania* 43 **F8**
Galich, *Russia* 48 **A6**
Galiche, *Bulgaria* 40 **C7**
Galicia □, *Spain* 34 **C3**
Galilee = Hagalil, *Israel* 75 **C4**
Galilee, L., *Australia* 94 **C4**
Galilee, Sea of = Yam Kinneret, *Israel* 75 **C4**
Galim, *Cameroon* 83 **D7**
Galinoporni, *Cyprus* 36 **D13**
Galion, *U.S.A.* 110 **F2**
Galiuro Mts., *U.S.A.* 115 **K8**
Galiwinku, *Australia* 94 **A2**
Gallabat, *Sudan* 81 **E4**
Gallan Hd., *U.K.* 14 **C1**
Gallarate, *Italy* 28 **C5**
Gallatin, *U.S.A.* 109 **G2**
Galle, *Sri Lanka* 66 **R12**
Gállego →, *Spain* 32 **D4**
Gallegos →, *Argentina* 128 **G3**
Galletti →, *Ethiopia* 81 **F5**
Galley Hd., *Ireland* 15 **E3**
Galliate, *Italy* 28 **C5**
Gallinas, Pta., *Colombia* 124 **A4**
Gallipoli = Gelibolu, *Turkey* 41 **F10**
Gallípoli, *Italy* 31 **B10**
Gallipolis, *U.S.A.* 108 **F4**
Gällivare, *Sweden* 8 **C19**
Gallneukirchen, *Austria* 26 **C7**
Gällö, *Sweden* 10 **B9**
Gallo, C., *Italy* 30 **D6**
Gallocanta, L. de, *Spain* 32 **E3**
Galloo I., *U.S.A.* 111 **C8**
Galloway, *U.K.* 14 **F4**
Galloway, Mull of, *U.K.* 14 **G4**
Gallup, *U.S.A.* 115 **J9**
Gallur, *Spain* 32 **D3**
Galoya, *Sri Lanka* 66 **Q12**
Galt, *U.S.A.* 116 **G5**
Galten, *Denmark* 11 **H3**
Galtür, *Austria* 26 **E3**
Galty Mts., *Ireland* 15 **D3**
Galtymore, *Ireland* 15 **D3**
Galva, *U.S.A.* 112 **E9**
Galve de Sorbe, *Spain* 32 **D1**
Galveston, *U.S.A.* 113 **L7**
Galveston B., *U.S.A.* 113 **L7**
Gálvez, *Argentina* 126 **C3**
Galway, *Ireland* 15 **C2**
Galway □, *Ireland* 15 **C2**
Galway B., *Ireland* 15 **C2**
Gam →, *Vietnam* 64 **B5**
Gamagōri, *Japan* 55 **G8**
Gamari, L., *Ethiopia* 81 **E5**
Gamawa, *Nigeria* 83 **C7**
Gamay, *Phil.* 61 **E6**
Gambaga, *Ghana* 83 **C4**
Gambat, *Pakistan* 68 **F3**
Gambela, *Ethiopia* 81 **F3**
Gambhir →, *India* 68 **F6**
Gambia ■, *W. Afr.* 82 **C1**
Gambia →, *W. Afr.* 82 **C1**
Gambier, *U.S.A.* 110 **F2**
Gambier, C., *Australia* 92 **B5**
Gambo, *Canada* 103 **C9**
Gamboli, *Pakistan* 68 **E3**
Gamboma, *Congo* 84 **E3**
Gamka →, *S. Africa* 88 **E3**
Gamkab →, *Namibia* 88 **D2**
Gamla Uppsala, *Sweden* 10 **E11**
Gamlakarleby = Kokkola, *Finland* 8 **E20**
Gamleby, *Sweden* 11 **G10**
Gammon →, *Canada* 105 **C9**
Gamo-Gofa □, *Ethiopia* 81 **F4**
Gamou, *Niger* 83 **C6**
Gamtoos →, *S. Africa* 88 **E4**
Gan, *France* 20 **E3**
Gan Goriama, Mts., *Cameroon* 83 **D7**
Gan Jiang →, *China* 59 **C11**
Ganado, *U.S.A.* 115 **J9**
Gananita, *Sudan* 80 **D3**
Gananoque, *Canada* 102 **D4**
Ganāveh, *Iran* 71 **D6**
Gäncä, *Azerbaijan* 49 **K8**
Gancheng, *China* 64 **C7**
Gand = Gent, *Belgium* 17 **C3**
Ganda, *Angola* 85 **G2**
Gandajika, *Dem. Rep. of the Congo* 84 **F4**
Gandak →, *India* 69 **G11**
Gandava, *Pakistan* 68 **E2**
Gander, *Canada* 103 **C9**
Gander L., *Canada* 103 **C9**
Ganderkesee, *Germany* 24 **B4**
Ganderowe Falls, *Zimbabwe* 87 **F2**
Gandesa, *Spain* 32 **D5**
Gandhi Sagar, *India* 68 **G6**
Gandhinagar, *India* 68 **H5**
Gandi, *Nigeria* 83 **C6**
Gandía, *Spain* 33 **G4**
Gandino, *Italy* 28 **C6**
Gando, Pta., *Canary Is.* 37 **G4**
Gandole, *Nigeria* 83 **D7**
Gâneb, *Mauritania* 82 **B2**
Ganedidalem = Gani, *Indonesia* 63 **E7**
Ganetti, *Sudan* 80 **D3**
Ganga →, *India* 69 **H14**
Ganga Sagar, *India* 69 **J13**
Gangafani, *Mali* 82 **C4**
Gangan →, *India* 69 **E8**
Ganganagar, *India* 68 **E5**
Gangapur, *India* 68 **F7**
Gangara, *Niger* 83 **C6**
Gangaw, *Burma* 67 **H19**
Gangdisê Shan, *China* 67 **D12**
Ganges = Ganga →, *India* 69 **H14**
Ganges, *Canada* 104 **D4**
Ganges, *France* 20 **E7**
Ganges, Mouths of the, *India* 69 **J14**
Gånghester, *Sweden* 11 **G7**
Gangi, *Italy* 31 **E7**
Gângiova, *Romania* 43 **G8**
Gangoh, *India* 68 **E7**
Gangroti, *India* 69 **D8**
Gangtok, *India* 67 **F16**
Gangu, *China* 56 **G3**
Gangyao, *China* 57 **B14**
Gani, *Indonesia* 63 **E7**
Ganj, *India* 69 **F8**
Ganluc, *China* 58 **C4**
Gannat, *France* 19 **F10**
Gannett Peak, *U.S.A.* 114 **E9**
Ganquan, *China* 56 **F5**
Gänserdorf, *Austria* 27 **C9**
Ganshui, *China* 58 **C6**
Gansu □, *China* 56 **G3**
Ganta, *Liberia* 82 **D3**
Gantheaume B., *Australia* 93 **E1**
Gantsevichi = Hantsavichy, *Belarus* 47 **F4**
Ganye, *Nigeria* 83 **D7**
Ganyem = Genyem, *Indonesia* 63 **E10**
Ganyu, *China* 57 **G10**
Ganyushkino, *Kazakstan* 49 **G9**
Ganzhou, *China* 59 **E10**
Gao, *Mali* 83 **B4**
Gao Xian, *China* 58 **C5**
Gao'an, *China* 59 **C10**
Gaochun, *China* 59 **B12**
Gaohe, *China* 59 **F9**
Gaohebu, *China* 59 **B11**
Gaokeng, *China* 59 **D9**
Gaolan Dao, *China* 59 **G9**
Gaoligong Shan, *China* 58 **E2**
Gaomi, *China* 57 **F10**
Gaoming, *China* 59 **F9**
Gaoping, *China* 56 **G7**
Gaotang, *China* 56 **F9**
Gaoua, *Burkina Faso* 82 **C4**
Gaoual, *Guinea* 82 **C2**
Gaoxiong = Kaohsiung, *Taiwan* 59 **F13**
Gaoyang, *China* 56 **E8**
Gaoyao, *China* 59 **F9**
Gaoyou, *China* 59 **A12**
Gaoyou Hu, *China* 57 **H10**
Gaoyuan, *China* 57 **F9**
Gaozhou, *China* 59 **G8**
Gap, *France* 21 **D10**
Gapan, *Phil.* 61 **D4**
Gapat →, *India* 69 **G10**
Gapuwiyak, *Australia* 94 **A2**
Gar, *China* 60 **C2**
Garabogazköl Aylagy, *Turkmenistan* 50 **E6**
Garachico, *Canary Is.* 37 **F3**
Garachiné, *Panama* 120 **E4**
Garafia, *Canary Is.* 37 **F2**
Garah, *Australia* 95 **D4**
Garajonay, *Canary Is.* 37 **F2**
Garango, *Burkina Faso* 83 **C4**
Garanhuns, *Brazil* 125 **E11**
Garautha, *India* 69 **G8**
Garawe, *Liberia* 82 **E3**
Garba Tula, *Kenya* 86 **B4**
Garberville, *U.S.A.* 114 **F2**
Garbiyang, *India* 69 **D9**
Garbsen, *Germany* 24 **C5**
Gard □, *France* 21 **D8**
Gard →, *France* 21 **E8**
Garda, L. di, *Italy* 28 **C7**
Gardanne, *France* 21 **E9**
Gårdby, *Sweden* 11 **H10**
Garde L., *Canada* 105 **A7**
Gardelegen, *Germany* 24 **C7**
Garden City, *Ga., U.S.A.* 109 **J5**
Garden City, *Kans., U.S.A.* 113 **G4**
Garden City, *Tex., U.S.A.* 113 **K4**
Garden Grove, *U.S.A.* 117 **M9**
Gardēz, *Afghan.* 68 **C3**
Gardhíki, *Greece* 38 **C3**
Gardiner, *Maine, U.S.A.* 109 **C11**
Gardiner, *Mont., U.S.A.* 114 **D8**
Gardiners I., *U.S.A.* 111 **E12**
Gardner, *U.S.A.* 111 **D13**
Gardner Canal, *Canada* 104 **C3**
Gardnerville, *U.S.A.* 116 **G7**
Gardno, Jezioro, *Poland* 44 **D4**
Gardo, *Somali Rep.* 74 **F4**
Gardone Val Trómpia, *Italy* 28 **C7**
Gárdony, *Hungary* 42 **C3**
Garešnica, *Croatia* 29 **C13**
Garéssio, *Italy* 28 **D5**
Garey, *U.S.A.* 117 **L6**
Garfield, *U.S.A.* 114 **C5**
Garforth, *U.K.* 12 **D6**
Gargaliánoi, *Greece* 38 **D3**
Gargan, Mt., *France* 20 **C5**
Gargouna, *Mali* 83 **B5**

Gargždai, *Lithuania* 44 C8
Garibaldi Prov. Park, *Canada* 104 D4
Gariep, L., *S. Africa* 88 E4
Garies, *S. Africa* 88 E2
Garigliano →, *Italy* 30 A6
Garissa, *Kenya* 86 C4
Garkida, *Nigeria* 83 C7
Garko, *Nigeria* 83 C6
Garland, *Tex., U.S.A.* 113 J6
Garland, *Utah, U.S.A.* 114 F7
Garlasco, *Italy* 28 C5
Garliava, *Lithuania* 44 D10
Garlin, *France* 20 E3
Garm, *Tajikistan* 50 F8
Garmāb, *Iran* 71 C8
Garmisch-Partenkirchen, *Germany* 25 H7
Garmo, Qullai = Kommunizma, Pik, *Tajikistan* 50 F8
Garmsār, *Iran* 71 C7
Garner, *U.S.A.* 112 D8
Garnett, *U.S.A.* 112 F7
Garo Hills, *India* 69 G14
Garoe, *Somali Rep.* 74 F4
Garonne →, *France* 20 C3
Garonne, Canal Latéral à la, *France* 20 D4
Garot, *India* 68 G6
Garoua, *Cameroon* 83 D7
Garpenberg, *Sweden* 10 D10
Garphyttan, *Sweden* 10 E8
Garrauli, *India* 69 G8
Garrel, *Germany* 24 C4
Garrigue = Garrigues, *France* 20 E7
Garrigues, *France* 20 E7
Garrison, *Mont., U.S.A.* 114 C7
Garrison, *N. Dak., U.S.A.* 112 B4
Garrison Res. = Sakakawea, L., *U.S.A.* 112 B4
Garron Pt., *U.K.* 15 A6
Garrovillas, *Spain* 35 F4
Garrucha, *Spain* 33 H3
Garry →, *U.K.* 14 E5
Garry, L., *Canada* 100 B9
Garsen, *Kenya* 86 C5
Gärsnäs, *Sweden* 11 J8
Garson L., *Canada* 105 B6
Gartempe →, *France* 20 B4
Gartz, *Germany* 24 B10
Garu, *Ghana* 83 C4
Garu, *India* 69 H11
Garub, *Namibia* 88 D2
Garut, *Indonesia* 63 G12
Garvão, *Portugal* 35 H2
Garvie Mts., *N.Z.* 91 L2
Garwa = Garoua, *Cameroon* 83 D7
Garwa, *India* 69 G10
Garwolin, *Poland* 45 G8
Gary, *U.S.A.* 108 E2
Garz, *Germany* 24 A9
Garzê, *China* 58 B3
Garzón, *Colombia* 124 C3
Gas-San, *Japan* 54 E10
Gasan Kuli = Esenguly, *Turkmenistan* 50 F6
Gascogne, *France* 20 E4
Gascogne, G. de, *Europe* 20 E2
Gascony = Gascogne, *France* 20 E4
Gascoyne →, *Australia* 93 D1
Gascoyne Junction, *Australia* 93 E2
Gascueña, *Spain* 32 E2
Gash, Wadi →, *Ethiopia* 81 D4
Gashagar, *Nigeria* 83 C7
Gashaka, *Nigeria* 83 D7
Gasherbrum, *Pakistan* 69 B7
Gashua, *Nigeria* 83 C7
Gaspé, *Canada* 103 C7
Gaspé, C. de, *Canada* 103 C7
Gaspé, Pén. de, *Canada* 103 C6
Gaspésie, Parc de Conservation de la, *Canada* 103 C6
Gassan, *Burkina Faso* 82 C4
Gassol, *Nigeria* 83 D7
Gasteiz = Vitoria-Gasteiz, *Spain* 32 C2
Gastonia, *U.S.A.* 109 H5
Gastoúni, *Greece* 38 D3
Gastoúri, *Greece* 38 B1
Gastre, *Argentina* 128 E3
Gästrikland, *Sweden* 10 D10
Gata, C., *Cyprus* 36 E12
Gata, C. de, *Spain* 33 J2
Gata, Sierra de, *Spain* 34 E4
Gataga →, *Canada* 104 B3
Gătaia, *Romania* 42 E6
Gatchina, *Russia* 46 C6
Gatehouse of Fleet, *U.K.* 14 G4
Gates, *U.S.A.* 110 C7
Gateshead, *U.K.* 12 C6
Gatesville, *U.S.A.* 113 K6
Gaths, *Zimbabwe* 87 G3
Gatico, *Chile* 126 A1
Gâtinais, *France* 19 D9
Gâtine, Hauteurs de, *France* 20 B3
Gatineau, *Canada* 111 A9
Gatineau →, *Canada* 102 C4
Gatineau, Parc Nat. de la, *Canada* 102 C4
Gattaran, *Phil.* 61 B4
Gattinara, *Italy* 28 C5
Gatton, *Australia* 95 D5
Gatun, L., *Panama* 120 E4
Gatyana, *S. Africa* 89 E4
Gau, *Fiji* 91 D8
Gaucín, *Spain* 35 J5
Gauer L., *Canada* 105 B9
Gauhati, *India* 67 F17
Gauja →, *Latvia* 9 H21
Gaula →, *Norway* 8 E14
Gauri Phanta, *India* 69 E9
Gausta, *Norway* 9 G13
Gauteng □, *S. Africa* 89 D4
Gāv Koshī, *Iran* 71 D8
Gāvakān, *Iran* 71 D7
Gavarnie, *France* 20 F3
Gavāter, *Iran* 71 E9
Gāvbandī, *Iran* 71 E7
Gavdhopoúla, *Greece* 36 E6
Gávdhos, *Greece* 36 E6
Gavi, *Italy* 28 D5
Gavião, *Portugal* 35 F3
Gaviota, *U.S.A.* 117 L6
Gāvkhūnī, Bāṭlāq-e, *Iran* 71 C7
Gävle, *Sweden* 10 D11
Gävleborgs län □, *Sweden* 10 C10
Gävlebukten, *Sweden* 10 D11
Gavorrano, *Italy* 28 F7
Gavray, *France* 18 D5
Gavrilov Yam, *Russia* 46 D10
Gávrion, *Greece* 38 D6
Gawachab, *Namibia* 88 D2
Gawilgarh Hills, *India* 66 J10
Gawu, *Nigeria* 83 D6
Gaxun Nur, *China* 60 B5
Gaya, *India* 69 G11
Gaya, *Niger* 83 C5
Gaya, *Nigeria* 83 C6
Gayéri, *Burkina Faso* 83 C5
Gaylord, *U.S.A.* 108 C3
Gayndah, *Australia* 95 D5
Gaysin = Haysyn, *Ukraine* 47 H5
Gayvoron = Hayvoron, *Ukraine* 47 H5
Gaza, *Gaza Strip* 75 D3
Gaza □, *Mozam.* 89 C5
Gaza Strip □, *Asia* 75 D3
Gazanjyk, *Turkmenistan* 71 B7
Gazaoua, *Niger* 83 C6
Gāzbor, *Iran* 71 D8
Gazi, *Dem. Rep. of the Congo* 86 B1
Gaziantep, *Turkey* 70 B3
Gazipaşa, *Turkey* 72 D5
Gbarnga, *Liberia* 82 D3
Gbekebo, *Nigeria* 83 D5
Gboko, *Nigeria* 83 D6
Gbongan, *Nigeria* 83 D5
Gcoverega, *Botswana* 88 B3
Gcuwa, *S. Africa* 89 E4
Gdańsk, *Poland* 44 D5
Gdańska, Zatoka, *Poland* 44 D6
Gdov, *Russia* 9 G22
Gdynia, *Poland* 44 D5
Geba →, *Guinea-Biss.* 82 C1
Gebe, *Indonesia* 63 D7
Gebeciler, *Turkey* 39 C12
Gebeit Mine, *Sudan* 80 C4
Gebel Abyad, *Sudan* 80 D2
Gebel Iweibid, *Egypt* 80 H8
Gebze, *Turkey* 41 F13
Gecha, *Ethiopia* 81 F4
Gedaref, *Sudan* 81 E4
Gedaref □, *Sudan* 81 E4
Gediz, *Turkey* 39 B11
Gediz →, *Turkey* 39 C8
Gedo, *Ethiopia* 81 F4
Gèdre, *France* 20 F4
Gedser, *Denmark* 11 K5
Geegully Cr. →, *Australia* 92 C3
Geel, *Belgium* 17 C4
Geelvink B. = Cenderwasih, Teluk, *Indonesia* 63 E9
Geelvink Chan., *Australia* 93 E1
Geesthacht, *Germany* 24 B6
Geidam, *Nigeria* 83 C7
Geikie →, *Canada* 105 B8
Geilenkirchen, *Germany* 24 E2
Geili, *Sudan* 81 D3
Geisingen, *Germany* 25 H4
Geislingen, *Germany* 25 G5
Geistown, *U.S.A.* 110 F6
Geita, *Tanzania* 86 C3
Gejiu, *China* 58 F4
Gel →, *Sudan* 81 F2
Gel, Meydān-e, *Iran* 71 D7
Gel River, *Sudan* 81 F2
Gela, *Italy* 31 E7
Gela, G. di, *Italy* 31 F7
Gelahun, *Liberia* 82 D2
Gelderland □, *Neths.* 17 B6
Geldern, *Germany* 24 D2
Geldrop, *Neths.* 17 C5
Geleen, *Neths.* 17 D5
Gelehun, *S. Leone* 82 D2
Gelembe, *Turkey* 39 B9
Gelemso, *Ethiopia* 81 F5
Gelendost, *Turkey* 72 C4
Gelendzhik, *Russia* 47 K10
Gelibolu, *Turkey* 41 F10
Gelibolu Yarımadası, *Turkey* 41 F10
Gelidonya Burnu, *Turkey* 72 D4
Gelnhausen, *Germany* 25 E5
Gelnica, *Slovak Rep.* 27 C13
Gelsenkirchen, *Germany* 24 D3
Gelting, *Germany* 24 A5
Gemas, *Malaysia* 65 L4
Gembloux, *Belgium* 17 D4
Gembu, *Nigeria* 83 D7
Gemena, *Dem. Rep. of the Congo* 84 D3
Gemerek, *Turkey* 70 B3
Gemla, *Sweden* 11 H8
Gemlik, *Turkey* 41 F13
Gemlik Körfezi, *Turkey* 41 F12
Gemona del Friuli, *Italy* 29 B10
Gemsa, *Egypt* 80 B3
Gemünden, *Germany* 25 E5
Genale →, *Ethiopia* 81 F4
Genç, *Turkey* 73 C9
Gençay, *France* 20 B4
Geneina, Gebel, *Egypt* 80 B3
General Acha, *Argentina* 126 D3
General Alvear, *Buenos Aires, Argentina* 126 D4
General Alvear, *Mendoza, Argentina* 126 D2
General Artigas, *Paraguay* 126 B4
General Belgrano, *Argentina* 126 D4
General Cabrera, *Argentina* 126 C3
General Cepeda, *Mexico* 118 B4
General Guido, *Argentina* 126 D4
General Juan Madariaga, *Argentina* 126 D4
General La Madrid, *Argentina* 126 D3
General MacArthur, *Phil.* 61 F6
General Martin Miguel de Güemes, *Argentina* 126 A3
General Paz, *Argentina* 126 B4
General Pico, *Argentina* 126 D3
General Pinedo, *Argentina* 126 B3
General Pinto, *Argentina* 126 C3
General Roca, *Argentina* 128 D3
General Santos, *Phil.* 61 H6
General Toshevo, *Bulgaria* 41 C12
General Trevino, *Mexico* 119 B5
General Trías, *Mexico* 118 B3
General Viamonte, *Argentina* 126 D3
General Villegas, *Argentina* 126 D3
Genesee, *Idaho, U.S.A.* 114 C5
Genesee, *Pa., U.S.A.* 110 E7
Genesee →, *U.S.A.* 110 C7
Geneseo, *Ill., U.S.A.* 112 E9
Geneseo, *N.Y., U.S.A.* 110 D7
Geneva = Genève, *Switz.* 25 J2
Geneva, *Ala., U.S.A.* 109 K3
Geneva, *N.Y., U.S.A.* 110 D8
Geneva, *Nebr., U.S.A.* 112 E6
Geneva, *Ohio, U.S.A.* 110 E4
Geneva, L. = Léman, L., *Europe* 19 F13
Geneva, L., *U.S.A.* 108 D1
Genève, *Switz.* 25 J2
Gengenbach, *Germany* 25 G4
Gengma, *China* 58 F2
Genichesk = Henichesk, *Ukraine* 47 J8
Genil →, *Spain* 35 H5
Genk, *Belgium* 17 D5
Genlis, *France* 19 E12
Gennargentu, Mti. del, *Italy* 30 B2
Gennes, *France* 18 E6
Genoa = Génova, *Italy* 28 D5
Genoa, *N.Y., U.S.A.* 111 D8
Genoa, *Nebr., U.S.A.* 112 E6
Genoa, *Nev., U.S.A.* 116 F7
Génova, *Italy* 28 D5
Génova, G. di, *Italy* 28 E6
Genriyetty, Ostrov, *Russia* 51 B16
Gent, *Belgium* 17 C3
Genteng, *Indonesia* 63 G12
Genthin, *Germany* 24 C8
Genyem, *Indonesia* 63 E10
Genzano di Lucánia, *Italy* 31 B9
Genzano di Roma, *Italy* 29 G9
Geoagiu, *Romania* 43 E8
Geographe B., *Australia* 93 F2
Geographe Chan., *Australia* 93 D1
Geokchay = Göyçay, *Azerbaijan* 49 K8
Georga, Zemlya, *Russia* 50 A5
George, *S. Africa* 88 E3
George →, *Canada* 103 A6
George, L., *Australia* 92 D3
George, L., *Uganda* 86 B3
George, L., *Fla., U.S.A.* 109 L5
George, L., *N.Y., U.S.A.* 111 C11
George Gill Ra., *Australia* 92 D5
George River = Kangiqsualujjuaq, *Canada* 101 C13
George Sound, *N.Z.* 91 L1
George Town, *Australia* 94 G4
George Town, *Bahamas* 120 B4
George Town, *Cayman Is.* 120 C3
George Town, *Malaysia* 65 K3
George V Land, *Antarctica* 5 C10
George VI Sound, *Antarctica* 5 D17
George West, *U.S.A.* 113 L5
Georgetown, *Australia* 94 B3
Georgetown, *Ont., Canada* 102 D4
Georgetown, *P.E.I., Canada* 103 C7
Georgetown, *Gambia* 82 C2
Georgetown, *Guyana* 124 B7
Georgetown, *Calif., U.S.A.* 116 G6
Georgetown, *Colo., U.S.A.* 114 G11
Georgetown, *Ky., U.S.A.* 108 F3
Georgetown, *N.Y., U.S.A.* 111 D9
Georgetown, *Ohio, U.S.A.* 108 F4
Georgetown, *S.C., U.S.A.* 109 J6
Georgetown, *Tex., U.S.A.* 113 K6
Georgia □, *U.S.A.* 109 K5
Georgia ■, *Asia* 49 J6
Georgia, Str. of, *Canada* 104 D4
Georgian B., *Canada* 102 C3
Georgina →, *Australia* 94 C2
Georgina I., *Canada* 110 B5
Georgiu-Dezh = Liski, *Russia* 47 G10
Georgiyevsk, *Russia* 49 H6
Georgsmarienhütte, *Germany* 24 C4
Gera, *Germany* 24 E8
Geraardsbergen, *Belgium* 17 D3
Geral, Serra, *Brazil* 127 B6
Geral de Goiás, Serra, *Brazil* 125 F9
Geraldine, *U.S.A.* 114 C8
Geraldton, *Australia* 93 E1
Geraldton, *Canada* 102 C2
Gérardmer, *France* 19 D13
Gercüş, *Turkey* 73 D9
Gerede, *Turkey* 72 B5
Gerês, Sierra do, *Portugal* 34 D3
Gereshk, *Afghan.* 66 D4
Geretsried, *Germany* 25 H7
Gérgal, *Spain* 33 H2
Gerik, *Malaysia* 65 K3
Gering, *U.S.A.* 112 E3
Gerlach, *U.S.A.* 114 F4
Gerlachovský štít, *Slovak Rep.* 27 B13
German Planina, *Macedonia* 40 D6
Germansen Landing, *Canada* 104 B4
Germantown, *U.S.A.* 113 M10
Germany ■, *Europe* 24 E6
Germencik, *Turkey* 39 D9
Germering, *Germany* 25 G7
Germersheim, *Germany* 25 F4
Germī, *Iran* 71 B6
Germiston, *S. Africa* 89 D4
Gernika-Lumo, *Spain* 32 B2
Gernsheim, *Germany* 25 F4
Gero, *Japan* 55 G8
Gerolzhofen, *Germany* 25 F6
Gerona = Girona, *Spain* 32 D7
Gerrard, *Canada* 104 C5
Gers □, *France* 20 E4
Gers →, *France* 20 D4
Gersfeld, *Germany* 24 E5
Gersthofen, *Germany* 25 G6
Gerzat, *France* 20 C7
Gerze, *Turkey* 72 B6
Geseke, *Germany* 24 D4
Geser, *Indonesia* 63 E8
Gesso →, *Italy* 28 D4
Gestro, Wabi →, *Ethiopia* 81 G5
Getafe, *Spain* 34 E7
Getinge, *Sweden* 11 H6
Gettysburg, *Pa., U.S.A.* 108 F7
Gettysburg, *S. Dak., U.S.A.* 112 C5
Getxo, *Spain* 32 B2
Getz Ice Shelf, *Antarctica* 5 D14
Gevaş, *Turkey* 73 C10
Gévaudan, *France* 20 D7
Gevgelija, *Macedonia* 40 E6
Gévora →, *Spain* 35 G4
Gewani, *Ethiopia* 81 E5
Gex, *France* 19 F13
Geyikli, *Turkey* 39 B8
Geyser, *U.S.A.* 114 C8
Geyserville, *U.S.A.* 116 G4
Geyve, *Turkey* 72 B4
Ghâbat el Arab = Wang Kai, *Sudan* 81 F2
Ghabeish, *Sudan* 81 E2
Ghaggar →, *India* 68 E6
Ghaghara →, *India* 69 G11
Ghaghat →, *Bangla.* 69 G13
Ghagra, *India* 69 H11
Ghagra →, *India* 69 F9
Ghalla, Wadi el →, *Sudan* 81 E2
Ghana ■, *W. Afr.* 83 D4
Ghansor, *India* 69 H9
Ghanzi, *Botswana* 88 C3
Gharb el Istiwa'iya □, *Sudan* 81 G3
Gharb Kordofân, *Sudan* 81 E2
Gharbîya, Es Sahrâ el, *Egypt* 80 B2
Ghardaïa, *Algeria* 78 B6
Ghârib, G., *Egypt* 80 B3
Gharig, *Sudan* 81 E2
Gharyān, *Libya* 79 B8
Ghat, *Libya* 79 D8
Ghatal, *India* 69 H12
Ghatampur, *India* 69 F9
Ghatsila, *India* 69 H12
Ghaṭṭī, *Si. Arabia* 70 D3
Ghawdex = Gozo, *Malta* 36 C1
Ghazal, Bahr el →, *Chad* 79 F9
Ghazâl, Bahr el →, *Sudan* 81 F3
Ghaziabad, *India* 68 E7
Ghazipur, *India* 69 G10
Ghaznī, *Afghan.* 68 C3
Ghaznī □, *Afghan.* 66 C6
Ghedi, *Italy* 28 C7
Ghelari, *Romania* 42 E7
Ghent = Gent, *Belgium* 17 C3
Gheorghe Gheorghiu-Dej = Oneşti, *Romania* 43 D11
Gheorgheni, *Romania* 43 D10
Gherla, *Romania* 43 C8
Ghidigeni, *Romania* 43 D12
Ghilarza, *Italy* 30 B1
Ghimeş-Făget, *Romania* 43 D11
Ghīnah, Wādī al →, *Si. Arabia* 70 D3
Ghisonaccia, *France* 21 F13
Ghisoni, *France* 21 F13
Ghizao, *Afghan.* 68 C1
Ghizar →, *Pakistan* 69 A5
Ghot Ogrein, *Egypt* 80 A2
Ghotaru, *India* 68 F4
Ghotki, *Pakistan* 68 E3
Ghowr □, *Afghan.* 66 C4
Ghudaf, W. al →, *Iraq* 70 C4
Ghudāmis, *Libya* 77 C4
Ghughri, *India* 69 H9
Ghugus, *India* 66 K11
Ghulam Mohammad Barrage, *Pakistan* 68 G3
Ghūrīān, *Afghan.* 66 B2
Gia Dinh, *Vietnam* 65 G6
Gia Lai = Plei Ku, *Vietnam* 64 F7
Gia Nghia, *Vietnam* 65 G6
Gia Ngoc, *Vietnam* 64 E7
Gia Vuc, *Vietnam* 64 E7
Giannutri, *Italy* 28 F8
Giant Forest, *U.S.A.* 116 J8
Giant Mts. = Krkonoše, *Czech Rep.* 26 A8
Giants Causeway, *U.K.* 15 A5
Giarabub = Al Jaghbūb, *Libya* 79 C10
Giarre, *Italy* 31 E8
Giaveno, *Italy* 28 C4
Gibara, *Cuba* 120 B4
Gibb River, *Australia* 92 C4
Gibbon, *U.S.A.* 112 E5
Gibe →, *Ethiopia* 81 F4
Gibellina Nuova, *Italy* 30 E5
Gibeon, *Namibia* 88 D2
Gibraleón, *Spain* 35 H4
Gibraltar ■, *Europe* 35 J5
Gibraltar, Str. of, *Medit. S.* 35 K5
Gibson Desert, *Australia* 92 D4
Gibsons, *Canada* 104 D4
Gibsonville, *U.S.A.* 116 F6
Giddings, *U.S.A.* 113 K6
Gidole, *Ethiopia* 81 F4
Giebnegáisi = Kebnekaise, *Sweden* 8 C18
Gien, *France* 19 E9
Giengen, *Germany* 25 G6
Giessen, *Germany* 24 E4
Gīfān, *Iran* 71 B8
Gifatin, Geziret, *Egypt* 80 B3
Gifhorn, *Germany* 24 C6
Gift Lake, *Canada* 104 B5
Gifu, *Japan* 55 G8
Gifu □, *Japan* 55 G8
Gigant, *Russia* 49 G5
Giganta, Sa. de la, *Mexico* 118 B2
Gigen, *Bulgaria* 41 C8
Gigha, *U.K.* 14 F3
Gíglio, *Italy* 28 F7
Gignac, *France* 20 E7
Gigüela →, *Spain* 35 F7
Gijón, *Spain* 34 B5
Gil I., *Canada* 104 C3
Gila →, *U.S.A.* 115 K6
Gila Bend, *U.S.A.* 115 K7
Gila Bend Mts., *U.S.A.* 115 K7
Gīlān □, *Iran* 71 B6
Gilău, *Romania* 43 D8
Gilbert →, *Australia* 94 B3
Gilbert Is., *Kiribati* 96 G9
Gilbert River, *Australia* 94 B3
Gilead, *U.S.A.* 111 B14
Gilf el Kebîr, Hadabat el, *Egypt* 80 C2
Gilford I., *Canada* 104 C3
Gilgil, *Kenya* 86 C4
Gilgit, *India* 69 B6
Gilgit →, *Pakistan* 69 B6
Giljeva Planina, *Serbia, Yug.* 40 C3
Gillam, *Canada* 105 B10
Gilleleje, *Denmark* 11 H6
Gillen, L., *Australia* 93 E3
Gillette, *U.S.A.* 112 C2
Gilliat, *Australia* 94 C3
Gillingham, *U.K.* 13 F8
Gilmer, *U.S.A.* 113 J7
Gilmore, L., *Australia* 93 F3
Gilo →, *Ethiopia* 81 F3
Gilort →, *Romania* 43 F8
Gilroy, *U.S.A.* 116 H5
Gimbi, *Ethiopia* 81 F4
Gimli, *Canada* 105 C9
Gimo, *Sweden* 10 D12
Gimone →, *France* 20 E5
Gimont, *France* 20 E4
Gin Gin, *Australia* 95 D5
Ginâh, *Egypt* 80 B3
Gineifa, *Egypt* 80 H8
Gingin, *Australia* 93 F2
Gingindlovu, *S. Africa* 89 D5
Ginir, *Ethiopia* 81 F5
Ginosa, *Italy* 31 B9
Ginzo de Limia = Xinzo de Limia, *Spain* 34 C3
Gióia, G. di, *Italy* 31 D8
Gióia del Colle, *Italy* 31 B9
Gióia Táuro, *Italy* 31 D8
Gioiosa Iónica, *Italy* 31 D9
Gioiosa Marea, *Italy* 31 D7
Gióna, Óros, *Greece* 38 C4
Giovi, Passo dei, *Italy* 28 D5
Giovinazzo, *Italy* 31 A9
Gir Hills, *India* 68 J4
Girab, *India* 68 F4
Girâfi, W. →, *Egypt* 75 F3
Giraltovce, *Slovak Rep.* 27 B14
Girard, *Kans., U.S.A.* 113 G7
Girard, *Ohio, U.S.A.* 110 E4
Girard, *Pa., U.S.A.* 110 E4
Girdle Ness, *U.K.* 14 D6
Giresun, *Turkey* 73 B8
Girga, *Egypt* 80 B3
Giri →, *India* 68 D7
Giridih, *India* 69 G12
Girifalco, *Italy* 31 D9
Girne = Kyrenia, *Cyprus* 36 D12
Giro, *Nigeria* 83 C5
Giromagny, *France* 19 E13
Girona, *Spain* 32 D7
Girona □, *Spain* 32 C7
Gironde □, *France* 20 D3
Gironde →, *France* 20 C2
Gironella, *Spain* 32 C6
Giru, *Australia* 94 B4
Girvan, *U.K.* 14 F4
Gisborne, *N.Z.* 91 H7
Gisenyi, *Rwanda* 86 C2
Gislaved, *Sweden* 11 G7
Gisors, *France* 19 C8

Gitega, Burundi 86 C2
Giuba →, Somali Rep. 74 G3
Giugliano in Campania, Italy 31 B7
Giulianova, Italy 29 F10
Giurgeni, Romania 43 F12
Giurgiu, Romania 43 G10
Giurgiu □, Romania 43 F10
Giurgiuleşti, Moldova 43 E13
Give, Denmark 11 J3
Givet, France 19 B11
Givors, France 21 C8
Givry, France 19 F11
Giyon, Ethiopia 81 F4
Giza = El Gîza, Egypt 80 J7
Gizhiga, Russia 51 C17
Gizhiginskaya Guba, Russia 51 C16
Giżycko, Poland 44 D8
Gizzeria, Italy 31 D9
Gjalicë e Lumës, Mal., Albania 40 D4
Gjegjan, Albania 40 E4
Gjirokastër, Albania 40 F4
Gjoa Haven, Canada 100 B10
Gjøvik, Norway 9 F14
Gjuhës, Kep i, Albania 40 F3
Glace Bay, Canada 103 C8
Glacier Bay National Park and Preserve, U.S.A. 104 B1
Glacier National Park, Canada 104 C5
Glacier National Park, U.S.A. 114 B7
Glacier Peak, U.S.A. 114 B3
Gladewater, U.S.A. 113 J7
Gladstone, Australia 94 C5
Gladstone, Canada 105 C9
Gladstone, U.S.A. 108 C2
Gladwin, U.S.A. 108 D3
Glafsfjorden, Sweden 10 E6
Głagów Małapolski, Poland 45 H8
Glåma = Glomma →, Norway 9 G14
Gláma, Iceland 8 D2
Glamis, U.S.A. 117 N11
Glamoč, Bos.-H. 29 D13
Glamsbjerg, Denmark 11 J4
Glarus, Switz. 25 H5
Glarus □, Switz. 25 J5
Glasco, Kans., U.S.A. 112 F6
Glasco, N.Y., U.S.A. 111 D11
Glasgow, U.K. 14 F4
Glasgow, Ky., U.S.A. 108 G3
Glasgow, Mont., U.S.A. 114 B10
Glasgow, City of □, U.K. 14 F4
Glaslyn, Canada 105 C7
Glastonbury, U.K. 13 F5
Glastonbury, U.S.A. 111 E12
Glauchau, Germany 24 E8
Glava, Sweden 10 E6
Glavice, Croatia 29 E13
Glazov, Russia 48 A11
Gleichen, Canada 104 C6
Gleisdorf, Austria 26 D8
Gleiwitz = Gliwice, Poland 45 H5
Glen, U.S.A. 111 B13
Glen Affric, U.K. 14 D3
Glen Canyon, U.S.A. 115 H8
Glen Canyon Dam, U.S.A. 115 H8
Glen Canyon National Recreation Area, U.S.A. 115 H8
Glen Coe, U.K. 14 E3
Glen Cove, U.S.A. 111 F11
Glen Garry, U.K. 14 D3
Glen Innes, Australia 95 D5
Glen Lyon, U.S.A. 111 E8
Glen Mor, U.K. 14 D4
Glen Moriston, U.K. 14 D4
Glen Robertson, Canada 111 A10
Glen Spean, U.K. 14 E4
Glen Ullin, U.S.A. 112 B4
Glénan, Îs. de, France 18 E3
Glencoe, Canada 110 D3
Glencoe, S. Africa 89 D5
Glencoe, U.S.A. 112 C7
Glendale, Ariz., U.S.A. 115 K7
Glendale, Calif., U.S.A. 117 L8
Glendale, Zimbabwe 87 F3
Glendive, U.S.A. 112 B2
Glendo, U.S.A. 112 D2
Glenfield, U.S.A. 111 C9
Glengarriff, Ireland 15 E2
Glenmont, U.S.A. 110 F2
Glenmorgan, Australia 95 D4
Glenn, U.S.A. 116 F4
Glennallen, U.S.A. 100 B5
Glennamaddy, Ireland 15 C3
Glenns Ferry, U.S.A. 114 E6
Glenore, Australia 94 B3
Glenreagh, Australia 95 E5
Glenrock, U.S.A. 114 E11
Glenrothes, U.K. 14 E5
Glens Falls, U.S.A. 111 C11
Glenside, U.S.A. 111 F9
Glenties, Ireland 15 B3
Glenville, U.S.A. 108 F5
Glenwood, Canada 103 C9
Glenwood, Ark., U.S.A. 113 H8
Glenwood, Iowa, U.S.A. 112 E7
Glenwood, Minn., U.S.A. 112 C7
Glenwood, Wash., U.S.A. 116 D5
Glenwood Springs, U.S.A. 114 G10
Glettinganes, Iceland 8 D7
Glifádha, Greece 38 D5
Glimåkra, Sweden 11 H8
Glina, Croatia 29 C13
Glinojeck, Poland 45 F7
Gliwice, Poland 45 H5
Globe, U.S.A. 115 K8
Glodeanu Siliştea, Romania 43 F11
Glodeni, Moldova 43 C12
Glödnitz, Austria 26 E7
Gloggnitz, Austria 26 D8
Głogów, Poland 45 G3
Głogówek, Poland 45 H4
Glomma →, Norway 9 G14
Glorieuses, Is., Ind. Oc. 89 A8
Glóssa, Greece 38 B5
Glossop, U.K. 12 D6
Gloucester, U.K. 13 F5
Gloucester, U.S.A. 111 D14
Gloucester I., Australia 94 C4
Gloucester Point, U.S.A. 108 G7
Gloucestershire □, U.K. 13 F5
Gloversville, U.S.A. 111 C10
Glovertown, Canada 103 C9
Głowno, Poland 45 G6
Głubczyce, Poland 45 H4
Glubokiy, Russia 49 F5
Glubokoye = Hlybokaye, Belarus 46 E4
Głuchołazy, Poland 45 H4
Glücksburg, Germany 24 A5
Glückstadt, Germany 24 B5
Glukhov = Hlukhiv, Ukraine 47 G7
Glusk, Belarus 47 F5
Głuszyca, Poland 45 H3
Glyngøre, Denmark 11 H2
Gmünd, Kärnten, Austria 26 E6
Gmünd, Niederösterreich, Austria 26 C8
Gmunden, Austria 26 D6
Gnarp, Sweden 10 B11
Gnesta, Sweden 10 E11
Gniew, Poland 44 E5
Gniewkowo, Poland 45 F5
Gniezno, Poland 45 F4
Gnjilane, Kosovo, Yug. 40 D5
Gnoien, Germany 24 B8
Gnosjö, Sweden 11 G7
Gnowangerup, Australia 93 F2
Go Cong, Vietnam 65 G6
Gō-no-ura, Japan 55 H4
Goa, India 66 M8
Goa □, India 66 M8
Goalpara, India 67 F17
Goaltor, India 69 H12
Goalundo Ghat, Bangla. 69 H13
Goaso, Ghana 82 D4
Goat Fell, U.K. 14 F3
Goba, Ethiopia 81 F4
Goba, Mozam. 89 D5
Gobabis, Namibia 88 C2
Göbel, Turkey 41 F12
Gobi, Asia 56 C6
Gobō, Japan 55 H7
Gobo, Sudan 81 F3
Göçbeyli, Turkey 39 B9
Goch, Germany 24 D2
Gochas, Namibia 88 C2
Godavari →, India 67 L13
Godavari Pt., India 67 L13
Godbout, Canada 103 C6
Godda, India 69 G12
Godech, Bulgaria 40 C7
Goderich, Canada 102 D3
Goderville, France 18 C7
Godfrey Ra., Australia 93 D2
Godhavn = Qeqertarsuaq, Greenland 4 C5
Godhra, India 68 H5
Gödöllő, Hungary 42 C4
Godoy Cruz, Argentina 126 C2
Gods →, Canada 102 A1
Gods L., Canada 102 B1
Gods River, Canada 105 C10
Godthåb = Nuuk, Greenland 101 B14
Godwin Austen = K2, Pakistan 69 B7
Goeie Hoop, Kaap die = Good Hope, C. of, S. Africa 88 E2
Goéland, L. au, Canada 102 C4
Goeree, Neths. 17 C3
Goes, Neths. 17 C3
Goffstown, U.S.A. 111 C13
Gogama, Canada 102 C3
Gogebic, L., U.S.A. 112 B10
Goggetti, Ethiopia 81 F4
Gogolin, Poland 45 H5
Gogonou, Benin 83 C5
Gogra = Ghaghara →, India 69 G11
Gogriâl, Sudan 81 F2
Gogti, Ethiopia 81 E5
Gohana, India 68 E7
Goharganj, India 68 H7
Goi →, India 68 H6
Goiânia, Brazil 125 G9
Goiás, Brazil 125 G8
Goiás □, Brazil 125 F9
Goio-Erê, Brazil 127 A5
Góis, Portugal 34 E2
Gojam □, Ethiopia 81 E4
Gojeb, Wabi →, Ethiopia 81 F4
Gojō, Japan 55 G7
Gojra, Pakistan 68 D5
Gökçeada, Turkey 41 F9
Gökçedağ, Turkey 39 B10
Gökçen, Turkey 39 C9
Gökçeören, Turkey 39 C10
Gökçeyazı, Turkey 39 B9
Gökırmak →, Turkey 72 B6
Gökova, Turkey 39 D10
Gökova Körfezi, Turkey 39 E9
Göksu →, Turkey 72 D6
Göksun, Turkey 72 C7
Gokteik, Burma 67 H20
Göktepe, Turkey 39 D10
Gokurt, Pakistan 68 E2
Gokwe, Zimbabwe 89 B4
Gola, India 69 E9
Golakganj, India 69 F13
Golan Heights = Hagolan, Syria 75 C4
Gołańcz, Poland 45 F4
Golāshkerd, Iran 71 E8
Golaya Pristen = Hola Pristan, Ukraine 47 J7
Gölbaşı, Adiyaman, Turkey 72 D7
Gölbaşı, Ankara, Turkey 72 C5
Golchikha, Russia 4 B12
Golconda, U.S.A. 114 F5
Gölcük, Kocaeli, Turkey 41 F13
Gölcük, Niğde, Turkey 72 C6
Gold, U.S.A. 110 E7
Gold Beach, U.S.A. 114 E1
Gold Coast, W. Afr. 83 E4
Gold Hill, U.S.A. 114 E2
Gold River, Canada 104 D3
Goldap, Poland 44 D9
Goldberg, Germany 24 B8
Golden, Canada 104 C5
Golden B., N.Z. 91 J4
Golden Gate, U.S.A. 114 H2
Golden Hinde, Canada 104 D3
Golden Lake, Canada 110 A7
Golden Vale, Ireland 15 D3
Goldendale, U.S.A. 114 D3
Goldfield, U.S.A. 115 H5
Goldsand L., Canada 105 B8
Goldsboro, U.S.A. 109 H7
Goldsmith, U.S.A. 113 K3
Goldsworthy, Australia 92 D2
Goldthwaite, U.S.A. 113 K5
Golegã, Portugal 35 F2
Goleniów, Poland 44 E1
Golestānak, Iran 71 D7
Goleta, U.S.A. 117 L7
Golfito, Costa Rica 120 E3
Golfo Aranci, Italy 30 B2
Gölgeli Dağları, Turkey 39 D10
Gölhisar, Turkey 39 D11
Goliad, U.S.A. 113 L6
Golija, Montenegro, Yug. 40 C2
Golija, Serbia, Yug. 40 C4
Golina, Poland 45 F5
Gölköy, Turkey 72 B7
Göllersdorf, Austria 26 C9
Gölmarmara, Turkey 39 C9
Golo →, France 21 F13
Gölova, Turkey 39 E12
Golpāyegān, Iran 71 C6
Gölpazarı, Turkey 72 B4
Golra, Pakistan 68 C5
Golspie, U.K. 14 D5
Golub-Dobrzyń, Poland 45 E6
Golubac, Serbia, Yug. 40 B5
Golyam Perelik, Bulgaria 41 E8
Golyama Kamchiya →, Bulgaria 41 C11
Goma, Dem. Rep. of the Congo 86 C2
Gomal Pass, Pakistan 68 D3
Gomati →, India 69 G10
Gombari, Dem. Rep. of the Congo 86 B2
Gombe, Nigeria 83 C7
Gömbe, Turkey 39 E11
Gombe □, Nigeria 83 C7
Gombe →, Tanzania 86 C3
Gombi, Nigeria 83 C7
Gomel = Homyel, Belarus 47 F6
Gomera, Canary Is. 37 F2
Gómez Palacio, Mexico 118 B4
Gomīshān, Iran 71 B7
Gommern, Germany 24 C7
Gomogomo, Indonesia 63 F8
Gomoh, India 67 H15
Gomotartsi, Bulgaria 40 B6
Gompa = Ganta, Liberia 82 D3
Gomphi, Greece 38 B3
Gonābād, Iran 71 C8
Gonaïves, Haiti 121 C5
Gonâve, G. de la, Haiti 121 C5
Gonâve, I. de la, Haiti 121 C5
Gonbad-e Kāvūs, Iran 71 B7
Gönc, Hungary 42 B6
Gonda, India 69 F9
Gondal, India 68 J4
Gonder, Ethiopia 81 E4
Gonder □, Ethiopia 81 E4
Gondia, India 66 J12
Gondola, Mozam. 87 F3
Gondomar, Portugal 34 D2
Gondrecourt-le-Château, France 19 D12
Gönen, Balıkesir, Turkey 41 F11
Gönen, Isparta, Turkey 39 D12
Gönen →, Turkey 41 F11
Gong Xian, China 58 C5
Gong'an, China 59 B9
Gongcheng, China 59 E8
Gongga Shan, China 58 C3
Gongguan, China 58 G7
Gonghe, China 60 C5
Gongola →, Nigeria 83 D7
Gongolgon, Australia 95 E4
Gongshan, China 58 D2
Gongtan, China 58 C7
Gongzhuling, China 57 C13
Goniadz, Poland 44 E9
Goniri, Nigeria 83 C7
Gonjo, China 58 B2
Gonnesa, Italy 30 C1
Gónnos, Greece 38 B4
Gonnosfanádiga, Italy 30 C1
Gonzaga, Phil. 61 B5
Gonzales, Calif., U.S.A. 116 J5
Gonzales, Tex., U.S.A. 113 L6
González Chaves, Argentina 126 D3
Good Hope, C. of, S. Africa 88 E2
Gooderham, Canada 110 B6
Goodhouse, S. Africa 88 D2
Gooding, U.S.A. 114 E6
Goodland, U.S.A. 112 F4
Goodlow, Canada 104 B4
Goodooga, Australia 95 D4
Goodsprings, U.S.A. 117 K11
Goole, U.K. 12 D7
Goomalling, Australia 93 F2
Goomeri, Australia 95 D5
Goonda, Mozam. 87 F3
Goondiwindi, Australia 95 D5
Goongarrie, L., Australia 93 F3
Goonyella, Australia 94 C4
Goose →, Canada 103 B7
Goose Creek, U.S.A. 109 J5
Goose L., U.S.A. 114 F3
Gop, India 66 H6
Gopalganj, India 69 F11
Göppingen, Germany 25 G5
Gor, Spain 35 H8
Góra, Dolnośląskie, Poland 45 G3
Góra, Mazowieckie, Poland 45 F7
Góra Kalwaria, Poland 45 G8
Gorakhpur, India 69 F10
Goražde, Bos.-H. 42 G3
Gorbatov, Russia 48 B6
Gorbea, Peña, Spain 32 B2
Gorda, U.S.A. 116 K5
Gorda, Pta., Canary Is. 37 F2
Gorda, Pta., Nic. 120 D3
Gordan B., Australia 92 B5
Gördes, Turkey 39 C10
Gordon, U.S.A. 112 D3
Gordon →, Australia 94 G4
Gordon L., Alta., Canada 105 B6
Gordon L., N.W.T., Canada 104 A6
Gordonvale, Australia 94 B4
Gore, Ethiopia 81 F4
Gore, N.Z. 91 M2
Gore Bay, Canada 102 C3
Görele, Turkey 73 B8
Goreme, Turkey 72 C6
Gorey, Ireland 15 D5
Gorg, Iran 71 D8
Gorgān, Iran 71 B7
Gorgona, Italy 28 E6
Gorgona, I., Colombia 124 C3
Gorgora, Ethiopia 81 E4
Gorgoram, Nigeria 83 C7
Gorham, U.S.A. 111 B13
Gori, Georgia 49 J7
Goriganga →, India 69 E9
Gorinchem, Neths. 17 C4
Goris, Armenia 73 C12
Goritsy, Russia 46 D9
Gorízia, Italy 29 C10
Gorj □, Romania 43 E8
Gorki = Horki, Belarus 46 E6
Gorki = Nizhniy Novgorod, Russia 48 B7
Gorkiy = Nizhniy Novgorod, Russia 48 B7
Gorkovskoye Vdkhr., Russia 48 B6
Gorlice, Poland 45 J8
Görlitz, Germany 24 D10
Gorlovka = Horlivka, Ukraine 47 H10
Gorman, U.S.A. 117 L8
Gorna Dzhumayo = Blagoevgrad, Bulgaria 40 D7
Gorna Oryakhovitsa, Bulgaria 41 C9
Gornja Radgona, Slovenia 29 B13
Gornja Tuzla, Bos.-H. 42 F3
Gornji Grad, Slovenia 29 B11
Gornji Milanovac, Serbia, Yug. 40 B4
Gornji Vakuf, Bos.-H. 42 G2
Gorno Ablanovo, Bulgaria 41 C9
Gorno-Altay □, Russia 50 D9
Gorno-Altaysk, Russia 50 D9
Gornyatskiy, Russia 49 F5
Gornyy, Saratov, Russia 48 E9
Gornyy, Sib., Russia 54 B6
Gorodenka = Horodenka, Ukraine 47 H3
Gorodets, Russia 48 B6
Gorodishche = Horodyshche, Ukraine 47 H6
Gorodishche, Russia 48 D7
Gorodnya = Horodnya, Ukraine 47 G6
Gorodok = Haradok, Belarus 46 E6
Gorodok = Horodok, Ukraine 47 H2
Gorodovikovsk, Russia 49 G5
Gorokhov = Horokhiv, Ukraine 47 G3
Gorokhovets, Russia 48 B6
Gorom Gorom, Burkina Faso 83 C4
Goromonzi, Zimbabwe 87 F3
Gorong, Kepulauan, Indonesia 63 E8
Gorongose →, Mozam. 89 C5
Gorongoza, Mozam. 87 F3
Gorongoza, Sa. da, Mozam. 87 F3
Gorontalo, Indonesia 63 D6
Goronyo, Nigeria 83 C6
Górowo Iławeckie, Poland 44 D7
Gorron, France 18 D6
Gorshechnoye, Russia 47 G10
Gort, Ireland 15 C3
Gortis, Greece 36 D6
Góry Bystrzyckie, Poland 45 H3
Goryachiy Klyuch, Russia 49 H4
Gorzkowice, Poland 45 G6
Górzno, Poland 45 E6
Gorzów Śląski, Poland 45 G5
Gorzów Wielkopolski, Poland 45 F2
Goshen, Calif., U.S.A. 116 J7
Goshen, Ind., U.S.A. 108 E3
Goshen, N.Y., U.S.A. 111 E10
Goshogawara, Japan 54 D10
Goslar, Germany 24 D6
Gospič, Croatia 29 D12
Gosport, U.K. 13 G6
Gossas, Senegal 82 C1
Gosse →, Australia 94 B1
Gossi, Mali 83 B4
Gossinga, Sudan 81 F2
Gostivar, Macedonia 40 E4
Gostyń, Poland 45 G4
Gostynin, Poland 45 F6
Göta älv →, Sweden 11 G5
Göta kanal, Sweden 11 F9
Götaland, Sweden 11 G8
Göteborg, Sweden 11 G5
Götene, Sweden 11 F7
Goteşti, Moldova 43 D13
Gotha, Germany 24 E6
Gothenburg = Göteborg, Sweden 11 G5
Gothenburg, U.S.A. 112 E4
Gothèye, Niger 83 C5
Gotland, Sweden 11 G12
Gotlands län □, Sweden 11 G12
Gotō-Rettō, Japan 55 H4
Gotse Delchev, Bulgaria 40 E7
Gotska Sandön, Sweden 9 G18
Götsu, Japan 55 G6
Gott Pk., Canada 104 C4
Góttero, Monte, Italy 28 D6
Göttingen, Germany 24 D5
Gottwald = Zmiyev, Ukraine 47 H9
Gottwaldov = Zlín, Czech Rep. 27 B10
Goubangzi, China 57 D11
Gouda, Neths. 17 B4
Goúdhoura, Ákra, Greece 36 E8
Goudiry, Senegal 82 C2
Goudoumaria, Niger 83 C7
Gouéké, Guinea 82 D3
Gough I., Atl. Oc. 2 G9
Gouin, Rés., Canada 102 C5
Gouitafla, Ivory C. 82 D3
Goulburn Is., Australia 94 A1
Goulia, Ivory C. 82 C3
Goulimine, Morocco 78 C3
Goumbou, Mali 82 B3
Gouménissa, Greece 40 F6
Goundam, Mali 82 B4
Goúra, Greece 38 D4
Gourbassi, Mali 82 C2
Gourdon, France 20 D5
Gouré, Niger 83 C7
Gourin, France 18 D3
Gourits →, S. Africa 88 E3
Gourma-Rharous, Mali 83 B4
Goúrnais, Greece 36 D7
Gournay-en-Bray, France 19 C8
Goursi, Burkina Faso 82 C4
Gouverneur, U.S.A. 111 B9
Gouviá, Greece 36 A3
Gouzon, France 19 F9
Governador Valadares, Brazil 125 G10
Governor's Harbour, Bahamas 120 A4
Govindgarh, India 69 G9
Gowan Ra., Australia 94 D4
Gowanda, U.S.A. 110 D6
Gower, U.K. 13 F3
Gowna, L., Ireland 15 C4
Goya, Argentina 126 B4
Göyçay, Azerbaijan 49 K8
Goyder Lagoon, Australia 95 D2
Goyllarisquisga, Peru 124 F3
Göynük, Antalya, Turkey 39 E12
Göynük, Bolu, Turkey 72 B4
Goz Beïda, Chad 79 F10
Goz Regeb, Sudan 81 D4
Gozdnica, Poland 45 G2
Gozo, Malta 36 C1
Graaff-Reinet, S. Africa 88 E3
Grabo, Ivory C. 82 D3
Grabow, Germany 24 B7
Grabów nad Prosną, Poland 45 G5
Gračac, Croatia 29 D12
Gračanica, Bos.-H. 42 F3
Graçay, France 19 E8
Gracias a Dios, C., Honduras 120 D3
Graciosa, I., Canary Is. 37 E6
Grad Sofiya □, Bulgaria 40 D7
Gradac, Montenegro, Yug. 40 C3
Gradačac, Bos.-H. 42 F3
Gradeška Planina, Macedonia 40 E6
Gradets, Bulgaria 41 D10
Gradišče, Slovenia 29 B12
Grădiştea de Munte, Romania 43 E8
Grado, Italy 29 C10
Grado, Spain 34 B4
Grady, U.S.A. 113 H3
Graeca, Lacul, Romania 43 F11
Grafenau, Germany 25 G9
Gräfenberg, Germany 25 F7
Grafham Water, U.K. 13 E7
Grafton, Australia 95 D5
Grafton, N. Dak., U.S.A. 112 A6
Grafton, W. Va., U.S.A. 108 F5
Graham, Canada 102 C1
Graham, U.S.A. 113 J5
Graham, Mt., U.S.A. 115 K9
Graham Bell, Ostrov = Greem-Bell, Ostrov, Russia 50 A7
Graham I., Canada 104 C2
Graham Land, Antarctica 5 C17
Grahamstown, S. Africa 88 E4
Grahamsville, U.S.A. 111 E10
Grahovo, Montenegro, Yug. 40 D2

Graie, Alpi, Europe 21 C11
Grain Coast, W. Afr. 82 E3
Grajaú, Brazil 125 E9
Grajaú →, Brazil 125 D10
Grajewo, Poland 44 E9
Gramada, Bulgaria 40 C6
Gramat, France 20 D5
Grammichele, Italy 31 E7
Grámmos, Óros, Greece 40 F4
Grampian, U.S.A. 110 F6
Grampian Highlands = Grampian Mts., U.K. 14 E5
Grampian Mts., U.K. 14 E5
Gramsh, Albania 40 F4
Gran Canaria, Canary Is. 37 G4
Gran Chaco, S. Amer. 126 B3
Gran Paradiso, Italy 28 C4
Gran Sasso d'Itália, Italy 29 F10
Granada, Nic. 120 D2
Granada, Spain 35 H7
Granada, U.S.A. 113 F3
Granada □, Spain 35 H7
Granadilla de Abona, Canary Is. 37 F3
Granard, Ireland 15 C4
Granbury, U.S.A. 113 J6
Granby, Canada 102 C5
Granby, U.S.A. 114 F11
Grand →, Canada 110 D5
Grand →, Mo., U.S.A. 112 F8
Grand →, S. Dak., U.S.A. 112 C4
Grand Bahama, Bahamas 120 A4
Grand Bank, Canada 103 C8
Grand Bassam, Ivory C. 82 D4
Grand Béréby, Ivory C. 82 E3
Grand-Bourg, Guadeloupe 121 C7
Grand Canal = Yun Ho →, China 57 E9
Grand Canyon, U.S.A. 115 H7
Grand Canyon National Park, U.S.A. 115 H7
Grand Cayman, Cayman Is. 120 C3
Grand Centre, Canada 105 C6
Grand Cess, Liberia 82 E3
Grand Coulee, U.S.A. 114 C4
Grand Coulee Dam, U.S.A. 114 C4
Grand Erg Occidental, Algeria 78 B6
Grand Erg Oriental, Algeria 78 B7
Grand Falls, Canada 103 C6
Grand Falls-Windsor, Canada 103 C8
Grand Forks, Canada 104 D5
Grand Forks, U.S.A. 112 B6
Grand Gorge, U.S.A. 111 D10
Grand Haven, U.S.A. 108 D2
Grand I., Mich., U.S.A. 108 B2
Grand I., N.Y., U.S.A. 110 D6
Grand Island, U.S.A. 112 E5
Grand Isle, La., U.S.A. 113 L9
Grand Isle, Vt., U.S.A. 111 B11
Grand Junction, U.S.A. 115 G9
Grand L., N.B., Canada 103 C6
Grand L., Nfld., Canada 103 C8
Grand L., Nfld., Canada 103 B7
Grand L., U.S.A. 113 L8
Grand Lahou, Ivory C. 82 D3
Grand Lake, U.S.A. 114 F11
Grand-Lieu, L. de, France 18 E5
Grand Manan I., Canada 103 D6
Grand Marais, Canada 112 B9
Grand Marais, U.S.A. 108 B3
Grand-Mère, Canada 102 C5
Grand Popo, Benin 83 D5
Grand Portage, U.S.A. 112 B10
Grand Prairie, U.S.A. 113 J6
Grand Rapids, Canada 105 C9
Grand Rapids, Mich., U.S.A. 108 D2
Grand Rapids, Minn., U.S.A. 112 B8
Grand St-Bernard, Col du, Europe 25 K3
Grand Teton, U.S.A. 114 E8
Grand Teton National Park, U.S.A. 114 D8
Grand Union Canal, U.K. 13 E7
Grand View, Canada 105 C8
Grandas de Salime, Spain 34 B4
Grande →, Jujuy, Argentina 126 A2
Grande →, Mendoza, Argentina 126 D2
Grande →, Bolivia 124 G6
Grande →, Bahia, Brazil 125 F10
Grande →, Minas Gerais, Brazil 125 H8
Grande, B., Argentina 128 G3
Grande, Rio →, U.S.A. 113 N6
Grande Baleine, R. de la →, Canada 102 A4
Grande Cache, Canada 104 C5
Grande-Entrée, Canada 103 C7
Grande Prairie, Canada 104 B5
Grande-Rivière, Canada 103 C7
Grande-Vallée, Canada 103 C6
Grandfalls, U.S.A. 113 K3
Grândola, Portugal 35 G2
Grandpré, France 19 C11
Grandview, U.S.A. 114 C4
Grandvilliers, France 19 C8
Graneros, Chile 126 C1
Grangemouth, U.K. 14 E5
Granger, U.S.A. 114 F9
Grängesberg, Sweden 10 D9
Grangeville, U.S.A. 114 D5
Granisle, Canada 104 C3
Granite City, U.S.A. 112 F9
Granite Falls, U.S.A. 112 C7
Granite L., Canada 103 C8
Granite Mt., U.S.A. 117 M10
Granite Pk., U.S.A. 114 D9
Graniteville, U.S.A. 111 B12
Granitola, C., Italy 30 E5
Granity, N.Z. 91 J3
Granja, Brazil 125 D10
Granja de Moreruela, Spain 34 D5
Granja de Torrehermosa, Spain 35 G5
Gränna, Sweden 11 F8
Granollers, Spain 32 D7
Gransee, Germany 24 B9
Grant, U.S.A. 112 E4
Grant, Mt., U.S.A. 114 G4
Grant City, U.S.A. 112 E7
Grant I., Australia 92 B5
Grant Range, U.S.A. 115 G6
Grantham, U.K. 12 E7
Grantown-on-Spey, U.K. 14 D5
Grants, U.S.A. 115 J10
Grants Pass, U.S.A. 114 E2
Grantsville, U.S.A. 114 F7
Granville, France 18 D5
Granville, N. Dak., U.S.A. 112 A4
Granville, N.Y., U.S.A. 111 C11
Granville, Ohio, U.S.A. 110 F2
Granville L., Canada 105 B8
Graskop, S. Africa 89 C5
Gräsö, Sweden 10 D12
Grass →, Canada 105 B9
Grass Range, U.S.A. 114 C9
Grass River Prov. Park, Canada 105 C8
Grass Valley, Calif., U.S.A. 116 F6
Grass Valley, Oreg., U.S.A. 114 D3
Grassano, Italy 31 B9
Grasse, France 21 E10
Grassflat, U.S.A. 110 F6
Grasslands Nat. Park, Canada 105 D7
Grassy, Australia 94 G3
Gråsten, Denmark 11 K3
Grästorp, Sweden 11 F6
Gratkorn, Austria 26 D8
Graubünden □, Switz. 25 J5
Graulhet, France 20 E5
Graus, Spain 32 C5
Grave, Pte. de, France 20 C2
Gravelbourg, Canada 105 D7
Gravelines, France 19 A9
's-Gravenhage, Neths. 17 B4
Gravenhurst, Canada 102 D4
Gravesend, Australia 95 D5
Gravesend, U.K. 13 F8
Gravina in Púglia, Italy 31 B9
Gravois, Pointe-à-, Haiti 121 C5
Gravone →, France 21 G12
Gray, France 19 E12
Grayling, U.S.A. 108 C3
Grays Harbor, U.S.A. 114 C1
Grays L., U.S.A. 114 E8
Grays River, U.S.A. 116 D3
Grayvoron, Russia 47 G8
Graz, Austria 26 D8
Grdelica, Serbia, Yug. 40 D6
Greasy L., Canada 104 A4
Great Abaco I., Bahamas 120 A4
Great Artesian Basin, Australia 94 C3
Great Australian Bight, Australia 93 F5
Great Bahama Bank, Bahamas 120 B4
Great Barrier I., N.Z. 91 G5
Great Barrier Reef, Australia 94 B4
Great Barrington, U.S.A. 111 D11
Great Basin, U.S.A. 114 G5
Great Basin Nat. Park, U.S.A. 114 G6
Great Bear →, Canada 100 B7
Great Bear L., Canada 100 B7
Great Belt = Store Bælt, Denmark 11 J4
Great Bend, Kans., U.S.A. 112 F5
Great Bend, Pa., U.S.A. 111 E9
Great Blasket I., Ireland 15 D1
Great Britain, Europe 6 E5
Great Codroy, Canada 103 C8
Great Dividing Ra., Australia 94 C4
Great Driffield = Driffield, U.K. 12 C7
Great Exuma I., Bahamas 120 B4
Great Falls, U.S.A. 114 C8
Great Fish = Groot Vis →, S. Africa 88 E4
Great Guana Cay, Bahamas 120 B4
Great Inagua I., Bahamas 121 B5
Great Indian Desert = Thar Desert, India 68 F5
Great Karoo, S. Africa 88 E3
Great Lake, Australia 94 G4
Great Lakes, N. Amer. 98 E11
Great Malvern, U.K. 13 E5
Great Miami →, U.S.A. 108 F3
Great Ormes Head, U.K. 12 D4
Great Ouse →, U.K. 12 E8
Great Palm I., Australia 94 B4
Great Plains, N. Amer. 106 A6
Great Ruaha →, Tanzania 86 D4
Great Sacandaga Res., U.S.A. 111 C10
Great Saint Bernard Pass = Grand St-Bernard, Col du, Europe 25 K3
Great Salt L., U.S.A. 114 F7
Great Salt Lake Desert, U.S.A. 114 F7
Great Salt Plains L., U.S.A. 113 G5
Great Sandy Desert, Australia 92 D3
Great Sangi = Sangihe, Pulau, Indonesia 63 D7
Great Scarcies →, S. Leone 82 D2
Great Skellig, Ireland 15 E1
Great Slave L., Canada 104 A5
Great Smoky Mts. Nat. Park, U.S.A. 109 H4
Great Snow Mt., Canada 104 B4
Great Stour = Stour →, U.K. 13 F9
Great Victoria Desert, Australia 93 E4
Great Wall, China 56 E5
Great Whernside, U.K. 12 C6
Great Yarmouth, U.K. 13 E9
Greater Antilles, W. Indies 121 C5
Greater London □, U.K. 13 F7
Greater Manchester □, U.K. 12 D5
Greater Sunda Is., Indonesia 62 F4
Grebbestad, Sweden 11 F5
Grebenka = Hrebenka, Ukraine 47 G7
Greco, C., Cyprus 36 E13
Greco, Mte., Italy 29 G10
Gredos, Sierra de, Spain 34 E6
Greece, U.S.A. 110 C7
Greece ■, Europe 38 B3
Greeley, Colo., U.S.A. 112 E2
Greeley, Nebr., U.S.A. 112 E5
Greem-Bell, Ostrov, Russia 50 A7
Green, U.S.A. 114 E2
Green →, Ky., U.S.A. 108 G2
Green →, Utah, U.S.A. 115 G9
Green B., U.S.A. 108 C2
Green Bay, U.S.A. 108 C2
Green Cove Springs, U.S.A. 109 L5
Green Lake, Canada 105 C7
Green Mts., U.S.A. 111 C12
Green River, Utah, U.S.A. 115 G8
Green River, Wyo., U.S.A. 114 F9
Green Valley, U.S.A. 115 L8
Greenbank, U.S.A. 116 B4
Greenbush, Mich., U.S.A. 110 B1
Greenbush, Minn., U.S.A. 112 A6
Greencastle, U.S.A. 108 F2
Greene, U.S.A. 111 D9
Greenfield, Calif., U.S.A. 116 J5
Greenfield, Calif., U.S.A. 117 K8
Greenfield, Ind., U.S.A. 108 F3
Greenfield, Iowa, U.S.A. 112 E7
Greenfield, Mass., U.S.A. 111 D12
Greenfield, Mo., U.S.A. 113 G8
Greenfield Park, Canada 111 A11
Greenland ■, N. Amer. 4 C5
Greenland Sea, Arctic 4 B7
Greenock, U.K. 14 F4
Greenore, Ireland 15 B5
Greenore Pt., Ireland 15 D5
Greenough, Australia 93 E1
Greenough →, Australia 93 E1
Greenough Pt., Canada 110 B3
Greenport, U.S.A. 111 E12
Greensboro, Ga., U.S.A. 109 J4
Greensboro, N.C., U.S.A. 109 G6
Greensboro, Vt., U.S.A. 111 B12
Greensburg, Ind., U.S.A. 108 F3
Greensburg, Kans., U.S.A. 113 G5
Greensburg, Pa., U.S.A. 110 F5
Greenstone Pt., U.K. 14 D3
Greenvale, Australia 94 B4
Greenville, Liberia 82 D3
Greenville, Ala., U.S.A. 109 K2
Greenville, Calif., U.S.A. 116 E6
Greenville, Maine, U.S.A. 109 C11
Greenville, Mich., U.S.A. 108 D3
Greenville, Miss., U.S.A. 113 J9
Greenville, Mo., U.S.A. 113 G9
Greenville, N.C., U.S.A. 109 H7
Greenville, N.H., U.S.A. 111 D13
Greenville, N.Y., U.S.A. 111 D10
Greenville, Ohio, U.S.A. 108 E3
Greenville, Pa., U.S.A. 110 E4
Greenville, S.C., U.S.A. 109 H4
Greenville, Tenn., U.S.A. 109 G4
Greenville, Tex., U.S.A. 113 J6
Greenwater Lake Prov. Park, Canada 105 C8
Greenwich, Conn., U.S.A. 111 E11
Greenwich, N.Y., U.S.A. 111 C11
Greenwich, Ohio, U.S.A. 110 E2
Greenwich □, U.K. 13 F8
Greenwood, Canada 104 D5
Greenwood, Ark., U.S.A. 113 H7
Greenwood, Ind., U.S.A. 108 F2
Greenwood, Miss., U.S.A. 113 J9
Greenwood, S.C., U.S.A. 109 H4
Greenwood, Mt., Australia 92 B5
Gregbe, Ivory C. 82 D3
Gregory, U.S.A. 112 D5
Gregory →, Australia 94 B2
Gregory, L., S. Austral., Australia 95 D2
Gregory, L., W. Austral., Australia 93 E2
Gregory Downs, Australia 94 B2
Gregory L., Australia 92 D4
Gregory Ra., Queens., Australia 94 B3
Gregory Ra., W. Austral., Australia 92 D3
Greiffenberg, Germany 24 B9
Greifswald, Germany 24 A9
Greifswalder Bodden, Germany 24 A9
Grein, Austria 26 C7
Greiz, Germany 24 E8
Gremikha, Russia 50 C4
Grenå, Denmark 11 H4
Grenada, U.S.A. 113 J10
Grenada ■, W. Indies 121 D7
Grenade, France 20 E5
Grenadier I., U.S.A. 111 B8
Grenadines, St. Vincent 121 D7
Grenchen, Switz. 25 H3
Grenen, Denmark 11 G4
Grenfell, Canada 105 C8
Grenoble, France 21 C9
Grenville, C., Australia 94 A3
Grenville Chan., Canada 104 C3
Gréoux-les-Bains, France 21 E9
Gresham, U.S.A. 116 E4
Gresik, Indonesia 63 G15
Gretna, U.K. 14 F5
Greven, Germany 24 C3
Grevená, Greece 40 F5
Grevená □, Greece 40 F5
Grevenbroich, Germany 24 D2
Grevenmacher, Lux. 17 E6
Grevesmühlen, Germany 24 B7
Grevestrand, Denmark 11 J6
Grey →, Canada 103 C8
Grey →, N.Z. 91 K3
Grey, C., Australia 94 A2
Grey Ra., Australia 95 D3
Greybull, U.S.A. 114 D9
Greymouth, N.Z. 91 K3
Greystones, Ireland 15 C5
Greytown, N.Z. 91 J5
Greytown, S. Africa 89 D5
Gribanovskiy, Russia 48 E5
Gribbell I., Canada 104 C3
Gribës, Mal i, Albania 40 F3
Gridley, U.S.A. 116 F5
Griekwastad, S. Africa 88 D3
Griesheim, Germany 25 F4
Grieskirchen, Austria 26 C6
Griffin, U.S.A. 109 J3
Griffith, Canada 110 A7
Griffith I., Canada 110 B4
Grignols, France 20 D3
Grigoriopol, Moldova 43 C14
Grimaylov = Hrymayliv, Ukraine 47 H4
Grimes, U.S.A. 116 F5
Grimma, Germany 24 D8
Grimmen, Germany 24 A9
Grimsay, U.K. 14 D1
Grimsby, Canada 110 C5
Grimsby, U.K. 12 D7
Grímsey, Iceland 8 C5
Grimshaw, Canada 104 B5
Grimslöv, Sweden 11 H8
Grimstad, Norway 9 G13
Grindelwald, Switz. 25 J4
Grindsted, Denmark 11 J2
Grindstone I., Canada 111 B8
Grindu, Romania 43 F11
Grinnell, U.S.A. 112 E8
Grintavec, Slovenia 29 B11
Gris-Nez, C., France 19 B8
Grisolles, France 20 E5
Grisons = Graubünden □, Switz. 25 J5
Grisslehamn, Sweden 10 D12
Grmeč Planina, Bos.-H. 29 D13
Groais I., Canada 103 B8
Grobiņa, Latvia 44 B8
Groblersdal, S. Africa 89 D4
Grobming, Austria 26 D6
Grocka, Serbia, Yug. 40 B4
Gródek, Poland 45 E10
Grodków, Poland 45 H4
Grodno = Hrodna, Belarus 46 F2
Grodzisk Mazowiecki, Poland 45 F7
Grodzisk Wielkopolski, Poland 45 F3
Grodzyanka = Hrodzyanka, Belarus 46 F5
Groesbeck, U.S.A. 113 K6
Groix, France 18 E3
Groix, Î. de, France 18 E3
Grójec, Poland 45 G7
Gronau, Niedersachsen, Germany 24 C5
Gronau, Nordrhein-Westfalen, Germany 24 C3
Grong, Norway 8 D15
Grönhögen, Sweden 11 H10
Groningen, Neths. 17 A6
Groningen □, Neths. 17 A6
Groom, U.S.A. 113 H4
Groot →, S. Africa 88 E3
Groot Berg →, S. Africa 88 E2
Groot-Brakrivier, S. Africa 88 E3
Groot Karasberge, Namibia 88 D2
Groot-Kei →, S. Africa 89 E4
Groot Vis →, S. Africa 88 E4
Grootdrink, S. Africa 88 D3
Groote Eylandt, Australia 94 A2
Grootfontein, Namibia 88 B2
Grootlaagte →, Africa 88 C3
Grootvloer →, S. Africa 88 E3
Gros C., Canada 104 A6
Gros Morne Nat. Park, Canada 103 C8
Grósio, Italy 28 B7
Grosne →, France 19 F11
Grossa, Pta., Spain 37 B8
Grossenbrode, Germany 24 A7
Grossenhain, Germany 24 D9
Grosser Arber, Germany 25 F9
Grosser Plöner See, Germany 24 A6
Grosseto, Italy 29 F8
Grossgerungs, Austria 26 C7
Grossglockner, Austria 26 D5
Groswater B., Canada 103 B8
Groton, Conn., U.S.A. 111 E12
Groton, N.Y., U.S.A. 111 D8
Groton, S. Dak., U.S.A. 112 C5
Grottáglie, Italy 31 B10
Grottaminarda, Italy 31 A8
Grottammare, Italy 29 F10
Grouard Mission, Canada 104 B5
Grouin, Pte. du, France 18 D5
Groundhog →, Canada 102 C3
Grouw, Neths. 17 A5
Grove City, U.S.A. 110 E4
Grove Hill, U.S.A. 109 K2
Groveland, U.S.A. 116 H6
Grover City, U.S.A. 117 K6
Groves, U.S.A. 113 L8
Groveton, U.S.A. 111 B13
Grožnjan, Croatia 29 C10
Groznyy, Russia 49 J7
Grubišno Polje, Croatia 42 E2
Grudovo, Bulgaria 41 D11
Grudusk, Poland 45 E7
Grudziądz, Poland 44 E5
Gruinard B., U.K. 14 D3
Gruissan, France 20 E7
Grumo Áppula, Italy 31 A9
Grums, Sweden 10 E7
Grünberg, Germany 24 E4
Gründau, Germany 25 E5
Grundy Center, U.S.A. 112 D8
Grünstadt, Germany 25 F4
Gruvberget, Sweden 10 C10
Gruver, U.S.A. 113 G4
Gruyères, Switz. 25 J3
Gruža, Serbia, Yug. 40 C4
Gryazi, Russia 47 F10
Gryazovets, Russia 46 C11
Grybów, Poland 45 J7
Grycksbo, Sweden 10 D9
Gryfice, Poland 44 E2
Gryfino, Poland 45 E1
Gryfów Śląski, Poland 45 G2
Grythyttan, Sweden 10 E8
Gstaad, Switz. 25 J3
Gua, India 67 H14
Gua Musang, Malaysia 65 K3
Guacanayabo, G. de, Cuba 120 B4
Guachípas →, Argentina 126 B2
Guadajoz →, Spain 35 H6
Guadalajara, Mexico 118 C4
Guadalajara, Spain 32 E1
Guadalajara □, Spain 32 E2
Guadalcanal, Solomon Is. 96 H8
Guadalcanal, Spain 35 G5
Guadalén →, Spain 35 G7
Guadales, Argentina 126 C2
Guadalete →, Spain 35 J4
Guadalimar →, Spain 35 G7
Guadalmena →, Spain 35 G8
Guadalmez →, Spain 35 G5
Guadalope →, Spain 32 D4
Guadalquivir →, Spain 35 J4
Guadalupe = Guadeloupe ■, W. Indies 121 C7
Guadalupe, Mexico 117 N10
Guadalupe, Spain 35 F5
Guadalupe, U.S.A. 117 L6
Guadalupe →, Mexico 117 N10
Guadalupe →, U.S.A. 113 L6
Guadalupe, Sierra de, Spain 35 F5
Guadalupe Bravos, Mexico 118 A3
Guadalupe I., Pac. Oc. 98 G8
Guadalupe Mts. Nat. Park, U.S.A. 113 K2
Guadalupe Peak, U.S.A. 113 K2
Guadalupe y Calvo, Mexico 118 B3
Guadarrama, Sierra de, Spain 34 E7
Guadauta, Georgia 49 J5
Guadeloupe ■, W. Indies 121 C7
Guadeloupe Passage, W. Indies 121 C7
Guadiamar →, Spain 35 J4
Guadiana →, Portugal 35 H3
Guadiana Menor →, Spain 35 H7
Guadiaro →, Spain 35 J5
Guadiato →, Spain 35 H5
Guadiela →, Spain 32 E2
Guadix, Spain 35 H7
Guafo, Boca del, Chile 128 E2
Guainía →, Colombia 124 C5
Guaíra, Brazil 127 A5
Guaíra □, Paraguay 126 B4
Guaitecas, Is., Chile 128 E2
Guajará-Mirim, Brazil 124 F5
Guajira, Pen. de la, Colombia 124 A4
Gualán, Guatemala 120 C2
Gualdo Tadino, Italy 29 E9
Gualeguay, Argentina 126 C4
Gualeguaychú, Argentina 126 C4
Gualequay →, Argentina 126 C4
Guam ■, Pac. Oc. 96 F6
Guaminí, Argentina 126 D3
Guamúchil, Mexico 118 B3
Guanabacoa, Cuba 120 B3
Guanacaste, Cordillera del, Costa Rica 120 D2
Guanaceví, Mexico 118 B3
Guanahani = San Salvador I., Bahamas 121 B5
Guanajay, Cuba 120 B3
Guanajuato, Mexico 118 C4
Guanajuato □, Mexico 118 C4
Guandacol, Argentina 126 B2
Guane, Cuba 120 B3
Guang'an, China 58 B6
Guangchang, China 59 D11
Guangde, China 59 B12
Guangdong □, China 59 F9
Guangfeng, China 59 C12
Guanghan, China 58 B5
Guangling, China 56 E8
Guangnan, China 58 E5
Guangning, China 59 F9
Guangrao, China 57 F10
Guangshui, China 59 B9
Guangshun, China 58 D6
Guangwu, China 56 F3
Guangxi Zhuangzu Zizhiqu □, China 58 F7
Guangyuan, China 58 A5
Guangze, China 59 D11
Guangzhou, China 59 F9
Guanipa →, Venezuela 124 B6

Guanling, *China* 58 E5
Guannan, *China* 57 G10
Guantánamo, *Cuba* 121 B4
Guantao, *China* 56 F8
Guanyang, *China* 59 E8
Guanyun, *China* 57 G10
Guápiles, *Costa Rica* 120 D3
Guaporé, *Brazil* 127 B5
Guaporé →, *Brazil* 122 E4
Guaqui, *Bolivia* 124 G5
Guara, Sierra de, *Spain* 32 C4
Guarapari, *Brazil* 127 A7
Guarapuava, *Brazil* 127 B5
Guaratinguetá, *Brazil* 127 A6
Guaratuba, *Brazil* 127 B6
Guarda, *Portugal* 34 E3
Guarda □, *Portugal* 34 E3
Guardafui, C. = Asir, Ras, *Somali Rep.* 74 E5
Guardamar del Segura, *Spain* 33 G4
Guardavalle, *Italy* 31 D9
Guárdia Sanframondi, *Italy* 31 A7
Guardiagrele, *Italy* 29 F11
Guardo, *Spain* 34 C6
Guareña, *Spain* 35 G4
Guareña →, *Spain* 34 D5
Guárico □, *Venezuela* 124 B5
Guarujá, *Brazil* 127 A6
Guarus, *Brazil* 127 A7
Guasave, *Mexico* 118 B3
Guasdualito, *Venezuela* 124 B4
Guastalla, *Italy* 28 D7
Guatemala, *Guatemala* 120 D1
Guatemala ■, *Cent. Amer.* 120 C1
Guaviare →, *Colombia* 122 C4
Guaxupé, *Brazil* 127 A6
Guayama, *Puerto Rico* 121 C6
Guayaquil, *Ecuador* 124 D3
Guayaquil, G. de, *Ecuador* 122 D2
Guaymas, *Mexico* 118 B2
Guba, *Dem. Rep. of the Congo* 87 E2
Guba, *Ethiopia* 81 E4
Gûbâl, Madîq, *Egypt* 80 B3
Gubat, *Phil.* 61 E6
Gúbbio, *Italy* 29 E9
Guben, *Germany* 24 D10
Gubin, *Poland* 45 G1
Gubio, *Nigeria* 83 C7
Gubkin, *Russia* 47 G9
Guča, *Serbia, Yug.* 40 C4
Gucheng, *China* 59 A8
Gudata = Guadauta, *Georgia* 49 J5
Gudbrandsdalen, *Norway* 9 F14
Guddu Barrage, *Pakistan* 66 E6
Gudenå →, *Denmark* 11 H4
Gudermes, *Russia* 49 J8
Gudhjem, *Denmark* 11 J8
Gudur, *India* 66 M11
Guebwiller, *France* 19 E14
Guecho = Getxo, *Spain* 32 B2
Guékédou, *Guinea* 82 D2
Guéle Mendouka, *Cameroon* 83 E7
Guelph, *Canada* 102 D3
Guéméné-Penfao, *France* 18 E5
Guéméné-sur-Scorff, *France* 18 D3
Guéné, *Benin* 83 C5
Guer, *France* 18 E4
Guérande, *France* 18 E4
Guéret, *France* 19 F8
Guérigny, *France* 19 E10
Guerneville, *U.S.A.* 116 G4
Guernica = Gernika-Lumo, *Spain* 32 B2
Guernsey, *U.K.* 13 H5
Guernsey, *U.S.A.* 112 D2
Guerrero □, *Mexico* 119 D5
Guessou-Sud, *Benin* 83 C5
Gueugnon, *France* 19 F11
Guéyo, *Ivory C.* 82 D3
Gughe, *Ethiopia* 81 F4
Gügher, *Iran* 71 D8
Guglionesi, *Italy* 29 G11
Guhakolak, Tanjung, *Indonesia* 63 G11
Gui Jiang →, *China* 59 F8
Guia, *Canary Is.* 37 F4
Guia de Isora, *Canary Is.* 37 F3
Guia Lopes da Laguna, *Brazil* 127 A4
Guiana, *S. Amer.* 122 C4
Guibéroua, *Ivory C.* 82 D3
Guichi, *China* 59 B11
Guider, *Cameroon* 83 D7
Guidiguir, *Niger* 83 C6
Guidimouni, *Niger* 83 C6
Guiding, *China* 58 D6
Guidong, *China* 59 D9
Guidónia-Montecélio, *Italy* 29 F9
Guiers, L. de, *Senegal* 82 B1
Guigang, *China* 58 F7
Guiglo, *Ivory C.* 82 D3
Guihulñgan, *Phil.* 61 F5
Guijá, *Mozam.* 89 C5
Guijuelo, *Spain* 34 E5
Guildford, *U.K.* 13 F7
Guilford, *U.S.A.* 111 E12
Guilin, *China* 59 E8
Guillaume-Delisle L., *Canada* 102 A4
Guillaumes, *France* 21 D10
Guillestre, *France* 21 D10
Guilvinec, *France* 18 E2
Güimar, *Canary Is.* 37 F3
Guimarães, *Portugal* 34 D2
Guimaras □, *Phil.* 61 F5
Guinda, *U.S.A.* 116 G4
Guinea, *Africa* 76 F4
Guinea ■, *W. Afr.* 82 C2
Guinea, Gulf of, *Atl. Oc.* 83 E5
Guinea-Bissau ■, *Africa* 82 C2
Güines, *Cuba* 120 B3
Guingamp, *France* 18 D3
Guinguinéo, *Senegal* 82 C1
Guipavas, *France* 18 D2
Guiping, *China* 59 F8
Guipúzcoa □, *Spain* 32 B2
Guir, *Mali* 82 B4
Guirel, *Mauritania* 82 B3
Güiria, *Venezuela* 124 A6
Guiscard, *France* 19 C10
Guise, *France* 19 C10
Guitiriz, *Spain* 34 B3
Guitri, *Ivory C.* 82 D3
Guiuan, *Phil.* 61 F6
Guixi, *China* 59 C11
Guiyang, *Guizhou, China* 58 D6
Guiyang, *Hunan, China* 59 E9
Guizhou □, *China* 58 D6
Gujan-Mestras, *France* 20 D2
Gujar Khan, *Pakistan* 68 C5
Gujarat □, *India* 68 H4
Gujiang, *China* 59 D10
Gujranwala, *Pakistan* 68 C6
Gujrat, *Pakistan* 68 C6
Gukovo, *Russia* 49 F5
Gulbarga, *India* 66 L10
Gulbene, *Latvia* 9 H22
Gulf, The, *Asia* 71 E6
Gulfport, *U.S.A.* 113 K10
Gulin, *China* 58 C5
Gulistan, *Pakistan* 68 D2
Gull Lake, *Canada* 105 C7
Gullbrandstorp, *Sweden* 11 H6
Gullspång, *Sweden* 11 F8
Güllük, *Turkey* 39 D9
Güllük Korfezi, *Turkey* 39 D9
Gulma, *Nigeria* 83 C5
Gulmarg, *India* 69 B6
Gülnar, *Turkey* 72 D5
Gülpınar, *Turkey* 39 B8
Gülşehir, *Turkey* 72 C6
Gulshad, *Kazakstan* 50 E8
Gulu, *Uganda* 86 B3
Gŭlŭbovo, *Bulgaria* 41 D9
Gulud, J., *Sudan* 81 E2
Gulwe, *Tanzania* 86 D4
Gulyaypole = Hulyaypole, *Ukraine* 47 J9
Gumal →, *Pakistan* 68 D4
Gumbaz, *Pakistan* 68 D3
Gumel, *Nigeria* 83 C6
Gumiel de Hizán, *Spain* 34 D7
Gumla, *India* 69 H11
Gumlu, *Australia* 94 B4
Gumma □, *Japan* 55 F9
Gummersbach, *Germany* 24 D3
Gummi, *Nigeria* 83 C6
Gümüldür, *Turkey* 39 C9
Gümüşçay, *Turkey* 41 F11
Gümüşhaciköy, *Turkey* 72 B6
Gümüşhane, *Turkey* 73 B8
Gümüşsu, *Turkey* 39 C11
Gumzai, *Indonesia* 63 F8
Guna, *Ethiopia* 81 F4
Guna, *India* 68 G7
Gundelfingen, *Germany* 25 G6
Güney, *Burdur, Turkey* 39 D11
Güney, *Denizli, Turkey* 39 C11
Güneydoğu Toroslar, *Turkey* 73 C9
Gunisao →, *Canada* 105 C9
Gunisao L., *Canada* 105 C9
Gunjyal, *Pakistan* 68 C4
Günlüce, *Turkey* 39 E10
Gunnarskog, *Sweden* 10 E6
Gunnbjørn Fjeld, *Greenland* 4 C6
Gunnebo, *Sweden* 11 G10
Gunnewin, *Australia* 95 D4
Gunnison, *Colo., U.S.A.* 115 G10
Gunnison, *Utah, U.S.A.* 114 G8
Gunnison →, *U.S.A.* 115 G9
Gunpowder, *Australia* 94 B2
Guntakal, *India* 66 M10
Guntersville, *U.S.A.* 109 H2
Guntong, *Malaysia* 65 K3
Guntur, *India* 67 L12
Gunungapi, *Indonesia* 63 F7
Gunungsitoli, *Indonesia* 62 D1
Günz →, *Germany* 25 G6
Gunza, *Angola* 84 G2
Günzburg, *Germany* 25 G6
Gunzenhausen, *Germany* 25 F6
Guo He →, *China* 57 H9
Guoyang, *China* 56 H9
Gupis, *Pakistan* 69 A5
Gura Humorului, *Romania* 43 C10
Gura-Teghii, *Romania* 43 E11
Gurag, *Ethiopia* 81 F4
Gurahonţ, *Romania* 42 D7
Gurdaspur, *India* 68 C6
Gurdon, *U.S.A.* 113 J8
Güre, *Balıkesir, Turkey* 39 B8
Güre, *Uşak, Turkey* 39 C11
Gurgaon, *India* 68 E7
Gürgentepe, *Turkey* 72 B7
Gurghiu, Munţii, *Romania* 43 D10
Gurgueia →, *Brazil* 125 E10
Gurha, *India* 68 G4
Guri, Embalse de, *Venezuela* 124 B6
Gurin, *Nigeria* 83 D7
Gurjaani, *Georgia* 49 K7
Gurk →, *Austria* 26 E7
Gurkha, *Nepal* 69 E11
Gurley, *Australia* 95 D4
Gurnet Point, *U.S.A.* 111 D14
Gürpınar, *Ist., Turkey* 41 F12
Gürpınar, *Van, Turkey* 73 C10
Gürsu, *Turkey* 41 F13
Gurué, *Mozam.* 87 F4
Gurun, *Malaysia* 65 K3
Gürün, *Turkey* 72 C7
Gurupá, *Brazil* 125 D8
Gurupá, I. Grande de, *Brazil* 125 D8
Gurupi, *Brazil* 125 F9
Gurupi →, *Brazil* 125 D9
Guruwe, *Zimbabwe* 89 B5
Guryev = Atyraū, *Kazakstan* 50 E6
Gus-Khrustalnyy, *Russia* 48 C5
Gusau, *Nigeria* 83 C6
Gusev, *Russia* 9 J20
Gushan, *China* 57 E12
Gushgy, *Turkmenistan* 50 F7
Gushi, *China* 59 A10
Gushiago, *Ghana* 83 D4
Gusinje, *Montenegro, Yug.* 40 D3
Gusinoozersk, *Russia* 51 D11
Gúspini, *Italy* 30 C1
Güssing, *Austria* 27 D9
Gustavsberg, *Sweden* 10 E12
Gustavus, *U.S.A.* 104 B1
Gustine, *U.S.A.* 116 H6
Güstrow, *Germany* 24 B8
Gusum, *Sweden* 11 F10
Guta = Kolárovo, *Slovak Rep.* 27 D10
Gütersloh, *Germany* 24 D4
Gutha, *Australia* 93 E2
Guthalungra, *Australia* 94 B4
Guthrie, *Okla., U.S.A.* 113 H6
Guthrie, *Tex., U.S.A.* 113 J4
Gutian, *China* 59 D12
Guttenberg, *U.S.A.* 112 D9
Gutu, *Zimbabwe* 89 B5
Guyana ■, *S. Amer.* 124 C7
Guyane française = French Guiana ■, *S. Amer.* 125 C8
Guyang, *China* 56 D6
Guyenne, *France* 20 D4
Guymon, *U.S.A.* 113 G4
Guyra, *Australia* 95 E5
Guyuan, *Hebei, China* 56 D8
Guyuan, *Ningxia Huizu, China* 56 G4
Güzelbahçe, *Turkey* 39 C8
Guzhang, *China* 58 C7
Guzhen, *China* 57 H9
Guzmán, L. de, *Mexico* 118 A3
Gvardeysk, *Russia* 9 J19
Gvardeyskoye, *Ukraine* 47 K8
Gwa, *Burma* 67 L19
Gwaai, *Zimbabwe* 87 F2
Gwabegar, *Australia* 95 E4
Gwadabawa, *Nigeria* 83 C6
Gwādar, *Pakistan* 66 G3
Gwagwada, *Nigeria* 83 C6
Gwalior, *India* 68 F8
Gwanara, *Nigeria* 83 D5
Gwanda, *Zimbabwe* 87 G2
Gwandu, *Nigeria* 83 C5
Gwane, *Dem. Rep. of the Congo* 86 B2
Gwaram, *Nigeria* 83 C7
Gwarzo, *Nigeria* 83 C6
Gwasero, *Nigeria* 83 D5
Gwda →, *Poland* 45 E3
Gweebarra B., *Ireland* 15 B3
Gweedore, *Ireland* 15 A3
Gweru, *Zimbabwe* 87 F2
Gwi, *Nigeria* 83 D6
Gwinn, *U.S.A.* 108 B2
Gwio Kura, *Nigeria* 83 C7
Gwoza, *Nigeria* 83 C7
Gwydir →, *Australia* 95 D4
Gwynedd □, *U.K.* 12 E3
Gyandzha = Gäncä, *Azerbaijan* 49 K8
Gyaring Hu, *China* 60 C4
Gydanskiy Poluostrov, *Russia* 50 C8
Gympie, *Australia* 95 D5
Gyomaendrőd, *Hungary* 42 D5
Gyöngyös, *Hungary* 42 C4
Győr, *Hungary* 42 C2
Győr-Moson-Sopron □, *Hungary* 42 C2
Gypsum Pt., *Canada* 104 A6
Gypsumville, *Canada* 105 C9
Gyueshevo, *Bulgaria* 40 D6
Gyula, *Hungary* 42 D6
Gyumri, *Armenia* 49 K6
Gyzylarbat, *Turkmenistan* 50 F6
Gyzyletrek, *Turkmenistan* 71 B7
Gzhatsk = Gagarin, *Russia* 46 E8

H

Ha 'Arava →, *Israel* 75 E4
Ha Coi, *Vietnam* 58 G6
Ha Dong, *Vietnam* 58 G5
Ha Giang, *Vietnam* 58 F5
Ha Tien, *Vietnam* 65 G5
Ha Tinh, *Vietnam* 64 C5
Ha Trung, *Vietnam* 64 C5
Haaksbergen, *Neths.* 17 B6
Haapsalu, *Estonia* 9 G20
Haarlem, *Neths.* 17 B4
Haast →, *N.Z.* 91 K2
Haast Bluff, *Australia* 92 D5
Hab →, *Pakistan* 68 G3
Hab Nadi Chauki, *Pakistan* 68 G2
Habaswein, *Kenya* 86 B4
Habay, *Canada* 104 B5
Ḩabbānīyah, *Iraq* 70 C4
Ḩabbānīyah, Hawr al, *Iraq* 73 F10
Habo, *Sweden* 11 G8
Haboro, *Japan* 54 B10
Ḩabshān, *U.A.E.* 71 F7
Hachenburg, *Germany* 24 E3
Hachijō-Jima, *Japan* 55 H9
Hachinohe, *Japan* 54 D10
Hachiōji, *Japan* 55 G9
Hachŏn, *N. Korea* 57 D15
Hacıbektaş, *Turkey* 72 C6
Hacılar, *Turkey* 72 C6
Hackås, *Sweden* 10 B8
Hackensack, *U.S.A.* 111 F10
Hackettstown, *U.S.A.* 111 F10
Hadali, *Pakistan* 68 C5
Hadarba, Ras, *Sudan* 80 C4
Hadarom □, *Israel* 75 E4
Hadd, Ra's al, *Oman* 74 C6
Hadejia, *Nigeria* 83 C7
Hadejia →, *Nigeria* 83 C7
Ḩadera, *Israel* 75 C3
Ḩadera, N. →, *Israel* 75 C3
Haderslev, *Denmark* 11 J3
Hadhramaut = Ḩaḑramawt, *Yemen* 74 D4
Hadibu, *Yemen* 74 E5
Hadım, *Turkey* 72 D5
Hadong, *S. Korea* 57 G14
Ḩaḑramawt, *Yemen* 74 D4
Ḩadrānīyah, *Iraq* 70 C4
Hadrian's Wall, *U.K.* 12 B5
Hadsten, *Denmark* 11 H4
Hadsund, *Denmark* 11 H4
Hadyach, *Ukraine* 47 G8
Haeju, *N. Korea* 57 E13
Haenam, *S. Korea* 57 G14
Haenertsburg, *S. Africa* 89 C4
Haerhpin = Harbin, *China* 57 B14
Hafar al Bāţin, *Si. Arabia* 70 D5
Hafik, *Turkey* 72 C7
Ḩafīrat al 'Aydā, *Si. Arabia* 70 E3
Ḩafit, *Oman* 71 F7
Hafizabad, *Pakistan* 68 C5
Haflong, *India* 67 G18
Hafnarfjörður, *Iceland* 8 D3
Haft Gel, *Iran* 71 D6
Hafun, Ras, *Somali Rep.* 74 E5
Hagalil, *Israel* 75 C4
Hagby, *Sweden* 11 H10
Hagen, *Germany* 24 D3
Hagenow, *Germany* 24 B7
Hagerman, *U.S.A.* 113 J2
Hagerstown, *U.S.A.* 108 F7
Hagersville, *Canada* 110 D4
Hagetmau, *France* 20 E3
Hagfors, *Sweden* 10 D7
Hagi, *Japan* 55 G5
Hagolan, *Syria* 75 C4
Hagondange, *France* 19 C13
Hags Hd., *Ireland* 15 D2
Hague, C. de la, *France* 18 C5
Hague, The = 's-Gravenhage, *Neths.* 17 B4
Haguenau, *France* 19 D14
Hai Duong, *Vietnam* 58 G6
Hai'an, *Guangdong, China* 59 G8
Hai'an, *Jiangsu, China* 59 A13
Haicheng, *Fujian, China* 59 E11
Haicheng, *Liaoning, China* 57 D12
Haidar Khel, *Afghan.* 68 C3
Haidargarh, *India* 69 F9
Haifa = Ḩefa, *Israel* 75 C4
Haifeng, *China* 59 F10
Haiger, *Germany* 24 E4
Haikou, *China* 60 D6
Ḩā'il, *Si. Arabia* 70 E4
Hailar, *China* 60 B6
Hailey, *U.S.A.* 114 E6
Haileybury, *Canada* 102 C4
Hailin, *China* 57 B15
Hailing Dao, *China* 59 G8
Hailong, *China* 57 C13
Hailuoto, *Finland* 8 D21
Haimen, *Guangdong, China* 59 F11
Haimen, *Jiangsu, China* 59 B13
Hainan □, *China* 60 E5
Hainaut □, *Belgium* 17 D4
Hainburg, *Austria* 27 C9
Haines, *Alaska, U.S.A.* 104 B1
Haines, *Oreg., U.S.A.* 114 D5
Haines City, *U.S.A.* 109 L5
Haines Junction, *Canada* 104 A1
Hainfeld, *Austria* 26 C8
Haining, *China* 59 B13
Haiphong, *Vietnam* 58 G6
Haitan Dao, *China* 59 E12
Haiti ■, *W. Indies* 121 C5
Haiya, *Sudan* 80 D4
Haiyan, *China* 59 B13
Haiyang, *China* 57 F11
Haiyuan, *Guangxi Zhuangzu, China* 58 F6
Haiyuan, *Ningxia Huizu, China* 56 F3
Haizhou, *China* 57 G10
Haizhou Wan, *China* 57 G10
Hajdú-Bihar □, *Hungary* 42 C6
Hajdúböszörmény, *Hungary* 42 C6
Hajdúdorog, *Hungary* 42 C6
Hajdúhadház, *Hungary* 42 C6
Hajdúnánás, *Hungary* 42 C6
Hajdúsámson, *Hungary* 42 C6
Hajdúszoboszló, *Hungary* 42 C6
Hajipur, *India* 69 G11
Ḩājjī Muḩsin, *Iraq* 70 C5
Ḩājjīābād, *Iran* 71 D7
Ḩājjīābād-e Zarrīn, *Iran* 71 C7
Hajnówka, *Poland* 45 F10
Hakansson, Mts., *Dem. Rep. of the Congo* 87 D2
Hakkâri, *Turkey* 70 B4
Hakkâri Dağları, *Turkey* 73 C10
Hakken-Zan, *Japan* 55 G7
Hakodate, *Japan* 54 D10
Hakos, *Namibia* 88 C2
Håksberg, *Sweden* 10 D9
Haku-San, *Japan* 55 F8
Hakui, *Japan* 55 F8
Hala, *Pakistan* 66 G6
Ḩalab, *Syria* 70 B3
Ḩalabjah, *Iraq* 70 C5
Halaib, *Sudan* 80 C4
Halasa, *Sudan* 81 E3
Hālat 'Ammār, *Si. Arabia* 70 D3
Halbā, *Lebanon* 75 A5
Halberstadt, *Germany* 24 D7
Halcombe, *N.Z.* 91 J5
Halcon, *Phil.* 63 B6
Halden, *Norway* 9 G14
Haldensleben, *Germany* 24 C7
Haldia, *India* 67 H16
Haldwani, *India* 69 E8
Hale →, *Australia* 94 C2
Halesowen, *U.K.* 13 E5
Haleyville, *U.S.A.* 109 H2
Half Assini, *Ghana* 82 D4
Halfmoon Bay, *N.Z.* 91 M2
Halfway →, *Canada* 104 B4
Halia, *India* 69 G10
Haliburton, *Canada* 102 C4
Halifax, *Australia* 94 B4
Halifax, *Canada* 103 D7
Halifax, *U.K.* 12 D6
Halifax, *U.S.A.* 110 F8
Halifax B., *Australia* 94 B4
Halifax I., *Namibia* 88 D2
Halīl →, *Iran* 71 E8
Halkirk, *U.K.* 14 C5
Hall Beach = Sanirajak, *Canada* 101 B11
Hall in Tirol, *Austria* 26 D4
Hall Pen., *Canada* 101 B13
Hall Pt., *Australia* 92 C3
Hallabro, *Sweden* 11 H9
Halland, *Sweden* 9 H15
Hallands län □, *Sweden* 11 H6
Hallands Väderö, *Sweden* 11 H6
Hallandsås, *Sweden* 11 H7
Hällbybrunn, *Sweden* 10 E10
Halle, *Belgium* 17 D4
Halle, *Nordrhein-Westfalen, Germany* 24 C4
Halle, *Sachsen-Anhalt, Germany* 24 D7
Hällefors, *Sweden* 10 E8
Hälleforsnäs, *Sweden* 10 E10
Hallein, *Austria* 26 D6
Hällekis, *Sweden* 11 F7
Hallen, *Sweden* 10 A8
Hallettsville, *U.S.A.* 113 L6
Hallim, *S. Korea* 57 H14
Hallingdalselvi →, *Norway* 9 F13
Hallock, *U.S.A.* 112 A6
Halls Creek, *Australia* 92 C4
Hallsberg, *Sweden* 10 E9
Hallstahammar, *Sweden* 10 E10
Hallstatt, *Austria* 26 D6
Hallstavik, *Sweden* 10 D12
Hallstead, *U.S.A.* 111 E9
Halmahera, *Indonesia* 63 D7
Halmeu, *Romania* 42 C8
Halmstad, *Sweden* 11 H6
Hals, *Denmark* 11 H4
Hälsingborg = Helsingborg, *Sweden* 11 H6
Hälsingland, *Sweden* 10 C10
Halstead, *U.K.* 13 F8
Haltern, *Germany* 24 D3
Halti, *Finland* 8 B19
Halton □, *U.K.* 12 D5
Haltwhistle, *U.K.* 12 C5
Ḩalul, *Qatar* 71 E7
Halvad, *India* 68 H4
Ḩalvān, *Iran* 71 C8
Ham, *France* 19 C10
Ham Tan, *Vietnam* 65 G6
Ham Yen, *Vietnam* 64 A5
Hamab, *Namibia* 88 D2
Hamad, *Sudan* 81 D3
Hamada, *Japan* 55 G6
Hamadān, *Iran* 71 C6
Hamadān □, *Iran* 71 C6
Hamāh, *Syria* 70 C3
Hamamatsu, *Japan* 55 G8
Hamar, *Norway* 9 F14
Hamâta, Gebel, *Egypt* 70 E2
Hambantota, *Sri Lanka* 66 R12
Hamber Prov. Park, *Canada* 104 C5
Hamburg, *Germany* 24 B5
Hamburg, *Ark., U.S.A.* 113 J9
Hamburg, *N.Y., U.S.A.* 110 D6
Hamburg, *Pa., U.S.A.* 111 F9
Hamburg □, *Germany* 24 B5
Ḩamḑ, W. al →, *Si. Arabia* 70 E3
Hamden, *U.S.A.* 111 E12
Hamdibey, *Turkey* 39 B9
Häme, *Finland* 9 F20
Hämeenlinna, *Finland* 9 F21
Hamélé, *Ghana* 82 C4
Hamelin Pool, *Australia* 93 E1
Hameln, *Germany* 24 C5
Hamerkaz □, *Israel* 75 C3
Hamersley Ra., *Australia* 92 D2
Hamhung, *N. Korea* 57 E14
Hami, *China* 60 B4
Hamilton, *Canada* 102 D4
Hamilton, *N.Z.* 91 G5
Hamilton, *U.K.* 14 F4

Hamilton, *Ala., U.S.A.* 109 H1
Hamilton, *Mont., U.S.A.* 114 C6
Hamilton, *N.Y., U.S.A.* 111 D9
Hamilton, *Ohio, U.S.A.* 108 F3
Hamilton, *Tex., U.S.A.* 113 K5
Hamilton →, *Australia* 94 C2
Hamilton City, *U.S.A.* 116 F4
Hamilton Inlet, *Canada* 103 B8
Hamilton Mt., *U.S.A.* 111 C10
Hamina, *Finland* 9 F22
Hamirpur, *H.P., India* 68 D7
Hamirpur, *Ut. P., India* 69 G9
Hamitabat, *Turkey* 41 E11
Hamlet, *U.S.A.* 109 H6
Hamlin = Hameln, *Germany* 24 C5
Hamlin, *N.Y., U.S.A.* 110 C7
Hamlin, *Tex., U.S.A.* 113 J4
Hamm, *Germany* 24 D3
Ḩammār, Hawr al, *Iraq* 70 D5
Hammarstrand, *Sweden* 10 A10
Hammelburg, *Germany* 25 E5
Hammeren, *Denmark* 11 J8
Hammerfest, *Norway* 8 A20
Hammerum, *Denmark* 11 H3
Hamminkeln, *Germany* 24 D2
Hammond, *Ind., U.S.A.* 108 E2
Hammond, *La., U.S.A.* 113 K9
Hammond, *N.Y., U.S.A.* 111 B9
Hammondsport, *U.S.A.* 110 D7
Hammonton, *U.S.A.* 108 F8
Hamneda, *Sweden* 11 H7
Hamoyet, Jebel, *Sudan* 80 D4
Hampden, *N.Z.* 91 L3
Hampshire □, *U.K.* 13 F6
Hampshire Downs, *U.K.* 13 F6
Hampton, *N.B., Canada* 103 C6
Hampton, *Ont., Canada* 110 C6
Hampton, *Ark., U.S.A.* 113 J8
Hampton, *Iowa, U.S.A.* 112 D8
Hampton, *N.H., U.S.A.* 111 D14
Hampton, *S.C., U.S.A.* 109 J5
Hampton, *Va., U.S.A.* 108 G7
Hampton Bays, *U.S.A.* 111 F12
Hampton Tableland, *Australia* 93 F4
Hamra, *Sweden* 10 C8
Hamrat esh Sheykh, *Sudan* 81 E2
Hamur, *Turkey* 73 C10
Hamyang, *S. Korea* 57 G14
Han Jiang →, *China* 59 F11
Han Shui, *China* 58 A7
Han Shui →, *China* 59 B10
Hanak, *Si. Arabia* 70 E3
Hanamaki, *Japan* 54 E10
Hanang, *Tanzania* 86 C4
Hanau, *Germany* 25 E4
Hanbogd = Ihbulag, *Mongolia* 56 C4
Hançalar, *Turkey* 39 C11
Hânceşti, *Moldova* 43 D13
Hancheng, *China* 56 G6
Hanchuan, *China* 59 B9
Hancock, *Mich., U.S.A.* 112 B10
Hancock, *N.Y., U.S.A.* 111 E9
Handa, *Japan* 55 G8
Handan, *China* 56 F8
Handeni, *Tanzania* 86 D4
Handlová, *Slovak Rep.* 27 C11
Handub, *Sudan* 80 D4
Handwara, *India* 69 B6
Hanegev, *Israel* 75 E4
Hanford, *U.S.A.* 116 J7
Hang Chat, *Thailand* 64 C2
Hang Dong, *Thailand* 64 C2
Hangang →, *S. Korea* 57 F14
Hangayn Nuruu, *Mongolia* 60 B4
Hangchou = Hangzhou, *China* 59 B13
Hanggin Houqi, *China* 56 D4
Hanggin Qi, *China* 56 E5
Hangu, *China* 57 E9
Hangzhou, *China* 59 B13
Hangzhou Wan, *China* 59 B13
Hanhongor, *Mongolia* 56 C3
Ḩanīdh, *Si. Arabia* 71 E6
Ḩanīsh, *Yemen* 74 E3
Haniska, *Slovak Rep.* 27 C14
Hanjiang, *China* 59 E12
Hankinson, *U.S.A.* 112 B6
Hanko, *Finland* 9 G20
Hankou, *China* 59 B10
Hanksville, *U.S.A.* 115 G8
Hanle, *India* 69 C8
Hanmer Springs, *N.Z.* 91 K4
Hann →, *Australia* 92 C4
Hann, Mt., *Australia* 92 C4
Hanna, *Canada* 104 C6
Hanna, *U.S.A.* 114 F10
Hannah B., *Canada* 102 B4
Hannibal, *Mo., U.S.A.* 112 F9
Hannibal, *N.Y., U.S.A.* 111 C8
Hannik, *Sudan* 80 D3
Hannover, *Germany* 24 C5
Hanö, *Sweden* 11 H8
Hanöbukten, *Sweden* 11 J8
Hanoi, *Vietnam* 58 G5
Hanover = Hannover, *Germany* 24 C5
Hanover, *Canada* 102 D3
Hanover, *S. Africa* 88 E3
Hanover, *N.H., U.S.A.* 111 C12
Hanover, *Ohio, U.S.A.* 110 F2
Hanover, *Pa., U.S.A.* 108 F7
Hanover, I., *Chile* 128 G2
Hansdiha, *India* 69 G12
Hanshou, *China* 59 C8
Hansi, *India* 68 E6
Hanstholm, *Denmark* 11 G2
Hantsavichy, *Belarus* 47 F4
Hanumangarh, *India* 68 E6
Hanyin, *China* 58 A7
Hanyuan, *China* 58 C4
Hanzhong, *China* 56 H4
Hanzhuang, *China* 57 G9
Haora, *India* 69 H13
Haoxue, *China* 59 B9
Haparanda, *Sweden* 8 D21
Happy, *U.S.A.* 113 H4
Happy Camp, *U.S.A.* 114 F2
Happy Valley-Goose Bay, *Canada* 103 B7
Hapsu, *N. Korea* 57 D15
Hapur, *India* 68 E7
Ḩaql, *Si. Arabia* 75 F3
Har, *Indonesia* 63 F8
Har-Ayrag, *Mongolia* 56 B5
Har Hu, *China* 60 C4
Har Us Nuur, *Mongolia* 60 B4
Har Yehuda, *Israel* 75 D3
Ḩaraḑ, *Si. Arabia* 74 C4
Haradok, *Belarus* 46 E6
Häradsbäck, *Sweden* 11 H8
Haranomachi, *Japan* 54 F10
Harare, *Zimbabwe* 87 F3
Harat, *Eritrea* 81 D4
Harbin, *China* 57 B14
Harbiye, *Turkey* 72 D7
Harbo, *Sweden* 10 D11
Harboør, *Denmark* 11 H2
Harbor Beach, *U.S.A.* 110 C2
Harbour Breton, *Canada* 103 C8
Harbour Deep, *Canada* 103 B8
Harburg, *Germany* 24 B5
Hårby, *Denmark* 11 J4
Harda, *India* 68 H7
Hardangerfjorden, *Norway* 9 F12
Hardangervidda, *Norway* 9 F12
Hardap Dam, *Namibia* 88 C2
Hardenberg, *Neths.* 17 B6
Harderwijk, *Neths.* 17 B5
Hardey →, *Australia* 92 D2
Hardin, *U.S.A.* 114 D10
Harding, *S. Africa* 89 E4
Harding Ra., *Australia* 92 C3
Hardisty, *Canada* 104 C6
Hardoi, *India* 69 F9
Hardwar = Haridwar, *India* 68 E8
Hardwick, *U.S.A.* 111 B12
Hardy, Pen., *Chile* 128 H3
Hare B., *Canada* 103 B8
Hareid, *Norway* 9 E12
Haren, *Germany* 24 C3
Harer, *Ethiopia* 81 F5
Harerge □, *Ethiopia* 81 F5
Hareto, *Ethiopia* 81 F4
Harfleur, *France* 18 C7
Hargeisa, *Somali Rep.* 74 F3
Harghita □, *Romania* 43 D10
Harghita, Munţii, *Romania* 43 D10
Hargshamn, *Sweden* 10 D12
Hari →, *Indonesia* 62 E2
Haria, *Canary Is.* 37 E6
Haridwar, *India* 68 E8
Harim, Jabal al, *Oman* 71 E8
Haringhata →, *Bangla.* 67 J16
Harīrūd →, *Asia* 66 A2
Härjedalen, *Sweden* 10 B7
Harlan, *Iowa, U.S.A.* 112 E7
Harlan, *Ky., U.S.A.* 109 G4
Hârlău, *Romania* 43 C11
Harlech, *U.K.* 12 E3
Harlem, *U.S.A.* 114 B9
Hårlev, *Denmark* 11 J6
Harlingen, *Neths.* 17 A5
Harlingen, *U.S.A.* 113 M6
Harlow, *U.K.* 13 F8
Harlowton, *U.S.A.* 114 C9
Harmancık, *Turkey* 39 B11
Harmånger, *Sweden* 10 C11
Harmil, *Eritrea* 81 D5
Harnai, *Pakistan* 68 D2
Harney Basin, *U.S.A.* 114 E4
Harney L., *U.S.A.* 114 E4
Harney Peak, *U.S.A.* 112 D3
Härnön, *Sweden* 10 B12
Härnösand, *Sweden* 10 B11
Haro, *Spain* 32 C2
Haroldswick, *U.K.* 14 A8
Harp L., *Canada* 103 A7
Harper, *Liberia* 82 E3
Harplinge, *Sweden* 11 H6
Harr, *Mauritania* 82 B2
Harrai, *India* 69 H8
Harrand, *Pakistan* 68 E4
Ḩarrat Khaybar, *Si. Arabia* 80 B5
Ḩarrat Nawāşīf, *Si. Arabia* 80 C5
Harricana →, *Canada* 102 B4
Harriman, *U.S.A.* 109 H3
Harrington Harbour, *Canada* 103 B8
Harris, *U.K.* 14 D2
Harris, Sd. of, *U.K.* 14 D1
Harris L., *Australia* 95 E2
Harris Pt., *Canada* 110 C2
Harrisburg, *Ill., U.S.A.* 113 G10
Harrisburg, *Nebr., U.S.A.* 112 E3
Harrisburg, *Pa., U.S.A.* 110 F8
Harrismith, *S. Africa* 89 D4
Harrison, *Ark., U.S.A.* 113 G8
Harrison, *Maine, U.S.A.* 111 B14
Harrison, *Nebr., U.S.A.* 112 D3
Harrison, C., *Canada* 103 B8
Harrison L., *Canada* 104 D4
Harrisonburg, *U.S.A.* 108 F6
Harrisonville, *U.S.A.* 112 F7
Harriston, *Canada* 110 C4
Harrisville, *Mich., U.S.A.* 110 B1
Harrisville, *N.Y., U.S.A.* 111 B9
Harrisville, *Pa., U.S.A.* 110 E5
Harrodsburg, *U.S.A.* 108 G3
Harrogate, *U.K.* 12 C6
Harrow □, *U.K.* 13 F7
Harrowsmith, *Canada* 111 B8
Harry S. Truman Reservoir, *U.S.A.* 112 F7
Harsefeld, *Germany* 24 B5
Harsewinkel, *Germany* 24 D4
Harsīn, *Iran* 70 C5
Hârşova, *Romania* 43 F12
Harstad, *Norway* 8 B17
Harsud, *India* 68 H7
Hart, *U.S.A.* 108 D2
Hartbees →, *S. Africa* 88 D3
Hartberg, *Austria* 26 D8
Hartford, *Conn., U.S.A.* 111 E12
Hartford, *Ky., U.S.A.* 108 G2
Hartford, *S. Dak., U.S.A.* 112 D6
Hartford, *Wis., U.S.A.* 112 D10
Hartford City, *U.S.A.* 108 E3
Hartland, *Canada* 103 C6
Hartland Pt., *U.K.* 13 F3
Hartlepool, *U.K.* 12 C6
Hartlepool □, *U.K.* 12 C6
Hartley Bay, *Canada* 104 C3
Hartmannberge, *Namibia* 88 B1
Hartney, *Canada* 105 D8
Hârtop, *Moldova* 43 D13
Harts →, *S. Africa* 88 D3
Hartselle, *U.S.A.* 109 H2
Hartshorne, *U.S.A.* 113 H7
Hartstown, *U.S.A.* 110 E4
Hartsville, *U.S.A.* 109 H5
Hartswater, *S. Africa* 88 D3
Hartwell, *U.S.A.* 109 H4
Harunabad, *Pakistan* 68 E5
Harvand, *Iran* 71 D7
Harvey, *Australia* 93 F2
Harvey, *Ill., U.S.A.* 108 E2
Harvey, *N. Dak., U.S.A.* 112 B5
Harwich, *U.K.* 13 F9
Haryana □, *India* 68 E7
Haryn →, *Belarus* 47 F4
Harz, *Germany* 24 D6
Harzgerode, *Germany* 24 D7
Hasa □, *Si. Arabia* 71 E6
Hasaheisa, *Sudan* 81 E3
Ḩasanābād, *Iran* 71 C7
Hasdo →, *India* 69 J10
Haselünne, *Germany* 24 C3
Hashimoto, *Japan* 55 G7
Hashtjerd, *Iran* 71 C6
Haskell, *U.S.A.* 113 J5
Hasköy, *Turkey* 41 E10
Haslach, *Germany* 25 G4
Hasle, *Denmark* 11 J8
Haslemere, *U.K.* 13 F7
Haslev, *Denmark* 11 J5
Hasparren, *France* 20 E2
Hassa, *Turkey* 72 D7
Hassela, *Sweden* 10 B10
Hasselt, *Belgium* 17 D5
Hassfurt, *Germany* 25 E6
Hassi Messaoud, *Algeria* 78 B7
Hässleholm, *Sweden* 11 H7
Hassloch, *Germany* 25 F4
Hästholmen, *Sweden* 11 F8
Hastings, *N.Z.* 91 H6
Hastings, *U.K.* 13 G8
Hastings, *Mich., U.S.A.* 108 D3
Hastings, *Minn., U.S.A.* 112 C8
Hastings, *Nebr., U.S.A.* 112 E5
Hästveda, *Sweden* 11 H7
Hat Yai, *Thailand* 65 J3
Hatanbulag = Ergel, *Mongolia* 56 C5
Hatay = Antalya, *Turkey* 72 D4
Hatch, *U.S.A.* 115 K10
Hatchet L., *Canada* 105 B8
Haţeg, *Romania* 42 E7
Hateruma-Shima, *Japan* 55 M1
Hatgal, *Mongolia* 60 A5
Hathras, *India* 68 F8
Hatia, *Bangla.* 67 H17
Ḩāţibah, Ra's, *Si. Arabia* 80 C4
Hato Mayor, *Dom. Rep.* 121 C6
Hatta, *India* 69 G8
Hatteras, C., *U.S.A.* 109 H8
Hattiesburg, *U.S.A.* 113 K10
Hatvan, *Hungary* 42 C4
Hau Bon = Cheo Reo, *Vietnam* 62 B3
Hau Duc, *Vietnam* 64 E7
Haugesund, *Norway* 9 G11
Haukipudas, *Finland* 8 D21
Haultain →, *Canada* 105 B7
Hauraki G., *N.Z.* 91 G5
Hausruck, *Austria* 26 C6
Haut Atlas, *Morocco* 78 B4
Haut-Rhin □, *France* 19 E14
Haut-Zaïre = Orientale □, *Dem. Rep. of the Congo* 86 B2
Haute-Corse □, *France* 21 F13
Haute-Garonne □, *France* 20 E5
Haute-Loire □, *France* 20 C7
Haute-Marne □, *France* 19 D12
Haute-Normandie □, *France* 18 C7
Haute-Saône □, *France* 19 E13
Haute-Savoie □, *France* 21 C10
Haute-Vienne □, *France* 20 C5
Hautes-Alpes □, *France* 21 D10
Hautes Fagnes = Hohe Venn, *Belgium* 17 D6
Hautes-Pyrénées □, *France* 20 F4
Hauteville-Lompnès, *France* 21 C9
Hautmont, *France* 19 B10
Hauts-de-Seine □, *France* 19 D9
Hauts Plateaux, *Algeria* 76 C4
Hauzenberg, *Germany* 25 G9
Havana = La Habana, *Cuba* 120 B3
Havana, *U.S.A.* 112 E9
Havant, *U.K.* 13 G7
Havârna, *Romania* 43 B11
Havasu, L., *U.S.A.* 117 L12
Havdhem, *Sweden* 11 G12
Havel →, *Germany* 24 C8
Havelian, *Pakistan* 68 B5
Havelock, *Canada* 102 D4
Havelock, *N.Z.* 91 J4
Havelock, *U.S.A.* 109 H7
Haverfordwest, *U.K.* 13 F3
Haverhill, *U.S.A.* 111 D13
Haverstraw, *U.S.A.* 111 E11
Håverud, *Sweden* 11 F6
Havirga, *Mongolia* 56 B7
Havířov, *Czech Rep.* 27 B11
Havlíčkův Brod, *Czech Rep.* 26 B8
Havneby, *Denmark* 11 J2
Havran, *Turkey* 39 B9
Havre, *U.S.A.* 114 B9
Havre-Aubert, *Canada* 103 C7
Havre-St.-Pierre, *Canada* 103 B7
Havsa, *Turkey* 41 E10
Havza, *Turkey* 72 B6
Haw →, *U.S.A.* 109 H6
Hawaii □, *U.S.A.* 106 H16
Hawaii I., *Pac. Oc.* 106 J17
Hawaiian Is., *Pac. Oc.* 106 H17
Hawaiian Ridge, *Pac. Oc.* 97 E11
Hawarden, *U.S.A.* 112 D6
Hawea, L., *N.Z.* 91 L2
Hawera, *N.Z.* 91 H5
Hawick, *U.K.* 14 F6
Hawk Junction, *Canada* 102 C3
Hawke B., *N.Z.* 91 H6
Hawkesbury, *Canada* 102 C5
Hawkesbury I., *Canada* 104 C3
Hawkesbury Pt., *Australia* 94 A1
Hawkinsville, *U.S.A.* 109 J4
Hawley, *Minn., U.S.A.* 112 B6
Hawley, *Pa., U.S.A.* 111 E9
Ḩawrān, W. →, *Iraq* 70 C4
Hawsh Mūssá, *Lebanon* 75 B4
Hawthorne, *U.S.A.* 114 G4
Hay →, *Australia* 94 C2
Hay →, *Canada* 104 A5
Hay, C., *Australia* 92 B4
Hay I., *Canada* 110 B4
Hay L., *Canada* 104 B5
Hay-on-Wye, *U.K.* 13 E4
Hay River, *Canada* 104 A5
Hay Springs, *U.S.A.* 112 D3
Haya = Tehoru, *Indonesia* 63 E7
Hayachine-San, *Japan* 54 E10
Hayange, *France* 19 C13
Haydarlı, *Turkey* 39 C12
Hayden, *U.S.A.* 114 F10
Haydon, *Australia* 94 B3
Hayes, *U.S.A.* 112 C4
Hayes →, *Canada* 102 A1
Hayes Creek, *Australia* 92 B5
Hayle, *U.K.* 13 G2
Hayling I., *U.K.* 13 G7
Haymana, *Turkey* 72 C5
Hayrabolu, *Turkey* 41 E11
Hays, *Canada* 104 C6
Hays, *U.S.A.* 112 F5
Haysyn, *Ukraine* 47 H5
Hayvoron, *Ukraine* 47 H5
Hayward, *Calif., U.S.A.* 116 H4
Hayward, *Wis., U.S.A.* 112 B9
Haywards Heath, *U.K.* 13 G7
Hazafon □, *Israel* 75 C4
Hazārān, Kūh-e, *Iran* 71 D8
Hazard, *U.S.A.* 108 G4
Hazaribag, *India* 69 H11
Hazaribag Road, *India* 69 G11
Hazebrouck, *France* 19 B9
Hazelton, *Canada* 104 B3
Hazelton, *U.S.A.* 112 B4
Hazen, *U.S.A.* 112 B4
Hazlehurst, *Ga., U.S.A.* 109 K4
Hazlehurst, *Miss., U.S.A.* 113 K9
Hazlet, *U.S.A.* 111 F10
Hazleton, *U.S.A.* 111 F9
Hazlett, L., *Australia* 92 D4
Hazro, *Turkey* 70 B4
He Xian, *Anhui, China* 59 B12
He Xian, *Guangxi Zhuangzu, China* 59 E8
Head of Bight, *Australia* 93 F5
Headlands, *Zimbabwe* 87 F3
Healdsburg, *U.S.A.* 116 G4
Healdton, *U.S.A.* 113 H6
Heany Junction, *Zimbabwe* 89 C4
Heard I., *Ind. Oc.* 3 G13
Hearne, *U.S.A.* 113 K6
Hearst, *Canada* 102 C3
Heart →, *U.S.A.* 112 B4
Heart's Content, *Canada* 103 C9
Heath Pt., *Canada* 103 C7
Heavener, *U.S.A.* 113 H7
Hebbronville, *U.S.A.* 113 M5
Hebei □, *China* 56 E9
Hebel, *Australia* 95 D4
Heber, *U.S.A.* 117 N11
Heber City, *U.S.A.* 114 F8
Heber Springs, *U.S.A.* 113 H9
Hebert, *Canada* 105 C7
Hebgen L., *U.S.A.* 114 D8
Hebi, *China* 56 G8
Hebrides, *U.K.* 6 D4
Hebrides, Sea of the, *U.K.* 14 D2
Hebron = Al Khalīl, *West Bank* 75 D4
Hebron, *Canada* 101 C13
Hebron, *N. Dak., U.S.A.* 112 B3
Hebron, *Nebr., U.S.A.* 112 E6
Heby, *Sweden* 10 E10
Hecate Str., *Canada* 104 C2
Heceta I., *U.S.A.* 104 B2
Hechi, *China* 58 E7
Hechingen, *Germany* 25 G4
Hechuan, *China* 58 B6
Hecla, *U.S.A.* 112 C5
Hecla I., *Canada* 105 C9
Hédé, *France* 18 D5
Hede, *Sweden* 10 B7
Hedemora, *Sweden* 10 D9
Hedensted, *Denmark* 11 J3
Hedesunda, *Sweden* 10 D10
Heerde, *Neths.* 17 B6
Heerenveen, *Neths.* 17 B5
Heerhugowaard, *Neths.* 17 B4
Heerlen, *Neths.* 17 D5
Ḩefa, *Israel* 75 C4
Ḩefa □, *Israel* 75 C4
Hefei, *China* 59 B11
Hefeng, *China* 59 C8
Hegalig, *Sudan* 81 E3
Hegang, *China* 60 B8
Heiban, *Sudan* 81 E3
Heichengzhen, *China* 56 F4
Heide, *Germany* 24 A5
Heidelberg, *Germany* 25 F4
Heidelberg, *S. Africa* 88 E3
Heidenau, *Germany* 24 E9
Heidenheim, *Germany* 25 G6
Heijing, *China* 58 E3
Heilbad Heiligenstadt, *Germany* 24 D6
Heilbron, *S. Africa* 89 D4
Heilbronn, *Germany* 25 F5
Heiligenblut, *Austria* 26 D5
Heiligenhafen, *Germany* 24 A6
Heilongjiang □, *China* 60 B7
Heilunkiang = Heilongjiang □, *China* 60 B7
Heimaey, *Iceland* 8 E3
Heinola, *Finland* 9 F22
Heinsberg, *Germany* 24 D2
Heinze Kyun, *Burma* 64 E1
Heishan, *China* 57 D12
Heishui, *Liaoning, China* 57 C10
Heishui, *Sichuan, China* 58 A4
Hejaz = Ḩijāz □, *Si. Arabia* 70 E3
Hejian, *China* 56 E9
Hejiang, *China* 58 C5
Hejin, *China* 56 G6
Hekımhan, *Turkey* 70 B3
Hekla, *Iceland* 8 E4
Hekou, *Guangdong, China* 59 F9
Hekou, *Yunnan, China* 58 F4
Hel, *Poland* 44 D5
Helagsfjället, *Sweden* 10 B6
Helan Shan, *China* 56 E3
Helechosa, *Spain* 35 F6
Helen Atoll, *Pac. Oc.* 63 D8
Helena, *Ark., U.S.A.* 113 H9
Helena, *Mont., U.S.A.* 114 C7
Helendale, *U.S.A.* 117 L9
Helensburgh, *U.K.* 14 E4
Helensville, *N.Z.* 91 G5
Helenvale, *Australia* 94 B4
Helgasjön, *Sweden* 11 H8
Helgeland, *Norway* 8 C15
Helgoland, *Germany* 24 A3
Heligoland = Helgoland, *Germany* 24 A3
Heligoland B. = Deutsche Bucht, *Germany* 24 A4
Heliopolis, *Egypt* 80 H7
Hella, *Iceland* 8 E3
Hellertown, *U.S.A.* 111 F9
Hellespont = Çanakkale Boğazı, *Turkey* 41 F10
Hellevoetsluis, *Neths.* 17 C4
Hellín, *Spain* 33 G3
Helmand □, *Afghan.* 66 D4
Helmand →, *Afghan.* 66 D2
Helme →, *Germany* 24 D7
Helmeringhausen, *Namibia* 88 D2
Helmond, *Neths.* 17 C5
Helmsdale, *U.K.* 14 C5
Helmsdale →, *U.K.* 14 C5
Helmstedt, *Germany* 24 C7
Helong, *China* 57 C15
Helper, *U.S.A.* 114 G8
Helsingborg, *Sweden* 11 H6
Helsinge, *Denmark* 11 H6
Helsingfors = Helsinki, *Finland* 9 F21
Helsingør, *Denmark* 11 H6
Helsinki, *Finland* 9 F21
Helska, Mierzeja, *Poland* 44 D5
Helston, *U.K.* 13 G2
Helvellyn, *U.K.* 12 C4
Helwân, *Egypt* 80 J7
Hemel Hempstead, *U.K.* 13 F7
Hemet, *U.S.A.* 117 M10
Hemingford, *U.S.A.* 112 D3
Hemmingford, *Canada* 111 A11
Hempstead, *U.S.A.* 113 K6
Hemse, *Sweden* 11 G12
Hemsön, *Sweden* 10 B12
Henån, *Sweden* 11 F5
Henan □, *China* 56 H8
Henares →, *Spain* 34 E7
Henashi-Misaki, *Japan* 54 D9
Hendaye, *France* 20 E2
Hendek, *Turkey* 72 B4

Henderson, Argentina 126 D3
Henderson, Ky., U.S.A. 108 G2
Henderson, N.C., U.S.A. 109 G6
Henderson, Nev., U.S.A. 117 J12
Henderson, Tenn., U.S.A. 109 H1
Henderson, Tex., U.S.A. 113 J7
Hendersonville, N.C., U.S.A. 109 H4
Hendersonville, Tenn., U.S.A. 109 G2
Hendījān, Iran 71 D6
Hendorābī, Iran 71 E7
Heng Jiang, China 58 C5
Heng Xian, China 58 F7
Hengcheng, China 56 E4
Hëngchun, Taiwan 59 F13
Hengdaohezi, China 57 B15
Hengelo, Neths. 17 B6
Hengfeng, China 59 C10
Hengshan, Hunan, China 59 D9
Hengshan, Shaanxi, China 56 F5
Hengshui, China 56 F8
Hengyang, China 59 D9
Henichesk, Ukraine 47 J8
Hénin-Beaumont, France 19 B9
Henlopen, C., U.S.A. 108 F8
Hennan, Sweden 10 B9
Hennebont, France 18 E3
Hennenman, S. Africa 88 D4
Hennessey, U.S.A. 113 G6
Hennigsdorf, Germany 24 C9
Henrietta, U.S.A. 113 J5
Henrietta, Ostrov = Genriyetty, Ostrov, Russia 51 B16
Henrietta Maria, C., Canada 102 A3
Henry, U.S.A. 112 E10
Henryetta, U.S.A. 113 H7
Henryville, Canada 111 A11
Hensall, Canada 110 C3
Henstedt-Ulzburg, Germany 24 B6
Hentiesbaai, Namibia 88 C1
Hentiyn Nuruu, Mongolia 60 B5
Henzada, Burma 67 L19
Hephaestia, Greece 39 B7
Heping, China 59 E10
Heppner, U.S.A. 114 D4
Hepu, China 58 G7
Hepworth, Canada 110 B3
Heqing, China 58 D3
Hequ, China 56 E6
Héraðsflói, Iceland 8 D6
Héraðsvötn →, Iceland 8 D4
Herald Cays, Australia 94 B4
Herāt, Afghan. 66 B3
Herāt □, Afghan. 66 B3
Hérault □, France 20 E7
Hérault →, France 20 E7
Herbault, France 18 E8
Herbert →, Australia 94 B4
Herberton, Australia 94 B4
Herbertsdale, S. Africa 88 E3
Herbignac, France 18 E4
Herborn, Germany 24 E4
Herby, Poland 45 H5
Herceg-Novi, Montenegro, Yug. 40 D2
Herchmer, Canada 105 B10
Herðubreið, Iceland 8 D5
Hereford, U.K. 13 E5
Hereford, U.S.A. 113 H3
Herefordshire □, U.K. 13 E5
Hereke, Turkey 41 F13
Herencia, Spain 35 F7
Herentals, Belgium 17 C4
Herford, Germany 24 C4
Héricourt, France 19 E13
Herington, U.S.A. 112 F6
Herisau, Switz. 25 H5
Hérisson, France 19 F9
Herkimer, U.S.A. 111 D10
Herlong, U.S.A. 116 E6
Herm, U.K. 13 H5
Hermann, U.S.A. 112 F9
Hermannsburg, Australia 92 D5
Hermannsburg, Germany 24 C6
Hermanus, S. Africa 88 E2
Herment, France 20 C6
Hermiston, U.S.A. 114 D4
Hermite, I., Chile 128 H3
Hermon, U.S.A. 111 B9
Hermon, Mt. = Shaykh, J. ash, Lebanon 75 B4
Hermosillo, Mexico 118 B2
Hernád →, Hungary 42 C6
Hernandarias, Paraguay 127 B5
Hernandez, U.S.A. 116 J6
Hernando, Argentina 126 C3
Hernando, U.S.A. 113 H10
Hernani, Spain 32 B3
Herndon, U.S.A. 110 F8
Herne, Germany 17 C7
Herne Bay, U.K. 13 F9
Herning, Denmark 11 H2
Heroica = Caborca, Mexico 118 A2
Heroica Nogales = Nogales, Mexico 118 A2
Heron Bay, Canada 102 C2
Herradura, Pta. de la, Canary Is. 37 F5
Herreid, U.S.A. 112 C4
Herrenberg, Germany 25 G4
Herrera, Spain 35 H6
Herrera de Alcántara, Spain 35 F3
Herrera de Pisuerga, Spain 34 C6
Herrera del Duque, Spain 35 F5
Herrestad, Sweden 11 F5
Herrin, U.S.A. 113 G10
Herriot, Canada 105 B8
Herrljunga, Sweden 11 F7
Hersbruck, Germany 25 F7
Hershey, U.S.A. 111 F8
Hersonissos, Greece 36 D7
Herstal, Belgium 17 D5
Hertford, U.K. 13 F7
Hertfordshire □, U.K. 13 F7
's-Hertogenbosch, Neths. 17 C5
Hertzogville, S. Africa 88 D4
Hervás, Spain 34 E5
Hervey B., Australia 94 C5
Herzberg, Brandenburg, Germany 24 D9
Herzberg, Niedersachsen, Germany 24 D6
Herzliyya, Israel 75 C3
Herzogenburg, Austria 26 C8
Ḥeşār, Fārs, Iran 71 D6
Ḥeşār, Markazī, Iran 71 C6
Hesdin, France 19 B9
Heshan, China 58 F7
Heshui, China 56 G5
Heshun, China 56 F7
Hesperia, U.S.A. 117 L9
Hesse = Hessen □, Germany 24 E4
Hessen □, Germany 24 E4
Hestra, Sweden 11 G7
Hetch Hetchy Aqueduct, U.S.A. 116 H5
Hettinger, U.S.A. 112 C3
Hettstedt, Germany 24 D7
Heuvelton, U.S.A. 111 B9
Heves, Hungary 42 C5
Heves □, Hungary 42 C5
Hewitt, U.S.A. 113 K6
Hexham, U.K. 12 C5
Hexi, Yunnan, China 58 E4
Hexi, Zhejiang, China 59 D12
Hexigten Qi, China 57 C9
Ḥeydarābād, Iran 71 D7
Heysham, U.K. 12 C5
Heyuan, China 59 F10
Heze, China 56 G8
Hezhang, China 58 D5
Hi Vista, U.S.A. 117 L9
Hialeah, U.S.A. 109 N5
Hiawatha, U.S.A. 112 F7
Hibbing, U.S.A. 112 B8
Hibbs B., Australia 94 G4
Hibernia Reef, Australia 92 B3
Hickman, U.S.A. 113 G10
Hickory, U.S.A. 109 H5
Hicks L., Canada 105 A9
Hicksville, U.S.A. 111 F11
Hida, Romania 43 C8
Hida-Gawa →, Japan 55 G8
Hida-Sammyaku, Japan 55 F8
Hidaka-Sammyaku, Japan 54 C11
Hidalgo, Mexico 119 C5
Hidalgo □, Mexico 119 C5
Hidalgo, Presa M., Mexico 118 B3
Hidalgo, Pta. del, Canary Is. 37 F3
Hidalgo del Parral, Mexico 118 B3
Hiddensee, Germany 24 A9
Hieflau, Austria 26 D7
Hiendelaencina, Spain 32 D2
Hierro, Canary Is. 37 G1
Higashiajima-San, Japan 54 F10
Higashiōsaka, Japan 55 G7
Higgins, U.S.A. 113 G4
Higgins Corner, U.S.A. 116 F5
High Atlas = Haut Atlas, Morocco 78 B4
High Bridge, U.S.A. 111 F10
High Level, Canada 104 B5
High Point, U.S.A. 109 H6
High Prairie, Canada 104 B5
High River, Canada 104 C6
High Tatra = Tatry, Slovak Rep. 27 B13
High Veld, Africa 76 J6
High Wycombe, U.K. 13 F7
Highland □, U.K. 14 D4
Highland Park, U.S.A. 108 D2
Highmore, U.S.A. 112 C5
Highrock L., Man., Canada 105 B8
Highrock L., Sask., Canada 105 B7
Higüey, Dom. Rep. 121 C6
Hihya, Egypt 80 H7
Hiiumaa, Estonia 9 G20
Híjar, Spain 32 D4
Ḥijāz □, Si. Arabia 70 E3
Hijo = Tagum, Phil. 61 H6
Hikari, Japan 55 H5
Hikmak, Ras el, Egypt 80 A2
Hiko, U.S.A. 116 H11
Hikone, Japan 55 G8
Hikurangi, N.Z. 91 F5
Hikurangi, Mt., N.Z. 91 H6
Hildburghausen, Germany 24 E6
Hildesheim, Germany 24 C5
Hill →, Australia 93 F2
Hill City, Idaho, U.S.A. 114 E6
Hill City, Kans., U.S.A. 112 F5
Hill City, S. Dak., U.S.A. 112 D3
Hill Island L., Canada 105 A7
Hillared, Sweden 11 G7
Hillcrest Center, U.S.A. 117 K8
Hillegom, Neths. 17 B4
Hillerød, Denmark 11 J6
Hillerstorp, Sweden 11 G7
Hillsboro, Kans., U.S.A. 112 F6
Hillsboro, N. Dak., U.S.A. 112 B6
Hillsboro, N.H., U.S.A. 111 C13
Hillsboro, Ohio, U.S.A. 108 F4
Hillsboro, Oreg., U.S.A. 116 E4
Hillsboro, Tex., U.S.A. 113 J6
Hillsborough, Grenada 121 D7
Hillsdale, Mich., U.S.A. 108 E3
Hillsdale, N.Y., U.S.A. 111 D11
Hillsport, Canada 102 C2
Hilo, U.S.A. 106 J17
Hilton, U.S.A. 110 C7
Hilton Head Island, U.S.A. 109 J5
Hilvan, Turkey 73 D8
Hilversum, Neths. 17 B5
Himachal Pradesh □, India 68 D7
Himalaya, Asia 69 E11
Himamaylan, Phil. 61 F5
Himarë, Albania 40 F3
Himatnagar, India 66 H8
Himeji, Japan 55 G7
Himi, Japan 55 F8
Himmerland, Denmark 11 H3
Ḥimş, Syria 75 A5
Ḥimş □, Syria 75 A6
Hinche, Haiti 121 C5
Hinchinbrook I., Australia 94 B4
Hinckley, U.K. 13 E6
Hinckley, U.S.A. 112 B8
Hindaun, India 68 F7
Hindsholm, Denmark 11 J4
Hindu Bagh, Pakistan 68 D2
Hindu Kush, Asia 66 B7
Hindubagh, Pakistan 66 D5
Hindupur, India 66 N10
Hines Creek, Canada 104 B5
Hinesville, U.S.A. 109 K5
Hinganghat, India 66 J11
Hingham, U.S.A. 114 B8
Hingir, India 69 J10
Hingoli, India 66 K10
Hinigaran, Phil. 61 F5
Hinis, Turkey 73 C9
Hinna = Imi, Ethiopia 81 F5
Hinna, Nigeria 83 C7
Hinnerup, Denmark 11 H4
Hinnøya, Norway 8 B16
Hinojosa del Duque, Spain 35 G5
Hinsdale, U.S.A. 111 D12
Hinterrhein →, Switz. 25 J5
Hinton, Canada 104 C5
Hinton, U.S.A. 108 G5
Hınzır Burnu, Turkey 72 D6
Hirado, Japan 55 H4
Hirakud Dam, India 67 J13
Hiran →, India 69 H8
Hirapur, India 69 G8
Hiratsuka, Japan 55 G9
Hirfanlı Barajı, Turkey 72 C5
Hiroo, Japan 54 C11
Hirosaki, Japan 54 D10
Hiroshima, Japan 55 G6
Hiroshima □, Japan 55 G6
Hirson, France 19 C11
Hirtshals, Denmark 11 G3
Hisar, India 68 E6
Hisarcık, Turkey 39 B11
Hisaria, Bulgaria 41 D8
Hisb →, Iraq 70 D5
Ḥismá, Si. Arabia 70 D3
Hispaniola, W. Indies 121 C5
Hīt, Iraq 70 C4
Hita, Japan 55 H5
Hitachi, Japan 55 F10
Hitchin, U.K. 13 F7
Hitoyoshi, Japan 55 H5
Hitra, Norway 8 E13
Hitzacker, Germany 24 B7
Hixon, Canada 104 C4
Ḥiyyon, N. →, Israel 75 E4
Hjalmar L., Canada 105 A7
Hjälmaren, Sweden 10 E9
Hjältevad, Sweden 11 G9
Hjo, Sweden 11 F8
Hjørring, Denmark 11 G3
Hjortkvarn, Sweden 11 F9
Hkakabo Razi, Burma 67 E20
Hlinsko, Czech Rep. 26 B8
Hlobane, S. Africa 89 D5
Hlohovec, Slovak Rep. 27 C10
Hlučín, Czech Rep. 27 B11
Hluhluwe, S. Africa 89 D5
Hlukhiv, Ukraine 47 G7
Hlyboka, Ukraine 47 H3
Hlybokaye, Belarus 46 E4
Hnúšt'a, Slovak Rep. 27 C12
Ho, Ghana 83 D5
Ho Chi Minh City = Thanh Pho Ho Chi Minh, Vietnam 65 G6
Ho Thuong, Vietnam 64 C5
Hoa Binh, Vietnam 58 G5
Hoa Da, Vietnam 65 G7
Hoa Hiep, Vietnam 65 G5
Hoai Nhon, Vietnam 64 E7
Hoang Lien Son, Vietnam 58 F4
Hoanib →, Namibia 88 B2
Hoare B., Canada 101 B13
Hoarusib →, Namibia 88 B2
Hobart, Australia 94 G4
Hobart, U.S.A. 113 H5
Hobbs, U.S.A. 113 J3
Hobbs Coast, Antarctica 5 D14
Hobe Sound, U.S.A. 109 M5
Hoboken, U.S.A. 111 F10
Hobro, Denmark 11 H3
Hoburgen, Sweden 11 H12
Hocalar, Turkey 39 C11
Hochfeld, Namibia 88 C2
Hochschwab, Austria 26 D8
Höchstadt, Germany 25 F6
Hockenheim, Germany 25 F4
Hodaka-Dake, Japan 55 F8
Hodgeville, Canada 105 C7
Hodgson, Canada 105 C9
Hódmezővásárhely, Hungary 42 D5
Hodna, Chott el, Algeria 78 A6
Hodonín, Czech Rep. 27 C10
Hoeamdong, N. Korea 57 C16
Hœdic, Î. de, France 18 E4
Hoek van Holland, Neths. 17 C4
Hoengsŏng, S. Korea 57 F14
Hoeryong, N. Korea 57 C15
Hoeyang, N. Korea 57 E14
Hof, Germany 25 E7
Hofgeismar, Germany 24 D5
Hofheim, Germany 25 E4
Hofmeyr, S. Africa 88 E4
Höfn, Iceland 8 D6
Hofors, Sweden 10 D10
Hofsjökull, Iceland 8 D4
Hōfu, Japan 55 G5
Hogan Group, Australia 95 F4
Höganäs, Sweden 11 H6
Hogarth, Mt., Australia 94 C2
Hoggar = Ahaggar, Algeria 78 D7
Högsäter, Sweden 11 F6
Högsby, Sweden 11 G10
Högsjö, Sweden 10 E9
Hogsty Reef, Bahamas 121 B5
Hoh →, U.S.A. 116 C2
Hohe Acht, Germany 25 E3
Hohe Tauern, Austria 26 D5
Hohe Venn, Belgium 17 D6
Hohenau, Austria 27 C9
Hohenems, Austria 26 D2
Hohenloher Ebene, Germany 25 F5
Hohenwald, U.S.A. 109 H2
Hohenwestedt, Germany 24 A5
Hoher Rhön = Rhön, Germany 24 E5
Hohhot, China 56 D6
Hóhlakas, Greece 36 D9
Hohoe, Ghana 83 D5
Hoi An, Vietnam 64 E7
Hoi Xuan, Vietnam 58 G5
Hoisington, U.S.A. 112 F5
Højer, Denmark 11 K2
Hōjō, Japan 55 H6
Hok, Sweden 11 G8
Hökensås, Sweden 11 G8
Hökerum, Sweden 11 G7
Hokianga Harbour, N.Z. 91 F4
Hokitika, N.Z. 91 K3
Hokkaidō □, Japan 54 C11
Hol-Hol, Djibouti 81 E5
Hola Pristan, Ukraine 47 J7
Holbæk, Denmark 11 J5
Holbrook, U.S.A. 115 J8
Holden, U.S.A. 114 G7
Holdenville, U.S.A. 113 H6
Holdrege, U.S.A. 112 E5
Holešov, Czech Rep. 27 B10
Holguín, Cuba 120 B4
Holíč, Slovak Rep. 27 C10
Holice, Czech Rep. 26 A8
Höljes, Sweden 10 D6
Hollabrunn, Austria 26 C9
Hollams Bird I., Namibia 88 C1
Holland, Mich., U.S.A. 108 D2
Holland, N.Y., U.S.A. 110 D6
Hollandale, U.S.A. 113 J9
Hollandia = Jayapura, Indonesia 63 E10
Holley, U.S.A. 110 C6
Hollfeld, Germany 25 F7
Hollidaysburg, U.S.A. 110 F6
Hollis, U.S.A. 113 H5
Hollister, Calif., U.S.A. 116 J5
Hollister, Idaho, U.S.A. 114 E6
Höllviken = Höllviksnäs, Sweden 11 J6
Höllviksnäs, Sweden 11 J6
Holly Hill, U.S.A. 109 L5
Holly Springs, U.S.A. 113 H10
Hollywood, U.S.A. 109 N5
Holman, Canada 100 A8
Hólmavík, Iceland 8 D3
Holmen, U.S.A. 112 D9
Holmes Reefs, Australia 94 B4
Holmsjö, Sweden 11 H9
Holmsjön, Västernorrland, Sweden 10 B10
Holmsjön, Västernorrland, Sweden 10 B9
Holmsland Klit, Denmark 11 J2
Holmsund, Sweden 8 E19
Holod, Romania 42 D7
Holroyd →, Australia 94 A3
Holstebro, Denmark 11 H2
Holsworthy, U.K. 13 G3
Holton, Canada 103 B8
Holton, U.S.A. 112 F7
Holtville, U.S.A. 117 N11
Holwerd, Neths. 17 A5
Holy I., Angl., U.K. 12 D3
Holy I., Northumb., U.K. 12 B6
Holyhead, U.K. 12 D3
Holyoke, Colo., U.S.A. 112 E3
Holyoke, Mass., U.S.A. 111 D12
Holyrood, Canada 103 C9
Holzkirchen, Germany 25 H7
Holzminden, Germany 24 D5
Homa Bay, Kenya 86 C3
Homalin, Burma 67 G19
Homand, Iran 71 C8
Homathko →, Canada 104 C4
Homberg, Germany 24 D5
Hombori, Mali 83 B4
Homburg, Germany 25 F3
Home B., Canada 101 B13
Home Hill, Australia 94 B4
Homedale, U.S.A. 114 E5
Homer, Alaska, U.S.A. 100 C4
Homer, La., U.S.A. 113 J8
Homer City, U.S.A. 110 F5
Homestead, Australia 94 C4
Homestead, U.S.A. 109 N5
Homewood, U.S.A. 116 F6
Homoine, Mozam. 89 C6
Homoljske Planina, Serbia, Yug. 40 B5
Homorod, Romania 43 D10
Homs = Ḥimş, Syria 75 A5
Homyel, Belarus 47 F6
Hon Chong, Vietnam 65 G5
Hon Me, Vietnam 64 C5
Honan = Henan □, China 56 H8
Honaz, Turkey 39 D11
Honbetsu, Japan 54 C11
Honcut, U.S.A. 116 F5
Honda Bay, Phil. 61 G3
Hondarribia, Spain 32 B3
Hondeklipbaai, S. Africa 88 E2
Hondo, Japan 55 H5
Hondo, U.S.A. 113 L5
Hondo →, Belize 119 D7
Honduras ■, Cent. Amer. 120 D2
Honduras, G. de, Caribbean 120 C2
Hønefoss, Norway 9 F14
Honesdale, U.S.A. 111 E9
Honey L., U.S.A. 116 E6
Honfleur, France 18 C7
Høng, Denmark 11 J5
Hong →, Vietnam 58 F5
Hong Gai, Vietnam 58 G6
Hong He →, China 56 H8
Hong Hu, China 59 C9
Hong Kong □, China 59 F10
Hong'an, China 59 B10
Hongch'ŏn, S. Korea 57 F14
Honghai Wan, China 59 F10
Honghe, China 58 F4
Honghu, China 59 C9
Hongjiang, China 58 D7
Hongliu He →, China 56 F5
Hongor, Mongolia 56 B7
Hongsa, Laos 64 C3
Hongshui He →, China 58 F7
Hongsŏng, S. Korea 57 F14
Hongtong, China 56 F6
Honguedo, Détroit d', Canada 103 C7
Hongwon, N. Korea 57 E14
Hongya, China 58 C4
Hongyuan, China 58 A4
Hongze Hu, China 57 H10
Honiara, Solomon Is. 96 H7
Honiton, U.K. 13 G4
Honjō, Japan 54 E10
Honkorâb, Ras, Egypt 80 C4
Honningsvåg, Norway 8 A21
Hönö, Sweden 11 G5
Honolulu, U.S.A. 106 H16
Hontoria del Pinar, Spain 32 D1
Hood, Mt., U.S.A. 114 D3
Hood, Pt., Australia 93 F2
Hood River, U.S.A. 114 D3
Hoodsport, U.S.A. 116 C3
Hooge, Germany 24 A4
Hoogeveen, Neths. 17 B6
Hoogezand-Sappemeer, Neths. 17 A6
Hooghly = Hugli →, India 69 J13
Hooghly-Chinsura = Chunchura, India 69 H13
Hook Hd., Ireland 15 D5
Hook I., Australia 94 C4
Hook of Holland = Hoek van Holland, Neths. 17 C4
Hooker, U.S.A. 113 G4
Hooker Creek, Australia 92 C5
Hoonah, U.S.A. 104 B1
Hooper Bay, U.S.A. 100 B3
Hoopeston, U.S.A. 108 E2
Hoopstad, S. Africa 88 D4
Höör, Sweden 11 J7
Hoorn, Neths. 17 B5
Hoover, U.S.A. 109 J2
Hoover Dam, U.S.A. 117 K12
Hooversville, U.S.A. 110 F6
Hop Bottom, U.S.A. 111 E9
Hopa, Turkey 73 B9
Hope, Canada 104 D4
Hope, Ariz., U.S.A. 117 M13
Hope, Ark., U.S.A. 113 J8
Hope, L., S. Austral., Australia 95 D2
Hope, L., W. Austral., Australia 93 F3
Hope I., Canada 110 B4
Hope Town, Bahamas 120 A4
Hopedale, Canada 103 A7
Hopedale, U.S.A. 111 D13
Hopefield, S. Africa 88 E2
Hopei = Hebei □, China 56 E9
Hopelchén, Mexico 119 D7
Hopetoun, Australia 93 F3
Hopetown, S. Africa 88 D3
Hopevale, Australia 94 B4
Hopewell, U.S.A. 108 G7
Hopfgarten, Austria 26 D5
Hopkins, L., Australia 92 D4
Hopkinsville, U.S.A. 109 G2
Hopland, U.S.A. 116 G3
Hoquiam, U.S.A. 116 D3
Horasan, Turkey 73 B10
Horažďovice, Czech Rep. 26 B6
Horb, Germany 25 G4
Hörby, Sweden 11 J7
Horcajo de Santiago, Spain 32 F1
Horden Hills, Australia 92 D5
Horezu, Romania 43 E8
Horgen, Switz. 25 H4
Horgoš, Serbia, Yug. 42 D4
Hořice, Czech Rep. 26 A8

Horinger, *China* 56 D6
Horki, *Belarus* 46 E6
Horlick Mts., *Antarctica* 5 E15
Horlivka, *Ukraine* 47 H10
Hormak, *Iran* 71 D9
Hormoz, *Iran* 71 E7
Hormoz, Jaz.-ye, *Iran* 71 E8
Hormozgān □, *Iran* 71 E8
Hormuz, Kūh-e, *Iran* 71 E7
Hormuz, Str. of, *The Gulf* 71 E8
Horn, *Austria* 26 C8
Horn, *Iceland* 8 C2
Horn, *Sweden* 11 G9
Horn →, *Canada* 104 A5
Horn, Cape = Hornos, C. de, *Chile* 122 J4
Horn Head, *Ireland* 15 A3
Horn I., *Australia* 94 A3
Horn Mts., *Canada* 104 A5
Hornachuelos, *Spain* 35 H5
Hornavan, *Sweden* 8 C17
Hornbeck, *U.S.A.* 113 K8
Hornbrook, *U.S.A.* 114 F2
Hornburg, *Germany* 24 C6
Horncastle, *U.K.* 12 D7
Horndal, *Sweden* 10 D10
Hornell, *U.S.A.* 110 D7
Hornell L., *Canada* 104 A5
Hornepayne, *Canada* 102 C3
Horní Planá, *Czech Rep.* 26 C7
Hornings Mills, *Canada* 110 B4
Hornitos, *U.S.A.* 116 H6
Hornos, C. de, *Chile* 122 J4
Hornoy-le-Bourg, *France* 19 C8
Hornsea, *U.K.* 12 D7
Hornslandet, *Sweden* 10 C11
Hörnum, *Germany* 24 A4
Horobetsu, *Japan* 54 C10
Horodenka, *Ukraine* 47 H3
Horodnya, *Ukraine* 47 G6
Horodok, *Khmelnytskyy, Ukraine* 47 H4
Horodok, *Lviv, Ukraine* 47 H2
Horodyshche, *Ukraine* 47 H6
Horokhiv, *Ukraine* 47 G3
Horovice, *Czech Rep.* 26 B6
Horqin Youyi Qianqi, *China* 57 A12
Horqueta, *Paraguay* 126 A4
Horred, *Sweden* 11 G6
Horse Creek, *U.S.A.* 112 E3
Horse Is., *Canada* 103 B8
Horsefly L., *Canada* 104 C4
Horseheads, *U.S.A.* 110 D8
Horsens, *Denmark* 11 J3
Horsham, *U.K.* 13 F7
Horšovský Týn, *Czech Rep.* 26 B5
Horten, *Norway* 9 G14
Hortobágy →, *Hungary* 42 C6
Horton, *U.S.A.* 112 F7
Horton →, *Canada* 100 B7
Horwood L., *Canada* 102 C3
Hosaina, *Ethiopia* 81 F4
Hose, Gunung-Gunung, *Malaysia* 62 D4
Ḩoseynābād, *Khuzestān, Iran* 71 C6
Ḩoseynābād, *Kordestān, Iran* 70 C5
Hoshangabad, *India* 68 H7
Hoshiarpur, *India* 68 D6
Hospet, *India* 66 M10
Hoste, I., *Chile* 128 H3
Hostens, *France* 20 D3
Hot, *Thailand* 64 C2
Hot Creek Range, *U.S.A.* 114 G6
Hot Springs, *Ark., U.S.A.* 113 H8
Hot Springs, *S. Dak., U.S.A.* 112 D3
Hotagen, *Sweden* 8 E16
Hotan, *China* 60 C2
Hotazel, *S. Africa* 88 D3
Hotchkiss, *U.S.A.* 115 G10
Hotham, C., *Australia* 92 B5
Hoting, *Sweden* 8 D17
Hotolisht, *Albania* 40 E4
Hotte, Massif de la, *Haiti* 121 C5
Hottentotsbaai, *Namibia* 88 D1
Houat, Î. de, *France* 18 E4
Houdan, *France* 19 D8
Houei Sai, *Laos* 58 G3
Houeillès, *France* 20 D4
Houffalize, *Belgium* 17 D5
Houghton, *Mich., U.S.A.* 112 B10
Houghton, *N.Y., U.S.A.* 110 D6
Houghton L., *U.S.A.* 108 C3
Houhora Heads, *N.Z.* 91 F4
Houlton, *U.S.A.* 109 B12
Houma, *U.S.A.* 113 L9
Houndé, *Burkina Faso* 82 C4
Hourtin, *France* 20 C2
Hourtin-Carcans, Étang d', *France* 20 C2
Housatonic →, *U.S.A.* 111 E11
Houston, *Canada* 104 C3
Houston, *Mo., U.S.A.* 113 G9
Houston, *Tex., U.S.A.* 113 L7
Hout →, *S. Africa* 89 C4
Houtkraal, *S. Africa* 88 E3
Houtman Abrolhos, *Australia* 93 E1
Hovd, *Mongolia* 60 B4
Hove, *U.K.* 13 G7
Hoveyzeh, *Iran* 71 D6
Hovmantorp, *Sweden* 11 H9
Hövsgöl, *Mongolia* 56 C5
Hövsgöl Nuur, *Mongolia* 60 A5
Hovsta, *Sweden* 10 E9
Howakil, *Eritrea* 81 D5
Howar, Wadi →, *Sudan* 81 D2
Howard, *Australia* 95 D5
Howard, *Pa., U.S.A.* 110 F7
Howard, *S. Dak., U.S.A.* 112 C6
Howe, *U.S.A.* 114 E7
Howe I., *Canada* 111 B8
Howell, *U.S.A.* 108 D4
Howick, *Canada* 111 A11
Howick, *S. Africa* 89 D5
Howick Group, *Australia* 94 A4
Howitt, L., *Australia* 95 D2
Howland I., *Pac. Oc.* 96 G10
Howrah = Haora, *India* 69 H13
Howth Hd., *Ireland* 15 C5
Höxter, *Germany* 24 D5
Hoy, *U.K.* 14 C5
Hoya, *Germany* 24 C5
Høyanger, *Norway* 9 F12
Hoyerswerda, *Germany* 24 D10
Hoylake, *U.K.* 12 D4
Hoyos, *Spain* 34 E4
Hpa-an = Pa-an, *Burma* 67 L20
Hpungan Pass, *Burma* 67 F20
Hradec Králové, *Czech Rep.* 26 A8
Hrádek, *Czech Rep.* 27 C9
Hranice, *Czech Rep.* 27 B10
Hrazdan, *Armenia* 49 K7
Hrebenka, *Ukraine* 47 G7
Hrodna, *Belarus* 46 F2
Hrodzyanka, *Belarus* 46 F5
Hron →, *Slovak Rep.* 27 D11
Hrubieszów, *Poland* 45 H10
Hrubý Jeseník, *Czech Rep.* 27 A10
Hrvatska = Croatia ■, *Europe* 29 C13
Hrymayliv, *Ukraine* 47 H4
Hsenwi, *Burma* 67 H20
Hsiamen = Xiamen, *China* 59 E12
Hsian = Xi'an, *China* 56 G5
Hsinchu, *Taiwan* 59 E13
Hsinhailien = Lianyungang, *China* 57 G10
Hsinying, *Taiwan* 59 F13
Hsopket, *Burma* 58 F2
Hsüchou = Xuzhou, *China* 57 G9
Hu Xian, *China* 56 G5
Hua Hin, *Thailand* 64 F2
Hua Xian, *Henan, China* 56 G8
Hua Xian, *Shaanxi, China* 56 G5
Hua'an, *China* 59 E11
Huab →, *Namibia* 88 B2
Huacheng, *China* 59 E10
Huachinera, *Mexico* 118 A3
Huacho, *Peru* 124 F3
Huade, *China* 56 D7
Huadian, *China* 57 C14
Huadu, *China* 59 F9
Huai He →, *China* 59 A12
Huai Yot, *Thailand* 65 J2
Huai'an, *Hebei, China* 56 D8
Huai'an, *Jiangsu, China* 57 H10
Huaibei, *China* 56 G9
Huaibin, *China* 59 A10
Huaide = Gongzhuling, *China* 57 C13
Huaidezhen, *China* 57 C13
Huaihua, *China* 58 D7
Huaiji, *China* 59 F9
Huainan, *China* 59 A11
Huaining, *China* 59 B11
Huairen, *China* 56 E7
Huairou, *China* 56 D9
Huaiyang, *China* 56 H8
Huaiyin, *China* 57 H10
Huaiyuan, *Anhui, China* 57 H9
Huaiyuan, *Guangxi Zhuangzu, China* 58 E7
Huajianzi, *China* 57 D13
Huajuapan de Leon, *Mexico* 119 D5
Hualapai Peak, *U.S.A.* 115 J7
Hualien, *Taiwan* 59 E13
Huallaga →, *Peru* 124 E3
Huambo, *Angola* 85 G3
Huan Jiang →, *China* 56 G5
Huan Xian, *China* 56 F4
Huancabamba, *Peru* 124 E3
Huancane, *Peru* 124 G5
Huancavelica, *Peru* 124 F3
Huancayo, *Peru* 124 F3
Huanchaca, *Bolivia* 124 H5
Huang Hai = Yellow Sea, *China* 57 G12
Huang He →, *China* 57 F10
Huang Xian, *China* 57 F11
Huangchuan, *China* 59 A10
Huanggang, *China* 59 B10
Huangguoshu, *China* 58 E5
Huangling, *China* 56 G5
Huanglong, *China* 56 G5
Huanglongtan, *China* 59 A8
Huangmei, *China* 59 B10
Huangpi, *China* 59 B10
Huangping, *China* 58 D6
Huangshan, *China* 59 C12
Huangshi, *China* 59 B10
Huangsongdian, *China* 57 C14
Huangyan, *China* 59 C13
Huangyangsi, *China* 59 D8
Huaning, *China* 58 E4
Huanjiang, *China* 58 E7
Huantai, *China* 57 F9
Huánuco, *Peru* 124 E3
Huaping, *China* 58 D3
Huaraz, *Peru* 124 E3
Huarmey, *Peru* 124 F3
Huarong, *China* 59 C9
Huascarán, *Peru* 122 D3
Huasco, *Chile* 126 B1
Huasco →, *Chile* 126 B1
Huasna, *U.S.A.* 117 K6
Huatabampo, *Mexico* 118 B3
Huauchinango, *Mexico* 119 C5
Huautla de Jiménez, *Mexico* 119 D5
Huaxi, *China* 58 D6
Huay Namota, *Mexico* 118 C4
Huayin, *China* 56 G6
Huayuan, *China* 58 C7
Huayun, *China* 58 B6
Huazhou, *China* 59 G8
Hubbard, *Ohio, U.S.A.* 110 E4
Hubbard, *Tex., U.S.A.* 113 K6
Hubbart Pt., *Canada* 105 B10
Hubei □, *China* 59 B9
Huch'ang, *N. Korea* 57 D14
Hucknall, *U.K.* 12 D6
Huddersfield, *U.K.* 12 D6
Hude, *Germany* 24 B4
Hudi, *Sudan* 80 D3
Hudiksvall, *Sweden* 10 C11
Hudson, *Canada* 102 B1
Hudson, *Mass., U.S.A.* 111 D13
Hudson, *N.Y., U.S.A.* 111 D11
Hudson, *Wis., U.S.A.* 112 C8
Hudson, *Wyo., U.S.A.* 114 E9
Hudson →, *U.S.A.* 111 F10
Hudson Bay, *Nunavut, Canada* 101 C11
Hudson Bay, *Sask., Canada* 105 C8
Hudson Falls, *U.S.A.* 111 C11
Hudson Mts., *Antarctica* 5 D16
Hudson Str., *Canada* 101 B13
Hudson's Hope, *Canada* 104 B4
Hue, *Vietnam* 64 D6
Huebra →, *Spain* 34 D4
Huedin, *Romania* 42 D8
Huehuetenango, *Guatemala* 120 C1
Huejúcar, *Mexico* 118 C4
Huélamo, *Spain* 32 E3
Huelgoat, *France* 18 D3
Huelma, *Spain* 35 H7
Huelva, *Spain* 35 H4
Huelva □, *Spain* 35 H4
Huelva →, *Spain* 35 H5
Huentelauquén, *Chile* 126 C1
Huércal-Overa, *Spain* 33 H3
Huerta, Sa. de la, *Argentina* 126 C2
Huertas, C. de las, *Spain* 33 G4
Huerva →, *Spain* 32 D4
Huesca, *Spain* 32 C4
Huesca □, *Spain* 32 C5
Huéscar, *Spain* 33 H2
Huetamo, *Mexico* 118 D4
Huete, *Spain* 32 E2
Hugh →, *Australia* 94 D1
Hughenden, *Australia* 94 C3
Hughes, *Australia* 93 F4
Hughesville, *U.S.A.* 111 E8
Hugli →, *India* 69 J13
Hugo, *Colo., U.S.A.* 112 F3
Hugo, *Okla., U.S.A.* 113 H7
Hugoton, *U.S.A.* 113 G4
Hui Xian = Huixian, *China* 56 G7
Hui Xian, *China* 56 H4
Hui'an, *China* 59 E12
Hui'anbu, *China* 56 F4
Huichang, *China* 59 E10
Huichapán, *Mexico* 119 C5
Huidong, *Guangdong, China* 59 F10
Huidong, *Sichuan, China* 58 D4
Huifa He →, *China* 57 C14
Huila, Nevado del, *Colombia* 124 C3
Huilai, *China* 59 F11
Huili, *China* 58 D4
Huimin, *China* 57 F9
Huinan, *China* 57 C14
Huinca Renancó, *Argentina* 126 C3
Huining, *China* 56 G3
Huinong, *China* 56 E4
Huisache, *Mexico* 118 C4
Huishui, *China* 58 D6
Huisne →, *France* 18 E7
Huiting, *China* 56 G9
Huitong, *China* 58 D7
Huixian, *China* 56 G7
Huixtla, *Mexico* 119 D6
Huize, *China* 58 D4
Huizhou, *China* 59 F10
Hukawng Valley, *Burma* 67 F20
Hukou, *China* 59 C11
Hukuntsi, *Botswana* 88 C3
Ḩulayfā', *Si. Arabia* 70 E4
Huld = Ulaanjirem, *Mongolia* 56 B3
Hulin He →, *China* 57 B12
Hull = Kingston upon Hull, *U.K.* 12 D7
Hull, *Canada* 102 C4
Hull →, *U.K.* 12 D7
Hulst, *Neths.* 17 C4
Hultsfred, *Sweden* 11 G9
Hulun Nur, *China* 60 B6
Hulyaypole, *Ukraine* 47 J9
Humahuaca, *Argentina* 126 A2
Humaitá, *Brazil* 124 E6
Humaitá, *Paraguay* 126 B4
Humansdorp, *S. Africa* 88 E3
Humara, J., *Sudan* 81 D3
Humbe, *Angola* 88 B1
Humber →, *U.K.* 12 D7
Humboldt, *Canada* 105 C7
Humboldt, *Iowa, U.S.A.* 112 D7
Humboldt, *Tenn., U.S.A.* 113 H10
Humboldt →, *U.S.A.* 114 F4
Humboldt Gletscher, *Greenland* 4 B4
Hume, *U.S.A.* 116 J8
Humenné, *Slovak Rep.* 27 C14
Hummelsta, *Sweden* 10 E10
Humphreys, Mt., *U.S.A.* 116 H8
Humphreys Peak, *U.S.A.* 115 J8
Humpolec, *Czech Rep.* 26 B8
Humptulips, *U.S.A.* 116 C3
Hūn, *Libya* 79 C9
Hun Jiang →, *China* 57 D13
Húnaflói, *Iceland* 8 D3
Hunan □, *China* 59 D9
Hunchun, *China* 57 C16
Hundested, *Denmark* 11 J5
Hundewali, *Pakistan* 68 D5
Hundred Mile House, *Canada* 104 C4
Hunedoara, *Romania* 42 E7
Hunedoara □, *Romania* 42 E7
Hünfeld, *Germany* 24 E5
Hung Yen, *Vietnam* 58 G6
Hungary ■, *Europe* 27 D12
Hungary, Plain of, *Europe* 6 F10
Hungerford, *Australia* 95 D3
Hŭngnam, *N. Korea* 57 E14
Hungt'ou Hsü, *Taiwan* 59 G13
Huni Valley, *Ghana* 82 D4
Hunneberg, *Sweden* 11 F6
Hunnebostrand, *Sweden* 11 F5
Hunsberge, *Namibia* 88 D2
Hunsrück, *Germany* 25 F3
Hunstanton, *U.K.* 12 E8
Hunte →, *Germany* 24 B4
Hunter, *U.S.A.* 111 D10
Hunter I., *Australia* 94 G3
Hunter I., *Canada* 104 C3
Hunters Road, *Zimbabwe* 87 F2
Hunterville, *N.Z.* 91 H5
Huntingburg, *U.S.A.* 108 F2
Huntingdon, *Canada* 102 C5
Huntingdon, *U.K.* 13 E7
Huntingdon, *U.S.A.* 110 F6
Huntington, *Ind., U.S.A.* 108 E3
Huntington, *Oreg., U.S.A.* 114 D5
Huntington, *Utah, U.S.A.* 114 G8
Huntington, *W. Va., U.S.A.* 108 F4
Huntington Beach, *U.S.A.* 117 M9
Huntington Station, *U.S.A.* 111 F11
Huntly, *N.Z.* 91 G5
Huntly, *U.K.* 14 D6
Huntsville, *Canada* 102 C4
Huntsville, *Ala., U.S.A.* 109 H2
Huntsville, *Tex., U.S.A.* 113 K7
Hunyani →, *Zimbabwe* 87 F3
Hunyuan, *China* 56 E7
Hunza →, *India* 69 B6
Huo Xian = Huozhou, *China* 56 F6
Huong Hoa, *Vietnam* 64 D6
Huong Khe, *Vietnam* 64 C5
Huonville, *Australia* 94 G4
Huoqiu, *China* 59 A11
Huoshan, *Anhui, China* 59 A12
Huoshan, *Anhui, China* 59 B11
Huoshao Dao = Lü-Tao, *Taiwan* 59 F13
Huozhou, *China* 56 F6
Hupeh = Hubei □, *China* 59 B9
Ḩūr, *Iran* 71 D8
Hurbanovo, *Slovak Rep.* 27 D11
Hurd, C., *Canada* 110 A3
Hure Qi, *China* 57 C11
Hurezani, *Romania* 43 F8
Hurghada, *Egypt* 80 B3
Hurley, *N. Mex., U.S.A.* 115 K9
Hurley, *Wis., U.S.A.* 112 B9
Huron, *Calif., U.S.A.* 116 J6
Huron, *Ohio, U.S.A.* 110 E2
Huron, *S. Dak., U.S.A.* 112 C5
Huron, L., *U.S.A.* 110 B2
Hurricane, *U.S.A.* 115 H7
Hurso, *Ethiopia* 81 F5
Hurunui →, *N.Z.* 91 K4
Hurup, *Denmark* 11 H2
Húsavík, *Iceland* 8 C5
Huşi, *Romania* 43 D13
Huskvarna, *Sweden* 11 G8
Hustadvika, *Norway* 8 E12
Hustontown, *U.S.A.* 110 F6
Hustopeče, *Czech Rep.* 27 C9
Husum, *Germany* 24 A5
Husum, *Sweden* 10 A13
Hutchinson, *Kans., U.S.A.* 113 F6
Hutchinson, *Minn., U.S.A.* 112 C7
Hutte Sauvage, L. de la, *Canada* 103 A7
Hüttenberg, *Austria* 26 E7
Hutton, Mt., *Australia* 95 D4
Huwun, *Ethiopia* 81 G5
Huy, *Belgium* 17 D5
Huzhou, *China* 59 B13
Hvalpsund, *Denmark* 11 H3
Hvammstangi, *Iceland* 8 D3
Hvar, *Croatia* 29 E13
Hvarski Kanal, *Croatia* 29 E13
Hvítá →, *Iceland* 8 D3
Hwachŏn-chŏsuji, *S. Korea* 57 E14
Hwang Ho = Huang He →, *China* 57 F10
Hwange, *Zimbabwe* 87 F2
Hwange Nat. Park, *Zimbabwe* 88 B4
Hyannis, *Mass., U.S.A.* 108 E10
Hyannis, *Nebr., U.S.A.* 112 E4
Hyargas Nuur, *Mongolia* 60 B4
Hybo, *Sweden* 10 C10
Hydaburg, *U.S.A.* 104 B2
Hyde Park, *U.S.A.* 111 E11
Hyden, *Australia* 93 F2
Hyder, *U.S.A.* 104 B2
Hyderabad, *India* 66 L11
Hyderabad, *Pakistan* 68 G3
Hyères, *France* 21 E10
Hyères, Îs. d', *France* 21 F10
Hyesan, *N. Korea* 57 D15
Hyland →, *Canada* 104 B3
Hyltebruk, *Sweden* 11 H7
Hymia, *India* 69 C8
Hyndman Peak, *U.S.A.* 114 E6
Hyōgo □, *Japan* 55 G7
Hyrum, *U.S.A.* 114 F8
Hysham, *U.S.A.* 114 C10
Hythe, *U.K.* 13 F9
Hyūga, *Japan* 55 H5
Hyvinge = Hyvinkää, *Finland* 9 F21
Hyvinkää, *Finland* 9 F21

I

I-n-Gall, *Niger* 83 B6
I-n-Oudad, *Algeria* 83 A5
I-n-Ouzzal, *Algeria* 83 A5
I-n-Tadreft, *Niger* 83 B6
Iablaniţa, *Romania* 42 F7
Iaco →, *Brazil* 124 E5
Iacobeni, *Romania* 43 C10
Iakora, *Madag.* 89 C8
Ialomiţa □, *Romania* 43 F12
Ialomiţa →, *Romania* 43 F12
Ialoveni, *Moldova* 43 D13
Ialpug →, *Moldova* 43 E13
Ianca, *Romania* 43 E12
Iara, *Romania* 43 D8
Iarda, *Ethiopia* 81 E4
Iargara, *Moldova* 43 D13
Iaşi, *Romania* 43 C12
Iaşi □, *Romania* 43 C12
Íasmos, *Greece* 41 E9
Ib →, *India* 69 J10
Iba, *Phil.* 61 D3
Ibadan, *Nigeria* 83 D5
Ibagué, *Colombia* 124 C3
Iballë, *Albania* 40 D4
Ibăneşti, *Botoşani, Romania* 43 B11
Ibăneşti, *Mureş, Romania* 43 D9
Ibar →, *Serbia, Yug.* 40 C4
Ibaraki □, *Japan* 55 F10
Ibarra, *Ecuador* 124 C3
Ibba, *Sudan* 81 G2
Ibba, Bahr el →, *Sudan* 81 F2
Ibbenbüren, *Germany* 24 C3
Ibembo, *Dem. Rep. of the Congo* 86 B1
Ibera, L., *Argentina* 126 B4
Iberian Peninsula, *Europe* 6 H5
Iberville, *Canada* 102 C5
Iberville, Lac d', *Canada* 102 A5
Ibi, *Nigeria* 83 D6
Ibi, *Spain* 33 G4
Ibiá, *Brazil* 125 G9
Ibiapaba, Sa. da, *Brazil* 125 D10
Ibicuí →, *Brazil* 127 B4
Ibicuy, *Argentina* 126 C4
Ibiza = Eivissa, *Spain* 37 C7
Íblei, Monti, *Italy* 31 E7
Ibo, *Mozam.* 87 E5
Ibonma, *Indonesia* 63 E8
Ibotirama, *Brazil* 125 F10
Ibrāhīm →, *Lebanon* 75 A4
'Ibrī, *Oman* 71 F8
Ibriktepe, *Turkey* 41 E10
Ibshawâi, *Egypt* 80 J7
Ibu, *Indonesia* 63 D7
Ibusuki, *Japan* 55 J5
Ica, *Peru* 124 F3
Iça →, *Brazil* 124 D5
Içana, *Brazil* 124 C5
Içana →, *Brazil* 124 C5
Içel = Mersin, *Turkey* 70 B2
Iceland ■, *Europe* 8 D4
Ich'ang = Yichang, *China* 59 B8
Ichchapuram, *India* 67 K14
Ichhawar, *India* 68 H7
Ichihara, *Japan* 55 G10
Ichikawa, *Japan* 55 G9
Ichilo →, *Bolivia* 124 G6
Ichinohe, *Japan* 54 D10
Ichinomiya, *Japan* 55 G8
Ichinoseki, *Japan* 54 E10
Ichnya, *Ukraine* 47 G7
Icod, *Canary Is.* 37 F3
Ida Grove, *U.S.A.* 112 D7
Idabel, *U.S.A.* 113 J7
Idaga Hamus, *Ethiopia* 81 E4
Idah, *Nigeria* 83 D6
Idaho □, *U.S.A.* 114 D7
Idaho City, *U.S.A.* 114 E6
Idaho Falls, *U.S.A.* 114 E7
Idanha-a-Nova, *Portugal* 34 F3
Idar-Oberstein, *Germany* 25 F3
Idfû, *Egypt* 80 C3
Ídhi Óros, *Greece* 36 D6
Ídhra, *Greece* 38 D5
Idi, *Indonesia* 62 C1
Idiofa, *Dem. Rep. of the Congo* 84 E3
Idkerberget, *Sweden* 10 D9
Idku, Bahra el, *Egypt* 80 H7
Idlib, *Syria* 70 C3
Idre, *Sweden* 10 C6
Idria, *U.S.A.* 116 J6
Idrija, *Slovenia* 29 C11
Idritsa, *Russia* 46 D5
Idutywa, *S. Africa* 89 E4
Ieper, *Belgium* 17 D2
Ierápetra, *Greece* 36 E7
Ierissós, *Greece* 40 F7
Ierissóu Kólpos, *Greece* 40 F7
Iernut, *Romania* 43 D9
Iesi, *Italy* 29 E10
Iésolo, *Italy* 29 C9
Ifach, Peñón de, *Spain* 33 G5
Ifakara, *Tanzania* 84 F7
'Ifāl, W. al →, *Si. Arabia* 70 D2

Ifanadiana, *Madag.* 89 C8
Ife, *Nigeria* 83 D5
Iférouâne, *Niger* 83 B6
Iffley, *Australia* 94 B3
Ifon, *Nigeria* 83 D6
Iforas, Adrar des, *Africa* 83 B5
Ifould, L., *Australia* 93 F5
Iganga, *Uganda* 86 B3
Igarapava, *Brazil* 125 H9
Igarka, *Russia* 50 C9
Igatimi, *Paraguay* 127 A4
Igbetti, *Nigeria* 83 D5
Igbo-Ora, *Nigeria* 83 D5
Igboho, *Nigeria* 83 D5
Igbor, *Nigeria* 83 D6
Iğdır, *Turkey* 73 C11
Igelfors, *Sweden* 11 F9
Iggesund, *Sweden* 10 C11
Iglésias, *Italy* 30 C1
Igloolik, *Canada* 101 B11
Igluligaarjuk, *Canada* 101 B10
Iglulik = Igloolik, *Canada* 101 B11
'Igma, Gebel el, *Egypt* 80 B3
Ignace, *Canada* 102 C1
İğneada, *Turkey* 41 E11
İğneada Burnu, *Turkey* 41 E12
Igoumenítsa, *Greece* 38 B2
Igra, *Russia* 48 B11
Iguaçu →, *Brazil* 127 B5
Iguaçu, Cat. del, *Brazil* 127 B5
Iguaçu Falls = Iguaçu, Cat. del, *Brazil* 127 B5
Iguala, *Mexico* 119 D5
Igualada, *Spain* 32 D6
Iguassu = Iguaçu →, *Brazil* 127 B5
Iguatu, *Brazil* 125 E11
Iharana, *Madag.* 89 A9
Ihbulag, *Mongolia* 56 C4
Iheya-Shima, *Japan* 55 L3
Ihiala, *Nigeria* 83 D6
Ihosy, *Madag.* 89 C8
Ihotry, Farihy, *Madag.* 89 C7
Ihugh, *Nigeria* 83 D6
Ii, *Finland* 8 D21
Ii-Shima, *Japan* 55 L3
Iida, *Japan* 55 G8
Iijoki →, *Finland* 8 D21
Iisalmi, *Finland* 8 E22
Iiyama, *Japan* 55 F9
Iizuka, *Japan* 55 H5
Ijebu-Igbo, *Nigeria* 83 D5
Ijebu-Ode, *Nigeria* 83 D5
IJmuiden, *Neths.* 17 B4
IJssel →, *Neths.* 17 B5
IJsselmeer, *Neths.* 17 B5
Ijuí, *Brazil* 127 B5
Ijuí →, *Brazil* 127 B4
Ikalamavony, *Madag.* 89 C8
Ikale, *Nigeria* 83 D6
Ikaluktutiak, *Canada* 100 B9
Ikang, *Nigeria* 83 E6
Ikara, *Nigeria* 83 C6
Ikare, *Nigeria* 83 D6
Ikaría, *Greece* 39 D8
Ikast, *Denmark* 11 H3
Ikeda, *Japan* 55 G6
Ikeja, *Nigeria* 83 D5
Ikela, *Dem. Rep. of the Congo* 84 E4
Ikerre-Ekiti, *Nigeria* 83 D6
Ikhtiman, *Bulgaria* 40 D7
Iki, *Japan* 55 H4
Ikimba L., *Tanzania* 86 C3
Ikire, *Nigeria* 83 D5
Ikizdere, *Turkey* 73 B9
Ikom, *Nigeria* 83 D6
Ikongo, *Madag.* 89 C8
Ikopa →, *Madag.* 89 B8
Ikot Ekpene, *Nigeria* 83 D6
Ikungu, *Tanzania* 86 C3
Ikurun, *Nigeria* 83 D5
Ila, *Nigeria* 83 D5
Ilagan, *Phil.* 61 C4
Ilaka, *Madag.* 89 B8
Īlām, *Iran* 70 C5
Ilam, *Nepal* 69 F12
Ilam □, *Iran* 70 C5
Ilan, *Taiwan* 59 E13
Ilanskiy, *Russia* 51 D10
Ilaro, *Nigeria* 83 D5
Ilatane, *Niger* 83 B5
Iława, *Poland* 44 E6
Ile →, *Kazakstan* 50 E8
Ile-à-la-Crosse, *Canada* 105 B7
Ile-à-la-Crosse, Lac, *Canada* 105 B7
Île-de-France □, *France* 19 D9
Ileanda, *Romania* 43 C8
Ilebo, *Dem. Rep. of the Congo* 84 E4
Ilek, *Russia* 50 D6
Ilero, *Nigeria* 83 D5
Ilesha, *Kwara, Nigeria* 83 D5
Ilesha, *Oyo, Nigeria* 83 D5
Ilford, *Canada* 105 B9
Ilfracombe, *Australia* 94 C3
Ilfracombe, *U.K.* 13 F3
Ilgaz, *Turkey* 72 B5
Ilgaz Dağları, *Turkey* 72 B5
Ilgın, *Turkey* 72 C4
Ílhavo, *Portugal* 34 E2
Ilhéus, *Brazil* 125 F11
Ili = Ile →, *Kazakstan* 50 E8
Ilia, *Romania* 42 E7
Ilia □, *Greece* 38 D3
Iliamna L., *U.S.A.* 100 C4
Iliç, *Turkey* 73 C8
Ilıca, *Turkey* 39 B9
Ilichevsk, *Azerbaijan* 73 C11
Iligan, *Phil.* 61 G6
Iligan Bay, *Phil.* 61 G6
Ilíkí, L., *Greece* 38 C5
Ilin I., *Phil.* 61 E4
Iliodhrómia, *Greece* 38 B5
Ilion, *U.S.A.* 111 D9
Ilirska-Bistrica, *Slovenia* 29 C11
Ilkeston, *U.K.* 12 E6
Ilkley, *U.K.* 12 D6
Illampu = Ancohuma, Nevada, *Bolivia* 122 E4
Illana B., *Phil.* 61 H5
Illapel, *Chile* 126 C1
Ille-et-Vilaine □, *France* 18 D5
Ille-sur-Têt, *France* 20 F6
Illéla, *Niger* 83 C6
Iller →, *Germany* 25 G5
Illertissen, *Germany* 25 G6
Illescas, *Spain* 34 E7
Illetas, *Spain* 37 B9
Illichivsk, *Ukraine* 47 J6
Illiers-Combray, *France* 18 D8
Illimani, Nevado, *Bolivia* 124 G5
Illinois □, *U.S.A.* 112 E10
Illinois →, *U.S.A.* 107 C8
Illium = Troy, *Turkey* 39 B8
Illizi, *Algeria* 78 C7
Illkirch-Graffenstaden, *France* 19 D14
Íllora, *Spain* 35 H7
Ilm →, *Germany* 24 D7
Ilmajoki, *Finland* 9 E20
Ilmen, Ozero, *Russia* 46 C6
Ilmenau, *Germany* 24 E6
Ilo, *Peru* 124 G4
Ilobu, *Nigeria* 83 D5
Iloilo, *Phil.* 61 F5
Ilora, *Nigeria* 83 D5
Ilorin, *Nigeria* 83 D5
Ilovatka, *Russia* 48 E7
Ilovlya, *Russia* 49 F7
Ilovlya →, *Russia* 49 F7
Iłowa, *Poland* 45 G2
Ilubabor □, *Ethiopia* 81 F4
Ilva Mică, *Romania* 43 C9
Ilwaco, *U.S.A.* 116 D2
Ilwaki, *Indonesia* 63 F7
Ilyichevsk = Illichivsk, *Ukraine* 47 J6
Iłża, *Poland* 45 G8
Iłzanka →, *Poland* 45 G8
Imabari, *Japan* 55 G6
Imaloto →, *Madag.* 89 C8
İmamoğlu, *Turkey* 72 D6
Imandra, Ozero, *Russia* 50 C4
Imanombo, *Madag.* 89 C8
Imari, *Japan* 55 H4
Imasa, *Sudan* 80 D4
Imathía □, *Greece* 40 F6
Imatra, *Finland* 46 B5
Imbil, *Australia* 95 D5
Iménas, *Mali* 83 B5
imeni 26 Bakinskikh Komissarov = Neftçala, *Azerbaijan* 71 B6
imeni 26 Bakinskikh Komissarov, *Turkmenistan* 71 B7
Imeri, Serra, *Brazil* 124 C5
Imerimandroso, *Madag.* 89 B8
Imi, *Ethiopia* 81 F5
Imishly = Imişli, *Azerbaijan* 49 L9
Imişli, *Azerbaijan* 49 L9
Imlay, *U.S.A.* 114 F4
Imlay City, *U.S.A.* 110 D1
Immaseri, *Sudan* 81 D2
Immenstadt, *Germany* 25 H6
Immingham, *U.K.* 12 D7
Immokalee, *U.S.A.* 109 M5
Imo □, *Nigeria* 83 D6
Imo →, *Nigeria* 83 E6
Ímola, *Italy* 29 D8
Imotski, *Croatia* 29 E14
Imperatriz, *Brazil* 125 E9
Impéria, *Italy* 28 E5
Imperial, *Canada* 105 C7
Imperial, *Calif., U.S.A.* 117 N11
Imperial, *Nebr., U.S.A.* 112 E4
Imperial Beach, *U.S.A.* 117 N9
Imperial Dam, *U.S.A.* 117 N12
Imperial Reservoir, *U.S.A.* 117 N12
Imperial Valley, *U.S.A.* 117 N11
Imperieuse Reef, *Australia* 92 C2
Impfondo, *Congo* 84 D3
Imphal, *India* 67 G18
Imphy, *France* 19 F10
Imranlı, *Turkey* 73 C8
İmroz = Gökçeada, *Turkey* 41 F9
İmroz, *Turkey* 41 F9
Imst, *Austria* 26 D3
Imuris, *Mexico* 118 A2
Imuruan B., *Phil.* 63 B5
In Akhmed, *Mali* 83 B4
In Aleï, *Mali* 82 B4
In Delimane, *Mali* 83 B5
In Guezzam, *Algeria* 83 B6
In Koufi, *Mali* 83 B5
In Salah, *Algeria* 78 C6
In Tallak, *Mali* 83 B5
In Tebezas, *Mali* 83 B5
Ina, *Japan* 55 G8
Inangahua, *N.Z.* 91 J3
Inanwatan, *Indonesia* 63 E8
Iñapari, *Peru* 124 F5
Inari, *Finland* 8 B22
Inarijärvi, *Finland* 8 B22
Inawashiro-Ko, *Japan* 54 F10
Inca, *Spain* 37 B9
Inca de Oro, *Chile* 126 B2
Incaguasi, *Chile* 126 B1
İnce Burun, *Turkey* 72 A6
Incekum Burnu, *Turkey* 72 D5
İncesu, *Turkey* 70 B2
Inch'ŏn, *S. Korea* 57 F14
Incio = Cruz de Incio, *Spain* 34 C3
İncirliova, *Turkey* 39 D9
Incline Village, *U.S.A.* 114 G4
Incomáti →, *Mozam.* 89 D5
Inda Silase, *Ethiopia* 81 E4
Indal, *Sweden* 10 B11
Indalsälven →, *Sweden* 10 B11
Indaw, *Burma* 67 G20
Indbir, *Ethiopia* 81 F4
Independence, *Calif., U.S.A.* 116 J8
Independence, *Iowa, U.S.A.* 112 D9
Independence, *Kans., U.S.A.* 113 G7
Independence, *Ky., U.S.A.* 108 F3
Independence, *Mo., U.S.A.* 112 F7
Independence Fjord, *Greenland* 4 A6
Independence Mts., *U.S.A.* 114 F5
Independenţa, *Romania* 43 E12
Index, *U.S.A.* 116 C5
India ■, *Asia* 66 K11
Indian →, *U.S.A.* 109 M5
Indian Cabins, *Canada* 104 B5
Indian Harbour, *Canada* 103 B8
Indian Head, *Canada* 105 C8
Indian Lake, *U.S.A.* 111 C10
Indian Ocean 52 K11
Indian Springs, *U.S.A.* 117 J11
Indiana, *U.S.A.* 110 F5
Indiana □, *U.S.A.* 108 F3
Indianapolis, *U.S.A.* 108 F2
Indianola, *Iowa, U.S.A.* 112 E8
Indianola, *Miss., U.S.A.* 113 J9
Indigirka →, *Russia* 51 B15
Inđija, *Serbia, Yug.* 42 E5
Indio, *U.S.A.* 117 M10
Indo-China, *Asia* 52 H14
Indonesia ■, *Asia* 62 F5
Indore, *India* 68 H6
Indramayu, *Indonesia* 63 G13
Indravati →, *India* 67 K12
Indre □, *France* 19 F8
Indre →, *France* 18 E7
Indre-et-Loire □, *France* 18 E7
Indulkana, *Australia* 95 D1
Indus →, *Pakistan* 68 G2
Indus, Mouth of the, *Pakistan* 68 H3
İnebolu, *Turkey* 72 B5
İnecik, *Turkey* 41 F11
İnegöl, *Turkey* 41 F13
Ineu, *Romania* 42 D6
Infantes = Villanueva de los Infantes, *Spain* 35 G7
Infiernillo, Presa del, *Mexico* 118 D4
Infiesto, *Spain* 34 B5
Ingelstad, *Sweden* 11 H8
Ingenio, *Canary Is.* 37 G4
Ingenio Santa Ana, *Argentina* 126 B2
Ingersoll, *Canada* 102 D3
Ingham, *Australia* 94 B4
Ingleborough, *U.K.* 12 C5
Inglewood, *Australia* 95 D5
Inglewood, *N.Z.* 91 H5
Inglewood, *U.S.A.* 117 M8
Ingólfshöfði, *Iceland* 8 E5
Ingolstadt, *Germany* 25 G7
Ingomar, *U.S.A.* 114 C10
Ingonish, *Canada* 103 C7
Ingore, *Guinea-Biss.* 82 C1
Ingraj Bazar, *India* 69 G13
Ingrid Christensen Coast, *Antarctica* 5 C6
Ingul → = Inhul →, *Ukraine* 47 J7
Ingulec = Inhulec, *Ukraine* 47 J7
Ingulets → = Inhulets →, *Ukraine* 47 J7
Inguri → = Enguri →, *Georgia* 49 J5
Ingushetia □, *Russia* 49 J7
Ingwavuma, *S. Africa* 89 D5
Inhaca, *Mozam.* 89 D5
Inhafenga, *Mozam.* 89 C5
Inhambane, *Mozam.* 89 C6
Inhambane □, *Mozam.* 89 C5
Inhaminga, *Mozam.* 87 F4
Inharrime, *Mozam.* 89 C6
Inharrime →, *Mozam.* 89 C6
Inhisar, *Turkey* 39 A12
Inhul →, *Ukraine* 47 J7
Inhulec, *Ukraine* 47 J7
Inhulets →, *Ukraine* 47 J7
Iniesta, *Spain* 33 F3
Ining = Yining, *China* 50 E9
Inírida →, *Colombia* 124 C5
Inishbofin, *Ireland* 15 C1
Inisheer, *Ireland* 15 C2
Inishfree B., *Ireland* 15 A3
Inishkea North, *Ireland* 15 B1
Inishkea South, *Ireland* 15 B1
Inishmaan, *Ireland* 15 C2
Inishmore, *Ireland* 15 C2
Inishowen Pen., *Ireland* 15 A4
Inishshark, *Ireland* 15 C1
Inishturk, *Ireland* 15 C1
Inishvickillane, *Ireland* 15 D1
Injibara, *Ethiopia* 81 E4
Injune, *Australia* 95 D4
Inklin →, *Canada* 104 B2
Inland Sea = Setonaikai, *Japan* 55 G6
Inle L., *Burma* 67 J20
Inlet, *U.S.A.* 111 C10
Inn →, *Austria* 26 C6
Innamincka, *Australia* 95 D3
Inner Hebrides, *U.K.* 14 E2
Inner Mongolia = Nei Monggol Zizhiqu □, *China* 56 D7
Inner Sound, *U.K.* 14 D3
Innerkip, *Canada* 110 C4
Innetalling I., *Canada* 102 A4
Innisfail, *Australia* 94 B4
Innisfail, *Canada* 104 C6
In'noshima, *Japan* 55 G6
Innsbruck, *Austria* 26 D4
Innviertel, *Austria* 26 C6
Inny →, *Ireland* 15 C4
Inongo, *Dem. Rep. of the Congo* 84 E3
İnönü, *Turkey* 39 B12
Inoucdjouac = Inukjuak, *Canada* 101 C12
Inowrocław, *Poland* 45 F5
Inpundong, *N. Korea* 57 D14
Inscription, C., *Australia* 93 E1
Insein, *Burma* 67 L20
Insjön, *Sweden* 10 D9
Ińsko, *Poland* 44 E2
Însurăţei, *Romania* 43 F12
Inta, *Russia* 50 C6
Intendente Alvear, *Argentina* 126 D3
İntepe, *Turkey* 39 A8
Interlaken, *Switz.* 25 J3
Interlaken, *U.S.A.* 111 D8
International Falls, *U.S.A.* 112 A8
Intiyaco, *Argentina* 126 B3
Întorsura Buzăului, *Romania* 43 E11
Inukjuak, *Canada* 101 C12
Inútil, B., *Chile* 128 G2
Inuvik, *Canada* 100 B6
Inveraray, *U.K.* 14 E3
Inverbervie, *U.K.* 14 E6
Invercargill, *N.Z.* 91 M2
Inverclyde □, *U.K.* 14 F4
Inverell, *Australia* 95 D5
Invergordon, *U.K.* 14 D4
Inverloch, *Australia* 95 F4
Invermere, *Canada* 104 C5
Inverness, *Canada* 103 C7
Inverness, *U.K.* 14 D4
Inverness, *U.S.A.* 109 L4
Inverurie, *U.K.* 14 D6
Investigator Group, *Australia* 95 E1
Inya, *Russia* 50 D9
Inyanga, *Zimbabwe* 87 F3
Inyangani, *Zimbabwe* 87 F3
Inyantue, *Zimbabwe* 88 B4
Inyo Mts., *U.S.A.* 116 J9
Inyokern, *U.S.A.* 117 K9
Inza, *Russia* 48 D8
Inzhavino, *Russia* 48 D6
Iō-Jima, *Japan* 55 J5
Ioánnina, *Greece* 38 B2
Ioánnina □, *Greece* 38 B2
Iola, *U.S.A.* 113 G7
Ion Corvin, *Romania* 43 F12
Iona, *U.K.* 14 E2
Ione, *U.S.A.* 116 G6
Ionia, *U.S.A.* 108 D3
Ionian Is. = Iónioi Nísoi, *Greece* 38 C2
Ionian Sea, *Medit. S.* 6 H9
Iónioi Nísoi, *Greece* 38 C2
Iónioi Nísoi □, *Greece* 38 C2
Íos, *Greece* 39 E7
Iowa □, *U.S.A.* 112 D8
Iowa →, *U.S.A.* 112 E9
Iowa City, *U.S.A.* 112 E9
Iowa Falls, *U.S.A.* 112 D8
Iowa Park, *U.S.A.* 113 J5
Ipala, *Tanzania* 86 C3
Ipameri, *Brazil* 125 G9
Ipáti, *Greece* 38 C4
Ipatinga, *Brazil* 125 G10
Ipatovo, *Russia* 49 H6
Ipel' →, *Europe* 27 D11
Ipiales, *Colombia* 124 C3
Ipin = Yibin, *China* 58 C5
Ípiros □, *Greece* 38 B2
Ipixuna, *Brazil* 124 E4
Ipoh, *Malaysia* 65 K3
Ippy, *C.A.R.* 84 C4
Ipsala, *Turkey* 41 F10
Ipsárion, Óros, *Greece* 41 F8
Ipswich, *Australia* 95 D5
Ipswich, *U.K.* 13 E9
Ipswich, *Mass., U.S.A.* 111 D14
Ipswich, *S. Dak., U.S.A.* 112 C5
Ipu, *Brazil* 125 D10
Iqaluit, *Canada* 101 B13
Iquique, *Chile* 124 H4
Iquitos, *Peru* 124 D4
Irabu-Jima, *Japan* 55 M2
Iracoubo, *Fr. Guiana* 125 B8
Īrafshān, *Iran* 71 E9
Irahuan, *Phil.* 61 G3
Iráklia, *Kikládhes, Greece* 39 E7
Iráklia, *Sérrai, Greece* 40 E7
Iráklion, *Greece* 36 D7
Iráklion □, *Greece* 36 D7
Irala, *Paraguay* 127 B5
Iran ■, *Asia* 71 C7
Iran, Gunung-Gunung, *Malaysia* 62 D4
Iran, Plateau of, *Asia* 52 F9
Iran Ra. = Iran, Gunung-Gunung, *Malaysia* 62 D4
Īrānshahr, *Iran* 71 E9
Irapuato, *Mexico* 118 C4
Iraq ■, *Asia* 70 C5
Irati, *Brazil* 127 B5
Irbes saurums, *Latvia* 44 A9
Irbid, *Jordan* 75 C4
Irbid □, *Jordan* 75 C5
Iregua →, *Spain* 32 C7
Ireland ■, *Europe* 15 C4
Irele, *Nigeria* 83 D6
Irgiz, Bolshaya →, *Russia* 48 D9
Irhyangdong, *N. Korea* 57 D15
Iri, *S. Korea* 57 G14
Irian Jaya □, *Indonesia* 63 E9
Irié, *Guinea* 82 D3
Iriga, *Phil.* 61 E5
Iringa, *Tanzania* 86 D4
Iringa □, *Tanzania* 86 D4
Iriomote-Jima, *Japan* 55 M1
Iriona, *Honduras* 120 C2
Iriri →, *Brazil* 125 D8
Irish Republic ■, *Europe* 15 C3
Irish Sea, *U.K.* 12 D3
Irkutsk, *Russia* 51 D11
Irlıganlı, *Turkey* 39 D11
Irma, *Canada* 105 C6
Irō-Zaki, *Japan* 55 G9
Iroise, Mer d', *France* 18 D2
Iron Gate = Portile de Fier, *Europe* 42 F7
Iron Mountain, *U.S.A.* 108 C1
Iron River, *U.S.A.* 112 B10
Irondequoit, *U.S.A.* 110 C7
Ironton, *Mo., U.S.A.* 113 G9
Ironton, *Ohio, U.S.A.* 108 F4
Ironwood, *U.S.A.* 112 B9
Iroquois, *Canada* 111 B9
Iroquois Falls, *Canada* 102 C3
Irosin, *Phil.* 61 E6
Irpin, *Ukraine* 47 G6
Irrara Cr. →, *Australia* 95 D4
Irrawaddy □, *Burma* 67 L19
Irrawaddy →, *Burma* 67 M19
Irrawaddy, Mouths of the, *Burma* 67 M19
Irricana, *Canada* 104 C6
Irsina, *Italy* 31 B9
Irtysh →, *Russia* 50 C7
Irumu, *Dem. Rep. of the Congo* 86 B2
Irún, *Spain* 32 B3
Irunea = Pamplona, *Spain* 32 C3
Irurzun, *Spain* 32 C3
Irvine, *U.K.* 14 F4
Irvine, *Calif., U.S.A.* 117 M9
Irvine, *Ky., U.S.A.* 108 G4
Irvinestown, *U.K.* 15 B4
Irving, *U.S.A.* 113 J6
Irvona, *U.S.A.* 110 F6
Irwin →, *Australia* 93 E1
Is, Jebel, *Sudan* 80 C4
Is-sur-Tille, *France* 19 E12
Isa, *Nigeria* 83 C6
Isa Khel, *Pakistan* 68 C4
Isaac →, *Australia* 94 C4
Isabel, *U.S.A.* 112 C4
Isabela, *Phil.* 61 H5
Isabela, I., *Mexico* 118 C3
Isabelia, Cord., *Nic.* 120 D2
Isabella Ra., *Australia* 92 D3
Isaccea, *Romania* 43 E13
Ísafjarðardjúp, *Iceland* 8 C2
Ísafjörður, *Iceland* 8 C2
Isagarh, *India* 68 G7
Isahaya, *Japan* 55 H5
Isaka, *Tanzania* 86 C3
Isakly, *Russia* 48 C10
Işalniţa, *Romania* 43 F8
Isan →, *India* 69 F9
Isana = Içana →, *Brazil* 124 C5
Isanlu Makutu, *Nigeria* 83 D6
Isar →, *Germany* 25 G8
Isarco →, *Italy* 29 B8
Ísari, *Greece* 38 D3
Íscar, *Spain* 34 D6
İscehisar, *Turkey* 39 C12
Íschia, *Italy* 30 B6
Isdell →, *Australia* 92 C3
Ise, *Japan* 55 G8
Ise-Wan, *Japan* 55 G8
Isefjord, *Denmark* 11 J5
Isel →, *Austria* 26 E5
Iseo, *Italy* 28 C7
Iseo, L. d', *Italy* 28 C7
Iseramagazi, *Tanzania* 86 C3
Isère □, *France* 21 C9
Isère →, *France* 21 D8
Iserlohn, *Germany* 24 D3
Isérnia, *Italy* 31 A7
Iseyin, *Nigeria* 83 D5
Isfahan = Eşfahān, *Iran* 71 C6
Ishëm, *Albania* 40 E3
Ishigaki-Shima, *Japan* 55 M2
Ishikari-Gawa →, *Japan* 54 C10
Ishikari-Sammyaku, *Japan* 54 C11
Ishikari-Wan, *Japan* 54 C10
Ishikawa □, *Japan* 55 F8
Ishim, *Russia* 50 D7
Ishim →, *Russia* 50 D8
Ishinomaki, *Japan* 54 E10
Ishioka, *Japan* 55 F10
Ishkuman, *Pakistan* 69 A5
Ishpeming, *U.S.A.* 108 B2
Isigny-sur-Mer, *France* 18 C5
Isıklar Dağı, *Turkey* 41 F11
Işıklı, *Turkey* 39 C11
Isil Kul, *Russia* 50 D8
Ísili, *Italy* 30 C2
Isiolo, *Kenya* 86 B4
Isiro, *Dem. Rep. of the Congo* 86 B2
Isisford, *Australia* 94 C3
İskenderun, *Turkey* 70 B3
İskenderun Körfezi, *Turkey* 72 D6
İskilip, *Turkey* 72 B6
Iskŭr →, *Bulgaria* 41 C8
Iskŭr, Yazovir, *Bulgaria* 40 D7

Iskut →, Canada 104 B2
Isla →, U.K. 14 E5
Isla Cristina, Spain 35 H3
Isla Vista, U.S.A. 117 L7
İslâhiye, Turkey 72 D7
Islam Headworks, Pakistan 68 E5
Islamabad, Pakistan 68 C5
Islamgarh, Pakistan 68 F4
Islamkot, Pakistan 68 G4
Islampur, India 69 G11
Island L., Canada 105 C10
Island Pond, U.S.A. 111 B13
Islands, B. of, Canada 103 C8
Islands, B. of, N.Z. 91 F5
Islay, U.K. 14 F2
Isle →, France 20 D3
Isle aux Morts, Canada 103 C8
Isle of Wight □, U.K. 13 G6
Isle Royale, U.S.A. 112 B10
Isle Royale National Park, U.S.A. 112 B10
Isleton, U.S.A. 116 G5
Ismail = Izmayil, Ukraine 47 K5
Ismâ'ilîya, Egypt 80 H8
Ismaning, Germany 25 G7
Isna, Egypt 80 B3
Isoanala, Madag. 89 C8
Isogstalo, India 69 B8
Ísola del Liri, Italy 29 G10
Ísola della Scala, Italy 28 C7
Ísola di Capo Rizzuto, Italy 31 D10
Isparta, Turkey 39 D12
Isperikh, Bulgaria 41 C10
Íspica, Italy 31 F7
Israel ■, Asia 75 D3
Isratu, Eritrea 81 D4
Issia, Ivory C. 82 D3
Issoire, France 20 C7
Issoudun, France 19 F8
Issyk-Kul, Ozero = Ysyk-Köl, Kyrgyzstan 50 E8
Ist, Croatia 29 D11
Istállós-kő, Hungary 42 B5
İstanbul, Turkey 41 E12
İstanbul □, Turkey 41 E12
İstanbul Boğazı, Turkey 41 E13
Istiaía, Greece 38 C5
Istok, Kosovo, Yug. 40 D4
Istokpoga, L., U.S.A. 109 M5
Istra, Croatia 29 C10
Istres, France 21 E8
Istria = Istra, Croatia 29 C10
Itá, Paraguay 126 B4
Itaberaba, Brazil 125 F10
Itabira, Brazil 125 G10
Itabirito, Brazil 127 A7
Itabuna, Brazil 125 F11
Itacaunas →, Brazil 125 E9
Itacoatiara, Brazil 124 D7
Itaipú, Représa de, Brazil 127 B5
Itaituba, Brazil 125 D7
Itajaí, Brazil 127 B6
Itajubá, Brazil 127 A6
Itaka, Tanzania 87 D3
Italy ■, Europe 7 G8
Itamaraju, Brazil 125 G11
Itampolo, Madag. 89 C7
Itandrano, Madag. 89 C8
Itapecuru-Mirim, Brazil 125 D10
Itaperuna, Brazil 127 A7
Itapetininga, Brazil 127 A6
Itapeva, Brazil 127 A6
Itapicuru →, Bahia, Brazil 125 F11
Itapicuru →, Maranhão, Brazil 125 D10
Itapipoca, Brazil 125 D11
Itapuá □, Paraguay 127 B4
Itaquari, Brazil 127 A7
Itaquí, Brazil 126 B4
Itararé, Brazil 127 A6
Itarsi, India 68 H7
Itatí, Argentina 126 B4
Itbayat, Phil. 61 A4
Itchen →, U.K. 13 G6
Itéa, Greece 38 C4
Itezhi Tezhi, L., Zambia 87 F2
Ithaca = Itháki, Greece 38 C2
Ithaca, U.S.A. 111 D8
Itháki, Greece 38 C2
Itiquira →, Brazil 125 G7
Itō, Japan 55 G9
Itoigawa, Japan 55 F8
Iton →, France 18 C8
Itonamas →, Bolivia 124 F6
Itri, Italy 30 A6
Itsa, Egypt 80 J7
Íttiri, Italy 30 B1
Ittoqqortoormiit, Greenland 4 B6
Itu, Brazil 127 A6
Itu, Nigeria 83 D6
Itu Aba I., S. China Sea 62 B4
Ituiutaba, Brazil 125 G9
Itumbiara, Brazil 125 G9
Ituna, Canada 105 C8
Itunge Port, Tanzania 87 D3
Iturbe, Argentina 126 A2
Ituri →, Dem. Rep. of the Congo 86 B2
Iturup, Ostrov, Russia 51 E15
Ituxi →, Brazil 124 E6
Ituyuro →, Argentina 126 A3
Itzehoe, Germany 24 B5
Ivahona, Madag. 89 C8
Ivaí →, Brazil 127 A5
Ivalo, Finland 8 B22
Ivalojoki →, Finland 8 B22
Ivanava, Belarus 47 F3
Ivančice, Czech Rep. 27 B9
Ivăneşti, Romania 43 D12
Ivangorod, Russia 46 C5
Ivanhoe, Calif., U.S.A. 116 J7
Ivanhoe, Minn., U.S.A. 112 C6
Ivanić Grad, Croatia 29 C13
Ivanjica, Serbia, Yug. 40 C4
Ivanjska, Bos.-H. 42 F2
Ivankoyskoye Vdkhr., Russia 46 D9
Ivano-Frankivsk, Ukraine 47 H3
Ivano-Frankovsk = Ivano-Frankivsk, Ukraine 47 H3
Ivanovo = Ivanava, Belarus 47 F3
Ivanovo, Russia 46 D11
Ivanšćica, Croatia 29 B13
Ivato, Madag. 89 C8
Ivatsevichy, Belarus 47 F3
Ivaylovgrad, Bulgaria 41 E10
Ivinheima →, Brazil 127 A5
Ivinhema, Brazil 127 A5
Ivohibe, Madag. 89 C8
Ivory Coast, W. Afr. 82 E4
Ivory Coast ■, Africa 82 D4
Ivösjön, Sweden 11 H8
Ivrea, Italy 28 C4
Ivrindi, Turkey 39 B9
Ivujivik, Canada 101 B12
Ivybridge, U.K. 13 G4
Iwaizumi, Japan 54 E10
Iwaki, Japan 55 F10
Iwakuni, Japan 55 G6
Iwamizawa, Japan 54 C10
Iwanai, Japan 54 C10
Iwata, Japan 55 G8
Iwate □, Japan 54 E10
Iwate-San, Japan 54 E10
Iwo, Nigeria 83 D5
Iwonicz-Zdrój, Poland 45 J8
Ixiamas, Bolivia 124 F5
Ixopo, S. Africa 89 E5
Ixtepec, Mexico 119 D5
Ixtlán del Río, Mexico 118 C4
Iyal Bakhit, Sudan 81 E2
Iyo, Japan 55 H6
Izabal, L. de, Guatemala 120 C2
Izamal, Mexico 119 C7
Izberbash, Russia 49 J8
Izbica, Poland 45 H10
Izbica Kujawska, Poland 45 F5
Izbiceni, Romania 43 G9
Izena-Shima, Japan 55 L3
Izgrev, Bulgaria 41 C10
Izhevsk, Russia 50 D6
Izmayil, Ukraine 47 K5
İzmir, Turkey 39 C9
İzmir □, Turkey 39 C9
İzmir Körfezi, Turkey 39 C8
İzmit = Kocaeli, Turkey 41 F13
Iznájar, Spain 35 H6
Iznalloz, Spain 35 H7
İznik, Turkey 72 B3
İznik Gölü, Turkey 41 F13
Izobil'nyy, Russia 49 H5
Izola, Slovenia 29 C10
Izra, Syria 75 C5
Iztochni Rodopi, Bulgaria 41 E9
Izu-Shotō, Japan 55 G10
Izúcar de Matamoros, Mexico 119 D5
Izumi-Sano, Japan 55 G7
Izumo, Japan 55 G6
Izyaslav, Ukraine 47 G4
Izyum, Ukraine 47 H9

J

Jaba, Ethiopia 81 F4
Jabal at Tā'ir, Red Sea 81 D5
Jabalón →, Spain 35 G6
Jabalpur, India 69 H8
Jabbūl, Syria 70 B3
Jabiru, Australia 92 B5
Jablah, Syria 70 C3
Jablanac, Croatia 29 D11
Jablanica, Bos.-H. 42 G2
Jablonec nad Nisou, Czech Rep. 26 A8
Jablonica, Slovak Rep. 27 C10
Jabłonowo Pomorskie, Poland 44 E6
Jablunkov, Czech Rep. 27 B11
Jaboatão, Brazil 125 E11
Jaboticabal, Brazil 127 A6
Jabukovac, Serbia, Yug. 40 B6
Jaca, Spain 32 C4
Jacareí, Brazil 127 A6
Jacarèzinho, Brazil 127 A6
Jackman, U.S.A. 109 C10
Jacksboro, U.S.A. 113 J5
Jackson, Ala., U.S.A. 109 K2
Jackson, Calif., U.S.A. 116 G6
Jackson, Ky., U.S.A. 108 G4
Jackson, Mich., U.S.A. 108 D3
Jackson, Minn., U.S.A. 112 D7
Jackson, Miss., U.S.A. 113 J9
Jackson, Mo., U.S.A. 113 G10
Jackson, N.H., U.S.A. 111 B13
Jackson, Ohio, U.S.A. 108 F4
Jackson, Tenn., U.S.A. 109 H1
Jackson, Wyo., U.S.A. 114 E8
Jackson B., N.Z. 91 K2
Jackson L., U.S.A. 114 E8
Jacksons, N.Z. 91 K3
Jackson's Arm, Canada 103 C8
Jacksonville, Ala., U.S.A. 109 J3
Jacksonville, Ark., U.S.A. 113 H8
Jacksonville, Calif., U.S.A. 116 H6
Jacksonville, Fla., U.S.A. 109 K5
Jacksonville, Ill., U.S.A. 112 F9
Jacksonville, N.C., U.S.A. 109 H7
Jacksonville, Tex., U.S.A. 113 K7
Jacksonville Beach, U.S.A. 109 K5
Jacmel, Haiti 121 C5
Jacob Lake, U.S.A. 115 H7
Jacobabad, Pakistan 68 E3
Jacobina, Brazil 125 F10
Jacques Cartier, Dét. de, Canada 103 C7
Jacques Cartier, Mt., Canada 103 C6
Jacques Cartier, Parc Prov., Canada 103 C5
Jacqueville, Ivory C. 82 D4
Jacuí →, Brazil 127 C5
Jacumba, U.S.A. 117 N10
Jacundá →, Brazil 125 D8
Jade, Germany 24 B4
Jadebusen, Germany 24 B4
Jadotville = Likasi, Dem. Rep. of the Congo 87 E2
Jadovnik, Serbia, Yug. 40 C3
Jadraque, Spain 32 E2
Jaén, Peru 124 E3
Jaén, Spain 35 H7
Jaén □, Spain 35 H7
Jafarabad, India 68 J4
Jaffa = Tel Aviv-Yafo, Israel 75 C3
Jaffna, Sri Lanka 66 Q12
Jaffrey, U.S.A. 111 D12
Jagadhri, India 68 D7
Jagadishpur, India 69 G11
Jagdalpur, India 67 K13
Jagersfontein, S. Africa 88 D4
Jaghīn →, Iran 71 E8
Jagodina, Serbia, Yug. 40 B5
Jagraon, India 66 D9
Jagst →, Germany 25 F5
Jagtial, India 66 K11
Jaguariaíva, Brazil 127 A6
Jaguaribe →, Brazil 125 D11
Jagüey Grande, Cuba 120 B3
Jahanabad, India 69 G11
Jahazpur, India 68 G6
Jahrom, Iran 71 D7
Jaijon, India 68 D7
Jailolo, Indonesia 63 D7
Jailolo, Selat, Indonesia 63 D7
Jaipur, India 68 F6
Jais, India 69 F9
Jaisalmer, India 68 F4
Jaisinghnagar, India 69 H8
Jaitaran, India 68 F5
Jaithari, India 69 H8
Jājarm, Iran 71 B8
Jajce, Bos.-H. 42 F2
Jakam →, India 68 H6
Jakarta, Indonesia 62 F3
Jakhal, India 68 E6
Jakhau, India 68 H3
Jakobstad = Pietarsaari, Finland 8 E20
Jakupica, Macedonia 40 E5
Jal, U.S.A. 113 J3
Jalālābād, Afghan. 68 B4
Jalalabad, India 69 F8
Jalalpur Jattan, Pakistan 68 C6
Jalama, U.S.A. 117 L6
Jalapa, Guatemala 120 D2
Jalapa Enríquez, Mexico 119 D5
Jalasjärvi, Finland 9 E20
Jalaun, India 69 F8
Jaldhaka →, Bangla. 69 F13
Jalesar, India 68 F8
Jaleswar, Nepal 69 F11
Jalgaon, India 66 J9
Jalībah, Iraq 70 D5
Jalingo, Nigeria 83 D7
Jalisco □, Mexico 118 D4
Jalkot, Pakistan 69 B5
Jallas →, Spain 34 C1
Jalna, India 66 K9
Jalón →, Spain 32 D3
Jalor, India 68 G5
Jalpa, Mexico 118 C4
Jalpaiguri, India 67 F16
Jaluit I., Marshall Is. 96 G8
Jalūlā, Iraq 70 C5
Jamaari, Nigeria 83 C6
Jamaica ■, W. Indies 120 C4
Jamalpur, Bangla. 67 G16
Jamalpur, India 69 G12
Jamalpurganj, India 69 H13
Jamanxim →, Brazil 125 D7
Jambi, Indonesia 62 E2
Jambi □, Indonesia 62 E2
Jambusar, India 68 H5
James →, S. Dak., U.S.A. 112 D6
James →, Va., U.S.A. 108 G7
James B., Canada 102 B3
James Ranges, Australia 92 D5
James Ross I., Antarctica 5 C18
Jamesabad, Pakistan 68 G3
Jamestown, S. Africa 88 E4
Jamestown, N. Dak., U.S.A. 112 B5
Jamestown, N.Y., U.S.A. 110 D5
Jamestown, Pa., U.S.A. 110 E4
Jamīlābād, Iran 71 C6
Jamiltepec, Mexico 119 D5
Jamira →, India 69 J13
Jämjö, Sweden 11 H9
Jamkhandi, India 66 L9
Jammerbugt, Denmark 11 G3
Jammu, India 68 C6
Jammu & Kashmir □, India 69 B7
Jamnagar, India 68 H4
Jamni →, India 69 G8
Jampur, Pakistan 68 E4
Jamrud, Pakistan 68 C4
Jämsä, Finland 9 F21
Jamshedpur, India 69 H12
Jamtara, India 69 H12
Jämtland, Sweden 8 E15
Jämtlands län □, Sweden 10 B7
Jan L., Canada 105 C8
Jan Mayen, Arctic 4 B7
Janakkala, Finland 9 F21
Janaúba, Brazil 125 G10
Jand, Pakistan 68 C5
Jandaq, Iran 71 C7
Jandia, Canary Is. 37 F5
Jandia, Pta. de, Canary Is. 37 F5
Jandola, Pakistan 68 C4
Jandowae, Australia 95 D5
Jándula →, Spain 35 G6
Janesville, U.S.A. 112 D10
Janga, Ghana 83 C4
Jangamo, Mozam. 89 C6
Janghai, India 69 G10
Janikowo, Poland 45 F5
Janīn, West Bank 75 C4
Janinà = Ioánnina □, Greece 38 B2
Janja, Bos.-H. 42 F4
Janjevo, Kosovo, Yug. 40 D5
Janjgir, India 69 J10
Janjina, Croatia 29 F14
Janjina, Madag. 89 C8
Janos, Mexico 118 A3
Jánoshalma, Hungary 42 D4
Jánosháza, Hungary 42 C2
Jánossomorja, Hungary 42 C2
Janów, Poland 45 H6
Janów Lubelski, Poland 45 H9
Janów Podlaski, Poland 45 F10
Janowiec Wielkopolski, Poland 45 F4
Januária, Brazil 125 G10
Janub Dârfûr □, Sudan 81 E2
Janub Kordofân □, Sudan 81 E3
Janubio, Canary Is. 37 F6
Janville, France 19 D8
Janzé, France 18 E5
Jaora, India 68 H6
Japan ■, Asia 55 G8
Japan, Sea of, Asia 54 E7
Japan Trench, Pac. Oc. 52 F18
Japen = Yapen, Indonesia 63 E9
Japla, India 69 G11
Japurá →, Brazil 122 D4
Jaquarão, Brazil 127 C5
Jaqué, Panama 120 E4
Jarābulus, Syria 70 B3
Jaraicejo, Spain 35 F5
Jaraíz de la Vera, Spain 34 E5
Jarama →, Spain 34 E7
Jaramānah, Syria 72 F7
Jarandilla, Spain 34 E5
Jaranwala, Pakistan 68 D5
Jarash, Jordan 75 C4
Järbo, Sweden 10 D10
Jardim, Brazil 126 A4
Jardín →, Spain 33 G2
Jardines de la Reina, Arch. de los, Cuba 120 B4
Jargalang, China 57 C12
Jargalant = Hovd, Mongolia 60 B4
Jari →, Brazil 125 D8
Jarīr, W. al →, Si. Arabia 70 E4
Järlåsa, Sweden 10 E11
Jarmen, Germany 24 B9
Järna, Dalarnas, Sweden 10 D8
Järna, Stockholm, Sweden 10 E11
Jarnac, France 20 C3
Jarny, France 19 C12
Jarocin, Poland 45 G4
Jaroměř, Czech Rep. 26 A8
Jarosław, Poland 45 H9
Järpås, Sweden 11 F6
Järpen, Sweden 10 A7
Jarrahdale, Australia 93 F2
Jarrahi →, Iran 71 D6
Jarres, Plaine des, Laos 64 C4
Jarso, Ethiopia 81 F4
Jartai, China 56 E3
Jarud Qi, China 57 B11
Järvenpää, Finland 9 F21
Jarvis, Canada 110 D4
Jarvis I., Pac. Oc. 97 H12
Jarvorník, Czech Rep. 27 A10
Järvsö, Sweden 10 C10
Jarwa, India 69 F10
Jaša Tomić, Serbia, Yug. 42 E5
Jasdan, India 68 H4
Jashpurnagar, India 69 H11
Jasidih, India 69 G12
Jasień, Poland 45 G2
Jāsimīyah, Iraq 70 C5
Jasin, Malaysia 65 L4
Jāsk, Iran 71 E8
Jasło, Poland 45 J8
Jasmund, Germany 24 A9
Jaso, India 69 G9
Jasper, Alta., Canada 104 C5
Jasper, Ont., Canada 111 B9
Jasper, Ala., U.S.A. 109 J2
Jasper, Fla., U.S.A. 109 K4
Jasper, Ind., U.S.A. 108 F2
Jasper, Tex., U.S.A. 113 K8
Jasper Nat. Park, Canada 104 C5
Jasrasar, India 68 F5
Jastarnia, Poland 44 D5
Jastrebarsko, Croatia 29 C12
Jastrowie, Poland 44 E3
Jastrzębie Zdrój, Poland 45 J5
Jász-Nagykun-Szolnok □, Hungary 42 C5
Jászapáti, Hungary 42 C5
Jászárokszállás, Hungary 42 C4
Jászberény, Hungary 42 C4
Jászkisér, Hungary 42 C5
Jászladány, Hungary 42 C5
Jataí, Brazil 125 G8
Jati, Pakistan 68 G3
Jatibarang, Indonesia 63 G13
Jatinegara, Indonesia 63 G12
Játiva = Xátiva, Spain 33 G4
Jättendal, Sweden 10 C11
Jaú, Brazil 127 A6
Jauja, Peru 124 F3
Jaunpur, India 69 G10
Java = Jawa, Indonesia 62 F3
Java Barat □, Indonesia 63 G12
Java Sea, Indonesia 62 E3
Java Tengah □, Indonesia 63 G14
Java Timur □, Indonesia 63 G15
Java Trench, Ind. Oc. 62 F3
Javalambre, Sa. de, Spain 32 E4
Jávea, Spain 33 G5
Javhlant = Ulyasutay, Mongolia 60 B4
Jawa, Indonesia 62 F3
Jawad, India 68 G6
Jawor, Poland 45 G3
Jaworzno, Poland 45 H6
Jaworzyna Śląska, Poland 45 H3
Jay Peak, U.S.A. 111 B12
Jaya, Puncak, Indonesia 63 E9
Jayanti, India 67 F16
Jayapura, Indonesia 63 E10
Jayawijaya, Pegunungan, Indonesia 63 E9
Jaynagar, India 67 F15
Jayrūd, Syria 70 C3
Jayton, U.S.A. 113 J4
Jāz Mūrīān, Hāmūn-e, Iran 71 E8
Jazīreh-ye Shīf, Iran 71 D6
Jazminal, Mexico 118 C4
Jazzīn, Lebanon 75 B4
Jean, U.S.A. 117 K11
Jean Marie River, Canada 104 A4
Jean Rabel, Haiti 121 C5
Jeanerette, U.S.A. 113 L9
Jeanette, Ostrov = Zhannetty, Ostrov, Russia 51 B16
Jeannette, U.S.A. 110 F5
Jebāl Bārez, Kūh-e, Iran 71 D8
Jebba, Nigeria 83 D5
Jebel, Bahr el →, Sudan 81 F3
Jebel Dud, Sudan 81 E3
Jebel Qerri, Sudan 81 D3
Jedburgh, U.K. 14 F6
Jedda = Jiddah, Si. Arabia 74 C2
Jeddore L., Canada 103 C8
Jedlicze, Poland 45 J8
Jędrzejów, Poland 45 H7
Jedwabne, Poland 45 E9
Jeetzel →, Germany 24 B7
Jefferson, Iowa, U.S.A. 112 D7
Jefferson, Ohio, U.S.A. 110 E4
Jefferson, Tex., U.S.A. 113 J7
Jefferson, Mt., Nev., U.S.A. 114 G5
Jefferson, Mt., Oreg., U.S.A. 114 D3
Jefferson City, Mo., U.S.A. 112 F8
Jefferson City, Tenn., U.S.A. 109 G4
Jeffersontown, U.S.A. 108 F3
Jeffersonville, U.S.A. 108 F3
Jeffrey City, U.S.A. 114 E10
Jega, Nigeria 83 C5
Jēkabpils, Latvia 9 H21
Jekyll I., U.S.A. 109 K5
Jelcz-Laskowice, Poland 45 G4
Jelenia Góra, Poland 45 H2
Jelgava, Latvia 9 H20
Jelgava □, Latvia 44 B10
Jelica, Serbia, Yug. 40 C4
Jelli, Sudan 81 F3
Jelšava, Slovak Rep. 27 C13
Jemaja, Indonesia 65 L5
Jemaluang, Malaysia 65 L4
Jember, Indonesia 63 H15
Jembongan, Malaysia 62 C5
Jena, Germany 24 E7
Jena, U.S.A. 113 K8
Jenbach, Austria 26 D4
Jenkins, U.S.A. 108 G4
Jenner, U.S.A. 116 G3
Jennings, U.S.A. 113 K8
Jepara, Indonesia 63 G14
Jequié, Brazil 125 F10
Jequitinhonha, Brazil 125 G10
Jequitinhonha →, Brazil 125 G11
Jerantut, Malaysia 65 L4
Jérémie, Haiti 121 C5
Jerez, Punta, Mexico 119 C5
Jerez de García Salinas, Mexico 118 C4
Jerez de la Frontera, Spain 35 J4
Jerez de los Caballeros, Spain 35 G4
Jericho = El Arīḥā, West Bank 75 D4
Jericho, Australia 94 C4
Jerichow, Germany 24 C8
Jerid, Chott = Djerid, Chott, Tunisia 78 B7
Jermyn, U.S.A. 111 E9
Jerome, U.S.A. 114 E6
Jerramungup, Australia 93 F2
Jersey, U.K. 13 H5
Jersey City, U.S.A. 111 F10
Jersey Shore, U.S.A. 110 E7
Jerseyville, U.S.A. 112 F9
Jerusalem, Israel 75 D4
Jervis Inlet, Canada 104 C4
Jerzu, Italy 30 C2
Jesenice, Slovenia 29 B11
Jeseník, Czech Rep. 27 A10

Jesenké, *Slovak Rep.* 27 C13
Jesi = Iesi, *Italy* 29 E10
Jesselton = Kota Kinabalu, *Malaysia* 62 C5
Jessnitz, *Germany* 24 D8
Jessore, *Bangla.* 67 H16
Jesup, *U.S.A.* 109 K5
Jesús Carranza, *Mexico* 119 D5
Jesús María, *Argentina* 126 C3
Jetmore, *U.S.A.* 113 F5
Jetpur, *India* 68 J4
Jeumont, *France* 19 B11
Jevnaker, *Norway* 9 F14
Jewett, *U.S.A.* 110 F3
Jewett City, *U.S.A.* 111 E13
Jeyḥūnābād, *Iran* 71 C6
Jeypore, *India* 67 K13
Jeziorak, Jezioro, *Poland* 44 E6
Jeziorany, *Poland* 44 E7
Jeziorka →, *Poland* 45 F8
Jha Jha, *India* 69 G12
Jhaarkand = Jharkhand □, *India* 69 H11
Jhabua, *India* 68 H6
Jhajjar, *India* 68 E7
Jhal, *Pakistan* 68 E2
Jhal Jhao, *Pakistan* 66 F4
Jhalawar, *India* 68 G7
Jhalida, *India* 69 H11
Jhalrapatan, *India* 68 G7
Jhang Maghiana, *Pakistan* 68 D5
Jhansi, *India* 69 G8
Jhargram, *India* 69 H12
Jharia, *India* 69 H12
Jharkhand □, *India* 69 H11
Jharsuguda, *India* 67 J14
Jhelum, *Pakistan* 68 C5
Jhelum →, *Pakistan* 68 D5
Jhilmilli, *India* 69 H10
Jhudo, *Pakistan* 68 G3
Jhunjhunu, *India* 68 E6
Ji-Paraná, *Brazil* 124 F6
Ji Xian, *Hebei, China* 56 F8
Ji Xian, *Henan, China* 56 G8
Ji Xian, *Shanxi, China* 56 F6
Jia Xian, *Henan, China* 56 H7
Jia Xian, *Shaanxi, China* 56 E6
Jiading, *China* 59 B13
Jiahe, *China* 59 E9
Jialing Jiang →, *China* 58 C6
Jiamusi, *China* 60 B8
Ji'an, *Jiangxi, China* 59 D10
Ji'an, *Jilin, China* 57 D14
Jianchang, *China* 57 D11
Jianchangying, *China* 57 D10
Jianchuan, *China* 58 D2
Jiande, *China* 59 C12
Jiang'an, *China* 58 C5
Jiangbei, *China* 58 C6
Jiangcheng, *China* 58 F3
Jiangchuan, *China* 58 E4
Jiangdi, *China* 58 D4
Jiangdu, *China* 59 A12
Jiange, *China* 58 A5
Jianghua, *China* 59 E8
Jiangjin, *China* 58 C6
Jiangkou, *China* 58 D7
Jiangle, *China* 59 D11
Jiangling, *China* 59 B9
Jiangmen, *China* 59 F9
Jiangning, *China* 59 B12
Jiangshan, *China* 59 C12
Jiangsu □, *China* 57 H11
Jiangxi □, *China* 59 D11
Jiangyan, *China* 59 A13
Jiangyin, *China* 59 B13
Jiangyong, *China* 59 E8
Jiangyou, *China* 58 B5
Jianhe, *China* 58 D7
Jianli, *China* 59 C9
Jianning, *China* 59 D11
Jian'ou, *China* 59 D12
Jianshi, *China* 58 B7
Jianshui, *China* 58 F4
Jianyang, *Fujian, China* 59 D12
Jianyang, *Sichuan, China* 58 B5
Jiao Xian = Jiaozhou, *China* 57 F11
Jiaohe, *Hebei, China* 56 E9
Jiaohe, *Jilin, China* 57 C14
Jiaojiang, *China* 59 C13
Jiaoling, *China* 59 E11
Jiaozhou, *China* 57 F11
Jiaozhou Wan, *China* 57 F11
Jiaozuo, *China* 56 G7
Jiashan, *China* 59 B13
Jiawang, *China* 57 G9
Jiaxiang, *China* 56 G9
Jiaxing, *China* 59 B13
Jiayi = Chiai, *Taiwan* 59 F13
Jiayu, *China* 59 C9
Jibiya, *Nigeria* 83 C6
Jibou, *Romania* 43 C8
Jibuti = Djibouti ■, *Africa* 81 E5
Jicarón, I., *Panama* 120 E3
Jičín, *Czech Rep.* 26 A8
Jiddah, *Si. Arabia* 74 C2
Jido, *India* 67 E19
Jieshou, *China* 56 H8
Jiexiu, *China* 56 F6
Jieyang, *China* 59 F11
Jigawa □, *Nigeria* 83 C6
Jiggalong, *Australia* 92 D3
Jigni, *India* 69 G8
Jihlava, *Czech Rep.* 26 B8
Jihlava →, *Czech Rep.* 27 C9
Jihočeský □, *Czech Rep.* 26 B7
Jihomoravský □, *Czech Rep.* 27 B9
Jijiga, *Ethiopia* 74 F3
Jikamshi, *Nigeria* 83 C6
Jikau, *Sudan* 81 F3
Jilin, *China* 57 C14
Jilin □, *China* 57 C13
Jiloca →, *Spain* 32 D3
Jilong = Chilung, *Taiwan* 59 E13
Jim Thorpe, *U.S.A.* 111 F9
Jima, *Ethiopia* 81 F4
Jimbolia, *Romania* 42 E5
Jimena de la Frontera, *Spain* 35 J5
Jiménez, *Mexico* 118 B4
Jimo, *China* 57 F11
Jin Jiang →, *China* 59 C10
Jin Xian = Jinzhou, *China* 56 E8
Jin Xian, *China* 57 E11
Jinan, *China* 56 F9
Jincheng, *China* 56 G7
Jinchuan, *China* 58 B4
Jind, *India* 68 E7
Jindřichův Hradec, *Czech Rep.* 26 B8
Jing He →, *China* 56 G5
Jing Shan, *China* 59 B8
Jing Xian, *China* 59 B12
Jing'an, *China* 59 C10
Jingbian, *China* 56 F5
Jingchuan, *China* 56 G4
Jingde, *China* 59 B12
Jingdezhen, *China* 59 C11
Jingdong, *China* 58 E3
Jinggangshan, *China* 59 D10
Jinggu, *China* 58 F3
Jinghai, *China* 56 E9
Jinghong, *China* 58 G3
Jingjiang, *China* 59 A13
Jingle, *China* 56 E6
Jingmen, *China* 59 B9
Jingning, *China* 56 G3
Jingpo Hu, *China* 57 C15
Jingshan, *China* 59 B9
Jingtai, *China* 56 F3
Jingxi, *China* 58 F6
Jingxing, *China* 56 E8
Jingyang, *China* 56 G5
Jingyu, *China* 57 C14
Jingyuan, *China* 56 F3
Jingzhou, *China* 58 D7
Jingziguan, *China* 56 H6
Jinhua, *China* 59 C12
Jining, *Nei Monggol Zizhiqu, China* 56 D7
Jining, *Shandong, China* 56 G9
Jinja, *Uganda* 86 B3
Jinjang, *Malaysia* 65 L3
Jinji, *China* 56 F4
Jinjiang, *Fujian, China* 59 E12
Jinjiang, *Yunnan, China* 58 D3
Jinjini, *Ghana* 82 D4
Jinkou, *China* 59 B10
Jinkouhe, *China* 58 C4
Jinmen Dao, *China* 59 E12
Jinnah Barrage, *Pakistan* 66 C7
Jinning, *China* 58 E4
Jinotega, *Nic.* 120 D2
Jinotepe, *Nic.* 120 D2
Jinping, *Guizhou, China* 58 D7
Jinping, *Yunnan, China* 58 F4
Jinsha, *China* 58 D6
Jinsha Jiang →, *China* 58 C5
Jinshan, *China* 59 B13
Jinshi, *China* 59 C8
Jintan, *China* 59 B12
Jinxi, *Jiangxi, China* 59 D11
Jinxi, *Liaoning, China* 57 D11
Jinxian, *China* 59 C11
Jinxiang, *China* 56 G9
Jinyang, *China* 58 D4
Jinyun, *China* 59 C13
Jinzhai, *China* 59 B10
Jinzhou, *Hebei, China* 56 E8
Jinzhou, *Liaoning, China* 57 D11
Jiparaná →, *Brazil* 124 E6
Jipijapa, *Ecuador* 124 D2
Jiquilpan, *Mexico* 118 D4
Jishan, *China* 56 G6
Jishou, *China* 58 C7
Jishui, *China* 59 D10
Jisr ash Shughūr, *Syria* 70 C3
Jitarning, *Australia* 93 F2
Jitra, *Malaysia* 65 J3
Jiu →, *Romania* 43 G8
Jiudengkou, *China* 56 E4
Jiujiang, *Guangdong, China* 59 F9
Jiujiang, *Jiangxi, China* 59 C10
Jiuling Shan, *China* 59 C10
Jiulong, *China* 58 C3
Jiutai, *China* 57 B13
Jiuxincheng, *China* 56 E8
Jiuyuhang, *China* 59 B12
Jixi, *Anhui, China* 59 B12
Jixi, *Heilongjiang, China* 57 B16
Jiyang, *China* 57 F9
Jiyuan, *China* 56 G7
Jīzān, *Si. Arabia* 74 D3
Jize, *China* 56 F8
Jizera →, *Czech Rep.* 26 A7
Jizl, W. →, *Si. Arabia* 80 B4
Jizl, Wādī al, *Si. Arabia* 70 E3
Jizō-Zaki, *Japan* 55 G6
Jizzakh, *Uzbekistan* 50 E7
Joaçaba, *Brazil* 127 B5
Joal Fadiout, *Senegal* 82 C1
João Pessoa, *Brazil* 125 E12
Joaquín V. González, *Argentina* 126 B3
Jobat, *India* 68 H6
Jobourg, Nez de, *France* 18 C5
Jódar, *Spain* 35 H7
Jodhpur, *India* 68 F5
Jodiya, *India* 68 H4
Jōetsu, *Japan* 55 F9
Jœuf, *France* 19 C12
Jofane, *Mozam.* 89 C5
Jogbani, *India* 69 F12
Jõgeva, *Estonia* 9 G22
Jogjakarta = Yogyakarta, *Indonesia* 62 F4
Johannesburg, *S. Africa* 89 D4
Johannesburg, *U.S.A.* 117 K9
Johansfors, *Sweden* 11 H9
Johilla →, *India* 69 H9
John Day, *U.S.A.* 114 D4
John Day →, *U.S.A.* 114 D3
John D'Or Prairie, *Canada* 104 B5
John H. Kerr Reservoir, *U.S.A.* 109 G6
John o' Groats, *U.K.* 14 C5
Johnnie, *U.S.A.* 117 J10
John's Ra., *Australia* 94 C1
Johnson, *Kans., U.S.A.* 113 G4
Johnson, *Vt., U.S.A.* 111 B12
Johnson City, *N.Y., U.S.A.* 111 D9
Johnson City, *Tenn., U.S.A.* 109 G4
Johnson City, *Tex., U.S.A.* 113 K5
Johnsonburg, *U.S.A.* 110 E6
Johnsondale, *U.S.A.* 117 K8
Johnson's Crossing, *Canada* 104 A2
Johnston, L., *Australia* 93 F3
Johnston Falls = Mambilima Falls, *Zambia* 87 E2
Johnston I., *Pac. Oc.* 97 F11
Johnstone Str., *Canada* 104 C3
Johnstown, *N.Y., U.S.A.* 111 C10
Johnstown, *Ohio, U.S.A.* 110 F2
Johnstown, *Pa., U.S.A.* 110 F6
Johor Baharu, *Malaysia* 65 M4
Jõhvi, *Estonia* 9 G22
Joigny, *France* 19 E10
Joinville, *Brazil* 127 B6
Joinville, *France* 19 D12
Joinville I., *Antarctica* 5 C18
Jojutla, *Mexico* 119 D5
Jokkmokk, *Sweden* 8 C18
Jökulsá á Bru →, *Iceland* 8 D6
Jökulsá á Fjöllum →, *Iceland* 8 C5
Jolfā, *Āzarbājān-e Sharqī, Iran* 70 B5
Jolfā, *Eşfahan, Iran* 71 C6
Joliet, *U.S.A.* 108 E1
Joliette, *Canada* 102 C5
Jolo, *Phil.* 61 J4
Jolon, *U.S.A.* 116 K5
Jomalig I., *Phil.* 61 D5
Jombang, *Indonesia* 63 G15
Jomda, *China* 58 B2
Jonava, *Lithuania* 9 J21
Jones Sound, *Canada* 4 B3
Jonesboro, *Ark., U.S.A.* 113 H9
Jonesboro, *La., U.S.A.* 113 J8
Jong →, *S. Leone* 82 D2
Jonglei, *Sudan* 81 F3
Jonglei □, *Sudan* 81 F3
Joniškis, *Lithuania* 9 H20
Jönköping, *Sweden* 11 G8
Jönköpings län □, *Sweden* 11 G8
Jonquière, *Canada* 103 C5
Jonsered, *Sweden* 11 G6
Jonzac, *France* 20 C3
Joplin, *U.S.A.* 113 G7
Jora, *India* 68 F6
Jordan, *Mont., U.S.A.* 114 C10
Jordan, *N.Y., U.S.A.* 111 C8
Jordan ■, *Asia* 75 E5
Jordan →, *Asia* 75 D4
Jordan Valley, *U.S.A.* 114 E5
Jordanów, *Poland* 45 J6
Jorhat, *India* 67 F19
Jörn, *Sweden* 8 D19
Jorong, *Indonesia* 62 E4
Jørpeland, *Norway* 9 G11
Jorquera →, *Chile* 126 B2
Jos, *Nigeria* 83 D6
Jos Plateau, *Nigeria* 83 D6
Jošanička Banja, *Serbia, Yug.* 40 C4
José Batlle y Ordóñez, *Uruguay* 127 C4
Joseni, *Romania* 43 D10
Joseph, L., *Nfld., Canada* 103 B6
Joseph, L., *Ont., Canada* 110 A5
Joseph Bonaparte G., *Australia* 92 B4
Joshinath, *India* 69 D8
Joshua Tree, *U.S.A.* 117 L10
Joshua Tree National Park, *U.S.A.* 117 M10
Josselin, *France* 18 E4
Jostedalsbreen, *Norway* 9 F12
Jotunheimen, *Norway* 9 F13
Joubertberge, *Namibia* 88 B1
Joué-lès-Tours, *France* 18 E7
Jourdanton, *U.S.A.* 113 L5
Joutseno, *Finland* 46 B5
Jovellanos, *Cuba* 120 B3
Joyeuse, *France* 21 D8
Józefów, *Lubelskie, Poland* 45 H10
Józefów, *Mazowieckie, Poland* 45 F8
Ju Xian, *China* 57 F10
Juan Aldama, *Mexico* 118 C4
Juan Bautista Alberdi, *Argentina* 126 C3
Juan de Fuca Str., *Canada* 116 B3
Juan de Nova, *Ind. Oc.* 89 B7
Juan Fernández, Arch. de, *Pac. Oc.* 122 G2
Juan José Castelli, *Argentina* 126 B3
Juan L. Lacaze, *Uruguay* 126 C4
Juankoski, *Finland* 8 E23
Juárez, *Argentina* 126 D4
Juárez, *Mexico* 117 N11
Juárez, Sierra de, *Mexico* 118 A1
Juàzeiro, *Brazil* 125 E10
Juàzeiro do Norte, *Brazil* 125 E11
Juba, *Sudan* 81 G3
Jubayl, *Lebanon* 75 A4
Jubbah, *Si. Arabia* 70 D4
Jubbal, *India* 68 D7
Jubbulpore = Jabalpur, *India* 69 H8
Jübek, *Germany* 24 A5
Jubga, *Russia* 49 H4
Jubilee L., *Australia* 93 E4
Juby, C., *Morocco* 78 C3
Júcar = Xúquer →, *Spain* 33 F4
Júcaro, *Cuba* 120 B4
Juchitán, *Mexico* 119 D5
Judaea = Har Yehuda, *Israel* 75 D3
Judenburg, *Austria* 26 D7
Judith →, *U.S.A.* 114 C9
Judith, Pt., *U.S.A.* 111 E13
Judith Gap, *U.S.A.* 114 C9
Juelsminde, *Denmark* 11 J4
Jugoslavia = Yugoslavia ■, *Europe* 40 C4
Juigalpa, *Nic.* 120 D2
Juillac, *France* 20 C5
Juist, *Germany* 24 B2
Juiz de Fora, *Brazil* 127 A7
Jujuy □, *Argentina* 126 A2
Julesburg, *U.S.A.* 112 E3
Juli, *Peru* 124 G5
Julia Cr. →, *Australia* 94 C3
Julia Creek, *Australia* 94 C3
Juliaca, *Peru* 124 G4
Julian, *U.S.A.* 117 M10
Julian Alps = Julijske Alpe, *Slovenia* 29 B11
Julian L., *Canada* 102 B4
Julianatop, *Surinam* 125 C7
Julianehåb = Qaqortoq, *Greenland* 101 B6
Jülich, *Germany* 24 E2
Julijske Alpe, *Slovenia* 29 B11
Julimes, *Mexico* 118 B3
Jullundur, *India* 68 D6
Julu, *China* 56 F8
Jumbo, *Zimbabwe* 87 F3
Jumbo Pk., *U.S.A.* 117 J12
Jumentos Cays, *Bahamas* 120 B4
Jumilla, *Spain* 33 G3
Jumla, *Nepal* 69 E10
Jumna = Yamuna →, *India* 69 G9
Junagadh, *India* 68 J4
Junction, *Tex., U.S.A.* 113 K5
Junction, *Utah, U.S.A.* 115 G7
Junction B., *Australia* 94 A1
Junction City, *Kans., U.S.A.* 112 F6
Junction City, *Oreg., U.S.A.* 114 D2
Junction Pt., *Australia* 94 A1
Jundah, *Australia* 94 C3
Jundiaí, *Brazil* 127 A6
Juneau, *U.S.A.* 104 B2
Junee, *Australia* 95 E4
Jungfrau, *Switz.* 25 J3
Junggar Pendi, *China* 60 B3
Jungshahi, *Pakistan* 68 G2
Juniata →, *U.S.A.* 110 F7
Junín, *Argentina* 126 C3
Junín de los Andes, *Argentina* 128 D2
Jūniyah, *Lebanon* 75 B4
Junlian, *China* 58 C5
Juntas, *Chile* 126 B2
Juntura, *U.S.A.* 114 E4
Jur, Nahr el →, *Sudan* 81 F2
Jura = Jura, Mts. du, *Europe* 19 F13
Jura = Schwäbische Alb, *Germany* 25 G5
Jura, *U.K.* 14 F3
Jura □, *France* 19 F12
Jura □, *Switz.* 25 H3
Jūra →, *Lithuania* 44 C9
Jura, Mts. du, *Europe* 19 F13
Jura, Sd. of, *U.K.* 14 F3
Jurbarkas, *Lithuania* 9 J20
Jurien, *Australia* 93 F2
Jurilovca, *Romania* 43 F13
Jūrmala, *Latvia* 9 H20
Jurong, *China* 59 B12
Juruá →, *Brazil* 122 D4
Juruena, *Brazil* 124 F7
Juruena →, *Brazil* 124 E7
Juruti, *Brazil* 125 D7
Jussey, *France* 19 E12
Justo Daract, *Argentina* 126 C2
Jutaí →, *Brazil* 124 D5
Jüterbog, *Germany* 24 D9
Juticalpa, *Honduras* 120 D2
Jutland = Jylland, *Denmark* 11 H3
Juventud, I. de la, *Cuba* 120 B3
Juvigny-sous-Andaine, *France* 18 D6
Jūy Zar, *Iran* 70 C5
Juye, *China* 56 G9
Juzennecourt, *France* 19 D11
Jvari, *Georgia* 49 J6
Jwaneng, *Botswana* 85 J4
Jyderup, *Denmark* 11 J5
Jylland, *Denmark* 11 H3
Jyväskylä, *Finland* 9 E21

K

K2, *Pakistan* 69 B7
Ka →, *Nigeria* 83 C5
Kaap Plateau, *S. Africa* 88 D3
Kaapkruis, *Namibia* 88 C1
Kaapstad = Cape Town, *S. Africa* 88 E2
Kaba, *Guinea* 82 C2
Kabaena, *Indonesia* 63 F6
Kabala, *S. Leone* 82 D2
Kabale, *Uganda* 86 C3
Kabalo, *Dem. Rep. of the Congo* 86 D2
Kabambare, *Dem. Rep. of the Congo* 86 C2
Kabango, *Dem. Rep. of the Congo* 87 D2
Kabanjahe, *Indonesia* 62 D1
Kabankalan, *Phil.* 61 G5
Kabara, *Mali* 82 B4
Kabardinka, *Russia* 47 K10
Kabardino-Balkar Republic = Kabardino-Balkaria □, *Russia* 49 J6
Kabardino-Balkaria □, *Russia* 49 J6
Kabarega Falls = Murchison Falls, *Uganda* 86 B3
Kabasalan, *Phil.* 61 H5
Kabba, *Nigeria* 83 D6
Kabetogama, *U.S.A.* 112 A8
Kabi, *Niger* 83 C7
Kabin Buri, *Thailand* 64 F3
Kabinakagami L., *Canada* 102 C3
Kabinda, *Dem. Rep. of the Congo* 84 F4
Kabna, *Sudan* 80 D3
Kabompo, *Zambia* 87 E1
Kabompo →, *Zambia* 85 G4
Kabondo, *Dem. Rep. of the Congo* 87 D2
Kabongo, *Dem. Rep. of the Congo* 86 D2
Kabot, *Guinea* 82 C2
Kabou, *Togo* 83 D5
Kabr, *Sudan* 81 E2
Kabūd Gonbad, *Iran* 71 B8
Kabugao, *Phil.* 61 B4
Kābul, *Afghan.* 68 B3
Kābul □, *Afghan.* 66 B6
Kābul →, *Pakistan* 68 C5
Kabunga, *Dem. Rep. of the Congo* 86 C2
Kaburuang, *Indonesia* 63 D7
Kabushiya, *Sudan* 81 D3
Kabwe, *Zambia* 87 E2
Kačanik, *Kosovo, Yug.* 40 D5
Kačerginė, *Lithuania* 44 D10
Kachchh, Gulf of, *India* 68 H3
Kachchh, Rann of, *India* 68 H4
Kachchhidhana, *India* 69 J8
Kachebera, *Zambia* 87 E3
Kachia, *Nigeria* 83 D6
Kachikau, *Botswana* 88 B3
Kachin □, *Burma* 58 D1
Kachira, L., *Uganda* 86 C3
Kachiry, *Kazakstan* 50 D8
Kachisi, *Ethiopia* 81 F4
Kachnara, *India* 68 H6
Kachot, *Cambodia* 65 G4
Kaçkar, *Turkey* 73 B9
Kadan, *Czech Rep.* 26 A6
Kadan Kyun, *Burma* 64 F2
Kadanai →, *Afghan.* 68 D1
Kadarkút, *Hungary* 42 D2
Kade, *Ghana* 83 D4
Kadi, *India* 68 H5
Kadınhanı, *Turkey* 72 C5
Kadiolo, *Mali* 82 C3
Kadipur, *India* 69 F10
Kadirli, *Turkey* 70 B3
Kadiyevka = Stakhanov, *Ukraine* 47 H10
Kadodo, *Sudan* 81 E2
Kadoka, *U.S.A.* 112 D4
Kadom, *Russia* 48 C6
Kadoma, *Zimbabwe* 87 F2
Kâdugli, *Sudan* 81 E2
Kaduna, *Nigeria* 83 C6
Kaduna □, *Nigeria* 83 C6
Kaduy, *Russia* 46 C9
Kaédi, *Mauritania* 82 B2
Kaélé, *Cameroon* 83 C7
Kaeng Khoï, *Thailand* 64 E3
Kaesŏng, *N. Korea* 57 F14
Kāf, *Si. Arabia* 70 D3
Kafan = Kapan, *Armenia* 70 B5
Kafanchan, *Nigeria* 83 D6
Kafareti, *Nigeria* 83 C7
Kaffrine, *Senegal* 82 C1
Kafin, *Nigeria* 83 D6
Kafin Madaki, *Nigeria* 83 C6
Kafinda, *Zambia* 87 E3
Kafirévs, Ákra, *Greece* 38 C6
Kafr el Battikh, *Egypt* 80 H7
Kafr el Dauwâr, *Egypt* 80 H7
Kafr el Sheikh, *Egypt* 80 H7
Kafue, *Zambia* 87 F2
Kafue →, *Zambia* 85 H5
Kafue Flats, *Zambia* 87 F2
Kafue Nat. Park, *Zambia* 87 F2
Kafulwe, *Zambia* 87 D2
Kaga, *Afghan.* 68 B4
Kaga Bandoro, *C.A.R.* 84 C3
Kagan, *Uzbekistan* 50 F7
Kagarko, *Nigeria* 83 D6
Kagawa □, *Japan* 55 G7
Kagera = Ziwa Maghariba □, *Tanzania* 86 C3
Kagera →, *Uganda* 86 C3
Kağızman, *Turkey* 70 B4
Kagmar, *Sudan* 81 E3
Kagoshima, *Japan* 55 J5
Kagoshima □, *Japan* 55 J5
Kagul = Cahul, *Moldova* 43 E13
Kahak, *Iran* 71 B6
Kahama, *Tanzania* 86 C3

Kahan, *Pakistan* 68 E3
Kahang, *Malaysia* 65 L4
Kahayan →, *Indonesia* 62 E4
Kahe, *Tanzania* 86 C4
Kahnūj, *Iran* 71 E8
Kahoka, *U.S.A.* 112 E9
Kahoolawe, *U.S.A.* 106 H16
Kahramanmaraş, *Turkey* 70 B3
Kâhta, *Turkey* 73 D8
Kahuta, *Pakistan* 68 C5
Kai, Kepulauan, *Indonesia* 63 F8
Kai Besar, *Indonesia* 63 F8
Kai Is. = Kai, Kepulauan, *Indonesia* 63 F8
Kai Kecil, *Indonesia* 63 F8
Kai Xian, *China* 58 B7
Kaiama, *Nigeria* 83 D5
Kaiapoi, *N.Z.* 91 K4
Kaieteur Falls, *Guyana* 124 B7
Kaifeng, *China* 56 G8
Kaihua, *China* 59 C12
Kaijiang, *China* 58 B6
Kaikohe, *N.Z.* 91 F4
Kaikoura, *N.Z.* 91 K4
Kaikoura Ra., *N.Z.* 91 J4
Kailahun, *S. Leone* 82 D2
Kaili, *China* 58 D6
Kailu, *China* 57 C11
Kailua Kona, *U.S.A.* 106 J17
Kaimana, *Indonesia* 63 E8
Kaimanawa Mts., *N.Z.* 91 H5
Kaimganj, *India* 69 F8
Kaimur Hills, *India* 69 G10
Kainab →, *Namibia* 88 D2
Kainji Dam, *Nigeria* 83 D5
Kainji Res., *Nigeria* 83 C5
Kainuu, *Finland* 8 D23
Kaipara Harbour, *N.Z.* 91 G5
Kaiping, *China* 59 F9
Kaipokok B., *Canada* 103 B8
Kaira, *India* 68 H5
Kairana, *India* 68 E7
Kaironi, *Indonesia* 63 E8
Kairouan, *Tunisia* 79 A8
Kaiserslautern, *Germany* 25 F3
Kaiserstuhl, *Germany* 25 G3
Kaitaia, *N.Z.* 91 F4
Kaitangata, *N.Z.* 91 M2
Kaithal, *India* 68 E7
Kaitu →, *Pakistan* 68 C4
Kaiyang, *China* 58 D6
Kaiyuan, *Liaoning, China* 57 C13
Kaiyuan, *Yunnan, China* 58 F4
Kajaani, *Finland* 8 D22
Kajabbi, *Australia* 94 C3
Kajana = Kajaani, *Finland* 8 D22
Kajang, *Malaysia* 65 L3
Kajaran, *Armenia* 73 C12
Kajiado, *Kenya* 86 C4
Kajo Kaji, *Sudan* 81 G3
Kajuru, *Nigeria* 83 C6
Kaka, *Sudan* 81 E3
Kakabeka Falls, *Canada* 102 C2
Kakadu Nat. Park, *Australia* 92 B5
Kakamas, *S. Africa* 88 D3
Kakamega, *Kenya* 86 B3
Kakanj, *Bos.-H.* 42 F3
Kakanui Mts., *N.Z.* 91 L3
Kakata, *Liberia* 82 D2
Kakdwip, *India* 69 J13
Kake, *Japan* 55 G6
Kake, *U.S.A.* 104 B2
Kakegawa, *Japan* 55 G9
Kakeroma-Jima, *Japan* 55 K4
Kakhib, *Russia* 49 J8
Kakhovka, *Ukraine* 47 J7
Kakhovske Vdskh., *Ukraine* 47 J7
Kakinada, *India* 67 L13
Kakisa →, *Canada* 104 A5
Kakisa L., *Canada* 104 A5
Kakogawa, *Japan* 55 G7
Kakwa →, *Canada* 104 C5
Kāl Gūsheh, *Iran* 71 D8
Kal Safīd, *Iran* 70 C5
Kala, *Nigeria* 83 C7
Kalaallit Nunaat = Greenland ■, *N. Amer.* 4 C5
Kalabagh, *Pakistan* 68 C4
Kalabahi, *Indonesia* 63 F6
Kalabáka, *Greece* 38 B3
Kalabana, *Mali* 82 C3
Kalach, *Russia* 48 E5
Kalach na Donu, *Russia* 49 F6
Kaladan →, *Burma* 67 J18
Kaladar, *Canada* 102 D4
Kalahari, *Africa* 88 C3
Kalahari Gemsbok Nat. Park, *S. Africa* 88 D3
Kalajoki, *Finland* 8 D20
Kālak, *Iran* 71 E8
Kalakamati, *Botswana* 89 C4
Kalakan, *Russia* 51 D12
K'alak'unlun Shank'ou = Karakoram Pass, *Pakistan* 69 B7
Kalam, *Pakistan* 69 B5
Kalama, *Dem. Rep. of the Congo* 86 C2
Kalama, *U.S.A.* 116 E4
Kalámai, *Greece* 38 D4
Kalamariá, *Greece* 40 F6
Kalamata = Kalámai, *Greece* 38 D4
Kalamazoo, *U.S.A.* 108 D3
Kalamazoo →, *U.S.A.* 108 D2
Kalambo Falls, *Tanzania* 87 D3
Kálamos, *Attikí, Greece* 38 C5
Kálamos, *Iónioi Nísoi, Greece* 38 C2
Kalan, *Turkey* 70 B3
Kalankalan, *Guinea* 82 C3
Kalannie, *Australia* 93 F2
Kalāntarī, *Iran* 71 C7
Kalao, *Indonesia* 63 F6
Kalaotoa, *Indonesia* 63 F6
Kälarne, *Sweden* 10 B10
Kalasin, *Thailand* 64 D4
Kalat, *Pakistan* 66 E5
Kalāteh, *Iran* 71 B7
Kalāteh-ye Ganj, *Iran* 71 E8
Kálathos, *Greece* 39 E10
Kalaus →, *Russia* 49 H7
Kalávrita, *Greece* 38 C4
Kalbarri, *Australia* 93 E1
Kale, *Antalya, Turkey* 39 E12
Kale, *Denizli, Turkey* 39 D10
Kalecik, *Turkey* 72 B5
Kalegauk Kyun, *Burma* 67 M20
Kalehe, *Dem. Rep. of the Congo* 86 C2
Kalema, *Tanzania* 86 C3
Kalemie, *Dem. Rep. of the Congo* 86 D2
Kalety, *Poland* 45 H5
Kalewa, *Burma* 67 H19
Kaleybar, *Iran* 70 B5
Kalgan = Zhangjiakou, *China* 56 D8
Kalgoorlie-Boulder, *Australia* 93 F3
Kali →, *India* 69 F8
Kali Sindh →, *India* 68 G6
Kaliakra, Nos, *Bulgaria* 41 C12
Kalianda, *Indonesia* 62 F3
Kalibo, *Phil.* 61 F5
Kalima, *Dem. Rep. of the Congo* 86 C2
Kalimantan □, *Indonesia* 62 E4
Kalimantan Barat □, *Indonesia* 62 E4
Kalimantan Selatan □, *Indonesia* 62 E5
Kalimantan Tengah □, *Indonesia* 62 E4
Kalimantan Timur □, *Indonesia* 62 D5
Kálimnos, *Greece* 39 D8
Kalimpong, *India* 69 F13
Kalinin = Tver, *Russia* 46 D8
Kaliningrad, *Russia* 9 J19
Kalininsk, *Russia* 48 E7
Kalinkavichy, *Belarus* 47 F5
Kalinkovichi = Kalinkavichy, *Belarus* 47 F5
Kalinovik, *Bos.-H.* 40 C2
Kalipetrovo, *Bulgaria* 41 B11
Kaliro, *Uganda* 86 B3
Kalirrákhi, *Greece* 41 F8
Kalispell, *U.S.A.* 114 B6
Kalisz, *Poland* 45 G5
Kalisz Pomorski, *Poland* 45 E2
Kaliua, *Tanzania* 86 D3
Kalívia Thorikoú, *Greece* 38 D5
Kalix, *Sweden* 8 D20
Kalix →, *Sweden* 8 D20
Kalka, *India* 68 D7
Kalkan, *Turkey* 39 E11
Kalkarindji, *Australia* 92 C5
Kalkaska, *U.S.A.* 108 C3
Kalkfeld, *Namibia* 88 C2
Kalkfontein, *Botswana* 88 C3
Kalkım, *Turkey* 39 B9
Kalkrand, *Namibia* 88 C2
Kållandsö, *Sweden* 11 F7
Kallavesi, *Finland* 8 E22
Källby, *Sweden* 11 F7
Kållered, *Sweden* 11 G6
Kallimasiá, *Greece* 39 C8
Kallinge, *Sweden* 11 H9
Kallithéa, *Greece* 38 D5
Kallmet, *Albania* 40 E3
Kalloní, *Greece* 39 B8
Kallonís, Kólpos, *Greece* 39 B8
Kallsjön, *Sweden* 8 E15
Kalmalo, *Nigeria* 83 C6
Kalmar, *Sweden* 11 H10
Kalmar län □, *Sweden* 11 G10
Kalmar sund, *Sweden* 11 H10
Kalmyk Republic = Kalmykia □, *Russia* 49 G8
Kalmykia □, *Russia* 49 G8
Kalmykovo, *Kazakstan* 50 E6
Kalna, *India* 69 H13
Kalnai, *India* 69 H10
Kalocsa, *Hungary* 42 D4
Kalofer, *Bulgaria* 41 D8
Kalokhorio, *Cyprus* 36 E12
Kaloko, *Dem. Rep. of the Congo* 86 D2
Kalol, *Gujarat, India* 68 H5
Kalol, *Gujarat, India* 68 H5
Kalolímnos, *Greece* 39 D9
Kalomo, *Zambia* 87 F2
Kalonerón, *Greece* 38 D3
Kalpi, *India* 69 F8
Kaltern = Caldaro, *Italy* 29 B8
Kaltungo, *Nigeria* 83 D7
Kalu, *Pakistan* 68 G2
Kaluga, *Russia* 46 E9
Kalulushi, *Zambia* 87 E2
Kalundborg, *Denmark* 11 J5
Kalush, *Ukraine* 47 H3
Kałuszyn, *Poland* 45 F8
Kalutara, *Sri Lanka* 66 R12
Kalvarija, *Lithuania* 44 D10
Kalyazin, *Russia* 46 D9
Kam, *Albania* 40 D4
Kam →, *Nigeria* 83 D7
Kama, *Dem. Rep. of the Congo* 86 C2
Kama →, *Russia* 50 D6
Kamachumu, *Tanzania* 86 C3
Kamaishi, *Japan* 54 E10
Kamalia, *Pakistan* 68 D5
Kaman, *India* 68 F6
Kaman, *Turkey* 72 C5
Kamanjab, *Namibia* 88 B2
Kamapanda, *Zambia* 87 E1
Kamaran, *Yemen* 74 D3
Kamativi, *Zimbabwe* 88 B4
Kamba, *Nigeria* 83 C5
Kambalda, *Australia* 93 F3
Kambar, *Pakistan* 68 F3
Kambia, *S. Leone* 82 D2
Kambolé, *Togo* 83 D5
Kambolé, *Zambia* 87 D3
Kambos, *Cyprus* 36 D11
Kambove, *Dem. Rep. of the Congo* 87 E2
Kamchatka, Poluostrov, *Russia* 51 D16
Kamchatka Pen. = Kamchatka, Poluostrov, *Russia* 51 D16
Kamchiya →, *Bulgaria* 41 C11
Kamen, *Russia* 50 D9
Kamen-Rybolov, *Russia* 54 B6
Kamenica, *Serbia, Yug.* 40 C6
Kamenica, *Serbia, Yug.* 40 B3
Kamenice nad Lipou, *Czech Rep.* 26 B8
Kamenjak, Rt, *Croatia* 29 D10
Kamenka = Kaminka, *Ukraine* 47 H7
Kamenka, *Kazakstan* 48 E10
Kamenka, *Penza, Russia* 48 D6
Kamenka, *Voronezh, Russia* 47 G10
Kamenka Bugskaya = Kamyanka-Buzka, *Ukraine* 47 G3
Kamenka Dneprovskaya = Kamyanka-Dniprovska, *Ukraine* 47 J8
Kamennomostskiy, *Russia* 49 H5
Kameno, *Bulgaria* 41 D11
Kamenolomini, *Russia* 49 G5
Kamensk-Shakhtinskiy, *Russia* 49 F5
Kamensk Uralskiy, *Russia* 50 D7
Kamenskiy, *Russia* 48 E7
Kamenskoye, *Russia* 51 C17
Kamenyak, *Bulgaria* 41 C10
Kamenz, *Germany* 24 D10
Kameoka, *Japan* 55 G7
Kamiah, *U.S.A.* 114 C5
Kamień Krajeński, *Poland* 44 E4
Kamień Pomorski, *Poland* 44 E1
Kamienna →, *Poland* 45 G8
Kamienna Góra, *Poland* 45 H3
Kamieńsk, *Poland* 45 G6
Kamieskroon, *S. Africa* 88 E2
Kamilukuak, L., *Canada* 105 A8
Kamin-Kashyrskyy, *Ukraine* 47 G3
Kamina, *Dem. Rep. of the Congo* 87 D2
Kaminak L., *Canada* 105 A10
Kaministiquia, *Canada* 102 C1
Kaminka, *Ukraine* 47 H7
Kaminoyama, *Japan* 54 E10
Kamiros, *Greece* 36 C9
Kamituga, *Dem. Rep. of the Congo* 86 C2
Kamla →, *India* 69 G12
Kamloops, *Canada* 104 C4
Kamnik, *Slovenia* 29 B11
Kamo, *Armenia* 49 K7
Kamo, *Japan* 54 F9
Kamoke, *Pakistan* 68 C6
Kamp →, *Austria* 26 C8
Kampala, *Uganda* 86 B3
Kampang Chhnang, *Cambodia* 65 F5
Kampar, *Malaysia* 65 K3
Kampar →, *Indonesia* 62 D2
Kampen, *Neths.* 17 B5
Kampene, *Dem. Rep. of the Congo* 84 E5
Kamphaeng Phet, *Thailand* 64 D2
Kampolombo, L., *Zambia* 87 E2
Kampong Saom, *Cambodia* 65 G4
Kampong Saom, Chaak, *Cambodia* 65 G4
Kampong To, *Thailand* 65 J3
Kampot, *Cambodia* 65 G5
Kampti, *Burkina Faso* 82 C4
Kampuchea = Cambodia ■, *Asia* 64 F5
Kampung Air Putih, *Malaysia* 65 K4
Kampung Jerangau, *Malaysia* 65 K4
Kampung Raja, *Malaysia* 65 K4
Kampungbaru = Tolitoli, *Indonesia* 63 D6
Kamrau, Teluk, *Indonesia* 63 E8
Kamsack, *Canada* 105 C8
Kamsai, *Guinea* 82 C2
Kamskoye Ustye, *Russia* 48 C9
Kamuchawie L., *Canada* 105 B8
Kamui-Misaki, *Japan* 54 C10
Kamyanets-Podilskyy, *Ukraine* 47 H4
Kamyanka-Buzka, *Ukraine* 47 G3
Kamyanka-Dniprovska, *Ukraine* 47 J8
Kāmyārān, *Iran* 70 C5
Kamyshin, *Russia* 48 E7
Kamyzyak, *Russia* 49 G9
Kan, *Sudan* 81 F3
Kanaaupscow, *Canada* 102 B4
Kanaaupscow →, *Canada* 101 C12
Kanab, *U.S.A.* 115 H7
Kanab →, *U.S.A.* 115 H7
Kanagi, *Japan* 54 D10
Kanairiktok →, *Canada* 103 A7
Kanália, *Greece* 38 B4
Kananga, *Dem. Rep. of the Congo* 84 F4
Kanash, *Russia* 48 C8
Kanaskat, *U.S.A.* 116 C5
Kanastraíon, Ákra = Paliouríon, Ákra, *Greece* 40 G7
Kanawha →, *U.S.A.* 108 F4
Kanazawa, *Japan* 55 F8
Kanchanaburi, *Thailand* 64 E2
Kanchenjunga, *Nepal* 69 F13
Kanchipuram, *India* 66 N11
Kańczuga, *Poland* 45 J9
Kandaghat, *India* 68 D7
Kandahar = Qandahār, *Afghan.* 66 D4
Kandalaksha, *Russia* 50 C4
Kandangan, *Indonesia* 62 E5
Kandanghaur, *Indonesia* 63 G13
Kandanos, *Greece* 36 D5
Kandava, *Latvia* 44 A9
Kandavu, *Fiji* 91 D8
Kandhíla, *Greece* 38 D4
Kandhkot, *Pakistan* 68 E3
Kandhla, *India* 68 E7
Kandi, *Benin* 83 C5
Kandi, *India* 69 H13
Kandiaro, *Pakistan* 68 F3
Kandıra, *Turkey* 72 B4
Kandla, *India* 68 H4
Kandreho, *Madag.* 89 B8
Kandy, *Sri Lanka* 66 R12
Kane, *U.S.A.* 110 E6
Kane Basin, *Greenland* 4 B4
Kanel, *Senegal* 82 B2
Kaneohe, *U.S.A.* 106 H16
Kanevskaya, *Russia* 49 G4
Kanfanar, *Croatia* 29 C10
Kang, *Botswana* 88 C3
Kangaba, *Mali* 82 C3
Kangal, *Turkey* 72 C7
Kangān, *Fārs, Iran* 71 E7
Kangān, *Hormozgān, Iran* 71 E8
Kangar, *Malaysia* 65 J3
Kangaré, *Mali* 82 C3
Kangaroo Mts., *Australia* 94 C3
Kangasala, *Finland* 9 F21
Kangāvar, *Iran* 71 C6
Kangding, *China* 58 B3
Kangdong, *N. Korea* 57 E14
Kangean, Kepulauan, *Indonesia* 62 F5
Kangean Is. = Kangean, Kepulauan, *Indonesia* 62 F5
Kangen →, *Sudan* 81 F3
Kanggye, *N. Korea* 57 D14
Kanggyŏng, *S. Korea* 57 F14
Kanghwa, *S. Korea* 57 F14
Kangikajik, *Greenland* 4 B6
Kangiqsliniq = Rankin Inlet, *Canada* 100 B10
Kangiqsualujjuaq, *Canada* 101 C13
Kangiqsujuaq, *Canada* 101 B12
Kangiqtugaapik = Clyde River, *Canada* 101 A13
Kangirsuk, *Canada* 101 B13
Kangnŭng, *S. Korea* 57 F15
Kangping, *China* 57 C12
Kangra, *India* 68 C7
Kangto, *India* 67 F18
Kanhar →, *India* 69 G10
Kani, *Ivory C.* 82 D3
Kaniama, *Dem. Rep. of the Congo* 86 D1
Kaniapiskau = Caniapiscau →, *Canada* 103 A6
Kaniapiskau, Res. = Caniapiscau, Rés. de, *Canada* 103 B6
Kanin, Poluostrov, *Russia* 50 C5
Kanin Nos, Mys, *Russia* 50 C5
Kanin Pen. = Kanin, Poluostrov, *Russia* 50 C5
Kaninë, *Albania* 40 F3
Kanjiža, *Serbia, Yug.* 42 D5
Kanjut Sar, *Pakistan* 69 A6
Kankaanpää, *Finland* 9 F20
Kankakee, *U.S.A.* 108 E2
Kankakee →, *U.S.A.* 108 E1
Kankan, *Guinea* 82 C3
Kankendy = Xankändi, *Azerbaijan* 70 B5
Kanker, *India* 67 J12
Kankossa, *Mauritania* 82 B2
Kankroli, *India* 68 G5
Kannapolis, *U.S.A.* 109 H5
Kannauj, *India* 69 F8
Kannod, *India* 66 H10
Kano, *Nigeria* 83 C6
Kano □, *Nigeria* 83 C6
Kan'onji, *Japan* 55 G6
Kanoroba, *Ivory C.* 82 D3
Kanowit, *Malaysia* 62 D4
Kanoya, *Japan* 55 J5
Kanpetlet, *Burma* 67 J18
Kanpur, *India* 69 F9
Kansas □, *U.S.A.* 112 F6
Kansas →, *U.S.A.* 112 F7
Kansas City, *Kans., U.S.A.* 112 F7
Kansas City, *Mo., U.S.A.* 112 F7
Kansenia, *Dem. Rep. of the Congo* 87 E2
Kansk, *Russia* 51 D10
Kansŏng, *S. Korea* 57 E15
Kansu = Gansu □, *China* 56 G3
Kantaphor, *India* 68 H7
Kantchari, *Burkina Faso* 83 C5
Kantché, *Niger* 83 C6
Kanté, *Togo* 83 D5
Kantemirovka, *Russia* 47 H10
Kantharalak, *Thailand* 64 E5
Kantli →, *India* 68 E6
Kantō □, *Japan* 55 F9
Kantō-Sanchi, *Japan* 55 G9
Kanturk, *Ireland* 15 D3
Kanuma, *Japan* 55 F9
Kanus, *Namibia* 88 D2
Kanye, *Botswana* 88 C4
Kanzenze, *Dem. Rep. of the Congo* 87 E2
Kanzi, Ras, *Tanzania* 86 D4
Kaohsiung, *Taiwan* 59 F13
Kaokoveld, *Namibia* 88 B1
Kaolack, *Senegal* 82 C1
Kaoshan, *China* 57 B13
Kapaa, *U.S.A.* 106 G15
Kapadvanj, *India* 68 H5
Kapaklı, *Turkey* 41 E11
Kapan, *Armenia* 70 B5
Kapanga, *Dem. Rep. of the Congo* 84 F4
Kapchagai = Qapshaghay, *Kazakstan* 50 E8
Kapela = Velika Kapela, *Croatia* 29 C12
Kapéllo, Ákra, *Greece* 38 E5
Kapema, *Dem. Rep. of the Congo* 87 E2
Kapfenberg, *Austria* 26 D8
Kapı Dağı, *Turkey* 41 F11
Kapiri Mposhi, *Zambia* 87 E2
Kapiskau →, *Canada* 102 B3
Kapit, *Malaysia* 62 D4
Kapiti I., *N.Z.* 91 J5
Kaplan, *U.S.A.* 113 K8
Kaplice, *Czech Rep.* 26 C7
Kapoe, *Thailand* 65 H2
Kapoeta, *Sudan* 81 G3
Kápolnásnyék, *Hungary* 42 C3
Kapos →, *Hungary* 42 D3
Kaposvár, *Hungary* 42 D2
Kapowsin, *U.S.A.* 116 D4
Kappeln, *Germany* 24 A5
Kappelshamn, *Sweden* 11 G12
Kapps, *Namibia* 88 C2
Kaprije, *Croatia* 29 E12
Kapsan, *N. Korea* 57 D15
Kapsukas = Marijampolė, *Lithuania* 9 J20
Kapuas →, *Indonesia* 62 E3
Kapuas Hulu, Pegunungan, *Malaysia* 62 D4
Kapuas Hulu Ra. = Kapuas Hulu, Pegunungan, *Malaysia* 62 D4
Kapulo, *Dem. Rep. of the Congo* 87 D2
Kapuni, *N.Z.* 91 H5
Kapurthala, *India* 68 D6
Kapuskasing, *Canada* 102 C3
Kapuskasing →, *Canada* 102 C3
Kapustin Yar, *Russia* 49 F7
Kaputar, *Australia* 95 E5
Kaputir, *Kenya* 86 B4
Kapuvár, *Hungary* 42 C2
Kara, *Russia* 50 C7
Karā, W. →, *Si. Arabia* 80 C5
Kara Ada, *Turkey* 39 E9
Kara Bogaz Gol, Zaliv = Garabogazköl Aylagy, *Turkmenistan* 50 E6
Kara Burun, *Turkey* 39 E9
Kara Kalpak Republic = Qoraqalpoghistan □, *Uzbekistan* 50 E6
Kara Kum, *Turkmenistan* 50 F6
Kara Sea, *Russia* 50 B7
Karaadilli, *Turkey* 39 C12
Karabiğa, *Turkey* 41 F11
Karabük, *Turkey* 72 B5
Karaburun, *Albania* 40 F3
Karaburun, *Turkey* 39 C8
Karabutak = Qarabutaq, *Kazakstan* 50 E7
Karacabey, *Turkey* 41 F12
Karacakılavuz, *Turkey* 41 E11
Karacaköy, *Turkey* 41 E12
Karacasu, *Turkey* 39 D10
Karachala = Qaraçala, *Azerbaijan* 49 L9
Karachayevsk, *Russia* 49 J5
Karachev, *Russia* 47 F8
Karachey-Cherkessia □, *Russia* 49 J5
Karachi, *Pakistan* 68 G2
Karad, *India* 66 L9
Karadirek, *Turkey* 39 C12
Karaga, *Ghana* 83 D4
Karaganda = Qaraghandy, *Kazakstan* 50 E8
Karagayly, *Kazakstan* 50 E8
Karaginskiy, Ostrov, *Russia* 51 D17
Karagola Road, *India* 69 G12
Karagüney Dağları, *Turkey* 72 B6
Karahallı, *Turkey* 39 C11
Karaikal, *India* 66 P11
Karaikkudi, *India* 66 P11
Karaisali, *Turkey* 72 D6
Karaj, *Iran* 71 C6
Karak, *Malaysia* 65 L4
Karakalpakstan = Qoraqalpoghistan □, *Uzbekistan* 50 E6
Karakelong, *Indonesia* 63 D7
Karakitang, *Indonesia* 63 D7
Karaklis = Vanadzor, *Armenia* 49 K7
Karakoçan, *Turkey* 73 C9
Karakol, *Kyrgyzstan* 50 E8
Karakoram Pass, *Pakistan* 69 B7
Karakoram Ra., *Pakistan* 69 B7
Karakurt, *Turkey* 73 B10
Karakuwisa, *Namibia* 88 B2
Karalon, *Russia* 51 D12
Karama, *Jordan* 75 D4
Karaman, *Balıkesir, Turkey* 39 B9
Karaman, *Konya, Turkey* 70 B2
Karamanlı, *Turkey* 39 D11

Karamay, *China* 60 B3
Karambu, *Indonesia* 62 E5
Karamea Bight, *N.Z.* 91 J3
Karamnasa →, *India* 69 G10
Karamürsel, *Turkey* 41 F13
Karand, *Iran* 70 C5
Karangana, *Mali* 82 C3
Karanganyar, *Indonesia* 63 G13
Karanjia, *India* 69 J11
Karankasso, *Burkina Faso* 82 C4
Karaova, *Turkey* 39 D9
Karapınar, *Turkey* 72 D5
Karasburg, *Namibia* 88 D2
Karasino, *Russia* 50 C9
Karasjok, *Norway* 8 B21
Karasu, *Turkey* 72 B4
Karasu →, *Turkey* 39 E12
Karasuk, *Russia* 50 D8
Karasuyama, *Japan* 55 F10
Karataş, *Adana, Turkey* 72 D6
Karataş, *Manisa, Turkey* 39 C10
Karataş Burnu, *Turkey* 72 D6
Karatau, Khrebet = Qarataū, *Kazakstan* 50 E7
Karatoprak, *Turkey* 39 D9
Karatsu, *Japan* 55 H5
Karaul, *Russia* 50 B9
Karauli, *India* 68 F7
Karavastasë, L. e, *Albania* 40 F3
Karávi, *Greece* 38 E5
Karavostasi, *Cyprus* 36 D11
Karawang, *Indonesia* 63 G12
Karawanken, *Europe* 26 E7
Karayazı, *Turkey* 73 C10
Karazhal, *Kazakstan* 50 E8
Karbalā', *Iraq* 70 C5
Kårböle, *Sweden* 10 C9
Karcag, *Hungary* 42 C5
Karcha →, *Pakistan* 69 B7
Karchana, *India* 69 G9
Karczew, *Poland* 45 F8
Kardam, *Bulgaria* 41 C12
Kardeljovo = Ploče, *Croatia* 29 E14
Kardhámila, *Greece* 39 C8
Kardhamíli, *Greece* 38 E4
Kardhítsa, *Greece* 38 B3
Kardhítsa □, *Greece* 38 B3
Kärdla, *Estonia* 9 G20
Kareeberge, *S. Africa* 88 E3
Kareha →, *India* 69 G12
Kareima, *Sudan* 80 D3
Karelia □, *Russia* 50 C4
Karelian Republic = Karelia □, *Russia* 50 C4
Karera, *India* 68 G8
Kārevāndar, *Iran* 71 E9
Kargasok, *Russia* 50 D9
Kargat, *Russia* 50 D9
Kargı, *Turkey* 72 B6
Kargil, *India* 69 B7
Kargopol, *Russia* 46 B10
Kargowa, *Poland* 45 F2
Karguéri, *Niger* 83 C7
Karhal, *India* 69 F8
Kariá, *Greece* 38 C2
Kariaí, *Greece* 41 F8
Karīān, *Iran* 71 E8
Karianga, *Madag.* 89 C8
Kariba, *Zimbabwe* 87 F2
Kariba, L., *Zimbabwe* 87 F2
Kariba Dam, *Zimbabwe* 87 F2
Kariba Gorge, *Zambia* 87 F2
Karibib, *Namibia* 88 C2
Karimata, Kepulauan, *Indonesia* 62 E3
Karimata, Selat, *Indonesia* 62 E3
Karimata Is. = Karimata, Kepulauan, *Indonesia* 62 E3
Karimnagar, *India* 66 K11
Karimunjawa, Kepulauan, *Indonesia* 62 F4
Karin, *Somali Rep.* 74 E4
Káristos, *Greece* 38 C6
Karīt, *Iran* 71 C8
Kariya, *Japan* 55 G8
Kariyangwe, *Zimbabwe* 89 B4
Karjala, *Finland* 46 A5
Karkaralinsk = Qarqaraly, *Kazakstan* 50 E8
Karkheh →, *Iran* 70 D5
Karkinitska Zatoka, *Ukraine* 47 K7
Karkinitskiy Zaliv = Karkinitska Zatoka, *Ukraine* 47 K7
Karkur Tohl, *Egypt* 80 C2
Karl Liebknecht, *Russia* 47 G8
Karl-Marx-Stadt = Chemnitz, *Germany* 24 E8
Karlholmsbruk, *Sweden* 10 D11
Karlino, *Poland* 44 D2
Karlivka, *Ukraine* 47 H8
Karlobag, *Croatia* 29 D12
Karlovac, *Croatia* 29 C12
Karlovka = Karlivka, *Ukraine* 47 H8
Karlovo, *Bulgaria* 41 D8
Karlovy Vary, *Czech Rep.* 26 A5
Karlsbad = Karlovy Vary, *Czech Rep.* 26 A5
Karlsborg, *Sweden* 11 F8
Karlshamn, *Sweden* 11 H8
Karlskoga, *Sweden* 10 E8
Karlskrona, *Sweden* 11 H9
Karlsruhe, *Germany* 25 F4
Karlstad, *Sweden* 10 E7
Karlstad, *U.S.A.* 112 A6
Karlstadt, *Germany* 25 F5
Karma, *Niger* 83 C5
Karmėlava, *Lithuania* 44 D11
Karmi'el, *Israel* 75 C4
Karnak, *Egypt* 79 C12
Karnal, *India* 68 E7
Karnali →, *Nepal* 69 E9
Karnaphuli Res., *Bangla.* 67 H18
Karnaprayag, *India* 69 D8
Karnataka □, *India* 66 N10
Karnes City, *U.S.A.* 113 L6
Karnische Alpen, *Europe* 26 E6
Karnobat, *Bulgaria* 41 D10
Kärnten □, *Austria* 26 E6
Karo, *Mali* 82 C4
Karoi, *Zimbabwe* 87 F2
Karonga, *Malawi* 87 D3
Karor, *Pakistan* 68 D4
Karora, *Sudan* 80 D4
Káros, *Greece* 39 E7
Karounga, *Mali* 82 B3
Karousádhes, *Greece* 38 B1
Karpacz, *Poland* 45 H2
Karpasia □, *Cyprus* 36 D13
Kárpathos, *Greece* 39 F9
Kárpathos, Stenón, *Greece* 39 F9
Karpenísion, *Greece* 38 C3
Karpuz Burnu = Apostolos Andreas, C., *Cyprus* 36 D13
Karpuzlu, *Turkey* 39 D9
Karratha, *Australia* 92 D2
Kars, *Turkey* 73 B10
Karsakpay, *Kazakstan* 50 E7
Karsha, *Kazakstan* 48 F10
Karshi = Qarshi, *Uzbekistan* 50 F7
Karsiyang, *India* 69 F13
Karsog, *India* 68 D7
Karst = Kras, *Croatia* 29 C10
Kartal, *Turkey* 41 F13
Kartál Óros, *Greece* 41 E9
Kartaly, *Russia* 50 D7
Kartapur, *India* 68 D6
Karthaus, *U.S.A.* 110 E6
Kartuzy, *Poland* 44 D5
Karufa, *Indonesia* 63 E8
Karumba, *Australia* 94 B3
Karumo, *Tanzania* 86 C3
Karumwa, *Tanzania* 86 C3
Kārūn →, *Iran* 71 D6
Karungu, *Kenya* 86 C3
Karup, *Denmark* 11 H3
Karviná, *Czech Rep.* 27 B11
Karwan →, *India* 68 F8
Karwar, *India* 66 M9
Karwi, *India* 69 G9
Kaş, *Turkey* 39 E11
Kasaba, *Turkey* 39 E11
Kasache, *Malawi* 87 E3
Kasai →, *Dem. Rep. of the Congo* 84 E3
Kasaï-Oriental □, *Dem. Rep. of the Congo* 86 D1
Kasaji, *Dem. Rep. of the Congo* 87 E1
Kasama, *Zambia* 87 E3
Kasan-dong, *N. Korea* 57 D14
Kasane, *Namibia* 88 B3
Kasanga, *Tanzania* 87 D3
Kasar, Ras, *Sudan* 80 D4
Kasaragod, *India* 66 N9
Kasba L., *Canada* 105 A8
Kāseh Garān, *Iran* 70 C5
Kasempa, *Zambia* 87 E2
Kasenga, *Dem. Rep. of the Congo* 87 E2
Kasese, *Uganda* 86 B3
Kasewa, *Zambia* 87 E2
Kasganj, *India* 69 F8
Kashabowie, *Canada* 102 C1
Kashaf, *Iran* 71 C9
Kāshān, *Iran* 71 C6
Kashechewan, *Canada* 102 B3
Kashgar = Kashi, *China* 60 C2
Kashi, *China* 60 C2
Kashimbo, *Dem. Rep. of the Congo* 87 E2
Kashin, *Russia* 46 D9
Kashipur, *India* 69 E8
Kashira, *Russia* 46 E10
Kashiwazaki, *Japan* 55 F9
Kashk-e Kohneh, *Afghan.* 66 B3
Kashkū'īyeh, *Iran* 71 D7
Kāshmar, *Iran* 71 C8
Kashmir, *Asia* 69 C7
Kashmor, *Pakistan* 68 E3
Kashpirovka, *Russia* 48 D9
Kashun Noerh = Gaxun Nur, *China* 60 B5
Kasiari, *India* 69 H12
Kasimov, *Russia* 48 C5
Kasinge, *Dem. Rep. of the Congo* 86 D2
Kasiruta, *Indonesia* 63 E7
Kaskaskia →, *U.S.A.* 112 G10
Kaskattama →, *Canada* 105 B10
Kaskinen, *Finland* 9 E19
Kaslo, *Canada* 104 D5
Kasmere L., *Canada* 105 B8
Kasongo, *Dem. Rep. of the Congo* 86 C2
Kasongo Lunda, *Dem. Rep. of the Congo* 84 F3
Kásos, *Greece* 39 F8
Kásos, Stenón, *Greece* 39 F8
Kaspi, *Georgia* 49 K7
Kaspichan, *Bulgaria* 41 C11
Kaspiysk, *Russia* 49 J8
Kaspiyskiy, *Russia* 49 H8
Kassab ed Doleib, *Sudan* 81 E3
Kassaba, *Egypt* 80 C2
Kassalâ, *Sudan* 81 D4
Kassalâ □, *Sudan* 81 D4
Kassándra, *Greece* 40 F7
Kassándrinon, *Greece* 40 F7
Kassel, *Germany* 24 D5
Kassinger, *Sudan* 80 D3
Kassiópi, *Greece* 36 A3
Kasson, *U.S.A.* 112 C8
Kastamonu, *Turkey* 72 B5
Kastav, *Croatia* 29 C11
Kastélli, *Greece* 36 D5
Kastéllion, *Greece* 36 D7
Kastellórizon = Megiste, *Greece* 39 E11
Kástellos, *Greece* 39 E9
Kastellou, Ákra, *Greece* 39 F9
Kasterlee, *Belgium* 17 C4
Kastlösa, *Sweden* 11 H10
Kastóri, *Greece* 38 D4
Kastoría, *Greece* 40 F5
Kastoría □, *Greece* 40 F5
Kastorías, Límni, *Greece* 40 F5
Kastornoye, *Russia* 47 G10
Kastós, *Greece* 38 C2
Kastrosikiá, *Greece* 38 B2
Kastsyukovichy, *Belarus* 46 F7
Kasulu, *Tanzania* 86 C3
Kasumi, *Japan* 55 G7
Kasumkent, *Russia* 49 K9
Kasungu, *Malawi* 87 E3
Kasur, *Pakistan* 68 D6
Kataba, *Zambia* 87 F2
Katagum, *Nigeria* 83 C7
Katahdin, Mt., *U.S.A.* 109 C11
Katako Kombe, *Dem. Rep. of the Congo* 86 C1
Katákolon, *Greece* 38 D3
Katale, *Tanzania* 86 C3
Katanda, *Katanga, Dem. Rep. of the Congo* 86 D1
Katanda, *Nord-Kivu, Dem. Rep. of the Congo* 86 C2
Katanga □, *Dem. Rep. of the Congo* 86 D2
Katangi, *India* 66 J11
Katanning, *Australia* 93 F2
Katastári, *Greece* 38 D2
Katavi Swamp, *Tanzania* 86 D3
Kateríni, *Greece* 40 F6
Katghora, *India* 69 H10
Katha, *Burma* 67 G20
Katherîna, Gebel, *Egypt* 70 D2
Katherine, *Australia* 92 B5
Katherine Gorge, *Australia* 92 B5
Kathi, *India* 68 J6
Kathiawar, *India* 68 H4
Kathikas, *Cyprus* 36 E11
Kathua, *India* 68 C6
Kati, *Mali* 82 C3
Katihar, *India* 69 G12
Katima Mulilo, *Zambia* 88 B3
Katimbira, *Malawi* 87 E3
Katingan = Mendawai →, *Indonesia* 62 E4
Katiola, *Ivory C.* 82 D3
Katlanovo, *Macedonia* 40 E5
Katmandu, *Nepal* 69 F11
Katni, *India* 69 H9
Káto Akhaïa, *Greece* 38 C3
Káto Arkhánai, *Greece* 36 D7
Káto Khorió, *Greece* 36 D7
Káto Pyrgos, *Cyprus* 36 D11
Káto Stavros, *Greece* 40 F7
Katokhí, *Greece* 38 C3
Katompe, *Dem. Rep. of the Congo* 86 D2
Katonga →, *Uganda* 86 B3
Katoúna, *Greece* 38 C3
Katowice, *Poland* 45 H6
Katrancı Dağı, *Turkey* 39 D12
Katrine, L., *U.K.* 14 E4
Katrineholm, *Sweden* 11 E10
Katsepe, *Madag.* 89 B8
Katsina, *Nigeria* 83 C6
Katsina □, *Nigeria* 83 C6
Katsina Ala, *Nigeria* 83 D6
Katsina Ala →, *Nigeria* 83 D6
Katsumoto, *Japan* 55 H4
Katsuura, *Japan* 55 G10
Katsuyama, *Japan* 55 F8
Kattaviá, *Greece* 36 D9
Kattegat, *Denmark* 11 H5
Katthammarsvik, *Sweden* 11 G12
Katul, J., *Sudan* 81 E2
Katumba, *Dem. Rep. of the Congo* 86 D2
Katungu, *Kenya* 86 C5
Katwa, *India* 69 H13
Katwijk, *Neths.* 17 B4
Kąty Wrocławskie, *Poland* 45 G3
Kauai, *U.S.A.* 106 H15
Kauai Channel, *U.S.A.* 106 H15
Kaub, *Germany* 25 E3
Kaufbeuren, *Germany* 25 H6
Kaufman, *U.S.A.* 113 J6
Kauhajoki, *Finland* 9 E20
Kaukauna, *U.S.A.* 108 C1
Kaukauveld, *Namibia* 88 C3
Kaunakakai, *U.S.A.* 106 H16
Kaunas, *Lithuania* 9 J20
Kaunia, *Bangla.* 69 G13
Kaunos, *Turkey* 39 E10
Kaura Namoda, *Nigeria* 83 C6
Kauru, *Nigeria* 83 C6
Kautokeino, *Norway* 8 B20
Kauwapur, *India* 69 F10
Kavacha, *Russia* 51 C17
Kavadarci, *Macedonia* 40 E6
Kavajë, *Albania* 40 E3
Kavak, *Turkey* 72 B7
Kavak Dağı, *Turkey* 39 D10
Kavaklı, *Turkey* 41 E11
Kavaklıdere, *Turkey* 39 D10
Kavalerovo, *Russia* 54 B7
Kavali, *India* 66 M12
Kavála, *Greece* 41 F8
Kavála □, *Greece* 41 E8
Kavála Kólpos, *Greece* 41 F8
Kavār, *Iran* 71 D7
Kavarna, *Bulgaria* 41 C12
Kavi, *India* 68 H5
Kavimba, *Botswana* 88 B3
Kavīr, Dasht-e, *Iran* 71 C7
Kavkaz, *Russia* 47 K9
Kävlinge, *Sweden* 11 J7
Kavos, *Greece* 36 B4
Kavoúsi, *Greece* 39 F7
Kaw, *Fr. Guiana* 125 C8
Kawa, *Sudan* 81 E3
Kawagama L., *Canada* 110 A6
Kawagoe, *Japan* 55 G9
Kawaguchi, *Japan* 55 G9
Kawambwa, *Zambia* 87 D2
Kawanoe, *Japan* 55 G6
Kawardha, *India* 69 J9
Kawasaki, *Japan* 55 G9
Kawasi, *Indonesia* 63 E7
Kawerau, *N.Z.* 91 H6
Kawhia Harbour, *N.Z.* 91 H5
Kawio, Kepulauan, *Indonesia* 63 D7
Kawnro, *Burma* 67 H21
Kawthaung, *Burma* 65 H2
Kawthoolei = Kayin □, *Burma* 67 L20
Kawthule = Kayin □, *Burma* 67 L20
Kaxholmen, *Sweden* 11 G8
Kaya, *Burkina Faso* 83 C4
Kayah □, *Burma* 67 K20
Kayalıköy Barajı, *Turkey* 41 E11
Kayan →, *Indonesia* 62 D5
Kaycee, *U.S.A.* 114 E10
Kayeli, *Indonesia* 63 E7
Kayenta, *U.S.A.* 115 H8
Kayes, *Mali* 82 C2
Kayı, *Turkey* 39 B12
Kayima, *S. Leone* 82 D2
Kayin □, *Burma* 67 L20
Kaymakçı, *Turkey* 39 C10
Kayoa, *Indonesia* 63 D7
Kayomba, *Zambia* 87 E1
Kaysatskoye, *Russia* 48 F8
Kayseri, *Turkey* 70 B2
Kaysville, *U.S.A.* 114 F8
Kaz Dağı, *Turkey* 39 B8
Kazachye, *Russia* 51 B14
Kazakstan ■, *Asia* 50 E7
Kazan, *Russia* 48 C9
Kazan →, *Canada* 105 A9
Kazan-Rettō, *Pac. Oc.* 96 E6
Kazanlŭk, *Bulgaria* 41 D9
Kazanskaya, *Russia* 48 F5
Kazatin = Kozyatyn, *Ukraine* 47 H5
Kazaure, *Nigeria* 83 C6
Kazbek, *Russia* 49 J7
Kāzerūn, *Iran* 71 D6
Kazi Magomed = Qazimämmäd, *Azerbaijan* 49 K9
Kazimierz Dolny, *Poland* 45 G8
Kazimierza Wielka, *Poland* 45 H7
Kazincbarcika, *Hungary* 42 B5
Kazlų Rūda, *Lithuania* 44 D10
Kaztalovka, *Kazakstan* 48 F9
Kazuno, *Japan* 54 D10
Kazym →, *Russia* 50 C7
Kcynia, *Poland* 45 F4
Ké-Macina, *Mali* 82 C3
Kéa, *Greece* 38 D6
Keady, *U.K.* 15 B5
Kearney, *U.S.A.* 112 E5
Kearny, *U.S.A.* 115 K8
Kearsarge, Mt., *U.S.A.* 111 C13
Keban, *Turkey* 73 C8
Keban Barajı, *Turkey* 70 B3
Kebbi □, *Nigeria* 83 C5
Kébi, *Ivory C.* 82 D3
Kebnekaise, *Sweden* 8 C18
Kebri Dehar, *Ethiopia* 74 F3
Kebumen, *Indonesia* 63 G13
Kecel, *Hungary* 42 D4
Kechika →, *Canada* 104 B3
Keçiborlu, *Turkey* 39 D12
Kecskemét, *Hungary* 42 D4
Kedada, *Ethiopia* 81 F4
Kėdainiai, *Lithuania* 9 J21
Kedarnath, *India* 69 D8
Kedgwick, *Canada* 103 C6
Kédhros Óros, *Greece* 36 D6
Kediri, *Indonesia* 62 F4
Kedjebi, *Ghana* 83 D5
Kédougou, *Senegal* 82 C2
Kędzierzyn-Koźle, *Poland* 45 H5
Keeler, *U.S.A.* 116 J9
Keeley L., *Canada* 105 C7
Keeling Is. = Cocos Is., *Ind. Oc.* 96 J1
Keelung = Chilung, *Taiwan* 59 E13
Keene, *Canada* 110 B6
Keene, *Calif., U.S.A.* 117 K8
Keene, *N.H., U.S.A.* 111 D12
Keene, *N.Y., U.S.A.* 111 B11
Keeper Hill, *Ireland* 15 D3
Keer-Weer, C., *Australia* 94 A3
Keeseville, *U.S.A.* 111 B11
Keetmanshoop, *Namibia* 88 D2
Keewatin, *Canada* 105 D10
Keewatin →, *Canada* 105 B8
Kefa □, *Ethiopia* 81 F4
Kefallinía, *Greece* 38 C2
Kefallinía □, *Greece* 38 C2
Kéfalos, *Greece* 39 E8
Kefamenanu, *Indonesia* 63 F6
Kefar Sava, *Israel* 75 C3
Keffi, *Nigeria* 83 D6
Keffin Hausa, *Nigeria* 83 C6
Keflavík, *Iceland* 8 D2
Keftya, *Ethiopia* 81 E4
Keg River, *Canada* 104 B5
Kegaska, *Canada* 103 B7
Keheili, *Sudan* 80 D3
Kehl, *Germany* 25 G3
Keighley, *U.K.* 12 D6
Keila, *Estonia* 9 G21
Keimoes, *S. Africa* 88 D3
Keita, *Niger* 83 C6
Keitele, *Finland* 8 E22
Keith, *U.K.* 14 D6
Keizer, *U.S.A.* 114 D2
Kejimkujik Nat. Park, *Canada* 103 D6
Kejserr Franz Joseph Fd., *Greenland* 4 B6
Kekri, *India* 68 G6
Kelam, *Ethiopia* 81 G4
Kelamet, *Eritrea* 81 D4
Kelan, *China* 56 E6
Kelang, *Malaysia* 65 L3
Kelantan →, *Malaysia* 65 J4
Këlcyrë, *Albania* 40 F4
Kelekçi, *Turkey* 39 D11
Keles, *Turkey* 41 G13
Keleti-főcsatorna, *Hungary* 42 C6
Kelheim, *Germany* 25 G7
Kelkit, *Turkey* 73 B8
Kelkit →, *Turkey* 72 B7
Kellerberrin, *Australia* 93 F2
Kellett, C., *Canada* 4 B1
Kelleys I., *U.S.A.* 110 E2
Kellogg, *U.S.A.* 114 C5
Kells = Ceanannus Mor, *Ireland* 15 C5
Kelmė, *Lithuania* 44 C9
Kelokedhara, *Cyprus* 36 E11
Kelowna, *Canada* 104 D5
Kelseyville, *U.S.A.* 116 G4
Kelso, *N.Z.* 91 L2
Kelso, *U.K.* 14 F6
Kelso, *U.S.A.* 116 D4
Keluang, *Malaysia* 65 L4
Kelvington, *Canada* 105 C8
Kem, *Russia* 50 C4
Kema, *Indonesia* 63 D7
Kemah, *Turkey* 70 B3
Kemaliye, *Erzincan, Turkey* 73 C8
Kemaliye, *Manisa, Turkey* 39 C10
Kemalpaşa, *Turkey* 39 C9
Kemaman, *Malaysia* 62 D2
Kemano, *Canada* 104 C3
Kemasik, *Malaysia* 65 K4
Kembolcha, *Ethiopia* 81 E4
Kemer, *Antalya, Turkey* 39 E12
Kemer, *Burdur, Turkey* 39 D12
Kemer, *Muğla, Turkey* 39 E11
Kemer Barajı, *Turkey* 39 D10
Kemerovo, *Russia* 50 D9
Kemi, *Finland* 8 D21
Kemi älv = Kemijoki →, *Finland* 8 D21
Kemijärvi, *Finland* 8 C22
Kemijoki →, *Finland* 8 D21
Kemmerer, *U.S.A.* 114 F8
Kemmuna = Comino, *Malta* 36 C1
Kemp, L., *U.S.A.* 113 J5
Kemp Land, *Antarctica* 5 C5
Kempt, L., *Canada* 102 C5
Kempten, *Germany* 25 H6
Kempton, *Australia* 94 G4
Kemptville, *Canada* 102 D4
Ken →, *India* 69 G9
Kenai, *U.S.A.* 100 B4
Kendai, *India* 69 H10
Kendal, *Indonesia* 63 G14
Kendal, *U.K.* 12 C5
Kendall, *U.S.A.* 109 N5
Kendall →, *Australia* 94 A3
Kendallville, *U.S.A.* 108 E3
Kendari, *Indonesia* 63 E6
Kendawangan, *Indonesia* 62 E4
Kende, *Nigeria* 83 C5
Kendrapara, *India* 67 J15
Këndrevicës, Maja e, *Albania* 40 F3
Kendrew, *S. Africa* 88 E3
Kene Thao, *Laos* 64 D3
Kenedy, *U.S.A.* 113 L6
Kenema, *S. Leone* 82 D2
Keng Kok, *Laos* 64 D5
Keng Tawng, *Burma* 67 J21
Keng Tung, *Burma* 58 G2
Kengeja, *Tanzania* 86 D4
Kenhardt, *S. Africa* 88 D3
Kéniéba, *Mali* 82 C2
Kenitra, *Morocco* 78 B4
Kenli, *China* 57 F10
Kenmare, *Ireland* 15 E2
Kenmare, *U.S.A.* 112 A3
Kenmare River, *Ireland* 15 E2
Kennebago Lake, *U.S.A.* 111 A14
Kennebec, *U.S.A.* 112 D5
Kennebec →, *U.S.A.* 109 D11
Kennebunk, *U.S.A.* 111 C14
Kennedy, *Zimbabwe* 88 B4
Kennedy Ra., *Australia* 93 D2
Kennedy Taungdeik, *Burma* 67 H18
Kenner, *U.S.A.* 113 L9
Kennet →, *U.K.* 13 F7
Kenneth Ra., *Australia* 93 D2

Kennett, *U.S.A.* 113 G9
Kennewick, *U.S.A.* 114 C4
Kenogami →, *Canada* 102 B3
Kenora, *Canada* 105 D10
Kenosha, *U.S.A.* 108 D2
Kensington, *Canada* 103 C7
Kent, *Ohio, U.S.A.* 110 E3
Kent, *Tex., U.S.A.* 113 K2
Kent, *Wash., U.S.A.* 116 C4
Kent □, *U.K.* 13 F8
Kent Group, *Australia* 94 F4
Kent Pen., *Canada* 100 B9
Kentaū, *Kazakstan* 50 E7
Kentland, *U.S.A.* 108 E2
Kenton, *U.S.A.* 108 E4
Kentucky □, *U.S.A.* 108 G3
Kentucky →, *U.S.A.* 108 F3
Kentucky L., *U.S.A.* 109 G2
Kentville, *Canada* 103 C7
Kentwood, *U.S.A.* 113 K9
Kenya ■, *Africa* 86 B4
Kenya, Mt., *Kenya* 86 C4
Keo Neua, Deo, *Vietnam* 64 C5
Keokuk, *U.S.A.* 112 E9
Keonjhargarh, *India* 69 J11
Kep, *Cambodia* 65 G5
Kep, *Vietnam* 64 B6
Kepez, *Turkey* 41 F10
Kepi, *Indonesia* 63 F9
Kępice, *Poland* 44 D3
Kępno, *Poland* 45 G4
Kepsut, *Turkey* 39 B10
Kerala □, *India* 66 P10
Kerama-Rettō, *Japan* 55 L3
Keran, *Pakistan* 69 B5
Keranyo, *Ethiopia* 81 F4
Kerao →, *Sudan* 81 E3
Keratéa, *Greece* 38 D5
Keraudren, C., *Australia* 92 C2
Kerava, *Finland* 9 F21
Kerch, *Ukraine* 47 K9
Kerchenskiy Proliv, *Black Sea* 47 K9
Kerchoual, *Mali* 83 B5
Kerempe Burnu, *Turkey* 72 A5
Keren, *Eritrea* 81 D4
Kerewan, *Gambia* 82 C1
Kerguelen, *Ind. Oc.* 3 G13
Keri, *Greece* 38 D2
Keri Kera, *Sudan* 81 E3
Kericho, *Kenya* 86 C4
Kerinci, *Indonesia* 62 E2
Kerki, *Turkmenistan* 50 F7
Kerkinítis, Límni, *Greece* 40 E7
Kérkira, *Greece* 36 A3
Kérkira □, *Greece* 38 B1
Kerkrade, *Neths.* 17 D6
Kerma, *Sudan* 80 D3
Kermadec Is., *Pac. Oc.* 96 L10
Kermadec Trench, *Pac. Oc.* 96 L10
Kermān, *Iran* 71 D8
Kerman, *U.S.A.* 116 J6
Kermān □, *Iran* 71 D8
Kermān, Bīābān-e, *Iran* 71 D8
Kermānshāh = Bākhtarān, *Iran* 70 C5
Kermen, *Bulgaria* 41 D10
Kermit, *U.S.A.* 113 K3
Kern →, *U.S.A.* 117 K7
Kernhof, *Austria* 26 D8
Kernow = Cornwall □, *U.K.* 13 G3
Kernville, *U.S.A.* 117 K8
Keroh, *Malaysia* 65 K3
Kérou, *Benin* 83 C5
Kérouane, *Guinea* 82 D3
Kerpen, *Germany* 24 E2
Kerrera, *U.K.* 14 E3
Kerrobert, *Canada* 105 C7
Kerrville, *U.S.A.* 113 K5
Kerry □, *Ireland* 15 D2
Kerry Hd., *Ireland* 15 D2
Kersa, *Ethiopia* 81 F5
Kerulen →, *Asia* 60 B6
Kerzaz, *Algeria* 78 C5
Kesagami →, *Canada* 102 B4
Kesagami L., *Canada* 102 B3
Keşan, *Turkey* 41 F10
Kesennuma, *Japan* 54 E10
Keshit, *Iran* 71 D8
Keşiş Dağ, *Turkey* 73 C8
Keskin, *Turkey* 72 C5
Kestell, *S. Africa* 89 D4
Kestenga, *Russia* 50 C4
Keswick, *U.K.* 12 C4
Keszthely, *Hungary* 42 D2
Ket →, *Russia* 50 D9
Keta, *Ghana* 83 D5
Keta Lagoon, *Ghana* 83 D5
Ketapang, *Indonesia* 62 E4
Ketchikan, *U.S.A.* 104 B2
Ketchum, *U.S.A.* 114 E6
Kete Krachi, *Ghana* 83 D4
Ketef, Khalîg Umm el, *Egypt* 70 F2
Keti Bandar, *Pakistan* 68 G2
Kétou, *Benin* 83 D5
Ketri, *India* 68 E6
Kętrzyn, *Poland* 44 D8
Kettering, *U.K.* 13 E7
Kettering, *U.S.A.* 108 F3
Kettle →, *Canada* 105 B11
Kettle Falls, *U.S.A.* 114 B4
Kettle Pt., *Canada* 110 C2
Kettleman City, *U.S.A.* 116 J7
Kęty, *Poland* 45 J6
Keuka L., *U.S.A.* 110 D7
Keuruu, *Finland* 9 E21
Kevelaer, *Germany* 24 D2
Kewanee, *U.S.A.* 112 E10
Kewaunee, *U.S.A.* 108 C2
Keweenaw B., *U.S.A.* 108 B1
Keweenaw Pen., *U.S.A.* 108 B2
Keweenaw Pt., *U.S.A.* 108 B2
Key Largo, *U.S.A.* 109 N5
Key West, *U.S.A.* 107 F10
Keyala, *Sudan* 81 G3
Keynsham, *U.K.* 13 F5
Keyser, *U.S.A.* 108 F6
Kezhma, *Russia* 51 D11
Kezi, *Zimbabwe* 89 C4
Kežmarok, *Slovak Rep.* 27 B13
Khabarovsk, *Russia* 51 E14
Khabr, *Iran* 71 D8
Khābūr →, *Syria* 70 C4
Khachmas = Xaçmaz, *Azerbaijan* 49 K9
Khachrod, *India* 68 H6
Khadari, W. el →, *Sudan* 81 E2
Khadro, *Pakistan* 68 F3
Khadyzhensk, *Russia* 49 H4
Khadzhilyangar, *India* 69 B8
Khaga, *India* 69 G9
Khagaria, *India* 69 G12
Khaipur, *Pakistan* 68 E5
Khair, *India* 68 F7
Khairabad, *India* 69 F9
Khairagarh, *India* 69 J9
Khairpur, *Pakistan* 68 F3
Khairpur Nathan Shah, *Pakistan* 68 F2
Khairwara, *India* 68 H5
Khaisor →, *Pakistan* 68 D3
Khajuri Kach, *Pakistan* 68 C3
Khakassia □, *Russia* 50 D9
Khakhea, *Botswana* 88 C3
Khalafābād, *Iran* 71 D6
Khalilabad, *India* 69 F10
Khalīlī, *Iran* 71 E7
Khalkhāl, *Iran* 71 B6
Khálki, *Dhodhekánisos, Greece* 39 E9
Khálki, *Thessalía, Greece* 38 B4
Khalkidhikí □, *Greece* 40 F7
Khalkís, *Greece* 38 C5
Khalmer-Sede = Tazovskiy, *Russia* 50 C8
Khalmer Yu, *Russia* 50 C7
Khalūf, *Oman* 74 C6
Kham Keut, *Laos* 64 C5
Khamaria, *India* 69 H9
Khambhaliya, *India* 68 H3
Khambhat, *India* 68 H5
Khambhat, G. of, *India* 66 J8
Khamilonísion, *Greece* 39 F8
Khamīr, *Iran* 71 E7
Khamir, *Yemen* 74 D3
Khamsa, *Egypt* 75 E1
Khan →, *Namibia* 88 C2
Khān Abū Shāmat, *Syria* 75 B5
Khān Azād, *Iraq* 70 C5
Khān Mujiddah, *Iraq* 70 C4
Khān Shaykhūn, *Syria* 70 C3
Khān Yūnis, *Gaza Strip* 75 D3
Khanai, *Pakistan* 68 D2
Khānaqīn, *Iraq* 70 C5
Khānbāghī, *Iran* 71 B7
Khandrá, *Greece* 39 F8
Khandwa, *India* 66 J10
Khandyga, *Russia* 51 C14
Khāneh, *Iran* 70 B5
Khanewal, *Pakistan* 68 D4
Khangah Dogran, *Pakistan* 68 D5
Khanh Duong, *Vietnam* 64 F7
Khaniá, *Greece* 36 D6
Khaniá □, *Greece* 36 D6
Khaniadhana, *India* 68 G8
Khaníon, Kólpos, *Greece* 36 D5
Khanka, L., *Asia* 51 E14
Khankendy = Xankändi, *Azerbaijan* 70 B5
Khanna, *India* 68 D7
Khanozai, *Pakistan* 68 D2
Khanpur, *Pakistan* 68 E4
Khanty-Mansiysk, *Russia* 50 C7
Khapalu, *Pakistan* 69 B7
Khapcheranga, *Russia* 51 E12
Kharabali, *Russia* 49 G8
Kharaghoda, *India* 68 H4
Kharagpur, *India* 69 H12
Khárakas, *Greece* 36 D7
Kharan Kalat, *Pakistan* 66 E4
Kharānaq, *Iran* 71 C7
Kharda, *India* 66 K9
Khardung La, *India* 69 B7
Khârga, El Wâhât-el, *Egypt* 80 B3
Khargon, *India* 66 J9
Khari →, *India* 68 G6
Kharian, *Pakistan* 68 C5
Kharit, Wadi el →, *Egypt* 80 C3
Khārk, Jazīreh-ye, *Iran* 71 D6
Kharkiv, *Ukraine* 47 H9
Kharkov = Kharkiv, *Ukraine* 47 H9
Kharmanli, *Bulgaria* 41 E9
Kharovsk, *Russia* 46 C11
Kharsawangarh, *India* 69 H11
Kharta, *Turkey* 72 B3
Khartoum = El Khartûm, *Sudan* 81 D3
Khasan, *Russia* 54 C5
Khasavyurt, *Russia* 49 J8
Khāsh, *Iran* 66 E2
Khashm el Girba, *Sudan* 81 E4
Khashum, *Sudan* 81 E2
Khashuri, *Georgia* 49 J6
Khaskovo, *Bulgaria* 41 E9
Khaskovo □, *Bulgaria* 41 E9
Khatanga, *Russia* 51 B11
Khatanga →, *Russia* 51 B11
Khatauli, *India* 68 E7
Khatra, *India* 69 H12
Khātūnābād, *Iran* 71 D7
Khatyrka, *Russia* 51 C18
Khavda, *India* 68 H3
Khaybar, Ḥarrat, *Si. Arabia* 70 E4
Khayelitsha, *S. Africa* 85 L3
Khāzimiyah, *Iraq* 70 C4
Khazzān Jabal al Awliyā, *Sudan* 81 D3
Khe Bo, *Vietnam* 64 C5
Khe Long, *Vietnam* 64 B5
Khed Brahma, *India* 66 G8
Khekra, *India* 68 E7
Khemarak Phouminville, *Cambodia* 65 G4
Khemisset, *Morocco* 78 B4
Khemmarat, *Thailand* 64 D5
Khenāmān, *Iran* 71 D8
Khenchela, *Algeria* 78 A7
Khersān →, *Iran* 71 D6
Khérson, *Greece* 40 E6
Kherson, *Ukraine* 47 J7
Khersónisos Akrotíri, *Greece* 36 D6
Kheta →, *Russia* 51 B11
Khewari, *Pakistan* 68 F3
Khilchipur, *India* 68 G7
Khiliomódhion, *Greece* 38 D4
Khilok, *Russia* 51 D12
Khimki, *Russia* 46 E9
Khíos, *Greece* 39 C8
Khíos □, *Greece* 39 C8
Khirsadoh, *India* 69 H8
Khiuma = Hiiumaa, *Estonia* 9 G20
Khiva, *Uzbekistan* 50 E7
Khīyāv, *Iran* 70 B5
Khlebarovo, *Bulgaria* 41 C10
Khlong Khlung, *Thailand* 64 D2
Khmelnik, *Ukraine* 47 H4
Khmelnitskiy = Khmelnytskyy, *Ukraine* 47 H4
Khmelnytskyy, *Ukraine* 47 H4
Khmer Rep. = Cambodia ■, *Asia* 64 F5
Khoai, Hon, *Vietnam* 65 H5
Khodoriv, *Ukraine* 47 H3
Khodzent = Khŭjand, *Tajikistan* 50 E7
Khojak Pass, *Afghan.* 68 D2
Khok Kloi, *Thailand* 65 H2
Khok Pho, *Thailand* 65 J3
Kholm, *Russia* 46 D6
Kholmsk, *Russia* 51 E15
Khomas Hochland, *Namibia* 88 C2
Khombole, *Senegal* 82 C1
Khomeyn, *Iran* 71 C6
Khomeynī Shahr, *Iran* 71 C6
Khomodino, *Botswana* 88 C3
Khon Kaen, *Thailand* 64 D4
Khong →, *Cambodia* 64 F5
Khong Sedone, *Laos* 64 E5
Khonuu, *Russia* 51 C15
Khoper →, *Russia* 48 F6
Khor el 'Atash, *Sudan* 81 E3
Khóra, *Greece* 38 D3
Khóra Sfakíon, *Greece* 36 D6
Khorāsān □, *Iran* 71 C8
Khorat = Nakhon Ratchasima, *Thailand* 64 E4
Khorat, Cao Nguyen, *Thailand* 64 E4
Khorixas, *Namibia* 88 C1
Khorol, *Ukraine* 47 H7
Khorramābād, *Khorāsān, Iran* 71 C8
Khorramābād, *Lorestān, Iran* 71 C6
Khorrāmshahr, *Iran* 71 D6
Khorugh, *Tajikistan* 50 F8
Khosravī, *Iran* 71 D6
Khosrowābād, *Khuzestān, Iran* 71 D6
Khosrowābād, *Kordestān, Iran* 70 C5
Khost, *Pakistan* 68 D2
Khosūyeh, *Iran* 71 D7
Khotyn, *Ukraine* 47 H4
Khouribga, *Morocco* 78 B4
Khowst, *Afghan.* 68 C3
Khoyniki, *Belarus* 47 G5
Khrami →, *Georgia* 49 K7
Khrenovoye, *Russia* 48 E5
Khrisoúpolis, *Greece* 41 F8
Khristianá, *Greece* 39 E7
Khrysokhou B., *Cyprus* 36 D11
Khtapodhiá, *Greece* 39 D7
Khu Khan, *Thailand* 64 E5
Khudzhand = Khŭjand, *Tajikistan* 50 E7
Khuff, *Si. Arabia* 70 E5
Khūgīānī, *Afghan.* 68 D2
Khuis, *Botswana* 88 D3
Khuiyala, *India* 68 F4
Khŭjand, *Tajikistan* 50 E7
Khujner, *India* 68 H7
Khulna, *Bangla.* 67 H16
Khulna □, *Bangla.* 67 H16
Khulo, *Georgia* 49 K6
Khumago, *Botswana* 88 C3
Khūnsorkh, *Iran* 71 E8
Khunti, *India* 69 H11
Khūr, *Iran* 71 C8
Khurai, *India* 68 G8
Khurayṣ, *Si. Arabia* 71 E6
Khureit, *Sudan* 81 E2
Khurīyā Murīyā, Jazā'ir, *Oman* 74 D6
Khurja, *India* 68 E7
Khūrmāl, *Iraq* 70 C5
Khurr, Wādī al, *Iraq* 70 C4
Khūsf, *Iran* 71 C8
Khush, *Afghan.* 66 C3
Khushab, *Pakistan* 68 C5
Khust, *Ukraine* 47 H2
Khuzdar, *Pakistan* 68 F2
Khūzestān □, *Iran* 71 D6
Khvāf, *Iran* 71 C9
Khvājeh, *Iran* 70 B5
Khvalynsk, *Russia* 48 D9
Khvānsār, *Iran* 71 D7
Khvatovka, *Russia* 48 D8
Khvor, *Iran* 71 C7
Khvorgū, *Iran* 71 E8
Khvormūj, *Iran* 71 D6
Khvoy, *Iran* 70 B5
Khvoynaya, *Russia* 46 C8
Khyber Pass, *Afghan.* 68 B4
Kiabukwa, *Dem. Rep. of the Congo* 87 D1
Kiama, *Australia* 95 E5
Kiamba, *Phil.* 61 H6
Kiambi, *Dem. Rep. of the Congo* 86 D2
Kiambu, *Kenya* 86 C4
Kiangara, *Madag.* 89 B8
Kiangsi = Jiangxi □, *China* 59 D11
Kiangsu = Jiangsu □, *China* 57 H11
Kiáton, *Greece* 38 C4
Kibæk, *Denmark* 11 H2
Kibanga Port, *Uganda* 86 B3
Kibara, *Tanzania* 86 C3
Kibare, Mts., *Dem. Rep. of the Congo* 86 D2
Kibombo, *Dem. Rep. of the Congo* 86 C2
Kibondo, *Tanzania* 86 C3
Kibre Mengist, *Ethiopia* 81 F4
Kibumbu, *Burundi* 86 C2
Kibungo, *Rwanda* 86 C3
Kibuye, *Burundi* 86 C2
Kibuye, *Rwanda* 86 C2
Kibwesa, *Tanzania* 86 D2
Kibwezi, *Kenya* 86 C4
Kicasalih, *Turkey* 41 E10
Kičevo, *Macedonia* 40 E4
Kichha, *India* 69 E8
Kichha →, *India* 69 E8
Kicking Horse Pass, *Canada* 104 C5
Kidal, *Mali* 83 B5
Kidderminster, *U.K.* 13 E5
Kidete, *Tanzania* 86 D4
Kidira, *Senegal* 82 C2
Kidnappers, C., *N.Z.* 91 H6
Kidsgrove, *U.K.* 12 D5
Kidston, *Australia* 94 B3
Kidugallo, *Tanzania* 86 D4
Kiel, *Germany* 24 A6
Kiel Canal = Nord-Ostsee-Kanal, *Germany* 24 A5
Kielce, *Poland* 45 H7
Kielder Water, *U.K.* 12 B5
Kieler Bucht, *Germany* 24 A6
Kiembara, *Burkina Faso* 82 C4
Kien Binh, *Vietnam* 65 H5
Kien Tan, *Vietnam* 65 G5
Kienge, *Dem. Rep. of the Congo* 87 E2
Kiessé, *Niger* 83 C5
Kiev = Kyyiv, *Ukraine* 47 G6
Kifaya, *Guinea* 82 C2
Kiffa, *Mauritania* 82 B2
Kifisiá, *Greece* 38 C5
Kifissós →, *Greece* 38 C5
Kifrī, *Iraq* 70 C5
Kigali, *Rwanda* 86 C3
Kigarama, *Tanzania* 86 C3
Kigelle, *Sudan* 81 F3
Kigoma □, *Tanzania* 86 D3
Kigoma-Ujiji, *Tanzania* 86 C2
Kigomasha, Ras, *Tanzania* 86 C4
Kığzı, *Turkey* 70 B4
Kihei, *U.S.A.* 106 H16
Kihnu, *Estonia* 9 G21
Kii-Sanchi, *Japan* 55 G8
Kii-Suidō, *Japan* 55 H7
Kikaiga-Shima, *Japan* 55 K4
Kikinda, *Serbia, Yug.* 42 E5
Kikládhes, *Greece* 38 E6
Kikládhes □, *Greece* 38 D6
Kikwit, *Dem. Rep. of the Congo* 84 E3
Kil, *Sweden* 10 E7
Kilafors, *Sweden* 10 C10
Kilar, *India* 68 C7
Kilauea Crater, *U.S.A.* 106 J17
Kilbrannan Sd., *U.K.* 14 F3
Kilchu, *N. Korea* 57 D15
Kilcoy, *Australia* 95 D5
Kildare, *Ireland* 15 C5
Kildare □, *Ireland* 15 C5
Kileikli, *Sudan* 81 E2
Kilfinnane, *Ireland* 15 D3
Kilgore, *U.S.A.* 113 J7
Kilibo, *Benin* 83 D5
Kilifi, *Kenya* 86 C4
Kilimanjaro, *Tanzania* 86 C4
Kilimanjaro □, *Tanzania* 86 C4
Kilimli, *Turkey* 72 B4
Kilindini, *Kenya* 86 C4
Kilis, *Turkey* 70 B3
Kiliya, *Ukraine* 47 K5
Kilkee, *Ireland* 15 D2
Kilkeel, *U.K.* 15 B5
Kilkenny, *Ireland* 15 D4
Kilkenny □, *Ireland* 15 D4
Kilkieran B., *Ireland* 15 C2
Kilkís, *Greece* 40 F6
Kilkís □, *Greece* 40 E6
Killala, *Ireland* 15 B2
Killala B., *Ireland* 15 B2
Killaloe, *Ireland* 15 D3
Killaloe Station, *Canada* 110 A7
Killarney, *Australia* 95 D5
Killarney, *Canada* 105 D9
Killarney, *Ireland* 15 D2
Killary Harbour, *Ireland* 15 C2
Killdeer, *U.S.A.* 112 B3
Killeberg, *Sweden* 11 H8
Killeen, *U.S.A.* 113 K6
Killin, *U.K.* 14 E4
Killíni, *Ilía, Greece* 38 D3
Killíni, *Korinthía, Greece* 38 D4
Killorglin, *Ireland* 15 D2
Killybegs, *Ireland* 15 B3
Kilmarnock, *U.K.* 14 F4
Kilmez, *Russia* 48 B10
Kilmez →, *Russia* 48 B10
Kilondo, *Tanzania* 87 D3
Kilosa, *Tanzania* 86 D4
Kilrush, *Ireland* 15 D2
Kilwa Kisiwani, *Tanzania* 87 D4
Kilwa Kivinje, *Tanzania* 87 D4
Kilwa Masoko, *Tanzania* 87 D4
Kilwinning, *U.K.* 14 F4
Kim, *U.S.A.* 113 G3
Kim →, *Cameroon* 83 D7
Kimaam, *Indonesia* 63 F9
Kimamba, *Tanzania* 86 D4
Kimball, *Nebr., U.S.A.* 112 E3
Kimball, *S. Dak., U.S.A.* 112 D5
Kimberley, *Australia* 92 C4
Kimberley, *Canada* 104 D5
Kimberley, *S. Africa* 88 D3
Kimberly, *U.S.A.* 114 E6
Kimch'aek, *N. Korea* 57 D15
Kimch'ŏn, *S. Korea* 57 F15
Kími, *Greece* 38 C6
Kimje, *S. Korea* 57 G14
Kimmirut, *Canada* 101 B13
Kímolos, *Greece* 38 E6
Kimovsk, *Moskva, Russia* 46 E9
Kimovsk, *Tula, Russia* 46 E10
Kimparana, *Mali* 82 C4
Kimpese, *Dem. Rep. of the Congo* 84 F2
Kimry, *Russia* 46 D9
Kimstad, *Sweden* 11 F9
Kinabalu, Gunong, *Malaysia* 62 C5
Kínaros, *Greece* 39 E8
Kinaskan L., *Canada* 104 B2
Kinbasket L., *Canada* 104 C5
Kincardine, *Canada* 102 D3
Kincolith, *Canada* 104 B3
Kinda, *Dem. Rep. of the Congo* 87 D2
Kindberg, *Austria* 26 D8
Kinde, *U.S.A.* 110 C2
Kinder Scout, *U.K.* 12 D6
Kindersley, *Canada* 105 C7
Kindia, *Guinea* 82 D2
Kindu, *Dem. Rep. of the Congo* 86 C2
Kinel, *Russia* 48 D10
Kineshma, *Russia* 48 B6
Kinesi, *Tanzania* 86 C3
King, L., *Australia* 93 F2
King, Mt., *Australia* 94 D4
King City, *U.S.A.* 116 J5
King Cr. →, *Australia* 94 C2
King Edward →, *Australia* 92 B4
King Frederick VI Land = Kong Frederik VI Kyst, *Greenland* 4 C5
King George B., *Falk. Is.* 128 G4
King George I., *Antarctica* 5 C18
King George Is., *Canada* 101 C11
King I. = Kadan Kyun, *Burma* 64 F2
King I., *Australia* 94 F3
King I., *Canada* 104 C3
King Leopold Ranges, *Australia* 92 C4
King of Prussia, *U.S.A.* 111 F9
King Sd., *Australia* 92 C3
King William I., *Canada* 100 B10
King William's Town, *S. Africa* 88 E4
Kingaok = Bathurst Inlet, *Canada* 100 B9
Kingaroy, *Australia* 95 D5
Kingfisher, *U.S.A.* 113 H6
Kingirbān, *Iraq* 70 C5
Kingisepp = Kuressaare, *Estonia* 9 G20
Kingisepp, *Russia* 46 C5
Kingman, *Ariz., U.S.A.* 117 K12
Kingman, *Kans., U.S.A.* 113 G5
Kingoonya, *Australia* 95 E2
Kingri, *Pakistan* 68 D3
Kings →, *U.S.A.* 116 J7
Kings Canyon National Park, *U.S.A.* 116 J8
King's Lynn, *U.K.* 12 E8
Kings Mountain, *U.S.A.* 109 H5
Kings Park, *U.S.A.* 111 F11
King's Peak, *U.S.A.* 114 F8
Kingsbridge, *U.K.* 13 G4
Kingsburg, *U.S.A.* 116 J7
Kingscourt, *Ireland* 15 C5
Kingsford, *U.S.A.* 108 C1
Kingsland, *U.S.A.* 109 K5
Kingsley, *U.S.A.* 112 D7
Kingsport, *U.S.A.* 109 G4
Kingston, *Canada* 102 D4
Kingston, *Jamaica* 120 C4
Kingston, *N.Z.* 91 L2
Kingston, *N.H., U.S.A.* 111 D13
Kingston, *N.Y., U.S.A.* 111 E11
Kingston, *Pa., U.S.A.* 111 E9
Kingston, *R.I., U.S.A.* 111 E13
Kingston Pk., *U.S.A.* 117 K11
Kingston upon Hull, *U.K.* 12 D7
Kingston upon Hull □, *U.K.* 12 D7
Kingston-upon-Thames □, *U.K.* 13 F7
Kingstown, *St. Vincent* 121 D7
Kingstree, *U.S.A.* 109 J6
Kingsville, *Canada* 102 D3

Kingsville, *U.S.A.* 113 M6
Kingussie, *U.K.* 14 D4
Kingwood, *U.S.A.* 113 K7
Kınık, *Antalya, Turkey* 39 E11
Kınık, *İzmir, Turkey* 39 B9
Kinistino, *Canada* 105 C7
Kinkala, *Congo* 84 E2
Kinki □, *Japan* 55 H8
Kinleith, *N.Z.* 91 H5
Kinmount, *Canada* 110 B6
Kinna, *Sweden* 11 G6
Kinnairds Hd., *U.K.* 14 D6
Kinnared, *Sweden* 11 G7
Kinnarodden, *Norway* 6 A11
Kinnarp, *Sweden* 11 F7
Kinneviken, *Sweden* 11 F7
Kinngait = Cape Dorset, *Canada* 101 B12
Kino, *Mexico* 118 B2
Kinoje →, *Canada* 102 B3
Kinomoto, *Japan* 55 G8
Kinoni, *Uganda* 86 C3
Kinoosao, *Canada* 105 B8
Kinross, *U.K.* 14 E5
Kinsale, *Ireland* 15 E3
Kinsale, Old Hd. of, *Ireland* 15 E3
Kinsha = Chang Jiang →, *China* 59 B13
Kinshasa, *Dem. Rep. of the Congo* 84 E3
Kinsley, *U.S.A.* 113 G5
Kinsman, *U.S.A.* 110 E4
Kinston, *U.S.A.* 109 H7
Kintampo, *Ghana* 83 D4
Kintore Ra., *Australia* 92 D4
Kintyre, *U.K.* 14 F3
Kintyre, Mull of, *U.K.* 14 F3
Kinushseo →, *Canada* 102 A3
Kinuso, *Canada* 104 B5
Kinyangiri, *Tanzania* 86 C3
Kinyeti, *Sudan* 81 G3
Kinzig →, *Germany* 25 G3
Kinzua, *U.S.A.* 110 E6
Kinzua Dam, *U.S.A.* 110 E6
Kióni, *Greece* 38 C2
Kiosk, *Canada* 102 C4
Kiowa, *Kans., U.S.A.* 113 G5
Kiowa, *Okla., U.S.A.* 113 H7
Kipahigan L., *Canada* 105 B8
Kipanga, *Tanzania* 86 D4
Kiparissía, *Greece* 38 D3
Kiparissiakós Kólpos, *Greece* 38 D3
Kipawa, L., *Canada* 102 C4
Kipembawe, *Tanzania* 86 D3
Kipengere Ra., *Tanzania* 87 D3
Kipili, *Tanzania* 86 D3
Kipini, *Kenya* 86 C5
Kipling, *Canada* 105 C8
Kippure, *Ireland* 15 C5
Kipushi, *Dem. Rep. of the Congo* 87 E2
Kirane, *Mali* 82 B2
Kiranomena, *Madag.* 89 B8
Kiraz, *Turkey* 39 C10
Kirazlı, *Turkey* 41 F10
Kirchhain, *Germany* 24 E4
Kirchheim, *Germany* 25 G5
Kirchheimbolanden, *Germany* 25 F3
Kirchschlag, *Austria* 27 D9
Kireç, *Turkey* 39 B10
Kirensk, *Russia* 51 D11
Kirghizia = Kyrgyzstan ■, *Asia* 50 E8
Kirghizstan = Kyrgyzstan ■, *Asia* 50 E8
Kiribati ■, *Pac. Oc.* 96 H10
Kırıkhan, *Turkey* 72 D7
Kırıkkale, *Turkey* 72 C5
Kirillov, *Russia* 46 C10
Kirin = Jilin, *China* 57 C14
Kirishi, *Russia* 46 C7
Kiritimati, *Kiribati* 97 G12
Kırka, *Turkey* 39 B12
Kırkağaç, *Turkey* 39 B9
Kirkby, *U.K.* 12 D5
Kirkby Lonsdale, *U.K.* 12 C5
Kirkcaldy, *U.K.* 14 E5
Kirkcudbright, *U.K.* 14 G4
Kirkee, *India* 66 K8
Kirkenes, *Norway* 8 B23
Kirkfield, *Canada* 110 B6
Kirkjubæjarklaustur, *Iceland* 8 E4
Kirkkonummi, *Finland* 9 F21
Kirkland Lake, *Canada* 102 C3
Kırklareli, *Turkey* 41 E11
Kırklareli □, *Turkey* 41 E11
Kirksville, *U.S.A.* 112 E8
Kirkūk, *Iraq* 70 C5
Kirkwall, *U.K.* 14 C6
Kirkwood, *S. Africa* 88 E4
Kirn, *Germany* 25 F3
Kirov, *Kaluga, Russia* 46 E8
Kirov, *Kirov, Russia* 50 D5
Kirovabad = Gäncä, *Azerbaijan* 49 K8
Kirovakan = Vanadzor, *Armenia* 49 K7
Kirovograd = Kirovohrad, *Ukraine* 47 H7
Kirovohrad, *Ukraine* 47 H7
Kirovsk = Babadayhan, *Turkmenistan* 50 F7
Kirovskiy, *Astrakhan, Russia* 49 H9
Kirovskiy, *Kamchatka, Russia* 51 D16
Kirovskiy, *Primorsk, Russia* 54 B6
Kirriemuir, *U.K.* 14 E5
Kirsanov, *Russia* 48 D6
Kırşehir, *Turkey* 70 B2
Kirtachi, *Niger* 83 C5
Kirthar Range, *Pakistan* 68 F2
Kirtland, *U.S.A.* 115 H9
Kiruna, *Sweden* 8 C19
Kirundu, *Dem. Rep. of the Congo* 86 C2
Kirya, *Russia* 48 C8
Kiryū, *Japan* 55 F9
Kisa, *Sweden* 11 G9
Kisaga, *Tanzania* 86 C3
Kisalaya, *Nic.* 120 D3
Kisalföld, *Hungary* 42 C2
Kisámou, Kólpos, *Greece* 36 D5
Kisanga, *Dem. Rep. of the Congo* 86 B2
Kisangani, *Dem. Rep. of the Congo* 86 B2
Kisar, *Indonesia* 63 F7
Kisarawe, *Tanzania* 86 D4
Kisarazu, *Japan* 55 G9
Kisbér, *Hungary* 42 C3
Kishanganga →, *Pakistan* 69 B5
Kishanganj, *India* 69 F13
Kishangarh, *Raj., India* 68 F6
Kishangarh, *Raj., India* 68 F4
Kishi, *Nigeria* 83 D5
Kishinev = Chişinău, *Moldova* 43 C13
Kishiwada, *Japan* 55 G7
Kishtwar, *India* 69 C6
Kisielice, *Poland* 44 E6
Kisii, *Kenya* 86 C3
Kisiju, *Tanzania* 86 D4
Kisir, *Turkey* 73 B10
Kisizi, *Uganda* 86 C2
Kiskomárom = Zalakomár, *Hungary* 42 D2
Kiskörei-víztároló, *Hungary* 42 C5
Kiskőrös, *Hungary* 42 D4
Kiskundorozsma, *Hungary* 42 D5
Kiskunfélegyháza, *Hungary* 42 D4
Kiskunhalas, *Hungary* 42 D4
Kiskunmajsa, *Hungary* 42 D4
Kislovodsk, *Russia* 49 J6
Kismayu = Chisimaio, *Somali Rep.* 77 G8
Kiso-Gawa →, *Japan* 55 G8
Kiso-Sammyaku, *Japan* 55 G8
Kisofukushima, *Japan* 55 G8
Kisoro, *Uganda* 86 C2
Kissidougou, *Guinea* 82 D2
Kissimmee, *U.S.A.* 109 L5
Kissimmee →, *U.S.A.* 109 M5
Kississing L., *Canada* 105 B8
Kissónerga, *Cyprus* 36 E11
Kissu, J., *Sudan* 80 C2
Kistanje, *Croatia* 29 E12
Kisújszállás, *Hungary* 42 C5
Kisumu, *Kenya* 86 C3
Kisvárda, *Hungary* 42 B7
Kiswani, *Tanzania* 86 C4
Kiswere, *Tanzania* 87 D4
Kit Carson, *U.S.A.* 112 F3
Kita, *Mali* 82 C3
Kitaibaraki, *Japan* 55 F10
Kitakami, *Japan* 54 E10
Kitakami-Gawa →, *Japan* 54 E10
Kitakami-Sammyaku, *Japan* 54 E10
Kitakata, *Japan* 54 F9
Kitakyūshū, *Japan* 55 H5
Kitale, *Kenya* 86 B4
Kitami, *Japan* 54 C11
Kitami-Sammyaku, *Japan* 54 B11
Kitangiri, L., *Tanzania* 86 C3
Kitaya, *Tanzania* 87 E5
Kitchener, *Canada* 102 D3
Kitee, *Finland* 46 A6
Kitega = Gitega, *Burundi* 86 C2
Kitengo, *Dem. Rep. of the Congo* 86 D1
Kitgum, *Uganda* 86 B3
Kíthira, *Greece* 38 E5
Kíthnos, *Greece* 38 D6
Kiti, *Cyprus* 36 E12
Kiti, C., *Cyprus* 36 E12
Kitimat, *Canada* 104 C3
Kitinen →, *Finland* 8 C22
Kitiyab, *Sudan* 81 D3
Kítros, *Greece* 40 F6
Kitsuki, *Japan* 55 H5
Kittakittaooloo, L., *Australia* 95 D2
Kittanning, *U.S.A.* 110 F5
Kittatinny Mts., *U.S.A.* 111 F10
Kittery, *U.S.A.* 109 D10
Kittilä, *Finland* 8 C21
Kitui, *Kenya* 86 C4
Kitwanga, *Canada* 104 B3
Kitwe, *Zambia* 87 E2
Kitzbühel, *Austria* 26 D5
Kitzbühler Alpen, *Austria* 26 D5
Kitzingen, *Germany* 25 F6
Kivarli, *India* 68 G5
Kivertsi, *Ukraine* 47 G3
Kividhes, *Cyprus* 36 E11
Kivik, *Sweden* 11 J8
Kivotós, *Greece* 40 F5
Kivu, L., *Dem. Rep. of the Congo* 86 C2
Kiyev = Kyyiv, *Ukraine* 47 G6
Kiyevskoye Vdkhr. = Kyyivske Vdskh., *Ukraine* 47 G6
Kıyıköy, *Turkey* 41 E12
Kiziguru, *Rwanda* 86 C3
Kızıl Adalar, *Turkey* 41 F13
Kızıl Irmak →, *Turkey* 72 B6
Kizil Jilga, *India* 69 B8
Kizil Yurt, *Russia* 49 J8
Kızılcabölük, *Turkey* 39 D11
Kızılcadağ, *Turkey* 39 D11
Kızılcahamam, *Turkey* 72 B5
Kızılhisar, *Turkey* 72 D3
Kızılırmak, *Turkey* 72 B5
Kızılkaya, *Turkey* 39 D12
Kızılören, *Turkey* 39 C12
Kızıltepe, *Turkey* 70 B4
Kizimkazi, *Tanzania* 86 D4
Kizlyar, *Russia* 49 J8
Kizyl-Arvat = Gyzylarbat, *Turkmenistan* 50 F6
Kjellerup, *Denmark* 11 H3
Kjölur, *Iceland* 8 D4
Kladanj, *Bos.-H.* 42 F3
Kladnica, *Serbia, Yug.* 40 C4
Kladno, *Czech Rep.* 26 A7
Kladovo, *Serbia, Yug.* 40 B6
Klaeng, *Thailand* 64 F3
Klagenfurt, *Austria* 26 E7
Klaipėda, *Lithuania* 9 J19
Klaipėda □, *Lithuania* 44 C8
Klaksvík, *Færoe Is.* 8 E9
Klamath →, *U.S.A.* 114 F1
Klamath Falls, *U.S.A.* 114 E3
Klamath Mts., *U.S.A.* 114 F2
Klamono, *Indonesia* 63 E8
Klanjec, *Croatia* 29 B12
Klappan →, *Canada* 104 B3
Klarälven →, *Sweden* 10 E7
Klässbol, *Sweden* 10 E6
Klatovy, *Czech Rep.* 26 B6
Klawer, *S. Africa* 88 E2
Klazienaveen, *Neths.* 17 B6
Klé, *Mali* 82 C3
Kłecko, *Poland* 45 F4
Kleczew, *Poland* 45 F5
Kleena Kleene, *Canada* 104 C4
Klein-Karas, *Namibia* 88 D2
Klekovača, *Bos.-H.* 29 D13
Klenoec, *Macedonia* 40 E4
Klenovec, *Slovak Rep.* 27 C12
Klerksdorp, *S. Africa* 88 D4
Kleszczele, *Poland* 45 F10
Kletnya, *Russia* 46 F7
Kletsk = Klyetsk, *Belarus* 47 F4
Kletskiy, *Russia* 49 F6
Kleve, *Germany* 24 D2
Klickitat, *U.S.A.* 114 D3
Klickitat →, *U.S.A.* 116 E5
Klidhes, *Cyprus* 36 D13
Klimovichi, *Belarus* 46 F6
Klin, *Russia* 46 D9
Klina, *Kosovo, Yug.* 40 D4
Klinaklini →, *Canada* 104 C3
Klintehamn, *Sweden* 11 G12
Klintsy, *Russia* 47 F7
Klip →, *S. Africa* 89 D4
Klipdale, *S. Africa* 88 E2
Klippan, *Sweden* 11 H7
Klipplaat, *S. Africa* 88 E3
Klisura, *Bulgaria* 41 D8
Kljajićevo, *Serbia, Yug.* 42 E4
Ključ, *Bos.-H.* 29 D13
Kłobuck, *Poland* 45 H5
Klockestrand, *Sweden* 10 B11
Kłodawa, *Poland* 45 F5
Kłodzko, *Poland* 45 H3
Klos, *Albania* 40 E4
Klosterneuburg, *Austria* 27 C9
Klosters, *Switz.* 25 J5
Klötze, *Germany* 24 C7
Klouto, *Togo* 83 D5
Kluane L., *Canada* 100 B6
Kluane Nat. Park, *Canada* 104 A1
Kluczbork, *Poland* 45 H5
Klukwan, *U.S.A.* 104 B1
Klyetsk, *Belarus* 47 F4
Klyuchevskaya, Gora, *Russia* 51 D17
Knäred, *Sweden* 11 H7
Knaresborough, *U.K.* 12 C6
Knee L., *Man., Canada* 102 A1
Knee L., *Sask., Canada* 105 B7
Knezha, *Bulgaria* 41 C8
Knić, *Serbia, Yug.* 40 C4
Knight Inlet, *Canada* 104 C3
Knighton, *U.K.* 13 E4
Knights Ferry, *U.S.A.* 116 H6
Knights Landing, *U.S.A.* 116 G5
Knin, *Croatia* 29 D13
Knislinge, *Sweden* 11 H8
Knittelfeld, *Austria* 26 D7
Knivsta, *Sweden* 10 E11
Knjaževac, *Serbia, Yug.* 40 C6
Knob, C., *Australia* 93 F2
Knock, *Ireland* 15 C3
Knockmealdown Mts., *Ireland* 15 D4
Knokke-Heist, *Belgium* 17 C3
Knossós, *Greece* 36 D7
Knowlton, *Canada* 111 A12
Knox, *U.S.A.* 108 E2
Knox Coast, *Antarctica* 5 C8
Knoxville, *Iowa, U.S.A.* 112 E8
Knoxville, *Pa., U.S.A.* 110 E7
Knoxville, *Tenn., U.S.A.* 109 H4
Knysna, *S. Africa* 88 E3
Knyszyn, *Poland* 44 E9
Ko Kha, *Thailand* 64 C2
Koartac = Quaqtaq, *Canada* 101 B13
Koba, *Indonesia* 63 F8
Kobarid, *Slovenia* 29 B10
Kobayashi, *Japan* 55 J5
Kobdo = Hovd, *Mongolia* 60 B4
Kōbe, *Japan* 55 G7
Kobelyaky, *Ukraine* 47 H8
København, *Denmark* 11 J6
Københavns Amtskommune □, *Denmark* 11 J6
Kobenni, *Mauritania* 82 B3
Kōbi-Sho, *Japan* 55 M1
Koblenz, *Germany* 25 E3
Kobo, *Ethiopia* 81 E4
Kobryn, *Belarus* 47 F3
Kobuleti, *Georgia* 49 K5
Kobylin, *Poland* 45 G4
Kobyłka, *Poland* 45 F8
Kobylkino, *Russia* 48 C6
Koca →, *Turkey* 41 F11
Kocabaş, *Turkey* 39 D11
Kocaeli, *Turkey* 41 F13
Kocaeli □, *Turkey* 41 F13
Kočane, *Serbia, Yug.* 40 C5
Kočani, *Macedonia* 40 E6
Koçarlı, *Turkey* 39 D9
Koceljevo, *Serbia, Yug.* 40 B3
Kočevje, *Slovenia* 29 C11
Koch Bihar, *India* 67 F16
Kochang, *S. Korea* 57 G14
Kochas, *India* 69 G10
Kocher →, *Germany* 25 F5
Kochi = Cochin, *India* 66 Q10
Kōchi, *Japan* 55 H6
Kōchi □, *Japan* 55 H6
Kochiu = Gejiu, *China* 58 F4
Kock, *Poland* 45 G9
Kodarma, *India* 69 G11
Kode, *Sweden* 11 G5
Kodiak, *U.S.A.* 100 C4
Kodiak I., *U.S.A.* 100 C4
Kodinar, *India* 68 J4
Kodok, *Sudan* 81 F3
Kodori →, *Georgia* 49 J5
Koedoesberge, *S. Africa* 88 E3
Koes, *Namibia* 88 D2
Kofçaz, *Turkey* 41 E11
Koffiefontein, *S. Africa* 88 D4
Kofiau, *Indonesia* 63 E7
Köflach, *Austria* 26 D8
Koforidua, *Ghana* 83 D4
Kōfu, *Japan* 55 G9
Koga, *Japan* 55 F9
Kogaluk →, *Canada* 103 A7
Køge, *Denmark* 11 J6
Køge Bugt, *Denmark* 11 J6
Kogi □, *Nigeria* 83 D6
Kogin Baba, *Nigeria* 83 D7
Koh-i-Khurd, *Afghan.* 68 C1
Koh-i-Maran, *Pakistan* 68 E2
Kohat, *Pakistan* 68 C4
Kohima, *India* 67 G19
Kohkīlūyeh va Būyer Aḥmadi □, *Iran* 71 D6
Kohler Ra., *Antarctica* 5 D15
Kohlu, *Pakistan* 68 E3
Kohtla-Järve, *Estonia* 9 G22
Koillismaa, *Finland* 8 D23
Koin-dong, *N. Korea* 57 D14
Koinare, *Bulgaria* 41 C8
Koindu, *S. Leone* 82 D2
Kojetín, *Czech Rep.* 27 B10
Kojŏ, *N. Korea* 57 E14
Kojonup, *Australia* 93 F2
Kojūr, *Iran* 71 B6
Koka, *Sudan* 80 C3
Kokand = Qŭqon, *Uzbekistan* 50 E8
Kokas, *Indonesia* 63 E8
Kokava, *Slovak Rep.* 27 C12
Kokchetav = Kökshetaū, *Kazakstan* 50 D7
Kokemäenjoki →, *Finland* 9 F19
Kokhma, *Russia* 48 B5
Koki, *Senegal* 82 B1
Kokkola, *Finland* 8 E20
Koko, *Nigeria* 83 C5
Koko Kyunzu, *Burma* 67 M18
Kokolopozo, *Ivory C.* 82 D3
Kokomo, *U.S.A.* 108 E2
Kokoro, *Niger* 83 C5
Koksan, *N. Korea* 57 E14
Kökshetaū, *Kazakstan* 50 D7
Koksoak →, *Canada* 101 C13
Kokstad, *S. Africa* 89 E4
Kokubu, *Japan* 55 J5
Kola, *Indonesia* 63 F8
Kola Pen. = Kolskiy Poluostrov, *Russia* 50 C4
Kolachi →, *Pakistan* 68 F2
Kolahoi, *India* 69 B6
Kolahun, *Liberia* 82 D2
Kolaka, *Indonesia* 63 E6
Kolar, *India* 66 N11
Kolar Gold Fields, *India* 66 N11
Kolaras, *India* 68 G6
Kolari, *Finland* 8 C20
Kolárovo, *Slovak Rep.* 27 D10
Kolašin, *Montenegro, Yug.* 40 D3
Kolayat, *India* 66 F8
Kolbäck, *Sweden* 10 E10
Kolbäcksån →, *Sweden* 10 E10
Kolbermoor, *Germany* 25 H8
Kolbuszowa, *Poland* 45 H8
Kolchugino = Leninsk-Kuznetskiy, *Russia* 50 D9
Kolchugino, *Russia* 46 D10
Kolda, *Senegal* 82 C2
Koldegi, *Sudan* 81 E3
Kolding, *Denmark* 11 J3
Kolepom = Dolak, Pulau, *Indonesia* 63 F9
Kolguyev, Ostrov, *Russia* 50 C5
Kolhapur, *India* 66 L9
Kolia, *Ivory C.* 82 D3
Kolín, *Czech Rep.* 26 A8
Kolind, *Denmark* 11 H4
Kolkas rags, *Latvia* 9 H20
Kolkata, *India* 69 H13
Kollam = Quilon, *India* 66 Q10
Kölleda, *Germany* 24 D7
Kollum, *Neths.* 17 A6
Kolmanskop, *Namibia* 88 D2
Köln, *Germany* 24 E2
Kolno, *Poland* 44 E8
Koło, *Poland* 45 F5
Kołobrzeg, *Poland* 44 D2
Kolokani, *Mali* 82 C3
Koloko, *Burkina Faso* 82 C3
Kololo, *Ethiopia* 81 F5
Kolomna, *Russia* 46 E10
Kolomyya, *Ukraine* 47 H3
Kolondiéba, *Mali* 82 C3
Kolonodale, *Indonesia* 63 E6
Kolonowskie, *Poland* 45 H5
Kolosib, *India* 67 G18
Kolpashevo, *Russia* 50 D9
Kolpino, *Russia* 46 C6
Kolpny, *Russia* 47 F9
Kolskiy Poluostrov, *Russia* 50 C4
Kolsva, *Sweden* 10 E9
Kolubara →, *Serbia, Yug.* 40 B4
Koluszki, *Poland* 45 G6
Kolwezi, *Dem. Rep. of the Congo* 87 E2
Kolyma →, *Russia* 51 C17
Kolymskoye Nagorye, *Russia* 51 C16
Kôm Hamâda, *Egypt* 80 H7
Kôm Ombo, *Egypt* 80 C3
Komadugu Gana →, *Nigeria* 83 C7
Komandorskiye Is. = Komandorskiye Ostrova, *Russia* 51 D17
Komandorskiye Ostrova, *Russia* 51 D17
Komárno, *Slovak Rep.* 27 D11
Komárom, *Hungary* 42 C3
Komárom-Esztergom □, *Hungary* 42 C3
Komatipoort, *S. Africa* 89 D5
Komatou Yialou, *Cyprus* 36 D13
Komatsu, *Japan* 55 F8
Komatsushima, *Japan* 55 H7
Kombissiri, *Burkina Faso* 83 C4
Kombori, *Burkina Faso* 82 C4
Kombóti, *Greece* 38 B3
Komen, *Slovenia* 29 C10
Komenda, *Ghana* 83 D4
Komi □, *Russia* 50 C6
Komiža, *Croatia* 29 E13
Komló, *Hungary* 42 D3
Kommunarsk = Alchevsk, *Ukraine* 47 H10
Kommunizma, Pik, *Tajikistan* 50 F8
Komodo, *Indonesia* 63 F5
Komoé →, *Ivory C.* 82 D4
Komoran, Pulau, *Indonesia* 63 F9
Komoro, *Japan* 55 F9
Komotini, *Greece* 41 E9
Komovi, *Montenegro, Yug.* 40 D3
Kompasberg, *S. Africa* 88 E3
Kompong Bang, *Cambodia* 65 F5
Kompong Cham, *Cambodia* 65 F5
Kompong Chhnang = Kampang Chhnang, *Cambodia* 65 F5
Kompong Chikreng, *Cambodia* 64 F5
Kompong Kleang, *Cambodia* 64 F5
Kompong Luong, *Cambodia* 65 G5
Kompong Pranak, *Cambodia* 64 F5
Kompong Som = Kampong Saom, *Cambodia* 65 G4
Kompong Som, Chhung = Kampong Saom, Chaak, *Cambodia* 65 G4
Kompong Speu, *Cambodia* 65 G5
Kompong Sralao, *Cambodia* 64 E5
Kompong Thom, *Cambodia* 64 F5
Kompong Trabeck, *Cambodia* 64 F5
Kompong Trabeck, *Cambodia* 65 G5
Kompong Trach, *Cambodia* 65 G5
Kompong Tralach, *Cambodia* 65 G5
Komrat = Comrat, *Moldova* 43 D13
Komsberg, *S. Africa* 88 E3
Komsomolets, Ostrov, *Russia* 51 A10
Komsomolsk, *Amur, Russia* 51 D14
Komsomolsk, *Ivanovo, Russia* 46 D11
Komsomolskiy, *Russia* 48 C7
Kömür Burnu, *Turkey* 39 C8
Kon Tum, *Vietnam* 64 E7
Kon Tum, Plateau du, *Vietnam* 64 E7
Kona, *Mali* 82 C4
Konakovo, *Russia* 46 D9
Konarhā □, *Afghan.* 66 B7
Konārī, *Iran* 71 D6
Konch, *India* 69 G8
Konde, *Tanzania* 86 C4
Kondiá, *Greece* 39 B7
Kondinin, *Australia* 93 F2
Kondoa, *Tanzania* 86 C4
Kondókali, *Greece* 36 A3
Kondopaga, *Russia* 46 A8
Kondratyevo, *Russia* 51 D10
Kondrovo, *Russia* 46 E8
Konduga, *Nigeria* 83 C7
Köneürgench, *Turkmenistan* 50 E6
Konevo, *Russia* 46 A10
Kong = Khong →, *Cambodia* 64 F5
Kong, *Ivory C.* 82 D4
Kong, Koh, *Cambodia* 65 G4
Kong Christian IX Land, *Greenland* 4 C6
Kong Christian X Land, *Greenland* 4 B6
Kong Frederik IX Land, *Greenland* 4 C5
Kong Frederik VI Kyst, *Greenland* 4 C5

Kong Frederik VIII Land, *Greenland* 4 B6
Kong Oscar Fjord, *Greenland* 4 B6
Kongeå →, *Denmark* 11 J2
Kongerslev, *Denmark* 11 H4
Kongju, *S. Korea* 57 F14
Konglu, *Burma* 67 F20
Kongola, *Namibia* 88 B3
Kongolo, *Kasai-Or., Dem. Rep. of the Congo* 86 D1
Kongolo, *Katanga, Dem. Rep. of the Congo* 86 D2
Kongor, *Sudan* 81 F3
Kongoussi, *Burkina Faso* 83 C4
Kongsberg, *Norway* 9 G13
Kongsvinger, *Norway* 9 F15
Kongwa, *Tanzania* 86 D4
Koni, *Dem. Rep. of the Congo* 87 E2
Koni, Mts., *Dem. Rep. of the Congo* 87 E2
Koniakari, *Mali* 82 C2
Koniecpol, *Poland* 45 H6
Königs Wusterhausen, *Germany* 24 C9
Königsberg = Kaliningrad, *Russia* 9 J19
Königsbrunn, *Germany* 25 G6
Königslutter, *Germany* 24 C6
Konin, *Poland* 45 F5
Konispol, *Albania* 40 G4
Kónitsa, *Greece* 38 A2
Konjic, *Bos.-H.* 42 G2
Konkiep, *Namibia* 88 D2
Konkouré →, *Guinea* 82 D2
Könnern, *Germany* 24 D7
Kono, *S. Leone* 82 D2
Konongo, *Ghana* 83 D4
Konosha, *Russia* 46 B11
Kōnosu, *Japan* 55 F9
Konotop, *Ukraine* 47 G7
Konsankoro, *Guinea* 82 D3
Końskie, *Poland* 45 G7
Konstancin-Jeziorna, *Poland* 45 F8
Konstantinovka = Kostyantynivka, *Ukraine* 47 H9
Konstantinovsk, *Russia* 49 G5
Konstantynów Łódźki, *Poland* 45 G6
Konstanz, *Germany* 25 H5
Kont, *Iran* 71 E9
Kontagora, *Nigeria* 83 C6
Kontcha, *Cameroon* 83 D7
Konya, *Turkey* 70 B2
Konya Ovası, *Turkey* 72 C5
Konz, *Germany* 25 F2
Konza, *Kenya* 86 C4
Koocanusa, L., *Canada* 114 B6
Kookynie, *Australia* 93 E3
Koolyanobbing, *Australia* 93 F2
Koonibba, *Australia* 95 E1
Koorda, *Australia* 93 F2
Kooskia, *U.S.A.* 114 C6
Kootenay →, *U.S.A.* 104 D5
Kootenay L., *Canada* 104 D5
Kootenay Nat. Park, *Canada* 104 C5
Kootjieskolk, *S. Africa* 88 E3
Kopanovka, *Russia* 49 G8
Kopaonik, *Yugoslavia* 40 C4
Kópavogur, *Iceland* 8 D3
Koper, *Slovenia* 29 C10
Kopervik, *Norway* 9 G11
Kopet Dagh, *Asia* 71 B8
Kopi, *Australia* 95 E2
Köping, *Sweden* 10 E10
Köpingsvik, *Sweden* 11 H10
Kopište, *Croatia* 29 F13
Koplik, *Albania* 40 D3
Köpmanholmen, *Sweden* 10 A12
Kopparberg, *Sweden* 10 E9
Koppeh Dāgh = Kopet Dagh, *Asia* 71 B8
Koppies, *S. Africa* 89 D4
Koppom, *Sweden* 10 E6
Koprivlen, *Bulgaria* 40 E7
Koprivnica, *Croatia* 29 B13
Kopřivnice, *Czech Rep.* 27 B11
Koprivshtitsa, *Bulgaria* 41 D8
Köprübaşı, *Turkey* 39 C10
Kopychyntsi, *Ukraine* 47 H3
Korab, *Macedonia* 40 E4
Korakiána, *Greece* 36 A3
Koral, *India* 68 J5
Korarou, L., *Mali* 82 B4
Korba, *India* 69 H10
Korbach, *Germany* 24 D4
Korbu, G., *Malaysia* 65 K3
Korce = Korçë, *Albania* 40 F4
Korçë, *Albania* 40 F4
Korčula, *Croatia* 29 F13
Korčulanski Kanal, *Croatia* 29 E13
Kord Kūy, *Iran* 71 B7
Kord Sheykh, *Iran* 71 D7
Kordestān □, *Iran* 70 C5
Kordofân, *Sudan* 79 F11
Koré Mayroua, *Niger* 83 C5
Korea, North ■, *Asia* 57 E14
Korea, South ■, *Asia* 57 G15
Korea Bay, *Korea* 57 E13
Korea Strait, *Asia* 57 H15
Korem, *Ethiopia* 81 E4
Korenevo, *Russia* 47 G8
Korenovsk, *Russia* 49 H4
Korets, *Ukraine* 47 G4
Korfantów, *Poland* 45 H4
Korgan, *Turkey* 72 B7
Korgus, *Sudan* 80 D3
Korhogo, *Ivory C.* 82 D3
Koribundu, *S. Leone* 82 D2
Korienzé, *Mali* 82 B4
Korinthía □, *Greece* 38 D4
Korinthiakós Kólpos, *Greece* 38 C4
Kórinthos, *Greece* 38 D4
Korioumé, *Mali* 82 B4
Koríssa, Límni, *Greece* 36 B3
Kōriyama, *Japan* 54 F10
Korkuteli, *Turkey* 39 D12
Kormakiti, C., *Cyprus* 36 D11
Körmend, *Hungary* 42 C1
Kornat, *Croatia* 29 E12
Korneshty = Corneşti, *Moldova* 43 C13
Korneuburg, *Austria* 27 C9
Kórnik, *Poland* 45 F4
Koro, *Fiji* 91 C8
Koro, *Ivory C.* 82 D3
Koro, *Mali* 82 C4
Koro Sea, *Fiji* 91 C9
Korocha, *Russia* 47 G9
Köroğlu Dağları, *Turkey* 72 B5
Korogwe, *Tanzania* 86 D4
Koronadal, *Phil.* 61 H6
Koróni, *Greece* 38 E3
Korónia, Límni, *Greece* 40 F7
Koronís, *Greece* 39 D7
Koronowo, *Poland* 45 E4
Koror, *Palau* 63 C8
Körös →, *Hungary* 42 D5
Köröstarcsa, *Hungary* 42 D6
Korosten, *Ukraine* 47 G5
Korostyshev, *Ukraine* 47 G5
Korotoyak, *Russia* 47 G10
Korraraika, Helodranon' i, *Madag.* 89 B7
Korsakov, *Russia* 51 E15
Korsberga, *Sweden* 11 G9
Korshunovo, *Russia* 51 D12
Korsør, *Denmark* 11 J5
Korsun Shevchenkovskiy, *Ukraine* 47 H6
Korsze, *Poland* 44 D8
Korti, *Sudan* 80 D3
Kortrijk, *Belgium* 17 D3
Korucu, *Turkey* 39 B9
Korwai, *India* 68 G8
Koryakskoye Nagorye, *Russia* 51 C18
Koryŏng, *S. Korea* 57 G15
Koryukovka, *Ukraine* 47 G7
Kos, *Greece* 39 E9
Kosa, *Ethiopia* 81 F4
Kosaya Gora, *Russia* 46 E9
Kościan, *Poland* 45 F3
Kościerzyna, *Poland* 44 D4
Kosciusko, *U.S.A.* 113 J10
Kosciuszko, Mt., *Australia* 95 F4
Kösély →, *Hungary* 42 C6
Kosha, *Sudan* 80 C3
Koshava, *Bulgaria* 40 B7
K'oshih = Kashi, *China* 60 C2
Koshiki-Rettō, *Japan* 55 J4
Kosi, *India* 68 F7
Kosi →, *India* 69 E8
Košice, *Slovak Rep.* 27 C14
Košický □, *Slovak Rep.* 27 C14
Kosjerić, *Serbia, Yug.* 40 B3
Köşk, *Turkey* 39 D10
Koskhinoú, *Greece* 36 C10
Koslan, *Russia* 50 C5
Kosŏng, *N. Korea* 57 E15
Kosovo □, *Yugoslavia* 40 D4
Kosovo Polje, *Kosovo, Yug.* 40 D5
Kosovska Kamenica, *Kosovo, Yug.* 40 D5
Kosovska Mitrovica, *Kosovo, Yug.* 40 D4
Kossou, L. de, *Ivory C.* 82 D3
Kosta, *Sweden* 11 H9
Kostajnica, *Croatia* 29 C13
Kostanjevica, *Slovenia* 29 C12
Kostenets, *Bulgaria* 40 D7
Koster, *S. Africa* 88 D4
Kôstî, *Sudan* 81 E3
Kostinbrod, *Bulgaria* 40 D7
Kostolac, *Serbia, Yug.* 40 B5
Kostopil, *Ukraine* 47 G4
Kostroma, *Russia* 46 D11
Kostromskoye Vdkhr., *Russia* 46 D11
Kostrzyn, *Lubuskie, Poland* 45 F1
Kostrzyn, *Wielkopolskie, Poland* 45 F4
Kostyantynivka, *Ukraine* 47 H9
Kostyukovichi = Kastsyukovichy, *Belarus* 46 F7
Koszalin, *Poland* 44 D3
Kőszeg, *Hungary* 42 C1
Kot Addu, *Pakistan* 68 D4
Kot Kapura, *India* 68 D6
Kot Moman, *Pakistan* 68 C5
Kot Sultan, *Pakistan* 68 D4
Kota, *India* 68 G6
Kota Baharu, *Malaysia* 65 J4
Kota Barrage, *India* 68 G6
Kota Belud, *Malaysia* 62 C5
Kota Kinabalu, *Malaysia* 62 C5
Kota Kubu Baharu, *Malaysia* 65 L3
Kota Tinggi, *Malaysia* 65 M4
Kotaagung, *Indonesia* 62 F2
Kotabaru, *Indonesia* 62 E5
Kotabumi, *Indonesia* 62 E2
Kotamobagu, *Indonesia* 63 D6
Kotcho L., *Canada* 104 B4
Kotdwara, *India* 69 E8
Kotel, *Bulgaria* 41 D10
Kotelnich, *Russia* 48 A9
Kotelnikovo, *Russia* 49 G6
Kotelnyy, Ostrov, *Russia* 51 B14
Kothari →, *India* 68 G6
Köthen, *Germany* 24 D7
Kothi, *Mad. P., India* 69 H10
Kothi, *Mad. P., India* 69 G9
Kotiro, *Pakistan* 68 F2
Kotka, *Finland* 9 F22
Kotlas, *Russia* 50 C5
Kotlenska Planina, *Bulgaria* 41 D10
Kotli, *Pakistan* 68 C5
Kotma, *India* 69 H9
Kotmul, *Pakistan* 69 B6
Koton-Karifi, *Nigeria* 83 D6
Kotonkoro, *Nigeria* 83 C6
Kotor, *Montenegro, Yug.* 40 D2
Kotor Varoš, *Bos.-H.* 42 F2
Kotoriba, *Croatia* 29 B13
Kotovo, *Russia* 48 E7
Kotovsk, *Russia* 48 D5
Kotovsk, *Ukraine* 47 J5
Kotputli, *India* 68 F7
Kotri, *Pakistan* 68 G3
Kótronas, *Greece* 38 E4
Kötschach-Mauthen, *Austria* 26 E6
Kotturu, *India* 66 M10
Kotuy →, *Russia* 51 B11
Kotzebue, *U.S.A.* 100 B3
Koudougou, *Burkina Faso* 82 C4
Koufonísi, *Greece* 36 E8
Koufonísia, *Greece* 39 E7
Kougaberge, *S. Africa* 88 E3
Kouibli, *Ivory C.* 82 D3
Kouilou →, *Congo* 84 E2
Koula Moutou, *Gabon* 84 E2
Koulen = Kulen, *Cambodia* 64 F5
Koulikoro, *Mali* 82 C3
Kouloúra, *Greece* 36 A3
Koúm-bournoú, Ákra, *Greece* 36 C10
Koumala, *Australia* 94 C4
Koumankou, *Mali* 82 C3
Koumbia, *Burkina Faso* 82 C4
Koumbia, *Guinea* 82 C2
Koumboum, *Guinea* 82 C2
Koumpenntoum, *Senegal* 82 C2
Koumra, *Chad* 79 G9
Koun-Fao, *Ivory C.* 82 D4
Koundara, *Guinea* 82 C2
Koundian, *Guinea* 82 C3
Koungheul, *Senegal* 82 C2
Kounradskiy, *Kazakstan* 50 E8
Kountze, *U.S.A.* 113 K7
Koupéla, *Burkina Faso* 83 C4
Kourémalé, *Mali* 82 C3
Kouris →, *Cyprus* 36 E11
Kourou, *Fr. Guiana* 125 B8
Kourouba, *Mali* 82 C2
Kouroukoto, *Mali* 82 C2
Kourouma, *Burkina Faso* 82 C4
Kourouninkoto, *Mali* 82 C3
Kouroussa, *Guinea* 82 C3
Koussanar, *Senegal* 82 C2
Koussané, *Mali* 82 C2
Koussane, *Senegal* 82 C2
Kousseri, *Cameroon* 79 F8
Koutiala, *Mali* 82 C3
Kouto, *Ivory C.* 82 D3
Kouvé, *Togo* 83 D5
Kouvola, *Finland* 9 F22
Kovačica, *Serbia, Yug.* 42 E5
Kovel, *Ukraine* 47 G3
Kovin, *Serbia, Yug.* 42 F5
Kovrov, *Russia* 48 B5
Kowal, *Poland* 45 F6
Kowalewo Pomorskie, *Poland* 45 E5
Kowanyama, *Australia* 94 B3
Kowloon, *H.K.* 59 F10
Kowŏn, *N. Korea* 57 E14
Köyceğiz, *Turkey* 39 E10
Köyceğiz Gölü, *Turkey* 39 E10
Koyulhisar, *Turkey* 72 B7
Koyunyeri, *Turkey* 41 F10
Koza, *Japan* 55 L3
Kozak, *Turkey* 39 B9
Kozan, *Turkey* 70 B2
Kozáni, *Greece* 40 F5
Kozáni □, *Greece* 40 F5
Kozara, *Bos.-H.* 29 D14
Kozarac, *Bos.-H.* 29 D13
Kozelets, *Ukraine* 47 G6
Kozelsk, *Russia* 46 E8
Kozhikode = Calicut, *India* 66 P9
Koziegłowy, *Poland* 45 H6
Kozienice, *Poland* 45 G8
Kozje, *Slovenia* 29 B12
Kozloduy, *Bulgaria* 40 C7
Kozlovets, *Bulgaria* 41 C9
Kozlovka, *Russia* 48 C9
Kozlu, *Turkey* 72 B4
Kozluk, *Turkey* 73 C9
Koźmin, *Poland* 45 G4
Kozmodemyansk, *Russia* 48 B8
Kożuchów, *Poland* 45 G2
Kozyatyn, *Ukraine* 47 H5
Kpabia, *Ghana* 83 D4
Kpalimé, *Togo* 83 D5
Kpandae, *Ghana* 83 D4
Kpessi, *Togo* 83 D5
Kra, Isthmus of = Kra, Kho Khot, *Thailand* 65 G2
Kra, Kho Khot, *Thailand* 65 G2
Kra Buri, *Thailand* 65 G2
Kraai →, *S. Africa* 88 E4
Krabi, *Thailand* 65 H2
Kracheh, *Cambodia* 64 F6
Kragan, *Indonesia* 63 G14
Kragerø, *Norway* 9 G13
Kragujevac, *Serbia, Yug.* 40 B4
Krajenka, *Poland* 45 E3
Krajina, *Bos.-H.* 29 D13
Krakatau = Rakata, Pulau, *Indonesia* 62 F3
Krakatoa = Rakata, Pulau, *Indonesia* 62 F3
Krakor, *Cambodia* 64 F5
Kraków, *Poland* 45 H6
Kralanh, *Cambodia* 64 F4
Králíky, *Czech Rep.* 27 A9
Kraljevo, *Serbia, Yug.* 40 C4
Královský Chlmec, *Slovak Rep.* 27 C14
Kralupy nad Vltavou, *Czech Rep.* 26 A7
Kramatorsk, *Ukraine* 47 H9
Kramfors, *Sweden* 10 B11
Kraniá, *Greece* 40 G5
Kranía Elassónas, *Greece* 38 B4
Kranídhion, *Greece* 38 D5
Kranj, *Slovenia* 29 B11
Kranjska Gora, *Slovenia* 29 B10
Krankskop, *S. Africa* 89 D5
Krapina, *Croatia* 29 B12
Krapina →, *Croatia* 29 C12
Krapkowice, *Poland* 45 H4
Kras, *Croatia* 29 C10
Kraskino, *Russia* 51 E14
Krāslava, *Latvia* 46 E4
Kraslice, *Czech Rep.* 26 A5
Krasnaya Gorbatka, *Russia* 48 C5
Krasnaya Polyana, *Russia* 49 J5
Kraśnik, *Poland* 45 H9
Krasnoarmeisk, *Ukraine* 47 H9
Krasnoarmeysk, *Russia* 48 E7
Krasnoarmeyskiy, *Russia* 49 G6
Krasnobrod, *Poland* 45 H10
Krasnodar, *Russia* 49 H4
Krasnodon, *Ukraine* 47 H10
Krasnogorskiy, *Russia* 48 B9
Krasnograd = Krasnohrad, *Ukraine* 47 H8
Krasnogvardeyskoye, *Russia* 49 H5
Krasnogvardyesk, *Ukraine* 47 K8
Krasnohrad, *Ukraine* 47 H8
Krasnokutsk, *Ukraine* 47 G8
Krasnolesnyy, *Russia* 47 G10
Krasnoperekopsk, *Ukraine* 47 J7
Krasnorechenskiy, *Russia* 54 B7
Krasnoselkup, *Russia* 50 C9
Krasnoslobodsk, *Mordvinia, Russia* 48 C6
Krasnoslobodsk, *Volgograd, Russia* 49 F7
Krasnoturinsk, *Russia* 50 D7
Krasnovodsk = Türkmenbashi, *Turkmenistan* 50 E6
Krasnoyarsk, *Russia* 51 D10
Krasnoye = Krasnyy, *Russia* 46 E6
Krasnozavodsk, *Russia* 46 D10
Krasny Sulin, *Russia* 47 J11
Krasnystaw, *Poland* 45 H10
Krasnyy, *Russia* 46 E6
Krasnyy Kholm, *Russia* 46 C9
Krasnyy Kut, *Russia* 48 E8
Krasnyy Liman, *Ukraine* 47 H9
Krasnýy Luch, *Ukraine* 47 H10
Krasnyy Profintern, *Russia* 46 D11
Krasnyy Yar, *Astrakhan, Russia* 49 G9
Krasnyy Yar, *Samara, Russia* 48 D10
Krasnyy Yar, *Volgograd, Russia* 48 E7
Krasnyye Baki, *Russia* 48 B7
Krasnyyoskolske Vdskh., *Ukraine* 47 H9
Kraszna →, *Hungary* 42 B7
Kratie = Kracheh, *Cambodia* 64 F6
Kratovo, *Macedonia* 40 D6
Krau, *Indonesia* 63 E10
Kravanh, Chuor Phnum, *Cambodia* 65 G4
Krefeld, *Germany* 24 D2
Krémaston, Límni, *Greece* 38 C3
Kremen, *Croatia* 29 D12
Kremenchug = Kremenchuk, *Ukraine* 47 H7
Kremenchuk, *Ukraine* 47 H7
Kremenchuksk Vdskh., *Ukraine* 47 H7
Kremenets, *Ukraine* 47 G3
Kremennaya, *Ukraine* 47 H10
Kremges = Svitlovodsk, *Ukraine* 47 H7
Kremmen, *Germany* 24 C9
Kremmling, *U.S.A.* 114 F10
Kremnica, *Slovak Rep.* 27 C11
Krems, *Austria* 26 C8
Kremsmünster, *Austria* 26 C7
Kretinga, *Lithuania* 9 J19
Krettsy, *Russia* 46 C7
Kreuzberg, *Germany* 25 E5
Kreuztal, *Germany* 24 E4
Kría Vrísi, *Greece* 40 F6
Kribi, *Cameroon* 83 E6
Krichem, *Bulgaria* 41 D8
Krichev = Krychaw, *Belarus* 46 F6
Krim, *Slovenia* 29 C11
Kriós, Ákra, *Greece* 36 D5
Krishna →, *India* 67 M12
Krishnanagar, *India* 69 H13
Kristdala, *Sweden* 11 G10
Kristiansand, *Norway* 9 G13
Kristianstad, *Sweden* 11 H8
Kristiansund, *Norway* 8 E12
Kristiinankaupunki, *Finland* 9 E19
Kristinehamn, *Sweden* 10 E8
Kristinestad = Kristiinankaupunki, *Finland* 9 E19
Kríti, *Greece* 36 D7
Kritsá, *Greece* 36 D7
Kriva →, *Macedonia* 40 D5
Kriva Palanka, *Macedonia* 40 D6
Krivaja →, *Bos.-H.* 42 F3
Krivelj, *Serbia, Yug.* 40 B6
Krivoy Rog = Kryvyy Rih, *Ukraine* 47 J7
Križevci, *Croatia* 29 B13
Krk, *Croatia* 29 C11
Krka →, *Slovenia* 29 C12
Krkonoše, *Czech Rep.* 26 A8
Krnov, *Czech Rep.* 27 A10
Krobia, *Poland* 45 G3
Krokeaí, *Greece* 38 E4
Krokek, *Sweden* 11 F10
Krokodil →, *Mozam.* 89 D5
Krokom, *Sweden* 10 A8
Krokowa, *Poland* 44 D5
Krolevets, *Ukraine* 47 G7
Kroměříž, *Czech Rep.* 27 B10
Krompachy, *Slovak Rep.* 27 C13
Kromy, *Russia* 47 F8
Kronach, *Germany* 25 E7
Krong Kaoh Kong, *Cambodia* 62 B2
Kronobergs län □, *Sweden* 11 H8
Kronprins Olav Kyst, *Antarctica* 5 C5
Kronshtadt, *Russia* 46 C5
Kroonstad, *S. Africa* 88 D4
Kröpelin, *Germany* 24 A7
Kropotkin, *Russia* 49 H5
Kropp, *Germany* 24 A5
Krosna, *Lithuania* 44 D10
Krośniewice, *Poland* 45 F6
Krosno, *Poland* 45 J8
Krosno Odrzańskie, *Poland* 45 F2
Krotoszyn, *Poland* 45 G4
Krotovka, *Russia* 48 D10
Kroussón, *Greece* 36 D6
Krrabë, *Albania* 40 E3
Krško, *Slovenia* 29 C12
Krstača, *Serbia, Yug.* 40 D4
Kruger Nat. Park, *S. Africa* 89 C5
Krugersdorp, *S. Africa* 89 D4
Kruisfontein, *S. Africa* 88 E3
Krujë, *Albania* 40 E3
Krulevshchina = Krulyewshchyna, *Belarus* 46 E4
Krulyewshchyna, *Belarus* 46 E4
Krumbach, *Germany* 25 G6
Krumë, *Albania* 40 D4
Krumovgrad, *Bulgaria* 41 E9
Krung Thep = Bangkok, *Thailand* 64 F3
Krupanj, *Serbia, Yug.* 40 B3
Krupina, *Slovak Rep.* 27 C12
Krupinica →, *Slovak Rep.* 27 C11
Krupki, *Belarus* 46 E5
Kruševac, *Serbia, Yug.* 40 C5
Kruševo, *Macedonia* 40 E5
Kruszwica, *Poland* 45 F5
Krychaw, *Belarus* 46 F6
Krymsk, *Russia* 47 K10
Krymskiy Poluostrov = Krymskyy Pivostriv, *Ukraine* 47 K8
Krymskyy Pivostriv, *Ukraine* 47 K8
Krynica, *Poland* 45 J7
Krynica Morska, *Poland* 44 D6
Krynki, *Poland* 45 E10
Kryvyy Rih, *Ukraine* 47 J7
Krzepice, *Poland* 45 H5
Krzeszów, *Poland* 45 H9
Krzna →, *Poland* 45 F10
Krzywiń, *Poland* 45 G3
Krzyż Wielkopolski, *Poland* 45 F2
Ksar el Kebir, *Morocco* 78 B4
Ksar es Souk = Er Rachidia, *Morocco* 78 B5
Książ Wielkopolski, *Poland* 45 F4
Kstovo, *Russia* 48 B7
Ku, W. el →, *Sudan* 81 E2
Kuala Belait, *Malaysia* 62 D4
Kuala Berang, *Malaysia* 65 K4
Kuala Dungun = Dungun, *Malaysia* 65 K4
Kuala Kangsar, *Malaysia* 65 K3
Kuala Kelawang, *Malaysia* 65 L4
Kuala Kerai, *Malaysia* 65 K4
Kuala Lipis, *Malaysia* 65 K4
Kuala Lumpur, *Malaysia* 65 L3
Kuala Nerang, *Malaysia* 65 J3
Kuala Pilah, *Malaysia* 65 L4
Kuala Rompin, *Malaysia* 65 L4
Kuala Selangor, *Malaysia* 65 L3
Kuala Sepetang, *Malaysia* 65 K3
Kuala Terengganu, *Malaysia* 65 K4
Kualajelai, *Indonesia* 62 E4
Kualakapuas, *Indonesia* 62 E4
Kualakurun, *Indonesia* 62 E4
Kualapembuang, *Indonesia* 62 E4
Kualasimpang, *Indonesia* 62 D1
Kuancheng, *China* 57 D10
Kuandang, *Indonesia* 63 D6
Kuandian, *China* 57 D13
Kuangchou = Guangzhou, *China* 59 F9
Kuanshan, *Taiwan* 59 F13
Kuantan, *Malaysia* 65 L4
Kuba = Quba, *Azerbaijan* 49 K9
Kuban →, *Russia* 47 K9
Kubenskoye, Ozero, *Russia* 46 C10
Kubokawa, *Japan* 55 H6
Kubrat, *Bulgaria* 41 C10
Kučevo, *Serbia, Yug.* 40 B5
Kucha Gompa, *India* 69 B7
Kuchaman, *India* 68 F6
Kuchenspitze, *Austria* 26 D3
Kuchinda, *India* 69 J11
Kuching, *Malaysia* 62 D4
Kuchino-eruba-Jima, *Japan* 55 J5
Kuchino-Shima, *Japan* 55 K4

Kuchinotsu, *Japan* 55 H5
Kuchl, *Austria* 26 D6
Kucing = Kuching, *Malaysia* 62 D4
Kuçovë, *Albania* 40 F3
Küçükbahçe, *Turkey* 39 C8
Küçükköy, *Turkey* 39 B8
Küçükkuyu, *Turkey* 39 B8
Küçükmenderes →, *Turkey* 39 D9
Kud →, *Pakistan* 68 F2
Kuda, *India* 66 H7
Kudat, *Malaysia* 62 C5
Kudirkos Naumiestis, *Lithuania* 44 D9
Kudowa-Zdrój, *Poland* 45 H3
Kudus, *Indonesia* 63 G14
Kudymkar, *Russia* 50 D6
Kueiyang = Guiyang, *China* 58 D6
Kufra Oasis = Al Kufrah, *Libya* 79 D10
Kufstein, *Austria* 26 D5
Kugluktuk, *Canada* 100 B8
Kugong I., *Canada* 102 A4
Kūhak, *Iran* 66 F3
Kuhan, *Pakistan* 68 E2
Kūhbonān, *Iran* 71 D8
Kūhestak, *Iran* 71 E8
Kuhin, *Iran* 71 B6
Kūhīrī, *Iran* 71 E9
Kuhnsdorf, *Austria* 26 E7
Kūhpāyeh, *Eşfahan, Iran* 71 C7
Kūhpāyeh, *Kermān, Iran* 71 D8
Kūhrān, Kūh-e, *Iran* 71 E8
Kui Buri, *Thailand* 65 F2
Kuiseb →, *Namibia* 88 B2
Kuito, *Angola* 85 G3
Kuiu I., *U.S.A.* 104 B2
Kujang, *N. Korea* 57 E14
Kujawsko-Pomorskie □, *Poland* 44 E5
Kuji, *Japan* 54 D10
Kujū-San, *Japan* 55 H5
Kukavica, *Serbia, Yug.* 40 D5
Kukawa, *Nigeria* 83 C7
Kukës, *Albania* 40 D4
Kukmor, *Russia* 48 B10
Kukup, *Malaysia* 65 M4
Kukvidze, *Russia* 48 E6
Kula, *Bulgaria* 40 C6
Kula, *Serbia, Yug.* 42 E4
Kula, *Turkey* 39 C10
Kulachi, *Pakistan* 68 D4
Kulai, *Malaysia* 65 M4
Kulal, Mt., *Kenya* 86 B4
Kulaly, Ostrov, *Kazakstan* 49 H10
Kulasekarappattinam, *India* 66 Q11
Kulautuva, *Lithuania* 44 D10
Kuldīga, *Latvia* 9 H19
Kuldīga □, *Latvia* 44 B8
Kuldja = Yining, *China* 50 E9
Kuldu, *Sudan* 81 E2
Kulebaki, *Russia* 48 C6
Kulen, *Cambodia* 64 F5
Kulen Vakuf, *Bos.-H.* 29 D13
Kulgam, *India* 69 C6
Kulgera, *Australia* 94 D1
Kulim, *Malaysia* 65 K3
Kulin, *Australia* 93 F2
Kullen, *Sweden* 11 H6
Kulmbach, *Germany* 25 E7
Kŭlob, *Tajikistan* 50 F7
Kulp, *Turkey* 73 C9
Kulpawn →, *Ghana* 83 D4
Kulsary, *Kazakstan* 50 E6
Kulti, *India* 69 H12
Kulu, *India* 68 D7
Kulu, *Turkey* 72 C5
Kulumbura, *Australia* 92 B4
Kulunda, *Russia* 50 D8
Kulungar, *Afghan.* 68 C3
Kūlvand, *Iran* 71 D7
Kulyab = Kŭlob, *Tajikistan* 50 F7
Kuma →, *Russia* 49 H8
Kumafşarı, *Turkey* 39 D11
Kumaganum, *Nigeria* 83 C7
Kumagaya, *Japan* 55 F9
Kumai, *Indonesia* 62 E4
Kumalar Dağı, *Turkey* 39 C12
Kumamba, Kepulauan, *Indonesia* 63 E9
Kumamoto, *Japan* 55 H5
Kumamoto □, *Japan* 55 H5
Kumanovo, *Macedonia* 40 D5
Kumara, *N.Z.* 91 K3
Kumarina, *Australia* 93 D2
Kumasi, *Ghana* 82 D4
Kumayri = Gyumri, *Armenia* 49 K6
Kumba, *Cameroon* 83 E6
Kumbağ, *Turkey* 41 F11
Kumbakonam, *India* 66 P11
Kumbarilla, *Australia* 95 D5
Kumbhraj, *India* 68 G7
Kumbia, *Australia* 95 D5
Kumbo, *Cameroon* 83 D7
Kŭmch'ŏn, *N. Korea* 57 E14
Kumdok, *India* 69 C8
Kume-Shima, *Japan* 55 L3
Kumeny, *Russia* 48 A9
Kumharsain, *India* 68 D7
Kŭmhwa, *S. Korea* 57 E14
Kumi, *Uganda* 86 B3
Kumkale, *Turkey* 41 G10
Kumla, *Sweden* 10 E9
Kumluca, *Turkey* 39 E12
Kummerower See, *Germany* 24 B8
Kumo, *Nigeria* 83 C7
Kumon Bum, *Burma* 67 F20
Kumylzhenskaya, *Russia* 48 F6
Kunágota, *Hungary* 42 D6
Kunashir, Ostrov, *Russia* 51 E15
Kunda, *Estonia* 9 G22
Kunda, *India* 69 G9
Kundar →, *Pakistan* 68 D3
Kundian, *Pakistan* 68 C4
Kundla, *India* 68 J4
Kunga →, *Bangla.* 69 J13
Kungälv, *Sweden* 11 G5
Kunghit I., *Canada* 104 C2
Kungrad = Qŭnghirot, *Uzbekistan* 50 E6
Kungsängen, *Sweden* 10 E11
Kungsbacka, *Sweden* 11 G6
Kungsgården, *Sweden* 10 D10
Kungshamn, *Sweden* 11 F5
Kungsör, *Sweden* 10 E10
Kungur, *Russia* 50 D6
Kunhar →, *Pakistan* 69 B5
Kunhegyes, *Hungary* 42 C5
Kuningan, *Indonesia* 63 G13
Kunlong, *Burma* 58 F2
Kunlun Shan, *Asia* 60 C3
Kunmadaras, *Hungary* 42 C5
Kunming, *China* 58 E4
Kunów, *Poland* 45 H8
Kunsan, *S. Korea* 57 G14
Kunshan, *China* 59 B13
Kunszentmárton, *Hungary* 42 D5
Kunszentmiklós, *Hungary* 42 C4
Kuntaur, *Senegal* 82 C2
Kununurra, *Australia* 92 C4
Kunwari →, *India* 69 F8
Kunya-Urgench = Köneürgench, *Turkmenistan* 50 E6
Künzelsau, *Germany* 25 F5
Kuopio, *Finland* 8 E22
Kupa →, *Croatia* 29 C13
Kupang, *Indonesia* 63 F6
Kupreanof I., *U.S.A.* 104 B2
Kupres, *Bos.-H.* 42 G2
Kupyansk, *Ukraine* 47 H9
Kupyansk-Uzlovoi, *Ukraine* 47 H9
Kuqa, *China* 60 B3
Kür →, *Azerbaijan* 73 C13
Kür Dili, *Azerbaijan* 71 B6
Kura = Kür →, *Azerbaijan* 73 C13
Kuranda, *Australia* 94 B4
Kuranga, *India* 68 H3
Kurashiki, *Japan* 55 G6
Kurayoshi, *Japan* 55 G6
Kürdämir, *Azerbaijan* 49 K9
Kurdistan, *Asia* 73 D10
Kŭrdzhali, *Bulgaria* 41 E9
Kure, *Japan* 55 G6
Küre, *Turkey* 72 B5
Küre Dağları, *Turkey* 72 B6
Kuressaare, *Estonia* 9 G20
Kurgan, *Russia* 50 D7
Kurganinsk, *Russia* 49 H5
Kurgannaya = Kurganinsk, *Russia* 49 H5
Kuri, *India* 68 F4
Kuria Maria Is. = Khurīyā Murīyā, Jazā'ir, *Oman* 74 D6
Kuridala, *Australia* 94 C3
Kurigram, *Bangla.* 67 G16
Kurikka, *Finland* 9 E20
Kuril Is. = Kurilskiye Ostrova, *Russia* 51 E15
Kuril Trench, *Pac. Oc.* 52 E19
Kurilsk, *Russia* 51 E15
Kurilskiye Ostrova, *Russia* 51 E15
Kurino, *Japan* 55 J5
Kurinskaya Kosa = Kür Dili, *Azerbaijan* 71 B6
Kurkur, *Egypt* 80 C3
Kurlovskiy, *Russia* 48 C5
Kurmuk, *Sudan* 81 E3
Kurnool, *India* 66 M11
Kuro-Shima, *Kagoshima, Japan* 55 J4
Kuro-Shima, *Okinawa, Japan* 55 M2
Kuror, J., *Sudan* 80 C3
Kurow, *N.Z.* 91 L3
Kurów, *Poland* 45 G9
Kurram →, *Pakistan* 68 C4
Kurrimine, *Australia* 94 B4
Kursavka, *Russia* 49 H6
Kurshskiy Zaliv, *Russia* 9 J19
Kursk, *Russia* 47 G9
Kuršumlija, *Serbia, Yug.* 40 C5
Kuršumlijska Banja, *Serbia, Yug.* 40 C5
Kurşunlu, *Bursa, Turkey* 41 F13
Kurşunlu, *Çankırı, Turkey* 72 B5
Kurtalan, *Turkey* 73 D9
Kurtbey, *Turkey* 41 E10
Kuru, *Sudan* 81 F2
Kuru, Bahr el →, *Sudan* 81 F2
Kuruçaşile, *Turkey* 72 B5
Kuruçay, *Turkey* 70 B3
Kuruktag, *China* 60 B3
Kuruman, *S. Africa* 88 D3
Kuruman →, *S. Africa* 88 D3
Kurume, *Japan* 55 H5
Kurun →, *Sudan* 81 F3
Kurunegala, *Sri Lanka* 66 R12
Kurya, *Russia* 50 C6
Kus Gölü, *Turkey* 41 F11
Kuşadası, *Turkey* 72 D2
Kuşadası Körfezi, *Turkey* 39 D8
Kusatsu, *Japan* 55 F9
Kusawa L., *Canada* 104 A1
Kusel, *Germany* 25 F3
Kushaka, *Nigeria* 83 C6
Kushalgarh, *India* 68 H6
Kushchevskaya, *Russia* 49 G4
Kusheriki, *Nigeria* 83 C6
Kushikino, *Japan* 55 J5
Kushima, *Japan* 55 J5
Kushimoto, *Japan* 55 H7
Kushiro, *Japan* 54 C12
Kushiro-Gawa →, *Japan* 54 C12
Kūshk, *Iran* 71 D8
Kushka = Gushgy, *Turkmenistan* 50 F7
Kūshkī, *Iran* 70 C5
Kushol, *India* 69 C7
Kushtia, *Bangla.* 67 H16
Kushum →, *Kazakstan* 48 F10
Kuskokwim B., *U.S.A.* 100 C3
Kusmi, *India* 69 H10
Kussharo-Ko, *Japan* 54 C12
Kustanay = Qostanay, *Kazakstan* 50 D7
Kut, Ko, *Thailand* 65 G4
Kütahya, *Turkey* 39 B12
Kütahya □, *Turkey* 39 B11
Kutaisi, *Georgia* 49 J6
Kutaraja = Banda Aceh, *Indonesia* 62 C1
Kutch, Gulf of = Kachchh, Gulf of, *India* 68 H3
Kutch, Rann of = Kachchh, Rann of, *India* 68 H4
Kutina, *Croatia* 29 C13
Kutiyana, *India* 68 J4
Kutjevo, *Croatia* 42 E2
Kutkashen, *Azerbaijan* 49 K8
Kutná Hora, *Czech Rep.* 26 B8
Kutno, *Poland* 45 F6
Kutse, *Botswana* 88 C3
Kutu, *Dem. Rep. of the Congo* 84 E3
Kutum, *Sudan* 81 E1
Kúty, *Slovak Rep.* 27 C10
Kuujjuaq, *Canada* 101 C13
Kuujjuarapik, *Canada* 102 A4
Kuŭp-tong, *N. Korea* 57 D14
Kuusamo, *Finland* 8 D23
Kuusankoski, *Finland* 9 F22
Kuvshinovo, *Russia* 46 D8
Kuwait = Al Kuwayt, *Kuwait* 70 D5
Kuwait ■, *Asia* 70 D5
Kuwana, *Japan* 55 G8
Kuwana →, *India* 69 F10
Kuybyshev = Samara, *Russia* 48 D10
Kuybyshev, *Russia* 50 D8
Kuybyshevo, *Ukraine* 47 J9
Kuybyshevskoye Vdkhr., *Russia* 48 C9
Kuye He →, *China* 56 E6
Kūyeh, *Iran* 70 B5
Kūysanjaq, *Iraq* 70 B5
Kuyucak, *Turkey* 39 D10
Kuyumba, *Russia* 51 C10
Kuzey Anadolu Dağları, *Turkey* 72 B7
Kuzmin, *Serbia, Yug.* 42 E4
Kuznetsk, *Russia* 48 D8
Kuzomen, *Russia* 50 C4
Kvænangen, *Norway* 8 A19
Kværndrup, *Denmark* 11 J4
Kvaløy, *Norway* 8 B18
Kvänum, *Sweden* 11 F7
Kvareli = Qvareli, *Georgia* 49 K7
Kvarner, *Croatia* 29 D11
Kvarnerič, *Croatia* 29 D11
Kvicksund, *Sweden* 10 E10
Kvillsfors, *Sweden* 11 G9
Kvismare kanal, *Sweden* 10 E9
Kvissleby, *Sweden* 10 B11
Kwa-Nobuhle, *S. Africa* 85 L5
Kwabhaca, *S. Africa* 89 E4
Kwakhanai, *Botswana* 88 C3
Kwakoegron, *Surinam* 125 B7
Kwale, *Kenya* 86 C4
Kwale, *Nigeria* 83 D6
KwaMashu, *S. Africa* 89 D5
Kwando →, *Africa* 88 B3
Kwangdaeri, *N. Korea* 57 D14
Kwangju, *S. Korea* 57 G14
Kwango →, *Dem. Rep. of the Congo* 84 E3
Kwangsi-Chuang = Guangxi Zhuangzu Zizhiqu □, *China* 58 F7
Kwangtung = Guangdong □, *China* 59 F9
Kwara □, *Nigeria* 83 D6
Kwataboahegan →, *Canada* 102 B3
Kwatisore, *Indonesia* 63 E8
KwaZulu Natal □, *S. Africa* 89 D5
Kweichow = Guizhou □, *China* 58 D6
Kwekwe, *Zimbabwe* 87 F2
Kwidzyn, *Poland* 44 E5
Kwiha, *Ethiopia* 81 E4
Kwinana New Town, *Australia* 93 F2
Kwisa →, *Poland* 45 G2
Kwoka, *Indonesia* 63 E8
Kwolla, *Nigeria* 83 D6
Kyabra Cr. →, *Australia* 95 D3
Kyaikto, *Burma* 64 D1
Kyakhta, *Russia* 51 D11
Kyancutta, *Australia* 95 E2
Kyaukpadaung, *Burma* 67 J19
Kyaukpyu, *Burma* 67 K18
Kyaukse, *Burma* 67 J20
Kybartai, *Lithuania* 44 D9
Kyburz, *U.S.A.* 116 G6
Kyelang, *India* 68 C7
Kyenjojo, *Uganda* 86 B3
Kyjov, *Czech Rep.* 27 B10
Kyle, *Canada* 105 C7
Kyle Dam, *Zimbabwe* 87 G3
Kyle of Lochalsh, *U.K.* 14 D3
Kyll →, *Germany* 25 F2
Kyllburg, *Germany* 25 E2
Kymijoki →, *Finland* 9 F22
Kynuna, *Australia* 94 C3
Kyō-ga-Saki, *Japan* 55 G7
Kyoga, L., *Uganda* 86 B3
Kyogle, *Australia* 95 D5
Kyom →, *Sudan* 81 F2
Kyongju, *S. Korea* 57 G15
Kyongpyaw, *Burma* 67 L19
Kyŏngsŏng, *N. Korea* 57 D15
Kyōto, *Japan* 55 G7
Kyōto □, *Japan* 55 G7
Kyparissovouno, *Cyprus* 36 D12
Kyperounda, *Cyprus* 36 E11
Kyrenia, *Cyprus* 36 D12
Kyrgyzstan ■, *Asia* 50 E8
Kyritz, *Germany* 24 C8
Kyrkhult, *Sweden* 11 H8
Kyrönjoki →, *Finland* 8 E19
Kystatyam, *Russia* 51 C13
Kysucké Nové Mesto, *Slovak Rep.* 27 B11
Kythréa, *Cyprus* 36 D12
Kyunhla, *Burma* 67 H19
Kyuquot Sound, *Canada* 104 D3
Kyurdamir = Kürdämir, *Azerbaijan* 49 K9
Kyūshū, *Japan* 55 H5
Kyūshū □, *Japan* 55 H5
Kyūshū-Sanchi, *Japan* 55 H5
Kyustendil, *Bulgaria* 40 D6
Kyusyur, *Russia* 51 B13
Kyyiv, *Ukraine* 47 G6
Kyyivske Vdskh., *Ukraine* 47 G6
Kyzyl, *Russia* 51 D10
Kyzyl Kum, *Uzbekistan* 50 E7
Kyzyl-Kyya, *Kyrgyzstan* 50 E8
Kzyl-Orda = Qyzylorda, *Kazakstan* 50 E7

L

La Albuera, *Spain* 35 G4
La Alcarria, *Spain* 32 E2
La Almarcha, *Spain* 32 F2
La Almunia de Doña Godina, *Spain* 32 D3
La Asunción, *Venezuela* 124 A6
La Baie, *Canada* 103 C5
La Banda, *Argentina* 126 B3
La Bañeza, *Spain* 34 C5
La Barca, *Mexico* 118 C4
La Barge, *U.S.A.* 114 E8
La Bastide-Puylaurent, *France* 20 D7
La Baule-Escoubiac, *France* 18 E4
La Belle, *U.S.A.* 109 M5
La Biche →, *Canada* 104 B4
La Biche, L., *Canada* 104 C6
La Bisbal d'Empordà, *Spain* 32 D8
La Bomba, *Mexico* 118 A1
La Brède, *France* 20 D3
La Bresse, *France* 19 D13
La Bureba, *Spain* 34 C7
La Calera, *Chile* 126 C1
La Campiña, *Spain* 35 H6
La Canal = Sa Canal, *Spain* 37 C7
La Cañiza = A Cañiza, *Spain* 34 C2
La Canourgue, *France* 20 D7
La Capelle, *France* 19 C10
La Carlota, *Argentina* 126 C3
La Carlota, *Phil.* 61 F5
La Carlota, *Spain* 35 H6
La Carolina, *Spain* 35 G7
La Cavalerie, *France* 20 D7
La Ceiba, *Honduras* 120 C2
La Chaise-Dieu, *France* 20 C7
La Chapelle d'Angillon, *France* 19 E9
La Chapelle-St-Luc, *France* 19 D11
La Chapelle-sur-Erdre, *France* 18 E5
La Charité-sur-Loire, *France* 19 E10
La Chartre-sur-le-Loir, *France* 18 E7
La Châtaigneraie, *France* 20 B3
La Châtre, *France* 19 F9
La Chaux-de-Fonds, *Switz.* 25 H2
La Chorrera, *Panama* 120 E4
La Ciotat, *France* 21 E9
La Clayette, *France* 19 F11
La Cocha, *Argentina* 126 B2
La Concepción = Ri-Aba, *Eq. Guin.* 83 E6
La Concepción, *Panama* 120 E3
La Concordia, *Mexico* 119 D6
La Coruña = A Coruña, *Spain* 34 B2
La Coruña □, *Spain* 34 B2
La Côte-St-André, *France* 21 C9
La Courtine-le-Trucq, *France* 20 C6
La Crau, *Bouches-du-Rhône, France* 21 E8
La Crau, *Var, France* 21 E10
La Crescent, *U.S.A.* 112 D9
La Crete, *Canada* 104 B5
La Crosse, *Kans., U.S.A.* 112 F5
La Crosse, *Wis., U.S.A.* 112 D9
La Cruz, *Costa Rica* 120 D2
La Cruz, *Mexico* 118 C3
La Désirade, *Guadeloupe* 121 C7
La Escondida, *Mexico* 118 C5
La Esmeralda, *Paraguay* 126 A3
La Esperanza, *Cuba* 120 B3
La Esperanza, *Honduras* 120 D2
La Estrada = A Estrada, *Spain* 34 C2
La Faouët, *France* 18 D3
La Fayette, *U.S.A.* 109 H3
La Fé, *Cuba* 120 B3
La Fère, *France* 19 C10
La Ferté-Bernard, *France* 18 D7
La Ferté-Gaucher, *France* 19 D10
La Ferté-Macé, *France* 18 D6
La Ferté-St-Aubin, *France* 19 E8
La Ferté-sous-Jouarre, *France* 19 D10
La Ferté-Vidame, *France* 18 D7
La Flèche, *France* 18 E6
La Follette, *U.S.A.* 109 G3
La Fregeneda, *Spain* 34 E4
La Fuente de San Esteban, *Spain* 34 E4
La Gacilly, *France* 18 E4
La Gineta, *Spain* 33 F2
La Grand-Combe, *France* 21 D8
La Grande, *U.S.A.* 114 D4
La Grande →, *Canada* 102 B5
La Grande Deux, Rés., *Canada* 102 B4
La Grande-Motte, *France* 21 E8
La Grande Quatre, Rés., *Canada* 102 B5
La Grande Trois, Rés., *Canada* 102 B4
La Grange, *Calif., U.S.A.* 116 H6
La Grange, *Ga., U.S.A.* 109 J3
La Grange, *Ky., U.S.A.* 108 F3
La Grange, *Tex., U.S.A.* 113 L6
La Grave, *France* 21 C10
La Guaira, *Venezuela* 124 A5
La Guardia = A Guarda, *Spain* 34 D2
La Gudiña = A Gudiña, *Spain* 34 C3
La Guerche-de-Bretagne, *France* 18 E5
La Guerche-sur-l'Aubois, *France* 19 F9
La Habana, *Cuba* 120 B3
La Haye-du-Puits, *France* 18 C5
La Horra, *Spain* 34 D7
La Independencia, *Mexico* 119 D6
La Isabela, *Dom. Rep.* 121 C5
La Jonquera, *Spain* 32 C7
La Junta, *U.S.A.* 113 F3
La Laguna, *Canary Is.* 37 F3
La Libertad, *Guatemala* 120 C1
La Libertad, *Mexico* 118 B2
La Ligua, *Chile* 126 C1
La Línea de la Concepción, *Spain* 35 J5
La Loche, *Canada* 105 B7
La Londe-les-Maures, *France* 21 E10
La Lora, *Spain* 34 C7
La Loupe, *France* 18 D8
La Louvière, *Belgium* 17 D4
La Machine, *France* 19 F10
La Maddalena, *Italy* 30 A2
La Malbaie, *Canada* 103 C5
La Mancha, *Spain* 33 F2
La Mariña, *Spain* 34 B3
La Martre, L., *Canada* 104 A5
La Mesa, *U.S.A.* 117 N9
La Misión, *Mexico* 118 A1
La Mothe-Achard, *France* 18 F5
La Motte, *France* 21 D10
La Motte-Chalançon, *France* 21 D9
La Motte-Servolex, *France* 21 C9
La Moure, *U.S.A.* 112 B5
La Muela, *Spain* 32 D3
La Mure, *France* 21 D9
La Negra, *Chile* 126 A1
La Oliva, *Canary Is.* 37 F6
La Orotava, *Canary Is.* 37 F3
La Oroya, *Peru* 124 F3
La Pacaudière, *France* 19 F10
La Palma, *Canary Is.* 37 F2
La Palma, *Panama* 120 E4
La Palma del Condado, *Spain* 35 H4
La Paloma, *Chile* 126 C1
La Pampa □, *Argentina* 126 D2
La Paragua, *Venezuela* 124 B6
La Paz, *Entre Ríos, Argentina* 126 C4
La Paz, *San Luis, Argentina* 126 C2
La Paz, *Bolivia* 124 G5
La Paz, *Honduras* 120 D2
La Paz, *Mexico* 118 C2
La Paz, *Phil.* 61 D4
La Paz Centro, *Nic.* 120 D2
La Pedrera, *Colombia* 124 D5
La Pérade, *Canada* 103 C5
La Perouse Str., *Asia* 54 B11
La Pesca, *Mexico* 119 C5
La Piedad, *Mexico* 118 C4
La Pine, *U.S.A.* 114 E3
La Plata, *Argentina* 126 D4
La Pobla de Lillet, *Spain* 32 C6
La Pocatière, *Canada* 103 C5
La Pola de Gordón, *Spain* 34 C5
La Porta, *France* 21 F13
La Porte, *Ind., U.S.A.* 108 E2
La Porte, *Tex., U.S.A.* 113 L7
La Presanella, *Italy* 28 B7
La Puebla = Sa Pobla, *Spain* 32 F8
La Puebla de Cazalla, *Spain* 35 H5
La Puebla de los Infantes, *Spain* 35 H5
La Puebla de Montalbán, *Spain* 34 F6
La Puebla del Río, *Spain* 35 H4
La Puerta de Segura, *Spain* 35 G8
La Purísima, *Mexico* 118 B2
La Push, *U.S.A.* 116 C2
La Quiaca, *Argentina* 126 A2
La Réole, *France* 20 D3
La Restinga, *Canary Is.* 37 G2
La Rioja, *Argentina* 126 B2
La Rioja □, *Argentina* 126 B2
La Rioja □, *Spain* 32 C2
La Robla, *Spain* 34 C5
La Roche-Bernard, *France* 18 E4
La Roche-Canillac, *France* 20 C5
La Roche-en-Ardenne, *Belgium* 17 D5
La Roche-sur-Foron, *France* 19 F13
La Roche-sur-Yon, *France* 18 F5
La Rochefoucauld, *France* 20 C4
La Rochelle, *France* 20 B2
La Roda, *Spain* 33 F2

La Roda de Andalucía, *Spain* 35 H6
La Romana, *Dom. Rep.* 121 C6
La Ronge, *Canada* 105 B7
La Rumorosa, *Mexico* 117 N10
La Sabina = Sa Savina, *Spain* 37 C7
La Sagra, *Spain* 33 H2
La Salle, *U.S.A.* 112 E10
La Sanabria, *Spain* 34 C4
La Santa, *Canary Is.* 37 E6
La Sarre, *Canada* 102 C4
La Scie, *Canada* 103 C8
La Selva, *Spain* 32 C7
La Selva Beach, *U.S.A.* 116 J5
La Selva del Camp, *Spain* 32 D6
La Serena, *Chile* 126 B1
La Serena, *Spain* 35 G5
La Seu d'Urgell, *Spain* 32 C6
La Seyne-sur-Mer, *France* 21 E9
La Sila, *Italy* 31 C9
La Solana, *Spain* 35 G7
La Soufrière, *St. Vincent* 121 D7
La Souterraine, *France* 19 F8
La Spézia, *Italy* 28 D6
La Suze-sur-Sarthe, *France* 18 E7
La Tagua, *Colombia* 124 C4
La Teste, *France* 20 D2
La Tortuga, *Venezuela* 121 D6
La Tour-du-Pin, *France* 21 C9
La Tranche-sur-Mer, *France* 18 F5
La Tremblade, *France* 20 C2
La Tuque, *Canada* 102 C5
La Unión, *Chile* 128 E2
La Unión, *El Salv.* 120 D2
La Unión, *Mexico* 118 D4
La Unión, *Spain* 33 H4
La Urbana, *Venezuela* 124 B5
La Vall d'Uixó, *Spain* 32 F4
La Vecilla de Curveño, *Spain* 34 C5
La Vega, *Dom. Rep.* 121 C5
La Vela de Coro, *Venezuela* 124 A5
La Veleta, *Spain* 35 H7
La Venta, *Mexico* 119 D6
La Ventura, *Mexico* 118 C4
La Voulte-sur-Rhône, *France* 21 D8
Laa an der Thaya, *Austria* 27 C9
Laaber, Grosse →, *Germany* 25 G8
Laage, *Germany* 24 B8
Laatzen, *Germany* 24 C5
Laba →, *Russia* 49 H4
Labasa, *Fiji* 91 C8
Labason, *Phil.* 61 G5
Labastide-Murat, *France* 20 D5
Labastide-Rouairoux, *France* 20 E6
Labbézenga, *Mali* 83 B5
Labe = Elbe →, *Europe* 24 B4
Labé, *Guinea* 82 C2
Laberge, L., *Canada* 104 A1
Labin, *Croatia* 29 C11
Labinsk, *Russia* 49 H5
Labis, *Malaysia* 65 L4
Łabiszyn, *Poland* 45 F4
Labo, *Phil.* 61 D5
Laboe, *Germany* 24 A6
Laborec →, *Slovak Rep.* 27 C14
Labouheyre, *France* 20 D3
Laboulaye, *Argentina* 126 C3
Labrador, *Canada* 103 B7
Labrador City, *Canada* 103 B6
Labrador Sea, *Atl. Oc.* 101 C14
Lábrea, *Brazil* 124 E6
Labruguière, *France* 20 E6
Labuan, *Malaysia* 62 C5
Labuan, Pulau, *Malaysia* 62 C5
Labuha, *Indonesia* 63 E7
Labuhan, *Indonesia* 63 G11
Labuhanbajo, *Indonesia* 63 F6
Labuk, Telok, *Malaysia* 62 C5
Labyrinth, L., *Australia* 95 E2
Labytnangi, *Russia* 50 C7
Laç, *Albania* 40 E3
Lac Bouchette, *Canada* 103 C5
Lac Édouard, *Canada* 102 C5
Lac La Biche, *Canada* 104 C6
Lac la Martre = Wha Ti, *Canada* 100 B8
Lac La Ronge Prov. Park, *Canada* 105 B7
Lac-Mégantic, *Canada* 103 C5
Lac Thien, *Vietnam* 64 F7
Lacanau, *France* 20 D2
Lacanau, Étang de, *France* 20 D2
Lacantúm →, *Mexico* 119 D6
Lacara →, *Spain* 35 G4
Lacaune, *France* 20 E6
Lacaune, Mts. de, *France* 20 E6
Laccadive Is. = Lakshadweep Is., *India* 52 H11
Lacepede Is., *Australia* 92 C3
Lacerdónia, *Mozam.* 87 F4
Lacey, *U.S.A.* 116 C4
Lachhmangarh, *India* 68 F6
Lachi, *Pakistan* 68 C4
Lachine, *Canada* 102 C5
Lachute, *Canada* 102 C5
Lackawanna, *U.S.A.* 110 D6
Lackawaxen, *U.S.A.* 111 E10
Lacolle, *Canada* 111 A11
Lacombe, *Canada* 104 C6
Lacona, *U.S.A.* 111 C8
Láconi, *Italy* 30 C2
Laconia, *U.S.A.* 111 C13
Lacq, *France* 20 E3
Ladakh Ra., *India* 69 C8
Lądek-Zdrój, *Poland* 45 H3
Ládhon →, *Greece* 38 D3
Ladik, *Turkey* 72 B6
Ladismith, *S. Africa* 88 E3
Ladíspoli, *Italy* 29 G9
Lādīz, *Iran* 71 D9
Ladnun, *India* 68 F6
Ladoga, L. = Ladozhskoye Ozero, *Russia* 46 B6
Ladozhskoye Ozero, *Russia* 46 B6
Lady Elliott I., *Australia* 94 C5
Lady Grey, *S. Africa* 88 E4
Ladybrand, *S. Africa* 88 D4
Ladysmith, *Canada* 104 D4
Ladysmith, *S. Africa* 89 D4
Ladysmith, *U.S.A.* 112 C9
Lae, *Papua N. G.* 96 H6
Laem Ngop, *Thailand* 65 F4
Laem Pho, *Thailand* 65 J3
Læsø, *Denmark* 11 G5
Læsø Rende, *Denmark* 11 G4
Lafayette, *Colo., U.S.A.* 112 F2
Lafayette, *Ind., U.S.A.* 108 E2
Lafayette, *La., U.S.A.* 113 K9
Lafayette, *Tenn., U.S.A.* 109 G2
Laferte →, *Canada* 104 A5
Lafia, *Nigeria* 83 D6
Lafiagi, *Nigeria* 83 D6
Lafleche, *Canada* 105 D7
Lafon, *Sudan* 81 F3
Lagan, *Sweden* 11 H7
Lagan →, *Sweden* 11 H6
Lagan →, *U.K.* 15 B6
Lagarfljót →, *Iceland* 8 D6
Lage, *Germany* 24 D4
Lågen →, *Oppland, Norway* 9 F14
Lågen →, *Vestfold, Norway* 9 G14
Lägerdorf, *Germany* 24 B5
Laghouat, *Algeria* 78 B6
Lagnieu, *France* 21 C9
Lagny-sur-Marne, *France* 19 D9
Lago, *Italy* 31 C9
Lagôa, *Portugal* 35 H2
Lagoa Vermelha, *Brazil* 127 B5
Lagoaça, *Portugal* 34 D4
Lagodekhi, *Georgia* 49 K8
Lagónegro, *Italy* 31 B8
Lagonoy G., *Phil.* 61 E5
Lagos, *Nigeria* 83 D5
Lagos, *Portugal* 35 H2
Lagos □, *Nigeria* 83 D5
Lagos de Moreno, *Mexico* 118 C4
Lagrange, *Australia* 92 C3
Lagrange B., *Australia* 92 C3
Laguardia, *Spain* 32 C2
Laguépie, *France* 20 D5
Laguna, *Brazil* 127 B6
Laguna, *U.S.A.* 115 J10
Laguna Beach, *U.S.A.* 117 M9
Laguna de Duera, *Spain* 34 D6
Laguna Limpia, *Argentina* 126 B4
Lagunas, *Chile* 126 A2
Lagunas, *Peru* 124 E3
Lahad Datu, *Malaysia* 63 C5
Lahad Datu, Teluk, *Malaysia* 63 D5
Lahan Sai, *Thailand* 64 E4
Lahanam, *Laos* 64 D5
Lahar, *India* 69 F8
Laharpur, *India* 69 F9
Lahat, *Indonesia* 62 E2
Lahewa, *Indonesia* 62 D1
Lāhījān, *Iran* 71 B6
Lahn →, *Germany* 25 E3
Lahnstein, *Germany* 25 E3
Laholm, *Sweden* 11 H7
Laholmsbukten, *Sweden* 11 H6
Lahore, *Pakistan* 68 D6
Lahr, *Germany* 25 G3
Lahri, *Pakistan* 68 E3
Lahti, *Finland* 9 F21
Lahtis = Lahti, *Finland* 9 F21
Laï, *Chad* 79 G9
Lai Chau, *Vietnam* 58 F4
Lai'an, *China* 59 A12
Laibin, *China* 58 F7
Laifeng, *China* 58 C7
L'Aigle, *France* 18 D7
Laignes, *France* 19 E11
L'Aiguillon-sur-Mer, *France* 20 B2
Laila = Laylá, *Si. Arabia* 74 C4
Laingsburg, *S. Africa* 88 E3
Lainio älv →, *Sweden* 8 C20
Lairg, *U.K.* 14 C4
Laishui, *China* 56 E8
Laissac, *France* 20 D6
Láives, *Italy* 29 B8
Laiwu, *China* 57 F9
Laixi, *China* 57 F11
Laiyang, *China* 57 F11
Laiyuan, *China* 56 E8
Laizhou, *China* 57 F10
Laizhou Wan, *China* 57 F10
Laja →, *Mexico* 118 C4
Lajere, *Nigeria* 83 C7
Lajes, *Brazil* 127 B5
Lajkovac, *Serbia, Yug.* 40 B4
Lajosmizse, *Hungary* 42 C4
Lak Sao, *Laos* 64 C5
Lakaband, *Pakistan* 68 D3
Lakamané, *Mali* 82 C3
Lake Alpine, *U.S.A.* 116 G7
Lake Andes, *U.S.A.* 112 D5
Lake Arthur, *U.S.A.* 113 K8
Lake Charles, *U.S.A.* 113 K8
Lake City, *Colo., U.S.A.* 115 G10
Lake City, *Fla., U.S.A.* 109 K4
Lake City, *Mich., U.S.A.* 108 C3
Lake City, *Minn., U.S.A.* 112 C8
Lake City, *Pa., U.S.A.* 110 D4
Lake City, *S.C., U.S.A.* 109 J6
Lake Cowichan, *Canada* 104 D4
Lake District, *U.K.* 12 C4
Lake Elsinore, *U.S.A.* 117 M9
Lake George, *U.S.A.* 111 C11
Lake Grace, *Australia* 93 F2
Lake Harbour = Kimmirut, *Canada* 101 B13
Lake Havasu City, *U.S.A.* 117 L12
Lake Hughes, *U.S.A.* 117 L8
Lake Isabella, *U.S.A.* 117 K8
Lake Jackson, *U.S.A.* 113 L7
Lake Junction, *U.S.A.* 114 D8
Lake King, *Australia* 93 F2
Lake Lenore, *Canada* 105 C8
Lake Louise, *Canada* 104 C5
Lake Mead National Recreation Area, *U.S.A.* 117 K12
Lake Mills, *U.S.A.* 112 D8
Lake Placid, *U.S.A.* 111 B11
Lake Pleasant, *U.S.A.* 111 C10
Lake Providence, *U.S.A.* 113 J9
Lake St. Peter, *Canada* 110 A6
Lake Superior Prov. Park, *Canada* 102 C3
Lake Village, *U.S.A.* 113 J9
Lake Wales, *U.S.A.* 109 M5
Lake Worth, *U.S.A.* 109 M5
Lakeba, *Fiji* 91 D9
Lakefield, *Canada* 102 D4
Lakehurst, *U.S.A.* 111 F10
Lakeland, *Australia* 94 B3
Lakeland, *U.S.A.* 109 M5
Lakeport, *Calif., U.S.A.* 116 F4
Lakeport, *Mich., U.S.A.* 110 C2
Lakeside, *Ariz., U.S.A.* 115 J9
Lakeside, *Calif., U.S.A.* 117 N10
Lakeside, *Nebr., U.S.A.* 112 D3
Lakeside, *Ohio, U.S.A.* 110 E2
Lakeview, *U.S.A.* 114 E3
Lakeville, *U.S.A.* 112 C8
Lakewood, *Colo., U.S.A.* 112 F2
Lakewood, *N.J., U.S.A.* 111 F10
Lakewood, *N.Y., U.S.A.* 110 D5
Lakewood, *Ohio, U.S.A.* 110 E3
Lakewood, *Wash., U.S.A.* 116 C4
Lakha, *India* 68 F4
Lakhaniá, *Greece* 36 D9
Lakhimpur, *India* 69 F9
Lakhnadon, *India* 69 H8
Lakhonpheng, *Laos* 64 E5
Lakhpat, *India* 68 H3
Läki, *Azerbaijan* 49 K8
Lakin, *U.S.A.* 113 G4
Lakitusaki →, *Canada* 102 B3
Lakki, *Pakistan* 68 C4
Lákkoi, *Greece* 36 D5
Lakonía □, *Greece* 38 E4
Lakonikós Kólpos, *Greece* 38 E4
Lakor, *Indonesia* 63 F7
Lakota, *Ivory C.* 82 D3
Lakota, *U.S.A.* 112 A5
Laksar, *India* 68 E8
Laksefjorden, *Norway* 8 A22
Lakselv, *Norway* 8 A21
Lakshadweep Is., *India* 52 H11
Lakshmanpur, *India* 69 H10
Lakshmikantapur, *India* 69 H13
Lala Ghat, *India* 67 G18
Lala Musa, *Pakistan* 68 C5
Lalago, *Tanzania* 86 C3
Lalapanzi, *Zimbabwe* 87 F3
Lalapaşa, *Turkey* 41 E10
Lalbenque, *France* 20 D5
L'Albufera, *Spain* 33 F4
Lalganj, *India* 69 G11
Lalgola, *India* 69 G13
Lālī, *Iran* 71 C6
Lalibela, *Ethiopia* 81 E4
Lalin, *China* 57 B14
Lalín, *Spain* 34 C2
Lalin He →, *China* 57 B13
Lalinde, *France* 20 D4
Lalitpur, *India* 69 G8
Lalkua, *India* 69 E8
Lalsot, *India* 68 F7
Lam, *Vietnam* 64 B6
Lam Pao Res., *Thailand* 64 D4
Lama Kara, *Togo* 83 D5
Lamaing, *Burma* 67 M20
Lamar, *Colo., U.S.A.* 112 F3
Lamar, *Mo., U.S.A.* 113 G7
Lamas, *Peru* 124 E3
Lamastre, *France* 21 D8
Lambach, *Austria* 26 C6
Lamballe, *France* 18 D4
Lambaréné, *Gabon* 84 E2
Lambay I., *Ireland* 15 C5
Lambert Glacier, *Antarctica* 5 D6
Lambert's Bay, *S. Africa* 88 E2
Lambesc, *France* 21 E9
Lambeth, *Canada* 110 D3
Lámbia, *Greece* 38 D3
Lambomakondro, *Madag.* 89 C7
Lambro →, *Italy* 28 C6
Lame, *Nigeria* 83 C6
Lame Deer, *U.S.A.* 114 D10
Lamego, *Portugal* 34 D3
Lamèque, *Canada* 103 C7
Lamesa, *U.S.A.* 113 J4
Lamía, *Greece* 38 C4
Lamitan, *Phil.* 61 H5
Lammermuir Hills, *U.K.* 14 F6
Lammhult, *Sweden* 11 G8
Lamoille →, *U.S.A.* 111 B11
Lamon B., *Phil.* 61 D5
Lamont, *Canada* 104 C6
Lamont, *Calif., U.S.A.* 117 K8
Lamont, *Wyo., U.S.A.* 114 E10
Lamotte-Beuvron, *France* 19 E9
Lampa, *Peru* 124 G4
Lampang, *Thailand* 64 C2
Lampasas, *U.S.A.* 113 K5
Lampazos de Naranjo, *Mexico* 118 B4
Lampertheim, *Germany* 25 F4
Lampeter, *U.K.* 13 E3
Lampman, *Canada* 105 D8
Lamprechtshausen, *Austria* 26 D5
Lampung □, *Indonesia* 62 F2
Lamta, *India* 69 H9
Lamu, *Kenya* 86 C5
Lamy, *U.S.A.* 115 J11
Lan Xian, *China* 56 E6
Lan Yu = Hung'ou Hsü, *Taiwan* 59 G13
Lanak La, *India* 69 B8
Lanak'o Shank'ou = Lanak La, *India* 69 B8
Lanao, L., *Phil.* 61 H6
Lanark, *Canada* 111 A8
Lanark, *U.K.* 14 F5
Lanbi Kyun, *Burma* 65 G2
Lancang, *China* 58 F2
Lancang Jiang →, *China* 58 G3
Lancashire □, *U.K.* 12 D5
Lancaster, *Canada* 111 A10
Lancaster, *U.K.* 12 C5
Lancaster, *Calif., U.S.A.* 117 L8
Lancaster, *Ky., U.S.A.* 108 G3
Lancaster, *N.H., U.S.A.* 111 B13
Lancaster, *N.Y., U.S.A.* 110 D6
Lancaster, *Ohio, U.S.A.* 108 F4
Lancaster, *Pa., U.S.A.* 111 F8
Lancaster, *S.C., U.S.A.* 109 H5
Lancaster, *Wis., U.S.A.* 112 D9
Lancaster Sd., *Canada* 101 A11
Lancelin, *Australia* 93 F2
Lanchow = Lanzhou, *China* 56 F2
Lanciano, *Italy* 29 F11
Lancun, *China* 57 F11
Łańcut, *Poland* 45 H9
Landau, *Bayern, Germany* 25 G8
Landau, *Rhld-Pfz., Germany* 25 F4
Landeck, *Austria* 26 D3
Lander, *U.S.A.* 114 E9
Lander →, *Australia* 92 D5
Landerneau, *France* 18 D2
Landeryd, *Sweden* 11 G7
Landes, *France* 20 D2
Landes □, *France* 20 E3
Landete, *Spain* 32 F3
Landi Kotal, *Pakistan* 68 B4
Landisburg, *U.S.A.* 110 F7
Landivisiau, *France* 18 D2
Landquart, *Switz.* 25 J5
Landrecies, *France* 19 B10
Land's End, *U.K.* 13 G2
Landsberg, *Germany* 25 G6
Landsborough Cr. →, *Australia* 94 C3
Landsbro, *Sweden* 11 G8
Landshut, *Germany* 25 G8
Landskrona, *Sweden* 11 J6
Landstuhl, *Germany* 25 F3
Landvetter, *Sweden* 11 G6
Lanesboro, *U.S.A.* 111 E9
Lanester, *France* 18 E3
Lanett, *U.S.A.* 109 J3
Lang Qua, *Vietnam* 64 A5
Lang Shan, *China* 56 D4
Lang Son, *Vietnam* 58 G6
Lang Suan, *Thailand* 65 H2
Langå, *Denmark* 11 H3
La'nga Co, *China* 67 D12
Langádhas, *Greece* 40 F7
Langádhia, *Greece* 38 D4
Långan →, *Sweden* 10 A8
Langano, L., *Ethiopia* 81 F4
Langar, *Iran* 71 C9
Langara I., *Canada* 104 C2
Långås, *Sweden* 11 H6
Langdai, *China* 58 D5
Langdon, *U.S.A.* 112 A5
Långe Jan = Ölands södra udde, *Sweden* 11 H10
Langeac, *France* 20 C7
Langeais, *France* 18 E7
Langeb Baraka →, *Sudan* 80 D4
Langeberg, *S. Africa* 88 E3
Langeberge, *S. Africa* 88 D3
Langeland, *Denmark* 11 K4
Langelands Bælt, *Denmark* 11 K4
Langen, *Hessen, Germany* 25 F4
Langen, *Niedersachsen, Germany* 24 B4
Langenburg, *Canada* 105 C8
Langeneß, *Germany* 24 A4
Langenlois, *Austria* 26 C8
Langeoog, *Germany* 24 B3
Langeskov, *Denmark* 11 J4
Länghem, *Sweden* 11 G7
Langhirano, *Italy* 28 D7
Langholm, *U.K.* 14 F5
Langjökull, *Iceland* 8 D3
Langkawi, Pulau, *Malaysia* 65 J2
Langklip, *S. Africa* 88 D3
Langkon, *Malaysia* 62 C5
Langlade, *St- P. & M.* 103 C8
Langley, *Canada* 116 A4
Langnau, *Switz.* 25 J3
Langogne, *France* 20 D7
Langon, *France* 20 D3
Langøya, *Norway* 8 B16
Langreo, *Spain* 34 B5
Langres, *France* 19 E12
Langres, Plateau de, *France* 19 E12
Langsa, *Indonesia* 62 D1
Långsele, *Sweden* 10 A11
Långshyttan, *Sweden* 10 D10
Langtry, *U.S.A.* 113 L4
Langu, *Thailand* 65 J2
Languedoc, *France* 20 E7
Languedoc-Roussillon □, *France* 20 E6
Langxi, *China* 59 B12
Langxiangzhen, *China* 56 E9
Langzhong, *China* 58 B5
Lanigan, *Canada* 105 C7
Lankao, *China* 56 G8
Länkäran, *Azerbaijan* 71 B6
Lanmeur, *France* 18 D3
Lannemezan, *France* 20 E4
Lannilis, *France* 18 D2
Lannion, *France* 18 D3
L'Annonciation, *Canada* 102 C5
Lanouaille, *France* 20 C5
Lanping, *China* 58 D2
Lansdale, *U.S.A.* 111 F9
Lansdowne, *Canada* 111 B8
Lansdowne, *India* 69 E8
Lansdowne House, *Canada* 102 B2
L'Anse, *U.S.A.* 108 B1
L'Anse au Loup, *Canada* 103 B8
L'Anse aux Meadows, *Canada* 103 B8
Lansford, *U.S.A.* 111 F9
Lanshan, *China* 59 E9
Lansing, *U.S.A.* 108 D3
Lanslebourg-Mont-Cenis, *France* 21 C10
Lanta Yai, Ko, *Thailand* 65 J2
Lantewa, *Nigeria* 83 C7
Lantian, *China* 56 G5
Lanus, *Argentina* 126 C4
Lanusei, *Italy* 30 C2
Lanuza, *Phil.* 61 G7
Lanxi, *China* 59 C12
Lanzarote, *Canary Is.* 37 F6
Lanzhou, *China* 56 F2
Lanzo Torinese, *Italy* 28 C4
Lao →, *Italy* 31 C8
Lao Bao, *Laos* 64 D6
Lao Cai, *Vietnam* 58 F4
Laoag, *Phil.* 61 B4
Laoang, *Phil.* 61 E6
Laoha He →, *China* 57 C11
Laohekou, *China* 59 A8
Laois □, *Ireland* 15 D4
Laon, *France* 19 C10
Laona, *U.S.A.* 108 C1
Laos ■, *Asia* 64 D5
Lapa, *Brazil* 127 B6
Lapai, *Nigeria* 83 D6
Lapalisse, *France* 19 F10
Lapeer, *U.S.A.* 108 D4
Lapeyrade, *France* 20 D3
Lapithos, *Cyprus* 36 D12
Lapland = Lappland, *Europe* 8 B21
Laporte, *U.S.A.* 111 E8
Lapovo, *Serbia, Yug.* 40 B5
Lappeenranta, *Finland* 9 F23
Lappland, *Europe* 8 B21
Laprida, *Argentina* 126 D3
Lapseki, *Turkey* 41 F10
Laptev Sea, *Russia* 51 B13
Lapua, *Finland* 8 E20
Lăpuş →, *Romania* 43 C8
Lapuş, Munţii, *Romania* 43 C8
Lăpuşna, *Moldova* 43 D13
Łapy, *Poland* 45 F9
Laqiya Arba'in, *Sudan* 80 C2
Laqiya Umran, *Sudan* 80 D2
L'Áquila, *Italy* 29 F10
Lār, *Āzarbājān-e Sharqī, Iran* 70 B5
Lār, *Fārs, Iran* 71 E7
Larabanga, *Ghana* 82 D4
Laragne-Montéglin, *France* 21 D9
Laramie, *U.S.A.* 112 E2
Laramie →, *U.S.A.* 114 F11
Laramie Mts., *U.S.A.* 112 E2
Laranjeiras do Sul, *Brazil* 127 B5
Larantuka, *Indonesia* 63 F6
Larat, *Indonesia* 63 F8
L'Arbresle, *France* 21 C8
Lärbro, *Sweden* 11 G12
Larde, *Mozam.* 87 F4
Larder Lake, *Canada* 102 C4
Lardhos, Ákra = Líndhos, Ákra, *Greece* 36 C10
Lardhos, Órmos, *Greece* 36 C10
Laredo, *Spain* 34 B7
Laredo, *U.S.A.* 113 M5
Laredo Sd., *Canada* 104 C3
Largentière, *France* 21 D8
L'Argentière-la-Bessée, *France* 21 D10
Largo, *U.S.A.* 109 M4
Largs, *U.K.* 14 F4
Lari, *Italy* 28 E7
Lariang, *Indonesia* 63 E5
Larimore, *U.S.A.* 112 B6
Lārīn, *Iran* 71 C7
Larino, *Italy* 29 G11
Lárisa, *Greece* 38 B4
Lárisa □, *Greece* 38 B4
Larkana, *Pakistan* 68 F3
Larnaca, *Cyprus* 36 E12
Larnaca Bay, *Cyprus* 36 E12
Larne, *U.K.* 15 B6
Larned, *U.S.A.* 112 F5
Laroquebrou, *France* 20 D6
Larose, *U.S.A.* 113 L9
Larrimah, *Australia* 92 C5
Larsen Ice Shelf, *Antarctica* 5 C17
Laruns, *France* 20 F3

Larvik, *Norway* 9 G14
Larzac, Causse du, *France* 20 E7
Las Alpujarras, *Spain* 33 J1
Las Animas, *U.S.A.* 112 F3
Las Anod, *Somali Rep.* 74 F4
Las Arenas, *Spain* 34 B6
Las Aves, Is., *W. Indies* 121 C7
Las Brenãs, *Argentina* 126 B3
Las Cabezas de San Juan, *Spain* 35 J5
Las Cejas, *Argentina* 128 B4
Las Chimeneas, *Mexico* 117 N10
Las Cruces, *U.S.A.* 115 K10
Las Flores, *Argentina* 126 D4
Las Heras, *Argentina* 126 C2
Las Lajas, *Argentina* 128 D2
Las Lomitas, *Argentina* 126 A3
Las Marismas, *Spain* 35 H4
Las Minas, *Spain* 33 G3
Las Navas de la Concepción, *Spain* 35 H5
Las Navas del Marqués, *Spain* 34 E6
Las Palmas, *Argentina* 126 B4
Las Palmas, *Canary Is.* 37 F4
Las Palmas →, *Mexico* 117 N10
Las Pedroñas, *Spain* 33 F2
Las Piedras, *Uruguay* 127 C4
Las Pipinas, *Argentina* 126 D4
Las Plumas, *Argentina* 128 E3
Las Rosas, *Argentina* 126 C3
Las Rozas, *Spain* 34 E7
Las Tablas, *Panama* 120 E3
Las Termas, *Argentina* 126 B3
Las Toscas, *Argentina* 126 B4
Las Truchas, *Mexico* 118 D4
Las Varillas, *Argentina* 126 C3
Las Vegas, *N. Mex., U.S.A.* 115 J11
Las Vegas, *Nev., U.S.A.* 117 J11
Lasarte, *Spain* 32 B2
Lascano, *Uruguay* 127 C5
Lash-e Joveyn, *Afghan.* 66 D2
Lashburn, *Canada* 105 C7
Lashio, *Burma* 67 H20
Lashkar, *India* 68 F8
Łasin, *Poland* 44 E6
Lasíthi, *Greece* 36 D7
Lasíthi □, *Greece* 36 D7
Läsjerd, *Iran* 71 C7
Lask, *Poland* 45 G6
Łaskarzew, *Poland* 45 G8
Laško, *Slovenia* 29 B12
Lassay-les-Châteaux, *France* 18 D6
Lassen Pk., *U.S.A.* 114 F3
Lassen Volcanic National Park, *U.S.A.* 114 F3
Last Mountain L., *Canada* 105 C7
Lastchance Cr. →, *U.S.A.* 116 E5
Lastoursville, *Gabon* 84 E2
Lastovo, *Croatia* 29 F13
Lastovski Kanal, *Croatia* 29 F14
Lat Yao, *Thailand* 64 E2
Latacunga, *Ecuador* 124 D3
Latakia = Al Lādhiqīyah, *Syria* 70 C2
Latchford, *Canada* 102 C4
Latehar, *India* 69 H11
Laterza, *Italy* 31 B9
Latham, *Australia* 93 E2
Lathen, *Germany* 24 C3
Lathi, *India* 68 F4
Lathrop Wells, *U.S.A.* 117 J10
Latiano, *Italy* 31 B10
Latina, *Italy* 30 A5
Latisana, *Italy* 29 C10
Latium = Lazio □, *Italy* 29 F9
Laton, *U.S.A.* 116 J7
Latorytsya →, *Slovak Rep.* 27 C14
Latouche Treville, C., *Australia* 92 C3
Latrobe, *Australia* 94 G4
Latrobe, *U.S.A.* 110 F5
Latrónico, *Italy* 31 B9
Latvia ■, *Europe* 9 H20
Lau, *Nigeria* 83 D7
Lau Group, *Fiji* 91 C9
Lauchhammer, *Germany* 24 D9
Lauda-Königshofen, *Germany* 25 F5
Lauenburg, *Germany* 24 B6
Lauf, *Germany* 25 F7
Laughlin, *U.S.A.* 115 J6
Laujar de Andarax, *Spain* 33 H2
Laukaa, *Finland* 9 E21
Launceston, *Australia* 94 G4
Launceston, *U.K.* 13 G3
Laune →, *Ireland* 15 D2
Launglon Bok, *Burma* 64 F1
Laupheim, *Germany* 25 G5
Laura, *Australia* 94 B3
Laureana di Borrello, *Italy* 31 D9
Laurel, *Miss., U.S.A.* 113 K10
Laurel, *Mont., U.S.A.* 114 D9
Laurencekirk, *U.K.* 14 E6
Laurens, *U.S.A.* 109 H4
Laurentian Plateau, *Canada* 103 B6
Lauria, *Italy* 31 B8
Laurie L., *Canada* 105 B8
Laurinburg, *U.S.A.* 109 H6
Laurium, *U.S.A.* 108 B1
Lausanne, *Switz.* 25 J2
Laut, *Indonesia* 65 K6
Laut, Pulau, *Indonesia* 62 E5
Laut Kecil, Kepulauan, *Indonesia* 62 E5
Lauterbach, *Germany* 24 E5
Lauterecken, *Germany* 25 F3
Lautoka, *Fiji* 91 C7
Lauzès, *France* 20 D5
Lavagh More, *Ireland* 15 B3
Lavagna, *Italy* 28 D6
Laval, *France* 18 D6
Lavalle, *Argentina* 126 B2
Lavant Station, *Canada* 111 A8
Lāvar Meydān, *Iran* 71 D7
Lávara, *Greece* 41 E10
Lavardac, *France* 20 D4
Lavaur, *France* 20 E5
Lavelanet, *France* 20 F5
Lavello, *Italy* 31 A8
Laverton, *Australia* 93 E3
Lavìs, *Italy* 28 B8
Lávkos, *Greece* 38 B5
Lavos, *Portugal* 34 E2
Lavradio, *Portugal* 35 G1
Lavras, *Brazil* 127 A7
Lavre, *Portugal* 35 G2
Lávrion, *Greece* 38 D6
Lávris, *Greece* 36 D6
Lavumisa, *Swaziland* 89 D5
Lawas, *Malaysia* 62 D5
Lawele, *Indonesia* 63 F6
Lawng Pit, *Burma* 67 G20
Lawqah, *Si. Arabia* 70 D4
Lawra, *Ghana* 82 C4
Lawrence, *N.Z.* 91 L2
Lawrence, *Kans., U.S.A.* 112 F7
Lawrence, *Mass., U.S.A.* 111 D13
Lawrenceburg, *Ind., U.S.A.* 108 F3
Lawrenceburg, *Tenn., U.S.A.* 109 H2
Lawrenceville, *Ga., U.S.A.* 109 J4
Lawrenceville, *Pa., U.S.A.* 110 E7
Laws, *U.S.A.* 116 H8
Lawton, *U.S.A.* 113 H5
Lawu, *Indonesia* 63 G14
Lawz, J. al, *Si. Arabia* 80 B4
Laxå, *Sweden* 11 F8
Laxford, L., *U.K.* 14 C3
Laxou, *France* 19 D13
Lay →, *France* 20 B2
Laylá, *Si. Arabia* 74 C4
Laylān, *Iraq* 70 C5
Layon →, *France* 18 E6
Layton, *U.S.A.* 114 F7
Laytonville, *U.S.A.* 114 G2
Lazarevac, *Serbia, Yug.* 40 B4
Lazarevskoye, *Russia* 49 J4
Lazarivo, *Madag.* 89 C8
Lazdijai, *Lithuania* 44 D10
Lazio □, *Italy* 29 F9
Lazo, *Moldova* 43 C13
Lazo, *Russia* 54 C6
Le Beausset, *France* 21 E9
Le Blanc, *France* 20 B5
Le Bleymard, *France* 20 D7
Le Bourgneuf-la-Fôret, *France* 18 D6
Le Bugue, *France* 20 D4
Le Canourgue = La Canourgue, *France* 20 D7
Le Cateau Cambrésis, *France* 19 B10
Le Caylar, *France* 20 E7
Le Chambon-Feugerolles, *France* 21 C8
Le Châtelet, *France* 19 F9
Le Chesne, *France* 19 C11
Le Cheylard, *France* 21 D8
Le Conquet, *France* 18 D2
Le Creusot, *France* 19 F11
Le Croisic, *France* 18 E4
Le Donjon, *France* 19 F10
Le Dorat, *France* 20 B5
Le François, *Martinique* 121 D7
Le Grand-Lucé, *France* 18 E7
Le Grand-Pressigny, *France* 18 F7
Le Grand-Quevilly, *France* 18 C8
Le Havre, *France* 18 C7
Le Lavandou, *France* 21 E10
Le Lion-d'Angers, *France* 18 E6
Le Louroux-Béconnais, *France* 18 E6
Le Luc, *France* 21 E10
Le Lude, *France* 18 E7
Le Mans, *France* 18 E7
Le Mars, *U.S.A.* 112 D6
Le Mayet-de-Montagne, *France* 19 F10
Le Mêle-sur-Sarthe, *France* 18 D7
Le Monastier-sur-Gazeille, *France* 20 D7
Le Monêtier-les-Bains, *France* 21 D10
Le Mont-Dore, *France* 20 C6
Le Mont-St-Michel, *France* 18 D5
Le Moule, *Guadeloupe* 121 C7
Le Muy, *France* 21 E10
Le Palais, *France* 18 E3
Le Perthus, *France* 20 F6
Le Puy-en-Velay, *France* 20 C7
Le Sueur, *U.S.A.* 112 C8
Le Teil, *France* 21 D8
Le Teilleul, *France* 18 D6
Le Theil, *France* 18 D7
Le Thillot, *France* 19 E13
Le Thuy, *Vietnam* 64 D6
Le Touquet-Paris-Plage, *France* 19 B8
Le Tréport, *France* 18 B8
Le Val-d'Ajol, *France* 19 E13
Le Verdon-sur-Mer, *France* 20 C2
Le Vigan, *France* 20 E7
Lea →, *U.K.* 13 F8
Leach, *Cambodia* 65 F4
Lead, *U.S.A.* 112 C3
Leader, *Canada* 105 C7
Leadville, *U.S.A.* 115 G10
Leaf →, *U.S.A.* 113 K10
Leaf Rapids, *Canada* 105 B9
Leamington, *Canada* 102 D3
Leamington, *U.S.A.* 114 G7
Leamington Spa = Royal Leamington Spa, *U.K.* 13 E6
Le'an, *China* 59 D10
Leandro Norte Alem, *Argentina* 127 B4
Leane, L., *Ireland* 15 D2
Learmonth, *Australia* 92 D1
Leask, *Canada* 105 C7
Leatherhead, *U.K.* 13 F7
Leavenworth, *Kans., U.S.A.* 112 F7
Leavenworth, *Wash., U.S.A.* 114 C3
Łeba, *Poland* 44 D4
Łeba →, *Poland* 44 D4
Lebach, *Germany* 25 F2
Lebak, *Phil.* 61 H6
Lebam, *U.S.A.* 116 D3
Lebane, *Serbia, Yug.* 40 D5
Lebanon, *Ind., U.S.A.* 108 E2
Lebanon, *Kans., U.S.A.* 112 F5
Lebanon, *Ky., U.S.A.* 108 G3
Lebanon, *Mo., U.S.A.* 113 G8
Lebanon, *N.H., U.S.A.* 111 C12
Lebanon, *Oreg., U.S.A.* 114 D2
Lebanon, *Pa., U.S.A.* 111 F8
Lebanon, *Tenn., U.S.A.* 109 G2
Lebanon ■, *Asia* 75 B5
Lebec, *U.S.A.* 117 L8
Lebedyan, *Russia* 47 F10
Lebedyn, *Ukraine* 47 G8
Lebel-sur-Quévillon, *Canada* 102 C4
Lebomboberge, *S. Africa* 89 C5
Lębork, *Poland* 44 D4
Lebrija, *Spain* 35 J4
Łebsko, Jezioro, *Poland* 44 D4
Lebu, *Chile* 126 D1
Leca da Palmeira, *Portugal* 34 D2
Lecce, *Italy* 31 B11
Lecco, *Italy* 28 C6
Lecco, L. di, *Italy* 28 C6
Lécera, *Spain* 32 D4
Lech, *Austria* 26 D3
Lech →, *Germany* 25 G6
Lechang, *China* 59 E9
Lechtaler Alpen, *Austria* 26 D3
Lecontes Mills, *U.S.A.* 110 E6
Lectoure, *France* 20 E4
Łęczna, *Poland* 45 G9
Łęczyca, *Poland* 45 F6
Ledesma, *Spain* 34 D5
Ledong, *China* 64 C7
Leduc, *Canada* 104 C6
Lee, *U.S.A.* 111 D11
Lee →, *Ireland* 15 E3
Lee Vining, *U.S.A.* 116 H7
Leech L., *U.S.A.* 112 B7
Leechburg, *U.S.A.* 110 F5
Leeds, *U.K.* 12 D6
Leeds, *U.S.A.* 109 J2
Leek, *Neths.* 17 A6
Leek, *U.K.* 12 D5
Leeman, *Australia* 93 E1
Leeper, *U.S.A.* 110 E5
Leer, *Germany* 24 B3
Leesburg, *U.S.A.* 109 L5
Leesville, *U.S.A.* 113 K8
Leetonia, *U.S.A.* 110 F4
Leeu Gamka, *S. Africa* 88 E3
Leeuwarden, *Neths.* 17 A5
Leeuwin, C., *Australia* 93 F2
Leeward Is., *Atl. Oc.* 121 C7
Lefka, *Cyprus* 36 D11
Lefkoniko, *Cyprus* 36 D12
Lefroy, *Canada* 110 B5
Lefroy, L., *Australia* 93 F3
Łeg →, *Poland* 45 H8
Leganés, *Spain* 34 E7
Legazpi, *Phil.* 61 E5
Lège-Cap-Ferret, *France* 20 D2
Lege Hida, *Ethiopia* 81 F5
Legendre I., *Australia* 92 D2
Leghorn = Livorno, *Italy* 28 E7
Legionowo, *Poland* 45 F7
Legnago, *Italy* 29 C8
Legnano, *Italy* 28 C5
Legnica, *Poland* 45 G3
Legrad, *Croatia* 29 B13
Leh, *India* 69 B7
Lehigh Acres, *U.S.A.* 109 M5
Lehighton, *U.S.A.* 111 F9
Lehliu, *Romania* 43 F11
Leho, *Sudan* 81 F3
Lehrte, *Germany* 24 C5
Lehututu, *Botswana* 88 C3
Lei Shui →, *China* 59 D9
Leiah, *Pakistan* 68 D4
Leibnitz, *Austria* 26 E8
Leibo, *China* 58 C4
Leicester, *U.K.* 13 E6
Leicester City □, *U.K.* 13 E6
Leicestershire □, *U.K.* 13 E6
Leichhardt →, *Australia* 94 B2
Leichhardt Ra., *Australia* 94 C4
Leiden, *Neths.* 17 B4
Leie →, *Belgium* 17 C3
Leifers = Láives, *Italy* 29 B8
Leimen, *Germany* 25 F4
Leine →, *Germany* 24 C5
Leinefelde, *Germany* 24 D6
Leinster, *Australia* 93 E3
Leinster □, *Ireland* 15 C4
Leinster, Mt., *Ireland* 15 D5
Leipalingis, *Lithuania* 44 D10
Leipzig, *Germany* 24 D8
Leiria, *Portugal* 34 F2
Leiria □, *Portugal* 34 F2
Leirvik, *Norway* 9 G11
Leishan, *China* 58 D7
Leisler, Mt., *Australia* 92 D4
Leith, *U.K.* 14 F5
Leith Hill, *U.K.* 13 F7
Leitha →, *Europe* 27 D10
Leitrim, *Ireland* 15 B3
Leitrim □, *Ireland* 15 B4
Leitza, *Spain* 32 B3
Leiyang, *China* 59 D9
Leizhou, *China* 59 G8
Leizhou Bandao, *China* 58 G7
Leizhou Wan, *China* 59 G8
Lek →, *Neths.* 17 C4
Leka, *Norway* 8 D14
Lekáni, *Greece* 41 E8
Lekbibaj, *Albania* 40 D3
Lekeitio, *Spain* 32 B2
Lekhainá, *Greece* 38 D3
Lekoui, *Burkina Faso* 82 C4
Leksand, *Sweden* 10 D9
Lékva Óros, *Greece* 36 D6
Leland, *Mich., U.S.A.* 108 C3
Leland, *Miss., U.S.A.* 113 J9
Lelång, *Sweden* 10 E6
Leleque, *Argentina* 128 E2
Lelystad, *Neths.* 17 B5
Lem, *Denmark* 11 H2
Lema, *Nigeria* 83 C5
Lema Shilindi, *Ethiopia* 81 G5
Léman, L., *Europe* 19 F13
Lemera, *Dem. Rep. of the Congo* 86 C2
Lemery, *Phil.* 61 E4
Lemhi Ra., *U.S.A.* 114 D7
Lemmer, *Neths.* 17 B5
Lemmon, *U.S.A.* 112 C3
Lemon Grove, *U.S.A.* 117 N9
Lemoore, *U.S.A.* 116 J7
Lempdes, *France* 20 C7
Lemvig, *Denmark* 11 H2
Lena →, *Russia* 51 B13
Lenart, *Slovenia* 29 B12
Lenartovce, *Slovak Rep.* 27 C13
Lencloître, *France* 18 F7
Léndas, *Greece* 36 E6
Lendava, *Slovenia* 29 B13
Lendeh, *Iran* 71 D6
Lendinara, *Italy* 29 C8
Lengerich, *Germany* 24 C3
Lenggong, *Malaysia* 65 K3
Lenggries, *Germany* 25 H7
Lengshuijiang, *China* 59 D8
Lengshuitan, *China* 59 D8
Lengua de Vaca, Pta., *Chile* 126 C1
Lengyeltóti, *Hungary* 42 D2
Lenhovda, *Sweden* 11 G9
Lenina, Kanal →, *Russia* 49 J7
Leninabad = Khŭjand, *Tajikistan* 50 E7
Leninakan = Gyumri, *Armenia* 49 K6
Leningrad = Sankt-Peterburg, *Russia* 46 C6
Lenino, *Ukraine* 47 K8
Leninogorsk, *Kazakstan* 50 D9
Leninsk, *Russia* 49 F7
Leninsk-Kuznetskiy, *Russia* 50 D9
Leninskoye, *Russia* 48 A8
Lenk, *Switz.* 25 J3
Lenkoran = Länkäran, *Azerbaijan* 71 B6
Lenmalu, *Indonesia* 63 E8
Lenne →, *Germany* 24 D3
Lennestadt, *Germany* 24 D4
Lennox, *U.S.A.* 112 D6
Lennoxville, *Canada* 111 A13
Leno, *Italy* 28 C7
Lenoir, *U.S.A.* 109 H5
Lenoir City, *U.S.A.* 109 H3
Lenore L., *Canada* 105 C8
Lenox, *U.S.A.* 111 D11
Lens, *France* 19 B9
Lensahn, *Germany* 24 A6
Lensk, *Russia* 51 C12
Lentekhi, *Georgia* 49 J6
Lenti, *Hungary* 42 D1
Lentini, *Italy* 31 E8
Lenwood, *U.S.A.* 117 L9
Lenya, *Burma* 62 B1
Lenzen, *Germany* 24 B7
Léo, *Burkina Faso* 82 C4
Leoben, *Austria* 26 D8
Leodhas = Lewis, *U.K.* 14 C2
Leola, *U.S.A.* 112 C5
Leominster, *U.K.* 13 E5
Leominster, *U.S.A.* 111 D13
Léon, *France* 20 E2
León, *Mexico* 118 C4
León, *Nic.* 120 D2
León, *Spain* 34 C5
Leon, *U.S.A.* 112 E8
León □, *Spain* 34 C5
Leon →, *U.S.A.* 113 K6
León, Montes de, *Spain* 34 C4
Leonardtown, *U.S.A.* 108 F7
Leonardville, *Namibia* 88 C2
Leonberg, *Germany* 25 G5
Leonding, *Austria* 26 C7
Leonessa, *Italy* 29 F9
Leonforte, *Italy* 31 E7
Leonídhion, *Greece* 38 D4
Leonora, *Australia* 93 E3
Leopoldina, *Brazil* 127 A7
Leopoldsburg, *Belgium* 17 C5
Leoti, *U.S.A.* 112 F4
Leova, *Moldova* 43 D13
Leoville, *Canada* 105 C7
Lepe, *Spain* 35 H3
Lepel = Lyepyel, *Belarus* 46 E5
Lepenoú, *Greece* 38 C3
Leping, *China* 59 C11
Lépo, L. do, *Angola* 88 B2
Lepontine, Alpi, *Italy* 28 B5
Leppävirta, *Finland* 9 E22
Lepsény, *Hungary* 42 D3
Lequeitio = Lekeitio, *Spain* 32 B2
Lercara Friddi, *Italy* 30 E6
Lerdo, *Mexico* 118 B4
Léré, *Chad* 83 D7
Léré, *Mali* 82 B4
Lere, *Bauchi, Nigeria* 83 D6
Lere, *Kaduna, Nigeria* 83 C6
Leribe, *Lesotho* 89 D4
Lérici, *Italy* 28 D6
Lérida = Lleida, *Spain* 32 D5
Lérins, Îs. de, *France* 21 E11
Lerma, *Spain* 34 C7
Léros, *Greece* 39 D8
Lérouville, *France* 19 D12
Lerum, *Sweden* 11 G6
Lerwick, *U.K.* 14 A7
Leş, *Romania* 42 D6
Les Abrets, *France* 21 C9
Les Andelys, *France* 18 C8
Les Borges Blanques, *Spain* 32 D5
Les Cayes, *Haiti* 121 C5
Les Essarts, *France* 18 F5
Les Herbiers, *France* 18 F5
Les Minquiers, Plateau des, *Chan. Is.* 18 D4
Les Pieux, *France* 18 C5
Les Ponts-de-Cé, *France* 18 E6
Les Riceys, *France* 19 E11
Les Sables-d'Olonne, *France* 20 B2
Les Vans, *France* 21 D8
Lesbos = Lésvos, *Greece* 39 B8
L'Escala, *Spain* 32 C8
Leshan, *China* 58 C4
Lésina, *Italy* 29 G12
Lésina, L. di, *Italy* 29 G12
Lesjöfors, *Sweden* 10 E8
Lesko, *Poland* 45 J9
Leskov I., *Antarctica* 5 B1
Leskovac, *Serbia, Yug.* 40 C5
Leskovik, *Albania* 40 F4
Leśna, *Poland* 45 G2
Lesneven, *France* 18 D2
Leśnica, *Poland* 45 H5
Lešnica, *Serbia, Yug.* 40 B3
Lesnoye, *Russia* 46 C8
Lesopilnoye, *Russia* 54 A7
Lesotho ■, *Africa* 89 D4
Lesozavodsk, *Russia* 51 E14
Lesparre-Médoc, *France* 20 C3
Lessay, *France* 18 C5
Lesse →, *Belgium* 17 D4
Lessebo, *Sweden* 11 H9
Lesser Antilles, *W. Indies* 121 D7
Lesser Slave L., *Canada* 104 B5
Lesser Sunda Is., *Indonesia* 63 F6
Lessines, *Belgium* 17 D3
Lester, *U.S.A.* 116 C5
Lestock, *Canada* 105 C8
Lesueur I., *Australia* 92 B4
Lésvos, *Greece* 39 B8
Leszno, *Poland* 45 G3
Letaba, *S. Africa* 89 C5
Letälven, *Sweden* 10 E8
Létavértes, *Hungary* 42 C6
Letchworth, *U.K.* 13 F7
Letea, Ostrov, *Romania* 43 E14
Lethbridge, *Canada* 104 D6
Lethem, *Guyana* 124 C7
Leti, Kepulauan, *Indonesia* 63 F7
Leti Is. = Leti, Kepulauan, *Indonesia* 63 F7
Letiahau →, *Botswana* 88 C3
Leticia, *Colombia* 124 D5
Leting, *China* 57 E10
Letjiesbos, *S. Africa* 88 E3
Letlhakane, *Botswana* 88 C4
Letlhakeng, *Botswana* 88 C3
Letong, *Indonesia* 62 D3
Letpadan, *Burma* 67 L19
Letpan, *Burma* 67 K19
Letsôk-aw Kyun, *Burma* 65 G2
Letterkenny, *Ireland* 15 B4
Leu, *Romania* 43 F9
Leucadia, *U.S.A.* 117 M9
Leucate, *France* 20 F7
Leucate, Étang de, *France* 20 F7
Leuk, *Switz.* 25 J3
Leuşeni, *Moldova* 43 D13
Leuser, G., *Indonesia* 62 D1
Leutkirch, *Germany* 25 H6
Leuven, *Belgium* 17 D4
Leuze-en-Hainaut, *Belgium* 17 D3
Lev Tolstoy, *Russia* 46 F10
Levádhia, *Greece* 38 C4
Levan, *Albania* 40 F3
Levanger, *Norway* 8 E14
Levant, Î. du, *France* 21 E10
Lévanto, *Italy* 28 D6
Lévanzo, *Italy* 30 D5
Levelland, *U.S.A.* 113 J3
Leven, *U.K.* 14 E6
Leven, L., *U.K.* 14 E5
Leven, Toraka, *Madag.* 89 A8
Leveque C., *Australia* 92 C3
Leverano, *Italy* 31 B10
Leverkusen, *Germany* 24 D3
Levice, *Slovak Rep.* 27 C11
Lévico Terme, *Italy* 29 C8
Levie, *France* 21 G13
Levier, *France* 19 F13
Levin, *N.Z.* 91 J5
Lévis, *Canada* 103 C5
Levis, L., *Canada* 104 A5

Levítha, Greece 39 D8
Levittown, N.Y., U.S.A. 111 F11
Levittown, Pa., U.S.A. 111 F10
Levka, Bulgaria 41 E10
Levkás, Greece 38 C2
Levkás □, Greece 38 C2
Levkímmi, Greece 36 B4
Levkímmi, Ákra, Greece 36 B4
Levkôsia = Nicosia, Cyprus 36 D12
Levoča, Slovak Rep. 27 B13
Levroux, France 19 F8
Levski, Bulgaria 41 C9
Levskigrad = Karlovo, Bulgaria 41 D8
Levuka, Fiji 91 C8
Lewes, U.K. 13 G8
Lewes, U.S.A. 108 F8
Lewin Brzeski, Poland 45 H4
Lewis, U.K. 14 C2
Lewis →, U.S.A. 116 E4
Lewis, Butt of, U.K. 14 C2
Lewis Ra., Australia 92 D4
Lewis Range, U.S.A. 114 C7
Lewis Run, U.S.A. 110 E6
Lewisburg, Pa., U.S.A. 110 F8
Lewisburg, Tenn., U.S.A. 109 H2
Lewisburg, W. Va., U.S.A. 108 G5
Lewisporte, Canada 103 C8
Lewiston, Idaho, U.S.A. 114 C5
Lewiston, Maine, U.S.A. 109 C11
Lewiston, N.Y., U.S.A. 110 C5
Lewistown, Mont., U.S.A. 114 C9
Lewistown, Pa., U.S.A. 110 F7
Lexington, Ill., U.S.A. 112 E10
Lexington, Ky., U.S.A. 108 F3
Lexington, Mich., U.S.A. 110 C2
Lexington, Mo., U.S.A. 112 F8
Lexington, N.C., U.S.A. 109 H5
Lexington, N.Y., U.S.A. 111 D10
Lexington, Nebr., U.S.A. 112 E5
Lexington, Ohio, U.S.A. 110 F2
Lexington, Tenn., U.S.A. 109 H1
Lexington, Va., U.S.A. 108 G6
Lexington Park, U.S.A. 108 F7
Leyburn, U.K. 12 C6
Leye, China 58 E6
Leyland, U.K. 12 D5
Leyre →, France 20 D2
Leyte □, Phil. 61 F6
Leyte Gulf, Phil. 61 F6
Leżajsk, Poland 45 H9
Lezay, France 20 B3
Lezhë, Albania 40 E3
Lezhi, China 58 B5
Lézignan-Corbières, France 20 E6
Lezoux, France 20 C7
Lgov, Russia 47 G8
Lhasa, China 60 D4
Lhazê, China 60 D3
Lhokkruet, Indonesia 62 D1
Lhokseumawe, Indonesia 62 C1
L'Hospitalet de Llobregat, Spain 32 D7
Li, Thailand 64 D2
Li Shui →, China 59 C9
Li Xian, Gansu, China 56 G3
Li Xian, Hebei, China 56 E8
Li Xian, Hunan, China 59 C8
Liádhoi, Greece 39 E8
Liancheng, China 59 E11
Lianga, Phil. 61 G7
Liangcheng,
Nei Monggol Zizhiqu, China 56 D7
Liangcheng, Shandong, China 57 G10
Liangdang, China 56 H4
Lianghe, China 58 E2
Lianghekou, China 58 C7
Liangping, China 58 B6
Liangpran, Indonesia 62 D4
Lianhua, China 59 D9
Lianjiang, Fujian, China 59 D12
Lianjiang, Guangdong, China 59 G8
Lianping, China 59 E10
Lianshan, China 59 E9
Lianshanguan, China 57 D12
Lianshui, China 57 H10
Lianyuan, China 59 D8
Lianyungang, China 57 G10
Lianzhou, China 59 E9
Liao He →, China 57 D11
Liaocheng, China 56 F8
Liaodong Bandao, China 57 E12
Liaodong Wan, China 57 D11
Liaoning □, China 57 D12
Liaoyang, China 57 D12
Liaoyuan, China 57 C13
Liaozhong, China 57 D12
Liapádhes, Greece 38 B1
Liard →, Canada 104 A4
Liard River, Canada 104 B3
Liari, Pakistan 68 G2
Libau = Liepāja, Latvia 9 H19
Libby, U.S.A. 114 B6
Libenge, Dem. Rep. of
the Congo 84 D3
Liberal, U.S.A. 113 G4
Liberec, Czech Rep. 26 A8
Liberia, Costa Rica 120 D2
Liberia ■, W. Afr. 82 D3
Liberty, Mo., U.S.A. 112 F7
Liberty, N.Y., U.S.A. 111 E10
Liberty, Pa., U.S.A. 110 E7
Liberty, Tex., U.S.A. 113 K7
Libiąż, Poland 45 H6
Lîbîya, Sahrâ', Africa 79 C10
Libo, China 58 E6
Libobo, Tanjung, Indonesia 63 E7
Libode, S. Africa 89 E4
Libohovë, Albania 40 F4
Libourne, France 20 D3
Libramont, Belgium 17 E5
Librazhd, Albania 40 E4
Libreville, Gabon 84 D1
Libya ■, N. Afr. 79 C9
Libyan Desert = Lîbîya, Sahrâ',
Africa 79 C10
Libyan Plateau = Ed-Déffa,
Egypt 80 A2
Licantén, Chile 126 D1
Licata, Italy 30 E6
Lice, Turkey 73 C9
Licheng, China 56 F7
Lichfield, U.K. 13 E6
Lichinga, Mozam. 87 E4
Lichtenburg, S. Africa 88 D4
Lichtenfels, Germany 25 E7
Lichuan, Hubei, China 58 B7
Lichuan, Jiangxi, China 59 D11
Licking →, U.S.A. 108 F3
Licosa, Punta, Italy 31 B7
Lida, Belarus 9 K21
Liden, Sweden 10 B10
Lidhoríkion, Greece 38 C4
Lidhult, Sweden 11 H7
Lidköping, Sweden 11 F7
Lido, Italy 29 C9
Lido, Niger 83 C5
Lido di Roma = Óstia, Lido di,
Italy 29 G9
Lidzbark, Poland 45 E6
Lidzbark Warmiński, Poland 44 D7
Liebenwalde, Germany 24 C9
Lieberose, Germany 24 D10
Liebig, Mt., Australia 92 D5
Liebling, Romania 42 E6
Liechtenstein ■, Europe 25 H5
Liège, Belgium 17 D5
Liège □, Belgium 17 D5
Liegnitz = Legnica, Poland 45 G3
Lienart, Dem. Rep. of the Congo 86 B2
Lienyünchiangshih =
Lianyungang, China 57 G10
Lienz, Austria 26 E5
Liepāja, Latvia 9 H19
Liepāja □, Latvia 44 B8
Liepājas ezers, Latvia 44 B8
Lier, Belgium 17 C4
Liernais, France 19 E11
Lieşti, Romania 43 E12
Liévin, France 19 B9
Lièvre →, Canada 102 C4
Liezen, Austria 26 D7
Liffey →, Ireland 15 C5
Lifford, Ireland 15 B4
Liffré, France 18 D5
Lifudzin, Russia 54 B7
Ligao, Phil. 61 E5
Lightning Ridge, Australia 95 D4
Lignano Sabbiadoro, Italy 29 C10
Ligny-en-Barrois, France 19 D12
Ligonier, U.S.A. 110 F5
Ligoúrion, Greece 38 D5
Ligueil, France 18 E7
Liguria □, Italy 28 D5
Ligurian Sea, Medit. S. 6 G7
Lihou Reefs and Cays, Australia 94 B5
Lihue, U.S.A. 106 H15
Lijiang, China 58 D3
Likasi, Dem. Rep. of the Congo 87 E2
Likenäs, Sweden 10 D8
Likhoslavl, Russia 46 D8
Likhovskoy, Russia 47 H11
Likoma I., Malawi 87 E3
Likumburu, Tanzania 87 D4
L'Île-Bouchard, France 18 E7
L'Île-Rousse, France 21 F12
Liling, China 59 D9
Lilla Edet, Sweden 11 F6
Lille, France 19 B10
Lille Bælt, Denmark 11 J3
Lillebonne, France 18 C7
Lillehammer, Norway 9 F14
Lillesand, Norway 9 G13
Lillhärdal, Sweden 10 C8
Lillian Pt., Australia 93 E4
Lillo, Spain 34 F7
Lillooet, Canada 104 C4
Lillooet →, Canada 104 D4
Lilongwe, Malawi 87 E3
Liloy, Phil. 63 C6
Lim →, Bos.-H. 40 C3
Lima, Indonesia 63 E7
Lima, Peru 124 F3
Lima, Mont., U.S.A. 114 D7
Lima, Ohio, U.S.A. 108 E3
Lima →, Portugal 34 D2
Liman, Indonesia 63 G14
Liman, Russia 49 H8
Limanowa, Poland 45 J7
Limassol, Cyprus 36 E12
Limavady, U.K. 15 A5
Limay →, Argentina 128 D3
Limay Mahuida, Argentina 126 D2
Limbach-Oberfrohna, Germany 24 E8
Limbang, Brunei 62 D5
Limbara, Mte., Italy 30 B2
Limbaži, Latvia 9 H21
Limbdi, India 68 H4
Limbe, Cameroon 83 E6
Limburg, Germany 25 E4
Limburg □, Belgium 17 C5
Limburg □, Neths. 17 C5
Limedsforsen, Sweden 10 D7
Limeira, Brazil 127 A6
Limenária, Greece 41 F8
Limerick, Ireland 15 D3
Limerick, U.S.A. 111 C14
Limerick □, Ireland 15 D3
Limestone, U.S.A. 110 D6
Limestone →, Canada 105 B10
Limfjorden, Denmark 11 H3
Limia = Lima →, Portugal 34 D2
Limín Khersonísou, Greece 39 F7
Limingen, Norway 8 D15
Limmared, Sweden 11 G7
Limmen Bight, Australia 94 A2
Limmen Bight →, Australia 94 B2
Límni, Greece 38 C5
Límnos, Greece 39 B7
Limoges, Canada 111 A9
Limoges, France 20 C5
Limón, Costa Rica 120 E3
Limon, U.S.A. 112 F3
Limone Piemonte, Italy 28 D4
Limousin, France 20 C5
Limousin, Plateaux du, France 20 C5
Limoux, France 20 E6
Limpopo →, Africa 89 D5
Limuru, Kenya 86 C4
Lin Xian, China 56 F6
Lin'an, China 59 B12
Linapacan I., Phil. 61 F3
Linapacan Str., Phil. 61 F3
Linares, Chile 126 D1
Linares, Mexico 119 C5
Linares, Spain 35 G7
Linaro, Capo, Italy 29 F8
Línas Mte., Italy 30 C1
Lincang, China 58 F3
Lincheng, China 56 F8
Linchuan, China 59 D11
Lincoln, Argentina 126 C3
Lincoln, N.Z. 91 K4
Lincoln, U.K. 12 D7
Lincoln, Calif., U.S.A. 116 G5
Lincoln, Ill., U.S.A. 112 E10
Lincoln, Kans., U.S.A. 112 F5
Lincoln, Maine, U.S.A. 109 C11
Lincoln, N.H., U.S.A. 111 B13
Lincoln, N. Mex., U.S.A. 115 K11
Lincoln, Nebr., U.S.A. 112 E6
Lincoln City, U.S.A. 114 D1
Lincoln Hav = Lincoln Sea,
Arctic 4 A5
Lincoln Sea, Arctic 4 A5
Lincolnshire □, U.K. 12 D7
Lincolnshire Wolds, U.K. 12 D7
Lincolnton, U.S.A. 109 H5
L'Incudine, France 21 G13
Lind, U.S.A. 114 C4
Linda, U.S.A. 116 F5
Lindau, Germany 25 H5
Linden, Guyana 124 B7
Linden, Ala., U.S.A. 109 J2
Linden, Calif., U.S.A. 116 G5
Linden, Tex., U.S.A. 113 J7
Lindenhurst, U.S.A. 111 F11
Lindesberg, Sweden 10 E9
Lindesnes, Norway 9 H12
Líndhos, Greece 36 C10
Líndhos, Ákra, Greece 36 C10
Lindi, Tanzania 87 D4
Lindi □, Tanzania 87 D4
Lindi →, Dem. Rep. of
the Congo 86 B2
Lindö, Sweden 11 F10
Lindome, Sweden 11 G6
Lindoso, Portugal 34 D2
Lindow, Germany 24 C8
Lindsay, Canada 102 D4
Lindsay, Calif., U.S.A. 116 J7
Lindsay, Okla., U.S.A. 113 H6
Lindsborg, U.S.A. 112 F6
Lindsdal, Sweden 11 H10
Linesville, U.S.A. 110 E4
Linfen, China 56 F6
Ling Xian, Hunan, China 59 D9
Ling Xian, Shandong, China 56 F9
Lingao, China 64 C7
Lingayen, Phil. 63 A6
Lingayen G., Phil. 61 C4
Lingbi, China 57 H9
Lingbo, Sweden 10 C10
Lingchuan, Guangxi Zhuangzu,
China 59 E8
Lingchuan, Shanxi, China 56 G7
Lingen, Germany 24 C3
Lingga, Indonesia 62 E2
Lingga, Kepulauan, Indonesia 62 E2
Lingga Arch. = Lingga,
Kepulauan, Indonesia 62 E2
Linghem, Sweden 11 F9
Lingle, U.S.A. 112 D2
Lingqiu, China 56 E8
Lingshan, China 58 F7
Lingshi, China 56 F6
Lingshou, China 56 E8
Lingshui, China 64 C8
Lingtai, China 56 G4
Linguère, Senegal 82 B1
Lingui, China 59 E8
Lingwu, China 56 E4
Lingyuan, China 57 D10
Lingyun, China 58 E6
Linhai, China 59 C13
Linhares, Brazil 125 G10
Linhe, China 56 D4
Linjiang, China 57 D14
Linköping, Sweden 11 F9
Linkou, China 57 B16
Linli, China 59 C8
Linnhe, L., U.K. 14 E3
Linqi, China 56 G7
Linqing, China 56 F8
Linqu, China 57 F10
Linru, China 56 G7
Lins, Brazil 127 A6
Linshui, China 58 B6
Linta →, Madag. 89 D7
Linth →, Switz. 25 H5
Linthal, Switz. 25 J5
Linton, Ind., U.S.A. 108 F2
Linton, N. Dak., U.S.A. 112 B4
Lintong, China 56 G5
Linwood, Canada 110 C4
Linwu, China 59 E9
Linxi, China 57 C10
Linxia, China 60 C5
Linxiang, China 59 C9
Linyanti →, Africa 88 B4
Linyi, China 57 G10
Linz, Austria 26 C7
Linz, Germany 24 E3
Linzhenzhen, China 56 F5
Linzi, China 57 F10
Lion, G. du, France 20 E7
Lionárisso, Cyprus 36 D13
Lioni, Italy 31 B8
Lions, G. of = Lion, G. du,
France 20 E7
Lion's Den, Zimbabwe 87 F3
Lion's Head, Canada 110 B3
Liozno = Lyozna, Belarus 46 E6
Lipa, Phil. 61 E4
Lipali, Mozam. 87 F4
Lipany, Slovak Rep. 27 B13
Lípari, Italy 31 D7
Lípari, I., Italy 31 D7
Lípari, Is. = Eólie, Ís., Italy 31 D7
Lipcani, Moldova 43 B11
Lipetsk, Russia 47 F10
Lipiany, Poland 45 E1
Liping, China 58 D7
Lipkany = Lipcani, Moldova 43 B11
Lipljan, Kosovo, Yug. 40 D5
Lipník nad Bečvou, Czech Rep. 27 B10
Lipno, Poland 45 F6
Lipova, Romania 42 D6
Lipovcy Manzovka, Russia 54 B6
Lipovets, Ukraine 47 H5
Lippe →, Germany 24 D2
Lippstadt, Germany 24 D4
Lipscomb, U.S.A. 113 G4
Lipsk, Poland 44 E10
Lipsko, Poland 45 G8
Lipsói, Greece 39 D8
Liptovský Hrádok, Slovak Rep. 27 B12
Liptovský Milkuláš, Slovak Rep. 27 B12
Lipu, China 59 E8
Lira, Uganda 86 B3
Liri →, Italy 30 A6
Liria = Llíria, Spain 33 F4
Lisala, Dem. Rep. of the Congo 84 D4
Lisboa, Portugal 35 G1
Lisboa □, Portugal 35 F1
Lisbon = Lisboa, Portugal 35 G1
Lisbon, N. Dak., U.S.A. 112 B6
Lisbon, N.H., U.S.A. 111 B13
Lisbon, Ohio, U.S.A. 110 F4
Lisbon Falls, U.S.A. 109 D10
Lisburn, U.K. 15 B5
Liscannor B., Ireland 15 D2
Liscia →, Italy 30 A2
Lishe Jiang →, China 58 E3
Lishi, China 56 F6
Lishu, China 57 C13
Lishui, Jiangsu, China 59 B12
Lishui, Zhejiang, China 59 C12
Lisianski I., Pac. Oc. 96 E10
Lisichansk = Lysychansk,
Ukraine 47 H10
Lisieux, France 18 C7
Liski, Russia 47 G10
L'Isle-Jourdain, Gers, France 20 E5
L'Isle-Jourdain, Vienne, France 20 B4
L'Isle-sur-la-Sorgue, France 21 E9
Lisle-sur-Tarn, France 20 E5
Lismore, Australia 95 D5
Lismore, Ireland 15 D4
Lista, Norway 9 G12
Lister, Mt., Antarctica 5 D11
Liston, Australia 95 D5
Listowel, Canada 102 D3
Listowel, Ireland 15 D2
Lit, Sweden 10 A8
Lit-et-Mixe, France 20 D2
Litang, Guangxi Zhuangzu,
China 58 F7
Litang, Sichuan, China 58 B3
Litang Qu →, China 58 C3
Litani →, Lebanon 75 B4
Litchfield, Calif., U.S.A. 116 E6
Litchfield, Conn., U.S.A. 111 E11
Litchfield, Ill., U.S.A. 112 F10
Litchfield, Minn., U.S.A. 112 C7
Liteni, Romania 43 C11
Líthinon, Ákra, Greece 36 E6
Lithuania ■, Europe 9 J20
Litija, Slovenia 29 B11
Lititz, U.S.A. 111 F8
Litókhoron, Greece 40 F6
Litoměřice, Czech Rep. 26 A7
Litomyšl, Czech Rep. 27 B9
Litschau, Austria 26 C8
Little Abaco I., Bahamas 120 A4
Little Barrier I., N.Z. 91 G5
Little Belt Mts., U.S.A. 114 C8
Little Blue →, U.S.A. 112 F6
Little Buffalo →, Canada 104 A6
Little Cayman, Cayman Is. 120 C3
Little Churchill →, Canada 105 B9
Little Colorado →, U.S.A. 115 H8
Little Current, Canada 102 C3
Little Current →, Canada 102 B3
Little Falls, Minn., U.S.A. 112 C7
Little Falls, N.Y., U.S.A. 111 C10
Little Fork →, U.S.A. 112 A8
Little Grand Rapids, Canada 105 C9
Little Humboldt →, U.S.A. 114 F5
Little Inagua I., Bahamas 121 B5
Little Karoo, S. Africa 88 E3
Little Lake, U.S.A. 117 K9
Little Laut Is. = Laut Kecil,
Kepulauan, Indonesia 62 E5
Little Mecatina = Petit-
Mécatina →, Canada 103 B8
Little Minch, U.K. 14 D2
Little Missouri →, U.S.A. 112 B3
Little Ouse →, U.K. 13 E9
Little Rann, India 68 H4
Little Red →, U.S.A. 113 H9
Little River, N.Z. 91 K4
Little Rock, U.S.A. 113 H8
Little Ruaha →, Tanzania 86 D4
Little Sable Pt., U.S.A. 108 D2
Little Scarcies →, S. Leone 82 D2
Little Sioux →, U.S.A. 112 E6
Little Smoky →, Canada 104 C5
Little Snake →, U.S.A. 114 F9
Little Valley, U.S.A. 110 D6
Little Wabash →, U.S.A. 108 G1
Little White →, U.S.A. 112 D4
Littlefield, U.S.A. 113 J3
Littlehampton, U.K. 13 G7
Littleton, U.S.A. 111 B13
Litvinov, Czech Rep. 26 A6
Liu He →, China 57 D11
Liu Jiang →, China 58 F7
Liuba, China 56 H4
Liucheng, China 58 E7
Liugou, China 57 D10
Liuhe, China 57 C13
Liuheng Dao, China 59 C14
Liujiang, China 58 E7
Liukang Tenggaja = Sabalana,
Kepulauan, Indonesia 63 F5
Liuli, Tanzania 87 E3
Liuwa Plain, Zambia 85 G4
Liuyang, China 59 C9
Liuzhou, China 58 E7
Liuzhuang, China 57 H11
Livada, Romania 42 C8
Livadherón, Greece 40 F5
Livadhia, Cyprus 36 E12
Livádhion, Greece 38 A4
Livarot, France 18 D7
Live Oak, Calif., U.S.A. 116 F5
Live Oak, Fla., U.S.A. 109 K4
Liveras, Cyprus 36 D11
Livermore, U.S.A. 116 H5
Livermore, Mt., U.S.A. 113 K2
Livermore Falls, U.S.A. 109 C11
Liverpool, Canada 103 D7
Liverpool, U.K. 12 D4
Liverpool, U.S.A. 111 C8
Liverpool Bay, U.K. 12 D4
Livigno, Italy 28 B7
Livingston, Guatemala 120 C2
Livingston, U.K. 14 F5
Livingston, Ala., U.S.A. 109 J1
Livingston, Calif., U.S.A. 116 H6
Livingston, Mont., U.S.A. 114 D8
Livingston, S.C., U.S.A. 109 J5
Livingston, Tenn., U.S.A. 109 G3
Livingston, Tex., U.S.A. 113 K7
Livingston, L., U.S.A. 113 K7
Livingston Manor, U.S.A. 111 E10
Livingstone, Zambia 87 F2
Livingstone Mts., Tanzania 87 D3
Livingstonia, Malawi 87 E3
Livno, Bos.-H. 42 G2
Livny, Russia 47 F9
Livonia, Mich., U.S.A. 108 D4
Livonia, N.Y., U.S.A. 110 D7
Livorno, Italy 28 E7
Livramento, Brazil 127 C4
Livron-sur-Drôme, France 21 D8
Liwale, Tanzania 87 D4
Liwiec →, Poland 45 F8
Lixi, China 58 D3
Lixian, China 58 B4
Lixoúrion, Greece 38 C2
Liyang, China 59 B12
Lizard I., Australia 94 A4
Lizard Pt., U.K. 13 H2
Lizzano, Italy 31 B10
Ljig, Serbia, Yug. 40 B4
Ljubija, Bos.-H. 29 D13
Ljubinje, Bos.-H. 40 D2
Ljubljana, Slovenia 29 B11
Ljubno, Slovenia 29 B11
Ljubovija, Serbia, Yug. 40 B3
Ljugarn, Sweden 11 G12
Ljung, Sweden 11 G7
Ljungan →, Sweden 10 B11
Ljungaverk, Sweden 10 B10
Ljungby, Sweden 9 H15
Ljungbyholm, Sweden 11 H10
Ljungdalen, Sweden 10 B6
Ljungsbro, Sweden 11 F9
Ljungskile, Sweden 11 F5
Ljusdal, Sweden 10 C10

Ljusfallshammar, *Sweden* 11 F9
Ljusnan →, *Sweden* 10 C11
Ljusne, *Sweden* 10 C11
Ljutomer, *Slovenia* 29 B13
Llagostera, *Spain* 32 D7
Llancanelo, Salina, *Argentina* 126 D2
Llandeilo, *U.K.* 13 F4
Llandovery, *U.K.* 13 F4
Llandrindod Wells, *U.K.* 13 E4
Llandudno, *U.K.* 12 D4
Llanelli, *U.K.* 13 F3
Llanes, *Spain* 34 B6
Llangollen, *U.K.* 12 E4
Llanidloes, *U.K.* 13 E4
Llano, *U.S.A.* 113 K5
Llano →, *U.S.A.* 113 K5
Llano Estacado, *U.S.A.* 113 J3
Llanos, *S. Amer.* 122 C3
Llanquihue, L., *Chile* 128 E1
Llanwrtyd Wells, *U.K.* 13 E4
Llebeig, C. des, *Spain* 37 B9
Lleida, *Spain* 32 D5
Lleida □, *Spain* 32 C6
Llentrisca, C., *Spain* 37 C7
Llera, *Mexico* 119 C5
Llerena, *Spain* 35 G5
Lleyn Peninsula, *U.K.* 12 E3
Llico, *Chile* 126 C1
Lliria, *Spain* 33 F4
Llobregat →, *Spain* 32 D7
Llodio, *Spain* 32 B2
Lloret de Mar, *Spain* 32 D7
Lloyd B., *Australia* 94 A3
Lloyd L., *Canada* 105 B7
Lloydminster, *Canada* 105 C7
Llucena del Cid, *Spain* 32 E4
Llucmajor, *Spain* 37 B9
Llullaillaco, Volcán, *S. Amer.* 126 A2
Lo →, *Vietnam* 64 B5
Loa, *U.S.A.* 115 G8
Loa →, *Chile* 126 A1
Loaita I., *S. China Sea* 62 B4
Loange →, *Dem. Rep. of the Congo* 84 E4
Loano, *Italy* 28 D5
Lobatse, *Botswana* 88 D4
Löbau, *Germany* 24 D10
Lobenstein, *Germany* 24 E7
Lobería, *Argentina* 126 D4
Löberöd, *Sweden* 11 J7
Łobez, *Poland* 44 E2
Lobito, *Angola* 85 G2
Lobo →, *Ivory C.* 82 D3
Lobos, *Argentina* 126 D4
Lobos, I., *Mexico* 118 B2
Lobos, I. de, *Canary Is.* 37 F6
Łobżenica, *Poland* 45 E4
Loc Binh, *Vietnam* 64 B6
Loc Ninh, *Vietnam* 65 G6
Locarno, *Switz.* 25 J4
Loch Baghasdail = Lochboisdale, *U.K.* 14 D1
Loch Garman = Wexford, *Ireland* 15 D5
Loch Nam Madadh = Lochmaddy, *U.K.* 14 D1
Lochaber, *U.K.* 14 E3
Locharbriggs, *U.K.* 14 F5
Lochboisdale, *U.K.* 14 D1
Loche, L. La, *Canada* 105 B7
Lochem, *Neths.* 17 B6
Loches, *France* 18 E7
Lochgilphead, *U.K.* 14 E3
Lochinver, *U.K.* 14 C3
Lochmaddy, *U.K.* 14 D1
Lochnagar, *Australia* 94 C4
Lochnagar, *U.K.* 14 E5
Łochów, *Poland* 45 F8
Lochy, L., *U.K.* 14 E4
Lock, *Australia* 95 E2
Lock Haven, *U.S.A.* 110 E7
Lockeford, *U.S.A.* 116 G5
Lockeport, *Canada* 103 D6
Lockerbie, *U.K.* 14 F5
Lockhart, *U.S.A.* 113 L6
Lockhart, L., *Australia* 93 F2
Lockhart River, *Australia* 94 A3
Lockney, *U.S.A.* 113 H4
Lockport, *U.S.A.* 110 C6
Locminé, *France* 18 E4
Locri, *Italy* 31 D9
Locronan, *France* 18 D2
Lod, *Israel* 75 D3
Lodeinoye Pole, *Russia* 46 B7
Lodève, *France* 20 E7
Lodge Bay, *Canada* 103 B8
Lodge Grass, *U.S.A.* 114 D10
Lodgepole Cr. →, *U.S.A.* 112 E2
Lodhran, *Pakistan* 68 E4
Lodi, *Italy* 28 C6
Lodi, *Calif., U.S.A.* 116 G5
Lodi, *Ohio, U.S.A.* 110 E3
Lodja, *Dem. Rep. of the Congo* 86 C1
Lodosa, *Spain* 32 C2
Lödöse, *Sweden* 11 F6
Lodwar, *Kenya* 86 B4
Łódź, *Poland* 45 G6
Łódzkie □, *Poland* 45 G6
Loei, *Thailand* 64 D3
Loengo, *Dem. Rep. of the Congo* 86 C2
Loeriesfontein, *S. Africa* 88 E2
Lofa →, *Liberia* 83 D2
Lofer, *Austria* 26 D5
Lofoten, *Norway* 8 B15
Lofsdalen, *Sweden* 10 B7
Lofsen →, *Sweden* 10 B7
Loftahammar, *Sweden* 11 G10
Loga, *Niger* 83 C5
Logan, *Iowa, U.S.A.* 112 E7
Logan, *Ohio, U.S.A.* 108 F4
Logan, *Utah, U.S.A.* 114 F8
Logan, *W. Va., U.S.A.* 108 G5
Logan, Mt., *Canada* 100 B5
Logandale, *U.S.A.* 117 J12
Logansport, *Ind., U.S.A.* 108 E2
Logansport, *La., U.S.A.* 113 K8
Logirim, *Sudan* 81 G3
Logo, *Sudan* 81 F3
Logone →, *Chad* 79 F9
Logroño, *Spain* 32 C2
Logrosán, *Spain* 35 F5
Løgstør, *Denmark* 11 H3
Løgumkloster, *Denmark* 11 J2
Lohals, *Denmark* 11 J4
Lohardaga, *India* 69 H11
Loharia, *India* 68 H6
Loharu, *India* 68 E6
Lohja, *Finland* 9 F21
Löhne, *Germany* 24 C4
Lohr, *Germany* 25 F5
Lohri Wah →, *Pakistan* 68 F2
Loi-kaw, *Burma* 67 K20
Loimaa, *Finland* 9 F20
Loir →, *France* 18 E6
Loir-et-Cher □, *France* 18 E8
Loire □, *France* 21 C8
Loire →, *France* 18 E4
Loire-Atlantique □, *France* 18 E5
Loiret □, *France* 19 E9
Loitz, *Germany* 24 B9
Loja, *Ecuador* 124 D3
Loja, *Spain* 35 H6
Loji = Kawasi, *Indonesia* 63 E7
Løjt Kirkeby, *Denmark* 11 J3
Lojung, *China* 58 E7
Loka, *Sudan* 81 G3
Lokandu, *Dem. Rep. of the Congo* 86 C2
Lokeren, *Belgium* 17 C3
Lokgwabe, *Botswana* 88 C3
Lokhvitsa, *Ukraine* 47 G7
Lokichokio, *Kenya* 86 B3
Lokitaung, *Kenya* 86 B4
Lokkan tekojärvi, *Finland* 8 C22
Løkken, *Denmark* 11 G3
Loknya, *Russia* 46 D6
Loko, *Nigeria* 83 D6
Lokoja, *Nigeria* 83 D6
Lokot, *Russia* 47 F8
Lol →, *Sudan* 81 F2
Lola, *Guinea* 82 D3
Lola, Mt., *U.S.A.* 116 F6
Lolibai, Gebel, *Sudan* 81 G3
Lolimi, *Sudan* 81 G3
Loliondo, *Tanzania* 86 C4
Lolland, *Denmark* 11 K5
Lollar, *Germany* 24 E4
Lolo, *U.S.A.* 114 C6
Lolodorf, *Cameroon* 83 E7
Lom, *Bulgaria* 40 C7
Lom →, *Bulgaria* 40 C7
Lom Kao, *Thailand* 64 D3
Lom Sak, *Thailand* 64 D3
Loma, *U.S.A.* 114 C8
Loma Linda, *U.S.A.* 117 L9
Lomami →, *Dem. Rep. of the Congo* 86 B1
Lomas de Zamóra, *Argentina* 126 C4
Lombadina, *Australia* 92 C3
Lombárdia □, *Italy* 28 C6
Lombardy = Lombárdia □, *Italy* 28 C6
Lombez, *France* 20 E4
Lomblen, *Indonesia* 63 F6
Lombok, *Indonesia* 62 F5
Lomé, *Togo* 83 D5
Lomela, *Dem. Rep. of the Congo* 84 E4
Lomela →, *Dem. Rep. of the Congo* 84 E4
Lomianki, *Poland* 45 F7
Lomma, *Sweden* 11 J7
Lommel, *Belgium* 17 C5
Lomond, *Canada* 104 C6
Lomond, L., *U.K.* 14 E4
Lomphat, *Cambodia* 64 F6
Lompobatang, *Indonesia* 63 F5
Lompoc, *U.S.A.* 117 L6
Łomża, *Poland* 45 E9
Loncoche, *Chile* 128 D2
Londa, *India* 66 M9
Londiani, *Kenya* 86 C4
Londinières, *France* 18 C8
London, *Canada* 102 D3
London, *U.K.* 13 F7
London, *Ky., U.S.A.* 108 G3
London, *Ohio, U.S.A.* 108 F4
London, Greater □, *U.K.* 13 F7
Londonderry, *U.K.* 15 B4
Londonderry □, *U.K.* 15 B4
Londonderry, C., *Australia* 92 B4
Londonderry, I., *Chile* 128 H2
Londres, *Argentina* 128 B3
Londrina, *Brazil* 127 A5
Lone Pine, *U.S.A.* 116 J8
Lonely Mine, *Zimbabwe* 89 B4
Long B., *U.S.A.* 109 J6
Long Beach, *Calif., U.S.A.* 117 M8
Long Beach, *N.Y., U.S.A.* 111 F11
Long Beach, *Wash., U.S.A.* 116 D2
Long Branch, *U.S.A.* 111 F11
Long Creek, *U.S.A.* 114 D4
Long Eaton, *U.K.* 12 E6
Long I., *Australia* 94 C4
Long I., *Bahamas* 121 B4
Long I., *Canada* 102 B4
Long I., *Ireland* 15 E2
Long I., *U.S.A.* 111 F11
Long Island Sd., *U.S.A.* 111 E12
Long L., *Canada* 102 C2
Long Lake, *U.S.A.* 111 C10
Long Point B., *Canada* 110 D4
Long Prairie →, *U.S.A.* 112 C7
Long Pt., *Canada* 110 D4
Long Range Mts., *Canada* 103 C8
Long Reef, *Australia* 92 B4
Long Spruce, *Canada* 105 B10
Long Str. = Longa, Proliv, *Russia* 4 C16
Long Thanh, *Vietnam* 65 G6
Long Xian, *China* 56 G4
Long Xuyen, *Vietnam* 65 G5
Longá, *Greece* 38 E3
Longa, Proliv, *Russia* 4 C16
Long'an, *China* 58 F6
Longarone, *Italy* 29 B9
Longbenton, *U.K.* 12 B6
Longboat Key, *U.S.A.* 109 M4
Longchang, *China* 58 C5
Longchi, *China* 58 C4
Longchuan, *Guangdong, China* 59 E10
Longchuan, *Yunnan, China* 58 E1
Longde, *China* 56 G4
Longeau, *France* 19 E12
Longford, *Australia* 94 G4
Longford, *Ireland* 15 C4
Longford □, *Ireland* 15 C4
Longhai, *China* 59 E11
Longhua, *China* 57 D9
Longhui, *China* 59 D8
Longido, *Tanzania* 86 C4
Longiram, *Indonesia* 62 E5
Longkou, *Jiangxi, China* 59 D10
Longkou, *Shandong, China* 57 F11
Longlac, *Canada* 102 C2
Longli, *China* 58 D6
Longlin, *China* 58 E5
Longling, *China* 58 E2
Longmeadow, *U.S.A.* 111 D12
Longmen, *China* 59 F10
Longming, *China* 58 F6
Longmont, *U.S.A.* 112 E2
Longnan, *China* 59 E10
Longnawan, *Indonesia* 62 D4
Longobucco, *Italy* 31 C9
Longquan, *China* 59 C12
Longreach, *Australia* 94 C3
Longshan, *China* 58 C7
Longsheng, *China* 59 E8
Longué-Jumelles, *France* 18 E6
Longueau, *France* 19 C9
Longueuil, *Canada* 111 A11
Longuyon, *France* 19 C12
Longvic, *France* 19 E12
Longview, *Tex., U.S.A.* 113 J7
Longview, *Wash., U.S.A.* 116 D4
Longwy, *France* 19 C12
Longxi, *China* 56 G3
Longyan, *China* 59 E11
Longyou, *China* 59 C12
Longzhou, *China* 58 F6
Lonigo, *Italy* 29 C8
Löningen, *Germany* 24 C3
Lonja →, *Croatia* 29 C13
Lonoke, *U.S.A.* 113 H9
Lonquimay, *Chile* 128 D2
Lons-le-Saunier, *France* 19 F12
Lönsboda, *Sweden* 11 H8
Looe, *U.K.* 13 G3
Lookout, C., *Canada* 102 A3
Lookout, C., *U.S.A.* 109 H7
Loolmalasin, *Tanzania* 86 C4
Loon →, *Alta., Canada* 104 B5
Loon →, *Man., Canada* 105 B8
Loon Lake, *Canada* 105 C7
Loongana, *Australia* 93 F4
Loop Hd., *Ireland* 15 D2
Lop Buri, *Thailand* 64 E3
Lop Nor = Lop Nur, *China* 60 B4
Lop Nur, *China* 60 B4
Lopare, *Bos.-H.* 42 F3
Lopatin, *Russia* 49 J8
Lopatina, Gora, *Russia* 51 D15
Lopaye, *Sudan* 81 F3
Lopez, *Phil.* 61 E5
Lopez, *U.S.A.* 111 E8
Lopez, C., *Gabon* 84 E1
Lopphavet, *Norway* 8 A19
Lora →, *Afghan.* 66 D4
Lora, Hāmūn-i-, *Pakistan* 66 E4
Lora Cr. →, *Australia* 95 D2
Lora del Río, *Spain* 35 H5
Lorain, *U.S.A.* 110 E2
Loralai, *Pakistan* 68 D3
Lorca, *Spain* 33 H3
Lord Howe I., *Pac. Oc.* 96 L7
Lord Howe Ridge, *Pac. Oc.* 96 L8
Lordsburg, *U.S.A.* 115 K9
Lorestan □, *Iran* 71 C6
Loreto, *Brazil* 125 E9
Loreto, *Italy* 29 E10
Loreto, *Mexico* 118 B2
Lorgues, *France* 21 E10
Lorhosso, *Burkina Faso* 82 C4
Lorient, *France* 18 E3
Lőrinci, *Hungary* 42 C4
Lormi, *India* 69 H9
Lorn, *U.K.* 14 E3
Lorn, Firth of, *U.K.* 14 E3
Lorovo, *Sudan* 81 G3
Lorovouno, *Cyprus* 36 D11
Lörrach, *Germany* 25 H3
Lorraine □, *France* 19 D13
Los, *Sweden* 10 C9
Los, Îles de, *Guinea* 82 D2
Los Alamos, *Calif., U.S.A.* 117 L6
Los Alamos, *N. Mex., U.S.A.* 115 J10
Los Altos, *U.S.A.* 116 H4
Los Andes, *Chile* 126 C1
Los Angeles, *Chile* 126 D1
Los Angeles, *U.S.A.* 117 M8
Los Angeles, Bahia de, *Mexico* 118 B2
Los Angeles Aqueduct, *U.S.A.* 117 K9
Los Banos, *U.S.A.* 116 H6
Los Barrios, *Spain* 35 J5
Los Blancos, *Argentina* 126 A3
Los Chiles, *Costa Rica* 120 D3
Los Corrales de Buelna, *Spain* 34 B6
Los Cristianos, *Canary Is.* 37 F3
Los Gallardos, *Spain* 33 H3
Los Gatos, *U.S.A.* 116 H5
Los Hermanos Is., *Venezuela* 121 D7
Los Islotes, *Canary Is.* 37 E6
Los Llanos de Aridane, *Canary Is.* 37 F2
Los Loros, *Chile* 126 B1
Los Lunas, *U.S.A.* 115 J10
Los Mochis, *Mexico* 118 B3
Los Monegros, *Spain* 32 D4
Los Nietos, *Spain* 33 H4
Los Olivos, *U.S.A.* 117 L6
Los Palacios, *Cuba* 120 B3
Los Palacios y Villafranca, *Spain* 35 H5
Los Reyes, *Mexico* 118 D4
Los Roques Is., *Venezuela* 121 D6
Los Santos de Maimona, *Spain* 35 G4
Los Teques, *Venezuela* 124 A5
Los Testigos, Is., *Venezuela* 124 A6
Los Vilos, *Chile* 126 C1
Los Yébenes, *Spain* 35 F7
Łosice, *Poland* 45 F9
Loskop Dam, *S. Africa* 89 D4
Løsning, *Denmark* 11 J3
Lossiemouth, *U.K.* 14 D5
Lostwithiel, *U.K.* 13 G3
Lot □, *France* 20 D5
Lot →, *France* 20 D4
Lot-et-Garonne □, *France* 20 D4
Lota, *Chile* 126 D1
Lotagipi Swamp, *Sudan* 81 G3
Loṭfābād, *Iran* 71 B8
Lothair, *S. Africa* 89 D5
Lotorp, *Sweden* 11 F9
Lötschbergtunnel, *Switz.* 25 J3
Löttorp, *Sweden* 11 G11
Lotung, *Taiwan* 59 E13
Loubomo, *Congo* 84 E2
Loudéac, *France* 18 D4
Loudi, *China* 59 D8
Loudonville, *U.S.A.* 110 F2
Loudun, *France* 18 E7
Loue →, *France* 19 E12
Louga, *Senegal* 82 B1
Loughborough, *U.K.* 12 E6
Loughrea, *Ireland* 15 C3
Loughros More B., *Ireland* 15 B3
Louhans, *France* 19 F12
Louis Trichardt, *S. Africa* 89 C4
Louis XIV, Pte., *Canada* 102 B4
Louisa, *U.S.A.* 108 F4
Louisbourg, *Canada* 103 C8
Louise I., *Canada* 104 C2
Louiseville, *Canada* 102 C5
Louisiade Arch., *Papua N. G.* 96 J7
Louisiana, *U.S.A.* 112 F9
Louisiana □, *U.S.A.* 113 K9
Louisville, *Ky., U.S.A.* 108 F3
Louisville, *Miss., U.S.A.* 113 J10
Louisville, *Ohio, U.S.A.* 110 F3
Loulay, *France* 20 B3
Loulé, *Portugal* 35 H3
Louny, *Czech Rep.* 26 A6
Loup City, *U.S.A.* 112 E5
Loups Marins, Lacs des, *Canada* 102 A5
Lourdes, *France* 20 E3
Lourinhã, *Portugal* 35 F1
Lousã, *Portugal* 34 E2
Louta, *Burkina Faso* 82 C4
Louth, *Ireland* 15 C5
Louth, *U.K.* 12 D7
Louth □, *Ireland* 15 C5
Loutrá Aidhipsoú, *Greece* 38 C5
Loutráki, *Greece* 38 D4
Louvain = Leuven, *Belgium* 17 D4
Louviers, *France* 18 C8
Louwsburg, *S. Africa* 89 D5
Lovat →, *Russia* 46 C6
Lovćen, *Montenegro, Yug.* 40 D2
Lovech, *Bulgaria* 41 C8
Lovech □, *Bulgaria* 41 C8
Loveland, *U.S.A.* 112 E2
Lovell, *U.S.A.* 114 D9
Lovelock, *U.S.A.* 114 F4
Lóvere, *Italy* 28 C7
Lövestad, *Sweden* 11 J7
Loviisa, *Finland* 9 F22
Loving, *U.S.A.* 113 J2
Lovington, *U.S.A.* 113 J3
Lovisa = Loviisa, *Finland* 9 F22
Lovosice, *Czech Rep.* 26 A7
Lovran, *Croatia* 29 C11
Lovrin, *Romania* 42 E5
Lövstabruk, *Sweden* 10 D11
Lövstabukten, *Sweden* 10 D11
Low, L., *Canada* 102 B4
Low Pt., *Australia* 93 F4
Low Tatra = Nízké Tatry, *Slovak Rep.* 27 C12
Lowa, *Dem. Rep. of the Congo* 86 C2
Lowa →, *Dem. Rep. of the Congo* 86 C2
Lowell, *U.S.A.* 111 D13
Lowellville, *U.S.A.* 110 E4
Löwen →, *Namibia* 88 D2
Lower Alkali L., *U.S.A.* 114 F3
Lower Arrow L., *Canada* 104 D5
Lower Austria = Niederösterreich □, *Austria* 26 C8
Lower California = Baja California, *Mexico* 118 A1
Lower Hutt, *N.Z.* 91 J5
Lower Lake, *U.S.A.* 116 G4
Lower Manitou L., *Canada* 105 D10
Lower Post, *Canada* 104 B3
Lower Red L., *U.S.A.* 112 B7
Lower Saxony = Niedersachsen □, *Germany* 24 C4
Lower Tunguska = Tunguska, Nizhnyaya →, *Russia* 51 C9
Lowestoft, *U.K.* 13 E9
Łowicz, *Poland* 45 F6
Lowville, *U.S.A.* 111 C9
Loxton, *S. Africa* 88 E3
Loyalton, *U.S.A.* 116 F6
Loyalty Is. = Loyauté, Is., *N. Cal.* 96 K8
Loyang = Luoyang, *China* 56 G7
Loyauté, Is., *N. Cal.* 96 K8
Loyev = Loyew, *Belarus* 47 G6
Loyew, *Belarus* 47 G6
Loyoro, *Uganda* 86 B3
Lož, *Slovenia* 29 C11
Lozère □, *France* 20 D7
Loznica, *Serbia, Yug.* 40 B3
Lozova, *Ukraine* 47 H9
Lü Shan, *China* 59 C11
Lü-Tao, *Taiwan* 59 F13
Luachimo, *Angola* 84 F4
Luajan →, *India* 69 G11
Lualaba →, *Dem. Rep. of the Congo* 86 B2
Luampa, *Zambia* 87 F1
Lu'an, *China* 59 B11
Luan Chau, *Vietnam* 58 G4
Luan He →, *China* 57 E10
Luan Xian, *China* 57 E10
Luancheng, *Guangxi Zhuangzu, China* 58 F7
Luancheng, *Hebei, China* 56 F8
Luanco, *Spain* 34 B5
Luanda, *Angola* 84 F2
Luang, Thale, *Thailand* 65 J3
Luang Prabang, *Laos* 58 H4
Luangwa, *Zambia* 87 F3
Luangwa →, *Zambia* 87 E3
Luangwa Valley, *Zambia* 87 E3
Luanne, *China* 57 D9
Luanping, *China* 57 D9
Luanshya, *Zambia* 87 E2
Luapula □, *Zambia* 87 E2
Luapula →, *Africa* 87 D2
Luarca, *Spain* 34 B4
Luashi, *Dem. Rep. of the Congo* 87 E1
Luau, *Angola* 84 G4
Lubaczów, *Poland* 45 H10
Lubań, *Poland* 45 G2
Lubana, Ozero = Lubānas Ezers, *Latvia* 9 H22
Lubānas Ezers, *Latvia* 9 H22
Lubang, *Phil.* 61 E4
Lubang Is., *Phil.* 63 B6
Lubartów, *Poland* 45 G9
Lubawa, *Poland* 44 E6
Lübbecke, *Germany* 24 C4
Lübben, *Germany* 24 D9
Lübbenau, *Germany* 24 D9
Lubbock, *U.S.A.* 113 J4
Lübeck, *Germany* 24 B6
Lübecker Bucht, *Germany* 24 A6
Lubefu, *Dem. Rep. of the Congo* 86 C1
Lubefu →, *Dem. Rep. of the Congo* 86 C1
Lubelskie □, *Poland* 45 G9
Lubero = Luofu, *Dem. Rep. of the Congo* 86 C2
Lubersac, *France* 20 C5
Lubicon L., *Canada* 104 B5
Lubień Kujawski, *Poland* 45 F6
Lubilash →, *Dem. Rep. of the Congo* 84 F4
Lubin, *Poland* 45 G3
Lublin, *Poland* 45 G9
Lubliniec, *Poland* 45 H5
Lubnān, Jabal, *Lebanon* 75 B4
Lubniewice, *Poland* 45 F2
Lubny, *Ukraine* 47 G7
Lubomierz, *Poland* 45 G2
Luboń, *Poland* 45 F3
Lubongola, *Dem. Rep. of the Congo* 86 C2
L'ubotín, *Slovak Rep.* 27 B13
Lubraniec, *Poland* 45 F5
Lubsko, *Poland* 45 G1
Lübtheen, *Germany* 24 B7
Lubuagan, *Phil.* 61 C4
Lubudi, *Dem. Rep. of the Congo* 84 F5
Lubudi →, *Dem. Rep. of the Congo* 87 D2
Lubuklinggau, *Indonesia* 62 E2
Lubuksikaping, *Indonesia* 62 D2
Lubumbashi, *Dem. Rep. of the Congo* 87 E2

Lubunda, *Dem. Rep. of the Congo* 86 D2
Lubungu, *Zambia* 87 E2
Lubuskie □, *Poland* 45 F2
Lubutu, *Dem. Rep. of the Congo* 86 C2
Luc An Chau, *Vietnam* 64 A5
Luc-en-Diois, *France* 21 D9
Lucan, *Canada* 110 C3
Lucania, Mt., *Canada* 100 B5
Lucas Channel, *Canada* 110 A3
Lucban, *Phil.* 61 D4
Lucca, *Italy* 28 E7
Lucé, *France* 18 D8
Luce Bay, *U.K.* 14 G4
Lucea, *Jamaica* 120 C4
Lucedale, *U.S.A.* 109 K1
Lucena, *Phil.* 61 E4
Lucena, *Spain* 35 H6
Lučenec, *Slovak Rep.* 27 C12
Lucera, *Italy* 31 A8
Lucerne = Luzern, *Switz.* 25 H4
Lucerne, *U.S.A.* 116 F4
Lucerne Valley, *U.S.A.* 117 L10
Lucero, *Mexico* 118 A3
Luchena →, *Spain* 33 H3
Lucheng, *China* 56 F7
Lucheringo →, *Mozam.* 87 E4
Lüchow, *Germany* 24 C7
Luchuan, *China* 59 F8
Lucia, *U.S.A.* 116 J5
Lucinda, *Australia* 94 B4
Luckau, *Germany* 24 D9
Luckenwalde, *Germany* 24 C9
Luckhoff, *S. Africa* 88 D3
Lucknow, *Canada* 110 C3
Lucknow, *India* 69 F9
Luçon, *France* 20 B2
Lüda = Dalian, *China* 57 E11
Luda Kamchiya →, *Bulgaria* 41 C11
Ludbreg, *Croatia* 29 B13
Lüdenscheid, *Germany* 24 D3
Lüderitz, *Namibia* 88 D2
Lüderitzbaai, *Namibia* 88 D2
Ludhiana, *India* 68 D6
Ludian, *China* 58 D4
Luding Qiao, *China* 58 C4
Lüdinghausen, *Germany* 24 D3
Ludington, *U.S.A.* 108 D2
Ludlow, *U.K.* 13 E5
Ludlow, *Calif., U.S.A.* 117 L10
Ludlow, *Pa., U.S.A.* 110 E6
Ludlow, *Vt., U.S.A.* 111 C12
Ludus, *Romania* 43 D9
Ludvika, *Sweden* 10 D9
Ludwigsburg, *Germany* 25 G5
Ludwigsfelde, *Germany* 24 C9
Ludwigshafen, *Germany* 25 F4
Ludwigslust, *Germany* 24 B7
Ludza, *Latvia* 46 D4
Lueki, *Dem. Rep. of the Congo* 86 C2
Luena, *Dem. Rep. of the Congo* 87 D2
Luena, *Zambia* 87 E3
Lüeyang, *China* 56 H4
Lufeng, *Guangdong, China* 59 F10
Lufeng, *Yunnan, China* 58 E4
Lufira →, *Dem. Rep. of the Congo* 87 D2
Lufkin, *U.S.A.* 113 K7
Lufupa, *Dem. Rep. of the Congo* 87 E1
Luga, *Russia* 46 C5
Luga →, *Russia* 46 C5
Lugano, *Switz.* 25 J4
Lugano, L. di, *Switz.* 28 C6
Lugansk = Luhansk, *Ukraine* 47 H10
Lugard's Falls, *Kenya* 86 C4
Lugela, *Mozam.* 87 F4
Lugenda →, *Mozam.* 87 E4
Lugh Ganana, *Somali Rep.* 74 G3
Lugnaquilla, *Ireland* 15 D5
Lugo, *Italy* 29 D8
Lugo, *Spain* 34 B3
Lugo □, *Spain* 34 C3
Lugoj, *Romania* 42 E6
Lugovoy = Qulan, *Kazakstan* 50 E8
Luhansk, *Ukraine* 47 H10
Luhe, *China* 59 A12
Luhe →, *Germany* 24 B6
Luhuo, *China* 58 B3
Luiana, *Angola* 88 B3
Luimneach = Limerick, *Ireland* 15 D3
Luing, *U.K.* 14 E3
Luino, *Italy* 28 C5
Luís Correia, *Brazil* 125 D10
Luitpold Coast, *Antarctica* 5 D1
Luiza, *Dem. Rep. of the Congo* 84 F4
Luizi, *Dem. Rep. of the Congo* 86 D2
Luján, *Argentina* 126 C4
Lujiang, *China* 59 B11
Lukang, *Taiwan* 59 E13
Lukanga Swamp, *Zambia* 87 E2
Lukavac, *Bos.-H.* 42 F3
Lukenie →, *Dem. Rep. of the Congo* 84 E3
Lukhisaral, *India* 69 G12
Lŭki, *Bulgaria* 41 E8
Lukolela, *Dem. Rep. of the Congo* 86 D1
Lukosi, *Zimbabwe* 87 F2
Lukovë, *Albania* 40 G3
Lukovit, *Bulgaria* 41 C8
Łuków, *Poland* 45 G9
Lukoyanov, *Russia* 48 C7
Lule älv →, *Sweden* 8 D19
Luleå, *Sweden* 8 D20
Lüleburgaz, *Turkey* 41 E11
Luliang, *China* 58 E4
Luling, *U.S.A.* 113 L6
Lulong, *China* 57 E10
Lulonga →, *Dem. Rep. of the Congo* 84 D3
Lulua →, *Dem. Rep. of the Congo* 84 E4
Lumajang, *Indonesia* 63 H15
Lumbala N'guimbo, *Angola* 85 G4
Lumberton, *U.S.A.* 109 H6
Lumbwa, *Kenya* 86 C4
Lumsden, *Canada* 105 C8
Lumsden, *N.Z.* 91 L2
Lumut, *Malaysia* 65 K3
Lumut, Tanjung, *Indonesia* 62 E3
Luna, *India* 68 H3
Lunan, *China* 58 E4
Lunavada, *India* 68 H5
Lunca, *Romania* 43 C10
Lunca Corbului, *Romania* 43 F9
Lund, *Sweden* 11 J7
Lundazi, *Zambia* 87 E3
Lunderskov, *Denmark* 11 J3
Lundi →, *Zimbabwe* 87 G3
Lundu, *Malaysia* 62 D3
Lundy, *U.K.* 13 F3
Lune →, *U.K.* 12 C5
Lüneburg, *Germany* 24 B6
Lüneburg Heath = Lüneburger Heide, *Germany* 24 B6
Lüneburger Heide, *Germany* 24 B6
Lunel, *France* 21 E8
Lünen, *Germany* 24 D3
Lunenburg, *Canada* 103 D7
Lunéville, *France* 19 D13
Lunga →, *Zambia* 87 E2
Lungi Airport, *S. Leone* 82 D2
Lunglei, *India* 67 H18
Luni, *India* 68 G5
Luni →, *India* 68 G4
Luninets = Luninyets, *Belarus* 47 F4
Luning, *U.S.A.* 114 G4
Lunino, *Russia* 48 D7
Luninyets, *Belarus* 47 F4
Lunkaransar, *India* 68 E5
Lunsemfwa →, *Zambia* 87 E3
Lunsemfwa Falls, *Zambia* 87 E2
Luo He →, *China* 56 G6
Luocheng, *China* 58 E7
Luochuan, *China* 56 G5
Luoci, *China* 58 E4
Luodian, *China* 58 E6
Luoding, *China* 59 F8
Luofu, *Dem. Rep. of the Congo* 86 C2
Luohe, *China* 56 H8
Luojiang, *China* 58 B5
Luonan, *China* 56 G6
Luoning, *China* 56 G6
Luoshan, *China* 59 A10
Luotian, *China* 59 B10
Luoxiao Shan, *China* 59 D10
Luoyang, *China* 56 G7
Luoyuan, *China* 59 D12
Luozigou, *China* 57 C16
Lupanshui, *China* 58 D5
Lupeni, *Romania* 43 E8
Lupilichi, *Mozam.* 87 E4
Łupków, *Poland* 45 J9
Lupoing, *China* 58 E5
Luquan, *China* 58 E4
Luque, *Paraguay* 126 B4
Lúras, *Italy* 30 B2
Luray, *U.S.A.* 108 F6
Lure, *France* 19 E13
Lurgan, *U.K.* 15 B5
Lusaka, *Zambia* 87 F2
Lusambo, *Dem. Rep. of the Congo* 86 C1
Lusangaye, *Dem. Rep. of the Congo* 86 C2
Luseland, *Canada* 105 C7
Lushan, *Henan, China* 56 H7
Lushan, *Sichuan, China* 58 B4
Lushi, *China* 56 G6
Lushnjë, *Albania* 40 F3
Lushoto, *Tanzania* 86 C4
Lushui, *China* 58 E2
Lüshun, *China* 57 E11
Lusignan, *France* 20 B4
Lusigny-sur-Barse, *France* 19 D11
Lusk, *U.S.A.* 112 D2
Lussac-les-Châteaux, *France* 20 B4
Lustenau, *Austria* 26 D2
Lūt, Dasht-e, *Iran* 71 D8
Luta = Dalian, *China* 57 E11
Lutherstadt Wittenberg, *Germany* 24 D8
Luton, *U.K.* 13 F7
Luton □, *U.K.* 13 F7
Lutselke, *Canada* 105 A6
Lutsk, *Ukraine* 47 G3
Lützow Holmbukta, *Antarctica* 5 C4
Lutzputs, *S. Africa* 88 D3
Luverne, *Ala., U.S.A.* 109 K2
Luverne, *Minn., U.S.A.* 112 D6
Luvua, *Dem. Rep. of the Congo* 87 D2
Luvua →, *Dem. Rep. of the Congo* 86 D2
Luvuvhu →, *S. Africa* 89 C5
Luwegu →, *Tanzania* 87 D4
Luwuk, *Indonesia* 63 E6
Luxembourg, *Lux.* 17 E6
Luxembourg □, *Belgium* 17 E5
Luxembourg ■, *Europe* 7 F7
Luxeuil-les-Bains, *France* 19 E13
Luxi, *Hunan, China* 59 C8
Luxi, *Yunnan, China* 58 E4
Luxi, *Yunnan, China* 58 E2
Luxor = El Uqsur, *Egypt* 80 B3
Luy-de-Béarn →, *France* 20 E3
Luy-de-France →, *France* 20 E3
Luyi, *China* 56 H8
Luz-St-Sauveur, *France* 20 F4
Luzern, *Switz.* 25 H4
Luzern □, *Switz.* 25 H3
Luzhai, *China* 58 E7
Luzhi, *China* 58 D5
Luzhou, *China* 58 C5
Luziânia, *Brazil* 125 G9
Lužnice →, *Czech Rep.* 26 B7
Luzon, *Phil.* 61 D4
Luzy, *France* 19 F10
Luzzi, *Italy* 31 C9
Lviv, *Ukraine* 47 H3
Lvov = Lviv, *Ukraine* 47 H3
Lwówek, *Poland* 45 F3
Lwówek Śląski, *Poland* 45 G2
Lyakhavichy, *Belarus* 47 F4
Lyakhovskiye, Ostrova, *Russia* 51 B15
Lyaki = Läki, *Azerbaijan* 49 K8
Lyal I., *Canada* 110 B3
Lyallpur = Faisalabad, *Pakistan* 68 D5
Lyaskovets, *Bulgaria* 41 C9
Lybster, *U.K.* 14 C5
Lycaonia, *Turkey* 72 D5
Lychen, *Germany* 24 B9
Lychkova, *Russia* 46 D7
Lycia, *Turkey* 39 E11
Lyckebyån →, *Sweden* 11 H9
Lycksele, *Sweden* 8 D18
Lycosura, *Greece* 38 D4
Lydda = Lod, *Israel* 75 D3
Lydenburg, *S. Africa* 89 D5
Lydia, *Turkey* 39 C10
Łydynia →, *Poland* 45 F7
Lyell, *N.Z.* 91 J4
Lyell I., *Canada* 104 C2
Lyepyel, *Belarus* 46 E5
Lygnern, *Sweden* 11 G6
Lykens, *U.S.A.* 111 F8
Lyman, *U.S.A.* 114 F8
Lyme B., *U.K.* 13 G4
Lyme Regis, *U.K.* 13 G5
Lymington, *U.K.* 13 G6
Łyna →, *Poland* 9 J19
Lynchburg, *U.S.A.* 108 G6
Lynd →, *Australia* 94 B3
Lynd Ra., *Australia* 95 D4
Lynden, *Canada* 110 C4
Lynden, *U.S.A.* 116 B4
Lyndhurst, *Australia* 95 E2
Lyndon →, *Australia* 93 D1
Lyndonville, *N.Y., U.S.A.* 110 C6
Lyndonville, *Vt., U.S.A.* 111 B12
Lyngen, *Norway* 8 B19
Lynher Reef, *Australia* 92 C3
Lynn, *U.S.A.* 111 D14
Lynn Lake, *Canada* 105 B8
Lynnwood, *U.S.A.* 116 C4
Lynton, *U.K.* 13 F4
Lyntupy, *Belarus* 9 J22
Lynx L., *Canada* 105 A7
Lyon, *France* 21 C8
Lyonnais, *France* 21 C8
Lyons = Lyon, *France* 21 C8
Lyons, *Ga., U.S.A.* 109 J4
Lyons, *Kans., U.S.A.* 112 F5
Lyons, *N.Y., U.S.A.* 110 C8
Lyons →, *Australia* 93 E2
Lyons Falls, *U.S.A.* 111 C9
Lyozna, *Belarus* 46 E6
Lys = Leie →, *Belgium* 17 C3
Lysá nad Labem, *Czech Rep.* 26 A7
Lysekil, *Sweden* 11 F5
Lyskovo, *Russia* 48 B7
Lystrup, *Denmark* 11 H4
Lysvik, *Sweden* 10 D7
Lysychansk, *Ukraine* 47 H10
Lytham St. Anne's, *U.K.* 12 D4
Lyttelton, *N.Z.* 91 K4
Lytton, *Canada* 104 C4
Lyuban, *Russia* 46 C6
Lyubertsy, *Russia* 46 E9
Lyubim, *Russia* 46 C11
Lyubimets, *Bulgaria* 41 E10
Lyuboml, *Ukraine* 47 G3
Lyubotyn, *Ukraine* 47 H8
Lyubytino, *Russia* 46 C7
Lyudinovo, *Russia* 46 F8

M

M.R. Gomez, Presa, *Mexico* 119 B5
Ma →, *Vietnam* 58 H5
Ma'adaba, *Jordan* 75 E4
Maamba, *Zambia* 88 B4
Ma'ān, *Jordan* 75 E4
Ma'ān □, *Jordan* 75 F5
Maanselkä, *Finland* 8 C23
Ma'anshan, *China* 59 B12
Maarianhamina, *Finland* 9 F18
Ma'arrat an Nu'mān, *Syria* 70 C3
Maas →, *Neths.* 17 C4
Maaseik, *Belgium* 17 C5
Maasin, *Phil.* 63 B6
Maastricht, *Neths.* 17 D5
Maave, *Mozam.* 89 C5
Mababe Depression, *Botswana* 88 B3
Mabalane, *Mozam.* 89 C5
Mabel L., *Canada* 104 C5
Mabenge, *Dem. Rep. of the Congo* 86 B1
Maberly, *Canada* 111 B8
Mabian, *China* 58 C4
Mabil, *Ethiopia* 81 E4
Mablethorpe, *U.K.* 12 D8
Mably, *France* 19 F11
Maboma, *Dem. Rep. of the Congo* 86 B2
Mabonto, *S. Leone* 82 D2
Mabrouk, *Mali* 83 B4
Mac Bac, *Vietnam* 65 H6
Macachín, *Argentina* 126 D3
Macaé, *Brazil* 127 A7
Macael, *Spain* 33 H2
McAlester, *U.S.A.* 113 H7
McAllen, *U.S.A.* 113 M5
MacAlpine L., *Canada* 100 B9
Macamic, *Canada* 102 C4
Macao = Macau □, *China* 59 F9
Macão, *Portugal* 35 F3
Macapá, *Brazil* 125 C8
McArthur →, *Australia* 94 B2
McArthur, Port, *Australia* 94 B2
Macau, *Brazil* 125 E11
Macau □, *China* 59 F9
McBride, *Canada* 104 C4
McCall, *U.S.A.* 114 D5
McCamey, *U.S.A.* 113 K3
McCammon, *U.S.A.* 114 E7
McCauley I., *Canada* 104 C2
McCleary, *U.S.A.* 116 C3
Macclenny, *U.S.A.* 109 K4
Macclesfield, *U.K.* 12 D5
M'Clintock Chan., *Canada* 100 A9
McClintock Ra., *Australia* 92 C4
McCloud, *U.S.A.* 114 F2
McCluer I., *Australia* 92 B5
McClure, *U.S.A.* 110 F7
McClure, L., *U.S.A.* 116 H6
M'Clure Str., *Canada* 4 B2
McClusky, *U.S.A.* 112 B4
McComb, *U.S.A.* 113 K9
McConaughy, L., *U.S.A.* 112 E4
McCook, *U.S.A.* 112 E4
McCreary, *Canada* 105 C9
McCullough Mt., *U.S.A.* 117 K11
McCusker →, *Canada* 105 B7
McDame, *Canada* 104 B3
McDermitt, *U.S.A.* 114 F5
McDonald, *U.S.A.* 110 F4
Macdonald, L., *Australia* 92 D4
McDonald Is., *Ind. Oc.* 3 G13
MacDonnell Ranges, *Australia* 92 D5
MacDowell L., *Canada* 102 B1
Macduff, *U.K.* 14 D6
Maceda, *Spain* 34 C3
Macedonia, *U.S.A.* 110 E3
Macedonia ■, *Europe* 40 E5
Maceió, *Brazil* 125 E11
Maceira, *Portugal* 34 F2
Macenta, *Guinea* 82 D3
Macerata, *Italy* 29 E10
McFarland, *U.S.A.* 117 K7
McFarlane →, *Canada* 105 B7
McGehee, *U.S.A.* 113 J9
McGill, *U.S.A.* 114 G6
Macgillycuddy's Reeks, *Ireland* 15 E2
McGraw, *U.S.A.* 111 D8
McGregor, *U.S.A.* 112 D9
McGregor Ra., *Australia* 95 D3
Mach, *Pakistan* 66 E5
Māch Kowr, *Iran* 71 E9
Machado = Jiparaná →, *Brazil* 124 E6
Machagai, *Argentina* 126 B3
Machakos, *Kenya* 86 C4
Machala, *Ecuador* 124 D3
Machanga, *Mozam.* 89 C6
Machattie, L., *Australia* 94 C2
Machault, *France* 19 C11
Machava, *Mozam.* 89 D5
Machece, *Mozam.* 87 F4
Machecoul, *France* 18 F5
Macheke, *Zimbabwe* 89 B5
Macheng, *China* 59 B10
Machero, *Spain* 35 F6
Machhu →, *India* 68 H4
Machias, *Maine, U.S.A.* 109 C12
Machias, *N.Y., U.S.A.* 110 D6
Machichi →, *Canada* 105 B10
Machico, *Madeira* 37 D3
Machilipatnam, *India* 67 L12
Machiques, *Venezuela* 124 A4
Machupicchu, *Peru* 124 F4
Machynlleth, *U.K.* 13 E4
Macia, *Mozam.* 89 D5
Maciejowice, *Poland* 45 G8
McIlwraith Ra., *Australia* 94 A3
Măcin, *Romania* 43 E13
Macina, *Mali* 82 C4
McInnes L., *Canada* 105 C10
McIntosh, *U.S.A.* 112 C4
McIntosh L., *Canada* 105 B8
Macintosh Ra., *Australia* 93 E4
Macintyre →, *Australia* 95 D5
Macizo Galaico, *Spain* 34 C3
Mackay, *Australia* 94 C4
Mackay, *U.S.A.* 114 E7
MacKay →, *Canada* 104 B6
Mackay, L., *Australia* 92 D4
McKay Ra., *Australia* 92 D3
McKeesport, *U.S.A.* 110 F5
McKellar, *Canada* 110 A5
McKenna, *U.S.A.* 116 D4
Mackenzie, *Canada* 104 B4
McKenzie, *U.S.A.* 109 G1
Mackenzie →, *Australia* 94 C4
Mackenzie →, *Canada* 100 B6
McKenzie →, *U.S.A.* 114 D2
Mackenzie Bay, *Canada* 4 B1
Mackenzie City = Linden, *Guyana* 124 B7
Mackenzie Mts., *Canada* 100 B6
Mackinaw City, *U.S.A.* 108 C3
McKinlay, *Australia* 94 C3
McKinlay →, *Australia* 94 C3
McKinley, Mt., *U.S.A.* 100 B4
McKinley Sea, *Arctic* 4 A7
McKinney, *U.S.A.* 113 J6
Mackinnon Road, *Kenya* 86 C4
McKittrick, *U.S.A.* 117 K7
Macklin, *Canada* 105 C7
McLaughlin, *U.S.A.* 112 C4
Maclean, *Australia* 95 D5
McLean, *U.S.A.* 113 H4
McLeansboro, *U.S.A.* 112 F10
Maclear, *S. Africa* 89 E4
McLennan, *Canada* 104 B5
McLeod →, *Canada* 104 C5
MacLeod, B., *Canada* 105 A7
McLeod, L., *Australia* 93 D1
MacLeod Lake, *Canada* 104 C4
McLoughlin, Mt., *U.S.A.* 114 E2
McMechen, *U.S.A.* 110 G4
McMinnville, *Oreg., U.S.A.* 114 D2
McMinnville, *Tenn., U.S.A.* 109 H3
McMurdo Sd., *Antarctica* 5 D11
McMurray = Fort McMurray, *Canada* 104 B6
McMurray, *U.S.A.* 116 B4
Macodoene, *Mozam.* 89 C6
Macomb, *U.S.A.* 112 E9
Macomer, *Italy* 30 B1
Mâcon, *France* 19 F11
Macon, *Ga., U.S.A.* 109 J4
Macon, *Miss., U.S.A.* 109 J1
Macon, *Mo., U.S.A.* 112 F8
Macossa, *Mozam.* 87 F3
Macoun L., *Canada* 105 B8
Macovane, *Mozam.* 89 C6
McPherson, *U.S.A.* 112 F6
McPherson Pk., *U.S.A.* 117 L7
McPherson Ra., *Australia* 95 D5
Macquarie →, *Australia* 95 E4
Macquarie Harbour, *Australia* 94 G4
Macquarie Is., *Pac. Oc.* 96 N7
MacRobertson Land, *Antarctica* 5 D6
Macroom, *Ireland* 15 E3
MacTier, *Canada* 110 A5
Macubela, *Mozam.* 87 F4
Macugnaga, *Italy* 28 C4
Macuiza, *Mozam.* 87 F3
Macusani, *Peru* 124 F4
Macuse, *Mozam.* 87 F4
Macuspana, *Mexico* 119 D6
Macusse, *Angola* 88 B3
Mada →, *Nigeria* 83 D6
Madadeni, *S. Africa* 89 D5
Madagali, *Nigeria* 83 C7
Madagascar ■, *Africa* 89 C8
Madā'in Sālih, *Si. Arabia* 70 E3
Madama, *Niger* 79 D8
Madame I., *Canada* 103 C7
Madan, *Bulgaria* 41 E8
Madaoua, *Niger* 83 C6
Madara, *Nigeria* 83 C7
Madaripur, *Bangla.* 67 H17
Madauk, *Burma* 67 L20
Madawaska, *Canada* 110 A7
Madawaska →, *Canada* 102 C4
Madaya, *Burma* 67 H20
Madbar, *Sudan* 81 F3
Maddalena, *Italy* 30 A2
Maddaloni, *Italy* 31 A7
Madeira, *Atl. Oc.* 37 D3
Madeira →, *Brazil* 122 D5
Madeleine, Îs. de la, *Canada* 103 C7
Maden, *Turkey* 73 C8
Madera, *Mexico* 118 B3
Madera, *Calif., U.S.A.* 116 J6
Madera, *Pa., U.S.A.* 110 F6
Madha, *India* 66 L9
Madhavpur, *India* 68 J3
Madhepura, *India* 69 F12
Madhubani, *India* 69 F12
Madhupur, *India* 69 G12
Madhya Pradesh □, *India* 68 J8
Madidi →, *Bolivia* 124 F5
Madikeri, *India* 66 N9
Madill, *U.S.A.* 113 H6
Madimba, *Dem. Rep. of the Congo* 84 E3
Ma'din, *Syria* 70 C3
Madina, *Mali* 82 C3
Madinani, *Ivory C.* 82 D3
Madingou, *Congo* 84 E2
Madirovalo, *Madag.* 89 B8
Madison, *Calif., U.S.A.* 116 G5
Madison, *Fla., U.S.A.* 109 K4
Madison, *Ind., U.S.A.* 108 F3
Madison, *Nebr., U.S.A.* 112 E6
Madison, *Ohio, U.S.A.* 110 E3
Madison, *S. Dak., U.S.A.* 112 D6
Madison, *Wis., U.S.A.* 112 D10
Madison →, *U.S.A.* 114 D8
Madison Heights, *U.S.A.* 108 G6
Madisonville, *Ky., U.S.A.* 108 G2
Madisonville, *Tex., U.S.A.* 113 K7
Madista, *Botswana* 88 C4
Madiun, *Indonesia* 62 F4
Madoc, *Canada* 110 B7
Madol, *Sudan* 81 F2

Madon →, *France* 19 D13
Madona, *Latvia* 9 H22
Madonie, *Italy* 30 E6
Madonna di Campíglio, *Italy* 28 B7
Madra Dağı, *Turkey* 39 B9
Madrakah, Ra's al, *Oman* 74 D6
Madras = Chennai, *India* 66 N12
Madras = Tamil Nadu □, *India* 66 P10
Madras, *U.S.A.* 114 D3
Madre, Laguna, *U.S.A.* 113 M6
Madre, Sierra, *Phil.* 61 C5
Madre de Dios →, *Bolivia* 122 E4
Madre de Dios, I., *Chile* 122 J3
Madre del Sur, Sierra, *Mexico* 119 D5
Madre Occidental, Sierra, *Mexico* 118 B3
Madre Oriental, Sierra, *Mexico* 118 C5
Madri, *India* 68 G5
Madrid, *Spain* 34 E7
Madrid, *U.S.A.* 111 B9
Madrid □, *Spain* 34 E7
Madridejos, *Spain* 35 F7
Madrigal de las Altas Torres, *Spain* 34 D6
Madrona, Sierra, *Spain* 35 G6
Madroñera, *Spain* 35 F5
Madu, *Sudan* 81 E2
Madura, *Australia* 93 F4
Madura, *Indonesia* 63 G15
Madura, Selat, *Indonesia* 63 G15
Madurai, *India* 66 Q11
Madurantakam, *India* 66 N11
Madzhalis, *Russia* 49 J8
Mae Chan, *Thailand* 64 B2
Mae Hong Son, *Thailand* 64 C2
Mae Khlong →, *Thailand* 64 F3
Mae Phrik, *Thailand* 64 D2
Mae Ramat, *Thailand* 64 D2
Mae Rim, *Thailand* 64 C2
Mae Sot, *Thailand* 64 D2
Mae Suai, *Thailand* 58 H2
Mae Tha, *Thailand* 64 C2
Maebashi, *Japan* 55 F9
Maella, *Spain* 32 D5
Maesteg, *U.K.* 13 F4
Maestra, Sierra, *Cuba* 120 B4
Maevatanana, *Madag.* 89 B8
Mafeking = Mafikeng, *S. Africa* 88 D4
Mafeking, *Canada* 105 C8
Maféré, *Ivory C.* 82 D4
Mafeteng, *Lesotho* 88 D4
Mafia I., *Tanzania* 86 D4
Mafikeng, *S. Africa* 88 D4
Mafra, *Brazil* 127 B6
Mafra, *Portugal* 35 G1
Mafungabusi Plateau, *Zimbabwe* 87 F2
Magadan, *Russia* 51 D16
Magadi, *Kenya* 86 C4
Magadi, L., *Kenya* 86 C4
Magaliesburg, *S. Africa* 89 D4
Magallanes, Estrecho de, *Chile* 122 J3
Magaluf, *Spain* 33 F7
Magangué, *Colombia* 124 B4
Magaria, *Niger* 83 C6
Magburaka, *S. Leone* 82 D2
Magdalen Is. = Madeleine, Îs. de la, *Canada* 103 C7
Magdalena, *Argentina* 126 D4
Magdalena, *Bolivia* 124 F6
Magdalena, *Mexico* 118 A2
Magdalena, *U.S.A.* 115 J10
Magdalena →, *Colombia* 122 B3
Magdalena →, *Mexico* 118 A2
Magdalena, B., *Mexico* 118 C2
Magdalena, Llano de la, *Mexico* 118 C2
Magdeburg, *Germany* 24 C7
Magdelaine Cays, *Australia* 94 B5
Magdub, *Sudan* 81 E2
Magee, *U.S.A.* 113 K10
Magelang, *Indonesia* 62 F4
Magellan's Str. = Magallanes, Estrecho de, *Chile* 122 J3
Magenta, *Italy* 28 C5
Magenta, L., *Australia* 93 F2
Magerøya, *Norway* 8 A21
Maggia →, *Switz.* 25 J4
Maggiorasca, Mte., *Italy* 28 D6
Maggiore, Lago, *Italy* 28 C5
Maghâgha, *Egypt* 80 B3
Maghama, *Mauritania* 82 B2
Magherafelt, *U.K.* 15 B5
Maghreb, *N. Afr.* 78 B5
Magione, *Italy* 29 E9
Magistralnyy, *Russia* 51 D11
Maglaj, *Bos.-H.* 42 F3
Magliano in Toscana, *Italy* 29 F8
Máglie, *Italy* 31 B11
Magnac-Laval, *France* 20 B5
Magnetic Pole (North) = North Magnetic Pole, *Canada* 4 B2
Magnetic Pole (South) = South Magnetic Pole, *Antarctica* 5 C9
Magnisía □, *Greece* 38 B5
Magnitogorsk, *Russia* 50 D6
Magnolia, *Ark., U.S.A.* 113 J8
Magnolia, *Miss., U.S.A.* 113 K9
Magny-en-Vexin, *France* 19 C8
Magog, *Canada* 103 C5
Magoro, *Uganda* 86 B3
Magosa = Famagusta, *Cyprus* 36 D12
Magouládhes, *Greece* 36 A3
Magoye, *Zambia* 87 F2
Magozal, *Mexico* 119 C5
Magpie, L., *Canada* 103 B7
Magrath, *Canada* 104 D6
Magre →, *Spain* 33 F4
Magrur, *Sudan* 81 E3
Magrur, Wadi →, *Sudan* 81 D2
Magta Lahjar, *Mauritania* 82 B2
Maguan, *China* 58 F5
Maguarinho, C., *Brazil* 125 D9
Magude, *Mozam.* 89 D5
Mağusa = Famagusta, *Cyprus* 36 D12
Maguse L., *Canada* 105 A9
Maguse Pt., *Canada* 105 A10
Magvana, *India* 68 H3
Magwe, *Burma* 67 J19
Magwe, *Sudan* 81 G3
Maha Sarakham, *Thailand* 64 D4
Mahābād, *Iran* 70 B5
Mahabharat Lekh, *Nepal* 69 E10
Mahabo, *Madag.* 89 C7
Mahadeo Hills, *India* 69 H8
Mahaffey, *U.S.A.* 110 F6
Mahagi, *Dem. Rep. of the Congo* 86 B3
Mahajamba →, *Madag.* 89 B8
Mahajamba, Helodranon' i, *Madag.* 89 B8
Mahajan, *India* 68 E5
Mahajanga, *Madag.* 89 B8
Mahajanga □, *Madag.* 89 B8
Mahajilo →, *Madag.* 89 B8
Mahakam →, *Indonesia* 62 E5
Mahalapye, *Botswana* 88 C4
Maḩallāt, *Iran* 71 C6
Māhān, *Iran* 71 D8
Mahan →, *India* 69 H10
Mahanadi →, *India* 67 J15
Mahananda →, *India* 69 G12
Mahanoro, *Madag.* 89 B8
Mahanoy City, *U.S.A.* 111 F8
Maharashtra □, *India* 66 J9
Mahari Mts., *Tanzania* 86 D3
Mahasham, W. →, *Egypt* 75 E3
Mahasoa, *Madag.* 89 C8
Mahasolo, *Madag.* 89 B8
Mahattat ash Shīdīyah, *Jordan* 75 F4
Mahattat 'Unayzah, *Jordan* 75 E4
Mahavavy →, *Madag.* 89 B8
Mahaxay, *Laos* 64 D5
Mahbubnagar, *India* 66 L10
Maḩḑah, *Oman* 71 E7
Mahdia, *Tunisia* 79 A8
Mahe, *India* 69 C8
Mahendragarh, *India* 68 E7
Mahenge, *Tanzania* 87 D4
Maheno, *N.Z.* 91 L3
Mahesana, *India* 68 H5
Maheshwar, *India* 68 H6
Mahgawan, *India* 69 F8
Mahi →, *India* 68 H5
Mahia Pen., *N.Z.* 91 H6
Mahilyow, *Belarus* 46 F6
Mahmiya, *Sudan* 81 D3
Mahmud Kot, *Pakistan* 68 D4
Mahmudia, *Romania* 43 E14
Mahmudiye, *Turkey* 39 B12
Mahmutbey, *Turkey* 41 E12
Mahnomen, *U.S.A.* 112 B7
Mahoba, *India* 69 G8
Mahón = Maó, *Spain* 37 B11
Mahone Bay, *Canada* 103 D7
Mahopac, *U.S.A.* 111 E11
Mahuta, *Nigeria* 83 C5
Mahuva, *India* 68 J4
Mahya Daği, *Turkey* 41 E11
Mai-Ndombe, L., *Dem. Rep. of the Congo* 84 E3
Mai-Sai, *Thailand* 58 G2
Maia, *Portugal* 34 D2
Maia, *Spain* 32 B3
Maials, *Spain* 32 D5
Maîche, *France* 19 E13
Maicurú →, *Brazil* 125 D8
Máida, *Italy* 31 D9
Maidan Khula, *Afghan.* 68 C3
Maidenhead, *U.K.* 13 F7
Maidstone, *Canada* 105 C7
Maidstone, *U.K.* 13 F8
Maiduguri, *Nigeria* 83 C7
Măieruş, *Romania* 43 E10
Maigatari, *Nigeria* 83 C6
Maignelay Montigny, *France* 19 C9
Maigo, *Phil.* 61 G5
Maigudo, *Ethiopia* 81 F4
Maihar, *India* 69 G9
Maijdi, *Bangla.* 67 H17
Maikala Ra., *India* 67 J12
Mailani, *India* 69 E9
Maillezais, *France* 20 B3
Mailsi, *Pakistan* 68 E5
Main →, *Germany* 25 F4
Main →, *U.K.* 15 B5
Mainburg, *Germany* 25 G7
Maine, *France* 18 D6
Maine □, *U.S.A.* 109 C11
Maine →, *Ireland* 15 D2
Maine-et-Loire □, *France* 18 E6
Maïne-Soroa, *Niger* 83 C7
Maingkwan, *Burma* 67 F20
Mainit, L., *Phil.* 61 G6
Mainland, *Orkney, U.K.* 14 C5
Mainland, *Shet., U.K.* 14 A7
Mainoru, *Australia* 94 A1
Mainpuri, *India* 69 F8
Maintal, *Germany* 25 E4
Maintenon, *France* 19 D8
Maintirano, *Madag.* 89 B7
Mainz, *Germany* 25 E4
Maipú, *Argentina* 126 D4
Maiquetía, *Venezuela* 124 A5
Máira →, *Italy* 28 D4
Mairabari, *India* 67 F18
Maisí, *Cuba* 121 B5
Maisí, Pta. de, *Cuba* 121 B5
Maitland →, *Canada* 110 C3
Maiyema, *Nigeria* 83 C5
Maiyuan, *China* 59 E11
Maiz, Is. del, *Nic.* 120 D3
Maizuru, *Japan* 55 G7
Majalengka, *Indonesia* 63 G13
Majene, *Indonesia* 63 E5
Majevica, *Bos.-H.* 42 F3
Maji, *Ethiopia* 81 F4
Majiang, *China* 58 D6
Majorca = Mallorca, *Spain* 37 B10
Maka, *Senegal* 82 C2
Makaha, *Zimbabwe* 89 B5
Makak, *Cameroon* 83 E7
Makalamabedi, *Botswana* 88 C3
Makale, *Indonesia* 63 E5
Makamba, *Burundi* 86 C2
Makari, *Cameroon* 83 C7
Makarikari = Makgadikgadi Salt Pans, *Botswana* 88 C4
Makarovo, *Russia* 51 D11
Makarska, *Croatia* 29 E14
Makaryev, *Russia* 48 B6
Makasar = Ujung Pandang, *Indonesia* 63 F5
Makasar, Selat, *Indonesia* 63 E5
Makasar, Str. of = Makasar, Selat, *Indonesia* 63 E5
Makat, *Kazakstan* 50 E6
Makedonija = Macedonia ■, *Europe* 40 E5
Makeni, *S. Leone* 82 D2
Makeyevka = Makiyivka, *Ukraine* 47 H9
Makgadikgadi Salt Pans, *Botswana* 88 C4
Makhachkala, *Russia* 49 J8
Makharadze = Ozurgeti, *Georgia* 49 K5
Makhmūr, *Iraq* 70 C4
Makian, *Indonesia* 63 D7
Makindu, *Kenya* 86 C4
Makinsk, *Kazakstan* 50 D8
Makiyivka, *Ukraine* 47 H9
Makkah, *Si. Arabia* 74 C2
Makkovik, *Canada* 103 A8
Makó, *Hungary* 42 D5
Mako, *Senegal* 82 C2
Makokou, *Gabon* 84 D2
Makongo, *Dem. Rep. of the Congo* 86 B2
Makoro, *Dem. Rep. of the Congo* 86 B2
Maków Mazowiecki, *Poland* 45 F8
Maków Podhalański, *Poland* 45 J6
Makrá, *Greece* 39 E7
Makrai, *India* 66 H10
Makran Coast Range, *Pakistan* 66 G4
Makrana, *India* 68 F6
Mákri, *Greece* 41 F9
Makriyialos, *Greece* 36 D7
Mākū, *Iran* 70 B5
Makunda, *Botswana* 88 C3
Makung, *Taiwan* 59 F12
Makurazaki, *Japan* 55 J5
Makurdi, *Nigeria* 83 D6
Makūyeh, *Iran* 71 D7
Makwassie, *S. Africa* 88 D4
Makwiro, *Zimbabwe* 89 B5
Mâl, *Mauritania* 82 B2
Mal B., *Ireland* 15 D2
Mala, Pta., *Panama* 120 E3
Mala Belozërka, *Ukraine* 47 J8
Mala Kapela, *Croatia* 29 D12
Mała Panew →, *Poland* 45 H4
Mala Vyska, *Ukraine* 47 H6
Malabang, *Phil.* 61 H6
Malabar Coast, *India* 66 P9
Malabo = Rey Malabo, *Eq. Guin.* 83 E6
Malabon, *Phil.* 61 D4
Malabu, *Nigeria* 83 D7
Malacca, Str. of, *Indonesia* 65 L3
Malacky, *Slovak Rep.* 27 C10
Malad City, *U.S.A.* 114 E7
Maladeta, *Spain* 32 C5
Maladzyechna, *Belarus* 46 E4
Málaga, *Spain* 35 J6
Málaga □, *Spain* 35 J6
Malagarasi, *Tanzania* 86 D3
Malagarasi →, *Tanzania* 86 D2
Malagasy Rep. = Madagascar ■, *Africa* 89 C8
Malagón, *Spain* 35 F7
Malagón →, *Spain* 35 H3
Malahide, *Ireland* 15 C5
Malaimbandy, *Madag.* 89 C8
Malakâl, *Sudan* 81 F3
Malakand, *Pakistan* 68 B4
Malakwal, *Pakistan* 68 C5
Malamala, *Indonesia* 63 E6
Malanda, *Australia* 94 B4
Malang, *Indonesia* 62 F4
Malangen, *Norway* 8 B18
Malanje, *Angola* 84 F3
Mälaren, *Sweden* 10 E11
Malargüe, *Argentina* 126 D2
Malartic, *Canada* 102 C4
Malaryta, *Belarus* 47 G3
Malatya, *Turkey* 70 B3
Malawi ■, *Africa* 87 E3
Malawi, L. = Nyasa, L., *Africa* 87 E3
Malay Pen., *Asia* 65 J3
Malaya Belozërka = Mala Belozërka, *Ukraine* 47 J8
Malaya Vishera, *Russia* 46 C7
Malaya Viska = Mala Vyska, *Ukraine* 47 H6
Malaybalay, *Phil.* 61 G6
Malāyer, *Iran* 71 C6
Malaysia ■, *Asia* 65 K4
Malazgirt, *Turkey* 70 B4
Malbaza, *Niger* 83 C6
Malbon, *Australia* 94 C3
Malbooma, *Australia* 95 E1
Malbork, *Poland* 44 D6
Malcésine, *Italy* 28 C7
Malchin, *Germany* 24 B8
Malchow, *Germany* 24 B8
Malcolm, *Australia* 93 E3
Malcolm, Pt., *Australia* 93 F3
Malczyce, *Poland* 45 G3
Maldah, *India* 69 G13
Maldegem, *Belgium* 17 C3
Malden, *Mass., U.S.A.* 111 D13
Malden, *Mo., U.S.A.* 113 G10
Malden I., *Kiribati* 97 H12
Maldives ■, *Ind. Oc.* 52 J11
Maldonado, *Uruguay* 127 C5
Maldonado, Punta, *Mexico* 119 D5
Malè, *Italy* 28 B7
Malé, *Maldives* 53 J11
Malé Karpaty, *Slovak Rep.* 27 C10
Maléa, Ákra, *Greece* 38 E5
Malegaon, *India* 66 J9
Malei, *Mozam.* 87 F4
Malek, *Sudan* 81 F3
Malek Kandī, *Iran* 70 B5
Malela, *Dem. Rep. of the Congo* 86 C2
Malema, *Mozam.* 87 E4
Máleme, *Greece* 36 D5
Maleny, *Australia* 95 D5
Målerås, *Sweden* 11 H9
Malerkotla, *India* 68 D6
Máles, *Greece* 36 D7
Malesherbes, *France* 19 D9
Maleshevska Planina, *Europe* 40 E7
Malesína, *Greece* 38 C5
Malestroit, *France* 18 E4
Malfa, *Italy* 31 D7
Malgobek, *Russia* 49 J7
Malgomaj, *Sweden* 8 D17
Malgrat = Malgrat de Mar, *Spain* 32 D7
Malgrat de Mar, *Spain* 32 D7
Malha, *Sudan* 81 D2
Malhargarh, *India* 68 G6
Malheur →, *U.S.A.* 114 D5
Malheur L., *U.S.A.* 114 E4
Mali, *Guinea* 82 C2
Mali ■, *Africa* 82 B4
Mali →, *Burma* 67 G20
Mali Kanal, *Serbia, Yug.* 42 E4
Mali Kyun, *Burma* 64 F2
Malibu, *U.S.A.* 117 L8
Maliku, *Indonesia* 63 E6
Malili, *Indonesia* 63 E6
Målilla, *Sweden* 11 G9
Malimba, Mts., *Dem. Rep. of the Congo* 86 D2
Malin Hd., *Ireland* 15 A4
Malin Pen., *Ireland* 15 A4
Malindi, *Kenya* 86 C5
Malines = Mechelen, *Belgium* 17 C4
Malino, *Indonesia* 63 D6
Malinyi, *Tanzania* 87 D4
Malipo, *China* 58 F5
Maliq, *Albania* 40 F4
Malita, *Phil.* 63 C7
Maliwun, *Burma* 62 B1
Maliya, *India* 68 H4
Maljenik, *Serbia, Yug.* 40 C5
Malkara, *Turkey* 41 F10
Małkinia Górna, *Poland* 45 F9
Malko Tŭrnovo, *Bulgaria* 41 E11
Mallaig, *U.K.* 14 D3
Mallaoua, *Niger* 83 C6
Mallawan, *India* 69 F9
Mallawi, *Egypt* 80 B3
Mallemort, *France* 21 E9
Málles Venosta, *Italy* 28 B7
Mállia, *Greece* 36 D7
Mallión, Kólpos, *Greece* 36 D7
Mallorca, *Spain* 37 B10
Mallorytown, *Canada* 111 B9
Mallow, *Ireland* 15 D3
Malmbäck, *Sweden* 11 G8
Malmberget, *Sweden* 8 C19
Malmédy, *Belgium* 17 D6
Malmesbury, *S. Africa* 88 E2
Malmköping, *Sweden* 10 E10
Malmö, *Sweden* 11 J6
Malmslätt, *Sweden* 11 F9
Malmyzh, *Russia* 48 B10
Malnaş, *Romania* 43 D10
Malo Konare, *Bulgaria* 41 D8
Maloarkhangelsk, *Russia* 47 F9
Malolos, *Phil.* 63 B6
Malombe L., *Malawi* 87 E4
Małomice, *Poland* 45 G2
Malomir, *Bulgaria* 41 D10
Malone, *U.S.A.* 111 B10
Malong, *China* 58 E4
Małopolskie □, *Poland* 45 J7
Malorad, *Bulgaria* 40 C7
Måløy, *Norway* 9 F11
Maloyaroslovets, *Russia* 46 E9
Malpartida, *Spain* 35 F4
Malpaso, *Canary Is.* 37 G1
Malpelo, I. de, *Colombia* 124 C2
Malpica de Bergantiños, *Spain* 34 B2
Malpur, *India* 68 H5
Malpura, *India* 68 F6
Mals = Málles Venosta, *Italy* 28 B7
Malta, *Idaho, U.S.A.* 114 E7
Malta, *Mont., U.S.A.* 114 B10
Malta ■, *Europe* 36 D2
Maltahöhe, *Namibia* 88 C2
Maltepe, *Turkey* 41 F13
Malton, *Canada* 110 C5
Malton, *U.K.* 12 C7
Maluku, *Indonesia* 63 E7
Maluku □, *Indonesia* 63 E7
Maluku Sea = Molucca Sea, *Indonesia* 63 E6
Malumfashi, *Nigeria* 83 C6
Malung, *Sweden* 10 D7
Malungsfors, *Sweden* 10 D7
Maluwe, *Ghana* 82 D4
Malvan, *India* 66 L8
Malvern, *U.S.A.* 113 H8
Malvern Hills, *U.K.* 13 E5
Malvinas, Is. = Falkland Is. □, *Atl. Oc.* 128 G5
Malý Dunaj →, *Slovak Rep.* 27 D11
Malya, *Tanzania* 86 C3
Malyn, *Ukraine* 47 G5
Malyy Lyakhovskiy, Ostrov, *Russia* 51 B15
Mama, *Russia* 51 D12
Mamadysh, *Russia* 48 C10
Mamanguape, *Brazil* 125 E11
Mamarr Mitlā, *Egypt* 75 E1
Mamasa, *Indonesia* 63 E5
Mambasa, *Dem. Rep. of the Congo* 86 B2
Mamberamo →, *Indonesia* 63 E9
Mambilima Falls, *Zambia* 87 E2
Mambirima, *Dem. Rep. of the Congo* 87 E2
Mambo, *Tanzania* 86 C4
Mambrui, *Kenya* 86 C5
Mamburao, *Phil.* 61 E4
Mameigwess L., *Canada* 102 B2
Mamers, *France* 18 D7
Mamfé, *Cameroon* 83 D6
Mammoth, *U.S.A.* 115 K8
Mammoth Cave National Park, *U.S.A.* 108 G3
Mamoré →, *Bolivia* 122 E4
Mamou, *Guinea* 82 C2
Mampatá, *Guinea-Biss.* 82 C2
Mampikony, *Madag.* 89 B8
Mampong, *Ghana* 83 D4
Mamry, Jezioro, *Poland* 44 D8
Mamuju, *Indonesia* 63 E5
Mamuno, *Botswana* 88 C3
Mamuras, *Albania* 40 E3
Man, *Ivory C.* 82 D3
Man, I. of, *U.K.* 12 C3
Man-Bazar, *India* 69 H12
Man Na, *Burma* 67 H20
Mana →, *Fr. Guiana* 125 B8
Manaar, G. of = Mannar, G. of, *Asia* 66 Q11
Manacapuru, *Brazil* 124 D6
Manacor, *Spain* 37 B10
Manado, *Indonesia* 63 D6
Managua, *Nic.* 120 D2
Managua, L. de, *Nic.* 120 D2
Manakara, *Madag.* 89 C8
Manali, *India* 68 C7
Manama = Al Manāmah, *Bahrain* 71 E6
Manambao →, *Madag.* 89 B7
Manambato, *Madag.* 89 A8
Manambolo →, *Madag.* 89 B7
Manambolosy, *Madag.* 89 B8
Mananara, *Madag.* 89 B8
Mananara →, *Madag.* 89 C8
Mananjary, *Madag.* 89 C8
Manankoro, *Mali* 82 C3
Manantenina, *Madag.* 89 C8
Manaos = Manaus, *Brazil* 124 D7
Manapire →, *Venezuela* 124 B5
Manapouri, *N.Z.* 91 L1
Manapouri, L., *N.Z.* 91 L1
Manaqil, *Sudan* 81 E3
Manār, Jabal, *Yemen* 74 E3
Manaravolo, *Madag.* 89 C8
Manas, *China* 60 B3
Manas →, *India* 67 F17
Manaslu, *Nepal* 69 E11
Manasquan, *U.S.A.* 111 F10
Manassa, *U.S.A.* 115 H11
Manaung, *Burma* 67 K18
Manaus, *Brazil* 124 D7
Manavgat, *Turkey* 72 D4
Manawan L., *Canada* 105 B8
Manay, *Phil.* 61 H7
Manbij, *Syria* 70 B3
Mancha Real, *Spain* 35 H7
Manche □, *France* 18 C5
Manchegorsk, *Russia* 50 C4
Manchester, *U.K.* 12 D5
Manchester, *Calif., U.S.A.* 116 G3
Manchester, *Conn., U.S.A.* 111 E12
Manchester, *Ga., U.S.A.* 109 J3
Manchester, *Iowa, U.S.A.* 112 D9
Manchester, *Ky., U.S.A.* 108 G4
Manchester, *N.H., U.S.A.* 111 D13
Manchester, *N.Y., U.S.A.* 110 D7
Manchester, *Pa., U.S.A.* 111 F8
Manchester, *Tenn., U.S.A.* 109 H2
Manchester, *Vt., U.S.A.* 111 C11
Manchester L., *Canada* 105 A7
Manchhar L., *Pakistan* 68 F2
Manchuria = Dongbei, *China* 57 D13

Manchurian Plain, *China* 52 E16
Manciano, *Italy* 29 F8
Mancifa, *Ethiopia* 81 F5
Mand →, *India* 69 J10
Mand →, *Iran* 71 D7
Manda, *Ludewe, Tanzania* 87 E3
Manda, *Mbeya, Tanzania* 86 D3
Manda, *Mbeya, Tanzania* 87 D3
Mandabé, *Madag.* 89 C7
Mandaguari, *Brazil* 127 A5
Mandah = Töhöm, *Mongolia* 56 B5
Mandal, *Norway* 9 G12
Mandala, Puncak, *Indonesia* 63 E10
Mandalay, *Burma* 67 J20
Mandale = Mandalay, *Burma* 67 J20
Mandalgarh, *India* 68 G6
Mandalgovi, *Mongolia* 56 B4
Mandalī, *Iraq* 70 C5
Mandan, *U.S.A.* 112 B4
Mandaon, *Phil.* 61 E5
Mandar, Teluk, *Indonesia* 63 E5
Mándas, *Italy* 30 C2
Mandaue, *Phil.* 61 F5
Mandelieu-la-Napoule, *France* 21 E10
Mandera, *Kenya* 86 B5
Mandi, *India* 68 D7
Mandi Dabwali, *India* 68 E6
Mandiana, *Guinea* 82 C3
Mandimba, *Mozam.* 87 E4
Mandioli, *Indonesia* 63 E7
Mandla, *India* 69 H9
Mandø, *Denmark* 11 J2
Mandorah, *Australia* 92 B5
Mandoto, *Madag.* 89 B8
Mandoúdhion, *Greece* 38 C5
Mándra, *Greece* 38 C5
Mandra, *Pakistan* 68 C5
Mandrákhi, *Greece* 39 E9
Mandrare →, *Madag.* 89 D8
Mandritsara, *Madag.* 89 B8
Mandronarivo, *Madag.* 89 C8
Mandsaur, *India* 68 G6
Mandurah, *Australia* 93 F2
Mandúria, *Italy* 31 B10
Mandvi, *India* 68 H3
Mandya, *India* 66 N10
Mandzai, *Pakistan* 68 D2
Mané, *Burkina Faso* 83 C4
Maneh, *Iran* 71 B8
Manengouba, Mts., *Cameroon* 83 E6
Manera, *Madag.* 89 C7
Manérbio, *Italy* 28 C7
Maneroo Cr. →, *Australia* 94 C3
Manfalût, *Egypt* 80 B3
Manfredónia, *Italy* 29 G12
Manfredónia, G. di, *Italy* 29 G13
Manga, *Burkina Faso* 83 C4
Manga, *Niger* 83 C7
Mangabeiras, Chapada das, *Brazil* 125 F9
Mangalia, *Romania* 43 G13
Mangalore, *India* 66 N9
Mangan, *India* 69 F13
Mangaung, *S. Africa* 85 K5
Mangawan, *India* 69 G9
Mangaweka, *N.Z.* 91 H5
Manggar, *Indonesia* 62 E3
Manggawitu, *Indonesia* 63 E8
Mangindrano, *Madag.* 89 A8
Mangkalihat, Tanjung, *Indonesia* 63 D5
Mangla, *Pakistan* 68 C5
Mangla Dam, *Pakistan* 69 C5
Manglaur, *India* 68 E7
Mangnai, *China* 60 C4
Mango, *Togo* 83 C5
Mangoche, *Malawi* 87 E4
Mangoky →, *Madag.* 89 C7
Mangole, *Indonesia* 63 E6
Mangombe, *Dem. Rep. of the Congo* 86 C2
Mangonui, *N.Z.* 91 F4
Mangoro →, *Madag.* 89 B8
Mangrol, *Mad. P., India* 68 J4
Mangrol, *Raj., India* 68 G6
Mangualde, *Portugal* 34 E3
Mangueira, L. da, *Brazil* 127 C5
Mangum, *U.S.A.* 113 H5
Mangyshlak Poluostrov, *Kazakstan* 50 E6
Manhattan, *U.S.A.* 112 F6
Manhiça, *Mozam.* 89 D5
Mania →, *Madag.* 89 B8
Maniago, *Italy* 29 B9
Manica, *Mozam.* 89 B5
Manica □, *Mozam.* 89 B5
Manicaland □, *Zimbabwe* 87 F3
Manicoré, *Brazil* 124 E6
Manicouagan →, *Canada* 103 C6
Manicouagan, Rés., *Canada* 103 B6
Maniema □, *Dem. Rep. of the Congo* 86 C2
Manīfah, *Si. Arabia* 71 E6
Manifold, C., *Australia* 94 C5
Maniganggo, *China* 58 B2
Manigotagan, *Canada* 105 C9
Manigotagan →, *Canada* 105 C9
Manihari, *India* 69 G12
Manihiki, *Cook Is.* 97 J11
Manika, Plateau de la, *Dem. Rep. of the Congo* 87 E2
Manikpur, *India* 69 G9
Manila, *Phil.* 61 D4
Manila, *U.S.A.* 114 F9
Manila B., *Phil.* 61 D4
Manimpé, *Mali* 82 C3
Maningrida, *Australia* 94 A1
Maninian, *Ivory C.* 82 C3
Manipur □, *India* 67 G19
Manipur →, *Burma* 67 H19
Manisa, *Turkey* 39 C9
Manisa □, *Turkey* 39 C9
Manistee, *U.S.A.* 108 C2
Manistee →, *U.S.A.* 108 C2
Manistique, *U.S.A.* 108 C2
Manito L., *Canada* 105 C7
Manitoba □, *Canada* 105 B9
Manitoba, L., *Canada* 105 C9
Manitou, *Canada* 105 D9
Manitou, L., *Canada* 103 B6
Manitou Is., *U.S.A.* 108 C3
Manitou Springs, *U.S.A.* 112 F2
Manitoulin I., *Canada* 102 C3
Manitouwadge, *Canada* 102 C2
Manitowoc, *U.S.A.* 108 C2
Manizales, *Colombia* 124 B3
Manja, *Madag.* 89 C7
Manjacaze, *Mozam.* 89 C5
Manjakandriana, *Madag.* 89 B8
Manjhand, *Pakistan* 68 G3
Manjil, *Iran* 71 B6
Manjimup, *Australia* 93 F2
Manjra →, *India* 66 K10
Mankato, *Kans., U.S.A.* 112 F5
Mankato, *Minn., U.S.A.* 112 C8
Mankayane, *Swaziland* 89 D5
Mankera, *Pakistan* 68 D4
Mankim, *Cameroon* 83 D7
Mankono, *Ivory C.* 82 D3
Mankota, *Canada* 105 D7
Manlay = Üydzin, *Mongolia* 56 B4
Manlleu, *Spain* 32 C7
Manmad, *India* 66 J9
Mann Ranges, *Australia* 93 E5
Manna, *Indonesia* 62 E2
Mannar, *Sri Lanka* 66 Q11
Mannar, G. of, *Asia* 66 Q11
Mannar I., *Sri Lanka* 66 Q11
Mannheim, *Germany* 25 F4
Manning, *Canada* 104 B5
Manning, *Oreg., U.S.A.* 116 E3
Manning, *S.C., U.S.A.* 109 J5
Manning Prov. Park, *Canada* 104 D4
Mannu →, *Italy* 30 C2
Mannu, C., *Italy* 30 B1
Mano, *S. Leone* 82 D2
Mano →, *Liberia* 82 D2
Mano River, *Liberia* 82 D2
Manoharpur, *India* 69 H11
Manokwari, *Indonesia* 63 E8
Manolás, *Greece* 38 C3
Manombo, *Madag.* 89 C7
Manono, *Dem. Rep. of the Congo* 86 D2
Manoppello, *Italy* 29 F11
Manosque, *France* 21 E9
Manotick, *Canada* 111 A9
Manouane →, *Canada* 103 C5
Manouane, L., *Canada* 103 B5
Manp'o, *N. Korea* 57 D14
Manpojin = Manp'o, *N. Korea* 57 D14
Manpur, *Mad. P., India* 68 H6
Manpur, *Mad. P., India* 69 H10
Manresa, *Spain* 32 D6
Mansa, *Gujarat, India* 68 H5
Mansa, *Punjab, India* 68 E6
Mansa, *Zambia* 87 E2
Månsåsen, *Sweden* 10 A8
Mansehra, *Pakistan* 68 B5
Mansel I., *Canada* 101 B11
Mansfield, *U.K.* 12 D6
Mansfield, *La., U.S.A.* 113 J8
Mansfield, *Mass., U.S.A.* 111 D13
Mansfield, *Ohio, U.S.A.* 110 F2
Mansfield, *Pa., U.S.A.* 110 E7
Mansfield, Mt., *U.S.A.* 111 B12
Mansilla de las Mulas, *Spain* 34 C5
Mansle, *France* 20 C4
Mansoa, *Guinea-Biss.* 82 C1
Manson Creek, *Canada* 104 B4
Manta, *Ecuador* 124 D2
Mantalingajan, Mt., *Phil.* 61 G2
Mantare, *Tanzania* 86 C3
Manteca, *U.S.A.* 116 H5
Manteo, *U.S.A.* 109 H8
Mantes-la-Jolie, *France* 19 D8
Manthani, *India* 66 K11
Manti, *U.S.A.* 114 G8
Mantiqueira, Serra da, *Brazil* 127 A7
Manton, *U.S.A.* 108 C3
Mantorp, *Sweden* 11 F9
Mántova, *Italy* 28 C7
Mänttä, *Finland* 9 E21
Mantua = Mántova, *Italy* 28 C7
Manturovo, *Russia* 48 A7
Manu, *Peru* 124 F4
Manu →, *Peru* 124 F4
Manua Is., *Amer. Samoa* 91 B14
Manuel Alves →, *Brazil* 125 F9
Manui, *Indonesia* 63 E6
Manukau, *N.Z.* 91 G5
Manuripi →, *Bolivia* 124 F5
Many, *U.S.A.* 113 K8
Manyara, L., *Tanzania* 86 C4
Manyas, *Turkey* 41 F11
Manych →, *Russia* 49 G5
Manych-Gudilo, Ozero, *Russia* 49 G6
Manyonga →, *Tanzania* 86 C3
Manyoni, *Tanzania* 86 D3
Manzai, *Pakistan* 68 C4
Manzala, Bahra el, *Egypt* 80 H7
Manzanares, *Spain* 35 F7
Manzaneda, *Spain* 34 C3
Manzanillo, *Cuba* 120 B4
Manzanillo, *Mexico* 118 D4
Manzanillo, Pta., *Panama* 120 E4
Manzano Mts., *U.S.A.* 115 J10
Manzarīyeh, *Iran* 71 C6
Manzhouli, *China* 60 B6
Manzini, *Swaziland* 89 D5
Mao, *Chad* 79 F9
Maó, *Spain* 37 B11
Maoke, Pegunungan, *Indonesia* 63 E9
Maolin, *China* 57 C12
Maoming, *China* 59 G8
Maopi T'ou, *China* 59 G13
Maouri, Dallol →, *Niger* 83 C5
Maoxian, *China* 58 B4
Maoxing, *China* 57 B13
Mapam Yumco, *China* 60 C3
Mapastepec, *Mexico* 119 D6
Mapia, Kepulauan, *Indonesia* 63 D8
Mapimí, *Mexico* 118 B4
Mapimí, Bolsón de, *Mexico* 118 B4
Maping, *China* 59 B9
Mapinga, *Tanzania* 86 D4
Mapinhane, *Mozam.* 89 C6
Maple Creek, *Canada* 105 D7
Maple Valley, *U.S.A.* 116 C4
Mapleton, *U.S.A.* 114 D2
Mapuera →, *Brazil* 124 D7
Mapulanguene, *Mozam.* 89 C5
Maputo, *Mozam.* 89 D5
Maputo □, *Mozam.* 89 D5
Maputo, B. de, *Mozam.* 89 D5
Maqiaohe, *China* 57 B16
Maqnā, *Si. Arabia* 70 D2
Maqueda, *Spain* 34 E6
Maquela do Zombo, *Angola* 84 F3
Maquinchao, *Argentina* 128 E3
Maquoketa, *U.S.A.* 112 D9
Mar, Serra do, *Brazil* 127 B6
Mar Chiquita, L., *Argentina* 126 C3
Mar del Plata, *Argentina* 126 D4
Mar Menor, *Spain* 33 H4
Mara, *Tanzania* 86 C3
Mara □, *Tanzania* 86 C3
Maraã, *Brazil* 124 D5
Marabá, *Brazil* 125 E9
Maracá, I. de, *Brazil* 125 C8
Maracaibo, *Venezuela* 124 A4
Maracaibo, L. de, *Venezuela* 122 C3
Maracaju, *Brazil* 127 A4
Maracay, *Venezuela* 124 A5
Maracena, *Spain* 35 H7
Maradi, *Niger* 83 C6
Marāgheh, *Iran* 70 B5
Marāh, *Si. Arabia* 70 E5
Marajó, I. de, *Brazil* 122 D6
Marākand, *Iran* 70 B5
Maralal, *Kenya* 86 B4
Maralinga, *Australia* 93 F5
Maramaraereğlisi, *Turkey* 41 F11
Marampa, *S. Leone* 82 D2
Maramureş □, *Romania* 43 C9
Maran, *Malaysia* 65 L4
Marana, *U.S.A.* 115 K8
Maranboy, *Australia* 92 B5
Maranchón, *Spain* 32 D2
Marand, *Iran* 70 B5
Marang, *Malaysia* 65 K4
Maranguape, *Brazil* 125 D11
Maranhão = São Luís, *Brazil* 125 D10
Maranhão □, *Brazil* 125 E9
Marano, L. di, *Italy* 29 C10
Maranoa →, *Australia* 95 D4
Marañón →, *Peru* 122 D3
Marão, *Mozam.* 89 C5
Maraş = Kahramanmaraş, *Turkey* 70 B3
Mărăşeşti, *Romania* 43 E12
Maratea, *Italy* 31 C8
Marateca, *Portugal* 35 G2
Marathasa □, *Cyprus* 36 E11
Marathókambos, *Greece* 39 D8
Marathon, *Australia* 94 C3
Marathon, *Canada* 102 C2
Marathón, *Greece* 38 C5
Marathon, *N.Y., U.S.A.* 111 D8
Marathon, *Tex., U.S.A.* 113 K3
Marathóvouno, *Cyprus* 36 D12
Maratua, *Indonesia* 63 D5
Maravatío, *Mexico* 118 D4
Marawi City, *Phil.* 61 G6
Marāwih, *U.A.E.* 71 E7
Marbella, *Spain* 35 J6
Marble Bar, *Australia* 92 D2
Marble Falls, *U.S.A.* 113 K5
Marblehead, *U.S.A.* 111 D14
Marburg, *Germany* 24 E4
Marcal →, *Hungary* 42 C2
Marcali, *Hungary* 42 D2
Marcaria, *Italy* 28 C7
Mărcăuţi, *Moldova* 43 B12
March, *U.K.* 13 E8
Marche, *France* 20 B5
Marche □, *Italy* 29 E10
Marche-en-Famenne, *Belgium* 17 D5
Marchena, *Spain* 35 H5
Marches = Marche □, *Italy* 29 E10
Marciana Marina, *Italy* 28 F7
Marcianise, *Italy* 31 A7
Marcigny, *France* 19 F11
Marcillat-en-Combraille, *France* 19 F9
Marck, *France* 19 B8
Marckolsheim, *France* 19 D14
Marco, *U.S.A.* 109 N5
Marcos Juárez, *Argentina* 126 C3
Mărculeşti, *Moldova* 43 C13
Marcus I. = Minami-Tori-Shima, *Pac. Oc.* 96 E7
Marcus Necker Ridge, *Pac. Oc.* 96 F9
Marcy, Mt., *U.S.A.* 111 B11
Mardan, *Pakistan* 68 B5
Mardin, *Turkey* 70 B4
Mårdsjön, *Sweden* 10 A9
Marécchia →, *Italy* 29 D9
Maree, L., *U.K.* 14 D3
Mareeba, *Australia* 94 B4
Mareetsane, *S. Africa* 88 D4
Maremma, *Italy* 29 F8
Maréna, *Mali* 82 C2
Maréna, *Mali* 82 C3
Marengo, *U.S.A.* 112 E8
Marennes, *France* 20 C2
Marenyi, *Kenya* 86 C4
Marerano, *Madag.* 89 C7
Maréttimo, *Italy* 30 E5
Mareuil, *France* 20 C4
Marfa, *U.S.A.* 113 K2
Marfa Pt., *Malta* 36 D1
Marganets = Marhanets, *Ukraine* 47 J8
Margaret →, *Australia* 92 C4
Margaret Bay, *Canada* 104 C3
Margaret L., *Canada* 104 B5
Margaret River, *Australia* 93 F2
Margarita, I. de, *Venezuela* 122 B4
Margarítion, *Greece* 38 B2
Margaritovo, *Russia* 54 C7
Margate, *S. Africa* 89 E5
Margate, *U.K.* 13 F9
Margeride, Mts. de la, *France* 20 D7
Margherita di Savóia, *Italy* 31 A9
Marghita, *Romania* 42 C7
Margonin, *Poland* 45 F4
Margosatubig, *Phil.* 61 H5
Mārgow, Dasht-e, *Afghan.* 66 D3
Marguerite, *Canada* 104 C4
Marhanets, *Ukraine* 47 J8
Mari El □, *Russia* 48 B8
Mari Indus, *Pakistan* 68 C4
Mari Republic = Mari El □, *Russia* 48 B8
María, Sa. de, *Spain* 33 H2
María Elena, *Chile* 126 A2
María Grande, *Argentina* 126 C4
Maria I., *N. Terr., Australia* 94 A2
Maria I., *Tas., Australia* 94 G4
Maria van Diemen, C., *N.Z.* 91 F4
Mariager, *Denmark* 11 H3
Mariager Fjord, *Denmark* 11 H4
Mariakani, *Kenya* 86 C4
Marian, *Australia* 94 C4
Marian L., *Canada* 104 A5
Mariana Trench, *Pac. Oc.* 52 H18
Marianao, *Cuba* 120 B3
Marianna, *Ark., U.S.A.* 113 H9
Marianna, *Fla., U.S.A.* 109 K3
Mariannelund, *Sweden* 11 G9
Mariánské Lázně, *Czech Rep.* 26 B5
Marias →, *U.S.A.* 114 C8
Mariato, Punta, *Panama* 120 E3
Mariazell, *Austria* 26 D8
Maribo, *Denmark* 11 K5
Maribor, *Slovenia* 29 B12
Marico →, *Africa* 88 C4
Maricopa, *Ariz., U.S.A.* 115 K7
Maricopa, *Calif., U.S.A.* 117 K7
Marîdî, *Sudan* 81 G2
Marîdî, Wadi →, *Sudan* 81 F2
Marié →, *Brazil* 124 D5
Marie Byrd Land, *Antarctica* 5 D14
Marie-Galante, *Guadeloupe* 121 C7
Mariecourt = Kangiqsujuaq, *Canada* 101 B12
Mariefred, *Sweden* 10 E11
Marieholm, *Sweden* 11 J7
Mariembourg, *Belgium* 17 D4
Marienbad = Mariánské Lázně, *Czech Rep.* 26 B5
Marienberg, *Germany* 24 E9
Mariental, *Namibia* 88 C2
Marienville, *U.S.A.* 110 E5
Mariestad, *Sweden* 11 F7
Marietta, *Ga., U.S.A.* 109 J3
Marietta, *Ohio, U.S.A.* 108 F5
Marieville, *Canada* 111 A11
Mariga →, *Nigeria* 83 C6
Marignane, *France* 21 E9
Marihatag, *Phil.* 61 G7
Mariinsk, *Russia* 50 D9
Mariinskiy Posad, *Russia* 48 B8
Marijampolė, *Lithuania* 9 J20
Marijampolės □, *Lithuania* 44 D10
Marília, *Brazil* 127 A6
Marín, *Spain* 34 C2
Marina, *U.S.A.* 116 J5
Marinduque, *Phil.* 63 B6
Marine City, *U.S.A.* 110 D2
Marineo, *Italy* 30 E6
Marinette, *U.S.A.* 108 C2
Maringá, *Brazil* 127 A5
Marinha Grande, *Portugal* 34 F2
Marino, *Italy* 29 G9
Marion, *Ala., U.S.A.* 109 J2
Marion, *Ill., U.S.A.* 113 G10
Marion, *Ind., U.S.A.* 108 E3
Marion, *Iowa, U.S.A.* 112 D9
Marion, *Kans., U.S.A.* 112 F6
Marion, *N.C., U.S.A.* 109 H5
Marion, *Ohio, U.S.A.* 108 E4
Marion, *S.C., U.S.A.* 109 H6
Marion, *Va., U.S.A.* 109 G5
Marion, L., *U.S.A.* 109 J5
Mariposa, *U.S.A.* 116 H7
Mariscal Estigarribia, *Paraguay* 126 A3
Maritime Alps = Maritimes, Alpes, *Europe* 21 D11
Maritimes, Alpes, *Europe* 21 D11
Maritsa = Évros →, *Greece* 72 B2
Maritsá, *Greece* 36 C10
Mariupol, *Ukraine* 47 J9
Marīvān, *Iran* 70 C5
Marj 'Uyūn, *Lebanon* 75 B4
Marka, *Si. Arabia* 80 D5
Markam, *China* 58 C2
Markaryd, *Sweden* 11 H7
Markazī □, *Iran* 71 C6
Markdale, *Canada* 110 B4
Marked Tree, *U.S.A.* 113 H9
Markelsdorfer Huk, *Germany* 24 A7
Market Drayton, *U.K.* 12 E5
Market Harborough, *U.K.* 13 E7
Market Rasen, *U.K.* 12 D7
Markham, *Canada* 110 C5
Markham, Mt., *Antarctica* 5 E11
Marki, *Poland* 45 F8
Markkleeberg, *Germany* 24 D8
Markleeville, *U.S.A.* 116 G7
Markoupoulon, *Greece* 38 D5
Markovac, *Serbia, Yug.* 40 B5
Markovo, *Russia* 51 C17
Markoye, *Burkina Faso* 83 C5
Marks, *Russia* 48 E8
Marksville, *U.S.A.* 113 K8
Markt Schwaben, *Germany* 25 G7
Marktoberdorf, *Germany* 25 H6
Marktredwitz, *Germany* 25 E8
Marl, *Germany* 24 D3
Marla, *Australia* 95 D1
Marlbank, *Canada* 110 B7
Marlboro, *Mass., U.S.A.* 111 D13
Marlboro, *N.Y., U.S.A.* 111 E11
Marlborough, *Australia* 94 C4
Marlborough, *U.K.* 13 F6
Marlborough Downs, *U.K.* 13 F6
Marle, *France* 19 C10
Marlin, *U.S.A.* 113 K6
Marlow, *Germany* 24 A8
Marlow, *U.S.A.* 113 H6
Marmagao, *India* 66 M8
Marmande, *France* 20 D4
Marmara, *Turkey* 41 F11
Marmara, Sea of = Marmara Denizi, *Turkey* 41 F12
Marmara Denizi, *Turkey* 41 F12
Marmara Gölü, *Turkey* 39 C10
Marmaris, *Turkey* 39 E10
Marmaris Limanı, *Turkey* 39 E10
Marmion, Mt., *Australia* 93 E2
Marmion L., *Canada* 102 C1
Marmolada, Mte., *Italy* 29 B8
Marmolejo, *Spain* 35 G6
Marmora, *Canada* 102 D4
Mármora, La, *Italy* 30 C2
Marnay, *France* 19 E12
Marne, *Germany* 24 B5
Marne □, *France* 19 D11
Marne →, *France* 19 D9
Marneuli, *Georgia* 49 K7
Maroala, *Madag.* 89 B8
Maroantsetra, *Madag.* 89 B8
Maroelaboom, *Namibia* 88 B2
Marofandilia, *Madag.* 89 C7
Marolambo, *Madag.* 89 C8
Maromandia, *Madag.* 89 A8
Marondera, *Zimbabwe* 87 F3
Maroni →, *Fr. Guiana* 125 B8
Marónia, *Greece* 41 F9
Maronne →, *France* 20 C5
Maroochydore, *Australia* 95 D5
Maros →, *Hungary* 42 D5
Marosakoa, *Madag.* 89 B8
Maroseranana, *Madag.* 89 B8
Maróstica, *Italy* 29 C8
Marotandrano, *Madag.* 89 B8
Marotaolano, *Madag.* 89 A8
Maroua, *Cameroon* 83 C7
Marovato, *Madag.* 89 B8
Marovoay, *Madag.* 89 B8
Marquard, *S. Africa* 88 D4
Marquesas Is. = Marquises, Is., *Pac. Oc.* 97 H14
Marquette, *U.S.A.* 108 B2
Marquise, *France* 19 B8
Marquises, Is., *Pac. Oc.* 97 H14
Marra, Djebel, *Sudan* 79 F10
Marra, Gebel, *Sudan* 81 F2
Marracuene, *Mozam.* 89 D5
Marradi, *Italy* 29 D8
Marrakech, *Morocco* 78 B4
Marratxi, *Spain* 32 F7
Marrawah, *Australia* 94 G3
Marree, *Australia* 95 D2
Marrero, *U.S.A.* 113 L9
Marrimane, *Mozam.* 89 C5
Marromeu, *Mozam.* 89 B6
Marroquí, Punta, *Spain* 35 K5
Marrubane, *Mozam.* 87 F4
Marrúbiu, *Italy* 30 C1
Marrupa, *Mozam.* 87 E4
Mars Hill, *U.S.A.* 109 B12
Marsá 'Alam, *Egypt* 80 B3
Marsá Matrûh, *Egypt* 80 A2
Marsá Sha'b, *Sudan* 80 C4
Marsabit, *Kenya* 86 B4
Marsala, *Italy* 30 E5
Marsalforn, *Malta* 36 C1
Mârşani, *Romania* 43 F9
Marsberg, *Germany* 24 D4
Marsciano, *Italy* 29 F9

Marseillan, *France* 20 E7
Marseille, *France* 21 E9
Marseilles = Marseille, *France* 21 E9
Marsh I., *U.S.A.* 113 L9
Marshall, *Liberia* 82 D2
Marshall, *Ark., U.S.A.* 113 H8
Marshall, *Mich., U.S.A.* 108 D3
Marshall, *Minn., U.S.A.* 112 C7
Marshall, *Mo., U.S.A.* 112 F8
Marshall, *Tex., U.S.A.* 113 J7
Marshall →, *Australia* 94 C2
Marshall Is. ■, *Pac. Oc.* 96 G9
Marshalltown, *U.S.A.* 112 D8
Marshbrook, *Zimbabwe* 89 B5
Marshfield, *Mo., U.S.A.* 113 G8
Marshfield, *Vt., U.S.A.* 111 B12
Marshfield, *Wis., U.S.A.* 112 C9
Marshūn, *Iran* 71 B6
Mársico Nuovo, *Italy* 31 B8
Märsta, *Sweden* 10 E11
Marstal, *Denmark* 11 K4
Marstrand, *Sweden* 11 G5
Mart, *U.S.A.* 113 K6
Marta →, *Italy* 29 F8
Martaban, *Burma* 67 L20
Martaban, G. of, *Burma* 67 L20
Martano, *Italy* 31 B11
Martapura, *Kalimantan, Indonesia* 62 E4
Martapura, *Sumatera, Indonesia* 62 E2
Marte, *Nigeria* 83 C7
Martel, *France* 20 D5
Martelange, *Belgium* 17 E5
Martellago, *Italy* 29 C9
Martés, Sierra, *Spain* 33 F4
Martfű, *Hungary* 42 C5
Martha's Vineyard, *U.S.A.* 111 E14
Martigné-Ferchaud, *France* 18 E5
Martigny, *Switz.* 25 J3
Martigues, *France* 21 E9
Martin, *Slovak Rep.* 27 B11
Martin, *S. Dak., U.S.A.* 112 D4
Martin, *Tenn., U.S.A.* 113 G10
Martín →, *Spain* 32 D4
Martin, L., *U.S.A.* 109 J3
Martina Franca, *Italy* 31 B10
Martinborough, *N.Z.* 91 J5
Martinez, *Calif., U.S.A.* 116 G4
Martinez, *Ga., U.S.A.* 109 J4
Martinique ■, *W. Indies* 121 D7
Martinique Passage, *W. Indies* 121 C7
Martínon, *Greece* 38 C5
Martinópolis, *Brazil* 127 A5
Martins Ferry, *U.S.A.* 110 F4
Martinsberg, *Austria* 26 C8
Martinsburg, *Pa., U.S.A.* 110 F6
Martinsburg, *W. Va., U.S.A.* 108 F7
Martinsicuro, *Italy* 29 F10
Martinsville, *Ind., U.S.A.* 108 F2
Martinsville, *Va., U.S.A.* 109 G6
Marton, *N.Z.* 91 J5
Martorell, *Spain* 32 D6
Martos, *Spain* 35 H7
Martuni, *Armenia* 49 K7
Maru, *Nigeria* 83 C6
Marudi, *Malaysia* 62 D4
Maruf, *Afghan.* 66 D5
Marugame, *Japan* 55 G6
Marunga, *Angola* 88 B3
Marungu, Mts., *Dem. Rep. of the Congo* 86 D3
Marv Dasht, *Iran* 71 D7
Marvast, *Iran* 71 D7
Marvejols, *France* 20 D7
Marvel Loch, *Australia* 93 F2
Marwar, *India* 68 G5
Mary, *Turkmenistan* 50 F7
Maryborough = Port Laoise, *Ireland* 15 C4
Maryborough, *Australia* 95 D5
Maryfield, *Canada* 105 D8
Maryland □, *U.S.A.* 108 F7
Maryland Junction, *Zimbabwe* 87 F3
Maryport, *U.K.* 12 C4
Mary's Harbour, *Canada* 103 B8
Marystown, *Canada* 103 C8
Marysville, *Canada* 104 D5
Marysville, *Calif., U.S.A.* 116 F5
Marysville, *Kans., U.S.A.* 112 F6
Marysville, *Mich., U.S.A.* 110 D2
Marysville, *Ohio, U.S.A.* 108 E4
Marysville, *Wash., U.S.A.* 116 B4
Maryville, *Mo., U.S.A.* 112 E7
Maryville, *Tenn., U.S.A.* 109 H4
Marzūq, *Libya* 79 C8
Masahunga, *Tanzania* 86 C3
Masai Steppe, *Tanzania* 86 C4
Masaka, *Uganda* 86 C3
Masalembo, Kepulauan, *Indonesia* 62 F4
Masalima, Kepulauan, *Indonesia* 62 F5
Masallı, *Azerbaijan* 73 C13
Masamba, *Indonesia* 63 E6
Masan, *S. Korea* 57 G15
Masandam, Ra's, *Oman* 71 E8
Masasi, *Tanzania* 87 E4
Masaya, *Nic.* 120 D2
Masba, *Nigeria* 83 C7
Masbate, *Phil.* 61 E5
Máscali, *Italy* 31 E8
Mascara, *Algeria* 78 A6
Mascota, *Mexico* 118 C4
Masela, *Indonesia* 63 F7
Maseru, *Lesotho* 88 D4
Mashaba, *Zimbabwe* 87 G3
Mashābīh, *Si. Arabia* 70 E3
Mashan, *China* 58 F7
Mashar, *Sudan* 81 F2
Mashegu, *Nigeria* 83 D6
Masherbrum, *Pakistan* 69 B7
Mashhad, *Iran* 71 B8
Mashi, *Nigeria* 83 C6
Mashīz, *Iran* 71 D8
Māshkel, Hāmūn-i-, *Pakistan* 66 E3
Mashki Chāh, *Pakistan* 66 E3
Mashonaland, *Zimbabwe* 85 H6
Mashonaland Central □, *Zimbabwe* 89 B5
Mashonaland East □, *Zimbabwe* 89 B5
Mashonaland West □, *Zimbabwe* 89 B4
Mashrakh, *India* 69 F11
Mashtaga = Maştağa, *Azerbaijan* 49 K10
Masindi, *Uganda* 86 B3
Masindi Port, *Uganda* 86 B3
Maşīrah, *Oman* 74 C6
Maşīrah, Khalīj, *Oman* 74 C6
Masisi, *Dem. Rep. of the Congo* 86 C2
Masjed Soleyman, *Iran* 71 D6
Mask, L., *Ireland* 15 C2
Maskin, *Oman* 71 F8
Maslen Nos, *Bulgaria* 41 D11
Maslinica, *Croatia* 29 E13
Masnou = El Masnou, *Spain* 32 D7
Masoala, Tanjon' i, *Madag.* 89 B9
Masoarivo, *Madag.* 89 B7
Masohi = Amahai, *Indonesia* 63 E7
Masomeloka, *Madag.* 89 C8
Mason, *Nev., U.S.A.* 116 G7
Mason, *Tex., U.S.A.* 113 K5
Mason City, *U.S.A.* 112 D8
Maspalomas, *Canary Is.* 37 G4
Maspalomas, Pta., *Canary Is.* 37 G4
Masqat, *Oman* 74 C6
Massa, *Italy* 28 D7
Massa Maríttima, *Italy* 28 E7
Massachusetts □, *U.S.A.* 111 D13
Massachusetts B., *U.S.A.* 111 D14
Massafra, *Italy* 31 B10
Massakory, *Chad* 79 F9
Massanella, *Spain* 37 B9
Massangena, *Mozam.* 89 C5
Massango, *Angola* 84 F3
Massat, *France* 20 F5
Massawa = Mitsiwa, *Eritrea* 81 D4
Massena, *U.S.A.* 111 B10
Massénya, *Chad* 79 F9
Masset, *Canada* 104 C2
Masseube, *France* 20 E4
Massiac, *France* 20 C7
Massif Central, *France* 20 D7
Massigui, *Mali* 82 C3
Massillon, *U.S.A.* 110 F3
Massinga, *Mozam.* 89 C6
Massingir, *Mozam.* 89 C5
Mässlingen, *Sweden* 10 B6
Masson, *Canada* 111 A9
Masson I., *Antarctica* 5 C7
Maştağa, *Azerbaijan* 49 K10
Mastanli = Momchilgrad, *Bulgaria* 41 E9
Masterton, *N.Z.* 91 J5
Mastic, *U.S.A.* 111 F12
Mástikho, Ákra, *Greece* 39 C8
Mastuj, *Pakistan* 69 A5
Mastung, *Pakistan* 66 E5
Mastūrah, *Si. Arabia* 80 C4
Masty, *Belarus* 46 F3
Masuda, *Japan* 55 G5
Masvingo, *Zimbabwe* 87 G3
Masvingo □, *Zimbabwe* 87 G3
Maşyāf, *Syria* 70 C3
Maszewo, *Poland* 44 E2
Mat →, *Albania* 40 E3
Matabeleland, *Zimbabwe* 85 H5
Matabeleland North □, *Zimbabwe* 87 F2
Matabeleland South □, *Zimbabwe* 87 G2
Matachel →, *Spain* 35 G4
Matachewan, *Canada* 102 C3
Matadi, *Dem. Rep. of the Congo* 84 F2
Matagalpa, *Nic.* 120 D2
Matagami, *Canada* 102 C4
Matagami, L., *Canada* 102 C4
Matagorda B., *U.S.A.* 113 L6
Matagorda I., *U.S.A.* 113 L6
Matak, *Indonesia* 65 L6
Mátala, *Greece* 36 E6
Matam, *Senegal* 82 B2
Matameye, *Niger* 83 C6
Matamoros, *Campeche, Mexico* 119 D6
Matamoros, *Coahuila, Mexico* 118 B4
Matamoros, *Tamaulipas, Mexico* 119 B5
Ma'ṭan as Sarra, *Libya* 79 D10
Matandu →, *Tanzania* 87 D3
Matane, *Canada* 103 C6
Matang, *China* 58 F5
Matankari, *Niger* 83 C5
Matanomadh, *India* 68 H3
Matanzas, *Cuba* 120 B3
Matapa, *Botswana* 88 C3
Matapan, C. = Taínaron, Ákra, *Greece* 38 E4
Matapédia, *Canada* 103 C6
Matara, *Sri Lanka* 66 S12
Mataram, *Indonesia* 62 F5
Matarani, *Peru* 124 G4
Mataranka, *Australia* 92 B5
Matarma, Râs, *Egypt* 75 E1
Mataró, *Spain* 32 D7
Matarraña →, *Spain* 32 D5
Mataruška Banja, *Serbia, Yug.* 40 C4
Matatiele, *S. Africa* 89 E4
Mataura, *N.Z.* 91 M2
Matehuala, *Mexico* 118 C4
Mateke Hills, *Zimbabwe* 87 G3
Matera, *Italy* 31 B9
Matese, Monti del, *Italy* 31 A7
Mátészalka, *Hungary* 42 C7
Matetsi, *Zimbabwe* 87 F2
Matfors, *Sweden* 10 B11
Matha, *France* 20 C3
Mathis, *U.S.A.* 113 L6
Mathráki, *Greece* 36 A3
Mathura, *India* 68 F7
Mati, *Phil.* 61 H7
Matiakoali, *Burkina Faso* 83 C5
Matiali, *India* 69 F13
Matías Romero, *Mexico* 119 D5
Matibane, *Mozam.* 87 E5
Matima, *Botswana* 88 C3
Matiri Ra., *N.Z.* 91 J4
Matjiesfontein, *S. Africa* 88 E3
Matla →, *India* 69 J13
Matlamanyane, *Botswana* 88 B4
Matli, *Pakistan* 68 G3
Matlock, *U.K.* 12 D6
Matna, *Sudan* 81 E4
Mato Grosso □, *Brazil* 125 F8
Mato Grosso, Planalto do, *Brazil* 122 E5
Mato Grosso do Sul □, *Brazil* 125 G8
Matochkin Shar, *Russia* 50 B6
Matopo Hills, *Zimbabwe* 87 G2
Matopos, *Zimbabwe* 87 G2
Matosinhos, *Portugal* 34 D2
Matour, *France* 19 F11
Matroosberg, *S. Africa* 88 E2
Maṭruḥ, *Oman* 74 C6
Matsena, *Nigeria* 83 C7
Matsesta, *Russia* 49 J4
Matsu Tao, *Taiwan* 59 E13
Matsue, *Japan* 55 G6
Matsumae, *Japan* 54 D10
Matsumoto, *Japan* 55 F9
Matsusaka, *Japan* 55 G8
Matsuura, *Japan* 55 H4
Matsuyama, *Japan* 55 H6
Mattagami →, *Canada* 102 B3
Mattancheri, *India* 66 Q10
Mattawa, *Canada* 102 C4
Matterhorn, *Switz.* 25 K3
Mattersburg, *Austria* 27 D9
Matthew Town, *Bahamas* 121 B5
Matthew's Ridge, *Guyana* 124 B6
Mattice, *Canada* 102 C3
Mattituck, *U.S.A.* 111 F12
Mattō, *Japan* 55 F8
Mattoon, *U.S.A.* 108 F1
Matuba, *Mozam.* 89 C5
Matucana, *Peru* 124 F3
Matūn = Khowst, *Afghan.* 68 C3
Maturín, *Venezuela* 124 B6
Matveyev Kurgan, *Russia* 47 J10
Matxitxako, C., *Spain* 32 B2
Mau, *Mad. P., India* 69 F8
Mau, *Ut. P., India* 69 G10
Mau, *Ut. P., India* 69 G9
Mau Escarpment, *Kenya* 86 C4
Mau Ranipur, *India* 69 G8
Maubeuge, *France* 19 B10
Maubourguet, *France* 20 E4
Maud, Pt., *Australia* 92 D1
Maudin Sun, *Burma* 67 M19
Maués, *Brazil* 124 D7
Mauganj, *India* 67 G12
Maughold Hd., *U.K.* 12 C3
Mauguio, *France* 20 E7
Maui, *U.S.A.* 106 H16
Maulamyaing = Moulmein, *Burma* 67 L20
Maule □, *Chile* 126 D1
Mauléon-Licharre, *France* 20 E3
Maumee, *U.S.A.* 108 E4
Maumee →, *U.S.A.* 108 E4
Maumere, *Indonesia* 63 F6
Maumusson, Pertuis de, *France* 20 C2
Maun, *Botswana* 88 C3
Mauna Kea, *U.S.A.* 106 J17
Mauna Loa, *U.S.A.* 106 J17
Maungmagan Kyunzu, *Burma* 64 E1
Maupin, *U.S.A.* 114 D3
Maure-de-Bretagne, *France* 18 E5
Maurepas, L., *U.S.A.* 113 K9
Maures, *France* 21 E10
Mauriac, *France* 20 C6
Maurice, L., *Australia* 93 E5
Mauricie, Parc Nat. de la, *Canada* 102 C5
Maurienne, *France* 21 C10
Mauritania ■, *Africa* 78 E3
Mauritius ■, *Ind. Oc.* 77 J9
Mauron, *France* 18 D4
Maurs, *France* 20 D6
Mauston, *U.S.A.* 112 D9
Mauterndorf, *Austria* 26 D6
Mauthen, *Austria* 26 E6
Mauvezin, *France* 20 E4
Mauzé-sur-le-Mignon, *France* 20 B3
Mavli, *India* 68 G5
Mavrovë, *Albania* 40 F3
Mavuradonha Mts., *Zimbabwe* 87 F3
Mawa, *Dem. Rep. of the Congo* 86 B2
Mawai, *India* 69 H9
Mawana, *India* 68 E7
Mawand, *Pakistan* 68 E3
Mawk Mai, *Burma* 67 J20
Mawlaik, *Burma* 67 H19
Mawlamyine = Moulmein, *Burma* 67 L20
Mawqaq, *Si. Arabia* 70 E4
Mawson Coast, *Antarctica* 5 C6
Max, *U.S.A.* 112 B4
Maxcanú, *Mexico* 119 C6
Maxesibeni, *S. Africa* 89 E4
Maxhamish L., *Canada* 104 B4
Maxixe, *Mozam.* 89 C6
Maxville, *Canada* 111 A10
Maxwell, *U.S.A.* 116 F4
Maxwelton, *Australia* 94 C3
May, C., *U.S.A.* 108 F8
May Pen, *Jamaica* 120 C4
Maya →, *Russia* 51 D14
Maya Mts., *Belize* 119 D7
Mayaguana, *Bahamas* 121 B5
Mayagüez, *Puerto Rico* 121 C6
Mayahi, *Niger* 83 C6
Mayals = Maials, *Spain* 32 D5
Mayāmey, *Iran* 71 B7
Mayang, *China* 58 D7
Mayanup, *Australia* 93 F2
Mayapan, *Mexico* 119 C7
Mayarí, *Cuba* 121 B4
Maybell, *U.S.A.* 114 F9
Maybole, *U.K.* 14 F4
Maychew, *Ethiopia* 81 E4
Maydān, *Iraq* 70 C5
Maydena, *Australia* 94 G4
Mayen, *Germany* 25 E3
Mayenne, *France* 18 D6
Mayenne □, *France* 18 D6
Mayenne →, *France* 18 E6
Mayer, *U.S.A.* 115 J7
Mayerthorpe, *Canada* 104 C5
Mayfield, *Ky., U.S.A.* 109 G1
Mayfield, *N.Y., U.S.A.* 111 C10
Mayhill, *U.S.A.* 115 K11
Maykop, *Russia* 49 H5
Maymyo, *Burma* 64 A1
Maynard, *Mass., U.S.A.* 111 D13
Maynard, *Wash., U.S.A.* 116 C4
Maynard Hills, *Australia* 93 E2
Mayne →, *Australia* 94 C3
Maynooth, *Ireland* 15 C5
Mayo, *Canada* 100 B6
Mayo □, *Ireland* 15 C2
Mayo Daga, *Nigeria* 83 D7
Mayo Faran, *Nigeria* 83 D7
Mayon Volcano, *Phil.* 61 E5
Mayor I., *N.Z.* 91 G6
Mayorga, *Spain* 34 C5
Mayotte, *Ind. Oc.* 85 G9
Mayraira Pt., *Phil.* 61 B4
Mayskiy, *Russia* 49 J7
Maysville, *U.S.A.* 108 F4
Mayu, *Indonesia* 63 D7
Mayville, *N. Dak., U.S.A.* 112 B6
Mayville, *N.Y., U.S.A.* 110 D5
Mayya, *Russia* 51 C14
Mazabuka, *Zambia* 87 F2
Mazagán = El Jadida, *Morocco* 78 B4
Mazagão, *Brazil* 125 D8
Mazamet, *France* 20 E6
Mazán, *Peru* 124 D4
Māzandarān □, *Iran* 71 B7
Mazapil, *Mexico* 118 C4
Mazara del Vallo, *Italy* 30 E5
Mazarrón, *Spain* 33 H3
Mazarrón, G. de, *Spain* 33 H3
Mazaruni →, *Guyana* 124 B7
Mazatán, *Mexico* 118 B2
Mazatenango, *Guatemala* 120 D1
Mazatlán, *Mexico* 118 C3
Mažeikiai, *Lithuania* 9 H20
Māzhān, *Iran* 71 C8
Mazīnān, *Iran* 71 B8
Mazoe, *Mozam.* 87 F3
Mazoe →, *Mozam.* 87 F3
Mazowe, *Zimbabwe* 87 F3
Mazowieckie □, *Poland* 45 F8
Mazrûb, *Sudan* 81 E2
Mazu Dao, *China* 59 D12
Mazurian Lakes = Mazurski, Pojezierze, *Poland* 44 E7
Mazurski, Pojezierze, *Poland* 44 E7
Mazyr, *Belarus* 47 F5
Mbaba, *Senegal* 82 C1
Mbabane, *Swaziland* 89 D5
Mbagne, *Mauritania* 82 B2
M'bahiakro, *Ivory C.* 82 D4
Mbaïki, *C.A.R.* 84 D3
Mbala, *Zambia* 87 D3
Mbalabala, *Zimbabwe* 89 C4
Mbale, *Uganda* 86 B3
Mbalmayo, *Cameroon* 83 E7
Mbam →, *Cameroon* 83 E7
Mbamba Bay, *Tanzania* 87 E3
Mbandaka, *Dem. Rep. of the Congo* 84 D3
Mbanga, *Cameroon* 83 E6
Mbanza Congo, *Angola* 84 F2
Mbanza Ngungu, *Dem. Rep. of the Congo* 84 F2
Mbarara, *Uganda* 86 C3
Mbashe →, *S. Africa* 89 E4
Mbatto, *Ivory C.* 82 D4
Mbenkuru →, *Tanzania* 87 D4
Mberengwa, *Zimbabwe* 87 G2
Mberengwa, Mt., *Zimbabwe* 87 G2
Mberubu, *Nigeria* 83 D6
Mbesuma, *Zambia* 87 E3
Mbeya, *Tanzania* 87 D3
Mbeya □, *Tanzania* 86 D3
M'bili, *Sudan* 81 F2
Mbinga, *Tanzania* 87 E4
Mbini □, *Eq. Guin.* 84 D2
Mboki, *C.A.R.* 81 F2
M'bonge, *Cameroon* 83 E6
Mboro, *Senegal* 82 B1
M'boukou Res., *Cameroon* 83 D7
Mboune, *Senegal* 82 C2
Mbour, *Senegal* 82 C1
Mbout, *Mauritania* 82 B2
Mbuji-Mayi, *Dem. Rep. of the Congo* 86 D1
Mbulu, *Tanzania* 86 C4
Mburucuyá, *Argentina* 126 B4
Mchinja, *Tanzania* 87 D4
Mchinji, *Malawi* 87 E3
Mdantsane, *S. Africa* 85 L5
Mead, L., *U.S.A.* 117 J12
Meade, *U.S.A.* 113 G4
Meadow Lake, *Canada* 105 C7
Meadow Lake Prov. Park, *Canada* 105 C7
Meadow Valley Wash →, *U.S.A.* 117 J12
Meadville, *U.S.A.* 110 E4
Meaford, *Canada* 102 D3
Mealhada, *Portugal* 34 E2
Mealy Mts., *Canada* 103 B8
Meander River, *Canada* 104 B5
Meares, C., *U.S.A.* 114 D2
Mearim →, *Brazil* 125 D10
Meath □, *Ireland* 15 C5
Meath Park, *Canada* 105 C7
Meaulne, *France* 19 F9
Meaux, *France* 19 D9
Mebechi-Gawa →, *Japan* 54 D10
Mecanhelas, *Mozam.* 87 F4
Mecca = Makkah, *Si. Arabia* 74 C2
Mecca, *U.S.A.* 117 M10
Mechanicsburg, *U.S.A.* 110 F8
Mechanicville, *U.S.A.* 111 D11
Mechara, *Ethiopia* 81 F5
Mechelen, *Belgium* 17 C4
Mecheria, *Algeria* 78 B5
Mechernich, *Germany* 24 E2
Mechetinskaya, *Russia* 49 G5
Mecidiye, *Turkey* 41 F10
Mecitözü, *Turkey* 72 B6
Mecklenburg-Vorpommern □, *Germany* 24 B8
Mecklenburger Bucht, *Germany* 24 A7
Meconta, *Mozam.* 87 E4
Mecsek, *Hungary* 42 D3
Meda, *Portugal* 34 E3
Medan, *Indonesia* 62 D1
Medanosa, Pta., *Argentina* 128 F3
Mede, *Italy* 28 C5
Médéa, *Algeria* 78 A6
Mededa, *Bos.-H.* 42 G4
Medellín, *Colombia* 124 B3
Medelpad, *Sweden* 10 B10
Medemblik, *Neths.* 17 B5
Mederdra, *Mauritania* 82 B1
Medford, *Mass., U.S.A.* 111 D13
Medford, *Oreg., U.S.A.* 114 E2
Medford, *Wis., U.S.A.* 112 C9
Medgidia, *Romania* 43 F13
Medi, *Sudan* 81 F3
Media Agua, *Argentina* 126 C2
Media Luna, *Argentina* 126 C2
Medianeira, *Brazil* 127 B5
Mediaş, *Romania* 43 D9
Medicina, *Italy* 29 D8
Medicine Bow, *U.S.A.* 114 F10
Medicine Bow Pk., *U.S.A.* 114 F10
Medicine Bow Ra., *U.S.A.* 114 F10
Medicine Hat, *Canada* 105 D6
Medicine Lake, *U.S.A.* 112 A2
Medicine Lodge, *U.S.A.* 113 G5
Medina = Al Madīnah, *Si. Arabia* 70 E3
Medina, *N. Dak., U.S.A.* 112 B5
Medina, *N.Y., U.S.A.* 110 C6
Medina, *Ohio, U.S.A.* 110 E3
Medina →, *U.S.A.* 113 L5
Medina de Pomar, *Spain* 34 C7
Medina de Ríoseco, *Spain* 34 D5
Medina del Campo, *Spain* 34 D6
Medina L., *U.S.A.* 113 L5
Medina Sidonia, *Spain* 35 J5
Medinaceli, *Spain* 32 D2
Medinipur, *India* 69 H12
Mediterranean Sea, *Europe* 6 H7
Médoc, *France* 20 C3
Medulin, *Croatia* 29 D10
Medveđa, *Serbia, Yug.* 40 D5
Medvedevo, *Russia* 48 B8
Medveditsa →, *Tver, Russia* 46 D9
Medveditsa →, *Volgograd, Russia* 48 F6
Medvedok, *Russia* 48 B10
Medvezhi, Ostrava, *Russia* 51 B17
Medvezhyegorsk, *Russia* 50 C4
Medway □, *U.K.* 13 F8
Medway →, *U.K.* 13 F8
Medzev, *Slovak Rep.* 27 C13
Medzilaborce, *Slovak Rep.* 27 B14
Medžitlija, *Macedonia* 40 F5
Meekatharra, *Australia* 93 E2
Meeker, *U.S.A.* 114 F10
Meelpaeg Res., *Canada* 103 C8
Meersburg, *Germany* 25 H5
Meerut, *India* 68 E7
Meeteetse, *U.S.A.* 114 D9
Mega, *Ethiopia* 81 G4
Megálo Khorío, *Greece* 39 E9
Megálo Petalí, *Greece* 38 D6
Megalópolis, *Greece* 38 D4

Meganísi, *Greece* 38 C2
Mégara, *Greece* 38 D5
Megasini, *India* 69 J12
Megdhova →, *Greece* 38 B3
Megève, *France* 21 C10
Meghalaya □, *India* 67 G17
Meghezez, *Ethiopia* 81 F4
Mégiscane, L., *Canada* 102 C4
Megiste, *Greece* 39 E11
Megra, *Russia* 46 B9
Mehadia, *Romania* 42 F7
Meharry, Mt., *Australia* 92 D2
Mehedeby, *Sweden* 10 D11
Mehedinţi □, *Romania* 42 F7
Meheisa, *Sudan* 80 D3
Mehlville, *U.S.A.* 112 F9
Mehndawal, *India* 69 F10
Mehr Jān, *Iran* 71 C7
Mehrābād, *Iran* 70 B5
Mehrān, *Iran* 70 C5
Mehrīz, *Iran* 71 D7
Mehun-sur-Yèvre, *France* 19 E9
Mei Jiang →, *China* 59 E11
Mei Xian, *China* 56 G4
Meicheng, *China* 59 C12
Meichengzhen, *China* 59 C8
Meichuan, *China* 59 B10
Meigu, *China* 58 C4
Meiktila, *Burma* 67 J19
Meinerzhagen, *Germany* 24 D3
Meiningen, *Germany* 24 E6
Meira, Serra de, *Spain* 34 B3
Meiringen, *Switz.* 25 J4
Meishan, *China* 58 B4
Meissen, *Germany* 24 D9
Meissner, *Germany* 24 D5
Meitan, *China* 58 D6
Meizhou, *China* 59 E11
Meja, *India* 69 G10
Mejillones, *Chile* 126 A1
Mekdela, *Ethiopia* 81 E4
Mekele, *Ethiopia* 81 E4
Mekhtar, *Pakistan* 66 D6
Meknès, *Morocco* 78 B4
Meko, *Nigeria* 83 D5
Mekong →, *Asia* 65 H6
Mekongga, *Indonesia* 63 E6
Mekrou →, *Benin* 83 C5
Mekvari = Kür →, *Azerbaijan* 73 C13
Mel, *Italy* 29 B9
Melagiri Hills, *India* 66 N10
Melaka, *Malaysia* 65 L4
Melalap, *Malaysia* 62 C5
Mélambes, *Greece* 36 D6
Melanesia, *Pac. Oc.* 96 H7
Melbourne, *U.S.A.* 109 L5
Melchor Múzquiz, *Mexico* 118 B4
Melchor Ocampo, *Mexico* 118 C4
Méldola, *Italy* 29 D9
Meldorf, *Germany* 24 A5
Melegnano, *Italy* 28 C6
Melenci, *Serbia, Yug.* 42 E5
Melenki, *Russia* 48 C5
Mélèzes →, *Canada* 102 A5
Melfi, *Italy* 31 B8
Melfort, *Canada* 105 C8
Melfort, *Zimbabwe* 87 F3
Melgaço, *Portugal* 34 C2
Melgar de Fernamental, *Spain* 34 C6
Melhus, *Norway* 8 E14
Melide, *Spain* 34 C2
Meligalá, *Greece* 38 D3
Melilla, *N. Afr.* 78 A5
Melilli, *Italy* 31 E8
Melipilla, *Chile* 126 C1
Mélissa, Ákra, *Greece* 36 D6
Mélissa Óros, *Greece* 39 D8
Melita, *Canada* 105 D8
Mélito di Porto Salvo, *Italy* 31 E8
Melitopol, *Ukraine* 47 J8
Melk, *Austria* 26 C8
Mellan Fryken, *Sweden* 10 E7
Mellansel, *Sweden* 8 E18
Mellbystrand, *Sweden* 11 H6
Melle, *France* 20 B3
Melle, *Germany* 24 C4
Mellen, *U.S.A.* 112 B9
Mellerud, *Sweden* 11 F6
Mellette, *U.S.A.* 112 C5
Mellid = Melide, *Spain* 34 C2
Mellieha, *Malta* 36 D1
Mellit, *Sudan* 81 E2
Mellrichstadt, *Germany* 24 E6
Melnik, *Bulgaria* 40 E7
Mělník, *Czech Rep.* 26 A7
Melo, *Uruguay* 127 C5
Melolo, *Indonesia* 63 F6
Melouprey, *Cambodia* 64 F5
Melrose, *U.K.* 14 F6
Melrose, *Minn., U.S.A.* 112 C7
Melrose, *N. Mex., U.S.A.* 113 H3
Melstone, *U.S.A.* 114 C10
Melsungen, *Germany* 24 D5
Melton Mowbray, *U.K.* 12 E7
Melun, *France* 19 D9
Melut, *Sudan* 81 E3
Melville, *Canada* 105 C8
Melville, C., *Australia* 94 A3
Melville, L., *Canada* 103 B8
Melville B., *Australia* 94 A2
Melville I., *Australia* 92 B5
Melville I., *Canada* 4 B2
Melville Pen., *Canada* 101 B11
Mélykút, *Hungary* 42 D4
Memaliaj, *Albania* 40 F3
Memba, *Mozam.* 87 E5
Memboro, *Indonesia* 63 F5
Membrilla, *Spain* 35 G7
Memel = Klaipėda, *Lithuania* 9 J19
Memel, *S. Africa* 89 D4
Memmingen, *Germany* 25 H6
Mempawah, *Indonesia* 62 D3
Memphis, *Egypt* 80 J7
Memphis, *Mich., U.S.A.* 110 D2
Memphis, *Tenn., U.S.A.* 113 H10
Memphis, *Tex., U.S.A.* 113 H4
Memphremagog, L., *U.S.A.* 111 B12
Mena, *Ukraine* 47 G7
Mena, *U.S.A.* 113 H7
Mena →, *Ethiopia* 81 F5
Menai Strait, *U.K.* 12 D3
Ménaka, *Mali* 83 B5
Menan = Chao Phraya →, *Thailand* 64 F3
Menarandra →, *Madag.* 89 D7
Menard, *U.S.A.* 113 K5
Menawashei, *Sudan* 81 E1
Mendawai →, *Indonesia* 62 E4
Mende, *France* 20 D7
Mendebo, *Ethiopia* 81 F4
Menden, *Germany* 24 D3
Menderes, *Turkey* 39 C9
Mendez, *Mexico* 119 B5
Mendhar, *India* 69 C6
Mendi, *Ethiopia* 81 F4
Mendip Hills, *U.K.* 13 F5
Mendocino, *U.S.A.* 114 G2
Mendocino, C., *U.S.A.* 114 F1
Mendota, *Calif., U.S.A.* 116 J6
Mendota, *Ill., U.S.A.* 112 E10
Mendoza, *Argentina* 126 C2
Mendoza □, *Argentina* 126 C2
Mene Grande, *Venezuela* 124 B4
Menemen, *Turkey* 39 C9
Menen, *Belgium* 17 D3
Menfi, *Italy* 30 E5
Mengdingjie, *China* 58 F2
Mengeš, *Slovenia* 29 B11
Menggala, *Indonesia* 62 E3
Menghai, *China* 58 G3
Mengíbar, *Spain* 35 H7
Mengjin, *China* 56 G7
Mengla, *China* 58 G3
Menglian, *China* 58 F2
Mengshan, *China* 59 E8
Mengyin, *China* 57 G9
Mengzhe, *China* 58 F3
Mengzi, *China* 58 F4
Menihek, *Canada* 103 B6
Menihek L., *Canada* 103 B6
Menin = Menen, *Belgium* 17 D3
Menlo Park, *U.S.A.* 116 H4
Menominee, *U.S.A.* 108 C2
Menominee →, *U.S.A.* 108 C2
Menomonie, *U.S.A.* 112 C9
Menongue, *Angola* 85 G3
Menorca, *Spain* 37 B11
Mentakab, *Malaysia* 65 L4
Mentawai, Kepulauan, *Indonesia* 62 E1
Menton, *France* 21 E11
Mentor, *U.S.A.* 110 E3
Menzies, *Australia* 93 E3
Meob B., *Namibia* 88 B2
Me'ona, *Israel* 75 B4
Meoqui, *Mexico* 118 B3
Mepaco, *Mozam.* 87 F3
Meppel, *Neths.* 17 B6
Meppen, *Germany* 24 C3
Mequinenza, *Spain* 32 D5
Mequinenza, Embalse de, *Spain* 32 D5
Mer, *France* 18 E8
Merabéllou, Kólpos, *Greece* 36 D7
Merak, *Indonesia* 63 F12
Meramangye, L., *Australia* 93 E5
Meran = Merano, *Italy* 29 B8
Merano, *Italy* 29 B8
Merate, *Italy* 28 C6
Merauke, *Indonesia* 63 F10
Merca, *Somali Rep.* 74 G3
Mercato Saraceno, *Italy* 29 E9
Merced, *U.S.A.* 116 H6
Merced →, *U.S.A.* 116 H6
Merced Pk., *U.S.A.* 116 H7
Mercedes, *Buenos Aires, Argentina* 126 C4
Mercedes, *Corrientes, Argentina* 126 B4
Mercedes, *San Luis, Argentina* 126 C2
Mercedes, *Uruguay* 126 C4
Mercedes, *U.S.A.* 113 M6
Merceditas, *Chile* 126 B1
Mercer, *N.Z.* 91 G5
Mercer, *U.S.A.* 110 E4
Mercer Island, *U.S.A.* 116 C4
Mercury, *U.S.A.* 117 J11
Mercy C., *Canada* 101 B13
Merdrignac, *France* 18 D4
Mere, *U.K.* 13 F5
Meredith, C., *Falk. Is.* 128 G4
Meredith, L., *U.S.A.* 113 H4
Merefa, *Ukraine* 47 H9
Merei, *Romania* 43 E11
Merga = Nukheila, *Sudan* 80 D2
Mergui, *Burma* 64 F2
Mergui Arch. = Myeik Kyunzu, *Burma* 65 G1
Meriç, *Turkey* 41 E10
Meriç →, *Turkey* 41 F10
Mérida, *Mexico* 119 C7
Mérida, *Spain* 35 G4
Mérida, *Venezuela* 124 B4
Mérida, Cord. de, *Venezuela* 122 C3
Meriden, *U.K.* 13 E6
Meriden, *U.S.A.* 111 E12
Meridian, *Calif., U.S.A.* 116 F5
Meridian, *Idaho, U.S.A.* 114 E5
Meridian, *Miss., U.S.A.* 109 J1
Mérignac, *France* 20 D3
Mérinaghène, *Senegal* 82 B1
Merinda, *Australia* 94 C4
Mering, *Germany* 25 G6
Meringa, *Nigeria* 83 C7
Merir, *Pac. Oc.* 63 D8
Merirumã, *Brazil* 125 C8
Merkel, *U.S.A.* 113 J5
Mermaid Reef, *Australia* 92 C2
Merowe, *Sudan* 80 D3
Merredin, *Australia* 93 F2
Merrick, *U.K.* 14 F4
Merrickville, *Canada* 111 B9
Merrill, *Oreg., U.S.A.* 114 E3
Merrill, *Wis., U.S.A.* 112 C10
Merrimack →, *U.S.A.* 111 D14
Merriman, *U.S.A.* 112 D4
Merritt, *Canada* 104 C4
Merritt Island, *U.S.A.* 109 L5
Merry I., *Canada* 102 A4
Merryville, *U.S.A.* 113 K8
Mersa Fatma, *Eritrea* 81 E5
Mersch, *Lux.* 17 E6
Merse →, *Italy* 29 E8
Mersea I., *U.K.* 13 F8
Merseburg, *Germany* 24 D7
Mersey →, *U.K.* 12 D4
Merseyside □, *U.K.* 12 D4
Mersin, *Turkey* 70 B2
Mersing, *Malaysia* 65 L4
Merta, *India* 68 F6
Merta Road, *India* 68 F5
Merthyr Tydfil, *U.K.* 13 F4
Merthyr Tydfil □, *U.K.* 13 F4
Mértola, *Portugal* 35 H3
Mertzon, *U.S.A.* 113 K4
Méru, *France* 19 C9
Meru, *Kenya* 86 B4
Meru, *Tanzania* 86 C4
Merville, *France* 19 B9
Méry-sur-Seine, *France* 19 D10
Merzifon, *Turkey* 72 B6
Merzig, *Germany* 25 F2
Mesa, *U.S.A.* 115 K8
Mesa Verde National Park, *U.S.A.* 115 H9
Mesagne, *Italy* 31 B10
Mesanagrós, *Greece* 36 C9
Mesaoría □, *Cyprus* 36 D12
Mesarás, Kólpos, *Greece* 36 D6
Meschede, *Germany* 24 D4
Mescit, *Turkey* 73 B9
Mesfinto, *Ethiopia* 81 E4
Mesgouez, L., *Canada* 102 B5
Meshchovsk, *Russia* 46 E8
Meshed = Mashhad, *Iran* 71 B8
Meshoppen, *U.S.A.* 111 E8
Meshra er Req, *Sudan* 81 F2
Mesilinka →, *Canada* 104 B4
Mesilla, *U.S.A.* 115 K10
Meslay-du-Maine, *France* 18 E6
Mesocco, *Switz.* 25 J5
Mesolóngion, *Greece* 38 C3
Mesopotamia = Al Jazirah, *Iraq* 70 C5
Mesopotamia, *U.S.A.* 110 E4
Mesopótamon, *Greece* 38 B2
Mesoraca, *Italy* 31 C9
Mésou Volímais = Volímai, *Greece* 38 D2
Mesquite, *U.S.A.* 115 H6
Messaad, *Algeria* 78 B6
Messac, *France* 18 E5
Messalo →, *Mozam.* 87 E4
Méssaména, *Cameroon* 83 E7
Messeue, *Greece* 38 D3
Messina, *Italy* 31 D8
Messina, *S. Africa* 89 C5
Messina, Str. di, *Italy* 31 D8
Messíni, *Greece* 38 D4
Messínia □, *Greece* 38 D3
Messiniakós Kólpos, *Greece* 38 E4
Messkirch, *Germany* 25 H5
Messonghi, *Greece* 36 B3
Mesta →, *Bulgaria* 40 E7
Mestá, Ákra, *Greece* 39 C7
Mestanza, *Spain* 35 G6
Mestre, *Italy* 29 C9
Mesudiye, *Turkey* 72 B7
Meta →, *S. Amer.* 122 C4
Meta Incognita Peninsula, *Canada* 101 B13
Metabetchouan, *Canada* 103 C5
Metairie, *U.S.A.* 113 L9
Metalici, Munţii, *Romania* 42 D7
Metaline Falls, *U.S.A.* 114 B5
Metallifere, Colline, *Italy* 28 E8
Metán, *Argentina* 126 B3
Metangula, *Mozam.* 87 E3
Metauro →, *Italy* 29 E10
Metema, *Ethiopia* 81 E4
Metengobalame, *Mozam.* 87 E3
Méthana, *Greece* 38 D5
Methóni, *Greece* 38 E3
Methven, *N.Z.* 91 K3
Metil, *Mozam.* 87 F4
Metkovets, *Bulgaria* 40 C7
Metković, *Croatia* 29 E14
Metlakatla, *U.S.A.* 100 C6
Metlika, *Slovenia* 29 C12
Metropolis, *U.S.A.* 113 G10
Métsovon, *Greece* 38 B3
Metu, *Ethiopia* 81 F4
Metz, *France* 19 C13
Metzingen, *Germany* 25 G5
Meulaboh, *Indonesia* 62 D1
Meung-sur-Loire, *France* 19 E8
Meureudu, *Indonesia* 62 C1
Meurthe →, *France* 19 D13
Meurthe-et-Moselle □, *France* 19 D13
Meuse □, *France* 19 C12
Meuse →, *Europe* 17 D5
Meuselwitz, *Germany* 24 D8
Mexia, *U.S.A.* 113 K6
Mexiana, I., *Brazil* 125 D9
Mexicali, *Mexico* 117 N11
Mexican Plateau, *Mexico* 98 G9
Mexican Water, *U.S.A.* 115 H9
México, *Mexico* 119 D5
Mexico, *Maine, U.S.A.* 111 B14
Mexico, *Mo., U.S.A.* 112 F9
Mexico, *N.Y., U.S.A.* 111 C8
México □, *Mexico* 119 D5
Mexico ■, *Cent. Amer.* 118 C4
Mexico, G. of, *Cent. Amer.* 119 C7
Mexico B., *U.S.A.* 111 C8
Meydān-e Naftūn, *Iran* 71 D6
Meydani, Ra's-e, *Iran* 71 E8
Meyenburg, *Germany* 24 B8
Meymac, *France* 20 C6
Meymaneh, *Afghan.* 66 B4
Meyrueis, *France* 20 D7
Meyssac, *France* 20 C5
Meyzieu, *France* 21 C8
Mezdra, *Bulgaria* 40 C7
Mèze, *France* 20 E7
Mezen, *Russia* 50 C5
Mezen →, *Russia* 50 C5
Mézenc, Mt., *France* 21 D8
Mezeş, Munţii, *Romania* 42 C8
Mezha →, *Russia* 46 E6
Mezhdurechenskiy, *Russia* 50 D7
Mézidon-Canon, *France* 18 C6
Mézières-en-Brenne, *France* 20 B5
Mézilhac, *France* 21 D8
Mézin, *France* 20 D4
Mezőberény, *Hungary* 42 D6
Mezőfalva, *Hungary* 42 D3
Mezőhegyes, *Hungary* 42 D5
Mezőkövácsháza, *Hungary* 42 D5
Mezőkövesd, *Hungary* 42 C5
Mézos, *France* 20 D2
Mezőtúr, *Hungary* 42 C5
Mezquital, *Mexico* 118 C4
Mezzolombardo, *Italy* 28 B8
Mfolozi →, *S. Africa* 89 D5
Mgeta, *Tanzania* 87 D4
Mglin, *Russia* 47 F7
Mhlaba Hills, *Zimbabwe* 87 F3
Mhow, *India* 68 H6
Miahuatlán, *Mexico* 119 D5
Miajadas, *Spain* 35 F5
Miami, *Fla., U.S.A.* 109 N5
Miami, *Okla., U.S.A.* 113 G7
Miami, *Tex., U.S.A.* 113 H4
Miami Beach, *U.S.A.* 109 N5
Mian Xian, *China* 56 H4
Mianchi, *China* 56 G6
Mīāndarreh, *Iran* 71 C7
Mīāndowāb, *Iran* 70 B5
Miandrivazo, *Madag.* 89 B8
Mīāneh, *Iran* 70 B5
Mianning, *China* 58 C4
Mianwali, *Pakistan* 68 C4
Mianyang, *China* 58 B5
Mianzhu, *China* 58 B5
Miaoli, *Taiwan* 59 E13
Miarinarivo, *Antananarivo, Madag.* 89 B8
Miarinarivo, *Toamasina, Madag.* 89 B8
Miariravaratra, *Madag.* 89 C8
Miass, *Russia* 50 D7
Miasteczko Krajeńskie, *Poland* 45 E4
Miastko, *Poland* 44 E3
Mica, *S. Africa* 89 C5
Micăsasa, *Romania* 43 D9
Michalovce, *Slovak Rep.* 27 C14
Michigan □, *U.S.A.* 108 C3
Michigan, L., *U.S.A.* 108 D2
Michigan City, *U.S.A.* 108 E2
Michika, *Nigeria* 83 C7
Michipicoten I., *Canada* 102 C2
Michoacan □, *Mexico* 118 D4
Michurin, *Bulgaria* 41 D11
Michurinsk, *Russia* 48 D5
Mico, Pta., *Nic.* 120 D3
Micronesia, *Pac. Oc.* 96 G7
Micronesia, Federated States of ■, *Pac. Oc.* 96 G7
Midai, *Indonesia* 65 L6
Midale, *Canada* 105 D8
Middelburg, *Neths.* 17 C3
Middelburg, *Eastern Cape, S. Africa* 88 E4
Middelburg, *Mpumalanga, S. Africa* 89 D4
Middelfart, *Denmark* 11 J3
Middelpos, *S. Africa* 88 E3
Middelwit, *S. Africa* 88 C4
Middle Alkali L., *U.S.A.* 114 F3
Middle Bass I., *U.S.A.* 110 E2
Middle East, *Asia* 52 F7
Middle Fork Feather →, *U.S.A.* 116 F5
Middle I., *Australia* 93 F3
Middle Loup →, *U.S.A.* 112 E5
Middle Sackville, *Canada* 103 D7
Middleboro, *U.S.A.* 111 E14
Middleburg, *Fla., U.S.A.* 109 K5
Middleburg, *N.Y., U.S.A.* 111 D10
Middleburg, *Pa., U.S.A.* 110 F7
Middlebury, *U.S.A.* 111 B11
Middlemount, *Australia* 94 C4
Middleport, *N.Y., U.S.A.* 110 C6
Middleport, *Ohio, U.S.A.* 108 F4
Middlesboro, *U.S.A.* 109 G4
Middlesbrough, *U.K.* 12 C6
Middlesbrough □, *U.K.* 12 C6
Middlesex, *Belize* 120 C2
Middlesex, *N.J., U.S.A.* 111 F10
Middlesex, *N.Y., U.S.A.* 110 D7
Middleton, *Australia* 94 C3
Middleton, *Canada* 103 D6
Middleton Cr. →, *Australia* 94 C3
Middletown, *U.K.* 15 B5
Middletown, *Calif., U.S.A.* 116 G4
Middletown, *Conn., U.S.A.* 111 E12
Middletown, *N.Y., U.S.A.* 111 E10
Middletown, *Ohio, U.S.A.* 108 F3
Middletown, *Pa., U.S.A.* 111 F8
Midhurst, *U.K.* 13 G7
Midī, *Yemen* 81 D5
Midi, Canal du →, *France* 20 E5
Midi d'Ossau, Pic du, *France* 20 F3
Midi-Pyrénées □, *France* 20 E5
Midland, *Canada* 102 D4
Midland, *Calif., U.S.A.* 117 M12
Midland, *Mich., U.S.A.* 108 D3
Midland, *Pa., U.S.A.* 110 F4
Midland, *Tex., U.S.A.* 113 K3
Midlands □, *Zimbabwe* 87 F2
Midleton, *Ireland* 15 E3
Midlothian, *U.S.A.* 113 J6
Midlothian □, *U.K.* 14 F5
Midongy, Tangorombohitr' i, *Madag.* 89 C8
Midongy Atsimo, *Madag.* 89 C8
Midou →, *France* 20 E3
Midouze →, *France* 20 E3
Midsayap, *Phil.* 61 H6
Midu, *China* 58 E3
Midway Is., *Pac. Oc.* 96 E10
Midway Wells, *U.S.A.* 117 N11
Midwest, *U.S.A.* 114 E10
Midwest City, *U.S.A.* 113 H6
Midyat, *Turkey* 70 B4
Midzŏr, *Bulgaria* 40 C6
Mie □, *Japan* 55 G8
Miechów, *Poland* 45 H7
Miedwie, Jezioro, *Poland* 45 E1
Międzybórz, *Poland* 45 G4
Międzychód, *Poland* 45 F2
Międzylesie, *Poland* 45 H3
Międzyrzec Podlaski, *Poland* 45 G9
Międzyrzecz, *Poland* 45 F2
Międzyzdroje, *Poland* 44 E1
Miejska Górka, *Poland* 45 G3
Miélan, *France* 20 E4
Mielec, *Poland* 45 H8
Mienga, *Angola* 88 B2
Miercurea-Ciuc, *Romania* 43 D10
Miercurea Sibiului, *Romania* 43 E8
Mieres, *Spain* 34 B5
Mieroszów, *Poland* 45 H3
Mieso, *Ethiopia* 81 F5
Mieszkowice, *Poland* 45 F1
Mifflintown, *U.S.A.* 110 F7
Mifraz Hefa, *Israel* 75 C4
Migennes, *France* 19 E10
Migliarino, *Italy* 29 D8
Miguel Alemán, Presa, *Mexico* 119 D5
Miguelturra, *Spain* 35 G7
Mihăileni, *Romania* 43 C11
Mihăileşti, *Romania* 43 F10
Mihailovca, *Moldova* 43 D13
Mihalgazi, *Turkey* 39 A12
Mihaliççık, *Turkey* 72 C4
Mihara, *Japan* 55 G6
Miheşu de Cîmpie, *Romania* 43 D9
Mijas, *Spain* 35 J6
Mikese, *Tanzania* 86 D4
Mikha-Tskhakaya = Senaki, *Georgia* 49 J6
Mikhailovka = Mykhaylivka, *Ukraine* 47 J8
Mikhaylov, *Russia* 46 E10
Mikhaylovgrad = Montana, *Bulgaria* 40 C7
Mikhaylovka, *Russia* 48 E6
Mikhnevo, *Russia* 46 E9
Mikínai, *Greece* 38 D4
Mikkeli, *Finland* 9 F22
Mikkwa →, *Canada* 104 B6
Mikniya, *Sudan* 81 D3
Mikołajki, *Poland* 44 E8
Míkonos, *Greece* 39 D7
Mikrí Préspa, Límni, *Greece* 40 F5
Mikrón Dhérion, *Greece* 41 E10
Mikstat, *Poland* 45 G4
Mikulov, *Czech Rep.* 27 C9
Mikumi, *Tanzania* 86 D4
Milaca, *U.S.A.* 112 C8
Milagro, *Ecuador* 124 D3
Milagros, *Phil.* 61 E5
Milan = Milano, *Italy* 28 C6
Milan, *Mo., U.S.A.* 112 E8
Milan, *Tenn., U.S.A.* 109 H1
Milange, *Mozam.* 87 F4
Milano, *Italy* 28 C6
Milanoa, *Madag.* 89 A8
Milâs, *Turkey* 39 D9
Mílatos, *Greece* 36 D7
Milazzo, *Italy* 31 D8
Milbank, *U.S.A.* 112 C6
Milbanke Sd., *Canada* 104 C3
Milden, *Canada* 105 C7

Mildenhall, *U.K.* 13 E8
Mildmay, *Canada* 110 B3
Mile, *China* 58 E4
Miléai, *Greece* 38 B5
Miles, *Australia* 95 D5
Miles City, *U.S.A.* 112 B2
Mileşti, *Moldova* 43 C13
Milestone, *Canada* 105 D8
Mileto, *Italy* 31 D9
Miletto, Mte., *Italy* 31 A7
Miletus, *Turkey* 39 D9
Milevsko, *Czech Rep.* 26 B7
Milford, *Calif., U.S.A.* 116 E6
Milford, *Conn., U.S.A.* 111 E11
Milford, *Del., U.S.A.* 108 F8
Milford, *Mass., U.S.A.* 111 D13
Milford, *N.H., U.S.A.* 111 D13
Milford, *Pa., U.S.A.* 111 E10
Milford, *Utah, U.S.A.* 115 G7
Milford Haven, *U.K.* 13 F2
Milford Sd., *N.Z.* 91 L1
Milḩ, Baḩr al, *Iraq* 70 C4
Milicz, *Poland* 45 G4
Milikapiti, *Australia* 92 B5
Miling, *Australia* 93 F2
Militello in Val di Catánia, *Italy* 31 E7
Milk →, *U.S.A.* 114 B10
Milk, Wadi el →, *Sudan* 80 D3
Milk River, *Canada* 104 D6
Mill I., *Antarctica* 5 C8
Mill Valley, *U.S.A.* 116 H4
Millárs →, *Spain* 32 F4
Millau, *France* 20 D7
Millbridge, *Canada* 110 B7
Millbrook, *Canada* 110 B6
Millbrook, *U.S.A.* 111 E11
Mille Lacs, L. des, *Canada* 102 C1
Mille Lacs L., *U.S.A.* 112 B8
Milledgeville, *U.S.A.* 109 J4
Millen, *U.S.A.* 109 J5
Millennium I. = Caroline I., *Kiribati* 97 H12
Miller, *U.S.A.* 112 C5
Millerovo, *Russia* 49 F5
Millersburg, *Ohio, U.S.A.* 110 F3
Millersburg, *Pa., U.S.A.* 110 F8
Millerton, *U.S.A.* 111 E11
Millerton L., *U.S.A.* 116 J7
Millevaches, Plateau de, *France* 20 C6
Millheim, *U.S.A.* 110 F7
Millington, *U.S.A.* 113 H10
Millinocket, *U.S.A.* 109 C11
Millmerran, *Australia* 95 D5
Millom, *U.K.* 12 C4
Mills L., *Canada* 104 A5
Millsboro, *U.S.A.* 110 G5
Milltown Malbay, *Ireland* 15 D2
Millville, *N.J., U.S.A.* 108 F8
Millville, *Pa., U.S.A.* 111 E8
Millwood L., *U.S.A.* 113 J8
Milna, *Croatia* 29 E13
Milne →, *Australia* 94 C2
Milo, *U.S.A.* 109 C11
Mílos, *Greece* 38 E6
Miłosław, *Poland* 45 F4
Milot, *Albania* 40 E3
Milparinka, *Australia* 95 D3
Miltenberg, *Germany* 25 F5
Milton, *N.S., Canada* 103 D7
Milton, *Ont., Canada* 110 C5
Milton, *N.Z.* 91 M2
Milton, *Calif., U.S.A.* 116 G6
Milton, *Fla., U.S.A.* 109 K2
Milton, *Pa., U.S.A.* 110 F8
Milton, *Vt., U.S.A.* 111 B11
Milton-Freewater, *U.S.A.* 114 D4
Milton Keynes, *U.K.* 13 E7
Milton Keynes □, *U.K.* 13 E7
Miluo, *China* 59 C9
Milverton, *Canada* 110 C4
Milwaukee, *U.S.A.* 108 D2
Milwaukee Deep, *Atl. Oc.* 121 C6
Milwaukie, *U.S.A.* 116 E4
Mim, *Ghana* 82 D4
Mimizan, *France* 20 D2
Mimoň, *Czech Rep.* 26 A7
Min Jiang →, *Fujian, China* 59 E12
Min Jiang →, *Sichuan, China* 58 C5
Min Xian, *China* 56 G3
Mina Pirquitas, *Argentina* 126 A2
Mīnā Su'ud, *Si. Arabia* 71 D6
Mīnā'al Aḩmadī, *Kuwait* 71 D6
Minago →, *Canada* 105 C9
Minaki, *Canada* 105 D10
Minamata, *Japan* 55 H5
Minami-Tori-Shima, *Pac. Oc.* 96 E7
Minas, *Uruguay* 127 C4
Minas, Sierra de las, *Guatemala* 120 C2
Minas Basin, *Canada* 103 C7
Minas de Rio Tinto = Minas de Riotinto, *Spain* 35 H4
Minas de Riotinto, *Spain* 35 H4
Minas Gerais □, *Brazil* 125 G9
Minatitlán, *Mexico* 119 D6
Minbu, *Burma* 67 J19
Minchinabad, *Pakistan* 68 D5
Mincio →, *Italy* 28 C7
Minčol, *Slovak Rep.* 27 B13
Mindanao, *Phil.* 61 H6
Mindanao Sea = Bohol Sea, *Phil.* 63 C6
Mindanao Trench, *Pac. Oc.* 61 F7
Mindel →, *Germany* 25 G6
Mindelheim, *Germany* 25 G6
Minden, *Canada* 110 B6
Minden, *Germany* 24 C4
Minden, *La., U.S.A.* 113 J8
Minden, *Nev., U.S.A.* 116 G7
Mindiptana, *Indonesia* 63 F10
Mindoro, *Phil.* 61 E4
Mindoro Str., *Phil.* 61 E4
Mine, *Japan* 55 G5
Minehead, *U.K.* 13 F4
Mineola, *N.Y., U.S.A.* 111 F11
Mineola, *Tex., U.S.A.* 113 J7
Mineral King, *U.S.A.* 116 J8
Mineral Wells, *U.S.A.* 113 J5
Mineralnyye Vody, *Russia* 49 H6
Minersville, *U.S.A.* 111 F8
Minerva, *U.S.A.* 110 F3
Minervino Murge, *Italy* 31 A9
Minetto, *U.S.A.* 111 C8
Mingäçevir, *Azerbaijan* 49 K8
Mingäçevir Su Anbarı, *Azerbaijan* 49 K8
Mingan, *Canada* 103 B7
Mingechaur = Mingäçevir, *Azerbaijan* 49 K8
Mingechaurskoye Vdkhr. = Mingäçevir Su Anbarı, *Azerbaijan* 49 K8
Mingela, *Australia* 94 B4
Mingenew, *Australia* 93 E2
Mingera Cr. →, *Australia* 94 C2
Minggang, *China* 59 A10
Mingguang, *China* 59 A11
Mingin, *Burma* 67 H19
Mingir, *Moldova* 43 D13
Minglanilla, *Spain* 33 F3
Minglun, *China* 58 E7
Mingo Junction, *U.S.A.* 110 F4
Mingorria, *Spain* 34 E6
Mingshan, *China* 58 B4
Mingteke Daban = Mintaka Pass, *Pakistan* 69 A6
Mingxi, *China* 59 D11
Mingyuegue, *China* 57 C15
Minho = Miño →, *Spain* 34 D2
Minhou, *China* 59 E12
Minićevo, *Serbia, Yug.* 42 G7
Minidoka, *U.S.A.* 114 E7
Minigwal, L., *Australia* 93 E3
Minilya →, *Australia* 93 D1
Minilya Roadhouse, *Australia* 93 D1
Minipi L., *Canada* 103 B7
Mink L., *Canada* 104 A5
Minkammen, *Sudan* 81 F3
Minna, *Nigeria* 83 D6
Minneapolis, *Kans., U.S.A.* 112 F6
Minneapolis, *Minn., U.S.A.* 112 C8
Minnedosa, *Canada* 105 C9
Minnesota □, *U.S.A.* 112 B8
Minnesota →, *U.S.A.* 112 C8
Minnewaukan, *U.S.A.* 112 A5
Minnipa, *Australia* 95 E2
Minnitaki L., *Canada* 102 C1
Mino, *Japan* 55 G8
Miño, *Spain* 34 B2
Miño →, *Spain* 34 D2
Minoa, *Greece* 39 F7
Minorca = Menorca, *Spain* 37 B11
Minot, *U.S.A.* 112 A4
Minqin, *China* 56 E2
Minqing, *China* 59 D12
Minsen, *Germany* 24 B3
Minsk, *Belarus* 46 F4
Mińsk Mazowiecki, *Poland* 45 F8
Mintabie, *Australia* 95 D1
Mintaka Pass, *Pakistan* 69 A6
Minto, *Canada* 103 C6
Minto, L., *Canada* 102 A5
Minton, *Canada* 105 D8
Minturn, *U.S.A.* 114 G10
Minturno, *Italy* 30 A6
Minûf, *Egypt* 80 H7
Minusinsk, *Russia* 51 D10
Minutang, *India* 67 E20
Minya el Qamh, *Egypt* 80 H7
Mionica, *Bos.-H.* 42 F3
Mionica, *Serbia, Yug.* 40 B4
Miquelon, *Canada* 102 C4
Miquelon, *St- P. & M.* 103 C8
Mir, *Niger* 83 C7
Mīr Kūh, *Iran* 71 E8
Mīr Shahdād, *Iran* 71 E8
Mira, *Italy* 29 C9
Mira, *Portugal* 34 E2
Mira →, *Portugal* 35 H2
Mira por vos Cay, *Bahamas* 121 B5
Mirabella Eclano, *Italy* 31 A7
Miraj, *India* 66 L9
Miram Shah, *Pakistan* 68 C4
Miramar, *Argentina* 126 D4
Miramar, *Mozam.* 89 C6
Miramas, *France* 21 E8
Mirambeau, *France* 20 C3
Miramichi, *Canada* 103 C6
Miramichi B., *Canada* 103 C7
Miramont-de-Guyenne, *France* 20 D4
Miranda, *Brazil* 125 H7
Miranda →, *Brazil* 124 G7
Miranda de Ebro, *Spain* 32 C2
Miranda do Corvo, *Portugal* 34 E2
Miranda do Douro, *Portugal* 34 D4
Mirande, *France* 20 E4
Mirandela, *Portugal* 34 D3
Mirándola, *Italy* 28 D8
Mirandópolis, *Brazil* 127 A5
Mirango, *Malawi* 87 E3
Mirano, *Italy* 29 C9
Miras, *Albania* 40 F4
Mirassol, *Brazil* 127 A6
Mirbāţ, *Oman* 74 D5
Mirear, *Egypt* 80 C4
Mirebeau, *Côte-d'Or, France* 19 E12
Mirebeau, *Vienne, France* 18 F7
Mirecourt, *France* 19 D13
Mirgorod = Myrhorod, *Ukraine* 47 H7
Miri, *Malaysia* 62 D4
Miriam Vale, *Australia* 94 C5
Miribel, *France* 19 G11
Mirim, L., *S. Amer.* 127 C5
Mirnyy, *Russia* 51 C12
Miroč, *Serbia, Yug.* 40 B6
Mirokhan, *Pakistan* 68 F3
Mirond L., *Canada* 105 B8
Mirosławiec, *Poland* 44 E3
Mirpur, *Pakistan* 69 C5
Mirpur Batoro, *Pakistan* 68 G3
Mirpur Bibiwari, *Pakistan* 68 E2
Mirpur Khas, *Pakistan* 68 G3
Mirpur Sakro, *Pakistan* 68 G2
Mirria, *Niger* 83 C6
Mirsk, *Poland* 45 H2
Mirtağ, *Turkey* 70 B4
Miryang, *S. Korea* 57 G15
Mirzaani, *Georgia* 49 K8
Mirzapur, *India* 69 G10
Mirzapur-cum-Vindhyachal = Mirzapur, *India* 69 G10
Misantla, *Mexico* 119 D5
Misawa, *Japan* 54 D10
Miscou I., *Canada* 103 C7
Mish'āb, Ra's al, *Si. Arabia* 71 D6
Mishan, *China* 60 B8
Mishawaka, *U.S.A.* 108 E2
Mishbih, Gebel, *Egypt* 80 C3
Mishima, *Japan* 55 G9
Misión, *Mexico* 117 N10
Misiones □, *Argentina* 127 B5
Misiones □, *Paraguay* 126 B4
Miskah, *Si. Arabia* 70 E4
Miskitos, Cayos, *Nic.* 120 D3
Miskolc, *Hungary* 42 B5
Misoke, *Dem. Rep. of the Congo* 86 C2
Misool, *Indonesia* 63 E8
Mişrātah, *Libya* 79 B9
Missanabie, *Canada* 102 C3
Missinaibi →, *Canada* 102 B3
Missinaibi L., *Canada* 102 C3
Mission, *Canada* 104 D4
Mission, *S. Dak., U.S.A.* 112 D4
Mission, *Tex., U.S.A.* 113 M5
Mission Beach, *Australia* 94 B4
Mission Viejo, *U.S.A.* 117 M9
Missirah, *Senegal* 82 C1
Missisa L., *Canada* 102 B2
Missisicabi →, *Canada* 102 B4
Mississagi →, *Canada* 102 C3
Mississauga, *Canada* 110 C5
Mississippi □, *U.S.A.* 113 J10
Mississippi →, *U.S.A.* 113 L10
Mississippi L., *Canada* 111 A8
Mississippi River Delta, *U.S.A.* 113 L9
Mississippi Sd., *U.S.A.* 113 K10
Missoula, *U.S.A.* 114 C7
Missouri □, *U.S.A.* 112 F8
Missouri →, *U.S.A.* 112 F9
Missouri City, *U.S.A.* 113 L7
Missouri Valley, *U.S.A.* 112 E7
Mist, *U.S.A.* 116 E3
Mistassibi →, *Canada* 103 B5
Mistassini, *Canada* 103 C5
Mistassini →, *Canada* 103 C5
Mistassini, L., *Canada* 102 B5
Mistastin L., *Canada* 103 A7
Mistelbach, *Austria* 27 C9
Misterbianco, *Italy* 31 E8
Mistinibi, L., *Canada* 103 A7
Mistretta, *Italy* 31 E7
Misty L., *Canada* 105 B8
Misurata = Mişrātah, *Libya* 79 B9
Mît Ghamr, *Egypt* 80 H7
Mitatib, *Sudan* 81 D4
Mitchell, *Australia* 95 D4
Mitchell, *Canada* 110 C3
Mitchell, *Nebr., U.S.A.* 112 E3
Mitchell, *Oreg., U.S.A.* 114 D3
Mitchell, *S. Dak., U.S.A.* 112 D6
Mitchell →, *Australia* 94 B3
Mitchell, Mt., *U.S.A.* 109 H4
Mitchell Ranges, *Australia* 94 A2
Mitchelstown, *Ireland* 15 D3
Mitha Tiwana, *Pakistan* 68 C5
Mithi, *Pakistan* 68 G3
Míthimna, *Greece* 39 B8
Mithrao, *Pakistan* 68 F3
Mitilíni, *Greece* 39 B8
Mitilinoí, *Greece* 39 D8
Mito, *Japan* 55 F10
Mitrofanovka, *Russia* 47 H10
Mitrovica = Kosovska Mitrovica, *Kosovo, Yug.* 40 D4
Mitsinjo, *Madag.* 89 B8
Mitsiwa, *Eritrea* 81 D4
Mitsiwa Channel, *Eritrea* 81 D5
Mitsukaidō, *Japan* 55 F9
Mittelberg, *Austria* 26 D3
Mittelfranken □, *Germany* 25 F6
Mittellandkanal →, *Germany* 24 C4
Mittenwalde, *Germany* 24 C9
Mittersill, *Austria* 26 D5
Mitterteich, *Germany* 25 F8
Mittimatalik = Pond Inlet, *Canada* 101 A12
Mittweida, *Germany* 24 E8
Mitú, *Colombia* 124 C4
Mitumba, *Tanzania* 86 D3
Mitumba, Mts., *Dem. Rep. of the Congo* 86 D2
Mitwaba, *Dem. Rep. of the Congo* 87 D2
Mityana, *Uganda* 86 B3
Mixteco →, *Mexico* 119 D5
Miyagi □, *Japan* 54 E10
Miyāh, W. el →, *Egypt* 80 C3
Miyāh, W. el →, *Syria* 70 C3
Miyake-Jima, *Japan* 55 G9
Miyako, *Japan* 54 E10
Miyako-Jima, *Japan* 55 M2
Miyako-Rettō, *Japan* 55 M2
Miyakonojō, *Japan* 55 J5
Miyani, *India* 68 J3
Miyanoura-Dake, *Japan* 55 J5
Miyazaki, *Japan* 55 J5
Miyazaki □, *Japan* 55 H5
Miyazu, *Japan* 55 G7
Miyet, Bahr el = Dead Sea, *Asia* 75 D4
Miyi, *China* 58 D4
Miyoshi, *Japan* 55 G6
Miyun, *China* 56 D9
Miyun Shuiku, *China* 57 D9
Mizan Teferi, *Ethiopia* 81 F4
Mizdah, *Libya* 79 B8
Mizen Hd., *Cork, Ireland* 15 E2
Mizen Hd., *Wick., Ireland* 15 D5
Mizhi, *China* 56 F6
Mizil, *Romania* 43 F11
Mizoram □, *India* 67 H18
Mizpe Ramon, *Israel* 75 E3
Mizusawa, *Japan* 54 E10
Mjällby, *Sweden* 11 H8
Mjöbäck, *Sweden* 11 G6
Mjölby, *Sweden* 11 F9
Mjörn, *Sweden* 11 G6
Mjøsa, *Norway* 9 F14
Mkata, *Tanzania* 86 D4
Mkokotoni, *Tanzania* 86 D4
Mkomazi, *Tanzania* 86 C4
Mkomazi →, *S. Africa* 89 E5
Mkulwe, *Tanzania* 87 D3
Mkumbi, Ras, *Tanzania* 86 D4
Mkushi, *Zambia* 87 E2
Mkushi River, *Zambia* 87 E2
Mkuze, *S. Africa* 89 D5
Mladá Boleslav, *Czech Rep.* 26 A7
Mladenovac, *Serbia, Yug.* 40 B4
Mlala Hills, *Tanzania* 86 D3
Mlange = Mulanje, *Malawi* 87 F4
Mlanje, Pic, *Malawi* 85 H7
Mlava →, *Serbia, Yug.* 40 B5
Mława, *Poland* 45 E7
Mlinište, *Bos.-H.* 29 D13
Mljet, *Croatia* 29 F14
Mljetski Kanal, *Croatia* 29 F14
Młynary, *Poland* 44 D6
Mmabatho, *S. Africa* 88 D4
Mme, *Cameroon* 83 D7
Mnichovo Hradiště, *Czech Rep.* 26 A7
Mo i Rana, *Norway* 8 C16
Moa, *Cuba* 121 B4
Moa, *Indonesia* 63 F7
Moa →, *S. Leone* 82 D2
Moab, *U.S.A.* 115 G9
Moala, *Fiji* 91 D8
Moama, *Australia* 95 F3
Moamba, *Mozam.* 89 D5
Moapa, *U.S.A.* 117 J12
Moate, *Ireland* 15 C4
Moba, *Dem. Rep. of the Congo* 86 D2
Mobārakābād, *Iran* 71 D7
Mobaye, *C.A.R.* 84 D4
Mobayi, *Dem. Rep. of the Congo* 84 D4
Moberley Lake, *Canada* 104 B4
Moberly, *U.S.A.* 112 F8
Mobile, *U.S.A.* 109 K1
Mobile B., *U.S.A.* 109 K2
Mobridge, *U.S.A.* 112 C4
Mobutu Sese Seko, L. = Albert, L., *Africa* 86 B3
Moc Chau, *Vietnam* 64 B5
Moc Hoa, *Vietnam* 65 G5
Mocabe Kasari, *Dem. Rep. of the Congo* 87 D2
Moçambique, *Mozam.* 87 F5
Moçâmedes = Namibe, *Angola* 85 H2
Mocanaqua, *U.S.A.* 111 E8
Mochudi, *Botswana* 88 C4
Mocimboa da Praia, *Mozam.* 87 E5
Mociu, *Romania* 43 D9
Möckeln, *Sweden* 11 H8
Mockfjärd, *Sweden* 10 D8
Moclips, *U.S.A.* 116 C2
Mocoa, *Colombia* 124 C3
Mococa, *Brazil* 127 A6
Mocorito, *Mexico* 118 B3
Moctezuma, *Mexico* 118 B3
Moctezuma →, *Mexico* 119 C5
Mocuba, *Mozam.* 87 F4
Mocúzari, Presa, *Mexico* 118 B3
Modane, *France* 21 C10
Modasa, *India* 68 H5
Modder →, *S. Africa* 88 D3
Modderrivier, *S. Africa* 88 D3
Módena, *Italy* 28 D7
Modena, *U.S.A.* 115 H7
Modesto, *U.S.A.* 116 H6
Módica, *Italy* 31 F7
Mödling, *Austria* 27 C9
Modo, *Sudan* 81 F3
Modra, *Slovak Rep.* 27 C10
Modriča, *Bos.-H.* 42 F3
Moebase, *Mozam.* 87 F4
Moëlan-sur-Mer, *France* 18 E3
Moengo, *Surinam* 125 B8
Moffat, *U.K.* 14 F5
Moga, *India* 68 D6
Mogadishu = Muqdisho, *Somali Rep.* 74 G4
Mogador = Essaouira, *Morocco* 78 B4
Mogadouro, *Portugal* 34 D4
Mogalakwena →, *S. Africa* 89 C4
Mogami-Gawa →, *Japan* 54 E10
Mogán, *Canary Is.* 37 G4
Mogaung, *Burma* 67 G20
Mogente = Moixent, *Spain* 33 G4
Mogho, *Ethiopia* 81 G5
Mogi das Cruzes, *Brazil* 127 A6
Mogi-Guaçu →, *Brazil* 127 A6
Mogi-Mirim, *Brazil* 127 A6
Mogielnica, *Poland* 45 G7
Mogige, *Ethiopia* 81 F4
Mogilev = Mahilyow, *Belarus* 46 F6
Mogilev-Podolskiy = Mohyliv-Podilskyy, *Ukraine* 47 H4
Mogilno, *Poland* 45 F4
Mogincual, *Mozam.* 87 F5
Mogliano Véneto, *Italy* 29 C9
Mogocha, *Russia* 51 D12
Mogok, *Burma* 67 H20
Mogollon Rim, *U.S.A.* 115 J8
Mógoro, *Italy* 30 C1
Mograt, *Sudan* 80 D3
Moguer, *Spain* 35 H4
Mogumber, *Australia* 93 F2
Mohács, *Hungary* 42 E3
Mohales Hoek, *Lesotho* 88 E4
Mohall, *U.S.A.* 112 A4
Moḩammadābād, *Iran* 71 B8
Mohammedia, *Morocco* 78 B4
Mohana →, *India* 69 G11
Mohanlalganj, *India* 69 F9
Mohave, L., *U.S.A.* 117 K12
Mohawk →, *U.S.A.* 111 D11
Moheda, *Sweden* 11 G8
Mohenjodaro, *Pakistan* 68 F3
Mohicanville Reservoir, *U.S.A.* 110 F3
Möhne →, *Germany* 24 D3
Mohoro, *Tanzania* 86 D4
Mohyliv-Podilskyy, *Ukraine* 47 H4
Moia, *Sudan* 81 F2
Moidart, L., *U.K.* 14 E3
Moineşti, *Romania* 43 D11
Moira →, *Canada* 110 B7
Moirans, *France* 21 C9
Moirans-en-Montagne, *France* 19 F12
Moíres, *Greece* 36 D6
Moisaküla, *Estonia* 9 G21
Moisie, *Canada* 103 B6
Moisie →, *Canada* 103 B6
Moissac, *France* 20 D5
Moita, *Portugal* 35 G2
Moixent, *Spain* 33 G4
Möja, *Sweden* 10 E12
Mojácar, *Spain* 33 H3
Mojados, *Spain* 34 D6
Mojave, *U.S.A.* 117 K8
Mojave Desert, *U.S.A.* 117 L10
Mojiang, *China* 58 F3
Mojjo →, *Ethiopia* 81 F5
Mojkovac, *Montenegro, Yug.* 40 D3
Mojo, *Bolivia* 126 A2
Mojo, *Ethiopia* 81 F4
Mojokerto, *Indonesia* 63 G15
Mokai, *N.Z.* 91 H5
Mokambo, *Dem. Rep. of the Congo* 87 E2
Mokameh, *India* 69 G11
Mokau, *N.Z.* 91 H5
Mokelumne →, *U.S.A.* 116 G5
Mokelumne Hill, *U.S.A.* 116 G6
Mokhós, *Greece* 36 D7
Mokhotlong, *Lesotho* 89 D4
Möklinta, *Sweden* 10 D10
Mokokchung, *India* 67 F19
Mokolo, *Cameroon* 83 C7
Mokolo →, *S. Africa* 89 C4
Mokp'o, *S. Korea* 57 G14
Mokra Gora, *Yugoslavia* 40 D4
Mokronog, *Slovenia* 29 C12
Moksha →, *Russia* 48 C6
Mokshan, *Russia* 48 D7
Mokwa, *Nigeria* 83 D6
Mol, *Belgium* 17 C5
Mola di Bari, *Italy* 31 A10
Molale, *Ethiopia* 81 E4
Moláoi, *Greece* 38 E4
Molara, *Italy* 30 B2
Molat, *Croatia* 29 D11
Molchanovo, *Russia* 50 D9
Mold, *U.K.* 12 D4
Moldava nad Bodvou, *Slovak Rep.* 27 C14
Moldavia = Moldova ■, *Europe* 43 C13
Moldavia, *Romania* 43 D12
Molde, *Norway* 8 E12
Moldova ■, *Europe* 43 C13
Moldova Nouă, *Romania* 42 F6
Moldoveanu, Vf., *Romania* 43 E9
Moldoviţa, *Romania* 43 C10
Mole →, *U.K.* 13 F7
Mole Creek, *Australia* 94 G4
Molepolole, *Botswana* 88 C4
Molfetta, *Italy* 31 A9
Molina de Aragón, *Spain* 32 E3
Molina de Segura, *Spain* 33 G3
Moline, *U.S.A.* 112 E9
Molinella, *Italy* 29 D8
Molinos, *Argentina* 126 B2
Moliro, *Dem. Rep. of the Congo* 86 D3

Moliterno, *Italy* 31 B8
Molkom, *Sweden* 10 E7
Mölle, *Sweden* 11 H6
Molledo, *Spain* 34 B6
Mollendo, *Peru* 124 G4
Mollerin, L., *Australia* 93 F2
Mollerussa, *Spain* 32 D5
Mollina, *Spain* 35 H6
Mölln, *Germany* 24 B6
Mölltorp, *Sweden* 11 F8
Mölnlycke, *Sweden* 11 G6
Molochansk, *Ukraine* 47 J8
Molochnoye, Ozero, *Ukraine* 47 J8
Molodechno = Maladzyechna, *Belarus* 46 E4
Molokai, *U.S.A.* 106 H16
Molopo →, *Africa* 88 D3
Mólos, *Greece* 38 C4
Molotov = Perm, *Russia* 50 D6
Molsheim, *France* 19 D14
Molson L., *Canada* 105 C9
Molteno, *S. Africa* 88 E4
Molu, *Indonesia* 63 F8
Molucca Sea, *Indonesia* 63 E6
Moluccas = Maluku, *Indonesia* 63 E7
Moma, *Dem. Rep. of the Congo* 86 C1
Moma, *Mozam.* 87 F4
Mombasa, *Kenya* 86 C4
Mombetsu, *Japan* 54 B11
Mombuey, *Spain* 34 C4
Momchilgrad, *Bulgaria* 41 E9
Momi, *Dem. Rep. of the Congo* 86 C2
Mompós, *Colombia* 124 B4
Møn, *Denmark* 11 K6
Mon □, *Burma* 67 L20
Mona, Canal de la, *W. Indies* 121 C6
Mona, Isla, *Puerto Rico* 121 C6
Mona, Pta., *Costa Rica* 120 E3
Monaca, *U.S.A.* 110 F4
Monaco ■, *Europe* 21 E11
Monadhliath Mts., *U.K.* 14 D4
Monadnock, Mt., *U.S.A.* 111 D12
Monaghan, *Ireland* 15 B5
Monaghan □, *Ireland* 15 B5
Monahans, *U.S.A.* 113 K3
Monapo, *Mozam.* 87 E5
Monar, L., *U.K.* 14 D3
Monarch Mt., *Canada* 104 C3
Monashee Mts., *Canada* 104 C5
Monasterevin, *Ireland* 15 C4
Monastir = Bitola, *Macedonia* 40 E5
Moncada, *Phil.* 61 D4
Moncalieri, *Italy* 28 D4
Moncalvo, *Italy* 28 C5
Moncão, *Portugal* 34 C2
Moncarapacho, *Portugal* 35 H3
Moncayo, Sierra del, *Spain* 32 D3
Mönchengladbach, *Germany* 24 D2
Monchique, *Portugal* 35 H2
Moncks Corner, *U.S.A.* 109 J5
Monclova, *Mexico* 118 B4
Moncontour, *France* 18 D4
Moncton, *Canada* 103 C7
Mondariz, *Spain* 34 C2
Mondego →, *Portugal* 34 E2
Mondego, C., *Portugal* 34 E2
Mondeodo, *Indonesia* 63 E6
Mondeville, *France* 18 C6
Mondolfo, *Italy* 29 E10
Mondoñedo, *Spain* 34 B3
Mondovì, *Italy* 28 D4
Mondragon, *Phil.* 61 E6
Mondragone, *Italy* 30 A6
Mondrain I., *Australia* 93 F3
Monemvasía, *Greece* 38 E5
Monessen, *U.S.A.* 110 F5
Monesterio, *Spain* 35 G4
Monestier-de-Clermont, *France* 21 D9
Monett, *U.S.A.* 113 G8
Moneymore, *U.K.* 15 B5
Monfalcone, *Italy* 29 C10
Monflanquin, *France* 20 D4
Monforte, *Portugal* 35 F3
Monforte de Lemos, *Spain* 34 C3
Mong Hsu, *Burma* 58 G2
Mong Kung, *Burma* 67 J20
Mong Nai, *Burma* 67 J20
Mong Pawk, *Burma* 67 H21
Mong Ping, *Burma* 58 G2
Mong Ton, *Burma* 67 J21
Mong Wa, *Burma* 67 J22
Mong Yai, *Burma* 67 H21
Mongalla, *Sudan* 81 F3
Mongers, L., *Australia* 93 E2
Monghyr = Munger, *India* 69 G12
Mongibello = Etna, *Italy* 31 E7
Mongo, *Chad* 79 F9
Mongo →, *S. Leone* 82 D2
Mongolia ■, *Asia* 51 E10
Mongonu, *Nigeria* 83 C7
Mongu, *Zambia* 85 H4
Môngua, *Angola* 88 B2
Monifieth, *U.K.* 14 E6
Monistrol-sur-Loire, *France* 21 C8
Monkey Bay, *Malawi* 87 E4
Monkey Mia, *Australia* 93 E1
Monkey River, *Belize* 119 D7
Mońki, *Poland* 44 E9
Monkoto, *Dem. Rep. of the Congo* 84 E4
Monkton, *Canada* 110 C3
Monmouth, *U.K.* 13 F5
Monmouth, *Ill., U.S.A.* 112 E9
Monmouth, *Oreg., U.S.A.* 114 D2
Monmouthshire □, *U.K.* 13 F5
Mono L., *U.S.A.* 116 H7
Monolith, *U.S.A.* 117 K8
Monólithos, *Greece* 36 C9
Monongahela, *U.S.A.* 110 F5
Monópoli, *Italy* 31 B10
Monor, *Hungary* 42 C4
Monóvar, *Spain* 33 G4
Monreal del Campo, *Spain* 32 E3
Monreale, *Italy* 30 D6
Monroe, *Ga., U.S.A.* 109 J4
Monroe, *La., U.S.A.* 113 J8
Monroe, *Mich., U.S.A.* 108 E4
Monroe, *N.C., U.S.A.* 109 H5
Monroe, *N.Y., U.S.A.* 111 E10
Monroe, *Utah, U.S.A.* 115 G7
Monroe, *Wash., U.S.A.* 116 C5
Monroe, *Wis., U.S.A.* 112 D10
Monroe City, *U.S.A.* 112 F9
Monroeton, *U.S.A.* 111 E8
Monroeville, *Ala., U.S.A.* 109 K2
Monroeville, *Pa., U.S.A.* 110 F5
Monrovia, *Liberia* 82 D2
Mons, *Belgium* 17 D3
Møns Klint, *Denmark* 11 K6
Monsaraz, *Portugal* 35 G3
Monse, *Indonesia* 63 E6
Monségur, *France* 20 D4
Monsélice, *Italy* 29 C8
Mönsterås, *Sweden* 11 G10
Mont Cenis, Col du, *France* 21 C10
Mont-de-Marsan, *France* 20 E3
Mont-Joli, *Canada* 103 C6
Mont-Laurier, *Canada* 102 C4
Mont-Louis, *Canada* 103 C6
Mont-roig del Camp, *Spain* 32 D5
Mont-St-Michel, Le = Le Mont-St-Michel, *France* 18 D5
Mont Tremblant, Parc Recr. du, *Canada* 102 C5
Montabaur, *Germany* 24 E3
Montagnac, *France* 20 E7
Montagnana, *Italy* 29 C8
Montagu, *S. Africa* 88 E3
Montagu I., *Antarctica* 5 B1
Montague, *Canada* 103 C7
Montague, I., *Mexico* 118 A2
Montague Ra., *Australia* 93 E2
Montague Sd., *Australia* 92 B4
Montaigu, *France* 18 F5
Montalbán, *Spain* 32 E4
Montalbano Iónico, *Italy* 31 B9
Montalbo, *Spain* 32 F2
Montalcino, *Italy* 29 E8
Montalegre, *Portugal* 34 D3
Montalto, *Italy* 31 D8
Montalto di Castro, *Italy* 29 F8
Montalto Uffugo, *Italy* 31 C9
Montalvo, *U.S.A.* 117 L7
Montamarta, *Spain* 34 D5
Montana, *Bulgaria* 40 C7
Montaña, *Peru* 124 E4
Montana □, *Bulgaria* 40 C7
Montana □, *U.S.A.* 114 C9
Montaña Clara, I., *Canary Is.* 37 E6
Montánchez, *Spain* 35 F4
Montargil, *Portugal* 35 F2
Montargis, *France* 19 E9
Montauban, *France* 20 D5
Montauk, *U.S.A.* 111 E13
Montauk Pt., *U.S.A.* 111 E13
Montbard, *France* 19 E11
Montbarrey, *France* 19 E12
Montbéliard, *France* 19 E13
Montblanc, *Spain* 32 D6
Montbrison, *France* 21 C8
Montcalm, Pic de, *France* 20 F5
Montceau-les-Mines, *France* 19 F11
Montcenis, *France* 21 B8
Montclair, *U.S.A.* 111 F10
Montcornet, *France* 19 C11
Montcuq, *France* 20 D5
Montdidier, *France* 19 C9
Monte Albán, *Mexico* 119 D5
Monte Alegre, *Brazil* 125 D8
Monte Azul, *Brazil* 125 G10
Monte Bello Is., *Australia* 92 D2
Monte-Carlo, *Monaco* 21 E11
Monte Caseros, *Argentina* 126 C4
Monte Comán, *Argentina* 126 C2
Monte Cristi, *Dom. Rep.* 121 C5
Monte Lindo →, *Paraguay* 126 A4
Monte Patria, *Chile* 126 C1
Monte Quemado, *Argentina* 126 B3
Monte Redondo, *Portugal* 34 F2
Monte Rio, *U.S.A.* 116 G4
Monte San Giovanni Campano, *Italy* 30 A6
Monte San Savino, *Italy* 29 E8
Monte Sant' Ángelo, *Italy* 29 G12
Monte Santu, C. di, *Italy* 30 B2
Monte Vista, *U.S.A.* 115 H10
Monteagudo, *Argentina* 127 B5
Montealegre del Castillo, *Spain* 33 G3
Montebello, *Canada* 102 C5
Montebello Iónico, *Italy* 31 E8
Montebelluna, *Italy* 29 C9
Montebourg, *France* 18 C5
Montecastrilli, *Italy* 29 F9
Montecatini Terme, *Italy* 28 E7
Montecito, *U.S.A.* 117 L7
Montecristo, *Italy* 28 F7
Montefalco, *Italy* 29 F9
Montefiascone, *Italy* 29 F9
Montefrío, *Spain* 35 H7
Montegiórgio, *Italy* 29 E10
Montego Bay, *Jamaica* 120 C4
Montehermoso, *Spain* 34 E4
Montejicar, *Spain* 35 H7
Montélimar, *France* 21 D8
Montella, *Italy* 31 B8
Montellano, *Spain* 35 J5
Montello, *U.S.A.* 112 D10
Montemor-o-Novo, *Portugal* 35 G2
Montemor-o-Velho, *Portugal* 34 E2
Montemorelos, *Mexico* 119 B5
Montendre, *France* 20 C3
Montenegro, *Brazil* 127 B5
Montenegro □, *Yugoslavia* 40 D3
Montenero di Bisáccia, *Italy* 29 G11
Montepuez, *Mozam.* 87 E4
Montepuez →, *Mozam.* 87 E5
Montepulciano, *Italy* 29 E8
Montereale, *Italy* 29 F10
Montereau-Faut-Yonne, *France* 19 D9
Monterey, *U.S.A.* 116 J5
Monterey B., *U.S.A.* 116 J5
Montería, *Colombia* 124 B3
Monteros, *Argentina* 126 B2
Monterotondo, *Italy* 29 F9
Monterrey, *Mexico* 118 B4
Montes Claros, *Brazil* 125 G10
Montesano, *U.S.A.* 116 D3
Montesano sulla Marcellana, *Italy* 31 B8
Montesárchio, *Italy* 31 A7
Montescaglioso, *Italy* 31 B9
Montesilvano, *Italy* 29 F11
Montevarchi, *Italy* 29 E8
Montevideo, *Uruguay* 127 C4
Montevideo, *U.S.A.* 112 C7
Montezuma, *U.S.A.* 112 E8
Montfaucon, *France* 18 E5
Montfaucon-d'Argonne, *France* 19 C12
Montfaucon-en-Velay, *France* 21 C8
Montfort, *France* 18 D5
Montfort-le-Gesnois, *France* 18 D7
Montgenèvre, *France* 21 D10
Montgomery = Sahiwal, *Pakistan* 68 D5
Montgomery, *U.K.* 13 E4
Montgomery, *Ala., U.S.A.* 109 J2
Montgomery, *Pa., U.S.A.* 110 E8
Montgomery, *W. Va., U.S.A.* 108 F5
Montgomery City, *U.S.A.* 112 F9
Montguyon, *France* 20 C3
Monthermé, *France* 19 C11
Monthey, *Switz.* 25 J2
Monthois, *France* 19 C11
Monti, *Italy* 30 B2
Monticelli d'Ongina, *Italy* 28 C6
Monticello, *Ark., U.S.A.* 113 J9
Monticello, *Fla., U.S.A.* 109 K4
Monticello, *Ind., U.S.A.* 108 E2
Monticello, *Iowa, U.S.A.* 112 D9
Monticello, *Ky., U.S.A.* 109 G3
Monticello, *Minn., U.S.A.* 112 C8
Monticello, *Miss., U.S.A.* 113 K9
Monticello, *N.Y., U.S.A.* 111 E10
Monticello, *Utah, U.S.A.* 115 H9
Montichiari, *Italy* 28 C7
Montier-en-Der, *France* 19 D11
Montignac, *France* 20 C5
Montigny-les-Metz, *France* 19 C13
Montigny-sur-Aube, *France* 19 E11
Montijo, *Portugal* 35 G2
Montijo, *Spain* 35 G4
Montilla, *Spain* 35 H6
Montivilliers, *France* 18 C7
Montluçon, *France* 19 F9
Montmagny, *Canada* 103 C5
Montmarault, *France* 19 F9
Montmartre, *Canada* 105 C8
Montmédy, *France* 19 C12
Montmélian, *France* 21 C10
Montmirail, *France* 19 D10
Montmoreau-St-Cybard, *France* 20 C4
Montmorillon, *France* 20 B4
Montmort-Lucy, *France* 19 D10
Monto, *Australia* 94 C5
Montoire-sur-le-Loir, *France* 18 E7
Montório al Vomano, *Italy* 29 F10
Montoro, *Spain* 35 G6
Montour Falls, *U.S.A.* 110 D8
Montoursville, *U.S.A.* 110 E8
Montpelier, *Idaho, U.S.A.* 114 E8
Montpelier, *Vt., U.S.A.* 111 B12
Montpellier, *France* 20 E7
Montpezat-de-Quercy, *France* 20 D5
Montpon-Ménestérol, *France* 20 D4
Montréal, *Canada* 102 C5
Montréal, *Aude, France* 20 E6
Montréal, *Gers, France* 20 E4
Montreal →, *Canada* 102 C3
Montreal L., *Canada* 105 C7
Montreal Lake, *Canada* 105 C7
Montredon-Labessonnié, *France* 20 E6
Montrésor, *France* 18 E8
Montret, *France* 19 F12
Montreuil, *Pas-de-Calais, France* 19 B8
Montreuil, *Seine-St-Denis, France* 19 D9
Montreuil-Bellay, *France* 18 E6
Montreux, *Switz.* 25 J2
Montrevel-en-Bresse, *France* 19 F12
Montrichard, *France* 18 E8
Montrose, *U.K.* 14 E6
Montrose, *Colo., U.S.A.* 115 G10
Montrose, *Pa., U.S.A.* 111 E9
Monts, Pte. des, *Canada* 103 C6
Montsalvy, *France* 20 D6
Montsant, Serra de, *Spain* 32 D6
Montsauche-les-Settons, *France* 19 E11
Montsec, Serra del, *Spain* 32 C5
Montserrat, *Spain* 32 D6
Montserrat ■, *W. Indies* 121 C7
Montuenga, *Spain* 34 D6
Montuiri, *Spain* 37 B9
Monywa, *Burma* 67 H19
Monza, *Italy* 28 C6
Monze, *Zambia* 87 F2
Monze, C., *Pakistan* 68 G2
Monzón, *Spain* 32 D5
Mooers, *U.S.A.* 111 B11
Mooi →, *S. Africa* 89 D5
Mooi River, *S. Africa* 89 D4
Moonah →, *Australia* 94 C2
Moonda, L., *Australia* 94 D3
Moonie, *Australia* 95 D5
Moonie →, *Australia* 95 D4
Moora, *Australia* 93 F2
Moorcroft, *U.S.A.* 112 C2
Moore →, *Australia* 93 F2
Moore, L., *Australia* 93 E2
Moore Park, *Australia* 94 C5
Moore Reefs, *Australia* 94 B4
Moorefield, *U.S.A.* 108 F6
Moores Res., *U.S.A.* 111 B13
Moorfoot Hills, *U.K.* 14 F5
Moorhead, *U.S.A.* 112 B6
Moormerland, *Germany* 24 B3
Moorpark, *U.S.A.* 117 L8
Moorreesburg, *S. Africa* 88 E2
Moosburg, *Germany* 25 G7
Moose →, *Canada* 102 B3
Moose →, *U.S.A.* 111 C9
Moose Creek, *Canada* 111 A10
Moose Factory, *Canada* 102 B3
Moose Jaw, *Canada* 105 C7
Moose Jaw →, *Canada* 105 C7
Moose Lake, *Canada* 105 C8
Moose Lake, *U.S.A.* 112 B8
Moose Mountain Prov. Park, *Canada* 105 D8
Moosehead L., *U.S.A.* 109 C11
Mooselookmeguntic L., *U.S.A.* 109 C10
Moosilauke, Mt., *U.S.A.* 111 B13
Moosomin, *Canada* 105 C8
Moosonee, *Canada* 102 B3
Moosup, *U.S.A.* 111 E13
Mopane, *S. Africa* 89 C4
Mopeia Velha, *Mozam.* 87 F4
Mopipi, *Botswana* 88 C3
Mopoi, *C.A.R.* 86 A2
Mopti, *Mali* 82 C4
Moqatta, *Sudan* 81 E4
Moqor, *Afghan.* 68 C2
Moquegua, *Peru* 124 G4
Mór, *Hungary* 42 C3
Mora, *Cameroon* 83 C7
Móra, *Portugal* 35 G2
Mora, *Spain* 35 F7
Mora, *Sweden* 10 C8
Mora, *Minn., U.S.A.* 112 C8
Mora, *N. Mex., U.S.A.* 115 J11
Mora →, *U.S.A.* 113 H2
Mora de Ebro = Mòra d'Ebre, *Spain* 32 D5
Mora de Rubielos, *Spain* 32 E4
Mòra d'Ebre, *Spain* 32 D5
Mòra la Nova, *Spain* 32 D5
Morača →, *Montenegro, Yug.* 40 D3
Moradabad, *India* 69 E8
Morafenobe, *Madag.* 89 B7
Morąg, *Poland* 44 E6
Moral de Calatrava, *Spain* 35 G7
Moraleja, *Spain* 34 E4
Moramanga, *Madag.* 89 B8
Moran, *Kans., U.S.A.* 113 G7
Moran, *Wyo., U.S.A.* 114 E8
Moranbah, *Australia* 94 C4
Morano Cálabro, *Italy* 31 C9
Morant Cays, *Jamaica* 120 C4
Morant Pt., *Jamaica* 120 C4
Morar, *India* 68 F8
Morar, L., *U.K.* 14 E3
Moratalla, *Spain* 33 G3
Moratuwa, *Sri Lanka* 66 R11
Morava →, *Slovak Rep.* 27 C9
Moravia, *U.S.A.* 111 D8
Moravian Hts. = Českomoravská Vrchovina, *Czech Rep.* 26 B8
Moravica →, *Serbia, Yug.* 40 C4
Moraviţa, *Romania* 42 E6
Moravská Třebová, *Czech Rep.* 27 B9
Moravské Budějovice, *Czech Rep.* 26 B8
Morawa, *Australia* 93 E2
Morawhanna, *Guyana* 124 B7
Moray □, *U.K.* 14 D5
Moray Firth, *U.K.* 14 D5
Morbach, *Germany* 25 F3
Morbegno, *Italy* 28 B6
Morbi, *India* 68 H4
Morbihan □, *France* 18 E4
Mörbylånga, *Sweden* 11 H10
Morcenx, *France* 20 D3
Morcone, *Italy* 31 A7
Mordelles, *France* 18 D5
Morden, *Canada* 105 D9
Mordoğan, *Turkey* 39 C8
Mordovian Republic = Mordvinia □, *Russia* 48 C7
Mordovo, *Russia* 48 D5
Mordvinia □, *Russia* 48 C7
Mordy, *Poland* 45 F9
Morea, *Greece* 6 H10
Moreau →, *U.S.A.* 112 C4
Morecambe, *U.K.* 12 C5
Morecambe B., *U.K.* 12 C5
Moree, *Australia* 95 D4
Morehead, *U.S.A.* 108 F4
Morehead City, *U.S.A.* 109 H7
Morel →, *India* 68 F7
Morelia, *Mexico* 118 D4
Morella, *Australia* 94 C3
Morella, *Spain* 32 E4
Morelos, *Mexico* 118 B3
Morelos □, *Mexico* 119 D5
Morena, *India* 68 F8
Morena, Sierra, *Spain* 35 G7
Moreni, *Romania* 43 F10
Moreno Valley, *U.S.A.* 117 M10
Moresby I., *Canada* 104 C2
Morestel, *France* 21 C9
Moreton I., *Australia* 95 D5
Moreuil, *France* 19 C9
Morey, *Spain* 37 B10
Morez, *France* 19 F13
Morgan, *U.S.A.* 114 F8
Morgan City, *U.S.A.* 113 L9
Morgan Hill, *U.S.A.* 116 H5
Morganfield, *U.S.A.* 108 G2
Morganton, *U.S.A.* 109 H5
Morgantown, *U.S.A.* 108 F6
Morgenzon, *S. Africa* 89 D4
Morges, *Switz.* 25 J2
Morghak, *Iran* 71 D8
Morgongåva, *Sweden* 10 E10
Morhange, *France* 19 D13
Morhar →, *India* 69 G11
Mori, *Italy* 28 C7
Moriarty, *U.S.A.* 115 J10
Moribaya, *Guinea* 82 D3
Morice L., *Canada* 104 C3
Moriki, *Nigeria* 83 C6
Morinville, *Canada* 104 C6
Morioka, *Japan* 54 E10
Moris, *Mexico* 118 B3
Morlaàs, *France* 20 E3
Morlaix, *France* 18 D3
Mörlunda, *Sweden* 11 G9
Mormanno, *Italy* 31 C8
Mormant, *France* 19 D9
Mornington, I., *Chile* 128 F1
Mornington I., *Australia* 94 B2
Mórnos →, *Greece* 38 C3
Moro, *Pakistan* 68 F2
Moro, *Sudan* 81 E3
Moro →, *Pakistan* 68 E2
Moro G., *Phil.* 61 H5
Morocco ■, *N. Afr.* 78 B4
Morogoro, *Tanzania* 86 D4
Morogoro □, *Tanzania* 86 D4
Moroleón, *Mexico* 118 C4
Morombe, *Madag.* 89 C7
Moron, *Argentina* 126 C4
Morón, *Cuba* 120 B4
Morón de Almazán, *Spain* 32 D2
Morón de la Frontera, *Spain* 35 H5
Morona →, *Peru* 124 D3
Morondava, *Madag.* 89 C7
Morondo, *Ivory C.* 82 D3
Morongo Valley, *U.S.A.* 117 L10
Moroni, *Comoros Is.* 77 H8
Moroni, *U.S.A.* 114 G8
Moronou, *Ivory C.* 82 D4
Morotai, *Indonesia* 63 D7
Moroto, *Uganda* 86 B3
Moroto Summit, *Kenya* 86 B3
Morozov, *Bulgaria* 41 D9
Morozovsk, *Russia* 49 F5
Morpeth, *U.K.* 12 B6
Morphou, *Cyprus* 36 D11
Morphou Bay, *Cyprus* 36 D11
Morrilton, *U.S.A.* 113 H8
Morrinhos, *Brazil* 125 G9
Morrinsville, *N.Z.* 91 G5
Morris, *Canada* 105 D9
Morris, *Ill., U.S.A.* 112 E10
Morris, *Minn., U.S.A.* 112 C7
Morris, *N.Y., U.S.A.* 111 D9
Morris, *Pa., U.S.A.* 110 E7
Morris, Mt., *Australia* 93 E5
Morrisburg, *Canada* 111 B9
Morristown, *Ariz., U.S.A.* 115 K7
Morristown, *N.J., U.S.A.* 111 F10
Morristown, *N.Y., U.S.A.* 111 B9
Morristown, *Tenn., U.S.A.* 109 G4
Morrisville, *N.Y., U.S.A.* 111 D9
Morrisville, *Pa., U.S.A.* 111 F10
Morrisville, *Vt., U.S.A.* 111 B12
Morro, Pta., *Chile* 126 B1
Morro Bay, *U.S.A.* 116 K6
Morro del Jable, *Canary Is.* 37 F5
Morro Jable, Pta. de, *Canary Is.* 37 F5
Morrosquillo, G. de, *Colombia* 120 E4
Mörrum, *Sweden* 11 H8
Morrumbene, *Mozam.* 89 C6
Mörrumsån →, *Sweden* 11 H8
Mors, *Denmark* 11 H2
Morshansk, *Russia* 48 D5
Mörsil, *Sweden* 10 A7
Mortagne →, *France* 19 D13
Mortagne-au-Perche, *France* 18 D7
Mortagne-sur-Gironde, *France* 20 C3
Mortagne-sur-Sèvre, *France* 18 F6
Mortain, *France* 18 D6
Mortara, *Italy* 28 C5
Morteau, *France* 19 E13
Morteros, *Argentina* 126 C3
Mortlach, *Canada* 105 C7
Morton, *Tex., U.S.A.* 113 J3
Morton, *Wash., U.S.A.* 116 D4
Morvan, *France* 19 E11
Morven, *Australia* 95 D4
Morvern, *U.K.* 14 E3

Moryń, *Poland* 45 F1
Morzine, *France* 19 F13
Mosalsk, *Russia* 46 E8
Mosbach, *Germany* 25 F5
Mošćenice, *Croatia* 29 C11
Mosciano Sant' Ángelo, *Italy* 29 F10
Moscos Is., *Burma* 64 E1
Moscow = Moskva, *Russia* 46 E9
Moscow, *Idaho, U.S.A.* 114 C5
Moscow, *Pa., U.S.A.* 111 E9
Mosel →, *Europe* 19 B14
Moselle = Mosel →, *Europe* 19 B14
Moselle □, *France* 19 D13
Moses Lake, *U.S.A.* 114 C4
Mosgiel, *N.Z.* 91 L3
Moshaweng →, *S. Africa* 88 D3
Moshi, *Tanzania* 86 C4
Moshupa, *Botswana* 88 C4
Mosina, *Poland* 45 F3
Mosjøen, *Norway* 8 D15
Moskenesøya, *Norway* 8 C15
Moskenstraumen, *Norway* 8 C15
Moskva, *Russia* 46 E9
Moskva →, *Russia* 46 E10
Moslavačka Gora, *Croatia* 29 C13
Mosomane, *Botswana* 88 C4
Mosonmagyaróvár, *Hungary* 42 C2
Mošorin, *Serbia, Yug.* 42 E5
Mospino, *Ukraine* 47 J9
Mosquera, *Colombia* 124 C3
Mosquero, *U.S.A.* 113 H3
Mosqueruela, *Spain* 32 E4
Mosquitia, *Honduras* 120 C3
Mosquito Coast = Mosquitia, *Honduras* 120 C3
Mosquito Creek L., *U.S.A.* 110 E4
Mosquito L., *Canada* 105 A8
Mosquitos, G. de los, *Panama* 120 E3
Moss, *Norway* 9 G14
Mossbank, *Canada* 105 D7
Mossburn, *N.Z.* 91 L2
Mosselbaai, *S. Africa* 88 E3
Mossendjo, *Congo* 84 E2
Mossingen, *Germany* 25 G5
Mossman, *Australia* 94 B4
Mossoró, *Brazil* 125 E11
Mossuril, *Mozam.* 87 E5
Most, *Czech Rep.* 26 A6
Mosta, *Malta* 36 D1
Mostaganem, *Algeria* 78 A6
Mostar, *Bos.-H.* 42 G2
Mostardas, *Brazil* 127 C5
Mostiska = Mostyska, *Ukraine* 47 H2
Móstoles, *Spain* 34 E7
Mosty = Masty, *Belarus* 46 F3
Mostyska, *Ukraine* 47 H2
Mosul = Al Mawşil, *Iraq* 70 B4
Mosŭlpo, *S. Korea* 57 H14
Mota, *Ethiopia* 81 E4
Mota del Cuervo, *Spain* 33 F2
Mota del Marqués, *Spain* 34 D5
Motagua →, *Guatemala* 120 C2
Motala, *Sweden* 11 F9
Motaze, *Mozam.* 89 C5
Moţca, *Romania* 43 C11
Moth, *India* 69 G8
Motherwell, *U.K.* 14 F5
Motihari, *India* 69 F11
Motilla del Palancar, *Spain* 33 F3
Motnik, *Slovenia* 29 B11
Motovun, *Croatia* 29 C10
Motozintla de Mendoza, *Mexico* 119 D6
Motril, *Spain* 35 J7
Motru, *Romania* 42 F7
Motru →, *Romania* 43 F8
Mott, *U.S.A.* 112 B3
Móttola, *Italy* 31 B10
Motueka, *N.Z.* 91 J4
Motueka →, *N.Z.* 91 J4
Motul, *Mexico* 119 C7
Mouchalagane →, *Canada* 103 B6
Moúdhros, *Greece* 39 B7
Mouding, *China* 58 E3
Moudjeria, *Mauritania* 82 B2
Moudon, *Switz.* 25 J2
Mouila, *Gabon* 84 E2
Moulianá, *Greece* 36 D7
Moulins, *France* 19 F10
Moulmein, *Burma* 67 L20
Moulouya, O. →, *Morocco* 78 B5
Moultrie, *U.S.A.* 109 K4
Moultrie, L., *U.S.A.* 109 J5
Mound City, *Mo., U.S.A.* 112 E7
Mound City, *S. Dak., U.S.A.* 112 C4
Moúnda, Ákra, *Greece* 38 C2
Moundou, *Chad* 79 G9
Moundsville, *U.S.A.* 110 G4
Moung, *Cambodia* 64 F4
Mount Airy, *U.S.A.* 109 G5
Mount Albert, *Canada* 110 B5
Mount Barker, *Australia* 93 F2
Mount Brydges, *Canada* 110 D3
Mount Burr, *Australia* 95 F3
Mount Carmel, *Ill., U.S.A.* 108 F2
Mount Carmel, *Pa., U.S.A.* 111 F8
Mount Charleston, *U.S.A.* 117 J11
Mount Clemens, *U.S.A.* 110 D2
Mount Coolon, *Australia* 94 C4
Mount Darwin, *Zimbabwe* 87 F3
Mount Desert I., *U.S.A.* 109 C11
Mount Dora, *U.S.A.* 109 L5
Mount Edziza Prov. Park, *Canada* 104 B2
Mount Fletcher, *S. Africa* 89 E4
Mount Forest, *Canada* 102 D3
Mount Garnet, *Australia* 94 B4
Mount Holly, *U.S.A.* 111 G10
Mount Holly Springs, *U.S.A.* 110 F7
Mount Hope, *Australia* 95 E2
Mount Isa, *Australia* 94 C2
Mount Jewett, *U.S.A.* 110 E6
Mount Kisco, *U.S.A.* 111 E11
Mount Laguna, *U.S.A.* 117 N10
Mount Larcom, *Australia* 94 C5
Mount Magnet, *Australia* 93 E2
Mount Maunganui, *N.Z.* 91 G6
Mount Molloy, *Australia* 94 B4
Mount Morgan, *Australia* 94 C5
Mount Morris, *U.S.A.* 110 D7
Mount Pearl, *Canada* 103 C9
Mount Penn, *U.S.A.* 111 F9
Mount Perry, *Australia* 95 D5
Mount Pleasant, *Iowa, U.S.A.* 112 E9
Mount Pleasant, *Mich., U.S.A.* 108 D3
Mount Pleasant, *Pa., U.S.A.* 110 F5
Mount Pleasant, *S.C., U.S.A.* 109 J6
Mount Pleasant, *Tenn., U.S.A.* 109 H2
Mount Pleasant, *Tex., U.S.A.* 113 J7
Mount Pleasant, *Utah, U.S.A.* 114 G8
Mount Pocono, *U.S.A.* 111 E9
Mount Rainier Nat. Park, *U.S.A.* 116 D5
Mount Revelstoke Nat. Park, *Canada* 104 C5
Mount Robson Prov. Park, *Canada* 104 C5
Mount Selinda, *Zimbabwe* 89 C5
Mount Shasta, *U.S.A.* 114 F2
Mount Signal, *U.S.A.* 117 N11
Mount Sterling, *Ill., U.S.A.* 112 F9
Mount Sterling, *Ky., U.S.A.* 108 F4
Mount Surprise, *Australia* 94 B3
Mount Union, *U.S.A.* 110 F7
Mount Upton, *U.S.A.* 111 D9
Mount Vernon, *Ill., U.S.A.* 108 F1
Mount Vernon, *Ind., U.S.A.* 112 F10
Mount Vernon, *N.Y., U.S.A.* 111 F11
Mount Vernon, *Ohio, U.S.A.* 110 F2
Mount Vernon, *Wash., U.S.A.* 116 B4
Mountain Ash, *U.K.* 13 F4
Mountain Center, *U.S.A.* 117 M10
Mountain City, *Nev., U.S.A.* 114 F6
Mountain City, *Tenn., U.S.A.* 109 G5
Mountain Dale, *U.S.A.* 111 E10
Mountain Grove, *U.S.A.* 113 G8
Mountain Home, *Ark., U.S.A.* 113 G8
Mountain Home, *Idaho, U.S.A.* 114 E6
Mountain Iron, *U.S.A.* 112 B8
Mountain Pass, *U.S.A.* 117 K11
Mountain View, *Ark., U.S.A.* 113 H8
Mountain View, *Calif., U.S.A.* 116 H4
Mountain View, *Hawaii, U.S.A.* 106 J17
Mountainair, *U.S.A.* 115 J10
Mountlake Terrace, *U.S.A.* 116 C4
Mountmellick, *Ireland* 15 C4
Mountrath, *Ireland* 15 D4
Moura, *Australia* 94 C4
Moura, *Brazil* 124 D6
Moura, *Portugal* 35 G3
Mourão, *Portugal* 35 G3
Mourdi, Dépression du, *Chad* 79 E10
Mourdiah, *Mali* 82 C3
Mourenx, *France* 20 E3
Mouri, *Ghana* 83 D4
Mourilyan, *Australia* 94 B4
Mourmelon-le-Grand, *France* 19 C11
Mourne →, *U.K.* 15 B4
Mourne Mts., *U.K.* 15 B5
Mourniaí, *Greece* 36 D6
Mournies = Mourniaí, *Greece* 36 D6
Mouscron, *Belgium* 17 D3
Moussoro, *Chad* 79 F9
Mouthe, *France* 19 F13
Moutier, *Switz.* 25 H3
Moûtiers, *France* 21 C10
Moutong, *Indonesia* 63 D6
Mouy, *France* 19 C9
Mouzáki, *Greece* 38 B3
Mouzon, *France* 19 C12
Movas, *Mexico* 118 B3
Moville, *Ireland* 15 A4
Mowandjum, *Australia* 92 C3
Moy →, *Ireland* 15 B2
Moyale, *Kenya* 81 G4
Moyamba, *S. Leone* 82 D2
Moyen Atlas, *Morocco* 78 B4
Moyne, L. le, *Canada* 103 A6
Moyo, *Indonesia* 62 F5
Moyobamba, *Peru* 124 E3
Moyyero →, *Russia* 51 C11
Moyynty, *Kazakstan* 50 E8
Mozambique = Moçambique, *Mozam.* 87 F5
Mozambique ■, *Africa* 87 F4
Mozambique Chan., *Africa* 89 B7
Mozdok, *Russia* 49 J7
Mozdūrān, *Iran* 71 B9
Mozhaysk, *Russia* 46 E9
Mozhga, *Russia* 48 B11
Mozhnābād, *Iran* 71 C9
Mozirje, *Slovenia* 29 B11
Mozyr = Mazyr, *Belarus* 47 F5
Mpanda, *Tanzania* 86 D3
Mpésoba, *Mali* 82 C3
Mphoengs, *Zimbabwe* 89 C4
Mpika, *Zambia* 87 E3
Mpulungu, *Zambia* 87 D3
Mpumalanga, *S. Africa* 89 D5
Mpumalanga □, *S. Africa* 89 B5
Mpwapwa, *Tanzania* 86 D4
Mqanduli, *S. Africa* 89 E4
Mqinvartsveri = Kazbek, *Russia* 49 J7
Mrągowo, *Poland* 44 E8
Mramor, *Serbia, Yug.* 40 C5
Mrkonjić Grad, *Bos.-H.* 42 F2
Mrkopalj, *Croatia* 29 C11
Mrocza, *Poland* 45 E4
Msambansovu, *Zimbabwe* 87 F3
M'sila →, *Algeria* 78 A6
Msoro, *Zambia* 87 E3
Msta →, *Russia* 46 C6
Mstislavl = Mstsislaw, *Belarus* 46 E6
Mstsislaw, *Belarus* 46 E6
Mszana Dolna, *Poland* 45 J7
Mszczonów, *Poland* 45 G7
Mtama, *Tanzania* 87 E4
Mtamvuna →, *S. Africa* 89 E5
Mtilikwe →, *Zimbabwe* 87 G3
Mtsensk, *Russia* 46 F9
Mtskheta, *Georgia* 49 K7
Mtubatuba, *S. Africa* 89 D5
Mtwalume, *S. Africa* 89 E5
Mtwara-Mikindani, *Tanzania* 87 E5
Mu Gia, Deo, *Vietnam* 64 D5
Mu Us Shamo, *China* 56 E5
Muang Chiang Rai = Chiang Rai, *Thailand* 58 H2
Muang Khong, *Laos* 64 E5
Muang Lamphun, *Thailand* 64 C2
Muang Pak Beng, *Laos* 58 H3
Muar, *Malaysia* 65 L4
Muarabungo, *Indonesia* 62 E2
Muaraenim, *Indonesia* 62 E2
Muarajuloi, *Indonesia* 62 E4
Muarakaman, *Indonesia* 62 E5
Muaratebo, *Indonesia* 62 E2
Muaratembesi, *Indonesia* 62 E2
Muaratewe, *Indonesia* 62 E4
Mubarakpur, *India* 69 F10
Mubarraz = Al Mubarraz, *Si. Arabia* 71 E6
Mubende, *Uganda* 86 B3
Mubi, *Nigeria* 83 C7
Mubur, Pulau, *Indonesia* 65 L6
Mucajaí →, *Brazil* 124 C6
Muchachos, Roque de los, *Canary Is.* 37 F2
Mücheln, *Germany* 24 D7
Muchinga Mts., *Zambia* 87 E3
Muchkapskiy, *Russia* 48 E6
Muchuan, *China* 58 C5
Muck, *U.K.* 14 E2
Muckadilla, *Australia* 95 D4
Mucur, *Turkey* 72 C6
Mucuri, *Brazil* 125 G11
Mucusso, *Angola* 88 B3
Muda, *Canary Is.* 37 F6
Mudanjiang, *China* 57 B15
Mudanya, *Turkey* 41 F12
Muddy Cr. →, *U.S.A.* 115 H8
Mudjatik →, *Canada* 105 B7
Mudurnu, *Turkey* 72 B4
Muecate, *Mozam.* 87 E4
Mueda, *Mozam.* 87 E4
Mueller Ra., *Australia* 92 C4
Muende, *Mozam.* 87 E3
Muerto, Mar, *Mexico* 119 D6
Mufu Shan, *China* 59 C10
Mufulira, *Zambia* 87 E2
Mufumbiro Range, *Africa* 86 C2
Mugardos, *Spain* 34 B2
Muge →, *Portugal* 35 F2
Múggia, *Italy* 29 C10
Mughal Sarai, *India* 69 G10
Mughayrā', *Si. Arabia* 70 D3
Mugi, *Japan* 55 H7
Mugia = Muxía, *Spain* 34 B1
Mugila, Mts., *Dem. Rep. of the Congo* 86 D2
Muğla, *Turkey* 39 D10
Muğla □, *Turkey* 39 D10
Muglad, *Sudan* 81 E2
Mŭglizh, *Bulgaria* 41 D9
Mugu, *Nepal* 69 E10
Muhammad, Ras, *Egypt* 70 E2
Muhammad Qol, *Sudan* 80 C4
Muhammadabad, *India* 69 F10
Muhesi →, *Tanzania* 86 D4
Mühlacker, *Germany* 25 G4
Mühldorf, *Germany* 25 G8
Mühlhausen, *Germany* 24 D6
Mühlig Hofmann fjell, *Antarctica* 5 D3
Mühlviertel, *Austria* 26 C7
Muhos, *Finland* 8 D22
Muhu, *Estonia* 9 G20
Muhutwe, *Tanzania* 86 C3
Muine Bheag, *Ireland* 15 D5
Muir, L., *Australia* 93 F2
Mujnak = Muynak, *Uzbekistan* 50 E6
Mukacheve, *Ukraine* 47 H2
Mukachevo = Mukacheve, *Ukraine* 47 H2
Mukah, *Malaysia* 62 D4
Mukandwara, *India* 68 G6
Mukawwa, Geziret, *Egypt* 80 C4
Mukawwar, *Sudan* 80 C4
Mukdahan, *Thailand* 64 D5
Mukden = Shenyang, *China* 57 D12
Mukerian, *India* 68 D6
Mukhtolovo, *Russia* 48 C6
Mukhtuya = Lensk, *Russia* 51 C12
Mukinbudin, *Australia* 93 F2
Mukishi, *Dem. Rep. of the Congo* 87 D1
Mukomuko, *Indonesia* 62 E2
Mukomwenze, *Dem. Rep. of the Congo* 86 D2
Muktsar, *India* 68 D6
Mukur = Moqor, *Afghan.* 68 C2
Mukutawa →, *Canada* 105 C9
Mukwela, *Zambia* 87 F2
Mula, *Spain* 33 G3
Mula →, *Pakistan* 68 F2
Mulange, *Dem. Rep. of the Congo* 86 C2
Mulanje, *Malawi* 87 F4
Mulchén, *Chile* 126 D1
Mulde →, *Germany* 24 D8
Mule Creek Junction, *U.S.A.* 112 D2
Muleba, *Tanzania* 86 C3
Mulejé, *Mexico* 118 B2
Muleshoe, *U.S.A.* 113 H3
Muletta, Gara, *Ethiopia* 81 F5
Mulgrave, *Canada* 103 C7
Mulhacén, *Spain* 35 H7
Mülheim, *Germany* 24 D2
Mulhouse, *France* 19 E14
Muli, *China* 58 D3
Muling, *China* 57 B16
Mull, *U.K.* 14 E3
Mull, Sound of, *U.K.* 14 E3
Mullaittivu, *Sri Lanka* 66 Q12
Mullen, *U.S.A.* 112 D4
Mullens, *U.S.A.* 108 G5
Muller, Pegunungan, *Indonesia* 62 D4
Mullet Pen., *Ireland* 15 B1
Mullewa, *Australia* 93 E2
Müllheim, *Germany* 25 H3
Mulligan →, *Australia* 94 D2
Mullingar, *Ireland* 15 C4
Mullins, *U.S.A.* 109 H6
Mullsjö, *Sweden* 11 G7
Mullumbimby, *Australia* 95 D5
Mulobezi, *Zambia* 87 F2
Mulroy B., *Ireland* 15 A4
Multan, *Pakistan* 68 D4
Mulumbe, Mts., *Dem. Rep. of the Congo* 87 D2
Mulungushi Dam, *Zambia* 87 E2
Mulvane, *U.S.A.* 113 G6
Mulwad, *Sudan* 80 D3
Mumbai, *India* 66 K8
Mumbwa, *Zambia* 87 F2
Mumra, *Russia* 49 H8
Mun →, *Thailand* 64 E5
Muna, *Indonesia* 63 F6
Munabao, *India* 68 G4
Munamagi, *Estonia* 9 H22
Münchberg, *Germany* 25 E7
Müncheberg, *Germany* 24 C10
München, *Germany* 25 G7
Munchen-Gladbach = Mönchengladbach, *Germany* 24 D2
Muncho Lake, *Canada* 104 B3
Munch'ŏn, *N. Korea* 57 E14
Muncie, *U.S.A.* 108 E3
Muncoonie, L., *Australia* 94 D2
Mundabbera, *Australia* 95 D5
Munday, *U.S.A.* 113 J5
Münden, *Germany* 24 D5
Mundiwindi, *Australia* 92 D3
Mundo →, *Spain* 33 G2
Mundo Novo, *Brazil* 125 F10
Mundra, *India* 68 H3
Mundrabilla, *Australia* 93 F4
Munera, *Spain* 33 F2
Mungallala, *Australia* 95 D4
Mungallala Cr. →, *Australia* 95 D4
Mungana, *Australia* 94 B3
Mungaoli, *India* 68 G8
Mungari, *Mozam.* 87 F3
Mungbere, *Dem. Rep. of the Congo* 86 B2
Mungeli, *India* 69 H9
Munger, *India* 69 G12
Munich = München, *Germany* 25 G7
Munising, *U.S.A.* 108 B2
Munka-Ljungby, *Sweden* 11 H6
Munkebo, *Denmark* 11 J4
Munkedal, *Sweden* 11 F5
Munkfors, *Sweden* 10 E7
Munku-Sardyk, *Russia* 51 D11
Münnerstadt, *Germany* 25 E6
Muñoz Gamero, Pen., *Chile* 128 G2
Munroe L., *Canada* 105 B9
Munsan, *S. Korea* 57 F14
Munster, *France* 19 D14
Munster, *Niedersachsen, Germany* 24 C6
Münster, *Nordrhein-Westfalen, Germany* 24 D3
Munster □, *Ireland* 15 D3
Muntadgin, *Australia* 93 F2
Muntele Mare, Vf., *Romania* 43 D8
Muntok, *Indonesia* 62 E3
Munyama, *Zambia* 87 F2
Munzur Dağları, *Turkey* 73 C8
Muong Beng, *Laos* 58 G3
Muong Boum, *Vietnam* 58 F4
Muong Et, *Laos* 64 B5
Muong Hai, *Laos* 58 G3
Muong Hiem, *Laos* 64 B4
Muong Houn, *Laos* 58 G3
Muong Hung, *Vietnam* 58 G4
Muong Kau, *Laos* 64 E5
Muong Khao, *Laos* 64 C4
Muong Khoua, *Laos* 58 G4
Muong Liep, *Laos* 64 C3
Muong May, *Laos* 64 E6
Muong Ngeun, *Laos* 58 G3
Muong Ngoi, *Laos* 58 G4
Muong Nhie, *Vietnam* 58 F4
Muong Nong, *Laos* 64 D6
Muong Ou Tay, *Laos* 58 F3
Muong Oua, *Laos* 64 C3
Muong Peun, *Laos* 58 G4
Muong Phalane, *Laos* 64 D5
Muong Phieng, *Laos* 64 C3
Muong Phine, *Laos* 64 D6
Muong Sai, *Laos* 58 G3
Muong Saiapoun, *Laos* 64 C3
Muong Sen, *Vietnam* 64 C5
Muong Sing, *Laos* 58 G3
Muong Son, *Laos* 58 G4
Muong Soui, *Laos* 64 C4
Muong Va, *Laos* 58 G4
Muong Xia, *Vietnam* 64 B5
Muonio, *Finland* 8 C20
Muonionjoki →, *Finland* 8 C20
Muping, *China* 57 F11
Mupoi, *Sudan* 81 F2
Muqaddam, Wadi →, *Sudan* 80 D3
Muqdisho, *Somali Rep.* 74 G4
Mur →, *Austria* 27 E9
Mur-de-Bretagne, *France* 18 D4
Muradiye, *Manisa, Turkey* 39 C9
Muradiye, *Van, Turkey* 73 C10
Murakami, *Japan* 54 E9
Murallón, Cerro, *Chile* 128 F2
Muranda, *Rwanda* 86 C2
Murang'a, *Kenya* 86 C4
Murashi, *Russia* 50 D5
Murat, *France* 20 C6
Murat →, *Turkey* 73 C9
Murat Dağı, *Turkey* 39 C11
Muratlı, *Turkey* 41 E11
Murato, *France* 21 F13
Murau, *Austria* 26 D7
Muravera, *Italy* 30 C2
Murayama, *Japan* 54 E10
Murça, *Portugal* 34 D3
Murchison →, *Australia* 93 E1
Murchison, Mt., *Antarctica* 5 D11
Murchison Falls, *Uganda* 86 B3
Murchison Ra., *Australia* 94 C1
Murchison Rapids, *Malawi* 87 F3
Murcia, *Spain* 33 G3
Murcia □, *Spain* 33 H3
Murdo, *U.S.A.* 112 D4
Murdoch Pt., *Australia* 94 A3
Mürefte, *Turkey* 41 F11
Mureş □, *Romania* 43 D9
Mureş →, *Romania* 42 D5
Mureşul = Mureş →, *Romania* 42 D5
Muret, *France* 20 E5
Murewa, *Zimbabwe* 89 B5
Murfreesboro, *N.C., U.S.A.* 109 G7
Murfreesboro, *Tenn., U.S.A.* 109 H2
Murgab = Murghob, *Tajikistan* 50 F8
Murgab →, *Turkmenistan* 71 B9
Murgenella, *Australia* 92 B5
Murgeni, *Romania* 43 D13
Murgha Kibzai, *Pakistan* 68 D3
Murghob, *Tajikistan* 50 F8
Murgon, *Australia* 95 D5
Muri, *India* 69 H11
Muria, *Indonesia* 63 G14
Muriaé, *Brazil* 127 A7
Murias de Paredes, *Spain* 34 C4
Muriel Mine, *Zimbabwe* 87 F3
Müritz, *Germany* 24 B8
Murka, *Kenya* 86 C4
Murliganj, *India* 69 G12
Murmansk, *Russia* 50 C4
Murnau, *Germany* 25 H7
Muro, *France* 21 F12
Muro, *Spain* 37 B10
Muro, C. de, *France* 21 G12
Muro de Alcoy, *Spain* 33 G4
Muro Lucano, *Italy* 31 B8
Murom, *Russia* 48 C6
Muroran, *Japan* 54 C10
Muros, *Spain* 34 C1
Muros y de Noya, Ría de, *Spain* 34 C1
Muroto, *Japan* 55 H7
Muroto-Misaki, *Japan* 55 H7
Murowana Goślina, *Poland* 45 F3
Murphy, *U.S.A.* 114 E5
Murphys, *U.S.A.* 116 G6
Murrat, *Sudan* 80 D2
Murrat Wells, *Sudan* 80 C3
Murray, *Ky., U.S.A.* 109 G1
Murray, *Utah, U.S.A.* 114 F8
Murray, L., *U.S.A.* 109 H5
Murray Harbour, *Canada* 103 C7
Murraysburg, *S. Africa* 88 E3
Murree, *Pakistan* 68 C5
Murrieta, *U.S.A.* 117 M9
Murro di Porco, Capo, *Italy* 31 F8
Murshid, *Sudan* 80 C3
Murshidabad, *India* 69 G13
Murska Sobota, *Slovenia* 29 B13
Murtle L., *Canada* 104 C5
Murtosa, *Portugal* 34 E2
Murungu, *Tanzania* 86 C3
Mururoa, *Pac. Oc.* 97 K14
Murwara, *India* 69 H9
Murwillumbah, *Australia* 95 D5
Mürz →, *Austria* 26 D8
Mürzzuschlag, *Austria* 26 D8
Muş, *Turkey* 70 B4
Mûsa, Gebel, *Egypt* 70 D2
Musa Khel, *Pakistan* 68 D3
Mūsa Qal'eh, *Afghan.* 66 C4
Musafirkhana, *India* 69 F9
Musala, *Bulgaria* 40 D7
Musala, *Indonesia* 62 D1
Musan, *N. Korea* 57 C15
Musangu, *Dem. Rep. of the Congo* 87 E1
Musasa, *Tanzania* 86 C3

Musay'īd, *Qatar* 71 E6
Muscat = Masqat, *Oman* 74 C6
Muscat & Oman = Oman ■, *Asia* 74 C6
Muscatine, *U.S.A.* 112 E9
Musgrave Harbour, *Canada* 103 C9
Musgrave Ranges, *Australia* 93 E5
Mushie, *Dem. Rep. of the Congo* 84 E3
Mushin, *Nigeria* 83 D5
Musi →, *Indonesia* 62 E2
Muskeg →, *Canada* 104 A4
Muskegon, *U.S.A.* 108 D2
Muskegon →, *U.S.A.* 108 D2
Muskegon Heights, *U.S.A.* 108 D2
Muskogee, *U.S.A.* 113 H7
Muskoka, L., *Canada* 110 B5
Muskwa →, *Canada* 104 B4
Muslīmiyah, *Syria* 70 B3
Musmar, *Sudan* 80 D4
Musofu, *Zambia* 87 E2
Musoma, *Tanzania* 86 C3
Musquaro, L., *Canada* 103 B7
Musquodoboit Harbour, *Canada* 103 D7
Musselburgh, *U.K.* 14 F5
Musselshell →, *U.S.A.* 114 C10
Mussidan, *France* 20 C4
Mussomeli, *Italy* 30 E6
Mussoorie, *India* 68 D8
Mussuco, *Angola* 88 B2
Mustafakemalpaşa, *Turkey* 41 F12
Mustang, *Nepal* 69 E10
Musters, L., *Argentina* 128 F3
Musudan, *N. Korea* 57 D15
Muszyna, *Poland* 45 J7
Mût, *Egypt* 80 B2
Mut, *Turkey* 70 B2
Mutanda, *Mozam.* 89 C5
Mutanda, *Zambia* 87 E2
Mutare, *Zimbabwe* 87 F3
Muting, *Indonesia* 63 F10
Mutoko, *Zimbabwe* 89 B5
Mutoray, *Russia* 51 C11
Mutshatsha, *Dem. Rep. of the Congo* 87 E1
Mutsu, *Japan* 54 D10
Mutsu-Wan, *Japan* 54 D10
Muttaburra, *Australia* 94 C3
Muttalip, *Turkey* 39 B12
Mutton I., *Ireland* 15 D2
Mutuáli, *Mozam.* 87 E4
Mutum Biyu, *Nigeria* 83 D7
Muweilih, *Egypt* 75 E3
Muxía, *Spain* 34 B1
Muy Muy, *Nic.* 120 D2
Muyinga, *Burundi* 86 C3
Muynak, *Uzbekistan* 50 E6
Muzaffarabad, *Pakistan* 69 B5
Muzaffargarh, *Pakistan* 68 D4
Muzaffarnagar, *India* 68 E7
Muzaffarpur, *India* 69 F11
Muzafirpur, *Pakistan* 68 D3
Muzhi, *Russia* 50 C7
Muzillac, *France* 18 E4
Muzūra, *Egypt* 80 J7
Mvôlô, *Sudan* 81 F2
Mvuma, *Zimbabwe* 87 F3
Mvurwi, *Zimbabwe* 87 F3
Mwadui, *Tanzania* 86 C3
Mwambo, *Tanzania* 87 E5
Mwandi, *Zambia* 87 F1
Mwanza, *Dem. Rep. of the Congo* 86 D2
Mwanza, *Tanzania* 86 C3
Mwanza, *Zambia* 87 F1
Mwanza □, *Tanzania* 86 C3
Mwaya, *Tanzania* 87 D3
Mweelrea, *Ireland* 15 C2
Mweka, *Dem. Rep. of the Congo* 84 E4
Mwenezi, *Zimbabwe* 87 G3
Mwenezi →, *Mozam.* 87 G3
Mwenga, *Dem. Rep. of the Congo* 86 C2
Mweru, L., *Zambia* 87 D2
Mweza Range, *Zimbabwe* 87 G3
Mwilambwe, *Dem. Rep. of the Congo* 86 D2
Mwimbi, *Tanzania* 87 D3
Mwinilunga, *Zambia* 87 E1
My Tho, *Vietnam* 65 G6
Myajlar, *India* 68 F4
Myanaung, *Burma* 67 K19
Myanmar = Burma ■, *Asia* 67 J20
Myaungmya, *Burma* 67 L19
Myeik Kyunzu, *Burma* 65 G1
Myers Chuck, *U.S.A.* 104 B2
Myerstown, *U.S.A.* 111 F8
Myingyan, *Burma* 67 J19
Myitkyina, *Burma* 67 G20
Myjava, *Slovak Rep.* 27 C10
Mykhaylivka, *Ukraine* 47 J8
Mykines, *Færoe Is.* 8 E9
Mykolayiv, *Ukraine* 47 J7
Mymensingh, *Bangla.* 67 G17
Mynydd Du, *U.K.* 13 F4
Mýrdalsjökull, *Iceland* 8 E4
Myrhorod, *Ukraine* 47 H7
Myrtle Beach, *U.S.A.* 109 J6
Myrtle Creek, *U.S.A.* 114 E2
Myrtle Point, *U.S.A.* 114 E1
Myrtou, *Cyprus* 36 D12
Mysia, *Turkey* 41 G11
Myślenice, *Poland* 45 J6
Myślibórz, *Poland* 45 F1
Mysłowice, *Poland* 45 H6
Mysore = Karnataka □, *India* 66 N10
Mysore, *India* 66 N10
Mystic, *U.S.A.* 111 E13
Myszków, *Poland* 45 H6
Myszyniec, *Poland* 44 E8
Mytishchi, *Russia* 46 E9
Mývatn, *Iceland* 8 D5
Mže →, *Czech Rep.* 26 B6
Mzimba, *Malawi* 87 E3
Mzimkulu →, *S. Africa* 89 E5
Mzimvubu →, *S. Africa* 89 E4
Mzuzu, *Malawi* 87 E3

N

Na Hearadh = Harris, *U.K.* 14 D2
Na Noi, *Thailand* 64 C3
Na Phao, *Laos* 64 D5
Na Sam, *Vietnam* 58 F6
Na San, *Vietnam* 64 B5
Naab →, *Germany* 25 F8
Na'am, *Sudan* 81 F2
Na'am →, *Sudan* 81 F2
Naantali, *Finland* 9 F19
Naas, *Ireland* 15 C5
Nababeep, *S. Africa* 88 D2
Nabadwip = Navadwip, *India* 69 H13
Nabari, *Japan* 55 G8
Nabawa, *Australia* 93 E1
Nabberu, L., *Australia* 93 E3
Nabburg, *Germany* 25 F8
Naberezhnyye Chelny, *Russia* 48 C11
Nabeul, *Tunisia* 79 A8
Nabha, *India* 68 D7
Nabīd, *Iran* 71 D8
Nabire, *Indonesia* 63 E9
Nabisar, *Pakistan* 68 G3
Nabisipi →, *Canada* 103 B7
Nabiswera, *Uganda* 86 B3
Nablus = Nābulus, *West Bank* 75 C4
Naboomspruit, *S. Africa* 89 C4
Nabou, *Burkina Faso* 82 C4
Nabua, *Phil.* 61 E5
Nābulus, *West Bank* 75 C4
Nacala, *Mozam.* 87 E5
Nacala-Velha, *Mozam.* 87 E5
Nacaome, *Honduras* 120 D2
Nacaroa, *Mozam.* 87 E4
Naches, *U.S.A.* 114 C3
Naches →, *U.S.A.* 116 D6
Nachicapau, L., *Canada* 103 A6
Nachingwea, *Tanzania* 87 E4
Nachna, *India* 68 F4
Náchod, *Czech Rep.* 26 A9
Nacimiento L., *U.S.A.* 116 K6
Naco, *Mexico* 118 A3
Nacogdoches, *U.S.A.* 113 K7
Nácori Chico, *Mexico* 118 B3
Nacozari, *Mexico* 118 A3
Nadi, *Sudan* 80 D3
Nadiad, *India* 68 H5
Nădlac, *Romania* 42 D5
Nador, *Morocco* 78 B5
Nadur, *Malta* 36 C1
Nadūshan, *Iran* 71 C7
Nadvirna, *Ukraine* 47 H3
Nadvornaya = Nadvirna, *Ukraine* 47 H3
Nadym, *Russia* 50 C8
Nadym →, *Russia* 50 C8
Nærbø, *Norway* 9 G11
Næstved, *Denmark* 11 J5
Nafada, *Nigeria* 83 C7
Naft-e Safīd, *Iran* 71 D6
Naftshahr, *Iran* 70 C5
Nafud Desert = An Nafūd, *Si. Arabia* 70 D4
Nag Hammâdi, *Egypt* 80 B3
Naga, *Phil.* 61 E5
Nagahama, *Japan* 55 G8
Nagai, *Japan* 54 E10
Nagaland □, *India* 67 G19
Nagano, *Japan* 55 F9
Nagano □, *Japan* 55 F9
Nagaoka, *Japan* 55 F9
Nagappattinam, *India* 66 P11
Nagar →, *Bangla.* 69 G13
Nagar Parkar, *Pakistan* 68 G4
Nagasaki, *Japan* 55 H4
Nagasaki □, *Japan* 55 H4
Nagato, *Japan* 55 G5
Nagaur, *India* 68 F5
Nagda, *India* 68 H6
Nagercoil, *India* 66 Q10
Nagina, *India* 69 E8
Nagīneh, *Iran* 71 C8
Nagir, *Pakistan* 69 A6
Naglarby, *Sweden* 10 D9
Nagod, *India* 69 G9
Nagold, *Germany* 25 G4
Nagold →, *Germany* 25 G4
Nagoorin, *Australia* 94 C5
Nagorno-Karabakh, *Azerbaijan* 70 B5
Nagornyy, *Russia* 51 D13
Nagoya, *Japan* 55 G8
Nagpur, *India* 66 J11
Nagua, *Dom. Rep.* 121 C6
Nagyatád, *Hungary* 42 D2
Nagyecsed, *Hungary* 42 C7
Nagykálló, *Hungary* 42 C6
Nagykanizsa, *Hungary* 42 D2
Nagykáta, *Hungary* 42 C4
Nagykőrös, *Hungary* 42 C4
Naha, *Japan* 55 L3
Nahan, *India* 68 D7
Nahanni Butte, *Canada* 104 A4
Nahanni Nat. Park, *Canada* 104 A4
Nahargarh, *Mad. P., India* 68 G6
Nahargarh, *Raj., India* 68 G7
Nahariyya, *Israel* 70 C2
Nahāvand, *Iran* 71 C6
Nahe →, *Germany* 25 F3
Nahîya, W. →, *Egypt* 80 B3
Naicá, *Mexico* 118 B3
Naicam, *Canada* 105 C8
Naikoon Prov. Park, *Canada* 104 C2
Naila, *Germany* 25 E7
Naimisharanya, *India* 69 F9
Nain, *Canada* 103 A7
Nā'īn, *Iran* 71 C7
Naini Tal, *India* 69 E8
Nainpur, *India* 66 H12
Naintré, *France* 18 F7
Nainwa, *India* 68 G6
Naipu, *Romania* 43 F10
Nairn, *U.K.* 14 D5
Nairobi, *Kenya* 86 C4
Naissaar, *Estonia* 9 G21
Naita, Mt., *Ethiopia* 81 F4
Naivasha, *Kenya* 86 C4
Naivasha, L., *Kenya* 86 C4
Najac, *France* 20 D5
Najafābād, *Iran* 71 C6
Najd, *Si. Arabia* 74 B3
Nájera, *Spain* 32 C2
Najerilla →, *Spain* 32 C2
Najibabad, *India* 68 E8
Najin, *N. Korea* 57 C16
Najmah, *Si. Arabia* 71 E6
Naju, *S. Korea* 57 G14
Nakadōri-Shima, *Japan* 55 H4
Nakalagba, *Dem. Rep. of the Congo* 86 B2
Nakaminato, *Japan* 55 F10
Nakamura, *Japan* 55 H6
Nakano, *Japan* 55 F9
Nakano-Shima, *Japan* 55 K4
Nakashibetsu, *Japan* 54 C12
Nakfa, *Eritrea* 81 D4
Nakhfar al Buşayyah, *Iraq* 70 D5
Nakhichevan = Naxçıvan, *Azerbaijan* 70 B5
Nakhichevan Republic = Naxçıvan □, *Azerbaijan* 50 F5
Nakhl, *Egypt* 75 F2
Nakhl-e Taqī, *Iran* 71 E7
Nakhodka, *Russia* 51 E14
Nakhon Nayok, *Thailand* 64 E3
Nakhon Pathom, *Thailand* 64 F3
Nakhon Phanom, *Thailand* 64 D5
Nakhon Ratchasima, *Thailand* 64 E4
Nakhon Sawan, *Thailand* 64 E3
Nakhon Si Thammarat, *Thailand* 65 H3
Nakhon Thai, *Thailand* 64 D3
Nakhtarana, *India* 68 H3
Nakina, *Canada* 102 B2
Nakło nad Notecią, *Poland* 45 E4
Nako, *Burkina Faso* 82 C4
Nakodar, *India* 68 D6
Nakskov, *Denmark* 11 K5
Naktong →, *S. Korea* 57 G15
Nakuru, *Kenya* 86 C4
Nakuru, L., *Kenya* 86 C4
Nakusp, *Canada* 104 C5
Nal, *Pakistan* 68 F2
Nal →, *Pakistan* 68 G1
Nalázi, *Mozam.* 89 C5
Nalchik, *Russia* 49 J6
Nałęczów, *Poland* 45 G9
Nalerigu, *Ghana* 83 C4
Nalgonda, *India* 66 L11
Nalhati, *India* 69 G12
Naliya, *India* 68 H3
Nallamalai Hills, *India* 66 M11
Nallıhan, *Turkey* 72 B4
Nalón →, *Spain* 34 B4
Nam Can, *Vietnam* 65 H5
Nam-ch'on, *N. Korea* 57 E14
Nam Co, *China* 60 C4
Nam Dinh, *Vietnam* 58 G6
Nam Du, Hon, *Vietnam* 65 H5
Nam Ngum Dam, *Laos* 64 C4
Nam-Phan, *Vietnam* 65 G6
Nam Phong, *Thailand* 64 D4
Nam Tha, *Laos* 58 G3
Nam Tok, *Thailand* 64 E2
Namacunde, *Angola* 88 B2
Namacurra, *Mozam.* 89 B6
Namak, Daryācheh-ye, *Iran* 71 C7
Namak, Kavir-e, *Iran* 71 C8
Namakzār, Daryācheh-ye, *Iran* 71 C9
Namaland, *Namibia* 88 C2
Namangan, *Uzbekistan* 50 E8
Namapa, *Mozam.* 87 E4
Namaqualand, *S. Africa* 88 E2
Namasagali, *Uganda* 86 B3
Namber, *Indonesia* 63 E8
Nambour, *Australia* 95 D5
Namche Bazar, *Nepal* 69 F12
Namchonjŏm = Nam-ch'on, *N. Korea* 57 E14
Namecunda, *Mozam.* 87 E4
Nameponda, *Mozam.* 87 F4
Náměšť nad Oslavou, *Czech Rep.* 27 B9
Námestovo, *Slovak Rep.* 27 B12
Nametil, *Mozam.* 87 F4
Namew L., *Canada* 105 C8
Namgia, *India* 69 D8
Namhkam, *Burma* 58 E1
Namib Desert, *Namibia* 88 C2
Namibe, *Angola* 85 H2
Namibe □, *Angola* 88 B1
Namibia ■, *Africa* 88 C2
Namibwoestyn = Namib Desert, *Namibia* 88 C2
Namīn, *Iran* 73 C13
Namlea, *Indonesia* 63 E7
Namoi →, *Australia* 95 E4
Nampa, *U.S.A.* 114 E5
Nampala, *Mali* 82 B3
Namp'o, *N. Korea* 57 E13
Nampō-Shotō, *Japan* 55 J10
Nampula, *Mozam.* 87 F4
Namrole, *Indonesia* 63 E7
Namse Shankou, *China* 67 E13
Namsen →, *Norway* 8 D14
Namsos, *Norway* 8 D14
Namtsy, *Russia* 51 C13
Namtu, *Burma* 67 H20
Namtumbo, *Tanzania* 87 E4
Namu, *Canada* 104 C3
Namur, *Belgium* 17 D4
Namur □, *Belgium* 17 D4
Namutoni, *Namibia* 88 B2
Namwala, *Zambia* 87 F2
Namwŏn, *S. Korea* 57 G14
Namysłów, *Poland* 45 G4
Nan, *Thailand* 64 C3
Nan →, *Thailand* 64 E3
Nan-ch'ang = Nanchang, *China* 59 C10
Nan Ling, *China* 59 E8
Nan Xian, *China* 59 C9
Nana, *Romania* 43 F11
Nana Kru, *Liberia* 82 E3
Nanaimo, *Canada* 104 D4
Nanam, *N. Korea* 57 D15
Nanan, *China* 59 E12
Nanango, *Australia* 95 D5
Nan'ao, *China* 59 F11
Nanao, *Japan* 55 F8
Nanbu, *China* 58 B6
Nanchang, *Jiangxi, China* 59 C10
Nanchang, *Kiangsi, China* 59 C10
Nancheng, *China* 59 D11
Nanching = Nanjing, *China* 59 A12
Nanchong, *China* 58 B6
Nanchuan, *China* 58 C6
Nancy, *France* 19 D13
Nanda Devi, *India* 69 D8
Nanda Kot, *India* 69 D9
Nandan, *China* 58 E6
Nandan, *Japan* 55 G7
Nanded, *India* 66 K10
Nandewar Ra., *Australia* 95 E5
Nandi, *Fiji* 91 C7
Nandigram, *India* 69 H12
Nandurbar, *India* 66 J9
Nandyal, *India* 66 M11
Nanfeng, *Guangdong, China* 59 F8
Nanfeng, *Jiangxi, China* 59 D11
Nanga-Eboko, *Cameroon* 83 E7
Nanga Parbat, *Pakistan* 69 B6
Nangade, *Mozam.* 87 E4
Nangapinoh, *Indonesia* 62 E4
Nangarhār □, *Afghan.* 66 B7
Nangatayap, *Indonesia* 62 E4
Nangeya Mts., *Uganda* 86 B3
Nangis, *France* 19 D10
Nangong, *China* 56 F8
Nanhua, *China* 58 E3
Nanhuang, *China* 57 F11
Nanhui, *China* 59 B13
Nanjeko, *Zambia* 87 F1
Nanji Shan, *China* 59 D13
Nanjian, *China* 58 E3
Nanjiang, *China* 58 A6
Nanjing, *Fujian, China* 59 E11
Nanjing, *Jiangsu, China* 59 A12
Nanjirinji, *Tanzania* 87 D4
Nankana Sahib, *Pakistan* 68 D5
Nankang, *China* 59 E10
Nanking = Nanjing, *China* 59 A12
Nankoku, *Japan* 55 H6
Nanling, *China* 59 B12
Nanning, *China* 58 F7
Nannup, *Australia* 93 F2
Nanpan Jiang →, *China* 58 E6
Nanpara, *India* 69 F9
Nanpi, *China* 56 E9
Nanping, *Fujian, China* 59 D12
Nanping, *Henan, China* 59 C9
Nanri Dao, *China* 59 E12
Nanripe, *Mozam.* 87 E4
Nansei-Shotō = Ryūkyū-rettō, *Japan* 55 M3
Nansen Sd., *Canada* 4 A3
Nanshan I., *S. China Sea* 62 B5
Nansio, *Tanzania* 86 C3
Nant, *France* 20 D7
Nanterre, *France* 19 D9
Nantes, *France* 18 E5
Nantiat, *France* 20 B5
Nanticoke, *U.S.A.* 111 E8
Nanton, *Canada* 104 C6
Nantong, *China* 59 A13
Nantou, *Taiwan* 59 F13
Nantua, *France* 19 F12
Nantucket I., *U.S.A.* 108 E10
Nantwich, *U.K.* 12 D5
Nanty Glo, *U.S.A.* 110 F6
Nanuque, *Brazil* 125 G10
Nanusa, Kepulauan, *Indonesia* 63 D7
Nanutarra Roadhouse, *Australia* 92 D2
Nanxi, *China* 58 C5
Nanxiong, *China* 59 E10
Nanyang, *China* 56 H7
Nanyi Hu, *China* 59 B12
Nanyuki, *Kenya* 86 B4
Nanzhang, *China* 59 B8
Nao, C. de la, *Spain* 33 G5
Naococane, L., *Canada* 103 B5
Náousa, *Imathía, Greece* 40 F6
Náousa, *Kikládhes, Greece* 39 D7
Naozhou Dao, *China* 59 G8
Napa, *U.S.A.* 116 G4
Napa →, *U.S.A.* 116 G4
Napanee, *Canada* 102 D4
Napanoch, *U.S.A.* 111 E10
Nape, *Laos* 64 C5
Nape Pass = Keo Neua, Deo, *Vietnam* 64 C5
Napier, *N.Z.* 91 H6
Napier Broome B., *Australia* 92 B4
Napier Pen., *Australia* 94 A2
Napierville, *Canada* 111 A11
Naples = Nápoli, *Italy* 31 B7
Naples, *U.S.A.* 109 M5
Napo, *China* 58 F5
Napo →, *Peru* 122 D3
Napoleon, *N. Dak., U.S.A.* 112 B5
Napoleon, *Ohio, U.S.A.* 108 E3
Nápoli, *Italy* 31 B7
Nápoli, G. di, *Italy* 31 B7
Napopo, *Dem. Rep. of the Congo* 86 B2
Naqâda, *Egypt* 80 B3
Naqadeh, *Iran* 73 D11
Naqb, Ra's an, *Jordan* 75 F4
Naqqāsh, *Iran* 71 C6
Nara, *Japan* 55 G7
Nara, *Mali* 82 B3
Nara □, *Japan* 55 G8
Nara Canal, *Pakistan* 68 G3
Nara Visa, *U.S.A.* 113 H3
Naraini, *India* 69 G9
Narasapur, *India* 67 L12
Narathiwat, *Thailand* 65 J3
Narayanganj, *Bangla.* 67 H17
Narayanpet, *India* 66 L10
Narbonne, *France* 20 E7
Narcea →, *Spain* 34 B4
Nardīn, *Iran* 71 B7
Nardò, *Italy* 31 B11
Narembeen, *Australia* 93 F2
Narendranagar, *India* 68 D8
Nares Str., *Arctic* 98 A13
Naretha, *Australia* 93 F3
Narew →, *Poland* 45 F7
Nari →, *Pakistan* 68 F2
Narin, *Afghan.* 66 A6
Narindra, Helodranon' i, *Madag.* 89 A8
Narita, *Japan* 55 G10
Närke, *Sweden* 10 E8
Narmada →, *India* 68 J5
Narman, *Turkey* 73 B9
Narmland, *Sweden* 9 F15
Narnaul, *India* 68 E7
Narni, *Italy* 29 F9
Naro, *Ghana* 82 C4
Naro Fominsk, *Russia* 46 E9
Narodnaya, *Russia* 6 B17
Narok, *Kenya* 86 C4
Narón, *Spain* 34 B2
Narowal, *Pakistan* 68 C6
Narrabri, *Australia* 95 E4
Narran →, *Australia* 95 D4
Narrogin, *Australia* 93 F2
Narrow Hills Prov. Park, *Canada* 105 C8
Narsimhapur, *India* 69 H8
Narsinghgarh, *India* 68 H7
Nartes, L. e, *Albania* 40 F3
Nartkala, *Russia* 49 J6
Naruto, *Japan* 55 G7
Narva, *Estonia* 46 C5
Narva →, *Russia* 9 G22
Narva Bay, *Estonia* 9 G19
Narvik, *Norway* 8 B17
Narvskoye Vdkhr., *Russia* 46 C5
Narwana, *India* 68 E7
Naryan-Mar, *Russia* 50 C6
Narym, *Russia* 50 D9
Naryn, *Kyrgyzstan* 50 E8
Nasa, *Norway* 8 C16
Nasarawa, *Nigeria* 83 D6
Năsăud, *Romania* 43 C9
Naseby, *N.Z.* 91 L3
Naselle, *U.S.A.* 116 D3
Naser, Buheirat en, *Egypt* 80 C3
Nashua, *Mont., U.S.A.* 114 B10
Nashua, *N.H., U.S.A.* 111 D13
Nashville, *Ark., U.S.A.* 113 J8
Nashville, *Ga., U.S.A.* 109 K4
Nashville, *Tenn., U.S.A.* 109 G2
Našice, *Croatia* 42 E3
Nasielsk, *Poland* 45 F7
Nasik, *India* 66 K8
Nasipit, *Phil.* 61 G6
Nasir, *Sudan* 81 F3
Nasirabad, *India* 68 F6
Nasirabad, *Pakistan* 68 E3
Naskaupi →, *Canada* 103 B7
Naso, *Italy* 31 D7
Naşrābād, *Iran* 71 C6
Naşriān-e Pā'īn, *Iran* 70 C5
Nass →, *Canada* 104 C3
Nassarawa □, *Nigeria* 83 D6
Nassau, *Bahamas* 120 A4
Nassau, *U.S.A.* 111 D11
Nassau, B., *Chile* 128 H3
Nasser, L. = Naser, Buheirat en, *Egypt* 80 C3
Nasser City = Kôm Ombo, *Egypt* 80 C3
Nassian, *Ivory C.* 82 D4
Nässjö, *Sweden* 11 G8

Nastapoka →, *Canada* 102 A4
Nastapoka, Is., *Canada* 102 A4
Nasugbu, *Phil.* 61 D4
Näsum, *Sweden* 11 H8
Näsviken, *Sweden* 10 C10
Nata, *Botswana* 88 C4
Nata →, *Botswana* 88 C4
Natal, *Brazil* 125 E11
Natal, *Indonesia* 62 D1
Natal, *S. Africa* 85 K6
Natalinci, *Serbia, Yug.* 42 F5
Naţanz, *Iran* 71 C6
Natashquan, *Canada* 103 B7
Natashquan →, *Canada* 103 B7
Natchez, *U.S.A.* 113 K9
Natchitoches, *U.S.A.* 113 K8
Nathdwara, *India* 68 G5
Nati, Pta., *Spain* 37 A10
Nation →, *Canada* 104 B4
National City, *U.S.A.* 117 N9
Natitingou, *Benin* 83 C5
Natividad, I., *Mexico* 118 B1
Natkyizin, *Burma* 64 E1
Natron, L., *Tanzania* 86 C4
Natrona Heights, *U.S.A.* 110 F5
Natrûn, W. el →, *Egypt* 80 H7
Nättraby, *Sweden* 11 H9
Natukanaoka Pan, *Namibia* 88 B2
Natuna Besar, Kepulauan, *Indonesia* 65 L7
Natuna Is. = Natuna Besar, Kepulauan, *Indonesia* 65 L7
Natuna Selatan, Kepulauan, *Indonesia* 65 L7
Natural Bridge, *U.S.A.* 111 B9
Naturaliste, C., *Australia* 94 G4
Nau Qala, *Afghan.* 68 B3
Naucelle, *France* 20 D6
Nauders, *Austria* 26 E3
Nauen, *Germany* 24 C8
Naugatuck, *U.S.A.* 111 E11
Naujaat = Repulse Bay, *Canada* 101 B11
Naujoji Akmenė, *Lithuania* 44 B9
Naumburg, *Germany* 24 D7
Nā'ūr at Tunayb, *Jordan* 75 D4
Nauru ■, *Pac. Oc.* 96 H8
Naushahra = Nowshera, *Pakistan* 66 C8
Naushahro, *Pakistan* 68 F3
Naushon I., *U.S.A.* 111 E14
Nauta, *Peru* 124 D4
Nautanwa, *India* 67 F13
Nautla, *Mexico* 119 C5
Nava, *Mexico* 118 B4
Nava, *Spain* 34 B5
Nava del Rey, *Spain* 34 D5
Navadwip, *India* 69 H13
Navahermosa, *Spain* 35 F6
Navahrudak, *Belarus* 46 F3
Navajo Reservoir, *U.S.A.* 115 H10
Navalcarnero, *Spain* 34 E6
Navalmoral de la Mata, *Spain* 34 F5
Navalvillar de Pela, *Spain* 35 F5
Navan = An Uaimh, *Ireland* 15 C5
Navapolatsk, *Belarus* 46 E5
Navarino, I., *Chile* 128 H3
Navarra □, *Spain* 32 C3
Navarre, *U.S.A.* 110 F3
Navarro →, *U.S.A.* 116 F3
Navas de San Juan, *Spain* 35 G7
Navasota, *U.S.A.* 113 K6
Navassa I., *W. Indies* 121 C5
Nävekvarn, *Sweden* 11 F10
Naver →, *U.K.* 14 C4
Navia, *Spain* 34 B4
Navia →, *Spain* 34 B4
Navia de Suarna, *Spain* 34 C3
Navibandar, *India* 68 J3
Navidad, *Chile* 126 C1
Naviraí, *Brazil* 127 A5
Navlakhi, *India* 68 H4
Navlya, *Russia* 47 F8
Năvodari, *Romania* 43 F13
Navoi = Nawoiy, *Uzbekistan* 50 E7
Navojoa, *Mexico* 118 B3
Navolato, *Mexico* 118 C3
Návpaktos, *Greece* 38 C3
Návplion, *Greece* 38 D4
Navrongo, *Ghana* 83 C4
Navsari, *India* 66 J8
Nawa Kot, *Pakistan* 68 E4
Nawab Khan, *Pakistan* 68 D3
Nawabganj, *Ut. P., India* 69 F9
Nawabganj, *Ut. P., India* 69 E8
Nawabshah, *Pakistan* 68 F3
Nawada, *India* 69 G11
Nawakot, *Nepal* 69 F11
Nawalgarh, *India* 68 F6
Nawanshahr, *India* 69 C6
Nawar, Dasht-i-, *Afghan.* 68 C3
Nawi, *Sudan* 80 D3
Nawoiy, *Uzbekistan* 50 E7
Naxçıvan, *Azerbaijan* 70 B5
Naxçıvan □, *Azerbaijan* 50 F5
Náxos, *Greece* 39 D7
Nay, *France* 20 E3
Nay, Mui, *Vietnam* 62 B3
Nāy Band, *Būshehr, Iran* 71 E7
Nāy Band, *Khorāsān, Iran* 71 C8
Nayakhan, *Russia* 51 C16
Nayarit □, *Mexico* 118 C4
Nayé, *Senegal* 82 C2
Nayong, *China* 58 D5
Nayoro, *Japan* 54 B11
Nayyāl, W. →, *Si. Arabia* 70 D3
Nazaré, *Brazil* 125 F11
Nazaré, *Portugal* 35 F1
Nazareth = Nazerat, *Israel* 75 C4
Nazareth, *U.S.A.* 111 F9
Nazas, *Mexico* 118 B4
Nazas →, *Mexico* 118 B4
Nazca, *Peru* 124 F4
Naze, The, *U.K.* 13 F9
Nazerat, *Israel* 75 C4
Nāzīk, *Iran* 70 B5
Nazilli, *Turkey* 39 D10
Nazko, *Canada* 104 C4
Nazko →, *Canada* 104 C4
Nazret, *Ethiopia* 81 F4
Nazwá, *Oman* 74 C6
Nchanga, *Zambia* 87 E2
Ncheu, *Malawi* 87 E3
Ndala, *Tanzania* 86 C3
Ndalatando, *Angola* 84 F2
Ndali, *Benin* 83 D5
Ndareda, *Tanzania* 86 C4
Ndélé, *C.A.R.* 84 C4
Ndikinimeki, *Cameroon* 83 E7
N'Dioum, *Senegal* 82 B2
Ndjamena, *Chad* 79 F8
Ndola, *Zambia* 87 E2
Ndoto Mts., *Kenya* 86 B4
Nduguti, *Tanzania* 86 C3
Néa Alikarnassós, *Greece* 39 F7
Néa Ankhíalos, *Greece* 38 B4
Néa Epídhavros, *Greece* 38 D5
Néa Flippiás, *Greece* 38 B2
Néa Ionia, *Greece* 38 B4
Néa Kallikrátia, *Greece* 40 F7
Néa Mákri, *Greece* 38 C5
Néa Moudhaniá, *Greece* 40 F7
Néa Péramos, *Attikí, Greece* 38 C5
Néa Péramos, *Kaválla, Greece* 41 F8
Néa Víssi, *Greece* 41 E10
Néa Zíkhna, *Greece* 40 E7
Neagh, Lough, *U.K.* 15 B5
Neah Bay, *U.S.A.* 116 B2
Neale, L., *Australia* 92 D5
Neamţ □, *Romania* 43 C11
Neápolis, *Kozáni, Greece* 40 F5
Neápolis, *Kríti, Greece* 36 D7
Neápolis, *Lakonía, Greece* 38 E5
Near Is., *U.S.A.* 100 C1
Neath, *U.K.* 13 F4
Neath Port Talbot □, *U.K.* 13 F4
Nebbou, *Burkina Faso* 83 C4
Nebelat el Hagana, *Sudan* 81 E2
Nebine Cr. →, *Australia* 95 D4
Nebitdag, *Turkmenistan* 50 F6
Nebo, *Australia* 94 C4
Nebolchy, *Russia* 46 C7
Nebraska □, *U.S.A.* 112 E5
Nebraska City, *U.S.A.* 112 E7
Nébrodi, Monti, *Italy* 31 E7
Necedah, *U.S.A.* 112 C9
Nechako →, *Canada* 104 C4
Neches →, *U.S.A.* 113 L8
Neckar →, *Germany* 25 F4
Necochea, *Argentina* 126 D4
Neda, *Spain* 34 B2
Nedelino, *Bulgaria* 41 E9
Nedelišće, *Croatia* 29 B13
Nédha →, *Greece* 38 D3
Needles, *Canada* 104 D5
Needles, *U.S.A.* 117 L12
Needles, The, *U.K.* 13 G6
Ñeembucú □, *Paraguay* 126 B4
Neemuch = Nimach, *India* 68 G6
Neenah, *U.S.A.* 108 C1
Neepawa, *Canada* 105 C9
Neftçala, *Azerbaijan* 71 B6
Neftegorsk, *Russia* 49 H4
Neftekumsk, *Russia* 49 H7
Nefyn, *U.K.* 12 E3
Négala, *Mali* 82 C3
Negapatam = Nagappattinam, *India* 66 P11
Negaunee, *U.S.A.* 108 B2
Negele, *Ethiopia* 81 F4
Negev Desert = Hanegev, *Israel* 75 E4
Negoiul, Vf., *Romania* 43 E9
Negombo, *Sri Lanka* 66 R11
Negotin, *Serbia, Yug.* 40 B6
Negotino, *Macedonia* 40 E6
Negra, Peña, *Spain* 34 C4
Negra, Pta., *Peru* 122 D2
Negrais, C. = Maudin Sun, *Burma* 67 M19
Negreşti, *Romania* 43 D12
Negreşti-Oaş, *Romania* 43 C8
Negril, *Jamaica* 120 C4
Negro →, *Argentina* 122 H4
Negro →, *Brazil* 122 D4
Negro →, *Uruguay* 127 C4
Negros, *Phil.* 61 G5
Negru Vodă, *Romania* 43 G13
Neguac, *Canada* 103 C6
Nehalem →, *U.S.A.* 116 E3
Nehāvand, *Iran* 71 C6
Nehbandān, *Iran* 71 D9
Nehoiu, *Romania* 43 E11
Nei Monggol Zizhiqu □, *China* 56 D7
Neijiang, *China* 58 C5
Neillsville, *U.S.A.* 112 C9
Neilton, *U.S.A.* 114 C2
Neiqiu, *China* 56 F8
Neiva, *Colombia* 124 C3
Neixiang, *China* 56 H6
Nejanilini L., *Canada* 105 B9
Nejd = Najd, *Si. Arabia* 74 B3
Nejo, *Ethiopia* 81 F4
Nekā, *Iran* 71 B7
Nekemte, *Ethiopia* 81 F4
Nêkheb, *Egypt* 80 B3
Neksø, *Denmark* 11 J9
Nelas, *Portugal* 34 E3
Nelia, *Australia* 94 C3
Nelidovo, *Russia* 46 D7
Neligh, *U.S.A.* 112 D5
Nelkan, *Russia* 51 D14
Nellore, *India* 66 M11
Nelson, *Canada* 104 D5
Nelson, *N.Z.* 91 J4
Nelson, *U.K.* 12 D5
Nelson, *Ariz., U.S.A.* 115 J7
Nelson, *Nev., U.S.A.* 117 K12
Nelson →, *Canada* 105 C9
Nelson, Estrecho, *Chile* 128 G2
Nelson Forks, *Canada* 104 B4
Nelson House, *Canada* 105 B9
Nelson L., *Canada* 105 B8
Nelspoort, *S. Africa* 88 E3
Nelspruit, *S. Africa* 89 D5
Néma, *Mauritania* 82 B3
Neman, *Russia* 9 J20
Neman →, *Lithuania* 9 J19
Neméa, *Greece* 38 D4
Nemeiben L., *Canada* 105 B7
Nemërçkë, Mal, *Albania* 40 F4
Nemira, Vf., *Romania* 43 D11
Némiscau, *Canada* 102 B4
Némiscau, L., *Canada* 102 B4
Nemours, *France* 19 D9
Nemšová, *Slovak Rep.* 27 C11
Nemunas = Neman →, *Lithuania* 9 J19
Nemuro, *Japan* 54 C12
Nemuro-Kaikyō, *Japan* 54 C12
Nen Jiang →, *China* 57 B13
Nenagh, *Ireland* 15 D3
Nenasi, *Malaysia* 65 L4
Nene →, *U.K.* 13 E8
Nénita, *Greece* 39 C8
Nenjiang, *China* 60 B7
Neno, *Malawi* 87 F3
Neodesha, *U.S.A.* 113 G7
Neokhórion, *Aitolía kai Akarnanía, Greece* 38 C3
Neokhórion, *Árta, Greece* 38 B2
Néon Karlovásion, *Greece* 39 D8
Néon Petrítsi, *Greece* 40 E7
Neosho, *U.S.A.* 113 G7
Neosho →, *U.S.A.* 113 H7
Nepal ■, *Asia* 69 F11
Nepalganj, *Nepal* 69 E9
Nepalganj Road, *India* 69 E9
Nephi, *U.S.A.* 114 G8
Nephin, *Ireland* 15 B2
Nepi, *Italy* 29 F9
Nepomuk, *Czech Rep.* 26 B6
Neptune, *U.S.A.* 111 F10
Nera →, *Italy* 29 F9
Nera →, *Romania* 42 F6
Nérac, *France* 20 D4
Nerang, *Australia* 95 D5
Neratovice, *Czech Rep.* 26 A7
Nerchinsk, *Russia* 51 D12
Nereju, *Romania* 43 E11
Nerekhta, *Russia* 46 D11
Néret, L., *Canada* 103 B5
Neretvanski Kanal, *Croatia* 29 E14
Neringa, *Lithuania* 9 J19
Nerja, *Spain* 35 J7
Nerl →, *Russia* 46 D11
Nerpio, *Spain* 33 G2
Nerva, *Spain* 35 H4
Nervi, *Italy* 28 D6
Neryungri, *Russia* 51 D13
Nescopeck, *U.S.A.* 111 E8
Nesebŭr, *Bulgaria* 41 D11
Ness, L., *U.K.* 14 D4
Ness City, *U.S.A.* 112 F5
Nesterov, *Poland* 47 G2
Nestórion, *Greece* 40 F5
Néstos →, *Greece* 41 E8
Nesvady, *Slovak Rep.* 27 D11
Nesvizh = Nyasvizh, *Belarus* 47 F4
Netanya, *Israel* 75 C3
Netarhat, *India* 69 H11
Nete →, *Belgium* 17 C4
Netherdale, *Australia* 94 C4
Netherlands ■, *Europe* 17 C5
Netherlands Antilles ■, *W. Indies* 124 A5
Neto →, *Italy* 31 C10
Netrang, *India* 68 J5
Nettancourt, *France* 19 D11
Nettetal, *Germany* 24 D2
Nettilling L., *Canada* 101 B12
Nettuno, *Italy* 30 A5
Netzahualcoyotl, Presa, *Mexico* 119 D6
Neu-Isenburg, *Germany* 25 E4
Neu-Ulm, *Germany* 25 G6
Neubrandenburg, *Germany* 24 B9
Neubukow, *Germany* 24 A7
Neuburg, *Germany* 25 G7
Neuchâtel, *Switz.* 25 J2
Neuchâtel □, *Switz.* 25 J2
Neuchâtel, Lac de, *Switz.* 25 J2
Neudau, *Austria* 26 D9
Neuenhagen, *Germany* 24 C9
Neuenhaus, *Germany* 24 C2
Neuf-Brisach, *France* 19 D14
Neufahrn, *Bayern, Germany* 25 G8
Neufahrn, *Bayern, Germany* 25 G7
Neufchâteau, *Belgium* 17 E5
Neufchâteau, *France* 19 D12
Neufchâtel-en-Bray, *France* 18 C8
Neufchâtel-sur-Aisne, *France* 19 C11
Neuhaus, *Germany* 24 B6
Neuillé-Pont-Pierre, *France* 18 E7
Neuilly-St-Front, *France* 19 C10
Neukalen, *Germany* 24 B8
Neumarkt, *Germany* 25 F7
Neumünster, *Germany* 24 A5
Neung-sur-Beuvron, *France* 19 E8
Neunkirchen, *Austria* 26 D9
Neunkirchen, *Germany* 25 F3
Neuquén, *Argentina* 128 D3
Neuquén □, *Argentina* 126 D2
Neuruppin, *Germany* 24 C8
Neusäss, *Germany* 25 G6
Neuse →, *U.S.A.* 109 H7
Neusiedl, *Austria* 27 D9
Neusiedler See, *Austria* 27 D9
Neuss, *Germany* 24 D2
Neussargues-Moissac, *France* 20 C7
Neustadt, *Bayern, Germany* 25 F8
Neustadt, *Bayern, Germany* 25 G7
Neustadt, *Bayern, Germany* 25 F6
Neustadt, *Bayern, Germany* 25 E7
Neustadt, *Brandenburg, Germany* 24 C8
Neustadt, *Hessen, Germany* 24 E5
Neustadt, *Niedersachsen, Germany* 24 C5
Neustadt, *Rhld-Pfz., Germany* 25 F4
Neustadt, *Sachsen, Germany* 24 D10
Neustadt, *Schleswig-Holstein, Germany* 24 A6
Neustadt, *Thüringen, Germany* 24 E7
Neustrelitz, *Germany* 24 B9
Neuvic, *France* 20 C6
Neuville-sur-Saône, *France* 21 C8
Neuvy-le-Roi, *France* 18 E7
Neuvy-St-Sépulchre, *France* 19 F8
Neuvy-sur-Barangeon, *France* 19 E9
Neuwerk, *Germany* 24 B4
Neuwied, *Germany* 24 E3
Neva →, *Russia* 46 C6
Nevada, *Iowa, U.S.A.* 112 D8
Nevada, *Mo., U.S.A.* 113 G7
Nevada □, *U.S.A.* 114 G5
Nevada City, *U.S.A.* 116 F6
Nevado, Cerro, *Argentina* 126 D2
Nevel, *Russia* 46 D5
Nevers, *France* 19 F10
Nevesinje, *Bos.-H.* 40 C2
Neville, *Canada* 105 D7
Nevinnomyssk, *Russia* 49 H6
Nevis, *St. Kitts & Nevis* 121 C7
Nevrokop = Gotse Delchev, *Bulgaria* 40 E7
Nevşehir, *Turkey* 70 B2
New →, *U.S.A.* 108 F5
New Aiyansh, *Canada* 104 B3
New Albany, *Ind., U.S.A.* 108 F3
New Albany, *Miss., U.S.A.* 113 H10
New Albany, *Pa., U.S.A.* 111 E8
New Amsterdam, *Guyana* 124 B7
New Angledool, *Australia* 95 D4
New Baltimore, *U.S.A.* 110 D2
New Bedford, *U.S.A.* 111 E14
New Berlin, *N.Y., U.S.A.* 111 D9
New Berlin, *Pa., U.S.A.* 110 F8
New Bern, *U.S.A.* 109 H7
New Bethlehem, *U.S.A.* 110 F5
New Bloomfield, *U.S.A.* 110 F7
New Boston, *U.S.A.* 113 J7
New Braunfels, *U.S.A.* 113 L5
New Brighton, *N.Z.* 91 K4
New Brighton, *U.S.A.* 110 F4
New Britain, *Papua N. G.* 96 H7
New Britain, *U.S.A.* 111 E12
New Brunswick, *U.S.A.* 111 F10
New Brunswick □, *Canada* 103 C6
New Bussa, *Nigeria* 83 D5
New Caledonia ■, *Pac. Oc.* 96 K8
New Castile = Castilla-La Mancha □, *Spain* 6 H5
New Castle, *Ind., U.S.A.* 108 F3
New Castle, *Pa., U.S.A.* 110 F4
New City, *U.S.A.* 111 E11
New Concord, *U.S.A.* 110 G3
New Cumberland, *U.S.A.* 110 F4
New Cuyama, *U.S.A.* 117 L7
New Delhi, *India* 68 E7
New Denver, *Canada* 104 D5
New Don Pedro Reservoir, *U.S.A.* 116 H6
New England, *U.S.A.* 112 B3
New England Ra., *Australia* 95 E5
New Forest, *U.K.* 13 G6
New Galloway, *U.K.* 14 F4
New Glasgow, *Canada* 103 C7
New Guinea, *Oceania* 52 K17
New Hamburg, *Canada* 110 C4
New Hampshire □, *U.S.A.* 111 C13
New Hampton, *U.S.A.* 112 D8
New Hanover, *S. Africa* 89 D5
New Hartford, *U.S.A.* 111 C9
New Haven, *Conn., U.S.A.* 111 E12
New Haven, *Mich., U.S.A.* 110 D2
New Hazelton, *Canada* 104 B3
New Hebrides = Vanuatu ■, *Pac. Oc.* 96 J8
New Holland, *U.S.A.* 111 F8
New Iberia, *U.S.A.* 113 K9
New Ireland, *Papua N. G.* 96 H7
New Jersey □, *U.S.A.* 108 E8
New Kensington, *U.S.A.* 110 F5
New Lexington, *U.S.A.* 108 F4
New Liskeard, *Canada* 102 C4
New London, *Conn., U.S.A.* 111 E12
New London, *Ohio, U.S.A.* 110 E2
New London, *Wis., U.S.A.* 112 C10
New Madrid, *U.S.A.* 113 G10
New Martinsville, *U.S.A.* 108 F5
New Meadows, *U.S.A.* 114 D5
New Melones L., *U.S.A.* 116 H6
New Mexico □, *U.S.A.* 115 J10
New Milford, *Conn., U.S.A.* 111 E11
New Milford, *Pa., U.S.A.* 111 E9
New Norcia, *Australia* 93 F2
New Norfolk, *Australia* 94 G4
New Orleans, *U.S.A.* 113 L9
New Philadelphia, *U.S.A.* 110 F3
New Plymouth, *N.Z.* 91 H5
New Plymouth, *U.S.A.* 114 E5
New Port Richey, *U.S.A.* 109 L4
New Providence, *Bahamas* 120 A4
New Quay, *U.K.* 13 E3
New Radnor, *U.K.* 13 E4
New Richmond, *Canada* 103 C6
New Richmond, *U.S.A.* 112 C8
New Roads, *U.S.A.* 113 K9
New Rochelle, *U.S.A.* 111 F11
New Rockford, *U.S.A.* 112 B5
New Romney, *U.K.* 13 G8
New Ross, *Ireland* 15 D5
New Salem, *U.S.A.* 112 B4
New Scone, *U.K.* 14 E5
New Siberian I. = Novaya Sibir, Ostrov, *Russia* 51 B16
New Siberian Is. = Novosibirskiye Ostrova, *Russia* 51 B15
New Smyrna Beach, *U.S.A.* 109 L5
New Town, *U.S.A.* 112 B3
New Tredegar, *U.K.* 13 F4
New Ulm, *U.S.A.* 112 C7
New Waterford, *Canada* 103 C7
New Westminster, *Canada* 116 A4
New York, *U.S.A.* 111 F11
New York □, *U.S.A.* 111 D9
New York Mts., *U.S.A.* 115 J6
New Zealand ■, *Oceania* 91 J6
Newaj →, *India* 68 G7
Newala, *Tanzania* 87 E4
Newark, *Del., U.S.A.* 108 F8
Newark, *N.J., U.S.A.* 111 F10
Newark, *N.Y., U.S.A.* 110 C7
Newark, *Ohio, U.S.A.* 110 F2
Newark-on-Trent, *U.K.* 12 D7
Newark Valley, *U.S.A.* 111 D8
Newberg, *U.S.A.* 114 D2
Newberry, *Mich., U.S.A.* 108 B3
Newberry, *S.C., U.S.A.* 109 H5
Newberry Springs, *U.S.A.* 117 L10
Newboro L., *Canada* 111 B8
Newbridge = Droichead Nua, *Ireland* 15 C5
Newburgh, *Canada* 110 B8
Newburgh, *U.S.A.* 111 E10
Newbury, *U.K.* 13 F6
Newbury, *N.H., U.S.A.* 111 B12
Newbury, *Vt., U.S.A.* 111 B12
Newburyport, *U.S.A.* 109 D10
Newcastle, *N.B., Canada* 103 C6
Newcastle, *Ont., Canada* 102 D4
Newcastle, *S. Africa* 89 D4
Newcastle, *U.K.* 15 B6
Newcastle, *Calif., U.S.A.* 116 G5
Newcastle, *Wyo., U.S.A.* 112 D2
Newcastle Emlyn, *U.K.* 13 E3
Newcastle Ra., *Australia* 92 C5
Newcastle-under-Lyme, *U.K.* 12 D5
Newcastle-upon-Tyne, *U.K.* 12 C6
Newcastle Waters, *Australia* 94 B1
Newcastle West, *Ireland* 15 D2
Newcomb, *U.S.A.* 111 C10
Newcomerstown, *U.S.A.* 110 F3
Newdegate, *Australia* 93 F2
Newell, *Australia* 94 B4
Newell, *U.S.A.* 112 C3
Newfane, *U.S.A.* 110 C6
Newfield, *U.S.A.* 111 D8
Newfound L., *U.S.A.* 111 C13
Newfoundland, *Canada* 98 E14
Newfoundland, *U.S.A.* 111 E9
Newfoundland □, *Canada* 103 B8
Newhall, *U.S.A.* 117 L8
Newhaven, *U.K.* 13 G8
Newkirk, *U.S.A.* 113 G6
Newlyn, *U.K.* 13 G2
Newman, *Australia* 92 D2
Newman, *U.S.A.* 116 H5
Newmarket, *Canada* 110 B5
Newmarket, *Ireland* 15 D2
Newmarket, *U.K.* 13 E8
Newmarket, *U.S.A.* 111 C14
Newnan, *U.S.A.* 109 J3
Newport, *Ireland* 15 C2
Newport, *I. of W., U.K.* 13 G6
Newport, *Newp., U.K.* 13 F5
Newport, *Ark., U.S.A.* 113 H9
Newport, *Ky., U.S.A.* 108 F3
Newport, *N.H., U.S.A.* 111 C12
Newport, *N.Y., U.S.A.* 111 C9
Newport, *Oreg., U.S.A.* 114 D1
Newport, *Pa., U.S.A.* 110 F7
Newport, *R.I., U.S.A.* 111 E13
Newport, *Tenn., U.S.A.* 109 H4
Newport, *Vt., U.S.A.* 111 B12
Newport, *Wash., U.S.A.* 114 B5
Newport □, *U.K.* 13 F4
Newport Beach, *U.S.A.* 117 M9
Newport News, *U.S.A.* 108 G7
Newport Pagnell, *U.K.* 13 E7
Newquay, *U.K.* 13 G2

Newry, *U.K.* 15 B5
Newton, *Ill., U.S.A.* 112 F10
Newton, *Iowa, U.S.A.* 112 E8
Newton, *Kans., U.S.A.* 113 F6
Newton, *Mass., U.S.A.* 111 D13
Newton, *Miss., U.S.A.* 113 J10
Newton, *N.C., U.S.A.* 109 H5
Newton, *N.J., U.S.A.* 111 E10
Newton, *Tex., U.S.A.* 113 K8
Newton Abbot, *U.K.* 13 G4
Newton Aycliffe, *U.K.* 12 C6
Newton Falls, *U.S.A.* 110 E4
Newton Stewart, *U.K.* 14 G4
Newtonmore, *U.K.* 14 D4
Newtown, *U.K.* 13 E4
Newtownabbey, *U.K.* 15 B6
Newtownards, *U.K.* 15 B6
Newtownbarry = Bunclody, *Ireland* 15 D5
Newtownstewart, *U.K.* 15 B4
Newville, *U.S.A.* 110 F7
Nexon, *France* 20 C5
Neya, *Russia* 48 A6
Neyrīz, *Iran* 71 D7
Neyshābūr, *Iran* 71 B8
Nezhin = Nizhyn, *Ukraine* 47 G6
Nezperce, *U.S.A.* 114 C5
Ngabang, *Indonesia* 62 D3
Ngabordamlu, Tanjung, *Indonesia* 63 F8
N'Gage, *Angola* 84 F3
Ngala, *Nigeria* 83 C7
Ngambé, *Cameroon* 83 D7
Ngambé, *Cameroon* 83 E7
Ngami Depression, *Botswana* . . 88 C3
Ngamo, *Zimbabwe* 87 F2
Ngangala, *Sudan* 81 G3
Nganglong Kangri, *China* 67 C12
Ngao, *Thailand* 64 C2
Ngaoundéré, *Cameroon* 84 C2
Ngapara, *N.Z.* 91 L3
Ngara, *Tanzania* 86 C3
Ngawi, *Indonesia* 63 G14
Nghia Lo, *Vietnam* 58 G5
Ngoboli, *Sudan* 81 G3
Ngoma, *Malawi* 87 E3
Ngomahura, *Zimbabwe* 87 G3
Ngomba, *Tanzania* 87 D3
Ngop, *Sudan* 81 F3
Ngoring Hu, *China* 60 C4
Ngorkou, *Mali* 82 B4
Ngorongoro, *Tanzania* 86 C4
Ngozi, *Burundi* 86 C2
Ngudu, *Tanzania* 86 C3
Nguigmi, *Niger* 79 F8
Nguila, *Cameroon* 83 E7
Nguiu, *Australia* 92 B5
Ngukurr, *Australia* 94 A1
Ngulu Atoll, *Pac. Oc.* 63 C9
Ngunga, *Tanzania* 86 C3
Nguru, *Nigeria* 83 C7
Nguru Mts., *Tanzania* 86 D4
Nguyen Binh, *Vietnam* 58 F5
Nha Trang, *Vietnam* 65 F7
Nhacoongo, *Mozam.* 89 C6
Nhamaabué, *Mozam.* 87 F4
Nhamundá →, *Brazil* 125 D7
Nhangulaze, L., *Mozam.* 89 C5
Nho Quan, *Vietnam* 58 G5
Nhulunbuy, *Australia* 94 A2
Nia-nia, *Dem. Rep. of the Congo* 86 B2
Niafounké, *Mali* 82 B4
Niagara Falls, *Canada* 102 D4
Niagara Falls, *U.S.A.* 110 C6
Niagara-on-the-Lake, *Canada* . 110 C5
Niah, *Malaysia* 62 D4
Niamey, *Niger* 83 C5
Niandan-Koro, *Guinea* 82 C3
Nianforando, *Guinea* 82 D2
Niangara, *Dem. Rep. of the Congo* 86 B2
Niangbo, *Ivory C.* 82 D3
Niangoloko, *Burkina Faso* 82 C4
Niantic, *U.S.A.* 111 E12
Niaro, *Sudan* 81 E3
Nias, *Indonesia* 62 D1
Niassa □, *Mozam.* 87 E4
Nibāk, *Si. Arabia* 71 E7
Nibe, *Denmark* 11 H3
Nicaragua ■, *Cent. Amer.* 120 D2
Nicaragua, L. de, *Nic.* 120 D2
Nicastro, *Italy* 31 D9
Nice, *France* 21 E11
Niceville, *U.S.A.* 109 K2
Nichicun, L., *Canada* 103 B5
Nichinan, *Japan* 55 J5
Nicholás, Canal, *W. Indies* 120 B3
Nicholasville, *U.S.A.* 108 G3
Nichols, *U.S.A.* 111 D8
Nicholson, *Australia* 92 C4
Nicholson, *U.S.A.* 111 E9
Nicholson →, *Australia* 94 B2
Nicholson L., *Canada* 105 A8
Nicholson Ra., *Australia* 93 E2
Nicholville, *U.S.A.* 111 B10
Nicobar Is., *Ind. Oc.* 52 J13
Nicola, *Canada* 104 C4
Nicolls Town, *Bahamas* 120 A4
Nicopolis, *Greece* 38 B2
Nicosia, *Cyprus* 36 D12
Nicosia, *Italy* 31 E7
Nicótera, *Italy* 31 D8
Nicoya, *Costa Rica* 120 D2
Nicoya, G. de, *Costa Rica* 120 E3
Nicoya, Pen. de, *Costa Rica* . . . 120 E2
Nidd →, *U.K.* 12 D6
Nidda, *Germany* 25 E5
Nidda →, *Germany* 25 E4
Nidwalden □, *Switz.* 25 J4
Nidzica, *Poland* 45 E7
Niebüll, *Germany* 24 A4
Nied →, *Germany* 19 C13
Niederaula, *Germany* 24 E5
Niederbayern □, *Germany* 25 G8
Niederbronn-les-Bains, *France* . 19 D14
Niedere Tauern, *Austria* 26 D7
Niederlausitz, *Germany* 24 D9
Niederösterreich □, *Austria* . . . 26 C8
Niedersachsen □, *Germany* . . . 24 C4
Niekerkshoop, *S. Africa* 88 D3
Niellé, *Ivory C.* 82 C3
Niemba, *Dem. Rep. of the Congo* 86 D2
Niemen = Neman →, *Lithuania* 9 J19
Niemodlin, *Poland* 45 H4
Nienburg, *Germany* 24 C5
Niepołomice, *Poland* 45 H7
Niers →, *Germany* 24 D1
Niesky, *Germany* 24 D10
Nieszawa, *Poland* 45 F5
Nieu Bethesda, *S. Africa* 88 E3
Nieuw Amsterdam, *Surinam* . . 125 B7
Nieuw Nickerie, *Surinam* 125 B7
Nieuwoudtville, *S. Africa* 88 E2
Nieuwpoort, *Belgium* 17 C2
Nieves, Pico de las, *Canary Is.* . 37 G4
Nièvre □, *France* 19 E10
Niga, *Mali* 82 C3
Niğde, *Turkey* 70 B2
Nigel, *S. Africa* 89 D4
Niger □, *Nigeria* 83 D6
Niger ■, *W. Afr.* 83 B7
Niger →, *W. Afr.* 83 D6
Niger Delta, *Africa* 83 E6
Nigeria ■, *W. Afr.* 83 D6
Nighasin, *India* 69 E9
Nightcaps, *N.Z.* 91 L2
Nigrita, *Greece* 40 F7
Nii-Jima, *Japan* 55 G9
Niigata, *Japan* 54 F9
Niigata □, *Japan* 55 F9
Niihama, *Japan* 55 H6
Niihau, *U.S.A.* 106 H14
Niimi, *Japan* 55 G6
Niitsu, *Japan* 54 F9
Nijar, *Spain* 33 J2
Nijil, *Jordan* 75 E4
Nijkerk, *Neths.* 17 B5
Nijmegen, *Neths.* 17 C5
Nijverdal, *Neths.* 17 B6
Nīk Pey, *Iran* 71 B6
Nike, *Nigeria* 83 D6
Nikiniki, *Indonesia* 63 F6
Nikísiani, *Greece* 41 F8
Nikítas, *Greece* 40 F7
Nikki, *Benin* 83 D5
Nikkō, *Japan* 55 F9
Nikolayev = Mykolayiv, *Ukraine* 47 J7
Nikolayevsk, *Russia* 48 E7
Nikolayevsk-na-Amur, *Russia* . 51 D15
Nikolsk, *Russia* 48 D8
Nikolskoye, *Russia* 51 D17
Nikopol, *Bulgaria* 41 C8
Nikopol, *Ukraine* 47 J8
Niksar, *Turkey* 72 B7
Nīkshahr, *Iran* 71 E9
Nikšić, *Montenegro, Yug.* 40 D2
Nîl, Nahr en →, *Africa* 80 H7
Nîl el Abyad →, *Sudan* 81 D3
Nîl el Azraq →, *Sudan* 81 D3
Nila, *Indonesia* 63 F7
Niland, *U.S.A.* 117 M11
Nile = Nîl, Nahr en →, *Africa* . 80 H7
Niles, *Mich., U.S.A.* 108 E2
Niles, *Ohio, U.S.A.* 110 E4
Nilüfer →, *Turkey* 41 F12
Nim Ka Thana, *India* 68 F6
Nimach, *India* 68 G6
Nimbahera, *India* 68 G6
Nîmes, *France* 21 E8
Nimfaíon, Ákra = Pínnes, Ákra, *Greece* 41 F8
Nimule, *Sudan* 81 G3
Nin, *Croatia* 29 D12
Nīnawá, *Iraq* 70 B4
Nindigully, *Australia* 95 D4
Nineveh = Nīnawá, *Iraq* 70 B4
Ning Xian, *China* 56 G4
Ning'an, *China* 57 B15
Ningbo, *China* 59 C13
Ningcheng, *China* 57 D10
Ningde, *China* 59 D12
Ningdu, *China* 59 D10
Ninggang, *China* 59 D9
Ningguo, *China* 59 B12
Ninghai, *China* 59 C13
Ninghua, *China* 59 D11
Ningi, *Nigeria* 83 C6
Ningjin, *China* 56 F8
Ningjing Shan, *China* 58 C2
Ninglang, *China* 58 D3
Ningling, *China* 56 G8
Ningming, *China* 58 F6
Ningnan, *China* 58 D4
Ningpo = Ningbo, *China* 59 C13
Ningqiang, *China* 56 H4
Ningshan, *China* 56 H5
Ningsia Hui A.R. = Ningxia Huizu Zizhiqu □, *China* 56 F4
Ningwu, *China* 56 E7
Ningxia Huizu Zizhiqu □, *China* 56 F4
Ningxiang, *China* 59 C9
Ningyang, *China* 56 G9
Ningyuan, *China* 59 E8
Ninh Binh, *Vietnam* 58 G5
Ninh Giang, *Vietnam* 64 B6
Ninh Hoa, *Vietnam* 64 F7
Ninh Ma, *Vietnam* 64 F7
Ninove, *Belgium* 17 D4
Nioaque, *Brazil* 127 A4
Niobrara, *U.S.A.* 112 D6
Niobrara →, *U.S.A.* 112 D6
Niono, *Mali* 82 C3
Nionsamoridougou, *Guinea* . . . 82 D3
Nioro du Rip, *Senegal* 82 C1
Nioro du Sahel, *Mali* 82 B3
Niort, *France* 20 B3
Nipawin, *Canada* 105 C8
Nipfjället, *Sweden* 10 C6
Nipigon, *Canada* 102 C2
Nipigon, L., *Canada* 102 C2
Nipishish L., *Canada* 103 B7
Nipissing, L., *Canada* 102 C4
Nipomo, *U.S.A.* 117 K6
Nipton, *U.S.A.* 117 K11
Niquelândia, *Brazil* 125 F9
Nīr, *Iran* 70 B5
Nirasaki, *Japan* 55 G9
Nirmal, *India* 66 K11
Nirmali, *India* 69 F12
Niš, *Serbia, Yug.* 40 C5
Nisa, *Portugal* 35 F3
Nisāb, *Si. Arabia* 70 D5
Nisāb, *Yemen* 74 E4
Nišava →, *Serbia, Yug.* 40 C5
Niscemi, *Italy* 31 E7
Nishinomiya, *Japan* 55 G7
Nishino'omote, *Japan* 55 J5
Nishiwaki, *Japan* 55 G7
Nísíros, *Greece* 39 E9
Niška Banja, *Serbia, Yug.* 40 C6
Niskibi →, *Canada* 102 A2
Nisko, *Poland* 45 H9
Nisporeni, *Moldova* 43 C13
Nisqually →, *U.S.A.* 116 C4
Nissáki, *Greece* 36 A3
Nissan →, *Sweden* 11 H6
Nissum Bredning, *Denmark* . . . 11 H2
Nissum Fjord, *Denmark* 11 H2
Nistru = Dnister →, *Europe* . . . 47 J6
Nisutlin →, *Canada* 104 A2
Nitchequon, *Canada* 103 B5
Niterói, *Brazil* 127 A7
Nith →, *Canada* 110 C4
Nith →, *U.K.* 14 F5
Nitra, *Slovak Rep.* 27 C11
Nitra →, *Slovak Rep.* 27 D11
Nitriansky □, *Slovak Rep.* 27 C11
Nittenau, *Germany* 25 F8
Niuafo'ou, *Tonga* 91 B11
Niue, *Cook Is.* 97 J11
Niulan Jiang →, *China* 58 D4
Niut, *Indonesia* 62 D4
Niutou Shan, *China* 59 C13
Niuzhuang, *China* 57 D12
Nivala, *Finland* 8 E21
Nivelles, *Belgium* 17 D4
Nivernais, *France* 19 E10
Niwas, *India* 69 H9
Nixon, *U.S.A.* 113 L6
Nizamabad, *India* 66 K11
Nizamghat, *India* 67 E19
Nizhne Kolymsk, *Russia* 51 C17
Nizhnegorskiy = Nyzhnohirskyy, *Ukraine* 47 K8
Nizhnekamsk, *Russia* 48 C10
Nizhneudinsk, *Russia* 51 D10
Nizhnevartovsk, *Russia* 50 C8
Nizhniy Chir, *Russia* 49 F6
Nizhniy Lomov, *Russia* 48 D6
Nizhniy Novgorod, *Russia* 48 B7
Nizhniy Tagil, *Russia* 50 D6
Nizhyn, *Ukraine* 47 G6
Nizina Mazowiecka, *Poland* 45 F8
Nizip, *Turkey* 70 B3
Nízké Tatry, *Slovak Rep.* 27 C12
Nízký Jeseník, *Czech Rep.* 27 B10
Nizza Monferrato, *Italy* 28 D5
Njakwa, *Malawi* 87 E3
Njanji, *Zambia* 87 E3
Njegoš, *Montenegro, Yug.* 40 D2
Njinjo, *Tanzania* 87 D4
Njombe, *Tanzania* 87 D3
Njombe →, *Tanzania* 86 D4
Njurundabommen, *Sweden* 10 B11
Nkambe, *Cameroon* 83 D7
Nkana, *Zambia* 87 E2
Nkandla, *S. Africa* 89 D5
Nkawkaw, *Ghana* 83 D4
Nkayi, *Zimbabwe* 87 F2
Nkhotakota, *Malawi* 87 E3
Nkongsamba, *Cameroon* 83 E6
Nkurenkuru, *Namibia* 88 B2
Nkwanta, *Ghana* 82 D4
Nmai →, *Burma* 58 F2
Noakhali = Maijdi, *Bangla.* 67 H17
Nobel, *Canada* 110 A4
Nobeoka, *Japan* 55 H5
Noblejas, *Spain* 34 F7
Noblesville, *U.S.A.* 108 E3
Noce →, *Italy* 28 B8
Nocera Inferiore, *Italy* 31 B7
Nocera Umbra, *Italy* 29 E9
Noci, *Italy* 31 B10
Nocona, *U.S.A.* 113 J6
Nocrich, *Romania* 43 E9
Noda, *Japan* 55 G9
Nogales, *Mexico* 118 A2
Nogales, *U.S.A.* 115 L8
Nogaro, *France* 20 E3
Nogat →, *Poland* 44 D6
Nōgata, *Japan* 55 H5
Nogent, *France* 19 D12
Nogent-le-Rotrou, *France* 18 D7
Nogent-sur-Seine, *France* 19 D10
Noggerup, *Australia* 93 F2
Noginsk, *Moskva, Russia* 46 E10
Noginsk, *Tunguska, Russia* 51 C10
Nogoa →, *Australia* 94 C4
Nogoyá, *Argentina* 126 C4
Nógrád □, *Hungary* 42 C4
Noguera Pallaresa →, *Spain* . . . 32 D5
Noguera Ribagorzana →, *Spain* 32 D5
Nohar, *India* 68 E6
Nohfelden, *Germany* 25 F3
Nohta, *India* 69 H8
Noia, *Spain* 34 C2
Noire, Montagne, *France* 20 E6
Noires, Mts., *France* 18 D3
Noirétable, *France* 20 C7
Noirmoutier, Î. de, *France* 18 F4
Noirmoutier-en-l'Île, *France* . . . 18 F4
Nojane, *Botswana* 88 C3
Nojima-Zaki, *Japan* 55 G9
Nok Kundi, *Pakistan* 66 E3
Nokaneng, *Botswana* 88 B3
Nokia, *Finland* 9 F20
Nokomis, *Canada* 105 C8
Nokomis L., *Canada* 105 B8
Nol, *Sweden* 11 G6
Nola, *C.A.R.* 84 D3
Nola, *Italy* 31 B7
Nolay, *France* 19 F11
Noli, C. di, *Italy* 28 D5
Nolinsk, *Russia* 48 B9
Noma Omuramba →, *Namibia* . 88 B3
Nombre de Dios, *Panama* 120 E4
Nome, *U.S.A.* 100 B3
Nomo-Zaki, *Japan* 55 H4
Nonacho L., *Canada* 105 A7
Nonancourt, *France* 18 D8
Nonda, *Australia* 94 C3
None, *Italy* 28 D4
Nong Chang, *Thailand* 64 E2
Nong Het, *Laos* 64 C4
Nong Khai, *Thailand* 64 D4
Nong'an, *China* 57 B13
Nongoma, *S. Africa* 89 D5
Nonoava, *Mexico* 118 B3
Nonoava →, *Mexico* 118 B3
Nonthaburi, *Thailand* 64 F3
Nontron, *France* 20 C4
Nonza, *France* 21 F13
Noonamah, *Australia* 92 B5
Noord Brabant □, *Neths.* 17 C5
Noord Holland □, *Neths.* 17 B4
Noordbeveland, *Neths.* 17 C3
Noordoostpolder, *Neths.* 17 B5
Noordwijk, *Neths.* 17 B4
Nootka I., *Canada* 104 D3
Nopiming Prov. Park, *Canada* . 105 C9
Nora, *Eritrea* 81 D5
Nora, *Sweden* 10 E9
Noralee, *Canada* 104 C3
Noranda = Rouyn-Noranda, *Canada* 102 C4
Norberg, *Sweden* 10 D9
Nórcia, *Italy* 29 F10
Norco, *U.S.A.* 117 M9
Nord □, *France* 19 B10
Nord-Kivu □, *Dem. Rep. of the Congo* 86 C2
Nord-Ostsee-Kanal, *Germany* . 24 A5
Nord-Pas-de-Calais □, *France* . 19 B9
Nordaustlandet, *Svalbard* 4 B9
Nordborg, *Denmark* 11 J3
Nordby, *Denmark* 11 J2
Norddeich, *Germany* 24 B3
Nordegg, *Canada* 104 C5
Norden, *Germany* 24 B3
Nordenham, *Germany* 24 B4
Norderney, *Germany* 24 B3
Norderstedt, *Germany* 24 B6
Nordfjord, *Norway* 9 F11
Nordfriesische Inseln, *Germany* 24 A4
Nordhausen, *Germany* 24 D6
Nordhorn, *Germany* 24 C3
Norðoyar, *Færoe Is.* 8 E9
Nordingrå, *Sweden* 10 B12
Nordjyllands Amtskommune □, *Denmark* 11 G4
Nordkapp, *Norway* 8 A21
Nordkapp, *Svalbard* 4 A9
Nordkinn = Kinnarodden, *Norway* 6 A11
Nordkinn-halvøya, *Norway* . . . 8 A22
Nördlingen, *Germany* 25 G6
Nordrhein-Westfalen □, *Germany* 24 D3
Nordstrand, *Germany* 24 A4
Nordvik, *Russia* 51 B12
Nore →, *Ireland* 15 D4
Norfolk, *Nebr., U.S.A.* 112 D6
Norfolk, *Va., U.S.A.* 108 G7
Norfolk □, *U.K.* 13 E8
Norfolk I., *Pac. Oc.* 96 K8
Norfork L., *U.S.A.* 113 G8
Norilsk, *Russia* 51 C9
Norma, Mt., *Australia* 94 C3
Normal, *U.S.A.* 112 E10
Norman, *U.S.A.* 113 H6
Norman →, *Australia* 94 B3
Norman Wells, *Canada* 100 B7
Normanby →, *Australia* 94 A3
Normandin, *Canada* 102 C5
Normanhurst, Mt., *Australia* . . . 93 E3
Normanton, *Australia* 94 B3
Normétal, *Canada* 102 C4
Norquay, *Canada* 105 C8
Norquinco, *Argentina* 128 E2
Norra Dellen, *Sweden* 10 C10
Norra Ulvön, *Sweden* 10 A12
Norrahammar, *Sweden* 11 G8
Norrbotten □, *Sweden* 8 C19
Nørre Åby, *Denmark* 11 J3
Nørre Alslev, *Denmark* 11 K5
Nørresundby, *Denmark* 11 G3
Norrhult, *Sweden* 11 G9
Norris Point, *Canada* 103 C8
Norristown, *U.S.A.* 111 F9
Norrköping, *Sweden* 11 F10
Norrland, *Sweden* 9 E16
Norrsundet, *Sweden* 10 D11
Norrtälje, *Sweden* 10 E12
Norseman, *Australia* 93 F3
Norsk, *Russia* 51 D14
Norte, Pta. del, *Canary Is.* 37 G2
Norte, Serra do, *Brazil* 124 F7
North, C., *Canada* 103 C7
North Adams, *U.S.A.* 111 D11
North Arm, *Canada* 104 A5
North Augusta, *U.S.A.* 109 J5
North Ayrshire □, *U.K.* 14 F4
North Bass I., *U.S.A.* 110 E2
North Battleford, *Canada* 105 C7
North Bay, *Canada* 102 C4
North Belcher Is., *Canada* 102 A4
North Bend, *Oreg., U.S.A.* 114 E1
North Bend, *Pa., U.S.A.* 110 E7
North Bend, *Wash., U.S.A.* 116 C5
North Bennington, *U.S.A.* 111 D11
North Berwick, *U.K.* 14 E6
North Berwick, *U.S.A.* 111 C14
North C., *Canada* 103 C7
North C., *N.Z.* 91 F4
North Canadian →, *U.S.A.* 113 H7
North Canton, *U.S.A.* 110 F3
North Cape = Nordkapp, *Norway* 8 A21
North Cape = Nordkapp, *Svalbard* 4 A9
North Caribou L., *Canada* 102 B1
North Carolina □, *U.S.A.* 109 H6
North Cascades National Park, *U.S.A.* 114 B3
North Channel, *Canada* 102 C3
North Channel, *U.K.* 14 F3
North Charleston, *U.S.A.* 109 J6
North Chicago, *U.S.A.* 108 D2
North Creek, *U.S.A.* 111 C11
North Dakota □, *U.S.A.* 112 B5
North Downs, *U.K.* 13 F8
North East, *U.S.A.* 110 D5
North East Frontier Agency = Arunachal Pradesh □, *India* . 67 F19
North East Lincolnshire □, *U.K.* 12 D7
North Eastern □, *Kenya* 86 B5
North Esk →, *U.K.* 14 E6
North European Plain, *Europe* . 6 E10
North Foreland, *U.K.* 13 F9
North Fork, *U.S.A.* 116 H7
North Fork American →, *U.S.A.* 116 G5
North Fork Feather →, *U.S.A.* . 116 F5
North Fork Grand →, *U.S.A.* . . 112 C3
North Fork Red →, *U.S.A.* 113 H5
North Frisian Is. = Nordfriesische Inseln, *Germany* 24 A4
North Gower, *Canada* 111 A9
North Hd., *Australia* 93 F1
North Henik L., *Canada* 105 A9
North Highlands, *U.S.A.* 116 G5
North Horr, *Kenya* 86 B4
North I., *Kenya* 86 B4
North I., *N.Z.* 91 H5
North Kingsville, *U.S.A.* 110 E4
North Knife →, *Canada* 105 B10
North Koel →, *India* 69 G10
North Korea ■, *Asia* 57 E14
North Lakhimpur, *India* 67 F19
North Lanarkshire □, *U.K.* 14 F5
North Las Vegas, *U.S.A.* 117 J11
North Lincolnshire □, *U.K.* 12 D7
North Little Rock, *U.S.A.* 113 H8
North Loup →, *U.S.A.* 112 E5
North Magnetic Pole, *Canada* . . 4 B2
North Minch, *U.K.* 14 C3
North Moose L., *Canada* 105 C8
North Myrtle Beach, *U.S.A.* 109 J6
North Nahanni →, *Canada* 104 A4
North Olmsted, *U.S.A.* 110 E3
North Ossetia □, *Russia* 49 J7
North Pagai, I. = Pagai Utara, Pulau, *Indonesia* 62 E2
North Palisade, *U.S.A.* 116 H8
North Platte, *U.S.A.* 112 E4
North Platte →, *U.S.A.* 112 E4
North Pole, *Arctic* . . . . . . 4 A
North Portal, *Canada* 105 D8
North Powder, *U.S.A.* 114 D5
North Pt., *U.S.A.* 110 A1
North Rhine Westphalia = Nordrhein-Westfalen □, *Germany* 24 D3
North River, *Canada* 103 B8
North Ronaldsay, *U.K.* 14 B6
North Saskatchewan →, *Canada* 105 C7
North Sea, *Europe* 6 D6
North Seal →, *Canada* 105 B9
North Somerset □, *U.K.* 13 F5

North Sporades = Vóriai Sporádhes, Greece 38 B5
North Sydney, Canada 103 C7
North Syracuse, U.S.A. 111 C8
North Taranaki Bight, N.Z. 91 H5
North Thompson →, Canada 104 C4
North Tonawanda, U.S.A. 110 C6
North Troy, U.S.A. 111 B12
North Truchas Pk., U.S.A. 115 J11
North Twin I., Canada 102 B4
North Tyne →, U.K. 12 B5
North Uist, U.K. 14 D1
North Vancouver, Canada 104 D4
North Vernon, U.S.A. 108 F3
North Wabasca L., Canada 104 B6
North Walsham, U.K. 12 E9
North-West □, S. Africa 88 D4
North West C., Australia 92 D1
North West Christmas I. Ridge, Pac. Oc. 97 G11
North West Frontier □, Pakistan 68 C4
North West Highlands, U.K. 14 D4
North West River, Canada 103 B7
North Western □, Zambia 87 E2
North Wildwood, U.S.A. 108 F8
North York Moors, U.K. 12 C7
North Yorkshire □, U.K. 12 C6
Northallerton, U.K. 12 C6
Northam, Australia 93 F2
Northam, S. Africa 88 C4
Northampton, Australia 93 E1
Northampton, U.K. 13 E7
Northampton, Mass., U.S.A. 111 D12
Northampton, Pa., U.S.A. 111 F9
Northamptonshire □, U.K. 13 E7
Northbridge, U.S.A. 111 D13
Northcliffe, Australia 93 F2
Northeast Providence Chan., W. Indies 120 A4
Northeim, Germany 24 D6
Northern □, Ghana 83 D4
Northern □, Malawi 87 E3
Northern □, Zambia 87 E3
Northern Areas □, Pakistan 69 A5
Northern Cape □, S. Africa 88 D3
Northern Circars, India 67 L13
Northern Indian L., Canada 105 B9
Northern Ireland □, U.K. 15 B5
Northern Light L., Canada 102 C1
Northern Marianas ■, Pac. Oc. 96 F6
Northern Province □, S. Leone 82 D2
Northern Province □, S. Africa 89 C4
Northern Territory □, Australia 92 D5
Northfield, Minn., U.S.A. 112 C8
Northfield, Vt., U.S.A. 111 B12
Northland □, N.Z. 91 F4
Northome, U.S.A. 112 B7
Northport, Ala., U.S.A. 109 J2
Northport, Wash., U.S.A. 114 B5
Northumberland □, U.K. 12 B6
Northumberland Is., Australia 94 C4
Northumberland Str., Canada 103 C7
Northville, U.S.A. 111 C10
Northwest Providence Channel, W. Indies 120 A4
Northwest Territories □, Canada 100 B9
Northwood, Iowa, U.S.A. 112 D8
Northwood, N. Dak., U.S.A. 112 B6
Norton, U.S.A. 112 F5
Norton, Zimbabwe 87 F3
Norton Sd., U.S.A. 100 B3
Nortorf, Germany 24 A5
Norwalk, Calif., U.S.A. 117 M8
Norwalk, Conn., U.S.A. 111 E11
Norwalk, Iowa, U.S.A. 112 E8
Norwalk, Ohio, U.S.A. 110 E2
Norway, Maine, U.S.A. 109 C10
Norway, Mich., U.S.A. 108 C2
Norway ■, Europe 8 E14
Norway House, Canada 105 C9
Norwegian Sea, Atl. Oc. 4 C8
Norwich, Canada 110 D4
Norwich, U.K. 13 E9
Norwich, Conn., U.S.A. 111 E12
Norwich, N.Y., U.S.A. 111 D9
Norwood, Canada 110 B7
Norwood, U.S.A. 111 B10
Noshiro, Japan 54 D10
Nosivka, Ukraine 47 G6
Nosovka = Nosivka, Ukraine 47 G6
Noşratābād, Iran 71 D8
Noss Hd., U.K. 14 C5
Nossebro, Sweden 11 F6
Nossob →, S. Africa 88 D3
Nossombougou, Mali 82 C3
Nosy Barren, Madag. 85 H8
Nosy Be, Madag. 85 G9
Nosy Boraha, Madag. 89 B8
Nosy Lava, Madag. 89 A8
Nosy Varika, Madag. 89 C8
Noteć →, Poland 45 F2
Notikewin →, Canada 104 B5
Notio Aigaio = Notios Aiyaíon □ 39 E7
Notios Aiyaíon □ 39 E7
Notios Evvoïkos Kólpos, Greece 38 C5
Noto, Italy 31 F8
Noto, G. di, Italy 31 F8
Notodden, Norway 9 G13
Notre Dame B., Canada 103 C8
Notre Dame de Koartac = Quaqtaq, Canada 101 B13
Notre-Dame-des-Bois, Canada 111 A13
Notre Dame d'Ivugivic = Ivujivik, Canada 101 B12
Notre-Dame-du-Nord, Canada 102 C4
Notsé, Togo 83 D5
Nottawasaga B., Canada 110 B4
Nottaway →, Canada 102 B4
Nottingham, U.K. 12 E6
Nottingham, City of □, U.K. 12 E6
Nottingham I., Canada 101 B12
Nottinghamshire □, U.K. 12 D6
Nottoway →, U.S.A. 108 G7
Notwane →, Botswana 88 C4
Nouâdhibou, Mauritania 78 D2
Nouâdhibou, Ras, Mauritania 78 D2
Nouakchott, Mauritania 82 B1
Nouâmghâr, Mauritania 82 B1
Nouméa, N. Cal. 96 K8
Nouna, Burkina Faso 82 C4
Noupoort, S. Africa 88 E3
Nouveau Comptoir = Wemindji, Canada 102 B4
Nouvelle-Amsterdam, I., Ind. Oc. 3 F13
Nouvelle-Calédonie = New Caledonia ■, Pac. Oc. 96 K8
Nouzonville, France 19 C11
Nová Baňa, Slovak Rep. 27 C11
Nová Bystřice, Czech Rep. 26 B8
Nova Casa Nova, Brazil 125 E10
Nova Esperança, Brazil 127 A5
Nova Friburgo, Brazil 127 A7
Nova Gaia = Cambundi-Catembo, Angola 84 G3
Nova Gorica, Slovenia 29 C10
Nova Gradiška, Croatia 42 E2
Nova Iguaçu, Brazil 127 A7
Nova Iorque, Brazil 125 E10
Nova Kakhovka, Ukraine 47 J7
Nova Lamego, Guinea-Biss. 82 C2
Nova Lima, Brazil 127 A7
Nova Lisboa = Huambo, Angola 85 G3
Nova Lusitânia, Mozam. 87 F3
Nova Mambone, Mozam. 89 C6
Nova Odesa, Ukraine 47 J6
Nová Paka, Czech Rep. 26 A8
Nova Pavova, Serbia, Yug. 42 F5
Nova Scotia □, Canada 103 C7
Nova Siri, Italy 31 B9
Nova Sofala, Mozam. 89 C5
Nova Varoš, Serbia, Yug. 40 C3
Nova Venécia, Brazil 125 G10
Nova Zagora, Bulgaria 41 D10
Novaci, Macedonia 40 E5
Novaci, Romania 43 E8
Novaféltria, Italy 29 E9
Novaleksandrovskaya = Novoaleksandrovsk, Russia 49 H5
Novannenskiy = Novoannenskiy, Russia 48 E6
Novar, Canada 110 A5
Novara, Italy 28 C5
Novato, U.S.A. 116 G4
Novaya Kakhovka = Nova Kakhovka, Ukraine 47 J7
Novaya Kazanka, Kazakstan 49 F9
Novaya Ladoga, Russia 46 B7
Novaya Lyalya, Russia 50 D7
Novaya Sibir, Ostrov, Russia 51 B16
Novaya Zemlya, Russia 50 B6
Nové Město, Slovak Rep. 27 C10
Nové Město na Moravě, Czech Rep. 26 B9
Nové Město nad Metují, Czech Rep. 27 A9
Nové Zámky, Slovak Rep. 27 C11
Novelda, Spain 33 G4
Novellara, Italy 28 D7
Noventa Vicentina, Italy 29 C8
Novgorod, Russia 46 C6
Novgorod-Severskiy = Novhorod-Siverskyy, Ukraine 47 G7
Novhorod-Siverskyy, Ukraine 47 G7
Novi Bečej, Serbia, Yug. 42 E5
Novi Iskar, Bulgaria 40 D7
Novi Kneževac, Serbia, Yug. 42 D5
Novi Lígure, Italy 28 D5
Novi Pazar, Bulgaria 41 C11
Novi Pazar, Serbia, Yug. 40 C4
Novi Sad, Serbia, Yug. 42 E4
Novi Slankamen, Serbia, Yug. 42 E5
Novi Travnik, Bos.-H. 42 F2
Novi Vinodolski, Croatia 29 C11
Novigrad, Istra, Croatia 29 C10
Novigrad, Zadar, Croatia 29 D12
Novigradsko More, Croatia 29 D12
Nôvo Hamburgo, Brazil 127 B5
Novo Mesto, Slovenia 29 C12
Novo Miloševo, Serbia, Yug. 42 E5
Novo Remanso, Brazil 125 E10
Novoaleksandrovsk, Russia 49 H5
Novoannenskiy, Russia 48 E6
Novoataysk, Russia 50 D9
Novoazovsk, Ukraine 47 J10
Novocheboksarsk, Russia 48 B8
Novocherkassk, Russia 49 G5
Novodevichye, Russia 48 D9
Novogrudok = Navahrudak, Belarus 46 F3
Novohrad-Volynskyy, Ukraine 47 G4
Novokachalinsk, Russia 54 B6
Novokazalinsk = Zhangaqazaly, Kazakstan 50 E7
Novokhopersk, Russia 48 E5
Novokuybyshevsk, Russia 48 D9
Novokuznetsk, Russia 50 D9
Novomirgorod, Ukraine 47 H6
Novomoskovsk, Russia 46 E10
Novomoskovsk, Ukraine 47 H8
Novopolotsk = Navapolatsk, Belarus 46 E5
Novorossiysk, Russia 47 K9
Novorybnoye, Russia 51 B11
Novorzhev, Russia 46 D5
Novosej, Albania 40 E4
Novoselytsya, Ukraine 47 H4
Novoshakhtinsk, Russia 47 J10
Novosibirsk, Russia 50 D9
Novosibirskiye Ostrova, Russia 51 B15
Novosil, Russia 47 F9
Novosokolniki, Russia 46 D6
Novotitarovskaya, Russia 49 H4
Novotroitsk, Russia 50 D6
Novoukrayinka, Ukraine 47 H6
Novouljanovsk, Russia 48 C9
Novouzensk, Russia 48 E9
Novovolynsk, Ukraine 47 G3
Novovoronezhskiy, Russia 47 G10
Novozybkov, Russia 47 F6
Novska, Croatia 29 C14
Novy Urengoy, Russia 50 C8
Nový Bor, Czech Rep. 26 A7
Novy Bug = Novyy Buh, Ukraine 47 J7
Nový Bydžov, Czech Rep. 26 A8
Novy Dwór Mazowiecki, Poland 45 F7
Nový Jičín, Czech Rep. 27 B11
Novyy Afon, Georgia 49 J5
Novyy Buh, Ukraine 47 J7
Novyy Oskol, Russia 47 G9
Novyy Port, Russia 50 C8
Now Shahr, Iran 71 B6
Nowa Deba, Poland 45 H8
Nowa Ruda, Poland 45 H3
Nowa Sarzyna, Poland 45 H9
Nowa Sól, Poland 45 G2
Nowata, U.S.A. 113 G7
Nowbarān, Iran 71 C6
Nowe, Poland 44 E5
Nowe Miasteczko, Poland 45 G2
Nowe Miasto, Poland 45 G7
Nowe Miasto Lubawskie, Poland 44 E6
Nowe Skalmierzyce, Poland 45 G4
Nowe Warpno, Poland 44 E1
Nowghāb, Iran 71 C8
Nowgong, Assam, India 67 F18
Nowgong, Mad. P., India 69 G8
Nowogard, Poland 44 E2
Nowogród, Poland 45 E8
Nowogród Bobrzanski, Poland 45 G2
Nowogrodziec, Poland 45 G2
Nowshera, Pakistan 66 C8
Nowy Dwór Gdański, Poland 44 D6
Nowy Sącz, Poland 45 J7
Nowy Staw, Poland 44 D6
Nowy Targ, Poland 45 J7
Nowy Tomyśl, Poland 45 F3
Nowy Wiśnicz, Poland 45 J7
Noxen, U.S.A. 111 E8
Noxon, U.S.A. 114 C6
Noyabr'sk, Russia 50 C8
Noyant, France 18 E7
Noyers, France 19 E10
Noyon, France 19 C9
Noyon, Mongolia 56 C2
Nozay, France 18 E5
Nqutu, S. Africa 89 D5
Nsanje, Malawi 87 F4
Nsawam, Ghana 83 D4
Nsomba, Zambia 87 E2
Nsukka, Nigeria 83 D6
Ntui, Cameroon 83 E7
Nu Jiang →, China 58 E2
Nu Shan, China 58 E2
Nuba Mts. = Nubah, Jibalan, Sudan 81 E3
Nubah, Jibalan, Sudan 81 E3
Nubia, Africa 76 D7
Nubian Desert = Nûbîya, Es Sahrâ en, Sudan 80 C3
Nûbîya, Es Sahrâ en, Sudan 80 C3
Nubledo, Spain 34 B5
Nuboai, Indonesia 63 E9
Nubra →, India 69 B7
Nucet, Romania 42 D7
Nueces →, U.S.A. 113 M6
Nueltin L., Canada 105 A9
Nueva Asunción □, Paraguay 126 A3
Nueva Carteya, Spain 35 H6
Nueva Gerona, Cuba 120 B3
Nueva Palmira, Uruguay 126 C4
Nueva Rosita, Mexico 118 B4
Nueva San Salvador, El Salv. 120 D2
Nueva Tabarca, Spain 33 G4
Nuéve de Julio, Argentina 126 D3
Nuevitas, Cuba 120 B4
Nuevo, G., Argentina 128 E4
Nuevo Casas Grandes, Mexico 118 A3
Nuevo Guerrero, Mexico 119 B5
Nuevo Laredo, Mexico 119 B5
Nuevo León □, Mexico 118 C5
Nuevo Rocafuerte, Ecuador 124 D3
Nugget Pt., N.Z. 91 M2
Nugrus, Gebel, Egypt 80 C3
Nuhaka, N.Z. 91 H6
Nuits-St-Georges, France 19 E11
Nukey Bluff, Australia 95 E2
Nukheila, Sudan 80 D2
Nukhuyb, Iraq 70 C4
Nuku'alofa, Tonga 91 E12
Nukus, Uzbekistan 50 E6
Nules, Spain 32 F4
Nullagine, Australia 92 D3
Nullagine →, Australia 92 D3
Nullarbor, Australia 93 F5
Nullarbor Plain, Australia 93 F4
Numalla, L., Australia 95 D3
Numan, Nigeria 83 D7
Numata, Japan 55 F9
Numatinna →, Sudan 81 F2
Numazu, Japan 55 G9
Numbulwar, Australia 94 A2
Numfoor, Indonesia 63 E8
Nunaksaluk I., Canada 103 A7
Nunap Isua, Greenland 101 C15
Nunavut □, Canada 101 B11
Nunda, U.S.A. 110 D7
Nungarin, Australia 93 F2
Nungo, Mozam. 87 E4
Nungwe, Tanzania 86 C3
Nunivak I., U.S.A. 100 B3
Nunkun, India 69 C7
Núoro, Italy 30 B2
Nūrābād, Iran 71 E8
Nure →, Italy 28 C6
Nuremberg = Nürnberg, Germany 25 F7
Nuri, Mexico 118 B3
Nurlat, Russia 48 C10
Nurmes, Finland 8 E23
Nürnberg, Germany 25 F7
Nurpur, Pakistan 68 D4
Nurra, La, Italy 30 B1
Nurran, L. = Terewah, L., Australia 95 D4
Nurrari Lakes, Australia 93 E5
Nurri, Italy 30 C2
Nürtingen, Germany 25 G5
Nurzec →, Poland 45 F9
Nus, Italy 28 C4
Nusa Barung, Indonesia 63 H15
Nusa Kambangan, Indonesia 63 G13
Nusa Tenggara Barat □, Indonesia 62 F5
Nusa Tenggara Timur □, Indonesia 63 F6
Nusaybin, Turkey 73 D9
Nushki, Pakistan 68 E2
Nuuk, Greenland 101 B14
Nuwakot, Nepal 69 E10
Nuweiba', Egypt 70 D2
Nuwerus, S. Africa 88 E2
Nuweveldberge, S. Africa 88 E3
Nuyts, C., Australia 93 F5
Nuyts, Pt., Australia 93 G2
Nuyts Arch., Australia 95 E1
Nxau-Nxau, Botswana 88 B3
Nyaake, Liberia 82 E3
Nyabing, Australia 93 F2
Nyack, U.S.A. 111 E11
Nyagan, Russia 50 C7
Nyahanga, Tanzania 86 C3
Nyahua, Tanzania 86 D3
Nyahururu, Kenya 86 B4
Nyainqentanglha Shan, China 60 C4
Nyakanazi, Tanzania 86 C3
Nyakrom, Ghana 83 D4
Nyâlâ, Sudan 81 E1
Nyamandhlovu, Zimbabwe 87 F2
Nyambiti, Tanzania 86 C3
Nyamlell, Sudan 81 F2
Nyamwaga, Tanzania 86 C3
Nyandekwa, Tanzania 86 C3
Nyanding →, Sudan 81 F3
Nyandoma, Russia 46 B11
Nyangana, Namibia 88 B3
Nyanguge, Tanzania 86 C3
Nyankpala, Ghana 83 D4
Nyanza, Rwanda 86 C2
Nyanza □, Kenya 86 C3
Nyanza-Lac, Burundi 86 C2
Nyaponges, Sudan 81 F3
Nyasa, L., Africa 87 E3
Nyasvizh, Belarus 47 F4
Nyazura, Zimbabwe 87 F3
Nyazwidzi →, Zimbabwe 87 G3
Nyborg, Denmark 11 J4
Nybro, Sweden 11 H9
Nyda, Russia 50 C8
Nyeri, Kenya 86 C4
Nyerol, Sudan 81 F3
Nyhammar, Sweden 10 D8
Nyinahin, Ghana 82 D4
Nyíradony, Hungary 42 C6
Nyírbátor, Hungary 42 C7
Nyíregyháza, Hungary 42 C6
Nykøbing, Storstrøm, Denmark 11 K5
Nykøbing, Vestsjælland, Denmark 11 J5
Nykøbing, Viborg, Denmark 11 H2
Nyköping, Sweden 11 F11
Nykroppa, Sweden 10 E8
Nykvarn, Sweden 10 E11
Nyland, Sweden 10 A11
Nylstroom, S. Africa 89 C4
Nymburk, Czech Rep. 26 A8
Nynäshamn, Sweden 11 F11
Nyoma Rap, India 69 C8
Nyoman = Neman →, Lithuania 9 J19
Nyon, Switz. 25 J2
Nyong →, Cameroon 83 E6
Nyons, France 21 D9
Nyou, Burkina Faso 83 C4
Nýrsko, Czech Rep. 26 B6
Nysa, Poland 45 H4
Nysa →, Europe 24 C10
Nysa Kłodzka →, Poland 45 H4
Nysäter, Sweden 10 E6
Nyssa, U.S.A. 114 E5
Nysted, Denmark 11 K5
Nyunzu, Dem. Rep. of the Congo 86 D2
Nyurba, Russia 51 C12
Nyzhnohirskyy, Ukraine 47 K8
Nzébéla, Guinea 82 D3
Nzega, Tanzania 86 C3
Nzérékoré, Guinea 82 D3
Nzeto, Angola 84 F2
Nzilo, Chutes de, Dem. Rep. of the Congo 87 E2
Nzo →, Ivory C. 82 D3
Nzubuka, Tanzania 86 C3

O

O Barco, Spain 34 C4
O Carballiño, Spain 34 C2
O Corgo, Spain 34 C3
O Pino, Spain 34 C2
O Porriño, Spain 34 C2
Ō-Shima, Japan 55 G9
Oa, Mull of, U.K. 14 F2
Oacoma, U.S.A. 112 D5
Oahe, L., U.S.A. 112 C4
Oahe Dam, U.S.A. 112 C4
Oahu, U.S.A. 106 H16
Oak Harbor, U.S.A. 116 B4
Oak Hill, U.S.A. 108 G5
Oak Ridge, U.S.A. 109 G3
Oak View, U.S.A. 117 L7
Oakan-Dake, Japan 54 C12
Oakdale, Calif., U.S.A. 116 H6
Oakdale, La., U.S.A. 113 K8
Oakes, U.S.A. 112 B5
Oakesdale, U.S.A. 114 C5
Oakey, Australia 95 D5
Oakfield, U.S.A. 110 C6
Oakham, U.K. 13 E7
Oakhurst, U.S.A. 116 H7
Oakland, U.S.A. 116 H4
Oakley, Idaho, U.S.A. 114 E7
Oakley, Kans., U.S.A. 112 F4
Oakover →, Australia 92 D3
Oakridge, U.S.A. 114 E2
Oakville, Canada 110 C5
Oakville, U.S.A. 116 D3
Oamaru, N.Z. 91 L3
Oancea, Romania 43 E12
Oasis, Calif., U.S.A. 117 M10
Oasis, Nev., U.S.A. 116 H9
Oates Land, Antarctica 5 C11
Oatlands, Australia 94 G4
Oatman, U.S.A. 117 K12
Oaxaca, Mexico 119 D5
Oaxaca □, Mexico 119 D5
Ob →, Russia 50 C7
Oba, Canada 102 C3
Obala, Cameroon 83 E7
Obama, Japan 55 G7
Oban, Nigeria 83 D6
Oban, U.K. 14 E3
Obbia, Somali Rep. 74 F4
Obera, Argentina 127 B4
Oberammergau, Germany 25 H7
Oberasbach, Germany 25 F6
Oberbayern □, Germany 25 G7
Oberdrauburg, Austria 26 E5
Oberfranken □, Germany 25 E7
Oberhausen, Germany 24 D2
Oberkirch, Germany 25 G4
Oberlausitz, Germany 24 D10
Oberlin, Kans., U.S.A. 112 F4
Oberlin, La., U.S.A. 113 K8
Oberlin, Ohio, U.S.A. 110 E2
Obernai, France 19 D14
Oberndorf, Germany 25 G4
Oberösterreich □, Austria 26 C7
Oberpfalz □, Germany 25 F8
Oberpfälzer Wald, Germany 25 F8
Oberstdorf, Germany 25 H6
Oberursel, Germany 25 E4
Oberwart, Austria 27 D9
Obi, Kepulauan, Indonesia 63 E7
Obi Is. = Obi, Kepulauan, Indonesia 63 E7
Obiaruku, Nigeria 83 D6
Óbidos, Brazil 125 D7
Óbidos, Portugal 35 F1
Obihiro, Japan 54 C11
Obilatu, Indonesia 63 E7
Obilnoye, Russia 49 G7
Obing, Germany 25 G8
Objat, France 20 C5
Obluchye, Russia 51 E14
Obninsk, Russia 46 E9
Obo, C.A.R. 86 A2
Oboa, Mt., Uganda 86 B3
Obock, Djibouti 81 E5
Oborniki, Poland 45 F3
Oborniki Śląskie, Poland 45 G3
Oboyan, Russia 47 G9
Obozerskaya = Obozerskiy, Russia 50 C5
Obozerskiy, Russia 50 C5
Obrenovac, Serbia, Yug. 40 B4
Obrovac, Croatia 29 D12
Obruk, Turkey 72 C5
Obrzycko, Poland 45 F3
Observatory Inlet, Canada 104 B3
Obshchi Syrt, Russia 6 E16
Obskaya Guba, Russia 50 C8
Obuasi, Ghana 83 D4
Obubra, Nigeria 83 D6
Obudu, Nigeria 83 D6
Obwalden □, Switz. 25 J4
Obzor, Bulgaria 41 D11

Ocala, U.S.A. 109 L4
Ocampo, Chihuahua, Mexico 118 B3
Ocampo, Tamaulipas, Mexico 119 C5
Ocaña, Spain 34 F7
Oconomowoc, U.S.A. 112 D10
Occidental, Cordillera, Colombia 122 C3
Ocean City, Md., U.S.A. 108 F8
Ocean City, N.J., U.S.A. 108 F8
Ocean City, Wash., U.S.A. 116 C2
Ocean Falls, Canada 104 C3
Ocean I. = Banaba, Kiribati 96 H8
Ocean Park, U.S.A. 116 D2
Oceano, U.S.A. 117 K6
Oceanport, U.S.A. 111 F10
Oceanside, U.S.A. 117 M9
Ochagavía, Spain 32 C3
Ochakiv, Ukraine 47 J6
Ochamchira, Georgia 49 J5
Ochil Hills, U.K. 14 E5
Ochsenfurt, Germany 25 F6
Ochsenhausen, Germany 25 G5
Ocilla, U.S.A. 109 K4
Ockelbo, Sweden 10 D10
Ocmulgee →, U.S.A. 109 K4
Ocna Mureş, Romania 43 D8
Ocna Sibiului, Romania 43 E9
Ocnele Mari, Romania 43 E9
Ocniţa, Moldova 43 B12
Oconee →, U.S.A. 109 K4
Oconto, U.S.A. 108 C2
Oconto Falls, U.S.A. 108 C1
Ocosingo, Mexico 119 D6
Ocotal, Nic. 120 D2
Ocotlán, Mexico 118 C4
Ocotlán de Morelos, Mexico 119 D5
Ocreza →, Portugal 35 F3
Öcsa, Hungary 42 C4
Octeville, France 18 C5
Oda, Ghana 83 D4
Ōda, Japan 55 G6
Oda, J., Sudan 80 C4
Ódáðahraun, Iceland 8 D5
Ödåkra, Sweden 11 H6
Odate, Japan 54 D10
Odawara, Japan 55 G9
Odda, Norway 9 F12
Odder, Denmark 11 J4
Odei →, Canada 105 B9
Odemira, Portugal 35 H2
Ödemiş, Turkey 39 C9
Odendaalsrus, S. Africa 88 D4
Odensbacken, Sweden 10 E9
Odense, Denmark 11 J4
Odenwald, Germany 25 F5
Oder →, Europe 24 B10
Oder-Havel Kanal, Germany 24 C10
Oderzo, Italy 29 C9
Odesa, Ukraine 47 J6
Ödeshög, Sweden 11 F8
Odessa = Odesa, Ukraine 47 J6
Odessa, Canada 111 B8
Odessa, Tex., U.S.A. 113 K3
Odessa, Wash., U.S.A. 114 C4
Odiakwe, Botswana 88 C4
Odiel →, Spain 35 H4
Odienné, Ivory C. 82 D3
Odintsovo, Russia 46 E9
Odiongan, Phil. 61 E4
Odobeşti, Romania 43 E12
Odolanów, Poland 45 G4
O'Donnell, U.S.A. 113 J4
Odorheiu Secuiesc, Romania 43 D10
Odoyevo, Russia 46 F9
Odra = Oder →, Europe 24 B10
Odra →, Spain 34 C6
Odžaci, Serbia, Yug. 42 E4
Odžak, Bos.-H. 42 E3
Odzi, Zimbabwe 89 B5
Odzi →, Zimbabwe 89 B5
Oebisfelde, Germany 24 C6
Oeiras, Brazil 125 E10
Oeiras, Portugal 35 G1
Oelrichs, U.S.A. 112 D3
Oelsnitz, Germany 25 E8
Oelwein, U.S.A. 112 D9
Oenpelli, Australia 92 B5
Oetz, Austria 26 D3
Of, Turkey 73 B9
Ofanto →, Italy 31 A9
Offa, Nigeria 83 D5
Offaly □, Ireland 15 C4
Offenbach, Germany 25 E4
Offenburg, Germany 25 G3
Offida, Italy 29 F10
Ofidhousa, Greece 39 E8
Ofotfjorden, Norway 8 B17
Ōfunato, Japan 54 E10
Oga, Japan 54 E9
Oga-Hantō, Japan 54 E9
Ogaden, Ethiopia 74 F3
Ōgaki, Japan 55 G8
Ogallala, U.S.A. 112 E4
Ogasawara Gunto, Pac. Oc. 52 G18
Ogbomosho, Nigeria 83 D5
Ogden, U.S.A. 114 F7
Ogdensburg, U.S.A. 111 B9
Ogeechee →, U.S.A. 109 K5
Ogilby, U.S.A. 117 N12
Oglio →, Italy 28 C7
Ogmore, Australia 94 C4
Ognon →, France 19 E12
Ogoja, Nigeria 83 D6
Ogoki, Canada 102 B2
Ogoki →, Canada 102 B2
Ogoki L., Canada 102 B2
Ogoki Res., Canada 102 B2
Ogooué →, Gabon 84 E1
Ogosta →, Bulgaria 40 C7
Ogowe = Ogooué →, Gabon 84 E1
Ogr = Sharafa, Sudan 81 E2
Ograźden, Macedonia 40 E6
Ogre, Latvia 9 H21
Ogrein, Sudan 80 D3
Ogulin, Croatia 29 C12
Ogun □, Nigeria 83 D5
Ogurchinskiy, Ostrov, Turkmenistan 71 B7
Oguta, Nigeria 83 D6
Ogwashi-Uku, Nigeria 83 D6
Ogwe, Nigeria 83 E6
Ohai, N.Z. 91 L2
Ohakune, N.Z. 91 H5
Ohata, Japan 54 D10
Ohau, L., N.Z. 91 L2
Ohio □, U.S.A. 110 F2
Ohio →, U.S.A. 108 G1
Ohře →, Czech Rep. 26 A7
Ohre →, Germany 24 C7
Ohrid, Macedonia 40 E4
Ohridsko Jezero, Macedonia 40 E4
Ohrigstad, S. Africa 89 C5
Öhringen, Germany 25 F5
Oi Qu, China 58 C2
Oiapoque, Brazil 125
Oikou, China 57 E9
Oil City, U.S.A. 110 E5
Oil Springs, Canada 110 D2
Oildale, U.S.A. 117 K7
Oinousa, Greece 39 C8
Oise □, France 19 C9
Oise →, France 19 C9
Ōita, Japan 55 H5
Ōita □, Japan 55 H5
Oiticica, Brazil 125 E10
Ojacaliente, Mexico 118 C4
Ojai, U.S.A. 117 L7
Ojinaga, Mexico 118 B4
Ojiya, Japan 55 F9
Ojos del Salado, Cerro, Argentina 126 B2
Oka →, Russia 48 B7
Okaba, Indonesia 63 F9
Okahandja, Namibia 88 C2
Okanagan L., Canada 104 D5
Okanogan, U.S.A. 114 B4
Okanogan →, U.S.A. 114 B4
Okány, Hungary 42 D6
Okaputa, Namibia 88 C2
Okara, Pakistan 68 D5
Okaukuejo, Namibia 88 B2
Okavango Swamps, Botswana 88 B3
Okaya, Japan 55 F9
Okayama, Japan 55 G6
Okayama □, Japan 55 G6
Okazaki, Japan 55 G8
Oke-Iho, Nigeria 83 D5
Okeechobee, U.S.A. 109 M5
Okeechobee, L., U.S.A. 109 M5
Okefenokee Swamp, U.S.A. 109 K4
Okehampton, U.K. 13 G4
Okene, Nigeria 83 D6
Oker →, Germany 24 C6
Okha, India 68 H3
Okha, Russia 51 D15
Ókhi Óros, Greece 38 C6
Okhotsk, Russia 51 D15
Okhotsk, Sea of, Asia 51 D15
Okhotskiy Perevoz, Russia 51 C14
Okhtyrka, Ukraine 47 G8
Oki-Shotō, Japan 55 F6
Okiep, S. Africa 88 D2
Okigwi, Nigeria 83 D6
Okija, Nigeria 83 D6
Okinawa □, Japan 55 L4
Okinawa-Guntō, Japan 55 L4
Okinawa-Jima, Japan 55 L4
Okino-erabu-Shima, Japan 55 L4
Okitipupa, Nigeria 83 D5
Oklahoma □, U.S.A. 113 H6
Oklahoma City, U.S.A. 113 H6
Okmulgee, U.S.A. 113 H7
Oknitsa = Ocniţa, Moldova 43 B12
Oko, W. →, Sudan 80 C4
Okolo, Uganda 86 B3
Okolona, U.S.A. 113 J10
Okombahe, Namibia 88 C2
Okonek, Poland 44 E3
Okotoks, Canada 104 C6
Okrika, Nigeria 83 E6
Oksibil, Indonesia 63 E10
Oktabrsk = Oktyabrsk, Kazakstan 50 E6
Oktyabrsk, Kazakstan 50 E6
Oktyabrsk, Russia 48 D9
Oktyabrskiy = Aktsyabrski, Belarus 47 F5
Oktyabrskiy, Russia 49 G5
Oktyabrskoy Revolyutsii, Ostrov, Russia 51 B10
Oktyabrskoye = Zhovtneve, Ukraine 47 J7
Okulovka, Russia 46 C7
Okuru, N.Z. 91 K2
Okushiri-Tō, Japan 54 C9
Okuta, Nigeria 83 D5
Okwa →, Botswana 88 C3
Ola, U.S.A. 113 H8
Ólafsfjörður, Iceland 8 C4
Ólafsvík, Iceland 8 D2
Olaine, Latvia 44 B10
Olancha, U.S.A. 117 J8
Olancha Pk., U.S.A. 117 J8
Olanchito, Honduras 120 C2
Öland, Sweden 11 H10
Ölands norra udde, Sweden 11 G11
Ölands södra udde, Sweden 11 H10
Olargues, France 20 E6
Olascoaga, Argentina 126 D3
Olathe, U.S.A. 112 F7
Olavarría, Argentina 126 D3
Oława, Poland 45 H4
Olbernhau, Germany 24 E9
Ólbia, Italy 30 B2
Ólbia, G. di, Italy 30 B2
Olching, Germany 25 G7
Olcott, U.S.A. 110 C6
Old Bahama Chan. = Bahama, Canal Viejo de, W. Indies 120 B4
Old Baldy Pk. = San Antonio, Mt., U.S.A. 117 L9
Old Castile = Castilla y Leon □, Spain 34 D6
Old Crow, Canada 100 B6
Old Dale, U.S.A. 117 L11
Old Dongola, Sudan 80 D3
Old Forge, N.Y., U.S.A. 111 C10
Old Forge, Pa., U.S.A. 111 E9
Old Perlican, Canada 103 C9
Old Shinyanga, Tanzania 86 C3
Old Speck Mt., U.S.A. 111 B14
Old Town, U.S.A. 109 C11
Old Washington, U.S.A. 110 F3
Old Wives L., Canada 105 C7
Oldbury, U.K. 13 F5
Oldcastle, Ireland 15 C4
Oldeani, Tanzania 86 C4
Oldenburg, Niedersachsen, Germany 24 B4
Oldenburg, Schleswig-Holstein, Germany 24 A6
Oldenzaal, Neths. 17 B6
Oldham, U.K. 12 D5
Oldman →, Canada 104 D6
Oldmeldrum, U.K. 14 D6
Olds, Canada 104 C6
Oldziyt, Mongolia 56 B5
Olean, U.S.A. 110 D6
Olecko, Poland 44 D9
Oléggio, Italy 28 C5
Oleiros, Portugal 34 F3
Oleiros, Spain 34 B2
Olekma →, Russia 51 C13
Olekminsk, Russia 51 C13
Oleksandriya, Kirovohrad, Ukraine 47 H7
Oleksandriya, Rivne, Ukraine 47 G4
Oleksandrovka, Ukraine 47 H7
Olema, U.S.A. 116 G4
Olenek, Russia 51 C12
Olenek →, Russia 51 B13
Olenino, Russia 46 D7
Oléron, Î. d', France 20 C2
Oleśnica, Poland 45 G4
Olesno, Poland 45 H5
Olevsk, Ukraine 47 G4
Olga, Russia 51 E14
Olga, L., Canada 102 C4
Olga, Mt., Australia 93 E5
Ølgod, Denmark 11 J2
Olhão, Portugal 35 H3
Olib, Croatia 29 D11
Oliena, Italy 30 B2
Oliete, Spain 32 D4
Olifants →, Africa 89 C5
Olifants →, Namibia 88 C2
Olifantshoek, S. Africa 88 D3
Ólimbos, Greece 39 F9
Ólimbos, Óros, Greece 40 F6
Olímpia, Brazil 127 A6
Olinda, Brazil 125 E12
Olite, Spain 32 C3
Oliva, Argentina 126 C3
Oliva, Spain 33 G4
Oliva, Punta del, Spain 34 B5
Oliva de la Frontera, Spain 35 G4
Olivares, Spain 32 F2
Olivehurst, U.S.A. 116 F5
Oliveira de Azeméis, Portugal 34 E2
Oliveira do Douro, Portugal 34 D2
Olivenza, Spain 35 G3
Oliver, Canada 104 D5
Oliver L., Canada 105 B8
Olivet, France 19 E8
Olkhovka, Russia 48 F7
Olkusz, Poland 45 H6
Ollagüe, Chile 126 A2
Olmedo, Spain 34 D6
Olmeto, France 21 G12
Olney, Ill., U.S.A. 108 F1
Olney, Tex., U.S.A. 113 J5
Olofström, Sweden 11 H8
Oloma, Cameroon 83 E7
Olomane →, Canada 103 B7
Olomouc, Czech Rep. 27 B10
Olonets, Russia 46 B7
Olongapo, Phil. 61 D4
Olonne-sur-Mer, France 20 B2
Oloron, Gave d' →, France 20 E2
Oloron-Ste-Marie, France 20 E3
Olot, Spain 32 C7
Olovo, Bos.-H. 42 F3
Olovyannaya, Russia 51 D12
Oloy →, Russia 51 C16
Olsberg, Germany 24 D4
Olshammar, Sweden 11 F8
Olshanka, Ukraine 47 H6
Olshany, Ukraine 47 G8
Olsztyn, Poland 44 E7
Olsztynek, Poland 44 E7
Olt □, Romania 43 F9
Olt →, Romania 43 G9
Olten, Switz. 25 H3
Olteniţa, Romania 43 F11
Olton, U.S.A. 113 H3
Oltu, Turkey 73 B9
Oluanpi, Taiwan 59 G13
Olula del Río, Spain 33 H2
Olur, Turkey 73 B10
Olutanga, Phil. 61 H5
Olvega, Spain 32 D2
Olvera, Spain 35 J5
Olymbos, Cyprus 36 D12
Olympia, Greece 38 D3
Olympia, U.S.A. 116 D4
Olympic Dam, Australia 95 E2
Olympic Mts., U.S.A. 116 C3
Olympic Nat. Park, U.S.A. 116 C3
Olympus, Cyprus 36 E11
Olympus, Mt. = Ólimbos, Óros, Greece 40 F6
Olympus, Mt. = Uludağ, Turkey 41 F13
Olympus, Mt., U.S.A. 116 C3
Olyphant, U.S.A. 111 E9
Om →, Russia 50 D8
Om Hajer, Eritrea 81 E4
Om Koi, Thailand 64 D2
Ōma, Japan 54 D10
Ōmachi, Japan 55 F8
Omae-Zaki, Japan 55 G9
Ōmagari, Japan 54 E10
Omagh, U.K. 15 B4
Omagh □, U.K. 15 B4
Omaha, U.S.A. 112 E7
Omak, U.S.A. 114 B4
Omalos, Greece 36 D5
Oman ■, Asia 74 C6
Oman, G. of, Asia 71 E8
Omaruru, Namibia 88 C2
Omaruru →, Namibia 88 C1
Omate, Peru 124 G4
Ombai, Selat, Indonesia 63 F6
Omboué, Gabon 84 E1
Ombrone →, Italy 28 F8
Omdurmân, Sudan 81 D3
Omegna, Italy 28 C5
Omemee, Canada 110 B6
Omeonga, Dem. Rep. of the Congo 86 C1
Ometepe, I. de, Nic. 120 D2
Ometepec, Mexico 119 D5
Ominato, Japan 54 D10
Omineca →, Canada 104 B4
Omiš, Croatia 29 E13
Omišalj, Croatia 29 C11
Omitara, Namibia 88 C2
Ōmiya, Japan 55 G9
Omme Å →, Denmark 11 J2
Ommen, Neths. 17 B6
Ömnögovĭ □, Mongolia 56 C3
Omo →, Ethiopia 81 F4
Omodeo, L., Italy 30 B1
Omodhos, Cyprus 36 E11
Omoko, Nigeria 83 D6
Omolon →, Russia 51 C16
Omono-Gawa →, Japan 54 E10
Omsk, Russia 50 D8
Omsukchan, Russia 51 C16
Ōmu, Japan 54 B11
Omul, Vf., Romania 43 E10
Omulew →, Poland 45 E8
Ōmura, Japan 55 H4
Omuramba Omatako →, Namibia 88 B2
Omuramba Ovambo →, Namibia 88 B2
Omurtag, Bulgaria 41 C10
Ōmuta, Japan 55 H5
Oña, Spain 34 C7
Onaga, U.S.A. 112 F6
Onalaska, U.S.A. 112 D9
Onancock, U.S.A. 108 G8
Onang, Indonesia 63 E5
Onaping L., Canada 102 C3
Oñati, Spain 32 B2
Onavas, Mexico 118 B3
Onawa, U.S.A. 112 D6
Oncócua, Angola 88 B1
Onda, Spain 32 F4
Ondaejin, N. Korea 57 D15
Ondangwa, Namibia 88 B2
Ondarroa, Spain 32 B2
Ondava →, Slovak Rep. 27 C14
Ondjiva, Angola 88 B2
Ondo, Nigeria 83 D5
Ondo □, Nigeria 83 D6
Öndörshil, Mongolia 56 B5
Öndverðarnes, Iceland 8 D1
One Tree, Australia 95 E3
Onega, Russia 50 C4
Onega →, Russia 6 C13
Onega, L. = Onezhskoye Ozero, Russia 46 B8
Oneida, U.S.A. 111 C9
Oneida L., U.S.A. 111 C9
O'Neill, U.S.A. 112 D5
Onekotan, Ostrov, Russia 51 E16
Onema, Dem. Rep. of the Congo 86 C1
Oneonta, U.S.A. 111 D9
Oneşti, Romania 43 D11
Onezhskoye Ozero, Russia 46 B8
Ongarue, N.Z. 91 H5
Ongers →, S. Africa 88 E3
Ongerup, Australia 93 F2
Ongjin, N. Korea 57 F13
Ongkharak, Thailand 64 E3
Ongniud Qi, China 57 C10
Ongoka, Dem. Rep. of the Congo 86 C2
Ongole, India 66 M12
Ongon = Havirga, Mongolia 56 B7
Oni, Georgia 49 J6
Onida, U.S.A. 112 C4
Onilahy →, Madag. 89 C7
Onitsha, Nigeria 83 D6
Onoda, Japan 55 G5
Onpyŏng-ni, S. Korea 57 H14
Ons, I. de, Spain 34 C2
Onslow, Australia 92 D2
Onslow B., U.S.A. 109 H7
Ontake-San, Japan 55 G8
Ontario, Calif., U.S.A. 117 L9
Ontario, Oreg., U.S.A. 114 D5
Ontario □, Canada 102 B2
Ontario, L., N. Amer. 110 C7
Ontinyent, Spain 33 G4
Ontonagon, U.S.A. 112 B10
Ontur, Spain 33 G3
Onyx, U.S.A. 117 K8
Oodnadatta, Australia 95 D2
Ooldea, Australia 93 F5
Oombulgurri, Australia 92 C4
Oorindi, Australia 94 C3
Oost-Vlaanderen □, Belgium 17 C3
Oostende, Belgium 17 C2
Oosterhout, Neths. 17 C4
Oosterschelde →, Neths. 17 C4
Oosterwolde, Neths. 17 B6
Ootacamund = Udagamandalam, India 66 P10
Ootsa L., Canada 104 C3
Opaka, Bulgaria 41 C10
Opala, Dem. Rep. of the Congo 86 C1
Opalenica, Poland 45 F3
Opan, Bulgaria 41 D9
Opanake, Sri Lanka 66 R12
Opasatika, Canada 102 C3
Opasquia Prov. Park, Canada 102 B1
Opatija, Croatia 29 C11
Opatów, Poland 45 H8
Opava, Czech Rep. 27 B10
Opelika, U.S.A. 109 J3
Opelousas, U.S.A. 113 K8
Opémisca, L., Canada 102 C5
Opheim, U.S.A. 114 B10
Ophthalmia Ra., Australia 92 D2
Opi, Nigeria 83 D6
Opinaca →, Canada 102 B4
Opinaca, Rés., Canada 102 B4
Opinnagau →, Canada 102 B3
Opiscoteo, L., Canada 103 B6
Opobo, Nigeria 83 E6
Opochka, Russia 46 D5
Opoczno, Poland 45 G7
Opol, Phil. 61 G6
Opole, Poland 45 H4
Opole Lubelskie, Poland 45 G8
Opolskie □, Poland 45 H5
Oponono L., Namibia 88 B2
Oporto = Porto, Portugal 34 D2
Opotiki, N.Z. 91 H6
Opp, U.S.A. 109 K2
Oppdal, Norway 9 E13
Óppido Mamertina, Italy 31 D8
Opportunity, U.S.A. 114 C5
Oprişor, Romania 42 F8
Oprtalj, Croatia 29 C10
Opua, N.Z. 91 F5
Opunake, N.Z. 91 H4
Opuwo, Namibia 88 B1
Opuzen, Croatia 29 E14
Ora, Cyprus 36 E12
Oracle, U.S.A. 115 K8
Oradea, Romania 42 C6
Öræfajökull, Iceland 8 D5
Orahovac, Kosovo, Yug. 40 D4
Orahovica, Croatia 42 E2
Orai, India 69 G8
Oraison, France 21 E9
Oral = Zhayyq →, Kazakstan 50 E6
Oral, Kazakstan 48 E10
Oran, Algeria 78 A5
Orange, France 21 D8
Orange, Calif., U.S.A. 117 M9
Orange, Mass., U.S.A. 111 D12
Orange, Tex., U.S.A. 113 K8
Orange, Va., U.S.A. 108 F6
Orange →, S. Africa 88 D2
Orange, C., Brazil 122 C5
Orange Cove, U.S.A. 116 J7
Orange Free State = Free State □, S. Africa 88 D4
Orange Grove, U.S.A. 113 M6
Orange Walk, Belize 119 D7
Orangeburg, U.S.A. 109 J5
Orangeville, Canada 102 D3
Orango, Guinea-Biss. 82 C1
Orani, Phil. 61 D4
Oranienburg, Germany 24 C9
Oranje = Orange →, S. Africa 88 D2
Oranje Vrystaat = Free State □, S. Africa 88 D4
Oranjemund, Namibia 88 D2
Oranjerivier, S. Africa 88 D3
Orapa, Botswana 85 J5
Orarak, Sudan 81 F3
Oras, Phil. 61 E6
Orašje, Bos.-H. 42 E3
Orăştie, Romania 43 E8
Oraşul Stalin = Braşov, Romania 43 E10
Orava →, Slovak Rep. 27 B12

Orava, Vodna nádriž, *Slovak Rep.* 27 B12
Oravița, *Romania* 42 E6
Orb →, *France* 20 E7
Orba →, *Italy* 28 D5
Ørbæk, *Denmark* 11 J4
Orbe, *Switz.* 25 J2
Orbec, *France* 18 C7
Orbetello, *Italy* 29 F8
Órbigo →, *Spain* 34 C5
Orbisonia, *U.S.A.* 110 F7
Orbyhus, *Sweden* 10 D11
Orcas I., *U.S.A.* 116 B4
Orce, *Spain* 33 H2
Orce →, *Spain* 33 H2
Orchard City, *U.S.A.* 115 G10
Orchies, *France* 19 B10
Orchila, I., *Venezuela* 121 D6
Órcia →, *Italy* 29 F8
Orco →, *Italy* 28 C4
Orcutt, *U.S.A.* 117 L6
Ord, *U.S.A.* 112 E5
Ord →, *Australia* 92 C4
Ord, Mt., *Australia* 92 C4
Ordenes = Ordes, *Spain* 34 B2
Orderville, *U.S.A.* 115 H7
Ordes, *Spain* 34 B2
Ording = St-Peter-Ording, *Germany* 24 A4
Ordos = Mu Us Shamo, *China* 56 E5
Ordu, *Turkey* 72 B7
Ordubad, *Azerbaijan* 73 C12
Orduña, *Álava, Spain* 32 C2
Orduña, *Granada, Spain* 35 H7
Ordway, *U.S.A.* 112 F3
Ordzhonikidze = Vladikavkaz, *Russia* 49 J7
Ordzhonikidze, *Ukraine* 47 J8
Ore, *Dem. Rep. of the Congo* 86 B2
Ore Mts. = Erzgebirge, *Germany* 24 E8
Orebić, *Croatia* 29 F14
Örebro, *Sweden* 10 E9
Örebro län □, *Sweden* 10 E8
Oregon, *U.S.A.* 112 D10
Oregon □, *U.S.A.* 114 E3
Oregon City, *U.S.A.* 116 E4
Öregrund, *Sweden* 10 D12
Öregrundsgrepen, *Sweden* 10 D12
Orekhov = Orikhiv, *Ukraine* 47 J8
Orekhovo-Zuyevo, *Russia* 46 E10
Orel, *Russia* 47 F9
Orel →, *Ukraine* 47 H8
Orellana, *Spain* 35 F5
Orellana, Canal de, *Spain* 35 F5
Orellana, Embalse de, *Spain* 35 F5
Orem, *U.S.A.* 114 F8
Ören, *Turkey* 39 D9
Orenburg, *Russia* 50 D6
Örencik, *Turkey* 39 B11
Orense = Ourense, *Spain* 34 C3
Orense □, *Spain* 34 C3
Orepuki, *N.Z.* 91 M1
Orestiás, *Greece* 41 E10
Orestos Pereyra, *Mexico* 118 B3
Øresund, *Europe* 11 J6
Orford Ness, *U.K.* 13 E9
Organà = Organyà, *Spain* 32 C6
Organos, Pta. de los, *Canary Is.* 37 F2
Organyà, *Spain* 32 C6
Orgaz, *Spain* 35 F7
Orgeyev = Orhei, *Moldova* 43 C13
Orhaneli, *Turkey* 41 G12
Orhaneli →, *Turkey* 41 G12
Orhangazi, *Turkey* 41 F13
Orhei, *Moldova* 43 C13
Orhon Gol →, *Mongolia* 60 A5
Ória, *Italy* 31 B10
Oriental, Cordillera, *Colombia* 122 C3
Orientale □, *Dem. Rep. of the Congo* 86 B2
Oriente, *Argentina* 126 D3
Orihuela, *Spain* 33 G4
Orihuela del Tremedal, *Spain* 32 E3
Orikhiv, *Ukraine* 47 J8
Orikum, *Albania* 40 F3
Orillia, *Canada* 102 D4
Orinoco →, *Venezuela* 122 C4
Orion, *Canada* 105 D6
Oriskany, *U.S.A.* 111 C9
Orissa □, *India* 67 K14
Orissaare, *Estonia* 9 G20
Oristano, *Italy* 30 C1
Oristano, G. di, *Italy* 30 C1
Orizaba, *Mexico* 119 D5
Orizare, *Bulgaria* 41 D11
Orjen, *Bos.-H.* 40 D2
Orjiva, *Spain* 35 J7
Orkanger, *Norway* 8 E13
Örkelljunga, *Sweden* 11 H7
Örken, *Sweden* 11 G9
Örkény, *Hungary* 42 C4
Orkla →, *Norway* 8 E13
Orkney, *S. Africa* 88 D4
Orkney □, *U.K.* 14 B5
Orkney Is., *U.K.* 14 B6
Orland, *U.S.A.* 116 F4
Orlando, *U.S.A.* 109 L5
Orlando, C. d', *Italy* 31 D7
Orléanais, *France* 19 E9
Orléans, *France* 19 E8
Orleans, *U.S.A.* 111 B12
Orléans, I. d', *Canada* 103 C5
Orlice →, *Czech Rep.* 26 A8
Orlov, *Slovak Rep.* 27 B13
Orlov Gay, *Russia* 48 E9
Orlová, *Czech Rep.* 27 B11
Orlovat, *Serbia, Yug.* 42 E5
Ormara, *Pakistan* 66 G4
Ormea, *Italy* 28 D4
Ormília, *Greece* 40 F7
Ormoc, *Phil.* 61 F6
Ormond, *N.Z.* 91 H6
Ormond Beach, *U.S.A.* 109 L5
Ormož, *Slovenia* 29 B13
Ormskirk, *U.K.* 12 D5
Ormstown, *Canada* 111 A11
Ornans, *France* 19 E13
Orne □, *France* 18 D7
Orne →, *France* 18 C6
Orneta, *Poland* 44 D7
Ornö, *Sweden* 10 E12
Örnsköldsvik, *Sweden* 10 A12
Oro, *N. Korea* 57 D14
Oro →, *Mexico* 118 B3
Oro Grande, *U.S.A.* 117 L9
Oro Valley, *U.S.A.* 115 K8
Orobie, Alpi, *Italy* 28 B6
Orocué, *Colombia* 124 C4
Orodara, *Burkina Faso* 82 C4
Orodo, *Nigeria* 83 D6
Orofino, *U.S.A.* 114 C5
Orol Dengizi = Aral Sea, *Asia* 50 E7
Oromocto, *Canada* 103 C6
Oron, *Nigeria* 83 E6
Orono, *Canada* 110 C6
Orono, *U.S.A.* 109 C11
Oronsay, *U.K.* 14 E2
Oropesa, *Spain* 34 F5
Oroquieta, *Phil.* 61 G5
Orosei, *Italy* 30 B2
Orosei, G. di, *Italy* 30 B2
Orosháza, *Hungary* 42 D5
Oroszlány, *Hungary* 42 C3
Orotukan, *Russia* 51 C16
Oroville, *Calif., U.S.A.* 116 F5
Oroville, *Wash., U.S.A.* 114 B4
Oroville, L., *U.S.A.* 116 F5
Orrefors, *Sweden* 11 H9
Orrviken, *Sweden* 10 A8
Orrville, *U.S.A.* 110 F3
Orsa, *Sweden* 10 C8
Orsara di Púglia, *Italy* 31 A8
Orsasjön, *Sweden* 10 C8
Orsha, *Belarus* 46 E6
Örsjö, *Sweden* 11 H9
Orsk, *Russia* 50 D6
Orșova, *Romania* 42 F7
Ørsted, *Denmark* 11 H4
Örsundsbro, *Sweden* 10 E11
Orta, L. d', *Italy* 28 C5
Orta Nova, *Italy* 31 A8
Ortaca, *Turkey* 39 E10
Ortakent, *Turkey* 39 D9
Ortaklar, *Turkey* 39 D9
Ortaköy, *Çorum, Turkey* 72 B6
Ortaköy, *Niğde, Turkey* 72 C6
Orte, *Italy* 29 F9
Ortegal, C., *Spain* 34 B3
Orthez, *France* 20 E3
Ortigueira, *Spain* 34 B3
Orting, *U.S.A.* 116 C4
Ortisei, *Italy* 29 B8
Ortles, *Italy* 28 B7
Ortón →, *Bolivia* 124 F5
Ortona, *Italy* 29 F11
Ortonville, *U.S.A.* 112 C6
Orūmīyeh, *Iran* 70 B5
Orūmīyeh, Daryācheh-ye, *Iran* 70 B5
Orune, *Italy* 30 B2
Oruro, *Bolivia* 124 G5
Orust, *Sweden* 11 F5
Oruzgān □, *Afghan.* 66 C5
Orvault, *France* 18 E5
Orvieto, *Italy* 29 F9
Orwell, *N.Y., U.S.A.* 111 C9
Orwell, *Ohio, U.S.A.* 110 E4
Orwell →, *U.K.* 13 F9
Orwigsburg, *U.S.A.* 111 F8
Oryakhovo, *Bulgaria* 40 C7
Orzinuovi, *Italy* 28 C6
Orzyc →, *Poland* 45 F8
Orzysz, *Poland* 44 E8
Osa →, *Poland* 44 E5
Osa, Pen. de, *Costa Rica* 120 E3
Osage, *U.S.A.* 112 D8
Osage →, *U.S.A.* 112 F9
Osage City, *U.S.A.* 112 F7
Ōsaka, *Japan* 55 G7
Osan, *S. Korea* 57 F14
Osawatomie, *U.S.A.* 112 F7
Osborne, *U.S.A.* 112 F5
Osby, *Sweden* 11 H7
Osceola, *Ark., U.S.A.* 113 H10
Osceola, *Iowa, U.S.A.* 112 E8
Oschatz, *Germany* 24 D9
Oschersleben, *Germany* 24 C7
Óschiri, *Italy* 30 B2
Oscoda, *U.S.A.* 110 B1
Osečina, *Serbia, Yug.* 40 B3
Ösel = Saaremaa, *Estonia* 9 G20
Osery, *Russia* 46 E10
Osgoode, *Canada* 111 A9
Osh, *Kyrgyzstan* 50 E8
Oshakati, *Namibia* 85 H3
Oshawa, *Canada* 102 D4
Oshigambo, *Namibia* 88 B2
Oshkosh, *Nebr., U.S.A.* 112 E3
Oshkosh, *Wis., U.S.A.* 112 C10
Oshmyany = Ashmyany, *Belarus* 9 J21
Oshnovīyeh, *Iran* 70 B5
Oshogbo, *Nigeria* 83 D5
Oshtorīnān, *Iran* 71 C6
Oshwe, *Dem. Rep. of the Congo* 84 E3
Osi, *Nigeria* 83 D6
Osieczna, *Poland* 45 G3
Osijek, *Croatia* 42 E3
Ósilo, *Italy* 30 B1
Ósimo, *Italy* 29 E10
Osintorf, *Belarus* 46 E6
Osipenko = Berdyansk, *Ukraine* 47 J9
Osipovichi = Asipovichy, *Belarus* 46 F5
Osiyan, *India* 68 F5
Osizweni, *S. Africa* 89 D5
Oskaloosa, *U.S.A.* 112 E8
Oskarshamn, *Sweden* 11 G10
Oskarström, *Sweden* 11 H6
Oskélanéo, *Canada* 102 C4
Öskemen, *Kazakstan* 50 E9
Oskol →, *Ukraine* 47 H9
Oslo, *Norway* 9 G14
Oslob, *Phil.* 61 G5
Oslofjorden, *Norway* 9 G14
Osmanabad, *India* 66 K10
Osmancık, *Turkey* 72 B6
Osmaniye, *Turkey* 70 B3
Osmanlı, *Turkey* 41 E10
Ösmo, *Sweden* 10 F11
Osnabrück, *Germany* 24 C4
Ośno Lubuskie, *Poland* 45 F1
Osoblaha, *Czech Rep.* 27 A10
Osogovska Planina, *Macedonia* 40 D6
Osor, *Italy* 29 D11
Osorio, *Brazil* 127 B5
Osorno, *Chile* 128 E2
Osorno, *Spain* 34 C6
Osoyoos, *Canada* 104 D5
Osøyro, *Norway* 9 F11
Ospika →, *Canada* 104 B4
Osprey Reef, *Australia* 94 A4
Oss, *Neths.* 17 C5
Ossa, Mt., *Australia* 94 G4
Óssa, Óros, *Greece* 38 B4
Ossa de Montiel, *Spain* 33 G2
Ossabaw I., *U.S.A.* 109 K5
Osse →, *France* 20 D4
Osse →, *Nigeria* 83 D6
Ossi, *Italy* 30 B1
Ossining, *U.S.A.* 111 E11
Ossipee, *U.S.A.* 111 C13
Ossokmanuan L., *Canada* 103 B7
Ossora, *Russia* 51 D17
Ostashkov, *Russia* 46 D7
Östavall, *Sweden* 10 B9
Oste →, *Germany* 24 B5
Ostend = Oostende, *Belgium* 17 C2
Oster, *Ukraine* 47 G6
Osterburg, *Germany* 24 C7
Osterburg, *U.S.A.* 110 F6
Osterburken, *Germany* 25 F5
Österbybruk, *Sweden* 10 D11
Österbymo, *Sweden* 11 G9
Österdalälven, *Sweden* 10 C7
Østerdalen, *Norway* 9 F14
Österfärnebo, *Sweden* 10 D10
Österforse, *Sweden* 10 A11
Östergötlands län □, *Sweden* 11 F9
Osterholz-Scharmbeck, *Germany* 24 B4
Østerild, *Denmark* 11 G2
Osterode, *Germany* 24 D6
Östersund, *Sweden* 10 A8
Östervåla, *Sweden* 10 D11
Ostfriesische Inseln, *Germany* 24 B3
Ostfriesland, *Germany* 24 B3
Östhammar, *Sweden* 10 D12
Óstia, Lido di, *Italy* 29 G9
Ostíglia, *Italy* 29 C8
Östmark, *Sweden* 10 D6
Östra Husby, *Sweden* 11 F10
Ostrava, *Czech Rep.* 27 B11
Ostróda, *Poland* 44 E6
Ostrogozhsk, *Russia* 47 G10
Ostroh, *Ukraine* 47 G4
Ostrołęka, *Poland* 45 E8
Ostrov, *Bulgaria* 41 C8
Ostrov, *Czech Rep.* 26 A5
Ostrov, *Romania* 43 F12
Ostrov, *Russia* 46 D5
Ostrów Lubelski, *Poland* 45 G9
Ostrów Mazowiecka, *Poland* 45 F8
Ostrów Wielkopolski, *Poland* 45 G4
Ostrowiec-Świętokrzyski, *Poland* 45 H8
Ostrožac, *Bos.-H.* 42 G2
Ostrzeszów, *Poland* 45 G4
Ostseebad Kühlungsborn, *Germany* 24 A7
Osttirol □, *Austria* 26 E5
Ostuni, *Italy* 31 B10
Osum →, *Albania* 40 F4
Osŭm →, *Bulgaria* 41 C8
Ōsumi-Kaikyō, *Japan* 55 J5
Ōsumi-Shotō, *Japan* 55 J5
Osun □, *Nigeria* 83 D5
Osuna, *Spain* 35 H5
Oswegatchie →, *U.S.A.* 111 B9
Oswego, *U.S.A.* 111 C8
Oswego →, *U.S.A.* 111 C8
Oswestry, *U.K.* 12 E4
Oświęcim, *Poland* 45 H6
Otaci, *Moldova* 43 B12
Otago □, *N.Z.* 91 L2
Otago Harbour, *N.Z.* 91 L3
Ōtake, *Japan* 55 G6
Otaki, *N.Z.* 91 J5
Otaru, *Japan* 54 C10
Otaru-Wan = Ishikari-Wan, *Japan* 54 C10
Otava →, *Czech Rep.* 26 B7
Otavalo, *Ecuador* 124 C3
Otavi, *Namibia* 88 B2
Otchinjau, *Angola* 88 B1
Otelec, *Romania* 42 E5
Otelnuk L., *Canada* 103 A6
Oțelu Roșu, *Romania* 42 E7
Otero de Rey = Outeiro de Rei, *Spain* 34 B3
Othello, *U.S.A.* 114 C4
Othonoí, *Greece* 38 B1
Óthris, Óros, *Greece* 38 B4
Otjiwarongo, *Namibia* 88 C2
Otmuchów, *Poland* 45 H4
Otočac, *Croatia* 29 D12
Otoineppu, *Japan* 54 B11
Otok, *Croatia* 29 E13
Otorohanga, *N.Z.* 91 H5
Otoskwin →, *Canada* 102 B2
Otra →, *Norway* 9 G13
Otradnyy, *Russia* 48 D10
Otranto, *Italy* 31 B11
Otranto, C. d', *Italy* 31 B11
Otranto, Str. of, *Italy* 31 B11
Otrokovice, *Czech Rep.* 27 B10
Otse, *S. Africa* 88 D4
Ōtsu, *Japan* 55 G7
Ōtsuki, *Japan* 55 G9
Ottawa = Outaouais →, *Canada* 102 C5
Ottawa, *Canada* 102 C4
Ottawa, *Ill., U.S.A.* 112 E10
Ottawa, *Kans., U.S.A.* 112 F7
Ottawa Is., *Canada* 101 C11
Ottélé, *Cameroon* 83 E7
Ottensheim, *Austria* 26 C7
Otter Cr. →, *U.S.A.* 111 B11
Otter L., *Canada* 105 B8
Otterndorf, *Germany* 24 B4
Otterup, *Denmark* 11 J4
Otterville, *Canada* 110 D4
Ottery St. Mary, *U.K.* 13 G4
Otto Beit Bridge, *Zimbabwe* 87 F2
Ottosdal, *S. Africa* 88 D4
Ottumwa, *U.S.A.* 112 E8
Otu, *Nigeria* 83 D5
Otukpa, *Nigeria* 83 D6
Oturkpo, *Nigeria* 83 D6
Otway, B., *Chile* 128 G2
Otwock, *Poland* 45 F8
Ötztaler Ache →, *Austria* 26 D3
Ötztaler Alpen, *Austria* 26 E3
Ou →, *Laos* 64 B4
Ou Neua, *Laos* 58 F3
Ou-Sammyaku, *Japan* 54 E10
Ouachita →, *U.S.A.* 113 K9
Ouachita, L., *U.S.A.* 113 H8
Ouachita Mts., *U.S.A.* 113 H7
Ouagadougou, *Burkina Faso* 83 C4
Ouahigouya, *Burkina Faso* 82 C4
Ouahran = Oran, *Algeria* 78 A5
Oualâta, *Mauritania* 82 B3
Ouallam, *Niger* 83 C5
Ouallene, *Algeria* 78 D6
Ouargaye, *Burkina Faso* 83 C5
Ouargla, *Algeria* 78 B7
Ouarkoye, *Burkina Faso* 82 C4
Ouarzazate, *Morocco* 78 B4
Ouassouas, *Mali* 83 B5
Ouatagouna, *Mali* 83 B5
Oubangi →, *Dem. Rep. of the Congo* 84 E3
Ouche →, *France* 19 E12
Ouddorp, *Neths.* 17 C3
Oude Rijn →, *Neths.* 17 B4
Oudeïka, *Mali* 83 B4
Oudenaarde, *Belgium* 17 D3
Oudon →, *France* 18 E6
Oudtshoorn, *S. Africa* 88 E3
Ouellé, *Ivory C.* 82 D4
Ouémé →, *Benin* 83 D5
Ouessa, *Burkina Faso* 82 C4
Ouessant, Î. d', *France* 18 D1
Ouesso, *Congo* 84 D3
Ouest, Pte. de l', *Canada* 103 C7
Ouezzane, *Morocco* 78 B4
Ougarou, *Burkina Faso* 83 C5
Oughterard, *Ireland* 15 C2
Ouidah, *Benin* 83 D5
Ouidi, *Niger* 83 C7
Ouistreham, *France* 18 C6
Oujda, *Morocco* 78 B5
Oujeft, *Mauritania* 82 A2
Oulainen, *Finland* 8 D21
Ould Yenjé, *Mauritania* 82 B2
Oullins, *France* 21 C8
Oulu, *Finland* 8 D21
Oulujärvi, *Finland* 8 D22
Oulujoki →, *Finland* 8 D21
Oulx, *Italy* 28 C3
Oum Chalouba, *Chad* 79 E10
Oum Hadjer, *Chad* 79 F9
Oumé, *Ivory C.* 82 D3
Ounasjoki →, *Finland* 8 C21
Ounguati, *Namibia* 88 C2
Ounianga Sérir, *Chad* 79 E10
Our →, *Lux.* 17 E6
Ouranópolis, *Greece* 40 F7
Ourârene, *Niger* 83 B6
Ouray, *U.S.A.* 115 G10
Ourcq →, *France* 19 C10
Ourense, *Spain* 34 C3
Ouricuri, *Brazil* 125 E10
Ourinhos, *Brazil* 127 A6
Ourique, *Portugal* 35 H2
Ouro Fino, *Brazil* 127 A6
Ouro-Ndia, *Mali* 82 B4
Ouro Prêto, *Brazil* 127 A7
Ouro Sogui, *Senegal* 82 B2
Oursi, *Burkina Faso* 83 C4
Ourthe →, *Belgium* 17 D5
Ouse →, *E. Susx., U.K.* 13 G8
Ouse →, *N. Yorks., U.K.* 12 D7
Oust, *France* 20 F5
Oust →, *France* 18 E4
Outaouais →, *Canada* 102 C5
Outardes →, *Canada* 103 C6
Outeiro de Rei, *Spain* 34 B3
Outer Hebrides, *U.K.* 14 D1
Outes = Serra de Outes, *Spain* 34 C2
Outjo, *Namibia* 88 C2
Outlook, *Canada* 105 C7
Outokumpu, *Finland* 8 E23
Outreau, *France* 19 B8
Ouvèze →, *France* 21 E8
Ouzouer-le-Marché, *France* 19 E8
Ovada, *Italy* 28 D5
Ovalau, *Fiji* 91 C8
Ovalle, *Chile* 126 C1
Ovamboland, *Namibia* 88 B2
Ovar, *Portugal* 34 E2
Overath, *Germany* 24 E3
Overflakkee, *Neths.* 17 C4
Overijssel □, *Neths.* 17 B6
Overland Park, *U.S.A.* 112 F7
Overton, *U.S.A.* 117 J12
Övertorneå, *Sweden* 8 C20
Överum, *Sweden* 11 F10
Ovid, *U.S.A.* 111 D8
Ovidiopol, *Ukraine* 47 J6
Ovidiu, *Romania* 43 F13
Oviedo, *Spain* 34 B5
Oviksfjällen, *Sweden* 10 A7
Oviši, *Latvia* 9 H19
Ovoot, *Mongolia* 56 B7
Övör Hangay □, *Mongolia* 56 B2
Ovoro, *Nigeria* 83 D6
Øvre Årdal, *Norway* 9 F12
Övre Fryken, *Sweden* 10 E7
Ovruch, *Ukraine* 47 G5
Owaka, *N.Z.* 91 M2
Owambo = Ovamboland, *Namibia* 88 B2
Owasco L., *U.S.A.* 111 D8
Owase, *Japan* 55 G8
Owatonna, *U.S.A.* 112 C8
Owbeh, *Afghan.* 66 B3
Owego, *U.S.A.* 111 D8
Owen Falls Dam, *Uganda* 86 B3
Owen Sound, *Canada* 102 D3
Owens →, *U.S.A.* 116 J9
Owens L., *U.S.A.* 117 J9
Owensboro, *U.S.A.* 108 G2
Owerri, *Nigeria* 83 D6
Owl →, *Canada* 105 B10
Owo, *Nigeria* 83 D6
Owosso, *U.S.A.* 108 D3
Owyhee, *U.S.A.* 114 F5
Owyhee →, *U.S.A.* 114 E5
Owyhee, L., *U.S.A.* 114 E5
Ox Mts. = Slieve Gamph, *Ireland* 15 B3
Öxarfjörður, *Iceland* 8 C5
Oxbow, *Canada* 105 D8
Oxelösund, *Sweden* 11 F11
Oxford, *N.Z.* 91 K4
Oxford, *U.K.* 13 F6
Oxford, *Mass., U.S.A.* 111 D13
Oxford, *Miss., U.S.A.* 113 H10
Oxford, *N.C., U.S.A.* 109 G6
Oxford, *N.Y., U.S.A.* 111 D9
Oxford, *Ohio, U.S.A.* 108 F3
Oxford L., *Canada* 105 C9
Oxfordshire □, *U.K.* 13 F6
Oxía, *Greece* 38 C3
Oxie, *Sweden* 11 J7
Oxílithos, *Greece* 38 C6
Oxnard, *U.S.A.* 117 L7
Oxsjövålen, *Sweden* 10 B7
Oxus = Amudarya →, *Uzbekistan* 50 E6
Oya, *Malaysia* 62 D4
Oyama, *Japan* 55 F9
Oyem, *Gabon* 84 D2
Oyen, *Canada* 105 C6
Oykel →, *U.K.* 14 D4
Oymyakon, *Russia* 51 C15
Oyo, *Nigeria* 83 D5
Oyo □, *Nigeria* 83 D5
Oyonnax, *France* 19 F12
Oyster Bay, *U.S.A.* 111 F11
Ōyübari, *Japan* 54 C11
Özalp, *Turkey* 73 C10
Ozamiz, *Phil.* 61 G5
Ozark, *Ala., U.S.A.* 109 K3
Ozark, *Ark., U.S.A.* 113 H8
Ozark, *Mo., U.S.A.* 113 G8
Ozark Plateau, *U.S.A.* 113 G9
Ozarks, L. of the, *U.S.A.* 112 F8
Ożarów, *Poland* 45 H8
Ózd, *Hungary* 42 B5
Ozernoye, *Russia* 48 E10
Ozette L., *U.S.A.* 116 B2
Ozieri, *Italy* 30 B2
Ozimek, *Poland* 45 H5
Ozinki, *Russia* 48 E9
Ozona, *U.S.A.* 113 K4
Ozorków, *Poland* 45 G6
Ozren, *Bos.-H.* 42 G3
Ozuluama, *Mexico* 119 C5
Ozun, *Romania* 43 E10
Ozurgeti, *Georgia* 49 K5

P

Pa, *Burkina Faso* 82 C4
Pa-an, *Burma* 67 L20
Pa Mong Dam, *Thailand* 64 D4
Pa Sak →, *Thailand* 62 B2
Paamiut, *Greenland* 4 C5
Paar →, *Germany* 25 G7
Paarl, *S. Africa* 88 E2
Pab Hills, *Pakistan* 68 F2
Pabbay, *U.K.* 14 D1
Pabianice, *Poland* 45 G6
Pabna, *Bangla.* 67 G16
Pabo, *Uganda* 86 B3
Pacaja →, *Brazil* 125 D8
Pacaraima, Sa., *S. Amer.* 122 C4
Pacasmayo, *Peru* 124 E3
Paceco, *Italy* 30 E5
Pachhar, *India* 68 G7
Pachino, *Italy* 31 F8
Pachitea →, *Peru* 124 E4
Pachmarhi, *India* 69 H8
Pachpadra, *India* 66 G8
Pachuca, *Mexico* 119 C5
Pacific, *Canada* 104 C3
Pacific-Antarctic Ridge, *Pac. Oc.* 97 M16
Pacific Grove, *U.S.A.* 116 J5
Pacific Ocean, *Pac. Oc.* 97 G14
Pacific Rim Nat. Park, *Canada* 116 B2
Pacifica, *U.S.A.* 116 H4
Pacitan, *Indonesia* 63 H14
Packwood, *U.S.A.* 116 D5
Pacov, *Czech Rep.* 26 B8
Pacy-sur-Eure, *France* 18 C8
Padaido, Kepulauan, *Indonesia* 63 E9
Padang, *Indonesia* 62 E2
Padang Endau, *Malaysia* 65 L4
Padangpanjang, *Indonesia* 62 E2
Padangsidempuan, *Indonesia* 62 D1
Padborg, *Denmark* 11 K3
Paddle Prairie, *Canada* 104 B5
Paddockwood, *Canada* 105 C7
Paderborn, *Germany* 24 D4
Padeş, Vf., *Romania* 42 E7
Padina, *Romania* 43 F12
Padma, *India* 69 G11
Pádova, *Italy* 29 C8
Padra, *India* 68 H5
Padrauna, *India* 69 F10
Padre I., *U.S.A.* 113 M6
Padrón, *Spain* 34 C2
Padstow, *U.K.* 13 G3
Padua = Pádova, *Italy* 29 C8
Paducah, *Ky., U.S.A.* 108 G1
Paducah, *Tex., U.S.A.* 113 H4
Padul, *Spain* 35 H7
Paengnyŏng-do, *S. Korea* 57 F13
Paeroa, *N.Z.* 91 G5
Paesana, *Italy* 28 D4
Pafúri, *Mozam.* 89 C5
Pag, *Croatia* 29 D12
Paga, *Ghana* 83 C4
Pagadian, *Phil.* 61 H5
Pagai Selatan, Pulau, *Indonesia* 62 E2
Pagai Utara, Pulau, *Indonesia* 62 E2
Pagalu = Annobón, *Atl. Oc.* 77 G4
Pagara, *India* 69 G9
Pagastikós Kólpos, *Greece* 38 B5
Pagatan, *Indonesia* 62 E5
Page, *U.S.A.* 115 H8
Pagėgiai, *Lithuania* 44 C8
Pago Pago, *Amer. Samoa* 91 B13
Pagosa Springs, *U.S.A.* 115 H10
Pagwa River, *Canada* 102 B2
Pahala, *U.S.A.* 106 J17
Pahang →, *Malaysia* 65 L4
Pahiatua, *N.Z.* 91 J5
Pahokee, *U.S.A.* 109 M5
Pahrump, *U.S.A.* 117 J11
Pahute Mesa, *U.S.A.* 116 H10
Pai, *Thailand* 64 C2
Paicines, *U.S.A.* 116 J5
Paide, *Estonia* 9 G21
Paignton, *U.K.* 13 G4
Paiho, *Taiwan* 59 F13
Päijänne, *Finland* 9 F21
Pailani, *India* 69 G9
Pailin, *Cambodia* 64 F4
Paimpol, *France* 18 D3
Painan, *Indonesia* 62 E2
Painesville, *U.S.A.* 110 E3
Paint Hills = Wemindji, *Canada* 102 B4
Paint L., *Canada* 105 B9
Painted Desert, *U.S.A.* 115 J8
Paintsville, *U.S.A.* 108 G4
País Vasco □, *Spain* 32 C2
Paisley, *Canada* 110 B3
Paisley, *U.K.* 14 F4
Paisley, *U.S.A.* 114 E3
Paita, *Peru* 124 E2
Paiva →, *Portugal* 34 D2
Paizhou, *China* 59 B9
Pajares, *Spain* 34 B5
Pajares, Puerto de, *Spain* 34 C5
Pajęczno, *Poland* 45 G5
Pak Lay, *Laos* 64 C3
Pak Phanang, *Thailand* 65 H3
Pak Sane, *Laos* 64 C4
Pak Song, *Laos* 64 E6
Pak Suong, *Laos* 58 H4
Pakaur, *India* 69 G12
Pakenham, *Canada* 111 A8
Pákhnes, *Greece* 36 D6
Pakhuis, *S. Africa* 88 E2
Pakistan ■, *Asia* 68 E4
Pakkading, *Laos* 64 C4
Pakokku, *Burma* 67 J19
Pakość, *Poland* 45 F5
Pakowki L., *Canada* 105 D6
Pakpattan, *Pakistan* 68 D5
Pakrac, *Croatia* 42 E2
Pakruojis, *Lithuania* 44 C10
Paks, *Hungary* 42 D3
Paktīā □, *Afghan.* 66 C6
Pakwach, *Uganda* 86 B3
Pakxe, *Laos* 64 E5
Pal Lahara, *India* 69 J11
Pala, *Chad* 79 G9
Pala, *Dem. Rep. of the Congo* 86 D2
Pala, *U.S.A.* 117 M9
Palabek, *Uganda* 86 B3
Palacios, *U.S.A.* 113 L6
Palafrugell, *Spain* 32 D8
Palagiano, *Italy* 31 B10
Palagonía, *Italy* 31 E7
Palagruža, *Croatia* 29 F13
Palaiókastron, *Greece* 36 D8
Palaiokhóra, *Greece* 36 D5
Pálairos, *Greece* 38 C2
Palaiseau, *France* 19 D9
Palam, *India* 66 K10
Palamás, *Greece* 38 B4
Palamòs, *Spain* 32 D8
Palampur, *India* 68 C7
Palamut, *Turkey* 39 C9
Palana, *Australia* 94 F4
Palana, *Russia* 51 D16
Palanan, *Phil.* 61 C5
Palanan Pt., *Phil.* 61 C5
Palandri, *Pakistan* 69 C5
Palanga, *Lithuania* 9 J19
Palangkaraya, *Indonesia* 62 E4
Palani Hills, *India* 66 P10
Palanpur, *India* 68 G5
Palapye, *Botswana* 88 C4
Palas, *Pakistan* 69 B5
Palas de Rei, *Spain* 34 C3
Palashi, *India* 69 H13
Palasponga, *India* 69 J11
Palatka, *Russia* 51 C16
Palatka, *U.S.A.* 109 L5
Palau, *Italy* 30 A2
Palau ■, *Pac. Oc.* 52 J17
Palauk, *Burma* 64 F2
Palawan, *Phil.* 61 G3
Palayankottai, *India* 66 Q10
Palazzo, Pte., *France* 21 F12
Palazzo San Gervásio, *Italy* 31 B8
Palazzolo Acréide, *Italy* 31 E7
Paldiski, *Estonia* 9 G21
Pale, *Bos.-H.* 42 G3
Paleleh, *Indonesia* 63 D6
Palembang, *Indonesia* 62 E2
Palencia, *Spain* 34 C6
Palencia □, *Spain* 34 C6
Palenque, *Mexico* 119 D6
Paleokastrítsa, *Greece* 36 A3
Paleometokho, *Cyprus* 36 D12
Palermo, *Italy* 30 D6
Palermo, *U.S.A.* 114 G3
Palestina, *Chile* 128 A3
Palestine, *Asia* 75 D4
Palestine, *U.S.A.* 113 K7
Palestrina, *Italy* 29 G9
Paletwa, *Burma* 67 J18
Palghat, *India* 66 P10
Palgrave, Mt., *Australia* 92 D2
Pali, *India* 68 G5
Palikir, *Micronesia* 96 G7
Palinuro, *Italy* 31 B8
Palinuro, C., *Italy* 31 B8
Palioúrion, Ákra, *Greece* 40 G7
Palisades Reservoir, *U.S.A.* 114 E8
Paliseul, *Belgium* 17 E5
Palitana, *India* 68 J4
Palizada, *Mexico* 119 D6
Palk Bay, *Asia* 66 Q11
Palk Strait, *Asia* 66 Q11
Palkānah, *Iraq* 70 C5
Palkot, *India* 69 H11
Palla Road = Dinokwe, *Botswana* 88 C4
Pallanza = Verbánia, *Italy* 28 C5
Pallarenda, *Australia* 94 B4
Pallasovka, *Russia* 48 E8
Pallës, Bishti i, *Albania* 40 E3
Pallinup →, *Australia* 93 F2
Pallisa, *Uganda* 86 B3
Pallu, *India* 68 E6
Palm Bay, *U.S.A.* 109 L5
Palm Beach, *U.S.A.* 109 M6
Palm Coast, *U.S.A.* 109 L5
Palm Desert, *U.S.A.* 117 M10
Palm Is., *Australia* 94 B4
Palm Springs, *U.S.A.* 117 M10
Palma, *Mozam.* 87 E5
Palma, B. de, *Spain* 37 B9
Palma de Mallorca, *Spain* 37 B9
Palma del Río, *Spain* 35 H5
Palma di Montechiaro, *Italy* 30 E6
Palma Soriano, *Cuba* 120 B4
Palmares, *Brazil* 125 E11
Palmarola, *Italy* 30 B5
Palmas, *Brazil* 127 B5
Palmas, C., *Liberia* 82 E3
Pálmas, G. di, *Italy* 30 D1
Palmdale, *U.S.A.* 117 L8
Palmeira das Missões, *Brazil* 127 B5
Palmeira dos Índios, *Brazil* 125 E11
Palmela, *Portugal* 35 G2
Palmer, *U.S.A.* 100 B5
Palmer →, *Australia* 94 B3
Palmer Arch., *Antarctica* 5 C17
Palmer Lake, *U.S.A.* 112 F2
Palmer Land, *Antarctica* 5 D18
Palmerston, *Canada* 110 C4
Palmerston, *N.Z.* 91 L3
Palmerston North, *N.Z.* 91 J5
Palmerton, *U.S.A.* 111 F9
Palmetto, *U.S.A.* 109 M4
Palmi, *Italy* 31 D8
Palmira, *Argentina* 126 C2
Palmira, *Colombia* 124 C3
Palmyra = Tudmur, *Syria* 70 C3
Palmyra, *Mo., U.S.A.* 112 F9
Palmyra, *N.J., U.S.A.* 111 F9
Palmyra, *N.Y., U.S.A.* 110 C7
Palmyra, *Pa., U.S.A.* 111 F8
Palmyra Is., *Pac. Oc.* 97 G11
Palo Alto, *U.S.A.* 116 H4
Palo Verde, *U.S.A.* 117 M12
Paloich, *Sudan* 81 E3
Palompon, *Phil.* 61 F6
Palopo, *Indonesia* 63 E6
Palos, C. de, *Spain* 33 H4
Palos de la Frontera, *Spain* 35 H4
Palos Verdes, *U.S.A.* 117 M8
Palos Verdes, Pt., *U.S.A.* 117 M8
Pålsboda, *Sweden* 10 E9
Palu, *Indonesia* 63 E5
Palu, *Turkey* 70 B3
Paluke, *Liberia* 82 D3
Paluzza, *Italy* 29 B10
Palwal, *India* 68 E7
Pama, *Burkina Faso* 83 C5
Pamanukan, *Indonesia* 63 G12
Pamiers, *France* 20 E5
Pamir, *Tajikistan* 50 F8
Pamlico →, *U.S.A.* 109 H7
Pamlico Sd., *U.S.A.* 109 H8
Pampa, *U.S.A.* 113 H4
Pampa de las Salinas, *Argentina* 126 C2
Pampanua, *Indonesia* 63 E6
Pampas, *Argentina* 126 D3
Pampas, *Peru* 124 F4
Pamphylia, *Turkey* 72 D4
Pamplona, *Colombia* 124 B4
Pamplona, *Spain* 32 C3
Pampoenpoort, *S. Africa* 88 E3
Pamukçu, *Turkey* 39 B9
Pamukkale, *Turkey* 39 D11
Pan Xian, *China* 58 E5
Pana, *U.S.A.* 112 F10
Panabo, *Phil.* 61 H6
Panaca, *U.S.A.* 115 H6
Panagyurishte, *Bulgaria* 41 D8
Panaitan, *Indonesia* 63 G11
Panaji, *India* 66 M8
Panamá, *Panama* 120 E4
Panama ■, *Cent. Amer.* 120 E4
Panamá, G. de, *Panama* 120 E4
Panama Canal, *Panama* 120 E4
Panama City, *U.S.A.* 109 K3
Panamint Range, *U.S.A.* 117 J9
Panamint Springs, *U.S.A.* 117 J9
Panão, *Peru* 124 E3
Panaon I., *Phil.* 61 F6
Panare, *Thailand* 65 J3
Panarea, *Italy* 31 D8
Panaro →, *Italy* 29 D8
Panay, *Phil.* 61 F5
Panay, G., *Phil.* 63 B6
Pančevo, *Serbia, Yug.* 42 F5
Panch'iao, *Taiwan* 59 E13
Panciu, *Romania* 43 E12
Pancorbo, Desfiladero, *Spain* 34 C7
Pâncota, *Romania* 42 D6
Panda, *Mozam.* 89 C5
Pandan, *Antique, Phil.* 61 F5
Pandan, *Catanduanes, Phil.* 61 D6
Pandegelang, *Indonesia* 63 G12
Pandhana, *India* 68 J7
Pandharpur, *India* 66 L9
Pando, *Uruguay* 127 C4
Pando, L. = Hope, L., *Australia* 95 D2
Pandokrátor, *Greece* 36 A3
Pandora, *Costa Rica* 120 E3
Pandrup, *Denmark* 11 G3
Panevėžys, *Lithuania* 9 J21
Panfilov, *Kazakstan* 50 E8
Panfilovo, *Russia* 48 E6
Pang-Long, *Burma* 67 H21
Pang-Yang, *Burma* 67 H21
Panga, *Dem. Rep. of the Congo* 86 B2
Pangaíon Óros, *Greece* 41 F8
Pangalanes, Canal des = Ampangalana, Lakandranon', *Madag.* 89 C8
Pangani, *Tanzania* 86 D4
Pangani →, *Tanzania* 86 D4
Pangfou = Bengbu, *China* 57 H9
Pangil, *Dem. Rep. of the Congo* 86 C2
Pangkah, Tanjung, *Indonesia* 63 G15
Pangkajene, *Indonesia* 63 E5
Pangkalanbrandan, *Indonesia* 62 D1
Pangkalanbuun, *Indonesia* 62 E4
Pangkalpinang, *Indonesia* 62 E3
Pangnirtung, *Canada* 101 B13
Pangong Tso, *India* 68 B8
Panguitch, *U.S.A.* 115 H7
Pangutaran Group, *Phil.* 61 H4
Panhandle, *U.S.A.* 113 H4
Pani Mines, *India* 68 H5
Pania-Mutombo, *Dem. Rep. of the Congo* 86 D1
Panikota I., *India* 68 J4
Panipat, *India* 68 E7
Panjal Range, *India* 68 C7
Panjang, Hon, *Vietnam* 65 H4
Panjgur, *Pakistan* 66 F4
Panjim = Panaji, *India* 66 M8
Panjin, *China* 57 D12
Panjinad Barrage, *Pakistan* 66 E7
Panjnad →, *Pakistan* 68 E4
Panjwai, *Afghan.* 68 D1
Pankshin, *Nigeria* 83 D6
Panmunjŏm, *N. Korea* 57 F14
Panna, *India* 69 G9
Panna Hills, *India* 69 G9
Pannawonica, *Australia* 92 D2
Pannirtuuq = Pangnirtung, *Canada* 101 B13
Pano Akil, *Pakistan* 68 F3
Pano Lefkara, *Cyprus* 36 E12
Pano Panayia, *Cyprus* 36 E11
Panorama, *Brazil* 127 A5
Pánormon, *Greece* 36 D6
Pansemal, *India* 68 J6
Panshan = Panjin, *China* 57 D12
Panshi, *China* 57 C14
Pantanal, *Brazil* 124 H7
Pantar, *Indonesia* 63 F6
Pante Macassar, *E. Timor* 63 F6
Pante Makasar = Pante Macassar, *E. Timor* 63 F6
Pantelleria, *Italy* 30 F4
Pantón, *Spain* 34 C3
Pánuco, *Mexico* 119 C5
Panyam, *Nigeria* 83 D6
Panyu, *China* 59 F9
Panzhihua, *China* 58 D3
Páola, *Italy* 31 C9
Paola, *Malta* 36 D2
Paola, *U.S.A.* 112 F7
Paonia, *U.S.A.* 115 G10
Paoting = Baoding, *China* 56 E8
Paot'ou = Baotou, *China* 56 D6
Paoua, *C.A.R.* 84 C3
Pápa, *Hungary* 42 C2
Papa Stour, *U.K.* 14 A7
Papa Westray, *U.K.* 14 B6
Papagayo →, *Mexico* 119 D5
Papagayo, G. de, *Costa Rica* 120 D2
Papakura, *N.Z.* 91 G5
Papantla, *Mexico* 119 C5
Papar, *Malaysia* 62 C5
Pápas, Ákra, *Greece* 38 C3
Papeete, *Tahiti* 97 J13
Papenburg, *Germany* 24 B3
Paphlagonia, *Turkey* 72 B5
Paphos, *Cyprus* 36 E11
Papien Chiang = Da →, *Vietnam* 58 G5
Papigochic →, *Mexico* 118 B3
Paposo, *Chile* 126 B1
Papoutsa, *Cyprus* 36 E12
Papua New Guinea ■, *Oceania* 96 H6
Papudo, *Chile* 126 C1
Papuk, *Croatia* 42 E2
Papun, *Burma* 67 K20
Papunya, *Australia* 92 D5
Pará = Belém, *Brazil* 125 D9
Pará □, *Brazil* 125 D8
Paraburdoo, *Australia* 92 D2
Paracale, *Phil.* 61 D5
Paracatu, *Brazil* 125 G9
Paracel Is., *S. China Sea* 62 A4
Parachinar, *Pakistan* 68 C4
Paraćin, *Serbia, Yug.* 40 C5
Paradas, *Spain* 35 H5
Paradela, *Spain* 34 C3
Paradhísi, *Greece* 36 C10
Paradip, *India* 67 J15
Paradise, *Calif., U.S.A.* 116 F5
Paradise, *Nev., U.S.A.* 117 J11
Paradise →, *Canada* 103 B8
Paradise Hill, *Canada* 105 C7
Paradise River, *Canada* 103 B8
Paradise Valley, *U.S.A.* 114 F5
Parado, *Indonesia* 63 F5
Paragould, *U.S.A.* 113 G9
Paragua →, *Venezuela* 124 B6
Paraguaçu →, *Brazil* 125 F11
Paraguaçu Paulista, *Brazil* 127 A5
Paraguaná, Pen. de, *Venezuela* 124 A5
Paraguarí, *Paraguay* 126 B4
Paraguarí □, *Paraguay* 126 B4
Paraguay ■, *S. Amer.* 126 A4
Paraguay →, *Paraguay* 126 B4
Paraíba = João Pessoa, *Brazil* 125 E12
Paraíba □, *Brazil* 125 E11
Paraíba do Sul →, *Brazil* 127 A7
Parainen, *Finland* 9 F20
Paraiso, *Mexico* 119 D6
Parak, *Iran* 71 E7
Parakhino Paddubye, *Russia* 46 C7
Parakou, *Benin* 83 D5
Paralimni, *Cyprus* 36 D12
Parálion-Astrous, *Greece* 38 D4
Paramaribo, *Surinam* 125 B7
Paramithiá, *Greece* 38 B2
Paramushir, Ostrov, *Russia* 51 D16
Paran →, *Israel* 75 E4
Paraná, *Argentina* 126 C3
Paraná, *Brazil* 125 F9
Paraná □, *Brazil* 127 A5
Paraná →, *Argentina* 126 C4
Paranaguá, *Brazil* 127 B6
Paranaíba, *Brazil* 125 G8
Paranaíba →, *Brazil* 125 H8
Paranapanema →, *Brazil* 127 A5
Paranapiacaba, Serra do, *Brazil* 127 A6
Paranas, *Phil.* 61 F6
Paranavaí, *Brazil* 127 A5
Parang, *Maguindanao, Phil.* 63 C6
Parang, *Sulu, Phil.* 61 J4
Parângul Mare, Vf., *Romania* 43 E8
Paraparaumu, *N.Z.* 91 J5
Parapóla, *Greece* 38 E5
Paraspóri, Ákra, *Greece* 39 F9
Paray-le-Monial, *France* 19 F11
Parbati →, *Mad. P., India* 68 G7
Parbati →, *Raj., India* 68 F7
Parbhani, *India* 66 K10
Parchim, *Germany* 24 B7
Parczew, *Poland* 45 G9
Pardes Hanna-Karkur, *Israel* 75 C3
Pardilla, *Spain* 34 D7
Pardo →, *Bahia, Brazil* 125 G11
Pardo →, *Mato Grosso, Brazil* 127 A5
Pardubice, *Czech Rep.* 26 A8
Pare, *Indonesia* 63 G15
Pare Mts., *Tanzania* 86 C4
Parecis, Serra dos, *Brazil* 124 F7
Paredes de Nava, *Spain* 34 C6
Paren, *Russia* 51 C17
Parent, *Canada* 102 C5
Parent, L., *Canada* 102 C4
Parentis-en-Born, *France* 20 D2
Parepare, *Indonesia* 63 E5
Parfino, *Russia* 46 D6
Párga, *Greece* 38 B2
Pargo, Pta. do, *Madeira* 37 D2
Pariaguán, *Venezuela* 124 B6
Paricutín, Cerro, *Mexico* 118 D4
Parigi, *Indonesia* 63 E6
Parika, *Guyana* 124 B7
Parikkala, *Finland* 46 B5
Parima, Serra, *Brazil* 124 C6
Parinari, *Peru* 124 D4
Pariñas, Pta., *S. Amer.* 122 D2
Parincea, *Romania* 43 D12
Parintins, *Brazil* 125 D7
Pariparit Kyun, *Burma* 67 M18
Paris, *Canada* 110 C4
Paris, *France* 19 D9
Paris, *Idaho, U.S.A.* 114 E8
Paris, *Ky., U.S.A.* 108 F3
Paris, *Tenn., U.S.A.* 109 G1
Paris, *Tex., U.S.A.* 113 J7
Paris, Ville de □, *France* 19 D9
Parish, *U.S.A.* 111 C8
Parishville, *U.S.A.* 111 B10
Park, *U.S.A.* 116 B4
Park City, *U.S.A.* 113 G6
Park Falls, *U.S.A.* 112 C9
Park Head, *Canada* 110 B3
Park Hills, *U.S.A.* 113 G9
Park Range, *U.S.A.* 114 G10
Park Rapids, *U.S.A.* 112 B7
Park River, *U.S.A.* 112 A6
Park Rynie, *S. Africa* 89 E5
Parkā Bandar, *Iran* 71 E8
Parkano, *Finland* 9 E20
Parker, *Ariz., U.S.A.* 117 L12
Parker, *Pa., U.S.A.* 110 E5
Parker Dam, *U.S.A.* 117 L12
Parkersburg, *U.S.A.* 108 F5
Parkfield, *U.S.A.* 116 K6
Parkhill, *Canada* 110 C3
Parkland, *U.S.A.* 116 C4
Parkston, *U.S.A.* 112 D6
Parksville, *Canada* 104 D4
Parla, *Spain* 34 E7
Pârliţa, *Moldova* 43 C12
Parma, *Italy* 28 D7
Parma, *Idaho, U.S.A.* 114 E5
Parma, *Ohio, U.S.A.* 110 E3
Parma →, *Italy* 28 D7
Parnaguá, *Brazil* 125 F10
Parnaíba, *Brazil* 125 D10
Parnaíba →, *Brazil* 122 D6
Parnassós, *Greece* 38 C4
Párnis, *Greece* 38 C5
Párnon Óros, *Greece* 38 D4
Pärnu, *Estonia* 9 G21
Páros, *Greece* 39 D7
Parowan, *U.S.A.* 115 H7
Parpaillon, *France* 21 D10
Parral, *Chile* 126 D1
Parras, *Mexico* 118 B4
Parrett →, *U.K.* 13 F4
Parris I., *U.S.A.* 109 J5
Parrsboro, *Canada* 103 C7
Parry I., *Canada* 110 A4
Parry Is., *Canada* 4 B2
Parry Sound, *Canada* 102 C4
Parsberg, *Germany* 25 F7
Parsęta →, *Poland* 44 D2
Parsnip →, *Canada* 104 B4
Parsons, *U.S.A.* 113 G7
Parsons Ra., *Australia* 94 A2
Partanna, *Italy* 30 E5
Parthenay, *France* 18 F6
Partinico, *Italy* 30 D6
Partizánske, *Slovak Rep.* 27 C11
Partridge I., *Canada* 102 A2
Paru →, *Brazil* 125 D8
Parvān □, *Afghan.* 66 B6
Parvatipuram, *India* 67 K13
Parvatsar, *India* 68 F6
Påryd, *Sweden* 11 H9
Parys, *S. Africa* 88 D4
Pas, Pta. des, *Spain* 37 C7
Pas-de-Calais □, *France* 19 B9
Pasada, *Spain* 34 B5
Pasadena, *Canada* 103 C8
Pasadena, *Calif., U.S.A.* 117 L8
Pasadena, *Tex., U.S.A.* 113 L7
Pasaje →, *Argentina* 126 B3

Paşalimanı, *Turkey* 41 F11
Pasay, *Phil.* 61 D4
Pascagoula, *U.S.A.* 113 K10
Pascagoula →, *U.S.A.* 113 K10
Paşcani, *Romania* 43 C11
Pasco, *U.S.A.* 114 C4
Pasco, Cerro de, *Peru* 124 F3
Pasco I., *Australia* 92 D2
Pascoag, *U.S.A.* 111 E13
Pascua, I. de, *Pac. Oc.* 97 K17
Pasewalk, *Germany* 24 B9
Pasfield L., *Canada* 105 B7
Pasha →, *Russia* 46 B7
Pashmakli = Smolyan, *Bulgaria* 41 E8
Pasinler, *Turkey* 73 C9
Pasir Mas, *Malaysia* 65 J4
Pasir Putih, *Malaysia* 65 K4
Pasirian, *Indonesia* 63 H15
Pasirkuning, *Indonesia* 62 E2
Påskallavik, *Sweden* 11 G10
Pasküh, *Iran* 71 E9
Pasłęk, *Poland* 44 D6
Pasłęka →, *Poland* 44 D6
Pasley, C., *Australia* 93 F3
Pašman, *Croatia* 29 E12
Pasni, *Pakistan* 66 G3
Paso Cantinela, *Mexico* 117 N11
Paso de Indios, *Argentina* 128 E3
Paso de los Libres, *Argentina* 126 B4
Paso de los Toros, *Uruguay* 126 C4
Paso Robles, *U.S.A.* 115 J3
Paspébiac, *Canada* 103 C6
Pasrur, *Pakistan* 68 C6
Passage West, *Ireland* 15 E3
Passaic, *U.S.A.* 111 F10
Passau, *Germany* 25 G9
Passero, C., *Italy* 31 F8
Passo Fundo, *Brazil* 127 B5
Passos, *Brazil* 125 H9
Passow, *Germany* 24 B10
Passy, *France* 21 C10
Pastavy, *Belarus* 9 J22
Pastaza →, *Peru* 124 D3
Pasto, *Colombia* 124 C3
Pastrana, *Spain* 32 E2
Pasuruan, *Indonesia* 63 G15
Pasym, *Poland* 44 E7
Pásztó, *Hungary* 42 C4
Patagonia, *Argentina* 122 H4
Patagonia, *U.S.A.* 115 L8
Patambar, *Iran* 71 D9
Patan, *Gujarat, India* 66 H8
Patan, *Maharashtra, India* 68 H5
Patani, *Indonesia* 63 D7
Pătârlagele, *Romania* 43 E11
Pataudi, *India* 68 E7
Patchogue, *U.S.A.* 111 F11
Patea, *N.Z.* 91 H5
Pategi, *Nigeria* 83 D6
Patensie, *S. Africa* 88 E3
Paterna, *Spain* 33 F4
Paternion, *Austria* 26 E6
Paternò, *Italy* 31 E7
Pateros, *U.S.A.* 114 B4
Paterson, *U.S.A.* 111 F10
Paterson Ra., *Australia* 92 D3
Pathankot, *India* 68 C6
Pathfinder Reservoir, *U.S.A.* 114 E10
Pathiu, *Thailand* 65 G2
Pathum Thani, *Thailand* 64 E3
Pati, *Indonesia* 63 G14
Patía →, *Colombia* 124 C3
Patiala, *Punjab, India* 68 D7
Patiala, *Ut. P., India* 69 F8
Patine Kouka, *Senegal* 82 C2
Patitírion, *Greece* 38 B5
Patkai Bum, *India* 67 F19
Pátmos, *Greece* 39 D8
Patna, *India* 69 G11
Patnos, *Turkey* 73 C10
Pato Branco, *Brazil* 127 B5
Patonga, *Uganda* 86 B3
Patos, *Albania* 40 F3
Patos, *Brazil* 125 E11
Patos, L. dos, *Brazil* 127 C5
Patos, Río de los →, *Argentina* 126 C2
Patos de Minas, *Brazil* 125 G9
Patquía, *Argentina* 126 C2
Pátrai, *Greece* 38 C3
Pátraikós Kólpos, *Greece* 38 C3
Patras = Pátrai, *Greece* 38 C3
Patrocínio, *Brazil* 125 G9
Patta, *Kenya* 86 C5
Pattada, *Italy* 30 B2
Pattani, *Thailand* 65 J3
Pattaya, *Thailand* 62 B2
Patten, *U.S.A.* 109 C11
Patterson, *Calif., U.S.A.* 116 H5
Patterson, *La., U.S.A.* 113 L9
Patterson, Mt., *U.S.A.* 116 G7
Patti, *Punjab, India* 68 D6
Patti, *Ut. P., India* 69 G10
Patti, *Italy* 31 D7
Pattoki, *Pakistan* 68 D5
Patton, *U.S.A.* 110 F6
Patuakhali, *Bangla.* 67 H17
Patuanak, *Canada* 105 B7
Patuca →, *Honduras* 120 C3
Patuca, Punta, *Honduras* 120 C3
Pătulele, *Romania* 42 F7
Pátzcuaro, *Mexico* 118 D4
Pau, *France* 20 E3
Pau, Gave de →, *France* 20 E2
Pauillac, *France* 20 C3
Pauk, *Burma* 67 J19
Paul I., *Canada* 103 A7
Paul Smiths, *U.S.A.* 111 B10
Paulatuk, *Canada* 100 B7
Paulhan, *France* 20 E7
Paulis = Isiro, *Dem. Rep. of the Congo* 86 B2
Paulistana, *Brazil* 125 E10
Paulo Afonso, *Brazil* 125 E11
Paulpietersburg, *S. Africa* 89 D5
Pauls Valley, *U.S.A.* 113 H6
Pauma Valley, *U.S.A.* 117 M10
Pauri, *India* 69 D8
Pāveh, *Iran* 70 C5
Pavelets, *Russia* 46 F10
Pavia, *Italy* 28 C6
Pavilion, *U.S.A.* 110 D6
Pavilly, *France* 18 C7
Pāvilosta, *Latvia* 9 H19
Pavlikeni, *Bulgaria* 41 C9
Pavlodar, *Kazakstan* 50 D8
Pavlograd = Pavlohrad, *Ukraine* 47 H8
Pavlohrad, *Ukraine* 47 H8
Pavlovo, *Russia* 48 C6
Pavlovsk, *Russia* 48 E5
Pavlovskaya, *Russia* 49 G4
Pavlovskiy-Posad, *Russia* 46 E10
Pavullo nel Frignano, *Italy* 28 D7
Pawayan, *India* 69 E9
Pawhuska, *U.S.A.* 113 G6
Pawling, *U.S.A.* 111 E11
Pawnee, *U.S.A.* 113 G6
Pawnee City, *U.S.A.* 112 E6
Pawtucket, *U.S.A.* 111 E13
Paximádhia, *Greece* 36 E6
Paxoí, *Greece* 38 B2
Paxton, *Ill., U.S.A.* 108 E1
Paxton, *Nebr., U.S.A.* 112 E4
Payakumbuh, *Indonesia* 62 E2
Payerne, *Switz.* 25 J2
Payette, *U.S.A.* 114 D5
Paymogo, *Spain* 35 H3
Payne Bay = Kangirsuk, *Canada* 101 B13
Payne L., *Canada* 101 C12
Paynes Find, *Australia* 93 E2
Paynesville, *Liberia* 82 D2
Paynesville, *U.S.A.* 112 C7
Pays de la Loire □, *France* 18 E6
Paysandú, *Uruguay* 126 C4
Payson, *U.S.A.* 115 J8
Paz →, *Guatemala* 120 D1
Paz, B. de la, *Mexico* 118 C2
Pāzanān, *Iran* 71 D6
Pazar, *Turkey* 73 B9
Pazarcık, *Turkey* 72 D7
Pazardzhik, *Bulgaria* 41 D8
Pazarköy, *Turkey* 39 B9
Pazarlar, *Turkey* 39 C11
Pazaryeri, *Turkey* 39 B11
Pazaryolu, *Turkey* 73 B9
Pazin, *Croatia* 29 C10
Pčinja →, *Macedonia* 40 E5
Pe Ell, *U.S.A.* 116 D3
Peabody, *U.S.A.* 111 D14
Peace →, *Canada* 104 B6
Peace Point, *Canada* 104 B6
Peace River, *Canada* 104 B5
Peach Springs, *U.S.A.* 115 J7
Peachland, *Canada* 104 D5
Peachtree City, *U.S.A.* 109 J3
Peak, The = Kinder Scout, *U.K.* 12 D6
Peak District, *U.K.* 12 D6
Peak Hill, *Australia* 93 E2
Peak Ra., *Australia* 94 C4
Peake Cr. →, *Australia* 95 D2
Peal de Becerro, *Spain* 35 H7
Peale, Mt., *U.S.A.* 115 G9
Pearblossom, *U.S.A.* 117 L9
Pearl →, *U.S.A.* 113 K10
Pearl City, *U.S.A.* 106 H16
Pearl Harbor, *U.S.A.* 106 H16
Pearl River, *U.S.A.* 111 E10
Pearsall, *U.S.A.* 113 L5
Peary Land, *Greenland* 4 A6
Pease →, *U.S.A.* 113 H5
Peawanuck, *Canada* 101 C11
Pebane, *Mozam.* 87 F4
Pebas, *Peru* 124 D4
Pebble Beach, *U.S.A.* 116 J5
Peć, *Kosovo, Yug.* 40 D4
Pécciolì, *Italy* 28 E7
Pechea, *Romania* 43 E12
Pechenga, *Russia* 50 C4
Pechenizhyn, *Ukraine* 47 H3
Pechiguera, Pta., *Canary Is.* 37 F6
Pechnezhskoye Vdkhr., *Ukraine* 47 G9
Pechora, *Russia* 50 C6
Pechora →, *Russia* 50 C6
Pechorskaya Guba, *Russia* 50 C6
Pecica, *Romania* 42 D6
Pecka, *Serbia, Yug.* 40 B3
Pécora, C., *Italy* 30 C1
Pečory, *Russia* 9 H22
Pecos, *U.S.A.* 113 K3
Pecos →, *U.S.A.* 113 L3
Pécs, *Hungary* 42 D3
Pedder, L., *Australia* 94 G4
Peddie, *S. Africa* 89 E4
Pedernales, *Dom. Rep.* 121 C5
Pedieos →, *Cyprus* 36 D12
Pedirka, *Australia* 95 D2
Pedra Azul, *Brazil* 125 G10
Pedreguer, *Spain* 33 G5
Pedreiras, *Brazil* 125 D10
Pedro Afonso, *Brazil* 125 E9
Pedro Cays, *Jamaica* 120 C4
Pedro de Valdivia, *Chile* 126 A2
Pedro Juan Caballero, *Paraguay* 127 A4
Pedro Muñoz, *Spain* 35 F8
Pedrógão Grande, *Portugal* 34 F2
Pee Dee →, *U.S.A.* 109 J6
Peebles, *U.K.* 14 F5
Peekskill, *U.S.A.* 111 E11
Peel, *U.K.* 12 C3
Peel →, *Canada* 100 B6
Peel Sound, *Canada* 100 A10
Peene →, *Germany* 24 A9
Peera Peera Poolanna L., *Australia* 95 D2
Peerless Lake, *Canada* 104 B6
Peers, *Canada* 104 C5
Pegasus Bay, *N.Z.* 91 K4
Peggau, *Austria* 26 D8
Pegnitz, *Germany* 25 F7
Pegnitz →, *Germany* 25 F6
Pego, *Spain* 33 G4
Pegu, *Burma* 67 L20
Pegu Yoma, *Burma* 67 K20
Pehčevo, *Macedonia* 40 E6
Pehlivanköy, *Turkey* 41 E10
Pehuajó, *Argentina* 126 D3
Pei Xian = Pizhou, *China* 56 G9
Peine, *Chile* 126 A2
Peine, *Germany* 24 C6
Peip'ing = Beijing, *China* 56 E9
Peipus, L. = Chudskoye, Ozero, *Russia* 9 G22
Peissenberg, *Germany* 25 H7
Peitz, *Germany* 24 D10
Peixe, *Brazil* 125 F9
Peixe →, *Brazil* 125 H8
Pek →, *Serbia, Yug.* 40 B5
Pekalongan, *Indonesia* 62 F3
Pekan, *Malaysia* 65 L4
Pekanbaru, *Indonesia* 62 D2
Pekang, *Taiwan* 59 F13
Pekin, *U.S.A.* 112 E10
Peking = Beijing, *China* 56 E9
Péla, *Guinea* 82 D3
Pelabuhan Kelang, *Malaysia* 65 L3
Pelabuhan Ratu, Teluk, *Indonesia* 63 G12
Pelabuhanratu, *Indonesia* 63 G12
Pélagos, *Greece* 38 B6
Pelaihari, *Indonesia* 62 E4
Pelat, Mt., *France* 21 D10
Pełczyce, *Poland* 45 E2
Peleaga, Vf., *Romania* 42 E7
Pelée, Mt., *Martinique* 121 D7
Pelee, Pt., *Canada* 102 D3
Pelee I., *Canada* 102 D3
Pelekech, *Kenya* 86 B4
Peleng, *Indonesia* 63 E6
Pélézi, *Ivory C.* 82 D3
Pelhřimov, *Czech Rep.* 26 B8
Pelican, *U.S.A.* 104 B1
Pelican L., *Canada* 105 C8
Pelican Narrows, *Canada* 105 B8
Pelješac, *Croatia* 29 F14
Pelkosenniemi, *Finland* 8 C22
Pella, *Greece* 40 F6
Pella, *S. Africa* 88 D2
Pella, *U.S.A.* 112 E8
Péllà □, *Greece* 40 F6
Pello, *Finland* 8 C21
Pellworm, *Germany* 24 A4
Pelly →, *Canada* 100 B6
Pelly Bay, *Canada* 101 B11
Peloponnese = Pelopónnisos □, *Greece* 38 D4
Pelopónnisos □, *Greece* 38 D4
Peloritani, Monti, *Italy* 31 D8
Pelorus Sd., *N.Z.* 91 J4
Pelotas, *Brazil* 127 C5
Pelotas →, *Brazil* 127 B5
Pelovo, *Bulgaria* 41 C8
Pelplin, *Poland* 44 E5
Pelvoux, Massif du, *France* 21 D10
Pemalang, *Indonesia* 63 G13
Pemanggil, Pulau, *Malaysia* 65 L5
Pematangsiantar, *Indonesia* 62 D1
Pemba, *Mozam.* 87 E5
Pemba, *Zambia* 87 F2
Pemba Channel, *Tanzania* 86 D4
Pemba I., *Tanzania* 86 D4
Pemberton, *Australia* 93 F2
Pemberton, *Canada* 104 C4
Pembina, *U.S.A.* 112 A6
Pembroke, *Canada* 102 C4
Pembroke, *U.K.* 13 F3
Pembrokeshire □, *U.K.* 13 F3
Pen-y-Ghent, *U.K.* 12 C5
Peña, Sierra de la, *Spain* 32 C4
Peña de Francia, Sierra de la, *Spain* 34 E4
Penafiel, *Portugal* 34 D2
Peñafiel, *Spain* 34 D6
Peñaflor, *Spain* 35 H5
Peñalara, *Spain* 34 E7
Penamacôr, *Portugal* 34 E3
Penang = Pinang, *Malaysia* 65 K3
Penápolis, *Brazil* 127 A6
Peñaranda de Bracamonte, *Spain* 34 E5
Peñarroya, *Spain* 32 E4
Peñarroya-Pueblonuevo, *Spain* 35 G5
Penarth, *U.K.* 13 F4
Peñas, C. de, *Spain* 34 B5
Penas, G. de, *Chile* 122 H3
Peñas de San Pedro, *Spain* 33 G3
Peñas del Chache, *Canary Is.* 37 E6
Peñausende, *Spain* 34 D5
Pench'i = Benxi, *China* 57 D12
Pend Oreille →, *U.S.A.* 114 B5
Pend Oreille, L., *U.S.A.* 114 C5
Pendálofon, *Greece* 40 F5
Pendembu, *Eastern, S. Leone* 82 D2
Pendembu, *Northern, S. Leone* 82 D2
Pender B., *Australia* 92 C3
Pendik, *Turkey* 41 F13
Pendjari →, *Benin* 83 C5
Pendleton, *U.S.A.* 114 D4
Pendra, *India* 69 H9
Penedo, *Brazil* 125 F11
Penetanguishene, *Canada* 102 D4
Penfield, *U.S.A.* 110 E6
Pengalengan, *Indonesia* 63 G12
Penge, *Kasai-Or., Dem. Rep. of the Congo* 86 D1
Penge, *Sud-Kivu, Dem. Rep. of the Congo* 86 C2
Penghu, *Taiwan* 59 F12
Penglai, *China* 57 F11
Pengshan, *China* 58 B4
Pengshui, *China* 58 C7
Penguin, *Australia* 94 G4
Pengxi, *China* 58 B5
Pengze, *China* 59 C11
Penhalonga, *Zimbabwe* 87 F3
Peniche, *Portugal* 35 F1
Penicuik, *U.K.* 14 F5
Penida, *Indonesia* 62 F5
Peninnes, Alpes = Pennine, Alpi, *Alps* 25 J3
Peninsular Malaysia □, *Malaysia* 65 L4
Peñíscola, *Spain* 32 E5
Penitente, Serra do, *Brazil* 125 E9
Penkridge, *U.K.* 12 E5
Penmarch, *France* 18 E2
Penmarch, Pte. de, *France* 18 E2
Penn Hills, *U.S.A.* 110 F5
Penn Yan, *U.S.A.* 110 D7
Penna, Punta della, *Italy* 29 F11
Pennant, *Canada* 105 C7
Penne, *Italy* 29 F10
Penner →, *India* 66 M12
Pennine, Alpi, *Alps* 25 J3
Pennines, *U.K.* 12 C5
Pennington, *U.S.A.* 116 F5
Pennington →, *Nigeria* 83 E6
Pennino, Mte., *Italy* 29 E9
Pennsburg, *U.S.A.* 111 F9
Pennsylvania □, *U.S.A.* 108 E7
Penny, *Canada* 104 C4
Peno, *Russia* 46 D7
Penobscot →, *U.S.A.* 109 C11
Penobscot B., *U.S.A.* 109 C11
Penong, *Australia* 93 F5
Penonomé, *Panama* 120 E3
Penrith, *U.K.* 12 C5
Penryn, *U.K.* 13 G2
Pensacola, *U.S.A.* 109 K2
Pensacola Mts., *Antarctica* 5 E1
Pense, *Canada* 105 C8
Penticton, *Canada* 104 D5
Pentland, *Australia* 94 C4
Pentland Firth, *U.K.* 14 C5
Pentland Hills, *U.K.* 14 F5
Penza, *Russia* 48 D7
Penzance, *U.K.* 13 G2
Penzberg, *Germany* 25 H7
Penzhino, *Russia* 51 C17
Penzhinskaya Guba, *Russia* 51 C17
Penzhou, *China* 58 B4
Penzlin, *Germany* 24 B9
Peoria, *Ariz., U.S.A.* 115 K7
Peoria, *Ill., U.S.A.* 112 E10
Pepacton Reservoir, *U.S.A.* 111 D10
Pepani →, *S. Africa* 88 D3
Pepel, *S. Leone* 82 D2
Peqin, *Albania* 40 E3
Pera Hd., *Australia* 94 A3
Perabumulih, *Indonesia* 62 E2
Perak →, *Malaysia* 65 K3
Perakhóra, *Greece* 38 C4
Perales de Alfambra, *Spain* 32 E4
Perales del Puerto, *Spain* 34 E4
Pérama, *Kérkira, Greece* 36 A3
Pérama, *Kríti, Greece* 36 D6
Peräpohjola, *Finland* 8 C22
Perast, *Montenegro, Yug.* 40 D2
Percé, *Canada* 103 C7
Perche, *France* 18 D8
Perchtoldsdorf, *Austria* 27 C9
Percival Lakes, *Australia* 92 D4
Percy, *France* 18 D5
Percy Is., *Australia* 94 C5
Perdido, Mte., *Spain* 32 C5
Perdu, Mt. = Perdido, Mte., *Spain* 32 C5
Pereira, *Colombia* 124 C3
Perelazovskiy, *Russia* 49 F6
Perenjori, *Australia* 93 E2
Peresecina, *Moldova* 43 C13
Pereslavl-Zalesskiy, *Russia* 46 D10
Peretu, *Romania* 43 F10
Pereyaslav-Khmelnytskyy, *Ukraine* 47 G6
Pérez, I., *Mexico* 119 C7
Perg, *Austria* 26 C7
Pergamino, *Argentina* 126 C3
Pergau →, *Malaysia* 65 K3
Pérgine Valsugana, *Italy* 29 B8
Pérgola, *Italy* 29 E9
Perham, *U.S.A.* 112 B7
Perhentian, Kepulauan, *Malaysia* 62 C2
Periam, *Romania* 42 D5
Péribonca →, *Canada* 103 C5
Péribonca, L., *Canada* 103 B5
Perico, *Argentina* 126 A2
Pericos, *Mexico* 118 B3
Périers, *France* 18 C5
Périgord, *France* 20 D4
Périgueux, *France* 20 C4
Perijá, Sierra de, *Colombia* 124 B4
Peristéra, *Greece* 38 B5
Peristerona →, *Cyprus* 36 D12
Perito Moreno, *Argentina* 128 F2
Perivol = Dragovishtitsa, *Bulgaria* 40 D6
Perkasie, *U.S.A.* 111 F9
Perković, *Croatia* 29 E13
Perlas, Arch. de las, *Panama* 120 E4
Perlas, Punta de, *Nic.* 120 D3
Perleberg, *Germany* 24 B7
Perlez, *Serbia, Yug.* 42 E5
Perm, *Russia* 50 D6
Përmet, *Albania* 40 F4
Pernambuco = Recife, *Brazil* 125 E12
Pernambuco □, *Brazil* 125 E11
Pernik, *Bulgaria* 40 D7
Peron Is., *Australia* 92 B5
Peron Pen., *Australia* 93 E1
Péronne, *France* 19 C9
Perosa Argentina, *Italy* 28 D4
Perow, *Canada* 104 C3
Perpendicular Pt., *Australia* 95 E5
Perpignan, *France* 20 F6
Perris, *U.S.A.* 117 M9
Perros-Guirec, *France* 18 D3
Perry, *Fla., U.S.A.* 109 K4
Perry, *Ga., U.S.A.* 109 J4
Perry, *Iowa, U.S.A.* 112 E7
Perry, *Okla., U.S.A.* 113 G6
Perryton, *U.S.A.* 113 G4
Perryville, *U.S.A.* 113 G10
Persan, *France* 19 C9
Persberg, *Sweden* 10 E8
Perşembe, *Turkey* 72 B7
Persepolis, *Iran* 71 D7
Pershotravensk, *Ukraine* 47 G4
Persia = Iran ■, *Asia* 71 C7
Persian Gulf = Gulf, The, *Asia* 71 E6
Perstorp, *Sweden* 11 H7
Pertek, *Turkey* 73 C8
Perth, *Australia* 93 F2
Perth, *Canada* 102 D4
Perth, *U.K.* 14 E5
Perth & Kinross □, *U.K.* 14 E5
Perth Amboy, *U.S.A.* 111 F10
Perth-Andover, *Canada* 103 C6
Pertuis, *France* 21 E9
Pertusato, C., *France* 21 G13
Peru, *Ind., U.S.A.* 108 E2
Peru, *N.Y., U.S.A.* 111 B11
Peru ■, *S. Amer.* 124 D4
Peru Basin, *Pac. Oc.* 97 J18
Peru-Chile Trench, *Pac. Oc.* 124 G3
Perúgia, *Italy* 29 E9
Perušić, *Croatia* 29 D12
Pervomaysk, *Russia* 48 C6
Pervomaysk, *Ukraine* 47 H6
Pervouralsk, *Russia* 50 D6
Pésaro, *Italy* 29 E9
Pescadores = Penghu, *Taiwan* 59 F12
Pescara, *Italy* 29 F11
Pescara →, *Italy* 29 F11
Peschanokopskoye, *Russia* 49 G5
Péscia, *Italy* 28 E7
Pescina, *Italy* 29 F10
Peshawar, *Pakistan* 68 B4
Peshkopi, *Albania* 40 E4
Peshtera, *Bulgaria* 41 D8
Peshtigo, *U.S.A.* 108 C2
Peski, *Russia* 48 E6
Pêso da Régua, *Portugal* 34 D3
Pesqueira, *Brazil* 125 E11
Pessac, *France* 20 D3
Pest □, *Hungary* 42 C4
Pestovo, *Russia* 46 C8
Pestravka, *Russia* 48 D9
Péta, *Greece* 38 B3
Petah Tiqwa, *Israel* 75 C3
Petalídhion, *Greece* 38 E3
Petaling Jaya, *Malaysia* 65 L3
Petaloudhes, *Greece* 36 C10
Petaluma, *U.S.A.* 116 G4
Pétange, *Lux.* 17 E5
Petaro, *Pakistan* 68 G3
Petatlán, *Mexico* 118 D4
Petauke, *Zambia* 87 E3
Petawawa, *Canada* 102 C4
Petén Itzá, L., *Guatemala* 120 C2
Peter I.s Øy, *Antarctica* 5 C16
Peter Pond L., *Canada* 105 B7
Peterbell, *Canada* 102 C3
Peterborough, *Canada* 102 D4
Peterborough, *U.K.* 13 E7
Peterborough, *U.S.A.* 111 D13
Peterborough □, *U.K.* 13 E7
Peterculter, *U.K.* 14 D6
Peterhead, *U.K.* 14 D7
Peterlee, *U.K.* 12 C6
Petermann Bjerg, *Greenland* 98 B17
Petermann Ranges, *Australia* 92 E5
Petersburg, *Alaska, U.S.A.* 100 C6
Petersburg, *Pa., U.S.A.* 110 F6
Petersburg, *Va., U.S.A.* 108 G7
Petersburg, *W. Va., U.S.A.* 108 F6
Petersfield, *U.K.* 13 F7
Petershagen, *Germany* 24 C4
Petília Policastro, *Italy* 31 C9
Petit Goâve, *Haiti* 121 C5
Petit Jardin, *Canada* 103 C8
Petit Lac Manicouagan, *Canada* 103 B6

Petit-Mécatina →, *Canada* 103 B8
Petit-Mécatina, I. du, *Canada* 103 B8
Petit Saint Bernard, Col du, *Italy* 21 C10
Petitcodiac, *Canada* 103 C6
Petite Baleine →, *Canada* 102 A4
Petite Saguenay, *Canada* 103 C5
Petitot →, *Canada* 104 A4
Petitsikapau L., *Canada* 103 B6
Petlad, *India* 68 H5
Peto, *Mexico* 119 C7
Petone, *N.Z.* 91 J5
Petorca, *Chile* 126 C1
Petoskey, *U.S.A.* 108 C3
Petra, *Jordan* 75 E4
Petra, *Spain* 37 B10
Petra, Ostrova, *Russia* 4 B13
Petra Velikogo, Zaliv, *Russia* 54 C6
Petrel = Petrer, *Spain* 33 G4
Petrella, Monte, *Italy* 30 A6
Petrer, *Spain* 33 G4
Petreto-Bicchisano, *France* 21 G12
Petrich, *Bulgaria* 40 E7
Petrified Forest National Park, *U.S.A.* 115 J9
Petrijanec, *Croatia* 29 B13
Petrikov = Pyetrikaw, *Belarus* 47 F5
Petrila, *Romania* 43 E8
Petrinja, *Croatia* 29 C13
Petrodvorets, *Russia* 46 C5
Petrograd = Sankt-Peterburg, *Russia* 46 C6
Petrolândia, *Brazil* 125 E11
Petrolia, *Canada* 102 D3
Petrolina, *Brazil* 125 E10
Petropavl, *Kazakstan* 50 D7
Petropavlovsk = Petropavl, *Kazakstan* 50 D7
Petropavlovsk-Kamchatskiy, *Russia* 51 D16
Petropavlovskiy = Akhtubinsk, *Russia* 49 F8
Petrópolis, *Brazil* 127 A7
Petroşani, *Romania* 43 E8
Petrova Gora, *Croatia* 29 C12
Petrovac, *Montenegro, Yug.* 40 D2
Petrovac, *Serbia, Yug.* 40 B5
Petrovaradin, *Serbia, Yug.* 42 E4
Petrovsk, *Russia* 48 D7
Petrovsk-Zabaykalskiy, *Russia* 51 D11
Petrovskaya, *Russia* 47 K9
Petrovskoye = Svetlograd, *Russia* 49 H6
Petrozavodsk, *Russia* 46 B8
Petrus Steyn, *S. Africa* 89 D4
Petrusburg, *S. Africa* 88 D4
Petzeck, *Austria* 26 E5
Peumo, *Chile* 126 C1
Peureulak, *Indonesia* 62 D1
Pevek, *Russia* 51 C18
Peveragno, *Italy* 28 D4
Peyrehorade, *France* 20 E2
Peyruis, *France* 21 D9
Pézenas, *France* 20 E7
Pezinok, *Slovak Rep.* 27 C10
Pfaffenhofen, *Germany* 25 G7
Pfarrkirchen, *Germany* 25 G8
Pfeffenhausen, *Germany* 25 G7
Pforzheim, *Germany* 25 G4
Pfullendorf, *Germany* 25 H5
Pfungstadt, *Germany* 25 F4
Phagwara, *India* 66 D9
Phaistós, *Greece* 36 D6
Phala, *Botswana* 88 C4
Phalera = Phulera, *India* 68 F6
Phalodi, *India* 68 F5
Phalsbourg, *France* 19 D14
Phan, *Thailand* 64 C2
Phan Rang, *Vietnam* 65 G7
Phan Ri = Hoa Da, *Vietnam* 65 G7
Phan Thiet, *Vietnam* 65 G7
Phanae, *Greece* 39 C7
Phanat Nikhom, *Thailand* 64 F3
Phangan, Ko, *Thailand* 65 H3
Phangnga, *Thailand* 65 H2
Phanom Sarakham, *Thailand* 64 F3
Phaphund, *India* 69 F8
Pharenda, *India* 69 F10
Pharr, *U.S.A.* 113 M5
Phatthalung, *Thailand* 65 J3
Phayao, *Thailand* 64 C2
Phelps, *U.S.A.* 110 D7
Phelps L., *Canada* 105 B8
Phenix City, *U.S.A.* 109 J3
Phet Buri, *Thailand* 64 F2
Phetchabun, *Thailand* 64 D3
Phetchabun, Thiu Khao, *Thailand* 64 E3
Phetchaburi = Phet Buri, *Thailand* 64 F2
Phi Phi, Ko, *Thailand* 65 J2
Phiafay, *Laos* 64 E6
Phibun Mangsahan, *Thailand* 64 E5
Phichai, *Thailand* 64 D3
Phichit, *Thailand* 64 D3
Philadelphia, *Miss., U.S.A.* 113 J10
Philadelphia, *N.Y., U.S.A.* 111 B9
Philadelphia, *Pa., U.S.A.* 111 G9
Philip, *U.S.A.* 112 C4
Philippeville, *Belgium* 17 D4
Philippi, *Greece* 41 E8
Philippi, *U.S.A.* 108 F5
Philippi L., *Australia* 94 C2
Philippines ■, *Asia* 61 F5
Philippolis, *S. Africa* 88 E4
Philippopolis = Plovdiv, *Bulgaria* 41 D8
Philipsburg, *Canada* 111 A11
Philipsburg, *Mont., U.S.A.* 114 C7
Philipsburg, *Pa., U.S.A.* 110 F6
Philipstown = Daingean, *Ireland* 15 C4
Philipstown, *S. Africa* 88 E3
Phillips, *U.S.A.* 112 C9
Phillipsburg, *Kans., U.S.A.* 112 F5
Phillipsburg, *N.J., U.S.A.* 111 F9
Philmont, *U.S.A.* 111 D11
Philomath, *U.S.A.* 114 D2
Phimai, *Thailand* 64 E4
Phitsanulok, *Thailand* 64 D3
Phnom Dangrek, *Thailand* 62 B2
Phnom Penh, *Cambodia* 65 G5
Phnum Penh = Phnom Penh, *Cambodia* 65 G5
Phoenicia, *U.S.A.* 111 D10
Phoenix, *Ariz., U.S.A.* 115 K7
Phoenix, *N.Y., U.S.A.* 111 C8
Phoenix Is., *Kiribati* 96 H10
Phoenixville, *U.S.A.* 111 F9
Phon, *Thailand* 64 E4
Phon Tiou, *Laos* 64 D5
Phong →, *Thailand* 64 D4
Phong Saly, *Laos* 58 G4
Phong Tho, *Vietnam* 64 A4
Phonhong, *Laos* 64 C4
Phonum, *Thailand* 65 H2
Phosphate Hill, *Australia* 94 C2
Photharam, *Thailand* 64 F2
Phra Nakhon Si Ayutthaya, *Thailand* 64 E3
Phra Thong, Ko, *Thailand* 65 H2
Phrae, *Thailand* 64 C3
Phrom Phiram, *Thailand* 64 D3
Phrygia, *Turkey* 72 C4
Phu Dien, *Vietnam* 64 C5
Phu Loi, *Laos* 64 B4
Phu Ly, *Vietnam* 58 G5
Phu Quoc, Dao, *Vietnam* 65 G4
Phu Tho, *Vietnam* 58 G5
Phuc Yen, *Vietnam* 58 G5
Phuket, *Thailand* 65 J2
Phuket, Ko, *Thailand* 65 J2
Phul, *India* 68 D6
Phulad, *India* 68 G5
Phulchari, *Bangla.* 69 G13
Phulera, *India* 68 F6
Phulpur, *India* 69 G10
Phum Phin, *Thailand* 65 H2
Piacenza, *Italy* 28 C6
Pian Cr. →, *Australia* 95 E4
Piana, *France* 21 F12
Pianella, *Italy* 29 F11
Pianosa, *Puglia, Italy* 29 F12
Pianosa, *Toscana, Italy* 28 F7
Piapot, *Canada* 105 D7
Pias, *Portugal* 35 G3
Piaseczno, *Poland* 45 F8
Piaski, *Poland* 45 G9
Piastów, *Poland* 45 F7
Piatra, *Romania* 43 G10
Piatra Neamţ, *Romania* 43 D11
Piatra Olt, *Romania* 43 F9
Piauí □, *Brazil* 125 E10
Piauí →, *Brazil* 125 E10
Piave →, *Italy* 29 C9
Piazza Ármerina, *Italy* 31 E7
Pibor →, *Sudan* 81 F3
Pibor Post, *Sudan* 81 F3
Picardie, *France* 19 C10
Picardie, Plaine de, *France* 19 C9
Picardy = Picardie, *France* 19 C10
Picayune, *U.S.A.* 113 K10
Picerno, *Italy* 31 B8
Pichhor, *India* 69 G8
Pichilemu, *Chile* 126 C1
Pichor, *India* 68 G8
Pickerel L., *Canada* 102 C1
Pickering, *U.K.* 12 C7
Pickering, Vale of, *U.K.* 12 C7
Pickle Lake, *Canada* 102 B1
Pickwick L., *U.S.A.* 109 H1
Pico Truncado, *Argentina* 128 F3
Picos, *Brazil* 125 E10
Picton, *Canada* 102 D4
Picton, *N.Z.* 91 J5
Pictou, *Canada* 103 C7
Picture Butte, *Canada* 104 D6
Picún Leufú, *Argentina* 128 D3
Pidurutalagala, *Sri Lanka* 66 R12
Piechowice, *Poland* 45 H2
Piedmont = Piemonte □, *Italy* 28 D5
Piedmont, *Ala., U.S.A.* 109 J3
Piedmont, *S.C., U.S.A.* 107 D10
Piedmonte Matese, *Italy* 31 A7
Piedra →, *Spain* 32 D3
Piedrabuena, *Spain* 35 G6
Piedrahita, *Spain* 34 E5
Piedralaves, *Spain* 34 E6
Piedras Blancas, *Spain* 34 B5
Piedras Negras, *Mexico* 118 B4
Piekary Śląskie, *Poland* 45 H5
Pieksämäki, *Finland* 9 E22
Piemonte □, *Italy* 28 D5
Pienaarsrivier, *S. Africa* 89 D4
Pieniężno, *Poland* 44 D7
Pieńsk, *Poland* 45 G2
Piercefield, *U.S.A.* 111 B10
Pierceland, *Canada* 105 C7
Piería □, *Greece* 40 F6
Pierpont, *U.S.A.* 110 E4
Pierre, *U.S.A.* 112 C4
Pierre-Buffière, *France* 20 C5
Pierre-de-Bresse, *France* 19 F12
Pierre E. Trudeau, Mt. = Logan, Mt., *Canada* 100 B5
Pierrefontaine-les-Varans, *France* 19 E13
Pierrefort, *France* 20 D6
Pierrelatte, *France* 21 D8
Pieštany, *Slovak Rep.* 27 C10
Piesting →, *Austria* 27 C9
Pieszyce, *Poland* 45 H3
Piet Retief, *S. Africa* 89 D5
Pietarsaari, *Finland* 8 E20
Pietermaritzburg, *S. Africa* 89 D5
Pietersburg, *S. Africa* 89 C4
Pietragalla, *Italy* 31 B8
Pietrasanta, *Italy* 28 E7
Pietroşiţa, *Romania* 43 E10
Pietrosul, Vf., *Maramureş, Romania* 43 C9
Pietrosul, Vf., *Suceava, Romania* 43 C10
Pieve di Cadore, *Italy* 29 B9
Pieve di Teco, *Italy* 28 D4
Pievepélago, *Italy* 28 D7
Pigadhítsa, *Greece* 40 G5
Pigeon L., *Canada* 110 B6
Piggott, *U.S.A.* 113 G9
Pigna, *Italy* 28 E4
Pigüe, *Argentina* 126 D3
Pihani, *India* 69 F9
Pihlajavesi, *Finland* 9 F23
Pijijiapan, *Mexico* 119 D6
Pikalevo, *Russia* 46 C8
Pikangikum Berens, *Canada* 105 C10
Pikes Peak, *U.S.A.* 112 F2
Piketberg, *S. Africa* 88 E2
Pikeville, *U.S.A.* 108 G4
Pikou, *China* 57 E12
Pikwitonei, *Canada* 105 B9
Piła, *Poland* 45 E3
Pila, *Spain* 33 G3
Pilaía, *Greece* 40 F6
Pilani, *India* 68 E6
Pilar, *Paraguay* 126 B4
Pilar de la Horadada, *Spain* 33 H4
Pilawa, *Poland* 45 G8
Pilaya →, *Bolivia* 124 H6
Pilbara, *Australia* 92 D2
Pilcomayo →, *Paraguay* 126 B4
Pilgrim's Rest, *S. Africa* 89 C5
Pilgrimstad, *Sweden* 10 B9
Píli, *Greece* 39 E9
Pilibhit, *India* 69 E8
Pilica →, *Poland* 45 G8
Pilion, *Greece* 38 B5
Pilis, *Hungary* 42 C4
Pilisvörösvár, *Hungary* 42 C3
Pilkhawa, *India* 68 E7
Pilliga, *Australia* 95 E4
Pílos, *Greece* 38 E3
Pilot Mound, *Canada* 105 D9
Pilot Point, *U.S.A.* 113 J6
Pilot Rock, *U.S.A.* 114 D4
Pilsen = Plzeň, *Czech Rep.* 26 B6
Pilštanj, *Slovenia* 29 B12
Piltene, *Latvia* 44 A8
Pilzno, *Poland* 45 J8
Pima, *U.S.A.* 115 K9
Pimenta Bueno, *Brazil* 124 F6
Pimentel, *Peru* 124 E3
Pina de Ebro, *Spain* 32 D4
Pinamalayan, *Phil.* 61 E4
Pinang, *Malaysia* 65 K3
Pinar, C. des, *Spain* 37 B10
Pinar del Río, *Cuba* 120 B3
Pınarbaşı, *Çanakkale, Turkey* 39 B8
Pınarbaşı, *Kayseri, Turkey* 72 C7
Pınarhisar, *Turkey* 41 E11
Pinatubo, Mt., *Phil.* 61 D3
Pincehely, *Hungary* 42 D3
Pinchang, *China* 58 B6
Pincher Creek, *Canada* 104 D6
Pinchi L., *Canada* 104 C4
Pinckneyville, *U.S.A.* 112 F10
Pińczów, *Poland* 45 H7
Pindar, *Australia* 93 E2
Pindi Gheb, *Pakistan* 68 C5
Pindiga, *Nigeria* 83 D7
Pindos Óros, *Greece* 38 B3
Pindus Mts. = Pindos Óros, *Greece* 38 B3
Pine →, *B.C., Canada* 104 B4
Pine →, *Sask., Canada* 105 B7
Pine, C., *Canada* 103 C9
Pine Bluff, *U.S.A.* 113 H9
Pine Bluffs, *U.S.A.* 112 E2
Pine City, *U.S.A.* 112 C8
Pine Cr. →, *U.S.A.* 110 E7
Pine Creek, *Australia* 92 B5
Pine Falls, *Canada* 105 C9
Pine Flat Res., *U.S.A.* 116 J7
Pine Grove, *U.S.A.* 111 F8
Pine Pass, *Canada* 104 B4
Pine Point, *Canada* 104 A6
Pine Ridge, *U.S.A.* 112 D3
Pine River, *Canada* 105 C8
Pine River, *U.S.A.* 112 B7
Pine Valley, *U.S.A.* 117 N10
Pinecrest, *U.S.A.* 116 G6
Pineda de Mar, *Spain* 32 D7
Pinedale, *Calif., U.S.A.* 116 J7
Pinedale, *Wyo., U.S.A.* 114 E9
Pinega →, *Russia* 50 C5
Pinehill, *Australia* 94 C4
Pinehouse L., *Canada* 105 B7
Pineimuta →, *Canada* 102 B1
Pinerolo, *Italy* 28 D4
Pineto, *Italy* 29 F11
Pinetop, *U.S.A.* 115 J9
Pinetown, *S. Africa* 89 D5
Pineville, *U.S.A.* 113 K8
Piney, *France* 19 D11
Ping →, *Thailand* 64 E3
Pingaring, *Australia* 93 F2
Pingba, *China* 58 D6
Pingbian, *China* 58 F4
Pingchuan, *China* 58 D3
Pingding, *China* 56 F7
Pingdingshan, *China* 56 H7
Pingdong, *Taiwan* 59 F13
Pingdu, *China* 57 F10
Pingelly, *Australia* 93 F2
Pingguo, *China* 58 F6
Pinghe, *China* 59 E11
Pinghu, *China* 59 B13
Pingjiang, *China* 59 C9
Pingle, *China* 59 E8
Pingli, *China* 58 A7
Pingliang, *China* 56 G4
Pinglu, *China* 56 E7
Pingluo, *China* 56 E4
Pingnan, *Fujian, China* 59 D12
Pingnan, *Guangxi Zhuangzu, China* 59 F8
Pingquan, *China* 57 D10
Pingrup, *Australia* 93 F2
Pingshan, *China* 58 C5
Pingtan, *China* 59 E12
Pingtang, *China* 58 E6
P'ingtung, *Taiwan* 59 F13
Pingwu, *China* 56 H3
Pingxiang, *Guangxi Zhuangzu, China* 58 F6
Pingxiang, *Jiangxi, China* 59 D9
Pingyao, *China* 56 F7
Pingyi, *China* 57 G9
Pingyin, *China* 56 F9
Pingyuan, *Guangdong, China* 59 E10
Pingyuan, *Shandong, China* 56 F9
Pingyuanjie, *China* 58 F4
Pinhal, *Brazil* 127 A6
Pinhal Novo, *Portugal* 35 G2
Pinheiro, *Brazil* 125 D9
Pinheiro Machado, *Brazil* 127 C5
Pinhel, *Portugal* 34 E3
Pini, *Indonesia* 62 D1
Piniós →, *Ilía, Greece* 38 D3
Piniós →, *Tríkkala, Greece* 38 B4
Pinjarra, *Australia* 93 F2
Pink Mountain, *Canada* 104 B4
Pinkafeld, *Austria* 27 D9
Pinnacles, *U.S.A.* 116 J5
Pinneberg, *Germany* 24 B5
Pínnes, Ákra, *Greece* 41 F8
Pinon Hills, *U.S.A.* 117 L9
Pinos, *Mexico* 118 C4
Pinos, Mt., *U.S.A.* 117 L7
Pinos Pt., *U.S.A.* 115 H3
Pinos Puente, *Spain* 35 H7
Pinotepa Nacional, *Mexico* 119 D5
Pinrang, *Indonesia* 63 E5
Pins, Pte. aux, *Canada* 110 D3
Pinsk, *Belarus* 47 F4
Pintados, *Chile* 124 H5
Pinyang, *China* 59 D13
Pinyug, *Russia* 50 C5
Pioche, *U.S.A.* 115 H6
Piombino, *Italy* 28 F7
Piombino, Canale di, *Italy* 28 F7
Pioner, Ostrov, *Russia* 51 B10
Pionki, *Poland* 45 G8
Piorini, L., *Brazil* 124 D6
Piotrków Trybunalski, *Poland* 45 G6
Piove di Sacco, *Italy* 29 C9
Pip, *Iran* 71 E9
Pipar, *India* 68 F5
Pipar Road, *India* 68 F5
Piparia, *Mad. P., India* 68 H8
Piparia, *Mad. P., India* 68 J7
Pipéri, *Greece* 38 B6
Pipestone, *U.S.A.* 112 D6
Pipestone →, *Canada* 102 B2
Pipestone Cr. →, *Canada* 105 D8
Piplan, *Pakistan* 68 C4
Piploda, *India* 68 H6
Pipmuacan, Rés., *Canada* 103 C5
Pippingarra, *Australia* 92 D2
Pipriac, *France* 18 E5
Piqua, *U.S.A.* 108 E3
Piquiri →, *Brazil* 127 A5
Pīr Sohrāb, *Iran* 71 E9
Pira, *Benin* 83 D5
Piracicaba, *Brazil* 127 A6
Piracuruca, *Brazil* 125 D10
Piræus = Piraiévs, *Greece* 38 D5
Piraiévs, *Greece* 38 D5
Pirajuí, *Brazil* 127 A6
Piram I., *India* 68 J5
Piran, *Slovenia* 29 C10
Pirané, *Argentina* 126 B4
Pirano = Piran, *Slovenia* 29 C10
Pirapora, *Brazil* 125 G10
Pirawa, *India* 68 G7
Pirdop, *Bulgaria* 41 D8
Pírgos, *Ilía, Greece* 38 D3
Pírgos, *Kríti, Greece* 39 F7
Pirgovo, *Bulgaria* 41 C9
Piribebuy, *Paraguay* 126 B4
Pirimapun, *Indonesia* 63 F9
Pirin Planina, *Bulgaria* 40 E7
Píríneos = Pyrénées, *Europe* 20 F4
Piripiri, *Brazil* 125 D10
Pirmasens, *Germany* 25 F3
Pirna, *Germany* 24 E9
Pirot, *Serbia, Yug.* 40 C6
Piru, *Indonesia* 63 E7
Piru, *U.S.A.* 117 L8
Piryatin = Pyryatyn, *Ukraine* 47 G7
Piryí, *Greece* 39 C7
Pisa, *Italy* 28 E7
Pisa →, *Poland* 45 E8
Pisagne, *Italy* 28 C7
Pisagua, *Chile* 124 G4
Pisarovina, *Croatia* 29 C12
Pisco, *Peru* 124 F3
Piscu, *Romania* 43 E12
Písek, *Czech Rep.* 26 B7
Pishan, *China* 60 C2
Pīshīn, *Iran* 71 E9
Pishin, *Pakistan* 68 D2
Pishin Lora →, *Pakistan* 68 E1
Pisidia, *Turkey* 72 D4
Pising, *Indonesia* 63 F6
Pismo Beach, *U.S.A.* 117 K6
Piso, L., *Liberia* 82 D2
Pissila, *Burkina Faso* 83 C4
Pissis, Cerro, *Argentina* 126 B2
Pissos, *France* 20 D3
Pissouri, *Cyprus* 36 E11
Pisticci, *Italy* 31 B9
Pistóia, *Italy* 28 E7
Pistol B., *Canada* 105 A10
Pisuerga →, *Spain* 34 D6
Pisz, *Poland* 44 E8
Pit →, *U.S.A.* 114 F2
Pita, *Guinea* 82 C2
Pitcairn I., *Pac. Oc.* 97 K14
Pite älv →, *Sweden* 8 D19
Piteå, *Sweden* 8 D19
Piterka, *Russia* 48 E8
Piteşti, *Romania* 43 F9
Pithapuram, *India* 67 L13
Pithara, *Australia* 93 F2
Píthion, *Greece* 41 E10
Pithiviers, *France* 19 D9
Pithoragarh, *India* 69 E9
Pithoro, *Pakistan* 68 G3
Pitigliano, *Italy* 29 F8
Pitkyaranta, *Russia* 46 B6
Pitlochry, *U.K.* 14 E5
Pitsilia □, *Cyprus* 36 E12
Pitt I., *Canada* 104 C3
Pittsburg, *Calif., U.S.A.* 116 G5
Pittsburg, *Kans., U.S.A.* 113 G7
Pittsburg, *Tex., U.S.A.* 113 J7
Pittsburgh, *U.S.A.* 110 F5
Pittsfield, *Ill., U.S.A.* 112 F9
Pittsfield, *Maine, U.S.A.* 109 C11
Pittsfield, *Mass., U.S.A.* 111 D11
Pittsfield, *N.H., U.S.A.* 111 C13
Pittston, *U.S.A.* 111 E9
Pittsworth, *Australia* 95 D5
Pituri →, *Australia* 94 C2
Piura, *Peru* 124 E2
Piva →, *Montenegro, Yug.* 40 C2
Piwniczna, *Poland* 45 J7
Pixley, *U.S.A.* 116 K7
Piyai, *Greece* 38 B3
Pizarra, *Spain* 35 J6
Pizhou, *China* 56 G9
Pizzo, *Italy* 31 D9
Placentia, *Canada* 103 C9
Placentia B., *Canada* 103 C9
Placer, *Masbate, Phil.* 61 F5
Placer, *Surigao N., Phil.* 61 G6
Placerville, *U.S.A.* 116 G6
Placetas, *Cuba* 120 B4
Plačkovica, *Macedonia* 40 E6
Plainfield, *N.J., U.S.A.* 111 F10
Plainfield, *Ohio, U.S.A.* 110 F3
Plainfield, *Vt., U.S.A.* 111 B12
Plains, *Mont., U.S.A.* 114 C6
Plains, *Tex., U.S.A.* 113 J3
Plainview, *Nebr., U.S.A.* 112 D6
Plainview, *Tex., U.S.A.* 113 H4
Plainwell, *U.S.A.* 108 D3
Plaisance, *France* 20 E4
Plaistow, *U.S.A.* 111 D13
Pláka, *Greece* 39 B7
Pláka, Ákra, *Greece* 36 D8
Plakenska Planina, *Macedonia* 40 E5
Planá, *Czech Rep.* 26 B5
Plana Cays, *Bahamas* 121 B5
Planada, *U.S.A.* 116 H6
Plancoët, *France* 18 D4
Plandište, *Serbia, Yug.* 42 E6
Plano, *U.S.A.* 113 J6
Plant City, *U.S.A.* 109 M4
Plaquemine, *U.S.A.* 113 K9
Plasencia, *Spain* 34 E4
Plaški, *Croatia* 29 C12
Plaster City, *U.S.A.* 117 N11
Plaster Rock, *Canada* 103 C6
Plastun, *Russia* 54 B8
Plasy, *Czech Rep.* 26 B6
Plata, Río de la, *S. Amer.* 126 C4
Plátani →, *Italy* 30 E6
Plátanos, *Greece* 36 D5
Plateau □, *Nigeria* 83 D6
Platí, Ákra, *Greece* 41 F8
Platte, *U.S.A.* 112 D5
Platte →, *Mo., U.S.A.* 112 F7
Platte →, *Nebr., U.S.A.* 112 E7
Platteville, *U.S.A.* 112 D9
Plattling, *Germany* 25 G8
Plattsburgh, *U.S.A.* 111 B11
Plattsmouth, *U.S.A.* 112 E7
Plau, *Germany* 24 B8
Plauen, *Germany* 24 E8
Plauer See, *Germany* 24 B8
Plav, *Montenegro, Yug.* 40 D3
Plavinas, *Latvia* 9 H21

Plavnica, *Montenegro, Yug.* 40 D3
Plavno, *Croatia* 29 D13
Plavsk, *Russia* 46 F9
Playa Blanca, *Canary Is.* 37 F6
Playa Blanca Sur, *Canary Is.* 37 F6
Playa de las Americas, *Canary Is.* 37 F3
Playa de Mogán, *Canary Is.* 37 G4
Playa del Inglés, *Canary Is.* 37 G4
Playa Esmerelda, *Canary Is.* 37 F5
Playgreen L., *Canada* 105 C9
Pleasant Bay, *Canada* 103 C7
Pleasant Hill, *U.S.A.* 116 H4
Pleasant Mount, *U.S.A.* 111 E9
Pleasanton, *Calif., U.S.A.* 116 H5
Pleasanton, *Tex., U.S.A.* 113 L5
Pleasantville, *N.J., U.S.A.* 108 F8
Pleasantville, *Pa., U.S.A.* 110 E5
Pléaux, *France* 20 C6
Plei Ku, *Vietnam* 64 F7
Plélan-le-Grand, *France* 18 D4
Pléneuf-Val-André, *France* 18 D4
Plenița, *Romania* 43 F8
Plenty →, *Australia* 94 C2
Plenty, B. of, *N.Z.* 91 G6
Plentywood, *U.S.A.* 112 A2
Plérin, *France* 18 D4
Plessisville, *Canada* 103 C5
Plestin-les-Grèves, *France* 18 D3
Pleszew, *Poland* 45 G4
Pleternica, *Croatia* 42 E2
Plétipi, L., *Canada* 103 B5
Pleven, *Bulgaria* 41 C8
Plevlja, *Montenegro, Yug.* 40 C3
Plevna, *Canada* 110 B8
Plješevica, *Croatia* 29 D12
Ploaghe, *Italy* 30 B1
Ploče, *Croatia* 29 E14
Płock, *Poland* 45 F6
Plöckenpass, *Italy* 29 B9
Plöckenstein, *Germany* 25 G9
Ploemeur, *France* 18 E3
Ploërmel, *France* 18 E4
Ploiești, *Romania* 43 F11
Plomárion, *Greece* 39 C8
Plombières-les-Bains, *France* 19 E13
Plomin, *Croatia* 29 C11
Plön, *Germany* 24 A6
Plonge, Lac la, *Canada* 105 B7
Płońsk, *Poland* 45 F7
Plopeni, *Romania* 43 E10
Plopișului, Munții, *Romania* 42 C7
Płoty, *Poland* 44 E2
Plouaret, *France* 18 D3
Plouay, *France* 18 E3
Ploučnice →, *Czech Rep.* 26 A7
Ploudalmézeau, *France* 18 D2
Plouescat, *France* 18 D2
Plougasnou, *France* 18 D3
Plougastel-Daoulas, *France* 18 D2
Plouguerneau, *France* 18 D2
Plouha, *France* 18 D4
Plouhinec, *France* 18 E2
Plovdiv, *Bulgaria* 41 D8
Plovdiv □, *Bulgaria* 41 D8
Plum, *U.S.A.* 110 F5
Plum I., *U.S.A.* 111 E12
Plumas, *U.S.A.* 116 F7
Plummer, *U.S.A.* 114 C5
Plumtree, *Zimbabwe* 87 G2
Plungė, *Lithuania* 9 J19
Pluvigner, *France* 18 E3
Plymouth, *U.K.* 13 G3
Plymouth, *Calif., U.S.A.* 116 G6
Plymouth, *Ind., U.S.A.* 108 E2
Plymouth, *Mass., U.S.A.* 111 E14
Plymouth, *N.C., U.S.A.* 109 H7
Plymouth, *N.H., U.S.A.* 111 C13
Plymouth, *Pa., U.S.A.* 111 E9
Plymouth, *Wis., U.S.A.* 108 D2
Plynlimon = Pumlumon Fawr, *U.K.* 13 E4
Plyusa, *Russia* 46 C5
Plyusa →, *Russia* 46 C5
Plyussa = Plyusa, *Russia* 46 C5
Plyussa → = Plyusa →, *Russia* 46 C5
Plzeň, *Czech Rep.* 26 B6
Pniewy, *Poland* 45 F3
Pô, *Burkina Faso* 83 C4
Po →, *Italy* 29 D9
Po, Foci del, *Italy* 29 D9
Po Hai = Bo Hai, *China* 57 E10
Pobé, *Benin* 83 D5
Pobé, *Burkina Faso* 83 C4
Pobeda, *Russia* 51 C15
Pobedy, Pik, *Kyrgyzstan* 50 E8
Pobiedziska, *Poland* 45 F4
Pobla de Segur, *Spain* 32 C5
Pobladura del Valle, *Spain* 34 C5
Pobra de Trives, *Spain* 34 C3
Pocahontas, *Ark., U.S.A.* 113 G9
Pocahontas, *Iowa, U.S.A.* 112 D7
Pocatello, *U.S.A.* 114 E7
Počátky, *Czech Rep.* 26 B8
Pochep, *Russia* 47 F7
Pochinki, *Russia* 48 C7
Pochinok, *Russia* 46 E7
Pöchlarn, *Austria* 26 C8
Pochutla, *Mexico* 119 D5
Pocito Casas, *Mexico* 118 B2
Pocking, *Germany* 25 G9
Pocomoke City, *U.S.A.* 108 F8
Poços de Caldas, *Brazil* 127 A6
Podbořany, *Czech Rep.* 26 A6
Poddębice, *Poland* 45 G5
Poděbrady, *Czech Rep.* 26 A8
Podensac, *France* 20 D3
Podenzano, *Italy* 28 D6
Podgorač, *Croatia* 42 E3
Podgorica, *Montenegro, Yug.* 40 D3
Podgorie, *Albania* 40 F4
Podilska Vysochyna, *Ukraine* 47 H4
Podkarpackie □, *Poland* 45 H9
Podkova, *Bulgaria* 41 E9
Podlapača, *Croatia* 29 D12
Podlaskie □, *Poland* 45 E10
Podoleni, *Romania* 43 D11
Podolínec, *Slovak Rep.* 27 B13
Podolsk, *Russia* 46 E9
Podor, *Senegal* 82 B1
Podporozhye, *Russia* 46 B8
Podu Iloaiei, *Romania* 43 C12
Podu Turcului, *Romania* 43 D12
Podujevo, *Kosovo, Yug.* 40 D5
Poel, *Germany* 24 B6
Pofadder, *S. Africa* 88 D2
Poggiardo, *Italy* 31 B11
Poggibonsi, *Italy* 28 E8
Póggio Mirteto, *Italy* 29 F9
Pogoanele, *Romania* 43 F12
Pogorzela, *Poland* 45 G4
Pogradec, *Albania* 40 F4
Pogranitšnyi, *Russia* 54 B5
Poh, *Indonesia* 63 E6
P'ohang, *S. Korea* 57 F15
Pohjanmaa, *Finland* 8 E20
Pohnpei, *Micronesia* 96 G7
Pohorelá, *Slovak Rep.* 27 C13
Pohořelice, *Czech Rep.* 27 C9
Pohorje, *Slovenia* 29 B12
Pohri, *India* 68 G6
Poiana Mare, *Romania* 42 G8
Poiana Ruscăi, Munții, *Romania* 42 E7
Poiana Stampei, *Romania* 43 C10
Poinsett, C., *Antarctica* 5 C8
Point Arena, *U.S.A.* 116 G3
Point Baker, *U.S.A.* 104 B2
Point Edward, *Canada* 102 D3
Point Hope, *U.S.A.* 100 B3
Point L., *Canada* 100 B8
Point Pedro, *Sri Lanka* 66 Q12
Point Pleasant, *N.J., U.S.A.* 111 F10
Point Pleasant, *W. Va., U.S.A.* 108 F4
Pointe-à-Pitre, *Guadeloupe* 121 C7
Pointe-Claire, *Canada* 111 A11
Pointe-Gatineau, *Canada* 111 A9
Pointe-Noire, *Congo* 84 E2
Poio, *Spain* 34 C2
Poirino, *Italy* 28 D4
Poisonbush Ra., *Australia* 92 D3
Poissonnier Pt., *Australia* 92 C2
Poitiers, *France* 18 F7
Poitou, *France* 20 B3
Poitou-Charentes □, *France* 20 B4
Poix-de-Picardie, *France* 19 C8
Poix-Terron, *France* 19 C11
Pojoaque, *U.S.A.* 115 J11
Pokaran, *India* 66 F7
Pokataroo, *Australia* 95 D4
Pokhara, *Nepal* 69 E10
Pokhvistnevo, *Russia* 48 D11
Poko, *Dem. Rep. of the Congo* 86 B2
Poko, *Sudan* 81 F3
Pokrov, *Russia* 46 E10
Pokrovsk = Engels, *Russia* 48 E8
Pokrovsk, *Russia* 51 C13
Pokrovskoye, *Russia* 47 J10
Pola = Pula, *Croatia* 29 D10
Pola, *Russia* 46 D7
Pola de Allande, *Spain* 34 B4
Pola de Lena, *Spain* 34 B5
Pola de Siero, *Spain* 34 B5
Pola de Somiedo, *Spain* 34 B4
Polacca, *U.S.A.* 115 J8
Polan, *Iran* 71 E9
Pol'ana, *Slovak Rep.* 27 C12
Poland ■, *Europe* 45 G3
Polanica-Zdrój, *Poland* 45 H3
Połaniec, *Poland* 45 H8
Polanów, *Poland* 44 D3
Polar Bear Prov. Park, *Canada* 102 A2
Polatlı, *Turkey* 72 C5
Polatsk, *Belarus* 46 E5
Polcura, *Chile* 126 D1
Połczyn-Zdrój, *Poland* 44 E3
Polessk, *Russia* 9 J19
Polesye = Pripet Marshes, *Europe* 47 F5
Polgar, *Hungary* 42 C6
Pŏlgyo-ri, *S. Korea* 57 G14
Poli, *Cameroon* 83 C7
Políaigos, *Greece* 38 E6
Policastro, G. di, *Italy* 31 C8
Police, *Poland* 44 E1
Polička, *Czech Rep.* 27 B9
Policoro, *Italy* 31 B9
Polignano a Mare, *Italy* 31 A9
Poligny, *France* 19 F12
Políkhnitas, *Greece* 39 B8
Polillo Is., *Phil.* 61 D4
Polillo Strait, *Phil.* 61 D4
Polis, *Cyprus* 36 D11
Polístena, *Italy* 31 D9
Políyiros, *Greece* 40 F7
Polk, *U.S.A.* 110 E5
Polkowice, *Poland* 45 G3
Polla, *Italy* 31 B8
Pollachi, *India* 66 P10
Pollença, *Spain* 37 B10
Pollença, B. de, *Spain* 37 B10
Póllica, *Italy* 31 B8
Pollino, Mte., *Italy* 31 C9
Polna, *Russia* 46 C5
Polnovat, *Russia* 50 C7
Pology, *Ukraine* 47 J9
Polonne, *Ukraine* 47 G4
Polonnoye = Polonne, *Ukraine* 47 G4
Polski Trŭmbesh, *Bulgaria* 41 C9
Polsko Kosovo, *Bulgaria* 41 C9
Polson, *U.S.A.* 114 C6
Poltár, *Slovak Rep.* 27 C12
Poltava, *Ukraine* 47 H8
Põltsamaa, *Estonia* 9 G21
Polunochnoye, *Russia* 50 C7
Põlva, *Estonia* 9 G22
Polynesia, *Pac. Oc.* 97 J11
Polynésie française = French Polynesia ■, *Pac. Oc.* 97 K13
Pomarance, *Italy* 28 E7
Pomaro, *Mexico* 118 D4
Pombal, *Portugal* 34 F2
Pómbia, *Greece* 36 E6
Pomene, *Mozam.* 89 C6
Pomeroy, *Ohio, U.S.A.* 108 F4
Pomeroy, *Wash., U.S.A.* 114 C5
Pomézia, *Italy* 30 A5
Pomichna, *Ukraine* 47 H6
Pomona, *Australia* 95 D5
Pomona, *U.S.A.* 117 L9
Pomorie, *Bulgaria* 41 D11
Pomorskie □, *Poland* 44 D5
Pomorskie, Pojezierze, *Poland* 44 E3
Pomos, *Cyprus* 36 D11
Pomos, C., *Cyprus* 36 D11
Pompano Beach, *U.S.A.* 109 M5
Pompei, *Italy* 31 B7
Pompey, *France* 19 D13
Pompeys Pillar, *U.S.A.* 114 D10
Pompton Lakes, *U.S.A.* 111 F10
Ponape = Pohnpei, *Micronesia* 96 G7
Ponask L., *Canada* 102 B1
Ponca, *U.S.A.* 112 D6
Ponca City, *U.S.A.* 113 G6
Ponce, *Puerto Rico* 121 C6
Ponchatoula, *U.S.A.* 113 K9
Poncheville, L., *Canada* 102 B4
Pond, *U.S.A.* 117 K7
Pond Inlet, *Canada* 101 A12
Pondicherry, *India* 66 P11
Ponds, I. of, *Canada* 103 B8
Ponferrada, *Spain* 34 C4
Pongo, Wadi →, *Sudan* 81 F2
Poniatowa, *Poland* 45 G9
Poniec, *Poland* 45 G3
Ponikva, *Slovenia* 29 B12
Ponnani, *India* 66 P9
Ponoka, *Canada* 104 C6
Ponorogo, *Indonesia* 63 G14
Pons = Ponts, *Spain* 32 D6
Pons, *France* 20 C3
Ponsul →, *Portugal* 34 F3
Pont-à-Mousson, *France* 19 D13
Pont-Audemer, *France* 18 C7
Pont-Aven, *France* 18 E3
Pont Canavese, *Italy* 28 C4
Pont-d'Ain, *France* 19 F12
Pont-de-Roide, *France* 19 E13
Pont-de-Salars, *France* 20 D6
Pont-de-Vaux, *France* 19 F11
Pont-de-Veyle, *France* 19 F11
Pont-du-Château, *France* 19 G10
Pont-l'Abbé, *France* 18 E2
Pont-l'Évêque, *France* 18 C7
Pont-St-Esprit, *France* 21 D8
Pont-St-Martin, *Italy* 28 C4
Pont-Ste-Maxence, *France* 19 C9
Pont-sur-Yonne, *France* 19 D10
Ponta do Sol, *Madeira* 37 D2
Ponta Grossa, *Brazil* 127 B5
Ponta Pora, *Brazil* 127 A4
Pontacq, *France* 20 E3
Pontailler-sur-Saône, *France* 19 E12
Pontarlier, *France* 19 F13
Pontassieve, *Italy* 29 E8
Pontaumur, *France* 20 C6
Pontcharra, *France* 21 C10
Pontchartrain L., *U.S.A.* 113 K10
Pontchâteau, *France* 18 E4
Ponte da Barca, *Portugal* 34 D2
Ponte de Sor, *Portugal* 35 F2
Ponte dell'Ólio, *Italy* 28 D6
Ponte di Legno, *Italy* 28 B7
Ponte do Lima, *Portugal* 34 D2
Ponte do Pungué, *Mozam.* 87 F3
Ponte-Leccia, *France* 21 F13
Ponte nelle Alpi, *Italy* 29 B9
Ponte Nova, *Brazil* 127 A7
Ponteareas, *Spain* 34 C2
Pontebba, *Italy* 29 B10
Ponteceso, *Spain* 34 B2
Pontecorvo, *Italy* 30 A6
Pontedeume, *Spain* 34 B2
Ponteix, *Canada* 105 D7
Pontevedra, *Spain* 34 C2
Pontevedra □, *Spain* 34 C2
Pontevedra, R. de →, *Spain* 34 C2
Pontevico, *Italy* 28 C7
Pontiac, *Ill., U.S.A.* 112 E10
Pontiac, *Mich., U.S.A.* 108 D4
Pontian Kecil, *Malaysia* 65 M4
Pontianak, *Indonesia* 62 E3
Pontine Is. = Ponziane, Ìsole, *Italy* 30 B5
Pontine Mts. = Kuzey Anadolu Dağları, *Turkey* 72 B7
Pontínia, *Italy* 30 A6
Pontivy, *France* 18 D4
Pontoise, *France* 19 C9
Ponton →, *Canada* 104 B5
Pontorson, *France* 18 D5
Pontrémoli, *Italy* 28 D6
Pontrieux, *France* 18 D3
Ponts, *Spain* 32 D6
Pontypool, *Canada* 110 B6
Pontypool, *U.K.* 13 F4
Ponza, *Italy* 30 B5
Ponziane, Ìsole, *Italy* 30 B5
Poochera, *Australia* 95 E1
Poole, *U.K.* 13 G6
Poole □, *U.K.* 13 G6
Poona = Pune, *India* 66 K8
Poopó, L. de, *Bolivia* 122 E4
Popayán, *Colombia* 124 C3
Poperinge, *Belgium* 17 D2
Popina, *Bulgaria* 41 B10
Poplar, *U.S.A.* 112 A2
Poplar →, *Canada* 105 C9
Poplar Bluff, *U.S.A.* 113 G9
Poplarville, *U.S.A.* 113 K10
Popocatépetl, Volcán, *Mexico* 119 D5
Popokabaka, *Dem. Rep. of the Congo* 84 F3
Pópoli, *Italy* 29 F10
Popovača, *Croatia* 29 C13
Popovo, *Bulgaria* 41 C10
Poppberg, *Germany* 25 F7
Poppi, *Italy* 29 E8
Poprad, *Slovak Rep.* 27 B13
Poprad →, *Slovak Rep.* 27 B13
Porali →, *Pakistan* 68 G2
Porbandar, *India* 66 J6
Porcher I., *Canada* 104 C2
Porcuna, *Spain* 35 H6
Porcupine →, *Canada* 105 B8
Porcupine →, *U.S.A.* 100 B5
Pordenone, *Italy* 29 C9
Pordim, *Bulgaria* 41 C8
Poreč, *Croatia* 29 C10
Poretskoye, *Russia* 48 C8
Pori, *Finland* 9 F19
Porí, *Greece* 38 F5
Porkhov, *Russia* 46 D5
Porlamar, *Venezuela* 124 A6
Porlezza, *Italy* 28 B6
Porma →, *Spain* 34 C5
Pornic, *France* 18 E4
Poronaysk, *Russia* 51 E15
Póros, *Greece* 38 D5
Poroshiri-Dake, *Japan* 54 C11
Poroszló, *Hungary* 42 C5
Poroto Mts., *Tanzania* 87 D3
Porpoise B., *Antarctica* 5 C9
Porquerolles, Î. de, *France* 21 F10
Porrentruy, *Switz.* 25 H3
Porreres, *Spain* 37 B10
Porsangen, *Norway* 8 A21
Porsgrunn, *Norway* 9 G13
Port Alberni, *Canada* 104 D4
Port Alfred, *S. Africa* 88 E4
Port Alice, *Canada* 104 C3
Port Allegany, *U.S.A.* 110 E6
Port Allen, *U.S.A.* 113 K9
Port Alma, *Australia* 94 C5
Port Angeles, *U.S.A.* 116 B3
Port Antonio, *Jamaica* 120 C4
Port Aransas, *U.S.A.* 113 M6
Port Arthur = Lüshun, *China* 57 E11
Port Arthur, *Australia* 94 G4
Port Arthur, *U.S.A.* 113 L8
Port au Choix, *Canada* 103 B8
Port au Port B., *Canada* 103 C8
Port-au-Prince, *Haiti* 121 C5
Port Austin, *U.S.A.* 110 B2
Port Bell, *Uganda* 86 B3
Port Bergé Vaovao, *Madag.* 89 B8
Port Blandford, *Canada* 103 C9
Port-Bouët, *Ivory C.* 82 D4
Port Bradshaw, *Australia* 94 A2
Port Burwell, *Canada* 110 D4
Port Canning, *India* 69 H13
Port-Cartier, *Canada* 103 B6
Port Chalmers, *N.Z.* 91 L3
Port Charlotte, *U.S.A.* 109 M4
Port Chester, *U.S.A.* 111 F11
Port Clements, *Canada* 104 C2
Port Clinton, *U.S.A.* 108 E4
Port Colborne, *Canada* 102 D4
Port Coquitlam, *Canada* 104 D4
Port Credit, *Canada* 110 C5
Port Curtis, *Australia* 94 C5
Port d'Alcúdia, *Spain* 37 B10
Port Dalhousie, *Canada* 110 C5
Port Darwin, *Australia* 92 B5
Port Darwin, *Falk. Is.* 128 G5
Port Davey, *Australia* 94 G4
Port-de-Bouc, *France* 21 E8
Port-de-Paix, *Haiti* 121 C5
Port de Pollença, *Spain* 37 B10
Port de Sóller, *Spain* 37 B9
Port Dickson, *Malaysia* 65 L3
Port Douglas, *Australia* 94 B4
Port Dover, *Canada* 110 D4
Port Edward, *Canada* 104 C2
Port Elgin, *Canada* 102 D3
Port Elizabeth, *S. Africa* 88 E4
Port Ellen, *U.K.* 14 F2
Port-en-Bessin, *France* 18 C6
Port Erin, *U.K.* 12 C3
Port Essington, *Australia* 92 B5
Port Etienne = Nouâdhibou, *Mauritania* 78 D2
Port Ewen, *U.S.A.* 111 E11
Port Fouâd = Bûr Fuad, *Egypt* 80 H8
Port Gamble, *U.S.A.* 116 C4
Port-Gentil, *Gabon* 84 E1
Port Germein, *Australia* 95 E2
Port Gibson, *U.S.A.* 113 K9
Port Glasgow, *U.K.* 14 F4
Port Harcourt, *Nigeria* 83 E6
Port Hardy, *Canada* 104 C3
Port Harrison = Inukjuak, *Canada* 101 C12
Port Hawkesbury, *Canada* 103 C7
Port Hedland, *Australia* 92 D2
Port Henry, *U.S.A.* 111 B11
Port Hood, *Canada* 103 C7
Port Hope, *Canada* 102 D4
Port Hope, *U.S.A.* 110 C2
Port Hope Simpson, *Canada* 103 B8
Port Hueneme, *U.S.A.* 117 L7
Port Huron, *U.S.A.* 110 D2
Port Iliç, *Azerbaijan* 73 C13
Port Jefferson, *U.S.A.* 111 F11
Port Jervis, *U.S.A.* 111 E10
Port-Joinville, *France* 18 F4
Port Katon, *Russia* 47 J10
Port Kelang = Pelabuhan Kelang, *Malaysia* 65 L3
Port Kenny, *Australia* 95 E1
Port-la-Nouvelle, *France* 20 E7
Port Lairge = Waterford, *Ireland* 15 D4
Port Laoise, *Ireland* 15 C4
Port Lavaca, *U.S.A.* 113 L6
Port Leyden, *U.S.A.* 111 C9
Port Loko, *S. Leone* 82 D2
Port Louis, *France* 18 E3
Port Louis, *Mauritius* 77 H9
Port Lyautey = Kenitra, *Morocco* 78 B4
Port McNeill, *Canada* 104 C3
Port Maria, *Jamaica* 120 C4
Port Matilda, *U.S.A.* 110 F6
Port Mellon, *Canada* 104 D4
Port-Menier, *Canada* 103 C7
Port Moody, *Canada* 116 A4
Port Morant, *Jamaica* 120 C4
Port Moresby, *Papua N. G.* 96 H6
Port Musgrave, *Australia* 94 A3
Port-Navalo, *France* 18 E4
Port Neches, *U.S.A.* 113 L8
Port Nolloth, *S. Africa* 88 D2
Port Nouveau-Québec = Kangiqsualujjuaq, *Canada* 101 C13
Port of Spain, *Trin. & Tob.* 121 D7
Port Orange, *U.S.A.* 109 L5
Port Orchard, *U.S.A.* 116 C4
Port Orford, *U.S.A.* 114 E1
Port Pegasus, *N.Z.* 91 M1
Port Perry, *Canada* 102 D4
Port Radium = Echo Bay, *Canada* 100 B8
Port Renfrew, *Canada* 104 D4
Port Roper, *Australia* 94 A2
Port Rowan, *Canada* 110 D4
Port Safaga = Bûr Safâga, *Egypt* 70 E2
Port Said = Bûr Sa'îd, *Egypt* 80 H8
Port St. Joe, *U.S.A.* 109 L3
Port St. Johns = Umzimvubu, *S. Africa* 89 E4
Port-St-Louis-du-Rhône, *France* 21 E8
Port St. Lucie, *U.S.A.* 109 M5
Port-Ste-Marie, *France* 20 D4
Port Sanilac, *U.S.A.* 110 C2
Port Severn, *Canada* 110 B5
Port Shepstone, *S. Africa* 89 E5
Port Simpson, *Canada* 104 C2
Port Stanley = Stanley, *Falk. Is.* 128 G5
Port Stanley, *Canada* 102 D3
Port Sudan = Bûr Sûdân, *Sudan* 80 D4
Port Sulphur, *U.S.A.* 113 L10
Port-sur-Saône, *France* 19 E13
Port Talbot, *U.K.* 13 F4
Port Taufiq = Bûr Taufiq, *Egypt* 80 J8
Port Townsend, *U.S.A.* 116 B4
Port-Vendres, *France* 20 F7
Port Vila, *Vanuatu* 96 J8
Port Washington, *U.S.A.* 108 D2
Port Weld = Kuala Sepetang, *Malaysia* 65 K3
Portadown, *U.K.* 15 B5
Portaferry, *U.K.* 15 B6
Portage, *Pa., U.S.A.* 110 F6
Portage, *Wis., U.S.A.* 112 D10
Portage La Prairie, *Canada* 105 D9
Portageville, *U.S.A.* 113 G10
Portalegre, *Portugal* 35 F3
Portalegre □, *Portugal* 35 F3
Portales, *U.S.A.* 113 H3
Portarlington, *Ireland* 15 C4
Portbou, *Spain* 32 C8
Portel, *Portugal* 35 G3
Porter L., *N.W.T., Canada* 105 A7
Porter L., *Sask., Canada* 105 B7
Porterville, *S. Africa* 88 E2
Porterville, *U.S.A.* 116 J8
Portes-lès-Valence, *France* 21 D8
Porthcawl, *U.K.* 13 F4
Porthill, *U.S.A.* 114 B5
Porthmadog, *U.K.* 12 E3
Portile de Fier, *Europe* 42 F7
Portimão, *Portugal* 35 H2
Portishead, *U.K.* 13 F5
Portiței, Gura, *Romania* 43 F14
Portknockie, *U.K.* 14 D6
Portland, *Canada* 111 B8
Portland, *Conn., U.S.A.* 111 E12
Portland, *Maine, U.S.A.* 101 D12
Portland, *Mich., U.S.A.* 108 D3
Portland, *Oreg., U.S.A.* 116 E4
Portland, *Pa., U.S.A.* 111 F9

Portland, *Tex., U.S.A.* 113 **M6**
Portland, I. of, *U.K.* 13 **G5**
Portland Bill, *U.K.* 13 **G5**
Portland Canal, *U.S.A.* 104 **B2**
Portmadoc = Porthmadog, *U.K.* 12 **E3**
Porto, *France* 21 **F12**
Porto, *Portugal* 34 **D2**
Porto □, *Portugal* 34 **D2**
Porto, G. de, *France* 21 **F12**
Pôrto Alegre, *Brazil* 127 **C5**
Porto Amboim = Gunza, *Angola* 84 **G2**
Porto Azzurro, *Italy* 28 **F7**
Porto Cristo, *Spain* 37 **B10**
Pôrto de Móz, *Brazil* 125 **D8**
Porto Empédocle, *Italy* 30 **E6**
Pôrto Esperança, *Brazil* 124 **G7**
Pôrto Franco, *Brazil* 125 **E9**
Pórto Lágos, *Greece* 41 **E9**
Porto Mendes, *Brazil* 127 **A5**
Porto Moniz, *Madeira* 37 **D2**
Pôrto Murtinho, *Brazil* 124 **H7**
Pôrto Nacional, *Brazil* 125 **F9**
Porto-Novo, *Benin* 83 **D5**
Porto Petro, *Spain* 37 **B10**
Porto San Giórgio, *Italy* 29 **E10**
Porto Sant' Elpídio, *Italy* 29 **E10**
Porto Santo, I. de, *Madeira* 78 **B2**
Porto Santo Stéfano, *Italy* 28 **F8**
Pôrto São José, *Brazil* 127 **A5**
Pôrto Seguro, *Brazil* 125 **G11**
Porto Tolle, *Italy* 29 **D9**
Porto Tórres, *Italy* 30 **B1**
Pôrto União, *Brazil* 127 **B5**
Pôrto Válter, *Brazil* 124 **E4**
Porto-Vecchio, *France* 21 **G13**
Pôrto Velho, *Brazil* 124 **E6**
Portobelo, *Panama* 120 **E4**
Portoferráio, *Italy* 28 **F7**
Portogruaro, *Italy* 29 **C9**
Portola, *U.S.A.* 116 **F6**
Portomaggiore, *Italy* 29 **D8**
Portoscuso, *Italy* 30 **C1**
Portovénere, *Italy* 28 **D6**
Portoviejo, *Ecuador* 124 **D2**
Portpatrick, *U.K.* 14 **G3**
Portree, *U.K.* 14 **D2**
Portrush, *U.K.* 15 **A5**
Portsmouth, *Domin.* 121 **C7**
Portsmouth, *U.K.* 13 **G6**
Portsmouth, *N.H., U.S.A.* 109 **D10**
Portsmouth, *Ohio, U.S.A.* 108 **F4**
Portsmouth, *R.I., U.S.A.* 111 **E13**
Portsmouth, *Va., U.S.A.* 108 **G7**
Portsmouth □, *U.K.* 13 **G6**
Portsoy, *U.K.* 14 **D6**
Portstewart, *U.K.* 15 **A5**
Porttipahtan tekojärvi, *Finland* 8 **B22**
Portugal ■, *Europe* 34 **F3**
Portugalete, *Spain* 32 **B1**
Portumna, *Ireland* 15 **C3**
Portville, *U.S.A.* 110 **D6**
Porvenir, *Chile* 128 **G2**
Porvoo, *Finland* 9 **F21**
Porzuna, *Spain* 35 **F6**
Posada, *Italy* 30 **B2**
Posada →, *Italy* 30 **B2**
Posadas, *Argentina* 127 **B4**
Posadas, *Spain* 35 **H5**
Poschiavo, *Switz.* 25 **J6**
Posets, *Spain* 32 **C5**
Poshan = Boshan, *China* 57 **F9**
Posht-e-Badam, *Iran* 71 **C7**
Posídhion, Ákra, *Greece* 40 **G7**
Posidium, *Greece* 39 **F9**
Poso, *Indonesia* 63 **E6**
Posong, *S. Korea* 57 **G14**
Posse, *Brazil* 125 **F9**
Possession I., *Antarctica* 5 **D11**
Pössneck, *Germany* 24 **E7**
Possum Kingdom L., *U.S.A.* 113 **J5**
Post, *U.S.A.* 113 **J4**
Post Falls, *U.S.A.* 114 **C5**
Postavy = Pastavy, *Belarus* 9 **J22**
Poste-de-la-Baleine = Kuujjuarapik, *Canada* 102 **A4**
Postmasburg, *S. Africa* 88 **D3**
Postojna, *Slovenia* 29 **C11**
Poston, *U.S.A.* 117 **M12**
Postville, *Canada* 103 **B8**
Potamós, *Andikíthira, Greece* 38 **F5**
Potamós, *Kíthira, Greece* 38 **E4**
Potchefstroom, *S. Africa* 88 **D4**
Potcoava, *Romania* 43 **F9**
Poteau, *U.S.A.* 113 **H7**
Poteet, *U.S.A.* 113 **L5**
Potenza, *Italy* 31 **B8**
Potenza →, *Italy* 29 **E10**
Potenza Picena, *Italy* 29 **E10**
Poteriteri, L., *N.Z.* 91 **M1**
Potgietersrus, *S. Africa* 89 **C4**
Poti, *Georgia* 49 **J5**
Potiskum, *Nigeria* 83 **C7**
Potlogi, *Romania* 43 **F10**
Potomac →, *U.S.A.* 108 **G7**
Potosí, *Bolivia* 124 **G5**
Potosi Mt., *U.S.A.* 117 **K11**
Pototan, *Phil.* 61 **F5**
Potrerillos, *Chile* 126 **B2**
Potsdam, *Germany* 24 **C9**
Potsdam, *U.S.A.* 111 **B10**
Pottenstein, *Germany* 25 **F7**
Pottersville, *U.S.A.* 111 **C11**
Pottery Hill = Abu Ballas, *Egypt* 80 **C2**
Pottstown, *U.S.A.* 111 **F9**
Pottsville, *U.S.A.* 111 **F8**
Pottuvil, *Sri Lanka* 66 **R12**
P'otzu, *Taiwan* 59 **F13**
Pouancé, *France* 18 **E5**
Pouce Coupé, *Canada* 104 **B4**
Poughkeepsie, *U.S.A.* 111 **E11**
Pouilly-sur-Loire, *France* 19 **E9**
Poulaphouca Res., *Ireland* 15 **C5**
Poulsbo, *U.S.A.* 116 **C4**
Poultney, *U.S.A.* 111 **C11**
Poulton-le-Fylde, *U.K.* 12 **D5**
Pouso Alegre, *Brazil* 127 **A6**
Pout, *Senegal* 82 **C1**
Pouthisat, *Cambodia* 64 **F4**
Pouzauges, *France* 18 **F6**
Pova de Sta. Iria, *Portugal* 35 **G1**
Považská Bystrica, *Slovak Rep.* 27 **B11**
Poverty B., *N.Z.* 91 **H7**
Povlen, *Serbia, Yug.* 40 **B3**
Póvoa de Lanhosa, *Portugal* 34 **D2**
Póvoa de Varzim, *Portugal* 34 **D2**
Povorino, *Russia* 48 **E6**
Povungnituk = Puvirnituq, *Canada* 101 **B12**
Powassan, *Canada* 102 **C4**
Poway, *U.S.A.* 117 **N9**
Powder →, *U.S.A.* 112 **B2**
Powder River, *U.S.A.* 114 **E10**
Powell, *U.S.A.* 114 **D9**
Powell, L., *U.S.A.* 115 **H8**
Powell River, *Canada* 104 **D4**
Powers, *U.S.A.* 108 **C2**
Powys □, *U.K.* 13 **E4**
Poyang Hu, *China* 59 **C11**
Poyarkovo, *Russia* 51 **E13**
Poysdorf, *Austria* 27 **C9**
Poza de la Sal, *Spain* 34 **C7**
Poza Rica, *Mexico* 119 **C5**
Pozanti, *Turkey* 72 **D6**
Požarevac, *Serbia, Yug.* 40 **B5**
Pozazal, Puerto, *Spain* 34 **C6**
Požega, *Croatia* 42 **E2**
Požega, *Serbia, Yug.* 40 **C4**
Poznań, *Poland* 45 **F3**
Pozo, *U.S.A.* 117 **K6**
Pozo Alcón, *Spain* 35 **H8**
Pozo Almonte, *Chile* 124 **H5**
Pozo Colorado, *Paraguay* 126 **A4**
Pozoblanco, *Spain* 35 **G6**
Pozzallo, *Italy* 31 **F7**
Pozzomaggiore, *Italy* 30 **B1**
Pozzuoli, *Italy* 31 **B7**
Pra →, *Ghana* 83 **D4**
Prabuty, *Poland* 44 **E6**
Prača, *Bos.-H.* 42 **G3**
Prachatice, *Czech Rep.* 26 **B6**
Prachin Buri, *Thailand* 64 **E3**
Prachuap Khiri Khan, *Thailand* 65 **G2**
Pradelles, *France* 20 **D7**
Prades, *France* 20 **F6**
Prado, *Brazil* 125 **G11**
Prado del Rey, *Spain* 35 **J5**
Præstø, *Denmark* 11 **J6**
Pragersko, *Slovenia* 29 **B12**
Prague = Praha, *Czech Rep.* 26 **A7**
Praha, *Czech Rep.* 26 **A7**
Prahecq, *France* 20 **B3**
Prahova □, *Romania* 43 **E10**
Prahova →, *Romania* 43 **F10**
Prahovo, *Serbia, Yug.* 40 **B6**
Praia, *C. Verde Is.* 77 **E1**
Práia a Mare, *Italy* 31 **C8**
Praid, *Romania* 43 **D10**
Prainha, *Amazonas, Brazil* 124 **E6**
Prainha, *Pará, Brazil* 125 **D8**
Prairie, *Australia* 94 **C3**
Prairie City, *U.S.A.* 114 **D4**
Prairie Dog Town Fork →, *U.S.A.* 113 **H5**
Prairie du Chien, *U.S.A.* 112 **D9**
Prairies, L. of the, *Canada* 105 **C8**
Pramánda, *Greece* 38 **B3**
Prampram, *Ghana* 83 **D5**
Pran Buri, *Thailand* 64 **F2**
Prang, *Ghana* 83 **D4**
Prapat, *Indonesia* 62 **D1**
Prasonísi, Ákra, *Greece* 36 **D9**
Prästmon, *Sweden* 10 **A11**
Praszka, *Poland* 45 **G5**
Prata, *Brazil* 125 **G9**
Pratabpur, *India* 69 **H10**
Pratapgarh, *Raj., India* 68 **G6**
Pratapgarh, *Ut. P., India* 69 **G9**
Prato, *Italy* 28 **E8**
Prátola Peligna, *Italy* 29 **F10**
Prats-de-Mollo-la-Preste, *France* 20 **F6**
Pratt, *U.S.A.* 113 **G5**
Prattville, *U.S.A.* 109 **J2**
Pravdinsk, *Russia* 48 **B6**
Pravets, *Bulgaria* 40 **D7**
Pravia, *Spain* 34 **B4**
Praya, *Indonesia* 62 **F5**
Pré-en-Pail, *France* 18 **D6**
Precordillera, *Argentina* 126 **C2**
Predáppio, *Italy* 29 **D8**
Predazzo, *Italy* 29 **B8**
Predeal, *Romania* 43 **E10**
Predejane, *Serbia, Yug.* 40 **D6**
Preeceville, *Canada* 105 **C8**
Preetz, *Germany* 24 **A6**
Pregrada, *Croatia* 29 **B12**
Preiļi, *Latvia* 9 **H22**
Preko, *Croatia* 29 **D12**
Prelog, *Croatia* 29 **B13**
Prémery, *France* 19 **E10**
Premià de Mar, *Spain* 32 **D7**
Premont, *U.S.A.* 113 **M5**
Premuda, *Croatia* 29 **D11**
Prentice, *U.S.A.* 112 **C9**
Prenzlau, *Germany* 24 **B9**
Preobrazheniye, *Russia* 54 **C6**
Preparis North Channel, *Ind. Oc.* 67 **M18**
Preparis South Channel, *Ind. Oc.* 67 **M18**
Přerov, *Czech Rep.* 27 **B10**
Prescott, *Canada* 102 **D4**
Prescott, *Ariz., U.S.A.* 115 **J7**
Prescott, *Ark., U.S.A.* 113 **J8**
Prescott Valley, *U.S.A.* 115 **J7**
Preservation Inlet, *N.Z.* 91 **M1**
Preševo, *Serbia, Yug.* 40 **D5**
Presho, *U.S.A.* 112 **D4**
Presicce, *Italy* 31 **C11**
Presidencia de la Plaza, *Argentina* 126 **B4**
Presidencia Roque Saenz Peña, *Argentina* 126 **B3**
Presidente Epitácio, *Brazil* 125 **H8**
Presidente Hayes □, *Paraguay* 126 **A4**
Presidente Prudente, *Brazil* 127 **A5**
Presidio, *Mexico* 118 **B4**
Presidio, *U.S.A.* 113 **L2**
Preslav, *Bulgaria* 41 **C10**
Preslavska Planina, *Bulgaria* 41 **C10**
Prešov, *Slovak Rep.* 27 **B14**
Prešovský □, *Slovak Rep.* 27 **B13**
Prespa, *Bulgaria* 41 **E8**
Prespa, L. = Prespansko Jezero, *Macedonia* 40 **F5**
Prespansko Jezero, *Macedonia* 40 **F5**
Presque I., *U.S.A.* 110 **D4**
Presque Isle, *U.S.A.* 109 **B12**
Prestatyn, *U.K.* 12 **D4**
Prestea, *Ghana* 82 **D4**
Presteigne, *U.K.* 13 **E5**
Přeštice, *Czech Rep.* 26 **B6**
Preston, *Canada* 110 **C4**
Preston, *U.K.* 12 **D5**
Preston, *Idaho, U.S.A.* 114 **E8**
Preston, *Minn., U.S.A.* 112 **D8**
Preston, C., *Australia* 92 **D2**
Prestonburg, *U.S.A.* 108 **G4**
Prestwick, *U.K.* 14 **F4**
Pretoria, *S. Africa* 89 **D4**
Preuilly-sur-Claise, *France* 18 **F7**
Préveza, *Greece* 38 **C2**
Préveza □, *Greece* 38 **B2**
Prey Veng, *Cambodia* 65 **G5**
Priazovskoye, *Ukraine* 47 **J8**
Pribilof Is., *U.S.A.* 100 **C2**
Priboj, *Serbia, Yug.* 40 **C3**
Příbram, *Czech Rep.* 26 **B7**
Price, *U.S.A.* 114 **G8**
Price I., *Canada* 104 **C3**
Prichard, *U.S.A.* 109 **K1**
Priego, *Spain* 32 **E2**
Priego de Córdoba, *Spain* 35 **H6**
Priekule, *Latvia* 9 **H19**
Prien, *Germany* 25 **H8**
Prienai, *Lithuania* 9 **J20**
Prieska, *S. Africa* 88 **D3**
Priest L., *U.S.A.* 114 **B5**
Priest River, *U.S.A.* 114 **B5**
Priest Valley, *U.S.A.* 116 **J6**
Prievidza, *Slovak Rep.* 27 **C11**
Prignitz, *Germany* 24 **B7**
Prijedor, *Bos.-H.* 29 **D13**
Prijepolje, *Serbia, Yug.* 40 **C3**
Prikaspiyskaya Nizmennost = Caspian Depression, *Eurasia* 49 **G9**
Prikro, *Ivory C.* 82 **D4**
Prikubanskaya Nizmennost, *Russia* 49 **H4**
Prilep, *Macedonia* 40 **E5**
Priluki = Pryluky, *Ukraine* 47 **G7**
Prime Seal I., *Australia* 94 **G4**
Primorsk, *Russia* 46 **B5**
Primorsko, *Bulgaria* 41 **D11**
Primorsko-Akhtarsk, *Russia* 47 **J10**
Primorskoye, *Ukraine* 47 **J9**
Primrose L., *Canada* 105 **C7**
Prince Albert, *Canada* 105 **C7**
Prince Albert, *S. Africa* 88 **E3**
Prince Albert Mts., *Antarctica* 5 **D11**
Prince Albert Nat. Park, *Canada* 105 **C7**
Prince Albert Pen., *Canada* 100 **A8**
Prince Albert Sd., *Canada* 100 **A8**
Prince Alfred, C., *Canada* 4 **B1**
Prince Charles I., *Canada* 101 **B12**
Prince Charles Mts., *Antarctica* 5 **D6**
Prince Edward I. □, *Canada* 103 **C7**
Prince Edward Is., *Ind. Oc.* 3 **G11**
Prince Edward Pt., *Canada* 110 **C8**
Prince George, *Canada* 104 **C4**
Prince of Wales, C., *U.S.A.* 98 **C3**
Prince of Wales I., *Australia* 94 **A3**
Prince of Wales I., *Canada* 100 **A10**
Prince of Wales I., *U.S.A.* 100 **C6**
Prince Patrick I., *Canada* 4 **B2**
Prince Regent Inlet, *Canada* 4 **B3**
Prince Rupert, *Canada* 104 **C2**
Princess Charlotte B., *Australia* 94 **A3**
Princess May Ranges, *Australia* 92 **C4**
Princess Royal I., *Canada* 104 **C3**
Princeton, *Canada* 104 **D4**
Princeton, *Calif., U.S.A.* 116 **F4**
Princeton, *Ill., U.S.A.* 112 **E10**
Princeton, *Ind., U.S.A.* 108 **F2**
Princeton, *Ky., U.S.A.* 108 **G2**
Princeton, *Mo., U.S.A.* 112 **E8**
Princeton, *N.J., U.S.A.* 111 **F10**
Princeton, *W. Va., U.S.A.* 108 **G5**
Principe, I. de, *Atl. Oc.* 76 **F4**
Principe da Beira, *Brazil* 124 **F6**
Prineville, *U.S.A.* 114 **D3**
Prins Harald Kyst, *Antarctica* 5 **D4**
Prinsesse Astrid Kyst, *Antarctica* 5 **D3**
Prinsesse Ragnhild Kyst, *Antarctica* 5 **D4**
Prinzapolca, *Nic.* 120 **D3**
Prior, C., *Spain* 34 **B2**
Priozersk, *Russia* 46 **B6**
Pripet = Prypyat →, *Europe* 47 **G6**
Pripet Marshes, *Europe* 47 **F5**
Pripyat Marshes = Pripet Marshes, *Europe* 47 **F5**
Pripyats = Prypyat →, *Europe* 47 **G6**
Prislop, Pasul, *Romania* 43 **C9**
Pristen, *Russia* 47 **G9**
Priština, *Kosovo, Yug.* 40 **D5**
Pritzwalk, *Germany* 24 **B8**
Privas, *France* 21 **D8**
Priverno, *Italy* 30 **A6**
Privolzhsk, *Russia* 48 **B5**
Privolzhskaya Vozvyshennost, *Russia* 48 **E7**
Privolzhskiy, *Russia* 48 **E8**
Privolzhye, *Russia* 48 **D9**
Priyutnoye, *Russia* 49 **G6**
Prizren, *Kosovo, Yug.* 40 **D4**
Prizzi, *Italy* 30 **E6**
Prnjavor, *Bos.-H.* 42 **F2**
Probolinggo, *Indonesia* 63 **G15**
Prochowice, *Poland* 45 **G3**
Proctor, *U.S.A.* 111 **C11**
Proddatur, *India* 66 **M11**
Prodhromos, *Cyprus* 36 **E11**
Proença-a-Nova, *Portugal* 34 **F3**
Profítis Ilías, *Greece* 36 **C9**
Profondeville, *Belgium* 17 **D4**
Progreso, *Coahuila, Mexico* 118 **B4**
Progreso, *Yucatán, Mexico* 119 **C7**
Prokhladnyy, *Russia* 49 **J7**
Prokletije, *Albania* 40 **D3**
Prokopyevsk, *Russia* 50 **D9**
Prokuplje, *Serbia, Yug.* 40 **C5**
Proletarsk, *Russia* 49 **G5**
Proletarskaya = Proletarsk, *Russia* 49 **G5**
Prome = Pyè, *Burma* 67 **K19**
Prophet →, *Canada* 104 **B4**
Prophet River, *Canada* 104 **B4**
Propriá, *Brazil* 125 **F11**
Propriano, *France* 21 **G12**
Proserpine, *Australia* 94 **C4**
Prosna →, *Poland* 45 **F4**
Prospect, *U.S.A.* 111 **C9**
Prosser, *U.S.A.* 114 **C4**
Prostějov, *Czech Rep.* 27 **B10**
Prostki, *Poland* 44 **E9**
Proston, *Australia* 95 **D5**
Proszowice, *Poland* 45 **H7**
Próti, *Greece* 38 **D3**
Provadiya, *Bulgaria* 41 **C11**
Provence, *France* 21 **E9**
Provence-Alpes-Côte d'Azur □, *France* 21 **D10**
Providence, *Ky., U.S.A.* 108 **G2**
Providence, *R.I., U.S.A.* 111 **E13**
Providence Bay, *Canada* 102 **C3**
Providence Mts., *U.S.A.* 117 **K11**
Providencia, I. de, *Colombia* 120 **D3**
Provideniya, *Russia* 51 **C19**
Provins, *France* 19 **D10**
Provo, *U.S.A.* 114 **F8**
Provost, *Canada* 105 **C6**
Prozor, *Bos.-H.* 42 **G2**
Prrenjas, *Albania* 40 **E4**
Prudhoe Bay, *U.S.A.* 100 **A5**
Prudhoe I., *Australia* 94 **C4**
Prud'homme, *Canada* 105 **C7**
Prudnik, *Poland* 45 **H4**
Prüm, *Germany* 25 **E2**
Prundu, *Romania* 43 **F11**
Pruszcz Gdański, *Poland* 44 **D5**
Pruszków, *Poland* 45 **F7**
Prut →, *Romania* 43 **E13**
Pruzhany, *Belarus* 47 **F3**
Prvič, *Croatia* 29 **D11**
Prydz B., *Antarctica* 5 **C6**
Pryluky, *Ukraine* 47 **G7**
Pryor, *U.S.A.* 113 **G7**
Prypyat →, *Europe* 47 **G6**
Przasnysz, *Poland* 45 **E7**
Przedbórz, *Poland* 45 **G6**
Przedecz, *Poland* 45 **F5**
Przemków, *Poland* 45 **G2**
Przemyśl, *Poland* 45 **J9**
Przeworsk, *Poland* 45 **H9**
Przewóz, *Poland* 45 **G1**
Przhevalsk = Karakol, *Kyrgyzstan* 50 **E8**
Przysucha, *Poland* 45 **G7**
Psakhná, *Greece* 38 **C5**
Psará, *Greece* 39 **C7**
Psathoúra, *Greece* 38 **B6**
Psel →, *Ukraine* 47 **H7**
Pserimos, *Greece* 39 **E9**
Psíra, *Greece* 36 **D7**
Pskov, *Russia* 46 **D5**
Pskovskoye, Ozero, *Russia* 46 **D5**
Psunj, *Croatia* 42 **E2**
Pteleón, *Greece* 38 **B4**
Ptich = Ptsich →, *Belarus* 47 **F5**
Ptolemaís, *Greece* 40 **F5**
Ptsich →, *Belarus* 47 **F5**
Ptuj, *Slovenia* 29 **B12**
Ptujska Gora, *Slovenia* 29 **B12**
Pu Xian, *China* 56 **F6**
Pua, *Thailand* 64 **C3**
Puán, *Argentina* 126 **D3**
Pu'an, *China* 58 **E5**
Puan, *S. Korea* 57 **G14**
Pubei, *China* 58 **F7**
Pucallpa, *Peru* 124 **E4**
Pucheng, *China* 59 **D12**
Pucheni, *Romania* 43 **E10**
Puchheim, *Germany* 25 **G7**
Púchov, *Slovak Rep.* 27 **B11**
Pucioasa, *Romania* 43 **E10**
Pučišća, *Croatia* 29 **E13**
Puck, *Poland* 44 **D5**
Pucka, Zatoka, *Poland* 44 **D5**
Puçol, *Spain* 33 **F4**
Pudasjärvi, *Finland* 8 **D22**
Puding, *China* 58 **D5**
Pudozh, *Russia* 46 **B9**
Pudukkottai, *India* 66 **P11**
Puebla, *Mexico* 119 **D5**
Puebla □, *Mexico* 119 **D5**
Puebla de Alcocer, *Spain* 35 **G5**
Puebla de Don Fadrique, *Spain* 33 **H2**
Puebla de Don Rodrigo, *Spain* 35 **F6**
Puebla de Guzmán, *Spain* 35 **H3**
Puebla de la Calzada, *Spain* 35 **G4**
Puebla de Sanabria, *Spain* 34 **C4**
Puebla de Trives = Pobra de Trives, *Spain* 34 **C3**
Pueblo, *U.S.A.* 112 **F2**
Pueblo Hundido, *Chile* 126 **B1**
Puelches, *Argentina* 126 **D2**
Puelén, *Argentina* 126 **D2**
Puente Alto, *Chile* 126 **C1**
Puente-Genil, *Spain* 35 **H6**
Puente la Reina, *Spain* 32 **C3**
Puenteareas = Ponteareas, *Spain* 34 **C2**
Puentedeume = Pontedeume, *Spain* 34 **B2**
Puentes de Garcia Rodriguez = As Pontes de García Rodríguez, *Spain* 34 **B3**
Pu'er, *China* 58 **F3**
Puerco →, *U.S.A.* 115 **J10**
Puerto, *Canary Is.* 37 **F2**
Puerto Aisén, *Chile* 128 **F2**
Puerto Ángel, *Mexico* 119 **D5**
Puerto Arista, *Mexico* 119 **D6**
Puerto Armuelles, *Panama* 120 **E3**
Puerto Ayacucho, *Venezuela* 124 **B5**
Puerto Barrios, *Guatemala* 120 **C2**
Puerto Bermejo, *Argentina* 126 **B4**
Puerto Bermúdez, *Peru* 124 **F4**
Puerto Bolívar, *Ecuador* 124 **D3**
Puerto Cabello, *Venezuela* 124 **A5**
Puerto Cabezas, *Nic.* 120 **D3**
Puerto Cabo Gracias á Dios, *Nic.* 120 **D3**
Puerto Carreño, *Colombia* 124 **B5**
Puerto Castilla, *Honduras* 120 **C2**
Puerto Chicama, *Peru* 124 **E3**
Puerto Coig, *Argentina* 128 **G3**
Puerto Cortés, *Costa Rica* 120 **E3**
Puerto Cortés, *Honduras* 120 **C2**
Puerto Cumarebo, *Venezuela* 124 **A5**
Puerto de Alcudia = Port d'Alcúdia, *Spain* 37 **B10**
Puerto de Andraitx, *Spain* 37 **B9**
Puerto de Cabrera, *Spain* 37 **B9**
Puerto de Gran Tarajal, *Canary Is.* 37 **F5**
Puerto de la Cruz, *Canary Is.* 37 **F3**
Puerto de Mazarrón, *Spain* 33 **H3**
Puerto de Pozo Negro, *Canary Is.* 37 **F6**
Puerto de Sóller = Port de Sóller, *Spain* 37 **B9**
Puerto de Somosierra, *Spain* 34 **D7**
Puerto del Carmen, *Canary Is.* 37 **F6**
Puerto del Rosario, *Canary Is.* 37 **F6**
Puerto Deseado, *Argentina* 128 **F3**
Puerto Escondido, *Mexico* 119 **D5**
Puerto Heath, *Bolivia* 124 **F5**
Puerto Inírida, *Colombia* 124 **C5**
Puerto Juárez, *Mexico* 119 **C7**
Puerto La Cruz, *Venezuela* 124 **A6**
Puerto Leguízamo, *Colombia* 124 **D4**
Puerto Limón, *Colombia* 124 **C4**
Puerto Lobos, *Argentina* 128 **E3**
Puerto Lumbreras, *Spain* 33 **H3**
Puerto Madryn, *Argentina* 128 **E3**
Puerto Maldonado, *Peru* 124 **F5**
Puerto Manotí, *Cuba* 120 **B4**
Puerto Mazarrón = Puerto de Mazarrón, *Spain* 33 **H3**
Puerto Montt, *Chile* 128 **E2**
Puerto Morazán, *Nic.* 120 **D2**
Puerto Morelos, *Mexico* 119 **C7**
Puerto Natales, *Chile* 128 **G2**
Puerto Padre, *Cuba* 120 **B4**
Puerto Páez, *Venezuela* 124 **B5**
Puerto Peñasco, *Mexico* 118 **A2**
Puerto Pinasco, *Paraguay* 126 **A4**
Puerto Plata, *Dom. Rep.* 121 **C5**
Puerto Pollensa = Port de Pollença, *Spain* 37 **B10**
Puerto Princesa, *Phil.* 61 **G3**
Puerto Quepos, *Costa Rica* 120 **E3**
Puerto Real, *Spain* 35 **J4**
Puerto Rico, *Canary Is.* 37 **G4**
Puerto Rico ■, *W. Indies* 121 **C6**
Puerto Rico Trench, *Atl. Oc.* 121 **C6**
Puerto San Julián, *Argentina* 128 **F3**
Puerto Sastre, *Paraguay* 126 **A4**
Puerto Serrano, *Spain* 35 **J5**
Puerto Suárez, *Bolivia* 124 **G7**
Puerto Vallarta, *Mexico* 118 **C3**

Puerto Wilches, *Colombia* 124 B4
Puertollano, *Spain* 35 G6
Pueyrredón, L., *Argentina* 128 F2
Puffin I., *Ireland* 15 E1
Pugachev, *Russia* 48 D9
Pugal, *India* 68 E5
Puge, *China* 58 D4
Puge, *Tanzania* 86 C3
Puget Sound, *U.S.A.* 114 C2
Puget-Théniers, *France* 21 E10
Púglia □, *Italy* 31 A9
Pugŏdong, *N. Korea* 57 C16
Pugu, *Tanzania* 86 D4
Pūgūnzī, *Iran* 71 E8
Pui, *Romania* 42 E8
Puieşti, *Romania* 43 D12
Puig Major, *Spain* 37 B9
Puigcerdà, *Spain* 32 C6
Puigmal, *Spain* 32 C7
Puigpunyent, *Spain* 37 B9
Puijiang, *China* 58 B4
Puisaye, Collines de la, *France* 19 E10
Puiseaux, *France* 19 D9
Pujehun, *S. Leone* 82 D2
Pujiang, *China* 59 C12
Pujols, *France* 20 D3
Pujon-chŏsuji, *N. Korea* 57 D14
Pukaki L., *N.Z.* 91 L3
Pukapuka, *Cook Is.* 97 J11
Pukaskwa Nat. Park, *Canada* 102 C2
Pukatawagan, *Canada* 105 B8
Pukchin, *N. Korea* 57 D13
Pukch'ŏng, *N. Korea* 57 D15
Pukë, *Albania* 40 D3
Pukekohe, *N.Z.* 91 G5
Pukhrayan, *India* 69 F8
Pukou, *China* 59 A12
Pula, *Croatia* 29 D10
Pula, *Italy* 30 C1
Pulacayo, *Bolivia* 124 H5
Pulandian, *China* 57 E11
Pularumpi, *Australia* 92 B5
Pulaski, *N.Y., U.S.A.* 111 C8
Pulaski, *Tenn., U.S.A.* 109 H2
Pulaski, *Va., U.S.A.* 108 G5
Pulau →, *Indonesia* 63 F9
Puławy, *Poland* 45 G8
Pulga, *U.S.A.* 116 F5
Pulicat L., *India* 66 N12
Pullman, *U.S.A.* 114 C5
Pulo-Anna, *Pac. Oc.* 63 D8
Pulog, Mt., *Phil.* 61 C4
Pułtusk, *Poland* 45 F8
Pülümür, *Turkey* 73 C8
Pumlumon Fawr, *U.K.* 13 E4
Puná, I., *Ecuador* 124 D2
Punakha, *Bhutan* 67 F16
Punasar, *India* 68 F5
Punata, *Bolivia* 124 G5
Punch, *India* 69 C6
Punch →, *Pakistan* 68 C5
Punda Maria, *S. Africa* 89 C5
Pune, *India* 66 K8
P'ungsan, *N. Korea* 57 D15
Pungue, Ponte de, *Mozam.* 87 F3
Puning, *China* 59 F11
Punjab □, *India* 68 D7
Punjab □, *Pakistan* 68 E6
Puno, *Peru* 124 G4
Punpun →, *India* 69 G11
Punta Alta, *Argentina* 128 D4
Punta Arenas, *Chile* 128 G2
Punta de Díaz, *Chile* 126 B1
Punta Gorda, *Belize* 119 D7
Punta Gorda, *U.S.A.* 109 M5
Punta Prieta, *Mexico* 118 B2
Punta Prima, *Spain* 37 B11
Punta Umbría, *Spain* 35 H4
Puntarenas, *Costa Rica* 120 E3
Punto Fijo, *Venezuela* 124 A4
Punxsatawney, *U.S.A.* 110 F6
Puqi, *China* 59 C9
Puquio, *Peru* 124 F4
Pur →, *Russia* 50 C8
Purace, Vol., *Colombia* 124 C3
Puračić, *Bos.-H.* 42 F3
Puralia = Puruliya, *India* 69 H12
Puranpur, *India* 69 E9
Purbeck, Isle of, *U.K.* 13 G6
Purcell, *U.S.A.* 113 H6
Purcell Mts., *Canada* 104 D5
Puri, *India* 67 K14
Purmerend, *Neths.* 17 B4
Purnia, *India* 69 G12
Pursat = Pouthisat, *Cambodia* 64 F4
Purukcahu, *Indonesia* 62 E4
Puruliya, *India* 69 H12
Purus →, *Brazil* 122 D4
Puruvesi, *Finland* 46 B5
Purvis, *U.S.A.* 113 K10
Pŭrvomay, *Bulgaria* 41 D9
Purwa, *India* 69 F9
Purwakarta, *Indonesia* 63 G12
Purwodadi, *Indonesia* 63 G14
Purwokerto, *Indonesia* 63 G13
Puryŏng, *N. Korea* 57 C15
Pusa, *India* 69 G11
Pusan, *S. Korea* 57 G15
Pushkin, *Russia* 46 C6
Pushkino, *Moskva, Russia* 46 D9
Pushkino, *Saratov, Russia* 48 E8
Püspökladány, *Hungary* 42 C6
Pustoshka, *Russia* 46 D5
Puszczykowo, *Poland* 45 F3
Putahow L., *Canada* 105 B8
Putao, *Burma* 67 F20
Putaruru, *N.Z.* 91 H5
Putbus, *Germany* 24 A9
Putian, *China* 59 E12
Putignano, *Italy* 31 B10
Puting, Tanjung, *Indonesia* 62 E4
Putlitz, *Germany* 24 B8
Putna, *Romania* 43 C10
Putna →, *Romania* 43 E12
Putnam, *U.S.A.* 111 E13
Putnok, *Hungary* 42 B5
Putorana, Gory, *Russia* 51 C10
Puttalam, *Sri Lanka* 66 Q11
Puttgarden, *Germany* 24 A7
Püttlingen, *Germany* 25 F2
Putumayo →, *S. Amer.* 122 D4
Putuo, *China* 59 C14
Putussibau, *Indonesia* 62 D4
Puvirnituq, *Canada* 101 B12
Puy-de-Dôme, *France* 20 C6
Puy-de-Dôme □, *France* 20 C7
Puy-l'Évêque, *France* 20 D5
Puyallup, *U.S.A.* 116 C4
Puyang, *China* 56 G8
Puylaurens, *France* 20 E6
Pūzeh Rīg, *Iran* 71 E8
Pwani □, *Tanzania* 86 D4
Pweto, *Dem. Rep. of the Congo* 87 D2
Pwllheli, *U.K.* 12 E3
Pyana →, *Russia* 48 C8
Pyapon, *Burma* 67 L19
Pyasina →, *Russia* 51 B9
Pyatigorsk, *Russia* 49 H6
Pyatykhatky, *Ukraine* 47 H7
Pydna, *Greece* 40 F6
Pyè, *Burma* 67 K19
Pyetrikaw, *Belarus* 47 F5
Pyhäjoki, *Finland* 8 D21
Pyinmana, *Burma* 67 K20
Pyla, C., *Cyprus* 36 E12
Pymatuning Reservoir, *U.S.A.* 110 E4
Pyŏktong, *N. Korea* 57 D13
Pyŏnggang, *N. Korea* 57 E14
P'yŏngt'aek, *S. Korea* 57 F14
P'yŏngyang, *N. Korea* 57 E13
Pyote, *U.S.A.* 113 K3
Pyramid L., *U.S.A.* 114 G4
Pyramid Pk., *U.S.A.* 117 J10
Pyramids, *Egypt* 80 J7
Pyrénées, *Europe* 20 F4
Pyrénées-Atlantiques □, *France* 20 E3
Pyrénées-Orientales □, *France* 20 F6
Pyryatyn, *Ukraine* 47 G7
Pyrzyce, *Poland* 45 E1
Pyskowice, *Poland* 45 H5
Pytalovo, *Russia* 46 D4
Pyu, *Burma* 67 K20
Pyzdry, *Poland* 45 F4

Q

Qaanaaq, *Greenland* 4 B4
Qabirri →, *Azerbaijan* 49 K8
Qachasnek, *S. Africa* 89 E4
Qa'el Jafr, *Jordan* 75 E5
Qa'emābād, *Iran* 71 D9
Qā'emshahr, *Iran* 71 B7
Qagan Nur, *China* 56 C8
Qahar Youyi Zhongqi, *China* 56 D7
Qahremānshahr = Bākhtarān, *Iran* 70 C5
Qaidam Pendi, *China* 60 C4
Qajarīyeh, *Iran* 71 D6
Qala, Ras il, *Malta* 36 C1
Qala-i-Jadid = Spīn Búldak, *Afghan.* 68 D2
Qala Viala, *Pakistan* 68 D2
Qala Yangi, *Afghan.* 68 B2
Qal'at al Akhḑar, *Si. Arabia* 70 E3
Qal'at Dīzah, *Iraq* 70 B5
Qal'at Şāliḩ, *Iraq* 70 D5
Qal'at Sukkar, *Iraq* 70 D5
Qalyûb, *Egypt* 80 H7
Qamani'tuaq = Baker Lake, *Canada* 100 B10
Qamdo, *China* 58 B1
Qamruddin Karez, *Pakistan* 68 D3
Qandahār, *Afghan.* 66 D4
Qandahār □, *Afghan.* 66 D4
Qapān, *Iran* 71 B7
Qapshaghay, *Kazakstan* 50 E8
Qaqortoq, *Greenland* 101 B6
Qâra, *Egypt* 80 B2
Qara Qash →, *India* 69 B8
Qarabutaq, *Kazakstan* 50 E7
Qaraçala, *Azerbaijan* 49 L9
Qaraghandy, *Kazakstan* 50 E8
Qārah, *Si. Arabia* 70 D4
Qarataū, *Kazakstan* 50 E8
Qarataū, *Kazakstan* 50 E7
Qardud, *Sudan* 81 E2
Qareh →, *Iran* 70 B5
Qareh Tekān, *Iran* 71 B6
Qarqan He →, *China* 60 C3
Qarqaraly, *Kazakstan* 50 E8
Qarrasa, *Sudan* 81 E3
Qarshi, *Uzbekistan* 50 F7
Qartabā, *Lebanon* 75 A4
Qaryat al Gharab, *Iraq* 70 D5
Qaryat al 'Ulyā, *Si. Arabia* 70 E5
Qasr 'Amra, *Jordan* 70 D3
Qaşr-e Qand, *Iran* 71 E9
Qasr Farâfra, *Egypt* 80 B2
Qatanā, *Syria* 75 B5
Qatar ■, *Asia* 71 E6
Qatlīsh, *Iran* 71 B8
Qattâra, *Egypt* 80 A2
Qattâra, Munkhafed el, *Egypt* 80 B2
Qattâra Depression = Qattâra, Munkhafed el, *Egypt* 80 B2
Qawām al Ḩamzah, *Iraq* 70 D5
Qāyen, *Iran* 71 C8
Qazaqstan = Kazakstan ■, *Asia* 50 E7
Qazimämmäd, *Azerbaijan* 49 K9
Qazvin, *Iran* 71 B6
Qeissan, *Sudan* 81 E3
Qena, *Egypt* 80 B3
Qena, W. →, *Egypt* 80 B3
Qeqertarsuaq, *Greenland* 101 B5
Qeqertarsuaq, *Greenland* 4 C5
Qeshlāq, *Iran* 70 C5
Qeshm, *Iran* 71 E8
Qeys, *Iran* 71 E7
Qezel Owzen →, *Iran* 71 B6
Qezi'ot, *Israel* 75 E3
Qi Xian, *China* 56 G8
Qian Gorlos, *China* 57 B13
Qian Xian, *China* 56 G5
Qiancheng, *China* 58 D7
Qianjiang, *Guangxi Zhuangzu, China* 58 F7
Qianjiang, *Hubei, China* 59 B9
Qianjiang, *Sichuan, China* 58 C7
Qianshan, *China* 59 B11
Qianwei, *China* 58 C4
Qianxi, *China* 58 D6
Qianyang, *Hunan, China* 59 D8
Qianyang, *Shaanxi, China* 56 G4
Qianyang, *Zhejiang, China* 59 B12
Qiaojia, *China* 58 D4
Qichun, *China* 59 B10
Qidong, *Hunan, China* 59 D9
Qidong, *Jiangsu, China* 59 B13
Qijiang, *China* 58 C6
Qikiqtarjuaq, *Canada* 101 B13
Qila Safed, *Pakistan* 66 E2
Qila Saifullāh, *Pakistan* 68 D3
Qilian Shan, *China* 60 C4
Qimen, *China* 59 C11
Qin He →, *China* 56 G7
Qin Jiang →, *Guangxi Zhuangzu, China* 58 F7
Qin Jiang →, *Jiangxi, China* 59 D10
Qin Ling = Qinling Shandi, *China* 56 H5
Qin'an, *China* 56 G3
Qing Xian, *China* 56 E9
Qingcheng, *China* 57 F9
Qingdao, *China* 57 F11
Qingfeng, *China* 56 G8
Qinghai □, *China* 60 C4
Qinghai Hu, *China* 60 C5
Qinghecheng, *China* 57 D13
Qinghemen, *China* 57 D11
Qingjian, *China* 56 F6
Qingjiang = Huaiyin, *China* 57 H10
Qingliu, *China* 59 D11
Qinglong, *China* 58 E5
Qingping, *China* 58 D6
Qingpu, *China* 59 B13
Qingshui, *China* 56 G4
Qingshuihe, *China* 56 E6
Qingtian, *China* 59 C13
Qingtongxia Shuiku, *China* 56 F3
Qingxi, *China* 58 D7
Qingxu, *China* 56 F7
Qingyang, *Anhui, China* 59 B11
Qingyang, *Gansu, China* 56 F4
Qingyi Jiang →, *China* 58 C4
Qingyuan, *Guangdong, China* 59 F9
Qingyuan, *Liaoning, China* 57 C13
Qingyuan, *Zhejiang, China* 59 D12
Qingyun, *China* 57 F9
Qingzhen, *China* 58 D6
Qinhuangdao, *China* 57 E10
Qinling Shandi, *China* 56 H5
Qinshui, *China* 56 G7
Qinyang = Jiyuan, *China* 56 G7
Qinyuan, *China* 56 F7
Qinzhou, *China* 58 G7
Qionghai, *China* 64 C8
Qionglai, *China* 58 B4
Qionglai Shan, *China* 58 B4
Qiongzhou Haixia, *China* 64 B8
Qiqihar, *China* 51 E13
Qirâiya, W. →, *Egypt* 75 E3
Qiryat Ata, *Israel* 75 C4
Qiryat Gat, *Israel* 75 D3
Qiryat Mal'akhi, *Israel* 75 D3
Qiryat Shemona, *Israel* 75 B4
Qiryat Yam, *Israel* 75 C4
Qishan, *China* 56 G4
Qitai, *China* 60 B3
Qiubei, *China* 58 E5
Qixia, *China* 57 F11
Qiyang, *China* 59 D8
Qızılağac Körfäzi, *Azerbaijan* 71 B6
Qojūr, *Iran* 70 B5
Qom, *Iran* 71 C6
Qomolangma Feng = Everest, Mt., *Nepal* 69 E12
Qomsheh, *Iran* 71 D6
Qoraqalpoghistan □, *Uzbekistan* 50 E6
Qorveh, *Iran* 73 E12
Qostanay, *Kazakstan* 50 D7
Qotūr, *Iran* 73 C11
Qu Jiang →, *China* 58 B6
Qu Xian, *China* 58 B6
Quabbin Reservoir, *U.S.A.* 111 D12
Quairading, *Australia* 93 F2
Quakenbrück, *Germany* 24 C3
Quakertown, *U.S.A.* 111 F9
Qualicum Beach, *Canada* 104 D4
Quamby, *Australia* 94 C3
Quan Long = Ca Mau, *Vietnam* 65 H5
Quanah, *U.S.A.* 113 H5
Quang Ngai, *Vietnam* 64 E7
Quang Tri, *Vietnam* 64 D6
Quang Yen, *Vietnam* 58 G6
Quannan, *China* 59 E10
Quantock Hills, *U.K.* 13 F4
Quanzhou, *Fujian, China* 59 E12
Quanzhou, *Guangxi Zhuangzu, China* 59 E8
Qu'Appelle, *Canada* 105 C8
Quaqtaq, *Canada* 101 B13
Quaraí, *Brazil* 126 C4
Quarré-les-Tombes, *France* 19 E11
Quarteira, *Portugal* 35 H2
Quartu Sant'Elena, *Italy* 30 C2
Quartzsite, *U.S.A.* 117 M12
Quatsino Sd., *Canada* 104 C3
Quba, *Azerbaijan* 49 K9
Qūchān, *Iran* 71 B8
Québec, *Canada* 103 C5
Québec □, *Canada* 103 C6
Quedlinburg, *Germany* 24 D7
Queen Alexandra Ra., *Antarctica* 5 E11
Queen Charlotte City, *Canada* 104 C2
Queen Charlotte Is., *Canada* 104 C2
Queen Charlotte Sd., *Canada* 104 C3
Queen Charlotte Strait, *Canada* 104 C3
Queen Elizabeth Is., *Canada* 98 B10
Queen Elizabeth Nat. Park, *Uganda* 86 C3
Queen Mary Land, *Antarctica* 5 D7
Queen Maud G., *Canada* 100 B9
Queen Maud Land, *Antarctica* 5 D3
Queen Maud Mts., *Antarctica* 5 E13
Queens Chan., *Australia* 92 C4
Queensland □, *Australia* 94 C3
Queenstown, *Australia* 94 G4
Queenstown, *N.Z.* 91 L2
Queenstown, *S. Africa* 88 E4
Queets, *U.S.A.* 116 C2
Queguay Grande →, *Uruguay* 126 C4
Queimadas, *Brazil* 125 F11
Quelimane, *Mozam.* 87 F4
Quellón, *Chile* 128 E2
Quelpart = Cheju do, *S. Korea* 57 H14
Queluz, *Portugal* 35 G1
Quemado, *N. Mex., U.S.A.* 115 J9
Quemado, *Tex., U.S.A.* 113 L4
Quemoy = Chinmen, *Taiwan* 59 E13
Quemú-Quemú, *Argentina* 126 D3
Quequén, *Argentina* 126 D4
Querétaro, *Mexico* 118 C4
Querétaro □, *Mexico* 118 C5
Querfurt, *Germany* 24 D7
Quérigut, *France* 20 F6
Querqueville, *France* 18 C5
Quesada, *Spain* 35 H7
Queshan, *China* 56 H8
Quesnel, *Canada* 104 C4
Quesnel →, *Canada* 104 C4
Quesnel L., *Canada* 104 C4
Questa, *U.S.A.* 115 H11
Questembert, *France* 18 E4
Quetico Prov. Park, *Canada* 102 C1
Quetta, *Pakistan* 68 D2
Quezaltenango, *Guatemala* 120 D1
Quezon City, *Phil.* 61 D4
Qufār, *Si. Arabia* 70 E4
Qui Nhon, *Vietnam* 64 F7
Quibaxe, *Angola* 84 F2
Quibdo, *Colombia* 124 B3
Quiberon, *France* 18 E3
Quiberon, Presqu'île de, *France* 18 E3
Quickborn, *Germany* 24 B5
Quiet L., *Canada* 104 A2
Quiindy, *Paraguay* 126 B4
Quila, *Mexico* 118 C3
Quilán, C., *Chile* 128 E2
Quilcene, *U.S.A.* 116 C4
Quilimarí, *Chile* 126 C1
Quilino, *Argentina* 126 C3
Quill Lakes, *Canada* 105 C8
Quillabamba, *Peru* 124 F4
Quillagua, *Chile* 126 A2
Quillaicillo, *Chile* 126 C1
Quillan, *France* 20 F6
Quillota, *Chile* 126 C1
Quilmes, *Argentina* 126 C4
Quilon, *India* 66 Q10
Quilpie, *Australia* 95 D3
Quilpué, *Chile* 126 C1
Quilua, *Mozam.* 87 F4
Quimilí, *Argentina* 126 B3
Quimper, *France* 18 E2
Quimperlé, *France* 18 E3
Quinault →, *U.S.A.* 116 C2
Quincy, *Calif., U.S.A.* 116 F6
Quincy, *Fla., U.S.A.* 109 K3
Quincy, *Ill., U.S.A.* 112 F9
Quincy, *Mass., U.S.A.* 111 D14
Quincy, *Wash., U.S.A.* 114 C4
Quines, *Argentina* 126 C2
Quinga, *Mozam.* 87 F5
Quingey, *France* 19 E12
Quinns Rocks, *Australia* 93 F2
Quintana de la Serena, *Spain* 35 G5
Quintana Roo □, *Mexico* 119 D7
Quintanar de la Orden, *Spain* 35 F7
Quintanar de la Sierra, *Spain* 32 D2
Quintanar del Rey, *Spain* 33 F3
Quintero, *Chile* 126 C1
Quintin, *France* 18 D4
Quinto, *Spain* 32 D4
Quípar →, *Spain* 33 G3
Quirihue, *Chile* 126 D1
Quirinópolis, *Brazil* 125 G8
Quiroga, *Spain* 34 C3
Quissac, *France* 21 E8
Quissanga, *Mozam.* 87 E5
Quissico, *Mozam.* 89 C5
Quitilipi, *Argentina* 126 B3
Quitman, *U.S.A.* 109 K4
Quito, *Ecuador* 124 D3
Quixadá, *Brazil* 125 D11
Quixaxe, *Mozam.* 87 F5
Qujing, *China* 58 E4
Qulan, *Kazakstan* 50 E8
Qul'ân, Jazâ'ir, *Egypt* 70 E2
Qumbu, *S. Africa* 89 E4
Quneitra, *Syria* 75 B4
Qŭnghirot, *Uzbekistan* 50 E6
Qu'nyido, *China* 58 B2
Quoin I., *Australia* 92 B4
Quoin Pt., *S. Africa* 88 E2
Qŭqon, *Uzbekistan* 50 E8
Qurein, *Sudan* 81 E3
Qurnat as Sawdā', *Lebanon* 75 A5
Qûs, *Egypt* 80 B3
Qusar, *Azerbaijan* 49 K9
Quşaybā', *Si. Arabia* 70 E4
Qusaybah, *Iraq* 70 C4
Quseir, *Egypt* 70 E2
Qūshchī, *Iran* 70 B5
Quthing, *Lesotho* 89 E4
Qūţīābād, *Iran* 71 C6
Quwo, *China* 56 G6
Quyang, *China* 56 E8
Quynh Nhai, *Vietnam* 64 B4
Quyon, *Canada* 111 A8
Quzhou, *China* 59 C12
Quzi, *China* 56 F4
Qvareli, *Georgia* 49 K7
Qytet Stalin = Kuçovë, *Albania* 40 F3
Qyzylorda, *Kazakstan* 50 E7

R

Ra, Ko, *Thailand* 65 H2
Raab, *Austria* 26 C6
Raahe, *Finland* 8 D21
Raalte, *Neths.* 17 B6
Raasay, *U.K.* 14 D2
Raasay, Sd. of, *U.K.* 14 D2
Rab, *Croatia* 29 D11
Raba, *Indonesia* 63 F5
Rába →, *Hungary* 42 C2
Raba →, *Poland* 45 H7
Rabaçal →, *Portugal* 34 D3
Rabah, *Nigeria* 83 C6
Rabai, *Kenya* 86 C4
Rabak, *Sudan* 81 E3
Rabastens, *France* 20 E5
Rabastens-de-Bigorre, *France* 20 E4
Rabat, *Malta* 36 D1
Rabat, *Morocco* 78 B4
Rabaul, *Papua N. G.* 96 H7
Rābigh, *Si. Arabia* 74 C2
Rabka, *Poland* 45 J6
Rabniţa, *Moldova* 43 C14
Rābor, *Iran* 71 D8
Rača, *Serbia, Yug.* 40 B4
Răcăciuni, *Romania* 43 D11
Răcăşdia, *Romania* 42 F6
Racconigi, *Italy* 28 D4
Race, C., *Canada* 103 C9
Rach Gia, *Vietnam* 65 G5
Rachid, *Mauritania* 82 B2
Raciąż, *Poland* 45 F7
Racibórz, *Poland* 45 H5
Racine, *U.S.A.* 108 D2
Rackerby, *U.S.A.* 116 F5
Radama, Nosy, *Madag.* 89 A8
Radama, Saikanosy, *Madag.* 89 A8
Radan, *Serbia, Yug.* 40 D5
Rădăuţi, *Romania* 43 C10
Rădăuţi-Prut, *Romania* 43 B11
Radbuza →, *Czech Rep.* 26 B6
Radcliff, *U.S.A.* 108 G3
Radeberg, *Germany* 24 D9
Radebeul, *Germany* 24 D9
Radeče, *Slovenia* 29 B12
Radekhiv, *Ukraine* 47 G3
Radekhov = Radekhiv, *Ukraine* 47 G3
Radenthein, *Austria* 26 E6
Radew →, *Poland* 44 D2
Radford, *U.S.A.* 108 G5
Radhanpur, *India* 68 H4
Radhwa, Jabal, *Si. Arabia* 70 E3
Radika →, *Macedonia* 40 E4
Radisson, *Qué., Canada* 102 B4
Radisson, *Sask., Canada* 105 C7
Radium Hot Springs, *Canada* 104 C5
Radlje ob Dravi, *Slovenia* 29 B12
Radnevo, *Bulgaria* 41 D9
Radnice, *Czech Rep.* 26 B6
Radnor Forest, *U.K.* 13 E4
Radolfzell, *Germany* 25 H4
Radom, *Poland* 45 G8
Radomir, *Bulgaria* 40 D6
Radomka →, *Poland* 45 G8
Radomsko, *Poland* 45 G6
Radomyshl, *Ukraine* 47 G5
Radomyśl Wielki, *Poland* 45 H8
Radoszyce, *Poland* 45 G7
Radoviš, *Macedonia* 40 E6

Radovljica, *Slovenia* 29 B11
Radstadt, *Austria* 26 D6
Radstock, C., *Australia* 95 E1
Răducăneni, *Romania* 43 D12
Raduša, *Macedonia* 40 D5
Radviliškis, *Lithuania* 9 J20
Radville, *Canada* 105 D8
Raḑwá, J., *Si. Arabia* 80 C4
Radymno, *Poland* 45 J9
Radzanów, *Poland* 45 F7
Radziejów, *Poland* 45 F5
Radzyń Chełmiński, *Poland* 44 E5
Radzyń Podlaski, *Poland* 45 G9
Rae, *Canada* 104 A5
Rae Bareli, *India* 69 F9
Rae Isthmus, *Canada* 101 B11
Raeren, *Belgium* 17 D6
Raeside, L., *Australia* 93 E3
Raetihi, *N.Z.* 91 H5
Rafaela, *Argentina* 126 C3
Rafah, *Gaza Strip* 75 D3
Rafai, *C.A.R.* 86 B1
Raffadali, *Italy* 30 E6
Raffili, *Sudan* 81 F2
Rafḩā, *Si. Arabia* 70 D4
Rafsanjān, *Iran* 71 D8
Raft Pt., *Australia* 92 C3
Râgâ, *Sudan* 81 F2
Raga →, *Sudan* 81 F2
Ragachow, *Belarus* 47 F6
Ragag, *Sudan* 81 E1
Ragama, *Sri Lanka* 66 R11
Ragged, Mt., *Australia* 93 F3
Raghunathpalli, *India* 69 H11
Raghunathpur, *India* 69 H12
Raglan, *N.Z.* 91 G5
Ragusa, *Italy* 31 F7
Raha, *Indonesia* 63 E6
Rahad, Nahr ed →, *Sudan* 81 E3
Rahaeng = Tak, *Thailand* 64 D2
Rahatgarh, *India* 69 H8
Rahden, *Germany* 24 C4
Raheita, *Eritrea* 81 E5
Rahimyar Khan, *Pakistan* 68 E4
Rāhjerd, *Iran* 71 C6
Rahon, *India* 68 D7
Raichur, *India* 66 L10
Raiganj, *India* 69 G13
Raigarh, *India* 67 J13
Raijua, *Indonesia* 63 F6
Raikot, *India* 68 D6
Railton, *Australia* 94 G4
Rainbow Lake, *Canada* 104 B5
Rainier, *U.S.A.* 116 D4
Rainier, Mt., *U.S.A.* 116 D5
Rainy L., *Canada* 105 D10
Rainy River, *Canada* 105 D10
Raippaluoto, *Finland* 8 E19
Raipur, *India* 67 J12
Ra'is, *Si. Arabia* 80 C4
Raisen, *India* 68 H8
Raisio, *Finland* 9 F20
Raj Nandgaon, *India* 67 J12
Raj Nilgiri, *India* 69 J12
Raja, Ujung, *Indonesia* 62 D1
Raja Ampat, Kepulauan, *Indonesia* 63 E7
Rajahmundry, *India* 67 L12
Rajang →, *Malaysia* 62 D4
Rajanpur, *Pakistan* 68 E4
Rajapalaiyam, *India* 66 Q10
Rajasthan □, *India* 68 F5
Rajasthan Canal, *India* 68 F5
Rajauri, *India* 69 C6
Rajgarh, *Mad. P., India* 68 G7
Rajgarh, *Raj., India* 68 F7
Rajgarh, *Raj., India* 68 E6
Rajgir, *India* 69 G11
Rajgród, *Poland* 44 E9
Rajkot, *India* 68 H4
Rajmahal Hills, *India* 69 G12
Rajpipla, *India* 66 J8
Rajpur, *India* 68 H6
Rajpura, *India* 68 D7
Rajshahi, *Bangla.* 67 G16
Rajshahi □, *Bangla.* 69 G13
Rajula, *India* 68 J4
Rakaia, *N.Z.* 91 K4
Rakaia →, *N.Z.* 91 K4
Rakan, Ra's, *Qatar* 71 E6
Rakaposhi, *Pakistan* 69 A6
Rakata, Pulau, *Indonesia* 62 F3
Rakhiv, *Ukraine* 47 H3
Rakhni, *Pakistan* 68 D3
Rakhni →, *Pakistan* 68 E3
Rakitnoye, *Russia* 54 B7
Rakitovo, *Bulgaria* 41 E8
Rakoniewice, *Poland* 45 F3
Rakops, *Botswana* 88 C3
Rakovica, *Croatia* 29 D12
Rakovník, *Czech Rep.* 26 A6
Rakovski, *Bulgaria* 41 D8
Rakvere, *Estonia* 9 G22
Raleigh, *U.S.A.* 109 H6
Ralja, *Serbia, Yug.* 40 B4
Ralls, *U.S.A.* 113 J4
Ralston, *U.S.A.* 110 E8
Ram →, *Canada* 104 A4
Rām Allāh, *West Bank* 75 D4
Rama, *Nic.* 120 D3
Ramacca, *Italy* 31 E7
Ramakona, *India* 69 J8
Ramales de la Victoria, *Spain* 34 B7
Raman, *Thailand* 65 J3
Ramanathapuram, *India* 66 Q11
Ramanetaka, B. de, *Madag.* 89 A8
Ramanujganj, *India* 69 H10
Ramat Gan, *Israel* 75 C3
Ramatlhabama, *S. Africa* 88 D4
Ramban, *India* 69 C6
Rambervillers, *France* 19 D13
Rambipuji, *Indonesia* 63 H15
Rambouillet, *France* 19 D8
Ramechhap, *Nepal* 69 F12
Ramenskoye, *Russia* 46 E10
Ramganga →, *India* 69 F8
Ramgarh, *Bihar, India* 69 H11
Ramgarh, *Raj., India* 68 F6
Ramgarh, *Raj., India* 68 F4
Rāmhormoz, *Iran* 71 D6
Ramīān, *Iran* 71 B7
Ramingining, *Australia* 94 A2
Ramla, *Israel* 75 D3
Ramlu, *Eritrea* 81 E5
Râmna →, *Romania* 43 E12
Ramnad = Ramanathapuram, *India* 66 Q11
Ramnagar, *Jammu & Kashmir, India* 69 C6
Ramnagar, *Ut. P., India* 69 E8
Ramnäs, *Sweden* 10 E10
Râmnicu Sărat, *Romania* 43 E12
Râmnicu Vâlcea, *Romania* 43 E9
Ramon, *Russia* 47 G10
Ramona, *U.S.A.* 117 M10
Ramonville-St-Agne, *France* 20 E5
Ramore, *Canada* 102 C3
Ramos →, *Nigeria* 83 D6
Ramotswa, *Botswana* 88 C4
Rampur, *H.P., India* 68 D7
Rampur, *Mad. P., India* 68 H5
Rampur, *Ut. P., India* 69 E8
Rampur Hat, *India* 69 G12
Rampura, *India* 68 G6
Ramrama Tola, *India* 69 J8
Ramree I., *Burma* 67 K19
Rāmsar, *Iran* 71 B6
Ramsey, *U.K.* 12 C3
Ramsey, *U.S.A.* 111 E10
Ramsey L., *Canada* 102 C3
Ramsgate, *U.K.* 13 F9
Ramsjö, *Sweden* 10 B9
Ramstein, *Germany* 25 F3
Ramtek, *India* 66 J11
Ramvik, *Sweden* 10 B11
Rana Pratap Sagar Dam, *India* 68 G6
Ranaghat, *India* 69 H13
Ranahu, *Pakistan* 68 G3
Ranau, *Malaysia* 62 C5
Rancagua, *Chile* 126 C1
Rance →, *France* 18 D5
Rancheria →, *Canada* 104 A3
Ranchester, *U.S.A.* 114 D10
Ranchi, *India* 69 H11
Rancho Cucamonga, *U.S.A.* 117 L9
Randalstown, *U.K.* 15 B5
Randan, *France* 19 F10
Randazzo, *Italy* 31 E7
Randers, *Denmark* 11 H4
Randers Fjord, *Denmark* 11 H4
Randfontein, *S. Africa* 89 D4
Randle, *U.S.A.* 116 D5
Randolph, *Mass., U.S.A.* 111 D13
Randolph, *N.Y., U.S.A.* 110 D6
Randolph, *Utah, U.S.A.* 114 F8
Randolph, *Vt., U.S.A.* 111 C12
Randsburg, *U.S.A.* 117 K9
Råne älv →, *Sweden* 8 D20
Rangae, *Thailand* 65 J3
Rangaunu B., *N.Z.* 91 F4
Rangeley, *U.S.A.* 111 B14
Rangeley L., *U.S.A.* 111 B14
Rangely, *U.S.A.* 114 F9
Ranger, *U.S.A.* 113 J5
Rangia, *India* 67 F17
Rangiora, *N.Z.* 91 K4
Rangitaiki →, *N.Z.* 91 G6
Rangitata →, *N.Z.* 91 K3
Rangkasbitung, *Indonesia* 63 G12
Rangon →, *Burma* 67 L20
Rangoon, *Burma* 67 L20
Rangpur, *Bangla.* 67 G16
Rangsit, *Thailand* 64 F3
Ranibennur, *India* 66 M9
Raniganj, *Ut. P., India* 69 F9
Raniganj, *W. Bengal, India* 67 H15
Ranikhet, *India* 69 E8
Raniwara, *India* 66 G8
Rāniyah, *Iraq* 70 B5
Ranka, *India* 69 H10
Ranken →, *Australia* 94 C2
Rankin, *U.S.A.* 113 K4
Rankin Inlet, *Canada* 100 B10
Rankweil, *Austria* 26 D2
Rannoch, L., *U.K.* 14 E4
Rannoch Moor, *U.K.* 14 E4
Ranobe, Helodranon' i, *Madag.* 89 C7
Ranohira, *Madag.* 89 C8
Ranomafana, *Toamasina, Madag.* 89 B8
Ranomafana, *Toliara, Madag.* 89 C8
Ranomena, *Madag.* 89 C8
Ranong, *Thailand* 65 H2
Ranotsara Nord, *Madag.* 89 C8
Rānsa, *Iran* 71 C6
Ransiki, *Indonesia* 63 E8
Rantabe, *Madag.* 89 B8
Rantauprapat, *Indonesia* 62 D1
Rantemario, *Indonesia* 63 E5
Rantoul, *U.S.A.* 108 E1
Ranum, *Denmark* 11 H3
Ranyah, W. →, *Si. Arabia* 80 C5
Raon l'Étape, *France* 19 D13
Raoping, *China* 59 F11
Raoyang, *China* 56 E8
Rapa, *Pac. Oc.* 97 K13
Rapallo, *Italy* 28 D6
Rapar, *India* 68 H4
Rāpch, *Iran* 71 E8
Raper, C., *Canada* 101 B13
Rapid City, *U.S.A.* 112 D3
Rapid River, *U.S.A.* 108 C2
Rapla, *Estonia* 9 G21
Rapti →, *India* 69 F10
Rapu Rapu I., *Phil.* 61 E6
Raqaba ez Zarqa →, *Sudan* 81 F2
Raquette →, *U.S.A.* 111 B10
Raquette Lake, *U.S.A.* 111 C10
Rarotonga, *Cook Is.* 97 K12
Ra's al 'Ayn, *Syria* 70 B4
Ra's al Khaymah, *U.A.E.* 71 E7
Râs el Mâ, *Mali* 82 B4
Ras Ghârib, *Egypt* 80 B3
Ras Mallap, *Egypt* 80 B3
Rasca, Pta. de la, *Canary Is.* 37 G3
Rășcani, *Moldova* 43 C12
Raseiniai, *Lithuania* 9 J20
Rashad, *Sudan* 81 E3
Rashîd, *Egypt* 80 H7
Rashîd, Masabb, *Egypt* 80 H7
Rashmi, *India* 68 G6
Rasht, *Iran* 71 B6
Rasi Salai, *Thailand* 64 E5
Raška, *Serbia, Yug.* 40 C4
Râsnov, *Romania* 43 E10
Rason L., *Australia* 93 E3
Rașova, *Romania* 43 F12
Rasovo, *Bulgaria* 40 C7
Rasra, *India* 69 G10
Rasskazovo, *Russia* 48 D5
Rast, *Romania* 43 G8
Rastatt, *Germany* 25 G4
Rastede, *Germany* 24 B4
Răstolița, *Romania* 43 D9
Rasul, *Pakistan* 68 C5
Raszków, *Poland* 45 G4
Rat Buri, *Thailand* 64 F2
Rat Islands, *U.S.A.* 100 C1
Rat L., *Canada* 105 B9
Ratangarh, *India* 68 E6
Rätansbyn, *Sweden* 10 B8
Raţāwī, *Iraq* 70 D5
Rath, *India* 69 G8
Rath Luirc, *Ireland* 15 D3
Rathdrum, *Ireland* 15 D5
Rathenow, *Germany* 24 C8
Rathkeale, *Ireland* 15 D3
Rathlin I., *U.K.* 15 A5
Rathmelton, *Ireland* 15 A4
Ratibor = Racibórz, *Poland* 45 H5
Rätikon, *Austria* 26 D2
Ratingen, *Germany* 24 D2
Ratlam, *India* 68 H6
Ratnagiri, *India* 66 L8
Ratodero, *Pakistan* 68 F3
Raton, *U.S.A.* 113 G2
Rattaphum, *Thailand* 65 J3
Ratten, *Austria* 26 D8
Rattray Hd., *U.K.* 14 D7
Rättvik, *Sweden* 10 D9
Ratz, Mt., *Canada* 104 B2
Ratzeburg, *Germany* 24 B6
Raub, *Malaysia* 65 L3
Rauch, *Argentina* 126 D4
Raudales de Malpaso, *Mexico* 119 D6
Raufarhöfn, *Iceland* 8 C6
Raufoss, *Norway* 9 F14
Raukumara Ra., *N.Z.* 91 H6
Rauma, *Finland* 9 F19
Raurkela, *India* 69 H11
Rausu-Dake, *Japan* 54 B12
Răut →, *Moldova* 43 C14
Rava-Ruska, *Poland* 47 G2
Rava Russkaya = Rava-Ruska, *Poland* 47 G2
Ravalli, *U.S.A.* 114 C6
Ravānsar, *Iran* 70 C5
Ravanusa, *Italy* 30 E6
Rāvar, *Iran* 71 D8
Ravena, *U.S.A.* 111 D11
Ravenna, *Italy* 29 D9
Ravenna, *Nebr., U.S.A.* 112 E5
Ravenna, *Ohio, U.S.A.* 110 E3
Ravensburg, *Germany* 25 H5
Ravenshoe, *Australia* 94 B4
Ravensthorpe, *Australia* 93 F3
Ravenswood, *Australia* 94 C4
Ravenswood, *U.S.A.* 108 F5
Ravi →, *Pakistan* 68 D4
Ravna Gora, *Croatia* 29 C11
Ravna Reka, *Serbia, Yug.* 40 B5
Ravne na Koroškem, *Slovenia* 29 B11
Rawa Mazowiecka, *Poland* 45 G7
Rawalpindi, *Pakistan* 68 C5
Rawāndūz, *Iraq* 70 B5
Rawang, *Malaysia* 65 L3
Rawene, *N.Z.* 91 F4
Rawicz, *Poland* 45 G3
Rawka →, *Poland* 45 F7
Rawlinna, *Australia* 93 F4
Rawlins, *U.S.A.* 114 F10
Rawlinson Ra., *Australia* 93 D4
Rawson, *Argentina* 128 E3
Raxaul, *India* 69 F11
Ray, *U.S.A.* 112 A3
Ray, C., *Canada* 103 C8
Rayadurg, *India* 66 M10
Rayagada, *India* 67 K13
Raychikhinsk, *Russia* 51 E13
Rāyen, *Iran* 71 D8
Rayleigh, *U.K.* 13 F8
Raymond, *Canada* 104 D6
Raymond, *Calif., U.S.A.* 116 H7
Raymond, *N.H., U.S.A.* 111 C13
Raymond, *Wash., U.S.A.* 116 D3
Raymondville, *U.S.A.* 113 M6
Raymore, *Canada* 105 C8
Rayón, *Mexico* 118 B2
Rayong, *Thailand* 64 F3
Rayville, *U.S.A.* 113 J9
Raz, Pte. du, *France* 18 D2
Razan, *Iran* 71 C6
Ražana, *Serbia, Yug.* 40 B3
Ražanj, *Serbia, Yug.* 40 C5
Razdelna, *Bulgaria* 41 C11
Razdel'naya = Rozdilna, *Ukraine* 47 J6
Razdolnoye, *Russia* 54 C5
Razdolnoye, *Ukraine* 47 K7
Razeh, *Iran* 71 C6
Razgrad, *Bulgaria* 41 C10
Razim, Lacul, *Romania* 43 F14
Razlog, *Bulgaria* 40 E7
Razmak, *Pakistan* 68 C3
Ré, Î. de, *France* 20 B2
Reading, *U.K.* 13 F7
Reading, *U.S.A.* 111 F9
Reading □, *U.K.* 13 F7
Realicó, *Argentina* 126 D3
Réalmont, *France* 20 E6
Ream, *Cambodia* 65 G4
Reata, *Mexico* 118 B4
Reay Forest, *U.K.* 14 C4
Rebais, *France* 19 D10
Rebi, *Indonesia* 63 F8
Rebiana, *Libya* 79 D10
Rebun-Tō, *Japan* 54 B10
Recanati, *Italy* 29 E10
Recaș, *Romania* 42 E6
Recco, *Italy* 28 D6
Recherche, Arch. of the, *Australia* 93 F3
Rechna Doab, *Pakistan* 68 D5
Rechytsa, *Belarus* 47 F6
Recife, *Brazil* 125 E12
Recklinghausen, *Germany* 17 C7
Reconquista, *Argentina* 126 B4
Recreo, *Argentina* 126 B2
Recz, *Poland* 45 E2
Red →, *La., U.S.A.* 113 K9
Red →, *N. Dak., U.S.A.* 100 C10
Red Bank, *U.S.A.* 111 F10
Red Bay, *Canada* 103 B8
Red Bluff, *U.S.A.* 114 F2
Red Bluff L., *U.S.A.* 113 K3
Red Cloud, *U.S.A.* 112 E5
Red Creek, *U.S.A.* 111 C8
Red Deer, *Canada* 104 C6
Red Deer →, *Alta., Canada* 105 C7
Red Deer →, *Man., Canada* 105 C8
Red Deer L., *Canada* 105 C8
Red Hook, *U.S.A.* 111 E11
Red Indian L., *Canada* 103 C8
Red L., *Canada* 105 C10
Red Lake, *Canada* 105 C10
Red Lake Falls, *U.S.A.* 112 B6
Red Lake Road, *Canada* 105 C10
Red Lodge, *U.S.A.* 114 D9
Red Mountain, *U.S.A.* 117 K9
Red Oak, *U.S.A.* 112 E7
Red Rock, *Canada* 102 C2
Red Rock, L., *U.S.A.* 112 E8
Red Rocks Pt., *Australia* 93 F4
Red Sea, *Asia* 74 C2
Red Slate Mt., *U.S.A.* 116 H8
Red Sucker L., *Canada* 102 B1
Red Tower Pass = Turnu Roșu, P., *Romania* 43 E9
Red Wing, *U.S.A.* 112 C8
Reda, *Poland* 44 D5
Redang, *Malaysia* 62 C2
Redange, *Lux.* 17 E5
Redcar, *U.K.* 12 C6
Redcar & Cleveland □, *U.K.* 12 C7
Redcliff, *Canada* 105 C6
Redcliffe, *Australia* 95 D5
Redcliffe, Mt., *Australia* 93 E3
Reddersburg, *S. Africa* 88 D4
Redding, *U.S.A.* 114 F2
Redditch, *U.K.* 13 E6
Redfield, *U.S.A.* 112 C5
Redford, *U.S.A.* 111 B11
Redkino, *Russia* 46 D9
Redlands, *U.S.A.* 117 M9
Redmond, *Oreg., U.S.A.* 114 D3
Redmond, *Wash., U.S.A.* 116 C4
Redon, *France* 18 E4
Redonda, *Antigua* 121 C7
Redondela, *Spain* 34 C2
Redondo, *Portugal* 35 G3
Redondo Beach, *U.S.A.* 117 M8
Redruth, *U.K.* 13 G2
Redvers, *Canada* 105 D8
Redwater, *Canada* 104 C6
Redwood, *U.S.A.* 111 B9
Redwood City, *U.S.A.* 116 H4
Redwood Falls, *U.S.A.* 112 C7
Redwood National Park, *U.S.A.* 114 F1
Ree, L., *Ireland* 15 C3
Reed, L., *Canada* 105 C8
Reed City, *U.S.A.* 108 D3
Reedley, *U.S.A.* 116 J7
Reedsburg, *U.S.A.* 112 D9
Reedsport, *U.S.A.* 114 E1
Reedsville, *U.S.A.* 110 F7
Reefton, *N.Z.* 91 K3
Rees, *Germany* 24 D2
Reese →, *U.S.A.* 114 F5
Refahiye, *Turkey* 73 C8
Reftele, *Sweden* 11 G7
Refugio, *U.S.A.* 113 L6
Rega →, *Poland* 44 D2
Regalbuto, *Italy* 31 E7
Regen, *Germany* 25 G9
Regen →, *Germany* 25 F8
Regensburg, *Germany* 25 F8
Regenstauf, *Germany* 25 F8
Reggâne = Zaouiet Reggâne, *Algeria* 78 C6
Reggello, *Italy* 29 E8
Réggio di Calábria, *Italy* 31 D8
Réggio nell'Emília, *Italy* 28 D7
Reghin, *Romania* 43 D9
Regina, *Canada* 105 C8
Regina Beach, *Canada* 105 C8
Registro, *Brazil* 127 A6
Reguengos de Monsaraz, *Portugal* 35 G3
Rehar →, *India* 69 H10
Rehli, *India* 69 H8
Rehoboth, *Namibia* 88 C2
Rehovot, *Israel* 75 D3
Reichenbach, *Germany* 24 E8
Reid, *Australia* 93 F4
Reidsville, *U.S.A.* 109 G6
Reigate, *U.K.* 13 F7
Reillo, *Spain* 32 F3
Reims, *France* 19 C11
Reina Adelaida, Arch., *Chile* 128 G2
Reinbek, *Germany* 24 B6
Reindeer →, *Canada* 105 B8
Reindeer I., *Canada* 105 C9
Reindeer L., *Canada* 105 B8
Reinga, C., *N.Z.* 91 F4
Reinosa, *Spain* 34 B6
Reitz, *S. Africa* 89 D4
Reivilo, *S. Africa* 88 D3
Rejaf, *Sudan* 81 G3
Rejmyre, *Sweden* 11 F9
Rejowiec Fabryczny, *Poland* 45 G10
Reka →, *Slovenia* 29 C11
Rekovac, *Serbia, Yug.* 40 C5
Reliance, *Canada* 105 A7
Rémalard, *France* 18 D7
Rembang, *Indonesia* 63 G14
Remedios, *Panama* 120 E3
Remeshk, *Iran* 71 E8
Remetea, *Romania* 43 D10
Remich, *Lux.* 17 E6
Remiremont, *France* 19 D13
Remo, *Ethiopia* 81 F5
Remontnoye, *Russia* 49 G6
Remoulins, *France* 21 E8
Remscheid, *Germany* 17 C7
Ren Xian, *China* 56 F8
Rende, *Italy* 31 C9
Rendína, *Greece* 38 B3
Rendsburg, *Germany* 24 A5
Renfrew, *Canada* 102 C4
Renfrewshire □, *U.K.* 14 F4
Rengat, *Indonesia* 62 E2
Rengo, *Chile* 126 C1
Renhua, *China* 59 E9
Renhuai, *China* 58 D6
Reni, *Ukraine* 47 K5
Renk, *Sudan* 81 E3
Rennell Sd., *Canada* 104 C2
Renner Springs, *Australia* 94 B1
Rennes, *France* 18 D5
Rennie L., *Canada* 105 A7
Reno, *U.S.A.* 116 F7
Reno →, *Italy* 29 D9
Renovo, *U.S.A.* 110 E7
Renqiu, *China* 56 E9
Rens, *Denmark* 11 K3
Renshou, *China* 58 C5
Rensselaer, *Ind., U.S.A.* 108 E2
Rensselaer, *N.Y., U.S.A.* 111 D11
Rentería, *Spain* 32 B3
Renton, *U.S.A.* 116 C4
Réo, *Burkina Faso* 82 C4
Reocín, *Spain* 34 B6
Reotipur, *India* 69 G10
Répcelak, *Hungary* 42 C2
Republic, *Mo., U.S.A.* 113 G8
Republic, *Wash., U.S.A.* 114 B4
Republican →, *U.S.A.* 112 F6
Repulse Bay, *Canada* 101 B11
Requena, *Peru* 124 E4
Requena, *Spain* 33 F3
Réquista, *France* 20 D6
Reşadiye = Datça, *Turkey* 39 E9
Reşadiye, *Turkey* 72 B7
Reşadiye Yarımadası, *Turkey* 39 E9
Resavica, *Serbia, Yug.* 40 B5
Resen, *Macedonia* 40 E5
Reserve, *U.S.A.* 115 K9
Resht = Rasht, *Iran* 71 B6
Resistencia, *Argentina* 126 B4
Reşiţa, *Romania* 42 E6
Resko, *Poland* 44 E2
Resolution I., *Canada* 101 B13
Resolution I., *N.Z.* 91 L1
Ressano Garcia, *Mozam.* 89 D5
Reston, *Canada* 105 D8
Reszel, *Poland* 44 D8
Retalhuleu, *Guatemala* 120 D1
Retenue, L. de, *Dem. Rep. of the Congo* 87 E2
Retezat, Munţii, *Romania* 42 E8

Retford, *U.K.* 12 D7
Rethel, *France* 19 C11
Rethem, *Germany* 24 C5
Réthímnon, *Greece* 36 D6
Réthímnon ☐, *Greece* 36 D6
Reti, *Pakistan* 68 E3
Retiche, Alpi, *Switz.* 25 J6
Retiers, *France* 18 E5
Retortillo, *Spain* 34 E4
Retournac, *France* 21 C8
Rétság, *Hungary* 42 C4
Réunion ■, *Ind. Oc.* 77 J9
Reus, *Spain* 32 D6
Reuterstadt Stavenhagen, *Germany* 24 B8
Reutlingen, *Germany* 25 G5
Reutte, *Austria* 26 D3
Reval = Tallinn, *Estonia* 9 G21
Revel, *France* 20 E6
Revelganj, *India* 69 G11
Revelstoke, *Canada* 104 C5
Reventazón, *Peru* 124 E2
Revigny-sur-Ornain, *France* 19 D11
Revillagigedo, Is. de, *Pac. Oc.* 118 D2
Revin, *France* 19 C11
Revúca, *Slovak Rep.* 27 C13
Revuè →, *Mozam.* 87 F3
Rewa, *India* 69 G9
Rewari, *India* 68 E7
Rexburg, *U.S.A.* 114 E8
Rey, *Iran* 71 C6
Rey, I. del, *Panama* 120 E4
Rey Malabo, *Eq. Guin.* 83 E6
Reyðarfjörður, *Iceland* 8 D6
Reyes, Pt., *U.S.A.* 116 H3
Reyhanlı, *Turkey* 72 D7
Reykjahlið, *Iceland* 8 D5
Reykjanes, *Iceland* 8 E2
Reykjavík, *Iceland* 8 D3
Reynolds Ra., *Australia* 92 D5
Reynoldsville, *U.S.A.* 110 E6
Reynosa, *Mexico* 119 B5
Rēzekne, *Latvia* 9 H22
Rezina, *Moldova* 43 C13
Rezovo, *Bulgaria* 41 D12
Rezvān, *Iran* 71 E8
Rgotina, *Serbia, Yug.* 40 B6
Rhamnus, *Greece* 38 C6
Rhayader, *U.K.* 13 E4
Rheda-Wiedenbrück, *Germany* 24 D4
Rhede, *Germany* 24 D2
Rhein →, *Europe* 17 C6
Rhein-Main-Donau-Kanal, *Germany* 25 F7
Rheinbach, *Germany* 24 E2
Rheine, *Germany* 24 C3
Rheinfelden, *Germany* 25 H3
Rheinhessen-Pfalz ☐, *Germany* 25 F3
Rheinland-Pfalz ☐, *Germany* 25 E2
Rheinsberg, *Germany* 24 B8
Rhin = Rhein →, *Europe* 17 C6
Rhine = Rhein →, *Europe* 17 C6
Rhinebeck, *U.S.A.* 111 E11
Rhineland-Palatinate = Rheinland-Pfalz ☐, *Germany* 25 E2
Rhinelander, *U.S.A.* 112 C10
Rhinns Pt., *U.K.* 14 F2
Rhino Camp, *Uganda* 86 B3
Rhir, Cap, *Morocco* 78 B4
Rho, *Italy* 28 C6
Rhode Island ☐, *U.S.A.* 111 E13
Rhodes = Ródhos, *Greece* 36 C10
Rhodesia = Zimbabwe ■, *Africa* 87 F3
Rhodope Mts. = Rhodopi Planina, *Bulgaria* 41 E8
Rhodopi Planina, *Bulgaria* 41 E8
Rhön, *Germany* 24 E5
Rhondda, *U.K.* 13 F4
Rhondda Cynon Taff ☐, *U.K.* 13 F4
Rhône ☐, *France* 21 C8
Rhône →, *France* 21 E8
Rhône-Alpes ☐, *France* 21 C9
Rhum, *U.K.* 14 E2
Rhyl, *U.K.* 12 D4
Ri-Aba, *Eq. Guin.* 83 E6
Riachão, *Brazil* 125 E9
Riangnom, *Sudan* 81 F3
Riaño, *Spain* 34 C6
Rians, *France* 21 E9
Riansáres →, *Spain* 35 F7
Riasi, *India* 69 C6
Riau ☐, *Indonesia* 62 D2
Riau, Kepulauan, *Indonesia* 62 D2
Riau Arch. = Riau, Kepulauan, *Indonesia* 62 D2
Riaza, *Spain* 34 D7
Riaza →, *Spain* 34 D7
Riba de Saelices, *Spain* 32 E2
Riba-Roja de Turia, *Spain* 33 F4
Ribadavia, *Spain* 34 C2
Ribadeo, *Spain* 34 B3
Ribadesella, *Spain* 34 B5
Ribado, *Nigeria* 83 D7
Ribao, *Cameroon* 83 D7
Ribas = Ribes de Freser, *Spain* 32 C7
Ribas do Rio Pardo, *Brazil* 125 H8
Ribble →, *U.K.* 12 D5
Ribe, *Denmark* 11 J2
Ribe Amtskommune ☐, *Denmark* 11 J2
Ribeauvillé, *France* 19 D14
Ribécourt-Dreslincourt, *France* 19 C9
Ribeira = Santa Uxía, *Spain* 34 C2
Ribeira Brava, *Madeira* 37 D2
Ribeirão Prêto, *Brazil* 127 A6
Ribemont, *France* 19 C10
Ribera, *Italy* 30 E6
Ribérac, *France* 20 C4
Riberalta, *Bolivia* 124 F5
Ribes de Freser, *Spain* 32 C7
Ribnica, *Slovenia* 29 C11
Ribnitz-Damgarten, *Germany* 24 A8
Ričany, *Czech Rep.* 26 B7
Riccarton, *N.Z.* 91 K4
Ríccia, *Italy* 31 A7
Riccione, *Italy* 29 E9
Rice, *U.S.A.* 117 L12
Rice L., *Canada* 110 B6
Rice Lake, *U.S.A.* 112 C9
Rich, C., *Canada* 110 B4
Richard Toll, *Senegal* 82 B1
Richards Bay, *S. Africa* 89 D5
Richardson →, *Canada* 105 B6
Richardson Lakes, *U.S.A.* 108 C10
Richardson Springs, *U.S.A.* 116 F5
Riche, C., *Australia* 93 F2
Richelieu, *France* 18 E7
Richey, *U.S.A.* 112 B2
Richfield, *U.S.A.* 115 G8
Richfield Springs, *U.S.A.* 111 D10
Richford, *U.S.A.* 111 B12
Richibucto, *Canada* 103 C7
Richland, *Ga., U.S.A.* 109 J3
Richland, *Wash., U.S.A.* 114 C4
Richland Center, *U.S.A.* 112 D9
Richlands, *U.S.A.* 108 G5
Richmond, *Australia* 94 C3
Richmond, *N.Z.* 91 J4
Richmond, *U.K.* 12 C6
Richmond, *Calif., U.S.A.* 116 H4
Richmond, *Ind., U.S.A.* 108 F3
Richmond, *Ky., U.S.A.* 108 G3
Richmond, *Mich., U.S.A.* 110 D2
Richmond, *Mo., U.S.A.* 112 F8
Richmond, *Tex., U.S.A.* 113 L7
Richmond, *Utah, U.S.A.* 114 F8
Richmond, *Va., U.S.A.* 108 G7
Richmond, *Vt., U.S.A.* 111 B12
Richmond Hill, *Canada* 110 C5
Richmond Ra., *Australia* 95 D5
Richwood, *U.S.A.* 108 F5
Ricla, *Spain* 32 D3
Ridder = Leninogorsk, *Kazakstan* 50 D9
Riddlesburg, *U.S.A.* 110 F6
Ridgecrest, *U.S.A.* 117 K9
Ridgefield, *Conn., U.S.A.* 111 E11
Ridgefield, *Wash., U.S.A.* 116 E4
Ridgeland, *U.S.A.* 109 J5
Ridgetown, *Canada* 102 D3
Ridgewood, *U.S.A.* 111 F10
Ridgway, *U.S.A.* 110 E6
Riding Mountain Nat. Park, *Canada* 105 C9
Ridley, Mt., *Australia* 93 F3
Riebeek-Oos, *S. Africa* 88 E4
Ried, *Austria* 26 C6
Riedlingen, *Germany* 25 G5
Riedstadt, *Germany* 25 F4
Rienza →, *Italy* 29 B8
Riesa, *Germany* 24 D9
Riesi, *Italy* 31 E7
Riet →, *S. Africa* 88 D3
Rietavas, *Lithuania* 44 C8
Rietbron, *S. Africa* 88 E3
Rietfontein, *Namibia* 88 C3
Rieti, *Italy* 29 F9
Rieupeyroux, *France* 20 D6
Riez, *France* 21 E10
Riffe L., *U.S.A.* 116 D4
Rifle, *U.S.A.* 114 G10
Rift Valley ☐, *Kenya* 86 B4
Rīga, *Latvia* 9 H21
Riga, G. of, *Latvia* 9 H20
Rigacikun, *Nigeria* 83 C6
Rīgān, *Iran* 71 D8
Rīgas Jūras Līcis = Riga, G. of, *Latvia* 9 H20
Rigaud, *Canada* 111 A10
Rigby, *U.S.A.* 114 E8
Rīgestān, *Afghan.* 66 D4
Riggins, *U.S.A.* 114 D5
Rignac, *France* 20 D6
Rigolet, *Canada* 103 B8
Rihand Dam, *India* 69 G10
Riihimäki, *Finland* 9 F21
Riiser-Larsen-halvøya, *Antarctica* 5 C4
Rijau, *Nigeria* 83 C6
Rijeka, *Croatia* 29 C11
Rijeka Crnojevića, *Montenegro, Yug.* 40 D3
Rijssen, *Neths.* 17 B6
Rike, *Ethiopia* 81 E4
Rikuzentakada, *Japan* 54 E10
Rila, *Bulgaria* 40 D7
Rila Planina, *Bulgaria* 40 D7
Riley, *U.S.A.* 114 E4
Rima →, *Nigeria* 83 C6
Rimah, Wadi ar →, *Si. Arabia* 70 E4
Rimavská Sobota, *Slovak Rep.* 27 C13
Rimbey, *Canada* 104 C6
Rimbo, *Sweden* 10 E12
Rimersburg, *U.S.A.* 110 E5
Rimforsa, *Sweden* 11 F9
Rimi, *Nigeria* 83 C6
Rímini, *Italy* 29 D9
Rimouski, *Canada* 103 C6
Rimrock, *U.S.A.* 116 D5
Rinca, *Indonesia* 63 F5
Rincón de la Victoria, *Spain* 35 J6
Rincón de Romos, *Mexico* 118 C4
Rinconada, *Argentina* 126 A2
Rind →, *India* 69 G9
Ringarum, *Sweden* 11 F10
Ringas, *India* 68 F6
Ringe, *Denmark* 11 J4
Ringim, *Nigeria* 83 C6
Ringkøbing, *Denmark* 11 H2
Ringkøbing Amtskommune ☐, *Denmark* 11 H2
Ringkøbing Fjord, *Denmark* 11 H2
Ringsjön, *Sweden* 11 J7
Ringsted, *Denmark* 11 J5
Ringvassøy, *Norway* 8 B18
Ringwood, *U.S.A.* 111 E10
Rinía, *Greece* 39 D7
Rinjani, *Indonesia* 62 F5
Rinteln, *Germany* 24 C5
Río, Punta del, *Spain* 33 J2
Rio Branco, *Brazil* 124 E5
Río Branco, *Uruguay* 127 C5
Río Bravo del Norte →, *Mexico* 119 B5
Rio Brilhante, *Brazil* 127 A5
Rio Claro, *Brazil* 127 A6
Rio Claro, *Trin. & Tob.* 121 D7
Río Colorado, *Argentina* 128 D4
Río Cuarto, *Argentina* 126 C3
Rio das Pedras, *Mozam.* 89 C6
Rio de Janeiro, *Brazil* 127 A7
Rio de Janeiro ☐, *Brazil* 127 A7
Rio do Sul, *Brazil* 127 B6
Río Gallegos, *Argentina* 128 G3
Rio Grande = Grande, Rio →, *U.S.A.* 113 N6
Río Grande, *Argentina* 128 G3
Rio Grande, *Brazil* 127 C5
Río Grande, *Mexico* 118 C4
Río Grande, *Nic.* 120 D3
Rio Grande City, *U.S.A.* 113 M5
Río Grande de Santiago →, *Mexico* 118 C3
Rio Grande do Norte ☐, *Brazil* 125 E11
Rio Grande do Sul ☐, *Brazil* 127 C5
Río Hato, *Panama* 120 E3
Río Lagartos, *Mexico* 119 C7
Rio Largo, *Brazil* 125 E11
Rio Maior, *Portugal* 35 F2
Rio Marina, *Italy* 28 F7
Río Mulatos, *Bolivia* 124 G5
Río Muni = Mbini ☐, *Eq. Guin.* 84 D2
Rio Negro, *Brazil* 127 B6
Rio Pardo, *Brazil* 127 C5
Rio Rancho, *U.S.A.* 115 J10
Río Segundo, *Argentina* 126 C3
Río Tercero, *Argentina* 126 C3
Rio Tinto, *Portugal* 34 D2
Rio Verde, *Brazil* 125 G8
Río Verde, *Mexico* 119 C5
Rio Vista, *U.S.A.* 116 G5
Ríobamba, *Ecuador* 124 D3
Ríohacha, *Colombia* 124 A4
Riom, *France* 20 C7
Riom-ès-Montagnes, *France* 20 C6
Rion-des-Landes, *France* 20 E3
Rionero in Vúlture, *Italy* 31 B8
Rioni →, *Georgia* 49 J5
Riós, *Spain* 34 D3
Ríosucio, *Colombia* 124 B3
Riou L., *Canada* 105 B7
Rioz, *France* 19 E13
Ripatransone, *Italy* 29 F10
Ripley, *Canada* 110 B3
Ripley, *Calif., U.S.A.* 117 M12
Ripley, *N.Y., U.S.A.* 110 D5
Ripley, *Tenn., U.S.A.* 113 H10
Ripley, *W. Va., U.S.A.* 108 F5
Ripoll, *Spain* 32 C7
Ripon, *U.K.* 12 C6
Ripon, *Calif., U.S.A.* 116 H5
Ripon, *Wis., U.S.A.* 108 D1
Riposto, *Italy* 31 E8
Risan, *Montenegro, Yug.* 40 D2
Riscle, *France* 20 E3
Rishā', W. ar →, *Si. Arabia* 70 E5
Rishiri-Tō, *Japan* 54 B10
Rishon le Ẕiyyon, *Israel* 75 D3
Risle →, *France* 18 C7
Rison, *U.S.A.* 113 J8
Risør, *Norway* 9 G13
Rita Blanca Cr. →, *U.S.A.* 113 H3
Riti, *Nigeria* 83 D6
Ritter, Mt., *U.S.A.* 116 H7
Rittman, *U.S.A.* 110 F3
Ritzville, *U.S.A.* 114 C4
Riva del Garda, *Italy* 28 C7
Riva Lígure, *Italy* 28 E4
Rivadavia, *Buenos Aires, Argentina* 126 D3
Rivadavia, *Mendoza, Argentina* 126 C2
Rivadavia, *Salta, Argentina* 126 A3
Rivadavia, *Chile* 126 B1
Rivarolo Canavese, *Italy* 28 C4
Rivas, *Nic.* 120 D2
Rive-de-Gier, *France* 21 C8
River Cess, *Liberia* 82 D3
River Jordan, *Canada* 116 B2
Rivera, *Argentina* 126 D3
Rivera, *Uruguay* 127 C4
Riverbank, *U.S.A.* 116 H6
Riverdale, *U.S.A.* 116 J7
Riverhead, *U.S.A.* 111 F12
Riverhurst, *Canada* 105 C7
Rivers, *Canada* 105 C8
Rivers ☐, *Nigeria* 83 E6
Rivers Inlet, *Canada* 104 C3
Riversdale, *S. Africa* 88 E3
Riverside, *U.S.A.* 117 M9
Riverton, *Canada* 105 C9
Riverton, *N.Z.* 91 M2
Riverton, *U.S.A.* 114 E9
Riverton Heights, *U.S.A.* 116 C4
Rives, *France* 21 C9
Rivesaltes, *France* 20 F6
Riviera, *U.S.A.* 117 K12
Riviera di Levante, *Italy* 28 D6
Riviera di Ponente, *Italy* 28 D5
Rivière-au-Renard, *Canada* 103 C7
Rivière-du-Loup, *Canada* 103 C6
Rivière-Pentecôte, *Canada* 103 C6
Rivière-Pilote, *Martinique* 121 D7
Rivière St. Paul, *Canada* 103 B8
Rivne, *Ukraine* 47 G4
Rívoli, *Italy* 28 C4
Rixheim, *France* 19 E14
Riyadh = Ar Riyāḍ, *Si. Arabia* 70 E5
Rize, *Turkey* 73 B9
Rizhao, *China* 57 G10
Rizokarpaso, *Cyprus* 36 D13
Rizzuto, C., *Italy* 31 D10
Rjukan, *Norway* 9 G13
Ro, *Greece* 39 E11
Roa, *Spain* 34 D7
Road Town, *Br. Virgin Is.* 121 C7
Roan Plateau, *U.S.A.* 114 G9
Roanne, *France* 19 F11
Roanoke, *Ala., U.S.A.* 109 J3
Roanoke, *Va., U.S.A.* 108 G6
Roanoke →, *U.S.A.* 109 H7
Roanoke I., *U.S.A.* 109 H8
Roanoke Rapids, *U.S.A.* 109 G7
Roatán, *Honduras* 120 C2
Robāt Sang, *Iran* 71 C8
Robbins I., *Australia* 94 G4
Róbbio, *Italy* 28 C5
Robe →, *Australia* 92 D2
Röbel, *Germany* 24 B8
Robert Lee, *U.S.A.* 113 K4
Robertsdale, *U.S.A.* 110 F6
Robertsganj, *India* 69 G10
Robertson, *S. Africa* 88 E2
Robertson I., *Antarctica* 5 C18
Robertson Ra., *Australia* 92 D3
Robertsport, *Liberia* 82 D2
Roberval, *Canada* 103 C5
Robeson Chan., *Greenland* 4 A4
Robesonia, *U.S.A.* 111 F8
Robi, *Ethiopia* 81 F4
Robinson, *U.S.A.* 108 F2
Robinson →, *Australia* 94 B2
Robinson Ra., *Australia* 93 E2
Robledo, *Spain* 33 G2
Roblin, *Canada* 105 C8
Roboré, *Bolivia* 124 G7
Robson, *Canada* 104 D5
Robson, Mt., *Canada* 104 C5
Robstown, *U.S.A.* 113 M6
Roca, C. da, *Portugal* 35 G1
Roca Partida, I., *Mexico* 118 D2
Rocamadour, *France* 20 D5
Rocas, I., *Brazil* 125 D12
Rocca San Casciano, *Italy* 29 D8
Roccadáspide, *Italy* 31 B8
Roccastrada, *Italy* 29 F8
Roccella Iónica, *Italy* 31 D9
Rocha, *Uruguay* 127 C5
Rochdale, *U.K.* 12 D5
Rochechouart, *France* 20 C4
Rochefort, *Belgium* 17 D5
Rochefort, *France* 20 C3
Rochefort-en-Terre, *France* 18 E4
Rochelle, *U.S.A.* 112 E10
Rocher River, *Canada* 104 A6
Rocheservière, *France* 18 F5
Rochester, *U.K.* 13 F8
Rochester, *Ind., U.S.A.* 108 E2
Rochester, *Minn., U.S.A.* 112 C8
Rochester, *N.H., U.S.A.* 111 C14
Rochester, *N.Y., U.S.A.* 110 C7
Rociu, *Romania* 43 F10
Rock →, *Canada* 104 A3
Rock Creek, *U.S.A.* 110 E4
Rock Falls, *U.S.A.* 112 E10
Rock Hill, *U.S.A.* 109 H5
Rock Island, *U.S.A.* 112 E9
Rock Rapids, *U.S.A.* 112 D6
Rock Sound, *Bahamas* 120 B4
Rock Springs, *Mont., U.S.A.* 114 C10
Rock Springs, *Wyo., U.S.A.* 114 F9
Rock Valley, *U.S.A.* 112 D6
Rockall, *Atl. Oc.* 6 D3
Rockdale, *Tex., U.S.A.* 113 K6
Rockdale, *Wash., U.S.A.* 116 C5
Rockefeller Plateau, *Antarctica* 5 E14
Rockford, *U.S.A.* 112 D10
Rockglen, *Canada* 105 D7
Rockhampton, *Australia* 94 C5
Rockingham, *Australia* 93 F2
Rockingham, *U.S.A.* 109 H6
Rockingham B., *Australia* 94 B4
Rocklake, *U.S.A.* 112 A5
Rockland, *Canada* 111 A9
Rockland, *Idaho, U.S.A.* 114 E7
Rockland, *Maine, U.S.A.* 109 C11
Rockland, *Mich., U.S.A.* 112 B10
Rocklin, *U.S.A.* 116 G5
Rockmart, *U.S.A.* 109 H3
Rockport, *Mass., U.S.A.* 111 D14
Rockport, *Mo., U.S.A.* 112 E7
Rockport, *Tex., U.S.A.* 113 L6
Rocksprings, *U.S.A.* 113 K4
Rockville, *Conn., U.S.A.* 111 E12
Rockville, *Md., U.S.A.* 108 F7
Rockwall, *U.S.A.* 113 J6
Rockwell City, *U.S.A.* 112 D7
Rockwood, *Canada* 110 C4
Rockwood, *Maine, U.S.A.* 109 C11
Rockwood, *Tenn., U.S.A.* 109 H3
Rocky Ford, *U.S.A.* 112 F3
Rocky Gully, *Australia* 93 F2
Rocky Harbour, *Canada* 103 C8
Rocky Island L., *Canada* 102 C3
Rocky Lane, *Canada* 104 B5
Rocky Mount, *U.S.A.* 109 H7
Rocky Mountain House, *Canada* 104 C6
Rocky Mountain National Park, *U.S.A.* 114 F11
Rocky Mts., *N. Amer.* 114 G10
Rocky Point, *Namibia* 88 B2
Rocroi, *France* 19 C11
Rod, *Pakistan* 66 E3
Rødby, *Denmark* 11 K5
Rødbyhavn, *Denmark* 11 K5
Roddickton, *Canada* 103 B8
Rødding, *Denmark* 11 J3
Rödeby, *Sweden* 11 H9
Rødekro, *Denmark* 11 J3
Rodenkirchen, *Germany* 24 B4
Rodez, *France* 20 D6
Rodholívas, *Greece* 40 F7
Rodhópi ☐, *Greece* 41 E9
Rodhopoú, *Greece* 36 D5
Ródhos, *Greece* 36 C10
Rodi Gargánico, *Italy* 29 G12
Rodna, *Romania* 43 C9
Rodnei, Munții, *Romania* 43 C9
Rodney, *Canada* 110 D3
Rodney, C., *N.Z.* 91 G5
Rodniki, *Russia* 48 B5
Rodonit, Kepi i, *Albania* 40 E3
Rodriguez, *Ind. Oc.* 3 E13
Roe →, *U.K.* 15 A5
Roebling, *U.S.A.* 111 F10
Roebourne, *Australia* 92 D2
Roebuck B., *Australia* 92 C3
Roermond, *Neths.* 17 C6
Roes Welcome Sd., *Canada* 101 B11
Roeselare, *Belgium* 17 D3
Rogachev = Ragachow, *Belarus* 47 F6
Rogačica, *Serbia, Yug.* 40 B3
Rogagua, L., *Bolivia* 124 F5
Rogaška Slatina, *Slovenia* 29 B12
Rogatec, *Slovenia* 29 B12
Rogatica, *Bos.-H.* 42 G4
Rogatyn, *Ukraine* 47 H3
Rogdhia, *Greece* 36 D7
Rogers, *U.S.A.* 113 G7
Rogers City, *U.S.A.* 108 C4
Rogersville, *Canada* 103 C6
Roggan →, *Canada* 102 B4
Roggan L., *Canada* 102 B4
Roggeveldberge, *S. Africa* 88 E3
Roggiano Gravina, *Italy* 31 C9
Rogliano, *France* 21 F13
Rogliano, *Italy* 31 C9
Rogoaguado, L., *Bolivia* 124 F5
Rogoźno, *Poland* 45 F3
Rogue →, *U.S.A.* 114 E1
Rohan, *France* 18 D4
Róhda, *Greece* 36 A3
Rohnert Park, *U.S.A.* 116 G4
Rohri, *Pakistan* 68 F3
Rohri Canal, *Pakistan* 68 F3
Rohtak, *India* 68 E7
Roi Et, *Thailand* 64 D4
Roja, *Latvia* 9 H20
Rojas, *Argentina* 126 C3
Rojiște, *Romania* 43 F8
Rojo, C., *Mexico* 119 C5
Rokan →, *Indonesia* 62 D2
Rokel →, *S. Leone* 82 D2
Rokiškis, *Lithuania* 9 J21
Rokitno, *Russia* 47 G8
Rokycany, *Czech Rep.* 26 B6
Rolândia, *Brazil* 127 A5
Rolla, *U.S.A.* 113 G9
Rolleston, *Australia* 94 C4
Rollingstone, *Australia* 94 B4
Rom, *Sudan* 81 F3
Roma, *Australia* 95 D4
Roma, *Italy* 29 G9
Roma, *Sweden* 11 G12
Roma, *U.S.A.* 113 M5
Romain C., *U.S.A.* 109 J6
Romaine, *Canada* 103 B7
Romaine →, *Canada* 103 B7
Roman, *Bulgaria* 40 C7
Roman, *Romania* 43 D11
Roman-Kosh, Gora, *Ukraine* 47 K8
Romanche →, *France* 21 C9
Romang, *Indonesia* 63 F7
Români, *Egypt* 75 E1
Romania ■, *Europe* 43 D10
Romanija, *Bos.-H.* 42 G3
Romano, Cayo, *Cuba* 120 B4
Romanovka = Basarabeasca, *Moldova* 43 D13
Romans-sur-Isère, *France* 21 C9
Romanshorn, *Switz.* 25 H5
Rombari, *Sudan* 81 G3
Romblon, *Phil.* 61 E5
Rome = Roma, *Italy* 29 G9
Rome, *Ga., U.S.A.* 109 H3
Rome, *N.Y., U.S.A.* 111 C9
Rome, *Pa., U.S.A.* 111 E8
Rometta, *Italy* 31 D8
Romilly-sur-Seine, *France* 19 D10
Romney, *U.S.A.* 108 F6
Romney Marsh, *U.K.* 13 F8
Romny, *Ukraine* 47 G7

Rømø, *Denmark* 11 J2
Romodan, *Ukraine* 47 G7
Romodanovo, *Russia* 48 C7
Romont, *Switz.* 25 J2
Romorantin-Lanthenay, *France* 19 E8
Romsdalen, *Norway* 9 E12
Romsey, *U.K.* 13 G6
Ron, *Vietnam* 64 D6
Rona, *U.K.* 14 D3
Ronan, *U.S.A.* 114 C6
Roncador, Cayos, *Caribbean* 120 D3
Roncador, Serra do, *Brazil* 125 F8
Ronciglione, *Italy* 29 F9
Ronco →, *Italy* 29 D9
Ronda, *Spain* 35 J5
Ronda, Serranía de, *Spain* 35 J5
Rondane, *Norway* 9 F13
Rondônia □, *Brazil* 124 F6
Rondonópolis, *Brazil* 125 G8
Rong, Koh, *Cambodia* 65 G4
Rong Jiang →, *China* 58 E7
Rong Xian, *Guangxi Zhuangzu, China* 59 F8
Rong Xian, *Sichuan, China* 58 C5
Rong'an, *China* 58 E7
Rongchang, *China* 58 C5
Ronge, L. la, *Canada* 105 B7
Rongjiang, *China* 58 E7
Rongshui, *China* 58 E7
Rønne, *Denmark* 11 J8
Ronne Ice Shelf, *Antarctica* 5 D18
Ronneby, *Sweden* 11 H9
Ronnebyån →, *Sweden* 11 H9
Rönneshytta, *Sweden* 11 F9
Ronsard, C., *Australia* 93 D1
Ronse, *Belgium* 17 D3
Roodepoort, *S. Africa* 89 D4
Roof Butte, *U.S.A.* 115 H9
Rooiboklaagte →, *Namibia* 88 C3
Roorkee, *India* 68 E7
Roosendaal, *Neths.* 17 C4
Roosevelt, *U.S.A.* 114 F8
Roosevelt →, *Brazil* 122 D4
Roosevelt, Mt., *Canada* 104 B3
Roosevelt I., *Antarctica* 5 D12
Ropczyce, *Poland* 45 H8
Roper →, *Australia* 94 A2
Roper Bar, *Australia* 94 A1
Roque Pérez, *Argentina* 126 D4
Roquefort, *France* 20 D3
Roquemaure, *France* 21 D8
Roquetas de Mar, *Spain* 33 J2
Roquetes, *Spain* 32 E5
Roquevaire, *France* 21 E9
Roraima □, *Brazil* 124 C6
Roraima, Mt., *Venezuela* 122 C4
Røros, *Norway* 9 E14
Rorschach, *Switz.* 25 H5
Rosa, *Zambia* 87 D3
Rosa, L., *Bahamas* 121 B5
Rosa, Monte, *Italy* 28 C4
Rosal de la Frontera, *Spain* 35 H3
Rosalia, *U.S.A.* 114 C5
Rosamond, *U.S.A.* 117 L8
Rosans, *France* 21 D9
Rosario, *Argentina* 126 C3
Rosário, *Brazil* 125 D10
Rosario, *Baja Calif., Mexico* 118 B1
Rosario, *Sinaloa, Mexico* 118 C3
Rosario, *Paraguay* 126 A4
Rosario de la Frontera, *Argentina* 126 B3
Rosario de Lerma, *Argentina* 126 A2
Rosario del Tala, *Argentina* 126 C4
Rosário do Sul, *Brazil* 127 C5
Rosarito, *Mexico* 117 N9
Rosarno, *Italy* 31 D8
Rosas = Roses, *Spain* 32 C8
Roscoe, *U.S.A.* 111 E10
Roscoff, *France* 18 D3
Roscommon, *Ireland* 15 C3
Roscommon □, *Ireland* 15 C3
Roscrea, *Ireland* 15 D4
Rose →, *Australia* 94 A2
Rose Blanche, *Canada* 103 C8
Rose Pt., *Canada* 104 C2
Rose Valley, *Canada* 105 C8
Roseau, *Domin.* 121 C7
Roseau, *U.S.A.* 112 A7
Rosebery, *Australia* 94 G4
Rosebud, *S. Dak., U.S.A.* 112 D4
Rosebud, *Tex., U.S.A.* 113 K6
Roseburg, *U.S.A.* 114 E2
Rosedale, *U.S.A.* 113 J9
Roseland, *U.S.A.* 116 G4
Rosemary, *Canada* 104 C6
Rosenberg, *U.S.A.* 113 L7
Rosendaël, *France* 19 A9
Rosenheim, *Germany* 25 H8
Roses, *Spain* 32 C8
Roses, G. de, *Spain* 32 C8
Roseto degli Abruzzi, *Italy* 29 F11
Rosetown, *Canada* 105 C7
Rosetta = Rashîd, *Egypt* 80 H7
Roseville, *Calif., U.S.A.* 116 G5
Roseville, *Mich., U.S.A.* 110 D2
Rosewood, *Australia* 95 D5
Roshkhvār, *Iran* 71 C8
Rosières-en-Santerre, *France* 19 C9
Rosignano Maríttimo, *Italy* 28 E7
Rosignol, *Guyana* 124 B7
Roşiori de Vede, *Romania* 43 F10
Rositsa, *Bulgaria* 41 C11
Rositsa →, *Bulgaria* 41 C9
Roskilde, *Denmark* 11 J6
Roskilde Amtskommune □, *Denmark* 11 J6
Roskovec, *Albania* 40 F3
Roslavl, *Russia* 46 F7
Rosmaninhal, *Portugal* 34 F3
Rosmead, *S. Africa* 88 E4
Røsnæs, *Denmark* 11 J4
Rosolini, *Italy* 31 F7
Rosporden, *France* 18 E3
Ross, *Australia* 94 G4
Ross, *N.Z.* 91 K3
Ross Béthio, *Mauritania* 82 B1
Ross I., *Antarctica* 5 D11
Ross Ice Shelf, *Antarctica* 5 E12
Ross L., *U.S.A.* 114 B3
Ross-on-Wye, *U.K.* 13 F5
Ross River, *Australia* 94 C1
Ross River, *Canada* 104 A2
Ross Sea, *Antarctica* 5 D11
Rossall Pt., *U.K.* 12 D4
Rossan Pt., *Ireland* 15 B3
Rossano, *Italy* 31 C9
Rossburn, *Canada* 105 C8
Rosseau, *Canada* 110 A5
Rosseau L., *Canada* 110 A5
Rosses, The, *Ireland* 15 A3
Rossignol, L., *Canada* 102 B5
Rossignol Res., *Canada* 103 D6
Rossland, *Canada* 104 D5
Rosslare, *Ireland* 15 D5
Rosslau, *Germany* 24 D8
Rosso, *Mauritania* 82 B1
Rosso, C., *France* 21 F12
Rossosh, *Russia* 47 G10
Røssvatnet, *Norway* 8 D16
Røst, *Norway* 8 C15
Rosthern, *Canada* 105 C7
Rostock, *Germany* 24 A8
Rostov, *Don, Russia* 47 J10
Rostov, *Yaroslavl, Russia* 46 D10
Rostrenen, *France* 18 D3
Roswell, *Ga., U.S.A.* 109 H3
Roswell, *N. Mex., U.S.A.* 113 J2
Rota, *Spain* 35 J4
Rotan, *U.S.A.* 113 J4
Rotenburg, *Hessen, Germany* 24 E5
Rotenburg, *Niedersachsen, Germany* 24 B5
Roth, *Germany* 25 F7
Rothaargebirge, *Germany* 24 D4
Rothenburg ob der Tauber, *Germany* 25 F6
Rother →, *U.K.* 13 G8
Rotherham, *U.K.* 12 D6
Rothes, *U.K.* 14 D5
Rothesay, *Canada* 103 C6
Rothesay, *U.K.* 14 F3
Roti, *Indonesia* 63 F6
Rotja, Pta., *Spain* 33 G6
Rotondo, Mte., *France* 21 F13
Rotoroa, L., *N.Z.* 91 J4
Rotorua, *N.Z.* 91 H6
Rotorua, L., *N.Z.* 91 H6
Rott →, *Germany* 25 G9
Rottenburg, *Germany* 25 G4
Rottenmann, *Austria* 26 D7
Rotterdam, *Neths.* 17 C4
Rotterdam, *U.S.A.* 111 D10
Rottne, *Sweden* 11 G8
Rottnest I., *Australia* 93 F2
Rottumeroog, *Neths.* 17 A6
Rottweil, *Germany* 25 G4
Rotuma, *Fiji* 96 J9
Roubaix, *France* 19 B10
Roudnice nad Labem, *Czech Rep.* 26 A7
Rouen, *France* 18 C8
Rouergue, *France* 20 D5
Rouillac, *France* 20 C3
Rouleau, *Canada* 105 C8
Round Mountain, *U.S.A.* 114 G5
Round Mt., *Australia* 95 E5
Round Rock, *U.S.A.* 113 K6
Roundup, *U.S.A.* 114 C9
Rousay, *U.K.* 14 B5
Rouses Point, *U.S.A.* 111 B11
Rouseville, *U.S.A.* 110 E5
Roussillon, *Isère, France* 21 C8
Roussillon, *Pyrénées-Or., France* 20 F6
Rouxville, *S. Africa* 88 E4
Rouyn-Noranda, *Canada* 102 C4
Rovaniemi, *Finland* 8 C21
Rovato, *Italy* 28 C7
Rovenki, *Ukraine* 47 H10
Rovereto, *Italy* 28 C8
Rovigo, *Italy* 29 C8
Rovinj, *Croatia* 29 C10
Rovno = Rivne, *Ukraine* 47 G4
Rovnoye, *Russia* 48 E8
Rovuma = Ruvuma →, *Tanzania* 87 E5
Row'ān, *Iran* 71 C6
Rowena, *Australia* 95 D4
Rowley Shoals, *Australia* 92 C2
Roxa, *Guinea-Biss.* 82 C1
Roxas, *Capiz, Phil.* 61 F5
Roxas, *Isabela, Phil.* 61 C4
Roxas, *Mind. Or., Phil.* 61 E4
Roxboro, *U.S.A.* 109 G6
Roxburgh, *N.Z.* 91 L2
Roxbury, *U.S.A.* 110 F7
Roxen, *Sweden* 11 F9
Roy, *Mont., U.S.A.* 114 C9
Roy, *N. Mex., U.S.A.* 113 H2
Roy, *Utah, U.S.A.* 114 F7
Royal Canal, *Ireland* 15 C4
Royal Leamington Spa, *U.K.* 13 E6
Royal Tunbridge Wells, *U.K.* 13 F8
Royan, *France* 20 C2
Roye, *France* 19 C9
Royston, *U.K.* 13 E7
Rožaj, *Montenegro, Yug.* 40 D4
Różan, *Poland* 45 F8
Rozay-en-Brie, *France* 19 D9
Rozdilna, *Ukraine* 47 J6
Rozhyshche, *Ukraine* 47 G3
Rožmitál pod Třemšínem, *Czech Rep.* 26 B6
Rožňava, *Slovak Rep.* 27 C13
Rozogi, *Poland* 44 E8
Rozoy-sur-Serre, *France* 19 C11
Rozzano, *Italy* 28 C6
Rrëshen, *Albania* 40 E3
Rrogozhine, *Albania* 40 E3
Rtanj, *Serbia, Yug.* 40 C5
Rtishchevo, *Russia* 48 D6
Rúa = A Rúa, *Spain* 34 C3
Ruacaná, *Namibia* 88 B1
Ruahine Ra., *N.Z.* 91 H6
Ruapehu, *N.Z.* 91 H5
Ruapuke I., *N.Z.* 91 M2
Ruâq, W. →, *Egypt* 75 F2
Rub' al Khālī, *Si. Arabia* 74 D4
Rubeho Mts., *Tanzania* 86 D4
Rubezhnoye = Rubizhne, *Ukraine* 47 H10
Rubh a' Mhail, *U.K.* 14 F2
Rubha Hunish, *U.K.* 14 D2
Rubha Robhanais = Lewis, Butt of, *U.K.* 14 C2
Rubí, *Spain* 32 D7
Rubicon →, *U.S.A.* 116 G5
Rubicone →, *Italy* 29 D9
Rubik, *Albania* 40 E3
Rubino, *Ivory C.* 82 D4
Rubio, *Venezuela* 124 B4
Rubizhne, *Ukraine* 47 H10
Rubtsovsk, *Russia* 50 D9
Ruby L., *U.S.A.* 114 F6
Ruby Mts., *U.S.A.* 114 F6
Rubyvale, *Australia* 94 C4
Rucheng, *China* 59 E9
Ruciane-Nida, *Poland* 44 E8
Rūd Sar, *Iran* 71 B6
Ruda, *Sweden* 11 G10
Ruda Śląska, *Poland* 45 H5
Rudall →, *Australia* 92 D3
Rüdersdorf, *Germany* 24 C9
Rudewa, *Tanzania* 87 E3
Rudkøbing, *Denmark* 11 K4
Rudna, *Poland* 45 G3
Rudnik, *Bulgaria* 41 D11
Rudnik, *Poland* 45 H9
Rudnik, *Serbia, Yug.* 40 B4
Rudnya, *Russia* 46 E6
Rudnyy, *Kazakstan* 50 D7
Rudo, *Bos.-H.* 42 G4
Rudolfa, Ostrov, *Russia* 50 A6
Rudolstadt, *Germany* 24 E7
Rudong, *China* 59 A13
Rudozem, *Bulgaria* 41 E8
Rudyard, *U.S.A.* 108 B3
Rue, *France* 19 B8
Rufa'a, *Sudan* 81 E3
Rufiji →, *Tanzania* 86 D4
Rufino, *Argentina* 126 C3
Rufisque, *Senegal* 82 C1
Rufunsa, *Zambia* 87 F2
Rugao, *China* 59 A13
Rugby, *U.K.* 13 E6
Rugby, *U.S.A.* 112 A5
Rügen, *Germany* 24 A9
Rugles, *France* 18 D7
Ruhengeri, *Rwanda* 86 C2
Ruhla, *Germany* 24 E6
Ruhland, *Germany* 24 D9
Ruhnu, *Estonia* 9 H20
Ruhr →, *Germany* 24 D2
Ruhuhu →, *Tanzania* 87 E3
Rui'an, *China* 59 D13
Ruichang, *China* 59 C10
Ruidoso, *U.S.A.* 115 K11
Ruijin, *China* 59 E10
Ruili, *China* 58 E1
Ruivo, Pico, *Madeira* 37 D3
Ruj, *Bulgaria* 40 D6
Rujen, *Macedonia* 40 D6
Rujm Tal'at al Jamā'ah, *Jordan* 75 E4
Ruk, *Pakistan* 68 F3
Rukhla, *Pakistan* 68 C4
Ruki →, *Dem. Rep. of the Congo* 84 E3
Rukwa □, *Tanzania* 86 D3
Rukwa, L., *Tanzania* 86 D3
Rulhieres, C., *Australia* 92 B4
Rum = Rhum, *U.K.* 14 E2
Rum Cay, *Bahamas* 121 B5
Rum Jungle, *Australia* 92 B5
Ruma, *Serbia, Yug.* 42 E4
Rumāḥ, *Si. Arabia* 70 E5
Rumania = Romania ■, *Europe* 43 D10
Rumaylah, *Iraq* 70 D5
Rumbêk, *Sudan* 81 F2
Rumburk, *Czech Rep.* 26 A7
Rumford, *U.S.A.* 109 C10
Rumia, *Poland* 44 D5
Rumilly, *France* 21 C9
Rumoi, *Japan* 54 C10
Rumonge, *Burundi* 86 C2
Rumson, *U.S.A.* 111 F11
Rumuruti, *Kenya* 86 B4
Runan, *China* 56 H8
Runanga, *N.Z.* 91 K3
Runaway, C., *N.Z.* 91 G6
Runcorn, *U.K.* 12 D5
Rundu, *Namibia* 88 B2
Rungwa, *Tanzania* 86 D3
Rungwa →, *Tanzania* 86 D3
Rungwe, *Tanzania* 87 D3
Rungwe, Mt., *Tanzania* 84 F6
Runka, *Nigeria* 83 C6
Runn, *Sweden* 10 D9
Runton Ra., *Australia* 92 D3
Ruokolahti, *Finland* 46 B5
Ruoqiang, *China* 60 C3
Rupa, *India* 67 F18
Rupar, *India* 68 D7
Rupat, *Indonesia* 62 D2
Rupea, *Romania* 43 D10
Rupen →, *India* 68 H4
Rupert, *U.S.A.* 114 E7
Rupert →, *Canada* 102 B4
Rupert B., *Canada* 102 B4
Rupert House = Waskaganish, *Canada* 102 B4
Rupsa, *India* 69 J12
Rur →, *Germany* 24 D1
Rurrenabaque, *Bolivia* 124 F5
Rus →, *Spain* 33 F2
Rusambo, *Zimbabwe* 87 F3
Rusape, *Zimbabwe* 87 F3
Ruschuk = Ruse, *Bulgaria* 41 C9
Ruse, *Bulgaria* 41 C9
Ruse □, *Bulgaria* 41 C10
Ruşeţu, *Romania* 43 F12
Rush, *Ireland* 15 C5
Rushan, *China* 57 F11
Rushden, *U.K.* 13 E7
Rushmore, Mt., *U.S.A.* 112 D3
Rushville, *Ill., U.S.A.* 112 E9
Rushville, *Ind., U.S.A.* 108 F3
Rushville, *Nebr., U.S.A.* 112 D3
Russas, *Brazil* 125 D11
Russell, *Canada* 105 C8
Russell, *Kans., U.S.A.* 112 F5
Russell, *N.Y., U.S.A.* 111 B9
Russell, *Pa., U.S.A.* 110 E5
Russell L., *Man., Canada* 105 B8
Russell L., *N.W.T., Canada* 104 A5
Russellkonda, *India* 67 K14
Russellville, *Ala., U.S.A.* 109 H2
Russellville, *Ark., U.S.A.* 113 H8
Russellville, *Ky., U.S.A.* 109 G2
Rüsselsheim, *Germany* 25 F4
Russi, *Italy* 29 D9
Russia ■, *Eurasia* 51 C11
Russian →, *U.S.A.* 116 G3
Russkoye Ustie, *Russia* 4 B15
Rust, *Austria* 27 D9
Rustam, *Pakistan* 68 B5
Rustam Shahr, *Pakistan* 68 F2
Rustavi, *Georgia* 49 K7
Rustenburg, *S. Africa* 88 D4
Ruston, *U.S.A.* 113 J8
Rutana, *Burundi* 86 C3
Rute, *Spain* 35 H6
Ruteng, *Indonesia* 63 F6
Ruth, *U.S.A.* 110 C2
Rutherford, *U.S.A.* 116 G4
Rutland, *U.S.A.* 111 C12
Rutland □, *U.K.* 13 E7
Rutland Water, *U.K.* 13 E7
Rutledge →, *Canada* 105 A6
Rutledge L., *Canada* 105 A6
Rutqa, W. →, *Syria* 73 E9
Rutshuru, *Dem. Rep. of the Congo* 86 C2
Ruvo di Púglia, *Italy* 31 A9
Ruvu, *Tanzania* 86 D4
Ruvu →, *Tanzania* 86 D4
Ruvuma □, *Tanzania* 87 E4
Ruvuma →, *Tanzania* 87 E5
Ruwais, *U.A.E.* 71 E7
Ruwenzori, *Africa* 86 B2
Ruya →, *Zimbabwe* 89 B5
Ruyigi, *Burundi* 86 C3
Ruyuan, *China* 59 E9
Ruzayevka, *Russia* 48 C7
Rŭzhevo Konare, *Bulgaria* 41 D8
Ružomberok, *Slovak Rep.* 27 B12
Rwanda ■, *Africa* 86 C3
Ryakhovo, *Bulgaria* 41 C10
Ryan, L., *U.K.* 14 G3
Ryazan, *Russia* 46 E10
Ryazhsk, *Russia* 46 F11
Rybache = Rybachye, *Kazakstan* 50 E9
Rybachye, *Kazakstan* 50 E9
Rybinsk, *Russia* 46 C10
Rybinskoye Vdkhr., *Russia* 46 C10
Rybnik, *Poland* 45 H5
Rybnitsa = Râbniţa, *Moldova* 43 C14
Rybnoye, *Russia* 46 E10
Rychnov nad Kněžnou, *Czech Rep.* 27 A9
Rychwał, *Poland* 45 F5
Rycroft, *Canada* 104 B5
Ryd, *Sweden* 11 H8
Rydaholm, *Sweden* 11 H8
Ryde, *U.K.* 13 G6
Ryderwood, *U.S.A.* 116 D3
Rydzyna, *Poland* 45 G3
Rye, *U.K.* 13 G8
Rye →, *U.K.* 12 C7
Rye Bay, *U.K.* 13 G8
Rye Patch Reservoir, *U.S.A.* 114 F4
Ryegate, *U.S.A.* 114 C9
Ryki, *Poland* 45 G8
Ryley, *Canada* 104 C6
Rylsk, *Russia* 47 G8
Rymanów, *Poland* 45 J8
Ryn, *Poland* 44 E8
Ryn Peski, *Kazakstan* 49 G9
Ryōtsu, *Japan* 54 E9
Rypin, *Poland* 45 E6
Ryssby, *Sweden* 11 H8
Ryūgasaki, *Japan* 55 G10
Ryūkyū Is. = Ryūkyū-rettō, *Japan* 55 M3
Ryūkyū-rettō, *Japan* 55 M3
Rzepin, *Poland* 45 F1
Rzeszów, *Poland* 45 H8
Rzhev, *Russia* 46 D8

S

Sa, *Thailand* 64 C3
Sa Canal, *Spain* 37 C7
Sa Conillera, *Spain* 37 C7
Sa Dec, *Vietnam* 65 G5
Sa Dragonera, *Spain* 37 B9
Sa Mesquida, *Spain* 37 B11
Sa Pobla, *Spain* 32 F8
Sa Savina, *Spain* 37 C7
Sa'ādatābād, *Fārs, Iran* 71 D7
Sa'ādatābād, *Hormozgān, Iran* 71 D7
Sa'ādatābād, *Kermān, Iran* 71 D7
Saale →, *Germany* 24 D7
Saaler Bodden, *Germany* 24 A8
Saalfeld, *Germany* 24 E7
Saalfelden, *Austria* 26 D5
Saane →, *Switz.* 25 H3
Saar →, *Europe* 17 E6
Saarbrücken, *Germany* 25 F2
Saarburg, *Germany* 25 F2
Saaremaa, *Estonia* 9 G20
Saarijärvi, *Finland* 9 E21
Saariselkä, *Finland* 8 B23
Saarland □, *Germany* 25 F2
Saarlouis, *Germany* 25 F2
Sab 'Ābar, *Syria* 70 C3
Saba, *W. Indies* 121 C7
Šabac, *Serbia, Yug.* 40 B3
Sabadell, *Spain* 32 D7
Sabah □, *Malaysia* 62 C5
Sabak Bernam, *Malaysia* 65 L3
Sabalān, Kūhhā-ye, *Iran* 70 B5
Sabalana, Kepulauan, *Indonesia* 63 F5
Sábana de la Mar, *Dom. Rep.* 121 C6
Sábanalarga, *Colombia* 124 A4
Sabang, *Indonesia* 62 C1
Săbăoani, *Romania* 43 C11
Sabará, *Brazil* 125 G10
Sabarmati →, *India* 68 H5
Sabattis, *U.S.A.* 111 B10
Sabáudia, *Italy* 30 A6
Saberania, *Indonesia* 63 E9
Sabhah, *Libya* 79 C8
Sabi →, *India* 68 E7
Sabidana, J., *Sudan* 80 D4
Sabie, *S. Africa* 89 D5
Sabinal, *Mexico* 118 A3
Sabinal, *U.S.A.* 113 L5
Sabiñánigo, *Spain* 32 C4
Sabinar, Punta del, *Spain* 33 J2
Sabinas, *Mexico* 118 B4
Sabinas →, *Mexico* 118 B4
Sabinas Hidalgo, *Mexico* 118 B4
Sabine →, *U.S.A.* 113 L8
Sabine L., *U.S.A.* 113 L8
Sabine Pass, *U.S.A.* 113 L8
Sabinov, *Slovak Rep.* 27 B14
Sabinsville, *U.S.A.* 110 E7
Sabirabad, *Azerbaijan* 49 K9
Sabkhet el Bardawîl, *Egypt* 75 D2
Sablayan, *Phil.* 61 E4
Sable, *Canada* 103 A6
Sable, C., *Canada* 103 D6
Sable, C., *U.S.A.* 107 E10
Sable I., *Canada* 103 D8
Sablé-sur-Sarthe, *France* 18 E6
Sabonkafi, *Niger* 83 C6
Sabor →, *Portugal* 34 D3
Sabou, *Burkina Faso* 82 C4
Sabres, *France* 20 D3
Sabrina Coast, *Antarctica* 5 C9
Sabugal, *Portugal* 34 E3
Sabulubbek, *Indonesia* 62 E1
Sabuncu, *Turkey* 39 B12
Sabzevār, *Iran* 71 B8
Sabzvārān, *Iran* 71 D8
Sac City, *U.S.A.* 112 D7
Sacedón, *Spain* 32 E2
Săcele, *Romania* 43 E10
Sachigo →, *Canada* 102 A2
Sachigo, L., *Canada* 102 B1
Sachkhere, *Georgia* 49 J6
Sachsen □, *Germany* 24 E9
Sachsen-Anhalt □, *Germany* 24 D7
Sacile, *Italy* 29 C9
Sackets Harbor, *U.S.A.* 111 C8
Sackville, *Canada* 103 C7
Saco, *Maine, U.S.A.* 109 D10
Saco, *Mont., U.S.A.* 114 B10
Sacramento, *U.S.A.* 116 G5
Sacramento →, *U.S.A.* 116 G5
Sacramento Mts., *U.S.A.* 115 K11
Sacramento Valley, *U.S.A.* 116 G5
Sacratif, C., *Spain* 35 J7
Săcueni, *Romania* 42 C7
Sada, *Spain* 34 B2
Sada-Misaki, *Japan* 55 H6
Sádaba, *Spain* 32 C3

Sadabad, India 68 F8
Sadani, Tanzania 86 D4
Sadao, Thailand 65 J3
Sadd el Aali, Egypt 80 C3
Saddle Mt., U.S.A. 116 E3
Sade, Nigeria 83 C7
Sadimi, Dem. Rep. of the Congo 87 D1
Sadiola, Mali 82 C2
Sa'dīyah, Hawr as, Iraq 73 F12
Sado, Japan 54 F9
Sado →, Portugal 35 G2
Sadon, Burma 67 G20
Sadon, Russia 49 J6
Sadra, India 68 H5
Sadri, India 68 G5
Sæby, Denmark 11 G4
Saegertown, U.S.A. 110 E4
Saelices, Spain 32 F2
Safaalan, Turkey 41 E12
Safaga, Egypt 80 B3
Şafājah, Si. Arabia 70 E3
Šafárikovo = Tornal'a, Slovak Rep. 27 C13
Säffle, Sweden 10 E6
Safford, U.S.A. 115 K9
Saffron Walden, U.K. 13 E8
Safi, Morocco 78 B4
Şafīābād, Iran 71 B8
Safīd Dasht, Iran 71 C6
Safīd Kūh, Afghan. 66 B3
Safīd Rūd →, Iran 71 B6
Safipur, India 69 F9
Safonovo, Russia 46 E7
Safranbolu, Turkey 72 B5
Saft Rashîn, Egypt 80 J7
Safwān, Iraq 70 D5
Sag Harbor, U.S.A. 111 F12
Saga, Japan 55 H5
Saga □, Japan 55 H5
Sagae, Japan 54 E10
Sagala, Mali 82 C3
Sagamore, U.S.A. 110 F5
Sagar, Karnataka, India 66 M9
Sagar, Mad. P., India 69 H8
Sagara, L., Tanzania 86 D3
Sagay, Phil. 61 F5
Saginaw, U.S.A. 108 D4
Saginaw →, U.S.A. 108 D4
Saginaw B., U.S.A. 108 D4
Sagleipie, Liberia 82 D3
Saglouc = Salluit, Canada 101 B12
Sagŏ-ri, S. Korea 57 G14
Sagone, France 21 F12
Sagone, G. de, France 21 F12
Sagres, Portugal 35 J2
Sagua la Grande, Cuba 120 B3
Saguache, U.S.A. 115 G10
Saguaro Nat. Park, U.S.A. 115 K8
Saguenay →, Canada 103 C5
Sagunt, Spain 32 F4
Sagunto = Sagunt, Spain 32 F4
Sagwara, India 68 H6
Sahaba, Sudan 80 D3
Sahagún, Spain 34 C5
Saḩam al Jawlān, Syria 75 C4
Sahamandrevo, Madag. 89 C8
Sahand, Kūh-e, Iran 70 B5
Sahara, Africa 78 D6
Saharan Atlas = Saharien, Atlas, Algeria 78 B6
Saharanpur, India 68 E7
Saharien, Atlas, Algeria 78 B6
Saharsa, India 69 G12
Sahasinaka, Madag. 89 C8
Sahaswan, India 69 E8
Sahel, Africa 78 E5
Sahel, Canal du, Mali 82 C3
Sahibganj, India 69 G12
Sāḩilīyah, Iraq 70 C4
Sahiwal, Pakistan 68 D5
Şaḩneh, Iran 70 C5
Sahuaripa, Mexico 118 B3
Sahuarita, U.S.A. 115 L8
Sahuayo, Mexico 118 C4
Šahy, Slovak Rep. 27 C11
Sai →, India 69 G10
Sai Buri, Thailand 65 J3
Sa'id Bundas, Sudan 79 G10
Sa'īdābād, Kermān, Iran 71 D7
Sa'īdābād, Semnān, Iran 71 B7
Sa'īdīyeh, Iran 71 B6
Saidpur, Bangla. 67 G16
Saidpur, India 69 G10
Saidu, Pakistan 69 B5
Saignes, France 20 C6
Saigon = Thanh Pho Ho Chi Minh, Vietnam 65 G6
Saijō, Japan 55 H6
Saikanosy Masoala, Madag. 89 B9
Saikhoa Ghat, India 67 F19
Saiki, Japan 55 H5
Sailana, India 68 H6
Saillans, France 21 D9
Sailolof, Indonesia 63 E8
Saimaa, Finland 9 F23
Saimbeyli, Turkey 72 D7
Şa'in Dezh, Iran 70 B5
St. Abb's Head, U.K. 14 F6
St-Affrique, France 20 E6
St-Agrève, France 21 C8
St-Aignan, France 18 E8
St. Alban's, Canada 103 C8
St. Albans, U.K. 13 F7
St. Albans, Vt., U.S.A. 111 B11
St. Albans, W. Va., U.S.A. 108 F5
St. Alban's Head, U.K. 13 G5
St. Albert, Canada 104 C6
St-Amand-en-Puisaye, France 19 E10
St-Amand-les-Eaux, France 19 B10
St-Amand-Montrond, France 19 F9
St-Amarin, France 19 E14
St-Amour, France 19 F12
St-André-de-Cubzac, France 20 D3
St-André-les-Alpes, France 21 E10
St. Andrew's, Canada 103 C8
St. Andrews, U.K. 14 E6
St-Anicet, Canada 111 A10
St. Ann B., Canada 103 C7
St. Ann's Bay, Jamaica 120 C4
St. Anthony, Canada 103 B8
St. Anthony, U.S.A. 114 E8
St. Antoine, Canada 103 C7
St-Antonin-Noble-Val, France 20 D5
St-Astier, France 20 C4
St-Aubin-du-Cormier, France 18 D5
St-Augustin →, Canada 103 B8
St-Augustin-Saguenay, Canada 103 B8
St. Augustine, U.S.A. 109 L5
St-Aulaye, France 20 C4
St. Austell, U.K. 13 G3
St-Avold, France 19 C13
St. Barbe, Canada 103 B8
St-Barthélemy, W. Indies 121 C7
St-Béat, France 20 F4
St. Bees Hd., U.K. 12 C4
St-Benoît-du-Sault, France 20 B5
St-Bonnet, France 21 D10
St-Brévin-les-Pins, France 18 E4
St-Brice-en-Coglès, France 18 D5
St. Bride's, Canada 103 C9
St. Brides B., U.K. 13 F2
St-Brieuc, France 18 D4
St-Calais, France 18 E7
St-Cast-le-Guildo, France 18 D4
St. Catharines, Canada 102 D4
St. Catherines I., U.S.A. 109 K5
St. Catherine's Pt., U.K. 13 G6
St-Céré, France 20 D5
St-Cergue, Switz. 25 J2
St-Cernin, France 20 C6
St-Chamond, France 21 C8
St. Charles, Ill., U.S.A. 108 E1
St. Charles, Mo., U.S.A. 112 F9
St. Charles, Va., U.S.A. 108 F7
St-Chély-d'Apcher, France 20 D7
St-Chinian, France 20 E6
St. Christopher-Nevis = St. Kitts & Nevis ■, W. Indies 121 C7
St-Ciers-sur-Gironde, France 20 C3
St. Clair, Mich., U.S.A. 110 D2
St. Clair, Pa., U.S.A. 111 F8
St. Clair →, U.S.A. 110 D2
St. Clair, L., Canada 102 D3
St. Clair, L., U.S.A. 110 D2
St. Clairsville, U.S.A. 110 F4
St-Claud, France 20 C4
St. Claude, Canada 105 D9
St-Claude, France 19 F12
St-Clet, Canada 111 A10
St. Cloud, Fla., U.S.A. 109 L5
St. Cloud, Minn., U.S.A. 112 C7
St. Cricq, C., Australia 93 E1
St. Croix, U.S. Virgin Is. 121 C7
St. Croix →, U.S.A. 112 C8
St. Croix Falls, U.S.A. 112 C8
St-Cyprien, France 20 F7
St-Cyr-sur-Mer, France 21 E9
St. David's, Canada 103 C8
St. David's, U.K. 13 F2
St. David's Head, U.K. 13 F2
St-Denis, France 19 D9
St-Dié, France 19 D13
St-Dizier, France 19 D11
St-Égrève, France 21 C9
St. Elias, Mt., U.S.A. 100 B5
St. Elias Mts., Canada 104 A1
St. Elias Mts., U.S.A. 100 C6
St-Eloy-les-Mines, France 19 F9
St-Émilion, France 20 D3
St-Étienne, France 21 C8
St-Étienne-de-Tinée, France 21 D10
St-Étienne-du-Rouvray, France 18 C8
St. Eugène, Canada 111 A10
St. Eustatius, W. Indies 121 C7
St-Fargeau, France 19 E10
St-Félicien, Canada 102 C5
St-Florent, France 21 F13
St-Florent, G. de, France 21 F13
St-Florent-sur-Cher, France 19 F9
St-Florentin, France 19 E10
St-Flour, France 20 C7
St. Francis, U.S.A. 112 F4
St. Francis →, U.S.A. 113 H9
St. Francis, C., S. Africa 88 E3
St. Francisville, U.S.A. 113 K9
St-François, L., Canada 111 A10
St-Fulgent, France 18 F5
St-Gabriel, Canada 102 C5
St. Gallen = Sankt Gallen, Switz. 25 H5
St-Galmier, France 19 G11
St-Gaudens, France 20 E4
St-Gaultier, France 18 F8
St-Gengoux-le-National, France 19 F11
St-Geniez-d'Olt, France 20 D6
St. George, Australia 95 D4
St. George, Canada 103 C6
St. George, S.C., U.S.A. 109 J5
St. George, Utah, U.S.A. 115 H7
St. George, C., Canada 103 C8
St. George, C., U.S.A. 109 L3
St. George Ra., Australia 92 C4
St. George's, Canada 103 C8
St-Georges, Canada 103 C5
St. George's, Grenada 121 D7
St. George's B., Canada 103 C8
St. Georges Basin, N.S.W., Australia 95 F5
St. Georges Basin, W. Austral., Australia 92 C4
St. George's Channel, Europe 15 E6
St-Georges-lès-Baillargeaux, France 20 B4
St-Germain-de-Calberte, France 20 D7
St-Germain-en-Laye, France 19 D9
St-Germain-Lembron, France 20 C7
St-Gervais-d'Auvergne, France 19 F9
St-Gervais-les-Bains, France 21 C10
St-Gildas, Pte. de, France 18 E4
St-Gilles, France 21 E8
St-Girons, Ariège, France 20 F5
St-Girons, Landes, France 20 E2
St. Gotthard P. = San Gottardo, P. del, Switz. 25 J4
St. Helena, U.S.A. 114 G2
St. Helena ■, Atl. Oc. 76 H3
St. Helena, Mt., U.S.A. 116 G4
St. Helena B., S. Africa 88 E2
St. Helens, Australia 94 G4
St. Helens, U.K. 12 D5
St. Helens, U.S.A. 116 E4
St. Helens, Mt., U.S.A. 116 D4
St. Helier, U.K. 13 H5
St-Herblain, France 18 E5
St-Hilaire-du-Harcouët, France 18 D5
St-Hippolyte, France 19 E13
St-Hippolyte-du-Fort, France 20 E7
St-Honoré-les-Bains, France 19 F10
St-Hubert, Belgium 17 D5
St-Hyacinthe, Canada 102 C5
St. Ignace, U.S.A. 108 C3
St. Ignace I., Canada 102 C2
St. Ignatius, U.S.A. 114 C6
St-Imier, Switz. 25 H2
St. Ives, U.K. 13 G2
St-James, France 18 D5
St. James, U.S.A. 112 D7
St-Jean →, Canada 103 B7
St-Jean, L., Canada 103 C5
St-Jean-d'Angély, France 20 C3
St-Jean-de-Braye, France 19 E8
St-Jean-de-Luz, France 20 E2
St-Jean-de-Maurienne, France 21 C10
St-Jean-de-Monts, France 18 F4
St-Jean-du-Gard, France 20 D7
St-Jean-en-Royans, France 21 C9
St-Jean-Pied-de-Port, France 20 E2
St-Jean-Port-Joli, Canada 103 C5
St-Jean-sur-Richelieu, Canada 102 C5
St-Jérôme, Canada 102 C5
St. John, Canada 103 C6
St. John, U.S.A. 113 G5
St. John →, Liberia 82 D2
St. John →, U.S.A. 109 C12
St. John, C., Canada 103 C8
St. John's, Antigua 121 C7
St. John's, Canada 103 C9
St. Johns, Ariz., U.S.A. 115 J9
St. Johns, Mich., U.S.A. 108 D3
St. Johns →, U.S.A. 109 K5
St. John's Pt., Ireland 15 B3
St. Johnsbury, U.S.A. 111 B12
St. Johnsville, U.S.A. 111 D10
St. Joseph, La., U.S.A. 113 K9
St. Joseph, Mo., U.S.A. 112 F7
St. Joseph →, U.S.A. 108 D2
St. Joseph, I., Canada 102 C3
St. Joseph, L., Canada 102 B1
St-Jovite, Canada 102 C5
St-Juéry, France 20 E6
St-Julien-Chapteuil, France 21 C8
St-Julien-de-Vouvantes, France 18 E5
St-Julien-en-Genevois, France 19 F13
St-Junien, France 20 C4
St-Just-en-Chaussée, France 19 C9
St-Just-en-Chevalet, France 20 C7
St. Kitts & Nevis ■, W. Indies 121 C7
St. Laurent, Canada 105 C9
St-Laurent-de-la-Salanque, France 20 F6
St-Laurent-du-Pont, France 21 C9
St-Laurent-en-Grandvaux, France 19 F12
St-Laurent-Médoc, France 20 C3
St. Lawrence, Australia 94 C4
St. Lawrence, Canada 103 C8
St. Lawrence →, Canada 103 C6
St. Lawrence, Gulf of, Canada 103 C7
St. Lawrence I., U.S.A. 100 B3
St. Leonard, Canada 103 C6
St-Léonard-de-Noblat, France 20 C5
St. Lewis →, Canada 103 B8
St-Lô, France 18 C5
St-Louis, France 19 E14
St. Louis, Senegal 82 B1
St. Louis, U.S.A. 112 F9
St. Louis →, U.S.A. 112 B8
St-Loup-sur-Semouse, France 19 E13
St. Lucia ■, W. Indies 121 D7
St. Lucia, L., S. Africa 89 D5
St. Lucia Channel, W. Indies 121 D7
St. Maarten, W. Indies 121 C7
St. Magnus B., U.K. 14 A7
St-Maixent-l'École, France 20 B3
St-Malo, France 18 D4
St-Malo, G. de, France 18 D4
St-Mandrier-sur-Mer, France 21 E9
St-Marc, Haiti 121 C5
St-Marcellin, France 21 C9
St-Marcouf, Îs., France 18 C5
St. Maries, U.S.A. 114 C5
St-Martin, W. Indies 121 C7
St. Martin, L., Canada 105 C9
St-Martin-de-Crau, France 21 E8
St-Martin-de-Ré, France 20 B2
St-Martin-d'Hères, France 21 C9
St-Martin-Vésubie, France 21 D11
St-Martory, France 20 E4
St. Marys, Australia 94 G4
St. Marys, Canada 110 C3
St. Mary's, Corn., U.K. 13 H1
St. Mary's, Orkney, U.K. 14 C6
St. Marys, Ga., U.S.A. 109 K5
St. Marys, Pa., U.S.A. 110 E6
St. Mary's, C., Canada 103 C9
St. Mary's B., Canada 103 C9
St. Marys Bay, Canada 103 D6
St-Mathieu, Pte., France 18 D2
St. Matthew I., U.S.A. 100 B2
St. Matthews, I. = Zadetkyi Kyun, Burma 65 G1
St-Maurice →, Canada 102 C5
St-Maximin-la-Ste-Baume, France 21 E9
St-Médard-en-Jalles, France 20 D3
St-Méen-le-Grand, France 18 D4
St-Mihiel, France 19 D12
St. Moritz, Switz. 25 J5
St-Nazaire, France 18 E4
St. Neots, U.K. 13 E7
St-Nicolas-de-Port, France 19 D13
St-Niklaas, Belgium 17 C4
St-Omer, France 19 B9
St-Palais-sur-Mer, France 20 C2
St-Pamphile, Canada 103 C6
St-Pardoux-la-Rivière, France 20 C4
St. Pascal, Canada 103 C6
St. Paul, Canada 104 C6
St-Paul, France 21 D10
St. Paul, Minn., U.S.A. 112 C8
St. Paul, Nebr., U.S.A. 112 E5
St-Paul →, Canada 103 B8
St. Paul →, Liberia 82 D2
St. Paul, I., Ind. Oc. 3 F13
St-Paul-de-Fenouillet, France 20 F6
St. Paul I., Canada 103 C7
St-Paul-lès-Dax, France 20 E2
St-Péray, France 21 D8
St. Peter, U.S.A. 112 C8
St-Peter-Ording, Germany 24 A4
St. Peter Port, U.K. 13 H5
St. Peters, N.S., Canada 103 C7
St. Peters, P.E.I., Canada 103 C7
St. Petersburg = Sankt-Peterburg, Russia 46 C6
St. Petersburg, U.S.A. 109 M4
St-Philbert-de-Grand-Lieu, France 18 E5
St-Pie, Canada 111 A12
St-Pierre, St- P. & M. 103 C8
St-Pierre, L., Canada 102 C5
St-Pierre-d'Oléron, France 20 C2
St-Pierre-en-Port, France 18 C7
St-Pierre et Miquelon □, St- P. & M. 103 C8
St-Pierre-le-Moûtier, France 19 F10
St-Pierre-sur-Dives, France 18 C6
St-Pol-de-Léon, France 18 D3
St-Pol-sur-Mer, France 19 A9
St-Pol-sur-Ternoise, France 19 B9
St-Pons, France 20 E6
St-Pourçain-sur-Sioule, France 19 F10
St-Priest, France 21 C8
St-Quay-Portrieux, France 18 D4
St. Quentin, Canada 103 C6
St-Quentin, France 19 C10
St-Rambert-d'Albon, France 21 C8
St-Raphaël, France 21 E10
St. Regis, U.S.A. 114 C6
St-Renan, France 18 D2
St-Saëns, France 18 C8
St-Savin, France 20 B4
St-Savinien, France 20 C3
St. Sebastien, Tanjon' i, Madag. 89 A8
St-Seine-l'Abbaye, France 19 E11
St-Sernin-sur-Rance, France 20 E6
St-Sever, France 20 E3
St-Siméon, Canada 103 C6
St. Simons I., U.S.A. 109 K5
St. Simons Island, U.S.A. 109 K5
St. Stephen, Canada 103 C6
St-Sulpice, France 20 E5
St-Sulpice-Laurière, France 20 B5
St-Sulpice-les-Feuilles, France 20 B5
St-Syprien = St-Cyprien, France 20 F7
St-Thégonnec, France 18 D3
St. Thomas, Canada 102 D3
St. Thomas I., U.S. Virgin Is. 121 C7
St-Tite, Canada 102 C5
St-Tropez, France 21 E10
St. Troud = St. Truiden, Belgium 17 D5
St. Truiden, Belgium 17 D5
St-Vaast-la-Hougue, France 18 C5
St-Valery-en-Caux, France 18 C7
St-Valéry-sur-Somme, France 19 B8
St-Vallier, France 19 F11
St-Vallier-de-Thiey, France 21 E10
St-Varent, France 18 F6
St-Vaury, France 20 B5
St. Vincent, Italy 28 C4
St. Vincent & the Grenadines ■, W. Indies 121 D7
St-Vincent-de-Tyrosse, France 20 E2
St. Vincent Passage, W. Indies 121 D7
St-Vith, Belgium 17 D6
St-Vivien-de-Médoc, France 20 C2
St. Walburg, Canada 105 C7
St-Yrieix-la-Perche, France 20 C5
Ste-Adresse, France 18 C7
Ste-Agathe-des-Monts, Canada 102 C5
Ste-Anne, L., Canada 103 B6
Ste-Anne-des-Monts, Canada 103 C6
Ste-Croix, Switz. 25 J2
Ste-Enimie, France 20 D7
Ste-Foy-la-Grande, France 20 D4
Ste. Genevieve, U.S.A. 112 G9
Ste-Hermine, France 20 B2
Ste-Livrade-sur-Lot, France 20 D4
Ste-Marguerite →, Canada 103 B6
Ste-Marie, Martinique 121 D7
Ste-Marie-aux-Mines, France 19 D14
Ste-Marie de la Madeleine, Canada 103 C5
Ste-Maure-de-Touraine, France 18 E7
Ste-Maxime, France 21 E10
Ste-Menehould, France 19 C11
Ste-Mère-Église, France 18 C5
Ste-Rose, Guadeloupe 121 C7
Ste. Rose du Lac, Canada 105 C9
Ste-Savine, France 19 D11
Ste-Sigolène, France 21 C8
Saintes, France 20 C3
Saintes, I. des, Guadeloupe 121 C7
Stes-Maries-de-la-Mer, France 21 E8
Saintfield, U.K. 15 B6
Saintonge, France 20 C3
Saipan, Pac. Oc. 96 F6
Sairang, India 67 H18
Sairecábur, Cerro, Bolivia 126 A2
Saitama □, Japan 55 F9
Saiteli = Kadınhanı, Turkey 72 C5
Saiţi, Moldova 43 D14
Saiyid, Pakistan 68 C5
Sajama, Bolivia 124 G5
Sajan, Serbia, Yug. 42 E5
Sajó →, Hungary 42 C6
Sajószentpéter, Hungary 42 B5
Sajum, India 69 C8
Sak →, S. Africa 88 E3
Sakaba, Nigeria 83 C6
Sakai, Japan 55 G7
Sakaide, Japan 55 G6
Sakaiminato, Japan 55 G6
Sakākah, Si. Arabia 70 D4
Sakakawea, L., U.S.A. 112 B4
Sakami →, Canada 102 B4
Sakami, L., Canada 102 B4
Sâkâne, 'Erg i-n, Mali 83 A4
Sakania, Dem. Rep. of the Congo 87 E2
Sakaraha, Madag. 89 C7
Sakarya, Turkey 72 B4
Sakarya →, Turkey 72 B4
Sakashima-Guntō, Japan 55 M2
Sakassou, Ivory C. 82 D3
Sakata, Japan 54 E9
Sakchu, N. Korea 57 D13
Sakeny →, Madag. 89 C8
Sakété, Benin 83 D5
Sakha □, Russia 51 C13
Sakhalin, Russia 51 D15
Sakhalinskiy Zaliv, Russia 51 D15
Şaki, Azerbaijan 49 K8
Šakiai, Lithuania 9 J20
Sakon Nakhon, Thailand 64 D5
Sakrand, Pakistan 68 F3
Sakri, India 69 F12
Sakrivier, S. Africa 88 E3
Sakskøbing, Denmark 11 K5
Sakti, India 69 H10
Sakuma, Japan 55 G8
Sakurai, Japan 55 G7
Saky, Ukraine 47 K7
Sal →, Russia 49 G5
Sala, Eritrea 81 D4
Šal'a, Slovak Rep. 27 C10
Sala, Sweden 10 E10
Sala →, Eritrea 81 D4
Sala Consilina, Italy 31 B8
Sala-y-Gómez, Pac. Oc. 97 K17
Salaberry-de-Valleyfield, Canada 102 C5
Saladas, Argentina 126 B4
Saladillo, Argentina 126 D4
Salado →, Buenos Aires, Argentina 126 D4
Salado →, La Pampa, Argentina 128 D3
Salado →, Santa Fe, Argentina 126 C3
Salado →, Mexico 113 M5
Salaga, Ghana 83 D4
Sālah, Syria 75 C5
Sălaj □, Romania 42 C8
Sálakhos, Greece 36 C9
Salala, Liberia 82 D2
Salala, Sudan 80 C4
Salālah, Oman 74 D5
Salamanca, Chile 126 C1
Salamanca, Spain 34 E5
Salamanca, U.S.A. 110 D6
Salamanca □, Spain 34 E5
Salāmatābād, Iran 70 C5
Salamis, Cyprus 36 D12
Salamís, Greece 38 D5
Salar de Atacama, Chile 126 A2
Salar de Uyuni, Bolivia 124 H5
Sălard, Romania 42 C7
Salas, Spain 34 B4
Salas de los Infantes, Spain 34 C7
Salatiga, Indonesia 63 G14
Salaverry, Peru 124 E3
Salawati, Indonesia 63 E8
Salaya, India 68 H3

Salayar, Indonesia 63 F6
Salazar →, Spain 32 C3
Salbris, France 19 E9
Salcia, Romania 43 G9
Sălciua, Romania 43 D8
Salcombe, U.K. 13 G4
Saldaña, Spain 34 C6
Saldanha, S. Africa 88 E2
Saldanha B., S. Africa 88 E2
Saldus, Latvia 9 H20
Saldus □, Latvia 44 B9
Sale, Italy 28 D5
Salé, Morocco 78 B4
Sale, U.K. 12 D5
Salekhard, Russia 50 C7
Salem, India 66 P11
Salem, Ill., U.S.A. 108 F1
Salem, Ind., U.S.A. 108 F2
Salem, Mass., U.S.A. 111 D14
Salem, Mo., U.S.A. 113 G9
Salem, N.H., U.S.A. 111 D13
Salem, N.J., U.S.A. 108 F8
Salem, N.Y., U.S.A. 111 C11
Salem, Ohio, U.S.A. 110 F4
Salem, Oreg., U.S.A. 114 D2
Salem, S. Dak., U.S.A. 112 D6
Salem, Va., U.S.A. 108 G5
Salemi, Italy 30 E5
Sälen, Sweden 10 C7
Salernes, France 21 E10
Salerno, Italy 31 B7
Salerno, G. di, Italy 31 B7
Salford, U.K. 12 D5
Salgir →, Ukraine 47 K8
Salgótarján, Hungary 42 B4
Salgueiro, Brazil 125 E11
Salibabu, Indonesia 63 D7
Salida, U.S.A. 106 C5
Salies-de-Béarn, France 20 E3
Salihli, Turkey 72 C3
Salihorsk, Belarus 47 F4
Salima, Malawi 85 G6
Salina, Italy 31 D7
Salina, Kans., U.S.A. 112 F6
Salina, Utah, U.S.A. 115 G8
Salina Cruz, Mexico 119 D5
Salinas, Brazil 125 G10
Salinas, Chile 126 A2
Salinas, Ecuador 124 D2
Salinas, U.S.A. 116 J5
Salinas →, Guatemala 119 D6
Salinas →, U.S.A. 116 J5
Salinas, B. de, Nic. 120 D2
Salinas, Pampa de las, Argentina 126 C2
Salinas Ambargasta, Argentina 126 B3
Salinas de Hidalgo, Mexico 118 C4
Salinas Grandes, Argentina 126 C3
Saline →, Ark., U.S.A. 113 J8
Saline →, Kans., U.S.A. 112 F6
Salines, Spain 37 B10
Salines, C. de ses, Spain 37 B10
Salinópolis, Brazil 125 D9
Salins-les-Bains, France 19 F12
Salir, Portugal 35 H2
Salisbury = Harare, Zimbabwe 87 F3
Salisbury, U.K. 13 F6
Salisbury, Md., U.S.A. 108 F8
Salisbury, N.C., U.S.A. 109 H5
Salisbury I., Canada 101 B12
Salisbury Plain, U.K. 13 F6
Săliște, Romania 43 E8
Salka, Nigeria 83 C5
Şalkhad, Syria 75 C5
Salla, Finland 8 C23
Sallanches, France 21 C10
Sallent, Spain 32 D6
Salles, France 20 D3
Salles-Curan, France 20 D6
Salling, Denmark 11 H2
Salliq, Canada 101 B11
Sallisaw, U.S.A. 113 H7
Sallom Junction, Sudan 80 D4
Salluit, Canada 101 B12
Salmās, Iran 70 B5
Salmerón, Spain 32 E2
Salmo, Canada 104 D5
Salmon, U.S.A. 114 D7
Salmon →, Canada 104 C4
Salmon →, U.S.A. 114 D5
Salmon Arm, Canada 104 C5
Salmon Gums, Australia 93 F3
Salmon River Mts., U.S.A. 114 D6
Salo, Finland 9 F20
Salò, Italy 28 C7
Salobreña, Spain 35 J7
Salome, U.S.A. 117 M13
Salon, India 69 F9
Salon-de-Provence, France 21 E9
Salonica = Thessaloníki, Greece 40 F6
Salonta, Romania 42 D6
Salor →, Spain 35 F3
Salou, Spain 32 D6
Salou, C. de, Spain 32 D6
Saloum →, Senegal 82 C1
Salpausselkä, Finland 9 F22
Salsacate, Argentina 126 C2
Salses, France 20 F6
Salsk, Russia 49 G5
Salso →, Italy 30 E6
Salsomaggiore Terme, Italy 28 D6
Salt, Spain 32 D7
Salt →, Canada 104 B6
Salt →, U.S.A. 115 K7
Salt Lake City, U.S.A. 114 F8
Salt Range, Pakistan 68 C5
Salta, Argentina 126 A2
Salta □, Argentina 126 A2
Saltara, Italy 29 E9
Saltash, U.K. 13 G3
Saltburn by the Sea, U.K. 12 C7
Saltcoats, U.K. 14 F4
Saltee Is., Ireland 15 D5
Saltfjellet, Norway 8 C16
Saltfjorden, Norway 8 C16
Saltholm, Denmark 11 J6
Saltillo, Mexico 118 B4
Salto, Argentina 126 C3
Salto, Uruguay 126 C4
Salto del Guaíra, Paraguay 127 A5
Salton City, U.S.A. 117 M11
Salton Sea, U.S.A. 117 M11
Saltpond, Ghana 83 D4
Saltsburg, U.S.A. 110 F5
Saltsjöbaden, Sweden 10 E12
Saluda →, U.S.A. 109 J5
Salûm, Egypt 80 A2
Salûm, Khâlig el, Egypt 80 A2
Salur, India 67 K13
Saluzzo, Italy 28 D4
Salvador, Brazil 125 F11
Salvador, Canada 105 C7
Salvador, L., U.S.A. 113 L9
Salvaterra de Magos, Portugal 35 F2
Sálvora, I. de, Spain 34 C2
Salween →, Burma 67 L20
Salyan, Azerbaijan 50 F5
Salza →, Austria 26 D7
Salzach →, Austria 26 C5
Salzburg, Austria 26 D6
Salzburg □, Austria 26 D6
Salzgitter, Germany 24 C6
Salzkotten, Germany 24 D4
Salzwedel, Germany 24 C7
Sam, India 68 F4
Sam Neua, Laos 58 G5
Sam Ngao, Thailand 64 D2
Sam Rayburn Reservoir, U.S.A. 113 K7
Sam Son, Vietnam 64 C5
Sam Teu, Laos 64 C5
Sama de Langreo = Langreo, Spain 34 B5
Samagaltay, Russia 51 D10
Samales Group, Phil. 61 J4
Samâlût, Egypt 80 B3
Samana, India 68 D7
Samana Cay, Bahamas 121 B5
Samandağı, Turkey 72 D6
Samandıra, Turkey 41 F13
Samanga, Tanzania 87 D4
Samangwa, Dem. Rep. of the Congo 86 C1
Samani, Japan 54 C11
Samanli Dağları, Turkey 41 F13
Samar, Phil. 61 F6
Samara, Russia 48 D10
Samara →, Russia 48 D10
Samara →, Ukraine 47 H8
Samaria = Shōmrōn, West Bank 75 C4
Samariá, Greece 36 D5
Samarinda, Indonesia 62 E5
Samarkand = Samarqand, Uzbekistan 50 F7
Samarqand, Uzbekistan 50 F7
Sāmarrā, Iraq 70 C4
Samastipur, India 69 G11
Şamaxi, Azerbaijan 49 K9
Samba, Dem. Rep. of the Congo 86 C2
Samba, India 69 C6
Sambalpur, India 67 J14
Sambar, Tanjung, Indonesia 62 E4
Sambas, Indonesia 62 D3
Sambava, Madag. 89 A9
Sambawizi, Zimbabwe 87 F2
Sambhal, India 69 E8
Sambhar, India 68 F6
Sambhar L., India 68 F6
Sambiase, Italy 31 D9
Sambir, Ukraine 47 H2
Sambor, Cambodia 64 F6
Samborombón, B., Argentina 126 D4
Sambuca di Sicília, Italy 30 E6
Samch'ŏk, S. Korea 57 F15
Samch'onp'o, S. Korea 57 G15
Same, Tanzania 86 C4
Samer, France 19 B8
Samfya, Zambia 87 E2
Sámi, Greece 38 C2
Şämkir, Azerbaijan 49 K8
Şamlı, Turkey 39 B9
Samnah, Si. Arabia 70 E3
Samo Alto, Chile 126 C1
Samoa ■, Pac. Oc. 91 B13
Samobor, Croatia 29 C12
Samoëns, France 19 F13
Samokov, Bulgaria 40 D7
Šamorín, Slovak Rep. 27 C10
Samorogouan, Burkina Faso 82 C4
Sámos, Greece 39 D8
Samoš, Serbia, Yug. 42 E5
Samos, Spain 34 C3
Sámos □, Greece 39 D8
Samothráki = Mathráki, Greece 36 A3
Samothráki, Évros, Greece 41 F9
Samothráki, Évros, Greece 41 F9
Samoylovka, Russia 48 E6
Sampa, Ghana 82 D4
Sampacho, Argentina 126 C3
Sampang, Indonesia 63 G15
Samper de Calanda, Spain 32 D4
Sampéyre, Italy 28 D4
Sampit, Indonesia 62 E4
Sampit, Teluk, Indonesia 62 E4
Samrong, Cambodia 64 E4
Samrong, Thailand 64 E3
Samsø, Denmark 11 J4
Samsø Bælt, Denmark 11 J4
Samsun, Turkey 72 B7
Samtredia, Georgia 49 J6
Samui, Ko, Thailand 65 H3
Samur →, Russia 49 K9
Samurskiy Khrebet, Russia 49 K8
Samusole, Dem. Rep. of the Congo 87 E1
Samut Prakan, Thailand 64 F3
Samut Songkhram →, Thailand 62 B1
Samwari, Pakistan 68 E2
San, Mali 82 C4
San →, Cambodia 64 F5
San →, Poland 45 H8
San Adrián, Spain 32 C3
San Adrián, C. de, Spain 34 B2
San Agustin, C., Phil. 61 H7
San Agustín de Valle Fértil, Argentina 126 C2
San Ambrosio, Pac. Oc. 122 F3
San Andreas, U.S.A. 116 G6
San Andres, Phil. 61 E6
San Andrés, I. de, Caribbean 120 D3
San Andrês del Rabanedo, Spain 34 C5
San Andres Mts., U.S.A. 115 K10
San Andrés Tuxtla, Mexico 119 D5
San Angelo, U.S.A. 113 K4
San Anselmo, U.S.A. 116 H4
San Antonio, Belize 119 D7
San Antonio, Chile 126 C1
San Antonio, Phil. 61 D4
San Antonio, N. Mex., U.S.A. 115 K10
San Antonio, Tex., U.S.A. 113 L5
San Antonio →, U.S.A. 113 L6
San Antonio, C., Argentina 126 D4
San Antonio, C., Cuba 120 B3
San Antonio, C. de, Spain 33 G5
San Antonio, Mt., U.S.A. 117 L9
San Antonio de los Baños, Cuba 120 B3
San Antonio de los Cobres, Argentina 126 A2
San Antonio Oeste, Argentina 128 E4
San Arcángelo, Italy 31 B9
San Ardo, U.S.A. 116 J6
San Augustín, Canary Is. 37 G4
San Augustine, U.S.A. 113 K7
San Bartolomé, Canary Is. 37 F6
San Bartolomé de Tirajana, Canary Is. 37 G4
San Bartolomeo in Galdo, Italy 31 A8
San Benedetto del Tronto, Italy 29 F10
San Benedetto Po, Italy 28 C7
San Benedicto, I., Mexico 118 D2
San Benito, U.S.A. 113 M6
San Benito →, U.S.A. 116 J5
San Benito Mt., U.S.A. 116 J6
San Bernardino, U.S.A. 117 L9
San Bernardino Mts., U.S.A. 117 L10
San Bernardino Str., Phil. 61 E6
San Bernardo, Chile 126 C1
San Bernardo, I. de, Colombia 124 B3
San Blas, Mexico 118 B3
San Blas, Arch. de, Panama 120 E4
San Blas, C., U.S.A. 109 L3
San Bonifacio, Italy 29 C8
San Borja, Bolivia 124 F5
San Buenaventura, Mexico 118 B4
San Carlos = Butuku-Luba, Eq. Guin. 83 E6
San Carlos = Sant Carles, Spain 37 B8
San Carlos, Argentina 126 C2
San Carlos, Chile 126 D1
San Carlos, Baja Calif. S., Mexico 118 C2
San Carlos, Coahuila, Mexico 118 B4
San Carlos, Nic. 120 D3
San Carlos, Neg. Occ., Phil. 61 F5
San Carlos, Pangasinan, Phil. 61 D4
San Carlos, Uruguay 127 C5
San Carlos, U.S.A. 115 K8
San Carlos, Venezuela 124 B5
San Carlos de Bariloche, Argentina 128 E2
San Carlos de Bolívar, Argentina 128 D4
San Carlos de la Rápita = Sant Carles de la Ràpita, Spain 32 E5
San Carlos del Zulia, Venezuela 124 B4
San Carlos L., U.S.A. 115 K8
San Cataldo, Italy 30 E6
San Celoni = Sant Celoni, Spain 32 D7
San Clemente, Chile 126 D1
San Clemente, Spain 33 F2
San Clemente, U.S.A. 117 M9
San Clemente I., U.S.A. 117 N8
San Cristóbal = Es Migjorn Gran, Spain 37 B11
San Cristóbal, Argentina 126 C3
San Cristóbal, Dom. Rep. 121 C5
San Cristóbal, Venezuela 124 B4
San Cristóbal de la Casas, Mexico 119 D6
San Damiano d'Asti, Italy 28 D5
San Daniele del Friuli, Italy 29 B10
San Diego, Calif., U.S.A. 117 N9
San Diego, Tex., U.S.A. 113 M5
San Diego, C., Argentina 128 G3
San Diego de la Unión, Mexico 118 C4
San Dimitri, Ras, Malta 36 C1
San Donà di Piave, Italy 29 C9
San Estanislao, Paraguay 126 A4
San Esteban de Gormaz, Spain 32 D1
San Felice Circeo, Italy 30 A6
San Felice sul Panaro, Italy 29 D8
San Felipe, Chile 126 C1
San Felipe, Mexico 118 A2
San Felipe, Venezuela 124 A5
San Felipe →, U.S.A. 117 M11
San Felix, Chile 126 B1
San Félix, Pac. Oc. 122 F2
San Fernando = Sant Ferran, Spain 37 C7
San Fernando, Chile 126 C1
San Fernando, Baja Calif., Mexico 118 B1
San Fernando, Tamaulipas, Mexico 119 C5
San Fernando, La Union, Phil. 61 C4
San Fernando, Pampanga, Phil. 61 D4
San Fernando, Spain 35 J4
San Fernando, Trin. & Tob. 121 D7
San Fernando, U.S.A. 117 L8
San Fernando de Apure, Venezuela 124 B5
San Fernando de Atabapo, Venezuela 124 C5
San Fernando di Púglia, Italy 31 A9
San Francisco, Argentina 126 C3
San Francisco, U.S.A. 116 H4
San Francisco →, U.S.A. 115 K9
San Francisco, Paso de, S. Amer. 126 B2
San Francisco de Macorís, Dom. Rep. 121 C5
San Francisco del Monte de Oro, Argentina 126 C2
San Francisco del Oro, Mexico 118 B3
San Francisco Javier = Sant Francesc de Formentera, Spain 37 C7
San Francisco Solano, Pta., Colombia 122 C3
San Fratello, Italy 31 D7
San Gabriel, Chile 126 C1
San Gabriel Mts., U.S.A. 117 L9
San Gavino Monreale, Italy 30 C1
San Gimignano, Italy 28 E8
San Giórgio di Nogaro, Italy 29 C10
San Giórgio Iónico, Italy 31 B10
San Giovanni Bianco, Italy 28 C6
San Giovanni in Fiore, Italy 31 C9
San Giovanni in Persiceto, Italy 29 D8
San Giovanni Rotondo, Italy 29 G12
San Giovanni Valdarno, Italy 29 E8
San Giuliano Terme, Italy 28 E7
San Gorgonio Mt., U.S.A. 117 L10
San Gottardo, P. del, Switz. 25 J4
San Gregorio, Uruguay 127 C4
San Gregorio, U.S.A. 116 H4
San Guiseppe Jato, Italy 30 E6
San Ignacio, Belize 119 D7
San Ignacio, Bolivia 124 G6
San Ignacio, Mexico 118 B2
San Ignacio, Paraguay 120 C2
San Ignacio, L., Mexico 118 B2
San Ildefonso, C., Phil. 61 C5
San Isidro, Argentina 126 C4
San Isidro, Phil. 61 H7
San Jacinto, U.S.A. 117 M10
San Jaime = Sant Jaume, Spain 37 B11
San Javier, Misiones, Argentina 127 B4
San Javier, Santa Fe, Argentina 126 C4
San Javier, Bolivia 124 G6
San Javier, Chile 126 D1
San Javier, Spain 33 H4
San Jeronimo Taviche, Mexico 119 D5
San Joaquin, U.S.A. 116 J6
San Joaquin →, U.S.A. 116 G5
San Joaquin Valley, U.S.A. 116 J6
San Jon, U.S.A. 113 H3
San Jordi = Sant Jordi, Spain 37 B9
San Jorge, Argentina 126 C3
San Jorge, Spain 37 C7
San Jorge, B. de, Mexico 118 A2
San Jorge, G., Argentina 128 F3
San Jorge, G. of, Argentina 122 H4
San José = San Josep, Spain 37 C7
San José, Costa Rica 120 E3
San José, Guatemala 120 D1
San José, Mexico 118 C2
San Jose, Mind. Occ., Phil. 61 E4
San Jose, Nueva Ecija, Phil. 61 D4
San Jose, U.S.A. 116 H5
San Jose →, U.S.A. 115 J10
San Jose de Buenavista, Phil. 63 B6
San José de Chiquitos, Bolivia 124 G6
San José de Feliciano, Argentina 126 C4
San José de Jáchal, Argentina 126 C2
San José de Mayo, Uruguay 126 C4
San José del Cabo, Mexico 118 C3
San José del Guaviare, Colombia 124 C4
San Josep, Spain 37 C7
San Juan, Argentina 126 C2
San Juan, Mexico 118 C4
San Juan, Phil. 61 F6
San Juan, Puerto Rico 121 C6
San Juan □, Argentina 126 C2
San Juan →, Argentina 126 C2
San Juan →, Nic. 120 D3
San Juan →, U.S.A. 115 H8
San Juan Bautista = Sant Joan Baptista, Spain 37 B8
San Juan Bautista, Paraguay 126 B4
San Juan Bautista, U.S.A. 116 J5
San Juan Bautista Valle Nacional, Mexico 119 D5
San Juan Capistrano, U.S.A. 117 M9
San Juan Cr. →, U.S.A. 116 J5
San Juan de Alicante, Spain 33 G4
San Juan de Guadalupe, Mexico 118 C4
San Juan de la Costa, Mexico 118 C2
San Juan de los Morros, Venezuela 124 B5
San Juan del Norte, Nic. 120 D3
San Juan del Norte, B. de, Nic. 120 D3
San Juan del Río, Mexico 119 C5
San Juan del Sur, Nic. 120 D2
San Juan I., U.S.A. 116 B3
San Juan Mts., U.S.A. 115 H10
San Just, Sierra de, Spain 32 E4
San Justo, Argentina 126 C3
San Kamphaeng, Thailand 64 C2
San Lázaro, C., Mexico 118 C2
San Lázaro, Sa., Mexico 118 C3
San Leandro, U.S.A. 116 H4
San Leonardo de Yagüe, Spain 32 D1
San Lorenzo = Sant Llorenç des Cardassar, Spain 37 B10
San Lorenzo, Argentina 126 C3
San Lorenzo, Ecuador 124 C3
San Lorenzo, Paraguay 126 B4
San Lorenzo →, Mexico 118 C3
San Lorenzo, I., Mexico 118 B2
San Lorenzo, Mte., Argentina 128 F2
San Lorenzo de la Parrilla, Spain 32 F2
San Lorenzo de Morunys = Sant Llorenç de Morunys, Spain 32 C6
San Lucas, Bolivia 124 H5
San Lucas, Baja Calif. S., Mexico 118 C3
San Lucas, Baja Calif. S., Mexico 118 B2
San Lucas, U.S.A. 116 J5
San Lucas, C., Mexico 118 C3
San Lúcido, Italy 31 C9
San Luis, Argentina 126 C2
San Luis, Cuba 120 B3
San Luis, Guatemala 120 C2
San Luis, Ariz., U.S.A. 115 K6
San Luis, Colo., U.S.A. 115 H11
San Luis □, Argentina 126 C2
San Luis, I., Mexico 118 B2
San Luis, Sierra de, Argentina 126 C2
San Luis de la Paz, Mexico 118 C4
San Luis Obispo, U.S.A. 117 K6
San Luis Potosí, Mexico 118 C4
San Luis Potosí □, Mexico 118 C4
San Luis Reservoir, U.S.A. 116 H5
San Luis Río Colorado, Mexico 118 A2
San Manuel, U.S.A. 115 K8
San Marco, C., Italy 30 C1
San Marco Argentano, Italy 31 C9
San Marco in Lámis, Italy 29 G12
San Marcos, Guatemala 120 D1
San Marcos, Mexico 118 B2
San Marcos, Calif., U.S.A. 117 M9
San Marcos, Tex., U.S.A. 113 L6
San Marino, San Marino 29 E9
San Marino ■, Europe 29 E9
San Martín, Argentina 126 C2
San Martin →, Bolivia 124 F6
San Martín, L., Argentina 128 F2
San Martín de la Vega, Spain 34 E7
San Martin de los Andes, Argentina 128 E2
San Martín de Valdeiglesias, Spain 34 E6
San Mateo = Sant Mateu, Baleares, Spain 37 B7
San Mateo = Sant Mateu, Valencia, Spain 32 E5
San Mateo, Phil. 61 C4
San Mateo, U.S.A. 116 H4
San Matías, Bolivia 124 G7
San Matías, G., Argentina 122 H4
San Miguel = Sant Miquel, Spain 37 B7
San Miguel, El Salv. 120 D2
San Miguel, Panama 120 E4
San Miguel, U.S.A. 116 K6
San Miguel →, Bolivia 124 F6
San Miguel de Tucumán, Argentina 126 B2
San Miguel del Monte, Argentina 126 D4
San Miguel I., U.S.A. 117 L6
San Miniato, Italy 28 E7
San Nicolás, Canary Is. 37 G4
San Nicolas, Phil. 61 B4
San Nicolás de los Arroyas, Argentina 126 C3
San Nicolas I., U.S.A. 117 M7
San Onofre, U.S.A. 117 M9
San Pablo, Bolivia 126 A2
San Pablo, Phil. 61 D4
San Pablo, U.S.A. 116 H4
San Páolo di Civitate, Italy 29 G12
San Pedro, Buenos Aires, Argentina 126 C4
San Pedro, Misiones, Argentina 127 B5
San Pedro, Chile 126 C1
San Pédro, Ivory C. 82 E3
San Pedro, Mexico 118 C2
San Pedro □, Paraguay 126 A4
San Pedro →, Chihuahua, Mexico 118 B3
San Pedro →, Nayarit, Mexico 118 C3
San Pedro →, U.S.A. 115 K8
San Pedro, Pta., Chile 126 B1
San Pedro, Sierra de, Spain 35 F4
San Pedro Channel, U.S.A. 117 M8
San Pedro de Atacama, Chile 126 A2
San Pedro de Jujuy, Argentina 126 A3
San Pedro de las Colonias, Mexico 118 B4
San Pedro de Macorís, Dom. Rep. 121 C6
San Pedro del Norte, Nic. 120 D3
San Pedro del Paraná, Paraguay 126 B4

San Pedro del Pinatar, *Spain* **33 H4**
San Pedro Mártir, Sierra, *Mexico* **118 A1**
San Pedro Mixtepec, *Mexico* **119 D5**
San Pedro Ocampo = Melchor Ocampo, *Mexico* **118 C4**
San Pedro Sula, *Honduras* **120 C2**
San Pietro, *Italy* **30 C1**
San Pietro Vernótico, *Italy* **31 B11**
San Quintín, *Mexico* **118 A1**
San Rafael, *Argentina* **126 C2**
San Rafael, *Calif., U.S.A.* **116 H4**
San Rafael, *N. Mex., U.S.A.* **115 J10**
San Rafael Mt., *U.S.A.* **117 L7**
San Rafael Mts., *U.S.A.* **117 L7**
San Ramón de la Nueva Orán, *Argentina* **126 A3**
San Remo, *Italy* **28 E4**
San Roque, *Argentina* **126 B4**
San Roque, *Spain* **35 J5**
San Rosendo, *Chile* **126 D1**
San Saba, *U.S.A.* **113 K5**
San Salvador, *El Salv.* **120 D2**
San Salvador, *Spain* **37 B10**
San Salvador de Jujuy, *Argentina* **126 A3**
San Salvador I., *Bahamas* **121 B5**
San Salvo, *Italy* **29 F11**
San Sebastián = Donostia-San Sebastián, *Spain* **32 B3**
San Sebastián, *Argentina* **128 G3**
San Sebastian de la Gomera, *Canary Is.* **37 F2**
San Serra = Son Serra, *Spain* **37 B10**
San Serverino Marche, *Italy* **29 E10**
San Severo, *Italy* **29 G12**
San Simeon, *U.S.A.* **116 K5**
San Simon, *U.S.A.* **115 K9**
San Stéfano di Cadore, *Italy* **29 B9**
San Stino di Livenza, *Italy* **29 C9**
San Telmo = Sant Telm, *Spain* **37 B9**
San Telmo, *Mexico* **118 A1**
San Tiburcio, *Mexico* **118 C4**
San Valentin, Mte., *Chile* **122 H3**
San Vicente de Alcántara, *Spain* **35 F3**
San Vicente de la Barquera, *Spain* **34 B6**
San Vincente del Raspeig, *Spain* **33 G4**
San Vincenzo, *Italy* **28 E7**
San Vito, *Costa Rica* **120 E3**
San Vito, *Italy* **30 C2**
San Vito, C., *Italy* **30 D5**
San Vito al Tagliamento, *Italy* **29 C9**
San Vito Chietino, *Italy* **29 F11**
San Vito dei Normanni, *Italy* **31 B10**
Sana', *Yemen* **74 D3**
Sana ✈, *Bos.-H.* **29 C13**
Sanaba, *Burkina Faso* **82 C4**
Şanāfīr, *Si. Arabia* **80 B3**
Sanaga ✈, *Cameroon* **83 E6**
Sanaloa, Presa, *Mexico* **118 C3**
Sanana, *Indonesia* **63 E7**
Sanand, *India* **68 H5**
Sanandaj, *Iran* **70 C5**
Sanandita, *Bolivia* **126 A3**
Sanary-sur-Mer, *France* **21 E9**
Sanawad, *India* **68 H7**
Sancellas = Sencelles, *Spain* **37 B9**
Sancergues, *France* **19 E9**
Sancerre, *France* **19 E9**
Sancerrois, Collines du, *France* **19 E9**
Sancha He ✈, *China* **58 D6**
Sanchahe, *China* **57 B14**
Sánchez, *Dom. Rep.* **121 C6**
Sanchor, *India* **68 G4**
Sancoins, *France* **19 F9**
Sancti Spíritus, *Cuba* **120 B4**
Sancy, Puy de, *France* **20 C6**
Sand ✈, *S. Africa* **89 C5**
Sand Hills, *U.S.A.* **112 D4**
Sand Springs, *U.S.A.* **113 G6**
Sanda, *Japan* **55 G7**
Sandakan, *Malaysia* **62 C5**
Sandan = Sambor, *Cambodia* **64 F6**
Sandanski, *Bulgaria* **40 E7**
Sandaré, *Mali* **82 C2**
Sandared, *Sweden* **11 G6**
Sandarne, *Sweden* **10 C11**
Sanday, *U.K.* **14 B6**
Sandefjord, *Norway* **9 G14**
Sanders, *U.S.A.* **115 J9**
Sanderson, *U.S.A.* **113 K3**
Sandersville, *U.S.A.* **109 J4**
Sandfire Roadhouse, *Australia* **92 C3**
Sandfly L., *Canada* **105 B7**
Sandfontein, *Namibia* **88 C2**
Sandhammaren, C., *Sweden* **11 J8**
Sandía, *Peru* **124 F5**
Sandıklı, *Turkey* **39 C12**
Sandila, *India* **69 F9**
Sandnes, *Norway* **9 G11**
Sandnessjøen, *Norway* **8 C15**
Sandoa, *Dem. Rep. of the Congo* **84 F4**
Sandomierz, *Poland* **45 H8**
Sândominic, *Romania* **43 D10**
Sandover ✈, *Australia* **94 C2**
Sandoway, *Burma* **67 K19**
Sandoy, *Færoe Is.* **8 F9**
Sandpoint, *U.S.A.* **114 B5**
Sandray, *U.K.* **14 E1**
Sandringham, *U.K.* **12 E8**
Sandstone, *Australia* **93 E2**
Sandu, *China* **58 E6**
Sandusky, *Mich., U.S.A.* **110 C2**
Sandusky, *Ohio, U.S.A.* **110 E2**
Sandvig, *Sweden* **11 J8**
Sandviken, *Sweden* **10 D10**
Sandwich, C., *Australia* **94 B4**
Sandwich B., *Canada* **103 B8**
Sandwich B., *Namibia* **88 C1**
Sandy, *Oreg., U.S.A.* **116 E4**
Sandy, *Pa., U.S.A.* **110 E6**
Sandy, *Utah, U.S.A.* **114 F8**
Sandy Bay, *Canada* **105 B8**
Sandy Bight, *Australia* **93 F3**
Sandy C., *Queens., Australia* **94 C5**
Sandy C., *Tas., Australia* **94 G3**
Sandy Cay, *Bahamas* **121 B4**
Sandy Cr. ✈, *U.S.A.* **114 F9**
Sandy L., *Canada* **102 B1**
Sandy Lake, *Canada* **102 B1**
Sandy Valley, *U.S.A.* **117 K11**
Sanford, *Fla., U.S.A.* **109 L5**
Sanford, *Maine, U.S.A.* **109 D10**
Sanford, *N.C., U.S.A.* **109 H6**
Sanford ✈, *Australia* **93 E2**
Sanford, Mt., *U.S.A.* **100 B5**
Sang-i-Masha, *Afghan.* **68 C2**
Sanga, *Mozam.* **87 E4**
Sanga ✈, *Congo* **84 E3**
Sangamner, *India* **66 K9**
Sangar, *Afghan.* **68 C1**
Sangar, *Russia* **51 C13**
Sangar Sarai, *Afghan.* **68 B4**
Sangaredi, *Guinea* **82 C2**
Sangarh ✈, *Pakistan* **68 D4**
Sangasso, *Mali* **82 C3**
Sangatte, *France* **19 B8**
Sangay, *Ecuador* **124 D3**
Sange, *Dem. Rep. of the Congo* **86 D2**
Sangeang, *Indonesia* **63 F5**
Sângeorz-Băi, *Romania* **43 C9**
Sanger, *U.S.A.* **116 J7**
Sângera, *Moldova* **43 D13**
Sangerhausen, *Germany* **24 D7**
Sanggan He ✈, *China* **56 E9**
Sanggau, *Indonesia* **62 D4**
Sanghar, *Pakistan* **68 F3**
Sangihe, Kepulauan, *Indonesia* **63 D7**
Sangihe, Pulau, *Indonesia* **63 D7**
Sangju, *S. Korea* **57 F15**
Sangkapura, *Indonesia* **62 F4**
Sangkhla, *Thailand* **64 E2**
Sangkulirang, *Indonesia* **62 D5**
Sangla, *Pakistan* **68 D5**
Sangli, *India* **66 L9**
Sangmélima, *Cameroon* **83 E7**
Sangod, *India* **68 G7**
Sangre de Cristo Mts., *U.S.A.* **113 G2**
Sangro ✈, *Italy* **29 F11**
Sangrur, *India* **68 D6**
Sangudo, *Canada* **104 C6**
Sangue ✈, *Brazil* **124 F7**
Sangüesa, *Spain* **32 C3**
Sanguinaires, Îs., *France* **21 G12**
Sangzhi, *China* **59 C8**
Sanhala, *Ivory C.* **82 C3**
Sanibel, *U.S.A.* **109 M4**
Sanirajak, *Canada* **101 B11**
Sanjawi, *Pakistan* **68 D3**
Sanje, *Uganda* **86 C3**
Sanjiang, *China* **58 E7**
Sanjo, *Japan* **54 F9**
Sankh ✈, *India* **69 H11**
Sankt Andrä, *Austria* **26 E7**
Sankt Augustin, *Germany* **24 E3**
Sankt Blasien, *Germany* **25 H4**
Sankt Gallen, *Switz.* **25 H5**
Sankt Gallen □, *Switz.* **25 H5**
Sankt Goar, *Germany* **25 E3**
Sankt Ingbert, *Germany* **25 F3**
Sankt Johann im Pongau, *Austria* **26 D6**
Sankt Johann in Tirol, *Austria* **26 D5**
Sankt-Peterburg, *Russia* **46 C6**
Sankt Pölten, *Austria* **26 C8**
Sankt Ulrich = Ortisei, *Italy* **29 B8**
Sankt Valentin, *Austria* **26 C7**
Sankt Veit an der Glan, *Austria* **26 E7**
Sankt Wendel, *Germany* **25 F3**
Sankt Wolfgang, *Austria* **26 D6**
Sankuru ✈, *Dem. Rep. of the Congo* **84 E4**
Sanliurfa, *Turkey* **70 B3**
Sanlúcar de Barrameda, *Spain* **35 J4**
Sanluri, *Italy* **30 C1**
Sânmartin, *Romania* **43 D10**
Sanmen, *China* **59 C13**
Sanmenxia, *China* **56 G6**
Sanming, *China* **59 D11**
Sannaspos, *S. Africa* **88 D4**
Sannicandro Gargánico, *Italy* **29 G12**
Sânnicolau Mare, *Romania* **42 D5**
Sannieshof, *S. Africa* **88 D4**
Sannīn, J., *Lebanon* **75 B4**
Sanniquellie, *Liberia* **82 D3**
Sannûr, W. ✈, *Egypt* **80 B3**
Sanok, *Poland* **45 J9**
Sanquhar, *U.K.* **14 F5**
Sansanding, *Mali* **82 C3**
Sansepolcro, *Italy* **29 E9**
Sansha, *China* **59 D13**
Sanshui, *China* **59 F9**
Sanski Most, *Bos.-H.* **29 D13**
Sansui, *China* **58 D7**
Sant Antoni Abat, *Spain* **37 C7**
Sant Boi de Llobregat, *Spain* **32 D7**
Sant Carles, *Spain* **37 B8**
Sant Carles de la Ràpita, *Spain* **32 E5**
Sant Celoni, *Spain* **32 D7**
Sant Feliu de Guíxols, *Spain* **32 D8**
Sant Feliu de Llobregat, *Spain* **32 D7**
Sant Ferran, *Spain* **37 C7**
Sant Francesc de Formentera, *Spain* **37 C7**
Sant Jaume, *Spain* **37 B11**
Sant Joan Baptista, *Spain* **37 B8**
Sant Jordi, *Spain* **37 B9**
Sant Jordi, G. de, *Spain* **32 E6**
Sant Llorenç de Morunys, *Spain* **32 C6**
Sant Llorenç des Cardassar, *Spain* **37 B10**
Sant Mateu, *Baleares, Spain* **37 B7**
Sant Mateu, *Valencia, Spain* **32 E5**
Sant Miquel, *Spain* **37 B7**
Sant Telm, *Spain* **37 B9**
Sant' Ágata Militello, *Italy* **31 D7**
Santa Agnés, *Spain* **37 B7**
Santa Ana, *Bolivia* **124 F5**
Santa Ana, *El Salv.* **120 D2**
Santa Ana, *Mexico* **118 A2**
Santa Ana, *U.S.A.* **117 M9**
Sant' Ángelo Lodigiano, *Italy* **28 C6**
Sant' Antíoco, *Italy* **30 C1**
Santa Barbara, *Chile* **126 D1**
Santa Barbara, *Honduras* **120 D2**
Santa Bárbara, *Mexico* **118 B3**
Santa Bárbara, *Spain* **32 E5**
Santa Barbara, *U.S.A.* **117 L7**
Santa Bárbara, Mt., *Spain* **33 H2**
Santa Barbara Channel, *U.S.A.* **117 L7**
Santa Barbara I., *U.S.A.* **117 M7**
Santa Catalina, Gulf of, *U.S.A.* **117 N9**
Santa Catalina, I., *Mexico* **118 B2**
Santa Catalina I., *U.S.A.* **117 M8**
Santa Catarina □, *Brazil* **127 B6**
Santa Catarina, I. de, *Brazil* **127 B6**
Santa Caterina di Pittinuri, *Italy* **30 B1**
Santa Caterina Villarmosa, *Italy* **31 E7**
Santa Cecília, *Brazil* **127 B5**
Santa Clara, *Cuba* **120 B4**
Santa Clara, *Calif., U.S.A.* **116 H5**
Santa Clara, *Utah, U.S.A.* **115 H7**
Santa Clara, El Golfo de, *Mexico* **118 A2**
Santa Clara de Olimar, *Uruguay* **127 C5**
Santa Clarita, *U.S.A.* **117 L8**
Santa Clotilde, *Peru* **124 D4**
Santa Coloma de Farners, *Spain* **32 D7**
Santa Coloma de Gramenet, *Spain* **32 D7**
Santa Comba, *Spain* **34 B2**
Santa Croce Camerina, *Italy* **31 F7**
Santa Croce di Magliano, *Italy* **29 G11**
Santa Cruz, *Argentina* **128 G3**
Santa Cruz, *Bolivia* **124 G6**
Santa Cruz, *Chile* **126 C1**
Santa Cruz, *Costa Rica* **120 D2**
Santa Cruz, *Madeira* **37 D3**
Santa Cruz, *Phil.* **61 D4**
Santa Cruz, *U.S.A.* **116 J4**
Santa Cruz ✈, *Argentina* **128 G3**
Santa Cruz de la Palma, *Canary Is.* **37 F2**
Santa Cruz de Mudela, *Spain* **35 G7**
Santa Cruz de Tenerife, *Canary Is.* **37 F3**
Santa Cruz del Norte, *Cuba* **120 B3**
Santa Cruz del Retamar, *Spain* **34 E6**
Santa Cruz del Sur, *Cuba* **120 B4**
Santa Cruz do Rio Pardo, *Brazil* **127 A6**
Santa Cruz do Sul, *Brazil* **127 B5**
Santa Cruz I., *U.S.A.* **117 M7**
Santa Cruz Is., *Solomon Is.* **96 J8**
Santa Domingo, Cay, *Bahamas* **120 B4**
Sant' Egídio alla Vibrata, *Italy* **29 F10**
Santa Elena, *Argentina* **126 C4**
Santa Elena, C., *Costa Rica* **120 D2**
Sant' Eufémia, G. di, *Italy* **31 D9**
Santa Eulàlia des Riu, *Spain* **37 C8**
Santa Fe, *Argentina* **126 C3**
Santa Fe, *Spain* **35 H7**
Santa Fe, *U.S.A.* **115 J11**
Santa Fé □, *Argentina* **126 C3**
Santa Fé do Sul, *Brazil* **125 H8**
Santa Filomena, *Brazil* **125 E9**
Santa Fiora, *Italy* **29 F8**
Santa Gertrudis, *Spain* **37 C7**
Santa Giustina, *Italy* **29 B9**
Santa Inês, *Brazil* **125 F11**
Santa Inés, *Spain* **35 G5**
Santa Inés, I., *Chile* **122 J3**
Santa Isabel = Rey Malabo, *Eq. Guin.* **83 E6**
Santa Isabel, *Argentina* **126 D2**
Santa Isabel, Pico, *Eq. Guin.* **83 E6**
Santa Isabel do Morro, *Brazil* **125 F8**
Santa Lucía, *Corrientes, Argentina* **126 B4**
Santa Lucía, *San Juan, Argentina* **126 C2**
Santa Lucía, *Spain* **33 H4**
Santa Lucía, *Uruguay* **126 C4**
Santa Lucia Range, *U.S.A.* **116 K5**
Santa Magdalena, I., *Mexico* **118 C2**
Santa Margarita, *Argentina* **126 D3**
Santa Margarita, *Spain* **37 B10**
Santa Margarita, *U.S.A.* **116 K6**
Santa Margarita ✈, *U.S.A.* **117 M9**
Santa Margarita, I., *Mexico* **118 C2**
Santa Margherita, *Italy* **30 D1**
Santa Margherita Ligure, *Italy* **28 D6**
Santa María, *Argentina* **126 B2**
Santa Maria, *Brazil* **127 B5**
Santa Maria, *Phil.* **61 C4**
Santa Maria, *U.S.A.* **117 L6**
Santa María ✈, *Mexico* **118 A3**
Santa María, B. de, *Mexico* **118 B3**
Santa Maria, C. de, *Portugal* **35 J3**
Santa Maria Cápua Vétere, *Italy* **31 A7**
Santa Maria da Feira, *Portugal* **34 E2**
Santa Maria da Vitória, *Brazil* **125 F10**
Santa Maria del Camí, *Spain* **37 B9**
Santa Maria di Léuca, C., *Italy* **31 C11**
Santa María la Real de Nieva, *Spain* **34 D6**
Santa Marinella, *Italy* **29 F8**
Santa Marta, *Colombia* **124 A4**
Santa Marta, Sierra Nevada de, *Colombia* **122 B3**
Santa Marta de Tormes, *Spain* **34 E5**
Santa Marta Grande, C., *Brazil* **127 B6**
Santa Marta Ortigueira, Ría de, *Spain* **34 B3**
Santa Maura = Levkás, *Greece* **38 C2**
Santa Monica, *U.S.A.* **117 M8**
Santa Olalla, *Huelva, Spain* **35 H4**
Santa Olalla, *Toledo, Spain* **34 E6**
Santa Paula, *U.S.A.* **117 L7**
Santa Pola, *Spain* **33 G4**
Santa Ponsa, *Spain* **37 B9**
Santa Rita, *U.S.A.* **115 K10**
Santa Rosa, *La Pampa, Argentina* **126 D3**
Santa Rosa, *San Luis, Argentina* **126 C2**
Santa Rosa, *Brazil* **127 B5**
Santa Rosa, *Calif., U.S.A.* **116 G4**
Santa Rosa, *N. Mex., U.S.A.* **113 H2**
Santa Rosa de Copán, *Honduras* **120 D2**
Santa Rosa de Río Primero, *Argentina* **126 C3**
Santa Rosa del Sara, *Bolivia* **124 G6**
Santa Rosa I., *Calif., U.S.A.* **117 M6**
Santa Rosa I., *Fla., U.S.A.* **109 K2**
Santa Rosa Range, *U.S.A.* **114 F5**
Santa Rosalía, *Mexico* **118 B2**
Santa Sylvina, *Argentina* **126 B3**
Santa Tecla = Nueva San Salvador, *El Salv.* **120 D2**
Santa Teresa, *Argentina* **126 C3**
Santa Teresa, *Australia* **94 C1**
Santa Teresa, *Mexico* **119 B5**
Santa Teresa di Riva, *Italy* **31 E8**
Santa Teresa Gallura, *Italy* **30 A2**
Santa Uxía, *Spain* **34 C2**
Santa Vitória do Palmar, *Brazil* **127 C5**
Santa Ynez ✈, *U.S.A.* **117 L6**
Santa Ynez Mts., *U.S.A.* **117 L6**
Santa Ysabel, *U.S.A.* **117 M10**
Santadi, *Italy* **30 C1**
Santaella, *Spain* **35 H6**
Santai, *China* **58 B5**
Santana, *Madeira* **37 D3**
Sântana, *Romania* **42 D6**
Santana, Coxilha de, *Brazil* **127 C4**
Santana do Livramento, *Brazil* **127 C4**
Santander, *Spain* **34 B7**
Santander Jiménez, *Mexico* **119 C5**
Santanyí, *Spain* **37 B10**
Santaquin, *U.S.A.* **114 G8**
Santarcángelo di Romagna, *Italy* **29 D9**
Santarém, *Brazil* **125 D8**
Santarém, *Portugal* **35 F2**
Santarém □, *Portugal* **35 F2**
Santaren Channel, *W. Indies* **120 B4**
Santee, *U.S.A.* **117 N10**
Santee ✈, *U.S.A.* **109 J6**
Santéramo in Colle, *Italy* **31 B9**
Santerno ✈, *Italy* **29 D8**
Santhià, *Italy* **28 C5**
Santiago, *Brazil* **127 B5**
Santiago, *Chile* **126 C1**
Santiago, *Panama* **120 E3**
Santiago, *Phil.* **61 C4**
Santiago □, *Chile* **126 C1**
Santiago ✈, *Mexico* **98 G9**
Santiago ✈, *Peru* **124 D3**
Santiago, Punta de, *Eq. Guin.* **83 E6**
Santiago de Compostela, *Spain* **34 C2**
Santiago de Cuba, *Cuba* **120 C4**
Santiago de los Cabelleros, *Dom. Rep.* **121 C5**
Santiago del Estero, *Argentina* **126 B3**
Santiago del Estero □, *Argentina* **126 B3**
Santiago del Teide, *Canary Is.* **37 F3**
Santiago do Cacém, *Portugal* **35 G2**
Santiago Ixcuintla, *Mexico* **118 C3**
Santiago Papasquiaro, *Mexico* **118 C3**
Santiaguillo, L. de, *Mexico* **118 C4**
Santiguila, *Mali* **82 C3**
Santillana, *Spain* **34 B6**
Santisteban del Puerto, *Spain* **35 G7**
Santo Amaro, *Brazil* **125 F11**
Santo Anastácio, *Brazil* **127 A5**
Santo André, *Brazil* **127 A6**
Santo Ângelo, *Brazil* **127 B5**
Santo Antônio do Içá, *Brazil* **124 D5**
Santo Antônio do Leverger, *Brazil* **125 G7**
Santo Domingo, *Dom. Rep.* **121 C6**
Santo Domingo, *Baja Calif., Mexico* **118 A1**
Santo Domingo, *Baja Calif. S., Mexico* **118 B2**
Santo Domingo, *Nic.* **120 D3**
Santo Domingo de la Calzada, *Spain* **32 C2**
Santo Domingo de los Colorados, *Ecuador* **124 D3**
Santo Domingo Pueblo, *U.S.A.* **115 J10**
Santo Stéfano di Camastro, *Italy* **31 D7**
Santo Tirso, *Portugal* **34 D2**
Santo Tomás, *Mexico* **118 A1**
Santo Tomás, *Peru* **124 F4**
Santo Tomé, *Argentina* **127 B4**
Santo Tomé de Guayana = Ciudad Guayana, *Venezuela* **124 B6**
Santomera, *Spain* **33 G3**
Santoña, *Spain* **34 B7**
Santoríni = Thíra, *Greece* **39 E7**
Santos, *Brazil* **127 A6**
Santos, Sierra de los, *Spain* **35 G5**
Santos Dumont, *Brazil* **127 A7**
Sanwer, *India* **68 H6**
Sanxenxo, *Spain* **34 C2**
Sanyuan, *China* **56 G5**
São Bartolomeu de Messines, *Portugal* **35 H2**
São Bernardo do Campo, *Brazil* **127 A6**
São Borja, *Brazil* **127 B4**
São Brás de Alportel, *Portugal* **35 H3**
São Carlos, *Brazil* **127 A6**
São Cristóvão, *Brazil* **125 F11**
São Domingos, *Brazil* **125 F9**
São Domingos, *Guinea-Biss.* **82 C1**
São Francisco, *Brazil* **125 G10**
São Francisco ✈, *Brazil* **122 E7**
São Francisco do Sul, *Brazil* **127 B6**
São Gabriel, *Brazil* **127 C5**
São Gonçalo, *Brazil* **127 A7**
Sao Hill, *Tanzania* **87 D4**
São João, *Guinea-Biss.* **82 C1**
São João da Boa Vista, *Brazil* **127 A6**
São João da Madeira, *Portugal* **34 E2**
São João da Pesqueira, *Portugal* **34 D3**
São João del Rei, *Brazil* **127 A7**
São João do Araguaia, *Brazil* **125 E9**
São João do Piauí, *Brazil* **125 E10**
São Joaquim, *Brazil* **127 B6**
São Jorge, Pta. de, *Madeira* **37 D3**
São José, *Brazil* **127 B5**
São José do Norte, *Brazil* **127 C5**
São José do Rio Prêto, *Brazil* **127 A6**
São José dos Campos, *Brazil* **127 A6**
São Leopoldo, *Brazil* **127 B5**
São Lourenço, *Brazil* **127 A6**
São Lourenço ✈, *Brazil* **125 G7**
São Lourenço, Pta. de, *Madeira* **37 D3**
São Lourenço do Sul, *Brazil* **127 C5**
São Luís, *Brazil* **125 D10**
São Luís Gonzaga, *Brazil* **127 B5**
São Marcos ✈, *Brazil* **125 G9**
São Marcos, B. de, *Brazil* **125 D10**
São Martinho da Cortiça, *Portugal* **34 E2**
São Mateus, *Brazil* **125 G11**
São Mateus do Sul, *Brazil* **127 B5**
São Miguel do Oeste, *Brazil* **127 B5**
São Paulo, *Brazil* **127 A6**
São Paulo □, *Brazil* **127 A6**
São Paulo, I., *Atl. Oc.* **2 D8**
São Paulo de Olivença, *Brazil* **124 D5**
São Pedro do Sul, *Portugal* **34 E2**
São Roque, *Madeira* **37 D3**
São Roque, C. de, *Brazil* **122 D7**
São Sebastião, I. de, *Brazil* **127 A6**
São Sebastião do Paraíso, *Brazil* **127 A6**
São Teotónio, *Portugal* **35 H2**
São Tomé, *Atl. Oc.* **76 F4**
São Tomé, C. de, *Brazil* **127 A7**
São Tomé & Principe ■, *Africa* **77 F4**
São Vicente, *Brazil* **127 A6**
São Vicente, *Madeira* **37 D2**
São Vicente, C. de, *Portugal* **35 H1**
Saona, I., *Dom. Rep.* **121 C6**
Saône ✈, *France* **19 G11**
Saône-et-Loire □, *France* **19 F11**
Saonek, *Indonesia* **63 E8**
Sápai, *Greece* **41 E9**
Sapanca, *Turkey* **72 B4**
Saparua, *Indonesia* **63 E7**
Sapele, *Nigeria* **83 D6**
Sapelo I., *U.S.A.* **109 K5**
Şaphane, *Turkey* **39 B11**
Sapiéntza, *Greece* **38 E3**
Sapone, *Burkina Faso* **83 C4**
Saposoa, *Peru* **124 E3**
Sapouy, *Burkina Faso* **83 C4**
Sapozhok, *Russia* **48 D5**
Sapphire, *Australia* **94 C4**
Sappho, *U.S.A.* **116 B2**
Sapporo, *Japan* **54 C10**
Sapri, *Italy* **31 B8**
Sapulpa, *U.S.A.* **113 H6**
Saqqez, *Iran* **70 B5**
Sar Dasht, *Iran* **71 C6**
Sar Gachīneh = Yāsūj, *Iran* **71 D6**
Sar Planina, *Macedonia* **40 E4**
Sara, *Burkina Faso* **82 C4**
Sara, *Phil.* **61 F5**
Sara Buri = Saraburi, *Thailand* **64 E3**
Sarāb, *Iran* **70 B5**
Sarabadi, *Iraq* **70 C5**
Saraburi, *Thailand* **64 E3**
Saradiya, *India* **68 J4**
Saraféré, *Mali* **82 B4**
Saragossa = Zaragoza, *Spain* **32 D4**
Saraguro, *Ecuador* **124 D3**
Sarai Naurang, *Pakistan* **68 C4**
Saraikela, *India* **69 H11**
Saraiu, *Romania* **43 F13**
Sarajevo, *Bos.-H.* **42 G3**
Sarakhs, *Turkmenistan* **71 B9**
Saran, Gunung, *Indonesia* **62 E4**
Saranac L., *U.S.A.* **111 B10**
Saranac Lake, *U.S.A.* **111 B10**
Saranda, *Tanzania* **86 D3**
Sarandë, *Albania* **40 G3**
Sarandí del Yi, *Uruguay* **127 C4**
Sarandí Grande, *Uruguay* **126 C4**
Sarangani B., *Phil.* **61 J6**
Sarangani Is., *Phil.* **61 J6**
Sarangarh, *India* **67 J13**

Saransk, *Russia* 48 C7
Sarapul, *Russia* 50 D6
Sarasota, *U.S.A.* 109 M4
Saratoga, *Calif., U.S.A.* 116 H4
Saratoga, *Wyo., U.S.A.* 114 F10
Saratoga Springs, *U.S.A.* 111 C11
Saratok, *Malaysia* 62 D4
Saratov, *Russia* 48 E7
Saravane, *Laos* 64 E6
Sarawak □, *Malaysia* 62 D4
Saray, *Tekirdağ, Turkey* 41 E11
Saray, *Van, Turkey* 73 C11
Saraya, *Guinea* 82 C2
Saraya, *Senegal* 82 C2
Saraycık, *Turkey* 39 B11
Sarayköy, *Turkey* 39 D10
Saraylar, *Turkey* 41 F11
Sarayönü, *Turkey* 72 C5
Sarbāz, *Iran* 71 E9
Sarbīsheh, *Iran* 71 C8
Sárbogárd, *Hungary* 42 D3
Sarca →, *Italy* 28 C7
Sarcelles, *France* 19 D9
Sarda →, *India* 67 F12
Sardarshahr, *India* 68 E6
Sardegna □, *Italy* 30 B1
Sardhana, *India* 68 E7
Sardina, Pta., *Canary Is.* 37 F4
Sardinia = Sardegna □, *Italy* 30 B1
Sardis, *Turkey* 39 C10
Sārdūīyeh = Dar Mazār, *Iran* 71 D8
S'Arenal, *Spain* 37 B9
Sarentino, *Italy* 29 B8
Saréyamou, *Mali* 82 B4
Sargasso Sea, *Atl. Oc.* 97 D20
Sargodha, *Pakistan* 68 C5
Sarh, *Chad* 79 G9
Sarhala, *Ivory C.* 82 D3
Sārī, *Iran* 71 B7
Sari d'Orcino, *France* 21 F12
Sária, *Greece* 39 F9
Saria, *India* 69 J10
Sariab, *Pakistan* 68 D2
Sarıbeyler, *Turkey* 39 B9
Sarıgöl, *Turkey* 72 C3
Sarıkamiş, *Turkey* 73 B10
Sarıkaya, *Turkey* 72 C6
Sarikei, *Malaysia* 62 D4
Sarıköy, *Turkey* 41 F11
Sarila, *India* 69 G8
Sarina, *Australia* 94 C4
Sariñena, *Spain* 32 D4
Sarita, *U.S.A.* 113 M6
Sariwŏn, *N. Korea* 57 E13
Sariyar Barajı, *Turkey* 72 B4
Sariyer, *Turkey* 41 E13
Sarju →, *India* 69 F9
Sark, *U.K.* 13 H5
Sarkad, *Hungary* 42 D6
Sarkari Tala, *India* 68 F4
Şarkışla, *Turkey* 72 C7
Şarköy, *Turkey* 41 F11
Sarlat-la-Canéda, *France* 20 D5
Sărmăşag, *Romania* 42 C7
Sărmaşu, *Romania* 43 D9
Sarmi, *Indonesia* 63 E9
Sarmiento, *Argentina* 128 F3
Sarmizegetusa, *Romania* 42 E7
Särna, *Sweden* 10 C7
Sarnano, *Italy* 29 E10
Sarnen, *Switz.* 25 J4
Sarnia, *Canada* 102 D3
Sarno, *Italy* 31 B7
Sarnthein = Sarentino, *Italy* 29 B8
Särö, *Sweden* 11 G5
Sarolangun, *Indonesia* 62 E2
Saronikós Kólpos, *Greece* 38 D5
Saronno, *Italy* 28 C6
Saros Körfezi, *Turkey* 41 F10
Sárospatak, *Hungary* 42 B6
Sarpsborg, *Norway* 9 G14
Sarracín, *Spain* 34 C7
Sarralbe, *France* 19 D14
Sarre = Saar →, *Europe* 17 E6
Sarre, *Italy* 28 C4
Sarre-Union, *France* 19 D14
Sarrebourg, *France* 19 D14
Sarreguemines, *France* 19 C14
Sarria, *Spain* 34 C3
Sarrión, *Spain* 32 E4
Sarro, *Mali* 82 C3
Sarstedt, *Germany* 24 C5
Sartène, *France* 21 G12
Sarthe □, *France* 18 D7
Sarthe →, *France* 18 E6
Sartilly, *France* 18 D5
Saruhanlı, *Turkey* 39 C9
Sărulești, *Romania* 43 F11
Saruna →, *Pakistan* 68 F2
Sárvár, *Hungary* 42 C1
Sarvar, *India* 68 F6
Sarvestān, *Iran* 71 D7
Särvfjället, *Sweden* 10 B7
Sárvíz →, *Hungary* 42 D3
Sary-Tash, *Kyrgyzstan* 50 F8
Sarych, Mys, *Ukraine* 47 K7
Saryshagan, *Kazakstan* 50 E8
Sarzana, *Italy* 28 D6
Sarzeau, *France* 18 E4
Sasan Gir, *India* 68 J4
Sasaram, *India* 69 G11
Sasebo, *Japan* 55 H4
Saser, *India* 69 B7
Saskatchewan □, *Canada* 105 C7
Saskatchewan →, *Canada* 105 C8
Saskatoon, *Canada* 105 C7
Saskylakh, *Russia* 51 B12
Sasolburg, *S. Africa* 89 D4
Sasovo, *Russia* 48 C5
Sassandra, *Ivory C.* 82 E3
Sassandra →, *Ivory C.* 82 E3
Sássari, *Italy* 30 B1
Sassnitz, *Germany* 24 A9
Sasso Marconi, *Italy* 29 D8
Sassocorvaro, *Italy* 29 E9
Sassoferrato, *Italy* 29 E9
Sasstown, *Liberia* 82 E3
Sassuolo, *Italy* 28 D7
Sástago, *Spain* 32 D4
Sasumua Dam, *Kenya* 86 C4
Sasyk, Ozero, *Ukraine* 47 K5
Sata-Misaki, *Japan* 55 J5
Satadougou, *Mali* 82 C2
Satakunta, *Finland* 9 F20
Satama-Soukoura, *Ivory C.* 82 D4
Satara, *India* 66 L8
Satara, *S. Africa* 89 C5
Satbarwa, *India* 69 H11
Såtenäs, *Sweden* 11 F6
Säter, *Sweden* 10 D9
Satevó, *Mexico* 118 B3
Satilla →, *U.S.A.* 109 K5
Satmala Hills, *India* 66 J9
Satna, *India* 69 G9
Šator, *Bos.-H.* 29 D13
Sátoraljaújhely, *Hungary* 42 B6
Satpura Ra., *India* 66 J10
Satrup, *Germany* 24 A5
Satsuna-Shotō, *Japan* 55 K5
Sattahip, *Thailand* 64 F3
Satu Mare, *Romania* 42 C7
Satu Mare □, *Romania* 42 C8
Satui, *Indonesia* 62 E5
Satun, *Thailand* 65 J3
Saturnina →, *Brazil* 124 F7
Sauce, *Argentina* 126 C4
Sauceda, *Mexico* 118 B4
Saucillo, *Mexico* 118 B3
Sauda, *Norway* 9 G12
Sauðarkrókur, *Iceland* 8 D4
Saudi Arabia ■, *Asia* 70 B3
Saugeen →, *Canada* 110 B3
Saugerties, *U.S.A.* 111 D11
Saugues, *France* 20 D7
Saugus, *U.S.A.* 117 L8
Saujon, *France* 20 C3
Sauk Centre, *U.S.A.* 112 C7
Sauk Rapids, *U.S.A.* 112 C7
Saulgau, *Germany* 25 G5
Saulieu, *France* 19 E11
Sault, *France* 21 D9
Sault Ste. Marie, *Canada* 102 C3
Sault Ste. Marie, *U.S.A.* 101 D11
Saumlaki, *Indonesia* 63 F8
Saumur, *France* 18 E6
Saunders C., *N.Z.* 91 L3
Saunders I., *Antarctica* 5 B1
Saunders Point, *Australia* 93 E4
Sauri, *Nigeria* 83 C6
Saurimo, *Angola* 84 F4
Sausalito, *U.S.A.* 116 H4
Sauveterre-de-Béarn, *France* 20 E3
Sauzé-Vaussais, *France* 20 B4
Savá, *Honduras* 120 C2
Sava, *Italy* 31 B10
Sava →, *Serbia, Yug.* 42 F5
Savage, *U.S.A.* 112 B2
Savage I. = Niue, *Cook Is.* 97 J11
Savage River, *Australia* 94 G4
Savai'i, *Samoa* 91 A12
Savalou, *Benin* 83 D5
Savane, *Mozam.* 87 F4
Savanna, *U.S.A.* 112 D9
Savanna-la-Mar, *Jamaica* 120 C4
Savannah, *Ga., U.S.A.* 109 J5
Savannah, *Mo., U.S.A.* 112 F7
Savannah, *Tenn., U.S.A.* 109 H1
Savannah →, *U.S.A.* 109 J5
Savannakhet, *Laos* 64 D5
Savant L., *Canada* 102 B1
Savant Lake, *Canada* 102 B1
Săvârşin, *Romania* 42 D7
Savaştepe, *Turkey* 39 B9
Savé, *Benin* 83 D5
Save →, *France* 20 E5
Save →, *Mozam.* 89 C5
Sāveh, *Iran* 71 C6
Savelugu, *Ghana* 83 D4
Savenay, *France* 18 E5
Săveni, *Romania* 43 C11
Saverdun, *France* 20 E5
Saverne, *France* 19 D14
Savigliano, *Italy* 28 D4
Savigny-sur-Braye, *France* 18 E7
Sávio →, *Italy* 29 D9
Šavnik, *Montenegro, Yug.* 40 D3
Savo, *Finland* 8 E22
Savoie □, *France* 21 C10
Savona, *Italy* 28 D5
Savona, *U.S.A.* 110 D7
Savonlinna, *Finland* 46 B5
Savoy = Savoie □, *France* 21 C10
Şavşat, *Turkey* 73 B10
Sävsjö, *Sweden* 11 G8
Savur, *Turkey* 70 B4
Sawahlunto, *Indonesia* 62 E2
Sawai, *Indonesia* 63 E7
Sawai Madhopur, *India* 68 G7
Sawang Daen Din, *Thailand* 64 D4
Sawankhalok, *Thailand* 64 D2
Sawara, *Japan* 55 G10
Sawatch Range, *U.S.A.* 115 G10
Sawel Mt., *U.K.* 15 B4
Sawi, *Thailand* 65 G2
Sawla, *Ghana* 82 D4
Sawmills, *Zimbabwe* 87 F2
Sawtooth Range, *U.S.A.* 114 E6
Sawu, *Indonesia* 63 F6
Sawu Sea, *Indonesia* 63 F6
Saxby →, *Australia* 94 B3
Saxmundham, *U.K.* 13 E9
Saxony = Sachsen □, *Germany* 24 E9
Saxony, Lower = Niedersachsen □, *Germany* 24 C4
Saxton, *U.S.A.* 110 F6
Say, *Mali* 82 C4
Say, *Niger* 83 C5
Saya, *Nigeria* 83 D5
Sayabec, *Canada* 103 C6
Sayaboury, *Laos* 64 C3
Sayán, *Peru* 124 F3
Sayan, Vostochnyy, *Russia* 51 D10
Sayan, Zapadnyy, *Russia* 51 D10
Saydā, *Lebanon* 75 B4
Sayhandulaan = Oldziyt, *Mongolia* 56 B5
Sayḩūt, *Yemen* 74 D5
Saykhin, *Kazakstan* 49 F8
Saynshand, *Mongolia* 60 B6
Sayre, *Okla., U.S.A.* 113 H5
Sayre, *Pa., U.S.A.* 111 E8
Sayreville, *U.S.A.* 111 F10
Sayula, *Mexico* 118 D4
Sayward, *Canada* 104 C3
Sazanit, *Albania* 40 F3
Sázava →, *Czech Rep.* 26 B7
Sazin, *Pakistan* 69 B5
Sazlika →, *Bulgaria* 41 E9
Scaër, *France* 18 D3
Scafell Pike, *U.K.* 12 C4
Scalea, *Italy* 31 C8
Scalloway, *U.K.* 14 A7
Scalpay, *U.K.* 14 D3
Scandia, *Canada* 104 C6
Scandiano, *Italy* 28 D7
Scandicci, *Italy* 29 E8
Scandinavia, *Europe* 8 E16
Scansano, *Italy* 29 F8
Scapa Flow, *U.K.* 14 C5
Scappoose, *U.S.A.* 116 E4
Scarámia, Capo, *Italy* 31 F7
Scarba, *U.K.* 14 E3
Scarborough, *Trin. & Tob.* 121 D7
Scarborough, *U.K.* 12 C7
Scariff I., *Ireland* 15 E1
Scarp, *U.K.* 14 C1
Scebeli, Wabi →, *Somali Rep.* 74 G3
Šćedro, *Croatia* 29 E13
Schaal See, *Germany* 24 B6
Schaffhausen, *Switz.* 25 H4
Schagen, *Neths.* 17 B4
Schaghticoke, *U.S.A.* 111 D11
Schärding, *Austria* 26 C6
Scharhörn, *Germany* 24 B4
Scheessel, *Germany* 24 B5
Schefferville, *Canada* 103 B6
Scheibbs, *Austria* 26 C8
Schelde →, *Belgium* 17 C4
Schell Creek Ra., *U.S.A.* 114 G6
Schellsburg, *U.S.A.* 110 F6
Schenectady, *U.S.A.* 111 D11
Schenevus, *U.S.A.* 111 D10
Scherfede, *Germany* 24 D5
Schesslitz, *Germany* 25 F7
Schiedam, *Neths.* 17 C4
Schiermonnikoog, *Neths.* 17 A6
Schiltigheim, *France* 19 D14
Schio, *Italy* 29 C8
Schladming, *Austria* 26 D6
Schlanders = Silandro, *Italy* 28 B7
Schlei →, *Germany* 24 A5
Schleiden, *Germany* 24 E2
Schleiz, *Germany* 24 E7
Schleswig, *Germany* 24 A5
Schleswig-Holstein □, *Germany* 24 A5
Schlüchtern, *Germany* 25 E5
Schmalkalden, *Germany* 24 E6
Schmölln, *Germany* 24 E8
Schneeberg, *Austria* 26 D8
Schneeberg, *Germany* 24 E8
Schneverdingen, *Germany* 24 B5
Schoharie, *U.S.A.* 111 D10
Schoharie →, *U.S.A.* 111 D10
Scholls, *U.S.A.* 116 E4
Schönberg, *Mecklenburg-Vorpommern, Germany* 24 B6
Schönberg, *Schleswig-Holstein, Germany* 24 A6
Schönebeck, *Germany* 24 C7
Schongau, *Germany* 25 H6
Schöningen, *Germany* 24 C6
Schopfheim, *Germany* 25 H3
Schorndorf, *Germany* 25 G5
Schortens, *Germany* 24 B3
Schouten I., *Australia* 94 G4
Schouten Is. = Supiori, *Indonesia* 63 E9
Schouwen, *Neths.* 17 C3
Schramberg, *Germany* 25 G4
Schrankogel, *Austria* 26 D4
Schreiber, *Canada* 102 C2
Schrems, *Austria* 26 C8
Schrobenhausen, *Germany* 25 G7
Schroffenstein, *Namibia* 88 D2
Schroon Lake, *U.S.A.* 111 C11
Schruns, *Austria* 26 D2
Schuler, *Canada* 105 C6
Schumacher, *Canada* 102 C3
Schurz, *U.S.A.* 114 G4
Schuyler, *U.S.A.* 112 E6
Schuylerville, *U.S.A.* 111 C11
Schuylkill →, *U.S.A.* 111 G9
Schuylkill Haven, *U.S.A.* 111 F8
Schwabach, *Germany* 25 F7
Schwaben □, *Germany* 25 G6
Schwäbisch Gmünd, *Germany* 25 G5
Schwäbisch Hall, *Germany* 25 F5
Schwäbische Alb, *Germany* 25 G5
Schwabmünchen, *Germany* 25 G6
Schwalmstadt, *Germany* 24 E5
Schwandorf, *Germany* 25 F8
Schwaner, Pegunungan, *Indonesia* 62 E4
Schwanewede, *Germany* 24 B4
Schwarmstedt, *Germany* 24 C5
Schwarze Elster →, *Germany* 24 D8
Schwarzenberg, *Germany* 24 E8
Schwarzrand, *Namibia* 88 D2
Schwarzwald, *Germany* 25 G4
Schwaz, *Austria* 26 D4
Schwechat, *Austria* 27 C9
Schwedt, *Germany* 24 B10
Schweinfurt, *Germany* 25 E6
Schweizer-Reneke, *S. Africa* 88 D4
Schwenningen = Villingen-Schwenningen, *Germany* 25 G4
Schwerin, *Germany* 24 B7
Schweriner See, *Germany* 24 B7
Schwetzingen, *Germany* 25 F4
Schwyz, *Switz.* 25 H4
Schwyz □, *Switz.* 25 H4
Sciacca, *Italy* 30 E6
Scicli, *Italy* 31 F7
Scilla, *Italy* 31 D8
Scilly, Isles of, *U.K.* 13 H1
Ścinawa, *Poland* 45 G3
Scione, *Greece* 40 G7
Scioto →, *U.S.A.* 108 F4
Scituate, *U.S.A.* 111 D14
Scobey, *U.S.A.* 112 A2
Scordia, *Italy* 31 E7
Scoresbysund = Ittoqqortoormiit, *Greenland* 4 B6
Scorniceşti, *Romania* 43 F9
Scotia, *Calif., U.S.A.* 114 F1
Scotia, *N.Y., U.S.A.* 111 D11
Scotia Sea, *Antarctica* 5 B18
Scotland, *Canada* 110 C4
Scotland □, *U.K.* 14 E5
Scott, C., *Australia* 92 B4
Scott City, *U.S.A.* 112 F4
Scott Glacier, *Antarctica* 5 C8
Scott I., *Antarctica* 5 C11
Scott Is., *Canada* 104 C3
Scott L., *Canada* 105 B7
Scott Reef, *Australia* 92 B3
Scottburgh, *S. Africa* 89 E5
Scottdale, *U.S.A.* 110 F5
Scottish Borders □, *U.K.* 14 F6
Scottsbluff, *U.S.A.* 112 E3
Scottsboro, *U.S.A.* 109 H3
Scottsburg, *U.S.A.* 108 F3
Scottsdale, *Australia* 94 G4
Scottsdale, *U.S.A.* 115 K7
Scottsville, *Ky., U.S.A.* 109 G2
Scottsville, *N.Y., U.S.A.* 110 C7
Scottville, *U.S.A.* 108 D2
Scranton, *U.S.A.* 111 E9
Scugog, L., *Canada* 110 B6
Sculeni, *Moldova* 43 C12
Scunthorpe, *U.K.* 12 D7
Scuol Schuls, *Switz.* 25 J6
Scutari = Üsküdar, *Turkey* 41 F13
Seabrook, L., *Australia* 93 F2
Seaford, *U.K.* 13 G8
Seaford, *U.S.A.* 108 F8
Seaforth, *Australia* 94 C4
Seaforth, *Canada* 110 C3
Seaforth, L., *U.K.* 14 D2
Seagraves, *U.S.A.* 113 J3
Seaham, *U.K.* 12 C6
Seal →, *Canada* 105 B10
Seal L., *Canada* 103 B7
Sealy, *U.S.A.* 113 L6
Searchlight, *U.S.A.* 117 K12
Searcy, *U.S.A.* 113 H9
Searles L., *U.S.A.* 117 K9
Seascale, *U.K.* 12 C4
Seaside, *Calif., U.S.A.* 116 J5
Seaside, *Oreg., U.S.A.* 116 E3
Seattle, *U.S.A.* 116 C4
Seaview Ra., *Australia* 94 B4
Sebago L., *U.S.A.* 111 C14
Sebago Lake, *U.S.A.* 111 C14
Sebastián Vizcaíno, B., *Mexico* 118 B2
Sebastopol = Sevastopol, *Ukraine* 47 K7
Sebastopol, *U.S.A.* 116 G4
Sebba, *Burkina Faso* 83 C5
Sebderat, *Eritrea* 81 D4
Sébékoro, *Mali* 82 C3
Seben, *Turkey* 72 B4
Sebeş, *Romania* 43 E8
Sebeşului, Munţii, *Romania* 43 E8
Sebewaing, *U.S.A.* 108 D4
Sebezh, *Russia* 46 D5
Sebha = Sabhah, *Libya* 79 C8
Sébi, *Mali* 82 B4
Şebinkarahisar, *Turkey* 73 B8
Sebiş, *Romania* 42 D7
Sebnitz, *Germany* 24 E10
Sebring, *Fla., U.S.A.* 109 M5
Sebring, *Ohio, U.S.A.* 110 F3
Sebringville, *Canada* 110 C3
Sebta = Ceuta, *N. Afr.* 78 A4
Sebuku, *Indonesia* 62 E5
Sebuku, Teluk, *Malaysia* 62 D5
Sečanj, *Serbia, Yug.* 42 E5
Secchia →, *Italy* 28 C8
Sechelt, *Canada* 104 D4
Sechura, Desierto de, *Peru* 124 E2
Seclin, *France* 19 B10
Secondigny, *France* 18 F6
Sečovce, *Slovak Rep.* 27 C14
Secretary I., *N.Z.* 91 L1
Secunderabad, *India* 66 L11
Security-Widefield, *U.S.A.* 112 F2
Sedalia, *U.S.A.* 112 F8
Sedan, *France* 19 C11
Sedan, *U.S.A.* 113 G6
Sedano, *Spain* 34 C7
Seddon, *N.Z.* 91 J5
Seddonville, *N.Z.* 91 J4
Sedé Boqér, *Israel* 75 E3
Sedeh, *Fārs, Iran* 71 D7
Sedeh, *Khorāsān, Iran* 71 C8
Séderon, *France* 21 D9
Sederot, *Israel* 75 D3
Sédhiou, *Senegal* 82 C1
Sedico, *Italy* 29 B9
Sedlčany, *Czech Rep.* 26 B7
Sedley, *Canada* 105 C8
Sedona, *U.S.A.* 115 J8
Sedova, Pik, *Russia* 50 B6
Sedro Woolley, *U.S.A.* 116 B4
Šeduva, *Lithuania* 44 C10
Sędziszów, *Poland* 45 H7
Sędziszów Małapolski, *Poland* 45 H8
Seebad Ahlbeck, *Germany* 24 B10
Seefeld in Tirol, *Austria* 26 D4
Seehausen, *Germany* 24 C7
Seeheim, *Namibia* 88 D2
Seeheim-Jugenheim, *Germany* 25 F4
Seeis, *Namibia* 88 C2
Seekoei →, *S. Africa* 88 E4
Seeley's Bay, *Canada* 111 B8
Seelow, *Germany* 24 C10
Sées, *France* 18 D7
Seesen, *Germany* 24 D6
Seevetal, *Germany* 24 B6
Sefadu, *S. Leone* 82 D2
Seferihisar, *Turkey* 39 C8
Séfeto, *Mali* 82 C3
Sefwi Bekwai, *Ghana* 82 D4
Segamat, *Malaysia* 65 L4
Şegarcea, *Romania* 43 F8
Ségbana, *Benin* 83 C5
Segbwema, *S. Leone* 82 D2
Seget, *Indonesia* 63 E8
Segonzac, *France* 20 C3
Segorbe, *Spain* 32 F4
Ségou, *Mali* 82 C3
Segovia = Coco →, *Cent. Amer.* 120 D3
Segovia, *Spain* 34 E6
Segovia □, *Spain* 34 E6
Segré, *France* 18 E6
Segre →, *Spain* 32 D5
Séguéla, *Ivory C.* 82 D3
Séguénéga, *Burkina Faso* 83 C4
Seguin, *U.S.A.* 113 L6
Segundo →, *Argentina* 126 C3
Segura →, *Spain* 33 G4
Segura, Sierra de, *Spain* 33 G2
Seh Konj, Kūh-e, *Iran* 71 D8
Seh Qal'eh, *Iran* 71 C8
Sehitwa, *Botswana* 88 C3
Sehore, *India* 68 H7
Sehwan, *Pakistan* 68 F2
Şeica Mare, *Romania* 43 D9
Seil, *U.K.* 14 E3
Seiland, *Norway* 8 A20
Seilhac, *France* 20 C5
Seiling, *U.S.A.* 113 G5
Seille →, *Moselle, France* 19 C13
Seille →, *Saône-et-Loire, France* 19 F11
Sein, Î. de, *France* 18 D2
Seinäjoki, *Finland* 9 E20
Seine →, *France* 18 C7
Seine, B. de la, *France* 18 C6
Seine-et-Marne □, *France* 19 D10
Seine-Maritime □, *France* 18 C7
Seine-St-Denis □, *France* 19 D9
Seini, *Romania* 43 C8
Seirijai, *Lithuania* 44 D10
Seistan = Sīstān, *Asia* 71 D9
Seistan, Daryācheh-ye = Sīstān, Daryācheh-ye, *Iran* 71 D9
Sejerø, *Denmark* 11 J5
Sejerø Bugt, *Denmark* 11 J5
Sejny, *Poland* 44 D10
Seka, *Ethiopia* 81 F4
Sekayu, *Indonesia* 62 E2
Seke, *Tanzania* 86 C3
Sekenke, *Tanzania* 86 C3
Seki, *Turkey* 39 E11
Sekondi-Takoradi, *Ghana* 82 E4
Sekota, *Ethiopia* 81 E4
Seksna, *Russia* 46 C10
Sekuma, *Botswana* 88 C3
Selah, *U.S.A.* 114 C3
Selama, *Malaysia* 65 K3
Selárgius, *Italy* 30 C2
Selaru, *Indonesia* 63 F8
Selb, *Germany* 25 E8
Selby, *U.K.* 12 D6
Selby, *U.S.A.* 112 C4
Selca, *Croatia* 29 E13
Selçuk, *Turkey* 39 D9
Selden, *U.S.A.* 112 F4
Sele →, *Italy* 31 B7

Selebi-Pikwe, *Botswana* 89 C4
Selemdzha →, *Russia* 51 D13
Selendi, *Manisa, Turkey* 39 C10
Selendi, *Manisa, Turkey* 39 C9
Selenga = Selenge Mörön →, *Asia* 60 A5
Selenge Mörön →, *Asia* 60 A5
Selenicë, *Albania* 40 F3
Selenter See, *Germany* 24 A6
Sélestat, *France* 19 D14
Seletan, Tanjung, *Indonesia* 62 E4
Selevac, *Serbia, Yug.* 40 B4
Sélibabi, *Mauritania* 82 B2
Seliger, Ozero, *Russia* 46 D7
Seligman, *U.S.A.* 115 J7
Şelim, *Turkey* 73 B10
Selîma, El Wâhât el, *Sudan* 80 C2
Selimiye, *Turkey* 39 D9
Selinda Spillway →, *Botswana* 88 B3
Selinoûs, *Greece* 38 D3
Selinsgrove, *U.S.A.* 110 F8
Selizharovo, *Russia* 46 D7
Selkirk, *Canada* 105 C9
Selkirk, *U.K.* 14 F6
Selkirk I., *Canada* 105 C9
Selkirk Mts., *Canada* 100 C8
Sellama, *Sudan* 81 E2
Selliá, *Greece* 36 D6
Sellières, *France* 19 F12
Sells, *U.S.A.* 115 L8
Sellye, *Hungary* 42 E2
Selma, *Ala., U.S.A.* 109 J2
Selma, *Calif., U.S.A.* 116 J7
Selma, *N.C., U.S.A.* 109 H6
Selmer, *U.S.A.* 109 H1
Selongey, *France* 19 E12
Selowandoma Falls, *Zimbabwe* 87 G3
Selpele, *Indonesia* 63 E8
Selsey Bill, *U.K.* 13 G7
Seltso, *Russia* 46 F8
Seltz, *France* 19 D15
Selu, *Indonesia* 63 F8
Sélune →, *France* 18 D5
Selva = La Selva del Camp, *Spain* 32 D6
Selva, *Argentina* 126 B3
Selvas, *Brazil* 122 D4
Selwyn L., *Canada* 105 B8
Selwyn Mts., *Canada* 100 B6
Selwyn Ra., *Australia* 94 C3
Seman →, *Albania* 40 F3
Semarang, *Indonesia* 62 F4
Sembabule, *Uganda* 86 C3
Şemdinli, *Turkey* 73 D11
Sémé, *Senegal* 82 B2
Semeih, *Sudan* 81 E3
Semenov, *Russia* 48 B7
Semenovka, *Chernihiv, Ukraine* 47 F7
Semenovka, *Kremenchuk, Ukraine* 47 H7
Semeru, *Indonesia* 63 H15
Semey, *Kazakstan* 50 D9
Semikarakorskiy, *Russia* 49 G5
Semiluki, *Russia* 47 G10
Seminoe Reservoir, *U.S.A.* 114 F10
Seminole, *Okla., U.S.A.* 113 H6
Seminole, *Tex., U.S.A.* 113 J3
Seminole Draw →, *U.S.A.* 113 J3
Semipalatinsk = Semey, *Kazakstan* 50 D9
Semirara Is., *Phil.* 61 F4
Semitau, *Indonesia* 62 D4
Semiyarka, *Kazakstan* 50 D8
Semiyarskoye = Semiyarka, *Kazakstan* 50 D8
Semmering P., *Austria* 26 D8
Semnān, *Iran* 71 C7
Semnān □, *Iran* 71 C7
Semporna, *Malaysia* 63 D5
Semuda, *Indonesia* 62 E4
Semur-en-Auxois, *France* 19 E11
Sen →, *Cambodia* 62 B3
Senā, *Iran* 71 D6
Sena, *Mozam.* 87 F4
Sena Madureira, *Brazil* 124 E5
Senador Pompeu, *Brazil* 125 E11
Senaki, *Georgia* 49 J6
Senanga, *Zambia* 85 H4
Senatobia, *U.S.A.* 113 H10
Sencelles, *Spain* 37 B9
Sendafa, *Ethiopia* 81 F4
Sendai, *Kagoshima, Japan* 55 J5
Sendai, *Miyagi, Japan* 54 E10
Sendai-Wan, *Japan* 54 E10
Senden, *Bayern, Germany* 25 G6
Senden, *Nordrhein-Westfalen, Germany* 24 D3
Sendhwa, *India* 68 J6
Sene →, *Ghana* 83 D4
Senec, *Slovak Rep.* 27 C10
Seneca, *U.S.A.* 109 H4
Seneca Falls, *U.S.A.* 111 D8
Seneca L., *U.S.A.* 110 D8
Senecaville L., *U.S.A.* 110 G3
Senegal ■, *W. Afr.* 82 C2
Sénégal →, *W. Afr.* 82 B1
Senegambia, *Africa* 76 E2
Senekal, *S. Africa* 89 D4
Senftenberg, *Germany* 24 D10
Senga Hill, *Zambia* 87 D3
Senge Khambab = Indus →, *Pakistan* 68 G2
Sengiley, *Russia* 48 D9
Sengua →, *Zimbabwe* 87 F2
Senhor-do-Bonfim, *Brazil* 125 F10
Senica, *Slovak Rep.* 27 C10
Senigállia, *Italy* 29 E10
Senio →, *Italy* 29 D9
Senirkent, *Turkey* 39 C12
Senise, *Italy* 31 B9
Senj, *Croatia* 29 D11
Senja, *Norway* 8 B17
Senkaku-Shotō, *Japan* 55 L1
Senlis, *France* 19 C9
Senmonorom, *Cambodia* 64 F6
Sennâr, *Sudan* 81 E3
Sennar □, *Sudan* 81 E3
Senneterre, *Canada* 102 C4
Senno, *Belarus* 46 E5
Sénnori, *Italy* 30 B1
Seno, *Laos* 64 D5
Senonches, *France* 18 D8
Senorbì, *Italy* 30 C2
Senožeče, *Slovenia* 29 C11
Sens, *France* 19 D10
Senta, *Serbia, Yug.* 42 E5
Sentani, *Indonesia* 63 E10
Sentery, *Dem. Rep. of the Congo* 86 D2
Sentinel, *U.S.A.* 115 K7
Šentjur, *Slovenia* 29 B12
Senya Beraku, *Ghana* 83 D4
Seo de Urgel = La Seu d'Urgell, *Spain* 32 C6
Seohara, *India* 69 E8
Seonath →, *India* 69 J10
Seondha, *India* 69 F8
Seoni, *India* 69 H8
Seoni Malwa, *India* 68 H8
Seoul = Sŏul, *S. Korea* 57 F14
Sepīdān, *Iran* 71 D7
Sepo-ri, *N. Korea* 57 E14
Sępólno Krajeńskie, *Poland* 44 E4
Sepone, *Laos* 64 D6
Sępopol, *Poland* 44 D8
Sept-Îles, *Canada* 103 B6
Septemvri, *Bulgaria* 41 D8
Sepúlveda, *Spain* 34 D7
Sequeros, *Spain* 34 E4
Sequim, *U.S.A.* 116 B3
Sequoia National Park, *U.S.A.* 116 J8
Serafimovich, *Russia* 48 F6
Seraing, *Belgium* 17 D5
Seraja, *Indonesia* 65 L7
Serakhis →, *Cyprus* 36 D11
Seram, *Indonesia* 63 E7
Seram Sea, *Indonesia* 63 E7
Seranantsara, *Madag.* 89 B8
Serang, *Indonesia* 63 G12
Serasan, *Indonesia* 65 L7
Seravezza, *Italy* 28 E7
Şerbettar, *Turkey* 41 E10
Serbia □, *Yugoslavia* 40 C5
Şercaia, *Romania* 43 E10
Serdo, *Ethiopia* 81 E5
Serdobsk, *Russia* 48 D7
Sered', *Slovak Rep.* 27 C10
Seredka, *Russia* 46 C5
Şereflikoçhisar, *Turkey* 72 C5
Seregno, *Italy* 28 C6
Seremban, *Malaysia* 65 L3
Serengeti Plain, *Tanzania* 86 C4
Serenje, *Zambia* 87 E3
Sereth = Siret →, *Romania* 43 E12
Sergach, *Russia* 48 C7
Sergen, *Turkey* 41 E11
Sergino, *Russia* 50 C7
Sergipe □, *Brazil* 125 F11
Sergiyev Posad, *Russia* 46 D10
Seria, *Brunei* 62 D4
Serian, *Malaysia* 62 D4
Seriate, *Italy* 28 C6
Seribu, Kepulauan, *Indonesia* 62 F3
Sérifontaine, *France* 19 C8
Sérifos, *Greece* 38 D6
Sérignan, *France* 20 E7
Sérigny →, *Canada* 103 A6
Serik, *Turkey* 72 D4
Seringapatam Reef, *Australia* 92 B3
Serinhisar, *Turkey* 39 D11
Sermaize-les-Bains, *France* 19 D11
Sermata, *Indonesia* 63 F7
Sérmide, *Italy* 29 D8
Sernovodsk, *Russia* 48 D10
Sernur, *Russia* 48 B9
Serock, *Poland* 45 F8
Serón, *Spain* 33 H2
Serós, *Spain* 32 D5
Serov, *Russia* 50 D7
Serowe, *Botswana* 88 C4
Serpa, *Portugal* 35 H3
Serpeddí, Punta, *Italy* 30 C2
Serpentara, *Italy* 30 C2
Serpentine Lakes, *Australia* 93 E4
Serpis →, *Spain* 33 G4
Serpukhov, *Russia* 46 E9
Serra de Outes, *Spain* 34 C2
Serra do Navio, *Brazil* 125 C8
Serra San Bruno, *Italy* 31 D9
Serradilla, *Spain* 34 F4
Sérrai, *Greece* 40 E7
Sérrai □, *Greece* 40 E7
Serramanna, *Italy* 30 C1
Serravalle Scrívia, *Italy* 28 D5
Serre-Ponçon, L. de, *France* 21 D10
Serres, *France* 21 D9
Serrezuela, *Argentina* 126 C2
Serrinha, *Brazil* 125 F11
Sersale, *Italy* 31 C9
Sertã, *Portugal* 34 F2
Sertanópolis, *Brazil* 127 A5
Sêrtar, *China* 58 A3
Serua, *Indonesia* 63 F8
Serui, *Indonesia* 63 E9
Serule, *Botswana* 88 C4
Sérvia, *Greece* 40 F6
Serzedelo, *Portugal* 34 D2
Sese Is., *Uganda* 86 C3
Sesepe, *Indonesia* 63 E7
Sesfontein, *Namibia* 88 B1
Sesheke, *Zambia* 88 B3
Sésia →, *Italy* 28 C5
Sesimbra, *Portugal* 35 G1
S'Espalmador, *Spain* 37 C7
S'Espardell, *Spain* 37 C7
Sessa Aurunca, *Italy* 30 A6
S'Estanyol, *Spain* 37 B9
Sestao, *Spain* 32 B2
Sesto Calende, *Italy* 28 C5
Sesto San Giovanni, *Italy* 28 C6
Sestri Levante, *Italy* 28 D6
Sestriere, *Italy* 28 D3
Sestroretsk, *Russia* 46 B6
Sestrunj, *Croatia* 29 D11
Sestu, *Italy* 30 C2
Setana, *Japan* 54 C9
Sète, *France* 20 E7
Sete Lagôas, *Brazil* 125 G10
Sétif, *Algeria* 78 A7
Seto, *Japan* 55 G8
Setonaikai, *Japan* 55 G6
Settat, *Morocco* 78 B4
Séttimo Torinese, *Italy* 28 C4
Setting L., *Canada* 105 C9
Settle, *U.K.* 12 C5
Settlement Pt., *Bahamas* 109 M6
Settlers, *S. Africa* 89 C4
Setúbal, *Portugal* 35 G2
Setúbal □, *Portugal* 35 G2
Setúbal, B. de, *Portugal* 35 G2
Seugne →, *France* 20 C3
Seul, Lac, *Canada* 102 B1
Seurre, *France* 19 F12
Sevan, *Armenia* 49 K7
Sevan, Ozero = Sevana Lich, *Armenia* 49 K7
Sevana Lich, *Armenia* 49 K7
Sevastopol, *Ukraine* 47 K7
Seven Sisters, *Canada* 104 C3
Sever →, *Spain* 35 F3
Sévérac-le-Château, *France* 20 D7
Severn →, *Canada* 102 A2
Severn →, *U.K.* 13 F5
Severn L., *Canada* 102 B1
Severnaya Zemlya, *Russia* 51 B10
Severo-Kurilsk, *Russia* 51 D16
Severo-Yeniseyskiy, *Russia* 51 C10
Severočeský □, *Czech Rep.* 26 A7
Severodonetsk = Syeverodonetsk, *Ukraine* 47 H10
Severodvinsk, *Russia* 50 C4
Severomoravský □, *Czech Rep.* 27 B10
Sevier, *U.S.A.* 115 G7
Sevier →, *U.S.A.* 115 G7
Sevier Desert, *U.S.A.* 114 G7
Sevier L., *U.S.A.* 114 G7
Sevilla, *Spain* 35 H5
Sevilla □, *Spain* 35 H5
Seville = Sevilla, *Spain* 35 H5
Sevlievo, *Bulgaria* 41 C9
Sevnica, *Slovenia* 29 B12
Sèvre-Nantaise →, *France* 18 E5
Sèvre-Niortaise →, *France* 20 B3
Sevsk, *Russia* 47 F8
Sewa →, *S. Leone* 82 D2
Sewani, *India* 68 E6
Seward, *Alaska, U.S.A.* 100 B5
Seward, *Nebr., U.S.A.* 112 E6
Seward, *Pa., U.S.A.* 110 F5
Seward Peninsula, *U.S.A.* 100 B3
Sewell, *Chile* 126 C1
Sewer, *Indonesia* 63 F8
Sewickley, *U.S.A.* 110 F4
Sexsmith, *Canada* 104 B5
Seychelles ■, *Ind. Oc.* 52 K9
Seyðisfjörður, *Iceland* 8 D6
Seydişehir, *Turkey* 72 D4
Seydvān, *Iran* 70 B5
Seyhan →, *Turkey* 70 B2
Seyhan Barajı, *Turkey* 72 D6
Seyitgazi, *Turkey* 39 B12
Seyitömer, *Turkey* 39 B11
Seym →, *Ukraine* 47 G7
Seymen, *Turkey* 41 E11
Seymour, *S. Africa* 89 E4
Seymour, *Conn., U.S.A.* 111 E11
Seymour, *Ind., U.S.A.* 108 F3
Seymour, *Tex., U.S.A.* 113 J5
Seyne, *France* 21 D10
Seyssel, *France* 21 C9
Sežana, *Slovenia* 29 C10
Sézanne, *France* 19 D10
Sezze, *Italy* 30 A6
Sfântu Gheorghe, *Covasna, Romania* 43 E10
Sfântu Gheorghe, *Tulcea, Romania* 43 F14
Sfântu Gheorghe, Braţul →, *Romania* 43 F14
Sfax, *Tunisia* 79 B8
Sha Xi →, *China* 59 D12
Sha Xian, *China* 59 D11
Shaanxi □, *China* 56 G5
Shaba = Katanga □, *Dem. Rep. of the Congo* 86 D2
Shabla, *Bulgaria* 41 C12
Shabogamo L., *Canada* 103 B6
Shabunda, *Dem. Rep. of the Congo* 86 C2
Shache, *China* 60 C2
Shackleton Ice Shelf, *Antarctica* 5 C8
Shackleton Inlet, *Antarctica* 5 E11
Shādegān, *Iran* 71 D6
Shadi, *China* 59 D10
Shadi, *India* 69 C7
Shadrinsk, *Russia* 50 D7
Shadyside, *U.S.A.* 110 G4
Shaffa, *Nigeria* 83 C7
Shafter, *U.S.A.* 117 K7
Shaftesbury, *U.K.* 13 F5
Shagamu, *Nigeria* 83 D5
Shagram, *Pakistan* 69 A5
Shah Alizai, *Pakistan* 68 E2
Shah Bunder, *Pakistan* 68 G2
Shahabad, *Punjab, India* 68 D7
Shahabad, *Raj., India* 68 G7
Shahabad, *Ut. P., India* 69 F8
Shahadpur, *Pakistan* 68 G3
Shahba, *Syria* 75 C5
Shahdād, *Iran* 71 D8
Shahdād, Namakzār-e, *Iran* 71 D8
Shahdadkot, *Pakistan* 68 F2
Shahdol, *India* 69 H9
Shahe, *China* 56 F8
Shahganj, *India* 69 F10
Shahgarh, *India* 66 F6
Shahjahanpur, *India* 69 F8
Shahpur, *India* 68 H7
Shahpur, *Baluchistan, Pakistan* 68 E3
Shahpur, *Punjab, Pakistan* 68 C5
Shahpur Chakar, *Pakistan* 68 F3
Shahpura, *Mad. P., India* 69 H9
Shahpura, *Raj., India* 68 G6
Shahr-e Bābak, *Iran* 71 D7
Shahr-e Kord, *Iran* 71 C6
Shāhrakht, *Iran* 71 C9
Shahrig, *Pakistan* 68 D2
Shahukou, *China* 56 D7
Shaikhabad, *Afghan.* 68 B3
Shajapur, *India* 68 H7
Shakargarh, *Pakistan* 68 C6
Shakawe, *Botswana* 88 B3
Shaker Heights, *U.S.A.* 110 E3
Shakhty, *Russia* 49 G5
Shakhunya, *Russia* 48 B8
Shaki, *Nigeria* 83 D5
Shākir, *Egypt* 80 B3
Shala, L., *Ethiopia* 81 F4
Shali, *Russia* 49 J7
Shallow Lake, *Canada* 110 B3
Shalqar, *Kazakstan* 50 E6
Shalskiy, *Russia* 46 B8
Shaluli Shan, *China* 58 B2
Shām, *Iran* 71 E8
Shām, Bādiyat ash, *Asia* 70 C3
Shamâl Bahr el Ghazal □, *Sudan* 81 F2
Shamâl Dârfûr □, *Sudan* 81 E2
Shamâl Kordofân □, *Sudan* 81 E3
Shamattawa, *Canada* 102 A1
Shamattawa →, *Canada* 102 A2
Shambe, *Sudan* 81 F3
Shambu, *Ethiopia* 81 F4
Shamīl, *Iran* 71 E8
Shamkhor = Şämkir, *Azerbaijan* 49 K8
Shāmkūh, *Iran* 71 C8
Shamli, *India* 68 E7
Shammar, Jabal, *Si. Arabia* 70 E4
Shamo = Gobi, *Asia* 56 C6
Shamo, L., *Ethiopia* 81 F4
Shamokin, *U.S.A.* 111 F8
Shamrock, *U.S.A.* 113 H4
Shamva, *Zimbabwe* 87 F3
Shan □, *Burma* 67 J21
Shan Xian, *China* 56 G9
Shanan →, *Ethiopia* 81 F5
Shanchengzhen, *China* 57 C13
Shāndak, *Iran* 71 D9
Shandon, *U.S.A.* 116 K6
Shandong □, *China* 57 G10
Shandong Bandao, *China* 57 F11
Shang Xian = Shangzhou, *China* 56 H5
Shanga, *Nigeria* 78 F6
Shangalowe, *Dem. Rep. of the Congo* 87 E2
Shangani, *Zimbabwe* 89 B4
Shangani →, *Zimbabwe* 87 F2
Shangbancheng, *China* 57 D10
Shangcheng, *China* 59 B10
Shangchuan Dao, *China* 59 G9
Shangdu, *China* 56 D7
Shanggao, *China* 59 C10
Shanghai, *China* 59 B13
Shanghai Shi □, *China* 59 B13
Shanghang, *China* 59 E11
Shanghe, *China* 57 F9
Shanglin, *China* 58 F7
Shangnan, *China* 56 H6
Shangqiu, *China* 56 G8
Shangrao, *China* 59 C11
Shangshui, *China* 60 C6
Shangsi, *China* 58 F6
Shangyou, *China* 59 E10
Shangyu, *China* 59 B13
Shangzhi, *China* 57 B14
Shangzhou, *China* 56 H5
Shanhetun, *China* 57 B14
Shani, *Nigeria* 83 C7
Shannon, *N.Z.* 91 J5
Shannon →, *Ireland* 15 D2
Shannon, Mouth of the, *Ireland* 15 D2
Shannon Airport, *Ireland* 15 D3
Shansi = Shanxi □, *China* 56 F7
Shantar, Ostrov Bolshoy, *Russia* 51 D14
Shantipur, *India* 69 H13
Shantou, *China* 59 F11
Shantung = Shandong □, *China* 57 G10
Shanwei, *China* 59 F10
Shanxi □, *China* 56 F7
Shanyang, *China* 56 H5
Shanyin, *China* 56 E7
Shaodong, *China* 59 D8
Shaoguan, *China* 59 E9
Shaoshan, *China* 59 D9
Shaowu, *China* 59 D11
Shaoxing, *China* 59 C13
Shaoyang, *Hunan, China* 59 D8
Shaoyang, *Hunan, China* 59 D8
Shap, *U.K.* 12 C5
Shapinsay, *U.K.* 14 B6
Shaqq el Gi'eifer →, *Sudan* 81 D2
Shaqra', *Si. Arabia* 70 E5
Shaqrā', *Yemen* 74 E4
Sharafa, *Sudan* 81 E2
Sharafkhāneh, *Iran* 70 B5
Sharbot Lake, *Canada* 111 B8
Shari, *Japan* 54 C12
Sharjah = Ash Shāriqah, *U.A.E.* 71 E7
Shark B., *Australia* 93 E1
Sharm el Sheikh, *Egypt* 80 B3
Sharon, *Mass., U.S.A.* 111 D13
Sharon, *Pa., U.S.A.* 110 E4
Sharon Springs, *Kans., U.S.A.* 112 F4
Sharon Springs, *N.Y., U.S.A.* 111 D10
Sharp Pt., *Australia* 94 A3
Sharpe L., *Canada* 102 B1
Sharpsville, *U.S.A.* 110 E4
Sharq el Istiwa'iya □, *Sudan* 81 G3
Sharya, *Russia* 48 A7
Shasha, *Ethiopia* 81 F4
Shashemene, *Ethiopia* 81 F4
Shashi, *Botswana* 89 C4
Shashi, *China* 59 B9
Shashi →, *Africa* 87 G2
Shasta, Mt., *U.S.A.* 114 F2
Shasta L., *U.S.A.* 114 F2
Shatawi, *Sudan* 81 E3
Shatsk, *Russia* 48 C5
Shatt al Arab = Arab, Shatt al →, *Asia* 71 D6
Shatura, *Russia* 46 E10
Shaumyani = Shulaveri, *Georgia* 49 K7
Shaunavon, *Canada* 105 D7
Shaver L., *U.S.A.* 116 H7
Shaw →, *Australia* 92 D2
Shaw I., *Australia* 94 C4
Shawanaga, *Canada* 110 A4
Shawangunk Mts., *U.S.A.* 111 E10
Shawano, *U.S.A.* 108 C1
Shawinigan, *Canada* 102 C5
Shawnee, *U.S.A.* 113 H6
Shay Gap, *Australia* 92 D3
Shayang, *China* 59 B9
Shaybārā, *Si. Arabia* 70 E3
Shayib el Banat, Gebel, *Egypt* 80 B3
Shaykh, J. ash, *Lebanon* 75 B4
Shaykh Miskīn, *Syria* 75 C5
Shaykh Sa'īd, *Iraq* 70 C5
Shchekino, *Russia* 46 E9
Shcherbakov = Rybinsk, *Russia* 46 C10
Shchigry, *Russia* 47 G9
Shchors, *Ukraine* 47 G6
Shchuchinsk, *Kazakstan* 50 D8
She Xian, *Anhui, China* 59 C12
She Xian, *Hebei, China* 56 F7
Shebekino, *Russia* 47 G9
Shebele = Scebeli, Wabi →, *Somali Rep.* 74 G3
Sheboygan, *U.S.A.* 108 D2
Shebshi Mts., *Nigeria* 83 D7
Shediac, *Canada* 103 C7
Sheelin, L., *Ireland* 15 C4
Sheep Haven, *Ireland* 15 A4
Sheerness, *U.K.* 13 F8
Sheet Harbour, *Canada* 103 D7
Sheffield, *U.K.* 12 D6
Sheffield, *Ala., U.S.A.* 109 H2
Sheffield, *Mass., U.S.A.* 111 D11
Sheffield, *Pa., U.S.A.* 110 E5
Shehojele, *Ethiopia* 81 E4
Shehong, *China* 58 B5
Sheikh Idris, *Sudan* 81 E3
Sheikhpura, *India* 69 G11
Shek Hasan, *Ethiopia* 81 E4
Shekhupura, *Pakistan* 68 D5
Sheki = Şaki, *Azerbaijan* 49 K8
Shelburne, *N.S., Canada* 103 D6
Shelburne, *Ont., Canada* 102 D3
Shelburne, *U.S.A.* 111 B11
Shelburne B., *Australia* 94 A3
Shelburne Falls, *U.S.A.* 111 D12
Shelby, *Mich., U.S.A.* 108 D2
Shelby, *Miss., U.S.A.* 113 J9
Shelby, *Mont., U.S.A.* 114 B8
Shelby, *N.C., U.S.A.* 109 H5
Shelby, *Ohio, U.S.A.* 110 F2
Shelbyville, *Ill., U.S.A.* 112 F10
Shelbyville, *Ind., U.S.A.* 108 F3
Shelbyville, *Ky., U.S.A.* 108 F3
Shelbyville, *Tenn., U.S.A.* 109 H2
Sheldon, *U.S.A.* 112 D7
Sheldrake, *Canada* 103 B7
Shelengo, Khawr →, *Sudan* 81 E2
Shelikhova, Zaliv, *Russia* 51 D16
Shell Lakes, *Australia* 93 E4
Shellbrook, *Canada* 105 C7
Shelon →, *Russia* 46 C6
Shelter I, *U.S.A.* 111 E12
Shelton, *Conn., U.S.A.* 111 E11
Shelton, *Wash., U.S.A.* 116 C3
Shemakha = Şamaxi, *Azerbaijan* 49 K9
Shëmri, *Albania* 40 D4

Shemsi, *Sudan* 80 D2
Shen Xian, *China* 56 F8
Shenandoah, *Iowa, U.S.A.* 112 E7
Shenandoah, *Pa., U.S.A.* 111 F8
Shenandoah, *Va., U.S.A.* 108 F6
Shenandoah →, *U.S.A.* 108 F7
Shenandoah National Park, *U.S.A.* 108 F6
Shenchi, *China* 56 E7
Shendam, *Nigeria* 83 D6
Shendî, *Sudan* 81 D3
Shenge, *S. Leone* 82 D2
Shengfang, *China* 56 E9
Shëngjergj, *Albania* 40 E4
Shëngjin, *Albania* 40 E3
Shengzhou, *China* 59 C13
Shenjingzi, *China* 57 B13
Shenmu, *China* 56 E6
Shennongjia, *China* 59 B8
Shenqiu, *China* 56 H8
Shensi = Shaanxi □, *China* 56 G5
Shenyang, *China* 57 D12
Shenzhen, *China* 59 F10
Sheo, *India* 68 F4
Sheopur Kalan, *India* 66 G10
Shepetivka, *Ukraine* 47 G4
Shepetovka = Shepetivka, *Ukraine* 47 G4
Sheppey, I. of, *U.K.* 13 F8
Shepton Mallet, *U.K.* 13 F5
Sheqi, *China* 56 H7
Sher Qila, *Pakistan* 69 A6
Sherab, *Sudan* 81 E1
Sherborne, *U.K.* 13 G5
Sherbro →, *S. Leone* 82 D2
Sherbro I., *S. Leone* 82 D2
Sherbrooke, *N.S., Canada* 103 C7
Sherbrooke, *Qué., Canada* 103 C5
Sherburne, *U.S.A.* 111 D9
Shereik, *Sudan* 80 D3
Shergarh, *India* 68 F5
Sherghati, *India* 69 G11
Sheridan, *Ark., U.S.A.* 113 H8
Sheridan, *Wyo., U.S.A.* 114 D10
Sheringham, *U.K.* 12 E9
Sherkin I., *Ireland* 15 E2
Sherkot, *India* 69 E8
Sherman, *U.S.A.* 113 J6
Sherpur, *India* 69 G10
Sherridon, *Canada* 105 B8
Sherwood Forest, *U.K.* 12 D6
Sherwood Park, *Canada* 104 C6
Sheslay →, *Canada* 104 B2
Shethanei L., *Canada* 105 B9
Shetland □, *U.K.* 14 A7
Shetland Is., *U.K.* 14 A7
Shetrunji →, *India* 68 J5
Shewa □, *Ethiopia* 81 F4
Shewa Gimira, *Ethiopia* 81 F4
Sheyenne →, *U.S.A.* 112 B6
Shibām, *Yemen* 74 D4
Shibata, *Japan* 54 F9
Shibecha, *Japan* 54 C12
Shibetsu, *Japan* 54 B11
Shibîn el Kôm, *Egypt* 80 H7
Shibîn el Qanâtir, *Egypt* 80 H7
Shibing, *China* 58 D7
Shibogama L., *Canada* 102 B2
Shibushi, *Japan* 55 J5
Shicheng, *China* 59 D11
Shickshinny, *U.S.A.* 111 E8
Shickshock Mts. = Chic-Chocs, Mts., *Canada* 103 C6
Shidao, *China* 57 F12
Shidian, *China* 58 E2
Shido, *Japan* 55 G7
Shiel, L., *U.K.* 14 E3
Shield, C., *Australia* 94 A2
Shīeli, *Kazakstan* 50 E7
Shifang, *China* 58 B5
Shiga □, *Japan* 55 G8
Shigu, *China* 58 D2
Shiguaigou, *China* 56 D6
Shihchiachuangi = Shijiazhuang, *China* 56 E8
Shijak, *Albania* 40 E3
Shijiazhuang, *China* 56 E8
Shijiu Hu, *China* 59 B12
Shikarpur, *India* 68 E8
Shikarpur, *Pakistan* 68 F3
Shikohabad, *India* 69 F8
Shikoku □, *Japan* 55 H6
Shikoku-Sanchi, *Japan* 55 H6
Shiliguri, *India* 67 F16
Shilka, *Russia* 51 D12
Shilka →, *Russia* 51 D13
Shillelagh, *Ireland* 15 D5
Shillington, *U.S.A.* 111 F9
Shillong, *India* 67 G17
Shilo, *West Bank* 75 C4
Shilong, *China* 59 F9
Shilou, *China* 56 F6
Shilovo, *Russia* 48 C5
Shimabara, *Japan* 55 H5
Shimada, *Japan* 55 G9
Shimane □, *Japan* 55 G6
Shimanovsk, *Russia* 51 D13
Shimen, *China* 59 C8
Shimenjie, *China* 59 C11
Shimian, *China* 58 C4
Shimizu, *Japan* 55 G9
Shimodate, *Japan* 55 F9
Shimoga, *India* 66 N9
Shimoni, *Kenya* 86 C4
Shimonoseki, *Japan* 55 H5
Shimpuru Rapids, *Angola* 88 B2
Shimsk, *Russia* 46 C6
Shin, L., *U.K.* 14 C4
Shinan, *China* 58 F7
Shinano-Gawa →, *Japan* 55 F9
Shināş, *Oman* 71 E8
Shīndand, *Afghan.* 66 C3
Shinglehouse, *U.S.A.* 110 E6
Shingū, *Japan* 55 H7
Shingwidzi, *S. Africa* 89 C5
Shinjō, *Japan* 54 E10
Shinkafe, *Nigeria* 83 C6
Shinshār, *Syria* 75 A5
Shinyanga, *Tanzania* 86 C3
Shinyanga □, *Tanzania* 86 C3
Shio-no-Misaki, *Japan* 55 H7
Shiogama, *Japan* 54 E10
Shiojiri, *Japan* 55 F8
Shipchenski Prokhod, *Bulgaria* 41 D9
Shiping, *China* 58 F4
Shippegan, *Canada* 103 C7
Shippensburg, *U.S.A.* 110 F7
Shippenville, *U.S.A.* 110 E5
Shiprock, *U.S.A.* 115 H9
Shiqian, *China* 58 D7
Shiqma, N. →, *Israel* 75 D3
Shiquan, *China* 56 H5
Shiquan He = Indus →, *Pakistan* 68 G2
Shīr Kūh, *Iran* 71 D7
Shiragami-Misaki, *Japan* 54 D10
Shirakawa, *Fukushima, Japan* 55 F10
Shirakawa, *Gifu, Japan* 55 F8
Shirane-San, *Gumma, Japan* 55 F9
Shirane-San, *Yamanashi, Japan* 55 G9
Shiraoi, *Japan* 54 C10
Shīrāz, *Iran* 71 D7
Shirbîn, *Egypt* 80 H7
Shire →, *Africa* 87 F4
Shiretoko-Misaki, *Japan* 54 B12
Shirinab →, *Pakistan* 68 D2
Shiriya-Zaki, *Japan* 54 D10
Shiroishi, *Japan* 54 F10
Shīrvān, *Iran* 71 B8
Shirwa, L. = Chilwa, L., *Malawi* 87 F4
Shishi, *China* 59 E12
Shishou, *China* 59 C9
Shitai, *China* 59 B11
Shivpuri, *India* 68 G7
Shixian, *China* 57 C15
Shixing, *China* 59 E10
Shiyan, *China* 59 A8
Shiyata, *Egypt* 80 B2
Shizhu, *China* 58 C7
Shizong, *China* 58 E5
Shizuishan, *China* 56 E4
Shizuoka, *Japan* 55 G9
Shizuoka □, *Japan* 55 G9
Shklov = Shklow, *Belarus* 46 E6
Shklow, *Belarus* 46 E6
Shkoder = Shkodër, *Albania* 40 D3
Shkodër, *Albania* 40 D3
Shkumbini →, *Albania* 40 E3
Shmidta, Ostrov, *Russia* 51 A10
Shō-Gawa →, *Japan* 55 F8
Shoal L., *Canada* 105 D9
Shoal Lake, *Canada* 105 C8
Shōdo-Shima, *Japan* 55 G7
Sholapur = Solapur, *India* 66 L9
Shologontsy, *Russia* 51 C12
Shōmrōn, *West Bank* 75 C4
Shoreham by Sea, *U.K.* 13 G7
Shori →, *Pakistan* 68 E3
Shorkot Road, *Pakistan* 68 D5
Shoshone, *Calif., U.S.A.* 117 K10
Shoshone, *Idaho, U.S.A.* 114 E6
Shoshone L., *U.S.A.* 114 D8
Shoshone Mts., *U.S.A.* 114 G5
Shoshong, *Botswana* 88 C4
Shoshoni, *U.S.A.* 114 E9
Shostka, *Ukraine* 47 G7
Shou Xian, *China* 59 A11
Shouchang, *China* 59 C12
Shouguang, *China* 57 F10
Shouning, *China* 59 D12
Shouyang, *China* 56 F7
Show Low, *U.S.A.* 115 J9
Shpola, *Ukraine* 47 H6
Shreveport, *U.S.A.* 113 J8
Shrewsbury, *U.K.* 13 E5
Shri Mohangarh, *India* 68 F4
Shrirampur, *India* 69 H13
Shropshire □, *U.K.* 13 E5
Shū, *Kazakstan* 50 E8
Shū →, *Kazakstan* 52 E10
Shuangbai, *China* 58 E3
Shuangcheng, *China* 57 B14
Shuangfeng, *China* 59 D9
Shuanggou, *China* 57 G9
Shuangjiang, *China* 58 F2
Shuangliao, *China* 57 C12
Shuangshanzi, *China* 57 D10
Shuangyang, *China* 57 C13
Shuangyashan, *China* 60 B8
Shubra Khit, *Egypt* 80 H7
Shucheng, *China* 59 B11
Shugozero, *Russia* 46 C8
Shuguri Falls, *Tanzania* 87 D4
Shuiji, *China* 59 D12
Shuiye, *China* 56 F8
Shujalpur, *India* 68 H7
Shukpa Kunzang, *India* 69 B8
Shulan, *China* 57 B14
Shulaveri, *Georgia* 49 K7
Shule, *China* 60 C2
Shumagin Is., *U.S.A.* 100 C4
Shumen, *Bulgaria* 41 C10
Shumerlya, *Russia* 48 C8
Shumikha, *Russia* 50 D7
Shunchang, *China* 59 D11
Shunde, *China* 59 F9
Shungay, *Kazakstan* 49 F8
Shuo Xian = Shuozhou, *China* 56 E7
Shuozhou, *China* 56 E7
Shūr →, *Fārs, Iran* 71 D7
Shūr →, *Kermān, Iran* 71 D8
Shūr →, *Yazd, Iran* 71 D7
Shūr Āb, *Iran* 71 C6
Shūr Gaz, *Iran* 71 D8
Shūrāb, *Iran* 71 C8
Shūrjestān, *Iran* 71 D7
Shurugwi, *Zimbabwe* 87 F3
Shūsf, *Iran* 71 D9
Shūsh, *Iran* 73 F13
Shūshtar, *Iran* 71 D6
Shuswap L., *Canada* 104 C5
Shuya, *Russia* 48 B5
Shuyang, *China* 57 G10
Shūzū, *Iran* 71 D7
Shwebo, *Burma* 67 H19
Shwegu, *Burma* 67 G20
Shweli →, *Burma* 67 H20
Shymkent, *Kazakstan* 50 E7
Shyok, *India* 69 B8
Shyok →, *Pakistan* 69 B6
Si Chon, *Thailand* 65 H2
Si Kiang = Xi Jiang →, *China* 59 F9
Si-ngan = Xi'an, *China* 56 G5
Si Prachan, *Thailand* 64 E3
Si Racha, *Thailand* 64 F3
Si Xian, *China* 57 H9
Siahaf →, *Pakistan* 68 E3
Siahan Range, *Pakistan* 66 F4
Siaksriindrapura, *Indonesia* 62 D2
Sialkot, *Pakistan* 68 C6
Siam = Thailand ■, *Asia* 64 E4
Sian = Xi'an, *China* 56 G5
Sianów, *Poland* 44 D3
Siantan, *Indonesia* 62 D3
Sīāreh, *Iran* 71 D9
Siargao I., *Phil.* 61 G7
Siari, *Pakistan* 69 B7
Siasi, *Phil.* 63 C6
Siasi I., *Phil.* 61 J4
Siátista, *Greece* 40 F5
Siau, *Indonesia* 63 D7
Šiauliai, *Lithuania* 9 J20
Šiauliai □, *Lithuania* 44 C10
Siazan = Siyäzän, *Azerbaijan* 49 K9
Sibâi, Gebel el, *Egypt* 70 E2
Sibayi, L., *S. Africa* 89 D5
Sibdu, *Sudan* 81 E2
Šibenik, *Croatia* 29 E12
Siberia, *Russia* 4 D13
Siberut, *Indonesia* 62 E1
Sibi, *Pakistan* 68 E2
Sibil = Oksibil, *Indonesia* 63 E10
Sibiti, *Congo* 84 E2
Sibiu, *Romania* 43 E9
Sibiu □, *Romania* 43 E9
Sibley, *U.S.A.* 112 D7
Sibolga, *Indonesia* 62 D1
Sibsagar, *India* 67 F19
Sibu, *Malaysia* 62 D4
Sibuco, *Phil.* 61 H5
Sibuguey B., *Phil.* 61 H5
Sibut, *C.A.R.* 84 C3
Sibutu, *Phil.* 63 D5
Sibutu Group, *Phil.* 61 J3
Sibutu Passage, *E. Indies* 63 D5
Sibuyan I., *Phil.* 61 E5
Sibuyan Sea, *Phil.* 61 E5
Sic, *Romania* 43 D8
Sicamous, *Canada* 104 C5
Siccus →, *Australia* 95 E2
Sichuan □, *China* 58 B5
Sichuan Pendi, *China* 58 B5
Sicilia, *Italy* 31 E7
Sicilia □, *Italy* 31 E7
Sicily = Sicilia, *Italy* 31 E7
Sicuani, *Peru* 124 F4
Šid, *Serbia, Yug.* 42 E4
Sidamo □, *Ethiopia* 81 G4
Sidaouet, *Niger* 83 B6
Sidári, *Greece* 36 A3
Siddhapur, *India* 68 H5
Siddipet, *India* 66 K11
Sidensjö, *Sweden* 10 A12
Sidéradougou, *Burkina Faso* 82 C4
Siderno, *Italy* 31 D9
Sidhauli, *India* 69 F9
Sídheros, Ákra, *Greece* 36 D8
Sidhi, *India* 69 G9
Sidhirókastron, *Greece* 40 E7
Sîdi Abd el Rahmân, *Egypt* 80 A2
Sîdi Barrâni, *Egypt* 80 A2
Sidi-bel-Abbès, *Algeria* 78 A5
Sidi Haneish, *Egypt* 80 A2
Sidi Ifni, *Morocco* 78 C3
Sidi Omar, *Egypt* 80 A1
Sidlaw Hills, *U.K.* 14 E5
Sidley, Mt., *Antarctica* 5 D14
Sidmouth, *U.K.* 13 G4
Sidmouth, C., *Australia* 94 A3
Sidney, *Canada* 104 D4
Sidney, *Mont., U.S.A.* 112 B2
Sidney, *N.Y., U.S.A.* 111 D9
Sidney, *Nebr., U.S.A.* 112 E3
Sidney, *Ohio, U.S.A.* 108 E3
Sidney Lanier, L., *U.S.A.* 109 H4
Sido, *Mali* 82 C3
Sidoarjo, *Indonesia* 63 G15
Sidon = Saydā, *Lebanon* 75 B4
Sidra, G. of = Surt, Khalīj, *Libya* 79 B9
Siedlce, *Poland* 45 F9
Sieg →, *Germany* 24 E3
Siegburg, *Germany* 24 E3
Siegen, *Germany* 24 E4
Siem Pang, *Cambodia* 64 E6
Siem Reap = Siemreab, *Cambodia* 64 F4
Siemiatycze, *Poland* 45 F9
Siemreab, *Cambodia* 64 F4
Siena, *Italy* 29 E8
Sieniawa, *Poland* 45 H9
Sieradz, *Poland* 45 G5
Sieraków, *Poland* 45 F3
Sierck-les-Bains, *France* 19 C13
Sierning, *Austria* 26 C7
Sierpc, *Poland* 45 F6
Sierra Blanca, *U.S.A.* 115 L11
Sierra Blanca Peak, *U.S.A.* 115 K11
Sierra City, *U.S.A.* 116 F6
Sierra Colorada, *Argentina* 128 E3
Sierra de Yeguas, *Spain* 35 H6
Sierra Gorda, *Chile* 126 A2
Sierra Leone ■, *W. Afr.* 82 D2
Sierra Madre, *Mexico* 119 D6
Sierra Mojada, *Mexico* 118 B4
Sierra Nevada, *Spain* 35 H7
Sierra Nevada, *U.S.A.* 116 H8
Sierra Vista, *U.S.A.* 115 L8
Sierraville, *U.S.A.* 116 F6
Sierre, *Switz.* 25 J3
Sifani, *Ethiopia* 81 E5
Sifié, *Ivory C.* 82 D3
Sífnos, *Greece* 38 E6
Sifton, *Canada* 105 C8
Sifton Pass, *Canada* 104 B3
Sigean, *France* 20 E6
Sighetu-Marmaţiei, *Romania* 43 C8
Sighişoara, *Romania* 43 D9
Sigli, *Indonesia* 62 C1
Siglufjörður, *Iceland* 8 C4
Sigmaringen, *Germany* 25 G5
Signa, *Italy* 28 E8
Signakhi = Tsnori, *Georgia* 49 K7
Signal, *U.S.A.* 117 L13
Signal Pk., *U.S.A.* 117 M12
Signy-l'Abbaye, *France* 19 C11
Sigsig, *Ecuador* 124 D3
Sigüenza, *Spain* 32 D2
Siguiri, *Guinea* 82 C3
Sigulda, *Latvia* 9 H21
Sihanoukville = Kampong Saom, *Cambodia* 65 G4
Sihora, *India* 69 H9
Sihui, *China* 59 F9
Siikajoki →, *Finland* 8 D21
Siilinjärvi, *Finland* 8 E22
Siirt, *Turkey* 73 D9
Sijarira Ra., *Zimbabwe* 87 F2
Sika, *India* 68 H3
Sikao, *Thailand* 65 J2
Sikar, *India* 68 F6
Sikasso, *Mali* 82 C3
Sikeston, *U.S.A.* 113 G10
Sikhote Alin, Khrebet, *Russia* 51 E14
Sikhote Alin Ra. = Sikhote Alin, Khrebet, *Russia* 51 E14
Sikiá., *Greece* 40 F7
Síkinos, *Greece* 39 E7
Sikkani Chief →, *Canada* 104 B4
Sikkim □, *India* 67 F16
Siklós, *Hungary* 42 E3
Sikotu-Ko, *Japan* 54 C10
Sil →, *Spain* 34 C3
Silacayoapan, *Mexico* 119 D5
Šilalė, *Lithuania* 44 C9
Silandro, *Italy* 28 B7
Silawad, *India* 68 J6
Silay, *Phil.* 61 F5
Silba, *Croatia* 29 D11
Silchar, *India* 67 G18
Şile, *Turkey* 41 E13
Siler City, *U.S.A.* 109 H6
Silgarhi Doti, *Nepal* 69 E9
Silghat, *India* 67 F18
Sili, *Burkina Faso* 82 C4
Silifke, *Turkey* 70 B2
Siliguri = Shiliguri, *India* 67 F16
Siling Co, *China* 60 C3
Silistea Nouă, *Romania* 43 F10
Silistra, *Bulgaria* 41 B11
Silivri, *Turkey* 41 E12
Siljan, *Sweden* 10 D8
Siljansnäs, *Sweden* 10 D8
Silkeborg, *Denmark* 11 H3
Silkwood, *Australia* 94 B4
Silla, *Spain* 33 F4
Sillajhuay, Cordillera, *Chile* 124 G5
Sillamäe, *Estonia* 9 G22
Sillé-le-Guillaume, *France* 18 D6
Silleda, *Spain* 34 C2
Silloth, *U.K.* 12 C4
Sílo, *Greece* 41 E9
Siloam Springs, *U.S.A.* 113 G7
Silopi, *Turkey* 73 D10
Silsbee, *U.S.A.* 113 K7
Siluko, *Nigeria* 83 D6
Šilutė, *Lithuania* 9 J19
Silva Porto = Kuito, *Angola* 85 G3
Silvan, *Turkey* 73 C9
Silvani, *India* 69 H8
Silver City, *U.S.A.* 115 K9
Silver Cr. →, *U.S.A.* 114 E4
Silver Creek, *U.S.A.* 110 D5
Silver L., *U.S.A.* 116 G6
Silver Lake, *Calif., U.S.A.* 117 K10
Silver Lake, *Oreg., U.S.A.* 114 E3
Silverdalen, *Sweden* 11 G9
Silverton, *Colo., U.S.A.* 115 H10
Silverton, *Tex., U.S.A.* 113 H4
Silves, *Portugal* 35 H2
Silvi Marina, *Italy* 29 F11
Silvies →, *U.S.A.* 114 E4
Silvrettahorn, *Switz.* 28 B7
Silwa Bahari, *Egypt* 80 C3
Silz, *Austria* 26 D3
Simaltala, *India* 69 G12
Simanggang = Bandar Sri Aman, *Malaysia* 62 D4
Simao, *China* 58 F3
Simard, L., *Canada* 102 C4
Şimareh →, *Iran* 73 F12
Simav, *Turkey* 39 B10
Simav →, *Turkey* 41 F12
Simav Dağları, *Turkey* 39 B10
Simba, *Tanzania* 86 C4
Simbach, *Germany* 25 G9
Simbirsk, *Russia* 48 C9
Simbo, *Tanzania* 86 C2
Simcoe, *Canada* 102 D3
Simcoe, L., *Canada* 102 D4
Simdega, *India* 69 H11
Simeonovgrad, *Bulgaria* 41 D9
Simeria, *Romania* 42 E8
Simeto →, *Italy* 31 E8
Simeulue, *Indonesia* 62 D1
Simferopol, *Ukraine* 47 K8
Sími, *Greece* 39 E9
Simi Valley, *U.S.A.* 117 L8
Simikot, *Nepal* 69 E9
Simitli, *Bulgaria* 40 E7
Simla, *India* 68 D7
Simlångsdalen, *Sweden* 11 H7
Şimleu-Silvaniei, *Romania* 42 C7
Simmern, *Germany* 25 F3
Simmie, *Canada* 105 D7
Simmler, *U.S.A.* 117 K7
Simnas, *Lithuania* 44 D10
Simojoki →, *Finland* 8 D21
Simojovel, *Mexico* 119 D6
Simonette →, *Canada* 104 B5
Simonstown, *S. Africa* 88 E2
Simontornya, *Hungary* 42 D3
Simplonpass, *Switz.* 25 J4
Simplontunnel, *Switz.* 25 J4
Simpson Desert, *Australia* 94 D2
Simpson Pen., *Canada* 101 B11
Simpungdong, *N. Korea* 57 D15
Simrishamn, *Sweden* 11 J8
Simsbury, *U.S.A.* 111 E12
Simushir, Ostrov, *Russia* 51 E16
Sin Cowe I., *S. China Sea* 62 C4
Sinabang, *Indonesia* 62 D1
Sinadogo, *Somali Rep.* 74 F4
Sinai = Es Sînâ', *Egypt* 75 F3
Sinai, Mt. = Mûsa, Gebel, *Egypt* 70 D2
Sinai Peninsula, *Egypt* 75 F3
Sinaia, *Romania* 43 E10
Sinaloa □, *Mexico* 118 C3
Sinaloa de Leyva, *Mexico* 118 B3
Sinalunga, *Italy* 29 E8
Sinan, *China* 58 D7
Sînandrei, *Romania* 42 E6
Sinarádhes, *Greece* 36 A3
Sincan, *Turkey* 72 B5
Sincanlı, *Turkey* 39 C12
Sincelejo, *Colombia* 124 B3
Sinch'ang, *N. Korea* 57 D15
Sinchang-ni, *N. Korea* 57 E14
Sinclair, *U.S.A.* 114 F10
Sinclair Mills, *Canada* 104 C4
Sinclair's B., *U.K.* 14 C5
Sinclairville, *U.S.A.* 110 D5
Sincorá, Serra do, *Brazil* 125 F10
Sind, *Pakistan* 68 G3
Sind □, *Pakistan* 68 G3
Sind →, *Jammu & Kashmir, India* 69 B6
Sind →, *Mad. P., India* 69 F8
Sind Sagar Doab, *Pakistan* 68 D4
Sindal, *Denmark* 11 G4
Sindangan, *Phil.* 61 G5
Sindangbarang, *Indonesia* 63 G12
Sinde, *Zambia* 87 F2
Sindelfingen, *Germany* 25 G4
Sındırgı, *Turkey* 39 B10
Sindou, *Burkina Faso* 82 C3
Sindri, *India* 69 H12
Sine →, *Senegal* 82 C1
Sinegorskiy, *Russia* 49 G5
Sinekli, *Turkey* 41 E12
Sinelnikovo = Synelnykove, *Ukraine* 47 H8
Sinendé, *Benin* 83 C5
Sines, *Portugal* 35 H2
Sines, C. de, *Portugal* 35 H2
Sineu, *Spain* 37 B10
Sinfra, *Ivory C.* 82 D3
Sing Buri, *Thailand* 64 E3
Singa, *Sudan* 81 E3
Singapore ■, *Asia* 65 M4
Singapore, Straits of, *Asia* 65 M5
Singaraja, *Indonesia* 62 F5
Singen, *Germany* 25 H4
Singida, *Tanzania* 86 C3
Singida □, *Tanzania* 86 D3
Singitikós Kólpos, *Greece* 40 F7
Singkaling Hkamti, *Burma* 67 G19
Singkang, *Indonesia* 63 E6
Singkawang, *Indonesia* 62 D3
Singkep, *Indonesia* 62 E2
Singleton, Mt., *N. Terr., Australia* 92 D5

Singleton, Mt., *W. Austral., Australia* 93 E2
Singö, *Sweden* 10 D12
Singoli, *India* 68 G6
Singora = Songkhla, *Thailand* 65 J3
Singosan, *N. Korea* 57 E14
Sinhung, *N. Korea* 57 D14
Sînî □, *Egypt* 75 F3
Siniátsikon, Óros, *Greece* 40 F5
Siniscóla, *Italy* 30 B2
Sinj, *Croatia* 29 E13
Sinjai, *Indonesia* 63 F6
Sinjajevina, *Montenegro, Yug.* 40 D3
Sinjār, *Iraq* 70 B4
Sinkat, *Sudan* 80 D4
Sinkiang Uighur = Xinjiang Uygur Zizhiqu □, *China* 60 B3
Sinmak, *N. Korea* 57 E14
Sínnai, *Italy* 30 C2
Sinnamary, *Fr. Guiana* 125 B8
Sinni →, *Italy* 31 B9
Sinnuris, *Egypt* 80 J7
Sinoie, Lacul, *Romania* 43 F13
Sinop, *Turkey* 72 A6
Sinor, *India* 68 J5
Sinp'o, *N. Korea* 57 E15
Sinsheim, *Germany* 25 F4
Sinsk, *Russia* 51 C13
Sintang, *Indonesia* 62 D4
Sinton, *U.S.A.* 113 L6
Sintra, *Portugal* 35 G1
Sinŭiju, *N. Korea* 57 D13
Sinyukha →, *Ukraine* 47 H6
Sinzig, *Germany* 24 E3
Sio →, *Hungary* 42 D3
Siocon, *Phil.* 61 H5
Siófok, *Hungary* 42 D3
Sion, *Switz.* 25 J3
Sion Mills, *U.K.* 15 B4
Sioux City, *U.S.A.* 112 D6
Sioux Falls, *U.S.A.* 112 D6
Sioux Lookout, *Canada* 102 B1
Sioux Narrows, *Canada* 105 D10
Sipalay, *Phil.* 61 G5
Šipan, *Croatia* 40 D1
Siping, *China* 57 C13
Sipiwesk L., *Canada* 105 B9
Šipovo, *Bos.-H.* 42 F2
Sipra →, *India* 68 H6
Sipura, *Indonesia* 62 E1
Siquia →, *Nic.* 120 D3
Siquijor, *Phil.* 61 G5
Siquirres, *Costa Rica* 120 D3
Şīr Banī Yās, *U.A.E.* 71 E7
Sir Edward Pellew Group, *Australia* 94 B2
Sir Graham Moore Is., *Australia* 92 B4
Sir James MacBrien, Mt., *Canada* 100 B7
Sira →, *Norway* 9 G12
Siracusa, *Italy* 31 E8
Sirajganj, *Bangla.* 69 G13
Sirakoro, *Mali* 82 C3
Şiran, *Turkey* 73 B8
Sirasso, *Ivory C.* 82 D3
Sirathu, *India* 69 G9
Sīrdān, *Iran* 71 B6
Sirdaryo = Syrdarya →, *Kazakstan* 50 E7
Sire, *Ethiopia* 81 F4
Siren, *U.S.A.* 112 C8
Sirer, *Spain* 37 C7
Siret, *Romania* 43 C11
Siret →, *Romania* 43 E12
Sirghāyā, *Syria* 75 B5
Şiria, *Romania* 42 D6
Sirino, Mte., *Italy* 31 B8
Sirmaur, *India* 69 G9
Sírna, *Greece* 39 E8
Şirnak, *Turkey* 73 D10
Sirohi, *India* 68 G5
Sironj, *India* 68 G7
Síros, *Greece* 38 D6
Sirretta Pk., *U.S.A.* 117 K8
Sīrrī, *Iran* 71 E7
Sirsa, *India* 68 E6
Sirsa →, *India* 69 F8
Siruela, *Spain* 35 G5
Sisak, *Croatia* 29 C13
Sisaket, *Thailand* 64 E5
Sisante, *Spain* 33 F2
Sisargas, Is., *Spain* 34 B2
Sishen, *S. Africa* 88 D3
Sishui, *Henan, China* 56 G7
Sishui, *Shandong, China* 57 G9
Sisipuk L., *Canada* 105 B8
Sisophon, *Cambodia* 64 F4
Sisseton, *U.S.A.* 112 C6
Sissonne, *France* 19 C10
Sīstān, *Asia* 71 D9
Sīstān, Daryācheh-ye, *Iran* 71 D9
Sīstān va Balūchestān □, *Iran* 71 E9
Sisteron, *France* 21 D9
Sisters, *U.S.A.* 114 D3
Siswa Bazar, *India* 69 F10
Sitakili, *Mali* 82 C2
Sitamarhi, *India* 69 F11
Sitampiky, *Madag.* 89 B8
Sitapur, *India* 69 F9
Siteki, *Swaziland* 89 D5
Sitges, *Spain* 32 D6
Sithoniá, *Greece* 40 F7
Sitía, *Greece* 36 D8
Sitka, *U.S.A.* 104 B1
Sitoti, *Botswana* 88 C3
Sitra, *Egypt* 80 B2
Sittang Myit →, *Burma* 67 L20
Sittard, *Neths.* 17 C5
Sittensen, *Germany* 24 B5
Sittingbourne, *U.K.* 13 F8
Sittona, *Eritrea* 81 E4
Sittoung = Sittang Myit →, *Burma* 67 L20
Sittwe, *Burma* 67 J18
Situbondo, *Indonesia* 63 G16
Siuna, *Nic.* 120 D3
Siuri, *India* 69 H12
Siutghiol, Lacul, *Romania* 43 F13
Sīvand, *Iran* 71 D7
Sivas, *Turkey* 70 B3
Sivaslı, *Turkey* 39 C11
Siverek, *Turkey* 70 B3
Sivrihisar, *Turkey* 72 C4
Sîwa, *Egypt* 80 B2
Sîwa, El Wâhât es, *Egypt* 80 B2
Siwa Oasis = Sîwa, El Wâhât es, *Egypt* 80 B2
Siwalik Range, *Nepal* 69 F10
Siwan, *India* 69 F11
Siwana, *India* 68 G5
Sixmilebridge, *Ireland* 15 D3
Sixth Cataract, *Sudan* 81 D3
Siyâl, Jazâ'ir, *Egypt* 80 C4
Siyäzän, *Azerbaijan* 49 K9
Siziwang Qi, *China* 56 D6
Sjælland, *Denmark* 11 J5
Sjællands Odde, *Denmark* 11 J5
Sjenica, *Serbia, Yug.* 40 C3
Sjöbo, *Sweden* 11 J7
Sjötofta, *Sweden* 11 G7
Sjötorp, *Sweden* 11 F8
Sjumen = Shumen, *Bulgaria* 41 C10
Sjuntorp, *Sweden* 11 F6
Skadarsko Jezero, *Montenegro, Yug.* 40 D3
Skadovsk, *Ukraine* 47 J7
Skælskør, *Denmark* 11 J5
Skærbæk, *Denmark* 11 J2
Skaftafell, *Iceland* 8 D5
Skagafjörður, *Iceland* 8 D4
Skagastølstindane, *Norway* 9 F12
Skagaströnd, *Iceland* 8 D3
Skagen, *Denmark* 11 G4
Skagern, *Sweden* 10 F8
Skagerrak, *Denmark* 11 G2
Skagit →, *U.S.A.* 116 B4
Skagway, *U.S.A.* 100 C6
Skala-Podilska, *Ukraine* 47 H4
Skala Podolskaya = Skala-Podilska, *Ukraine* 47 H4
Skalat, *Ukraine* 47 H3
Skalbmierz, *Poland* 45 H7
Skälderviken, *Sweden* 11 H6
Skalica, *Slovak Rep.* 27 C10
Skallingen, *Denmark* 11 J2
Skalni Dol = Kamenyak, *Bulgaria* 41 C10
Skanderborg, *Denmark* 11 H3
Skåne, *Sweden* 11 J7
Skåne län □, *Sweden* 11 H7
Skaneateles, *U.S.A.* 111 D8
Skaneateles L., *U.S.A.* 111 D8
Skänninge, *Sweden* 11 F9
Skanör med Falsterbo, *Sweden* 11 J6
Skantzoúra, *Greece* 38 B6
Skara, *Sweden* 11 F7
Skärblacka, *Sweden* 11 F9
Skardu, *Pakistan* 69 B6
Skåre, *Sweden* 10 E7
Skärhamn, *Sweden* 11 G5
Skarszewy, *Poland* 44 D5
Skaryszew, *Poland* 45 G8
Skarżysko-Kamienna, *Poland* 45 G7
Skattkärr, *Sweden* 10 E7
Skattungbyn, *Sweden* 10 C8
Skawina, *Poland* 45 J6
Skebobruk, *Sweden* 10 E12
Skeena →, *Canada* 104 C2
Skeena Mts., *Canada* 104 B3
Skegness, *U.K.* 12 D8
Skeldon, *Guyana* 124 B7
Skeleton Coast Park, *Namibia* 88 C1
Skellefte älv →, *Sweden* 8 D19
Skellefteå, *Sweden* 8 D19
Skelleftehamn, *Sweden* 8 D19
Skender Vakuf, *Bos.-H.* 42 F2
Skerries, The, *U.K.* 12 D3
Skhíza, *Greece* 38 E3
Skhoinoúsa, *Greece* 39 E7
Ski, *Norway* 9 G14
Skíathos, *Greece* 38 B5
Skibbereen, *Ireland* 15 E2
Skiddaw, *U.K.* 12 C4
Skidegate, *Canada* 104 C2
Skídhra, *Greece* 40 F6
Skien, *Norway* 9 G13
Skierniewice, *Poland* 45 G7
Skikda, *Algeria* 78 A7
Skillingaryd, *Sweden* 11 G8
Skillinge, *Sweden* 11 J8
Skilloura, *Cyprus* 36 D12
Skinári, Ákra, *Greece* 38 D2
Skinnskatteberg, *Sweden* 10 E9
Skipton, *U.K.* 12 D5
Skirmish Pt., *Australia* 94 A1
Skiropoúla, *Greece* 38 C6
Skíros, *Greece* 38 C6
Skivarp, *Sweden* 11 J7
Skive, *Denmark* 11 H3
Skjálfandafljót →, *Iceland* 8 D5
Skjálfandi, *Iceland* 8 C5
Skjern, *Denmark* 11 J2
Skoczów, *Poland* 45 J5
Škofja Loka, *Slovenia* 29 B11
Skoghall, *Sweden* 10 E7
Skogstorp, *Sweden* 10 E10
Skoki, *Poland* 45 F4
Skole, *Ukraine* 47 H2
Skópelos, *Greece* 38 B5
Skopí, *Greece* 36 D8
Skopin, *Russia* 46 F10
Skopje, *Macedonia* 40 D5
Skórcz, *Poland* 44 E5
Skørping, *Denmark* 11 H3
Skövde, *Sweden* 11 F7
Skovorodino, *Russia* 51 D13
Skowhegan, *U.S.A.* 109 C11
Skradin, *Croatia* 29 E12
Skrea, *Sweden* 11 H6
Skrunda, *Latvia* 44 B9
Skrwa →, *Poland* 45 F6
Skull, *Ireland* 15 E2
Skultorp, *Sweden* 11 F7
Skultuna, *Sweden* 10 E10
Skunk →, *U.S.A.* 112 E9
Skuodas, *Lithuania* 9 H19
Skurup, *Sweden* 11 J7
Skutskär, *Sweden* 10 D11
Skvyra, *Ukraine* 47 H5
Skwierzyna, *Poland* 45 F2
Skye, *U.K.* 14 D2
Skykomish, *U.S.A.* 114 C3
Skyros = Skíros, *Greece* 38 C6
Skyttorp, *Sweden* 10 D11
Slættaratindur, *Færoe Is.* 8 E9
Slagelse, *Denmark* 11 J5
Slamet, *Indonesia* 63 G13
Slaney →, *Ireland* 15 D5
Slangberge, *S. Africa* 88 E3
Slănic, *Romania* 43 E10
Slano, *Croatia* 40 D1
Slantsy, *Russia* 46 C5
Slaný, *Czech Rep.* 26 A7
Śląskie □, *Poland* 45 H6
Slätbaken, *Sweden* 11 F10
Slate Is., *Canada* 102 C2
Slatina, *Croatia* 42 E2
Slatina, *Romania* 43 F9
Slatina Timiş, *Romania* 42 E7
Slatington, *U.S.A.* 111 F9
Slaton, *U.S.A.* 113 J4
Slave →, *Canada* 104 A6
Slave Coast, *W. Afr.* 83 D5
Slave Lake, *Canada* 104 B6
Slave Pt., *Canada* 104 A5
Slavgorod, *Russia* 50 D8
Slavinja, *Serbia, Yug.* 40 C6
Slavkov u Brna, *Czech Rep.* 27 B9
Slavonija, *Europe* 42 E2
Slavonski Brod, *Croatia* 42 E3
Slavuta, *Ukraine* 47 G4
Slavyanka, *Russia* 54 C5
Slavyanovo, *Bulgaria* 41 C8
Slavyansk = Slovyansk, *Ukraine* 47 H9
Slavyansk-na-Kubani, *Russia* 47 K10
Sława, *Poland* 45 G3
Slawharad, *Belarus* 46 F6
Sławno, *Poland* 44 D3
Sławoborze, *Poland* 44 E2
Sleaford, *U.K.* 12 D7
Sleaford B., *Australia* 95 E2
Sleat, Sd. of, *U.K.* 14 D3
Sleeper Is., *Canada* 101 C11
Sleepy Eye, *U.S.A.* 112 C7
Slemon L., *Canada* 104 A5
Ślesin, *Poland* 45 F5
Slide Mt., *U.S.A.* 111 E10
Slidell, *U.S.A.* 113 K10
Sliema, *Malta* 36 D2
Slieve Aughty, *Ireland* 15 C3
Slieve Bloom, *Ireland* 15 C4
Slieve Donard, *U.K.* 15 B6
Slieve Gamph, *Ireland* 15 B3
Slieve Gullion, *U.K.* 15 B5
Slieve Mish, *Ireland* 15 D2
Slievenamon, *Ireland* 15 D4
Sligeach = Sligo, *Ireland* 15 B3
Sligo, *Ireland* 15 B3
Sligo, *U.S.A.* 110 E5
Sligo □, *Ireland* 15 B3
Sligo B., *Ireland* 15 B3
Slippery Rock, *U.S.A.* 110 E4
Slite, *Sweden* 11 G12
Sliven, *Bulgaria* 41 D10
Slivnitsa, *Bulgaria* 40 D7
Sljeme, *Croatia* 29 C12
Sloan, *U.S.A.* 117 K11
Sloansville, *U.S.A.* 111 D10
Slobozia, *Moldova* 43 D14
Slobozia, *Argeş, Romania* 43 F10
Slobozia, *Ialomiţa, Romania* 43 F12
Slocan, *Canada* 104 D5
Słomniki, *Poland* 45 H7
Slonim, *Belarus* 47 F3
Slough, *U.K.* 13 F7
Slough □, *U.K.* 13 F7
Sloughhouse, *U.S.A.* 116 G5
Slovak Rep. ■, *Europe* 27 C13
Slovakia = Slovak Rep. ■, *Europe* 27 C13
Slovakian Ore Mts. = Slovenské Rudohorie, *Slovak Rep.* 27 C12
Slovenia ■, *Europe* 29 C11
Slovenija = Slovenia ■, *Europe* 29 C11
Slovenj Gradec, *Slovenia* 29 B12
Slovenska Bistrica, *Slovenia* 29 B12
Slovenske Konjice, *Slovenia* 29 B12
Slovenské Rudohorie, *Slovak Rep.* 27 C12
Slovyansk, *Ukraine* 47 H9
Słubice, *Poland* 45 F1
Sluch →, *Ukraine* 47 G4
Sluis, *Neths.* 17 C3
Slŭnchev Bryag, *Bulgaria* 41 D11
Slunj, *Croatia* 29 C12
Słupca, *Poland* 45 F4
Słupia →, *Poland* 44 D3
Słupsk, *Poland* 44 D4
Slurry, *S. Africa* 88 D4
Slutsk, *Belarus* 47 F4
Slyne Hd., *Ireland* 15 C1
Slyudyanka, *Russia* 51 D11
Småland, *Sweden* 11 G9
Smålandsfarvandet, *Denmark* 11 J5
Smålandsstenar, *Sweden* 11 G7
Smalltree L., *Canada* 105 A8
Smallwood Res., *Canada* 103 B7
Smarhon, *Belarus* 46 E4
Smarje, *Slovenia* 29 B12
Smartt Syndicate Dam, *S. Africa* 88 E3
Smartville, *U.S.A.* 116 F5
Smeaton, *Canada* 105 C8
Smedby, *Sweden* 11 H10
Smederevo, *Serbia, Yug.* 40 B4
Smederevska Palanka, *Serbia, Yug.* 40 B4
Smedjebacken, *Sweden* 10 D9
Smela = Smila, *Ukraine* 47 H6
Smerwick Harbour, *Ireland* 15 D1
Smethport, *U.S.A.* 110 E6
Smidovich, *Russia* 51 E14
Śmigiel, *Poland* 45 F3
Smila, *Ukraine* 47 H6
Smilyan, *Bulgaria* 41 E8
Smith, *Canada* 104 B6
Smith Center, *U.S.A.* 112 F5
Smith Sund, *Greenland* 4 B4
Smithburne →, *Australia* 94 B3
Smithers, *Canada* 104 C3
Smithfield, *S. Africa* 89 E4
Smithfield, *N.C., U.S.A.* 109 H6
Smithfield, *Utah, U.S.A.* 114 F8
Smiths Falls, *Canada* 102 D4
Smithton, *Australia* 94 G4
Smithville, *Canada* 110 C5
Smithville, *U.S.A.* 113 K6
Smoky →, *Canada* 104 B5
Smoky Bay, *Australia* 95 E1
Smoky Hill →, *U.S.A.* 112 F6
Smoky Hills, *U.S.A.* 112 F5
Smoky Lake, *Canada* 104 C6
Smøla, *Norway* 8 E13
Smolensk, *Russia* 46 E7
Smolikas, Óros, *Greece* 40 F4
Smolník, *Slovak Rep.* 27 C13
Smolyan, *Bulgaria* 41 E8
Smooth Rock Falls, *Canada* 102 C3
Smoothstone L., *Canada* 105 C7
Smorgon = Smarhon, *Belarus* 46 E4
Smulţi, *Romania* 43 E12
Smyadovo, *Bulgaria* 41 C11
Smygehamn, *Sweden* 11 J7
Smyrna = İzmir, *Turkey* 39 C9
Smyrna, *U.S.A.* 108 F8
Snæfell, *Iceland* 8 D6
Snaefell, *U.K.* 12 C3
Snæfellsjökull, *Iceland* 8 D2
Snake →, *U.S.A.* 114 C4
Snake Range, *U.S.A.* 114 G6
Snake River Plain, *U.S.A.* 114 E7
Snasahögarna, *Sweden* 10 A6
Snåsavatnet, *Norway* 8 D14
Snedsted, *Denmark* 11 H2
Sneek, *Neths.* 17 A5
Sneeuberge, *S. Africa* 88 E3
Snejbjerg, *Denmark* 11 H2
Snelling, *U.S.A.* 116 H6
Snezhnoye, *Ukraine* 47 J10
Snežnik, *Slovenia* 29 C11
Śniadowo, *Poland* 45 E8
Śniardwy, Jezioro, *Poland* 44 E8
Śnieżka, *Europe* 26 A8
Snigirevka = Snihurivka, *Ukraine* 47 J7
Snihurivka, *Ukraine* 47 J7
Snina, *Slovak Rep.* 27 C15
Snizort, L., *U.K.* 14 D2
Snøhetta, *Norway* 9 E13
Snohomish, *U.S.A.* 116 C4
Snoul, *Cambodia* 65 F6
Snow Hill, *U.S.A.* 108 F8
Snow Lake, *Canada* 105 C8
Snow Mt., *Calif., U.S.A.* 116 F4
Snow Mt., *Maine, U.S.A.* 111 A14
Snow Shoe, *U.S.A.* 110 E7
Snowbird L., *Canada* 105 A8
Snowdon, *U.K.* 12 D3
Snowdrift →, *Canada* 105 A6
Snowflake, *U.S.A.* 115 J8
Snowshoe Pk., *U.S.A.* 114 B6
Snowville, *U.S.A.* 114 F7
Snowy Mt., *U.S.A.* 111 C10
Snug Corner, *Bahamas* 121 B5
Snyatyn, *Ukraine* 47 H3
Snyder, *Okla., U.S.A.* 113 H5
Snyder, *Tex., U.S.A.* 113 J4
Soahanina, *Madag.* 89 B7
Soalala, *Madag.* 89 B8
Soaloka, *Madag.* 89 B8
Soamanonga, *Madag.* 89 C7
Soan →, *Pakistan* 68 C4
Soanierana-Ivongo, *Madag.* 89 B8
Soanindraniny, *Madag.* 89 B8
Şoarş, *Romania* 43 E9
Soavina, *Madag.* 89 C8
Soavinandriana, *Madag.* 89 B8
Soba, *Nigeria* 83 C6
Sobat, Nahr →, *Sudan* 81 F3
Soběslav, *Czech Rep.* 26 B7
Sobhapur, *India* 68 H8
Sobinka, *Russia* 46 E11
Sobótka, *Poland* 45 H3
Sobra, *Croatia* 29 F14
Sobradinho, Represa de, *Brazil* 125 E10
Sobral, *Brazil* 125 D10
Sobrance, *Slovak Rep.* 27 C15
Sobreira Formosa, *Portugal* 34 F3
Soc Giang, *Vietnam* 58 F6
Soc Trang, *Vietnam* 65 H5
Soča →, *Europe* 26 E6
Socastee, *U.S.A.* 109 J6
Sochaczew, *Poland* 45 F7
Soch'e = Shache, *China* 60 C2
Sochi, *Russia* 49 J4
Société, Is. de la, *Pac. Oc.* 97 J12
Society Is. = Société, Is. de la, *Pac. Oc.* 97 J12
Socompa, Portezuelo de, *Chile* 126 A2
Socorro, *N. Mex., U.S.A.* 115 J10
Socorro, *Tex., U.S.A.* 115 L10
Socorro, I., *Mexico* 118 D2
Socotra, *Yemen* 74 E5
Socovos, *Spain* 33 G3
Socuéllamos, *Spain* 33 F2
Soda L., *U.S.A.* 115 J5
Soda Plains, *India* 69 B8
Soda Springs, *U.S.A.* 114 E8
Sodankylä, *Finland* 8 C22
Soddy-Daisy, *U.S.A.* 109 H3
Söderala, *Sweden* 10 C10
Söderbärke, *Sweden* 10 D9
Söderfors, *Sweden* 10 D11
Söderhamn, *Sweden* 10 C11
Söderköping, *Sweden* 11 F10
Södermanland, *Sweden* 9 G17
Södermanlands län □, *Sweden* 10 E10
Södertälje, *Sweden* 10 E11
Sodiri, *Sudan* 81 E2
Sodo, *Ethiopia* 81 F4
Södra Dellen, *Sweden* 10 C10
Södra Finnskoga, *Sweden* 10 D6
Södra Sandby, *Sweden* 11 J7
Södra Ulvön, *Sweden* 10 B12
Södra Vi, *Sweden* 11 G9
Sodražica, *Slovenia* 29 C11
Sodus, *U.S.A.* 110 C7
Soekmekaar, *S. Africa* 89 C4
Soest, *Germany* 24 D4
Soest, *Neths.* 17 B5
Sofádhes, *Greece* 38 B4
Sofala □, *Mozam.* 89 B5
Sofara, *Mali* 82 C4
Sofia = Sofiya, *Bulgaria* 40 D7
Sofia →, *Madag.* 89 B8
Sofievka, *Ukraine* 47 H7
Sofikón, *Greece* 38 D5
Sofiya, *Bulgaria* 40 D7
Sofiya □, *Bulgaria* 40 D7
Sōfu-Gan, *Japan* 55 K10
Sogakofe, *Ghana* 83 D5
Sogamoso, *Colombia* 124 B4
Sogār, *Iran* 71 E8
Sögel, *Germany* 24 C3
Sogndalsfjøra, *Norway* 9 F12
Søgne, *Norway* 9 G12
Sognefjorden, *Norway* 9 F11
Söğüt, *Bilecik, Turkey* 39 A12
Söğüt, *Burdur, Turkey* 39 D11
Söğüt Dağı, *Turkey* 39 D11
Söğütköy, *Turkey* 39 E10
Sŏgwipo, *S. Korea* 57 H14
Soh, *Iran* 71 C6
Sohâg, *Egypt* 80 B3
Sohagpur, *India* 68 H8
Sŏhori, *N. Korea* 57 D15
Soignies, *Belgium* 17 D4
Soin, *Burkina Faso* 82 C4
Soira, *Eritrea* 81 E4
Soissons, *France* 19 C10
Sōja, *Japan* 55 G6
Sojat, *India* 68 G5
Sok →, *Russia* 48 D10
Sokal, *Ukraine* 47 G3
Söke, *Turkey* 39 D9
Sokelo, *Dem. Rep. of the Congo* 87 D1
Sokhós, *Greece* 40 F7
Sokhumi, *Georgia* 49 J5
Soko Banja, *Serbia, Yug.* 40 C5
Sokodé, *Togo* 83 D5
Sokol, *Russia* 46 C11
Sokolac, *Bos.-H.* 42 G3
Sokółka, *Poland* 44 E10
Sokolo, *Mali* 82 C3
Sokolo, *Mali* 82 C3
Sokolov, *Czech Rep.* 26 A5
Sokołów Małpolski, *Poland* 45 H9
Sokołów Podlaski, *Poland* 45 F9
Sokoły, *Poland* 45 F9
Sokoto, *Nigeria* 83 C6
Sokoto □, *Nigeria* 83 C6
Sokoto →, *Nigeria* 83 C5
Sol Iletsk, *Russia* 50 D6
Sola →, *Poland* 45 H6
Solai, *Kenya* 86 B4
Solan, *India* 68 D7
Solano, *Phil.* 61 C4
Solapur, *India* 66 L9
Solca, *Romania* 43 C10
Solda Gölü, *Turkey* 39 D11

Soldăneşti, *Moldova* 43 C13
Soldotna, *U.S.A.* 100 B4
Soléa □, *Cyprus* 36 D12
Solec Kujawski, *Poland* 45 E5
Soledad, *Colombia* 124 A4
Soledad, *U.S.A.* 116 J5
Soledad, *Venezuela* 124 B6
Solent, The, *U.K.* 13 G6
Solenzara, *France* 21 G13
Solesmes, *France* 19 B10
Solfonn, *Norway* 9 F12
Solhan, *Turkey* 70 B4
Soligorsk = Salihorsk, *Belarus* 47 F4
Solihull, *U.K.* 13 E6
Solikamsk, *Russia* 50 D6
Solila, *Madag.* 89 C8
Solimões = Amazonas →, *S. Amer.* 122 D5
Solin, *Croatia* 29 E13
Solingen, *Germany* 24 D3
Sollebrunn, *Sweden* 11 F6
Sollefteå, *Sweden* 10 A11
Sollentuna, *Sweden* 10 E11
Sóller, *Spain* 37 B9
Sollerön, *Sweden* 10 D8
Solling, *Germany* 24 D5
Solnechnogorsk, *Russia* 46 D9
Solo →, *Indonesia* 63 G15
Solofra, *Italy* 31 B7
Sologne, *France* 19 E8
Solok, *Indonesia* 62 E2
Sololá, *Guatemala* 120 D1
Solomon, N. Fork →, *U.S.A.* 112 F5
Solomon, S. Fork →, *U.S.A.* 112 F5
Solomon Is. ■, *Pac. Oc.* 96 H7
Solon, *China* 60 B7
Solon Springs, *U.S.A.* 112 B9
Solor, *Indonesia* 63 F6
Solotcha, *Russia* 46 E10
Solothurn, *Switz.* 25 H3
Solothurn □, *Switz.* 25 H3
Solsona, *Spain* 32 C6
Solt, *Hungary* 42 D4
Šolta, *Croatia* 29 E13
Solṭānābād, *Khorāsān, Iran* 71 C8
Solṭānābād, *Khorāsān, Iran* 71 B8
Soltau, *Germany* 24 C5
Soltsy, *Russia* 46 C6
Solunska Glava, *Macedonia* 40 E5
Solvang, *U.S.A.* 117 L6
Solvay, *U.S.A.* 111 C8
Sölvesborg, *Sweden* 11 H8
Solway Firth, *U.K.* 12 C4
Solwezi, *Zambia* 87 E2
Sōma, *Japan* 54 F10
Soma, *Turkey* 39 B9
Somabhula, *Zimbabwe* 89 B4
Somali Pen., *Africa* 76 F8
Somali Rep. ■, *Africa* 74 F4
Somalia = Somali Rep. ■, *Africa* 74 F4
Sombernon, *France* 19 E11
Sombor, *Serbia, Yug.* 42 E4
Sombra, *Canada* 110 D2
Sombrerete, *Mexico* 118 C4
Sombrero, *Anguilla* 121 C7
Şomcuta Mare, *Romania* 43 C8
Somdari, *India* 68 G5
Somers, *U.S.A.* 114 B6
Somerset, *Ky., U.S.A.* 108 G3
Somerset, *Mass., U.S.A.* 111 E13
Somerset, *Pa., U.S.A.* 110 F5
Somerset □, *U.K.* 13 F5
Somerset East, *S. Africa* 88 E4
Somerset I., *Canada* 100 A10
Somerset West, *S. Africa* 88 E2
Somersworth, *U.S.A.* 111 C14
Somerton, *U.S.A.* 115 K6
Somerville, *U.S.A.* 111 F10
Someş →, *Romania* 42 C7
Someşul Mare →, *Romania* 43 C8
Somme □, *France* 19 C9
Somme →, *France* 19 B8
Somme, B. de la, *France* 18 B8
Sommen, *Jönköping, Sweden* 11 F8
Sommen, *Östergötland, Sweden* 11 F9
Sommepy-Tahure, *France* 19 C11
Sömmerda, *Germany* 24 D7
Sommesous, *France* 19 D11
Sommières, *France* 21 E8
Somnath, *India* 68 J4
Somogy □, *Hungary* 42 D2
Somogyszob, *Hungary* 42 D2
Somoto, *Nic.* 120 D2
Sompolno, *Poland* 45 F5
Somport, Puerto de, *Spain* 32 C4
Son →, *India* 69 G11
Son Ha, *Vietnam* 64 E7
Son Hoa, *Vietnam* 64 F7
Son La, *Vietnam* 58 G4
Son Serra, *Spain* 37 B10
Son Servera, *Spain* 32 F8
Son Tay, *Vietnam* 58 G5
Soná, *Panama* 120 E3
Sonamarg, *India* 69 B6
Sonamukhi, *India* 69 H12
Sonar →, *India* 69 G8
Sŏnch'ŏn, *N. Korea* 57 E13
Sondags →, *S. Africa* 88 E4
Sóndalo, *Italy* 28 B7
Sondar, *India* 69 C6
Sønder Felding, *Denmark* 11 J2
Sønder Omme, *Denmark* 11 J2
Sønderborg, *Denmark* 11 K3
Sønderjyllands Amtskommune □, *Denmark* 11 J3
Sondershausen, *Germany* 24 D6
Sóndrio, *Italy* 28 B6
Sone, *Mozam.* 87 F3
Sonepur, *India* 67 J13
Song, *Nigeria* 83 D7
Song, *Thailand* 64 C3
Song Cau, *Vietnam* 64 F7
Song Xian, *China* 56 G7
Songch'ŏn, *N. Korea* 57 E14
Songea, *Tanzania* 87 E4
Songeons, *France* 19 C8
Songhua Hu, *China* 57 C14
Songhua Jiang →, *China* 60 B8
Songjiang, *China* 59 B13
Songjin, *N. Korea* 57 D15
Songjŏng-ni, *S. Korea* 57 G14
Songkan, *China* 58 C6
Songkhla, *Thailand* 65 J3
Songming, *China* 58 E4
Songnim, *N. Korea* 57 E13
Songo, *Mozam.* 85 H6
Songo, *Sudan* 79 G10
Songpan, *China* 58 A4
Songtao, *China* 58 C7
Songwe, *Dem. Rep. of the Congo* 86 C2
Songwe →, *Africa* 87 D3
Songxi, *China* 59 D12
Songzi, *China* 59 B8
Sonhat, *India* 69 H10
Sonid Youqi, *China* 56 C7
Sonipat, *India* 68 E7
Sonkach, *India* 68 H7
Sonkovo, *Russia* 46 D9
Sonmiani, *Pakistan* 68 G2
Sonmiani B., *Pakistan* 68 G2
Sonnino, *Italy* 30 A6
Sono →, *Brazil* 125 E9
Sonoma, *U.S.A.* 116 G4
Sonora, *Calif., U.S.A.* 116 H6
Sonora, *Tex., U.S.A.* 113 K4
Sonora □, *Mexico* 118 B2
Sonora →, *Mexico* 118 B2
Sonoran Desert, *U.S.A.* 117 L12
Sonoyta, *Mexico* 118 A2
Sonqor, *Iran* 73 E12
Sŏnsan, *S. Korea* 57 F15
Sonseca, *Spain* 35 F7
Sonsonate, *El Salv.* 120 D2
Sonsorol Is., *Pac. Oc.* 63 C8
Sonstorp, *Sweden* 11 F9
Sonthofen, *Germany* 25 H6
Soochow = Suzhou, *China* 59 B13
Sooke, *Canada* 116 B3
Sop Hao, *Laos* 58 G5
Sop Prap, *Thailand* 64 D2
Sopelana, *Spain* 32 B2
Sopi, *Indonesia* 63 D7
Sopo, Nahr →, *Sudan* 81 F2
Sopot, *Bulgaria* 41 D8
Sopot, *Poland* 44 D5
Sopot, *Serbia, Yug.* 40 B4
Sopotnica, *Macedonia* 40 E5
Sopron, *Hungary* 42 C1
Sopur, *India* 69 B6
Sør-Rondane, *Antarctica* 5 D4
Sora, *Italy* 29 G10
Sorah, *Pakistan* 68 F3
Söråker, *Sweden* 10 B11
Sorano, *Italy* 29 F8
Soraon, *India* 69 G9
Sorbas, *Spain* 33 H2
Sörbygden, *Sweden* 10 B10
Sore, *France* 20 D3
Sorel, *Canada* 102 C5
Soresina, *Italy* 28 C6
Sörforsa, *Sweden* 10 C10
Sórgono, *Italy* 30 B2
Sorgues, *France* 21 D8
Sorgun, *Turkey* 72 C6
Soria, *Spain* 32 D2
Soria □, *Spain* 32 D2
Soriano, *Uruguay* 126 C4
Soriano nel Cimino, *Italy* 29 F9
Sorkh, Kuh-e, *Iran* 71 C8
Sorø, *Denmark* 11 J5
Soro, *Guinea* 82 C3
Soroca, *Moldova* 43 B13
Sorocaba, *Brazil* 127 A6
Soroki = Soroca, *Moldova* 43 B13
Sorol Atoll, *Pac. Oc.* 63 C10
Sorong, *Indonesia* 63 E8
Soroní, *Greece* 36 C10
Soroti, *Uganda* 86 B3
Sørøya, *Norway* 8 A20
Sørøysundet, *Norway* 8 A20
Sorraia →, *Portugal* 35 G2
Sorrell, *Australia* 94 G4
Sorrento, *Italy* 31 B7
Sorsele, *Sweden* 8 D17
Sörsjön, *Sweden* 10 C7
Sorso, *Italy* 30 B1
Sorsogon, *Phil.* 61 E6
Sortavala, *Russia* 46 B6
Sortino, *Italy* 31 E8
Sortland, *Norway* 8 B16
Sorvizhi, *Russia* 48 B9
Sos = Sos del Rey Católico, *Spain* 32 C3
Sos del Rey Católico, *Spain* 32 C3
Sŏsan, *S. Korea* 57 F14
Soscumica, L., *Canada* 102 B4
Sösdala, *Sweden* 11 H7
Sosna →, *Russia* 47 F10
Sosnovka, *Kirov, Russia* 48 B10
Sosnovka, *Tambov, Russia* 48 D5
Sosnovyy Bor, *Russia* 46 C5
Sosnowiec, *Poland* 45 H6
Sospel, *France* 21 E11
Sossus Vlei, *Namibia* 88 C2
Šoštanj, *Slovenia* 29 B12
Sŏsura, *N. Korea* 57 C16
Sot →, *India* 69 F8
Sotkamo, *Finland* 8 D23
Soto del Barco, *Spain* 34 B4
Soto la Marina →, *Mexico* 119 C5
Soto y Amío, *Spain* 34 C5
Sotrondio, *Spain* 34 B5
Sotuta, *Mexico* 119 C7
Souanké, *Congo* 84 D2
Soubré, *Ivory C.* 82 D3
Souderton, *U.S.A.* 111 F9
Soúdha, *Greece* 36 D6
Soúdhas, Kólpos, *Greece* 36 D6
Souflíon, *Greece* 41 E10
Soufrière, *St. Lucia* 121 D7
Souillac, *France* 20 D5
Souilly, *France* 19 C12
Soukhouma, *Laos* 64 E5
Sŏul, *S. Korea* 57 F14
Soulac-sur-Mer, *France* 20 C2
Soulougou, *Burkina Faso* 83 C5
Soultz-sous-Forêts, *France* 19 D14
Sound, The = Øresund, *Europe* 11 J6
Sound, The, *U.K.* 13 G3
Soúnion, Ákra, *Greece* 38 D6
Sources, Mt. aux, *Lesotho* 89 D4
Soure, *Brazil* 125 D9
Soure, *Portugal* 34 E2
Souris, *Man., Canada* 105 D8
Souris, *P.E.I., Canada* 103 C7
Souris →, *Canada* 112 A5
Sourou →, *Africa* 82 C4
Soúrpi, *Greece* 38 B4
Sousa, *Brazil* 125 E11
Sousel, *Portugal* 35 G3
Sousse, *Tunisia* 79 A8
Soustons, *France* 20 E2
Sout →, *S. Africa* 88 E2
South Africa ■, *Africa* 88 E3
South America 122 E5
South Atlantic Ocean 122 H7
South Aulatsivik I., *Canada* 103 A7
South Ayrshire □, *U.K.* 14 F4
South Baldy, *U.S.A.* 115 J10
South Bass I., *U.S.A.* 110 E2
South Bend, *Ind., U.S.A.* 108 E2
South Bend, *Wash., U.S.A.* 116 D3
South Boston, *U.S.A.* 109 G6
South Branch, *Canada* 103 C8
South Brook, *Canada* 103 C8
South Carolina □, *U.S.A.* 109 J5
South Charleston, *U.S.A.* 108 F5
South China Sea, *Asia* 62 C4
South Dakota □, *U.S.A.* 112 C5
South Deerfield, *U.S.A.* 111 D12
South Downs, *U.K.* 13 G7
South East C., *Australia* 94 G4
South East Is., *Australia* 93 F3
South Esk →, *U.K.* 14 E6
South Foreland, *U.K.* 13 F9
South Fork American →, *U.S.A.* 116 G5
South Fork Feather →, *U.S.A.* 116 F5
South Fork Grand →, *U.S.A.* 112 C3
South Fork Republican →, *U.S.A.* 112 E4
South Georgia, *Antarctica* 122 J7
South Gloucestershire □, *U.K.* 13 F5
South Hadley, *U.S.A.* 111 D12
South Haven, *U.S.A.* 108 D2
South Henik, L., *Canada* 105 A9
South Honshu Ridge, *Pac. Oc.* 96 E6
South Horr, *Kenya* 86 B4
South I., *Kenya* 86 B4
South I., *N.Z.* 91 L3
South Indian Lake, *Canada* 105 B9
South Invercargill, *N.Z.* 91 M2
South Knife →, *Canada* 105 B10
South Koel →, *India* 69 H11
South Korea ■, *Asia* 57 G15
South Lake Tahoe, *U.S.A.* 116 G6
South Lanarkshire □, *U.K.* 14 F5
South Loup →, *U.S.A.* 112 E5
South Magnetic Pole, *Antarctica* 5 C9
South Milwaukee, *U.S.A.* 108 D2
South Molton, *U.K.* 13 F4
South Moose L., *Canada* 105 C8
South Nahanni →, *Canada* 104 A4
South Nation →, *Canada* 111 A9
South Natuna Is. = Natuna Selatan, Kepulauan, *Indonesia* 65 L7
South Negril Pt., *Jamaica* 120 C4
South Orkney Is., *Antarctica* 5 C18
South Ossetia □, *Georgia* 49 J7
South Pagai, I. = Pagai Selatan, Pulau, *Indonesia* 62 E2
South Paris, *U.S.A.* 111 B14
South Pittsburg, *U.S.A.* 109 H3
South Platte →, *U.S.A.* 112 E4
South Pole, *Antarctica* 5 E
South Porcupine, *Canada* 102 C3
South Portland, *U.S.A.* 109 D10
South Pt., *U.S.A.* 110 B1
South River, *Canada* 102 C4
South River, *U.S.A.* 111 F10
South Ronaldsay, *U.K.* 14 C6
South Sandwich Is., *Antarctica* 5 B1
South Saskatchewan →, *Canada* 105 C7
South Seal →, *Canada* 105 B9
South Shetland Is., *Antarctica* 5 C18
South Shields, *U.K.* 12 C6
South Sioux City, *U.S.A.* 112 D6
South Taranaki Bight, *N.Z.* 91 H5
South Thompson →, *Canada* 104 C4
South Twin I., *Canada* 102 B4
South Tyne →, *U.K.* 12 C5
South Uist, *U.K.* 14 D1
South West Africa = Namibia ■, *Africa* 88 C2
South West C., *Australia* 94 G4
South Williamsport, *U.S.A.* 110 E8
South Yorkshire □, *U.K.* 12 D6
Southampton, *Canada* 102 D3
Southampton, *U.K.* 13 G6
Southampton, *U.S.A.* 111 F12
Southampton □, *U.K.* 13 G6
Southampton I., *Canada* 101 B11
Southaven, *U.S.A.* 113 H9
Southbank, *Canada* 104 C3
Southbridge, *N.Z.* 91 K4
Southbridge, *U.S.A.* 111 D12
Southend, *Canada* 105 B8
Southend-on-Sea, *U.K.* 13 F8
Southend-on-Sea □, *U.K.* 13 F8
Southern □, *Malawi* 87 F4
Southern □, *S. Leone* 82 D2
Southern □, *Zambia* 87 F2
Southern Alps, *N.Z.* 91 K3
Southern Cross, *Australia* 93 F2
Southern Indian L., *Canada* 105 B9
Southern Ocean, *Antarctica* 5 C6
Southern Pines, *U.S.A.* 109 H6
Southern Uplands, *U.K.* 14 F5
Southington, *U.S.A.* 111 E12
Southland □, *N.Z.* 91 L1
Southold, *U.S.A.* 111 E12
Southport, *Australia* 95 D5
Southport, *U.K.* 12 D4
Southport, *Fla., U.S.A.* 109 K3
Southport, *N.Y., U.S.A.* 110 D8
Southwest C., *N.Z.* 91 M1
Southwold, *U.K.* 13 E9
Soutpansberg, *S. Africa* 89 C4
Souvigny, *France* 19 F10
Sovata, *Romania* 43 D10
Soverato, *Italy* 31 D9
Sovetsk, *Kaliningd., Russia* 9 J19
Sovetsk, *Kirov, Russia* 48 B9
Sovetskaya Gavan = Vanino, *Russia* 51 E15
Sovicille, *Italy* 29 E8
Soweto, *S. Africa* 89 D4
Sōya-Kaikyō = La Perouse Str., *Asia* 54 B11
Sōya-Misaki, *Japan* 54 B10
Soyaux, *France* 20 C4
Sozh →, *Belarus* 47 F6
Sozopol, *Bulgaria* 41 D11
Spa, *Belgium* 17 D5
Spain ■, *Europe* 7 H5
Spalding, *U.K.* 12 E7
Spangler, *U.S.A.* 110 F6
Spanish, *Canada* 102 C3
Spanish Fork, *U.S.A.* 114 F8
Spanish Town, *Jamaica* 120 C4
Sparks, *U.S.A.* 116 F7
Sparreholm, *Sweden* 10 E10
Sparta = Spárti, *Greece* 38 D4
Sparta, *Mich., U.S.A.* 108 D3
Sparta, *N.J., U.S.A.* 111 E10
Sparta, *Wis., U.S.A.* 112 D9
Spartanburg, *U.S.A.* 109 H5
Spartansburg, *U.S.A.* 110 E5
Spárti, *Greece* 38 D4
Spartivento, C., *Calabria, Italy* 31 E9
Spartivento, C., *Sard., Italy* 30 D1
Sparwood, *Canada* 104 D6
Spas-Demensk, *Russia* 46 E7
Spas-Klepiki, *Russia* 46 E11
Spassk Dalniy, *Russia* 51 E14
Spassk-Ryazanskiy, *Russia* 46 E11
Spátha, Ákra, *Greece* 36 D5
Spatsizi →, *Canada* 104 B3
Spatsizi Plateau Wilderness Park, *Canada* 104 B3
Spean →, *U.K.* 14 E4
Spearfish, *U.S.A.* 112 C3
Spearman, *U.S.A.* 113 G4
Speculator, *U.S.A.* 111 C10
Speia, *Moldova* 43 D14
Speightstown, *Barbados* 121 D8
Speke Gulf, *Tanzania* 86 C3
Spello, *Italy* 29 F9
Spencer, *Idaho, U.S.A.* 114 D7
Spencer, *Iowa, U.S.A.* 112 D7
Spencer, *N.Y., U.S.A.* 111 D8
Spencer, *Nebr., U.S.A.* 112 D5
Spencer B., *Namibia* 88 D1
Spencerville, *Canada* 111 B9
Spences Bridge, *Canada* 104 C4
Spennymoor, *U.K.* 12 C6
Spenser Mts., *N.Z.* 91 K4
Spentrup, *Denmark* 11 H4
Sperkhiós →, *Greece* 38 C4
Sperrin Mts., *U.K.* 15 B5
Spessart, *Germany* 25 F5
Spétsai, *Greece* 38 D5
Spey →, *U.K.* 14 D5
Speyer, *Germany* 25 F4
Spezand, *Pakistan* 68 E2
Spezzano Albanese, *Italy* 31 C9
Spiekeroog, *Germany* 24 B3
Spiez, *Switz.* 25 J3
Spíli, *Greece* 36 D6
Spilimbergo, *Italy* 29 B9
Spīn Būldak, *Afghan.* 68 D2
Spinalónga, *Greece* 36 D7
Spinazzola, *Italy* 31 B9
Spineni, *Romania* 43 F9
Spirit Lake, *U.S.A.* 116 D4
Spirit River, *Canada* 104 B5
Spiritwood, *Canada* 105 C7
Spišská Nová Ves, *Slovak Rep.* 27 C13
Spišské Podhradie, *Slovak Rep.* 27 B13
Spital, *Austria* 26 D7
Spithead, *U.K.* 13 G6
Spittal an der Drau, *Austria* 26 E6
Spitzbergen = Svalbard, *Arctic* 4 B8
Spjelkavik, *Norway* 9 E12
Split, *Croatia* 29 E13
Split L., *Canada* 105 B9
Split Lake, *Canada* 105 B9
Splitski Kanal, *Croatia* 29 E13
Splügenpass, *Switz.* 25 J5
Spofford, *U.S.A.* 113 L4
Spokane, *U.S.A.* 114 C5
Spoleto, *Italy* 29 F9
Spooner, *U.S.A.* 112 C9
Sporyy Navolok, Mys, *Russia* 50 B7
Sprague, *U.S.A.* 114 C5
Spratly I., *S. China Sea* 62 C4
Spratly Is., *S. China Sea* 62 C4
Spray, *U.S.A.* 114 D4
Spreča →, *Bos.-H.* 42 F3
Spree →, *Germany* 24 C9
Spreewald, *Germany* 24 D9
Spremberg, *Germany* 24 D10
Sprengisandur, *Iceland* 8 D5
Spring City, *U.S.A.* 111 F9
Spring Creek, *U.S.A.* 114 F6
Spring Garden, *U.S.A.* 116 F6
Spring Hill, *U.S.A.* 109 L4
Spring Mts., *U.S.A.* 115 H6
Spring Valley, *U.S.A.* 117 N10
Springbok, *S. Africa* 88 D2
Springboro, *U.S.A.* 110 E4
Springdale, *Canada* 103 C8
Springdale, *U.S.A.* 113 G7
Springe, *Germany* 24 C5
Springer, *U.S.A.* 113 G2
Springerville, *U.S.A.* 115 J9
Springfield, *Canada* 110 D4
Springfield, *N.Z.* 91 K3
Springfield, *Colo., U.S.A.* 113 G3
Springfield, *Ill., U.S.A.* 112 F10
Springfield, *Mass., U.S.A.* 111 D12
Springfield, *Mo., U.S.A.* 113 G8
Springfield, *Ohio, U.S.A.* 108 F4
Springfield, *Oreg., U.S.A.* 114 D2
Springfield, *Tenn., U.S.A.* 109 G2
Springfield, *Vt., U.S.A.* 111 C12
Springfontein, *S. Africa* 88 E4
Springhill, *Canada* 103 C7
Springhill, *U.S.A.* 113 J8
Springhouse, *Canada* 104 C4
Springs, *S. Africa* 89 D4
Springsure, *Australia* 94 C4
Springvale, *U.S.A.* 111 C14
Springville, *Calif., U.S.A.* 116 J8
Springville, *N.Y., U.S.A.* 110 D6
Springville, *Utah, U.S.A.* 114 F8
Springwater, *U.S.A.* 110 D7
Spruce-Creek, *U.S.A.* 110 F6
Spruce Mt., *U.S.A.* 111 B12
Spur, *U.S.A.* 113 J4
Spurn Hd., *U.K.* 12 D8
Spuž, *Montenegro, Yug.* 40 D3
Spuzzum, *Canada* 104 D4
Squam L., *U.S.A.* 111 C13
Squamish, *Canada* 104 D4
Square Islands, *Canada* 103 B8
Squillace, G. di, *Italy* 31 D9
Squinzano, *Italy* 31 B11
Squires, Mt., *Australia* 93 E4
Srbac, *Bos.-H.* 42 E2
Srbica, *Kosovo, Yug.* 40 D4
Srbija = Serbia □, *Yugoslavia* 40 C5
Srbobran, *Serbia, Yug.* 42 E4
Sre Ambel, *Cambodia* 65 G4
Sre Khtum, *Cambodia* 65 F6
Sre Umbell = Sre Ambel, *Cambodia* 65 G4
Srebrenica, *Bos.-H.* 42 F4
Sredinny Ra. = Sredinnyy Khrebet, *Russia* 51 D16
Sredinnyy Khrebet, *Russia* 51 D16
Središče, *Slovenia* 29 B13
Sredna Gora, *Bulgaria* 41 D8
Srednekolymsk, *Russia* 51 C16
Sredni Rodopi, *Bulgaria* 41 E8
Srednogorie, *Bulgaria* 41 D8
Śrem, *Poland* 45 F4
Sremska Mitrovica, *Serbia, Yug.* 42 F4
Sremski Karlovci, *Serbia, Yug.* 42 E4
Srepok →, *Cambodia* 64 F6
Sretensk, *Russia* 51 D12
Sri Lanka ■, *Asia* 66 R12
Srikakulam, *India* 67 K13
Srinagar, *India* 69 B6
Środa Śląska, *Poland* 45 G3
Środa Wielkopolski, *Poland* 45 F4
Srpska Crnja, *Serbia, Yug.* 42 E5
Srpski Itebej, *Serbia, Yug.* 42 E5
Staaten →, *Australia* 94 B3
Staberhuk, *Germany* 24 A7
Stade, *Germany* 24 B5
Stadskanaal, *Neths.* 17 A6
Stadtallendorf, *Germany* 24 E5
Stadthagen, *Germany* 24 C5
Stadtlohn, *Germany* 24 D2
Stadtroda, *Germany* 24 E7
Staffa, *U.K.* 14 E2
Staffanstorp, *Sweden* 11 J7
Stafford, *U.K.* 12 E5
Stafford, *U.S.A.* 113 G5
Stafford Springs, *U.S.A.* 111 E12

Sulejówek, *Poland* 45 F8
Süleymanlı, *Turkey* 39 C9
Sulima, *S. Leone* 82 D2
Sulina, *Romania* 43 E14
Sulina, Braţul →, *Romania* 43 E14
Sulingen, *Germany* 24 C4
Suliţa, *Romania* 43 C11
Sulitjelma, *Norway* 8 C17
Sułkowice, *Poland* 45 J6
Sullana, *Peru* 124 D2
Süller, *Turkey* 39 C11
Sullivan, *Ill., U.S.A.* 112 F10
Sullivan, *Ind., U.S.A.* 108 F2
Sullivan, *Mo., U.S.A.* 112 F9
Sullivan Bay, *Canada* 104 C3
Sullivan I. = Lanbi Kyun, *Burma* 65 G2
Sully-sur-Loire, *France* 19 E9
Sulmierzyce, *Poland* 45 G4
Sulmona, *Italy* 29 F10
Süloğlu, *Turkey* 41 E10
Sulphur, *La., U.S.A.* 113 K8
Sulphur, *Okla., U.S.A.* 113 H6
Sulphur Pt., *Canada* 104 A6
Sulphur Springs, *U.S.A.* 113 J7
Sultan, *Canada* 102 C3
Sultan, *U.S.A.* 116 C5
Sultan Dağları, *Turkey* 72 C4
Sultanhisar, *Turkey* 39 D10
Sultaniça, *Turkey* 41 F10
Sultaniye, *Turkey* 41 F12
Sultanpur, *Mad. P., India* 68 H8
Sultanpur, *Punjab, India* 68 D6
Sultanpur, *Ut. P., India* 69 F10
Sulu Arch., *Phil.* 61 J4
Sulu Sea, *E. Indies* 61 G4
Sülüklü, *Turkey* 72 C5
Sululta, *Ethiopia* 81 F4
Suluova, *Turkey* 72 B6
Suluq, *Libya* 79 B10
Sulzbach, *Germany* 25 F3
Sulzbach-Rosenberg, *Germany* 25 F7
Sulzberger Ice Shelf, *Antarctica* 5 D10
Sumalata, *Indonesia* 63 D6
Sumampa, *Argentina* 126 B3
Sumatera □, *Indonesia* 62 D2
Sumatera Barat □, *Indonesia* 62 E2
Sumatera Utara □, *Indonesia* 62 D1
Sumatra = Sumatera □, *Indonesia* 62 D2
Sumba, *Indonesia* 63 F5
Sumba, Selat, *Indonesia* 63 F5
Sumbawa, *Indonesia* 62 F5
Sumbawa Besar, *Indonesia* 62 F5
Sumbawanga □, *Tanzania* 84 F6
Sumbe, *Angola* 84 G2
Sumburgh Hd., *U.K.* 14 B7
Sumdeo, *India* 69 D8
Sumdo, *India* 69 B8
Sumedang, *Indonesia* 63 G12
Sümeg, *Hungary* 42 D2
Sumeih, *Sudan* 81 F2
Šumen = Shumen, *Bulgaria* 41 C10
Sumenep, *Indonesia* 63 G15
Sumgait = Sumqayıt, *Azerbaijan* 49 K9
Summer L., *U.S.A.* 114 E3
Summerland, *Canada* 104 D5
Summerside, *Canada* 103 C7
Summersville, *U.S.A.* 108 F5
Summerville, *Ga., U.S.A.* 109 H3
Summerville, *S.C., U.S.A.* 109 J5
Summit Lake, *Canada* 104 C4
Summit Peak, *U.S.A.* 115 H10
Sumner, *Iowa, U.S.A.* 112 D8
Sumner, *Wash., U.S.A.* 116 C4
Sumoto, *Japan* 55 G7
Šumperk, *Czech Rep.* 27 B9
Sumqayıt, *Azerbaijan* 49 K9
Sumter, *U.S.A.* 109 J5
Sumy, *Ukraine* 47 G8
Sun City, *Ariz., U.S.A.* 115 K7
Sun City, *Calif., U.S.A.* 117 M9
Sun City Center, *U.S.A.* 109 M4
Sun Lakes, *U.S.A.* 115 K8
Sun Valley, *U.S.A.* 114 E6
Sunagawa, *Japan* 54 C10
Sunan, *N. Korea* 57 E13
Sunart, L., *U.K.* 14 E3
Sunburst, *U.S.A.* 114 B8
Sunbury, *U.S.A.* 111 F8
Sunchales, *Argentina* 126 C3
Suncho Corral, *Argentina* 126 B3
Sunch'ŏn, *S. Korea* 57 G14
Suncook, *U.S.A.* 111 C13
Sunda, Selat, *Indonesia* 62 F3
Sunda Is., *Indonesia* 52 K14
Sunda Str. = Sunda, Selat, *Indonesia* 62 F3
Sundance, *Canada* 105 B10
Sundance, *U.S.A.* 112 C2
Sundar Nagar, *India* 68 D7
Sundarbans, The, *Asia* 67 J16
Sundargarh, *India* 67 H14
Sundays = Sondags →, *S. Africa* 88 E4
Sunderland, *Canada* 110 B5
Sunderland, *U.K.* 12 C6
Sundre, *Canada* 104 C6
Sunds, *Denmark* 11 H3
Sundsvall, *Sweden* 10 B11
Sundsvallsbukten, *Sweden* 10 B11
Sung Hei, *Vietnam* 65 G6
Sungai Kolok, *Thailand* 65 J3
Sungai Lembing, *Malaysia* 65 L4
Sungai Petani, *Malaysia* 65 K3
Sungaigerong, *Indonesia* 62 E2
Sungailiat, *Indonesia* 62 E3
Sungaipenuh, *Indonesia* 62 E2
Sungari = Songhua Jiang →, *China* 60 B8
Sunghua Chiang = Songhua Jiang →, *China* 60 B8
Sungikai, *Sudan* 81 E2
Sungurlu, *Turkey* 72 B6
Sunja, *Croatia* 29 C13
Sunland Park, *U.S.A.* 115 L10
Sunnansjö, *Sweden* 10 D8
Sunndalsøra, *Norway* 9 E13
Sunne, *Sweden* 10 E7
Sunnemo, *Sweden* 10 E7
Sunnyside, *U.S.A.* 114 C3
Sunnyvale, *U.S.A.* 116 H4
Suntar, *Russia* 51 C12
Sunyani, *Ghana* 82 D4
Suomenselkä, *Finland* 8 E21
Suomussalmi, *Finland* 8 D23
Suoyarvi, *Russia* 46 A7
Supai, *U.S.A.* 115 H7
Supaul, *India* 69 F12
Superior, *Ariz., U.S.A.* 115 K8
Superior, *Mont., U.S.A.* 114 C6
Superior, *Nebr., U.S.A.* 112 E5
Superior, *Wis., U.S.A.* 112 B8
Superior, L., *N. Amer.* 102 C2
Supetar, *Croatia* 29 E13
Suphan Buri, *Thailand* 64 E3
Suphan Dağı, *Turkey* 70 B4
Supiori, *Indonesia* 63 E9
Supraśl, *Poland* 45 E10
Supraśl →, *Poland* 45 E9
Supung Shuiku, *China* 57 D13
Sūq Suwayq, *Si. Arabia* 70 E3
Suqian, *China* 57 H10
Sūr, *Lebanon* 75 B4
Şūr, *Oman* 74 C6
Sur, Pt., *U.S.A.* 116 J5
Sura →, *Russia* 48 C8
Surab, *Pakistan* 68 E2
Surabaja = Surabaya, *Indonesia* 62 F4
Surabaya, *Indonesia* 62 F4
Surahammar, *Sweden* 10 E10
Suraia, *Romania* 43 E12
Surakarta, *Indonesia* 62 F4
Surakhany, *Azerbaijan* 49 K10
Šurany, *Slovak Rep.* 27 C11
Surat, *Australia* 95 D4
Surat, *India* 66 J8
Surat Thani, *Thailand* 65 H2
Suratgarh, *India* 68 E5
Suraż, *Poland* 45 F9
Surazh, *Belarus* 46 E6
Surazh, *Russia* 47 F7
Surduc, *Romania* 43 C8
Surduc Pasul, *Romania* 43 E8
Surdulica, *Serbia, Yug.* 40 D6
Surendranagar, *India* 68 H4
Surf, *U.S.A.* 117 L6
Surgères, *France* 20 B3
Surgut, *Russia* 50 C8
Sùria, *Spain* 32 D6
Suriapet, *India* 66 L11
Surigao, *Phil.* 61 G6
Surigao Strait, *Phil.* 61 F6
Surin, *Thailand* 64 E4
Surin Nua, Ko, *Thailand* 65 H1
Surinam ■, *S. Amer.* 125 C7
Suriname = Surinam ■, *S. Amer.* 125 C7
Suriname →, *Surinam* 125 B7
Sūrmaq, *Iran* 71 D7
Sürmene, *Turkey* 73 B9
Surovikino, *Russia* 49 F6
Surrey □, *U.K.* 13 F7
Sursand, *India* 69 F11
Sursar →, *India* 69 F12
Sursee, *Switz.* 25 H4
Sursk, *Russia* 48 D7
Surskoye, *Russia* 48 C8
Surt, *Libya* 79 B9
Surt, Khalīj, *Libya* 79 B9
Surtanahu, *Pakistan* 68 F4
Surte, *Sweden* 11 G6
Surtsey, *Iceland* 8 E3
Sürüç, *Turkey* 73 D8
Suruga-Wan, *Japan* 55 G9
Susa, *Italy* 28 C4
Suså →, *Denmark* 11 J5
Sušac, *Croatia* 29 F13
Susak, *Croatia* 29 D11
Susaki, *Japan* 55 H6
Sūsangerd, *Iran* 71 D6
Susanville, *U.S.A.* 114 F3
Susch, *Switz.* 25 J6
Suşehri, *Turkey* 73 B8
Sušice, *Czech Rep.* 26 B6
Susleni, *Moldova* 43 C13
Susner, *India* 68 H7
Susong, *China* 59 B11
Susquehanna, *U.S.A.* 111 E9
Susquehanna →, *U.S.A.* 111 G8
Susques, *Argentina* 126 A2
Sussex, *Canada* 103 C6
Sussex, *U.S.A.* 111 E10
Sussex, E. □, *U.K.* 13 G8
Sussex, W. □, *U.K.* 13 G7
Sustut →, *Canada* 104 B3
Susuman, *Russia* 51 C15
Susunu, *Indonesia* 63 E8
Susurluk, *Turkey* 39 B10
Susuz, *Turkey* 73 B10
Susz, *Poland* 44 E6
Sütçüler, *Turkey* 72 D4
Şuţeşti, *Romania* 43 E12
Sutherland, *S. Africa* 88 E3
Sutherland, *U.S.A.* 112 E4
Sutherland Falls, *N.Z.* 91 L1
Sutherlin, *U.S.A.* 114 E2
Suthri, *India* 68 H3
Sutlej →, *Pakistan* 68 E4
Sutter, *U.S.A.* 116 F5
Sutter Creek, *U.S.A.* 116 G6
Sutton, *Canada* 111 A12
Sutton, *Nebr., U.S.A.* 112 E6
Sutton, *W. Va., U.S.A.* 108 F5
Sutton →, *Canada* 102 A3
Sutton Coldfield, *U.K.* 13 E6
Sutton in Ashfield, *U.K.* 12 D6
Sutton L., *Canada* 102 B3
Suttor →, *Australia* 94 C4
Suttsu, *Japan* 54 C10
Suva, *Fiji* 91 D8
Suva Gora, *Macedonia* 40 E5
Suva Planina, *Serbia, Yug.* 40 C6
Suva Reka, *Kosovo, Yug.* 40 D4
Suvorov, *Russia* 46 E9
Suvorov Is. = Suwarrow Is., *Cook Is.* 97 J11
Suvorovo, *Bulgaria* 41 C11
Suwałki, *Poland* 44 D9
Suwannaphum, *Thailand* 64 E4
Suwannee →, *U.S.A.* 109 L4
Suwanose-Jima, *Japan* 55 K4
Suwarrow Is., *Cook Is.* 97 J11
Suwayq aş Şuqban, *Iraq* 70 D5
Suweis, Khalîg el, *Egypt* 80 J8
Suweis, Qanâ es, *Egypt* 80 H8
Suwŏn, *S. Korea* 57 F14
Suzdal, *Russia* 46 D11
Suzhou, *Anhui, China* 56 H9
Suzhou, *Jiangsu, China* 59 B13
Suzu, *Japan* 55 F8
Suzu-Misaki, *Japan* 55 F8
Suzuka, *Japan* 55 G8
Suzzara, *Italy* 28 D7
Svalbard, *Arctic* 4 B8
Svalöv, *Sweden* 11 J7
Svaneke, *Denmark* 11 J9
Svängsta, *Sweden* 11 H8
Svanskog, *Sweden* 10 E6
Svappavaara, *Sweden* 8 C19
Svärdsjö, *Sweden* 10 D9
Svartå, *Sweden* 10 E8
Svartisen, *Norway* 8 C15
Svartvik, *Sweden* 10 B11
Svatove, *Ukraine* 47 H10
Svatovo = Svatove, *Ukraine* 47 H10
Svay Chek, *Cambodia* 64 F4
Svay Rieng, *Cambodia* 65 G5
Svealand □, *Sweden* 10 D9
Svedala, *Sweden* 11 J7
Sveg, *Sweden* 10 B8
Svendborg, *Denmark* 11 J4
Svenljunga, *Sweden* 11 G7
Svenstavik, *Sweden* 10 B8
Svenstrup, *Denmark* 11 H3
Sverdlovsk = Yekaterinburg, *Russia* 50 D7
Sverdlovsk, *Ukraine* 47 H10
Sverdrup Is., *Canada* 4 B3
Svetac, *Croatia* 29 E12
Sveti Nikola, Prokhad, *Europe* 40 C6
Sveti Nikole, *Macedonia* 40 E5
Sveti Rok, *Croatia* 29 D12
Svetlaya, *Russia* 54 A9
Svetlogorsk = Svyetlahorsk, *Belarus* 47 F5
Svetlograd, *Russia* 49 H6
Svetlovodsk = Svitlovodsk, *Ukraine* 47 H7
Svidník, *Slovak Rep.* 27 B14
Svilaja Planina, *Croatia* 29 E13
Svilajnac, *Serbia, Yug.* 40 B5
Svilengrad, *Bulgaria* 41 E10
Svir →, *Russia* 46 B7
Sviritsa, *Russia* 46 B7
Svishtov, *Bulgaria* 41 C9
Svislach, *Belarus* 47 F3
Svitava →, *Czech Rep.* 27 B9
Svitavy, *Czech Rep.* 27 B9
Svitlovodsk, *Ukraine* 47 H7
Svobodnyy, *Russia* 51 D13
Svoge, *Bulgaria* 40 D7
Svolvær, *Norway* 8 B16
Svratka →, *Czech Rep.* 27 B9
Svrljig, *Serbia, Yug.* 40 C6
Svyetlahorsk, *Belarus* 47 F5
Swabian Alps = Schwäbische Alb, *Germany* 25 G5
Swainsboro, *U.S.A.* 109 J4
Swakop →, *Namibia* 88 C2
Swakopmund, *Namibia* 88 C1
Swale →, *U.K.* 12 C6
Swan →, *Australia* 93 F2
Swan →, *Canada* 105 C8
Swan Hills, *Canada* 104 C5
Swan Is., *W. Indies* 120 C3
Swan L., *Canada* 105 C8
Swan Peak, *U.S.A.* 114 C7
Swan Ra., *U.S.A.* 114 C7
Swan River, *Canada* 105 C8
Swanage, *U.K.* 13 G6
Swansea, *Australia* 94 G4
Swansea, *Canada* 110 C5
Swansea, *U.K.* 13 F4
Swansea □, *U.K.* 13 F3
Swar →, *Pakistan* 69 B5
Swartberge, *S. Africa* 88 E3
Swartmodder, *S. Africa* 88 D3
Swartnossob →, *Namibia* 88 C2
Swartruggens, *S. Africa* 88 D4
Swarzędz, *Poland* 45 F4
Swastika, *Canada* 102 C3
Swatow = Shantou, *China* 59 F11
Swaziland ■, *Africa* 89 D5
Sweden ■, *Europe* 9 G16
Swedru, *Ghana* 83 D4
Sweet Home, *U.S.A.* 114 D2
Sweetgrass, *U.S.A.* 114 B8
Sweetwater, *Nev., U.S.A.* 116 G7
Sweetwater, *Tenn., U.S.A.* 109 H3
Sweetwater, *Tex., U.S.A.* 113 J4
Sweetwater →, *U.S.A.* 114 E10
Swellendam, *S. Africa* 88 E3
Swider →, *Poland* 45 F8
Świdnica, *Poland* 45 H3
Świdnik, *Poland* 45 G9
Świdwin, *Poland* 44 E2
Świebodzice, *Poland* 45 H3
Świebodzin, *Poland* 45 F2
Świecie, *Poland* 44 E5
Swierzawa, *Poland* 45 G2
Świętokrzyskie □, *Poland* 45 H7
Świętokrzyskie, Góry, *Poland* 45 H7
Swift Current, *Canada* 105 C7
Swiftcurrent →, *Canada* 105 C7
Swilly, L., *Ireland* 15 A4
Swindon, *U.K.* 13 F6
Swindon □, *U.K.* 13 F6
Swinemünde = Świnoujście, *Poland* 44 E1
Swinford, *Ireland* 15 C3
Świnoujście, *Poland* 44 E1
Switzerland ■, *Europe* 25 J4
Swords, *Ireland* 15 C5
Swoyerville, *U.S.A.* 111 E9
Syasstroy, *Russia* 46 B7
Sychevka, *Russia* 46 E8
Syców, *Poland* 45 G4
Sydenham →, *Canada* 110 D2
Sydney, *Canada* 103 C7
Sydney L., *Canada* 105 C10
Sydney Mines, *Canada* 103 C7
Sydprøven = Alluitsup Paa, *Greenland* 4 C5
Sydra, G. of = Surt, Khalīj, *Libya* 79 B9
Syeverodonetsk, *Ukraine* 47 H10
Syke, *Germany* 24 C4
Sykesville, *U.S.A.* 110 E6
Syktyvkar, *Russia* 50 C6
Sylacauga, *U.S.A.* 109 J2
Sylarna, *Sweden* 8 E15
Sylhet, *Bangla.* 67 G17
Sylhet □, *Bangla.* 67 G17
Sylt, *Germany* 24 A4
Sylvan Beach, *U.S.A.* 111 C9
Sylvan Lake, *Canada* 104 C6
Sylvania, *U.S.A.* 109 J5
Sylvester, *U.S.A.* 109 K4
Sym, *Russia* 50 C9
Symón, *Mexico* 118 C4
Synelnykove, *Ukraine* 47 H8
Synnott Ra., *Australia* 92 C4
Syracuse, *Kans., U.S.A.* 113 G4
Syracuse, *N.Y., U.S.A.* 111 C8
Syracuse, *Nebr., U.S.A.* 112 E6
Syrdarya →, *Kazakstan* 50 E7
Syria ■, *Asia* 70 C3
Syrian Desert = Shām, Bādiyat ash, *Asia* 70 C3
Sysslebäck, *Sweden* 10 D6
Syzran, *Russia* 48 D9
Szabolcs-Szatmár-Bereg □, *Hungary* 42 B6
Szadek, *Poland* 45 G5
Szamocin, *Poland* 45 E4
Szamos →, *Hungary* 42 B7
Szamotuły, *Poland* 45 F3
Száraz →, *Hungary* 42 D6
Szarvas, *Hungary* 42 D5
Százhalombatta, *Hungary* 42 C3
Szczawnica, *Poland* 45 J7
Szczebrzeszyn, *Poland* 45 H9
Szczecin, *Poland* 44 E1
Szczecinek, *Poland* 44 E3
Szczeciński, Zalew = Stettiner Haff, *Germany* 24 B10
Szczekociny, *Poland* 45 H6
Szczucin, *Poland* 45 H8
Szczuczyn, *Poland* 44 E9
Szczyrk, *Poland* 45 J6
Szczytna, *Poland* 45 H3
Szczytno, *Poland* 44 E7
Szechwan = Sichuan □, *China* 58 B5
Szécsény, *Hungary* 42 B4
Szeged, *Hungary* 42 D5
Szeghalom, *Hungary* 42 C6
Székesfehérvár, *Hungary* 42 C3
Szekszárd, *Hungary* 42 D3
Szendrő, *Hungary* 42 B5
Szentendre, *Hungary* 42 C4
Szentes, *Hungary* 42 D5
Szentgotthárd, *Hungary* 42 D1
Szentlőrinc, *Hungary* 42 D3
Szerencs, *Hungary* 42 B6
Szigetszentmiklós, *Hungary* 42 C4
Szigetvár, *Hungary* 42 D2
Szikszó, *Hungary* 42 B5
Szklarska Poreba, *Poland* 45 H2
Szkwa →, *Poland* 45 E8
Szlichtyngowa, *Poland* 45 G3
Szob, *Hungary* 42 C3
Szolnok, *Hungary* 42 C5
Szombathely, *Hungary* 42 C1
Szprotawa, *Poland* 45 G2
Sztum, *Poland* 44 E6
Sztutowo, *Poland* 44 D6
Szubin, *Poland* 45 E4
Szydłowiec, *Poland* 45 G7
Szypliszki, *Poland* 44 D10

T

Ta Khli Khok, *Thailand* 64 E3
Ta Lai, *Vietnam* 65 G6
Tab, *Hungary* 42 D3
Tabacal, *Argentina* 126 A3
Tabaco, *Phil.* 61 E5
Tabagné, *Ivory C.* 82 D4
Ţābah, *Si. Arabia* 70 E4
Tabankort, *Niger* 83 B5
Ţabas, *Khorāsān, Iran* 71 C9
Ţabas, *Khorāsān, Iran* 71 C8
Tabasará, Serranía de, *Panama* 120 E3
Tabasco □, *Mexico* 119 D6
Tabāsīn, *Iran* 71 D8
Tabatinga, Serra da, *Brazil* 125 F10
Taber, *Canada* 104 D6
Taberg, *Sweden* 11 G8
Taberg, *U.S.A.* 111 C9
Tabla, *Niger* 83 C5
Tablas I., *Phil.* 61 E5
Tablas Strait, *Phil.* 61 E4
Table B. = Tafelbaai, *S. Africa* 88 E2
Table B., *Canada* 103 B8
Table Mt., *S. Africa* 88 E2
Table Rock L., *U.S.A.* 113 G8
Tabletop, Mt., *Australia* 94 C4
Tábor, *Czech Rep.* 26 B7
Tabora, *Tanzania* 86 D3
Tabora □, *Tanzania* 86 D3
Tabou, *Ivory C.* 82 E3
Tabrīz, *Iran* 70 B5
Tabuaeran, *Kiribati* 97 G12
Tabuenca, *Spain* 32 D3
Tabūk, *Si. Arabia* 70 D3
Täby, *Sweden* 10 E12
Tacámbaro de Codallos, *Mexico* 118 D4
Tacheng, *China* 60 B3
Tach'i, *Taiwan* 59 E13
Tachia, *Taiwan* 59 E13
Tach'ing Shan = Daqing Shan, *China* 56 D6
Tachov, *Czech Rep.* 26 B5
Tácina →, *Italy* 31 D9
Tacloban, *Phil.* 61 F6
Tacna, *Peru* 124 G4
Tacoma, *U.S.A.* 116 C4
Tacuarembó, *Uruguay* 127 C4
Tademaït, Plateau du, *Algeria* 78 C6
Tadio, L., *Ivory C.* 82 D3
Tadjoura, *Djibouti* 81 E5
Tadjoura, Golfe de, *Djibouti* 81 E5
Tadmor, *N.Z.* 91 J4
Tadoule, L., *Canada* 105 B9
Tadoussac, *Canada* 103 C6
Tadzhikistan = Tajikistan ■, *Asia* 50 F8
Taechŏn-ni, *S. Korea* 57 F14
Taegu, *S. Korea* 57 G15
Taegwan, *N. Korea* 57 D13
Taejŏn, *S. Korea* 57 F14
Tafalla, *Spain* 32 C3
Tafar, *Sudan* 81 F2
Tafelbaai, *S. Africa* 88 E2
Tafermaar, *Indonesia* 63 F8
Tafí Viejo, *Argentina* 126 B2
Tafīhān, *Iran* 71 D7
Tafiré, *Ivory C.* 82 D3
Tafo, *Ghana* 83 D4
Tafresh, *Iran* 71 C6
Taft, *Iran* 71 D7
Taft, *Phil.* 61 F6
Taft, *U.S.A.* 117 K7
Taftān, Kūh-e, *Iran* 71 D9
Taga Dzong, *Bhutan* 67 F16
Taganrog, *Russia* 47 J10
Taganrogskiy Zaliv, *Russia* 47 J10
Tagânt, *Mauritania* 82 B2
Tagatay, *Phil.* 61 D4
Tagbilaran, *Phil.* 61 G5
Tággia, *Italy* 28 E4
Tagish, *Canada* 104 A2
Tagish L., *Canada* 104 A2
Tagliacozzo, *Italy* 29 F10
Tagliamento →, *Italy* 29 C10
Táglio di Po, *Italy* 29 D9
Tago, *Phil.* 61 G7
Tagomago, *Spain* 37 B8
Tagourãret, *Mauritania* 82 B3
Taguatinga, *Brazil* 125 F10
Tagudin, *Phil.* 61 C4
Tagum, *Phil.* 61 H6
Tagus = Tejo →, *Europe* 35 F2
Tahakopa, *N.Z.* 91 M2
Tahan, Gunong, *Malaysia* 65 K4
Tahat, *Algeria* 78 D7
Tāherī, *Iran* 71 E7
Tahiti, *Pac. Oc.* 97 J13
Tahlequah, *U.S.A.* 113 H7
Tahoe, L., *U.S.A.* 116 G6
Tahoe City, *U.S.A.* 116 F6
Tahoka, *U.S.A.* 113 J4
Taholah, *U.S.A.* 116 C2
Tahoua, *Niger* 83 C6
Tahrūd, *Iran* 71 D8
Tahsis, *Canada* 104 D3
Tahta, *Egypt* 80 B3
Tahtaköprü, *Turkey* 41 G13
Tahtalı Dağları, *Turkey* 72 C7
Tahulandang, *Indonesia* 63 D7
Tahuna, *Indonesia* 63 D7
Taï, *Ivory C.* 82 D3
Tai Hu, *China* 59 B12
Tai Shan, *China* 57 F9
Tai'an, *China* 57 F9

Taxco de Alarcón, *Mexico* 119 D5
Taxila, *Pakistan* 68 C5
Tay →, *U.K.* 14 E5
Tay, Firth of, *U.K.* 14 E5
Tay, L., *Australia* 93 F3
Tay, L., *U.K.* 14 E4
Tay Ninh, *Vietnam* 65 G6
Tayabamba, *Peru* 124 E3
Tayabas Bay, *Phil.* 61 E4
Taylakova, *Russia* 50 D8
Taylakovy = Taylakova, *Russia* 50 D8
Taylor, *Canada* 104 B4
Taylor, *Nebr., U.S.A.* 112 E5
Taylor, *Pa., U.S.A.* 111 E9
Taylor, *Tex., U.S.A.* 113 K6
Taylor, Mt., *U.S.A.* 115 J10
Taylorville, *U.S.A.* 112 F10
Taymā, *Si. Arabia* 70 E3
Taymyr, Oz., *Russia* 51 B11
Taymyr, Poluostrov, *Russia* 51 B11
Tayport, *U.K.* 14 E6
Tayshet, *Russia* 51 D10
Taytay, *Phil.* 61 F3
Taz →, *Russia* 50 C8
Taza, *Morocco* 78 B5
Tāzah Khurmātū, *Iraq* 70 C5
Tazawa-Ko, *Japan* 54 E10
Tazin, *Canada* 105 B7
Tazin L., *Canada* 105 B7
Tazovskiy, *Russia* 50 C8
Tbilisi, *Georgia* 49 K7
Tchad = Chad ■, *Africa* 79 F8
Tchad, L., *Chad* 79 F8
Tchaourou, *Benin* 83 D5
Tch'eng-tou = Chengdu, *China* 58 B5
Tchentlo L., *Canada* 104 B4
Tchetti, *Benin* 83 D5
Tchibanga, *Gabon* 84 E2
Tchien, *Liberia* 82 D3
Tchin Tabaraden, *Niger* 83 B6
Tch'ong-k'ing = Chongqing, *China* 58 C6
Tczew, *Poland* 44 D5
Te Anau, *N.Z.* 91 L1
Te Anau, L., *N.Z.* 91 L1
Te Aroha, *N.Z.* 91 G5
Te Awamutu, *N.Z.* 91 H5
Te Kuiti, *N.Z.* 91 H5
Te-n-Dghâmcha, Sebkhet, *Mauritania* 82 B1
Te Puke, *N.Z.* 91 G6
Te Waewae B., *N.Z.* 91 M1
Teaca, *Romania* 43 D9
Teague, *U.S.A.* 113 K6
Teano, *Italy* 31 A7
Teapa, *Mexico* 119 D6
Teba, *Spain* 35 J6
Tebakang, *Malaysia* 62 D4
Teberda, *Russia* 49 J5
Tébessa, *Algeria* 78 A7
Tebicuary →, *Paraguay* 126 B4
Tebingtinggi, *Indonesia* 62 D1
Tebintingii, *Indonesia* 62 E2
Tebulos, *Georgia* 49 J7
Tecate, *Mexico* 117 N10
Tecer Dağları, *Turkey* 72 C7
Tech →, *France* 20 F7
Techiman, *Ghana* 82 D4
Techirghiol, *Romania* 43 F13
Tecka, *Argentina* 128 E2
Tecomán, *Mexico* 118 D4
Tecopa, *U.S.A.* 117 K10
Tecoripa, *Mexico* 118 B3
Tecuala, *Mexico* 118 C3
Tecuci, *Romania* 43 E12
Tecumseh, *Canada* 110 D2
Tecumseh, *Mich., U.S.A.* 108 D4
Tecumseh, *Okla., U.S.A.* 113 H6
Tedzhen = Tejen, *Turkmenistan* 50 F7
Tees →, *U.K.* 12 C6
Tees B., *U.K.* 12 C6
Teeswater, *Canada* 110 C3
Tefé, *Brazil* 124 D6
Tefenni, *Turkey* 39 D11
Tegal, *Indonesia* 62 F3
Tegernsee, *Germany* 25 H7
Teggiano, *Italy* 31 B8
Tegid, L. = Bala, L., *U.K.* 12 E4
Tegina, *Nigeria* 83 C6
Tegucigalpa, *Honduras* 120 D2
Teguidda i-n-Tessoum, *Niger* 83 B6
Tehachapi, *U.S.A.* 117 K8
Tehachapi Mts., *U.S.A.* 117 L8
Tehamiyam, *Sudan* 80 D4
Tehilla, *Sudan* 80 D4
Téhini, *Ivory C.* 82 D4
Tehoru, *Indonesia* 63 E7
Tehrān, *Iran* 71 C6
Tehri, *India* 69 D8
Tehuacán, *Mexico* 119 D5
Tehuantepec, *Mexico* 119 D5
Tehuantepec, G. de, *Mexico* 119 D5
Tehuantepec, Istmo de, *Mexico* 119 D6
Teide, *Canary Is.* 37 F3
Teifi →, *U.K.* 13 E3
Teign →, *U.K.* 13 G4
Teignmouth, *U.K.* 13 G4
Teiuş, *Romania* 43 D8
Teixeira Pinto, *Guinea-Biss.* 82 C1
Tejam, *India* 69 E9
Tejen, *Turkmenistan* 50 F7
Tejen →, *Turkmenistan* 71 B9
Tejo →, *Europe* 35 F2
Tejon Pass, *U.S.A.* 117 L8
Tekamah, *U.S.A.* 112 E6
Tekapo, L., *N.Z.* 91 K3
Tekax, *Mexico* 119 C7
Teke, *Turkey* 41 E13
Tekeli, *Kazakstan* 50 E8
Tekeze →, *Ethiopia* 81 E4
Tekija, *Serbia, Yug.* 40 B6
Tekirdağ, *Turkey* 41 F11
Tekirdağ □, *Turkey* 41 E11
Tekirova, *Turkey* 39 E12
Tekkali, *India* 67 K14
Tekke, *Turkey* 72 B7
Tekman, *Turkey* 73 C9
Tekoa, *U.S.A.* 114 C5
Tel Aviv-Yafo, *Israel* 75 C3
Tel Lakhish, *Israel* 75 D3
Tel Megiddo, *Israel* 75 C4
Tela, *Honduras* 120 C2
Telanaipura = Jambi, *Indonesia* 62 E2
Telavi, *Georgia* 49 J7
Telč, *Czech Rep.* 26 B8
Telciu, *Romania* 43 C9
Telde, *Canary Is.* 37 G4
Telegraph Creek, *Canada* 104 B2
Telekhany = Tsyelyakhany, *Belarus* 47 F3
Telemark, *Norway* 9 G12
Telén, *Argentina* 126 D2
Teleneşti, *Moldova* 43 C13
Teleng, *Iran* 71 E9
Teleño, *Spain* 34 C4
Teleorman □, *Romania* 43 G10
Teleorman →, *Romania* 43 G10
Teles Pires →, *Brazil* 122 D5
Telescope Pk., *U.S.A.* 117 J9
Teletaye, *Mali* 83 B5
Telfer Mine, *Australia* 92 C3
Telford, *U.K.* 13 E5
Telford and Wrekin □, *U.K.* 12 E5
Telfs, *Austria* 26 D4
Télimélé, *Guinea* 82 C2
Teljo, J., *Sudan* 81 E2
Telkwa, *Canada* 104 C3
Tell City, *U.S.A.* 108 G2
Tellicherry, *India* 66 P9
Telluride, *U.S.A.* 115 H10
Teloloapán, *Mexico* 119 D5
Telpos Iz, *Russia* 6 C17
Telsen, *Argentina* 128 E3
Telšiai, *Lithuania* 9 H20
Telšiai □, *Lithuania* 44 C9
Teltow, *Germany* 24 C9
Teluk Anson = Teluk Intan, *Malaysia* 65 K3
Teluk Betung = Tanjungkarang Telukbetung, *Indonesia* 62 F3
Teluk Intan, *Malaysia* 65 K3
Telukbutun, *Indonesia* 65 K7
Telukdalem, *Indonesia* 62 D1
Tema, *Ghana* 83 D5
Temax, *Mexico* 119 C7
Temba, *S. Africa* 89 D4
Tembagapura, *Indonesia* 63 E9
Tembe, *Dem. Rep. of the Congo* 86 C2
Tembleque, *Spain* 34 F7
Temblor Range, *U.S.A.* 117 K7
Teme →, *U.K.* 13 E5
Temecula, *U.S.A.* 117 M9
Temerloh, *Malaysia* 62 D2
Teminabuan, *Indonesia* 63 E8
Temir, *Kazakstan* 50 E6
Temirtau, *Kazakstan* 50 D8
Temirtau, *Russia* 50 D9
Temiscamie →, *Canada* 103 B5
Témiscaming, *Canada* 102 C4
Témiscamingue, L., *Canada* 102 C4
Temnikov, *Russia* 48 C6
Temo →, *Italy* 30 B1
Temosachic, *Mexico* 118 B3
Tempe, *U.S.A.* 115 K8
Témpio Pausánia, *Italy* 30 B2
Tempiute, *U.S.A.* 116 H11
Temple, *U.S.A.* 113 K6
Temple B., *Australia* 94 A3
Templemore, *Ireland* 15 D4
Templeton, *U.S.A.* 116 K6
Templeton →, *Australia* 94 C2
Templin, *Germany* 24 B9
Tempoal, *Mexico* 119 C5
Temryuk, *Russia* 47 K9
Temska →, *Serbia, Yug.* 40 C6
Temuco, *Chile* 128 D2
Temuka, *N.Z.* 91 L3
Tenabo, *Mexico* 119 C6
Tenaha, *U.S.A.* 113 K7
Tenakee Springs, *U.S.A.* 104 B1
Tenali, *India* 67 L12
Tenancingo, *Mexico* 119 D5
Tenango, *Mexico* 119 D5
Tenasserim, *Burma* 65 F2
Tenasserim □, *Burma* 64 F2
Tenby, *U.K.* 13 F3
Tenda, Colle di, *France* 21 D11
Tendaho, *Ethiopia* 81 E5
Tende, *France* 21 D11
Tendelti, *Sudan* 81 E3
Tendrovskaya Kosa, *Ukraine* 47 J6
Tendukhera, *India* 69 H8
Teneida, *Egypt* 80 B2
Tenenkou, *Mali* 82 C4
Ténéré, *Niger* 83 B7
Tenerife, *Canary Is.* 37 F3
Tenerife, Pico, *Canary Is.* 37 G1
Teng Xian, *Guangxi Zhuangzu, China* 59 F8
Teng Xian, *Shandong, China* 57 G9
Tengah □, *Indonesia* 63 E6
Tengah, Kepulauan, *Indonesia* 62 F5
Tengchong, *China* 58 E2
Tengchowfu = Penglai, *China* 57 F11
Tenggara □, *Indonesia* 63 E6
Tenggarong, *Indonesia* 62 E5
Tenggol, Pulau, *Malaysia* 65 K4
Tengiz, Ozero, *Kazakstan* 50 D7
Tenhult, *Sweden* 11 G8
Tenino, *U.S.A.* 116 D4
Tenkasi, *India* 66 Q10
Tenke, *Katanga, Dem. Rep. of the Congo* 87 E2
Tenke, *Katanga, Dem. Rep. of the Congo* 87 E2
Tenkodogo, *Burkina Faso* 83 C4
Tenna →, *Italy* 29 E10
Tennant Creek, *Australia* 94 B1
Tennessee □, *U.S.A.* 109 H2
Tennessee →, *U.S.A.* 108 G1
Teno, Pta. de, *Canary Is.* 37 F3
Tenom, *Malaysia* 62 C5
Tenosique, *Mexico* 119 D6
Tenryū-Gawa →, *Japan* 55 G8
Tenterden, *U.K.* 13 F8
Tenterfield, *Australia* 95 D5
Teo, *Spain* 34 C2
Teófilo Otoni, *Brazil* 125 G10
Tepa, *Indonesia* 63 F7
Tepalcatepec →, *Mexico* 118 D4
Tepecik, *Bursa, Turkey* 41 F12
Tepecik, *Kütahya, Turkey* 39 B11
Tepehuanes, *Mexico* 118 B3
Tepelenë, *Albania* 40 F4
Tepetongo, *Mexico* 118 C4
Tepic, *Mexico* 118 C4
Teplá, *Czech Rep.* 26 B5
Teplice, *Czech Rep.* 26 A6
Tepoca, C., *Mexico* 118 A2
Tequila, *Mexico* 118 C4
Ter →, *Spain* 32 C8
Ter Apel, *Neths.* 17 B7
Téra, *Niger* 83 C5
Tera →, *Spain* 34 D5
Teraina, *Kiribati* 97 G11
Terakeka, *Sudan* 81 F3
Téramo, *Italy* 29 F10
Terazit, Massif de, *Niger* 83 A6
Tercan, *Turkey* 73 C9
Tercero →, *Argentina* 126 C3
Terebovlya, *Ukraine* 47 H3
Teregova, *Romania* 42 E7
Tereida, *Sudan* 81 E3
Terek →, *Russia* 49 J8
Tereshka →, *Russia* 48 E8
Teresina, *Brazil* 125 E10
Terespol, *Poland* 45 F10
Terewah, L., *Australia* 95 D4
Terges →, *Portugal* 35 H3
Tergnier, *France* 19 C10
Terlizzi, *Italy* 31 A9
Terme, *Turkey* 72 B7
Termez = Termiz, *Uzbekistan* 50 F7
Términi Imerese, *Italy* 30 E6
Términos, L. de, *Mexico* 119 D6
Termiz, *Uzbekistan* 50 F7
Térmoli, *Italy* 29 F12
Ternate, *Indonesia* 63 D7
Terneuzen, *Neths.* 17 C3
Terney, *Russia* 51 E14
Terni, *Italy* 29 F9
Ternitz, *Austria* 26 D9
Ternopil, *Ukraine* 47 H3
Ternopol = Ternopil, *Ukraine* 47 H3
Terpní, *Greece* 40 F7
Terra Bella, *U.S.A.* 117 K7
Terra Nova Nat. Park, *Canada* 103 C9
Terrace, *Canada* 104 C3
Terrace Bay, *Canada* 102 C2
Terracina, *Italy* 30 A6
Terralba, *Italy* 30 C1
Terranova = Ólbia, *Italy* 30 B2
Terrasini, *Italy* 30 D6
Terrassa, *Spain* 32 D7
Terrasson-la-Villedieu, *France* 20 C5
Terre Haute, *U.S.A.* 108 F2
Terrebonne B., *U.S.A.* 113 L9
Terrell, *U.S.A.* 113 J6
Terrenceville, *Canada* 103 C9
Terry, *U.S.A.* 112 B2
Terryville, *U.S.A.* 111 E11
Terschelling, *Neths.* 17 A5
Tersko-Kumskiy Kanal →, *Russia* 49 H7
Tertenía, *Italy* 30 C2
Terter → = Tärtär →, *Azerbaijan* 49 K8
Teruel, *Spain* 32 E3
Teruel □, *Spain* 32 E4
Tervel, *Bulgaria* 41 C11
Tervola, *Finland* 8 C21
Tešanj, *Bos.-H.* 42 F3
Teseney, *Eritrea* 81 D4
Tesha →, *Russia* 48 C6
Teshio, *Japan* 54 B10
Teshio-Gawa →, *Japan* 54 B10
Tešica, *Serbia, Yug.* 40 C5
Tesiyn Gol →, *Mongolia* 60 A4
Teslić, *Bos.-H.* 42 F2
Teslin, *Canada* 104 A2
Teslin →, *Canada* 104 A2
Teslin L., *Canada* 104 A2
Tessalit, *Mali* 83 A5
Tessaoua, *Niger* 83 C6
Tessin, *Germany* 24 A8
Tessit, *Mali* 83 B5
Test →, *U.K.* 13 G6
Testa del Gargano, *Italy* 29 G13
Testigos, Is. Las, *Venezuela* 121 D7
Tét, *Hungary* 42 C2
Têt →, *France* 20 F7
Tetachuck L., *Canada* 104 C3
Tetas, Pta., *Chile* 126 A1
Tete, *Mozam.* 87 F3
Tete □, *Mozam.* 87 F3
Teterev →, *Ukraine* 47 G6
Teterow, *Germany* 24 B8
Teteven, *Bulgaria* 41 D8
Tethul →, *Canada* 104 A6
Tetiyev, *Ukraine* 47 H5
Teton →, *U.S.A.* 114 C8
Tétouan, *Morocco* 78 A4
Tetovo, *Macedonia* 40 D4
Tetyushi, *Russia* 48 C9
Teuco →, *Argentina* 126 B3
Teulada, *Italy* 30 D1
Teulon, *Canada* 105 C9
Teun, *Indonesia* 63 F7
Teutoburger Wald, *Germany* 24 C4
Tevere →, *Italy* 29 G9
Teverya, *Israel* 75 C4
Teviot →, *U.K.* 14 F6
Tewantin, *Australia* 95 D5
Tewkesbury, *U.K.* 13 F5
Texada I., *Canada* 104 D4
Texarkana, *Ark., U.S.A.* 113 J8
Texarkana, *Tex., U.S.A.* 113 J7
Texas, *Australia* 95 D5
Texas □, *U.S.A.* 113 K5
Texas City, *U.S.A.* 113 L7
Texel, *Neths.* 17 A4
Texline, *U.S.A.* 113 G3
Texoma, L., *U.S.A.* 113 J6
Teykovo, *Russia* 46 D11
Teza →, *Russia* 48 B5
Tezin, *Afghan.* 68 B3
Teziutlán, *Mexico* 119 D5
Tezpur, *India* 67 F18
Tezzeron L., *Canada* 104 C4
Tha-anne →, *Canada* 105 A10
Tha Deua, *Laos* 64 D4
Tha Deua, *Laos* 64 C3
Tha Pla, *Thailand* 64 D3
Tha Rua, *Thailand* 64 E3
Tha Sala, *Thailand* 65 H2
Tha Song Yang, *Thailand* 64 D1
Thaba Putsoa, *Lesotho* 89 D4
Thabana Ntlenyana, *Lesotho* 89 D4
Thabazimbi, *S. Africa* 89 C4
Thādiq, *Si. Arabia* 70 E5
Thai Binh, *Vietnam* 58 G6
Thai Muang, *Thailand* 65 H2
Thai Nguyen, *Vietnam* 58 G5
Thailand ■, *Asia* 64 E4
Thailand, G. of, *Asia* 65 G3
Thakhek, *Laos* 64 D5
Thal, *Pakistan* 68 C4
Thal Desert, *Pakistan* 68 D4
Thala La = Hkakabo Razi, *Burma* 67 E20
Thalabarivat, *Cambodia* 64 F5
Thallon, *Australia* 95 D4
Thalwil, *Switz.* 25 H4
Thames, *N.Z.* 91 G5
Thames →, *Canada* 102 D3
Thames →, *U.K.* 13 F8
Thames →, *U.S.A.* 111 E12
Thames Estuary, *U.K.* 13 F8
Thamesford, *Canada* 110 C4
Thamesville, *Canada* 110 D3
Than, *India* 68 H4
Than Uyen, *Vietnam* 64 B4
Thana Gazi, *India* 68 F7
Thandla, *India* 68 H6
Thane, *India* 66 K8
Thanesar, *India* 68 D7
Thanet, I. of, *U.K.* 13 F9
Thangool, *Australia* 94 C5
Thanh Hoa, *Vietnam* 64 C5
Thanh Hung, *Vietnam* 65 H5
Thanh Pho Ho Chi Minh, *Vietnam* 65 G6
Thanh Thuy, *Vietnam* 64 A5
Thanjavur, *India* 66 P11
Thann, *France* 19 E14
Thano Bula Khan, *Pakistan* 68 G2
Thaolinta L., *Canada* 105 A9
Thaon-les-Vosges, *France* 19 D13
Thap Sakae, *Thailand* 65 G2
Thap Than, *Thailand* 64 E2
Thar Desert, *India* 68 F5
Tharad, *India* 68 G4
Thargomindah, *Australia* 95 D3
Tharrawaddy, *Burma* 67 L19
Tharthār, Mileh, *Iraq* 70 C4
Tharthār, W. ath →, *Iraq* 70 C4
Thasopoúla, *Greece* 41 F8
Thásos, *Greece* 41 F8
That Khe, *Vietnam* 58 F6
Thatcher, *Ariz., U.S.A.* 115 K9
Thatcher, *Colo., U.S.A.* 113 G2
Thaton, *Burma* 67 L20
Thau, Bassin de, *France* 20 E7
Thaungdut, *Burma* 67 G19
Thayer, *U.S.A.* 113 G9
Thayetmyo, *Burma* 67 K19
Thazi, *Burma* 67 J20
The Alberga →, *Australia* 95 D2
The Bight, *Bahamas* 121 B4
The Dalles, *U.S.A.* 114 D3
The English Company's Is., *Australia* 94 A2
The Frome →, *Australia* 95 D2
The Great Divide = Great Dividing Ra., *Australia* 94 C4
The Hague = 's-Gravenhage, *Neths.* 17 B4
The Hamilton →, *Australia* 95 D2
The Macumba →, *Australia* 95 D2
The Neales →, *Australia* 95 D2
The Officer →, *Australia* 93 E5
The Pas, *Canada* 105 C8
The Range, *Zimbabwe* 87 F3
The Salt L., *Australia* 95 E3
The Sandheads, *India* 69 J13
The Stevenson →, *Australia* 95 D2
The Warburton →, *Australia* 95 D2
The Woodlands, *U.S.A.* 113 K7
Thebes = Thívai, *Greece* 38 C5
Thebes, *Egypt* 80 B3
Thedford, *Canada* 110 C3
Thedford, *U.S.A.* 112 E4
Theebine, *Australia* 95 D5
Thekulthili L., *Canada* 105 A7
Thelon →, *Canada* 105 A8
Thénezay, *France* 18 F6
Thenon, *France* 20 C5
Theodore, *Australia* 94 C5
Theodore, *Canada* 105 C8
Theodore, *U.S.A.* 109 K1
Theodore Roosevelt National Memorial Park, *U.S.A.* 112 B3
Theodore Roosevelt Res., *U.S.A.* 115 K8
Thepha, *Thailand* 65 J3
Thérain →, *France* 19 C9
Theresa, *U.S.A.* 111 B9
Thermaïkós Kólpos, *Greece* 40 F6
Thermí, *Greece* 39 B8
Thermopolis, *U.S.A.* 114 E9
Thermopylae P., *Greece* 38 C4
Thesprotía □, *Greece* 38 B2
Thessalía □, *Greece* 38 B4
Thessalon, *Canada* 102 C3
Thessaloníki, *Greece* 40 F6
Thessaloníki □, *Greece* 40 F7
Thessaloniki, Gulf of = Thermaïkós Kólpos, *Greece* 40 F6
Thessaly = Thessalía □, *Greece* 38 B4
Thetford, *U.K.* 13 E8
Thetford Mines, *Canada* 103 C5
Theun →, *Laos* 64 C5
Theunissen, *S. Africa* 88 D4
Thevenard, *Australia* 95 E1
Thiámis →, *Greece* 38 B2
Thiberville, *France* 18 C7
Thibodaux, *U.S.A.* 113 L9
Thicket Portage, *Canada* 105 B9
Thief River Falls, *U.S.A.* 112 A6
Thiel Mts., *Antarctica* 5 E16
Thiene, *Italy* 29 C8
Thiérache, *France* 19 C10
Thiers, *France* 20 C7
Thiès, *Senegal* 82 C1
Thiesi, *Italy* 30 B1
Thiet, *Sudan* 81 F2
Thika, *Kenya* 86 C4
Thikombia, *Fiji* 91 B9
Thille-Boubacar, *Senegal* 82 B1
Thimphu, *Bhutan* 67 F16
Þingvallavatn, *Iceland* 8 D3
Thionville, *France* 19 C13
Thíra, *Greece* 39 E7
Thirasía, *Greece* 39 E7
Third Cataract, *Sudan* 80 D3
Thirsk, *U.K.* 12 C6
Thiruvananthapuram = Trivandrum, *India* 66 Q10
Thisted, *Denmark* 11 H2
Thívai, *Greece* 38 C5
Thiviers, *France* 20 C4
Thizy, *France* 19 F11
Þjórsá →, *Iceland* 8 E3
Thlewiaza →, *Man., Canada* 105 B8
Thlewiaza →, *N.W.T., Canada* 105 A10
Thmar Puok, *Cambodia* 64 F4
Tho Vinh, *Vietnam* 64 C5
Thoa →, *Canada* 105 A7
Thoen, *Thailand* 64 D2
Thoeng, *Thailand* 64 C3
Thohoyandou, *S. Africa* 85 J6
Tholdi, *Pakistan* 69 B7
Thomas, *U.S.A.* 113 H5
Thomas, L., *Australia* 95 D2
Thomaston, *U.S.A.* 109 J3
Thomasville, *Ala., U.S.A.* 109 K2
Thomasville, *Ga., U.S.A.* 109 K4
Thomasville, *N.C., U.S.A.* 109 H5
Thompson, *Canada* 105 B9
Thompson, *U.S.A.* 111 E9
Thompson →, *Canada* 104 C4
Thompson →, *U.S.A.* 112 F8
Thompson Falls, *U.S.A.* 114 C6
Thompson Pk., *U.S.A.* 114 F2
Thompson Springs, *U.S.A.* 115 G9
Thompsontown, *U.S.A.* 110 F7
Thomson, *U.S.A.* 109 J4
Thomson →, *Australia* 94 C3
Thomson's Falls = Nyahururu, *Kenya* 86 B4
Thônes, *France* 21 C10
Thonon-les-Bains, *France* 19 F13
Thorez, *Ukraine* 47 H10
Þórisvatn, *Iceland* 8 D4
Thornaby on Tees, *U.K.* 12 C6
Thornbury, *Canada* 110 B4
Thorne, *U.K.* 12 D7
Thornhill, *Canada* 104 C3
Thorold, *Canada* 110 C5

Þórshöfn, *Iceland* 8 C6
Thouarcé, *France* 18 E6
Thouars, *France* 18 F6
Thouet →, *France* 18 E6
Thouin, C., *Australia* 92 D2
Thousand Oaks, *U.S.A.* 117 L8
Thrace, *Turkey* 41 F10
Thrakikón Pélagos, *Greece* 41 F8
Three Forks, *U.S.A.* 114 D8
Three Gorges Dam, *China* 59 B8
Three Hills, *Canada* 104 C6
Three Hummock I., *Australia* 94 G3
Three Points, C., *Ghana* 82 E4
Three Rivers, *Calif., U.S.A.* 116 J8
Three Rivers, *Tex., U.S.A.* 113 L5
Three Sisters, *U.S.A.* 114 D3
Three Springs, *Australia* 93 E2
Throssell, L., *Australia* 93 E3
Throssell Ra., *Australia* 92 D3
Thuan Hoa, *Vietnam* 65 H5
Thubun Lakes, *Canada* 105 A6
Thueyts, *France* 21 D8
Thuin, *Belgium* 17 D4
Thuir, *France* 20 F6
Thule = Qaanaaq, *Greenland* 4 B4
Thun, *Switz.* 25 J3
Thunder B., *U.S.A.* 110 B1
Thunder Bay, *Canada* 102 C2
Thunersee, *Switz.* 25 J3
Thung Song, *Thailand* 65 H2
Thunkar, *Bhutan* 67 F17
Thuong Tra, *Vietnam* 64 D6
Thur →, *Switz.* 25 H5
Thurgau □, *Switz.* 25 H5
Thüringen □, *Germany* 24 D6
Thüringer Wald, *Germany* 24 E6
Thurles, *Ireland* 15 D4
Thurn P., *Austria* 26 D5
Thurrock □, *U.K.* 13 F8
Thursday I., *Australia* 94 A3
Thurso, *Canada* 102 C4
Thurso, *U.K.* 14 C5
Thurso →, *U.K.* 14 C5
Thurston I., *Antarctica* 5 D16
Thury-Harcourt, *France* 18 D6
Thutade L., *Canada* 104 B3
Thy, *Denmark* 11 H2
Thyborøn, *Denmark* 11 H2
Thyolo, *Malawi* 87 F4
Thysville = Mbanza Ngungu, *Dem. Rep. of the Congo* 84 F2
Ti-n-Amzi →, *Niger* 83 B5
Ti-n-Barraouene, O. →, *Africa* 83 B5
Ti-n-Zaouatene, *Algeria* 83 B5
Ti Tree, *Australia* 94 C1
Tiadiaye, *Senegal* 82 C1
Tian Shan, *Asia* 60 B3
Tianchang, *China* 59 A12
Tiandeng, *China* 58 F6
Tiandong, *China* 58 F6
Tian'e, *China* 58 E6
Tianhe, *China* 58 E7
Tianjin, *China* 57 E9
Tiankoura, *Burkina Faso* 82 C4
Tianlin, *China* 58 E6
Tianmen, *China* 59 B9
Tianquan, *China* 58 B4
Tianshui, *China* 56 G3
Tiantai, *China* 59 C13
Tianyang, *China* 58 F6
Tianzhen, *China* 56 D8
Tianzhu, *China* 58 D7
Tianzhuangtai, *China* 57 D12
Tiaret, *Algeria* 78 A6
Tiassalé, *Ivory C.* 82 D4
Tibagi, *Brazil* 127 A5
Tibagi →, *Brazil* 127 A5
Tibati, *Cameroon* 83 D7
Tibe, *Ethiopia* 81 F4
Tiber = Tevere →, *Italy* 29 G9
Tiberias = Teverya, *Israel* 75 C4
Tiberias, L. = Yam Kinneret, *Israel* 75 C4
Tibesti, *Chad* 79 D9
Tibet = Xizang Zizhiqu □, *China* 60 C3
Tibet, Plateau of, *Asia* 52 F12
Tibiao, *Phil.* 61 F5
Tibiri, *Niger* 83 C6
Ţibleş, Vf., *Romania* 43 C9
Ţibleşului, Munţii, *Romania* 43 C9
Tibnī, *Syria* 70 C3
Tibooburra, *Australia* 95 D3
Tibro, *Sweden* 11 F8
Tiburón, I., *Mexico* 118 B2
Ticao I., *Phil.* 61 E5
Tichît, *Mauritania* 82 B3
Ticho, *Ethiopia* 81 F4
Ticino □, *Switz.* 25 J4
Ticino →, *Italy* 25 K5
Ticleni, *Romania* 43 F8
Ticonderoga, *U.S.A.* 111 C11
Ticul, *Mexico* 119 C7
Tidaholm, *Sweden* 11 F7
Tidan, *Sweden* 11 F8
Tiddim, *Burma* 67 H18
Tidioute, *U.S.A.* 110 E5
Tidjikja, *Mauritania* 82 B2
Tidore, *Indonesia* 63 D7
Tiébissou, *Ivory C.* 82 D3
Tiel, *Neths.* 17 C5
Tiel, *Senegal* 82 C1
Tieling, *China* 57 C12
Tielt, *Belgium* 17 C3
Tien Shan = Tian Shan, *Asia* 60 B3
Tien-tsin = Tianjin, *China* 57 E9
Tien Yen, *Vietnam* 64 B6
T'ienching = Tianjin, *China* 57 E9
Tienen, *Belgium* 17 D4
Tiénigbé, *Ivory C.* 82 D3
Tientsin = Tianjin, *China* 57 E9
Tieri, *Australia* 94 C4
Tierp, *Sweden* 10 D11
Tierra Amarilla, *Chile* 126 B1
Tierra Amarilla, *U.S.A.* 115 H10
Tierra Colorada, *Mexico* 119 D5
Tierra de Barros, *Spain* 35 G4
Tierra de Campos, *Spain* 34 C6
Tierra del Fuego, I. Gr. de, *Argentina* 122 J4
Tiétar →, *Spain* 34 F4
Tieté →, *Brazil* 127 A5
Tiffin, *U.S.A.* 108 E4
Tiflis = Tbilisi, *Georgia* 49 K7
Tifton, *U.S.A.* 109 K4
Tifu, *Indonesia* 63 E7
Tighina, *Moldova* 43 D14
Tigil, *Russia* 51 D16
Tignish, *Canada* 103 C7
Tigray □, *Ethiopia* 81 E4
Tigre →, *Peru* 124 D4
Tigre →, *Venezuela* 124 B6
Tigris = Dijlah, Nahr →, *Asia* 70 D5
Tigveni, *Romania* 43 E9
Tigyaing, *Burma* 67 H20
Tîh, Gebel el, *Egypt* 80 B3
Tijara, *India* 68 F7
Tijuana, *Mexico* 117 N9
Tikal, *Guatemala* 120 C2
Tikamgarh, *India* 69 G8
Tikaré, *Burkina Faso* 83 C4
Tikhoretsk, *Russia* 49 H5
Tikhvin, *Russia* 46 C7
Tiko, *Cameroon* 83 E6
Tikrīt, *Iraq* 70 C4
Tiksi, *Russia* 51 B13
Tilamuta, *Indonesia* 63 D6
Tilburg, *Neths.* 17 C5
Tilbury, *Canada* 102 D3
Tilbury, *U.K.* 13 F8
Tilcara, *Argentina* 126 A2
Tilden, *U.S.A.* 112 D6
Tilemses, *Niger* 83 B5
Tilemsi, Vallée du, *Mali* 83 B5
Tilhar, *India* 69 F8
Tilichiki, *Russia* 51 C17
Tílissos, *Greece* 36 D7
Till →, *U.K.* 12 B5
Tillabéri, *Niger* 83 C5
Tillamook, *U.S.A.* 114 D2
Tillberga, *Sweden* 10 E10
Tillia, *Niger* 83 B5
Tillsonburg, *Canada* 102 D3
Tillyeria □, *Cyprus* 36 D11
Tilogne, *Senegal* 82 B2
Tílos, *Greece* 39 E9
Tilsit = Sovetsk, *Russia* 9 J19
Tilt →, *U.K.* 14 E5
Tilton, *U.S.A.* 111 C13
Tiltonsville, *U.S.A.* 110 F4
Tim, *Denmark* 11 H2
Timagami, L., *Canada* 102 C3
Timaru, *N.Z.* 91 L3
Timashevo, *Russia* 48 D10
Timashevsk, *Russia* 49 H4
Timau, *Kenya* 86 B4
Timbákion, *Greece* 36 D6
Timbedgha, *Mauritania* 82 B3
Timber Creek, *Australia* 92 C5
Timber Lake, *U.S.A.* 112 C4
Timber Mt., *U.S.A.* 116 H10
Timbo, *Guinea* 82 C2
Timbo, *Liberia* 82 D3
Timbuktu = Tombouctou, *Mali* 82 B4
Timeiaouine, *Algeria* 83 A5
Timétrine, Mts., *Mali* 83 B4
Timfi Óros, *Greece* 38 B2
Timfristós, Óros, *Greece* 38 C3
Timi, *Cyprus* 36 E11
Tîmia, *Niger* 83 B6
Timimoun, *Algeria* 78 C6
Timirist, Râs, *Mauritania* 82 B1
Timiş = Tamis →, *Serbia, Yug.* 42 F5
Timiş □, *Romania* 42 E6
Timişoara, *Romania* 42 E6
Timmersdala, *Sweden* 11 F7
Timmins, *Canada* 102 C3
Timok →, *Serbia, Yug.* 40 B6
Timor, *Indonesia* 63 F7
Timor Sea, *Ind. Oc.* 92 B4
Timor Timur = East Timor ■, *Asia* 63 F7
Timrå, *Sweden* 10 B11
Tin Can Bay, *Australia* 95 D5
Tin Ethisane, *Mali* 83 B4
Tin Gornai, *Mali* 83 B4
Tin Mt., *U.S.A.* 116 J9
Tina →, *S. Africa* 89 E4
Tîna, Khalîg el, *Egypt* 80 A3
Tinaca Pt., *Phil.* 61 J6
Tinajo, *Canary Is.* 37 E6
Tinca, *Romania* 42 D6
Tindal, *Australia* 92 B5
Tindouf, *Algeria* 78 C4
Tinée →, *France* 21 E11
Tineo, *Spain* 34 B4
Ting Jiang →, *China* 59 E11
Tinggi, Pulau, *Malaysia* 65 L5
Tinglev, *Denmark* 11 K3
Tingo Maria, *Peru* 124 E3
Tingrela, *Ivory C.* 82 C3
Tingsryd, *Sweden* 11 H9
Tingstäde, *Sweden* 11 G12
Tinh Bien, *Vietnam* 65 G5
Tinnevelly = Tirunelveli, *India* 66 Q10
Tinogasta, *Argentina* 126 B2
Tínos, *Greece* 39 D7
Tiñoso, C., *Spain* 33 H3
Tinpahar, *India* 69 G12
Tintina, *Argentina* 126 B3
Tintioulé, *Guinea* 82 C3
Tinto →, *Spain* 35 H4
Tioga, *N. Dak., U.S.A.* 112 A3
Tioga, *Pa., U.S.A.* 110 E7
Tioman, Pulau, *Malaysia* 65 L5
Tione di Trento, *Italy* 28 B7
Tionesta, *U.S.A.* 110 E5
Tior, *Sudan* 81 F3
Tipongpani, *India* 67 F19
Tipperary, *Ireland* 15 D3
Tipperary □, *Ireland* 15 D4
Tipton, *Calif., U.S.A.* 116 J7
Tipton, *Iowa, U.S.A.* 112 E9
Tipton Mt., *U.S.A.* 117 K12
Tiptonville, *U.S.A.* 113 G10
Tīrān, *Iran* 71 C6
Tīrān, *Si. Arabia* 80 B3
Tiranë, *Albania* 40 E3
Tirano, *Italy* 28 B7
Tiraspol, *Moldova* 43 D14
Tirdout, *Mali* 83 B4
Tire, *Turkey* 39 C9
Tirebolu, *Turkey* 73 B8
Tiree, *U.K.* 14 E2
Tiree, Passage of, *U.K.* 14 E2
Tîrgovişte = Târgovişte, *Romania* 43 F10
Tîrgu-Jiu = Târgu-Jiu, *Romania* 43 E8
Tîrgu Mureş = Târgu Mureş, *Romania* 43 D9
Tirich Mir, *Pakistan* 66 A7
Tiriolo, *Italy* 31 D9
Tiriro, *Guinea* 82 C3
Tírnavos, *Greece* 38 B4
Tirodi, *India* 66 J11
Tirol □, *Austria* 26 D3
Tirschenreuth, *Germany* 25 F8
Tirso →, *Italy* 30 C1
Tirstrup, *Denmark* 11 H4
Tiruchchirappalli, *India* 66 P11
Tirunelveli, *India* 66 Q10
Tirupati, *India* 66 N11
Tiruppur, *India* 66 P10
Tiruvannamalai, *India* 66 N11
Tisa, *India* 68 C7
Tisa →, *Serbia, Yug.* 42 E5
Tisdale, *Canada* 105 C8
Tishomingo, *U.S.A.* 113 H6
Tisjön, *Sweden* 10 D7
Tisnaren, *Sweden* 11 F9
Tišnov, *Czech Rep.* 27 B9
Tisovec, *Slovak Rep.* 27 C12
Tisza = Tisa →, *Serbia, Yug.* 42 E5
Tiszaföldvár, *Hungary* 42 D5
Tiszafüred, *Hungary* 42 C5
Tiszalök, *Hungary* 42 B6
Tiszavasvári, *Hungary* 42 C6
Tit-Ary, *Russia* 51 B13
Titaguas, *Spain* 32 F3
Titao, *Burkina Faso* 83 C4
Titel, *Serbia, Yug.* 42 E5
Tithwal, *Pakistan* 69 B5
Titicaca, L., *S. Amer.* 122 E4
Titisee, *Germany* 25 H4
Titiwa, *Nigeria* 83 C7
Tito, *Italy* 31 B8
Titograd = Podgorica, *Montenegro, Yug.* 40 D3
Titova Korenica, *Croatia* 29 D12
Titu, *Romania* 43 F10
Titule, *Dem. Rep. of the Congo* 86 B2
Titusville, *Fla., U.S.A.* 109 L5
Titusville, *Pa., U.S.A.* 110 E5
Tivaouane, *Senegal* 82 C1
Tivat, *Montenegro, Yug.* 40 D2
Tiverton, *U.K.* 13 G4
Tívoli, *Italy* 29 G9
Tiyo, *Eritrea* 81 E5
Tizi-Ouzou, *Algeria* 78 A6
Tizimín, *Mexico* 119 C7
Tjæreborg, *Denmark* 11 J2
Tjällmo, *Sweden* 11 F9
Tjeggelvas, *Sweden* 8 C17
Tjirebon = Cirebon, *Indonesia* 62 F3
Tjörn, *Sweden* 11 F5
Tkibuli = Tqibuli, *Georgia* 49 J6
Tkvarcheli = Tqvarcheli, *Georgia* 49 J5
Tlacotalpan, *Mexico* 119 D5
Tlahualilo, *Mexico* 118 B4
Tlaquepaque, *Mexico* 118 C4
Tlaxcala, *Mexico* 119 D5
Tlaxcala □, *Mexico* 119 D5
Tlaxiaco, *Mexico* 119 D5
Tlemcen, *Algeria* 78 B5
Tłuszcz, *Poland* 45 F8
Tlyarata, *Russia* 49 J8
To Bong, *Vietnam* 64 F7
Toad →, *Canada* 104 B4
Toad River, *Canada* 104 B3
Toamasina, *Madag.* 89 B8
Toamasina □, *Madag.* 89 B8
Toay, *Argentina* 126 D3
Toba, *China* 58 B1
Toba, *Japan* 55 G8
Toba, Danau, *Indonesia* 62 D1
Toba Kakar, *Pakistan* 68 D3
Toba Tek Singh, *Pakistan* 68 D5
Tobago, *Trin. & Tob.* 121 D7
Tobarra, *Spain* 33 G3
Tobelo, *Indonesia* 63 D7
Tobermory, *Canada* 102 C3
Tobermory, *U.K.* 14 E2
Tobi, *Pac. Oc.* 63 D8
Tobin, *U.S.A.* 116 F5
Tobin, L., *Australia* 92 D4
Tobin L., *Canada* 105 C8
Toblach = Dobbiaco, *Italy* 29 B9
Toboali, *Indonesia* 62 E3
Tobol →, *Russia* 50 D7
Toboli, *Indonesia* 63 E6
Tobolsk, *Russia* 50 D7
Tobor, *Senegal* 82 C1
Tobruk = Tubruq, *Libya* 79 B10
Tobyhanna, *U.S.A.* 111 E9
Tobyl = Tobol →, *Russia* 50 D7
Tocantinópolis, *Brazil* 125 E9
Tocantins □, *Brazil* 125 F9
Tocantins →, *Brazil* 122 D6
Toccoa, *U.S.A.* 109 H4
Toce →, *Italy* 28 C5
Tochi →, *Pakistan* 68 C4
Tochigi, *Japan* 55 F9
Tochigi □, *Japan* 55 F9
Tocina, *Spain* 35 H5
Töcksfors, *Sweden* 10 E5
Toconao, *Chile* 126 A2
Tocopilla, *Chile* 126 A1
Tocuyo →, *Venezuela* 124 A5
Todd →, *Australia* 94 C2
Todeli, *Indonesia* 63 E6
Todenyang, *Kenya* 86 B4
Todgarh, *India* 68 G5
Todi, *Italy* 29 F9
Todos os Santos, B. de, *Brazil* 125 F11
Todos Santos, *Mexico* 118 C2
Todtnau, *Germany* 25 H3
Toe Hd., *U.K.* 14 D1
Toecé, *Burkina Faso* 83 C4
Tofield, *Canada* 104 C6
Tofino, *Canada* 104 D3
Tofua, *Tonga* 91 D11
Tōgane, *Japan* 55 G10
Togba, *Mauritania* 82 B2
Togian, Kepulauan, *Indonesia* 63 E6
Togliatti, *Russia* 48 D9
Togo ■, *W. Afr.* 83 D5
Togtoh, *China* 56 D6
Tohma →, *Turkey* 72 C7
Tōhoku □, *Japan* 54 E10
Töhöm, *Mongolia* 56 B5
Toinya, *Sudan* 81 F2
Toiyabe Range, *U.S.A.* 114 G5
Tojikiston = Tajikistan ■, *Asia* 50 F8
Tojo, *Indonesia* 63 E6
Tōjō, *Japan* 55 G6
Tok, *U.S.A.* 100 B5
Tok-do, *Japan* 55 F5
Tokachi-Dake, *Japan* 54 C11
Tokachi-Gawa →, *Japan* 54 C11
Tokaj, *Hungary* 42 B6
Tokala, *Indonesia* 63 E6
Tōkamachi, *Japan* 55 F9
Tokanui, *N.Z.* 91 M2
Tokar, *Sudan* 80 D4
Tokara-Rettō, *Japan* 55 K4
Tokarahi, *N.Z.* 91 L3
Tokashiki-Shima, *Japan* 55 L3
Tokat, *Turkey* 72 B7
Tŏkch'ŏn, *N. Korea* 57 E14
Tokeland, *U.S.A.* 116 D3
Tokelau Is., *Pac. Oc.* 96 H10
Tokmak, *Kyrgyzstan* 50 E8
Tokmak, *Ukraine* 47 J8
Toko Ra., *Australia* 94 C2
Tokoro-Gawa →, *Japan* 54 B12
Tokuno-Shima, *Japan* 55 L4
Tokushima, *Japan* 55 G7
Tokushima □, *Japan* 55 H7
Tokuyama, *Japan* 55 G5
Tōkyō, *Japan* 55 G9
Tolaga Bay, *N.Z.* 91 H7
Tolbukhin = Dobrich, *Bulgaria* 41 C11
Toledo, *Brazil* 127 A5
Toledo, *Spain* 34 F6
Toledo, *Ohio, U.S.A.* 108 E4
Toledo, *Oreg., U.S.A.* 114 D2
Toledo, *Wash., U.S.A.* 114 C2
Toledo, Montes de, *Spain* 35 F6
Toledo Bend Reservoir, *U.S.A.* 113 K8
Tolentino, *Italy* 29 E10
Tolfa, *Italy* 29 F8
Tolga, *Australia* 94 B4
Toliara, *Madag.* 89 C7
Toliara □, *Madag.* 89 C8
Tolima, *Colombia* 124 C3
Tolitoli, *Indonesia* 63 D6
Tolkmicko, *Poland* 44 D6
Tollarp, *Sweden* 11 J7
Tollensesee, *Germany* 24 B9
Tollhouse, *U.S.A.* 116 H7
Tolmachevo, *Russia* 46 C5
Tolmezzo, *Italy* 29 B10
Tolmin, *Slovenia* 29 B10
Tolna, *Hungary* 42 D3
Tolna □, *Hungary* 42 D3
Tolo, Teluk, *Indonesia* 63 E6
Tolochin = Talachyn, *Belarus* 46 E5
Tolosa, *Spain* 32 B2
Tolox, *Spain* 35 J6
Toluca, *Mexico* 119 D5
Tom Burke, *S. Africa* 89 C4
Tom Price, *Australia* 92 D2
Toma, *Burkina Faso* 82 C4
Tomah, *U.S.A.* 112 D9
Tomahawk, *U.S.A.* 112 C10
Tomai, *Moldova* 43 D13
Tomakomai, *Japan* 54 C10
Tomales, *U.S.A.* 116 G4
Tomales B., *U.S.A.* 116 G3
Tomar, *Portugal* 35 F2
Tómaros, Óros, *Greece* 38 B2
Tomarza, *Turkey* 72 C6
Tomaszów Lubelski, *Poland* 45 H10
Tomaszów Mazowiecki, *Poland* 45 G7
Tomatlán, *Mexico* 118 D3
Tombadonkéa, *Guinea* 82 C2
Tombador, Serra do, *Brazil* 124 F7
Tombe, *Sudan* 81 F3
Tombigbee →, *U.S.A.* 109 K2
Tombouctou, *Mali* 82 B4
Tombstone, *U.S.A.* 115 L8
Tombua, *Angola* 88 B1
Tomé, *Chile* 126 D1
Tomelilla, *Sweden* 11 J7
Tomelloso, *Spain* 35 F7
Tomini, *Indonesia* 63 D6
Tomini, Teluk, *Indonesia* 63 E6
Tominian, *Mali* 82 C4
Tomiño, *Spain* 34 D2
Tomintoul, *U.K.* 14 D5
Tomislavgrad, *Bos.-H.* 42 G2
Tomkinson Ranges, *Australia* 93 E4
Tommot, *Russia* 51 D13
Tomnop Ta Suos, *Cambodia* 65 G5
Tomo →, *Colombia* 124 B5
Toms Place, *U.S.A.* 116 H8
Toms River, *U.S.A.* 111 G10
Tomsk, *Russia* 50 D9
Tomtabacken, *Sweden* 11 G8
Tona, *Spain* 32 D7
Tonalá, *Mexico* 119 D6
Tonale, Passo del, *Italy* 28 B7
Tonantins, *Brazil* 124 D5
Tonasket, *U.S.A.* 114 B4
Tonawanda, *U.S.A.* 110 D6
Tonbridge, *U.K.* 13 F8
Tondano, *Indonesia* 63 D6
Tondela, *Portugal* 34 E2
Tønder, *Denmark* 11 K2
Tondi Kiwindi, *Niger* 83 C5
Tondibi, *Mali* 83 B4
Tondoro, *Namibia* 88 B2
Tone →, *Australia* 93 F2
Tone-Gawa →, *Japan* 55 F9
Tonekābon, *Iran* 71 B6
Tong Xian, *China* 56 E9
Tongā, *Sudan* 81 F3
Tonga ■, *Pac. Oc.* 91 D11
Tonga Trench, *Pac. Oc.* 96 J10
Tongaat, *S. Africa* 89 D5
Tong'an, *China* 59 E12
Tongareva, *Cook Is.* 97 H12
Tongatapu Group, *Tonga* 91 E12
Tongbai, *China* 59 A9
Tongcheng, *Anhui, China* 59 B11
Tongcheng, *Hubei, China* 59 C9
Tongchŏn-ni, *N. Korea* 57 E14
Tongchuan, *China* 56 G5
Tongdao, *China* 58 D7
Tongeren, *Belgium* 17 D5
Tonggu, *China* 59 C10
Tongguan, *China* 56 G6
Tonghai, *China* 58 E4
Tonghua, *China* 57 D13
Tongjiang, *China* 58 B6
Tongjosŏn Man, *N. Korea* 57 E15
Tongking, G. of = Tonkin, G. of, *Asia* 60 E5
Tongliang, *China* 58 C6
Tongliao, *China* 57 C12
Tongling, *China* 59 B11
Tonglu, *China* 59 C12
Tongnae, *S. Korea* 57 G15
Tongnan = Anyue, *China* 58 B5
Tongobory, *Madag.* 89 C7
Tongoy, *Chile* 126 C1
Tongren, *China* 58 D7
Tongres = Tongeren, *Belgium* 17 D5
Tongsa Dzong, *Bhutan* 67 F17
Tongue, *U.K.* 14 C4
Tongue →, *U.S.A.* 112 B2
Tongwei, *China* 56 G3
Tongxiang, *China* 59 B13
Tongxin, *China* 56 F3
Tongyang, *N. Korea* 57 E14
Tongyu, *China* 57 B12
Tongzi, *China* 58 C6
Tonj, *Sudan* 81 F2
Tonj →, *Sudan* 81 F2
Tonk, *India* 68 F6
Tonkawa, *U.S.A.* 113 G6
Tonkin = Bac Phan, *Vietnam* 64 B5
Tonkin, G. of, *Asia* 60 E5
Tonle Sap, *Cambodia* 64 F4
Tonnay-Charente, *France* 20 C3
Tonneins, *France* 20 D4
Tonnerre, *France* 19 E10
Tönning, *Germany* 24 A4
Tono, *Japan* 54 E10
Tonopah, *U.S.A.* 115 G5
Tonosí, *Panama* 120 E3
Tons →, *Haryana, India* 68 D7
Tons →, *Ut. P., India* 69 F10
Tønsberg, *Norway* 9 G14
Tonya, *Turkey* 73 B8
Toobanna, *Australia* 94 B4
Toodyay, *Australia* 93 F2
Tooele, *U.S.A.* 114 F7
Toompine, *Australia* 95 D3
Toora-Khem, *Russia* 51 D10

Toowoomba, Australia 95 D5
Top Springs, Australia 92 C5
Topalu, Romania 43 F13
Topaz, U.S.A. 116 G7
Topeka, U.S.A. 112 F7
Topl'a →, Slovak Rep. 27 C14
Topley, Canada 104 C3
Toplica →, Serbia, Yug. 40 C5
Toplița, Romania 43 D10
Topocalma, Pta., Chile 126 C1
Topock, U.S.A. 117 L12
Topola, Serbia, Yug. 40 B4
Topolčani, Macedonia 40 E5
Topol'čany, Slovak Rep. 27 C11
Topolnitsa →, Bulgaria 41 D8
Topolobampo, Mexico 118 B3
Topoloveni, Romania 43 F10
Topolovgrad, Bulgaria 41 D10
Topolvățu Mare, Romania 42 E6
Toppenish, U.S.A. 114 C3
Topraisar, Romania 43 F13
Topusko, Croatia 29 C12
Torà, Spain 32 D6
Tora Kit, Sudan 81 E3
Toraka Vestale, Madag. 89 B7
Torata, Peru 124 G4
Torbalı, Turkey 39 C9
Torbat-e Heydārīyeh, Iran 71 C8
Torbat-e Jām, Iran 71 C9
Torbay, Canada 103 C9
Torbay □, U.K. 13 G4
Torbjörntorp, Sweden 11 F7
Tordesillas, Spain 34 D6
Töreboda, Sweden 11 F8
Torekov, Sweden 11 H6
Torellò, Spain 32 C7
Toreno, Spain 34 C4
Torfaen □, U.K. 13 F4
Torgau, Germany 24 D8
Torgelow, Germany 24 B10
Torhamn, Sweden 11 H9
Torhout, Belgium 17 C3
Tori, Ethiopia 81 F3
Tori-Shima, Japan 55 J10
Torigni-sur-Vire, France 18 C6
Torija, Spain 32 E1
Torin, Mexico 118 B2
Torino, Italy 28 C4
Torit, Sudan 81 G3
Torkamān, Iran 70 B5
Torkovichi, Russia 46 C6
Tormac, Romania 42 E6
Tormes →, Spain 34 D4
Tornado Mt., Canada 104 D6
Tornal'a, Slovak Rep. 27 C13
Torne älv →, Sweden 8 D21
Torneå = Tornio, Finland 8 D21
Torneträsk, Sweden 8 B18
Tornio, Finland 8 D21
Tornionjoki →, Finland 8 D21
Tornquist, Argentina 126 D3
Toro, Baleares, Spain 37 B11
Toro, Zamora, Spain 34 D5
Torö, Sweden 11 F11
Toro, Cerro del, Chile 126 B2
Toro Pk., U.S.A. 117 M10
Törökszentmiklós, Hungary 42 C5
Toronîos Kólpos, Greece 40 F7
Toronto, Canada 102 D4
Toronto, U.S.A. 110 F4
Toropets, Russia 46 D6
Tororo, Uganda 86 B3
Toros Dağları, Turkey 70 B2
Torpa, India 69 H11
Torquay, U.K. 13 G4
Torquemada, Spain 34 C6
Torrance, U.S.A. 117 M8
Torrão, Portugal 35 G2
Torre Annunziata, Italy 31 B7
Torre de Moncorvo, Portugal 34 D3
Torre del Campo, Spain 35 H7
Torre del Greco, Italy 31 B7
Torre del Mar, Spain 35 J6
Torre-Pacheco, Spain 33 H4
Torre Péllice, Italy 28 D4
Torreblanca, Spain 32 E5
Torrecampo, Spain 35 G6
Torrecilla en Cameros, Spain 32 C2
Torredembarra, Spain 32 D6
Torredonjimeno, Spain 35 H7
Torrejón de Ardoz, Spain 34 E7
Torrejoncillo, Spain 34 F4
Torrelaguna, Spain 34 E7
Torrelavega, Spain 34 B6
Torremaggiore, Italy 29 G12
Torremolinos, Spain 35 J6
Torrens Cr. →, Australia 94 C4
Torrens Creek, Australia 94 C4
Torrent, Spain 33 F4
Torrenueva, Spain 35 G7
Torreón, Mexico 118 B4
Torreperogil, Spain 35 G7
Torres, Brazil 127 B5
Torres, Mexico 118 B2
Torres Novas, Portugal 35 F2
Torres Strait, Australia 96 H6
Torres Vedras, Portugal 35 F1
Torrevieja, Spain 33 H4
Torrey, U.S.A. 115 G8
Torridge →, U.K. 13 G3
Torridon, L., U.K. 14 D3
Torrijos, Spain 34 F6
Tørring, Denmark 11 J3
Torrington, Conn., U.S.A. 111 E11
Torrington, Wyo., U.S.A. 112 D2
Torroella de Montgrì, Spain 32 C8
Torrox, Spain 35 J7
Torsås, Sweden 11 H9
Torsby, Sweden 10 D6
Torshälla, Sweden 10 E10
Tórshavn, Færoe Is. 8 E9
Torslanda, Sweden 11 G5
Torsö, Sweden 11 F7
Tortola, Br. Virgin Is. 121 C7
Tórtoles de Esgueva, Spain 34 D6
Tortolì, Italy 30 C2
Tortona, Italy 28 D5
Tortorici, Italy 31 D7
Tortosa, Spain 32 E5
Tortosa, C., Spain 32 E5
Tortosendo, Portugal 34 E3
Tortue, I. de la, Haiti 121 B5
Tortum, Turkey 73 B9
Ţorūd, Iran 71 C7
Torul, Turkey 73 B8
Toruń, Poland 45 E5
Tory I., Ireland 15 A3
Torysa →, Slovak Rep. 27 C14
Torzhok, Russia 46 D8
Torzym, Poland 45 F2
Tosa, Japan 55 H6
Tosa-Shimizu, Japan 55 H6
Tosa-Wan, Japan 55 H6
Toscana □, Italy 28 E8
Toscano, Arcipelago, Italy 28 F7
Toshkent, Uzbekistan 50 E7
Tosno, Russia 46 C6
Tossa de Mar, Spain 32 D7
Tösse, Sweden 11 F6
Tostado, Argentina 126 B3
Tostedt, Germany 24 B5
Tostón, Pta. de, Canary Is. 37 F5
Tosu, Japan 55 H5
Tosya, Turkey 72 B6
Toszek, Poland 45 H5
Totana, Spain 33 H3
Totebo, Sweden 11 G10
Toteng, Botswana 88 C3
Tôtes, France 18 C8
Tótkomlós, Hungary 42 D5
Totma, Russia 50 C5
Totnes, U.K. 13 G4
Totness, Surinam 125 B7
Toto, Nigeria 83 D6
Totonicapán, Guatemala 120 D1
Totten Glacier, Antarctica 5 C8
Tottenham, Canada 110 B5
Tottori, Japan 55 G7
Tottori □, Japan 55 G7
Touaret, Niger 83 A6
Touba, Ivory C. 82 D3
Touba, Senegal 82 C1
Toubkal, Djebel, Morocco 78 B4
Toucy, France 19 E10
Tougan, Burkina Faso 82 C4
Touggourt, Algeria 78 B7
Tougouri, Burkina Faso 83 C4
Tougué, Guinea 82 C2
Toukoto, Mali 82 C3
Toul, France 19 D12
Toulepleu, Ivory C. 82 D3
Toulon, France 21 E9
Toulouse, France 20 E5
Toummo, Niger 79 D8
Toumodi, Ivory C. 82 D3
Tounan, Taiwan 59 F13
Toungo, Nigeria 83 D7
Toungoo, Burma 67 K20
Touques →, France 18 C7
Touraine, France 18 E7
Tourane = Da Nang, Vietnam 64 D7
Tourcoing, France 19 B10
Touriñán, C., Spain 34 B1
Tournai, Belgium 17 D3
Tournan-en-Brie, France 19 D9
Tournay, France 20 E4
Tournon-St-Martin, France 18 F7
Tournon-sur-Rhône, France 21 C8
Tournus, France 19 F11
Tours, France 18 E7
Toussora, Mt., C.A.R. 84 C4
Touws →, S. Africa 88 E3
Touwsrivier, S. Africa 88 E3
Tovarkovskiy, Russia 46 F10
Tovuz, Azerbaijan 49 K7
Towada, Japan 54 D10
Towada-Ko, Japan 54 D10
Towanda, U.S.A. 111 E8
Towang, India 67 F17
Tower, U.S.A. 112 B8
Towerhill Cr. →, Australia 94 C3
Towner, U.S.A. 112 A4
Townsend, U.S.A. 114 C8
Townshend I., Australia 94 C5
Townsville, Australia 94 B4
Towson, U.S.A. 108 F7
Towuti, Danau, Indonesia 63 E6
Toya-Ko, Japan 54 C10
Toyama, Japan 55 F8
Toyama □, Japan 55 F8
Toyama-Wan, Japan 55 F8
Toyohashi, Japan 55 G8
Toyokawa, Japan 55 G8
Toyonaka, Japan 55 G7
Toyooka, Japan 55 G7
Toyota, Japan 55 G8
Tozeur, Tunisia 78 B7
Tqibuli, Georgia 49 J6
Tqvarcheli, Georgia 49 J5
Trá Li = Tralee, Ireland 15 D2
Tra On, Vietnam 65 H5
Trabancos →, Spain 34 D5
Traben-Trarbach, Germany 25 F3
Trabzon, Turkey 73 B8
Tracadie, Canada 103 C7
Tracy, Calif., U.S.A. 116 H5
Tracy, Minn., U.S.A. 112 C7
Tradate, Italy 28 C5
Trade Town, Liberia 82 D3
Trafalgar, C., Spain 35 J4
Traian, Brăila, Romania 43 E12
Traian, Tulcea, Romania 43 E13
Trail, Canada 104 D5
Trainor L., Canada 104 A4
Trákhonas, Cyprus 36 D12
Tralee, Ireland 15 D2
Tralee B., Ireland 15 D2
Tramore, Ireland 15 D4
Tramore B., Ireland 15 D4
Tran Ninh, Cao Nguyen, Laos 64 C4
Tranås, Sweden 11 F8
Tranbjerg, Denmark 11 H4
Trancas, Argentina 126 B2
Trancoso, Portugal 34 E3
Tranebjerg, Denmark 11 J4
Tranemo, Sweden 11 G7
Trang, Thailand 65 J2
Trangahy, Madag. 89 B7
Trangan, Indonesia 63 F8
Trångsviken, Sweden 10 A7
Trani, Italy 31 A9
Tranoroa, Madag. 89 C8
Tranqueras, Uruguay 127 C4
Transantarctic Mts., Antarctica 5 E12
Transilvania, Romania 43 D9
Transilvanian Alps = Carpații Meridionali, Romania 43 E9
Transtrand, Sweden 10 C7
Transtrandsfjällen, Sweden 10 C6
Transvaal, S. Africa 85 K5
Transylvania = Transilvania, Romania 43 D9
Trápani, Italy 30 D5
Trapper Pk., U.S.A. 114 D6
Trarza, Mauritania 82 B2
Trasacco, Italy 29 G10
Trăscău, Munții, Romania 43 D8
Trasimeno, L., Italy 29 E9
Träslövsläge, Sweden 11 G6
Trasvase Tajo-Segura, Canal de, Spain 32 E2
Trat, Thailand 65 F4
Tratani →, Pakistan 68 E3
Traun, Austria 26 C7
Traunreut, Germany 25 H8
Traunsee, Austria 26 D6
Traunstein, Germany 25 H8
Travemünde, Germany 24 B6
Travers, Mt., N.Z. 91 K4
Traverse City, U.S.A. 108 C3
Travis, L., U.S.A. 113 K5
Travnik, Bos.-H. 42 F2
Trbovlje, Slovenia 29 B12
Trébbia →, Italy 28 C6
Trebel →, Germany 24 B9
Trébeurden, France 18 D3
Třebíč, Czech Rep. 26 B8
Trebinje, Bos.-H. 40 D2
Trebisacce, Italy 31 C9
Trebišnjica →, Bos.-H. 40 D2
Trebišov, Slovak Rep. 27 C14
Trebižat →, Bos.-H. 29 E14
Trebnje, Slovenia 29 C12
Třeboň, Czech Rep. 26 B7
Trebonne, Australia 94 B4
Trebujena, Spain 35 J4
Trecate, Italy 28 C5
Tregaron, U.K. 13 E4
Tregnago, Italy 29 C8
Tregrosse Is., Australia 94 B5
Tréguier, France 18 D3
Trégunc, France 18 E3
Treherne, Canada 105 D9
Tréia, Italy 29 E10
Treignac, France 20 C5
Treinta y Tres, Uruguay 127 C5
Treis-karden, Germany 25 E3
Treklyano, Bulgaria 40 D6
Trelawney, Zimbabwe 89 B5
Trélazé, France 18 E6
Trelew, Argentina 128 E3
Trélissac, France 20 C4
Trelleborg, Sweden 11 J7
Tremadog Bay, U.K. 12 E3
Trémiti, Italy 29 F12
Tremonton, U.S.A. 114 F7
Tremp, Spain 32 C5
Trenche →, Canada 102 C5
Trenčiansky □, Slovak Rep. 27 C11
Trenčín, Slovak Rep. 27 C11
Trenggalek, Indonesia 63 H14
Trenque Lauquen, Argentina 126 D3
Trent →, Canada 110 B7
Trent →, U.K. 12 D7
Trentino-Alto Adige □, Italy 29 B8
Trento, Italy 28 B8
Trenton, Canada 102 D4
Trenton, Mo., U.S.A. 112 E8
Trenton, N.J., U.S.A. 111 F10
Trenton, Nebr., U.S.A. 112 E4
Trepassey, Canada 103 C9
Trepuzzi, Italy 31 B11
Tres Arroyos, Argentina 126 D3
Três Corações, Brazil 127 A6
Três Lagoas, Brazil 125 H8
Tres Lomas, Argentina 126 D3
Tres Marías, Islas, Mexico 118 C3
Tres Montes, C., Chile 128 F1
Tres Pinos, U.S.A. 116 J5
Três Pontas, Brazil 127 A6
Tres Puentes, Chile 126 B1
Tres Puntas, C., Argentina 128 F3
Três Rios, Brazil 127 A7
Tres Valles, Mexico 119 D5
Tresco, U.K. 13 H1
Treska →, Macedonia 40 E5
Treskavica, Bos.-H. 42 G3
Trespaderne, Spain 34 C7
Trets, France 21 E9
Treuchtlingen, Germany 25 G6
Treuenbrietzen, Germany 24 C8
Trevi, Italy 29 F9
Treviglio, Italy 28 C6
Trevínca, Peña, Spain 34 C4
Treviso, Italy 29 C9
Trévoux, France 21 C8
Trgovište, Serbia, Yug. 40 D6
Triabunna, Australia 94 G4
Triánda, Greece 36 C10
Triangle, Zimbabwe 89 C5
Triaucourt-en-Argonne, France 19 D12
Tribal Areas □, Pakistan 68 C4
Tribsees, Germany 24 A8
Tribulation, C., Australia 94 B4
Tribune, U.S.A. 112 F4
Tricárico, Italy 31 B9
Tricase, Italy 31 C11
Trichinopoly = Tiruchchirappalli, India 66 P11
Trichur, India 66 P10
Trier, Germany 25 F2
Trieste, Italy 29 C10
Trieste, G. di, Italy 29 C10
Trieux →, France 18 D3
Triggiano, Italy 31 A9
Triglav, Slovenia 29 B10
Trigno →, Italy 29 F11
Trigueros, Spain 35 H4
Tríkeri, Greece 38 B5
Trikhonis, Límni, Greece 38 C3
Tríkkala, Greece 38 B3
Tríkkala □, Greece 38 B3
Trikomo, Cyprus 36 D12
Trikora, Puncak, Indonesia 63 E9
Trilj, Croatia 29 E13
Trillo, Spain 32 E2
Trim, Ireland 15 C5
Trincomalee, Sri Lanka 66 Q12
Trindade, Brazil 125 G9
Trindade, I., Atl. Oc. 2 F8
Třinec, Czech Rep. 27 B11
Trinidad, Bolivia 124 F6
Trinidad, Cuba 120 B4
Trinidad, Trin. & Tob. 121 D7
Trinidad, Uruguay 126 C4
Trinidad, U.S.A. 113 G2
Trinidad →, Mexico 119 D5
Trinidad & Tobago ■, W. Indies 121 D7
Trinitápoli, Italy 31 A9
Trinity, Canada 103 C9
Trinity, U.S.A. 113 K7
Trinity →, Calif., U.S.A. 114 F2
Trinity →, Tex., U.S.A. 113 L7
Trinity B., Canada 103 C9
Trinity Is., U.S.A. 100 C4
Trinity Range, U.S.A. 114 F4
Trinkitat, Sudan 80 D4
Trino, Italy 28 C5
Trinway, U.S.A. 110 F2
Trionto, C., Italy 31 C9
Triora, Italy 28 D4
Tripoli = Tarābulus, Lebanon 75 A4
Tripoli = Tarābulus, Libya 79 B8
Trípolis, Greece 38 D4
Tripolitania, N. Afr. 79 B8
Tripura □, India 67 H18
Tripylos, Cyprus 36 E11
Trischen, Germany 24 A4
Tristan da Cunha, Atl. Oc. 77 K2
Trisul, India 69 D8
Trivandrum, India 66 Q10
Trivento, Italy 29 G11
Trnava, Slovak Rep. 27 C10
Trnavský □, Slovak Rep. 27 C10
Troarn, France 18 C6
Trochu, Canada 104 C6
Trodely I., Canada 102 B4
Troezen, Greece 38 D5
Trogir, Croatia 29 E13
Troglav, Croatia 29 E13
Tróia, Italy 31 A8
Troilus, L., Canada 102 B5
Troina, Italy 31 E7
Trois-Pistoles, Canada 103 C6
Trois-Rivières, Canada 102 C5
Troisdorf, Germany 24 E3
Troitsk, Russia 50 D7
Troitsko Pechorsk, Russia 50 C6
Trölladyngja, Iceland 8 D5
Trollhättan, Sweden 11 F6
Trollheimen, Norway 8 E13
Trombetas →, Brazil 125 D7
Tromsø, Norway 8 B18
Trona, U.S.A. 117 K9
Tronador, Mte., Argentina 128 E2
Trøndelag, Norway 8 D14
Trondheim, Norway 8 E14
Trondheimsfjorden, Norway 8 E14
Trönninge, Sweden 11 H6
Tronto →, Italy 29 F10
Troodos, Cyprus 36 E11
Troon, U.K. 14 F4
Tropea, Italy 31 D8
Tropic, U.S.A. 115 H7
Tropojë, Albania 40 D4
Trosa, Sweden 11 F11
Trostan, U.K. 15 A5
Trostberg, Germany 25 G8
Trostyanets, Ukraine 47 G8
Trout →, Canada 104 A5
Trout L., N.W.T., Canada 104 A4
Trout L., Ont., Canada 105 C10
Trout Lake, Canada 104 B6
Trout Lake, U.S.A. 116 E5
Trout River, Canada 103 C8
Trout Run, U.S.A. 110 E7
Trouville-sur-Mer, France 18 C7
Trowbridge, U.K. 13 F5
Troy, Turkey 39 B8
Troy, Ala., U.S.A. 109 K3
Troy, Kans., U.S.A. 112 F7
Troy, Mo., U.S.A. 112 F9
Troy, Mont., U.S.A. 114 B6
Troy, N.Y., U.S.A. 111 D11
Troy, Ohio, U.S.A. 108 E3
Troy, Pa., U.S.A. 111 E8
Troyan, Bulgaria 41 D8
Troyes, France 19 D11
Trpanj, Croatia 29 E14
Trstenik, Serbia, Yug. 40 C5
Trubchevsk, Russia 47 F7
Truchas Peak, U.S.A. 113 H2
Trucial States = United Arab Emirates ■, Asia 71 F7
Truckee, U.S.A. 116 F6
Trudfront, Russia 49 H8
Trudovoye, Russia 54 C6
Trujillo, Honduras 120 C2
Trujillo, Peru 124 E3
Trujillo, Spain 35 F5
Trujillo, U.S.A. 113 H2
Trujillo, Venezuela 124 B4
Truk, Micronesia 96 G7
Trumann, U.S.A. 113 H9
Trumansburg, U.S.A. 111 D8
Trumbull, Mt., U.S.A. 115 H7
Trŭn, Bulgaria 40 D6
Trun, France 18 D7
Trung-Phan = Annam, Vietnam 64 E7
Truro, Canada 103 C7
Truro, U.K. 13 G2
Truskavets, Ukraine 47 H2
Trŭstenik, Bulgaria 41 C8
Trustrup, Denmark 11 H4
Trutch, Canada 104 B4
Truth or Consequences, U.S.A. 115 K10
Trutnov, Czech Rep. 26 A8
Truxton, U.S.A. 111 D8
Truyère →, France 20 D6
Tryavna, Bulgaria 41 D9
Tryonville, U.S.A. 110 E5
Trzcianka, Poland 45 E3
Trzciel, Poland 45 F2
Trzcińsko Zdrój, Poland 45 F1
Trzebiatów, Poland 44 D2
Trzebiez, Poland 44 E1
Trzebnica, Poland 45 G4
Trzemeszno, Poland 45 F4
Tržič, Slovenia 29 B11
Tsagan Aman, Russia 49 G8
Tsamandás, Greece 38 B2
Tsandi, Namibia 88 B1
Tsaratanana, Madag. 89 B8
Tsaratanana, Mt. de, Madag. 89 A8
Tsarevo = Michurin, Bulgaria 41 D11
Tsarevo, Bulgaria 41 D9
Tsaritsáni, Greece 38 B4
Tsau, Botswana 88 C3
Tsebrykove, Ukraine 47 J6
Tselinograd = Astana, Kazakstan 50 D8
Tses, Namibia 88 D2
Tsetserleg, Mongolia 60 B5
Tsévié, Togo 83 D5
Tshabong, Botswana 88 D3
Tshane, Botswana 88 C3
Tshela, Dem. Rep. of the Congo 84 E2
Tshesebe, Botswana 89 C4
Tshibeke, Dem. Rep. of the Congo 86 C2
Tshibinda, Dem. Rep. of the Congo 86 C2
Tshikapa, Dem. Rep. of the Congo 84 F4
Tshilenge, Dem. Rep. of the Congo 86 D1
Tshinsenda, Dem. Rep. of the Congo 87 E2
Tshofa, Dem. Rep. of the Congo 86 D2
Tshwane, Botswana 88 C3
Tsigara, Botswana 88 C4
Tsihombe, Madag. 89 D8
Tsiigehtchic, Canada 100 B6
Tsimlyansk, Russia 49 G6
Tsimlyansk Res. = Tsimlyanskoye Vdkhr., Russia 49 F6
Tsimlyanskoye Vdkhr., Russia 49 F6
Tsinan = Jinan, China 56 F9
Tsineng, S. Africa 88 D3
Tsínga, Greece 41 E8
Tsinghai = Qinghai □, China 60 C4
Tsingtao = Qingdao, China 57 F11
Tsinjoarivo, Madag. 89 B8
Tsinjomitondraka, Madag. 89 B8
Tsiroanomandidy, Madag. 89 B8
Tsiteli-Tsqaro, Georgia 49 K8

Tsitondroina, *Madag.* 89 C8
Tsivilsk, *Russia* 48 C8
Tsivory, *Madag.* 89 C8
Tskhinvali, *Georgia* 49 J7
Tsna →, *Russia* 48 C6
Tsnori, *Georgia* 49 K7
Tso Moriri, L., *India* 69 C8
Tsobis, *Namibia* 88 B2
Tsodilo Hill, *Botswana* 88 B3
Tsogttsetsiy = Baruunsuu, *Mongolia* 56 C3
Tsolo, *S. Africa* 89 E4
Tsomo, *S. Africa* 89 E4
Tsu, *Japan* 55 G8
Tsu L., *Canada* 104 A6
Tsuchiura, *Japan* 55 F10
Tsuen Wan, *H.K.* 59 F10
Tsugaru-Kaikyō, *Japan* 54 D10
Tsumeb, *Namibia* 88 B2
Tsumis, *Namibia* 88 C2
Tsuruga, *Japan* 55 G8
Tsurugi-San, *Japan* 55 H7
Tsuruoka, *Japan* 54 E9
Tsushima, *Gifu, Japan* 55 G8
Tsushima, *Nagasaki, Japan* 55 G4
Tsuyama, *Japan* 55 G7
Tsvetkovo, *Ukraine* 47 H6
Tsyelyakhany, *Belarus* 47 F3
Tua →, *Portugal* 34 D3
Tual, *Indonesia* 63 F8
Tuam, *Ireland* 15 C3
Tuamotu Arch. = Tuamotu Is., *Pac. Oc.* 97 J13
Tuamotu Is., *Pac. Oc.* 97 J13
Tuamotu Ridge, *Pac. Oc.* 97 K14
Tuanfeng, *China* 59 B10
Tuanxi, *China* 58 D6
Tuao, *Phil.* 61 C4
Tuapse, *Russia* 49 H4
Tuatapere, *N.Z.* 91 M1
Tuba City, *U.S.A.* 115 H8
Tuban, *Indonesia* 63 G15
Tubani, *Botswana* 88 C3
Tubarão, *Brazil* 127 B6
Tūbās, *West Bank* 75 C4
Tubas →, *Namibia* 88 C2
Tübingen, *Germany* 25 G5
Tubruq, *Libya* 79 B10
Tubuai Is., *Pac. Oc.* 97 K13
Tuc Trung, *Vietnam* 65 G6
Tucacas, *Venezuela* 124 A5
T'uch'ang, *Taiwan* 59 E13
Tuchodi →, *Canada* 104 B4
Tuchola, *Poland* 44 E4
Tuchów, *Poland* 45 J8
Tuckanarra, *Australia* 93 E2
Tucson, *U.S.A.* 115 K8
Tucumán □, *Argentina* 126 B2
Tucumcari, *U.S.A.* 113 H3
Tucupita, *Venezuela* 124 B6
Tucuruí, *Brazil* 125 D9
Tucuruí, Reprêsa de, *Brazil* 125 D9
Tuczno, *Poland* 45 E3
Tudela, *Spain* 32 C3
Tudmur, *Syria* 70 C3
Tudor, L., *Canada* 103 A6
Tudora, *Romania* 43 C11
Tuella →, *Portugal* 34 D3
Tugela →, *S. Africa* 89 D5
Tuguegarao, *Phil.* 61 C4
Tugur, *Russia* 51 D14
Tui, *Spain* 34 C2
Tuineje, *Canary Is.* 37 F5
Tukangbesi, Kepulauan, *Indonesia* 63 F6
Tukarak I., *Canada* 102 A4
Tukayyid, *Iraq* 70 D5
Tûkh, *Egypt* 80 H7
Tukobo, *Ghana* 82 D4
Tuktoyaktuk, *Canada* 100 B6
Tukums, *Latvia* 9 H20
Tukums □, *Latvia* 44 B10
Tukuyu, *Tanzania* 87 D3
Tula, *Hidalgo, Mexico* 119 C5
Tula, *Tamaulipas, Mexico* 119 C5
Tula, *Nigeria* 83 D7
Tula, *Russia* 46 E9
Tulancingo, *Mexico* 119 C5
Tulare, *Serbia, Yug.* 40 D5
Tulare, *U.S.A.* 116 J7
Tulare Lake Bed, *U.S.A.* 116 K7
Tularosa, *U.S.A.* 115 K10
Tulbagh, *S. Africa* 88 E2
Tulcán, *Ecuador* 124 C3
Tulcea, *Romania* 43 E13
Tulcea □, *Romania* 43 E13
Tulchyn, *Ukraine* 47 H5
Tüleh, *Iran* 71 C7
Tulemalu L., *Canada* 105 A9
Tulgheş, *Romania* 43 D10
Tuli, *Zimbabwe* 87 G2
Tulia, *U.S.A.* 113 H4
Tuliszków, *Poland* 45 F5
Tulita, *Canada* 100 B7
Ţūlkarm, *West Bank* 75 C4
Tulla, *Ireland* 15 D3
Tullahoma, *U.S.A.* 109 H2
Tullamore, *Ireland* 15 C4
Tulle, *France* 20 C5
Tulln, *Austria* 26 C9
Tullow, *Ireland* 15 D5
Tullus, *Sudan* 81 E1
Tully, *Australia* 94 B4
Tully, *U.S.A.* 111 D8
Tulnici, *Romania* 43 E11
Tulovo, *Bulgaria* 41 D9
Tulsa, *U.S.A.* 113 G7
Tulsequah, *Canada* 104 B2
Tulu Milki, *Ethiopia* 81 F4
Tulu Welel, *Ethiopia* 81 F3
Tulua, *Colombia* 124 C3
Tulucești, *Romania* 43 E13
Tulun, *Russia* 51 D11
Tulungagung, *Indonesia* 63 H14
Tuma, *Russia* 46 E11
Tuma →, *Nic.* 120 D3
Tumaco, *Colombia* 124 C3
Tumatumari, *Guyana* 124 B7
Tumba, *Sweden* 10 E11
Tumba, L., *Dem. Rep. of the Congo* 84 E3
Tumbarumba, *Australia* 95 F4
Tumbaya, *Argentina* 126 A2
Tumbes, *Peru* 124 D2
Tumbur, *Sudan* 81 G3
Tumbwe, *Dem. Rep. of the Congo* 87 E2
Tumd Youqi, *China* 56 D6
Tumen, *China* 57 C15
Tumen Jiang →, *China* 57 C16
Tumeremo, *Venezuela* 124 B6
Tumkur, *India* 66 N10
Tump, *Pakistan* 66 F3
Tumpat, *Malaysia* 65 J4
Tumu, *Ghana* 82 C4
Tumucumaque, Serra, *Brazil* 122 C5
Tumwater, *U.S.A.* 116 C4
Tuna, *India* 68 H4
Tunadal, *Sweden* 10 B11
Tunas de Zaza, *Cuba* 120 B4
Tunbridge Wells = Royal Tunbridge Wells, *U.K.* 13 F8
Tunçbilek, *Turkey* 39 B11
Tunceli, *Turkey* 73 C8
Tundla, *India* 68 F8
Tundubai, *Sudan* 80 D2
Tunduru, *Tanzania* 87 E4
Tundzha →, *Bulgaria* 41 E10
Tungabhadra →, *India* 66 M11
Tungaru, *Sudan* 81 E3
Tungla, *Nic.* 120 D3
Tungsha Tao, *Taiwan* 59 G11
Tungshih, *Taiwan* 59 E13
Tungsten, *Canada* 104 A3
Tunguska, Nizhnyaya →, *Russia* 51 C9
Tunguska, Podkamennaya →, *Russia* 51 C10
Tunica, *U.S.A.* 113 H9
Tunis, *Tunisia* 78 A7
Tunisia ■, *Africa* 78 B6
Tunja, *Colombia* 124 B4
Tunkhannock, *U.S.A.* 111 E9
Tunliu, *China* 56 F7
Tunnsjøen, *Norway* 8 D15
Tunø, *Denmark* 11 J4
Tunungayualok I., *Canada* 103 A7
Tununirusiq = Arctic Bay, *Canada* 101 A11
Tunuyán, *Argentina* 126 C2
Tunuyán →, *Argentina* 126 C2
Tuo Jiang →, *China* 58 C5
Tuolumne, *U.S.A.* 116 H6
Tuolumne →, *U.S.A.* 116 H5
Tūp Āghāj, *Iran* 70 B5
Tupã, *Brazil* 127 A5
Tupelo, *U.S.A.* 109 H1
Tupik, *Russia* 46 E7
Tupinambaranas, *Brazil* 124 D7
Tupiza, *Bolivia* 126 A2
Tupižnica, *Serbia, Yug.* 40 C6
Tupman, *U.S.A.* 117 K7
Tupper, *Canada* 104 B4
Tupper Lake, *U.S.A.* 111 B10
Tupungato, Cerro, *S. Amer.* 126 C2
Tuquan, *China* 57 B11
Túquerres, *Colombia* 124 C3
Tura, *Russia* 51 C11
Turabah, *Si. Arabia* 70 D4
Turabah, *Si. Arabia* 80 C5
Tūrān, *Iran* 71 C8
Turan, *Russia* 51 D10
Ţurayf, *Si. Arabia* 70 D3
Turbacz, *Poland* 45 J7
Turbe, *Bos.-H.* 42 F2
Turčianske Teplice, *Slovak Rep.* 27 C11
Turcoaia, *Romania* 43 E13
Turda, *Romania* 43 D8
Turek, *Poland* 45 F5
Turen, *Venezuela* 124 B5
Turfan = Turpan, *China* 60 B3
Turfan Depression = Turpan Hami, *China* 52 E12
Turgeon →, *Canada* 102 C4
Tŭrgovishte, *Bulgaria* 41 C10
Turgut, *Turkey* 39 D10
Turgutlu, *Turkey* 39 C9
Turgwe →, *Zimbabwe* 89 C5
Turhal, *Turkey* 72 B7
Turia →, *Spain* 33 F4
Turiaçu, *Brazil* 125 D9
Turiaçu →, *Brazil* 125 D9
Turiec →, *Slovak Rep.* 27 B11
Turin = Torino, *Italy* 28 C4
Turkana, L., *Africa* 86 B4
Türkeli, *Turkey* 41 F11
Turkestan = Türkistan, *Kazakstan* 50 E7
Túrkeve, *Hungary* 42 C5
Turkey ■, *Eurasia* 72 C7
Turkey Creek, *Australia* 92 C4
Turki, *Russia* 48 D6
Türkistan, *Kazakstan* 50 E7
Türkmenbashi, *Turkmenistan* 50 E6
Turkmenistan ■, *Asia* 50 F6
Türkmenli, *Turkey* 39 B8
Türkoğlu, *Turkey* 72 D7
Turks & Caicos Is. ■, *W. Indies* 121 B5
Turks Island Passage, *W. Indies* 121 B5
Turku, *Finland* 9 F20
Turkwel →, *Kenya* 86 B4
Turlock, *U.S.A.* 116 H6
Turnagain →, *Canada* 104 B3
Turnagain, C., *N.Z.* 91 J6
Turneffe Is., *Belize* 119 D7
Turner, *U.S.A.* 114 B9
Turner Pt., *Australia* 94 A1
Turner Valley, *Canada* 104 C6
Turners Falls, *U.S.A.* 111 D12
Turnhout, *Belgium* 17 C4
Türnitz, *Austria* 26 D8
Turnor L., *Canada* 105 B7
Turnov, *Czech Rep.* 26 A8
Tŭrnovo = Veliko Tŭrnovo, *Bulgaria* 41 C9
Turnu Măgurele, *Romania* 43 G9
Turnu Roşu, P., *Romania* 43 E9
Turobin, *Poland* 45 H9
Turpan, *China* 60 B3
Turpan Hami, *China* 52 E12
Turrës, Kala e, *Albania* 40 E3
Turriff, *U.K.* 14 D6
Tursāq, *Iraq* 70 C5
Tursi, *Italy* 31 B9
Turtle Head I., *Australia* 94 A3
Turtle Is., *S. Leone* 82 D2
Turtle L., *Canada* 105 C7
Turtle Lake, *U.S.A.* 112 B4
Turtleford, *Canada* 105 C7
Turukhansk, *Russia* 51 C9
Turzovka, *Slovak Rep.* 27 B11
Tuscaloosa, *U.S.A.* 109 J2
Tuscánia, *Italy* 29 F8
Tuscany = Toscana □, *Italy* 28 E8
Tuscarawas →, *U.S.A.* 110 F3
Tuscarora Mt., *U.S.A.* 110 F7
Tuscola, *Ill., U.S.A.* 108 F1
Tuscola, *Tex., U.S.A.* 113 J5
Tuscumbia, *U.S.A.* 109 H2
Tuskegee, *U.S.A.* 109 J3
Tustin, *U.S.A.* 117 M9
Tuszyn, *Poland* 45 G6
Tutak, *Turkey* 73 C10
Tutayev, *Russia* 46 D10
Tuticorin, *India* 66 Q11
Tutin, *Serbia, Yug.* 40 D4
Tutóia, *Brazil* 125 D10
Tutong, *Brunei* 62 D4
Tutova →, *Romania* 43 D12
Tutrakan, *Bulgaria* 41 B10
Tuttle Creek L., *U.S.A.* 112 F6
Tuttlingen, *Germany* 25 H4
Tutuala, *Indonesia* 63 F7
Tutuila, *Amer. Samoa* 91 B13
Tutume, *Botswana* 85 J5
Tutun, *Egypt* 80 J7
Tututepec, *Mexico* 119 D5
Tuva □, *Russia* 51 D10
Tuvalu ■, *Pac. Oc.* 96 H9
Tuxer Alpen, *Austria* 26 D4
Tuxpan, *Mexico* 119 C5
Tuxtla Gutiérrez, *Mexico* 119 D6
Tuy = Tui, *Spain* 34 C2
Tuy An, *Vietnam* 64 F7
Tuy Duc, *Vietnam* 65 F6
Tuy Hoa, *Vietnam* 64 F7
Tuy Phong, *Vietnam* 65 G7
Tuya L., *Canada* 104 B2
Tuyen Hoa, *Vietnam* 64 D6
Tuyen Quang, *Vietnam* 58 G5
Tūysarkān, *Iran* 71 C6
Tuz Gölü, *Turkey* 72 C5
Ţūz Khurmātū, *Iraq* 70 C5
Tuzi, *Montenegro, Yug.* 40 D3
Tuzla, *Bos.-H.* 42 F3
Tuzlov →, *Russia* 47 J10
Tuzluca, *Turkey* 73 B10
Tvååker, *Sweden* 11 G6
Tvardiţa, *Moldova* 43 D13
Tver, *Russia* 46 D8
Tvrdošin, *Slovak Rep.* 27 B12
Tvrdošovce, *Slovak Rep.* 27 C11
Tvŭrditsa, *Bulgaria* 41 D9
Twain, *U.S.A.* 116 E5
Twain Harte, *U.S.A.* 116 G6
Twardogóra, *Poland* 45 G4
Tweed, *Canada* 110 B7
Tweed →, *U.K.* 14 F6
Tweed Heads, *Australia* 95 D5
Tweedsmuir Prov. Park, *Canada* 104 C3
Twentynine Palms, *U.S.A.* 117 L10
Twillingate, *Canada* 103 C9
Twin Bridges, *U.S.A.* 114 D7
Twin Falls, *Canada* 103 B7
Twin Falls, *U.S.A.* 114 E6
Twin Valley, *U.S.A.* 112 B6
Twinsburg, *U.S.A.* 110 E3
Twistringen, *Germany* 24 C4
Twitchell Reservoir, *U.S.A.* 117 L6
Two Harbors, *U.S.A.* 112 B9
Two Hills, *Canada* 104 C6
Two Rivers, *U.S.A.* 108 C2
Two Rocks, *Australia* 93 F2
Tyachiv, *Ukraine* 47 H2
Tychy, *Poland* 45 H5
Tyczyn, *Poland* 45 J9
Tykocin, *Poland* 45 E9
Tyler, *Minn., U.S.A.* 112 C6
Tyler, *Tex., U.S.A.* 113 J7
Tyligul →, *Ukraine* 47 J6
Týn nad Vltavou, *Czech Rep.* 26 B7
Tynda, *Russia* 51 D13
Tyndall, *U.S.A.* 112 D6
Tyne →, *U.K.* 12 C6
Tyne & Wear □, *U.K.* 12 B6
Týnec nad Sázavou, *Czech Rep.* 26 B7
Tynemouth, *U.K.* 12 B6
Tyre = Sūr, *Lebanon* 75 B4
Tyrifjorden, *Norway* 9 F14
Tyringe, *Sweden* 11 H7
Tyrnyauz, *Russia* 49 J6
Tyrol = Tirol □, *Austria* 26 D3
Tyrone, *U.S.A.* 110 F6
Tyrone □, *U.K.* 15 B4
Tyrrell L., *Canada* 105 A7
Tyrrhenian Sea, *Medit. S.* 6 G8
Tysfjorden, *Norway* 8 B17
Tystberga, *Sweden* 11 F11
Tytuvėnai, *Lithuania* 44 C10
Tyub Karagan, Mys, *Kazakstan* 49 H10
Tyuleni, Ostrova, *Kazakstan* 49 H10
Tyuleniy, *Russia* 49 H8
Tyuleniy, Mys, *Azerbaijan* 49 K10
Tyumen, *Russia* 50 D7
Tywi →, *U.K.* 13 F3
Tywyn, *U.K.* 13 E3
Tzaneen, *S. Africa* 89 C5
Tzermiádhes, *Greece* 36 D7
Tzoumérka, Óros, *Greece* 38 B3
Tzukong = Zigong, *China* 58 C5

U

U Taphao, *Thailand* 64 F3
U.S.A. = United States of America ■, *N. Amer.* 106 C7
Uatumã →, *Brazil* 124 D7
Uaupés, *Brazil* 124 D5
Uaupés →, *Brazil* 124 C5
Uaxactún, *Guatemala* 120 C2
Ub, *Serbia, Yug.* 40 B4
Ubá, *Brazil* 127 A7
Uba, *Nigeria* 83 C7
Ubaitaba, *Brazil* 125 F11
Ubangi = Oubangi →, *Dem. Rep. of the Congo* 84 E3
Ubauro, *Pakistan* 68 E3
Ubaye →, *France* 21 D10
Ubayyiḍ, W. al →, *Iraq* 70 C4
Ube, *Japan* 55 H5
Úbeda, *Spain* 35 G7
Uberaba, *Brazil* 125 G9
Uberlândia, *Brazil* 125 G9
Überlingen, *Germany* 25 H5
Ubiaja, *Nigeria* 83 D6
Ubolratna Res., *Thailand* 64 D4
Ubombo, *S. Africa* 89 D5
Ubon Ratchathani, *Thailand* 64 E5
Ubondo, *Dem. Rep. of the Congo* 86 C2
Ubort →, *Belarus* 47 F5
Ubrique, *Spain* 35 J5
Ubundu, *Dem. Rep. of the Congo* 86 C2
Ucayali →, *Peru* 122 D3
Uchab, *Namibia* 88 B2
Uchiura-Wan, *Japan* 54 C10
Uchquduq, *Uzbekistan* 50 E7
Uchte, *Germany* 24 C4
Uchur →, *Russia* 51 D14
Uckermark, *Germany* 24 B9
Ucluelet, *Canada* 104 D3
Uda →, *Russia* 51 D14
Udagamandalam, *India* 66 P10
Udainagar, *India* 68 H7
Udaipur, *India* 68 G5
Udaipur Garhi, *Nepal* 69 F12
Udala, *India* 69 J12
Udbina, *Croatia* 29 D12
Uddeholm, *Sweden* 10 D7
Uddevalla, *Sweden* 11 F5
Uddjaur, *Sweden* 8 D17
Uden, *Neths.* 17 C5
Udgir, *India* 66 K10
Udhampur, *India* 69 C6
Udi, *Nigeria* 83 D6
Údine, *Italy* 29 B10
Udmurtia □, *Russia* 50 D6
Udon Thani, *Thailand* 64 D4
Udupi, *India* 66 N9
Udvoy Balkan, *Bulgaria* 41 D10
Udzungwa Range, *Tanzania* 87 D4
Ueckermünde, *Germany* 24 B10
Ueda, *Japan* 55 F9
Uedineniya, Os., *Russia* 4 B12
Uele →, *Dem. Rep. of the Congo* 84 D4
Uelen, *Russia* 51 C19
Uelzen, *Germany* 24 C6
Uetersen, *Germany* 24 B5
Uetze, *Germany* 24 C6
Ufa, *Russia* 50 D6
Uffenheim, *Germany* 25 F6
Ugab →, *Namibia* 88 C1
Ugalla →, *Tanzania* 86 D3
Uganda ■, *Africa* 86 B3
Ugento, *Italy* 31 C11
Ugep, *Nigeria* 83 D6
Ughelli, *Nigeria* 83 D6
Ugie, *S. Africa* 89 E4
Ugíjar, *Spain* 35 J7
Ugine, *France* 21 C10
Uglegorsk, *Russia* 51 E15
Uglich, *Russia* 46 D10
Ugljan, *Croatia* 29 D12
Ugljane, *Croatia* 29 E13
Ugra →, *Russia* 46 E9
Ugŭrchin, *Bulgaria* 41 C8
Uh →, *Slovak Rep.* 27 C15
Uherské Hradiště, *Czech Rep.* 27 B10
Uherský Brod, *Czech Rep.* 27 B10
Úhlava →, *Czech Rep.* 26 B6
Uhlenhorst, *Namibia* 88 C2
Uhrichsville, *U.S.A.* 110 F3
Uibhist a Deas = South Uist, *U.K.* 14 D1
Uibhist a Tuath = North Uist, *U.K.* 14 D1
Uig, *U.K.* 14 D2
Uíge, *Angola* 84 F2
Uijŏngbu, *S. Korea* 57 F14
Ŭiju, *N. Korea* 57 D13
Uinta Mts., *U.S.A.* 114 F8
Uis, *Namibia* 88 B2
Uitenhage, *S. Africa* 88 E4
Uithuizen, *Neths.* 17 A6
Ujazd, *Poland* 45 H5
Újfehértó, *Hungary* 42 C6
Ujh →, *India* 68 C6
Ujhani, *India* 69 F8
Uji-guntō, *Japan* 55 J4
Ujjain, *India* 68 H6
Ujście, *Poland* 45 E3
Újszász, *Hungary* 42 C5
Ujung Pandang, *Indonesia* 63 F5
Uka, *Russia* 51 D17
Ukara I., *Tanzania* 86 C3
Uke-Shima, *Japan* 55 K4
Ukerewe I., *Tanzania* 86 C3
Ukholovo, *Russia* 48 D5
Ukhrul, *India* 67 G19
Ukhta, *Russia* 50 C6
Ukiah, *U.S.A.* 116 F3
Ukki Fort, *India* 69 C7
Ukmergė, *Lithuania* 9 J21
Ukraine ■, *Europe* 47 H7
Ukwi, *Botswana* 88 C3
Ulaan-Uul, *Mongolia* 56 B6
Ulaanbaatar, *Mongolia* 51 E11
Ulaangom, *Mongolia* 60 A4
Ulaanjirem, *Mongolia* 56 B3
Ulamba, *Dem. Rep. of the Congo* 87 D1
Ulan Bator = Ulaanbaatar, *Mongolia* 51 E11
Ulan Erge, *Russia* 49 G7
Ulan Khol, *Russia* 49 H8
Ulan Ude, *Russia* 51 D11
Ulanów, *Poland* 45 H9
Ulaş, *Sivas, Turkey* 72 C7
Ulaş, *Tekirdağ, Turkey* 41 E11
Ulaya, *Morogoro, Tanzania* 86 D4
Ulaya, *Tabora, Tanzania* 86 C3
Ulcinj, *Montenegro, Yug.* 40 E3
Ulco, *S. Africa* 88 D3
Ulefoss, *Norway* 9 G13
Ulëz, *Albania* 40 E3
Ulfborg, *Denmark* 11 H2
Ulhasnagar, *India* 66 K8
Uliastay = Ulyasutay, *Mongolia* 60 B4
Ulithi Atoll, *Pac. Oc.* 63 B9
Uljma, *Serbia, Yug.* 42 E6
Ulla →, *Spain* 34 C2
Ullapool, *U.K.* 14 D3
Ullared, *Sweden* 11 G6
Ulldecona, *Spain* 32 E5
Ullswater, *U.K.* 12 C5
Ullŭng-do, *S. Korea* 55 F5
Ulm, *Germany* 25 G5
Ulmarra, *Australia* 95 D5
Ulmeni, *Buzău, Romania* 43 E11
Ulmeni, *Maramureş, Romania* 43 C8
Ulonguè, *Mozam.* 87 E3
Ulricehamn, *Sweden* 11 G7
Ulrika, *Sweden* 11 F9
Ulsan, *S. Korea* 57 G15
Ulsta, *U.K.* 14 A7
Ulster □, *U.K.* 15 B5
Ulstrem, *Bulgaria* 41 D10
Ulubat Gölü, *Turkey* 41 F12
Ulubey, *Turkey* 39 C11
Uluborlu, *Turkey* 39 C12
Uluçinar, *Turkey* 72 D6
Uludağ, *Turkey* 41 F13
Uludere, *Turkey* 73 D10
Uluguru Mts., *Tanzania* 86 D4
Ulukışla, *Turkey* 72 D6
Ulungur He →, *China* 60 B3
Uluru = Ayers Rock, *Australia* 93 E5
Uluru Nat. Park, *Australia* 93 E5
Ulutau, *Kazakstan* 50 E7
Ulva, *U.K.* 14 E2
Ulverston, *U.K.* 12 C4
Ulverstone, *Australia* 94 G4
Ulya, *Russia* 51 D15
Ulyanovsk = Simbirsk, *Russia* 48 C9
Ulyasutay, *Mongolia* 60 B4
Ulysses, *U.S.A.* 113 G4
Umag, *Croatia* 29 C10
Umala, *Bolivia* 124 G5
Uman, *Ukraine* 47 H6
Umaria, *India* 67 H12
Umarkot, *Pakistan* 66 G6
Umarpada, *India* 68 J5
Umatilla, *U.S.A.* 114 D4
Umbagog L., *U.S.A.* 111 B13
Umbakumba, *Australia* 94 A2

Umbértide, *Italy* 29 E9
Umbrella Mts., *N.Z.* 91 L2
Umbria □, *Italy* 29 F9
Ume älv →, *Sweden* 8 E19
Umeå, *Sweden* 8 E19
Umera, *Indonesia* 63 E7
Umfuli →, *Zimbabwe* 87 F2
Umgusa, *Zimbabwe* 87 F2
Umim Urümah, *Si. Arabia* 80 B4
Umka, *Serbia, Yug.* 40 B4
Umkomaas, *S. Africa* 89 E5
Umlazi, *S. Africa* 85 L6
Umm ad Daraj, J., *Jordan* 75 C4
Umm al Qaywayn, *U.A.E.* 71 E7
Umm al Qittayn, *Jordan* 75 C5
Umm Arda, *Sudan* 81 D3
Umm Bāb, *Qatar* 71 E6
Umm Badr, *Sudan* 81 E2
Umm Baiyud, *Sudan* 81 E3
Umm Bel, *Sudan* 81 E2
Umm Birkah, *Si. Arabia* 80 B4
Umm Boim, *Sudan* 81 E2
Umm Dam, *Sudan* 81 E3
Umm Debi, *Sudan* 81 E3
Umm Dubban, *Sudan* 81 D3
Umm el Fahm, *Israel* 75 C4
Umm Gafala, *Sudan* 81 E2
Umm Gimala, *Sudan* 81 E2
Umm Inderaba, *Sudan* 80 D3
Umm Keddada, *Sudan* 81 E2
Umm Koweika, *Sudan* 81 E3
Umm Lajj, *Si. Arabia* 70 E3
Umm Merwa, *Sudan* 80 D3
Umm Qantur, *Sudan* 81 E3
Umm Qurein, *Sudan* 81 F2
Umm Ruwaba, *Sudan* 81 E3
Umm Saiyala, *Sudan* 81 E3
Umm Shanqa, *Sudan* 81 E2
Umm Shutur, *Sudan* 81 F3
Umm Sidr, *Sudan* 81 E2
Umm Zehetir, *Egypt* 80 J8
Umnak I., *U.S.A.* 100 C3
Umniati →, *Zimbabwe* 87 F2
Umpqua →, *U.S.A.* 114 E1
Umreth, *India* 68 H5
Umtata, *S. Africa* 89 E4
Umuahia, *Nigeria* 83 D6
Umuarama, *Brazil* 127 A5
Umurbey, *Turkey* 41 F10
Umvukwe Ra., *Zimbabwe* 87 F3
Umzimvubu, *S. Africa* 89 E4
Umzingwane →, *Zimbabwe* 87 G2
Umzinto, *S. Africa* 89 E5
Una, *India* 68 J4
Una →, *Bos.-H.* 29 D13
Unac →, *Bos.-H.* 29 D13
Unadilla, *U.S.A.* 111 D9
Unalakleet, *U.S.A.* 100 B3
Unalaska, *U.S.A.* 100 C3
Unalaska I., *U.S.A.* 100 C3
'Unayzah, *Si. Arabia* 70 E4
'Unāzah, J., *Asia* 70 C3
Uncastillo, *Spain* 32 C3
Uncía, *Bolivia* 124 G5
Uncompahgre Peak, *U.S.A.* 115 G10
Uncompahgre Plateau, *U.S.A.* 115 G9
Unden, *Sweden* 11 F8
Undersaker, *Sweden* 10 A7
Unecha, *Russia* 47 F7
Ungava, Pén. d', *Canada* 101 C12
Ungava B., *Canada* 101 C13
Ungeny = Ungheni, *Moldova* 43 C12
Unggi, *N. Korea* 57 C16
Ungheni, *Moldova* 43 C12
Unguala →, *Ethiopia* 81 F5
Ungwatiri, *Sudan* 81 D4
Uni, *Russia* 48 B10
União da Vitória, *Brazil* 127 B5
Uničov, *Czech Rep.* 27 B10
Uniejów, *Poland* 45 G5
Unije, *Croatia* 29 D11
Unimak I., *U.S.A.* 100 C3
Union, *Miss., U.S.A.* 113 J10
Union, *Mo., U.S.A.* 112 F9
Union, *S.C., U.S.A.* 109 H5
Union City, *Calif., U.S.A.* 116 H4
Union City, *N.J., U.S.A.* 111 F10
Union City, *Pa., U.S.A.* 110 E5
Union City, *Tenn., U.S.A.* 113 G10
Union Gap, *U.S.A.* 114 C3
Union Springs, *U.S.A.* 109 J3
Uniondale, *S. Africa* 88 E3
Uniontown, *U.S.A.* 108 F6
Unionville, *U.S.A.* 112 E8
Unirea, *Romania* 43 F12
United Arab Emirates ■, *Asia* 71 F7
United Kingdom ■, *Europe* 7 E5
United States of America ■, *N. Amer.* 106 C7
Unity, *Canada* 105 C7
Universales, Mtes., *Spain* 32 E3
University Park, *U.S.A.* 115 K10
Unjha, *India* 68 H5
Unna, *Germany* 24 D3
Unnao, *India* 69 F9
Uno, Ilha, *Guinea-Biss.* 82 C1
Unst, *U.K.* 14 A8
Unstrut →, *Germany* 24 D7
Unterfranken □, *Germany* 25 F5
Unterschleissheim, *Germany* 25 G7
Unuk →, *Canada* 104 B2
Ünye, *Turkey* 72 B7
Unzha, *Russia* 48 A7
Unzha →, *Russia* 48 B6
Uozu, *Japan* 55 F8
Upata, *Venezuela* 124 B6
Upemba, L., *Dem. Rep. of the Congo* 87 D2
Upernavik, *Greenland* 4 B5
Upington, *S. Africa* 88 D3
Upleta, *India* 68 J4
Upolu, *Samoa* 91 A13
Upper □, *Ghana* 83 C4
Upper Alkali L., *U.S.A.* 114 F3
Upper Arrow L., *Canada* 104 C5
Upper Austria = Oberösterreich □, *Austria* 26 C7
Upper Foster L., *Canada* 105 B7
Upper Hutt, *N.Z.* 91 J5
Upper Klamath L., *U.S.A.* 114 E3
Upper Lake, *U.S.A.* 116 F4
Upper Musquodoboit, *Canada* 103 C7
Upper Red L., *U.S.A.* 112 A7
Upper Sandusky, *U.S.A.* 108 E4
Upper Volta = Burkina Faso ■, *Africa* 82 C4
Upphärad, *Sweden* 11 F6
Uppland, *Sweden* 10 E11
Upplands-Väsby, *Sweden* 10 E11
Uppsala, *Sweden* 10 E11
Uppsala län □, *Sweden* 10 D11
Upshi, *India* 69 C7
Upstart, C., *Australia* 94 B4
Upton, *U.S.A.* 112 C2
Ur, *Iraq* 70 D5
Urad Qianqi, *China* 56 D5
Urakawa, *Japan* 54 C11
Ural = Zhayyq →, *Kazakstan* 50 E6
Ural Mts. = Uralskie Gory, *Eurasia* 50 D6
Uralsk = Oral, *Kazakstan* 48 E10
Uralskie Gory, *Eurasia* 50 D6
Urambo, *Tanzania* 86 D3
Urandangi, *Australia* 94 C2
Uranium City, *Canada* 105 B7
Uraricoera →, *Brazil* 124 C6
Urawa, *Japan* 55 G9
Uray, *Russia* 50 C7
'Uray'irah, *Si. Arabia* 71 E6
Urbana, *Ill., U.S.A.* 108 E1
Urbana, *Ohio, U.S.A.* 108 E4
Urbánia, *Italy* 29 E9
Urbel →, *Spain* 34 C7
Urbino, *Italy* 29 E9
Urbión, Picos de, *Spain* 32 C2
Urcos, *Peru* 124 F4
Urdinarrain, *Argentina* 126 C4
Urdos, *France* 20 F3
Urdzhar, *Kazakstan* 50 E9
Ure →, *U.K.* 12 C6
Uren, *Russia* 48 B7
Ures, *Mexico* 118 B2
Urfa = Sanliurfa, *Turkey* 70 B3
Urganch, *Uzbekistan* 50 E7
Urgench = Urganch, *Uzbekistan* 50 E7
Ürgüp, *Turkey* 70 B2
Uri, *India* 69 B6
Uri □, *Switz.* 25 J4
Uribia, *Colombia* 124 A4
Uricani, *Romania* 42 E8
Uriondo, *Bolivia* 126 A3
Urique, *Mexico* 118 B3
Urique →, *Mexico* 118 B3
Urk, *Neths.* 17 B5
Urla, *Turkey* 39 C8
Urlaţi, *Romania* 43 F11
Urmia = Orūmīyeh, *Iran* 70 B5
Urmia, L. = Orūmīyeh, Daryācheh-ye, *Iran* 70 B5
Uroševac, *Kosovo, Yug.* 40 D5
Urshult, *Sweden* 11 H8
Uruaçu, *Brazil* 125 F9
Uruapan, *Mexico* 118 D4
Urubamba →, *Peru* 124 F4
Uruçara, *Brazil* 124 D7
Uruçuí, *Brazil* 125 E10
Uruguai →, *Brazil* 127 B5
Uruguaiana, *Brazil* 126 B4
Uruguay ■, *S. Amer.* 126 C4
Uruguay →, *S. Amer.* 126 C4
Urumchi = Ürümqi, *China* 50 E9
Ürümqi, *China* 50 E9
Urup →, *Russia* 49 H5
Urup, Ostrov, *Russia* 51 E16
Uryupinsk, *Russia* 48 E5
Urzhum, *Russia* 48 B9
Urziceni, *Romania* 43 F11
Usa →, *Russia* 50 C6
Uşak, *Turkey* 39 C11
Uşak □, *Turkey* 39 C11
Usakos, *Namibia* 88 C2
Ušće, *Serbia, Yug.* 40 C4
Usedom, *Germany* 24 B10
Useless Loop, *Australia* 93 E1
'Usfān, *Si. Arabia* 80 C4
Ush-Tobe, *Kazakstan* 50 E8
Ushakova, Ostrov, *Russia* 4 A12
Ushant = Ouessant, Î. d', *France* 18 D1
Ushashi, *Tanzania* 86 C3
Ushat, *Sudan* 81 F2
'Ushayrah, *Si. Arabia* 80 C5
Ushibuka, *Japan* 55 H5
Ushuaia, *Argentina* 128 G3
Ushumun, *Russia* 51 D13
Usk, *Canada* 104 C3
Usk →, *U.K.* 13 F5
Uska, *India* 69 F10
Üsküdar, *Turkey* 41 F13
Uslar, *Germany* 24 D5
Usman, *Russia* 47 F10
Usoke, *Tanzania* 86 D3
Usolye Sibirskoye, *Russia* 51 D11
Usoro, *Nigeria* 83 D6
Uspallata, P. de, *Argentina* 126 C2
Uspenskiy, *Kazakstan* 50 E8
Ussel, *France* 20 C6
Usson-du-Poitou, *France* 20 B4
Ussuri →, *Asia* 54 A7
Ussuriysk, *Russia* 51 E14
Ussurka, *Russia* 54 B6
Ust-Aldan = Batamay, *Russia* 51 C13
Ust-Amginskoye = Khandyga, *Russia* 51 C14
Ust-Bolsheretsk, *Russia* 51 D16
Ust-Buzulukskaya, *Russia* 48 E6
Ust-Chaun, *Russia* 51 C18
Ust-Donetskiy, *Russia* 49 G5
Ust-Ilimpeya = Yukta, *Russia* 51 C11
Ust-Ilimsk, *Russia* 51 D11
Ust-Ishim, *Russia* 50 D8
Ust-Kamchatsk, *Russia* 51 D17
Ust-Kamenogorsk = Öskemen, *Kazakstan* 50 E9
Ust-Khayryuzovo, *Russia* 51 D16
Ust-Kut, *Russia* 51 D11
Ust-Kuyga, *Russia* 51 B14
Ust-Labinsk, *Russia* 49 H4
Ust-Luga, *Russia* 46 C5
Ust-Maya, *Russia* 51 C14
Ust-Mil, *Russia* 51 D14
Ust-Nera, *Russia* 51 C15
Ust-Nyukzha, *Russia* 51 D13
Ust-Olenek, *Russia* 51 B12
Ust-Omchug, *Russia* 51 C15
Ust-Port, *Russia* 50 C9
Ust-Tsilma, *Russia* 50 C6
Ust Urt = Ustyurt Plateau, *Asia* 50 E6
Ustaritz, *France* 20 E2
Uster, *Switz.* 25 H4
Ústí nad Labem, *Czech Rep.* 26 A7
Ústí nad Orlicí, *Czech Rep.* 27 B9
Ústica, *Italy* 30 D6
Ustinov = Izhevsk, *Russia* 50 D6
Ustka, *Poland* 44 D3
Ustroń, *Poland* 45 J5
Ustrzyki Dolne, *Poland* 45 J9
Ustyurt Plateau, *Asia* 50 E6
Ustyuzhna, *Russia* 46 C9
Usu, *China* 60 B3
Usuki, *Japan* 55 H5
Usulután, *El Salv.* 120 D2
Usumacinta →, *Mexico* 119 D6
Usumbura = Bujumbura, *Burundi* 86 C2
Usure, *Tanzania* 86 C3
Usutuo →, *Mozam.* 89 D5
Uta, *Indonesia* 63 E9
Utah □, *U.S.A.* 114 G8
Utah L., *U.S.A.* 114 F8
Utansjö, *Sweden* 10 B11
Utarni, *India* 68 F4
Utatlan, *Guatemala* 120 C1
Ute Creek →, *U.S.A.* 113 H3
Utebo, *Spain* 32 D3
Utena, *Lithuania* 9 J21
Utete, *Tanzania* 86 D4
Uthai Thani, *Thailand* 64 E3
Uthal, *Pakistan* 68 G2
Utiariti, *Brazil* 124 F7
Utica, *N.Y., U.S.A.* 111 C9
Utica, *Ohio, U.S.A.* 110 F2
Utiel, *Spain* 33 F3
Utikuma L., *Canada* 104 B5
Utö, *Sweden* 10 F12
Utopia, *Australia* 94 C1
Utraula, *India* 69 F10
Utrecht, *Neths.* 17 B5
Utrecht, *S. Africa* 89 D5
Utrecht □, *Neths.* 17 B5
Utrera, *Spain* 35 H5
Utsjoki, *Finland* 8 B22
Utsunomiya, *Japan* 55 F9
Uttar Pradesh □, *India* 69 F9
Uttaradit, *Thailand* 64 D3
Uttaranchal □, *India* 69 D8
Uttoxeter, *U.K.* 12 E6
Uummannarsuaq = Nunap Isua, *Greenland* 101 C15
Uusikaarlepyy, *Finland* 8 E20
Uusikaupunki, *Finland* 9 F19
Uva, *Russia* 48 B11
Uvac →, *Serbia, Yug.* 40 C3
Uvalde, *U.S.A.* 113 L5
Uvarovo, *Russia* 48 E6
Uvat, *Russia* 50 D7
Uvinza, *Tanzania* 86 D3
Uvira, *Dem. Rep. of the Congo* 86 C2
Uvs Nuur, *Mongolia* 60 A4
'Uwairidh, Ḥarrat al, *Si. Arabia* 70 E3
Uwajima, *Japan* 55 H6
Uweinat, Jebel, *Sudan* 80 C1
Uxbridge, *Canada* 110 B5
Uxin Qi, *China* 56 E5
Uxmal, *Mexico* 119 C7
Üydzin, *Mongolia* 56 B4
Uyo, *Nigeria* 83 D6
Üyüklü Tepe, *Turkey* 39 D9
Uyûn Mûsa, *Egypt* 75 F1
Uyuni, *Bolivia* 124 H5
Uzbekistan ■, *Asia* 50 E7
Uzen, Bolshoi →, *Kazakstan* 49 F9
Uzen, Mal →, *Kazakstan* 49 F9
Uzerche, *France* 20 C5
Uzès, *France* 21 D8
Uzh →, *Ukraine* 47 G6
Uzhgorod = Uzhhorod, *Ukraine* 47 H2
Uzhhorod, *Ukraine* 47 H2
Užice, *Serbia, Yug.* 40 C3
Uzlovaya, *Russia* 46 F10
Üzümlü, *Turkey* 39 E11
Uzunköprü, *Turkey* 41 E10
Uzunkuyu, *Turkey* 39 C8

V

Vaal →, *S. Africa* 88 D3
Vaal Dam, *S. Africa* 89 D4
Vaalwater, *S. Africa* 89 C4
Vaasa, *Finland* 8 E19
Vabre, *France* 20 E6
Vác, *Hungary* 42 C4
Vacaria, *Brazil* 127 B5
Vacaville, *U.S.A.* 116 G5
Vaccarès, Étang de, *France* 21 E8
Vach = Vakh →, *Russia* 50 C8
Vache, Î. à, *Haiti* 121 C5
Väckelsång, *Sweden* 11 H8
Väddö, *Sweden* 10 D12
Väderstad, *Sweden* 11 F8
Vadnagar, *India* 68 H5
Vado Lígure, *Italy* 28 D5
Vadodara, *India* 68 H5
Vadsø, *Norway* 8 A23
Vadstena, *Sweden* 11 F8
Vaduz, *Liech.* 25 H5
Værøy, *Norway* 8 C15
Vágar, *Færoe Is.* 8 E9
Vaggeryd, *Sweden* 11 G8
Vagney, *France* 19 D13
Vagnhärad, *Sweden* 11 F11
Vagos, *Portugal* 34 E2
Vågsfjorden, *Norway* 8 B17
Váh →, *Slovak Rep.* 27 D11
Vahsel B., *Antarctica* 5 D1
Váï, *Greece* 36 D8
Vaigach, *Russia* 50 B6
Vaiges, *France* 18 D6
Vaihingen, *Germany* 25 G4
Vail, *U.S.A.* 106 C5
Vailly-sur-Aisne, *France* 19 C10
Vaisali →, *India* 69 F8
Vaison-la-Romaine, *France* 21 D9
Vakarel, *Bulgaria* 40 D7
Vakfikebir, *Turkey* 73 B8
Vakh →, *Russia* 50 C8
Vakhtan, *Russia* 48 B8
Vál, *Hungary* 42 C3
Val-de-Marne □, *France* 19 D9
Val-d'Isère, *France* 21 C10
Val-d'Oise □, *France* 19 C9
Val-d'Or, *Canada* 102 C4
Val Marie, *Canada* 105 D7
Valaam, *Russia* 46 B6
Valadares, *Portugal* 34 D2
Valahia, *Romania* 43 F9
Valais □, *Switz.* 25 J3
Valais, Alpes du, *Switz.* 25 J3
Valandovo, *Macedonia* 40 E6
Valašské Meziříčí, *Czech Rep.* 27 B10
Valáxa, *Greece* 38 C6
Vålberg, *Sweden* 10 E7
Valbo, *Sweden* 10 D10
Valbondione, *Italy* 28 B7
Vâlcani, *Romania* 42 D5
Vâlcea □, *Romania* 43 F9
Valcheta, *Argentina* 128 E3
Valdagno, *Italy* 29 C8
Valdahon, *France* 19 E13
Valday, *Russia* 46 D7
Valdayskaya Vozvyshennost, *Russia* 46 D7
Valdeazogues →, *Spain* 35 G6
Valdecañas, Embalse de, *Spain* 34 F5
Valdemarsvik, *Sweden* 11 F10
Valdemoro, *Spain* 34 E7
Valdepeñas, *Spain* 35 G7
Valderaduey →, *Spain* 34 D5
Valdérice, *Italy* 30 D5
Valderrobres, *Spain* 32 E5
Valdés, Pen., *Argentina* 122 H4
Valdez, *U.S.A.* 100 B5
Valdivia, *Chile* 128 D2
Valdobbiádene, *Italy* 29 C8
Valdosta, *U.S.A.* 109 K4
Valdoviño, *Spain* 34 B2
Valdres, *Norway* 9 F13
Vale, *Georgia* 49 K6
Vale, *U.S.A.* 114 E5
Vale of Glamorgan □, *U.K.* 13 F4
Valea lui Mihai, *Romania* 42 C7
Valea Mărului, *Romania* 43 E12
Valemount, *Canada* 104 C5
Valença, *Brazil* 125 F11
Valença, *Portugal* 34 C2
Valença do Piauí, *Brazil* 125 E10
Valençay, *France* 19 E8
Valence = Valence d'Agen, *France* 20 D4
Valence, *France* 21 D8
Valence d'Agen, *France* 20 D4
Valencia, *Spain* 33 F4
Valencia, *U.S.A.* 115 J10
Valencia, *Venezuela* 124 A5
Valencia □, *Spain* 33 F4
Valencia, G. de, *Spain* 33 F5
Valencia de Alcántara, *Spain* 35 F3
Valencia de Don Juan, *Spain* 34 C5
Valencia I., *Ireland* 15 E1
Valenciennes, *France* 19 B10
Văleni, *Romania* 43 F9
Vălenii de Munte, *Romania* 43 E11
Valensole, *France* 21 E9
Valentigney, *France* 19 E13
Valentim, Sa. do, *Brazil* 125 E10
Valentin, *Russia* 54 C7
Valentine, *U.S.A.* 113 K2
Valenza, *Italy* 28 C5
Valera, *Venezuela* 124 B4
Valga, *Estonia* 9 H22
Valguarnera Caropepe, *Italy* 31 E7
Valier, *U.S.A.* 114 B7
Valinco, G. de, *France* 21 G12
Valjevo, *Serbia, Yug.* 40 B3
Valka, *Latvia* 9 H21
Valkeakoski, *Finland* 9 F20
Valkenswaard, *Neths.* 17 C5
Vall de Uxó = La Vall d'Uixó, *Spain* 32 F4
Valla, *Sweden* 10 E10
Valladolid, *Mexico* 119 C7
Valladolid, *Spain* 34 D6
Valladolid □, *Spain* 34 D6
Vallata, *Italy* 31 A8
Valldemossa, *Spain* 37 B9
Valle d'Aosta □, *Italy* 28 C4
Valle de Arán, *Spain* 32 C5
Valle de la Pascua, *Venezuela* 124 B5
Valle de las Palmas, *Mexico* 117 N10
Valle de Santiago, *Mexico* 118 C4
Valle de Suchil, *Mexico* 118 C4
Valle de Zaragoza, *Mexico* 118 B3
Valle Fértil, Sierra del, *Argentina* 126 C2
Valle Hermoso, *Mexico* 119 B5
Valledupar, *Colombia* 124 A4
Vallehermoso, *Canary Is.* 37 F2
Vallejo, *U.S.A.* 116 G4
Vallenar, *Chile* 126 B1
Vallentuna, *Sweden* 10 E12
Valleraugue, *France* 20 D7
Vallet, *France* 18 E5
Valletta, *Malta* 36 D2
Valley Center, *U.S.A.* 117 M9
Valley City, *U.S.A.* 112 B6
Valley Falls, *Oreg., U.S.A.* 114 E3
Valley Falls, *R.I., U.S.A.* 111 E13
Valley Springs, *U.S.A.* 116 G6
Valley View, *U.S.A.* 111 F8
Valley Wells, *U.S.A.* 117 K11
Valleyview, *Canada* 104 B5
Valli di Comácchio, *Italy* 29 D9
Vallimanca, Arroyo, *Argentina* 126 D4
Vallo della Lucánia, *Italy* 31 B8
Vallon-Pont-d'Arc, *France* 21 D8
Vallorbe, *Switz.* 25 J2
Valls, *Spain* 32 D6
Valmaseda = Balmaseda, *Spain* 32 B1
Valmiera, *Latvia* 9 H21
Valnera, *Spain* 34 B7
Valognes, *France* 18 C5
Valona = Vlorë, *Albania* 40 F3
Valongo, *Portugal* 34 D2
Valozhyn, *Belarus* 46 E4
Valpaços, *Portugal* 34 D3
Valparaíso, *Chile* 126 C1
Valparaíso, *Mexico* 118 C4
Valparaiso, *U.S.A.* 108 E2
Valparaíso □, *Chile* 126 C1
Valpovo, *Croatia* 42 E3
Valréas, *France* 21 D9
Vals, *Switz.* 25 J5
Vals →, *S. Africa* 88 D4
Vals, Tanjung, *Indonesia* 63 F9
Vals-les-Bains, *France* 21 D8
Valsad, *India* 66 J8
Valtellina, *Italy* 28 B6
Valuyki, *Russia* 47 G10
Valverde, *Canary Is.* 37 G2
Valverde del Camino, *Spain* 35 H4
Valverde del Fresno, *Spain* 34 E4
Vama, *Romania* 43 C10
Vamdrup, *Denmark* 11 J3
Våmhus, *Sweden* 10 C8
Vammala, *Finland* 9 F20
Vámos, *Greece* 36 D6
Van, *Turkey* 70 B4
Van, L. = Van Gölü, *Turkey* 70 B4
Van Alstyne, *U.S.A.* 113 J6
Van Blommestein Meer, *Surinam* 125 C7
Van Buren, *Canada* 103 C6
Van Buren, *Ark., U.S.A.* 113 H7
Van Buren, *Maine, U.S.A.* 109 B11
Van Buren, *Mo., U.S.A.* 113 G9
Van Canh, *Vietnam* 64 F7
Van Diemen, C., *N. Terr., Australia* 92 B5
Van Diemen, C., *Queens., Australia* 94 B2
Van Diemen G., *Australia* 92 B5
Van Gölü, *Turkey* 70 B4
Van Horn, *U.S.A.* 113 K2
Van Ninh, *Vietnam* 64 F7
Van Rees, Pegunungan, *Indonesia* 63 E9
Van Wert, *U.S.A.* 108 E3
Van Yen, *Vietnam* 58 G5
Vanadzor, *Armenia* 49 K7
Vanavara, *Russia* 51 C11
Vancouver, *Canada* 104 D4
Vancouver, *U.S.A.* 116 E4
Vancouver, C., *Australia* 93 G2
Vancouver I., *Canada* 104 D3
Vandalia, *Ill., U.S.A.* 112 F10

Vandalia, *Mo., U.S.A.* 112 F9
Vandenburg, *U.S.A.* 117 L6
Vanderbijlpark, *S. Africa* 89 D4
Vandergrift, *U.S.A.* 110 F5
Vanderhoof, *Canada* 104 C4
Vanderkloof Dam, *S. Africa* 88 E3
Vanderlin I., *Australia* 94 B2
Vänern, *Sweden* 11 F7
Vänersborg, *Sweden* 11 F6
Vang Vieng, *Laos* 64 C4
Vanga, *Kenya* 86 C4
Vangaindrano, *Madag.* 89 C8
Vanguard, *Canada* 105 D7
Vanino, *Russia* 51 E15
Vânju Mare, *Romania* 42 F7
Vanna, *Norway* 8 A18
Vännäs, *Sweden* 8 E18
Vannes, *France* 18 E4
Vanoise, *France* 21 C10
Vanrhynsdorp, *S. Africa* 88 E2
Vansbro, *Sweden* 10 D8
Vansittart B., *Australia* 92 B4
Vantaa, *Finland* 9 F21
Vanua Balavu, *Fiji* 91 C9
Vanua Levu, *Fiji* 91 C8
Vanuatu ■, *Pac. Oc.* 96 J8
Vanwyksvlei, *S. Africa* 88 E3
Vanzylsrus, *S. Africa* 88 D3
Vapnyarka, *Ukraine* 47 H5
Var □, *France* 21 E10
Var →, *France* 21 E11
Vara, *Sweden* 11 F6
Varades, *France* 18 E5
Varáita →, *Italy* 28 D4
Varallo, *Italy* 28 C5
Varanasi, *India* 69 G10
Varangerfjorden, *Norway* 8 A23
Varangerhalvøya, *Norway* 8 A23
Varano, Lago di, *Italy* 29 G12
Varaždin, *Croatia* 29 B13
Varazze, *Italy* 28 D5
Varberg, *Sweden* 11 G6
Vardar = Axiós →, *Greece* 40 F6
Varde, *Denmark* 11 J2
Varde Å →, *Denmark* 11 J2
Vardø, *Norway* 8 A24
Varel, *Germany* 24 B4
Varella, Mui, *Vietnam* 64 F7
Varėna, *Lithuania* 9 J21
Varennes-sur-Allier, *France* 19 F10
Varennes-Vauzelles, *France* 19 E10
Vareš, *Bos.-H.* 42 F3
Varese, *Italy* 28 C5
Vârfurile, *Romania* 42 D7
Vårgårda, *Sweden* 11 F6
Varginha, *Brazil* 127 A6
Vargön, *Sweden* 11 F6
Varillas, *Chile* 126 A1
Varkaus, *Finland* 9 E22
Värmdölandet, *Sweden* 10 E12
Värmeln, *Sweden* 10 E6
Värmlands Bro, *Sweden* 10 E7
Värmlands län □, *Sweden* 10 E6
Varna, *Bulgaria* 41 C11
Varna □, *Bulgaria* 41 C11
Värnamo, *Sweden* 11 G8
Varnsdorf, *Czech Rep.* 26 A7
Várpalota, *Hungary* 42 C3
Vars, *Canada* 111 A9
Vars, *France* 21 D10
Varto, *Turkey* 73 C9
Varvarin, *Serbia, Yug.* 40 C5
Varysburg, *U.S.A.* 110 D6
Varzaneh, *Iran* 71 C7
Varzi, *Italy* 28 D6
Varzo, *Italy* 28 B5
Varzy, *France* 19 E10
Vas □, *Hungary* 42 C1
Vasa Barris →, *Brazil* 125 F11
Vásárosnamény, *Hungary* 42 B7
Vascão →, *Portugal* 35 H3
Vaşcău, *Romania* 42 D7
Vascongadas = País Vasco □, *Spain* 32 C2
Vasht = Khāsh, *Iran* 66 E2
Vasilevichi, *Belarus* 47 F5
Vasilikón, *Greece* 38 C5
Vasilkov = Vasylkiv, *Ukraine* 47 G6
Vaslui, *Romania* 43 D12
Vaslui □, *Romania* 43 D12
Väsman, *Sweden* 10 D9
Vassar, *Canada* 105 D9
Vassar, *U.S.A.* 108 D4
Västerås, *Sweden* 10 E10
Västerbotten, *Sweden* 8 D18
Västerdalälven →, *Sweden* 10 D8
Västergötland, *Sweden* 11 F7
Västerhaninge, *Sweden* 10 E12
Västervik, *Sweden* 11 G10
Västmanland, *Sweden* 9 G16
Västmanlands län □, *Sweden* 10 E10
Vasto, *Italy* 29 F11
Västra Götalands Län □, *Sweden* 11 F6
Vasvár, *Hungary* 42 C1
Vasylkiv, *Ukraine* 47 G6
Vatan, *France* 19 E8
Vatersay, *U.K.* 14 E1
Váthia, *Greece* 38 E4
Vatican City ■, *Europe* 29 G9
Vaticano, C., *Italy* 31 D8
Vatili, *Cyprus* 36 D12
Vatin, *Serbia, Yug.* 42 E6
Vatnajökull, *Iceland* 8 D5
Vatoa, *Fiji* 91 D9
Vatólakkos, *Greece* 36 D5
Vatoloha, *Madag.* 89 B8
Vatomandry, *Madag.* 89 B8
Vatra-Dornei, *Romania* 43 C10
Vatrak →, *India* 68 H5
Vättern, *Sweden* 11 F8
Vaucluse □, *France* 21 E9
Vaucouleurs, *France* 19 D12
Vaud □, *Switz.* 25 J2
Vaughn, *Mont., U.S.A.* 114 C8
Vaughn, *N. Mex., U.S.A.* 115 J11
Vaujours L., *Canada* 102 A5
Vaupés = Uaupés →, *Brazil* 124 C5
Vaupes □, *Colombia* 124 C4
Vauvert, *France* 21 E8
Vauxhall, *Canada* 104 C6
Vav, *India* 68 G4
Vavatenina, *Madag.* 89 B8
Vava'u, *Tonga* 91 D12
Vavoua, *Ivory C.* 82 D3
Vawkavysk, *Belarus* 47 F3
Vaxholm, *Sweden* 10 E12
Växjö, *Sweden* 11 H8
Våxtorp, *Sweden* 11 H7
Vaygach, Ostrov, *Russia* 50 C6
Váyia, *Greece* 38 C5
Váyia, Ákra, *Greece* 36 C10
Vechelde, *Germany* 24 C6
Vechta, *Germany* 24 C4
Vechte →, *Neths.* 17 B6
Vecsés, *Hungary* 42 C4
Veddige, *Sweden* 11 G6
Vedea →, *Romania* 43 G10
Vedia, *Argentina* 126 C3
Vedum, *Sweden* 11 F7
Veendam, *Neths.* 17 A6
Veenendaal, *Neths.* 17 B5
Vefsna →, *Norway* 8 D15
Vega, *Norway* 8 D14
Vega, *U.S.A.* 113 H3
Vegadeo, *Spain* 34 B3
Vegorrítis, Límni, *Greece* 40 F5
Vegreville, *Canada* 104 C6
Veinge, *Sweden* 11 H7
Veisiejai, *Lithuania* 44 D10
Vejbystrand, *Sweden* 11 H6
Vejen, *Denmark* 11 J3
Vejer de la Frontera, *Spain* 35 J5
Vejle, *Denmark* 11 J3
Vejle Amtskommune □, *Denmark* 11 J3
Vejle Fjord, *Denmark* 11 J3
Vela Luka, *Croatia* 29 F13
Velas, C., *Costa Rica* 120 D2
Velasco, Sierra de, *Argentina* 126 B2
Velay, Mts. du, *France* 20 D7
Velbert, *Germany* 24 D3
Velddrif, *S. Africa* 88 E2
Velebit Planina, *Croatia* 29 D12
Velebitski Kanal, *Croatia* 29 D11
Veleka →, *Bulgaria* 41 D11
Velencei-tó, *Hungary* 42 C3
Velenje, *Slovenia* 29 B12
Veles, *Macedonia* 40 E5
Velestínon, *Greece* 38 B4
Vélez-Málaga, *Spain* 35 J6
Vélez Rubio, *Spain* 33 H2
Velhas →, *Brazil* 125 G10
Velika, *Croatia* 42 E2
Velika Gorica, *Croatia* 29 C13
Velika Kapela, *Croatia* 29 C12
Velika Kladuša, *Bos.-H.* 29 C12
Velika Kruša, *Kosovo, Yug.* 40 D4
Velika Morava →, *Serbia, Yug.* 40 B5
Velika Plana, *Serbia, Yug.* 40 B5
Velikaya →, *Russia* 46 D5
Velikaya Kema, *Russia* 54 B8
Velikaya Lepetikha, *Ukraine* 47 J7
Veliké Kapušany, *Slovak Rep.* 27 C15
Velike Lašče, *Slovenia* 29 C11
Veliki Jastrebac, *Serbia, Yug.* 40 C5
Veliki Kanal, *Serbia, Yug.* 42 E4
Veliki Popović, *Serbia, Yug.* 40 B5
Velikiye Luki, *Russia* 46 D6
Veliko Gradište, *Serbia, Yug.* 40 B5
Veliko Tŭrnovo, *Bulgaria* 41 C9
Velikonda Range, *India* 66 M11
Vélingara, *Senegal* 82 C2
Vélingara, *Senegal* 82 B2
Velingrad, *Bulgaria* 40 D7
Velino, Mte., *Italy* 29 F10
Velizh, *Russia* 46 E6
Velké Karlovice, *Czech Rep.* 27 B11
Velké Meziříčí, *Czech Rep.* 26 B9
Vel'ký Javorník, *Slovak Rep.* 27 B11
Vel'ký Krtíš, *Slovak Rep.* 27 C12
Vel'ký Meder, *Slovak Rep.* 27 D10
Vel'ký Tribeč, *Slovak Rep.* 27 C11
Velletri, *Italy* 30 A5
Vellinge, *Sweden* 11 J6
Vellmar, *Germany* 24 D5
Vellore, *India* 66 N11
Velsk, *Russia* 46 B11
Velten, *Germany* 24 C9
Velva, *U.S.A.* 112 A4
Velvendós, *Greece* 40 F6
Vemb, *Denmark* 11 H2
Vemdalen, *Sweden* 10 B7
Ven, *Sweden* 11 J6
Venaco, *France* 21 F13
Venado Tuerto, *Argentina* 126 C3
Venafro, *Italy* 31 A7
Venarey-les-Laumes, *France* 19 E11
Venaría, *Italy* 28 C4
Venčane, *Serbia, Yug.* 40 B4
Vence, *France* 21 E11
Vendas Novas, *Portugal* 35 G2
Vendée □, *France* 18 F5
Vendée →, *France* 18 F5
Vendéen, Bocage, *France* 20 B2
Vendeuvre-sur-Barse, *France* 19 D11
Vendôme, *France* 18 E8
Vendrell = El Vendrell, *Spain* 32 D6
Vendsyssel, *Denmark* 11 G4
Venelles, *France* 21 E9
Véneta, L., *Italy* 29 C9
Véneto □, *Italy* 29 C9
Venev, *Russia* 46 E10
Venézia, *Italy* 29 C9
Venézia, G. di, *Italy* 29 C10
Venezuela ■, *S. Amer.* 124 B5
Venezuela, G. de, *Venezuela* 122 B3
Vengurla, *India* 66 M8
Venice = Venézia, *Italy* 29 C9
Venice, *U.S.A.* 109 M4
Vénissieux, *France* 21 C8
Venjansjön, *Sweden* 10 D8
Venkatapuram, *India* 67 K12
Venlo, *Neths.* 17 C6
Vennesla, *Norway* 9 G12
Venosa, *Italy* 31 B8
Venray, *Neths.* 17 C6
Venta, *Lithuania* 44 B9
Venta →, *Latvia* 44 A8
Venta de Baños, *Spain* 34 D6
Venta de Cardeña = Cardeña, *Spain* 35 G6
Ventana, Punta de la, *Mexico* 118 C3
Ventana, Sa. de la, *Argentina* 126 D3
Ventersburg, *S. Africa* 88 D4
Venterstad, *S. Africa* 88 E4
Ventimíglia, *Italy* 28 E4
Ventnor, *U.K.* 13 G6
Ventotène, *Italy* 30 B6
Ventoux, Mt., *France* 21 D9
Ventspils, *Latvia* 9 H19
Ventspils □, *Latvia* 44 A8
Ventuarí →, *Venezuela* 124 C5
Ventucopa, *U.S.A.* 117 L7
Ventura, *U.S.A.* 117 L7
Vera, *Argentina* 126 B3
Vera, *Spain* 33 H3
Veracruz, *Mexico* 119 D5
Veracruz □, *Mexico* 119 D5
Veraval, *India* 68 J4
Verbánia, *Italy* 28 C5
Verbicaro, *Italy* 31 C8
Verbier, *Switz.* 25 J3
Vercelli, *Italy* 28 C5
Verchovchevo, *Ukraine* 47 H8
Verdalsøra, *Norway* 8 E14
Verde →, *Argentina* 128 E3
Verde →, *Goiás, Brazil* 125 G8
Verde →, *Mato Grosso do Sul, Brazil* 125 H8
Verde →, *Chihuahua, Mexico* 118 B3
Verde →, *Oaxaca, Mexico* 119 D5
Verde →, *Veracruz, Mexico* 118 C4
Verde →, *Paraguay* 126 A4
Verde →, *U.S.A.* 106 D4
Verde, Cay, *Bahamas* 120 B4
Verde Island Pass, *Phil.* 61 E4
Verden, *Germany* 24 C5
Verdhikoúsa, *Greece* 38 B3
Verdi, *U.S.A.* 116 F7
Verdon →, *France* 21 E9
Verdun, *France* 19 C12
Verdun-sur-le-Doubs, *France* 19 F12
Vereeniging, *S. Africa* 89 D4
Verga, C., *Guinea* 82 C2
Vergara, *Uruguay* 127 C5
Vergato, *Italy* 28 D8
Vergemont Cr. →, *Australia* 94 C3
Vergennes, *U.S.A.* 111 B11
Vergt, *France* 20 C4
Verín, *Spain* 34 D3
Verkhnedvinsk = Vyerkhnyadzvinsk, *Belarus* 46 E4
Verkhnevilyuysk, *Russia* 51 C13
Verkhniy Baskunchak, *Russia* 49 F8
Verkhovye, *Russia* 47 F9
Verkhoyansk, *Russia* 51 C14
Verkhoyansk Ra. = Verkhoyanskiy Khrebet, *Russia* 51 C13
Verkhoyanskiy Khrebet, *Russia* 51 C13
Vermenton, *France* 19 E10
Vermilion, *Canada* 105 C6
Vermilion, *U.S.A.* 110 E2
Vermilion →, *Alta., Canada* 105 C6
Vermilion →, *Qué., Canada* 102 C5
Vermilion, B., *U.S.A.* 113 L9
Vermilion Bay, *Canada* 105 D10
Vermilion L., *U.S.A.* 112 B8
Vermillion, *U.S.A.* 112 D6
Vermont □, *U.S.A.* 111 C12
Vermosh, *Albania* 40 D3
Vernal, *U.S.A.* 114 F9
Vernalis, *U.S.A.* 116 H5
Vernazza, *Italy* 28 D6
Verner, *Canada* 102 C3
Verneuil-sur-Avre, *France* 18 D7
Verneukpan, *S. Africa* 88 E3
Vernier, *Switz.* 25 J2
Vérnio, *Italy* 28 D8
Vernon, *Canada* 104 C5
Vernon, *France* 18 C8
Vernon, *U.S.A.* 113 H5
Vernonia, *U.S.A.* 116 E3
Vernouillet, *France* 18 D8
Vero Beach, *U.S.A.* 109 M5
Véroia, *Greece* 40 F6
Véroli, *Italy* 29 G10
Verona, *Canada* 111 B8
Verona, *Italy* 28 C7
Verona, *U.S.A.* 112 D10
Verrès, *Italy* 28 C4
Versailles, *France* 19 D9
Versmold, *Germany* 24 C4
Vert, C., *Senegal* 82 C1
Vertou, *France* 18 E5
Vertus, *France* 19 D11
Verulam, *S. Africa* 89 D5
Verviers, *Belgium* 17 D5
Vervins, *France* 19 C10
Veržej, *Slovenia* 29 B13
Verzy, *France* 19 C11
Vescovato, *France* 21 F13
Veselí nad Lužnicí, *Czech Rep.* 26 B7
Veselie, *Bulgaria* 41 D11
Veselovskoye Vdkhr., *Russia* 49 G5
Veshenskaya, *Russia* 48 F5
Vesle →, *France* 19 C10
Vesoul, *France* 19 E13
Vessigebro, *Sweden* 11 H6
Vesterålen, *Norway* 8 B16
Vestfjorden, *Norway* 8 C15
Vestmannaeyjar, *Iceland* 8 E3
Vestsjællands Amtskommune □, *Denmark* 11 J5
Vestspitsbergen, *Svalbard* 4 B8
Vestvågøy, *Norway* 8 B15
Vesuvio, *Italy* 31 B7
Vesuvius, Mt. = Vesuvio, *Italy* 31 B7
Vesyegonsk, *Russia* 46 C9
Veszprém, *Hungary* 42 C2
Veszprém □, *Hungary* 42 C2
Vésztő, *Hungary* 42 D6
Vetlanda, *Sweden* 11 G9
Vetluga, *Russia* 48 B7
Vetlugu →, *Russia* 48 B8
Vetluzhskiy, *Kostroma, Russia* 48 A7
Vetluzhskiy, *Nizhniy Novgorod, Russia* 48 B7
Vetovo, *Bulgaria* 41 C10
Vetralla, *Italy* 29 F9
Vetren, *Bulgaria* 41 D8
Vettore, Mte., *Italy* 29 F10
Veurne, *Belgium* 17 C2
Veveno →, *Sudan* 81 F3
Vevey, *Switz.* 25 J2
Vévi, *Greece* 40 F5
Veynes, *France* 21 D9
Veys, *Iran* 71 D6
Vézelay, *France* 19 E10
Vézelise, *France* 19 D13
Vézère →, *France* 20 D4
Vezhen, *Bulgaria* 41 D8
Vezirköprü, *Turkey* 72 B6
Vezzani, *France* 21 F13
Vi Thanh, *Vietnam* 65 H5
Viacha, *Bolivia* 124 G5
Viadana, *Italy* 28 D7
Viamão, *Brazil* 127 C5
Viana, *Brazil* 125 D10
Viana, *Spain* 32 C2
Viana do Alentejo, *Portugal* 35 G3
Viana do Bolo, *Spain* 34 C3
Viana do Castelo, *Portugal* 34 D2
Viana do Castelo □, *Portugal* 34 D2
Vianden, *Lux.* 17 E6
Viangchan = Vientiane, *Laos* 64 D4
Vianópolis, *Brazil* 125 G9
Viar →, *Spain* 35 H5
Viaréggio, *Italy* 28 E7
Viaur →, *France* 20 D5
Vibble, *Sweden* 11 G12
Vibo Valéntia, *Italy* 31 D9
Viborg, *Denmark* 11 H3
Viborg Amtskommune □, *Denmark* 11 H3
Vibraye, *France* 18 D7
Vic, *Spain* 32 D7
Vic, Étang de, *France* 20 E7
Vic-en-Bigorre, *France* 20 E4
Vic-Fézensac, *France* 20 E4
Vic-le-Comte, *France* 19 G10
Vic-sur-Cère, *France* 20 D6
Vícar, *Spain* 33 J2
Vicenza, *Italy* 29 C8
Vich = Vic, *Spain* 32 D7
Vichada →, *Colombia* 124 C5
Vichuga, *Russia* 48 B5
Vichy, *France* 19 F10
Vicksburg, *Ariz., U.S.A.* 117 M13
Vicksburg, *Miss., U.S.A.* 113 J9
Vico, *France* 21 F12
Vico, L. di, *Italy* 29 F9
Vico del Gargano, *Italy* 29 G12
Vicovu de Sus, *Romania* 43 C10
Victor, *India* 68 J4
Victor, *U.S.A.* 110 D7
Victoria = Labuan, *Malaysia* 62 C5
Victoria, *Argentina* 126 C3
Victoria, *Canada* 104 D4
Victoria, *Chile* 128 D2
Victoria, *Guinea* 82 C2
Victoria, *Malta* 36 C1
Victoria, *Phil.* 61 D4
Victoria, *Romania* 43 E9
Victoria, *Kans., U.S.A.* 112 F5
Victoria, *Tex., U.S.A.* 113 L6
Victoria →, *Australia* 92 C4
Victoria, Grand L., *Canada* 102 C4
Victoria, L., *Africa* 86 C3
Victoria, Mt., *Burma* 67 J18
Victoria Beach, *Canada* 105 C9
Victoria de Durango = Durango, *Mexico* 118 C4
Victoria de las Tunas, *Cuba* 120 B4
Victoria Falls, *Zimbabwe* 87 F2
Victoria Harbour, *Canada* 110 B5
Victoria I., *Canada* 100 A8
Victoria L., *Canada* 103 C8
Victoria Ld., *Antarctica* 5 D11
Victoria Nile →, *Uganda* 86 B3
Victoria River, *Australia* 92 C5
Victoria Str., *Canada* 100 B9
Victoria West, *S. Africa* 88 E3
Victorias, *Phil.* 61 F5
Victoriaville, *Canada* 103 C5
Victorica, *Argentina* 126 D2
Victorville, *U.S.A.* 117 L9
Vicuña, *Chile* 126 C1
Vicuña Mackenna, *Argentina* 126 C3
Vidal, *U.S.A.* 117 L12
Vidal Junction, *U.S.A.* 117 L12
Vidalia, *U.S.A.* 109 J4
Vidauban, *France* 21 E10
Videbæk, *Denmark* 11 H2
Videle, *Romania* 43 F10
Vídho, *Greece* 36 A3
Vidigueira, *Portugal* 35 G3
Vidin, *Bulgaria* 40 C6
Vidio, C., *Spain* 34 B4
Vidisha, *India* 68 H7
Vidra, *Romania* 43 E11
Viduša, *Bos.-H.* 40 D2
Vidzy, *Belarus* 9 J22
Viechtach, *Germany* 25 F8
Viedma, *Argentina* 128 E4
Viedma, L., *Argentina* 128 F2
Vieira do Minho, *Portugal* 34 D2
Vielha, *Spain* 32 C5
Viella = Vielha, *Spain* 32 C5
Vielsalm, *Belgium* 17 D5
Vienenburg, *Germany* 24 D6
Vieng Pou Kha, *Laos* 58 G3
Vienna = Wien, *Austria* 27 C9
Vienna, *Ill., U.S.A.* 113 G10
Vienna, *Mo., U.S.A.* 112 F9
Vienne, *France* 21 C8
Vienne □, *France* 20 B4
Vienne →, *France* 18 E7
Vientiane, *Laos* 64 D4
Vientos, Paso de los, *Caribbean* 121 C5
Viernheim, *Germany* 25 F4
Viersen, *Germany* 24 D2
Vierwaldstättersee, *Switz.* 25 J4
Vierzon, *France* 19 E9
Vieste, *Italy* 29 G13
Vietnam ■, *Asia* 64 C6
Vieux-Boucau-les-Bains, *France* 20 E2
Vif, *France* 21 C9
Vigan, *Phil.* 61 C4
Vigévano, *Italy* 28 C5
Vigia, *Brazil* 125 D9
Vigía Chico, *Mexico* 119 D7
Víglas, Ákra, *Greece* 36 D9
Vignemale, *France* 20 F3
Vigneulles-lès-Hattonchâtel, *France* 19 D12
Vignola, *Italy* 28 D8
Vigo, *Spain* 34 C2
Vigo, Ría de, *Spain* 34 C2
Vigsø Bugt, *Denmark* 11 G2
Vihiers, *France* 18 E6
Vihowa, *Pakistan* 68 D4
Vihowa →, *Pakistan* 68 D4
Vijayawada, *India* 67 L12
Vijosë →, *Albania* 40 F3
Vík, *Iceland* 8 E4
Vika, *Sweden* 10 D8
Vikarbyn, *Sweden* 10 D9
Vikeke, *E. Timor* 63 F7
Viken, *Skåne, Sweden* 11 H6
Viken, *Västra Götaland, Sweden* 11 F8
Viking, *Canada* 104 C6
Vikmanshyttan, *Sweden* 10 D9
Vikna, *Norway* 8 D14
Vila da Maganja, *Mozam.* 87 F4
Vila de João Belo = Xai-Xai, *Mozam.* 89 D5
Vila de Rei, *Portugal* 34 F2
Vila do Bispo, *Portugal* 35 H2
Vila do Conde, *Portugal* 34 D2
Vila Franca de Xira, *Portugal* 35 G2
Vila Gamito, *Mozam.* 87 E3
Vila Gomes da Costa, *Mozam.* 89 C5
Vila Machado, *Mozam.* 87 F3
Vila Mouzinho, *Mozam.* 87 E3
Vila Nova de Famalicão, *Portugal* 34 D2
Vila Nova de Fos Côa, *Portugal* 34 D3
Vila Nova de Foscôa = Vila Nova de Fos Côa, *Portugal* 34 D3
Vila Nova de Gaia, *Portugal* 34 D2
Vila Nova de Ourém, *Portugal* 34 F2
Vila Pouca de Aguiar, *Portugal* 34 D3
Vila Real, *Portugal* 34 D3
Vila Real □, *Portugal* 34 D3
Vila-real de los Infantes, *Spain* 32 F4
Vila Real de Santo António, *Portugal* 35 H3
Vila Vasco da Gama, *Mozam.* 87 E3
Vila Velha, *Brazil* 127 A7
Vila Viçosa, *Portugal* 35 G3
Vilafranca del Maestrat, *Spain* 32 E4
Vilafranca del Penedès, *Spain* 32 D6
Vilagarcía de Arousa, *Spain* 34 C2
Vilaine →, *France* 18 E4
Vilanandro, Tanjona, *Madag.* 89 B7

Vilanculos, *Mozam.* 89 C6
Vilanova de Castelló, *Spain* 33 F4
Vilanova i la Geltrú, *Spain* 32 D6
Vilar Formosa, *Portugal* 34 E4
Vilaseca, *Spain* 32 D6
Vilaseca-Salou = Vilaseca, *Spain* 32 D6
Vilbjerg, *Denmark* 11 H2
Vilches, *Spain* 35 G7
Vileyka, *Belarus* 46 E4
Vilhelmina, *Sweden* 8 D17
Vilhena, *Brazil* 124 F6
Viliga, *Russia* 51 C16
Viliya →, *Lithuania* 9 J21
Viljandi, *Estonia* 9 G21
Vilkaviškis, *Lithuania* 44 D10
Vilkija, *Lithuania* 44 C10
Vilkitskogo, Proliv, *Russia* 51 B11
Vilkovo = Vylkove, *Ukraine* 47 K5
Villa Abecia, *Bolivia* 126 A2
Villa Ahumada, *Mexico* 118 A3
Villa Ana, *Argentina* 126 B4
Villa Ángela, *Argentina* 126 B3
Villa Bella, *Bolivia* 124 F5
Villa Bens = Tarfaya, *Morocco* 78 C3
Villa Cañás, *Argentina* 126 C3
Villa Cisneros = Dakhla, *W. Sahara* 78 D2
Villa Colón, *Argentina* 126 C2
Villa Constitución, *Argentina* 126 C3
Villa de María, *Argentina* 126 B3
Villa del Rio, *Spain* 35 H6
Villa Dolores, *Argentina* 126 C2
Villa Frontera, *Mexico* 118 B4
Villa Guillermina, *Argentina* 126 B4
Villa Hayes, *Paraguay* 126 B4
Villa Iris, *Argentina* 126 D3
Villa Juárez, *Mexico* 118 B4
Villa María, *Argentina* 126 C3
Villa Mazán, *Argentina* 126 B2
Villa Minozzo, *Italy* 28 D7
Villa Montes, *Bolivia* 126 A3
Villa Ocampo, *Argentina* 126 B4
Villa Ocampo, *Mexico* 118 B3
Villa Ojo de Agua, *Argentina* 126 B3
Villa San Giovanni, *Italy* 31 D8
Villa San José, *Argentina* 126 C4
Villa San Martín, *Argentina* 126 B3
Villa Santina, *Italy* 29 B9
Villa Unión, *Mexico* 118 C3
Villablino, *Spain* 34 C4
Villacarlos, *Spain* 37 B11
Villacarriedo, *Spain* 34 B7
Villacarrillo, *Spain* 35 G7
Villacastín, *Spain* 34 E6
Villach, *Austria* 26 E6
Villacidro, *Italy* 30 C1
Villada, *Spain* 34 C6
Villadiego, *Spain* 34 C6
Villadóssola, *Italy* 28 B5
Villafeliche, *Spain* 32 D3
Villafranca, *Spain* 32 C3
Villafranca de los Barros, *Spain* 35 G4
Villafranca de los Caballeros, *Baleares, Spain* 37 B10
Villafranca de los Caballeros, *Toledo, Spain* 35 F7
Villafranca del Cid = Vilafranca del Maestrat, *Spain* 32 E4
Villafranca del Panadés = Vilafranca del Penedès, *Spain* 32 D6
Villafranca di Verona, *Italy* 28 C7
Villafranca Tirrena, *Italy* 31 D8
Villagrán, *Mexico* 119 C5
Villaguay, *Argentina* 126 C4
Villaharta, *Spain* 35 G6
Villahermosa, *Mexico* 119 D6
Villahermosa, *Spain* 33 G2
Villaines-la-Juhel, *France* 18 D6
Villajoyosa, *Spain* 33 G4
Villalba, *Spain* 34 B3
Villalba de Guardo, *Spain* 34 C6
Villalón de Campos, *Spain* 34 C5
Villalpando, *Spain* 34 D5
Villaluenga, *Spain* 34 E7
Villamanán, *Spain* 34 C5
Villamartín, *Spain* 35 J5
Villamayor de Santiago, *Spain* 32 F2
Villamblard, *France* 20 C4
Villanova Monteleone, *Italy* 30 B1
Villanueva, *U.S.A.* 113 H2
Villanueva de Castellón = Vilanova de Castelló, *Spain* 33 F4
Villanueva de Córdoba, *Spain* 35 G6
Villanueva de la Fuente, *Spain* 33 G2
Villanueva de la Serena, *Spain* 35 G5
Villanueva de la Sierra, *Spain* 34 E4
Villanueva de los Castillejos, *Spain* 35 H3
Villanueva de los Infantes, *Spain* 35 G7
Villanueva del Arzobispo, *Spain* 33 G2
Villanueva del Fresno, *Spain* 35 G3
Villanueva y Geltrú = Vilanova i la Geltrú, *Spain* 32 D6
Villaputzu, *Italy* 30 C2
Villaquilambre, *Spain* 34 C5
Villar del Arzobispo, *Spain* 32 F4
Villar del Rey, *Spain* 35 F4
Villard-de-Lans, *France* 21 C9
Villarramiel, *Spain* 34 C6
Villarreal = Vila-real de los Infantes, *Spain* 32 F4
Villarrica, *Chile* 128 D2
Villarrica, *Paraguay* 126 B4
Villarrobledo, *Spain* 33 F2
Villarroya de la Sierra, *Spain* 32 D3
Villarrubia de los Ojos, *Spain* 35 F7
Villars-les-Dombes, *France* 19 F12
Villasayas, *Spain* 32 D2
Villaseca de los Gamitos = Villaseco de los Gamitos, *Spain* 34 D4
Villaseco de los Gamitos, *Spain* 34 D4
Villasimíus, *Italy* 30 C2
Villastar, *Spain* 32 E3
Villatobas, *Spain* 34 F7
Villavicencio, *Argentina* 126 C2
Villavicencio, *Colombia* 124 C4
Villaviciosa, *Spain* 34 B5
Villazón, *Bolivia* 126 A2
Ville-Marie, *Canada* 102 C4
Ville Platte, *U.S.A.* 113 K8
Villedieu-les-Poêles, *France* 18 D5
Villefort, *France* 20 D7
Villefranche-de-Lauragais, *France* 20 E5
Villefranche-de-Rouergue, *France* 20 D6
Villefranche-du-Périgord, *France* 20 D5
Villefranche-sur-Saône, *France* 21 C8
Villel, *Spain* 32 E3
Villemur-sur-Tarn, *France* 20 E5
Villena, *Spain* 33 G4
Villenauxe-la-Grande, *France* 19 D10
Villenave-d'Ornon, *France* 20 D3
Villeneuve-d'Ascq, *France* 19 B10
Villeneuve-l'Archevêque, *France* 19 D10
Villeneuve-lès-Avignon, *France* 21 E8
Villeneuve-sur-Allier, *France* 19 F10
Villeneuve-sur-Lot, *France* 20 D4
Villeneuve-sur-Yonne, *France* 19 D10
Villeréal, *France* 20 D4
Villers-Bocage, *France* 18 C6
Villers-Cotterêts, *France* 19 C10
Villers-sur-Mer, *France* 18 C6
Villersexel, *France* 19 E13
Villerupt, *France* 19 C12
Villeurbanne, *France* 21 C8
Villiers, *S. Africa* 89 D4
Villingen-Schwenningen, *Germany* 25 G4
Vilna, *Canada* 104 C6
Vilnius, *Lithuania* 9 J21
Vils, *Austria* 26 D3
Vils →, *Bayern, Germany* 25 G9
Vils →, *Bayern, Germany* 25 F7
Vilsbiburg, *Germany* 25 G8
Vilshofen, *Germany* 25 G9
Vilusi, *Montenegro, Yug.* 40 D2
Vilvoorde, *Belgium* 17 D4
Vilyuy →, *Russia* 51 C13
Vilyuysk, *Russia* 51 C13
Vimianzo, *Spain* 34 B1
Vimioso, *Portugal* 34 D4
Vimmerby, *Sweden* 11 G9
Vimoutiers, *France* 18 D7
Vimperk, *Czech Rep.* 26 B6
Viña del Mar, *Chile* 126 C1
Vinarós, *Spain* 32 E5
Vincennes, *U.S.A.* 108 F2
Vincent, *U.S.A.* 117 L8
Vinchina, *Argentina* 126 B2
Vindelälven →, *Sweden* 8 E18
Vindeln, *Sweden* 8 D18
Vinderup, *Denmark* 11 H2
Vindhya Ra., *India* 68 H7
Vineland, *U.S.A.* 108 F8
Vineuil, *France* 18
Vinga, *Romania* 42 D6
Vingåker, *Sweden* 10 E9
Vinh, *Vietnam* 64 C5
Vinh Linh, *Vietnam* 64 D6
Vinh Long, *Vietnam* 65 G5
Vinh Yen, *Vietnam* 58 G5
Vinhais, *Portugal* 34 D3
Vinica, *Croatia* 29 B13
Vinica, *Macedonia* 40 E6
Vinica, *Slovenia* 29 C12
Vinita, *U.S.A.* 113 G7
Vinkovci, *Croatia* 42 E3
Vinnitsa = Vinnytsya, *Ukraine* 47 H5
Vinnytsya, *Ukraine* 47 H5
Vinslöv, *Sweden* 11 H7
Vintjärn, *Sweden* 10 D10
Vinton, *Calif., U.S.A.* 116 F6
Vinton, *Iowa, U.S.A.* 112 D8
Vinton, *La., U.S.A.* 113 K8
Vinţu de Jos, *Romania* 43 D8
Viöl, *Germany* 24 A5
Vipava, *Slovenia* 29 C10
Vipiteno, *Italy* 29 B8
Vir, *Croatia* 29 D12
Virac, *Phil.* 61 E6
Virachei, *Cambodia* 64 F6
Virago Sd., *Canada* 104 C2
Viramgam, *India* 68 H5
Viranşehir, *Turkey* 70 B3
Virawah, *Pakistan* 68 G4
Virbalis, *Lithuania* 44 D9
Virden, *Canada* 105 D8
Vire, *France* 18 D6
Vire →, *France* 18 C5
Vírgenes, C., *Argentina* 128 G3
Virgin →, *U.S.A.* 115 H6
Virgin Gorda, *Br. Virgin Is.* 121 C7
Virgin Is. (British) ■, *W. Indies* 121 C7
Virgin Is. (U.S.) ■, *W. Indies* 121 C7
Virginia, *S. Africa* 88 D4
Virginia, *U.S.A.* 112 B8
Virginia □, *U.S.A.* 108 G7
Virginia Beach, *U.S.A.* 108 G8
Virginia City, *Mont., U.S.A.* 114 D8
Virginia City, *Nev., U.S.A.* 116 F7
Virginia Falls, *Canada* 104 A3
Virginiatown, *Canada* 102 C4
Virje, *Croatia* 29 B13
Viroqua, *U.S.A.* 112 D9
Virovitica, *Croatia* 42 E2
Virpazar, *Montenegro, Yug.* 40 D3
Virpur, *India* 68 J4
Virserum, *Sweden* 11 G9
Virton, *Belgium* 17 E5
Virudunagar, *India* 66 Q10
Vis, *Croatia* 29 E13
Visalia, *U.S.A.* 116 J7
Visayan Sea, *Phil.* 61 F5
Visby, *Sweden* 11 G12
Viscount Melville Sd., *Canada* 4 B2
Visé, *Belgium* 17 D5
Višegrad, *Bos.-H.* 42 G4
Viseu, *Brazil* 125 D9
Viseu, *Portugal* 34 E3
Viseu □, *Portugal* 34 E3
Vişeu de Sus, *Romania* 43 C9
Vishakhapatnam, *India* 67 L13
Vişina, *Romania* 43 G9
Vişineşti, *Moldova* 43 D13
Visingsö, *Sweden* 11 F8
Viskafors, *Sweden* 11 G6
Viskan →, *Sweden* 11 G6
Viški Kanal, *Croatia* 29 E13
Vislanda, *Sweden* 11 H8
Visnagar, *India* 68 H5
Višnja Gora, *Slovenia* 29 C11
Viso, Mte., *Italy* 28 D4
Viso del Marqués, *Spain* 35 G7
Visoko, *Bos.-H.* 42 G3
Visokoi I., *Antarctica* 5 B1
Visp, *Switz.* 25 J3
Vissefjärda, *Sweden* 11 H9
Visselhövede, *Germany* 24 C5
Vissenbjerg, *Denmark* 11 J4
Vista, *U.S.A.* 117 M9
Vistonikos, Ormos = Vistonís, Límni, *Greece* 41 E9
Vistonís, Límni, *Greece* 41 E9
Vistula = Wisła →, *Poland* 44 D5
Vit →, *Bulgaria* 41 C8
Vitanje, *Slovenia* 29 B12
Vitebsk = Vitsyebsk, *Belarus* 46 E6
Viterbo, *Italy* 29 F9
Vitez, *Bos.-H.* 42 F2
Viti Levu, *Fiji* 91 C7
Vitigudino, *Spain* 34 D4
Vitim, *Russia* 51 D12
Vitim →, *Russia* 51 D12
Vitina, *Bos.-H.* 29 E14
Vitína, *Greece* 38 D4
Vítkov, *Czech Rep.* 27 B10
Vitória, *Brazil* 125 H10
Vitória da Conquista, *Brazil* 125 F10
Vitória de São Antão, *Brazil* 125 E11
Vitoria-Gasteiz, *Spain* 32 C2
Vitré, *France* 18 D5
Vitry-le-François, *France* 19 D11
Vitry-sur-Seine, *France* 19 D9
Vitsand, *Sweden* 10 D7
Vitsi, Óros, *Greece* 40 F5
Vitsyebsk, *Belarus* 46 E6
Vittaryd, *Sweden* 11 H7
Vitteaux, *France* 19 E11
Vittel, *France* 19 D12
Vittória, *Italy* 31 F7
Vittório Véneto, *Italy* 29 C9
Vittsjö, *Sweden* 11 H7
Viveiro, *Spain* 34 B3
Vivian, *U.S.A.* 113 J8
Viviers, *France* 21 D8
Vivonne, *France* 20 B4
Vizcaíno, Desierto de, *Mexico* 118 B2
Vizcaíno, Sierra, *Mexico* 118 B2
Vizcaya □, *Spain* 32 B2
Vize, *Turkey* 41 E11
Vizianagaram, *India* 67 K13
Vizille, *France* 21 C9
Viziňada, *Croatia* 29 C10
Viziru, *Romania* 43 E12
Vizzini, *Italy* 31 E7
Vlaardingen, *Neths.* 17 C4
Vlădeasa, Vf., *Romania* 42 D7
Vladičin Han, *Serbia, Yug.* 40 D6
Vladikavkaz, *Russia* 49 J7
Vladimir, *Russia* 46 D11
Vladimir Volynskiy = Volodymyr-Volynskyy, *Ukraine* 47 G3
Vladimirci, *Serbia, Yug.* 40 B3
Vladimirovac, *Serbia, Yug.* 42 E5
Vladimirovka, *Russia* 49 F8
Vladimirovo, *Bulgaria* 40 C7
Vladimorvka, *Kazakstan* 48 E10
Vladislavovka, *Ukraine* 47 K8
Vladivostok, *Russia* 51 E14
Vlăhiţa, *Romania* 43 D10
Vlakhiótis, *Greece* 38 E4
Vlasenica, *Bos.-H.* 42 F3
Vlašić, *Bos.-H.* 42 F2
Vlašim, *Czech Rep.* 26 B7
Vlasinsko Jezero, *Serbia, Yug.* 40 D6
Vlasotince, *Serbia, Yug.* 40 D6
Vlieland, *Neths.* 17 A4
Vlissingen, *Neths.* 17 C3
Vlorë, *Albania* 40 F3
Vlorës, Gjiri i, *Albania* 40 F3
Vltava →, *Czech Rep.* 26 A7
Vo Dat, *Vietnam* 65 G6
Vobarno, *Italy* 28 C7
Voćin, *Croatia* 42 E2
Vöcklabruck, *Austria* 26 C6
Vodice, *Croatia* 29 E12
Vodňany, *Czech Rep.* 26 B7
Vodnjan, *Croatia* 29 D10
Voe, *U.K.* 14 A7
Vogel Pk., *Nigeria* 83 D7
Vogelkop = Doberai, Jazirah, *Indonesia* 63 E8
Vogelsberg, *Germany* 24 E5
Voghera, *Italy* 28 D6
Vohibinany, *Madag.* 89 B8
Vohilava, *Madag.* 89 C8
Vohimarina = Iharana, *Madag.* 89 A9
Vohimena, Tanjon' i, *Madag.* 89 D8
Vohipeno, *Madag.* 89 C8
Voi, *Kenya* 86 C4
Void-Vacon, *France* 19 D12
Voineşti, *Iaşi, Romania* 43 C12
Voineşti, *Prahova, Romania* 43 E10
Voiotía □, *Greece* 38 C5
Voiron, *France* 21 C9
Voisey B., *Canada* 103 A7
Voitsberg, *Austria* 26 D8
Vojens, *Denmark* 11 J3
Vojmsjön, *Sweden* 8 D17
Vojnić, *Croatia* 29 C12
Vojnik, *Italy* 29 B12
Vojvodina □, *Serbia, Yug.* 42 E5
Vokhtoga, *Russia* 46 C11
Volary, *Czech Rep.* 26 C6
Volborg, *U.S.A.* 112 C2
Volcano Is. = Kazan-Rettō, *Pac. Oc.* 96 E6
Volchansk = Vovchansk, *Ukraine* 47 G9
Volchya →, *Ukraine* 47 H8
Volda, *Norway* 9 E12
Volga, *Russia* 46 C10
Volga →, *Russia* 49 G9
Volga Hts. = Privolzhskaya Vozvyshennost, *Russia* 48 E7
Volgo-Baltiyskiy Kanal, *Russia* 46 B9
Volgo-Donskoy Kanal, *Russia* 49 F7
Volgodonsk, *Russia* 49 G6
Volgograd, *Russia* 49 F7
Volgogradskoye Vdkhr., *Russia* 48 E8
Volgorechensk, *Russia* 48 B5
Volímai, *Greece* 38 D2
Volintiri, *Moldova* 43 D14
Volissós, *Greece* 39 C7
Volkach, *Germany* 25 F6
Völkermarkt, *Austria* 26 E7
Volkhov, *Russia* 46 C7
Volkhov →, *Russia* 46 B7
Völklingen, *Germany* 25 F2
Volkovysk = Vawkavysk, *Belarus* 47 F3
Volksrust, *S. Africa* 89 D4
Volnansk, *Ukraine* 47 H8
Volnovakha, *Ukraine* 47 J9
Volochanka, *Russia* 51 B10
Volodarsk, *Russia* 48 B6
Volodymyr-Volynskyy, *Ukraine* 47 G3
Vologda, *Russia* 46 C10
Volokolamsk, *Russia* 46 D8
Volokonovka, *Russia* 47 G9
Vólos, *Greece* 38 B4
Volosovo, *Russia* 46 C5
Volovets, *Ukraine* 47 H2
Volovo, *Russia* 46 F10
Volozhin = Valozhyn, *Belarus* 46 E4
Volsk, *Russia* 48 D8
Volta □, *Ghana* 83 D5
Volta →, *Ghana* 83 D5
Volta, L., *Ghana* 83 D5
Volta Blanche = White Volta →, *Ghana* 83 D4
Volta Redonda, *Brazil* 127 A7
Voltaire, C., *Australia* 92 B4
Volterra, *Italy* 28 E7
Voltri, *Italy* 28 D5
Volturno →, *Italy* 30 A6
Vólvi, L., *Greece* 40 F7
Volyně, *Czech Rep.* 26 B6
Volzhsk, *Russia* 48 C9
Volzhskiy, *Russia* 49 F7
Vondrozo, *Madag.* 89 C8
Vónitsa, *Greece* 38 C2
Vopnafjörður, *Iceland* 8 D6
Vorarlberg □, *Austria* 26 D2
Vóras Óros, *Greece* 40 F5
Vorbasse, *Denmark* 11 J3
Vorchdorf, *Austria* 26 C6
Vorderrhein →, *Switz.* 25 J5
Vordingborg, *Denmark* 11 J5
Vorë, *Albania* 40 E3
Voreio Aigaio = Vórios Aiyaíon □, *Greece* 39 C7
Voreppe, *France* 21 C9
Vóriai Sporádhes, *Greece* 38 B5
Vórios Aiyaíon □, *Greece* 39 C7
Vórios Evvoïkos Kólpos, *Greece* 38 C5
Vorkuta, *Russia* 50 C7
Vormsi, *Estonia* 9 G20
Vorona →, *Russia* 48 E6
Voronezh, *Russia* 47 G10
Voronezh, *Ukraine* 47 G7
Voronezh →, *Russia* 47 G10
Vorontsovo-Aleksandrovskoye = Zelenokumsk, *Russia* 49 H6
Voroshilovgrad = Luhansk, *Ukraine* 47 H10
Voroshilovsk = Alchevsk, *Ukraine* 47 H10
Vórroi, *Greece* 38 F6
Vorskla →, *Ukraine* 47 H8
Võrts Järv, *Estonia* 9 G22
Võru, *Estonia* 9 H22
Vosges, *France* 19 D14
Vosges □, *France* 19 D13
Voskopojë, *Albania* 40 F4
Voskresensk, *Russia* 46 E10
Voskresenskoye, *Russia* 48 B7
Voss, *Norway* 9 F12
Vostok I., *Kiribati* 97 J12
Votice, *Czech Rep.* 26 B7
Votsuri-Shima, *Japan* 55 M1
Vouga →, *Portugal* 34 E2
Vouillé, *France* 18 F7
Voúxa, Ákra, *Greece* 36 D5
Vouzela, *Portugal* 34 E2
Vouziers, *France* 19 C11
Vovchansk, *Ukraine* 47 G9
Vozhe, Ozero, *Russia* 46 B10
Vozhega, *Russia* 46 B11
Voznesensk, *Ukraine* 47 J6
Voznesenye, *Russia* 46 B8
Vrå, *Denmark* 11 G3
Vráble, *Slovak Rep.* 27 C11
Vraćevšnica, *Serbia, Yug.* 40 B4
Vrakhnéïka, *Greece* 38 C3
Vrancea □, *Romania* 43 E11
Vrancei, Munţii, *Romania* 43 E11
Vrangelya, Ostrov, *Russia* 51 B19
Vranica, *Bos.-H.* 42 G2
Vranje, *Serbia, Yug.* 40 D5
Vranjska Banja, *Serbia, Yug.* 40 D6
Vranov nad Topl'ou, *Slovak Rep.* 27 C14
Vransko, *Slovenia* 29 B11
Vransko Jezero, *Croatia* 29 E12
Vrapčište, *Macedonia* 40 E4
Vratsa, *Bulgaria* 40 C7
Vrbas, *Serbia, Yug.* 42 E4
Vrbas →, *Bos.-H.* 42 E2
Vrbnik, *Croatia* 29 C11
Vrbovec, *Croatia* 29 C13
Vrbovsko, *Croatia* 29 C12
Vrchlabí, *Czech Rep.* 26 A8
Vrede, *S. Africa* 89 D4
Vredefort, *S. Africa* 88 D4
Vreden, *Germany* 24 C2
Vredenburg, *S. Africa* 88 E2
Vredendal, *S. Africa* 88 E2
Vretstorp, *Sweden* 10 E8
Vrgorac, *Croatia* 29 E14
Vrhnika, *Slovenia* 29 C11
Vridi, *Ivory C.* 82 D4
Vrigstad, *Sweden* 11 G8
Vrindavan, *India* 68 F7
Vríses, *Greece* 36 D6
Vrnograč, *Bos.-H.* 29 C12
Vrondádhes, *Greece* 39 C8
Vrpolje, *Croatia* 42 E3
Vršac, *Serbia, Yug.* 42 E6
Vrsacki Kanal, *Serbia, Yug.* 42 E5
Vrútky, *Slovak Rep.* 27 B11
Vryburg, *S. Africa* 88 D3
Vryheid, *S. Africa* 89 D5
Vsetín, *Czech Rep.* 27 B11
Vu Liet, *Vietnam* 64 C5
Vŭcha →, *Bulgaria* 41 D8
Vučitrn, *Kosovo, Yug.* 40 D4
Vukovar, *Croatia* 42 E3
Vulcan, *Canada* 104 C6
Vulcan, *Romania* 43 E8
Vulcaneşti, *Moldova* 43 E13
Vulcano, *Italy* 31 D7
Vŭlchedruma, *Bulgaria* 40 C7
Vulkaneshty = Vulcaneşti, *Moldova* 43 E13
Vunduzi →, *Mozam.* 87 F3
Vung Tau, *Vietnam* 65 G6
Vŭrbitsa, *Bulgaria* 41 D10
Vurshets, *Bulgaria* 40 C7
Vutcani, *Romania* 43 D12
Vuya, *Sudan* 81 F2
Vyartsilya, *Russia* 46 A6
Vyatka = Kirov, *Russia* 50 D5
Vyatka →, *Russia* 48 C10
Vyatskiye Polyany, *Russia* 48 B10
Vyazemskiy, *Russia* 51 E14
Vyazma, *Russia* 46 E8
Vyazniki, *Russia* 48 B6
Vyborg, *Russia* 46 B5
Vychegda →, *Russia* 50 C5
Vychodné Beskydy, *Europe* 27 B15
Východočeský □, *Czech Rep.* 26 E8
Vyerkhnyadzvinsk, *Belarus* 46 E4
Vyksa, *Russia* 48 C6
Vylkove, *Ukraine* 47 K5
Vynohradiv, *Ukraine* 47 H2
Vyrnwy, L., *U.K.* 12 E4
Vyshniy Volochek, *Russia* 46 D8
Vyshzha = imeni 26 Bakinskikh Komissarov, *Turkmenistan* 71 B7
Vyškov, *Czech Rep.* 27 B9
Vysoké Mýto, *Czech Rep.* 27 B9
Vysokovsk, *Russia* 46 D9
Vyšší Brod, *Czech Rep.* 26 C7
Vytegra, *Russia* 46 B9

W

W.A.C. Bennett Dam, *Canada* 104 B4
Wa, *Ghana* 82 C4
Waal →, *Neths.* 17 C5
Waalwijk, *Neths.* 17 C5
Waat, *Sudan* 81 F3
Wabana, *Canada* 103 C9

Wabasca →, Canada 104 B5
Wabasca-Desmarais, Canada 104 B6
Wabash, U.S.A. 108 E3
Wabash →, U.S.A. 108 G1
Wabi →, Ethiopia 81 F5
Wabigoon L., Canada 105 D10
Wabowden, Canada 105 C9
Wąbrzeźno, Poland 45 E5
Wabu Hu, China 59 A11
Wabuk Pt., Canada 102 A2
Wabush, Canada 103 B6
Wąchock, Poland 45 G8
Wächtersbach, Germany 25 E5
Waco, U.S.A. 113 K6
Waconichi, L., Canada 102 B5
Wad Ban Naqa, Sudan 81 D3
Wad Banda, Sudan 81 E2
Wad el Haddad, Sudan 81 E3
Wad en Nau, Sudan 81 E3
Wad Hamid, Sudan 81 D3
Wad Medanî, Sudan 81 E3
Wad Thana, Pakistan 68 F2
Wadai, Africa 76 E5
Wadayama, Japan 55 G7
Waddeneilanden, Neths. 17 A5
Waddenzee, Neths. 17 A5
Waddington, U.S.A. 111 B9
Waddington, Mt., Canada 104 C3
Waddy Pt., Australia 95 C5
Wadebridge, U.K. 13 G3
Wadena, Canada 105 C8
Wadena, U.S.A. 112 B7
Wädenswil, Switz. 25 H4
Wadern, Germany 25 F2
Wadeye, Australia 92 B4
Wadhams, Canada 104 C3
Wādī as Sīr, Jordan 75 D4
Wadi Gemâl, Egypt 80 C4
Wadi Halfa, Sudan 80 C3
Wadian, China 59 A9
Wadlew, Poland 45 G6
Wadowice, Poland 45 J6
Wadsworth, Nev., U.S.A. 114 G4
Wadsworth, Ohio, U.S.A. 110 E3
Waegwan, S. Korea 57 G15
Wafangdian, China 57 E11
Wafrah, Si. Arabia 70 D5
Wageningen, Neths. 17 C5
Wager B., Canada 101 B11
Waghete, Indonesia 63 E9
Wagin, Australia 93 F2
Wagner, U.S.A. 112 D5
Wagon Mound, U.S.A. 113 G2
Wagoner, U.S.A. 113 H7
Wągrowiec, Poland 45 F4
Wah, Pakistan 68 C5
Wahai, Indonesia 63 E7
Wahiawa, U.S.A. 106 H15
Wâḥid, Egypt 75 E1
Wahnai, Afghan. 68 C1
Wahni, Ethiopia 81 E4
Wahoo, U.S.A. 112 E6
Wahpeton, U.S.A. 112 B6
Waiau →, N.Z. 91 K4
Waibeem, Indonesia 63 E8
Waiblingen, Germany 25 G5
Waidhofen an der Thaya, Austria 26 C8
Waidhofen an der Ybbs, Austria 26 D7
Waigeo, Indonesia 63 E8
Waihi, N.Z. 91 G5
Waihou →, N.Z. 91 G5
Waika, Dem. Rep. of the Congo 86 C2
Waikabubak, Indonesia 63 F5
Waikari, N.Z. 91 K4
Waikato →, N.Z. 91 G5
Waikokopu, N.Z. 91 H6
Waikouaiti, N.Z. 91 L3
Wailuku, U.S.A. 106 H16
Waimakariri →, N.Z. 91 K4
Waimate, N.Z. 91 L3
Wainganga →, India 66 K11
Waingapu, Indonesia 63 F6
Waini →, Guyana 124 B7
Wainwright, Canada 105 C6
Waiouru, N.Z. 91 H5
Waipara, N.Z. 91 K4
Waipawa, N.Z. 91 H6
Waipiro, N.Z. 91 H7
Waipu, N.Z. 91 F5
Waipukurau, N.Z. 91 J6
Wairakei, N.Z. 91 H6
Wairarapa, L., N.Z. 91 J5
Wairoa, N.Z. 91 H6
Waitaki →, N.Z. 91 L3
Waitara, N.Z. 91 H5
Waitsburg, U.S.A. 114 C5
Waiuku, N.Z. 91 G5
Wajima, Japan 55 F8
Wajir, Kenya 86 B5
Waka, Ethiopia 81 F4
Wakasa, Japan 55 G7
Wakasa-Wan, Japan 55 G7
Wakatipu, L., N.Z. 91 L2
Wakaw, Canada 105 C7
Wakayama, Japan 55 G7
Wakayama □, Japan 55 H7
Wake Forest, U.S.A. 109 H6
Wake I., Pac. Oc. 96 F8
WaKeeney, U.S.A. 112 F5
Wakefield, N.Z. 91 J4
Wakefield, U.K. 12 D6
Wakefield, Mass., U.S.A. 111 D13
Wakefield, Mich., U.S.A. 112 B10
Wakkanai, Japan 54 B10
Wakkerstroom, S. Africa 89 D5
Wakre, Indonesia 63 E8
Wakuach, L., Canada 103 A6
Walamba, Zambia 87 E2
Wałbrzych, Poland 45 H3
Walbury Hill, U.K. 13 F6
Walcheren, Neths. 17 C3
Walcott, U.S.A. 114 F10
Wałcz, Poland 45 E3
Waldbröl, Germany 24 E3
Waldburg Ra., Australia 93 D2
Waldeck, Germany 24 D5
Walden, Colo., U.S.A. 114 F10
Walden, N.Y., U.S.A. 111 E10
Waldkirch, Germany 25 G3
Waldkirchen, Germany 25 G9
Waldkraiburg, Germany 25 G8
Waldport, U.S.A. 114 D1
Waldron, U.S.A. 113 H7
Waldviertel, Austria 26 C8
Walebing, Australia 93 F2
Walembele, Ghana 82 C4
Walensee, Switz. 25 H5
Wales □, U.K. 13 E3
Walewale, Ghana 83 C4
Walgett, Australia 95 E4
Walgreen Coast, Antarctica 5 D15
Walker, U.S.A. 112 B7
Walker, L., Canada 103 B6
Walker L., Canada 105 C9
Walker L., U.S.A. 114 G4
Walkerston, Australia 94 C4
Walkerton, Canada 102 D3
Wall, U.S.A. 112 D3
Walla Walla, U.S.A. 114 C4
Wallace, Idaho, U.S.A. 114 C6
Wallace, N.C., U.S.A. 109 H7
Wallaceburg, Canada 102 D3
Wallachia = Valahia, Romania 43 F9
Wallal, Australia 95 D4
Wallam Cr. →, Australia 95 D4
Wallambin, L., Australia 93 F2
Wallangarra, Australia 95 D5
Walldürn, Germany 25 F5
Wallenhorst, Germany 24 C4
Wallenpaupack, L., U.S.A. 111 E9
Wallingford, U.S.A. 111 E12
Wallis & Futuna, Is., Pac. Oc. 96 J10
Wallowa, U.S.A. 114 D5
Wallowa Mts., U.S.A. 114 D5
Walls, U.K. 14 A7
Wallula, U.S.A. 114 C4
Wallumbilla, Australia 95 D4
Walmsley, L., Canada 105 A7
Walney, I. of, U.K. 12 C4
Walnut Creek, U.S.A. 116 H4
Walnut Ridge, U.S.A. 113 G9
Walpole, Australia 93 F2
Walpole, U.S.A. 111 D13
Wals, Austria 26 D5
Walsall, U.K. 13 E6
Walsenburg, U.S.A. 113 G2
Walsh, U.S.A. 113 G3
Walsh →, Australia 94 B3
Walsrode, Germany 24 C5
Walterboro, U.S.A. 109 J5
Walters, U.S.A. 113 H5
Waltershausen, Germany 24 E6
Waltham, U.S.A. 111 D13
Waltman, U.S.A. 114 E10
Walton, U.S.A. 111 D9
Walton-on-the-Naze, U.K. 13 F9
Walvis Bay, Namibia 88 C1
Walvisbaai = Walvis Bay, Namibia 88 C1
Wamba, Dem. Rep. of the Congo 86 B2
Wamba, Kenya 86 B4
Wamba, Nigeria 83 D6
Wamego, U.S.A. 112 F6
Wamena, Indonesia 63 E9
Wamsutter, U.S.A. 114 F9
Wamulan, Indonesia 63 E7
Wan Xian, China 56 E8
Wana, Pakistan 68 C3
Wanaaring, Australia 95 D3
Wanaka, N.Z. 91 L2
Wanaka L., N.Z. 91 L2
Wan'an, China 59 D10
Wanapitei L., Canada 102 C3
Wandel Sea = McKinley Sea, Arctic 4 A7
Wandérama, Ivory C. 82 D4
Wanderer, Zimbabwe 87 F3
Wandhari, Pakistan 68 F2
Wanding, China 58 E2
Wandoan, Australia 95 D4
Wanfu, China 57 D12
Wang →, Thailand 64 D2
Wang Kai, Sudan 81 F2
Wang Noi, Thailand 64 E3
Wang Saphung, Thailand 64 D3
Wang Thong, Thailand 64 D3
Wanga, Dem. Rep. of the Congo 86 B2
Wangal, Indonesia 63 F8
Wanganui, N.Z. 91 H5
Wangary, Australia 95 E2
Wangcang, China 58 A6
Wangcheng, China 59 C9
Wangdu, China 56 E8
Wangen, Germany 25 H5
Wangerooge, Germany 24 B3
Wangi, Kenya 86 C5
Wangiwangi, Indonesia 63 F6
Wangjiang, China 59 B11
Wangmo, China 58 E6
Wangolodougou, Ivory C. 82 D3
Wangqing, China 57 C15
Wankaner, India 68 H4
Wanless, Canada 105 C8
Wannian, China 59 C11
Wanning, China 64 C8
Wanon Niwat, Thailand 64 D4
Wanquan, China 56 D8
Wanrong, China 56 G6
Wanshan, China 58 D7
Wanshengchang, China 58 C6
Wantage, U.K. 13 F6
Wanyuan, China 58 A7
Wanzai, China 59 C10
Wapakoneta, U.S.A. 108 E3
Wapato, U.S.A. 114 C3
Wapawekka L., Canada 105 C8
Wapikopa L., Canada 102 B2
Wapiti →, Canada 104 B5
Wappingers Falls, U.S.A. 111 E11
Wapsipinicon →, U.S.A. 112 E9
Warab □, Sudan 81 F2
Warangal, India 66 L11
Waraseoni, India 69 J9
Waratah, Australia 94 G4
Warburg, Germany 24 D5
Warburton, Australia 93 E4
Warburton Ra., Australia 93 E4
Ward, N.Z. 91 J5
Ward →, Australia 95 D4
Ward Mt., U.S.A. 116 H8
Warden, S. Africa 89 D4
Wardha, India 66 J11
Wardha →, India 66 K11
Ware, Canada 104 B3
Ware, U.S.A. 111 D12
Waregem, Belgium 17 D3
Wareham, U.S.A. 111 E14
Waremme, Belgium 17 D5
Waren, Germany 24 B8
Warendorf, Germany 24 D4
Warialda, Australia 95 D5
Wariap, Indonesia 63 E8
Warin Chamrap, Thailand 64 E5
Warka, Poland 45 G8
Warkopi, Indonesia 63 E8
Warm Springs, U.S.A. 115 G5
Warman, Canada 105 C7
Warmbad, Namibia 88 D2
Warmbad, S. Africa 89 C4
Warmińsko-Mazurskie □, Poland 44 D8
Warminster, U.K. 13 F5
Warminster, U.S.A. 111 F9
Warnemünde, Germany 24 A8
Warner Mts., U.S.A. 114 F3
Warner Robins, U.S.A. 109 J4
Warnow →, Germany 24 A8
Waroona, Australia 93 F2
Warrego →, Australia 95 E4
Warrego Ra., Australia 94 C4
Warren, Ark., U.S.A. 113 J8
Warren, Mich., U.S.A. 108 D4
Warren, Minn., U.S.A. 112 A6
Warren, Ohio, U.S.A. 110 E4
Warren, Pa., U.S.A. 110 E5
Warrenpoint, U.K. 15 B5
Warrensburg, Mo., U.S.A. 112 F8
Warrensburg, N.Y., U.S.A. 111 C11
Warrenton, S. Africa 88 D3
Warrenton, U.S.A. 116 D3
Warri, Nigeria 83 D6
Warrina, Australia 95 D2
Warrington, U.K. 12 D5
Warrington, U.S.A. 109 K2
Warrington □, U.K. 12 D5
Warroad, U.S.A. 112 A7
Warruwi, Australia 94 A1
Warsa, Indonesia 63 E9
Warsak Dam, Pakistan 68 B4
Warsaw = Warszawa, Poland 45 F8
Warsaw, Ind., U.S.A. 108 E3
Warsaw, N.Y., U.S.A. 110 D6
Warsaw, Ohio, U.S.A. 110 F3
Warstein, Germany 24 D4
Warszawa, Poland 45 F8
Warta, Poland 45 G5
Warta →, Poland 45 F1
Warthe = Warta →, Poland 45 F1
Waru, Indonesia 63 E8
Warwick, Australia 95 D5
Warwick, U.K. 13 E6
Warwick, N.Y., U.S.A. 111 E10
Warwick, R.I., U.S.A. 111 E13
Warwickshire □, U.K. 13 E6
Wasaga Beach, Canada 110 B4
Wasagaming, Canada 105 C9
Wasatch Ra., U.S.A. 114 F8
Wasbank, S. Africa 89 D5
Wasco, Calif., U.S.A. 117 K7
Wasco, Oreg., U.S.A. 114 D3
Wase, Nigeria 83 D6
Waseca, U.S.A. 112 C8
Wasekamio L., Canada 105 B7
Wash, The, U.K. 12 E8
Washago, Canada 110 B5
Washburn, N. Dak., U.S.A. 112 B4
Washburn, Wis., U.S.A. 112 B9
Washim, India 66 J10
Washington, U.K. 12 C6
Washington, D.C., U.S.A. 108 F7
Washington, Ga., U.S.A. 109 J4
Washington, Ind., U.S.A. 108 F2
Washington, Iowa, U.S.A. 112 E9
Washington, Mo., U.S.A. 112 F9
Washington, N.C., U.S.A. 109 H7
Washington, N.J., U.S.A. 111 F10
Washington, Pa., U.S.A. 110 F4
Washington, Utah, U.S.A. 115 H7
Washington □, U.S.A. 114 C3
Washington, Mt., U.S.A. 111 B13
Washington Court House, U.S.A. 108 F4
Washington I., U.S.A. 108 C2
Washougal, U.S.A. 116 E4
Wasian, Indonesia 63 E8
Wasilków, Poland 45 E10
Wasilla, U.S.A. 100 B5
Wasior, Indonesia 63 E8
Waskaganish, Canada 102 B4
Waskaiowaka, L., Canada 105 B9
Waskesiu Lake, Canada 105 C7
Wasserburg, Germany 25 G8
Wasserkuppe, Germany 24 E5
Wassy, France 19 D11
Waswanipi, Canada 102 C4
Waswanipi, L., Canada 102 C4
Watampone, Indonesia 63 E6
Water Park Pt., Australia 94 C5
Water Valley, U.S.A. 113 H10
Waterberge, S. Africa 89 C4
Waterbury, Conn., U.S.A. 111 E11
Waterbury, Vt., U.S.A. 111 B12
Waterbury L., Canada 105 B8
Waterdown, Canada 110 C5
Waterford, Canada 110 D4
Waterford, Ireland 15 D4
Waterford, Calif., U.S.A. 116 H6
Waterford, Pa., U.S.A. 110 E5
Waterford □, Ireland 15 D4
Waterford Harbour, Ireland 15 D5
Waterhen L., Canada 105 C9
Waterloo, Belgium 17 D4
Waterloo, Ont., Canada 102 D3
Waterloo, Qué., Canada 111 A12
Waterloo, S. Leone 82 D2
Waterloo, Ill., U.S.A. 112 F9
Waterloo, Iowa, U.S.A. 112 D8
Waterloo, N.Y., U.S.A. 110 D8
Watersmeet, U.S.A. 112 B10
Waterton Lakes Nat. Park, U.S.A. 114 B7
Watertown, Conn., U.S.A. 111 E11
Watertown, N.Y., U.S.A. 111 C9
Watertown, S. Dak., U.S.A. 112 C6
Watertown, Wis., U.S.A. 112 D10
Waterval-Boven, S. Africa 89 D5
Waterville, Canada 111 A13
Waterville, Maine, U.S.A. 109 C11
Waterville, N.Y., U.S.A. 111 D9
Waterville, Pa., U.S.A. 110 E7
Waterville, Wash., U.S.A. 114 C3
Watervliet, U.S.A. 111 D11
Wates, Indonesia 63 G14
Watford, Canada 110 D3
Watford, U.K. 13 F7
Watford City, U.S.A. 112 B3
Wathaman →, Canada 105 B8
Wathaman L., Canada 105 B8
Watheroo, Australia 93 F2
Wating, China 56 G4
Watkins Glen, U.S.A. 110 D8
Watling I. = San Salvador I., Bahamas 121 B5
Watonga, U.S.A. 113 H5
Watrous, Canada 105 C7
Watrous, U.S.A. 113 H2
Watsa, Dem. Rep. of the Congo 86 B2
Watseka, U.S.A. 108 E2
Watson, Australia 93 F5
Watson, Canada 105 C8
Watson Lake, Canada 104 A3
Watsontown, U.S.A. 110 E8
Watsonville, U.S.A. 116 J5
Wattiwarriganna Cr. →, Australia 95 D2
Wattwil, Switz. 25 H5
Watuata = Batuata, Indonesia 63 F6
Watubela, Kepulauan, Indonesia 63 E8
Watubela Is. = Watubela, Kepulauan, Indonesia 63 E8
Wau = Wâw, Sudan 81 F2
Waubamik, Canada 110 A4
Waubay, U.S.A. 112 C6
Wauchope, Australia 94 C1
Wauchula, U.S.A. 109 M5
Waukarlycarly, L., Australia 92 D3
Waukegan, U.S.A. 108 D2
Waukesha, U.S.A. 108 D1
Waukon, U.S.A. 112 D9
Waupaca, U.S.A. 112 C10
Waupun, U.S.A. 112 D10
Waurika, U.S.A. 113 H6
Wausau, U.S.A. 112 C10
Wautoma, U.S.A. 112 C10
Wauwatosa, U.S.A. 108 D2
Waveney →, U.K. 13 E9
Waverley, N.Z. 91 H5
Waverly, Iowa, U.S.A. 112 D8
Waverly, N.Y., U.S.A. 111 E8
Wavre, Belgium 17 D4
Wâw, Sudan 81 F2
Wâw al Kabīr, Libya 79 C9
Wawa, Canada 102 C3
Wawa, Nigeria 83 D5
Wawa, Sudan 80 C3
Wawanesa, Canada 105 D9
Wawona, U.S.A. 116 H7
Waxahachie, U.S.A. 113 J6
Way, L., Australia 93 E3
Waycross, U.S.A. 109 K4
Wayi, Sudan 81 F3
Wayland, U.S.A. 110 D7
Wayne, Nebr., U.S.A. 112 D6
Wayne, W. Va., U.S.A. 108 F4
Waynesboro, Ga., U.S.A. 109 J4
Waynesboro, Miss., U.S.A. 109 K1
Waynesboro, Pa., U.S.A. 108 F7
Waynesboro, Va., U.S.A. 108 F6
Waynesburg, U.S.A. 108 F5
Waynesville, U.S.A. 109 H4
Waynoka, U.S.A. 113 G5
Wazirabad, Pakistan 68 C6
Wda →, Poland 44 E5
We, Indonesia 62 C1
Weald, The, U.K. 13 F8
Wear →, U.K. 12 C6
Weatherford, Okla., U.S.A. 113 H5
Weatherford, Tex., U.S.A. 113 J6
Weaverville, U.S.A. 114 F2
Webb City, U.S.A. 113 G7
Webequie, Canada 102 B2
Webo = Nyaake, Liberia 82 E3
Webster, Mass., U.S.A. 111 D13
Webster, N.Y., U.S.A. 110 C7
Webster, S. Dak., U.S.A. 112 C6
Webster City, U.S.A. 112 D8
Webster Springs, U.S.A. 108 F5
Weda, Indonesia 63 D7
Weda, Teluk, Indonesia 63 D7
Weddell I., Falk. Is. 128 G4
Weddell Sea, Antarctica 5 D1
Wedel, Germany 24 B5
Wedemark, Germany 24 C5
Wedgeport, Canada 103 D6
Wedza, Zimbabwe 87 F3
Wee Waa, Australia 95 E4
Weed, U.S.A. 114 F2
Weed Heights, U.S.A. 116 G7
Weedsport, U.S.A. 111 C8
Weedville, U.S.A. 110 E6
Weenen, S. Africa 89 D5
Weener, Germany 24 B3
Weert, Neths. 17 C5
Węgierska-Górka, Poland 45 J6
Węgliniec, Poland 45 G2
Węgorzewo, Poland 44 D8
Węgorzyno, Poland 44 E2
Węgrów, Poland 45 F9
Wehda □, Sudan 81 F3
Wei He →, Hebei, China 56 F8
Wei He →, Shaanxi, China 56 G6
Weichang, China 57 D9
Weichuan, China 56 G7
Weida, Germany 24 E8
Weiden, Germany 25 F8
Weifang, China 57 F10
Weihai, China 57 F12
Weil, Germany 25 H3
Weilburg, Germany 24 E4
Weilheim, Germany 25 H7
Weimar, Germany 24 E7
Weinan, China 56 G5
Weingarten, Germany 25 F4
Weinheim, Germany 25 F4
Weining, China 58 D5
Weipa, Australia 94 A3
Weir →, Australia 95 D4
Weir →, Canada 105 B10
Weir River, Canada 105 B10
Weirton, U.S.A. 110 F4
Weiser, U.S.A. 114 D5
Weishan, Shandong, China 57 G9
Weishan, Yunnan, China 58 E3
Weissenburg, Germany 25 F6
Weissenfels, Germany 24 D7
Weisswasser, Germany 24 D10
Weitra, Austria 26 C7
Weixi, China 58 D2
Weixin, China 58 D5
Weiyuan, China 56 G3
Weiz, Austria 26 D8
Weizhou Dao, China 58 G7
Wejherowo, Poland 44 D5
Wekusko L., Canada 105 C9
Welch, U.S.A. 108 G5
Weldya, Ethiopia 81 E4
Welega □, Ethiopia 81 F3
Welkite, Ethiopia 81 F4
Welkom, S. Africa 88 D4
Welland, Canada 102 D4
Welland →, U.K. 13 E7
Wellesley Is., Australia 94 B2
Wellingborough, U.K. 13 E7
Wellington, Canada 110 C7
Wellington, N.Z. 91 J5
Wellington, S. Africa 88 E2
Wellington, Somst., U.K. 13 G4
Wellington, Telford & Wrekin, U.K. 13 E5
Wellington, Colo., U.S.A. 112 E2
Wellington, Kans., U.S.A. 113 G6
Wellington, Nev., U.S.A. 116 G7
Wellington, Ohio, U.S.A. 110 E2
Wellington, Tex., U.S.A. 113 H4
Wellington, I., Chile 122 H3
Wells, U.K. 13 F5
Wells, Maine, U.S.A. 111 C14
Wells, N.Y., U.S.A. 111 C10
Wells, Nev., U.S.A. 114 F6
Wells, L., Australia 93 E3
Wells, Mt., Australia 92 C4
Wells Gray Prov. Park, Canada 104 C4
Wells-next-the-Sea, U.K. 12 E8
Wells River, U.S.A. 111 B12

Wellsboro, *U.S.A.* 110 E7
Wellsburg, *U.S.A.* 110 F4
Wellsville, *N.Y., U.S.A.* 110 D7
Wellsville, *Ohio, U.S.A.* 110 F4
Wellsville, *Utah, U.S.A.* 114 F8
Wellton, *U.S.A.* 115 K6
Welmel, Wabi →, *Ethiopia* 81 F5
Welo □, *Ethiopia* 81 E4
Wels, *Austria* 26 C7
Welshpool, *U.K.* 13 E4
Welwyn Garden City, *U.K.* 13 F7
Wem, *U.K.* 12 E5
Wembere →, *Tanzania* 86 C3
Wemindji, *Canada* 102 B4
Wen Xian, *China* 56 G7
Wenatchee, *U.S.A.* 114 C3
Wenchang, *China* 64 C8
Wencheng, *China* 59 D13
Wenchi, *Ghana* 82 D4
Wenchow = Wenzhou, *China* 59 D13
Wenchuan, *China* 58 B4
Wenden, *U.S.A.* 117 M13
Wendeng, *China* 57 F12
Wendesi, *Indonesia* 63 E8
Wendo, *Ethiopia* 81 F4
Wendover, *U.S.A.* 114 F6
Weng'an, *China* 58 D6
Wengcheng, *China* 59 E9
Wengyuan, *China* 59 E10
Wenjiang, *China* 58 B4
Wenling, *China* 59 C13
Wenlock →, *Australia* 94 A3
Wenshan, *China* 58 F5
Wenshang, *China* 56 G9
Wenshui, *China* 56 F7
Wensleydale, *U.K.* 12 C6
Wensu, *China* 60 B3
Wensum →, *U.K.* 12 E8
Wentzel L., *Canada* 104 B6
Wenut, *Indonesia* 63 E8
Wenxi, *China* 56 G6
Wenxian, *China* 56 H3
Wenzhou, *China* 59 D13
Weott, *U.S.A.* 114 F2
Wepener, *S. Africa* 88 D4
Werda, *Botswana* 88 D3
Werdau, *Germany* 24 E8
Werder, *Germany* 24 C8
Werdohl, *Germany* 24 D3
Wereilu, *Ethiopia* 81 E4
Weri, *Indonesia* 63 E8
Werneck, *Germany* 25 F6
Wernigerode, *Germany* 24 D6
Werra →, *Germany* 24 D5
Wertach →, *Germany* 25 G6
Wertheim, *Germany* 25 F5
Wertingen, *Germany* 25 G6
Wesel, *Germany* 24 D2
Weser →, *Germany* 24 B4
Weser-Ems □, *Germany* 24 C3
Weserbergland, *Germany* 24 C5
Wesiri, *Indonesia* 63 F7
Weslemkoon L., *Canada* 110 A7
Wesleyville, *Canada* 103 C9
Wesleyville, *U.S.A.* 110 D4
Wessel, C., *Australia* 94 A2
Wessel Is., *Australia* 94 A2
Wesselburen, *Germany* 24 A4
Wessington Springs, *U.S.A.* 112 C5
West, *U.S.A.* 113 K6
West →, *U.S.A.* 111 D12
West Baines →, *Australia* 92 C4
West Bank □, *Asia* 75 C4
West Bend, *U.S.A.* 108 D1
West Bengal □, *India* 69 H13
West Berkshire □, *U.K.* 13 F6
West Beskids = Západné Beskydy, *Europe* 27 B12
West Branch, *U.S.A.* 108 C3
West Branch Susquehanna →, *U.S.A.* 111 F8
West Bromwich, *U.K.* 13 E6
West Burra, *U.K.* 14 A7
West Canada Cr. →, *U.S.A.* 111 C10
West Cape Howe, *Australia* 93 G2
West Chazy, *U.S.A.* 111 B11
West Chester, *U.S.A.* 111 G9
West Columbia, *U.S.A.* 113 L7
West Covina, *U.S.A.* 117 L9
West Des Moines, *U.S.A.* 112 E8
West Dunbartonshire □, *U.K.* 14 F4
West End, *Bahamas* 120 A4
West Falkland, *Falk. Is.* 122 J4
West Fargo, *U.S.A.* 112 B6
West Farmington, *U.S.A.* 110 E4
West Fjord = Vestfjorden, *Norway* 8 C15
West Fork Trinity →, *U.S.A.* 113 J6
West Frankfort, *U.S.A.* 112 G10
West Hartford, *U.S.A.* 111 E12
West Haven, *U.S.A.* 111 E12
West Hazleton, *U.S.A.* 111 F9
West Helena, *U.S.A.* 113 H9
West Hurley, *U.S.A.* 111 E10
West Ice Shelf, *Antarctica* 5 C7
West Indies, *Cent. Amer.* 121 D7
West Jordan, *U.S.A.* 114 F8
West Lorne, *Canada* 110 D3
West Lothian □, *U.K.* 14 F5
West Lunga →, *Zambia* 87 E1
West Memphis, *U.S.A.* 113 H9
West Midlands □, *U.K.* 13 E6
West Mifflin, *U.S.A.* 110 F5
West Milton, *U.S.A.* 110 E8
West Monroe, *U.S.A.* 113 J8
West Newton, *U.S.A.* 110 F5
West Nicholson, *Zimbabwe* 87 G2
West Palm Beach, *U.S.A.* 109 M5
West Plains, *U.S.A.* 113 G9
West Point, *N.Y., U.S.A.* 111 E11
West Point, *Nebr., U.S.A.* 112 E6
West Point, *Va., U.S.A.* 108 G7
West Pt. = Ouest, Pte. de l', *Canada* 103 C7
West Road →, *Canada* 104 C4
West Rutland, *U.S.A.* 111 C11
West Schelde = Westerschelde →, *Neths.* 17 C3
West Seneca, *U.S.A.* 110 D6
West Siberian Plain, *Russia* 52 C11
West Sussex □, *U.K.* 13 G7
West-Terschelling, *Neths.* 17 A5
West Valley City, *U.S.A.* 114 F8
West Virginia □, *U.S.A.* 108 F5
West-Vlaanderen □, *Belgium* 17 D2
West Walker →, *U.S.A.* 116 G7
West Yellowstone, *U.S.A.* 114 D8
West Yorkshire □, *U.K.* 12 D6
Westall Pt., *Australia* 95 E1
Westbrook, *U.S.A.* 109 D10
Westbury, *Australia* 94 G4
Westby, *U.S.A.* 112 A2
Westend, *U.S.A.* 117 K9
Westerland, *Germany* 9 J13
Westerly, *U.S.A.* 111 E13
Western □, *Ghana* 82 D4
Western □, *Kenya* 86 B3
Western □, *S. Leone* 82 D2
Western □, *Zambia* 87 F1
Western Australia □, *Australia* 93 E2
Western Cape □, *S. Africa* 88 E3
Western Dvina = Daugava →, *Latvia* 9 H21
Western Ghats, *India* 66 N9
Western Isles □, *U.K.* 14 D1
Western Sahara ■, *Africa* 78 D3
Western Samoa = Samoa ■, *Pac. Oc.* 91 B13
Westernport, *U.S.A.* 108 F6
Westerschelde →, *Neths.* 17 C3
Westerstede, *Germany* 24 B3
Westerwald, *Germany* 24 E3
Westfield, *Mass., U.S.A.* 111 D12
Westfield, *N.Y., U.S.A.* 110 D5
Westfield, *Pa., U.S.A.* 110 E7
Westhill, *U.K.* 14 D6
Westhope, *U.S.A.* 112 A4
Westland Bight, *N.Z.* 91 K3
Westlock, *Canada* 104 C6
Westmar, *Australia* 95 D4
Westmeath □, *Ireland* 15 C4
Westminster, *U.S.A.* 108 F7
Westmont, *U.S.A.* 110 F6
Westmorland, *U.S.A.* 117 M11
Weston, *Oreg., U.S.A.* 114 D4
Weston, *W. Va., U.S.A.* 108 F5
Weston I., *Canada* 102 B4
Weston-super-Mare, *U.K.* 13 F5
Westover, *U.S.A.* 110 F6
Westport, *Canada* 111 B8
Westport, *Ireland* 15 C2
Westport, *N.Z.* 91 J3
Westport, *N.Y., U.S.A.* 111 B11
Westport, *Oreg., U.S.A.* 116 D3
Westport, *Wash., U.S.A.* 116 D2
Westray, *Canada* 105 C8
Westray, *U.K.* 14 B5
Westree, *Canada* 102 C3
Westville, *U.S.A.* 116 F6
Westwood, *U.S.A.* 114 F3
Wetar, *Indonesia* 63 F7
Wetaskiwin, *Canada* 104 C6
Wete, *Tanzania* 84 F7
Wetherby, *U.K.* 12 D6
Wethersfield, *U.S.A.* 111 E12
Wetteren, *Belgium* 17 D3
Wetzlar, *Germany* 24 E4
Wewoka, *U.S.A.* 113 H6
Wexford, *Ireland* 15 D5
Wexford □, *Ireland* 15 D5
Wexford Harbour, *Ireland* 15 D5
Weyburn, *Canada* 105 D8
Weyer Markt, *Austria* 26 D7
Weyhe, *Germany* 24 C4
Weyib →, *Ethiopia* 81 F5
Weymouth, *Canada* 103 D6
Weymouth, *U.K.* 13 G5
Weymouth, *U.S.A.* 111 D14
Weymouth, C., *Australia* 94 A3
Wha Ti, *Canada* 100 B8
Whakatane, *N.Z.* 91 G6
Whale →, *Canada* 103 A6
Whale Cove, *Canada* 105 A10
Whales, B. of, *Antarctica* 5 D12
Whalsay, *U.K.* 14 A8
Whangamomona, *N.Z.* 91 H5
Whangarei, *N.Z.* 91 F5
Whangarei Harb., *N.Z.* 91 F5
Wharfe →, *U.K.* 12 D6
Wharfedale, *U.K.* 12 C5
Wharton, *N.J., U.S.A.* 111 F10
Wharton, *Pa., U.S.A.* 110 E6
Wharton, *Tex., U.S.A.* 113 L6
Wheatland, *Calif., U.S.A.* 116 F5
Wheatland, *Wyo., U.S.A.* 112 D2
Wheatley, *Canada* 110 D2
Wheaton, *Md., U.S.A.* 108 F7
Wheaton, *Minn., U.S.A.* 112 C6
Wheelbarrow Pk., *U.S.A.* 116 H10
Wheeler, *Oreg., U.S.A.* 114 D2
Wheeler, *Tex., U.S.A.* 113 H4
Wheeler →, *Canada* 103 A6
Wheeler L., *U.S.A.* 109 H2
Wheeler Pk., *N. Mex., U.S.A.* 115 H11
Wheeler Pk., *Nev., U.S.A.* 115 G6
Wheeler Ridge, *U.S.A.* 117 L8
Wheeling, *U.S.A.* 110 F4
Whernside, *U.K.* 12 C5
Whiskey Jack L., *Canada* 105 B8
Whistleduck Cr. →, *Australia* 94 C2
Whistler, *Canada* 104 C4
Whitby, *Canada* 110 C6
Whitby, *U.K.* 12 C7
White →, *Ark., U.S.A.* 113 J9
White →, *Ind., U.S.A.* 108 F2
White →, *S. Dak., U.S.A.* 112 D5
White →, *Tex., U.S.A.* 113 J4
White →, *Utah, U.S.A.* 114 F9
White →, *Vt., U.S.A.* 111 C12
White →, *Wash., U.S.A.* 116 C4
White, L., *Australia* 92 D4
White B., *Canada* 103 C8
White Bird, *U.S.A.* 114 D5
White Butte, *U.S.A.* 112 B3
White City, *U.S.A.* 114 E2
White Hall, *U.S.A.* 112 F9
White Haven, *U.S.A.* 111 E9
White Horse, Vale of, *U.K.* 13 F6
White I., *N.Z.* 91 G6
White L., *Canada* 111 A8
White L., *U.S.A.* 113 L8
White Mountain Peak, *U.S.A.* 115 G4
White Mts., *Calif., U.S.A.* 116 H8
White Mts., *N.H., U.S.A.* 111 B13
White Nile = Nîl el Abyad →, *Sudan* 81 D3
White Nile Dam = Khazzān Jabal al Awliyā, *Sudan* 81 D3
White Otter L., *Canada* 102 C1
White Pass, *U.S.A.* 116 D5
White Plains, *U.S.A.* 111 E11
White River, *Canada* 102 C2
White River, *S. Africa* 89 D5
White River, *U.S.A.* 112 D4
White Rock, *Canada* 116 A4
White Russia = Belarus ■, *Europe* 46 F4
White Sea = Beloye More, *Russia* 50 C4
White Sulphur Springs, *Mont., U.S.A.* 114 C8
White Sulphur Springs, *W. Va., U.S.A.* 108 G5
White Swan, *U.S.A.* 116 D6
White Volta →, *Ghana* 83 D4
Whitecliffs, *N.Z.* 91 K3
Whitecourt, *Canada* 104 C5
Whiteface Mt., *U.S.A.* 111 B11
Whitefield, *U.S.A.* 111 B13
Whitefish, *U.S.A.* 114 B6
Whitefish L., *Canada* 105 A7
Whitefish Point, *U.S.A.* 108 B3
Whitegull, L., *Canada* 103 A7
Whitehall, *Mich., U.S.A.* 108 D2
Whitehall, *Mont., U.S.A.* 114 D7
Whitehall, *N.Y., U.S.A.* 111 C11
Whitehall, *Wis., U.S.A.* 112 C9
Whitehaven, *U.K.* 12 C4
Whitehorse, *Canada* 104 A1
Whitemark, *Australia* 94 G4
Whiteplains, *Liberia* 82 D2
Whiteriver, *U.S.A.* 115 K9
Whitesand →, *Canada* 104 A5
Whitesands, *S. Africa* 88 E3
Whitesboro, *N.Y., U.S.A.* 111 C9
Whitesboro, *Tex., U.S.A.* 113 J6
Whiteshell Prov. Park, *Canada* 105 D9
Whitesville, *U.S.A.* 110 D7
Whiteville, *U.S.A.* 109 H6
Whitewater, *U.S.A.* 108 D1
Whitewater Baldy, *U.S.A.* 115 K9
Whitewater L., *Canada* 102 B2
Whitewood, *Australia* 94 C3
Whitewood, *Canada* 105 C8
Whithorn, *U.K.* 14 G4
Whitianga, *N.Z.* 91 G5
Whitman, *U.S.A.* 111 D14
Whitney, *Canada* 102 C4
Whitney, Mt., *U.S.A.* 116 J8
Whitney Point, *U.S.A.* 111 D9
Whitstable, *U.K.* 13 F9
Whitsunday I., *Australia* 94 C4
Whittier, *U.S.A.* 117 M8
Wholdaia L., *Canada* 105 A8
Whyalla, *Australia* 95 E2
Wiarton, *Canada* 102 D3
Wiawso, *Ghana* 82 D4
Wiay, *U.K.* 14 D1
Wiązów, *Poland* 45 H4
Wibaux, *U.S.A.* 112 B2
Wichian Buri, *Thailand* 64 E3
Wichita, *U.S.A.* 113 G6
Wichita Falls, *U.S.A.* 113 J5
Wick, *U.K.* 14 C5
Wicked Pt., *Canada* 110 C7
Wickenburg, *U.S.A.* 115 K7
Wickepin, *Australia* 93 F2
Wickham, *Australia* 92 D2
Wickham, C., *Australia* 94 F3
Wickliffe, *U.S.A.* 110 E3
Wicklow, *Ireland* 15 D5
Wicklow □, *Ireland* 15 D5
Wicklow Hd., *Ireland* 15 D6
Wicklow Mts., *Ireland* 15 C5
Widawa, *Poland* 45 G5
Widawka →, *Poland* 45 G5
Widgeegoara Cr. →, *Australia* 95 D4
Widgiemooltha, *Australia* 93 F3
Widnes, *U.K.* 12 D5
Więcbork, *Poland* 45 E4
Wiehl, *Germany* 24 E3
Wiek, *Germany* 24 A9
Wielbark, *Poland* 44 E7
Wieleń, *Poland* 45 F3
Wielichowo, *Poland* 45 F3
Wieliczka, *Poland* 45 J7
Wielkopolskie □, *Poland* 45 F4
Wieluń, *Poland* 45 G5
Wien, *Austria* 27 C9
Wiener Neustadt, *Austria* 27 D9
Wieprz →, *Poland* 45 G8
Wieprza →, *Poland* 44 D3
Wieruszów, *Poland* 45 G5
Wiesbaden, *Germany* 25 E4
Wiesental, *Germany* 25 F4
Wiesloch, *Germany* 25 F4
Wiesmoor, *Germany* 24 B3
Wieżyca, *Poland* 44 D5
Wigan, *U.K.* 12 D5
Wiggins, *Colo., U.S.A.* 112 E2
Wiggins, *Miss., U.S.A.* 113 K10
Wight, I. of □, *U.K.* 13 G6
Wigry, Jezioro, *Poland* 44 D10
Wigston, *U.K.* 13 E6
Wigton, *U.K.* 12 C4
Wigtown, *U.K.* 14 G4
Wigtown B., *U.K.* 14 G4
Wil, *Switz.* 25 H5
Wilamowice, *Poland* 45 J6
Wilber, *U.S.A.* 112 E6
Wilberforce, *Canada* 110 A6
Wilberforce, C., *Australia* 94 A2
Wilburton, *U.S.A.* 113 H7
Wilcox, *U.S.A.* 110 E6
Wildbad, *Germany* 25 G4
Wildeshausen, *Germany* 24 C4
Wildon, *Austria* 26 E8
Wildrose, *U.S.A.* 117 J9
Wildspitze, *Austria* 26 E3
Wilga →, *Poland* 45 G8
Wilge →, *S. Africa* 89 D4
Wilhelm II Coast, *Antarctica* 5 C7
Wilhelmsburg, *Austria* 26 C8
Wilhelmshaven, *Germany* 24 B4
Wilhelmstal, *Namibia* 88 C2
Wilkes-Barre, *U.S.A.* 111 E9
Wilkie, *Canada* 105 C7
Wilkinsburg, *U.S.A.* 110 F5
Wilkinson Lakes, *Australia* 93 E5
Willapa B., *U.S.A.* 114 C2
Willapa Hills, *U.S.A.* 116 D3
Willard, *N.Y., U.S.A.* 110 D8
Willard, *Ohio, U.S.A.* 110 E2
Willcox, *U.S.A.* 115 K9
Willemstad, *Neth. Ant.* 121 D6
Willet, *U.S.A.* 111 D9
William →, *Canada* 105 B7
William 'Bill' Dannely Res., *U.S.A.* 109 J2
William Creek, *Australia* 95 D2
Williams, *Australia* 93 F2
Williams, *Ariz., U.S.A.* 115 J7
Williams, *Calif., U.S.A.* 116 F4
Williams Harbour, *Canada* 103 B8
Williams Lake, *Canada* 104 C4
Williamsburg, *Ky., U.S.A.* 109 G3
Williamsburg, *Pa., U.S.A.* 110 F6
Williamsburg, *Va., U.S.A.* 108 G7
Williamson, *N.Y., U.S.A.* 110 C7
Williamson, *W. Va., U.S.A.* 108 G4
Williamsport, *U.S.A.* 110 E7
Williamston, *U.S.A.* 109 H7
Williamstown, *Ky., U.S.A.* 108 F3
Williamstown, *Mass., U.S.A.* 111 D11
Williamstown, *N.Y., U.S.A.* 111 C9
Willimantic, *U.S.A.* 111 E12
Willingboro, *U.S.A.* 108 E8
Willis Group, *Australia* 94 B5
Williston, *S. Africa* 88 E3
Williston, *Fla., U.S.A.* 109 L4
Williston, *N. Dak., U.S.A.* 112 A3
Williston L., *Canada* 104 B4
Willits, *U.S.A.* 114 G2
Willmar, *U.S.A.* 112 C7
Willoughby, *U.S.A.* 110 E3
Willow Bunch, *Canada* 105 D7
Willow L., *Canada* 104 A5
Willow Wall, The, *China* 57 C12
Willowick, *U.S.A.* 110 E3
Willowlake →, *Canada* 104 A4
Willowmore, *S. Africa* 88 E3
Willows, *U.S.A.* 116 F4
Willowvale = Gatyana, *S. Africa* 89 E4
Wills, L., *Australia* 92 D4
Wills Cr. →, *Australia* 94 C3
Willsboro, *U.S.A.* 111 B11
Wilmette, *U.S.A.* 108 D2
Wilmington, *Del., U.S.A.* 108 F8
Wilmington, *N.C., U.S.A.* 109 H7
Wilmington, *Ohio, U.S.A.* 108 F4
Wilmington, *Vt., U.S.A.* 111 D12
Wilmslow, *U.K.* 12 D5
Wilsall, *U.S.A.* 114 D8
Wilson, *N.C., U.S.A.* 109 H7
Wilson, *N.Y., U.S.A.* 110 C6
Wilson, *Pa., U.S.A.* 111 F9
Wilson →, *Australia* 92 C4
Wilson Bluff, *Australia* 93 F4
Wilson Inlet, *Australia* 93 G2
Wilster, *Germany* 24 B5
Wilton, *U.S.A.* 112 B4
Wilton →, *Australia* 94 A1
Wiltshire □, *U.K.* 13 F6
Wiltz, *Lux.* 17 E5
Wiluna, *Australia* 93 E3
Wimborne Minster, *U.K.* 13 G6
Wimereux, *France* 19 B8
Winam G., *Kenya* 86 C3
Winburg, *S. Africa* 88 D4
Winchendon, *U.S.A.* 111 D12
Winchester, *U.K.* 13 F6
Winchester, *Conn., U.S.A.* 111 E11
Winchester, *Idaho, U.S.A.* 114 C5
Winchester, *Ind., U.S.A.* 108 E3
Winchester, *Ky., U.S.A.* 108 G3
Winchester, *N.H., U.S.A.* 111 D12
Winchester, *Nev., U.S.A.* 117 J11
Winchester, *Tenn., U.S.A.* 109 H2
Winchester, *Va., U.S.A.* 108 F6
Wind →, *U.S.A.* 114 E9
Wind River Range, *U.S.A.* 114 E9
Windau = Ventspils, *Latvia* 9 H19
Windber, *U.S.A.* 110 F6
Winder, *U.S.A.* 109 J4
Windermere, *U.K.* 12 C5
Windhoek, *Namibia* 88 C2
Windischgarsten, *Austria* 26 D7
Windom, *U.S.A.* 112 D7
Windorah, *Australia* 94 D3
Window Rock, *U.S.A.* 115 J9
Windrush →, *U.K.* 13 F6
Windsor, *N.S., Canada* 103 D7
Windsor, *Ont., Canada* 102 D3
Windsor, *U.K.* 13 F7
Windsor, *Colo., U.S.A.* 112 E2
Windsor, *Conn., U.S.A.* 111 E12
Windsor, *Mo., U.S.A.* 112 F8
Windsor, *N.Y., U.S.A.* 111 D9
Windsor, *Vt., U.S.A.* 111 C12
Windsor & Maidenhead □, *U.K.* 13 F7
Windsorton, *S. Africa* 88 D3
Windward Is., *W. Indies* 121 D7
Windward Passage = Vientos, Paso de los, *Caribbean* 121 C5
Winefred L., *Canada* 105 B6
Winejok, *Sudan* 81 F2
Winfield, *U.S.A.* 113 G6
Wingate Mts., *Australia* 92 B5
Wingham, *Canada* 102 D3
Winisk, *Canada* 102 A2
Winisk →, *Canada* 102 A2
Winisk L., *Canada* 102 B2
Wink, *U.S.A.* 113 K3
Winkler, *Canada* 105 D9
Winklern, *Austria* 26 E5
Winlock, *U.S.A.* 116 D4
Winneba, *Ghana* 83 D4
Winnebago, L., *U.S.A.* 108 D1
Winnecke Cr. →, *Australia* 92 C5
Winnemucca, *U.S.A.* 114 F5
Winnemucca L., *U.S.A.* 114 F4
Winnett, *U.S.A.* 114 C9
Winnfield, *U.S.A.* 113 K8
Winnibigoshish, L., *U.S.A.* 112 B7
Winnipeg, *Canada* 105 D9
Winnipeg →, *Canada* 105 C9
Winnipeg, L., *Canada* 105 C9
Winnipeg Beach, *Canada* 105 C9
Winnipegosis, *Canada* 105 C9
Winnipegosis L., *Canada* 105 C9
Winnipesaukee, L., *U.S.A.* 111 C13
Winnisquam L., *U.S.A.* 111 C13
Winnsboro, *La., U.S.A.* 113 J9
Winnsboro, *S.C., U.S.A.* 109 H5
Winnsboro, *Tex., U.S.A.* 113 J7
Winokapau, L., *Canada* 103 B7
Winona, *Minn., U.S.A.* 112 C9
Winona, *Miss., U.S.A.* 113 J10
Winooski, *U.S.A.* 111 B11
Winooski →, *U.S.A.* 111 B11
Winschoten, *Neths.* 17 A7
Winsen, *Germany* 24 B6
Winsford, *U.K.* 12 D5
Winslow, *Ariz., U.S.A.* 115 J8
Winslow, *Wash., U.S.A.* 116 C4
Winsted, *U.S.A.* 111 E11
Winston-Salem, *U.S.A.* 109 G5
Winter Garden, *U.S.A.* 109 L5
Winter Haven, *U.S.A.* 109 M5
Winter Park, *U.S.A.* 109 L5
Winterberg, *Germany* 24 D4
Winterhaven, *U.S.A.* 117 N12
Winters, *U.S.A.* 116 G5
Wintersville, *U.S.A.* 110 F4
Winterswijk, *Neths.* 17 C6
Winterthur, *Switz.* 25 H4
Winthrop, *U.S.A.* 114 B3
Winton, *Australia* 94 C3
Winton, *N.Z.* 91 M2
Wipper →, *Germany* 24 D7
Wirrulla, *Australia* 95 E1
Wisbech, *U.K.* 13 E8
Wisconsin □, *U.S.A.* 112 C10
Wisconsin →, *U.S.A.* 112 D9
Wisconsin Rapids, *U.S.A.* 112 C10
Wisdom, *U.S.A.* 114 D7
Wishaw, *U.K.* 14 F5
Wishek, *U.S.A.* 112 B5
Wisła, *Poland* 45 J5
Wisła →, *Poland* 44 D5
Wisłok →, *Poland* 45 H9
Wisłoka →, *Poland* 45 H8
Wismar, *Germany* 24 B7
Wisner, *U.S.A.* 112 E6
Wissant, *France* 19 B8
Wissembourg, *France* 19 C14

Wisznice, Poland 45 G10
Witbank, S. Africa 89 D4
Witdraai, S. Africa 88 D3
Witham, U.K. 13 F8
Witham →, U.K. 12 E7
Withernsea, U.K. 12 D8
Witkowo, Poland 45 F4
Witney, U.K. 13 F6
Witnica, Poland 45 F1
Witnossob →, Namibia 88 D3
Wittdün, Germany 24 A4
Witten, Germany 24 D3
Wittenberge, Germany 24 B7
Wittenburg, Germany 24 B7
Wittenheim, France 19 E14
Wittenoom, Australia 92 D2
Wittingen, Germany 24 C6
Wittlich, Germany 25 F2
Wittmund, Germany 24 B3
Wittow, Germany 24 A9
Wittstock, Germany 24 B8
Witvlei, Namibia 88 C2
Witzenhausen, Germany 24 D5
Wkra →, Poland 45 F7
Władysławowo, Poland 44 D5
Wleń, Poland 45 G2
Wlingi, Indonesia 63 H15
Włocławek, Poland 45 F6
Włodawa, Poland 45 G10
Włoszczowa, Poland 45 H6
Woburn, U.S.A. 111 D13
Wodian, China 56 H7
Wodzisław Śląski, Poland 45 H5
Wœrth, France 19 D14
Woinbogoin, China 58 A2
Woippy, France 19 C13
Wojcieszow, Poland 45 H2
Wokam, Indonesia 63 F8
Woking, U.K. 13 F7
Wokingham □, U.K. 13 F7
Wolbrom, Poland 45 H6
Wołczyn, Poland 45 G5
Woldegk, Germany 24 B9
Wolf →, Canada 104 A2
Wolf Creek, U.S.A. 114 C7
Wolf L., Canada 104 A2
Wolf Point, U.S.A. 112 A2
Wolfe I., Canada 102 D4
Wolfeboro, U.S.A. 111 C13
Wolfen, Germany 24 D8
Wolfenbüttel, Germany 24 C6
Wolfratshausen, Germany 25 H7
Wolfsberg, Austria 26 E7
Wolfsburg, Germany 24 C6
Wolgast, Germany 24 A9
Wolhusen, Switz. 25 H4
Wolin, Poland 44 E1
Wollaston, Is., Chile 128 H3
Wollaston L., Canada 105 B8
Wollaston Lake, Canada 105 B8
Wollaston Pen., Canada 100 B8
Wolmaransstad, S. Africa 88 D4
Wolmirstedt, Germany 24 C7
Wołomin, Poland 45 F8
Wołów, Poland 45 G3
Wolseley, S. Africa 88 E2
Wolsey, U.S.A. 112 C5
Wolstenholme, C., Canada 98 C12
Wolsztyn, Poland 45 F3
Wolvega, Neths. 17 B6
Wolverhampton, U.K. 13 E5
Wondai, Australia 95 D5
Wongan Hills, Australia 93 F2
Wŏnju, S. Korea 57 F14
Wonosari, Indonesia 63 G14
Wonosobo, Indonesia 63 G13
Wonowon, Canada 104 B4
Wŏnsan, N. Korea 57 E14
Wood Buffalo Nat. Park, Canada 104 B6
Wood Is., Australia 92 C3
Wood L., Canada 105 B8
Woodah I., Australia 94 A2
Woodbourne, U.S.A. 111 E10
Woodbridge, Canada 110 C5
Woodbridge, U.K. 13 E9
Woodburn, U.S.A. 114 D2
Woodenbong, Australia 95 D5
Woodend, Australia 95 F3
Woodford, Australia 95 D5
Woodfords, U.S.A. 116 G7
Woodlake, U.S.A. 116 J7
Woodland, Calif., U.S.A. 116 G5
Woodland, Maine, U.S.A. 109 C12
Woodland, Pa., U.S.A. 110 F6
Woodland, Wash., U.S.A. 116 E4
Woodland Caribou Prov. Park, Canada 105 C10
Woodridge, Canada 105 D9
Woodroffe, Mt., Australia 93 E5
Woods, L., Australia 94 B1
Woods, L. of the, Canada 105 D10
Woodstock, Australia 94 B4
Woodstock, N.B., Canada 103 C6
Woodstock, Ont., Canada 102 D3
Woodstock, U.K. 13 F6
Woodstock, Ill., U.S.A. 112 D10
Woodstock, Vt., U.S.A. 111 C12
Woodsville, U.S.A. 111 B13
Woodville, N.Z. 91 J5
Woodville, Miss., U.S.A. 113 K9
Woodville, Tex., U.S.A. 113 K7
Woodward, U.S.A. 113 G5
Woody, U.S.A. 117 K8
Woody →, Canada 105 C8
Wooler, U.K. 12 B5
Woolgoolga, Australia 95 E5
Woonsocket, R.I., U.S.A. 111 E13
Woonsocket, S. Dak., U.S.A. 112 C5
Wooramel →, Australia 93 E1
Wooramel Roadhouse, Australia 93 E1
Wooster, U.S.A. 110 F3
Worcester, S. Africa 88 E2
Worcester, U.K. 13 E5
Worcester, Mass., U.S.A. 111 D13
Worcester, N.Y., U.S.A. 111 D10
Worcestershire □, U.K. 13 E5
Wörgl, Austria 26 D5
Workington, U.K. 12 C4
Worksop, U.K. 12 D6
Workum, Neths. 17 B5
Worland, U.S.A. 114 D10
Wormhout, France 19 B9
Worms, Germany 25 F4
Worsley, Canada 104 B5
Wörth, Germany 25 F8
Wortham, U.S.A. 113 K6
Wörther See, Austria 26 E7
Worthing, U.K. 13 G7
Worthington, Minn., U.S.A. 112 D7
Worthington, Pa., U.S.A. 110 F5
Wosi, Indonesia 63 E7
Wou-han = Wuhan, China 59 B10
Wousi = Wuxi, China 59 B13
Wowoni, Indonesia 63 E6
Wrangel I. = Vrangelya, Ostrov, Russia 51 B19
Wrangell, U.S.A. 104 B2
Wrangell Mts., U.S.A. 100 B5
Wrath, C., U.K. 14 C3
Wray, U.S.A. 112 E3
Wrekin, The, U.K. 13 E5
Wrens, U.S.A. 109 J4
Wrexham, U.K. 12 D4
Wrexham □, U.K. 12 D5
Wriezen, Germany 24 C10
Wright = Paranas, Phil. 61 F6
Wright, U.S.A. 112 D2
Wright Pt., Canada 110 C3
Wrightson Mt., U.S.A. 115 L8
Wrightwood, U.S.A. 117 L9
Wrigley, Canada 100 B7
Wrocław, Poland 45 G4
Wronki, Poland 45 F3
Września, Poland 45 F4
Wschowa, Poland 45 G3
Wu Jiang →, China 58 C6
Wu'an, China 56 F8
Wubin, Australia 93 F2
Wubu, China 56 F6
Wuchang, China 57 B14
Wucheng, China 56 F9
Wuchuan, Guangdong, China 59 G8
Wuchuan, Guizhou, China 58 C7
Wuchuan, Nei Monggol Zizhiqu, China 56 D6
Wudi, China 57 F9
Wuding, China 58 E4
Wuding He →, China 56 F6
Wudinna, Australia 95 E2
Wudu, China 56 H3
Wufeng, China 59 B8
Wugang, China 59 D8
Wugong Shan, China 59 D9
Wuhan, China 59 B10
Wuhe, China 57 H9
Wuhsi = Wuxi, China 59 B13
Wuhu, China 59 B12
Wujiang, China 59 B13
Wukari, Nigeria 83 D6
Wulajie, China 57 B14
Wulanbulang, China 56 D6
Wular L., India 69 B6
Wulehe, Ghana 83 D5
Wulian, China 57 G10
Wuliang Shan, China 58 E3
Wuliaru, Indonesia 63 F8
Wuling Shan, China 58 C7
Wulong, China 58 C6
Wulumuchi = Ürümqi, China 50 E9
Wum, Cameroon 83 D7
Wuming, China 58 F7
Wun Rog, Sudan 81 F2
Wundowie, Australia 93 F2
Wuning, China 59 C10
Wunnummin L., Canada 102 B2
Wunsiedel, Germany 25 E8
Wunstorf, Germany 24 C5
Wuntho, Burma 67 H19
Wuping, China 59 E11
Wuppertal, Germany 24 D3
Wuppertal, S. Africa 88 E2
Wuqing, China 57 E9
Wurtsboro, U.S.A. 111 E10
Würzburg, Germany 25 F5
Wurzen, Germany 24 D8
Wushan, China 56 G3
Wushishi, Nigeria 83 D6
Wusuli Jiang = Ussuri →, Asia 54 A7
Wutach →, Germany 25 H4
Wutai, China 56 E7
Wuting = Huimin, China 57 F9
Wutong, China 59 E8
Wutonghaolai, China 57 C11
Wutongqiao, China 58 C4
Wuwei, Anhui, China 59 B11
Wuwei, Gansu, China 60 C5
Wuxi, Jiangsu, China 59 B13
Wuxi, Sichuan, China 58 B7
Wuxiang, China 56 F7
Wuxuan, China 58 F7
Wuxue, China 59 C10
Wuyang, China 56 H7
Wuyi, Hebei, China 56 F8
Wuyi, Zhejiang, China 59 C12
Wuyi Shan, China 59 D11
Wuyishan, China 59 D12
Wuyo, Nigeria 83 C7
Wuyuan, Jiangxi, China 59 C11
Wuyuan, Nei Monggol Zizhiqu, China 56 D5
Wuzhai, China 56 E6
Wuzhi Shan, China 64 C7
Wuzhong, China 56 E4
Wuzhou, China 59 F8
Wyaaba Cr. →, Australia 94 B3
Wyalkatchem, Australia 93 F2
Wyalusing, U.S.A. 111 E8
Wyandotte, U.S.A. 108 D4
Wyandra, Australia 95 D4
Wyara, L., Australia 95 D3
Wye →, U.K. 13 F5
Wyemandoo, Australia 93 E2
Wyk, Germany 24 A4
Wymondham, U.K. 13 E9
Wymore, U.S.A. 112 E6
Wyndham, Australia 92 C4
Wyndham, N.Z. 91 M2
Wynne, U.S.A. 113 H9
Wynyard, Australia 94 G4
Wynyard, Canada 105 C8
Wyola L., Australia 93 E5
Wyoming, Canada 110 D2
Wyoming □, U.S.A. 114 E10
Wyomissing, U.S.A. 111 F9
Wyrzysk, Poland 45 E4
Wyśmierzyce, Poland 45 G7
Wysoka, Poland 45 E4
Wysokie, Poland 45 H9
Wysokie Mazowieckie, Poland 45 F9
Wyszków, Poland 45 F8
Wyszogród, Poland 45 F7
Wytheville, U.S.A. 108 G5
Wyżyna Małopolska, Poland 45 H7

X

Xaçmaz, Azerbaijan 49 K9
Xai-Xai, Mozam. 89 D5
Xainza, China 60 C3
Xangongo, Angola 88 B2
Xankändi, Azerbaijan 70 B5
Xanlar, Azerbaijan 49 K8
Xanten, Germany 24 D2
Xánthi, Greece 41 E8
Xánthi □, Greece 41 E8
Xanthos, Turkey 39 E11
Xanxerê, Brazil 127 B5
Xapuri, Brazil 124 F5
Xar Moron He →, China 57 C11
Xarrë, Albania 40 G4
Xátiva, Spain 33 G4
Xau, L., Botswana 88 C3
Xavantina, Brazil 127 A5
Xenia, U.S.A. 108 F4
Xeropotamos →, Cyprus 36 E11
Xertigny, France 19 D13
Xhora, S. Africa 89 E4
Xhumo, Botswana 88 C3
Xi Jiang →, China 59 F9
Xi Xian, Henan, China 59 A10
Xi Xian, Shanxi, China 56 F6
Xia Xian, China 56 G6
Xiachengzi, China 57 B16
Xiachuan Dao, China 59 G9
Xiaguan, China 60 D5
Xiajiang, China 59 D10
Xiajin, China 56 F9
Xiamen, China 59 E12
Xi'an, China 56 G5
Xian Xian, China 56 E9
Xianfeng, China 58 C7
Xiang Jiang →, China 59 C9
Xiangcheng, Henan, China 56 H8
Xiangcheng, Henan, China 56 H7
Xiangcheng, Sichuan, China 58 C2
Xiangdu, China 58 F6
Xiangfan, China 59 A9
Xianggang = Hong Kong □, China 59 F10
Xianghuang Qi, China 56 C7
Xiangning, China 56 G6
Xiangquan, China 56 F7
Xiangquan He = Sutlej →, Pakistan 68 E4
Xiangshan, China 59 C13
Xiangshui, China 57 G10
Xiangtan, China 59 D9
Xiangxiang, China 59 D9
Xiangyin, China 59 C9
Xiangyun, China 58 E3
Xiangzhou, China 58 F7
Xianju, China 59 C13
Xianning, China 59 C10
Xianshui He →, China 58 B3
Xiantao, China 59 B9
Xianyang, China 56 G5
Xianyou, China 59 E12
Xiao Hinggan Ling, China 60 B7
Xiao Xian, China 56 G9
Xiaofeng, China 59 B12
Xiaogan, China 59 B9
Xiaojin, China 58 B4
Xiaolan, China 59 F9
Xiaoshan, China 59 B13
Xiaoyi, China 56 F6
Xiapu, China 59 D12
Xiawa, China 57 C11
Xiayi, China 56 G9
Xichang, China 58 D4
Xichong, China 58 B5
Xichou, China 58 E5
Xichuan, China 56 H6
Xide, China 58 C4
Xiemahe, China 59 B8
Xieng Khouang, Laos 64 C4
Xifei He →, China 56 H9
Xifeng, Gansu, China 56 G4
Xifeng, Guizhou, China 58 D6
Xifeng, Liaoning, China 57 C13
Xifengzhen = Xifeng, China 56 G4
Xigazê, China 60 D3
Xihe, China 56 G3
Xihua, China 56 H8
Xilaganí, Greece 41 F9
Xiliao He →, China 57 C12
Xilin, China 58 E5
Xilókastron, Greece 38 C4
Xime, Guinea-Biss. 82 C2
Ximeng, China 58 F2
Xin Jiang →, China 59 C11
Xin Xian = Xinzhou, China 56 E7
Xinavane, Mozam. 89 D5
Xinbin, China 57 D13
Xincai, China 59 A10
Xinchang, China 59 C13
Xincheng, Guangxi Zhuangzu, China 58 E7
Xincheng, Jiangxi, China 59 D10
Xindu, China 58 B5
Xinfeng, Guangdong, China 59 E10
Xinfeng, Jiangxi, China 59 D11
Xinfeng, Jiangxi, China 59 E10
Xinfengjiang Skuiku, China 59 F10
Xing Xian, China 56 E6
Xing'an, Guangxi Zhuangzu, China 59 E8
Xingan, Jiangxi, China 59 D10
Xingcheng, China 57 D11
Xingguo, China 59 D10
Xinghe, China 56 D7
Xinghua, China 57 H10
Xinghua Wan, China 59 E12
Xinglong, China 57 D9
Xingning, China 59 E10
Xingping, China 56 G5
Xingren, China 58 E5
Xingshan, China 59 B8
Xingtai, China 56 F8
Xingu →, Brazil 122 D5
Xingwen, China 58 C5
Xingyang, China 56 G7
Xinhe, China 56 F8
Xinhua, China 59 D8
Xinhuang, China 58 D7
Xinhui, China 59 F9
Xining, China 60 C5
Xinjian, China 59 C10
Xinjiang, China 56 G6
Xinjiang Uygur Zizhiqu □, China 60 B3
Xinjie, China 58 D3
Xinjin = Pulandian, China 57 E11
Xinjin, China 58 B4
Xinkai He →, China 57 C12
Xinle, China 56 E8
Xinlitun, China 57 D12
Xinlong, China 58 B3
Xinmin, China 57 D12
Xinning, China 59 D8
Xinping, China 58 E3
Xinshao, China 59 D8
Xintai, China 57 G9
Xintian, China 59 E9
Xinxian, China 59 B10
Xinxiang, China 56 G7
Xinxing, China 59 F9
Xinyang, China 59 A10
Xinye, China 59 A9
Xinyi, China 59 F8
Xinyu, China 59 D10
Xinzhan, China 57 C14
Xinzheng, China 56 G7
Xinzhou, Hubei, China 59 B10
Xinzhou, Shanxi, China 56 E7
Xinzo de Limia, Spain 34 C3
Xiongyuecheng, China 57 D12
Xiping, Henan, China 56 H8
Xiping, Henan, China 56 H6
Xiping, Zhejiang, China 59 C12
Xique-Xique, Brazil 125 F10
Xisha Qundao = Paracel Is., S. China Sea 62 A4
Xishui, Guizhou, China 58 C6
Xishui, Hubei, China 59 B10
Xitole, Guinea-Biss. 82 C2
Xiu Shui →, China 59 C10
Xiuning, China 59 C12
Xiuren, China 59 E8
Xiushan, China 58 C7
Xiushui, China 59 C10
Xiuwen, China 58 D6
Xiuyan, China 57 D12
Xixabangma Feng, China 67 E14
Xixia, China 56 H6
Xixiang, China 56 H4
Xiyang, China 56 F7
Xizang Zizhiqu □, China 60 C3
Xlendi, Malta 36 C1
Xu Jiang →, China 59 D11
Xuan Loc, Vietnam 65 G6
Xuan'en, China 58 C7
Xuanhan, China 58 B6
Xuanhua, China 56 D8
Xuanwei, China 58 C5
Xuanzhou, China 59 B12
Xuchang, China 56 G7
Xudat, Azerbaijan 49 K9
Xuefeng Shan, China 59 D8
Xuejiaping, China 59 B8
Xun Jiang →, China 59 F8
Xun Xian, China 56 G8
Xundian, China 58 E4
Xunwu, China 59 E10
Xunyang, China 56 H5
Xunyi, China 56 G5
Xupu, China 59 D8
Xúquer →, Spain 33 F4
Xushui, China 56 E8
Xuwen, China 59 G8
Xuyen Moc, Vietnam 65 G6
Xuyong, China 58 C5
Xuzhou, China 57 G9
Xylophagou, Cyprus 36 E12

Y

Ya Xian, China 64 C7
Yaamba, Australia 94 C5
Ya'an, China 58 C4
Yabassi, Cameroon 83 E6
Yabelo, Ethiopia 81 G4
Yablanitsa, Bulgaria 41 C8
Yablonovy Ra. = Yablonovyy Khrebet, Russia 51 D12
Yablonovyy Khrebet, Russia 51 D12
Yabrai Shan, China 56 E2
Yabrūd, Syria 75 B5
Yacheng, China 64 C7
Yacuiba, Bolivia 126 A3
Yacuma →, Bolivia 124 F5
Yadgir, India 66 L10
Yadkin →, U.S.A. 109 H5
Yadrin, Russia 48 C8
Yaeyama-Rettō, Japan 55 M1
Yagaba, Ghana 83 C4
Yağcılar, Turkey 39 B10
Yagodnoye, Russia 51 C15
Yahila, Dem. Rep. of the Congo 86 B1
Yahk, Canada 104 D5
Yahotyn, Ukraine 47 G6
Yahuma, Dem. Rep. of the Congo 84 D4
Yahyalı, Turkey 72 C6
Yaita, Japan 55 F9
Yaiza, Canary Is. 37 F6
Yajiang, China 58 B3
Yajua, Nigeria 83 C7
Yakima, U.S.A. 114 C3
Yakima →, U.S.A. 114 C3
Yako, Burkina Faso 82 C4
Yakobi I., U.S.A. 104 B1
Yakoruda, Bulgaria 40 D7
Yakovlevka, Russia 54 B6
Yaku-Shima, Japan 55 J5
Yakumo, Japan 54 C10
Yakutat, U.S.A. 100 C6
Yakutia = Sakha □, Russia 51 C13
Yakutsk, Russia 51 C13
Yala, Thailand 65 J3
Yale, U.S.A. 110 C2
Yalgoo, Australia 93 E2
Yalinga, C.A.R. 84 C4
Yalkubul, Punta, Mexico 119 C7
Yalleroi, Australia 94 C4
Yalobusha →, U.S.A. 113 J9
Yalong Jiang →, China 58 D3
Yalova, Turkey 41 F13
Yalta, Ukraine 47 K8
Yalu Jiang →, China 57 E13
Yalvaç, Turkey 72 C4
Yam Ha Melah = Dead Sea, Asia 75 D4
Yam Kinneret, Israel 75 C4
Yamada, Japan 55 H5
Yamagata, Japan 54 E10
Yamagata □, Japan 54 E10
Yamaguchi, Japan 55 G5
Yamaguchi □, Japan 55 G5
Yamal, Poluostrov, Russia 50 B8
Yamal Pen. = Yamal, Poluostrov, Russia 50 B8
Yamanashi □, Japan 55 G9
Yamba, Australia 95 D5
Yambarran Ra., Australia 92 C5
Yambéring, Guinea 82 C2
Yâmbiô, Sudan 81 G2
Yambol, Bulgaria 41 D10
Yamdena, Indonesia 63 F8
Yame, Japan 55 H5
Yamethin, Burma 67 J20
Yamma-Yamma, L., Australia 95 D3
Yamoussoukro, Ivory C. 82 D3
Yampa →, U.S.A. 114 F9
Yampi Sd., Australia 92 C3
Yampil, Moldova 47 H5
Yampol = Yampil, Moldova 47 H5
Yamrat, Nigeria 83 C6
Yamrukchal = Botev, Bulgaria 41 D8
Yamuna →, India 69 G9
Yamunanagar, India 68 D7
Yamzho Yumco, China 60 D4
Yan, Nigeria 83 C7
Yana →, Russia 51 B14

Yanagawa, Japan 55 H5
Yanai, Japan 55 H6
Yan'an, China 56 F5
Yanbian, China 58 D3
Yanbu 'al Baḩr, Si. Arabia 70 F3
Yanchang, China 56 F6
Yancheng, Henan, China 56 H8
Yancheng, Jiangsu, China 57 H11
Yanchep Beach, Australia 93 F2
Yanchi, China 56 F4
Yanchuan, China 56 F6
Yandoon, Burma 67 L19
Yanfeng, China 58 E3
Yanfolila, Mali 82 C3
Yang Xian, China 56 H4
Yang-Yang, Senegal 82 B1
Yangambi, Dem. Rep. of the Congo 86 B1
Yangbi, China 58 E2
Yangcheng, China 56 G7
Yangch'ü = Taiyuan, China 56 F7
Yangchun, China 59 F8
Yanggao, China 56 D7
Yanggu, China 56 F8
Yangjiang, China 59 G8
Yangliuqing, China 57 E9
Yangon = Rangoon, Burma 67 L20
Yangping, China 59 B8
Yangpingguan, China 56 H4
Yangquan, China 56 F7
Yangshan, China 59 E9
Yangshuo, China 59 E8
Yangtse = Chang Jiang →, China 59 B13
Yangtze Kiang = Chang Jiang →, China 59 B13
Yangxin, China 59 C10
Yangyang, S. Korea 57 E15
Yangyuan, China 56 D8
Yangzhong, China 59 A12
Yangzhou, China 59 A12
Yanhe, China 58 C7
Yanji, China 57 C15
Yanjin, China 58 C5
Yanjing, China 58 C2
Yankton, U.S.A. 112 D6
Yanonge, Dem. Rep. of the Congo 86 B1
Yanqi, China 60 B3
Yanqing, China 56 D8
Yanshan, Hebei, China 57 E9
Yanshan, Jiangxi, China 59 C11
Yanshan, Yunnan, China 58 F5
Yanshou, China 57 B15
Yantabulla, Australia 95 D4
Yantai, China 57 F11
Yanting, China 58 B5
Yantra →, Bulgaria 41 C9
Yanwa, China 58 D2
Yanyuan, China 58 D3
Yanzhou, China 56 G9
Yao Xian, China 56 G5
Yao Yai, Ko, Thailand 65 J2
Yao'an, China 58 E3
Yaodu, China 58 A5
Yaoundé, Cameroon 83 E7
Yaowan, China 57 G10
Yap I., Pac. Oc. 96 G5
Yapen, Indonesia 63 E9
Yapen, Selat, Indonesia 63 E9
Yapero, Indonesia 63 E9
Yappar →, Australia 94 B3
Yaqui →, Mexico 118 B2
Yar-Sale, Russia 50 C8
Yaraka, Australia 94 C3
Yaransk, Russia 48 B8
Yarbasan, Turkey 39 C10
Yardımcı Burnu, Turkey 39 E12
Yare →, U.K. 13 E9
Yaremcha, Ukraine 47 H3
Yarensk, Russia 50 C5
Yarfa, Si. Arabia 80 C4
Yarí →, Colombia 124 D4
Yarkand = Shache, China 60 C2
Yarker, Canada 111 B8
Yarkhun →, Pakistan 69 A5
Yarmouth, Canada 103 D6
Yarmūk →, Syria 75 C4
Yaroslavl, Russia 46 D10
Yarqa, W. →, Egypt 75 F2
Yarra Yarra Lakes, Australia 93 E2
Yarraman, Australia 95 D5
Yartsevo, Sib., Russia 51 C10
Yartsevo, Smolensk, Russia 46 E7
Yarumal, Colombia 124 B3
Yasawa Group, Fiji 91 C7
Yaselda, Belarus 47 F4
Yashi, Nigeria 83 C6
Yashikera, Nigeria 83 D5
Yashkul, Russia 49 G7
Yasin, Pakistan 69 A5
Yasinovataya, Ukraine 47 H9
Yasinski, L., Canada 102 B4
Yasinya, Ukraine 47 H3
Yasothon, Thailand 64 E5
Yāsūj, Iran 71 D6
Yatağan, Turkey 39 D10
Yatakala, Niger 83 C5
Yates Center, U.S.A. 113 G7
Yathkyed L., Canada 105 A9
Yatsushiro, Japan 55 H5
Yatta Plateau, Kenya 86 C4
Yavari →, Peru 124 D4
Yávaros, Mexico 118 B3
Yavatmal, India 66 J11
Yavne, Israel 75 D3
Yavoriv, Ukraine 47 H2
Yavorov = Yavoriv, Ukraine 47 H2
Yavuzeli, Turkey 72 D7
Yawatahama, Japan 55 H6
Yawri B., S. Leone 82 D2
Yaxi, China 58 D6
Yazd, Iran 71 D7
Yazd □, Iran 71 D7
Yazd-e Khvāst, Iran 71 D7
Yazıköy, Turkey 39 E9
Yazman, Pakistan 68 E4
Yazoo →, U.S.A. 113 J9
Yazoo City, U.S.A. 113 J9
Ybbs, Austria 26 C8
Yding Skovhøj, Denmark 11 J3
Ye Xian = Laizhou, China 57 F10
Ye Xian, China 56 H7
Yebyu, Burma 64 E2
Yechŏn, S. Korea 57 F15
Yecla, Spain 33 G3
Yécora, Mexico 118 B3
Yedintsy = Edineţ, Moldova 43 B12
Yedseram →, Nigeria 83 C7
Yefremov, Russia 46 F10
Yeghegnadzor, Armenia 73 C11
Yegorlyk →, Russia 49 G5
Yegorlykskaya, Russia 49 G5
Yegoryevsk, Russia 46 E10
Yegros, Paraguay 126 B4
Yehuda, Midbar, Israel 75 D4
Yei, Sudan 81 G3
Yei, Nahr →, Sudan 81 F3
Yejmiadzin, Armenia 49 K7
Yekaterinburg, Russia 50 D7
Yekaterinodar = Krasnodar, Russia 49 H4
Yelabuga, Russia 48 C11
Yelan, Russia 48 E6
Yelarbon, Australia 95 D5
Yelatma, Russia 48 C5
Yelets, Russia 47 F10
Yélimané, Mali 82 B2
Yelizavetgrad = Kirovohrad, Ukraine 47 H7
Yell, U.K. 14 A7
Yell Sd., U.K. 14 A7
Yellow Sea, China 57 G12
Yellowhead Pass, Canada 104 C5
Yellowknife, Canada 104 A6
Yellowknife →, Canada 104 A6
Yellowstone →, U.S.A. 112 B3
Yellowstone L., U.S.A. 114 D8
Yellowstone National Park, U.S.A. 114 D9
Yelnya, Russia 46 E7
Yelsk, Belarus 47 G5
Yelwa, Nigeria 83 C5
Yemen ■, Asia 74 E3
Yen Bai, Vietnam 58 G5
Yenagoa, Nigeria 83 E6
Yenakiyeve, Ukraine 47 H10
Yenakiyevo = Yenakiyeve, Ukraine 47 H10
Yenangyaung, Burma 67 J19
Yenbo = Yanbu 'al Baḩr, Si. Arabia 70 F3
Yende Millimou, Guinea 82 D2
Yendéré, Burkina Faso 82 C4
Yendi, Ghana 83 D4
Yéni, Niger 83 C5
Yenice, Ankara, Turkey 72 C5
Yenice, Aydın, Turkey 39 D10
Yenice, Çanakkale, Turkey 39 B9
Yenice, Edirne, Turkey 41 F10
Yenice →, Turkey 72 D6
Yenifoça, Turkey 39 C8
Yenihisar, Turkey 39 D9
Yeniköy, Bursa, Turkey 41 F13
Yeniköy, Çanakkale, Turkey 39 B8
Yeniköy, Kütahya, Turkey 39 C11
Yenipazar, Turkey 39 D10
Yenisaía, Greece 41 E8
Yenişehir, Turkey 41 F13
Yenisey →, Russia 50 B9
Yeniseysk, Russia 51 D10
Yeniseyskiy Zaliv, Russia 50 B9
Yennádhi, Greece 36 C9
Yenne, France 21 C9
Yenotayevka, Russia 49 G8
Yenyuka, Russia 51 D13
Yeo →, U.K. 13 G5
Yeo, L., Australia 93 E3
Yeo I., Canada 110 A3
Yeola, India 66 J9
Yeoryioúpolis, Greece 36 D6
Yeovil, U.K. 13 G5
Yepes, Spain 34 F7
Yeppoon, Australia 94 C5
Yeráki, Greece 38 D4
Yerbent, Turkmenistan 50 F6
Yerbogachen, Russia 51 C11
Yerevan, Armenia 49 K7
Yerington, U.S.A. 114 G4
Yerkesik, Turkey 39 D10
Yerköy, Turkey 72 C6
Yermak, Kazakstan 50 D8
Yermo, U.S.A. 117 L10
Yerólakkos, Cyprus 36 D12
Yeropol, Russia 51 C17
Yeropótamos →, Greece 36 D6
Yeroskipos, Cyprus 36 E11
Yershov, Russia 48 E9
Yerushalayim = Jerusalem, Israel 75 D4
Yerville, France 18 C7
Yes Tor, U.K. 13 G4
Yesan, S. Korea 57 F14
Yeşilhisar, Turkey 72 C6
Yeşilırmak →, Turkey 72 B7
Yeşilkent, Turkey 72 D7
Yeşilköy, Turkey 41 F12
Yeşilova, Turkey 39 D11
Yeşilyurt, Manisa, Turkey 39 C10
Yeşilyurt, Muğla, Turkey 39 D10
Yesnogorsk, Russia 46 E9
Yeso, U.S.A. 113 H2
Yessentuki, Russia 49 H6
Yessey, Russia 51 C11
Yeste, Spain 33 G2
Yetman, Australia 95 D5
Yeu, Î. d', France 18 F4
Yevlakh = Yevlax, Azerbaijan 49 K8
Yevlax, Azerbaijan 49 K8
Yevpatoriya, Ukraine 47 K7
Yeya →, Russia 47 J10
Yeysk, Russia 47 J10
Yezd = Yazd, Iran 71 D7
Yezerishche, Belarus 46 E5
Yhati, Paraguay 126 B4
Yhú, Paraguay 127 B4
Yi →, Uruguay 126 C4
Yi 'Allaq, G., Egypt 75 E2
Yi He →, China 57 G10
Yi Xian, Anhui, China 59 C11
Yi Xian, Hebei, China 56 E8
Yi Xian, Liaoning, China 57 D11
Yialí, Greece 39 E9
Yialiás →, Cyprus 36 D12
Yi'allaq, G., Egypt 80 A3
Yialousa, Cyprus 36 D13
Yiáltra, Greece 38 C4
Yianisádhes, Greece 36 D8
Yiannitsa, Greece 40 F6
Yibin, China 58 C5
Yichang, China 59 B8
Yicheng, Henan, China 59 B9
Yicheng, Shanxi, China 56 G6
Yichuan, China 56 F6
Yichun, Heilongjiang, China 60 B7
Yichun, Jiangxi, China 59 D10
Yidu, China 57 F10
Yidun, China 58 B2
Yifag, Ethiopia 81 E4
Yifeng, China 59 C10
Yihuang, China 59 D11
Yijun, China 56 G5
Yıldız Dağları, Turkey 41 E11
Yıldızeli, Turkey 72 C7
Yiliang, Yunnan, China 58 D5
Yiliang, Yunnan, China 58 E4
Yilong, China 58 B6
Yimen, China 58 E4
Yimianpo, China 57 B15
Yinchuan, China 56 E4
Yindarlgooda, L., Australia 93 F3
Ying He →, China 56 H9
Ying Xian, China 56 E7
Yingcheng, China 59 B9
Yingde, China 59 E9
Yingjiang, China 58 E1
Yingjing, China 58 C4
Yingkou, China 57 D12
Yingshan, Henan, China 59 B9
Yingshan, Hubei, China 59 B10
Yingshan, Sichuan, China 58 B6
Yingshang, China 59 A11
Yingtan, China 59 C11
Yining, China 50 E9
Yinjiang, China 58 C7
Yinmabin, Burma 67 H19
Yiofiros →, Greece 36 D7
Yioúra, Nótios Aiyaíon, Greece 38 D6
Yioúra, Thessalía, Greece 38 B6
Yipinglang, China 58 E3
Yirba Muda, Ethiopia 81 F4
Yirga Alem, Ethiopia 81 F4
Yirol, Sudan 81 F3
Yirrkala, Australia 94 A2
Yishan, China 58 E7
Yishui, China 57 G10
Yíthion, Greece 38 E4
Yitong, China 57 C13
Yiwu, China 59 C13
Yixing, China 59 B12
Yiyang, Henan, China 56 G7
Yiyang, Hunan, China 59 C9
Yiyang, Jiangxi, China 59 C11
Yizhang, China 59 E9
Yizheng, China 59 A12
Yli-Kitka, Finland 8 C23
Ylitornio, Finland 8 C20
Ylivieska, Finland 8 D21
Yngaren, Sweden 11 F10
Yoakum, U.S.A. 113 L6
Yobe □, Nigeria 83 C7
Yog Pt., Phil. 63 B6
Yogan, Togo 83 D5
Yoğuntaş, Turkey 41 E11
Yogyakarta, Indonesia 62 F4
Yoho Nat. Park, Canada 104 C5
Yojoa, L. de, Honduras 120 D2
Yŏju, S. Korea 57 F14
Yokadouma, Cameroon 84 D2
Yokkaichi, Japan 55 G8
Yoko, Cameroon 83 D7
Yokohama, Japan 55 G9
Yokosuka, Japan 55 G9
Yokote, Japan 54 E10
Yola, Nigeria 83 D7
Yolaina, Cordillera de, Nic. 120 D3
Yoloten, Turkmenistan 71 B9
Yom →, Thailand 62 A2
Yonago, Japan 55 G6
Yonaguni-Jima, Japan 55 M1
Yŏnan, N. Korea 57 F14
Yonezawa, Japan 54 F10
Yong Peng, Malaysia 65 L4
Yong Sata, Thailand 65 J2
Yongamp'o, N. Korea 57 E13
Yong'an, China 59 E11
Yongcheng, China 56 H9
Yŏngch'ŏn, S. Korea 57 G15
Yongchuan, China 58 C5
Yongchun, China 59 E12
Yongde, China 58 E2
Yongdeng, China 56 F2
Yongding, China 59 E11
Yŏngdŏk, S. Korea 57 F15
Yŏngdŭngpo, S. Korea 57 F14
Yongfeng, China 59 D10
Yongfu, China 58 E7
Yonghe, China 56 F6
Yŏnghŭng, N. Korea 57 E14
Yongji, China 56 G6
Yongjia, China 59 C13
Yŏngju, S. Korea 57 F15
Yongkang, Yunnan, China 58 E2
Yongkang, Zhejiang, China 59 C13
Yongnian, China 56 F8
Yongning, Guangxi Zhuangzu, China 58 F7
Yongning, Ningxia Huizu, China 56 E4
Yongping, China 58 E2
Yongqing, China 56 E9
Yongren, China 58 D3
Yongshan, China 58 C4
Yongsheng, China 58 D3
Yongshun, China 58 C7
Yongtai, China 59 E12
Yŏngwŏl, S. Korea 57 F15
Yongxin = Jinggangshan, China 59 D10
Yongxing, China 59 D9
Yongxiu, China 59 C10
Yongzhou, China 59 D8
Yonibana, S. Leone 82 D2
Yonkers, U.S.A. 111 F11
Yonne □, France 19 E10
Yonne →, France 19 D9
York, Australia 93 F2
York, U.K. 12 D6
York, Ala., U.S.A. 113 J10
York, Nebr., U.S.A. 112 E6
York, Pa., U.S.A. 108 F7
York, C., Australia 94 A3
York, City of □, U.K. 12 D6
York, Kap, Greenland 4 B4
York, Vale of, U.K. 12 C6
York Haven, U.S.A. 110 F8
York Sd., Australia 92 C4
Yorkshire Wolds, U.K. 12 C7
Yorkton, Canada 105 C8
Yorkville, U.S.A. 116 G3
Yoro, Honduras 120 C2
Yoron-Jima, Japan 55 L4
Yorosso, Mali 82 C4
Yos Sudarso, Pulau = Dolak, Pulau, Indonesia 63 F9
Yosemite National Park, U.S.A. 116 H7
Yosemite Village, U.S.A. 116 H7
Yoshkar Ola, Russia 48 B8
Yŏsu, S. Korea 57 G14
Yotvata, Israel 75 F4
You Jiang →, China 58 F6
You Xian, China 59 D9
Youbou, Canada 116 B2
Youghal, Ireland 15 E4
Youghal B., Ireland 15 E4
Youkounkoun, Guinea 82 C2
Young, Canada 105 C7
Young, Uruguay 126 C4
Youngstown, Canada 105 C6
Youngstown, N.Y., U.S.A. 110 C5
Youngstown, Ohio, U.S.A. 110 E4
Youngsville, U.S.A. 110 E5
Youngwood, U.S.A. 110 F5
Youxi, China 59 D12
Youyang, China 58 C7
Youyu, China 56 D7
Yozgat, Turkey 72 C6
Ypané →, Paraguay 126 A4
Yport, France 18 C7
Ypres = Ieper, Belgium 17 D2
Yreka, U.S.A. 114 F2
Yssingeaux, France 21 C8
Ystad, Sweden 11 J7
Ysyk-Köl, Kyrgyzstan 50 E8
Ythan →, U.K. 14 D7
Ytterhogdal, Sweden 10 B8
Ytyk-Kyuyel, Russia 51 C14
Yu Jiang →, China 58 F7
Yu Xian = Yuzhou, China 56 G7
Yu Xian, Hebei, China 56 E8
Yu Xian, Shanxi, China 56 E7
Yuan Jiang →, Hunan, China 59 C8
Yuan Jiang →, Yunnan, China 58 F4
Yuan'an, China 59 B8
Yuanjiang, Hunan, China 59 C9
Yuanjiang, Yunnan, China 58 F4
Yüanli, Taiwan 59 E13
Yüanlin, Taiwan 59 F13
Yuanling, China 59 C8
Yuanmou, China 58 E3
Yuanqu, China 56 G6
Yuanyang, Henan, China 56 G7
Yuanyang, Yunnan, China 58 F4
Yuba →, U.S.A. 116 F5
Yuba City, U.S.A. 116 F5
Yūbari, Japan 54 C10
Yubdo, Ethiopia 81 F4
Yūbetsu, Japan 54 B11
Yubo, Sudan 81 F2
Yucatán □, Mexico 119 C7
Yucatán, Canal de, Caribbean 120 B2
Yucatán, Península de, Mexico 98 H11
Yucatán Basin, Cent. Amer. 98 H11
Yucatan Str. = Yucatán, Canal de, Caribbean 120 B2
Yucca, U.S.A. 117 L12
Yucca Valley, U.S.A. 117 L10
Yucheng, China 56 F9
Yuci, China 56 F7
Yudu, China 59 E10
Yuechi, China 58 B6
Yuendumu, Australia 92 D5
Yueqing, China 59 C13
Yueqing Wan, China 59 D13
Yuexi, Anhui, China 59 B11
Yuexi, Sichuan, China 58 C4
Yueyang, China 59 C9
Yugan, China 59 C11
Yugoslavia ■, Europe 40 C4
Yuhuan, China 59 C13
Yuhuan Dao, China 59 C13
Yujiang, China 59 C11
Yukhnov, Russia 46 E8
Yukon →, U.S.A. 100 B3
Yukon Territory □, Canada 100 B6
Yüksekova, Turkey 73 D11
Yukta, Russia 51 C11
Yukuhashi, Japan 55 H5
Yulara, Australia 93 E5
Yule →, Australia 92 D2
Yuleba, Australia 95 D4
Yuli, Nigeria 83 D7
Yuli, Taiwan 59 F13
Yulin, Guangxi Zhuangzu, China 59 F8
Yülin, Hainan, China 65 C7
Yulin, Shaanxi, China 56 E5
Yuma, Ariz., U.S.A. 117 N12
Yuma, Colo., U.S.A. 112 E3
Yuma, B. de, Dom. Rep. 121 C6
Yumbe, Uganda 86 B3
Yumbi, Dem. Rep. of the Congo 86 C2
Yumen, China 60 C4
Yumurtalık, Turkey 72 D6
Yun Gui Gaoyuan, China 58 E3
Yun Ho →, China 57 E9
Yun Ling, China 58 D2
Yun Xian, Hubei, China 59 A8
Yun Xian, Yunnan, China 58 E3
Yuna, Australia 93 E2
Yunak, Turkey 72 C4
Yunan, China 59 F8
Yuncheng, Henan, China 56 G8
Yuncheng, Shanxi, China 56 G6
Yunfu, China 59 F9
Yungas, Bolivia 124 G5
Yungay, Chile 126 D1
Yunhe, China 59 C12
Yunkai Dashan, China 59 F8
Yunlin, Taiwan 59 F13
Yunlong, China 58 E2
Yunmeng, China 59 B9
Yunnan □, China 58 E4
Yunquera de Henares, Spain 32 E1
Yunt Dağı, Turkey 39 C9
Yunxi, China 56 H6
Yunxiao, China 59 F11
Yuping, China 58 D7
Yupyongdong, N. Korea 57 D15
Yuqing, China 58 D6
Yurga, Russia 50 D9
Yurimaguas, Peru 124 E3
Yuryev-Polskiy, Russia 46 D10
Yuryevets, Russia 48 B6
Yuscarán, Honduras 120 D2
Yushan, China 59 C12
Yushanzhen, China 58 C7
Yushe, China 56 F7
Yushu, Jilin, China 57 B14
Yushu, Qinghai, China 60 C4
Yusufeli, Turkey 73 B9
Yutai, China 56 G9
Yutian, China 57 E9
Yuxarı Qarabağ = Nagorno-Karabakh, Azerbaijan 70 B5
Yuxi, China 58 E4
Yuyao, China 59 B13
Yuzawa, Japan 54 E10
Yuzha, Russia 48 B6
Yuzhno-Sakhalinsk, Russia 51 E15
Yuzhou, China 56 G7
Yvelines □, France 19 D8
Yverdon-les-Bains, Switz. 25 J2
Yvetot, France 18 C7
Yzeure, France 19 F10

Z

Zaanstad, Neths. 17 B4
Zāb al Kabīr →, Iraq 70 C4
Zāb aş Şagīr →, Iraq 70 C4
Žabalj, Serbia, Yug. 42 E5
Žabari, Serbia, Yug. 40 B5
Zabarjad, Egypt 80 C4
Zabaykalsk, Russia 51 E12
Zabki, Poland 45 F8
Ząbkowice Śląskie, Poland 45 H3

Žabljak, Montenegro, Yug. 40 C3
Zabłudów, Poland 45 F9
Żabno, Poland 45 H7
Zābol, Iran 71 D9
Zābolī, Iran 71 E9
Zabré, Burkina Faso 83 C4
Zábřeh, Czech Rep. 27 B9
Zabrze, Poland 45 H5
Zabzuga, Ghana 83 D5
Zacapa, Guatemala 120 D2
Zacapu, Mexico 118 D4
Zacatecas, Mexico 118 C4
Zacatecas □, Mexico 118 C4
Zacatecoluca, El Salv. 120 D2
Zachary, U.S.A. 113 K9
Zachodnio-Pomorskie □, Poland 44 E2
Zacoalco, Mexico 118 C4
Zacualtipán, Mexico 119 C5
Zadar, Croatia 29 D12
Zadawa, Nigeria 83 C7
Zadetkyi Kyun, Burma 65 G1
Zadonsk, Russia 47 F10
Zafarqand, Iran 71 C7
Zafora, Greece 39 E8
Zafra, Spain 35 G4
Żagań, Poland 45 G2
Zagaoua, Chad 79 E10
Žagarė, Lithuania 44 B10
Zagazig, Egypt 80 H7
Zāgheh, Iran 71 C6
Zaglivérion, Greece 40 F7
Zagnanado, Benin 83 D5
Zagorá, Greece 38 B5
Zagorje, Slovenia 29 B11
Zagórów, Poland 45 F4
Zagorsk = Sergiyev Posad, Russia 46 D10
Zagórz, Poland 45 J9
Zagreb, Croatia 29 C12
Zāgros, Kūhhā-ye, Iran 71 C6
Zagros Mts. = Zāgros, Kūhhā-ye, Iran 71 C6
Žagubica, Serbia, Yug. 40 B5
Zaguinaso, Ivory C. 82 C3
Zagyva →, Hungary 42 C5
Zāhedān, Fārs, Iran 71 D7
Zāhedān, Sīstān va Balūchestān, Iran 71 D9
Zahlah, Lebanon 75 B4
Zahna, Germany 24 D8
Záhony, Hungary 42 B7
Zainsk, Russia 48 C11
Zaïre = Congo →, Africa 84 F2
Zaječar, Serbia, Yug. 40 C6
Zaka, Zimbabwe 89 C5
Zakamensk, Russia 51 D11
Zakataly = Zaqatala, Azerbaijan 49 K8
Zakháro, Greece 38 D3
Zakhodnaya Dzvina = Daugava →, Latvia 9 H21
Zākhū, Iraq 70 B4
Zákinthos, Greece 38 D2
Zákinthos □, Greece 38 D2
Zakopane, Poland 45 J6
Zakroczym, Poland 45 F7
Zákros, Greece 36 D8
Zala, Ethiopia 81 F4
Zala □, Hungary 42 D1
Zala →, Hungary 42 D2
Zalaegerszeg, Hungary 42 D1
Zalakomár, Hungary 42 D2
Zalalövő, Hungary 42 D1
Zalamea de la Serena, Spain 35 G5
Zalamea la Real, Spain 35 H4
Zalău, Romania 42 C8
Žalec, Slovenia 29 B12
Zaleshchiki = Zalishchyky, Ukraine 47 H3
Zalew Wiślany, Poland 44 D6
Zalewo, Poland 44 E6
Zalingei, Sudan 79 F10
Zalishchyky, Ukraine 47 H3
Zama L., Canada 104 B5
Zambeke, Dem. Rep. of the Congo 86 B2
Zambeze →, Africa 87 F4
Zambezi = Zambeze →, Africa 87 F4
Zambezi, Zambia 85 G4
Zambezia □, Mozam. 87 F4
Zambia ■, Africa 87 F2
Zamboanga, Phil. 61 H5
Zambrów, Poland 45 F9
Zametchino, Russia 48 D6
Zamfara □, Nigeria 83 C6
Zamfara →, Nigeria 83 C5
Zamora, Mexico 118 D4
Zamora, Spain 34 D5
Zamora □, Spain 34 D5
Zamość, Poland 45 H10
Zamtang, China 58 A3
Zan, Ghana 83 D4
Záncara →, Spain 33 F1
Zandvoort, Neths. 17 B4
Zanesville, U.S.A. 110 G2
Zangābād, Iran 70 B5
Zangue →, Mozam. 87 F4
Zanjān, Iran 71 B6
Zanjān □, Iran 71 B6
Zanjān →, Iran 71 B6
Zannone, Italy 30 B6
Zante = Zákinthos, Greece 38 D2
Zanthus, Australia 93 F3
Zanzibar, Tanzania 86 D4
Zaouiet El-Kala = Bordj Omar Driss, Algeria 78 C7
Zaouiet Reggâne, Algeria 78 C6
Zaoyang, China 59 A9
Zaozhuang, China 57 G9
Zap Suyu = Zāb al Kabīr →, Iraq 70 C4
Zapadna Morava →, Serbia, Yug. 40 C5
Zapadnaya Dvina = Daugava →, Latvia 9 H21
Zapadnaya Dvina, Russia 46 D7
Západné Beskydy, Europe 27 B12
Zapadni Rodopi, Bulgaria 40 E7
Západočeský □, Czech Rep. 26 B6
Zapala, Argentina 128 D2
Zapaleri, Cerro, Bolivia 126 A2
Zapata, U.S.A. 113 M5
Zapatón →, Spain 35 F4
Zaporizhzhya, Ukraine 47 J8
Zaporozhye = Zaporizhzhya, Ukraine 47 J8
Zaqatala, Azerbaijan 49 K8
Zara, Turkey 70 B3
Zaragoza, Coahuila, Mexico 118 B4
Zaragoza, Nuevo León, Mexico 119 C5
Zaragoza, Spain 32 D4
Zaragoza □, Spain 32 D4
Zarand, Kermān, Iran 71 D8
Zarand, Markazī, Iran 71 C6
Zărandului, Munţii, Romania 42 D7
Zaranj, Afghan. 66 D2
Zarasai, Lithuania 9 J22
Zarate, Argentina 126 C4
Zarautz, Spain 32 B2
Zaraysk, Russia 46 E10
Zard, Kūh-e, Iran 71 C6
Zāreh, Iran 71 C6
Zari, Nigeria 83 C7
Zaria, Nigeria 83 C6
Żarki, Poland 45 H6
Zárkon, Greece 38 B4
Zarneh, Iran 70 C5
Zărneşti, Romania 43 E10
Zarós, Greece 36 D6
Żarów, Poland 45 H3
Zarqā', Nahr az →, Jordan 75 C4
Zarrīn, Iran 71 C7
Zaruma, Ecuador 124 D3
Żary, Poland 45 G2
Zarza de Granadilla, Spain 34 E4
Zarzis, Tunisia 79 B8
Zas, Spain 34 B2
Zaskar →, India 69 B7
Zaskar Mts., India 69 C7
Zastron, S. Africa 88 E4
Žatec, Czech Rep. 26 A6
Zaterechnyy, Russia 49 H7
Zator, Poland 45 J6
Zavala, Bos.-H. 40 D1
Zavāreh, Iran 71 C7
Zave, Zimbabwe 89 B5
Zavetnoye, Russia 49 G6
Zavidovići, Bos.-H. 42 F3
Zavitinsk, Russia 51 D13
Zavodovski, I., Antarctica 5 B1
Zavolzhsk, Russia 48 B6
Zavolzhye, Russia 48 B6
Zawadzkie, Poland 45 H5
Zawichost, Poland 45 H8
Zawidów, Poland 45 G2
Zawiercie, Poland 45 H6
Zāwiyat al Bayḑā = Al Bayḑā, Libya 79 B10
Zâwyet Shammas, Egypt 80 A2
Zâwyet Um el Rakham, Egypt 80 A2
Zâwyet Ungeîla, Egypt 80 A2
Zāyā, Iraq 70 C5
Zāyandeh →, Iran 71 C7
Zaysan, Kazakstan 50 E9
Zaysan, Oz., Kazakstan 50 E9
Zayü, China 58 C1
Zazafotsy, Madag. 89 C8
Zázrivá, Slovak Rep. 27 B12
Zbarazh, Ukraine 47 H3
Zbąszyń, Poland 45 F2
Zbąszynek, Poland 45 F2
Zblewo, Poland 44 E5
Žďár nad Sázavov, Czech Rep. 26 B8
Zdolbuniv, Ukraine 47 G4
Ždrelo, Serbia, Yug. 40 B5
Zduńska Wola, Poland 45 G5
Zduny, Poland 45 G4
Zeballos, Canada 104 D3
Zebediela, S. Africa 89 C4
Zebila, Ghana 83 C4
Zeebrugge, Belgium 17 C3
Zeehan, Australia 94 G4
Zeeland □, Neths. 17 C3
Zeerust, S. Africa 88 D4
Zefat, Israel 75 C4
Zege, Ethiopia 81 E4
Zeggerene, Iracher, Mali 83 B5
Zégoua, Mali 82 C3
Zehdenick, Germany 24 C9
Zeil, Mt., Australia 92 D5
Zeila, Somali Rep. 74 E3
Zeist, Neths. 17 B5
Zeitz, Germany 24 D8
Żelechów, Poland 45 G8
Zelengora, Bos.-H. 40 C2
Zelenodolsk, Russia 48 C9
Zelenogorsk, Russia 46 B5
Zelenograd, Russia 46 D9
Zelenogradsk, Russia 9 J19
Zelenokumsk, Russia 49 H6
Železná Ruda, Czech Rep. 26 B6
Železnik, Serbia, Yug. 40 B4
Zelienople, U.S.A. 110 F4
Želiezovce, Slovak Rep. 27 C11
Zelina, Croatia 29 C13
Zell, Baden-W., Germany 25 H3
Zell, Rhld-Pfz., Germany 25 E3
Zell am See, Austria 26 D5
Zella-Mehlis, Germany 24 E6
Zelów, Poland 45 G6
Zeltweg, Austria 26 D7
Zémio, C.A.R. 86 A2
Zempléni-hegység, Hungary 42 B6
Zemplínska šírava, Slovak Rep. 27 C15
Zemun, Serbia, Yug. 40 B4
Zengbé, Cameroon 83 D7
Zengcheng, China 59 F9
Zenica, Bos.-H. 42 F2
Žepče, Bos.-H. 42 F3
Zeraf, Bahr ez →, Sudan 81 F3
Zerbst, Germany 24 D8
Żerków, Poland 45 F4
Zermatt, Switz. 25 J3
Zernez, Switz. 25 J6
Zernograd, Russia 49 G5
Zerqan, Albania 40 E4
Zestaponi, Georgia 49 J6
Zetel, Germany 24 B3
Zeulenroda, Germany 24 E7
Zeven, Germany 24 B5
Zevenaar, Neths. 17 C6
Zévio, Italy 28 C8
Zeya, Russia 51 D13
Zeya →, Russia 51 D13
Zeytinbaği, Turkey 41 F12
Zeytindağ, Turkey 39 C9
Zghartā, Lebanon 75 A4
Zgierz, Poland 45 G6
Zgorzelec, Poland 45 G2
Zguriţa, Moldova 43 B13
Zhabinka, Belarus 47 F3
Zhailma, Kazakstan 50 D7
Zhambyl = Taraz, Kazakstan 50 E8
Zhangaly, Kazakstan 49 G10
Zhangaqazaly, Kazakstan 50 E7
Zhangbei, China 56 D8
Zhangguangcai Ling, China 57 B15
Zhangjiakou, China 56 D8
Zhangping, China 59 E11
Zhangpu, China 59 E11
Zhangshu, China 59 C10
Zhangwu, China 57 C12
Zhangye, China 60 C5
Zhangzhou, China 59 E11
Zhanhua, China 57 F10
Zhanjiang, China 59 G8
Zhannetty, Ostrov, Russia 51 B16
Zhanyi, China 58 E4
Zhanyu, China 57 B12
Zhao Xian, China 56 F8
Zhao'an, China 59 F11
Zhaocheng, China 56 F6
Zhaojue, China 58 C4
Zhaoping, China 59 E8
Zhaoqing, China 59 F9
Zhaotong, China 58 D4
Zhaoyuan, Heilongjiang, China 57 B13
Zhaoyuan, Shandong, China 57 F11
Zharkovskiy, Russia 46 E7
Zhashkiv, Ukraine 47 H6
Zhashui, China 56 H5
Zhayyq →, Kazakstan 50 E6
Zhdanov = Mariupol, Ukraine 47 J9
Zhecheng, China 56 G8
Zhegao, China 59 B11
Zhejiang □, China 59 C13
Zheleznogorsk, Russia 47 F8
Zheleznogorsk-Ilimskiy, Russia 51 D11
Zheltyye Vody = Zhovti Vody, Ukraine 47 H7
Zhen'an, China 56 H5
Zhenba, China 58 A6
Zhenfeng, China 58 E5
Zheng'an, China 58 C6
Zhengding, China 56 E8
Zhenghe, China 59 D12
Zhengyang, China 59 A10
Zhengyangguan, China 59 A11
Zhengzhou, China 56 G7
Zhenhai, China 59 C13
Zhenjiang, China 59 A12
Zhenkang, China 58 F2
Zhenlai, China 57 B12
Zhenning, China 58 D5
Zhenping, Henan, China 56 H7
Zhenping, Shaanxi, China 58 B7
Zhenxiong, China 58 D5
Zhenyuan, Gansu, China 56 G4
Zhenyuan, Guizhou, China 58 D7
Zherdevka, Russia 48 E5
Zherong, China 59 D12
Zhetiqara, Kazakstan 50 D7
Zhezqazghan, Kazakstan 50 E7
Zhicheng, China 59 B8
Zhidan, China 56 F5
Zhigansk, Russia 51 C13
Zhigulevsk, Russia 48 D9
Zhijiang, Hubei, China 59 B8
Zhijiang, Hunan, China 58 D7
Zhijin, China 58 D5
Zhilinda, Russia 51 C12
Zhirnovsk, Russia 48 E7
Zhitomir = Zhytomyr, Ukraine 47 G5
Zhizdra, Russia 46 F8
Zhlobin, Belarus 47 F6
Zhmerinka = Zhmerynka, Ukraine 47 H5
Zhmerynka, Ukraine 47 H5
Zhob, Pakistan 68 D3
Zhob →, Pakistan 68 C3
Zhodino = Zhodzina, Belarus 46 E5
Zhodzina, Belarus 46 E5
Zhokhova, Ostrov, Russia 51 B16
Zhongdian, China 58 D2
Zhongdong, China 58 F6
Zhongdu, China 58 E7
Zhongning, China 56 F3
Zhongshan, Guangdong, China 59 F9
Zhongshan, Guangxi Zhuangzu, China 59 E8
Zhongtiao Shan, China 56 G6
Zhongwei, China 56 F3
Zhongxiang, China 59 B9
Zhongyang, China 56 F6
Zhoucun, China 57 F9
Zhouning, China 59 D12
Zhoushan, China 59 B14
Zhoushan Dao, China 59 C14
Zhouzhi, China 56 G5
Zhovti Vody, Ukraine 47 H7
Zhovtneve, Ukraine 47 J7
Zhovtnevoye = Zhovtneve, Ukraine 47 J7
Zhu Jiang →, China 59 F9
Zhuanghe, China 57 E12
Zhucheng, China 57 G10
Zhugqu, China 56 H3
Zhuhai, China 59 F9
Zhuji, China 59 C13
Zhukovka, Russia 46 F7
Zhumadian, China 56 H8
Zhuo Xian = Zhuozhou, China 56 E8
Zhuolu, China 56 D8
Zhuozhou, China 56 E8
Zhuozi, China 56 D7
Zhushan, China 59 A8
Zhuxi, China 58 A7
Zhuzhou, China 59 D9
Zhytomyr, Ukraine 47 G5
Zi Shui →, China 59 C9
Žiar nad Hronom, Slovak Rep. 27 C11
Zīārān, Iran 71 B6
Ziarat, Pakistan 68 D2
Zibo, China 57 F10
Zichang, China 56 F5
Zidarovo, Bulgaria 41 D11
Ziębice, Poland 45 H4
Zielona Góra, Poland 45 G2
Zierikzee, Neths. 17 C3
Ziesar, Germany 24 C8
Zifta, Egypt 80 H7
Zigey, Chad 79 F9
Zigong, China 58 C5
Ziguinchor, Senegal 82 C1
Zihuatanejo, Mexico 118 D4
Zijin, China 59 F10
Zile, Turkey 72 B6
Žilina, Slovak Rep. 27 B11
Žilinský □, Slovak Rep. 27 B12
Zillah, Libya 79 C9
Zillertaler Alpen, Austria 26 D4
Zima, Russia 51 D11
Zimapán, Mexico 119 C5
Zimba, Zambia 87 F2
Zimbabwe, Zimbabwe 87 G3
Zimbabwe ■, Africa 87 F3
Zimi, S. Leone 82 D2
Zimnicea, Romania 43 G10
Zimovniki, Russia 49 G6
Zinder, Niger 83 C6
Zinga, Tanzania 87 D4
Zingst, Germany 24 A8
Ziniaré, Burkina Faso 83 C4
Zinnowitz, Germany 24 A9
Zion National Park, U.S.A. 115 H7
Zirbitzkogel, Austria 26 D7
Zirc, Hungary 42 C2
Žiri, Slovenia 29 B11
Žirje, Croatia 29 E12
Zirl, Austria 26 D4
Zirndorf, Germany 25 F6
Ziros, Greece 36 D8
Zirreh, Gowd-e, Afghan. 66 E3
Zisterdorf, Austria 27 C9
Zitácuaro, Mexico 118 D4
Žitava →, Slovak Rep. 27 C11
Žitište, Serbia, Yug. 42 E5
Zitong, China 58 B5
Zítsa, Greece 38 B2
Zittau, Germany 24 E10
Zitundo, Mozam. 89 D5
Živinice, Bos.-H. 42 F3
Ziwa Maghariba □, Tanzania 86 C3
Ziway, L., Ethiopia 81 F4
Zixi, China 59 D11
Zixing, China 59 E9
Ziyang, Shaanxi, China 56 H5
Ziyang, Sichuan, China 58 B5
Ziyuan, China 59 D8
Ziyun, China 58 E6
Zizhong, China 58 C5
Zlarin, Croatia 29 E12
Zlatar, Croatia 29 B13
Zlatar, Serbia, Yug. 40 C3
Zlataritsa, Bulgaria 41 C9
Zlaté Moravce, Slovak Rep. 27 C11
Zlatibor, Serbia, Yug. 40 C3
Zlatitsa, Bulgaria 41 D8
Zlatna, Romania 43 D8
Zlatna Panega, Bulgaria 41 C8
Zlatni Pyasŭtsi, Bulgaria 41 C12
Zlatograd, Bulgaria 41 E9
Zlatoust, Russia 50 D6
Zletovo, Macedonia 40 E6
Zlín, Czech Rep. 27 B10
Złocieniec, Poland 44 E3
Złoczew, Poland 45 G5
Zlot, Serbia, Yug. 40 B5
Złotoryja, Poland 45 G2
Złotów, Poland 44 E4
Zmeinogorsk, Kazakstan 50 D9
Żmigród, Poland 45 G3
Zmiyev, Ukraine 47 H9
Znamenka = Znamyanka, Ukraine 47 H7
Znamyanka, Ukraine 47 H7
Żnin, Poland 45 F4
Znojmo, Czech Rep. 26 C9
Zobeyrī, Iran 70 C5
Zobia, Dem. Rep. of the Congo 86 B2
Zoetermeer, Neths. 17 B4
Zogang, China 58 C1
Zogno, Italy 28 C6
Zogqên, China 58 A2
Zolochev = Zolochiv, Ukraine 47 H3
Zolochiv, Ukraine 47 H3
Zolotonosha, Ukraine 47 H7
Zomba, Malawi 87 F4
Zongo, Dem. Rep. of the Congo 84 D3
Zonguldak, Turkey 72 B4
Zongyang, China 59 B11
Zonqor Pt., Malta 36 D2
Zonza, France 21 G13
Zorgo, Burkina Faso 83 C4
Zorita, Spain 35 F5
Zorleni, Romania 43 D12
Zornitsa, Bulgaria 41 D10
Zorritos, Peru 124 D2
Żory, Poland 45 H5
Zorzor, Liberia 82 D3
Zossen, Germany 24 C9
Zou Xiang, China 56 G9
Zouan-Hounien, Ivory C. 82 D3
Zouar, Chad 79 D9
Zouérate = Zouîrât, Mauritania 78 D3
Zouîrât, Mauritania 78 D3
Zourika, Niger 83 B6
Zourma, Burkina Faso 83 C4
Zoushan Dao, China 59 B14
Zoutkamp, Neths. 17 A6
Zrenjanin, Serbia, Yug. 42 E5
Zuarungu, Ghana 83 C4
Zuba, Nigeria 83 D6
Zubayr, Yemen 81 D5
Zubtsov, Russia 46 D8
Zuénoula, Ivory C. 82 D3
Zuera, Spain 32 D4
Zufār, Oman 74 D5
Zug □, Switz. 25 H4
Zugdidi, Georgia 49 J5
Zugersee, Switz. 25 H4
Zugspitze, Germany 25 H6
Zuid-Holland □, Neths. 17 C4
Zuidbeveland, Neths. 17 C3
Zuidhorn, Neths. 17 A6
Zújar, Spain 35 H8
Zújar →, Spain 35 G5
Żukowo, Poland 44 D5
Zula, Eritrea 81 D4
Zülpich, Germany 24 E2
Zumaia, Spain 32 B2
Zumárraga, Spain 32 B2
Zumbo, Mozam. 87 F3
Zummo, Nigeria 83 D7
Zumpango, Mexico 119 D5
Zungeru, Nigeria 83 D6
Zunhua, China 57 D9
Zuni, U.S.A. 115 J9
Zunyi, China 58 D6
Zuo Jiang →, China 58 F6
Zuozhou, China 58 F6
Županja, Croatia 42 E3
Žur, Kosovo, Yug. 40 D4
Zurbātīyah, Iraq 70 C5
Zürich, Switz. 25 H4
Zürich □, Switz. 25 H4
Zürichsee, Switz. 25 H4
Żuromin, Poland 45 E6
Žut, Croatia 29 E12
Zutphen, Neths. 17 B6
Zuwārah, Libya 79 B8
Zūzan, Iran 71 C8
Žužemberk, Slovenia 29 C11
Zvenigorodka = Zvenyhorodka, Ukraine 47 H6
Zvenyhorodka, Ukraine 47 H6
Zverinogolovskoye, Russia 50 D7
Zvezdets, Bulgaria 41 D11
Zvishavane, Zimbabwe 87 G3
Zvolen, Slovak Rep. 27 C12
Zvonce, Serbia, Yug. 40 D6
Zvornik, Bos.-H. 42 F4
Zwedru = Tchien, Liberia 82 D3
Zweibrücken, Germany 25 F3
Zwenkau, Germany 24 D8
Zwettl, Austria 26 C8
Zwickau, Germany 24 E8
Zwierzyniec, Poland 45 H9
Zwiesel, Germany 25 F9
Zwoleń, Poland 45 G8
Zwolle, Neths. 17 B6
Zwolle, U.S.A. 113 K8
Żychlin, Poland 45 F6
Żyrardów, Poland 45 F7
Zyryan, Kazakstan 50 E9
Zyryanka, Russia 51 C16
Zyryanovsk = Zyryan, Kazakstan 50 E9
Żywiec, Poland 45 J6
Zyyi, Cyprus 36 E12

KEY TO WORLD MAP PAGES

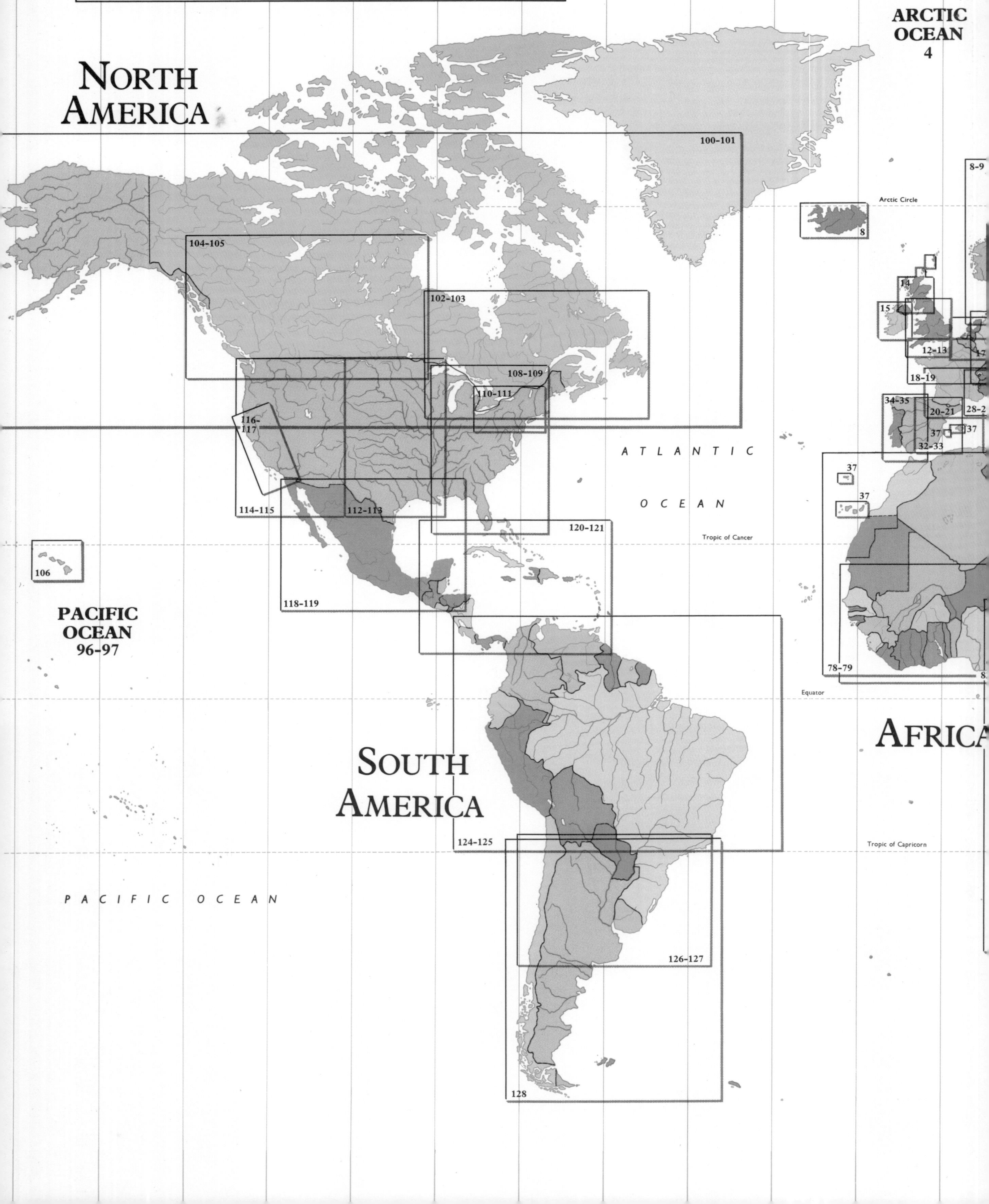

NORTH AMERICA
ARCTIC OCEAN 4
100-101
8-9
Arctic Circle
8
104-105
14
15
102-103
12-13
17
108-109
18-19
110-111
34-35
20-21
116-117
37
32-33
ATLANTIC OCEAN
37
37
114-115
112-113
120-121
Tropic of Cancer
106
118-119
PACIFIC OCEAN 96-97
78-79
Equator
SOUTH AMERICA
124-125
Tropic of Capricorn
PACIFIC OCEAN
126-127
128